A STUDENT'S GUIDE TO THE FEDERAL RULES OF CIVIL PROCEDURE

2022–2023 Edition

STEVEN BAICKER-McKEE
Joseph A. Katarincic Chair of Legal Process and Civil Procedure
Associate Professor of Law
Duquesne University School of Law

WILLIAM M. JANSSEN
Professor of Law
Charleston School of Law

WEST ACADEMIC PUBLISHING

444 Cedar Street, Suite 700
St. Paul, MN 55101
1-877-888-1330

Printed in the United States of America

ISBN: 978-0-314-17948-7

FEDERAL RULES OF CIVIL PROCEDURE AT A GLANCE

PREFACE TO THE 2022–2023 EDITION OF
A STUDENT'S GUIDE
TO THE FEDERAL RULES OF CIVIL PROCEDURE

This is the 25th edition of *A Student's Guide to the Federal Rules of Civil Procedure*. Students learning the Federal Rules of Civil Procedure have relied on this book to help learn the intricacies of those Rules and, importantly, the connection each Rule bears to practice. Here's how:

Each Rule is reprinted in its full, current text. After that text, two overview sections follow. The first we've titled "**How This Rule Fits In**," and it supplies law students with an orientation to the goal of each Rule and its role in the process of federal civil litigation generally. This section orients students to the stage of litigation that Rule is addressing and how—from a macro perspective—that Rule serves its purpose. The second post-text section, "**The Architecture of This Rule**," helps with a recurring, frustrating problem that exasperates many law students: how to make sense of a Rule's organization when its structure is long, multi-parted, and not at all obvious. This section offers an organizing approach for each of the longer Rules, explaining how the subparts of each Rule can be grouped together in a way that aids in understanding. After that section, our treatment of each Rule drills down into the details in an easily recognizable pattern, summarizing the purpose of each subpart and then offering insights into how lawyers and the courts use that subpart in federal practice. We collect those insights in sections called "**Practicing Law Under This Subpart.**"

The *Student's Guide* also contains other important resources essential to any law student's understanding of the Civil Rules:

- **Getting Started:** to help guide you through the foundational concepts of federal judicial power and how that power operates, including personal jurisdiction, subject-matter jurisdiction (with removal and remand), venue, the *Erie* Doctrine, and preclusion (*res judicata/collateral estoppel*).
- **Multidistrict Litigation ("MDL"):** with an introduction to MDL practice and the full text of the MDL statute.
- **Appellate Practice:** with a summary overview of federal appellate procedure.
- **Judiciary Code (Title 28):** with the full text of those federal statutes most often needed by the student of federal civil procedure.
- **U.S. Constitution:** with the full text of the federal Constitution.

Each edition of the *Student's Guide* is updated annually. This edition reflects new federal **case law** and up-to-date versions of all **Rule and statutory text** (capturing all Rule amendments).

We hope the *Student's Guide* will help you navigate your way through learning federal civil practice. But please tell us what you think. We welcome your comments and suggestions for enhancing the *Student's Guide*. Send us your thoughts; our contact information is printed on the author biography page that follows. Thank you!

THE AUTHORS

Additional *Civil Procedure* Study Aids
from Professors Janssen and Baicker-McKee
West Academic Publishing

Mastering Multiple Choice for Federal Civil Procedure

230 multiple choice practice questions, with easy-to-understand answers and explanations. Accompanied with strategies and techniques for success, and reference charts to decode questions by topic.
Now in its FOURTH EDITION.

Federal Civil Procedure Logic Maps

A collection of logic maps—in full-color—that graphically illustrate the structure and operation of most core concepts in federal civil practice, including the function of the Federal Rules of Civil Procedure.
THIRD EDITION expected in the summer of 2022.

ABOUT THE AUTHORS

STEVEN BAICKER-McKEE is the Joseph A. Katarincic Chair of Legal Process and Civil Procedure and an Associate Professor at the Duquesne University School of Law teaching civil procedure, litigation skills simulation courses, environmental law, environmental litigation, and energy law. Mr. Baicker-McKee has been honored by the students of his law school as their "Professor of the Year." He is a co-author of *Learning Civil Procedure*, the *Federal Civil Rules Handbook*, *Mastering Multiple Choice for Federal Civil Procedure*, Volume 12B of *Wright and Miller's Federal Practice and Procedure*, *Practicing Civil Discovery*, and the *Federal Litigator*, as well as numerous articles and book chapters. Before joining the faculty at Duquesne, Mr. Baicker-McKee practiced for more than 20 years as a litigator at Babst Calland in Pittsburgh, Pennsylvania, serving on the firm's Operating Committee and Board of Directors. While at Babst Calland, Mr. Baicker-McKee was recognized as one of the Outstanding Lawyers of America and elected to the Academy of Trial Lawyers.

Mr. Baicker-McKee received his B.A. from Yale University, then spent the next several years building fine furniture and custom cabinets in Charlottesville, Virginia before attending law school. Mr. Baicker-McKee received his J.D. from Marshall-Wythe School of Law, College of William and Mary, where he was on the Board of Editors of the *William and Mary Law Review*. He served a two-year clerkship with the Honorable Glenn E. Mencer of the United States District Court for the Western District of Pennsylvania, to whom he is forever indebted.

Mr. Baicker-McKee resides in Pittsburgh, Pennsylvania with his wife, Carol, and her love and support have been invaluable in every endeavor in Mr. Baicker-McKee's professional career.

WILLIAM M. JANSSEN is a Professor of Law at the Charleston School of Law in Charleston, South Carolina. Mr. Janssen teaches courses in civil procedure, products liability, mass torts, and first amendment law. He has been honored several times by the students of his law school as their "Professor of the Year." The author of various book chapters, articles, and bar review materials on civil procedure, Mr. Janssen is also the sole author of *Federal Civil Procedure Logic Maps*, an illustrative resource for learning federal civil practice; a co-author of the *Federal Civil Rules Handbook*, *Mastering Multiple Choice for Federal Civil Procedure,* Volume 12B of *Wright and Miller's Federal Practice and Procedure,* and *Practicing Civil Discovery;* and a contributing author to *Attorney-Client Privilege in the United States*. Before his appointment to the faculty in Charleston, Mr. Janssen was a litigation partner, the Chair of Life Sciences Practices, and a member of the Executive Committee at the Midatlantic law firm of Saul Ewing LLP, with whom he practiced for almost 17 years. He focused his private practice in pharmaceutical and medical device risk management and litigation. Mr. Janssen is a member of the International Association of Defense Counsel and the Food and Drug Law Institute.

Mr. Janssen graduated from Saint Joseph's University in Philadelphia and The American University, Washington College of Law, in Washington, D.C. He served as Executive Editor of the *American University Law Review* and as a member of the Moot Court Board. After law school, Mr. Janssen clerked for the Honorable James McGirr Kelly, on the United States District Court for the Eastern District of Pennsylvania, and for the Honorable Joseph F. Weis, Jr., on the United States Court of Appeals for the Third Circuit.

Mr. Janssen resides in Charleston, South Carolina, with his wife Mary Kay, to whom he dedicates his work on the *Student's Guide*.

About the Authors

* * *

The authors welcome any comments or suggestions about this book. Their telephone contacts and email addresses are provided below.

CONTACT *THE* AUTHORS:

PROF. STEVEN BAICKER-MCKEE
(412) 396-2258
baickermckees@duq.edu

PROF. WILLIAM M. JANSSEN
(843) 377-2442
wjanssen@charlestonlaw.edu

SUMMARY OF CONTENTS

TABLE OF CONTENTS

A STUDENT'S GUIDE TO THE FEDERAL RULES OF CIVIL PROCEDURE

2022–2023 Edition

PART I

MULTIPLE CHOICE PRACTICE *for* LAW STUDENTS

Why Multiple Choice?

Law students are often tested in ways that are much different than undergraduate college students. Most first-year law school final examinations pose complex, fact-rich hypotheticals about which one or more essay or short-answer questions are asked. This type of testing paradigm enables the professor not only to assess students' mastery of the black-letter law they learned over the course of the law school class, but also the critical ability of students to apply that learned law in a practical context that simulates law practice. This type of mastery in an applied setting is a dominant testing approach for 1L civil procedure as well.

But that is not the only manner of testing.

Learning how to comfortably, confidently approach law school level multiple choice questions is also an essential test-taking skill. First, most first-year law school classes will incorporate a set of multiple choice questions in final examinations, so performing well in this testing environment is often necessary to perform well in 1L courses. Second, most U.S. jurisdictions require law school graduates to pass a bar examination for admission to practice, and a core component of that exam is a full-day, 200-question multiple choice test called the Multistate Bar Examination (MBE). So, in aspiring to optimal grade performance in your law school classes and in beginning the long, rigorous work to prepare to take the MBE, honing your success in taking multiple choice questions is an important testing skill.

This Part of the *Student's Guide* offers you a preview of what law school/MBE type multiple choice questions look like for civil procedure. We've included 8 civil procedure multiple choice questions, followed by the answers (with explanations) for each of those questions. Try your hand at these samples, and begin to acquire a comfort with a testing approach that you are likely to encounter often over the next 3½ years.

Some Tips and Trips

Succeeding with multiple choice questions often hinges on more than just your command of the substantive material itself. Multiple choice questions feel (and often are) tricky, feel confusing or unpredictable, and may require a discriminating level of concentration and analysis that is different from other testing paradigms. Unlike essays and short-answer questions, with multiple choice questions, you know that one of the available choices is *the* answer. To be an effective testing device, the multiple choice questions must then present the test-taker with other, wrong choices that appear to be alluringly attractive as a correct answer. Thus, well written multiple choice questions are just plain tough. Here are a few strategies to bear in mind as you start to prepare to take multiple choice questions:

- *Practice with Time Constraints:* Most law school and MBE multiple choice questions are built for a very particular time constraint—1 minutes 48 seconds per question. This allows bar takers to complete 100 MBE questions during a 3-hour morning testing session, and a second set of 100 MBE questions during a 3-hour testing session after lunch. When you practice, hold yourself to this time standard so that you become accustomed to that pace.
- *Practice with Groups of Questions:* Like any other conditioning exercise, try to practice answering multiple choice questions in the manner in which you will encounter them in a testing setting. Don't practice one at a time—practice in groups (perhaps five or ten questions in a sitting, all answered under a sensible time constraint). Doing so helps to condition your mind for the speed and efficiency of actual testing environments.

- *Always Zero in on the "Call-of-the-Question":* One recurring technique for framing multiple choice questions in a manner that makes them challenging is to supply answer choices that are—truly—correct statements of the black-letter law, yet do not squarely answer the question posed. Bear in mind that testing technique. Avoid choosing those accurate, but nonresponsive, answers by first reading the "call-of-the-question" (that is, the particular legal question that is being asked). This way, you will zero in on not merely correct statements of the law, but more critically, a correct *and responsive* answer to the posed question.
- *Be Suspicious of Absolutes:* Another frequent testing technique is to supply answers that contain broad statements of the law that are sometimes (or even often) correct, but not uniformly so. An answer choice that contains terminology that is absolutist (like, "always" and "never") should raise a red flag in your mind. Few principles in the law can be described in such absolute terms, and you should be on guard against choices framed in that manner.
- *Check the Answers and Explanations:* Getting a practice multiple choice question right is a victory, but you want to also make sure it wasn't an accident. Always be sure to read through the explanations supplied with the practice answers so that you understand not only why the one selection was right, but also why the other three selections were wrong. This added step, when carefully taken, will help grow your command of the material.

Sample Multiple Choice Questions for Civil Procedure

Q1. Arizona enacted a statute that provided that anyone driving on the State's roads shall be deemed to consent to personal jurisdiction for any accidents occurring on those roads, and shall be deemed to consent to notice by publication in a newspaper of general circulation in the county where the accident occurred. Driver, domiciled in Ohio, was in an accident with Bicyclist in Tucson, Arizona. Bicyclist sued Driver in federal court in Arizona. Bicyclist published notice of the suit in accordance with the statute. Driver did not see the notices, and default judgment was entered against Driver. At the time of the accident, Driver was just passing through Arizona on his way to California for a work conference, and has no contacts with Arizona other than this one incident. When Bicyclist tried to collect on the judgment, Driver challenged notice and personal jurisdiction.

How will the court likely rule?

(A) It will rule that Driver did not receive adequate notice and that deemed consent under the statute is constitutionally ineffective.

(B) It will rule that Driver did not receive adequate notice and that deemed consent under the statute is constitutionally effective.

(C) It will rule that Driver did receive adequate notice and that deemed consent under the statute is constitutionally ineffective.

(D) It will rule that Driver did receive adequate notice and that deemed consent under the statute is constitutionally effective.

See ANSWER on Page 6

Q2. Seller refurbished speedboats for resale from his home in Kitty Hawk, North Carolina. One summer, Buyer noticed Seller's roadside advertisement while driving his family to Florida for vacation. On his way back from vacation, Buyer purchased a refurbished speedboat from Seller, agreeing to make three yearly payments for the purchase. The next year, Seller relocated to Pawley's Island, South Carolina. Buyer paid the first of his three installments, but failed to pay the second or third installments. Seller then filed a lawsuit against Buyer in South Carolina State court. Several months later, Seller saw Buyer having lunch with a business client at a restaurant in Pawley's Island.

If Seller is able to have Buyer served with a complaint and summons before Buyer finishes his lunch, would the South Carolina State court have proper jurisdiction over Buyer?

(A) Yes, but only because Seller is now a citizen of South Carolina.

(B) Yes, but only if Buyer was lunching in South Carolina voluntarily.

(C) No, unless Buyer has sufficient other minimum contacts with South Carolina.

(D) No, unless Buyer is a citizen of South Carolina.

See ANSWER on Page 6

Q3. Buyer and Seller enter into a contract that contained a forum selection clause, reading: "The parties to this contract agree that any action under this contract shall be brought in the federal district court for the Western District of Pennsylvania. The parties hereby consent to, and waive any objections to, personal jurisdiction, subject-matter jurisdiction, and venue in that forum." Buyer filed a complaint in federal court in Pennsylvania, and the Seller filed a motion challenging personal jurisdiction and subject-matter jurisdiction.

Which of the following best describes the effect of this contract clause?

(A) Seller's consent will be effective to establish both personal jurisdiction and subject-matter jurisdiction.

(B) Seller's consent will be effective to establish personal jurisdiction but not as to subject-matter jurisdiction.

(C) Seller's consent will be effective to establish subject-matter jurisdiction but not as to personal jurisdiction.

(D) Seller's consent will not be effective to establish either subject-matter jurisdiction or personal jurisdiction.

See ANSWER on Page 7

Q4. Rider, domiciled in North Dakota, was injured on a bicycle trip in Wyoming when his bicycle malfunctioned. The bicycle was manufactured by Bicycle Company, and Rider purchased it from Store in South Dakota while on a business trip. Rider sued both Bicycle Company and Store in federal court in the District of North Dakota (the only district in that State). Bicycle Company was a Delaware corporation, with its principal place of business in Michigan; it had no activities or property in North Dakota. Store was a North Dakota corporation with its principal place of business in North Dakota. It was a retail chain, with sister stores in South Dakota.

Is venue proper in the District of North Dakota?

(A) Yes, because Rider resides in North Dakota.

(B) Yes, because Store resides in North Dakota.

(C) No, because Bicycle Company's citizenship is not relevant in a venue analysis.

(D) No, because Bicycle Company does not reside in North Dakota and the sale and accident occurred outside North Dakota.

See ANSWER on Page 7

Q5. Three Partners co-owned a hardware store in Arkansas. Two of the Partners conspired to force the third Partner out of the business. That owner, Partner 3, brought a lawsuit against the two conspiring owners (Partner 1 and Partner 2) in Arkansas federal court. Partner 1 and Partner 2 filed a counterclaim against Partner 3 and, also, crossclaimed against one another.

Which of the following Partners has filed an untimely answer in that federal lawsuit?

(A) Partner 1, who filed an answer 58 days after being sent a waiver of service request, which he had timely returned with his waiver consent.

(B) Partner 2, who filed an answer 21 days after being served by personal delivery with original process.

(C) Partner 3, who filed an answer 20 days after receiving notice that his motion to dismiss Partner 1's counterclaim had been denied by the court.

(D) Partner 1, who filed an answer to Partner 2's crossclaim 18 days after being served with the pleading that contained it.

See ANSWER on Page 8

Q6. Firm bought and sold securities for its customers. Broker was a longstanding Firm employee and one of its most talented securities traders. A messy dispute with a wealthy customer over a trade that had been negligently executed by Broker caused Firm to lose several million dollars. Firm fired Broker. Broker then filed a lawsuit invoking the court's diversity jurisdiction against Firm, asserting breach of several terms of the employment contract. In discovery, Broker's attorney issued a broad request to inspect all electronically stored information in Firm's possession relating to Broker or any of Broker's clients.

Which, among the following, would be Firm's best argument in resisting Broker's discovery demand?

(A) Information that is electronically stored is not discoverable in federal court.

(B) Broker failed to designate the form for the production of the electronically stored information.

(C) Broker's demand exceeds the numerical maximum set in the Federal Rules of Civil Procedure for allowable requests for inspection.

(D) The requested electronically stored information is not reasonably accessible.

See ANSWER on Page 8

Q7. Orchestra entered into a contract with Violinist, a famous musician, to play with Orchestra for 5 seasons. In the middle of the second season, Violinist refused to perform, stating publicly that Orchestra's music director and conductor were "incompetent philistines." Orchestra sued Violinist in federal court for damages for defamation and for specific performance of the contract. Ten days after filing her answer to the complaint, Violinist filed and served a jury trial demand.

Does Violinist have a right to a jury trial?

(A) Yes, as to both claims.

(B) Yes, as to the defamation claim but not as to the contract claim.

(C) Yes, as to the contract claim but not as to the defamation claim.

(D) No, as to both claims.

See ANSWER on Page 8

Q8. Inmate brought a civil rights action against Prison in federal court under 42 U.S.C. § 1983, claiming he did not receive proper medical care. Prison moved for summary judgment, arguing that Prisoner did not have sufficient evidence to establish deliberate indifference, the legal standard for this type of prisoner civil rights action. The court denied the motion, finding genuine disputes as to material facts. At trial, Prison made a Rule 50 motion at the close of Inmate's case, and the court denied the motion, ruling that Inmate had introduced sufficient evidence to support the claim. Prison renewed the Rule 50 motion for judgment as a matter of law at the conclusion of all testimony and evidence, which the court denied. The jury returned a verdict in favor of Inmate, and Prison appealed, contending on appeal that the evidence presented at trial did not satisfy the requirements for deliberate indifference.

May the appellate court hear the appeal?

(A) Yes, because Prison preserved the issue by filing a Rule 56 motion for summary judgment.

(B) Yes, because Prison preserved the issue by filing a Rule 50 motion after Inmate had been fully heard on the issue.

(C) Yes, because Prison preserved the issue by renewing its Rule 50 motion at the close of the record.

(D) No, because Prison failed to renew the Rule 50 motion again after trial.

See ANSWER on Page 9

ANSWERS *to* Sample Multiple Choice Questions *for* Civil Procedure

Q1. **Answer (A) is wrong:** In *Hess v. Pawloski*, 274 U.S. 352 (1927), the U.S. Supreme Court held that a statute that implied consent to personal jurisdiction when a motorist used the State's roads was constitutional. *See also Elkhart Eng'g Corp. v. Dornier Werke*, 343 F.2d 861, 865–66 (5th Cir. 1965). Therefore, the Arizona court likely has personal jurisdiction over Driver.

Answer (B) is the best choice: As explained in Answer (A), the deemed consent in the statute was constitutional. In *Mullane v. Central Hanover Bank & Trust Co.*, 339 U.S. 306 (1950), however, the U.S. Supreme Court held that the Constitution does not require actual notice, but it does require notice "reasonably calculated under all the circumstances, to apprise interested parties of the action and give them an opportunity to object." Simply publishing notice in a local newspaper is not reasonably calculated to put an out of State driver on notice of the lawsuit. Therefore, while the Arizona court would likely rule that Driver had consented to an exercise of personal jurisdiction, it would also likely rule that Bicyclist failed to give Driver adequate notice. *See also Banks v. Leon,* 975 F. Supp. 815 (W.D. Va. 1997).

Answers (C) and (D) are wrong: As explained in Answers (A) and (B), the Arizona court would likely rule that Driver had consented to an exercise of personal jurisdiction, but that Bicyclist failed to give Driver adequate notice.

Q2. **Answer (A) is wrong:** In assessing whether personal jurisdiction satisfies the U.S. Constitution's Due Process Clause, the contacts of the plaintiff with the forum are not dispositive. The proper inquiry focuses on the defendant's contacts with the State, not the plaintiff's contacts. *See Keeton v. Hustler Magazine, Inc.*, 465 U.S. 770, 779 (1984).

Answer (B) is the best choice: The U.S. Supreme Court has confirmed that transient (or "tag") jurisdiction satisfies with the Due Process Clause, at least so long as it is exercised over someone who is voluntarily and knowingly within the forum. *See Burnham v. Superior Ct. of Cal.*, 495 U.S. 604, 616–622 (1990) (plurality); *id.* at 639–40 (Brennan, J., concurring).

Answer (C) is wrong: Were Buyer to have minimum contacts with South Carolina, that, too, might be a basis for the South Carolina courts' exercise of personal jurisdiction. But, as explained in Answer (B), such minimum contacts are not essential if transient personal jurisdiction exists.

Answer (D) is wrong: Like in Answer (C), Buyer's citizenship in South Carolina could support domicile-based personal jurisdiction. But, again as noted in Answer (B), Buyer's domicile is not essential to South Carolina's assertion of personal jurisdiction over Buyer if transient jurisdiction exists.

Q3. **Answer (A) is wrong:** A forum selection clause is a provision included in many contracts where the contracting parties identify the forum where all or part of any contract-related dispute must be litigated. Parties can consent to personal jurisdiction in such a contract clause unless enforcement of the clause would be fundamentally unfair. *See Carnival Cruise Lines, Inc. v. Shute,* 499 U.S. 585, 600–01 (1991). However, subject-matter jurisdiction is a structural constitutional limitation on the type of cases federal courts are authorized to handle, and the parties cannot create subject-matter jurisdiction by waiver, stipulation, or consent. *See Ins. Corp. of Ireland, Ltd. v. Compagnie des Bauxites de Guinee,* 456 U.S. 694, 702 (1982). Therefore, Seller's agreement to the forum selection clause may invest the Pennsylvania court with personal jurisdiction, but it will not affect the court's subject-matter jurisdiction analysis.

Answer (B) is the best choice: As explained in Answer (A), the court will likely enforce the parties' agreement as to personal jurisdiction, but will conduct its subject-matter jurisdiction analysis without regard to Seller's consent.

Answer (C) is wrong: As explained in Answer (A), consent is relevant to the personal jurisdiction analysis, but not the subject-matter analysis.

Answer (D) is wrong: As explained in Answer (A), consent is relevant to the personal jurisdiction analysis, but not the subject-matter analysis.

Q4. **Answer (A) is wrong:** 28 U.S.C. § 1391(b)(1) authorizes venue based on the *defendants'* residence if all of the defendants reside in the same State. As explained in Answer (D), none of the venue provisions in 28 U.S.C. § 1391 authorize venue based on the *plaintiff's* residence.

Answer (B) is wrong: For venue purposes, residence for individuals is their place of domicile. *See* 28 U.S.C. § 1391(c)(1). For corporations, residence varies on litigating posture—when plaintiffs, corporations are deemed residents of their principal place of business; when defendants, corporations are deemed residents of any judicial district in which they are subject to personal jurisdiction regarding the dispute. *See* 28 U.S.C. § 1391(c)(2). Because North Dakota has only one district, a corporate defendant will be deemed to reside in North Dakota if its contacts with North Dakota would support personal jurisdiction. *See* 28 U.S.C. § 1391(c)(2). Because Bicycle Company has no contacts with North Dakota, it does not reside there. Accordingly, residence based venue is not proper because *all* defendants do not reside in North Dakota. It is improper to conduct this analysis on a party-by-party basis; residence-based venue requires all defendants to reside in the same State. As discussed further in Answer (D), the second option—where a substantial part of the operative events occurred—will also not permit venue in North Dakota.

Answer (C) is wrong: A defendant's *citizenship* is critical to the diversity-based subject-matter jurisdiction analysis. But for venue purposes, it is a corporate defendant's *residence* (that is, amenability to personal jurisdiction) that will establish venue. Here, however, those attributes align. A corporate defendant is subject to general ("all-purpose") personal jurisdiction in those forums where it was incorporated and where it maintains its principal place of business. *See Goodyear Dunlop Tires Ops., S.A. v. Brown*, 564 U.S. 915, 924 (2011) (listing both as "paradigm" forums for general jurisdiction). But here those citizenship attributes (and, thus, residence for venue purposes) do not point to North Dakota. As explained in Answer (B), since residence-based venue must be proper as to *all* defendants, venue is not proper in North Dakota.

Answer (D) is the best choice: Venue in federal court is governed by 28 U.S.C. § 1391. Absent a special federal law providing otherwise, federal venue is proper: (1) in any judicial district where defendants reside, so long as all defendants are residents of that State, or (2) in a judicial district where a substantial part of the events or omissions giving rise to the claim occurred (or where a substantial part of the property that is the subject of the lawsuit is situated). *See* 28 U.S.C. § 1391(b)(1)–(b)(2). If neither of those formulas would locate a proper venue, then venue will be proper in any judicial district where any defendant would be subject to the court's personal jurisdiction regarding the lawsuit. *See* 28 U.S.C. § 1391(b)(3). As explained in Answer (B), the defendants do not all reside in North Dakota, so residence-based venue is not proper there. Likewise, the accident occurred in Wyoming and the sale occurred in South Dakota. None of the facts suggest any events or omissions in North Dakota, so venue is not proper there under § 1391(b)(2). Therefore, venue is not proper in North Dakota.

Q5. **Answer (A) is wrong:** Federal civil litigants who agree to waive formal service of process are rewarded under the Rules with a response time of 60 days from the date the request for waiver was sent. *See* Rule 12(a)(1)(A)(ii). Because Partner 1 answered within the required 60 days, that answer was timely.

Answer (B) is wrong: Federal civil litigants who have not waived service, but are instead served traditionally with original process, have 21 days from service to file their answers. *See* Rule 12(a)(1)(A)(i). Because Partner 2 answered within that 21-day period, that answer was timely.

Answer (C) is the best choice: Plaintiffs are required under the Rules to file an answer to counterclaims. *See* Rule 12(a)(1)(B). The time for filing any answer is suspended by the filing of a timely motion to dismiss. *See* Rule 12(a)(4). If the court denies that motion, the moving party then has 14 days from the date of the court's action to file an answer. *See* Rule 12(a)(4)(A). Because Partner 3's answer to the counterclaim was filed outside that 14-day period, it was untimely.

Answer (D) is wrong: Co-defendants are required under the Rules to file an answer to crossclaims. *See* Rule 12(a)(1)(B). The time for filing such an answer is 21 days after service of the pleading that contained the crossclaim. *See* Rule 12(a)(1)(B). Because Partner 1's answer to the crossclaim was filed within this 21-day period, it was timely.

Q6. **Answer (A) is wrong:** Early on, litigants had contended that electronically stored information ought not to be subject to discovery at all. It is now expressly clear that electronically stored information is, indeed, discoverable as a category. *See* Rule 34(a)(1)(A).

Answer (B) is wrong: The Rules permit a requesting party to designate a preferred form for the production of electronically stored information. *See* Rule 34(b)(1)(C). But even if no preferred form of production is expressed, the responding party is under a duty to make electronically stored information available for inspection, and must state the form or forms in which it will make that material available. *See* Rule 34(b)(2)(D).

Answer (C) is wrong: The Rules install numerical maximums for certain discovery, such as a limit on the number of interrogatories, *see* Rule 33(a)(1), and a limit on the number of depositions, *see* Rule 30(a)(2)(A)(i). But there is no numerical maximum for requests for inspection.

Answer (D) is the best choice: A party is relieved of its burden to produce electronically stored information from sources that it identifies to be not reasonably accessible because of undue burden or cost. *See* Rule 26(b)(2)(B). Were such an objection asserted, the requesting party may respond by filing with the court a motion to compel the production of the requested discovery, notwithstanding its associated burden and cost. *See id.*

Q7. **Answer (A) is wrong:** As explained in Answer (B), Violinist has no right to a jury trial as to the specific performance claim.

Answer (B) is the best choice: Under Rule 38 of the Federal Rules of Civil Procedure and the Seventh Amendment of the U.S. Constitution, parties have the right to jury trial for any claims that were common law claims (generally those seeking money damages) at the time that the Seventh Amendment was ratified in 1791. A defamation allegation seeking money damages is a common law claim. But specific performance is an equitable claim, so Violinist has no right to a jury trial for that claim. *See, e.g., Klein v. Shell Oil Co.,* 386 F.2d 659, 663 (8th Cir. 1967); *Rosenblatt v. Baer,* 383 U.S. 75 (1966). Under Rule 38, a party preserves the right to a jury trial by filing and serving a demand within 14 days of the last pleading addressing the issue (which, typically, is the answer to the complaint).

Answer (C) is wrong: As explained in Answer (B), Violinist has a right to a jury trial for the defamation claim, but no right to a jury trial as to the specific performance claim.

Answer (D) is wrong: As explained in Answer (B), Violinist has a right to a jury trial for the defamation claim.

Q8. **Answer (A) is wrong:** For issues regarding the sufficiency of the evidence, a party may not appeal a denial of a summary judgment motion without also raising the issue under Rule 50. *See Ortiz v. Jordan*, 131 S. Ct. 884, 891–92 (2011).

Answer (B) is wrong: In order to preserve for appeal an issue relating to the sufficiency of evidence, a party must both file a motion for judgment as a matter of law during trial under Rule 50(a), and then renew the motion *after trial* under Rule 50(b). *See Unitherm Food Servs., Inc. v. Swift-Eckrich, Inc.*, 546 U.S. 394, 396 (2006). Here, Prison filed a Rule 50(a) motion twice during trial, but failed to file a Rule 50(b) motion after the verdict.

Answer (C) is wrong: As explained in Answer (B), Prison failed to file a Rule 50(b) motion after trial, and therefore did not preserve the issue it sought to raise on appeal related to the sufficiency of the evidence.

Answer (D) is the best choice: As explained in Answer (B), Prison failed to file a Rule 50(b) motion after trial, and therefore did not preserve the issue it sought to raise on appeal related to the sufficiency of the evidence.

PART II

GETTING STARTED: JUDICIAL POWER, WHERE THE RULES FIT IN, JURISDICTION, NOTICE, VENUE, *ERIE*, AND PRECLUSION

Table of Sections

A. FEDERAL CIVIL PRACTICE: HOW EVERYTHING FITS TOGETHER

§ 2.1a Federal Judicial Power

This *Student's Guide* is primarily a learning tool for the Federal Rules of Civil Procedure (referred to, throughout this *Guide*, as the "Rules"). The Rules establish the manner in which civil law is practiced in the Nation's federal trial courts. But those procedures cannot be fully understood without first learning how the Rules fit in.

Federal civil practice is governed by the Rules, to be sure. But the procedures for practicing law in the federal courts are governed not just by the Rules. The U.S. Constitution imposes limits on how federal courts may operate. Also, laws enacted by the U.S. Congress set additional standards and procedures for federal civil litigation. Case law interpreting and applying principles of federal civil practice add still another source of procedural requirements. Each district has local procedural rules that apply only to cases pending in that district, and many judges have additional procedures (often called "Chambers Rules") that apply only in their cases. All in all, learning how to practice successfully in the Nation's federal trial courts requires a comfortable knowledge of all these sources of procedural law and how those sources function together to empower the federal judiciary.

So, this *Student's Guide* begins not with the Rules themselves.

We begin, instead, with federal judicial power.

Judicial power is the lawful authority of a court to act. Litigants come to the courts to have their civil disputes resolved. They hope to obtain from the courts a judgment that will grant them the remedy they seek, be binding on all parties, and be enforceable throughout the United States. Obviously, this hope starts with a court that possesses the legal right to act on the lawsuit. In other words, there must be a court that may lawfully exercise its judicial power.

The authority of the federal courts to act begins with the U.S. Constitution. In the landmark 1878 case of *Pennoyer v. Neff*, the Supreme Court famously identified two threshold requirements for judicial proceedings to be constitutionally valid: the defendant (or the defendant's property) must be brought within the court's jurisdiction ("personal jurisdiction") and the tribunal must be "competent" by "the law of its creation" to rule "upon the subject-matter of the suit" ("subject-matter jurisdiction"). *Pennoyer v. Neff*, 95 U.S. 714, 733 (1878). Over the years, the law has evolved on how these two predicates for judicial power—"personal" and "subject-matter" jurisdiction—operate. But the law has remained constant on one point. When the court's jurisdiction is missing, it "cannot proceed at all" and is, instead, authorized to take only two actions: to declare that jurisdiction is absent and to dismiss the case. *Ex Parte McCardle*, 74 U.S. 506, 514 (1868). *See also Ruhrgas AG v. Marathon Oil Co.*, 526 U.S. 574, 577 (1999) ("Jurisdiction to resolve cases on the merits requires both authority over the category of claim in suit (subject-matter jurisdiction) and authority over the parties (personal jurisdiction), so that the court's decision will bind them.").

An example is helpful. Suppose Bob Bicyclist was struck in California by a car negligently driven by Clara Cardriver. Assume Bicyclist was a California citizen and Cardriver was a New York citizen. If Bicyclist sues Cardriver for negligence—a State law tort claim—in federal court in California, that court would need "personal" jurisdiction over Cardriver in order to render a binding, enforceable judgment against her in Bicyclist's lawsuit. Because Cardriver was, at the time, driving in California (and doing so, allegedly, negligently), the California federal court is likely to possess "personal" jurisdiction over Cardriver—assuming Cardriver is given proper notice of Bicyclist's lawsuit and an appropriate opportunity to appear and defend against Bicyclist's claims.

The California court would also need subject-matter jurisdiction over Bicyclist's State law tort claim. Federal courts are courts of limited jurisdiction, meaning that they cannot hear every type of dispute. Rather, they only have the constitutional authority to adjudicate certain categories of disputes. One such category, discussed in detail below, is diversity-based federal jurisdiction—the authority to adjudicate certain claims between citizens of different States. Diversity jurisdiction might supply the federal court with the "subject-matter" jurisdiction needed to hear Bicyclist's case.

In addition to "personal" and "subject-matter" jurisdiction, "venue" is a third prerequisite for the lawful exercise of judicial power. The "venue" requirements are imposed by statutory (not constitutional) law, and expect that the court selected for the lawsuit have some logical connection to the dispute. "Venue" would determine which of the federal trial courts in California could hear this lawsuit. If the accident occurred in Southern California, "venue" would likely be proper in the federal court encompassing that geographic area—namely, the United States District Court for the Southern District of California.

Because Bicyclist is asserting a State law claim, the federal court would also need to decide what law to apply—federal law or State law. That question may be controlled by the "*Erie* doctrine," an analysis found in a Supreme Court case involving the Erie Railroad Company and a host of cases interpreting *Erie*. In Bicyclist's lawsuit, the federal court would likely apply federal court procedures but California's tort law.

Perhaps this is not Bicyclist's first lawsuit against Cardriver. What if Bicyclist had sued Cardriver in an earlier lawsuit, but only to recover the value of his now-destroyed bicycle? Could Bicyclist bring a later, second lawsuit against Cardriver, this time for personal injuries he sustained in the incident? Here, the California federal court would need to determine if Bicyclist's first lawsuit has "precluded" his ability to sue Cardriver a second time. In this lawsuit, the federal court may well rule that principles of res judicata (or "claim preclusion") deprive Bicyclist of his right to sue Cardriver again concerning the same accident.

These important concepts of federal judicial power—jurisdiction, notice, venue, the *Erie* doctrine, and preclusion theory—are not fully addressed by the Rules. In fact, Rule 82 provides that the Rules neither increase nor limit a district court's power and obligations in the areas of jurisdiction and venue. Rather, these concepts are rooted in the U.S. Constitution, federal statutes, and case law. Each will be discussed below. But first—now oriented to how other sources of law influence federal civil practice—we will introduce the Rules themselves.

§ 2.1b Where the Rules Fit In

What the Rules Are

The *Federal Rules of Civil Procedure* ("Rules") took effect on Friday, September 16, 1938. They established the manner of practice for civil litigation in the federal trial courts. The Rules are national in scope. They apply in all federal districts, to all federal trial judges, and for all civil actions and proceedings (except where specifically exempted by the Rules themselves). *See* Rule 1 and Rule 81. This result—a nationally uniform system of federal procedures—was one of the important objectives of adopting the Rules in the first place.

The constitutionality of the Rules flows from the authority granted Congress in Article III of the U.S. Constitution to establish a federal judiciary. *See Hanna v. Plumer*, 380 U.S. 460, 472 (1965) ("For the constitutional provision for a federal court system (augmented by the Necessary and Proper Clause) carries with it congressional power to make rules governing the practice and pleading in those courts . . ."). Where one of the Rules squarely addresses a matter of procedure, and that Rule is found to be both constitutional and in accordance with Congress's direct or delegated rulemaking authority, that Rule will govern—notwithstanding any contrary State law. *See Gasperini v. Ctr. for Humanities, Inc.*, 518 U.S. 415, 428 n.7 (1996). None of the Rules has ever been declared to be invalid.

Today, the Rules are supplemented in nearly all federal districts with a set of "Local Rules," and many individual federal judges have supplemented them further by adopting "Chambers Policies" or "Standing Orders." But none of those locally-adopted procedures are permitted to be inconsistent with the Rules. *See* Rule 83(a)(1). Moreover, many States have used the Rules as a template for crafting their own State procedures, and State courts often refer to the Rules as an important resource for interpreting their own State rules. *See Laffitte v. Bridgestone Corp.*, 674 S.E.2d 154, 162 n.10 (S.C. 2009) (federal decisions interpreting a federal Rule (which State rule mirrors) accepted as "persuasive authority" in correctly interpreting that State rule).

For all of these reasons, learning the Rules and how to use them is essential training for every American law student.

How the Rules Came to Be

Federal trial courts are located within the boundaries of the various States, territories, and the District of Columbia.[1] For many years before the Rules were drafted, federal practice followed the *Conformity Act of 1872*, which instructed that federal practice, pleadings, and other proceedings had to generally conform "as near as may be" to the practice, pleadings, and other proceedings governing practice in the State courts of the particular State within which each federal court was located. *See generally Nudd v. Burrows*, 91 U.S. 426, 441–42 (1875). This approach to federal practice had the effect of more closely aligning each federal court's procedures to its host State's procedures, but in doing so, it allowed for federal procedures to differ—sometimes significantly—from one federal district to the next. Thus, how a lawyer practiced civil litigation in federal court in Boston might be quite different from the norms that prevailed in federal court in Richmond.

The Rules were drafted to correct this anomaly. The goal was ambitious—to craft a single, nationally uniform set of procedures to govern civil litigation in every federal trial court across the Nation. In 1934, Congress enacted the *Rules Enabling Act* which delegated to the U.S. Supreme Court the task of preparing the new federal rules of civil practice. *See* 28 U.S.C. §§ 2071–72. The Court, in turn, commissioned a distinguished group of lawyers and law professors to actually draft the Rules; their handiwork was then adopted by the Court about three years later in December 1937, reported to Congress in January 1938, and took effect in September 1938. For background reading on the drafting of the Rules, *see* generally Charles E. Clark, *The Proposed Federal Rules of Civil Procedure*, 22 A.B.A. J. 447 (1936); Charles E. Clark, *The New Federal Rules of Civil Procedure: The Last Phase—Underlying Philosophy Embodied in Some of the Basic Provisions of the New Procedure*, 23 A.B.A. J. 976 (1937).

As drafted, the Rules were destined to do far more than simply unify federal practice across the country. As one of the principal co-drafters of the Rules explained on the eve of the Rules taking effect: "The rules are really so simple that it is hard for those who are familiar with the technique of the modern litigation to appreciate how simple they are." Edson R. Sunderland, *The New Federal Rules*, 45 W. Va. L. Q. 5, 30 (1938). The Rules were prepared with a master, defining purpose: "to eliminate technical matters by removing the basis for technical objections, to make it as difficult as impossible, for cases to go off on procedural points, and to make litigation as inexpensive, as practicable and as convenient, as can be done." *Id.* In scope, effect, and influence on the practice of civil litigation in America, the Rules were nothing short of revolutionary.

Amending the Rules

In the many decades that have followed their promulgation, the Rules have been amended on numerous occasions to meet new challenges, address unforeseen developments and technological advances, and resolve shortcomings later discovered. The process for amending the Rules is not unlike the process by which they were originally drafted. Congress directed the creation of a "Judicial Conference of the United States," a body of federal judges from throughout the country to continuously study the operation and effect of the Rules in practice, and to recommend to the U.S. Supreme Court revisions to those Rules as may be "desirable to promote simplicity in procedure, fairness in administration, the just determination of litigation, and the elimination of unjustifiable expense and delay." *See* 28 U.S.C. § 331. The work of the Conference is coordinated through committees on the various sets of federal rules, and those committees, in turn, make recommendations to the Conference. Before Rules are adopted, public consideration and comment is invited on prospective drafts. Only after the committees, the Conference, and the U.S. Supreme Court are all satisfied that an amendment

---

[1] Only two of the federal districts span outside the boundary of the States in which they sit—the District of Wyoming encompasses territory in Montana and Idaho (because the district includes all of Yellowstone National Park) and the District of Hawai'i encompasses other Pacific Island territories of the United States. Every other federal district court lies entirely within a single State or territory.

is in order, will a revision to the Rules be delivered to Congress for legislative consideration. Congress, however, need not formally act on the proposed amendments. Under the terms of the *Rules Enabling Act*, Rule amendments take effect on December 1 of the year of submission *unless* Congress acts legislatively to modify or block them. *See* 28 U.S.C. § 2074. Recent amendments to the Rules are summarized in Part III of this text.

The text of the Rules that appear in this *Student's Guide* reprints the current (and soon to be in-force) language of each of the Federal Rules of Civil Procedure. The past 20 years have marked an unusually active period of Rule amendments:

- **Organizational Deponent Amendments (2020)** (which imposes on parties the duty to confer in good faith about the matters for examination before or promptly after requesting to depose an organization);
- **Electronic Filing & Service, Class Action, and Enforcement Amendments (2018)** (which mandated electronic filing (subject to certain exceptions), adjusted the electronic service procedures, modified the procedures for class action settlements and certain class action appeals, and extended the "automatic stay" period for enforcing civil judgments and permitted further stays upon the posting of a bond or other security);
- **Technical Amendments (2016 & 2017)** (which resolved certain drafting ambiguities, and which eliminated the 3-extra-day extension rule for electronic filings);
- **Discovery Amendments (2015)** (which promoted the "proportionality" standard for the scope of allowable discovery, revised procedures for production requests, and sought to encourage more active judicial case management and cooperation among the parties);
- **Subpoena Amendments (2013)** (which adjusted civil subpoena powers);
- **Summary Judgment Amendments (2010)** (which restructured the summary judgment rule and codified certain common law summary judgment practices);
- **Expert Amendments (2010)** (which installed new expert disclosure obligations and extended work product protection to certain expert materials);
- **Time Computation Amendments (2009)** (which revised certain time deadlines and redesigned the approach for computing time);
- **"Restyling" Amendments (2007)** (which gave the Rules a top-to-bottom rewrite for clarity, consistency, and simplicity);
- **Privacy Amendments (2007)** (which authorized the redaction of certain personal-identifying information);
- **Discovery of Electronic Data Amendments (2006)** (which formalized disclosure and discovery of electronically-stored information);
- **Intervention in Constitution Challenges (2006)** (which collected provisions requiring notice, certification, and a right of intervention for constitutional challenges to federal or State laws);
- **Disclosure Statements (2002)** (which imposed a disclosure statement obligation on nongovernmental corporate litigants).

B. FEDERAL PERSONAL JURISDICTION

§ 2.2 Personal Jurisdiction—Introduction

Personal jurisdiction protects a litigant's individual liberty interest. It constrains a court's ability to rule by ensuring, among other goals, that the court's act of ruling in the lawsuit will not offend "traditional notions of fair play and substantial justice." *Ins. Corp. of Ireland v. Compagnie des Bauxites de Guinee*, 456 U.S. 694, 702 (1982) (quoting *International Shoe Co. v. Washington*, 326 U.S. 310, 316 (1945) (citation omitted)). In this way, personal jurisdiction represents an individual right enjoyed by litigants to be treated in a manner that is not constitutionally unfair.

Subject-matter jurisdiction is quite different. Subject-matter jurisdiction is a *structural* limitation on a court's ability to act. Courts are empowered to rule by the laws that supply them with their judicial authority. In the federal system, those empowering laws come from two sources—Article III of the U.S. Constitution and the federal Judiciary Code enacted by the U.S. Congress. Thus, federal courts are constrained to act only so far as the Constitution and Congress permits. This constraint, then, is not merely a safeguard for individuals against an unfair tribunal, but rather a fixed, structural boundary over which no federal judge may pass. *Id.* at 702–03. *See Mansfield, C. & L. M. R. Co. v. Swan*, 111 U.S. 379, 382 (1884) ("the rule, springing from the nature and limits of the judicial power of the United States, is inflexible and without exception").

One would think, then, that learning about subject-matter jurisdiction—the fixed, inflexible, and without-exception brand of jurisdiction—should come first. Curiously, though, law students are often taught personal jurisdiction first in their study of civil procedure, usually because that journey offers students exposure to a number of other "learning moments" that their professors believe will enhance their mastery of the law. In any event, it is not jurisprudentially unsound to focus on personal jurisdiction first. In 1999, the Supreme Court ruled that there is "no unyielding . . . hierarchy" among types of jurisdiction and that, while it may be customary to examine a court's subject-matter jurisdiction first, a court does not necessarily act improperly by choosing to start with personal jurisdiction. *Ruhrgas AG v. Marathon Oil Co.*, 526 U.S. 574, 578 (1999). Because many law students' study of civil procedure begins with personal jurisdiction, it is to there that we will first turn.

§ 2.3 Personal Jurisdiction Types: *In Personam* and *In Rem*

Personal jurisdiction is the court's authority to exert its coercive judicial power over certain persons, entities, or things. It is a *litigant*-focused brand of jurisdiction. It requires an examination of whether it is lawful and fair for the court to issue a ruling that binds *these* particular persons, *these* particular entities, or *these* particular things (or parcels of property).

The law has traditionally recognized two types of personal jurisdiction: *in personam* jurisdiction (where the court's power rests on its authority over a defendant's person) and *in rem* jurisdiction (where the court's power rests on its authority over a defendant's property located within the territory of the court). *See Shaffer v. Heitner*, 433 U.S. 186, 199 (1977). The requirements for exercising these types of personal jurisdiction are described below.

Note, however, that personal jurisdiction under one or the other of these types must exist as to each claim in a lawsuit. If the court lacks personal jurisdiction over the defendant (or property) as to certain of the lawsuit's claims, it will likely be required to dismiss those claims (absent the defendant's consent or a waiver of the defendant's right to object). One exception, recognized by some federal courts, provides a caveat to this all-claims requirement. If the federal court finds that it possesses personal jurisdiction as to certain claims in the lawsuit, it might nonetheless be permitted to exercise "pendent" personal jurisdiction as to the remaining claims in the lawsuit so long as they arise out of the same "common nucleus of operative facts" as the claims for which personal jurisdiction exists. *See Picot v. Weston*, 780 F.3d 1206, 1211 (9th Cir. 2015).

§ 2.4 Personal Jurisdiction Requirements: The Two-Step Personal Jurisdiction Inquiry

A two-step inquiry is needed to determine whether a court may exercise personal jurisdiction over a particular defendant. First, the court must have been granted authority by its legislature to act against the particular defendant (the "legislative" step). Second, the court's use of that legislatively-granted authority must not offend the United States Constitution (the "constitutional" step). Unless both of these steps are met, the court will lack personal jurisdiction over that defendant and, absent the defendant's consent or waiver, may not proceed to bind the defendant with a judicial ruling. *See*

United Techs. Corp. v. Mazer, 556 F.3d 1260, 1275 n.15 (11th Cir. 2009) (because personal jurisdiction failed under the legislative step, court did not proceed on to consider the constitutional step).

How to Challenge Personal Jurisdiction

A judge's exercise of personal jurisdiction can be challenged by filing a pre-answer motion to dismiss on that ground, by raising (and thereafter dutifully preserving) that objection in a responsive pleading, or in certain circumstances by collateral attack following a default. *See* Rule 12(b)(2).

Burden of Proving Personal Jurisdiction

Ordinarily, the party invoking the court's personal jurisdiction bears the burden of demonstrating that it exists. Thus, that burden typically falls on the plaintiff, but usually is not triggered unless and until the defendant contests the court's right to exercise personal jurisdiction. The nature of the burden and how it is carried depends on the manner of the defendant's challenge. *See* Rule 12(b)(2).

Jurisdictional Discovery

On occasion, a party may contend that its adversary is, alone, in possession of the facts needed to show that sufficient forum-related contacts exist (or do not exist) to allow personal jurisdiction. In such circumstances the presiding judge may grant limited discovery so that the seeking party can endeavor to obtain that jurisdictional evidence. Before authorizing such discovery, judges normally require the seeking party to propose more than a hopeful fishing expedition. Instead, that party ordinarily must make a good faith showing that its targeted discovery might lead to facts confirming the existence of personal jurisdiction over the adversary.

§ 2.4a Personal Jurisdiction Requirements: The "Legislative" Step

The first step in establishing personal jurisdiction is satisfying the legislature's requirements for the exercise of judicial power over the particular defendant. Each legislature is entitled to determine how much personal jurisdiction authority to impart to its courts.

PRACTICING LAW WITH THIS PRINCIPLE

State-Granted Power: Resident Defendants

State legislatures often grant their courts very broad judicial authority over defendants who reside within their borders. (For personal jurisdiction purposes, "reside" means more than temporary presence—it generally means citizenship.) South Carolina is a good example. Its legislature grants the South Carolina courts the authority to exercise personal jurisdiction over any cause of action against a defendant who is domiciled in the State, is organized under the laws of the State, maintains its principal place of business in the State, or is doing business in the State. *See* S.C. Code § 36–2–802.

State-Granted Power: Non-Resident Defendants

When the defendant does not reside within the State's borders, the grant of personal jurisdiction by the State legislatures is (and must be) more tightly constrained. These grants, often called "long-arm statutes," can vary greatly by State. Florida is a good example of this type of authority. Its legislature permits the Florida courts to exercise personal jurisdiction over a non-resident defendant as to a cause of action arising from nine different categories of Florida-related behavior, including: operating a business in Florida, committing a tort in Florida, breaching a contract in Florida, or insuring a person located in Florida. *See* Fla. Stat. § 48.193(1)(a).

State-Granted Power: "Unenumerated" Authority

Other State legislatures grant their courts "unenumerated" judicial authority, permitting those courts to exercise personal jurisdiction to the greatest extent that the U.S. Constitution will tolerate. Wyoming is a good example of this type of "unenumerated" grant. *See* Wyo. Stat. 5–1–

107(a) ("A Wyoming court may exercise jurisdiction on any basis not inconsistent with the Wyoming or United States constitution.").

Federally-Granted Power

The allowable personal jurisdiction reach of the federal courts is set out in Rule 4(k) of the Federal Rules of Civil Procedure, which is discussed in greater detail in the Rules section of this text. By way of overview, that Rule grants the federal courts the right to exercise personal jurisdiction in four circumstances:

- *Borrowed State Statute:* when the State courts in the State where the federal court is located would be able to exercise personal jurisdiction over the defendant; or
- *Congress Allows:* when Congress, by federal statute, permits the federal court to exercise personal jurisdiction over the defendant; or
- *The 100-Mile Bulge Rule:* when the defendant is joined into the lawsuit by Rule 14 (third-party practice) or Rule 19 (required party joinder) and served within a federal district that is not more than 100 miles from where the lawsuit is pending; or
- *National-Contacts Personal Jurisdiction:* when the defendant is being sued for a claim arising under federal law and is not subject to the personal jurisdiction of any individual U.S. State's courts, so long as exercising personal jurisdiction would be consistent with the federal Constitution and federal laws.

§ 2.4b Personal Jurisdiction Requirements: The "Constitutional" Step

The second step in establishing personal jurisdiction—the "constitutional" step—is satisfied if the court's exercise of its legislatively-granted personal jurisdiction authority will not offend the due process guarantee memorialized in the U.S. Constitution. Thus, the Constitution acts as the outer limit of a court's personal jurisdiction authority: courts may make full use of the personal jurisdiction authority granted them by their legislatures, but only so long as doing so would not offend constitutional due process.

PRACTICING LAW WITH THIS PRINCIPLE

Two Different Due Process Clauses

The Constitution contains two Due Process Clauses. The first, in the Fifth Amendment, imposes the due process constraint when federal courts rule. The second, in the Fourteenth Amendment, imposes the same[2] constraint when State courts rule.

The Meaning of "Due Process"

The Due Process Clauses ordinarily bar a court from reaching out to render a binding judgment against anyone with whom the sovereign has no contacts, ties, or other relations. *See Int'l Shoe Co. v. Washington*, 326 U.S. 310, 319 (1945). In this way, the Clauses are understood as protecting litigants from being burdened by the chore of having to travel to a distant or inconvenient forum in order to see that justice is done. *See World-Wide Volkswagen Corp. v. Woodson*, 444 U.S. 286, 292 (1980). But inconvenience, alone, does not answer this inquiry. Indeed, jurisdiction might be prohibited even when the defendant would actually be inconvenienced only slightly (or not at all) and even when the chosen forum has a strong interest in applying its law and can do so efficiently. *See Bristol-Myers Squibb Co. v. Superior Court*, 137 S. Ct. 1773 (2017). This is so because of the territorial limitations on each State's sovereignty: each State has the sovereign authority to try cases in its own courts and the companion power to limit the encroaching reach of sister States into its borders. *See id.* at 1780. Courts must have

[2] Courts have long assumed that the Fifth Amendment Due Process Clause and the Fourteenth Amendment Due Process Clause operate identically. The Supreme Court, though, has not yet squarely confirmed this assumption. *See, e.g., Bristol-Myers Squibb Co. v. Superior Court*, 137 S. Ct. 1173, 1783–84 (2017); *Omni Capital Int'l, Ltd. v. Rudolf Wolff & Co.*, 484 U.S. 97, 102 n.5 (1987).

constitutionally adequate personal jurisdiction over every party or thing over which they will act. Consequently, due process must be satisfied as to everyone in the lawsuit. *See Rush v. Savchuk*, 444 U.S. 320, 332 (1980).

Consequences of Violating Due Process

If a court were to violate the constitutional due process limit on its personal jurisdiction and issue a ruling nonetheless, that decision would be void in the place where it was entered and not entitled to full faith and credit (including enforcement) anywhere else. *See World-Wide Volkswagen Corp.*, 444 U.S. at 291.

Can Be Waived or Forfeited

Because personal jurisdiction is a litigant protection (and not a structural constraint, like subject-matter jurisdiction), it can be waived by the parties or forfeited by a failure to properly or timely assert it. *See Insurance Corp. of Ireland v. Compagnie des Bauxites de Guinee*, 456 U.S. 694, 703 (1982).

§ 2.5 Personal Jurisdiction Type: *In Personam* Jurisdiction

When a court rests its exercise of personal jurisdiction on its authority over a defendant's person, it is invoking *in personam* personal jurisdiction. This type of personal jurisdiction can be exercised over natural persons (people) or entities (like corporations, partnerships, and other sorts of associations). When a court issues a lawful judgment *in personam*, that ruling is a binding one that may be enforced against the defendant wherever that defendant (or that defendant's property) may be found. *See Shaffer v. Heitner*, 433 U.S. 186, 210 (1977) ("The Full Faith and Credit Clause, after all, makes the valid in personam judgment of one State enforceable in all other States.").

Exercises of *in personam* personal jurisdiction satisfy the "constitutional" step when the court's use of its coercive authority over the defendant is not fundamentally unfair or unreasonable. The methods for testing this constitutionality are found principally in case law, and may be grouped into three classes: (1) where the party consents to personal jurisdiction; (2) where the party is served with original process while voluntarily present in the State where the court is sitting; or (3) where the party has a sufficient connection (or "contacts") with that State to deem jurisdiction proper.

PRACTICING LAW WITH THIS PRINCIPLE

Method #1—Consent to Jurisdiction

Because personal jurisdiction is intended to ensure that a party will not be obligated to litigate in an unfair or unreasonable forum, the parties are entitled to a voice in making that assessment. They are usually allowed to surrender this protection if they find it in their interests to do so, and they may *lose* this protection involuntarily if they fail to properly or timely assert it. *See Insurance Corp. of Ireland v. Compagnie des Bauxites de Guinee*, 456 U.S. 694, 704–05 (1982). *Plaintiffs* ordinarily cannot complain about the court's exercise of personal jurisdiction over them. After all, plaintiffs selected where to file their lawsuit, and are therefore deemed to have consented to the personal jurisdiction of the court where they filed. *See Adam v. Saenger*, 303 U.S. 59, 67–68 (1938). In other contexts, the consent inquiry can be more nuanced:

(1) *Consent by Advance Agreement:* By prior agreement or contract, parties can consent to a court's personal jurisdiction (though, be reminded: they *cannot* consent to subject-matter jurisdiction). *See National Equipment Rental, Ltd. v. Szukhent,* 375 U.S. 311, 315–16 (1964). This is true even where the forum the parties have selected would not otherwise have had personal jurisdiction over those parties. These sorts of agreements—often referred to as "forum selection clauses"—are routinely included in many business contracts; by including such clauses, the contracting parties negotiate, at the outset of their agreement, for the place where any future dispute under the contract will be heard and resolved. *See Burger King Corp. v. Rudzewicz*, 471 U.S. 462, 472 n.14 (1985). These clauses are generally upheld so long as they are contractually valid, absent some extraordinary circumstance. *See Atlantic Marine Const. Co. v. U.S. Dist. Ct. for W. Dist. of Texas*, 571 U.S.

49, 62 (2013). A consent clause like this might, for example, be invalid when there was substantially unequal bargaining power or duress among the parties that gave one side an unconstitutionally unfair advantage in choosing the jurisdiction or if there was no rational link between the chosen forum and the parties or their cause of action (*e.g.*, in a contract made in Georgia and to be performed by Georgians entirely in Georgia, the clause selects the Pacific Island of Guam as the forum for any litigation).

(2) *Consent by Waiver:* A party can also consent to the court's exercise of personal jurisdiction by not timely, properly objecting to the court's authority. *See* Rules 12(b)(2), 12(g), and 12(h)(1). This sort of consent can be done intentionally (where the party is willing to have the court proceed when personal jurisdiction would otherwise be improper) or unintentionally (by neglectfully failing to raise an objection, or failing to do so properly or timely). *See Insurance Corp. of Ireland*, 456 U.S. at 704–05.

(3) *Consent by Counterclaiming:* A plaintiff sued on a counterclaim may be deemed to have consented to personal jurisdiction on that counterclaim by the act of filing that plaintiff's original complaint. *See Adam,* 303 U.S. at 67–68. Conversely, a defendant is usually not deemed to have consented to personal jurisdiction when it both objects to personal jurisdiction but also simultaneously asserts some affirmative claim for relief (like, for instance, a counterclaim against the plaintiff).

(4) *Consent for the Limited Purpose of Determining Jurisdiction:* A party who objects to a court's personal jurisdiction is always deemed to have consented to that court's jurisdiction for the limited purpose of having that court determine whether personal jurisdiction exists. *See Insurance Corp. of Ireland,* 456 U.S. at 706.

Method #2—In-State Service (Transient or "Tag") Jurisdiction

A defendant served with original process while physically present within a State is normally subject to the personal jurisdiction of the State and federal trial courts within that State. *See Pennoyer v. Neff*, 95 U.S. 714, 733 (1878). It is irrelevant whether the defendant lives within the State or was just passing through; personal jurisdiction is present in such cases simply because the defendant was properly served within the State's physical territory. *See Burnham v. Superior Ct.,* 495 U.S. 604, 619 (1990) (plurality opinion). Of course, the served defendant must have been in the State voluntarily and not improperly enticed there by a fraud. Thus, drugging a person and driving her into the State or alarming a person into coming with a concocted tale of an urgent family illness will likely make an ensuing in-State "tag" of that person insufficient to confer personal jurisdiction.

- *Reasonableness/Fairness Inquiry:* The Supreme Court's most detailed discussion of "tag" jurisdiction appeared in a 1990 opinion. Although all nine Justices agreed in that case that "tag" jurisdiction was constitutionally proper, one nuance divided them. Four Justices believed that the longstanding "pedigree" of "tag" jurisdiction supplies automatic constitutional validation, without any further inquiry into reasonableness or fairness. *See Burnham,* 495 U.S. at 621 (plurality, by Scalia, J.). Four other Justices resisted that view, and would perform an "independent inquiry" into the reasonableness and fairness of exercising "tag"-based personal jurisdiction in each individual case, albeit with three narrowing caveats—"tag" is considered to be "consistent" with a defendant's "reasonable expectations," is "entitled to a strong presumption" of constitutionality, and, "as a rule," ought to be understood as satisfying due process. *See id.* at 629–39 (Brennan, J., concurring). Because neither view received support from a majority of the Court, the necessity for a separate case-specific inquiry into reasonableness / fairness remains uncertain nationally.

- *"Tagging" a Corporation:* Although it is discussed only sporadically in the case law, some courts have ruled that personal jurisdiction cannot be acquired over a corporation by "tagging" one of its officers who might be visiting the forum State. Those courts often reason that because corporations are recognized as a legal entity, separate and apart from their owners and employees, "tagging" a corporate officer cannot confer personal jurisdiction over the corporation. *See, e.g., Martinez v. Aero Caribbean*, 764 F.3d 1062, 1067–70 (9th Cir. 2014). *But see Northern Light Tech., Inc. v. Northern Lights Club*, 236 F.3d 57, 64 n.10 (1st Cir. 2001) (finding personal jurisdiction over corporate defendant based on tag of its officer). Bear in mind, however, the important distinction between a jurisdiction-conferring "tag" on a corporate officer (which some courts reject) and a Rules-compliant service of process on a corporate officer (which Rule 4 requires).

- *"Tagging" an Unincorporated Entity:* The availability of "tag" for acquiring personal jurisdiction over partnerships, limited liability companies, associations, and other unincorporated entities is even less frequently discussed. Some courts permit a jurisdiction-conferring "tag" on such entities' senior employees, perhaps because the company separateness that is a hallmark of corporations may not exist in unincorporated settings; other courts disagree.
- *Being "Tagged" While Contesting Personal Jurisdiction:* It is now settled that a litigant's act of contesting a federal court's personal jurisdiction will not, itself, constitute a waiver of those objections. For similar policy reasons, it would seem that a litigant's personal appearance in court for the purpose of arguing against personal jurisdiction should likewise not compromise those objections by affording the opponent a "tag" opportunity. No case law seems to have squarely confronted this question (beyond that case law that recognizes that a "special appearance" is not a waiver or consent to personal jurisdiction). Perhaps the case law silence is because the answer is so necessarily clear: to allow a jurisdiction-conferring "tag" on the arguing litigant would render illusory the Rules' procedures for how to properly contest personal jurisdiction.
- *"Tag" and the Legislative Authority Step:* Although the constitutionality of "tag" jurisdiction now seems well settled, the first consideration in every personal jurisdiction inquiry—the legislative step—must also be met. Here, a wrinkle emerges. Although some States have expressly codified "tag" jurisdiction as a legislatively authorized means for acquiring jurisdiction, others have not done so—but may recognize "tag" as a matter of common law.

Method #3—Contacts-Based Jurisdiction

Defendants who neither consent to personal jurisdiction in a State nor are served with original process while there may still be subject to that State's personal jurisdiction when they have adequate "contacts" (or connections) with that State to meet the Constitution's due process mandate. Two types of contacts-based personal jurisdiction exist—specific personal jurisdiction and general personal jurisdiction.

(1) ***Specific Jurisdiction:*** Personal jurisdiction is permitted over a defendant who has certain "minimum contacts" with the forum that the court's exercise of its judicial authority over that defendant would not offend "traditional notions of fair play and substantial justice." *See Int'l Shoe Co. v. Washington*, 326 U.S. 310, 316 (1945). This is "case-specific" and "conduct-linked" personal jurisdiction. It exists only where the cause of action at issue "aris[es] out of or relate[s] to" the defendant's purposeful actions directed into the forum. *See Daimler AG v. Bauman*, 571 U.S. 117, 122 (2014). *See generally Bristol-Myers Squibb Co. v. Superior Court*, 137 S. Ct. 1781 (2017) (defendant's unrelated connections with the forum will not support specific jurisdiction). A defendant who engages in such purposeful connections with the forum should reasonably foresee that it could be held to account in that forum should its behavior give rise to or relate to a cause of action there. *See World-Wide Volkswagen Corp. v. Woodson*, 444 U.S. 286, 297 (1980). In other words, a defendant's act of intentionally, purposefully choosing to connect with a forum can supply the requisite due process for a court in that forum to act in a lawsuit that arises from or relates to that connection. The test for specific personal jurisdiction is thus a two-part inquiry: (a) minimum contacts and (b) traditional notions of fair play and substantial justice.

- *"Minimum Contacts":* The first inquiry in assessing specific personal jurisdiction is the "minimum contacts" one. This inquiry is not wholly (or even principally) quantitative. Even a modest number of contacts with the forum (or even just one) might be sufficient. Rather than volume, this inquiry is really a qualitative one. The defendant must have engaged in some behavior through which it "purposefully avail[ed] itself of the privilege of conducting activities within the forum State, thus invoking the benefits and protections" of that State's laws. *Hanson v. Denckla*, 357 U.S. 235, 253 (1958). If it did so, *and* if the cause of action *arose out of* or *relates to* that behavior, then the defendant is deemed to have been placed on "fair warning" that it could be sued there. *See Burger King Corp. v. Rudzewicz*, 471 U.S. 462, 472–73 (1985).
  - *"Purposeful Availment":* To qualify as "minimum contacts," the connection must be *purposeful, with the forum*, and *by the defendant*. *See Walden v. Fiore*, 571 U.S. 277, 283–86 (2014). The contacts must be "the defendant's own choice" and "show that the defendant deliberately 'reached out beyond' its home—by, for example, 'exploi[ting] a market' in the forum State or entering a contractual relationship centered there." *See Ford Motor Co. v. Montana Eighth Jud. Dist. Ct.*, ___ U.S. ___, 141 S. Ct. 1017, 1025 (2021). A defendant's purposeful availment of the forum is understood as a "privilege" which, when enjoyed, invokes the "benefits and protections" of that forum's laws. *See J. McIntyre Mach., Ltd. v. Nicastro*, 564 U.S. 873, 880 (2011). That, in turn, triggers a reciprocal obligation to return there to litigate a related dispute. *See Int'l Shoe Co.*, 326 U.S. at 319. *See also Ford Motor Co.*, 141 S. Ct. at 1029–30 (enjoying benefits and protections "creates reciprocal obligations"). Thus, neither "random," "fortuitous," or "attenuated" contacts, nor the unilateral acts of some third-party, will be enough to establish "minimum contacts." *See Burger King Corp.*, 471 U.S. at 475.
    - *Physical Contacts Not Always Necessary:* The connection needed to satisfy the "minimum contacts" test need not always be an in-person, physical one. *See Walden*, 571 U.S. at 283. For example, contracting in a manner that deliberately "reaches out" to create "continuing relationships and obligations" with another State's citizens might suffice, even in the absence of physical presence. *See Burger King Corp.*, 471 U.S. at 473–76.
    - *Contracting with a Forum Resident:* The mere existence of a contract with a forum resident cannot, alone, fulfill the purposeful availment obligation. *See Burger King Corp.*, 471 U.S. at 478–79. Nor will the mere inclusion in that contract of a choice-of-law clause (which selects a particular forum's substantial law to apply). Instead, courts look behind the fact of contracting to assess whether the agreement's negotiations, its terms, its contemplated future consequences, and the parties' actual course of dealing reveal that the defendant purposefully availed itself of the forum. *See id.*
    - *Placing Products in the "Stream of Commerce":* The Supreme Court has twice considered whether, and under what circumstances, the act of placing products into the "stream of commerce" can supply the purposeful availment needed to satisfy specific jurisdiction. Both times, the Court was unable to produce a majority opinion. *See J. McIntyre Machinery, Ltd. v. Nicastro,* 564 U.S. 873 (2011); *Asahi Metal Industry Co. v. Superior Ct.,* 480 U.S. 102 (1987). Three views divided the Court. Under the first view, specific jurisdiction would require that the defendant not only place the product in the stream of commerce but also undertake additional conduct revealing "an intent or purpose to serve the market in the forum state." *See Asahi Metal Industry,* 480 U.S. at 112 (O'Connor., J., "awareness-plus" test). Under the second view, a defendant's placement of the product in the stream of commerce would alone suffice for specific jurisdiction, provided the defendant was "aware that the

final product is being marketed in the forum State." *See id.* at 117 (Brennan, J., "mere awareness" test). Under the third view, purposeful availment would be assessed by examining the volume, value, and hazardous character of the products. *See id.* at 122 (Stevens, J.). In the Court's most recent (albeit unsuccessful) try, the decisive fifth and sixth votes skirted the issue by emphasizing that, at a minimum, "stream" theory could not rest on "a single, isolated sale." *See J. McIntyre Machinery, Ltd,* 564 U.S. at 888 (Breyer & Alito, JJ., concurring). Because there is no definitive ruling from the Supreme Court on "stream" theory, its formulation varies by circuit and by State.

- *Contacts with the Forum by the Plaintiff:* The "minimum contacts" inquiry focuses on whether the *defendant* has purposefully availed itself of the forum and, for that reason, is now exposed to personal jurisdiction there. There is no companion requirement that the *plaintiff* also have "minimum contacts" with the forum. *See Keeton v. Hustler Mag., Inc.*, 465 U.S. 770, 779 (1984). (Nor should there be, as the plaintiff consents to the judge's jurisdiction by choosing to file there, *see Adam v. Saenger*, 303 U.S. 59, 67–68 (1938)). Nor does the fact that a plaintiff *has* meaningful contacts with the forum mean that specific personal jurisdiction will necessarily exist there. *See Walden*, 571 U.S. at 284–86. Obviously, though, a plaintiff's location in the forum is not irrelevant: a defendant who purposefully reaches into the plaintiff's home forum in order to engage with that plaintiff there is the quintessential example of specific jurisdiction.

o *"Arises out of" or "Relates to":* In addition to forum contacts purposefully made by the defendant, "minimum contacts" also requires that the lawsuit "arise out of" or "relate to" the defendant's involvement with the forum. *See Goodyear Dunlop Tires Ops., S.A. v. Brown*, 564 U.S. 915, 919 (2011) ("specific jurisdiction is confined to adjudication of 'issues deriving from, or connected with, the very controversy that establishes jurisdiction' ") (citation omitted).

- "*Arises out of*" is self-explanatory—it is satisfied where the lawsuit's claims are causally connected to the defendant's purposeful activities in the forum (*i.e.*, the defendant's in-State activities actually produced the plaintiff's injury or loss).

- "*Relates to*" is less clear—it is satisfied by something less than a causal connection, though the Supreme Court has been quick to emphasize that this "does not mean anything goes." *Ford Motor Co.*, 141 S. Ct. at 1026. Thus, a plaintiff injured in her home State while using a defendant's product could sue there if that defendant had marketed, sold, and serviced the product in that State, even if the plaintiff had acquired the product outside the State. *Id.* at 1026–32. But a plaintiff injured in her home State by a defendant's product marketed, sold, and serviced in that State could not sue in another State merely because other plaintiffs, allegedly injured in the same way by the same product, were suing there. *See Bristol-Myers Squibb Co.*, 137 S. Ct. at 1781 ("What is needed—and what is missing here—is a connection between the forum and the specific claims at issue."). Although the reach of this "relates to" path remains uncertain, one conclusion seems very clear—even a hearty volume of contacts, without connectedness, will not suffice for specific jurisdiction. *See id.* ("When there is no [arising from/relates to] connection, specific jurisdiction is lacking regardless of the extent of a defendant's unconnected activities in the State.").

o *"Virtual" Contacts (Internet Activities):* The Supreme Court has yet to decide in any comprehensive manner how Internet activities count in a "minimum contacts" analysis. Lower courts, however, have not struggled much in this context. Merely posting on the Internet or creating Internet-accessible information is generally not sufficient to confer specific personal jurisdiction. Rather, "something more" has always been required. Although courts have used different terminology ("aiming," "targeting," "directing," "intentionality"), this "something more" seems generally to equate to the purposeful availment inquiry.

- *"Traditional Notions of Fair Play and Substantial Justice":* The second of the two specific personal jurisdiction inquiries considers whether an exercise of jurisdiction would "offend traditional notions of fair play and substantial justice." This inquiry is separate but *in addition to* the "minimum contacts" inquiry discussed above. Thus, even if a defendant has qualifying "minimum contacts" with the forum, if the exercise of jurisdiction there would prove so pulverizingly difficult—so oppressive that it would offend traditional notions of fair play and substantial justice—specific personal jurisdiction would be improper. *See Burger King Corp.,* 471 U.S. at 476–78. The Supreme Court has supplied a non-exhaustive list of factors for use in making this fairness assessment. *See World-Wide Volkswagen Corp.,* 444 U.S. at 292. Those fairness factors are:

  (1) The defendant's burden in litigating in the forum court;

  (2) The forum State's interest in having the litigation in its own courts;

  (3) The plaintiff's interest in litigating in its chosen forum;

  (4) The interstate judicial system's interest in the most effective resolution of the entire litigation; and

  (5) The shared several States' interest in furthering substantive social policies.

  In lawsuits involving foreign nationals, the Court added the further precaution that "[g]reat care and reserve should be exercised when extending our notions of personal jurisdiction into the international field." *See Asahi Metal Indus. Co.*, 480 U.S. at 115.

- *Burdens of Proof:* It is the duty of the party asserting a claim (usually the plaintiff) to demonstrate that the court enjoys personal jurisdiction over each defendant. Particularly in the absence of an evidentiary hearing, a plaintiff's burden can be met simply by a prima facie demonstration of jurisdiction. (Even when that prima facie case is opposed, courts typically resolve all factual disputes in favor of the plaintiff.) If the court is satisfied that a defendant is shown to have had sufficient "minimum contacts" with a State, the burden then shifts to the defendant to make "a compelling case" demonstrating why the court's exercise of personal jurisdiction would be unjust. *See Burger King Corp.,* 471 U.S. at 477.

(2) ***General Jurisdiction:*** Unlike specific personal jurisdiction, general personal jurisdiction is *not* case-specific or conduct-linked. Indeed, to satisfy general personal jurisdiction, a defendant's contacts are not required to have any connection at all to the cause of action. When general jurisdiction exists over a defendant in a particular forum, that forum may hear and rule upon any claim against that defendant wherever it may have arisen. *See Bristol-Myers Squibb Co. v. Superior Ct.*, 582 U.S. ___, 137 S. Ct. 1773, 1780 (2017). For this reason, general jurisdiction has been dubbed "all-purpose" jurisdiction. *See Goodyear Dunlop Tires Ops., S.A. v. Brown*, 564 U.S. 915, 919 (2011). But this "sweeping" adjudicative breadth carries with it an important, corresponding limit. General jurisdiction may only be exercised in a forum where a defendant's contacts are so "continuous and systematic," "so constant and pervasive," as "to render [the defendant] essentially at home" there. *See Daimler AG v. Bauman*, 571 U.S. 117, 122 (2014); *Goodyear Dunlop Tires Ops, S.A.*, 564 U.S. at 919. This test invites an inquiry into more than just the magnitude of a defendants contacts with a forum; it instead compels "an appraisal of a corporation's activities in their entirety, nationwide and worldwide." *See Daimler AG*, 571 U.S. at 139 n.20. Due to its narrow availability, this brand of personal jurisdiction has come to play a

reduced role in contemporary litigation. Nonetheless, general jurisdiction persists to achieve one very important objective: to ensure that plaintiffs always have "at least one clear and certain forum" where they can sue any defendant. *See Daimler AG*, 571 U.S. at 139.

- *How Much Is Enough?:* The Court has supplied clues, but no definitive measure for testing where a defendant is "at home" or "essentially at home." For individuals, the Court has labeled domicile as the "home" for natural persons—their "paradigm forum" for general jurisdiction. For corporations, that paradigm forum (their "home") appears to be both the place of incorporation and the principal place of business. *See Goodyear Dunlop Tire Ops.*, 564 U.S. at 924. But, in "an exceptional case," defendants can be "essentially" at home in a location that is not their actual home. The Court has cited its decision in *Perkins v. Benquet Consolidated Mining Co.*, 342 U.S. 437 (1952), as "the textbook case" of such an instance. *See Goodyear Dunlop Tire Ops.*, 564 U.S. at 927–28. In *Perkins*, wartime necessity required a Philippine mining company to cease its home operations and conduct all its business activities in Ohio. Although the cause of action in that case had nothing to do with Ohio, the Court ruled that the company could be sued there under general personal jurisdiction.
- *How Much Isn't Enough?:* The Court has emphasized that the magnitude of contacts with the forum, alone, is not the sole focus of general jurisdiction; rather, that contact volume must be appraised in its entirety to assess whether it renders the defendant "essentially at home" there. *Cf. Daimler AG*, 571 U.S. at 139 n.20 ("A corporation that operates in many places can scarcely be deemed at home in all of them."). Conducting this inquiry, the Court has rebuffed all recent attempts at asserting general personal jurisdiction against a company at locations other than its place of incorporation or principal place of business. *See BNSF Rwy. Co.*, 137 S. Ct. at 1559 (more than 2,000 miles of permanent, in-forum railroad track and 2,100 in-forum employees not sufficient); *Daimler AG*, 571 U.S. at 138–39 (doing business (even in substantial volume) in forum not sufficient); *Goodyear Dunlop Tire Ops.*, 564 U.S. at 921–29 (2011) (delivering tens of thousands of tires into forum not sufficient); *Helicopteros Nacionales de Colombia, S.A. v. Hall*, 466 U.S. 408, 418 (1984) (mere purchases (even at regular intervals) and training sessions in forum not sufficient). In fact, the Court's measuring stick for general jurisdiction outside the "paradigm" forums seems to be how closely (or not) a case's facts mirror those in *Perkins*. *See Goodyear Dunlop Tire Ops., S.A.*, 564 U.S. at 929 ("Unlike the defendant in *Perkins*, whose sole wartime business activity was conducted in Ohio, petitioners are in no sense at home in North Carolina.").
- *No "Traditional Notions of Fair Play" Inquiry:* Unlike specific jurisdiction, there is no second-stage inquiry for general personal jurisdiction. The "traditional notions of fair play and substantial justice" factors are immaterial to this type of jurisdiction. Because general jurisdiction exists only where a defendant is "genuinely at home," inquiring whether it would be fair and reasonable to expect the defendant to litigate there is considered "superfluous." *See Daimler AG*, 571 U.S. at 139 n.20.

(3) ***Connecting Specific Jurisdiction and General Jurisdiction:*** Over the years, courts and scholars have endeavored to connect, or align, specific jurisdiction with general jurisdiction in a manner that would plot those two types of jurisdiction on a type of continuum. Lawyers often argued personal jurisdiction relying on just that understanding (*e.g.*, "Your Honor, as we've shown, there are insufficient contacts here to support specific jurisdiction, and, of course, if there are not enough contacts for specific jurisdiction, then there could not possibly be enough for general jurisdiction"). The Supreme Court's recent personal jurisdiction case law belies this sort of analysis. Specific (or "case-linked") jurisdiction is anchored to connectedness—some injury, loss, or obligation must have been caused by or must relate to the defendant's purposefully-availing activities with that forum. In contrast, general (or "all-purpose") jurisdiction is anchored to pinpointing where the defendant is at (or "essentially" at) home. The inquiries ask different questions. Accordingly, exercising specific jurisdiction over a defendant might be possible where

general jurisdiction is not, just as exercising general jurisdiction over a defendant might be possible where specific jurisdiction is not. *Cf. Bristol-Myers Squibb Co.*, 137 S. Ct. at 1778 (noting lower courts' decision that general jurisdiction was lacking, then turning to assess specific jurisdiction); *Goodyear Dunlop Tire Ops.*, 564 U.S. at 919–20 (noting that specific jurisdiction was lacking, then turning to examine general jurisdiction). *See generally Helicopteros Nacionales de Colombia, S.A.*, 466 U.S. at 415–16 (parties concede claims did not arise out of or relate to contacts with the forum, so Court "must explore" whether forum contacts "constitute the kind of continuous and systematic" contacts required of general jurisdiction).

- *No Middle Ground Between Specific and General Jurisdiction:* Embracing similar reasoning, a few courts had earlier supposed that some middle jurisdictional possibility lay between specific and general jurisdiction, a conceptual area where a combination of *some connectedness* between contacts and cause of action (but not enough for specific jurisdiction) and *some heavier* volume of contacts (but not enough for general jurisdiction) could justify a court's exercise of its judicial power. The Supreme Court seems to have now rejected this possibility as "elid[ing] the essential difference between case-linked (specific) and all-purpose (general) jurisdiction." *See Goodyear Dunlop Tire Ops.*, 564 U.S. at 927. *See also id.* at 919–20 (chiding the lower court for "[c]onfusing or blending general and specific jurisdictional inquiries").

Jurisdictional Discovery

Sometimes a plaintiff will allege that the defendant alone has possession of the facts needed to show the sufficient forum-related contacts to support personal jurisdiction. In such circumstances a court may grant limited discovery so that the plaintiff can endeavor to obtain that jurisdictional evidence. Before authorizing such discovery, courts normally require plaintiff to propose more than a hopeful fishing expedition. Instead, plaintiffs ordinarily must make a good faith showing that their targeted discovery might lead to facts confirming the existence of personal jurisdiction over the defendant. If jurisdictional discovery is allowed, it will take place within the Rules governing discovery discussed later in this text.

§ 2.6 Personal Jurisdiction Type: *In Rem* Jurisdiction

When a court rests its exercise of personal jurisdiction on its authority over property within its territory, it is invoking either *in rem* or *quasi in rem* personal jurisdiction. When a judge rests the exercise of personal jurisdiction on authority over property within the court's territory, the judge is invoking either *in rem* or *quasi in rem* personal jurisdiction. In such cases, the resulting judgment is understood as operating directly on the property itself. The difference between these two types of property-based jurisdiction hinges on whom the judge's judgment will affect. A judgment *in rem* generally affects (and binds) the interests of all persons everywhere who might claim an interest in the property. *See Hanson v. Denckla*, 357 U.S. 235, 246 n.12 (1958) ("affects the interests of all persons in designated property"); *Becher v. Contoure Labs.*, 279 U.S. 388, 391 (1929) ("binds all the world"). Conversely, a judgment *quasi in rem* affects only the interests of particular persons. *See Shaffer v. Heitner*, 433 U.S. 186, 199 n.17 (1977); *Hanson v. Denckla*, 357 U.S. 235, 246 n.12 (1958). *In rem* is discussed in this section; *quasi in rem* in discussed in the next.

PRACTICING LAW WITH THIS PRINCIPLE

Objective of *In Rem* Actions

The goal in *in rem* proceedings is ordinarily to determine the ownership of (*i.e.*, title to) property that is located within the territory of the court. Such jurisdiction is commonly invoked in admiralty (where a vessel is seized), in bankruptcy (where debtor assets are seized), and in civil condemnation (where instrumentality of a crime is seized by the government).

Limited Effect of *In Rem* Judgments

The effect of a judgment *in rem* is necessarily limited to the property that has been seized and on which the jurisdiction rests. Such a judgment imposes no personal liability on the property's owner (because that owner has not been brought within the court's *in personam* reach). *See Shaffer*, 433 U.S. at 199. Accordingly, unlike *in personam* judgments, a judgment *in rem* cannot be enforced elsewhere under the Constitution's Full Faith and Credit Clause.

Prerequisites for Exercising *In Rem* Jurisdiction

Although *in rem* case law can often be old and sparse, the following general prerequisites to the exercise of *in rem* jurisdiction appear common:

(1) *Property With Value:* Because jurisdiction cannot be invoked to perform a useless act and because *in rem* jurisdiction is constrained to the value of the property in question, that property must have some value.

(2) *Property Located in the Forum:* A court's *in rem* authority rests on its ability to exercise physical power over the property at issue; consequently, the property in question must lie within the territorial jurisdiction (*i.e.*, within the reach) of the tribunal. *See Hanson*, 357 U.S. at 246, 250. The consequence of the property's later removal from the forum, following proper initiation of the *in rem* lawsuit, can be less clear.

(3) *Property Seized By the Court:* The court must acquire effective control of the property in question by a judicial seizure. *See United States v. Ursery*, 518 U.S. 267, 277 (1996). The timing of this seizure is important: it must occur at the outset of the litigation, since doing so serves the companion goal of ensuring notice to those having a custodial interest in the property. *See Pennoyer v. Neff*, 95 U.S. 714, 727 (1877). The manner of accomplishing the seizure will depend on the nature of the property seized; actual, physical possession by the court is not always necessary (it may instead be sufficient for the court to effectively interfere with control over the property). *See United States v. James Daniel Good Real Prop.*, 510 U.S. 43, 57–58 (1993). For example, seizing a tract of land might be accomplished by a judicial order directing the local land records office to freeze the property's title, pending the outcome of the lawsuit. Seizing intangible property, like shares of stock, might be achieved by an order directing the appropriate authority to halt trading in those shares. Conversely, if the property is jewelry or a vehicle, the court might direct the U.S. Marshal to take physical custody of the property. Some courts have held that this prerequisite of seizure can be excused with litigants' consent or by waiver.

(4) *Lawful Notice Given:* Proper notice of the seizure must be given. *See Shaffer*, 433 U.S. at 206. The requisite notice must meet both constitutional requirements (fixed by the Due Process Clause) and service requirements (set by Rule 4). Although, at one time, posting physical notice "upon the thing itself" would likely suffice in most *in rem* cases, the Constitution today is more nuanced—the manner of notice will be examined more particularly to assess "its ability to inform people of the pendency of proceedings that affect their interests." *See Greene v. Lindsey*, 456 U.S. 444, 451–56 (1982).

(5) *Constitutionally Proper:* Reasoning that, at base, *in rem* judgments do not really act *against property*, but rather act *against the owner's interest in that property*, the standard for assessing whether an exercise of *in rem* jurisdiction comports with constitutional due process is the same standard used to assess the exercise of jurisdiction over persons and their interests generally—namely, the specific jurisdiction test (discussed above). *See Shaffer*, 433 U.S. at 212. Because *in rem* lawsuits endeavor to definitively determine the title owner of property that is both located within the court's territory and by then seized by the court, it "would be unusual" for that court to lack such jurisdiction under this standard. *See id.* at 207–08.

Additional Prerequisite for Federal Courts

In addition to the general prerequisites noted above, Rule 4(n) limits the circumstances under which federal courts may exercise *in rem* jurisdiction. Federal courts may invoke *in rem* jurisdiction when some federal statute permits it. In that situation, the appropriate notice to claimants is that set by the applicable statute (or by following the relevant provisions of the federal service of process rule, Rule 4). Otherwise, federal courts may use *in rem* only upon a showing that *in personam* jurisdiction cannot be not obtained in the forum "by reasonable efforts" under Rule 4. In that latter circumstance, *in rem* jurisdiction is obtained by seizing the property "under the circumstances and in the manner" provided by the applicable State law.

No Dueling Exercises of *In Rem* Jurisdiction

If two *in rem* (or *quasi in rem*) actions are filed against the same property, one in State court and the other in federal court, the court first to acquire its jurisdiction or first to assume control of the property is entitled to proceed and the other court must yield. *See Princess Lida of Thurn & Taxis v. Thompson*, 305 U.S. 456, 466–67 (1939). If the first court is federal, it may, if necessary, issue an order restraining the further prosecution of the State proceeding. *See Mandeville v. Canterbury*, 318 U.S. 47, 48–49 (1943). Relatedly, after one court establishes *in rem* jurisdiction over property, no second court will assume *in rem* jurisdiction over the same property. *See Marshall v. Marshall,* 547 U.S. 293, 311 (2006).

§ 2.7 Personal Jurisdiction Type: *Quasi In Rem* Jurisdiction

Like *in rem* jurisdiction, *quasi in rem* personal jurisdiction rests on the court's authority over property within its territory. As noted earlier, unlike a judgment *in rem*, a judgment *quasi in rem* affects only the interests of the particular parties in the lawsuit. *See Shaffer v. Heitner*, 433 U.S. 186, 199 n.17 (1977).

PRACTICING LAW WITH THIS PRINCIPLE

Two Types of *Quasi In Rem* Actions

The law recognizes two types of *quasi in rem* lawsuits, each with different goals.

The first type (commonly labeled "***Quasi In Rem* Type #1**") is ordinarily a title fight between competing claimants to the same property, where the litigants each seek to persuade the court that (a) their claim to the property is superior to that of their opponents and (b) their opponents' claims should be declared extinguished. *See Shaffer*, 433 U.S. at 199 n.17; *Hanson v. Denckla*, 357 U.S. 235, 246 n.12 (1958). The difference, then, between this first type and *in rem* lawsuits is merely the scope of the resulting judgment (*i.e.*, binds the litigants only *versus* binds the world).

The second type (commonly labeled "***Quasi In Rem* Type #2**") is much different. It involves no competing claims to title, but rather rests on the presumption that the defendant is the one, true, lawful owner of the property in question. A plaintiff's objective in this second type of *quasi in rem* is to win the property in order to satisfy some claim that the plaintiff has against the defendant (a claim which, incidentally, might have no relationship of any kind to the seized property). *See Shaffer*, 433 U.S. at 199 n.17. Functionally, this second *quasi in rem* type is a means for collecting on a debt or other obligation, and had been used principally when the debtor was outside the court's reach but his or her property was not. Today, for constitutional reasons (discussed below), that use is often unavailable. But the strategic value of this second type of *quasi in rem* persists—when available, it may dramatically encumber a defendant's in-forum assets in a way that could prompt great urgency in seeing to it that the pending lawsuit (or at least the property's seizure) is expeditiously resolved. *See Shaffer*, 433 U.S. at 191–92 n.7 (*quasi in rem* used to seize stock shares belonging to individual officers and directors of corporation, valued collectively at time of seizure in May 1974 at approximately $1.2 million).

Limited Effect of *Quasi in Rem* Judgments

The effect of a judgment *quasi in rem* is limited to the property that has been seized and on which the jurisdiction rests, just as is true with *in rem* judgments. *Quasi in rem* judgments impose no personal liability on the property's owner and will not trigger the Constitution's Full Faith and Credit Clause in a way that would allow enforcement elsewhere of any judgment shortfall.

Prerequisites for Exercising *Quasi in Rem* Jurisdiction

The *in rem* discussion above listed five jurisdictional prerequisites, an additional prerequisite when litigating in federal court, and the no-dueling-jurisdiction principle. All apply in *quasi in rem* lawsuits as well.

Nuances in *Quasi In Rem Type #2* Lawsuits

Lawsuits filed as *in rem* or *quasi in rem type #1* actions proceed similarly. But *quasi in rem type #2* actions are meaningfully different in nature, which implicates several noteworthy nuances for practice:

(a) *Importance of Defendant's Ownership:* Settled ownership is central to *quasi in rem type #2* lawsuits: whereas *in rem* and *quasi in rem type #1* lawsuits are endeavoring to discern who the rightful owner of the seized property is, *quasi in rem type #2* lawsuits are premised on a conviction that the property owner's identity is already clearly known.

(b) *Importance of the Seized Property's Value:* In most *quasi in rem type #2* lawsuits, the endgame is liquidating the defendant's seized asset to generate funds that will then be used to pay off a debt or obligation owed to the plaintiff. Thus, the convertible value of the seized asset assumes special importance. That importance is accentuated by two attributes of *quasi in rem* litigation: first, the defendant's potential exposure is limited to the value of the seized asset and, as noted above, there is no full-faith-and-credit transferability. Ergo, if a plaintiff's claim is worth, say, $500,000, but the only in-forum asset of the defendant is a $4,000 used car, the attractiveness of *quasi in rem type #2* disappears.

(c) *Formidable Constitutional Hurdle:* Some have described *quasi in rem type #2* lawsuits as "basically a halfway house between *in rem* and *in personam* jurisdiction"—they are not really actions against the seized property, but in truth are actions against the person of the defendant using the expedient of her in-forum property to acquire an adjudicative power against her that, because of her lack of forum presence, would not otherwise exist. Predictably, then, a *quasi in rem type #2* lawsuit's comportment with constitutional due process is tested using the *International Shoe* specific jurisdiction analysis (discussed earlier). *See Shaffer*, 433 U.S. at 212. That standard requires that the defendant not only have purposeful contacts with the forum, but also that those purposeful contacts give rise or relate to the lawsuit's claims. This will pose a formidable, often unsurmountable obstacle when the seized property in a *quasi in rem type #2* lawsuit has no connection to the plaintiff's claim. *See id.* at 208–09.

   i. *Then, Why Ever Consider Quasi In Rem Type #2?* If property-based *quasi in rem type #2* lawsuits are tested by (and limited by) the same person-based standards as *in personam* lawsuits, why would a litigant ever want to pursue the former if the latter was feasible? After all, *quasi in rem type #2* lawsuits are constrained in ways *in personam* judgments are not—they are limited by the value of the seized asset and non-transferable under full faith and credit principles. Often, litigation strategy supplies the answer to this query: by encumbering an opponent's valuable, in-forum property in a *quasi in rem* proceeding, an opponent (who otherwise may lie outside the court's reach) may be coaxed into consenting to the forum's exercise of *in personam* jurisdiction in order to have that encumbered property released. As noted above, however, because the *International Shoe* standards govern, the opportunity for such *quasi in rem type #2* lawsuits is far more restricted than before.

   ii. *Not a Hurdle When Merely Enforcing Lawful Judgments:* The *International Shoe* test is not implicated when a plaintiff, who has already fully litigated her claim against the defendant elsewhere in a court of competent jurisdiction, is merely seeking to enforce that out-of-State judgment against the defendant's assets located in the forum. Such enforcement is ensured by the Constitution's Full Faith and Credit Clause; to that use the *International Shoe* test poses no impediment. *See Shaffer*, 433 U.S. at 210, n.36.

Defendant's Default-or-Submit Dilemma: Threatened with the loss of its property, a defendant in a *quasi in rem type #2* lawsuit might desire to come into the forum to defend against that claim on its merits, but doing so places the defendant at peril. By appearing in the forum to defend, that defendant may be vulnerable there to being "tagged" with service of process, which would confer *in personam* jurisdiction and expose the defendant to personal liability for the full amount of the claim—and that judgment would be entitled to full-faith-and-credit transferability. Some courts have rescued defendants from this "default-or-submit" dilemma by allowing them to make a "limited appearance" in the forum to defend against the *quasi in rem type #2* claim, immune from "tag" jurisdiction. *See United States v. First Nat. City Bank,* 379 U.S. 378, 390 (1965) (surveying case law).

§ 2.8 Personal Jurisdiction Wrap-Up: The Notice Requirement for Personal Jurisdiction

By exercising personal jurisdiction, a court exerts its coercive authority over the parties to the lawsuit and may (assuming all other prerequisites for invoking judicial power are met) render a final, binding, and enforceable civil judgment. Personal jurisdiction principles assesses when that authority over the litigants is possible. A further, albeit unsurprising precondition to personal jurisdiction is that the parties over whom the judge proposes to exercise this judicial power be given appropriate notice of that fact and an opportunity to appear and be heard.

PRACTICING LAW WITH THIS PRINCIPLE

Notice as a Precondition for Exercising Personal Jurisdiction

Proper notice is considered a prerequisite to the exercise of personal jurisdiction authority. *See BNSF Ry. Co. v. Tyrrell*, 581 U.S. ___, 137 S. Ct. 1549, 1556 (2017); *Omni Cap. Int'l, Ltd. v. Rudolf Wolff & Co.*, 484 U.S. 97, 104 (1987). More precisely, proper notice (through service of original process) is the procedural event by which a court asserts its coercive authority over a defending party. *See Mississippi Pub. Corp. v. Murphree*, 326 U.S. 438, 444–45 (1946). This relationship between personal jurisdiction and notice has historical lineage. At common law, a court would acquire personal jurisdiction over a defendant through a writ of *capias ad respondendum*, whereupon the sheriff would take the defendant into custody and bring him before the tribunal. *See Murphy Bros. v. Michetti Pipe Stringing, Inc.*, 526 U.S. 344, 350–51 (1999). Thus, in a very tangible sense, exercising judicial authority was "grounded" on a court's actual, physical "power over the defendant's person" or the defendant's property. *See Int'l Shoe Co. v. Washington*, 326 U.S. 310, 316 (1945). Notice, through service of original process, is "the contemporary counterpart to that writ." *See Murphy Bros.*, 526 U.S. at 350. Proper personal jurisdiction, then, remains merely inchoate until notice is accomplished: "Accordingly, one becomes a party officially, and is required to take action in that capacity, only upon service of a summons or other authority-asserting measure stating the time within which the party served must appear and defend." *See id.*

Notice Must, First, Satisfy the U.S. Constitution

The U.S. Constitution's Due Process Clause has long required appropriate notice in civil lawsuits. *See Pennoyer v. Neff*, 95 U.S. 714 (1877). Notice is considered essential to due process because it facilitates the Constitution's "fundamental requisite" of the defendant's right to an opportunity to be heard: "This right to be heard has little reality or worth unless one is informed that the matter is pending and can choose for himself whether to appear or default, acquiesce or contest." *See Mullane v. Cent. Hanover Bank & Tr. Co.*, 339 U.S. 306, 314 (1950).

Interestingly, given the paramount importance it assigns to proper notice, the U.S. Supreme Court has never ruled that *actually* receiving notice is constitutionally indispensable. *See Jones v. Flowers*, 547 U.S. 220, 226 (2006); *Dusenbery v. United States*, 534 U.S. 161, 171 (2002). Sometimes, actual notice may be impractical or even impossible. But "a mere gesture" or idle attempt at notice will violate due process. *See Mullane*, 339 U.S. at 315. Instead, the means chosen to impart notice "must be such as one desirous of actually informing the absentee might reasonably adopt to accomplish it," or, in an often-recounted phrase, "reasonably calculated, under all the circumstances, to apprise interested parties of the pendency of the action and afford them an opportunity to present their objections." *See id.* To meet this standard, the notice method must either "in itself [be] reasonably certain to inform those affected" or, if that is not possible, must not be "substantially less likely to bring home notice than other of the feasible and customary substitutes." *See id.* Actual, in-hand delivery of written notice to defendants while they are present within the forum "is the classic form of notice" and is "always adequate in any type of proceeding." *See id.* at 313. Whether different means of delivery will satisfy due process will depend on "the practicalities and peculiarities" of each case. *See id.* at 314–15. Few bright-line constitutional guideposts exist. However, the Court has determined that notice, even if originally proper at the time it was given, may be rendered inadequate if the sender comes to learn the notice failed; in such a case, due process may require a further attempt at notice if, under the circumstances of the case, a further attempt would be reasonable. *See Jones*, 547 U.S. at 229–30.

Notice Must, Second, Also Satisfy the Federal Rules

In addition to being constitutionally adequate, notice in a federal lawsuit must also meet the federal service requirements set out in Rule 4, which are discussed in depth later in this text. Thus, showing that the defendant received actual notice of the lawsuit or that constitutional due process was otherwise met will usually not excuse a failure to satisfy the Rule requirements for proper federal service of process.

Notice Obligation May Be Waived

Because they are intended to safeguard a defendant's interests, a defendant can voluntarily surrender or involuntarily lose an otherwise meritorious challenge to improper service by consent, waiver, or failure to properly and timely assert (and then press) that objection. Indeed, the Rules codify a procedure for formally inviting a defendant to waive formal notice through service of process, in exchange for an extended time to respond to the serving party's complaint.

C. FEDERAL SUBJECT-MATTER JURISDICTION, REMOVAL, AND REMAND

§ 2.9 Subject-Matter Jurisdiction in Federal District Courts—Introduction

Jurisdiction over persons or things ("personal jurisdiction"), discussed above, defines the limits of a court's reach to require a defendant to appear and defend a lawsuit or the court's reach over property that is the subject of a lawsuit. Subject-matter jurisdiction, by contrast, limits the kind of cases a court may hear, irrespective of where the affected persons or pieces of property may be found. Thus, if a person is served with process within the State where a court sits, the court likely has personal jurisdiction over that person. But if the cause of action is of a kind that a federal court cannot hear, the court would still lack subject-matter jurisdiction and the court would lack the constitutional authority to adjudicate the case. Subject-matter jurisdiction must be satisfied *as to each claim in a case* before a federal court will hear that claim.

As part of the compromise between States' rights and federal rights, the Constitution established a federal court system with *limited* subject-matter jurisdiction, only empowered to hear those specific categories of cases authorized in the Constitution. *See* U.S. CONST. art. III, sec. 2. It then permitted Congress to attend to the details of the federal court system, and Congress accordingly enacted a series of federal statutes addressing, among other things, the federal courts' subject-matter jurisdiction. Although there are a number of congressionally-sanctioned subject-matter categories, this *Student's Guide* will focus on the two most prominent categories: cases arising under federal laws (federal question or "arising under" jurisdiction, discussed in Section 2.10) and cases involving citizens of different States (diversity jurisdiction, discussed in Section 2.11). Before turning to these categories, a few general jurisdictional concepts are important.

- *Original vs. Supplemental Jurisdiction:* In order to bring a case into federal court in the first instance, there must be at least one claim that possesses "original" subject-matter jurisdiction (such as federal question or diversity jurisdiction). Given one claim with original jurisdiction, other claims that are sufficiently related to the claim with original subject-matter jurisdiction may, under appropriate circumstances, be included in the lawsuit through the exercise of "supplemental jurisdiction," even though those other claims might not themselves qualify for original subject-matter jurisdiction. *See* Section 2.12 for a discussion of supplemental jurisdiction.

- *Duty to Demonstrate Jurisdiction:* Because they possess only *limited* subject-matter jurisdiction, federal courts must first be persuaded that they have the judicial power to proceed in a pending lawsuit. The burden of demonstrating that the requirements of federal subject-matter jurisdiction are met rests on the party seeking to invoke the court's jurisdiction. *See Kokkonen v. Guardian Life Insurance Co. of America,* 511 U.S. 375, 377 (1994). In the initial instance, Rule 8(a)(1) requires a plaintiff filing a complaint in federal court to set forth, in that complaint, the basis for the court's subject-matter jurisdiction.

- *Well-Pleaded Complaint:* In general, the basis for original subject-matter jurisdiction must be found in the claims set forth in the complaint. *See Caterpillar Inc. v. Williams,* 482 U.S. 386, 392 (1987). The basis for subject-matter jurisdiction cannot be based on an anticipated federal law defense or matter set forth in the answer or other pleadings. *See Aetna Health, Inc. v. Davila,* 542 U.S. 200, 207 (2004). The term "well-pleaded complaint" can be misleading. It is a term of art, not a critique on the drafting skill of the plaintiff. It simply means that in assessing whether federal subject-matter jurisdiction is present or not, the court will examine only those allegations that would be found in a properly asserted statement of the plaintiff's own claim (and not, as noted above, in some prediction of a defendant's defense or claims). *See Franchise Tax Bd. v. Construction Laborers Vacation Trust for So. Cal.,* 463 U.S. 1, 27–28 (1983).

  The effect of the well-pleaded complaint rule is to restrict the scope of federal question jurisdiction. It is always possible, and often happens, that important federal issues will be injected into a lawsuit on the defendant's side of the case (for example, a federal defense to a plaintiff's State law cause of action). Such defendant-triggered federal issues, even if central to the outcome of a case, will not typically confer federal question jurisdiction—not because there is no federal question, but because the federal question arises only in a defense and not in the plaintiff's well-pleaded complaint. *See, e.g., Metropolitan Life Ins. Co. v. Taylor,* 481 U.S. 58, 63 (1987).

- *Jurisdiction to Determine Jurisdiction:* A federal court that lacks subject-matter jurisdiction lacks authority to decide a case, and most rulings the court makes before realizing it lacks subject-matter jurisdiction are void. This is one obvious, necessary exception. If someone challenges the federal court's subject-matter jurisdiction, the court always possesses the jurisdiction to decide whether it has jurisdiction (even if the ultimate answer is "no"). *See United States v. Ruiz,* 536 U.S. 622, 628 (2007).

- *Consent:* Unlike personal jurisdiction, subject-matter jurisdiction cannot be obtained through consent of the parties. *See Insurance Corp. of Ireland, Ltd. v. Compagnie des Bauxites de Guinee,* 456 U.S. 694, 702 (1982). The rationale is that the limits on a federal district court's subject-matter jurisdiction are grounded in the constitutional balance of federal and State judicial power, and it is not the prerogative of the parties to enter into agreements that have the effect of upsetting that balance. Moreover, because the parties cannot confer subject-matter jurisdiction on the court by consent, there is no time limit on objections to subject-matter jurisdiction. Instead, lack of subject-matter jurisdiction can be raised at any time, and the court must determine whether it has subject-matter jurisdiction whenever the question arises, either on motion of a party or on its own. *See Bender v. Williamsport Area School Dist.*, 475 U.S. 534, 541 (1986).

§ 2.10 Subject-Matter Jurisdiction in Federal District Courts: Federal Question Jurisdiction

The most common form of federal subject-matter jurisdiction is federal question jurisdiction under 28 U.S.C. § 1331, which extends to "all civil actions arising under the Constitution, laws, or treaties of the United States." This form of subject-matter jurisdiction is sometimes referred to as "arising under jurisdiction" because the phrase "arising under" appears in both this statute and Article III of the U.S. Constitution and because it captures the concept that the claim must actually be found in the federal law, rather than simply loosely depending on the federal law. Federal question jurisdiction typically accounts for more than half the cases filed in federal courts. The purpose of federal question jurisdiction is to promote the uniform application of federal laws across the country—the interpretation of a federal statute should be the same in Texas and in Maine.

The vast majority of federal question claims are those that seek a federal remedy for a violation of a right created by a federal law (found in a federal statute). *See Merrell Dow Pharm., Inc. v. Thompson*, 478 U.S. 804, 808 (1986). In this category of claims, the federal law in question establishes private rights of action (that is, the law actually authorizes the plaintiff to bring the sort of claim now pending before the court). For example, 42 U.S.C. § 1983 authorizes an action against any person who, under color of law, deprives another person of "any rights, privileges, or immunities secured by the Constitution and laws." If an employee working for a State agency believes that the agency's medical leave policies violate her constitutional rights, she may bring a claim under § 1983, and a federal district court would have federal question jurisdiction over her claim. *See Monell v. Dep't of Soc. Serv. of New York*, 436 U.S. 658 (1978).

There is, however, a second, narrow category of federal question claims where a State remedy is being sought for a violation of a State law *but* the resolution of that claim will "necessarily raise a stated federal issue, actually disputed and substantial, which a federal forum may entertain without disturbing any congressionally approved balance of federal and state judicial responsibilities." *Gunn v. Minton*, 568 U.S. 251, 258 (2013). In other words, if, to resolve the plaintiff's State law claim, the court must determine matters of federal law with broad national implications, a federal court might be able to exercise federal question jurisdiction even though the plaintiff's claim arises under State law. Consider, for example, a woman who asserts that a medicine that she took while pregnant harmed her child. She might contend that the medicine was improperly labeled in violation of the Federal Food, Drug, and Cosmetics Act (FDCA). While that federal act might authorize government agents to impose fines or penalties against a non-compliant medicine manufacturer, the FDCA does not create a private cause of action. Consequently, the woman must endeavor to sue the medicine manufacturer under State tort law, but might rest her State tort law claim on the argument that the manufacturer was negligent *because* it violated the federal FDCA by improperly labeling its medicine. Is that enough to convert her State tort law claim into one qualifying for federal question jurisdiction? *See Merrell Dow Pharm., Inc.*, 478 U.S. at 805–17 (holding that it is not, as explained in the discussion below).

PRACTICING LAW WITH THIS PRINCIPLE

Constitutional Violations

Although most federal question cases involve claims arising under a federal statute, a plaintiff can, under the right circumstances, bring a claim simply alleging that the defendant violated the plaintiff's constitutional rights. *See, e.g., Bivens v. Six Unknown Named Agents of Federal Bureau of Narcotics,* 403 U.S. 388, 395–96 (1971).

Declining to Plead a Federal Claim: Complete Preemption

Ordinarily, the plaintiff has control of the counts in the complaint and may therefore avoid federal question jurisdiction simply by forgoing claims based on federal law. *See Caterpillar Inc.*

v. Williams, 482 U.S. 386, 389 (1987). However, in areas where federal law has completely preempted State law, a plaintiff cannot avoid the federal question by pleading only State law. *See Beneficial Nat. Bank v. Anderson,* 539 U.S. 1, 8 (2003).

State Claims That Depend on Federal Law

The mere fact that the court will be required to resolve some federal issue in the course of deciding a plaintiff's State law claims is, alone, not enough to trigger federal question subject-matter jurisdiction. *See Empire Healthchoice Assur., Inc. v. McVeigh*, 547 U.S. 677, 701 (2006) ("it takes more than a federal element to open the arising under door") (cleaned up). Instead, when a federal issue is embedded within a State claim, federal question jurisdiction will exist over that State law claim only if the federal issue is:

(1) Necessarily raised by the claim pressed in the plaintiff's lawsuit;

(2) Actually disputed by the parties;

(3) Substantial to the federal system as a whole (and not just substantial in the eyes of the particular parties to the lawsuit); *and*

(4) Capable of being resolved in federal court without causing a disruption in the federal-State balance approved by Congress (or will it, instead, trigger an enormous shift of case volume from State courts into federal court without some clear indication from Congress that such was their intent).

See Gunn v. Minton, 568 U.S. 251, 256–65 (2013); *Grable & Sons Metal Prods., Inc. v. Darue Eng'g & Mfg.*, 545 U.S. 308, 312–20 (2005). Consequently, while this second type of federal subject-matter jurisdiction exists, it represents a "special and small category." *See Gunn,* 568 U.S. at 258.

Weak Federal Claims

The probability of defeat on the merits does not, by itself, strip a plaintiff's claim of federal question jurisdiction. *See Bell v. Hood,* 327 U.S. 678, 682 (1946).

Amount in Controversy

Unlike diversity jurisdiction, Section 1331 does not contain any requirement that federal question cases satisfy a specific dollar amount. Thus, if a case arose under the federal civil rights laws, and the amount at issue was only ten dollars, the case would still qualify for federal question jurisdiction.

Exclusive vs. Concurrent Subject-Matter Jurisdiction

Many statutes create exclusive jurisdiction in the federal district courts (specifying that a claim under the statute must be brought in a federal court, sometimes specifying which particular federal court). If a federal statute is silent as to whether a claim it creates lies within exclusive federal jurisdiction or instead is subject to the concurrent jurisdiction of federal and State trial courts, the jurisdiction is concurrent, not exclusive. *Tafflin v. Levitt*, 493 U.S. 455, 458–59 (1990).

Specific Jurisdictional Statutes

In addition to the broad jurisdictional grant of Section 1331, a number of federal statutes establish federal subject-matter jurisdiction over specific categories of federal law claims. For example, 28 U.S.C. § 1337 authorizes federal courts to hear civil actions arising under federal laws regulating commerce. In the same fashion, 28 U.S.C. § 1338 provides subject-matter jurisdiction over claims arising under federal patent law and 28 U.S.C. § 1343 authorizes a federal court to hear claims alleging violations of federally guaranteed civil rights. When one of those specific jurisdictional grants applies, a plaintiff must bring its action under that section, and all of the conditions and limitations of an action under that specific jurisdictional grant will apply.

§ 2.11 Subject-Matter Jurisdiction in Federal District Courts: Diversity Jurisdiction

After federal question jurisdiction, the most common form of federal subject-matter jurisdiction is diversity jurisdiction under 28 U.S.C. § 1332. Diversity jurisdiction permits a federal district court to hear State law causes of action if two basic requirements are fulfilled: no plaintiff may be a citizen of the same State as any defendant; and the amount in controversy must exceed $75,000, exclusive of interest and costs. Somewhere around thirty percent of the cases in federal court are founded on diversity jurisdiction, but a larger percentage of jurisdictional complexities arise in this area.

The purpose of diversity jurisdiction was to protect out-of-State parties from favoritism by judges toward local parties. For example, suppose a Connecticut company wanted to sue an Alabama company for breach of contract, and, for reasons of personal jurisdiction or venue, had to bring its lawsuit in Alabama. The Connecticut company might fear that the Alabama State court judge might have a relationship with the Alabama company, or perhaps its lawyer, that could influence the course or outcome of the lawsuit. Perhaps the company's CEO and the judge belong to the same country club. Perhaps the lawyer made a sizeable contribution to the judge's election campaign. To foster fair treatment of all citizens, the Constitution authorized the federal courts to hear disputes between citizens of different States, with the idea that federal courts, with appointed federal judges, would provide a "more level playing field" for adjudicating such disputes.

PRACTICING LAW WITH THIS PRINCIPLE

The First Diversity Requirement: Complete Diversity of Citizenship

To qualify under Section 1332, the parties' diversity must be "complete." *See Strawbridge v. Curtiss*, 7 U.S. (3 Cranch.) 267, 268 (1806) (Marshall, C.J.). Applying the "versus test" is a simple way to remember this requirement—every party on the left side of the "v." must have a citizenship that is different from every party on the right side of the "v." *See Lincoln Prop. Co. v. Roche*, 546 U.S. 81, 89 (2005) ("we have read the statutory formulation 'between . . . citizens of different States' to require complete diversity between all plaintiffs and all defendants"). The test only compares plaintiffs to defendants, however; there is no requirement that multiple plaintiffs have citizenships different from one another or that defendants have citizenships different from their fellow defendants. Complete diversity is evaluated across the complete complaint, and not on a count-by-count basis. *See Exxon Mobil Corp. v. Allapattah Servs., Inc.*, 545 U.S. 546, 553 (2005). Thus, in a case where a plaintiff files a two-count complaint against two defendants (the first count against one defendant and the second count against the other defendant), the court will not have diversity jurisdiction over either count unless the plaintiff is not a citizen of the same State as either defendant.

Citizenship of an Individual

An individual is a citizen of an American State if the individual is: (1) an American citizen; and (2) domiciled in the State (because individuals are not normally considered "citizens" of States). A person's domicile is the person's "true, fixed, and permanent home," where the person intends to reside indefinitely, and to where the person intends to return. *See Vlandis v. Kline,* 412 U.S. 441, 454 (1973). An individual is a domicile, and thus citizen, of only one State at any point in time. *See Wachovia Bank v. Schmidt,* 546 U.S. 303, 318 (2006). If an individual changes *residence*, the individual's *domicile* will not change unless the individual intends to reside in the new State indefinitely.

- *Citizenship of Decedents, Infants, and Incompetents:* For diversity purposes, parties acting as representatives of decedents' estates, infants, or incompetent persons shall be deemed to take the citizenship of the estate or persons whom they represent.

Citizenship of Corporations

A corporation is a citizen of two places: both (1) the State where it is incorporated; and (2) the State where it has its principal place of business. Generally, a corporation is only incorporated in one State. A corporation's principal place of business for purposes of diversity jurisdiction is the corporate "nerve center," typically the corporation's headquarters. *See Hertz Corp. v. Friend,* 559 U.S. 77, 92–93 (2010). Thus, depending on the particular facts of incorporation and location of business operations, a corporation will typically be a citizen of one or two States for diversity purposes. If a corporation has citizenship in more than one jurisdiction, the opposing party must be diverse from *all* the corporation's citizenships or complete diversity is not established.

Citizenship of Unincorporated Associations

For diversity purposes, unincorporated associations such as partnerships, limited liability companies, joint ventures, and labor unions are citizens of every State in which one or more of their members is a citizen. *See Carden v. Arkoma Assocs.,* 494 U.S. 185, 195–96 (1990). Thus, for very large unincorporated entities, such as national labor unions with members in every State, diversity of citizenship is unlikely to exist between the entity and its opponent in a lawsuit. When the case involves class litigation, however, an unincorporated association is treated like a corporation, and is a citizen of the State where it has its principal place of business and the State under whose laws it is organized.

Citizenship of Trusts

When a trust is the party, the trust is deemed a citizen of every State in which any of its members is a citizen. *See Americold Realty Trust v. Conagra Foods, Inc.,* 136 S. Ct. 1012, 1017 (2016). When the trustee is the party, the trust takes the citizenship of the trustee.

Citizenship of Indian Tribes and Tribal Corporations

Most courts have concluded that Indian tribes are not citizens of a State for the purposes of Section 1332. In contrast, tribal corporations are normally treated as equivalent to State corporations for purposes of diversity jurisdiction.

District of Columbia, Puerto Rico, and U.S. Territories and Possessions

For purposes of diversity jurisdiction, the District of Columbia, Puerto Rico, the Virgin Islands, Guam, and America's other territories and possessions are treated as American States. Thus, persons domiciled in those places will typically be treated as citizens of those "States" for diversity purposes.

Alienage Jurisdiction

There are a variety of rules that apply when a case includes parties that are not American citizens:

(1) Complete diversity will exist when the parties on one side are citizens of American States and the opposing parties are citizens or subjects of foreign countries;

(2) Complete diversity will exist when the parties that are American citizens are citizens of different States and additional parties are citizens or subjects of foreign countries;

(3) Complete diversity will exist when a foreign country is a plaintiff suing citizens of American States;

(4) Diversity jurisdiction is not available when citizens or subjects of one foreign country are suing citizens or subjects of another foreign country;

(5) American citizens domiciled abroad may not sue or be sued in a federal district court on the basis of diversity jurisdiction. *See Newman-Green, Inc. v. Alfonzo-Larrain,* 490 U.S. 826, 828 (1989);

(6) If an American citizen is also a citizen of a foreign country, the only citizenship that will be evaluated for purposes of diversity jurisdiction is the individual's American citizenship; and

(7) The federal courts may not exercise diversity jurisdiction in a suit between a citizen of an American State and a "legal resident alien" who is domiciled in the same State.

Likewise, "aliens" permanently resident in the United States and domiciled in different States may not use diversity jurisdiction to sue one another in a district court.

Suits Involving the United States

Section 1332 does not create subject-matter jurisdiction for suits involving the United States. However, Sections 1345 and 1346 address subject-matter jurisdiction for such suits.

Timing of Citizenship

The parties must be diverse at the time the lawsuit is filed. It is irrelevant that the parties may not have been diverse at the time the cause of action arose, or that a party diverse at the time of filing acquires a non-diverse citizenship later on during the course of the lawsuit. Thus, if a citizen of New York seeks to sue another New York citizen in federal district court over a State cause of action, the plaintiff could create diversity of citizenship by making a genuine change of domicile from New York to another jurisdiction prior to filing suit.

When a case arrives in federal district court through the process of removal (discussed below), the analysis of jurisdiction is made as of the date the removal petition was filed. *See Pullman Co. v. Jenkins,* 305 U.S. 534, 537 (1939). Some courts require that complete diversity have existed at both the time the complaint was filed and at the time the removal petition was filed.

Curing Defects in Diversity

A lack of complete diversity when the case was filed can be cured by dismissal of the non-diverse party under Rule 21. *See Caterpillar, Inc. v. Lewis,* 519 U.S. 61, 64 (1996). Conversely, if a party who was not diverse at the time the case was filed subsequently changes citizenship and becomes diverse, the original defect in diversity jurisdiction is not cured. *See Grupo Dataflux v. Atlas Global Group, L.P.,* 541 U.S. 567, 575 (2004).

Realignment of Parties

The requirement of complete diversity means that the alignment of parties (*i.e.*, as plaintiffs or defendants) may be crucial to a determination of the existence of federal subject-matter jurisdiction. Normally it is the plaintiff who provides the initial alignment of parties in the complaint by listing each party as a plaintiff or a defendant. However, because the plaintiff is not a disinterested party, the court has authority to re-align the parties to reflect accurately the parties whose interests coincide and those parties whose interests conflict with the first group of parties. *See City of Indianapolis v. Chase Nat'l Bank,* 314 U.S. 63, 69 (1941).

The Second Diversity Requirement: Amount in Controversy

Diversity jurisdiction requires not only that the parties be citizens of different States, but also that the matter in controversy exceed $75,000, exclusive of interest and costs. The word "exceed" is not extraneous; unless the amount in controversy, exclusive of interests and costs, is $75,000.01 or more, diversity jurisdiction cannot be invoked. The time at which the amount in controversy is measured is the date that the suit is filed. Later events that may reduce the amount recoverable do not nullify diversity jurisdiction that was proper at the time of filing.

- *Recovery of Less than $75,000.01:* If a plaintiff initially seeks more than $75,000 but ultimately recovers less, the amount in controversy requirement is not defeated.

"Legal Certainty" Test

In the ordinary case, determination of the amount in controversy is made by reference to the plaintiff's prayer for relief. Unliquidated claims—claims that do not have a precisely calculable value such as pain and suffering—for more than $75,000 will normally be taken at face value as satisfying the amount in controversy requirement, provided they are pleaded in good faith. Only where it is certain—based on the liquidated nature of the claim, the manifestly frivolous nature of the prayer for relief, or a statutory limitation on damages recoverable—that the plaintiff cannot possibly recover the jurisdictional amount, will the court disregard the plaintiff's prayer. *St. Paul Mercury Indem. Co. v. Red Cab Co.*, 303 U.S. 283, 289 (1938).

Burden of Proof

If the amount in controversy is at issue, it is normally the plaintiff's burden to demonstrate that the requirement is met. An exception arises when a plaintiff originally files suit in State court and the defendant removes the case to federal court. In that circumstance, if it is unclear whether the plaintiff's claim meets the amount in controversy requirement, the burden of proving the existence of the jurisdictional amount is shifted to the defendant who removed the case. *See McNutt v. General Motors Acceptance Corp.,* 298 U.S. 178, 189 (1936).

Jurisdictional Amount in Equity Cases

Because lawsuits seeking equitable relief typically do not entail monetary damages, a straightforward measurement against the $75,000 threshold is not possible. In general, courts will consider the amount in controversy requirement satisfied if either the benefit to the plaintiff of the equitable relief or the cost to or burden on the defendant to comply with the relief exceeds $75,000. *See, e.g., Glenwood Light & Water Co. v. Mutual Light, Heat & Power Co.,* 239 U.S. 121, 125–26 (1915). Thus, for example, if a landowner sought an injunction prohibiting a nearby company from discharging pollutants into a stream that was carrying the pollutants into the landowner's pond and killing the fish, the amount in controversy requirement could be satisfied if the value to the landowner of obtaining the injunction would exceed $75,000 or the burden to the company—perhaps measured by the cost of installing new pollution control equipment—would exceed $75,000.

Aggregation of Claims

If a plaintiff has more than one claim against a defendant, questions arise as to whether the plaintiff may add the value of the claims together to satisfy the amount in controversy requirement. If a plaintiff has multiple claims against the same defendant, the rule is simple and generous; a single plaintiff may aggregate the amount in controversy from all claims against a single defendant, no matter how dissimilar the claims are. Thus, if one plaintiff has two different, unrelated claims against one defendant, each totaling $40,000, the plaintiff may aggregate those amounts in controversy such that each claim qualifies for diversity jurisdiction (assuming the parties are diverse in citizenship). Likewise, if the plaintiff has one claim against a defendant seeking $80,000 and another claim against the same defendant seeking $15,000, the amount in controversy requirement is satisfied for each claim. This rule applies regardless of the number of defendants in the case. Thus, if one plaintiff sues two defendants and asserts two claims against defendant number 1, the plaintiff may aggregate the amount in controversy from those two claims to satisfy the amount in controversy requirement for both claims against defendant number 1.

Aggregation of the amount in controversy for claims involving multiple plaintiffs or defendants is much more limited. Where a single plaintiff seeks to aggregate the amount in controversy from claims against more than one defendant, aggregation is permitted only if the claims against the defendants involve joint liability. Many tort claims involve such joint liability. For example, if a plaintiff sued two defendants in a three-car pileup seeking a total of $80,000, it is quite likely that each defendant's share of liability would be below $75,000 (and thus would not satisfy the amount in controversy requirement on its own), and there is a mathematical certainty that both claims could not exceed $75,000. Because the plaintiff has the potential to recover the full $80,000 from either defendant under the principles of joint and several liability, however, the courts consider the amount in controversy requirement satisfied as to both claims.

The circumstances where two or more plaintiffs can aggregate the amount in controversy for their claims to satisfy the jurisdictional amount are even narrower, and do not frequently occur. Two plaintiffs may aggregate the amount in controversy for their claims only if the claims are truly joint, such as in the case of joint ownership of the property that is the subject of the lawsuit. *See, e.g., Snyder v. Harris,* 394 U.S. 332, 334 (1969). For example, if two plaintiffs each jointly owned an automobile worth $80,000 and they sued a defendant alleging that the defendant had destroyed the automobile completely, the plaintiffs could aggregate their individual claims to satisfy the jurisdictional amount even though they could not each recover in excess of $75,000. But if the allegation was that the two plaintiffs each suffered $40,000 in personal injuries when another driver collided with their automobile, they could not aggregate the amount in controversy for their claims because the claims would be seen as distinct—even if the injuries occurred in the same accident.

These aggregation rules only pertain to attempts to aggregate damages from different claims. They do not apply to adding up different elements of damages from one claim. Thus, for example, if the plaintiff was in a car accident with one defendant and sustained both damages to her car and injuries to her body, she would not need to apply aggregation rules—if those damages added up to more than $75,000, her negligence claim would satisfy the amount in controversy requirement on its own. Conversely, if the plaintiff's only harm was $40,000 in damages to her car, she could not bring a claim for negligence and another claim for battery, then aggregate the $40,000 from each claim. She would only be entitled to recover the $40,000 one time, so cannot aggregate those amounts.

Diversity Jurisdiction in Class Actions

The Class Action Fairness Act established relaxed requirements for diversity jurisdiction over class actions. Diversity jurisdiction will lie if the aggregate amount in controversy exceeds $5,000,000, exclusive of interest and costs and: (a) any member of a class of plaintiffs is a citizen of an American State different from the American State of citizenship of any defendant; (b) any member of a class of plaintiffs is a foreign country or a citizen or subject of a foreign country and any defendant is a citizen of an American State; or (c) any member of a class of plaintiffs is a citizen of an American State and any defendant is a foreign country or a citizen or subject of a foreign country.

Declining Diversity Jurisdiction in Class Actions: Even if a class action has met the requirements for diversity jurisdiction, the federal district courts may refrain from hearing such a class lawsuit. The court has discretion to decline to exercise diversity jurisdiction when two requirements are met and some other prudential considerations are weighed. The first of the two requirements is that more than one-third and less than two-thirds of the total membership of a plaintiff class consists of citizens of the State in which the action was originally filed. The second requirement is that the "primary" defendants are citizens of the State in which the action was originally filed. In addition to the existence of those two requirements, the court must also weigh the following factors:

(a) whether the claims in question involve matters of national or interstate interest;

(b) whether the claims will be controlled by the law of the State where the case was originally filed or by the law of another State or States;

(c) whether the plaintiffs have, through artful pleading, sought to avoid federal subject-matter jurisdiction;

(d) whether the action was filed in a court with a clear relationship with the plaintiffs, the underlying events, or the defendants;

(e) whether the number of class plaintiffs who are citizens of the State in which the case was filed is substantially larger than the number of plaintiffs from any other State, and the citizenship of other plaintiffs is dispersed among a significant variety of other States; and

(f) whether during the three years prior to filing the instant action, another class action has been filed asserting similar claims, without regard to whether the claims were asserted on behalf of the identical plaintiffs.

Local Controversy Exception: Although this statutory exception typically gives the district court the discretion to exercise or decline to exercise subject-matter jurisdiction, the district court is ***required*** to decline to exercise jurisdiction if all of the following elements are met: (1) more than two-thirds of class plaintiffs are citizens of the State of original filing; (2) at least one defendant is a citizen of the State where the suit was originally filed and is both a subject of "significant" relief sought by the plaintiff class and a party whose alleged conduct is a "significant" basis for the plaintiffs' cause of action; (3) principal injuries in the case were incurred in the State of original filing; and (4) there has been no filing of a lawsuit in the last three years based on the same or similar allegations by the same or other plaintiffs against any of the same defendants.

Home State Exception: Likewise, a district court is ***required*** to decline to exercise jurisdiction if: two-thirds or more of the plaintiff class are citizens of the State of original filing; *and* "primary defendants" are also citizens of that same State.

Diversity Jurisdiction in Mass Actions

Many mass actions are treated as the equivalent of class actions for purposes of diversity jurisdiction. The definition of a mass action is a civil action in which one hundred or more persons each seek monetary relief and a joint trial because their claims involve a single event or occurrence that gave rise to the cause of action. Mass actions which meet that definition are deemed eligible for treatment as class actions only if they meet the additional requirement that each plaintiff's individual claim is in excess of $75,000.

Exceptions for Domestic Relations and Probate Cases

Federal courts routinely do not exercise diversity jurisdiction over cases in which divorce, child custody, or matters of probate are at issue. *See Markham v. Allen,* 326 U.S. 490, 494 (1946). However, these exceptions to the application of diversity jurisdiction are construed narrowly. Thus, if a case involved a dispute over property arising out of a divorce decree previously granted, the federal court might hear the case if the requirements of diversity jurisdiction were otherwise satisfied. *See Ankenbrandt v. Richards,* 504 U.S. 689, 695 (1992).

Manipulation of Diversity Jurisdiction

The diversity provisions of 28 U.S.C. § 1332 are modified by 28 U.S.C. § 1359, governing collusive invocation of jurisdiction. Section 1359 provides that if a party, "by assignment or otherwise," has been "improperly or collusively . . . joined" to invoke jurisdiction, the federal district court will not have jurisdiction. *See Kramer v. Caribbean Mills, Inc.,* 394 U.S. 823, 827 (1969). Thus, a plaintiff who wants to sue a defendant in federal court but who is a citizen of the same State as a defendant may not create diversity jurisdiction by assigning the claim to another person who is diverse from the defendant. Conversely, a plaintiff cannot join a nondiverse defendant for the sole purpose of destroying complete diversity, as addressed below in the discussion of removal.

§ 2.12 Subject-Matter Jurisdiction in Federal District Courts: Requirements for Supplemental Jurisdiction

Once a case is properly in federal court, through an exercise of at least one form of original subject-matter jurisdiction, efficiency may dictate that other related claims—such as counterclaims or crossclaims—be adjudicated at the same time in that same case. Supplemental jurisdiction, authorized by Congress at 28 U.S.C. § 1367, authorizes district courts to exercise subject-matter jurisdiction over certain such related claims. To achieve this objective, supplemental jurisdiction has two relatively simple threshold requirements. First, there must be one claim over which the court has original subject-matter jurisdiction. Second, the claim over which the court is asked to assert supplemental jurisdiction must arise out of the same "case or controversy" as the claim with original jurisdiction.

♦ ***Example:*** Suppose that a New York plaintiff had two causes of action against a New York defendant arising out of the same conduct: one arising under federal antitrust law, the other under State law. Federal antitrust claims are within the exclusive subject-matter jurisdiction of federal district courts. The State claim, by contrast, does not qualify for diversity jurisdiction because both parties are New York citizens. Without supplemental jurisdiction, the plaintiff would have to prosecute two separate suits, one in federal court and the other in State court, and incur all the extra time and money such suits would entail for both the parties and the taxpayers. Supplemental jurisdiction would lie over the State law claim, eliminating these diseconomies.

PRACTICING LAW WITH THIS PRINCIPLE

Prerequisite for Supplemental Jurisdiction

As its name suggests, supplemental jurisdiction is not an independent basis for satisfying the requirements of federal subject-matter jurisdiction in the same way as federal question jurisdiction or diversity jurisdiction. Instead, claims based on supplemental jurisdiction must be able to attach themselves to some other claim that can satisfy original federal subject-matter jurisdiction through, *e.g.*, federal question jurisdiction or diversity jurisdiction.

Same Case or Controversy

Supplemental jurisdiction can only be effective for claims that are "so related" to one another that they "form part of the same case or controversy." Thus, to "piggy-back" into federal court under supplemental jurisdiction, a claim that lacks an independent basis for subject-matter jurisdiction must be deemed part of the same constitutional "case" as some other claim in that lawsuit that does enjoy independent subject-matter jurisdiction. Determining whether that relationship exists focuses on the similarity and overlap between the witnesses and evidence relevant to the respective claims. *See United Mine Workers of Am. v. Gibbs,* 383 U.S. 715, 725 (1966) (explaining that the Constitution authorizes jurisdiction over a "case," and that claims that arise out of a "common nucleus of operative fact" and would be expected to be tried together are part of a single "case").

No Amount in Controversy Requirement

To qualify for supplemental jurisdiction, a claim need not satisfy any amount in controversy requirement.

Can Apply to Both Joined Claims and Joined (and Intervening) Parties

When its requirements are met, supplemental jurisdiction may be used to bring both new claims and new parties into a federal lawsuit.

Supplemental Jurisdiction's Statutory Disqualifier

Supplemental jurisdiction is subject to a limitation that is designed to prevent clever plaintiffs from circumventing the requirement of complete diversity of citizenship. If an adversary is a citizen of the same State as the plaintiff, naming that adversary as a defendant would destroy complete diversity of citizenship. To maneuver around that restriction, a clever plaintiff could name only the diverse adversaries as defendants, hoping that one of those defendants would then join the non-diverse defendant into the case. The plaintiff could then assert its own claim against that non-diverse defendant under the court's supplemental jurisdiction. The supplemental jurisdiction statute prevents this ploy. *See* 28 U.S.C. § 1367(b). It prohibits the exercise of supplemental jurisdiction when all four of the following conditions are met:

(1) the claims that independently qualify for federal subject-matter jurisdiction do so *solely* on the basis of diversity jurisdiction; *and*

(2) the claims that do not independently qualify for federal subject-matter jurisdiction are brought by a plaintiff (*e.g.,* not by a defendant or third-party defendant); *and*

(3) those claims are brought *either*:

  (a) by the original plaintiff, and are asserted against parties joined into the lawsuit under Rule 14 (impleader), Rule 19 (required party joinder), Rule 20 (permissive party joinder), or Rule 24 (intervention); *or*

(b) by someone proposing to join into the lawsuit as a co-plaintiff under Rule 19 (required party joinder) or Rule 24 (intervention); *and*

(4) exercising supplemental jurisdiction over such claims would be "inconsistent with the jurisdictional requirements of section 1332."

Supplemental Jurisdiction's Implied Case Law Disqualifier

In 2005, the Supreme Court considered a purported "drafting gap" in the wording of Section 1367(b). See *Exxon Mobil Corp. v. Allapattah Servs., Inc.*, 545 U.S. 546, 562–65 (2005). The statute expressly disqualifies for supplemental jurisdiction certain claims by an original plaintiff against a nondiverse *defendant* who was joined permissively to the lawsuit under Rule 20, yet does not disqualify for supplemental jurisdiction a claim by a nondiverse party who proposes to permissively join the lawsuit as a *co-plaintiff* under Rule 20. See 28 U.S.C. § 1367(b). The Court suggested (but did not expressly hold) that a "contamination theory" view of the complete diversity principle would cure that "drafting gap." Under this analysis, if another plaintiff was added to a complaint over which the court had diversity jurisdiction, as permitted by Rule 20 (for example, by amendment under Rule 15), Section 1367(b) would not block the "drafting gap," exercise of supplemental jurisdiction over claims brought by the nondiverse, permissively added Rule 20 plaintiff, but the presence of that nondiverse Rule 20 plaintiff would defeat all the litigants' ability to satisfy the complete diversity rule. This would in turn either compel the dismissal of the lawsuit entirely or at least the severing (under Rule 21) of the claims involving the newly added, nondiverse plaintiff.

Court's Discretion

Even if supplemental jurisdiction exists under 28 U.S.C. §§ 1367(a) and (b), the district judge still enjoys substantial discretion to decline to hear supplemental claims in appropriate circumstances. *See* 28 U.S.C. § 1367(c). *See also Carlsbad Tech, Inc. v. HIF Bio, Inc.,* 556 U.S. 635, 639 (2009).

The four circumstances in which a federal court might choose to decline to exercise supplemental jurisdiction (and, thus, dismiss a claim that otherwise qualifies for supplemental jurisdiction) are:

(1) *Difficult Questions of State Law:* District courts may decline to exercise supplemental jurisdiction if State courts would be better able to untangle a "novel or complex" question of State law. However, federal courts generally employ § 1367(c)(1) only in unusual cases involving the greatest difficulty in applying State law.

(2) *Non-Diverse State Claim Predominates:* The court may decline to exercise supplemental jurisdiction over a State law claim when that claim predominates over the claims which formed the original basis of the court's subject-matter jurisdiction.

(3) *Original Counts Dismissed:* The court may decline to exercise supplemental jurisdiction when it has dismissed all the claims over which it had original jurisdiction. *See Arbaugh v. Y&H Corp.*, 546 U.S. 500, 514 (2006). Courts give substantial weight to the point in the case at which the dismissal occurred. If the federal court dismissed the original jurisdiction claims at the outset of the case, it would probably dismiss the supplemental claims immediately. *Carnegie-Mellon University v. Cohill,* 484 U.S. 343, 350 (1988). If, however, the federal court proceeded through much of the litigation and had informed itself of the merits of the supplemental claims, then the court would be more likely to retain jurisdiction over the supplemental claims.

Under one circumstance, this discretion to dismiss becomes mandatory. If the basis for dismissing the claims which the plaintiff brought under the court's original jurisdiction was a determination that original jurisdiction was lacking, the court is required to dismiss the claims as to which the plaintiff has asserted the court's supplemental jurisdiction too (because the first requirement for supplemental jurisdiction—at least one claim with original jurisdiction—would never have been satisfied).

(4) *Other Exceptional Circumstances:* The court has discretion to dismiss supplemental claims in circumstances not anticipated by Congress, although courts rarely exercise this discretion.

When Supplemental Jurisdiction Fails—Tolling a Statute of Limitations

A party's hope to acquire supplemental jurisdiction over a State-law claim may fail; the court could, for example, disagree that Section 1367 provides such jurisdiction or the court might believe it best to exercise its discretion not to hear the claim. In such cases, the State-law claim will be dismissed, leaving the claimant with the option of refiling the dismissed claim in State court. To preserve that right, Congress directed that the statute of limitations applicable to the dismissed claim is deemed "tolled" (that is, "suspended" like a stopped-clock) during the time it was pending in federal court *and* then for a further 30 days following its dismissal by the federal judge. *See* 28 U.S.C. § 1367(d); *Artis v. District of Columbia*, 138 S. Ct. 594 (2018).

§ 2.13 Removal

Removal is not a separate type of subject-matter jurisdiction. Instead, it is a tool reserved for defendants, allowing them (under certain circumstances) to make use of the same subject-matter jurisdiction principles discussed above. Removal permits a defendant to override a plaintiff's choice of a State court forum, and to relocate the lawsuit to federal court. Removal is only available when a federal court would have subject-matter jurisdiction over the dispute. The removal process is controlled by federal law.

PRACTICING LAW WITH THIS PRINCIPLE

Congress's Removal Statutes

There are several removal statutes. The most relevant for law students are the three general removal statutes: 28 U.S.C. § 1441 (governing removal for diversity cases, most federal questions, and non-diverse claims joined with federal questions); 28 U.S.C. § 1446 (establishing the procedure for accomplishing removal); and 28 U.S.C. §§ 1447–49 (setting procedures after removal).

The general right of removal is subject to such exceptions as Congress may create from time to time. *See* 28 U.S.C. § 1441(a); *Breuer v. Jim's Concrete of Brevard, Inc.*, 538 U.S. 691, 694 (2003). Congress has, on occasion, enacted specific removal statutes that apply only in particular circumstances, such as removal in lawsuits against federal officers or agencies (28 U.S.C. §§ 1442, 1442(a), and 1444); and removal in lawsuits where a defendant might not be able to assert a federal civil right in a State court (28 U.S.C. § 1443). In other contexts, Congress has foreclosed the right of removal, as it did, for example, in 28 U.S.C. § 1445, for suits against railroads under the Federal Employers' Liability Act and suits arising under State workers' compensation laws.

Threshold Removal Requirement: Federal Subject-Matter Jurisdiction Must Exist

Removal is possible only when at least one claim filed by the plaintiff falls within the original subject-matter jurisdiction of the federal district court. *See Jefferson County v. Acker,* 527 U.S. 423, 430 (1999).

- *Time for Testing if Subject-Matter Jurisdiction Exists:* The presence or absence of federal subject-matter jurisdiction is evaluated at the time a notice of removal is filed. *See Caterpillar Inc. v. Lewis,* 519 U.S. 61, 73 (1996). However, when subject-matter jurisdiction is based on diversity of citizenship, jurisdiction must exist *both* at the time the State court action was begun *and* at the time the notice of removal was filed.

- *Exception—Post-Removal Cures:* If at the time a case is removed subject-matter jurisdiction is lacking, but the plaintiff subsequently amends the complaint in a way that then establishes valid subject-matter jurisdiction, the defect that existed at the time of removal may be ignored. *See Caterpillar Inc. v. Lewis,* 519 U.S. 61, 64 (1996).

- *Burden of Proving Federal Subject-Matter Jurisdiction:* The party seeking removal carries the burden of establishing that all jurisdictional requirements for removal are met. The statutory right to remove is narrowly construed. Where a doubt exists, a district court will resolve it by sending the lawsuit back to State court (this process, called "remand," is discussed below.)
- *When State Court Lacks Jurisdiction:* The federal district court may hear a removed case even if the State court from which the case was removed lacked jurisdiction to proceed with the lawsuit. *See* 28 U.S.C. § 1441(f). (Unresolved, however, is whether venue in the State court must have been proper prior to removal.)

Other Preliminary Removal Limitations

Congress has established other removal constraints that govern this State-to-federal court shifting procedure:

- *Removal Is a Defendant's Option Only:* Only defendants can exercise the option of removal. *See* 28 U.S.C. § 1441(a). (Plaintiffs already had their opportunity to make the federal/State forum choice at the time they selected where to file their lawsuit.)
  - *"Defendant" Defined:* For purposes of the general removal statute, "defendant" is understood to mean the *original* defendant or defendants: those parties defending against the original plaintiff's claims. Other parties are not "defendants" within the meaning of this statute and, consequently, may not exercise the option of removal—even though those parties might find themselves in a defending position on certain claims (like, for example, the original plaintiff "defending" against a counterclaim or a Rule 13(h) additional party brought in to "defend" against a counterclaim). *See Home Depot U.S.A., Inc. v. Jackson*, 139 S. Ct. 1743, 1747–50 (2019). Consequently, parties defending against counterclaims, crossclaims, or third-party impleader claims have no right, based on that "defending" status alone, to remove cases (with one exception: when the basis for removal is a third-party claim against a foreign country, 28 U.S.C. § 1441(d)).
- *Removal from State Courts Only:* Under Congress's general removal statute, the lawsuit must have been pending in State court at the time the removal notice was filed. The statute provides no authority to remove a case pending in other sorts of tribunals (such as in State administrative agencies).
- *Removal to the Local Federal District Court Only:* Removed cases go to only one locale when they arrive into the federal system: to the federal district (or division) encompassing the location where the State court is sitting. *See* 28 U.S.C. § 1441(a). Thus, a case removed from a Pennsylvania State trial court in Pittsburgh, Pennsylvania would be sent to the United States District Court for the Western District of Pennsylvania (the federal district court that encompasses the city of Pittsburgh).
- *Blocking Removal by Careful Claim Selection:* Plaintiffs can ordinarily foreclose the possibility of removal by electing not to plead claims that would be removal-eligible. Note, however, that in the rare instance that the plaintiff's State law claims are completely preempted by federal law, the lawsuit might still be removable. *See Metropolitan Life Ins. Co. v. Taylor,* 481 U.S. 58, 65–66 (1987).

Removals Based on Federal Question Jurisdiction

A defendant may remove any case that is based on the Constitution, laws, or treaties of the United States, if the federal court would have original subject-matter jurisdiction over the claim. *See* 28 U.S.C. § 1441(c). In general, this authorizes removal of cases that could have been filed originally in federal district court pursuant to 28 U.S.C. § 1331 (governing "arising under" subject-matter jurisdiction), unless Congress provides otherwise.

Removals Based on Diversity of Citizenship Jurisdiction

A defendant may also remove any case where the parties meet the requirements of diversity of citizenship jurisdiction (namely, complete diversity and a qualifying amount in controversy). But these types of removals are limited by one important exception. Diversity-based removals are not generally available if the defendant (who might otherwise qualify under the diversity requirements) is being sued at "home"—that is, in a forum where that defendant is a citizen. *See* 28 U.S.C. § 1441(b)(2). Note, this "home-defendant" exception might not apply where the defendant removes the case in the often very narrow time window between filing and the moment that defendant is formally served with process. *See Encompass Ins. Co. v. Stone Mansion Rest. Inc.*, 902 F.3d 147, 152 (3d Cir. 2018) (construing Section 1441(b)(2)'s "properly joined and served as defendants" statutory phrasing). Diversity-based removals also implicate other issues:

- *Fraudulent Joinder:* A plaintiff may join a nondiverse defendant for the purpose of attempting to block removal of an otherwise diverse claim, but may do so only so long as there exists a legitimate basis for the joinder. Otherwise, the doctrine of "fraudulent joinder" permits the court to disregard the citizenship of the nondiverse defendant in testing subject-matter jurisdiction. The standard for fraudulent joinder is not always clear, but likely exists where the plaintiff engages in "outright fraud" in pleading jurisdictional allegations, where there is no colorable basis for the claim against the nondiverse defendant, or where the plaintiff joins a nondiverse defendant who has no joint, several, or alternative liability with a diverse defendant, and there is no connection between the claims against the diverse and nondiverse defendants.
- *Fictitious Names Disregarded:* When the applicable State procedure allows lawsuits against defendants identified by fictitious names (*e.g., General Motors v. John Doe, Mary Roe, and Jane Coe),* the citizenship of such defendants will be disregarded in testing for diversity. *See* 28 U.S.C. § 1441(b)(1).
- *Post-Removal Events Affecting Diversity Requirements:* The courts are divided on the question of whether a case that was properly removed on the basis of diversity jurisdiction must be remanded to State court when events occurring after removal would have defeated removal had those events occurred prior to removal.
- *Amount in Controversy:* If the complaint states no amount in controversy, the defendant can assert one in its notice of removal, provided it does so plausibly (evidence establishing that assertion is only required if it is challenged). *See Dart Cherokee Basin Operating Co., LLC v. Owens*, 135 S. Ct. 547, 554 (2014).

Removal of Multiparty, Multiforum Wrongful Death Actions

Original federal subject-matter jurisdiction extends to certain civil actions arising from a single accident where at least 75 natural persons have died at a discrete location, provided minimal diversity and the other provisions of the Multiparty, Multiforum Jurisdiction statute are satisfied. *See* 28 U.S.C. § 1369. Under certain circumstances, those actions—when filed in a State court—may be removed. *See* 28 U.S.C. § 1441(e)(1).

Removal of Lawsuits Against Foreign Countries

Lawsuits against foreign countries or their agents, filed originally in a State court, may be removed regardless of whether the suit was based on a federal question or State law. *See* 28 U.S.C. § 1441(d). This removal right is vested in the foreign country and is substantially unqualified. *See id.* Moreover, the time limit for filing for removal may be extended, for good cause shown, beyond the 30-day limit imposed routinely on more conventional removal petitions. *See id.* It is the defendant's burden to demonstrate good cause for a delay in filing. However, while a foreign country's right to remove is unrestricted if filed within the 30-day limit, removals filed outside that period are subject to the discretion of the district court. Foreign sovereigns, as defendants, do not waive whatever sovereign immunity defenses they may enjoy under federal law by filing for removal. When removal is sought under this right, the court must try the case without a jury.

Joinder of Both Removable and "Non-Removable" Claims

Plaintiffs may allege multiple claims, only some of which are removable. When the basis for removal in such a case is the presence of a federal question, the process is clear. Defendants may remove the lawsuit in its entirety. *See* 28 U.S.C. § 1441(c)(1). Once in federal court, however, the judge must sever all nonremovable claims (those that lack either original or supplemental subject-matter jurisdiction) and then remand those severed claims back to the State court from which they were removed. *See* 28 U.S.C. § 1441(c)(2). However, when the basis for removal would be diversity of citizenship only, there is no statutory authority permitting a removal where a portion of the claims satisfy the diversity requirements and other portions do not.

Removal by States and Effect on Their Eleventh Amendment Immunity

The Eleventh Amendment to the U.S. Constitution affords American States a substantial degree of immunity against lawsuits in federal district courts. It is unclear whether an American State, sued originally in a State court but electing to remove the dispute to federal court, waives its Eleventh Amendment immunity by doing so.

Forum Selection Clauses

An otherwise valid forum selection clause that limits jurisdiction exclusively to a non-federal court is likely enforceable, notwithstanding that the parties would otherwise be eligible for federal diversity jurisdiction. It is unclear whether the same result follows if a case was eligible for federal question jurisdiction (particularly exclusive federal question jurisdiction).

§ 2.14 Removal: Removal Procedure

When eligible to do so, defendants may remove a State court lawsuit to federal district court by filing a timely "notice of removal" with the appropriate federal court. No motion practice or court order is necessary. Instead, the proper filing and service of a "notice of removal" will accomplish the task.

PRACTICING LAW WITH THIS PRINCIPLE

Notice of Removal—Its Contents, and Rule 11

A "notice of removal" is ordinarily a very simple form. *See* Notice of Removal of Civil Action—General Form, 14 Fed. Proc. Forms § 58:53 (sample). It should contain a concise statement of the grounds upon which removal is based and should be accompanied by copies of "all process, pleadings, and orders served upon" the defendant who is seeking the removal. *See* 28 U.S.C. § 1446(a). Notices of removal are expressly subject to the ethical lawyering provisions of Rule 11, which permits the sanctioning of inappropriate pleadings and motions. *See id.* There is no rule prohibiting a party from filing more than one notice of removal, provided that each is timely and meets the requirements of Rule 11.

Notice of Removal—Where Filed

The notice of removal must be filed in the particular district court that encompasses the territory within which the State lawsuit is pending.

Notice of Removal—Service and Effect

The defendants must give written notice to all adverse parties "promptly" after filing the notice of removal. A copy of the notice must also be filed with the clerk of the State court where the lawsuit had been pending. Upon such filing, removal is complete (no motion or judicial act is necessary). The State court is immediately divested of its jurisdiction over the lawsuit (and must, in the language of the statute, "proceed no further" on the lawsuit), and jurisdiction is correspondingly immediately invested in the federal court. *See* 28 U.S.C. § 1446(d). *See also Roman Catholic Archdiocese of San Juan v. Acevedo Feliciano*, 140 S. Ct. 676, 700 (2020).

Notice of Removal—Unanimous Consent Required

Under the general removal statute, all defendants who have been both joined and served in the lawsuit must "join in or consent to the removal" for it to be proper. *See* 28 U.S.C. § 1446(a)(2). Some courts have required that each defendant must individually confirm to the court, either personally or through counsel, its consent. Other courts have held that the required unanimity may be shown less formally. If the case is removable due to the presence of a federal question, but includes other, non-removable counts, this consent requirement is satisfied by the consent of those defendants sued on the federal question; consent by the defendants sued only on the non-removable counts is not necessary. *See* 28 U.S.C. § 1441(c)(2).

- *Unjoined/Unserved Defendants:* Consent need only be obtained from those defendants already joined and served in the lawsuit. Thus, removal does not ordinarily depend on consent from later-joined or later-served defendants.
- *Class Action Exception:* In cases involving class actions eligible for removal, *any* defendant may seek removal "without consent of all defendants." *See* 28 U.S.C. § 1453(b).
- *Nominal Party Exception:* Consent is not required from nominal parties (parties with no immediately apparent personal stake in the litigation). Whether a party is "nominal" is, however, not always clear.

Notice of Removal—Time for Filing

Generally, a removal-eligible defendant has 30 days to file a notice of removal. *See* 28 U.S.C. § 1446(b). This 30-day period ordinarily runs from the defendant's receipt—"through service or otherwise"—of a copy of the initial pleading setting out the claim. This facially straight-forward directive, however, is sometimes mired in complexity. For example, the initial pleading will have been filed in a State court where averments about citizenship diversity or the presence of a federal question may well have been irrelevant and unnecessary; consequently, the initial pleading may not yet contain enough information to confirm whether the lawsuit is truly removable. In other cases, multiple defendants may be named, but not all served at the same time, or the applicable State law might permit a lawsuit to be filed by a "writ," with a complaint to follow sometime later. Notwithstanding these context variants, some timing rules are settled:

- *When Removability Is Clear:* If removability is clear from the initial pleading, the 30-day period runs from the defendant's receipt of that pleading (through service or otherwise).
- *When Removability Is Clear but There Is Only Partial Service:* If removability is clear, but (in accordance with State law) the defendant has only been served with a summons and the initial pleading is filed with the court, the 30-day period runs from service of that summons. However, if State law permits (or requires) that only a summons be served initially and then, later, a complaint is furnished to the defendant, the 30-day period runs from the date the defendant receives the complaint. *See Murphy Bros., Inc. v. Michetti Pipe Stringing, Inc.*, 526 U.S. 344, 354 (1999). Alternatively, if the complaint is filed without immediate service on the defendant, the 30-day period runs from service of the summons on the defendant. *See id.*
- *When Service Is Waived:* If a defendant has, pursuant to State law, voluntarily waived the formal requirements of service of process, the 30-day period will run on the occurrence of some other event, such as the date waiver of service becomes effective. *See id.* at 350.
- *When an Advance "Courtesy" Copy Is Delivered:* Absent a waiver of service, the 30-day period will not begin to run when a "courtesy" copy of the pleading is supplied, where formal service, as directed by State law, has not yet been accomplished. *See id.* at 356.

- *When Multiple Defendants Are Named:* In a multi-defendant lawsuit, each defendant has 30 days "after receipt by service on" that defendant to file a notice of removal. Thus, later-served defendants have a later running time in which to file their notices. (In such a case, those defendants who were served earlier may join in or consent to the removal, even if they had not earlier filed timely notices of removal themselves.)
- *When Service Is Made on a Statutory Agent:* When service is authorized on an agent designated by statute (such as when the local secretary of State is authorized to be served on defendant's behalf), the 30-day period runs from the date the defendant receives notice that such service has been made.
- *When Removability Is NOT Clear:* If the "case stated" in the initial pleading does not disclose a basis for removal, the 30-day period begins to run when the defendant receives "through service or otherwise" information from which, for the first time, the defendant can ascertain that the lawsuit is—or has become—removable. *See* 28 U.S.C. § 1446(b)(3). Such information can come from an amended pleading, a motion, an order, or other paper (such as discovery responses, settlement proposals, or correspondence). It is common practice to relieve the defendant of the chore of "guessing" at removal eligibility or independently investigating the question. Instead, the defendant's time limit for removal should begin to run only where it is clear, from consulting appropriate documents, that removal is possible.
    - *1-Year Outside Time Limit:* If the basis for removal is subject-matter jurisdiction based on diversity of citizenship, the right to remove on the basis of this "after-acquired eligibility" expires if not filed within one year after commencement of the lawsuit. *See* 28 U.S.C. § 1446(c)(1). Courts usually measure "commencement" for this purpose by referencing the relevant State court's commencement rules.
    - *Bad Faith Exception:* But this 1-year cap will not apply where a plaintiff acted in "bad faith" to prevent a defendant's removal, such as where a plaintiff deliberately failed to disclose the true amount in controversy in order to block removal. See 28 U.S.C. § 1446(c).
    - *Waiver Exception:* If a defendant fails to remove within the 1-year time limit, but the plaintiff fails to raise a timeliness objection, the 1-year limit will be deemed waived.
    - *Class Action Exception:* The 1-year limit does not apply to the removal of class actions (though class action defendants must, nevertheless, still remove within 30 days of notice of removal eligibility). See 28 U.S.C. § 1453(b).
- *Sources of Information to Reveal Removability:* There is some case law restricting the sources of information to show that the lawsuit is removable. When the defendant attempts to remove within the original 30-day period from filing, sources may be broader (including sources of the defendant's own creation). However, when the defendant is attempting to show later that an originally unremovable case has *become* removable, sources may be narrower (excluding defendant-generated information).
- *Premature Removals:* If a defendant files a notice of removal after the case is filed, but before formal service on that defendant, and then takes no further action on removal after being served, it appears that such a filing can qualify as a timely removal.
- *Foreign Sovereigns as Defendants:* When the removing defendant is a foreign sovereign within the meaning of the Foreign Sovereign Immunities Act, 28 U.S.C. § 1441(d), the 30-day removal period may be extended by the district court for cause shown. *See* 28 U.S.C. § 1605.

Notice of Removal—Eligibility for Removal in Diversity Cases

In assessing whether a case is removable on the basis of diversity, the general rule is that the amount the plaintiff demands in the initial pleading is considered to be the amount in controversy—so long as it is made in good faith and is not, to a legal certainty, overstated. *See* 28 U.S.C. § 1446(c)(2).

- *Nonmonetary Relief:* If the initial pleading seeks only nonmonetary relief, the defendant's notice of removal may assert a qualifying amount in controversy. *See id.*
- *Monetary Relief That Is Uncapped or Without Sum-Certain:* If the initial pleading seeks monetary relief, but State procedure did not permit a plea for a sum-certain or, alternatively, allows recovery of damages greater than the amount sought in the initial pleading, the defendant's notice of removal may assert a qualifying amount in controversy. *See id.*
- *Monetary Relief That Qualifies Even When Unpleaded:* If the initial pleading requests monetary relief in an amount less than the jurisdictional requirement, removal may still be appropriate if the district court finds that the lawsuit seeks relief that actually qualifies under the amount in controversy requirement (tested under a preponderance of the evidence standard). *See id.*
- *After-Acquired Information:* Where the initial pleading does not disclose a qualifying amount in controversy, but subsequent information comes to light demonstrating that the requirement is satisfied, removal may be proper. *See* 28 U.S.C. § 1446(c)(3).

Notice of Removal—Amendments

A notice of removal may be amended to correct defective allegations of removal jurisdiction. *See* 28 U.S.C. § 1653. Courts may permit such amendments even when made beyond the 30-day removal period. However, if the amendment is not merely corrective, but proposes instead to raise new allegations, the amendment must be rejected.

Notification to State Court and Other Parties

Defendants seeking removal must "promptly" notify the State court and other parties through filing and service of copies of the notice of removal. *See* 28 U.S.C. § 1446(d).

No Bond Required

Formerly, defendants seeking removal were required to post a bond to cover the plaintiff's costs if the federal court determined that removal was inappropriate. Congress amended the removal statutes to delete this requirement. Note, however, that a defendant who wrongfully removes a lawsuit to federal court may still be subject to sanctions under Rule 11 or imposition of costs and expenses following a remand. *See* 28 U.S.C. § 1447(c).

Remedy for Inappropriate Removal

If the federal court determines that removal was inappropriate, it may remand part or all of the case to the State court. Dismissal is *not* ordinarily an appropriate remedy.

§ 2.14a Removal Procedure: Special Removal Procedures in Class Actions

Congress enacted the Class Action Fairness Act (CAFA) in 2005. This federal law created greater opportunity for class actions pending in State court to be removed to federal court and, if thereafter remanded back to State court, greater opportunity for appellate review of that decision to remand. *See* 28 U.S.C. §§ 1332(d)(1), 1453(a).

PRACTICING LAW WITH THIS PRINCIPLE

How CAFA Modified the Usual Removal Requirements

The Class Action Fairness Act modified several of the usual requirements and procedures for removal for the class action context. (Note: CAFA assigned special definitions to the terms "class," "class action," "class certification order," and "class members," and those special definitions apply when interpreting the Act. *See* 28 U.S.C. §§ 1332(d), 1453, 1711–15.)

- *Diversity of Citizenship:* CAFA relaxes the requirement of complete diversity by permitting the exercise of diversity-based federal subject-matter jurisdiction if any single class member is diverse from the class opponents. *See* 28 U.S.C. § 1332(d)(2).
- *Amount in Controversy:* CAFA also relaxes the amount-in-controversy requirement, by permitting a diversity-based removal if the individual claims of *all* class members—when aggregated together—exceed $5,000,000, exclusive of interest and costs. *See* 28 U.S.C. § 1332(d)(2), (d)(6). Although this figure is obviously larger than the usual more-than-$75,000 threshold, the aggregation effect makes removal more tenable for many classes. (A full summary of all of CAFA's requirements appears with Rule 23 below.)
- *1-Year Outside Limitation on Removal of Diversity Cases:* The 1-year outside time limit on after-acquired removability in diversity cases does not apply to class actions under CAFA. *See* 28 U.S.C. § 1453(b).
- *"Home-Defendant" Bar:* CAFA also lifts the usual prohibition that bars defendants from diversity-based removals when they are citizens of the State where the lawsuit is pending. *See* 28 U.S.C. § 1453(b).
- *Unanimous Consent:* CAFA also permits removal on the basis of a single defendant's request; the usual requirement of defendant unanimity is excused. *See id.*
- *Appellate Review Prohibition:* As explained below, remand decisions are largely immune from appellate review. This bar not apply under CAFA. *See* 28 U.S.C. § 1453(c). Instead, CAFA allows appeal from either grants or denials of remand motions, as well as orders issued *sua sponte*, with the following procedures:
    - o *Appeal by Permission, Not by Right:* The appeals court may (but need not) hear such an appeal. *See id.*
    - o *10 Days to Apply:* Parties seeking review of a decision granting or denying remand must apply to the appeals court within 10 days of entry of the order. *See id.*
    - o *60 Days to Rule:* If the appeals court elects to hear the appeal, it must rule within 60 days. The 60-day period begins to run from the date that the appeals court grants the petition to appeal. The period may be extended, however, upon the parties' consent (for "any period of time") or upon court order, issued for good cause shown (for 10 days). If the appeals court fails to rule within the prescribed time, the appeal is deemed denied. *See id.*

Class Actions That Do Not Fall Within CAFA

CAFA excludes from its specially-tailored removal procedures a few categories of class actions: (1) those "solely" involving certain claims under federal securities laws; and (2) those "solely" involving claims arising under State corporate laws governing the internal affairs or governance of State-chartered corporations. *See* 28 U.S.C. § 1453(d).

§ 2.15 Removal: Post-Removal Procedures and Remand

Once a case has been removed to a federal district court, that court may issue orders and process (including allowing joinder of additional parties) and may retrieve the State court record. If the removal is found to be improper, the court may also order the lawsuit sent back ("remanded") to State court.

PRACTICING LAW WITH THIS PRINCIPLE

Post-Removal Authority to Issue Orders and Process

Following removal, the federal district court has the authority to issue orders and process necessary to bring parties within its jurisdiction. *See* 28 U.S.C. § 1447(a).

Post-Removal Service of Process

At the time of removal, service of process might not yet be complete on all defendants. In such a circumstance, the federal district court is authorized to permit completion of service begun in the State proceeding or, alternatively, to issue its own service on any as-yet-unserved defendants. *See* 28 U.S.C. § 1448. Defendants who are so served may challenge the removal (by seeking remand, if appropriate). *See id.* This authority confers no additional rights on the plaintiff.

Post-Removal Joinder of Non-Diverse Parties

The district court may refuse the joinder of non-diverse parties whose presence would destroy the court's subject-matter jurisdiction, or the court may grant such a joinder and then remand the lawsuit back to State court. *See* 28 U.S.C. § 1447(e). Factors the district court may weigh include whether the joinder's purpose was to defeat federal jurisdiction, whether the movant has been dilatory in seeking the joinder, whether significant prejudice would follow from denying the joinder, and other, case-peculiar considerations.

Post-Removal Retrieval of the State Court Case Record

The district court is authorized to obtain all the court records of a removed case either by requiring the removing party to supply copies or by issuing a writ of certiorari to the State court to retrieve the records directly. *See* 28 U.S.C. § 1447(b). If the district court chooses the first option, that party's failure to comply may permit the federal court to remand the case back to State court. If the State court fails to supply the record, following a proper request and payment or tender of proper fees, the district court is authorized to re-create the record "by affidavit or otherwise." *See* 28 U.S.C. § 1449.

Remand—Generally

Removal occurs immediately (as explained above); it requires no motion or court order, and takes effect upon the notice of removal. A litigant who believes the removal to be improper must thereafter request the federal judge to return the lawsuit to State court by a process known as "remand." *See* 28 U.S.C. § 1447(c). Removal is improper (and remand necessary) if federal subject-matter jurisdiction does not exist over the removed case or because the procedural requirements for removal were not followed.

Remand—On Jurisdictional Grounds

Subject-matter jurisdiction defects cannot be consented to or waived. If federal subject-matter jurisdiction is absent, the removed lawsuit *must* be remanded back to State court. A motion for remand on this basis may be made at any time prior to final judgment in the case. *See* 28 U.S.C. § 1447(c).

Remand—On Non-Jurisdictional Grounds

When removal is defective for any other, non-jurisdictional reason (such as, for example, failure to remove in a timely manner or to have the consent of all defendants), the district court will also remand back to State court—provided a motion for remand is made within 30 days after the filing of the notice of removal. *See* 28 U.S.C. § 1447(c).

- *Violation of the "Home-Defendant" Bar:* In diversity cases, removal is not permitted when a defendant is a citizen of the State where the lawsuit is then pending. *See* 28 U.S.C. § 1441(b)(2). Courts are divided on whether a removal that violates this home-defendant bar is a non-jurisdictional defect (which must be filed within 30 days of removal) or a jurisdictional defect (which may be filed at any time prior to final judgment). *See Lively v. Wild Oats Markets, Inc.*, 456 F.3d 933, 942 (9th Cir. 2006) (noting division, and view that substantial majority favor non-jurisdictional defect view).

Remand—On Other Grounds

Other grounds justifying removal—ones falling outside this jurisdictional/non-jurisdictional classification—may exist, such as asking the district court to exercise its discretion to abstain from deciding the dispute. *See Quackenbush v. Allstate Ins. Co.,* 517 U.S. 706, 712 (1996). It is unclear whether such remands must be sought within the 30-day period following removal.

Burden of Proof, and Resolving Doubts

The burden of proving that removal is appropriate falls on the party seeking removal. Removal statutes are construed strictly, and doubts are usually resolved in favor of remand.

Remand by the Court *Sua Sponte*

If the federal district court notices its own lack of subject-matter jurisdiction, the court need not wait for a motion to remand to be filed by a party. Instead, the court must remand the case on its own initiative. *See* 28 U.S.C. § 1447(c). Such action must be taken any time the court notices its lack of subject-matter jurisdiction (up until final judgment). If, however, the basis for remand is not a lack of subject-matter jurisdiction but merely a non-jurisdictional procedural defect, *sua sponte* remands (that is, remands in the absence of some party's motion) are improper.

Remanding in Part

Partial remands are required when a lawsuit, removed on the basis of the presence of a federal question, also includes nonremovable claims. In such instances, the district court must sever the nonremovable claims and remand those back to State court. *See* 28 U.S.C. § 1441(c).

Remand Only, No Dismissals

A district court has authority only to remand a case that has been removed improperly; it usually has no authority to dismiss such a case. *See Int'l Primate Protection League v. Administrators of Tulane Educ'l Fund,* 500 U.S. 72, 89 (1991).

Discretion to Impose Costs and Fees

When remanding a case back to State court, the district court may impose costs and actual expenses, "including attorney fees," where such an award would be appropriate. *See* 28 U.S.C. § 1447(c). The power to consider a motion for costs and fees continues even if the underlying case has already been remanded to State court.

Remand Logistics

When the district court remands a case, the federal clerk of court will send a certified copy of the notice of remand to the clerk of the relevant State court. *See* 28 U.S.C. § 1447(c). Jurisdiction remains with the district court until that mailing occurs. However, once it occurs, that mailing divests the federal district court of its jurisdiction over the case. If remand is based on a failure of federal subject-matter jurisdiction, the remand becomes effective even earlier, *i.e.,* at the time the order is entered. Once remand is effective, jurisdiction re-vests in the State court.

Remand—No Appeal or Reconsideration of Most Remand Orders

Subject to a few exceptions, an order by the federal court to remand a lawsuit back to State court for either lack of subject-matter jurisdiction or a procedural defect is not reviewable. 28 U.S.C. § 1447(d); *Kircher v. Putnam Funds Trust,* 547 U.S. 633, 640 (2006). This prohibition was designed to reduce the mischief caused by lawsuits ricocheting back and forth between two different court systems. Instead, Congress prescribed that most remand orders are to be made by the district courts and, once made, are final and conclusive. *See Ex parte Pa. Co.*, 137 U.S. 451, 454 (1890). This prohibition is broad—no review is allowed by direct appeal, by writ of mandamus, or even by reconsideration by the issuing trial judges themselves. *See Kircher v. Putnam Funds Trust,* 547 U.S. 633, 640 (2006). Review is barred even when the order of remand is "manifestly, inarguably erroneous." *See In re Norfolk Southern Rwy. Co.,* 756 F.3d 282, 287 (4th Cir. 2014). This bar may also prevent a second effort at removal by the same parties on similar grounds.

Notwithstanding the sweeping, seemingly absolutist language of this no-review prohibition, there are exceptions. Some of the most important of these exceptions follow:

(1) *Denials of Remand:* Only a decision to *grant* remand falls within the prohibition. Orders that deny remand are reviewable on appeal.

(2) *Statutory Exceptions:* Congress itself has enacted a few statutory exceptions to its no-review prohibition. *See* 28 U.S.C. § 1447(d).

(3) *Remand Based on Grounds Other than Subject-Matter Jurisdiction or Procedural Defect*: A court retains the authority to examine whether the basis for remand falls within a non-reviewable category (namely, defect either in subject-matter jurisdiction or in removal procedure). *See Powerex Corp. v. Reliant Energy Servs., Inc.,* 551 U.S. 224 (2007). If it does, review of any type is almost always foreclosed, absent some exception. *See id.* (This is true even if the ruling is mixed with considerations that appear to fall outside the scope of the prohibition.)

However, when the ground for remand falls outside these non-reviewable categories, review of the remand decision may be possible either in the district court that granted it or upon appellate review. *See Quackenbush v. Allstate Ins. Co.,* 517 U.S. 706, 712 (1996). Examples of such reviewable grounds for remand include: a remand based on either a motion of a party or the court's own motion that asserts a procedural defect, but does so more than 30 days after removal; a *sua sponte* remand by the district court based only on a procedural defect in removal (not a defect in subject-matter jurisdiction); a remand based on the discretionary authority of the Declaratory Judgment Act; a remand issued by a magistrate judge; a remand based on the district court's discretionary authority under 28 U.S.C. § 1441(c); a discretionary remand of claims within a district court's supplemental jurisdiction under 28 U.S.C. § 1367(c); a remand based on defendants' waiver of their arbitration rights; a remand issued after the district judge erroneously refused to recuse; a remand of a class action that is expressly appealable under the Class Action Fairness Act; a remand granted as enforcement of a valid forum selection clause; a remand made where the Supreme Court has clarified a party's right to remove in the period between the original remand decision and a party's second attempt to remove; a remand under circumstances in which, if a federal court did not review an order that determines a claim for attorney fees, no court would be able to review it because the State court would lack jurisdiction to do so; an erroneous holding that multiple efforts to remove were barred even where changed allegations of fact demonstrate that subject-matter jurisdiction is satisfied; and a district court's decision to abstain from deciding State questions. *See, e.g., Carlsbad Tech., Inc. v. HIF Bio, Inc.,* 556 U.S. 635, 640 (2009) (remand based on § 1367(c) is appealable); *Quackenbush v. Allstate Ins. Co.,* 517 U.S. 706, 712 (1996) (remand based on abstention is appealable). Finally, the appeals court may properly look at the "objective merits" of the remand order to determine the appropriateness of an award of costs and fees under § 1447(c).

(4) *Orders Following Non-Diverse Joinder:* The district court must remand if it permits a non-diverse joinder that destroys its subject-matter jurisdiction. *See* 28 U.S.C. § 1447(e). It appears that such a remand is considered a jurisdictional ruling and, thus, is non-reviewable. If, however, a district court decides to retain a case and *not* remand following a non-diverse joinder, that decision seems reviewable.

(5) *Remands in Class Actions:* A district court decisions granting or denying remand in class actions may be appealed to the appropriate court of appeals. *See* 28 U.S.C. § 1435(c). Such appeals must be made within 7 days of entry of the original order. The appellate court must then decide such an appeal within 60 days of the filing of the appeal, unless this time is extended upon all parties' consent or the court extends time (for up to 10 days) for good cause shown. If the appellate court does not act within the prescribed time, the appeal is automatically denied. *See id.*

D. FEDERAL VENUE

§ 2.16 Venue

Venue sets the appropriate federal districts in which a particular case should be heard. Venue requirements are distinct from, and in addition to, jurisdictional prerequisites. State courts are also subject to the venue requirements established by their respective legislatures, and such requirements may differ significantly from the federal venue statutes. For federal courts, however, the only venue requirements that must be met are those enacted by Congress. *See Leroy v. Great Western United Corp.*, 443 U.S. 173, 184 (1979). Venue is concerned with litigation convenience; thus, like personal jurisdiction, it can be waived.

PRACTICING LAW WITH THIS PRINCIPLE

Making Sense of Power Concepts: Subject-Matter Jurisdiction, Personal Jurisdiction, and Venue

These are three separate prerequisites for civil litigation, and must not be confused. Each is required for a court to act. Subject-matter jurisdiction has its foundations in the U.S. Constitution and is used to determine whether a case can be heard in the federal court system. Venue is a legislative (non-constitutional) constraint, and zeroes in on which particular federal districts, if any, may host that case. Personal jurisdiction resolves who the court may exercise its coercive, judicial power over when it hosts that case—an inquiry that is both legislative (the statutory step) and constitutional (the due process step). *See generally Neirbo Co. v. Bethlehem Shipbuilding Corp., Ltd.*, 308 U.S. 165, 167–68 (1939).

Venue Options in Federal Court

Congress's general venue statute, Section 1391(b), creates two options for satisfying venue in most cases, plus a third option that may be used by a plaintiff *if* neither of the first two options is available. Keep that limitation in mind: this statute does not ordinarily give a plaintiff three choices, but only two—the third is reserved for only where the first two options cannot be used to establish a venue anywhere.

- *Where Defendant Resides:* venue lies in any judicial ***district*** where any defendant resides, provided that all defendants reside in the same ***State***. (The meaning of "resides" for venue purposes is discussed below.)
- *Where Substantial Events or Omissions Occurred:* venue lies in any judicial district in which a substantial part of the relevant events or omissions giving rise to the claim occurred, or where a substantial part of the property that is the subject of the action is found (*e.g.*, in a tort case, where the damage occurred or the wrongful act was done).
- *Where Any Defendant Is Subject to Personal Jurisdiction:* if, and only if, neither of the above two venue options are available, venue will lie in any judicial district in which any defendant is subject to personal jurisdiction at the time a suit is filed.

Federal Judicial Districts

State borders matter greatly in questions of jurisdiction. For venue questions, however, the important boundary is that which exists between federal judicial districts. Districts are established by Congress. In less populous States, the entire State may be a single district; more populous States are often divided in several (as many as four) different Districts (New York, for example, is divided into the Eastern, Western, Southern, and Northern Districts).

- *Federal "Divisions":* Sometimes, a federal judicial district will be further divided into smaller geographic areas, called "divisions." For example, the United States District Court for the Eastern District of Virginia is subdivided into four "divisions": the Alexandria Division; the Norfolk Division; the Richmond Division; and the Newport News Division. Local rules of a federal district court might supplement venue statutes by requiring that a case be filed not only within the proper judicial "district," but also within the appropriate "division" within that district.

Defining "Resides"

To apply the first venue option (where the defendant resides), Congress had to define "resides" for venue purposes, which it did in 28 U.S.C. § 1391(c):

- *Residence for Natural Persons:* A natural person's residence is deemed to be the judicial district in which that person is domiciled. *See* 28 U.S.C. § 1391(c)(1). Typically, a natural person has only one domicile (and thus, for venue purposes, only one residence), notwithstanding that the person in question may actually have homes in several different States. This definition of residence applies to citizens as well as aliens lawfully admitted for permanent residence in the United States.
- *Residence for Entities That May Sue or Be Sued in Their Own Names:* Congress provided two different definitions of "resides" for entities that may sue or be sued in their own names (such as corporations, partnerships, etc.):
    - For entities that are defendants, "resides" means any judicial district in which that entity would be subject to the personal jurisdiction of the federal court. *See id.* § 1391(c)(2). But there is a caveat for some corporations—
        - If the defendant is a corporation subject to personal jurisdiction in a particular State *and* if that State has more than one federal district, the corporation "resides" in that district where its contacts would subject it to personal jurisdiction (had that district been its own State) or, if none, where the corporation has its most significant contacts. *See id.* § 1391(d).
    - For entities that are plaintiffs, "resides" means the judicial district encompassing the plaintiff's principal place of business. *See id.* § 1391(c)(2).
- *Defendants Not Resident in the United States:* Defendants not resident in the United States may be sued in any judicial district. *See* 28 U.S.C. § 1391(c)(3). Further, if such non-resident defendants are co-defendants with parties who are resident in the United States, only the residence of the United States-based defendants may be taken into account in determining the appropriateness of venue. *See* 28 U.S.C. § 1391(c)(3). However, if the defendant is lawfully admitted for permanent residence in the United States (*i.e.*, a "green-card" holder), he or she is deemed to "reside" for venue purposes in the place of his or her domicile. *See* 28 U.S.C. § 1391(c)(1).

Counterclaims and Crossclaims

Generally speaking, only plaintiffs have the burden of satisfying requirements of venue. Counterclaims, crossclaims, and similar actions normally do not raise venue questions. This approach, then, is quite different from the one that applies in jurisdictional analyses, for which every count in a case must satisfy some form of both personal and subject-matter jurisdiction.

Consent to Venue

Venue, like personal jurisdiction, is a waivable protection for defendants against an inconvenient forum. If parties consent to personal jurisdiction in a particular district or State, it appears settled that they also consent to venue there. Moreover, if the plaintiff files suit in a federal judicial district where venue is improper, the court may still hear that case if the defendant does not object to venue. *See, e.g., Leroy v. Great Western United Corp.*, 443 U.S. 173, 180 (1979).

Venue and Removal

If a claim is removed from a State court to a federal district court, Section 1391 does not apply. Instead, proper venue in a removed case is the federal district encompassing the place where the State claim was pending at the time of removal. *See* 28 U.S.C. § 1441(a). However, a party who sought removal of a claim does not thereby waive a challenge to venue. That challenge is preserved and may be raised in federal court.

Remedy for Improper Venue

If the court, on timely objection of a party, finds venue to be defective, the court may dismiss the action, with the consequence that the plaintiff might refile the same claim in an appropriate venue elsewhere (if the action is not otherwise barred). This can raise significant time-bar problems for a plaintiff. To mitigate these problems, Congress allows a federal district court, on finding venue to be faulty, to *transfer* the lawsuit to a judicial district or division where venue is proper. *See* 28 U.S.C. § 1406. The court's discretion to employ this transfer remedy is broad, constrained only by "the interest of justice." *See Ritzen Group, Inc. v. Jackson Masonry, LLC*, 140 S. Ct. 582, 590 n.3 (2020).

Special Venue over the United States, Its Agencies, and Its Officers

Three venue possibilities are available if the United States, a federal agency, or a federal officer acting in an official capacity is a defendant. (Note, however, that these additional possibilities are available *only against federal defendants in a case*; Section 1391(e) specifically provides that if non-federal parties are also defendants, venue as to them must be satisfied under § 1391(a) or (b), or some other specific venue statute.)

(1) A *Single Defendant's Residence:* venue will lie in a judicial district where a single defendant in the action resides. *See* 28 U.S.C. § 1391(e). Thus, the United States, its agencies, or officers can be sued in a judicial district where some other defendant resides. That would be true even if the federal officer, for example, did not reside in that district and did no business there; or

(2) *Location of Events or Property:* venue will lie in a judicial district where "a substantial part of the events or omissions giving rise to the claim occurred, or a substantial part of property that is the subject of the action is situated," *see id.*; or

(3) *Plaintiff's Residence:* venue will lie in a judicial district where a single plaintiff resides, provided that the cause of action does not involve real property, *see id.*

(4) *Nationwide Personal Jurisdiction Over Federal Agencies and Officers:* To ensure that the broad venue authority of this section is not nullified by problems of personal jurisdiction, Section 1391(e) also provides that the federal district court shall be able, by certified mail, to obtain personal jurisdiction over federal agencies and officers not found within the State in which the court sits.

(5) *Personal Suits Against Federal Officers:* The venue opportunities provided by Section 1391(e) as to federal officers are available only when the officers are sued in their official capacities. If they are sued personally for money damages, Section 1391(e) is not applicable. *See Stafford v. Briggs,* 444 U.S. 527, 542 (1980).

Special Venue over Foreign Countries

Section 1391(f) prescribes the venue when foreign countries or their agencies are defendants. Four possibilities for venue exist, depending on whether the lawsuit is against the foreign sovereign itself, its agency, or its shipping or cargo. These possibilities are:

(1) *Location of Events or Property:* venue will lie in a judicial district where a substantial portion of the events giving rise to the claim occurred, or where a substantial part of property that is the subject of the claim is located;

(2) *Location of Vessel or Cargo:* venue will lie in any judicial district where a vessel or cargo belonging to a foreign State is located. This venue possibility is available only if the claim arose under 28 U.S.C. § 1605(b), governing suits in admiralty against foreign countries;

(3) *Location of Agency That Is Doing Business:* if the defendant is an agency or instrumentality of the foreign country, as described in 28 U.S.C. § 1603(b), venue will lie in any judicial district in which the agency is licensed to do business or is doing business. Privately owned non-American corporations do not fit within the description of a foreign country's instrumentality as defined by Section 1603(b). For Section 1603(b) to apply, the foreign country itself, not merely its citizens, must be the majority owner of an instrumentality; or

(4) *Venue in the District of Columbia:* if the defendant is a foreign country itself or a political subdivision of a foreign country, venue may be satisfied in the United States District Court for the District of Columbia.

Special Venue over Admiralty, Maritime, or Prize Cases

The general venue provisions of Section 1391, discussed above, do not extend to cases in federal district court arising under federal admiralty or maritime law. *See* 28 U.S.C. § 1390(b).

§ 2.17 Intra-Federal "Convenience" Venue Changes (and Forum Non Conveniens)

On occasion, a court that *has* proper venue in a case may find that it is less ideally suited to hear and resolve that case than some different court. Venue changes based on "convenience" may be proper in such cases. When the more appropriate forum is another federal district court, the original court may dismiss the lawsuit (less likely), or transfer it (more likely) to the new federal forum. If, however, the more appropriate forum is not another federal court (*e.g.,* a tribunal in a foreign nation), the original court can only dismiss, invoking the forum non conveniens doctrine, and thereupon encourage the parties to litigate their dispute in that, or some other, new forum. The original court enjoys wide discretion in making "convenience" venue change assessments.

PRACTICING LAW WITH THIS PRINCIPLE

Relationship to Jurisdiction and Venue

Intra-federal convenience transfers and forum non conveniens arise ordinarily only when the federal court actually possesses personal jurisdiction (*in personam* or *in rem*), subject-matter jurisdiction, and lawful venue over the dispute—but that the court is being invited nonetheless to exercise its discretion to step aside and allow it to be heard elsewhere. *See American Dredging Co. v. Miller,* 510 U.S. 443, 453 (1994).

Timing

Usually, a motion to dismiss or transfer to another federal district, or to dismiss under the forum non conveniens doctrine, will normally be made by the parties early in the litigation. A motion made after judgment will not be granted; motions made after trial are also unlikely to succeed. Typically, a court will not rule on forum non conveniens until it first determines whether its jurisdiction and venue are proper. *See Gulf Oil Corp. v. Gilbert,* 330 U.S. 501, 504 (1947). But that is not an absolute rule; when a forum non conveniens analysis will more certainly and expeditiously resolve the question of the most appropriate forum, a court may bypass jurisdiction questions to do so. *See Sinochem Int'l Co. v. Malaysia Int'l Shipping Corp.*, 549 U.S. 422, 432 (2007).

- *Sua Sponte Forum Non Conveniens:* Forum non conveniens is ordinarily raised by a party, not by the court on its own initiate. But, provided it affords notice to all parties and an opportunity to be heard, a *sua sponte* forum non conveniens dismissal can be proper. *See Wong v. PartyGaming Ltd.*, 589 F.3d 821, 830 (6th Cir. 2009).

Intra-Federal Transfers (Rather than Dismissals)

When the more convenient, appropriate forum is simply a different federal court, Congress has supplied an efficient remedy. The original court may *transfer* the case to a different federal district court in which the case "might have been brought or . . . to which all parties have consented." *See* 28 U.S.C. § 1404. *See also Ritzen Group, Inc. v. Jackson Masonry, LLC*, 140 S. Ct. 582, 590 n.3 (2020). Because a transferred case is not dismissed, transfer usually creates no statute of limitations problems. *See Ferens v. John Deere Co.,* 494 U.S. 516, 526 (1990). It also affords district courts somewhat more flexibility in assessing whether to relocate the case. *See Piper Aircraft v. Reyno,* 454 U.S. 235, 253 (1981). Transfer is now the standard remedy in cases where it can be applied. *See Quackenbush v. Allstate Ins. Co.,* 517 U.S. 706, 722 (1996). However, this transfer option may be used only between federal districts. *See Atlantic Marine Const. Co. v. U.S. Dist. Court for W. Dist. of Texas*, 134 S. Ct. 568, 580. If the more convenient, appropriate forum lies outside the United States, the only remedy available is a forum non conveniens dismissal of the action, with an opportunity for the plaintiff to file the claim elsewhere. *See Quackenbush,* 517 U.S. at 722. This remedy can create practical problems for plaintiffs, so courts often condition a grant of a defendant's motion to dismiss for forum non conveniens on the defendant's assent to submit to jurisdiction in the new forum and waiver of any challenge on statute of limitations grounds.

- *Transfers by Consent:* If parties consent to personal jurisdiction in a particular district or State, they may also consent to venue there. *See* 28 U.S.C. § 1404(a).

- *Partial Transfers:* It is uncertain whether the transfer of an entire case is required, or whether a district court may properly choose to transfer only a portion of a case.

- *Transfers to Certain Territories:* Transfers are not permitted to the district courts for Guam, the Northern Marianas, and the Virgin Islands. *See* 28 U.S.C. § 1404(d).

Forum Non Conveniens—Requirement of an Adequate Alternative Forum

A case may not be dismissed on forum non conveniens grounds unless an adequate alternative forum exists. *See Gulf Oil Corp. v. Gilbert,* 330 U.S. 501, 506–07 (1947). The defendant has the burden of demonstrating the availability of such a forum. Even if the plaintiff's choice of forum seems strained, that choice will not be overruled (assuming no problems with jurisdiction and venue exist) until the trial court makes the threshold determination that a different forum choice exists. If there is no other such forum, the court will retain the case.

Evaluating the adequacy of an alternative forum requires an assessment of whether the defendants are subject to service of process there, whether the alternative forum will actually hear the case, and whether jurisdiction will lie over the defendant. *See Piper Aircraft Co. v. Reyno,* 454 U.S. 235, 255 n.22 (1981). If there is some question about jurisdiction in the proposed alternative forum, the moving defendant can usually eliminate the issue by stipulating to jurisdiction in that forum.

A development in some foreign jurisdictions has added a new wrinkle to the question of the availability of an alternative forum in foreign countries. Some countries, apparently concerned about the use of forum non conveniens in United States courts, have enacted legislation providing that if one of their citizens files a suit in, *e.g.*, a United States court, the courts of the plaintiff's home country are closed to that plaintiff on that cause of action. These laws apply to circumstances where, prior to the filing in the United States, the plaintiff's home court would otherwise have had concurrent jurisdiction. In such circumstances, it may be possible to conclude that the foreign court, in the most literal sense, is no longer an available forum.

If the proposed alternative forum is found in another country, the trial court hearing the forum non conveniens motion will, in addition to questions of jurisdiction and service of process, also examine whether the foreign court has the capacity to provide an adequate remedy. *See Piper Aircraft Co.,* 454 U.S. at 254.

A foreign court may also be "inadequate" because the cause of action would be barred by a foreign statute of limitations. A defendant's willingness and ability to waive the statute of limitations defense in a foreign court may help alleviate that concern, but only if the foreign forum permits waiver of a statute of limitations defense. The issue can be complicated further if it is shown that the party who chose the original forum deliberately delayed filing suit so as to ensure that the case would be time-barred elsewhere. In extreme cases, there may even be questions about the integrity of a particular foreign court.

When the court believes that another forum would be more appropriate but yet retains some concern over whether a case will actually be heard in the foreign court, the court's dismissal order could invite the parties to return if that need arises.

The probability that a foreign court will not apply American substantive law is usually not weighed heavily in determining the adequacy of an alternative forum. *See Piper Aircraft Co.,* 454 U.S. at 247. However, the result may be different in cases where distinctions in procedural law preclude a reasonable opportunity for the plaintiff to present a case.

Forum Non Conveniens—Deference to Plaintiff's Choice of Forum

Normally, the court will give substantial deference to a plaintiff's choice of forum. *See Koster v. (American) Lumbermens Mut. Cas. Co.*, 330 U.S. 518, 524 (1947). *See generally Gulf Oil Corp. v. Gilbert*, 330 U.S. 501, 508 (1947) ("[U]nless the balance is strongly in favor of the defendant, the plaintiff's choice of forum should rarely be disturbed.").

Thus, for a defendant to prevail on a forum non conveniens motion, the defendant must demonstrate that the plaintiff's choice of forum is significantly inappropriate, notwithstanding the existence of satisfactory jurisdiction and venue. This deference means that when the court is weighing the public and private interests (discussed below), the plaintiff's choice of forum will not be defeated by a mere preponderance of interests favoring dismissal; instead the weighing factors must tilt heavily in favor of trial in the alternative forum. In all cases, the trial court's discretion in weighing factors may not be used to nullify the deference to which a plaintiff's choice of forum is entitled. (Of course, this question of deference is never reached unless the defendant first establishes that an adequate, alternative forum exists.)

- *Exception—Plaintiff Does Not Reside in District:* If the plaintiff does not reside in the judicial district where the case was filed, the plaintiff's choice of forum receives less deference. *See Piper Aircraft Co. v. Reyno,* 454 U.S. 235, 255–56 (1981) (when plaintiff chooses her home forum, "it is reasonable to assume that this choice is convenient," but when plaintiff's choice is not her home, "this assumption is much less reasonable").
- *Exception—Non-American Plaintiffs:* American plaintiffs receive substantially more deference in their choices of a forum than do non-American plaintiffs. *See Reyno,* 454 U.S. at 256. However, "less deference" is not the same as no deference, and a foreign plaintiff's choice of forum is still entitled to some respect.
- *Exception—Certain Declaratory Judgment Plaintiffs:* If the plaintiff who has chosen the forum is seeking declaratory relief, with a "bad faith" motive of taking advantage of the true plaintiff in a strategic race-to-judgment, the declaratory judgment plaintiff's choice of forum might receive little deference.

- *Exception—Identical Lawsuits in Different Venues:* If an unusual case involves identical lawsuits filed in different venues, there is no deference to either plaintiff's choice of forum.
- *Modification—Corporate Plaintiffs in International Business:* If the plaintiff is an American corporation with substantial experience in international business transactions that is suing on a cause of action that arose outside the United States, it appears that such a plaintiff will receive less deference than would, for example, an individual American plaintiff suing on a personal injury incurred while on vacation outside the United States.

Forum Non Conveniens—Judicial Discretion in Weighing Convenience Factors

Once a trial court identifies an adequate alternative forum where the defendants will be subject to jurisdiction, the court will weigh public and private interest factors in determining whether to grant or deny the forum non conveniens motion. This weighing is obviously a highly fact-dependent inquiry, and must be assessed on a case-by-case basis. *See Van Cauwenberghe v. Biard,* 486 U.S. 517, 529 (1988). The court enjoys significant discretion. *See Piper Aircraft v. Reyno,* 454 U.S. 235, 257 (1981). However, failure to weigh all the public or private interest factors implicated in a particular case can be abuse of discretion. Should the court grant the motion, it has discretion to impose conditions on its ruling.

Forum Non Conveniens—Public Interest Factors

The public interest factors include: (1) having local disputes settled locally; (2) avoiding problems of applying foreign law; and (3) avoiding burdening jurors with cases that have no impact on their community. *See Piper Aircraft v. Reyno,* 454 U.S. 235, 258 n.6 (1981); *Gulf Oil Corp. v. Gilbert,* 330 U.S. 501, 508–09 (1947). In some cases there may also be questions about the enforceability of a judgment that the court would render if it retained the case.

- *Local Disputes:* The desire to settle local disputes locally (or, alternatively, the desire to avoid imposing distant disputes on a local court) takes into account questions such as local court congestion.
- *Application of Foreign Law:* Courts may be reluctant to take cases in which they will be obligated to apply the law of another jurisdiction, though this consideration normally is not dispositive.
- *Burdening Jurors with Cases of No Local Interest:* This factor implicates two interests: whether local citizens should have to carry the burden of trying a case unrelated to their community and whether the citizenry of another area has a greater interest in the outcome of a case.
- *Enforceability of a Judgment:* If enforcement of a prospective judgment could require further litigation outside the United States, the court may weigh that factor in determining whether the case should be heard in the United States in the first instance. This consideration would carry particular weight if there is a significant possibility that the judgment would be unenforceable, thus potentially reducing the American judicial proceeding to a waste of time and judicial resources.
- *Public Policy:* In unusual cases, courts may retain a particular lawsuit because public policy favors an American forum for such a suit.
- *Pending Litigation in a Foreign Forum:* The existence of concurrent litigation in a foreign court is *not* a factor arguing in favor of dismissing a case on forum non conveniens grounds.

Forum Non Conveniens—Private Interest Factors

Private interest factors include: (1) ease of access to evidence; (2) the cost for witnesses to attend trial; (3) the availability of compulsory process; and (4) other factors that might shorten trial or make it less expensive. *See Piper Aircraft v. Reyno,* 454 U.S. 235, 258 n.6 (1981); *Gulf Oil Corp. v. Gilbert,* 330 U.S. 501, 508–09 (1947). For the most part, these factors assess the impact of forum selection on the ability of parties to prove their case. If a plaintiff's choice of forum—or the defendant's proposed alternative—substantially affects a party's ability to put forward witnesses and evidence, the court will be inclined to weigh that consideration heavily. *See Reyno,* 454 U.S. at 259.

Venue Convenience and Forum Selection Clauses

Parties can agree in advance to resolve their disputes in a particular venue through a forum selection clause included in an agreement between them, and if they do so, a later forum non conveniens assertion is unlikely to succeed. *See Stewart Org., Inc. v. Ricoh Corp.,* 487 U.S. 22, 29 (1988). In such a contest, the moving party will bear a heavy burden, since a valid forum selection clause must be given "controlling weight in all but the most exception cases." *See id.* at 33. Neither plaintiff's choice of filing location nor the private interest factors will merit consideration by the court in such a case. *See Atlantic Marine Const. Co. v. U.S. Dist. Court for W. Dist. of Texas,* 134 S. Ct. 568, 581–82 (2013). Ordinarily, a court confronted with a valid forum selection clause will grant a motion for an intra-federal transfer for convenience, if available, or dismiss, if a transfer option is not available. *See id.* at 579.

E. THE *ERIE* DOCTRINE

§ 2.18 The *Erie* Problem—Introduction

Federal district courts do not just preside over disputes involving federal law. They are often called upon—properly—to hear State law disputes (that is, disputes arising under a State's constitution, statutes, or common law) when diversity of citizenship jurisdiction, 28 U.S.C. § 1332, or supplemental jurisdiction, 28 U.S.C. § 1367, is invoked.[3] In such instances, where the federal court is essentially sitting as a substitute State court tribunal, what law should it apply? Attempting to answer this question is a chore that has bewitched federal courts for years. This is the "*Erie*" problem.

Bear in mind, from the outset, that this dilemma is not a matter of jurisdiction. To the contrary, the federal court only comes upon an "*Erie*" problem (*i.e.,* which law to apply) if it has the lawful right to preside over the dispute in the first place (jurisdiction and venue). To better understand the "*Erie*" problem, we should first understand its namesake.

§ 2.19 The Case: *Erie R.R. Co. v. Tompkins*

Mr. Tompkins was a Pennsylvania citizen who was injured in Pennsylvania by a passing freight train as he walked alongside a railroad right-of-way. *See Erie R.R. Co. v. Tompkins,* 304 U.S. 64, 69 (1938). Pennsylvania had no statutory law setting the duty of care owed by the railroad to Mr. Tompkins, but the Railroad insisted that the State supreme court had answered that question in its common law. Under that case law, Mr. Tompkins was considered a trespasser, to whom the railroad owed only a minimal duty of care (namely, to avoid wantonly or willfully injuring him). Litigating under such a standard, Mr. Tompkins' chance of success was slim. So, instead of filing a lawsuit in a Pennsylvania State court, he filed in a federal court in New York (the State where the railroad was incorporated), arguing that, in the absence of any *enacted* Pennsylvania law on point, the New York federal court should feel free to exercise its own independent judgment as to what the law should be (that is, to create "general" common law). The federal court accepted this invitation. It then decided that when a right-of-way was in "open and notorious" use by the public, the law ought to impose upon

---

[3] While the original *Erie* doctrine developed in the context of cases based on the diversity jurisdiction of federal district courts, it appears now to be applied also to cases in which district courts have supplemental jurisdiction over non-diverse state claims. *See Felder v. Casey,* 487 U.S. 131, 151 (1988) (*Erie* also applies to claims based on predecessors to supplemental jurisdiction).

the railroad a duty of care, and, as such, Mr. Tompkins ought to be able to sue the railroad for negligence. Applying this freshly-announced law, the New York jury found the railroad breached its assumed duty, and awarded Mr. Tompkins damages. *See id.* at 68.

The U.S. Supreme Court reversed. It abolished (as unconstitutional!) an older body of its own precedent that had permitted federal courts to create "general" common law when there was no on-point enacted State law, and instead directed federal trial courts hearing diversity cases to apply the same substantive State law that a State court hearing the same case would have used (which included that State's unenacted (decisional) law). *See id.* at 71. As later authority would explain it, the decision in *Erie* rested on several important premises (later coined "the twin aims of *Erie*"): (1) claimants should not be encouraged to "shop" for a federal forum in the hope of improving their chances of success by changing the law to be applied; and (2) laws should not be applied inequitably merely because the courthouse has changed from a State one to a federal one. *See Hanna v. Plumer,* 380 U.S. 460, 467–68 (1965).

The impact of the *Erie* ruling was immediate and lasting. Federal courts would, in the future, have to apply State common law as well as State enacted law in diversity cases. Abolition of federal general common law meant that the constitutionally suspect practice of creating a body of federal substantive law to compete with State common law was at an end: federal courts hearing State claims, the Court had ruled, lack constitutional authority to substitute federal common law of their own creation for a State's common law that would otherwise control the outcome of that case. This reduced the temptation to engage in forum shopping: once federal general common law was abolished, lawyers lost an important motivation for filing in federal district court (*i.e.,* to obtain different substantive law than a State court would apply). Consider Mr. Tompkins and his attorney: their case valuation would now—post-*Erie*—be much different (he would be a trespasser, owed only a very modest duty of care, regardless of where the case was tried).

Before we leave *Erie*, a bit more scene-setting is useful. The Court in *Erie* was interpreting a law enacted by the first Congress in 1789, as they were forming the lower federal courts. That law, known today as the Rules of Decision Act, instructed that, unless federal law provided otherwise, the "laws of the several States shall be regarded as rules of decision in civil cases" tried in the federal courts. *See* 28 U.S.C. § 1652. In other words, federal judges, in diversity cases, were directed by Congress to apply State substantive law (the "rules of decision"), until told otherwise.

But new and knotty problems emerged in the wake of *Erie*. *See Shady Grove Orthopedic Assocs., P.A. v. Allstate Ins. Co.*, 559 U.S. 393, 398 (2010) (noting "*Erie*'s murky waters"). It is to those problems, which continue to confound courts and practitioners, that this discussion now turns.

§ 2.20 Distinguishing Between Substance and Procedure

The uncertainties that followed in the wake of *Erie* were largely practical ones. They were foreshadowed in a concurrence written by one of the justices at the end of the *Erie* opinion. Justice Reed agreed with *Erie*'s holding, but worried in his concurrence about its reach: would federal courts still remain free to apply their own rules of *procedure*—even in diversity cases? He thought so. *See Erie R.R. Co.,* 304 U.S. at 90 (Reed, J., concurring) ("No one doubts federal power over procedure."). What seemed to him obvious at the time has become muddled in the years that passed.

Substantive law and procedural law differ in important ways (as least theoretically). Substantive law sets the "rules of decision" by which a court determines whether a litigant's rights have been violated and to what remedies that litigant may be entitled. Procedural law establishes the "manner and means" for adjudicating and enforcing those rights and remedies (whatever they may be). *See Shady Grove Orthopedic Assocs., P.A.*, 559 U.S. at 407. A few examples are useful.

In a negligence lawsuit, most States allow plaintiffs to recover upon showing that they were owed a duty by the defendant, that this duty was breached by the defendant, and that the breach proximately caused them to suffer an injury or loss. This is substantive law—the substantive elements that will be applied to resolve plaintiffs' claim (in other words, the "rule of decision"). The defendant might defeat this claim by demonstrating (if the applicable law permitted it) that plaintiffs were contributorily negligent or assumed a risk. This, too, is substantive law—a substantive defense.

By contrast, procedural law governs the manner and means of litigating—such as, the form and timing for court submissions, how allegations in a pleading need to be prepared, when new parties can be joined, how discovery is conducted, how evidence is admitted, when motions are timely, and the like. These procedures help direct the course of a lawsuit. What does *Erie* require? Must federal courts, when they sit in diversity, apply both a State's substantive law and its procedural law? What if the State court system requires that all pleadings include highly detailed allegations of fact and a recital of all witnesses and their knowledge? Must the federal judge (who would otherwise apply the far more lenient federal "notice" pleading standards) adjust how she tests pleadings when she hears that diversity case? If the answer is "yes," the hope for a nationally-uniform body of federal procedure might be in vain.

Some answers in this thicket seem reasonably clear.

First, in working through an *Erie* issue, the distinction between substantive law and procedural law matters under *Erie*. Since the Rules of Decision Act was enacted in 1789, it has been quite clear that federal courts must apply State substantive law in diversity cases. *See* 28 U.S.C. § 1652. No similar mandate directs federal courts to replicate a State's litigation procedures. Thus, when federal courts sit in diversity and are called upon by *Erie* to resolve a State law claim, they must apply State substantive law but they generally continue to apply federal procedural law. *See Gasperini v. Center for Humanities, Inc.*, 518 U.S. 415, 427 & n.7 (1996).

Second, Congress, however, also may, consistent with the Rules of Decision Act, supplant State substantive law with a body of federal *enacted* law (not decisional law) that supersedes State substantive law. Thus, for example, Congress may enact a law requiring a medical device manufacturer to abide by certain standards set by the federal Food and Drug Administration, and in so doing displace (or "preempt") competing State law which would have established a different set of standards. *See Riegel v. Medtronic, Inc.*, 552 U.S. 312, 322–25 (2008).

Third, Congress also has the authority to promulgate federal procedural law, *see Shady Grove Orthopedic Assocs., P.A.*, 559 U.S. at 406, and when it does so validly, that law displaces competing State procedural law, *see Gasperini*, 518 U.S. at 427 n.7. In 1934, Congress did just that by enacting the Rules Enabling Act which permitted the creation of a uniform body of rules of procedure for the federal judiciary. *See* 28 U.S.C. §§ 2071–72. The Federal Rules of Civil Procedure, drafted under the authority granted by this Act, took effect in 1938.

Fourth, federal procedural law might displace some, but not quite all, of a State's procedural law. In such cases, an *Erie* collision can be avoided if, on closer inspection, the court finds that there is no true conflict between the two laws, *see Walker v. Armco Steel Corp.*, 446 U.S. 740, 751 (1980), or if the interests of both can be simultaneously, harmoniously accommodated, *see Gasperini*, 518 U.S. at 436–37.

These broad, theoretical anchors of clarity are helpful. But they cannot obscure the multitude of *Erie* questions that still remained. How can a law be reliably classified as "substantive" or "procedural"? Procedural laws, after all, can have a reverberating substantive effect. Consider a federal procedure that requires that a lawsuit be dismissed if it is not served within 90 days after filing. A local State procedure might permit a longer, 120-day service period. If an unserved federal diversity lawsuit is dismissed after 91 days, hasn't that federal procedure had an indisputably substantive effect (and, importantly for *Erie* purposes, one that differs from State procedure)? This nuance prompted the Supreme Court to once observe that "[c]lassification of a law as 'substantive' or 'procedural' for *Erie* purposes is sometimes a challenging endeavor." *See Gasperini*, 518 U.S. at 427.

A myriad of other *Erie*-related questions arose as new situations were encountered. What if the federal procedures at issue weren't statutes or rules (like those adopted under the Rules Enabling Act), but judge-made law? Should State law apply then? Under what circumstances? Should the Federal Rules of Procedure always displace State procedures, or should there be the possibility of exceptions?

§ 2.21 How the *Erie* Doctrine Seems to Operate Today

When even the U.S. Supreme Court describes *Erie* as "murky waters," a fair degree of caution should precede any attempt to map the operation of *Erie* and its progeny. To be sure, the Supreme Court has supplied some benchmarks, but uncertainty persists at the margins. Remember, as you work through this discussion, the whole *Erie* business only applies when a federal court is serving as a substitute State tribunal (principally, in diversity cases).

A. When the State Law Is Truly Substantive Law

This much is certain. The federal courts must apply State substantive law (the "rule of decision"), unless the U.S. Constitution, an Act of Congress, or a U.S. treaty otherwise supplants ("preempts") that State law. *See* Rules of Decision Act, 28 U.S.C. § 1652. And federal courts may not craft "general" federal common law to supplant a State's substantive common law. *See Erie R.R. Co.,* 304 U.S. at 77–78. So, in diversity cases, applicable State laws that establish a party's "rights" or "remedies" will govern in federal court, unless they have been preempted by federal law.

B. When a State's Procedural Law Clashes with a Federal Rule of Procedure

In its 1934 Rules Enabling Act, Congress delegated to the U.S. Supreme Court the authority to promulgate the rules of practice and procedure that would guide the federal judiciary. *See* 28 U.S.C. §§ 2071–72. (For further reading on the rulemaking process, *see* Section 2.1b above.) Four years later in 1938, the Federal Rules of Civil Procedure took effect. A collision between these new Rules and the evolving *Erie* doctrine was inevitable. The Court tackled this issue comprehensively in 1965 in *Hanna v. Plumer,* 380 U.S. 460, 465–73 (1965).

The plaintiff in *Hanna* served the defendant by leaving a copy of the summons and complaint with the defendant's spouse at the defendant's residence. This was lawful service under Rule 4 of the Federal Rules of Civil Procedure. However, under State procedure, service was not proper because, under the circumstances of the case, State law required that the defendant be served differently. Ergo, a collision existed between the Federal Rules and a competing State procedure.

To resolve that collision, the *Hanna* Court introduced a two-step analysis:

The first step was to determine if the federal rule at issue was valid—that is, lawfully made. This, in turn, involved two inquiries. The contested rule had to be valid under the Rules Enabling Act, since Congress had only authorized the U.S. Supreme Court to create federal rules that were truly procedural (that is, which did not alter substantive rights). *See id.* at 464–65. The contested rule also had to be valid under Article III of the U.S. Constitution, which only permitted Congress to set the practice and procedure for federal litigation. *See id.* at 472. Both validity tests had to be satisfied. In *Hanna*, because Rule 4 was unquestionably procedural (*i.e.,* setting the means for serving process on a defendant), it comported with both the Rules Enabling Act and the U.S. Constitution. (None of the Rules has ever been found to violate this validity test.)

The second step was to determine if the federal rule at issue could be harmonized with State procedure (for example, if they addressed different concerns), or whether the federal and State procedures were locked in inescapable conflict. Thus, in a later case, the Court assessed whether Rule 3 of the Federal Rules of Civil Procedure (which directed that a federal case is "commenced" by filing a complaint) inescapably conflicted with a State law that held that its statutes of limitation continued to run until a defendant was served with the complaint. The unanimous Court there held that the federal law (which merely defined commencement) was not in direct conflict with the State law (which set the tolling rules for its limitations periods). *See Walker v. Armco Steel Corp.,* 446 U.S. 740 (1980). Of course, that sort of "harmonizing" wasn't possible in *Hanna*—the federal rule permitted a type of service that the State law forbade. Because federal Rule 4 was valid and unavoidably collided with the State procedure, the federal rule prevailed and the State procedure was displaced. *See Hanna,* 380 U.S. at 468.

This two-step inquiry now guides the *Erie* question when a federal rule is involved. If the federal rule at issue inescapably conflicts with State procedure, only one question remains: is that rule a valid one (namely, a lawful exercise of rule-making power under the Rules Enabling Act and the U.S. Constitution)? If a valid rule conflicts inescapably with State procedure, the federal rule governs. *See Shady Grove Orthopedic Associates, P.A.*, 559 U.S. at 404–07.

C. When a State's Procedural Law Clashes with a Federal Procedural Statute

The same analysis applies when the conflict involves a federal statute. Congress delegated rulemaking authority to the U.S. Supreme Court, but Congress may also enact procedural laws directly. When it does so, the *Erie* path is again straightforward. Federal courts are bound to apply the procedural law enacted by Congress, provided that Congress acted within its constitutional authority and its law is squarely relevant to the issue before the district court. *See Stewart Org., Inc. v. Ricoh Corp.*, 487 U.S. 22, 26 (1988).

D. When a State's Procedural Law Clashes with Federal Procedural Case Law (or When There is No Inescapable Conflict)

If it is federal procedural *case law* that is causing the conflict with State procedures, or if there is no inescapable conflict at all and federal and State law might be applied together, the *Erie* choice that emerges is at its murkiest. In those instances, should the federal court apply the State procedure?

The analysis seems to require a three-part inquiry.

First, the court must inquire whether applying the State law could be "outcome determinative"—that is, would it "significantly affect the result of a litigation for a federal court to disregard a law of a State that would be controlling in an action upon the same claim by the same parties in a State court?" *See Guaranty Trust Co. v. York*, 326 U.S. 99, 109 (1945); *see also Gasperini*, 518 U.S. at 428–30. If the choice between these laws would indeed be outcome-affecting, the inquiry continues on to the next step. Note, the Court has rejected the view that the "outcome determinative" test should be applied mechanically, so as to reflexively always prefer State law over federal law. *See Gasperini*, 518 U.S. at 428; *Hanna*, 380 U.S. at 468.

Second, the court will next assess whether the so-called "twin aims" of *Erie* are implicated by the choice—that is, whether choosing to apply (or not apply) that State law, would encourage forum shopping or cause an inequitable administration of the law. *See Gasperini*, 518 U.S. at 428; *Hanna*, 380 U.S. at 468. If it would, then the analysis continues to a final step.

Third, the court must then weigh the competing federal and State interests. *See Byrd v. Blue Ridge Rural Elec. Co-op., Inc.*, 356 U.S. 525, 533–39 (1958). In doing so, it must be borne in mind that the federal courts are "an independent system for administering justice to litigants who properly invoke [their] jurisdiction," and that State laws should not be permitted to routinely "alter the essential character or function of a federal court" or to "disrupt[ ] the federal system of allocating functions between judge and jury." *See id.* at 537–40. Accordingly, a weak (or nonexistent) State interest might cause the federal court to ignore the State procedure at issue, while a strong State interest—that is, one "bound up" with "State-created rights and obligations"—may weigh heavily in favor of applying that State procedure. *See id.* at 535. Moreover, if a State's law is found to be anchored to a dominant State interest and can be applied in a manner "without disrupting the federal system" (*i.e.*, the two procedures can be accommodated harmoniously), the federal court might properly do so. *See Gasperini*, 518 U.S. at 436–38.

How, precisely, to conduct this sort of delicate weighing of competing governmental interests is not yet well understood. Indeed, in the very case where this balancing framework was announced, the Court had no challenging weighing task to perform. Instead, the Court found that the State had no particular policy interest in its procedural law, and certainly none that was "bound up" with important State concerns. *See Byrd*, 356 U.S. at 535–36.

§ 2.22 Finding the State Law to Apply

A. Which State's Law?

The original goal of *Erie* was to ensure that federal district courts apply the same substantive law that a State court would use. In *Erie* itself, application of that rule meant that a federal district court sitting in New York would apply the same substantive law that a New York State trial court would use. But this did not necessarily mean the substantive law of New York.

Mr. Tompkins' injury occurred in Pennsylvania, but the lawsuit was filed in a federal district court in New York. If the case had been heard in a State court in New York, the State court would have had to decide whether to use New York substantive law (the law of the State where the case was filed), Pennsylvania substantive law (the law of the State where the incident and injury occurred), or the substantive law of some other State. On the facts of *Erie,* it was clear at the time the case was heard that a New York State court would have applied the substantive law of Pennsylvania (because the accident giving rise to the lawsuit occurred in Pennsylvania). Because a New York court would have used Pennsylvania law, the duty of the federal district court in New York under the *Erie* doctrine—to apply the same law that a State court would use—was to use Pennsylvania law.

The question of *which* State's substantive law to apply is not an *Erie* question, but one addressed by a different body of jurisprudence known as "conflict of laws" or "choice of law." That jurisprudence is beyond the scope of this *Student's Guide* and often covered in a semester-long elective course in law school called "Conflicts of Law."

B. Using the Law the State Court Would Use

In cases where a federal district court recognizes that it is obligated to apply State law on an issue, a question remains as to how to identify the *content* of the State law. Of course, if the State has clear constitutional or statutory law on the matter, or if its highest court has spoken on the matter definitively, then the process is easy. *See C.I.R. v. Bosch's Estate,* 387 U.S. 456, 465 (1967). The question becomes more difficult, however, when the State law is unclear. It would then become the unenviable task of the federal court to discern what the State law "is" (and not what the federal judge thinks it ought to be). *See Klaxon Co. v. Stentor Electric Mfg. Co.,* 313 U.S. 487, 497 (1941); *West v. American Tel. & Tel. Co.,* 311 U.S. 223, 236 (1940).

To address the problems raised by this situation, three distinct approaches have evolved.

First, the federal court could abstain from deciding the case and direct the parties to re-file their lawsuit in State court. This approach has the advantage of protecting against an errant federal "guess" about the content of State law, but it also ignores "the virtually unflagging obligation of the federal courts to exercise the jurisdiction given them." *See Colorado River Water Conservation Dist. v. United States*, 424 U.S. 800, 817 (1976). *See also id.* at 813 (abstaining "is the exception, not the rule," reserved only for "exceptional circumstances").

Second, the federal court could "certify" the uncertain question of State law to that State's high court with the request that the State high court supply the definitive answer to the question. Certification carries with it the prospect of guidance from a definitive source to an unresolved State-law question, but its promise has always been limited by some real-world obstacles. The process is an expensive one, obligating litigants to brief and argue an issue before yet another court. It also causes delay, with the federal litigation held in abeyance as the State court ponders the certified question. The State's certification statute may not necessarily require its supreme court to answer a question from a federal court (and if it does, there is no assurance the answer will precisely match the federal case's needs). Finally, not all States have certification statutes, so this option may not even be available. *See generally* Geri J. Yonover, *A Kinder, Gentler* Erie*: Reining in the Use of Certification,* 47 ARK. L. REV. 305, 314–16 (1994) (most but not all jurisdictions have certification statutes).

Third, and most frequently, the federal courts undertake to "predict" what the State high court would do, using the tools they have available. The federal courts may consult a variety of sources in performing this task, including: analogous decisions by the State high court; reported decisions from lower State courts or federal courts; trends in neighboring States; and even legal scholarship and the American Law Institutes' well regarded *Restatements of Law*. This path for discerning the content of State law, while frequently used, is also the one fraught with the greatest risk for error. *See Bogy v. Ford Motor Co.,* 538 F.3d 352, 355 (5th Cir. 2008) (when State law is unclear, federal court "must make an *Erie* guess"). And were the federal court to "predict" incorrectly, the litigants are often without a remedy for correction. Thus, for example, if a federal court "predicts" that a State high court would resolve a question in a certain way, that judgment is likely to be final—even if State court later, in a different case, definitively resolves the very same question in the opposite manner. *See Deweerth v. Baldinger*, 38 F.3d 1266, 1274 (2d Cir. 1994).

§ 2.23 The Residue of Federal Common Law

Although *general* federal common law was abolished by *Erie*, specific federal common law persists. In a "few" and "restricted" settings, federal courts still retain the power to "create" a body of judge-made substantive law (that is, binding rules of decision, a power quite different from merely interpreting, construing, or applying a federal law). *See Atherton v. FDIC*, 519 U.S. 213, 218 (1997). Those limited law-creating settings include disputes between States, *see Hinderlider v. La Plata River & Cherry Creek Ditch Co.*, 304 U.S. 92 (1938); disputes involving interstate bodies of water, *Florida v. Georgia*, 138 S. Ct. 2502, 2513 (2018); disputes involving foreign nations, *see Banco Nacional de Cuba v. Sabbatino*, 376 U.S. 398 (1964); disputes by Native Americans to sue to enforce aboriginal land rights, *see Oneida Cty. v. Oneida Indian Nations of N.Y. State*, 470 U.S. 226, 235–36 (1985); disputes involving federal contractors and civil liability of federal officials, *see Boyle v. United Technologies Corp.*, 487 U.S. 500 (1988); and disputes in admiralty, *see Rodriguez v. FDIC*, 140 S. Ct. 713, 717 (2020). Thus, post-*Erie* opportunities for substantive lawmaking by federal courts exist still, but they are limited and narrow; the Supreme Court has explained why: "Judicial lawmaking in the form of federal common law plays a necessarily modest role under a Constitution that vests the federal government's 'legislative Powers' in Congress and reserves most other regulatory authority to the States." *Rodriguez*, 140 S. Ct. at 717.

F. PRECLUSION (RES JUDICATA AND COLLATERAL ESTOPPEL)

§ 2.24 Introduction

The doctrine of "preclusion" addresses the question of whether the entry of a judgment in an earlier lawsuit should foreclose the ability to litigate all, or part, of a later lawsuit. The doctrine is grounded in policies of judicial economy, fairness, and finality. *See Baldwin v. Iowa State Traveling Men's Ass'n*, 283 U.S. 522, 525–26 (1931) ("Public policy dictates that there be an end of litigation; that those who have contested an issue shall be bound by the result of the contest; and that matters once tried shall be considered forever settled as between the parties.").

As it is classically understood, preclusion encompasses two primary concepts: res judicata (or "claim preclusion") and collateral estoppel (or "issue preclusion"). Although both are preclusion principles, they operate differently. If res judicata/claim preclusion applies, a plaintiff who lost a lawsuit will likely be precluded from later raising claims which were, or could have been, litigated in the earlier lawsuit. If collateral estoppel/issue preclusion applies, a particular issue that was decided in an earlier litigation may be treated as already decided for the purposes of a later litigation, without the need of further proof.

Preclusion principles owe their existence almost entirely to judge-made law. *See Taylor v. Sturgell,* 553 U.S. 880, 891 (2008). Legislative impacts on these doctrines is limited, and constitutional considerations arise only in circumstances where use of the doctrines might have the potential to limit the due process right of an interested party (such as when preclusion is applied against someone who had not yet had a fair opportunity to be heard in court). *See South Central Bell Tel. Co. v. Alabama,* 526 U.S. 160, 168 (1999).

Finally, a few words about preclusion terminology. First, the emergence of "claim" and "issue" preclusion as more modern terms for res judicata and collateral estoppel is both helpful and confusing. Obvious, these new terms have the advantage of being far more descriptive than their antecedents (and that's good for law students, lawyers, and judges alike). The new terminology is being used today with increasing frequency. *See Yeager v. United States,* 557 U.S. 110, 119 n.4 (2009); *Kircher v. Putnam Funds Trust,* 547 U.S. 633 n.14 (2006). But not all courts do so, and students need to be familiar with the historic terms as well. Second, some older case precedent had the unfortunate habit of referring to both res judicata and collateral estoppel collectively, under an umbrella-like use of the term "res judicata." *See Migra v. Warren City School Dist. Bd. of Educ.,* 465 U.S. 75, 77 n.1 (1984). Because the two types of preclusion operate differently, knowing which particular type is implicated in a lawsuit is not just important but potentially determinative.

§ 2.25 Res Judicata (also known as "Claim Preclusion")

Res judicata (or "claim preclusion") terminates a litigant's right to sue entirely. If it applies, the litigant is denied the opportunity to re-litigate a claim that he or she actually litigated earlier (or had the right and ability to litigate earlier). For res judicata to apply, three elements must generally be met: claim identity, party identity, and a final, valid judgment on the merits. *See Cromwell v. Sac County,* 94 U.S. 351 (1876).

PRACTICING LAW WITH THIS PRINCIPLE

Threshold Requirement: An Earlier Litigation

Res judicata (claim preclusion) can only ever apply where the present lawsuit bears a certain relationship to a prior lawsuit that has already been decided. If there has been no prior litigation, there can be no res judicata. (Importantly, it is the second court—not the court that first heard the case and entered a judgment—that will decide the applicability of the first judgment to other cases. *See Phillips Petroleum Co. v. Shutts,* 472 U.S. 797, 805 (1985) ("[A] court adjudicating a dispute may not be able to predetermine the res judicata effect of its own judgment.")).

Element #1—Identity of the Claims

First, the "claim" in the present lawsuit must be the same "claim" as the one litigated in the earlier lawsuit. Courts generally hold that claims need not be literally identical in all respects to meet this first element of res judicata. But courts over the years struggled to articulate the standards for testing whether two claims are identical.

Some courts defined "claim" using a "single, unitary wrongful act" test, which would test whether the claims in question arose from the same factual event (*e.g.,* the same vehicular accident). Under that view, a claim for a shoulder injury and a claim for a leg injury, both resulting from the same car crash, would qualify as the same claim. Thus, if the injured motorist sued for the shoulder injury only, that motorist would likely be foreclosed from bringing a second, later lawsuit to sue the same defendant for the leg injury. Other courts applied a "primary rights" test, which would inquire whether the legal right allegedly invaded was identical or different among the claims. Thus, if that same injured motorist sued for physical injuries, but neglected to sue for damage to her vehicle, she could likely do so in separate lawsuits (noting that the right of personal integrity is different from the right of property ownership). *See generally Carter v. Hinkle,* 52 S.E.2d 135, 138 (Va. 1949) (discussing early theories of claim identity). An earlier approach limited claim identity to only lawsuits asserting the very same *theory of recovery*, a view now almost often abandoned.

Today, many courts have settled on a more functional standard for claim identity, asking whether the "underlying facts" in the claims of the original lawsuit and the later lawsuit are "related in time, space, origin, or motivation, whether they form a convenient trial unit, and whether their treatment as a unit conforms to the parties' expectations or business understanding or usage." *See Interoceanica Corp. v. Sound Pilots, Inc.*, 107 F.3d 86, 90 (2d Cir. 1997) (citation omitted). *See also Lucky Brand Dungarees, Inc. v. Marcel Fashions Group, Inc.*, 140 S. Ct. 1589, 1594–95 (2020) (" 'aris[e] from same transaction' " or "involve a 'common nucleus of operative facts' "). This so-called "transactional" standard for claim identity produces a more flexible, case-nuanced inquiry to the first res judicata element. Of course, claims based on events that post-date the filing of the original action will ordinarily not be precluded. *See Lucky Brand Dungarees, Inc.*, 140 S. Ct. at 1596; *Whole Women's Health v. Hellerstedt*, 136 S. Ct. 2292, 2305 (2016). Applying this "transactional" inquiry, the patient's informed consent lawsuit against her doctor in the example above is likely to result in a finding of claim identity. The court would likely reason that the patient's first lawsuit (for surgical error producing a loss of vision) and her second lawsuit (for lack of informed consent producing a loss of vision) were related in time, space, origin, and motivation, would have formed a convenient trial package, and treating them as an indivisible unit would have conformed to the parties' expectations and prevailing litigation norms.

Element #2—Identity of the Parties

The second element for res judicata requires that the parties in the second lawsuit be identical to (or in privity with) the parties in the first lawsuit. The rationale for this element is self-evident: litigants can only be barred for litigating *again* if they, in fact, actually had litigated *before*. Usually, this element is easy to discern. If two pedestrians, walking along the same sidewalk, are injured by the same out-of-control motorist, the outcome in the first pedestrian's personal injury lawsuit will, of course, not bar the second pedestrian's personal injury lawsuit. Even though both pedestrians' claims arose from the same occurrence, the obvious difference between the parties would preclude application of res judicata. *See Cooper v. Harris*, 137 S. Ct. 1455, 1467 (2017) ("One person's lawsuit generally does not bar another's, no matter how similar they are in substance.").

For purposes of this second requirement for res judicata, parties who are actually the same persons or business entities are clearly "identical." But sometimes persons who are different but who share a common interest may be treated as "identical" because the law considers them to be in "privity" with the earlier litigant. *See id.* ("when plaintiffs in two cases have a special relationship, a judgment against one can indeed bind both"). Examples include: (1) where the nonparty succeeded to the interest of a party (for example, by purchasing whatever interest the party may have had after completion of the first litigation); (2) where the nonparty, though technically not participating in the first lawsuit, nevertheless controlled one party's litigation in that suit (for example, if the nonparty is an insurance company for a party); (3) where the nonparty shared a property interest with the party; (4) where the party and nonparty had an agent-principal relationship; (5) where the nonparty's interests were otherwise "adequately represented" by the original party; or (6) where the nonparty agrees to be bound by the outcome of the earlier litigation.

Element #3—Valid, Final Judgment on the Merits

The third and final element for res judicata requires that the first litigation must have proceeded to a valid, final judgment on the merits.

A judgment is valid when it is entered by a court competent to do so. A belief (even if well founded) that the judgment is wrongly decided is not enough to deprive it of validity for purposes of res judicata, so long as the deciding court possessed the judicial power to rule. *See City of Arlington v. F.C.C.*, 569 U.S. 290, 297 (2013).

A judgment is final when a trial judge enters judgment, so that the parties are then in a position to appeal it or enforce the outcome. *See Clay v. United States*, 537 U.S. 522, 526 (2003). Conversely, there might not be a final judgment when the case is settled prior to judgment (unless the settlement is reduced by the court to a judgment or decree), nor is judgment finality likely present any time the court makes an important but interlocutory ruling.

A judgment must also be on the merits. A jury verdict or bench trial judgment will obviously meet this requirement. Usually, cases terminated under Rule 12(b)(6)—for failure to state a claim upon which relief can be granted—are considered judgments on the merits for purposes of res judicata. *See Federated Dept. Stores, Inc. v. Moitie,* 452 U.S. 394, 399 n.3 (1981). But dismissals on jurisdictional grounds usually have a very narrow preclusive effect—they will only foreclose a relitigation of the contested jurisdictional issue. If the claimant subsequently files a second lawsuit alleging a different theory of recovery, or files in a different, appropriate forum, the original dismissal will normally not block the second lawsuit. *See Semtek Int'l Inc. v. Lockheed Martin Corp.,* 531 U.S. 497, 503–04 (2001).

There are unusual situations where a judgment may be valid, final, and on the merits, yet still not be given res judicata effect because applying preclusion would conflict with some other, important legal principle. *See Lytle v. Household Mfg., Inc.,* 494 U.S. 545, 555–56 (1990).

The Reach of Res Judicata

When it applies, res judicata bars the re-litigation of not only those claims that were actually litigated in the prior lawsuit, but also those claims that could have been litigated in the prior lawsuit. *See Cromwell v. Sac County,* 94 U.S. 351 (1876). This is why, in the example above, the motorist's second lawsuit for injury to his leg is likely precluded by the motorist's first lawsuit against the same driver for injury to the shoulder. Assuming the injuries were sustained in the same collision and known at the time of the first lawsuit, the motorist's decision *not* to sue for the additional injury causes an inefficient use of judicial resources and an undue unfairness to the defendant.

If, however, a claim is not asserted in the first lawsuit because asserting it there would have been improper (such as, for example, where exclusive jurisdiction over that claim existed only in a different forum), res judicata is unlikely to apply. *See Marrese v. American Academy of Orthopaedic Surgeons,* 470 U.S. 373, 382 (1985).

Invoking Res Judicata

In federal court, res judicata is expressly denominated as an affirmative defense. *See* Rule 8(c). Consequently, a defendant seeking to use res judicata to preclude a plaintiff's claim must affirmatively plead the defense. Failure to do so may result in waiver of the defense.

Res Judicata and Defenses

Whether res judicata could be used to bar *defenses* that could have been brought earlier but weren't had perplexed the lower federal courts. The U.S. Supreme Court has now tepidly suggested that "defense preclusion" as "standalone category of res judicata" does not exist, at least not in a context "unmoored from the two guideposts of issue preclusion and claim preclusion." *See also Lucky Brand Dungarees, Inc. v. Marcel Fashions Group, Inc.*, 140 S. Ct. 1589, 1595 (2020) ("our case law indicates that any such preclusion of defenses must, at a minimum, satisfy the strictures of issue preclusion and claim preclusion").

Res Judicata and Counterclaims

In federal court, res judicata is not always applied to potential counterclaims by defendants, for various reasons. But be forewarned, however. Although *preclusion* principles might not cause a later bar, the operation of the Rules may. Rule 13(a) provides that counterclaims deemed "compulsory" must be asserted or are lost—not by operation of preclusion principles, but as a consequence of the Rule's compulsory counterclaim obligation. *See* Rule 13(a). By operation of this Rule, failure to assert a compulsory counterclaim usually results in a judicial refusal to hear the claim in subsequent litigation.

Res Judicata and the Full Faith and Credit Guarantee

Full faith and credit is a constitutional principle controlling the circumstances when courts of one State must enforce the judicial decisions of another State. *See* U.S. Const. art. IV, § 1. This concept implicates res judicata. If the res judicata principles of the State in which a judgment was rendered would require other courts in that same State to treat the judgment as preclusive, full faith and credit will generally require the courts of other States to give that judgment the same effect. Analogous rules usually require federal courts to give similar deference to the final judgments of State courts of competent jurisdiction. *See Durfee v. Duke,* 375 U.S. 106, 109–11 (1963).

Res Judicata and Judicial Power

In general, when a court hears a case over which it lacks jurisdiction, a timely and proper challenge to the resulting judgment may render that judgment a nullity. *See, e.g.,* Rule 12(b)(1)–(b)(2); Rule 60(b)(4). When, however, that judgment is fully final—either because no appeal was taken or appeals have been exhausted—res judicata may bar consideration of any later challenge to the judgment, even if jurisdiction was lacking. *See Kontrick v. Ryan,* 540 U.S. 443, 456 n.9 (2007).

§ 2.26 Collateral Estoppel (also known as "Issue Preclusion")

Collateral estoppel (or "issue preclusion") forecloses the relitigation of some specific issue (fact or law) that has been litigated earlier. *See Herrera v. Wyoming*, 139 S. Ct. 1686, 1697 (2019). If it applies, the precluded issue is considered as having been already established for the purposes of the later lawsuit, with no further proof needed on the point. For collateral estoppel to apply, four elements must generally be met: issue identity, actual prior litigation of the issue, a ruling that necessarily decided the issue, and a final, valid judgment on the merits. *See generally B&B Hardware, Inc. v. Hargis Indus., Inc.*, 575 U.S. 138, 148 (2015). In addition, collateral estoppel principles may only be invoked by and may only be invoked against appropriate parties.

PRACTICING LAW WITH THIS PRINCIPLE

Threshold Requirement: An Earlier Litigation

As with res judicata, collateral estoppel can only ever apply where the issue in question bears a certain relationship to a prior lawsuit's resolution of an earlier issue.

Element #1—Identical Issues

Res judicata had required that there be identical "claims" between the first and second lawsuits. In contrast, collateral estoppel requires only that one or more "issues" be identical between the original and later lawsuits. An "issue" for this purpose is "a right, question, or fact distinctly put in issue and directly determined." *See Southern Pacific R.R. v. U.S.*, 168 U.S. 1, 48 (1897). Testing for issue identity can pose a knotty inquiry, but usually examines the degree of overlap between the evidence and arguments, whether new evidence or argument involves the application of the same rule of law, whether pretrial preparation in the first action reasonably could be expected to embrace the matter in the later case, and how closely the two claims relate to one another. Note, however, that the underlying subject matters of the original and later lawsuits need not be identical, so long as the issue in question is.

Element #2—Actually, Vigorously Litigated

Unlike res judicata, collateral estoppel will not bar litigation of an issue that was not actually raised in a prior proceeding (even if it could have been raised there). *See Regions Hosp. v. Shalala,* 522 U.S. 448, 461 (1998). For example, in a breach of contract lawsuit, a defendant who litigates the meaning of one clause of the agreement is not barred, in a second lawsuit alleging a later breach under the same contract, from litigating the meaning of a different clause. For this reason, collateral estoppel generally will not apply in default judgments: no issues, in a default context, are actually litigated. Moreover, for collateral estoppel to apply, the issue must have been litigated with some vigor. Issues raised in some passing, casual way, but which did not significantly engage the attention of the litigants, are usually not precluded because to do so may prove unfair.

Element #3—Necessarily Decided

Collateral estoppel will not apply unless the issue decided in the first lawsuit was necessary or essential to the judgment there. *See Rios v. Rios*, 373 S.W.2d 386, 388–39 (Tex. Ct. Civ. App. 1963). Thus, in the breach of contract example above, if the defendant was found not liable merely because the plaintiff was found to have breached, other issues decided in that litigation (such as, for example, whether good consideration existed) would not have been necessary or essential to the judgment. Similarly, if a jury finds for a plaintiff without explaining which (or both) of two distinct grounds is the basis for its verdict, a defendant may retain the right to challenge those same grounds if they arise as issues in subsequent litigation. Conversely, if a jury expressly finds for a plaintiff on two distinct grounds, both of which were vigorously litigated and both of which were decided in the plaintiff's favor, both may be treated as eligible for collateral estoppel in subsequent lawsuits. In sum, collateral estoppel is inapplicable if a later court cannot discern whether the particular issue litigated earlier was necessary or essential to the prior outcome.

Element #4—Valid, Final Judgment on the Merits

Finally, collateral estoppel applies only to issues resolved in cases decided on their merits with a judgment that was valid and final. *See Yeager v. United States,* 557 U.S. 110, 119 (2009). The meaning of this fourth element tracks the meaning of the same element as discussed with res judicata above.

Who May Raise Collateral Estoppel, and Whom May It Be Asserted Against

Historically, res judicata had required that, before any "claims" are precluded, it must first be shown that the parties in the second lawsuit were identical to (or in privity with) parties in the first lawsuit. At one time, a similar requirement of identical parties also applied to collateral estoppel and its preclusion of "issues." This identity requirement was referred to as collateral estoppel's "mutuality" requirement (*i.e.,* collateral estoppel could not apply unless it applied mutually to all parties in the lawsuit). *See Blonder-Tongue Labs., Inc. v. University of Illinois Found.*, 402 U.S. 313, 320–21 (1971). Today, however, most jurisdictions have abandoned or substantially weakened the "mutuality" prerequisite for collateral estoppel.

Of course, when "mutuality" is actually present (that is, when the parties in the second lawsuit are the same parties who litigated the first lawsuit), they are eligible to assert collateral estoppel, provided all of the doctrine's other requirements are satisfied. But when "mutuality" is absent, when the parties to the second lawsuit are not identical to those in the first, collateral estoppel still might bar an issue's re-litigation when the court determines that it would be fair to do so:

- *Defensive Nonmutual Collateral Estoppel:* "Defensive" nonmutual collateral estoppel would apply the doctrine in favor of a defendant who is trying, in a second lawsuit, to use preclusion defensively—as a shield—to repel a plaintiff's attack. For example, suppose plaintiff sues defendant for patent infringement, and suppose that defendant's defense is that plaintiff's patent is legally invalid. If defendant wins the case on that ground (patent invalidity), the matter is obviously res judicata as between the two litigating parties. But if the same plaintiff later files a second lawsuit against a different defendant, asserting once again that the same patent had been infringed, most American courts permit the use of collateral estoppel to bar that plaintiff from re-litigating the issue of patent infringement—even though the parties were not identical. Those courts reason that this sort of "defensive" use of nonmutual collateral estoppel is fair because the plaintiff who is being precluded had a full and fair opportunity to litigate the patent validity issue in the first lawsuit. *See Blonder-Tongue Labs., Inc. v. University of Illinois Found.*, 402 U.S. 313, 328–29 (1971).
- *Offensive Nonmutual Collateral Estoppel:* "Offensive" nonmutual collateral estoppel would apply the doctrine in favor of a plaintiff who is trying, in a second lawsuit, to use preclusion offensively—as a sword—to strike down a defense raised by a defendant. This is the more troublesome use of doctrine. In a well-known case decided by the

Supreme Court, defendants had previously been sued by the Securities and Exchange Commission for making false proxy statements. *See Parklane Hosiery Co., Inc. v. Shore,* 439 U.S. 322 (1979). The Commission sought an injunction, and the defendants lost the lawsuit. Subsequently a class of shareholders sued the defendants on the same grounds and sought collateral estoppel based on the earlier court's finding that the proxy statements had been false and misleading. In contrast to defensive nonmutual collateral estoppel, this case was an attempt to use the defendants' prior loss as a sword with which to produce a second unfavorable result against those defendants.

The Court ruled that, at least sometimes, nonmutual collateral estoppel may be used offensively. However, before such a use, the Court directed lower federal courts to examine all the circumstances of a case to ensure fairness. Specifically, the Court suggested that courts examine: (1) whether the plaintiff seeking offensive nonmutual collateral estoppel could have participated in the previous lawsuit; (2) whether the defendant had a fair chance to litigate the issue with knowledge of the fact that the same issue might arise in subsequent litigation; (3) whether the judgment in the litigation for which collateral estoppel is sought was inconsistent with (or dissimilar to) results in any litigation which had taken place still earlier; and (4) whether, in the previous lawsuit, procedural limitations had prevented the defendants from offering some evidence or otherwise defending themselves in ways now open in the later litigation. *See id.* at 329–32.

- *Nonmutuality and the United States:* Although the United States is as vulnerable as any other party to the application of collateral estoppel when mutuality is present, it is settled that nonmutual collateral estoppel (defensive or offensive) may not be applied against the United States. *See United States v. Mendoza,* 464 U.S. 154, 162 (1984).

Applicability to Issues of Both Law and Fact

Older cases doubted whether collateral estoppel was applicable to issues of law as well as fact. While some jurisdictions may still recognize that limitation, the clear trend in most circumstances is that collateral estoppel may apply to issues of both law and fact. *See Montana v. United States,* 440 U.S. 147, 162 (1979).

Exceptions

Even where all the elements of collateral estoppel are satisfied, it is still possible that a court may be persuaded that applying the doctrine is unfair in particular circumstances. For example, courts are reluctant to impose collateral estoppel where the affected party might not reasonably have appreciated the risk that collateral estoppel would apply in subsequent cases. Also, when the law or facts of a situation undergo material change between the first lawsuit and the second one, it might be unfair to impose collateral estoppel on issues decided in the first lawsuit. *See Herrera v. Wyoming,* 139 S. Ct. 1686, 1697 (2019); *Montana v. United States,* 440 U.S. 147, 159 (1979). Collateral estoppel will also typically be inapplicable to situations where a district court judgment is not appealable. *See Kircher v. Putnam Funds Trust,* 547 U.S. 633, 641–42 (2006).

Invoking Collateral Estoppel

Collateral estoppel, like res judicata, is an enumerated affirmative defense in federal practice. *See* Rule 8(c). Generally, like all other affirmative defenses, collateral estoppel must be pleaded or it may be deemed waived.

Collateral Estoppel and the Full Faith and Credit Guarantee

Full faith and credit applies to matters of collateral estoppel. Thus, if the courts of a jurisdiction where a case was decided would treat an issue from that judgment as collaterally estopped, other State and federal courts have a duty to give the issue the same status.

PART III

USING THIS *STUDENT'S GUIDE*

How This *Student's Guide* Helps You Learn Civil Procedure

This *Student's Guide to the Federal Rules of Civil Procedure* is your source for the text of the Federal Rules of Civil Procedure. The text of those Rules appears on the following pages, Rule by Rule. But at the end of each Rule's text, the *Student's Guide* gives you a "decoder ring" of sorts to help you master each of those Rules. You'll find three resources after each Rule:

- ***How The Rule Fits In:*** This first discussion follows immediately after the text of each Rule. It orients you to the Rule in its federal civil procedure context—how it "fits in" to the practice of law in federal courts. This discussion will explain the Rule's importance and function from a macro perspective, and will enable you to see the role that Rule plays in civil litigation. It offers a great starting point for your mastery of that Rule's content.
- ***The Architecture of This Rule:*** This next discussion diagrams the Rule for you, which is especially helpful with long, dense Rule text. This should aid you in making sense of the Rule's structure and organization. You'll see how the Rule's parts fit together.
- ***How This Rule Works in Practice:*** Finally, this last discussion, always the longest, disassembles the Rule, subpart by subpart, and discusses how each subpart actually operates in federal civil practice. Consider this discussion the bridge between learning "theory" and seeing "practice."

The Rule-by-Rule treatment occupies the largest volume of the *Student's Guide*, but the other parts are worth your attention as well. Aside from the Rule-by-Rule treatment, this text offers six other features that you will find helpful in your study of Civil Procedure:

- ***Federal Power, Jurisdiction, Notice, Venue, Erie Doctrine, and Preclusion:*** These foundational principles of federal civil litigation are each likely covered in some depth in your law school Civil Procedure class. They certainly will become critically important to you as you practice law. But these are not comprehensively treated by the Rules themselves. It's content every civil litigator needs to know, but the concepts emanate from sources other than the Federal Rules of Civil Procedure. All of those concepts are discussed in depth—in Part II, §§ 2.1a and 2.2–2.26.
- ***The Story of the Federal Rules of Civil Procedure:*** The history of the Federal Rules of Civil Procedure is a fascinating one and a worthwhile read. That background will also help you understand the evolutionary process of the rulemaking—in Part II, § 2.1b.
- ***Multidistrict Litigation:*** This important, non-Rules-based lawsuit centralization tool is described, along with Congress's enacting statute—in Part VI.
- ***Federal Appellate Procedure:*** The details and nuances of federal civil appeals are beyond the scope of this *Student's Guide*, but every civil litigator needs to know the basics. An orientation to federal appellate procedure is a valuable caboose to your learning of Civil Procedure—in Part VII.
- ***Federal Statutes:*** A select number of federal statutes, appearing in the Judiciary Title (Title 28) of the U.S. Code, are routinely used by civil litigators—in Part VIII.
- ***U.S. Constitution:*** Every reprinting of the Rules ought to be accompanied by the full text of the federal Constitution—in Part IX.

Keeping Current in Federal Practice

The procedures governing federal civil litigation are highly dynamic, with changes in the text of the Rules themselves and in critically important interpretative case law arriving each year. The

Student's Guide contains the current text of the Rules and the most recent, core national case law as of the date each edition is printed. (For a discussion of the Rules amendment process, see Part II, § 2.1b.)

To acquire a sense for how ever-changing the Rules have been over just the past 20 years, take a peek at this list of Rule amendments:

- **Entity Deposition Amendments (2020)** (which expand pre-deposition obligations for those requesting to depose representatives of an entity party);
- **Electronic Filing & Service, Class Action Procedure, and Stay-of-Proceedings Amendments (2018)** (which compelled electronic filing by most attorneys, revised the class action notice, approval, and appeal requirements, and altered the post-judgment stay procedures);
- **Technical Amendments (2016 & 2017)** (which resolved certain drafting ambiguities, and which eliminated the 3-extra-day extension rule for electronic filings);
- **Managerial Judging & Proportionality-in-Discovery Amendments (2015)** (which imposed more active case-management responsibilities on judges and established a "proportionality" standard for the scope of allowable discovery);
- **Subpoena Amendments (2013)** (which adjusted civil subpoena powers);
- **Summary Judgment Amendments (2010)** (which restructured the summary judgment rule and codified certain common law summary judgment practices);
- **Expert Amendments (2010)** (which installed new expert disclosure obligations and extended work product protection to certain expert materials);
- **Time Computation Amendments (2009)** (which revised certain time deadlines and redesigned the approach for computing time);
- **"Restyling" Amendments (2007)** (which gave the Rules a top-to-bottom rewrite for clarity, consistency, and simplicity);
- **Privacy Amendments (2007)** (which authorized the redaction of certain personal-identifying information);
- **Discovery of Electronic Data Amendments (2006)** (which formalized disclosure and discovery of electronically-stored information);
- **Intervention in Constitution Challenges (2006)** (which collected provisions requiring notice, certification, and a right of intervention for constitutional challenges to federal or State laws);
- **Disclosure Statements (2002)** (which imposed a disclosure statement obligation on nongovernmental corporate litigants).

PART IV

FEDERAL RULES OF CIVIL PROCEDURE WITH STUDY ADVICE AND AUTHOR COMMENTARY

Rules Effective September 16, 1938

Including Amendments Effective December 1, 2020

Research Note

Rule requirements, case law applications, commentary, and references to treatises and law reviews are available in Wright, Miller, et al., Federal Practice and Procedure, *Volumes 4 to 20.*

Use WESTLAW® *to find cases citing or applying rules.* WESTLAW *may also be used to search for terms in court rules or to update court rules. See the US-RULES and US-ORDERS SCOPE screens for detailed descriptive information and search tips.*

Table of Rules

I. SCOPE OF RULES—FORM OF ACTION

II. COMMENCING AN ACTION; SERVICE OF PROCESS, PLEADINGS, MOTIONS, AND ORDERS

III. PLEADINGS AND MOTIONS

IV. PARTIES

V. DEPOSITIONS AND DISCOVERY

VI. TRIALS

SUPPLEMENTAL RULES FOR ADMIRALTY OR MARITIME CLAIMS AND ASSET FORFEITURE ACTIONS

APPENDIX OF FORMS

[An editorial note regarding the now-abrogated Appendix of Forms appears in Part V, below.]

I. SCOPE OF RULES—FORM OF ACTION

RULE 1

SCOPE AND PURPOSE

These rules govern the procedure in all civil actions and proceedings in the United States district courts, except as stated in Rule 81. They should be construed, administered, and employed by the court and the parties to secure the just, speedy, and inexpensive determination of every action and proceeding.

[Amended December 29, 1948, effective October 20, 1949; February 28, 1966, effective July 1, 1966; April 22, 1993, effective December 1, 1993; April 30, 2007, effective December 1, 2007; April 29, 2015, effective December 1, 2015.]

UNDERSTANDING RULE 1

HOW RULE 1 FITS IN

The study of Civil Procedure involves, in most law schools, an intensive focus on the Federal Rules of Civil Procedure. Why is that?

There are many reasons. First, the Federal Rules of Civil Procedure are (obviously) national in reach—they govern the procedure that will be used in litigating civil cases in every federal trial court in America. For that reason alone, lawyers-in-training will need to learn them. Second, the Federal Rules are comprehensive in scope; most types of litigating tools that a civil trial lawyer would want to use (or would likely encounter other lawyers using) are addressed by the Federal Rules. Thus, those Rules offer an ideal teaching vehicle for learning the "ins" and "outs" of civil litigation generally. Third, although the Federal Rules do not apply in State courts, many States have modeled their own State court rules on all or some of the Federal Rules. So, knowing how civil procedure works in federal court is likely to offer useful insights into how the same sorts of procedures work in local State courts. Fourth, most bar examinations test on a test-taker's mastery of federal civil practice, which makes sense, given that most bar exams rely, at least in part, on national testing devices (like the Uniform Bar Examination and the Multistate Bar Examination's multiple choice questions) to grade applicants who are seeking admission in that State to become licensed to practice law. There are other reasons, too, but suffice it to say that learning the Federal Rules of Civil Procedure is today an essential component of most every law student's journey from classroom to courtroom.

The story of the Federal Rules of Civil Procedure is a fascinating one. In the very year the U.S. Constitution was ratified, the first Congress enacted the Judiciary Act of 1789 which authorized federal courts to prepare rules for practice in their courtrooms, so long as those procedures were not "repugnant to the laws of the United States." 1 Stat. 73, 83. But that first Congress also enacted a "Conformity Act," which instructed that, until further notice, each federal court was to conform its "writs and executions" in all "suits at common law" to match those used or allowed in the State where that federal court was sitting. 1 Stat. 93, 93. The story was a bit different for suits in equity. For those types of disputes, Congress directed the Supreme Court to prepare a special set of equity rules. 1 Stat. 275, 276. So, early on, there was countrywide federal uniformity of procedure in equity suits, but not in "suits at common law." In "suits at common law," the procedures in the federal courts were not uniform at all, but varied State by State.

As the Nation grew in size, in population, and in legal complexity, these State-by-State variations became increasingly troublesome. After a lengthy, sometimes pitched battle in the federal legislature, Congress finally passed the Rules Enabling Act of 1934, directing the Supreme Court to merge law cases and equity claims into a single, unified type of civil case that would be litigated in a single type of federal tribunal which would apply a uniform set of federal procedures. 48 Stat. 1064. To aid in this imposing task, the Supreme Court appointed a committee of distinguished jurists, academics, and practitioners who labored for months drafting the new procedures. The Supreme Court adopted a revised version of the new procedures in December 1937, and submitted that finished version to Congress in January 1938. Congress took no action to block the new procedures from taking effect, and, at long last, the effective date arrived on Friday, September 16, 1938. The Federal Rules of Civil Procedure had been born.

The rule-drafting task was not done, however, and is not finished still. The Federal Rules of Civil Procedure have been amended more than thirty times already, as the Supreme Court and its various rule-advising committees have tinkered with the Rules to resolve weaknesses, correct imprecisions, and add innovative procedures to meet new litigation realities. That constantly evolving process is unlikely ever to end. For law students, practitioners, scholars, and judges alike, this perpetual "work-in-progress" nature of the Rules means that mastering federal civil practice will remain an always moving target. Whatever their role (learning, litigating, teaching, or presiding), all lawyers must keep pace with the dynamic nature of federal practice and remain ever vigilant in adapting to the Rules as they change.

THE ARCHITECTURE OF RULE 1

For a Rule spanning just two sentences, Rule 1 accomplishes quite a bit. Structurally, it accomplishes two objectives. Its first sentence sets the reach of the Federal Rules of Civil Procedure—they are to apply to "all civil actions and proceedings" in the federal trial courts. The few, fairly narrow exceptions are listed in Rule 81. The second sentence installs the "touchstones" of the Federal Rules of Civil Procedure—the just, speedy, and inexpensive resolution of federal civil cases. The parties and federal judges are called upon to construe, administer, and use the Rules to achieve those three touchstones.

HOW RULE 1 WORKS IN PRACTICE

Status and Validity of the Federal Rules

The Rules have the force and effect of law. They enjoy "presumptive validity." *See Burlington No. R. Co. v. Woods*, 480 U.S. 1, 6 (1987). Nevertheless, although promulgated by the United States Supreme Court, a Federal Rule may still be challenged as inconsistent with either the rulemaking power delegated by Congress to the Supreme Court under the Rules Enabling Act or the U.S. Constitution. *See Mississippi Pub. Corp. v. Murphree,* 326 U.S. 438, 444 (1946). To date, no Rule has ever been declared invalid.

The Advisory Committee and Its Committee Notes

To help draft the original Federal Rules of Civil Procedure, the Supreme Court appointed an Advisory Committee on Rules comprising a panel of judges, attorneys, and law professors. This consultative tradition continues today, in the form of the Judicial Conference of the United States' Advisory Committee on Civil Rules, which considers and recommends amendments to the Rules. The members of the Advisory Committee have included federal and State judges, practicing attorneys, law professors, and Department of Justice representatives.

Both the original Advisory Committee and its successors have published "Notes" as an aid in construing and interpreting the particular purpose and intent of each Rule and its amendments. The Committee Notes are only guides; the Notes neither are a part of the Rules nor have they been approved by the Supreme Court. However, in practice, the Notes have assumed the force of a veritable legislative history to the Rules and their amendments. The Notes can be cited as formidable (though non-binding) authority for construing the Rules.

Where the Rules Apply

The Rules apply to all civil cases in all federal district courts of the United States. *See Ashcroft v. Iqbal,* 556 U.S. 662, 684 (2009). They do not apply to the federal appeals courts, to the federal tax court, to certain "specialized proceedings" listed in Rule 81, or in federal criminal cases. By special congressional act, the Rules have been extended to the United States District Court for the District of Columbia, and to the territorial/insular courts of Guam, the Northern Mariana Islands, Puerto Rico, and the Virgin Islands.

But the Rules Are Not All-Encompassing

The Rules set out many of the powers of federal trial courts, but the absence of a particular authority in the Rules does not necessarily foreclose it. For example, courts enjoy the "inherent power" to respond reasonably to "problems and needs" arising in the course of administering justice (provided that power is not exercised in a manner contrary to an express grant or constraint found in a Rule or statute). *See Dietz v. Bouldin*, 136 S. Ct. 1885, 1891–93 (2016).

Rules to Be Harmonized Together

The Rules were designed to be "interdependent." Thus, in interpreting them, courts seek to "harmonize" the Rules with one another, and will only allow one Rule to take precedence over another where a truly irreconcilable conflict arises.

Touchstones—"Just," "Speedy," and "Inexpensive"

Aside from defining when the Rules apply, Rule 1 also fixes the broad objectives of the Federal Rules of Civil Procedure: they are to be construed, administered, and employed so as to achieve the "just, speedy, and inexpensive determination of every action." This admonition applies also to Local Rules promulgated to supplement the national Rules.

Often cited, these goals have been lauded by the Supreme Court as "the touchstones of federal procedure," *Brown Shoe Co. v. United States,* 370 U.S. 294, 306 (1962); and as a "paramount command," *Dietz v. Bouldin*, 136 S. Ct. 1885, 1891 (2016). The text of Rule 1 emphasizes the trial courts' affirmative duty to exercise the procedural authority the Rules bestow so as to resolve civil litigation fairly and without undue cost or delay. This affirmative duty is shared by practicing attorneys, as officers of the court. To realize Rule l's goals of "just, speedy, and inexpensive" determinations of federal cases, the parties are expected to work diligently to follow the Rules and the courts are called upon to resolutely enforce the Rules, otherwise the Rules—and the laudable objectives they seek—will become illusory. Broadly understood, the Rules encourage the cooperative and proportional use of procedure, and discourage "over-use, misuse, and abuse of procedural tools that increase costs and result in delay." *See* Rule 1 advisory comm. note (2015). They favor decisions on the merits, rather than ones based on mere technicalities. *See Schiavone v. Fortune*, 477 U.S. 21, 27 (1986).

The courts have quoted these touchstones as guidance for construing and interpreting the Rules. In finding a Rule's meaning, the touchstones of Rule 1 disfavor any interpretation that will cause confusion or that sets a trap for the unwary. So pervasive is the Rule 1 mission that it has been cited as authority for preventing a litigant from flouting the "spirit" of the Rules, even where the litigant's conduct might otherwise comport with the Rule's literal meaning. Examples of federal courts citing and relying on Rule 1 to achieve these objectives are legion.

This simple Rule is a reminder that form should not be exalted over substance. Yet, the Rules' flexibility is certainly not unbounded. Rule 1's touchstones cannot be used, for example, to rescue a filing by distorting its deficient (but clearly pleaded) content into something that it is not, under the banner of liberality.

RULE 2

ONE FORM OF ACTION

There is one form of action—the civil action.

[Amended April 30, 2007, effective December 1, 2007.]

UNDERSTANDING RULE 2

HOW RULE 2 FITS IN

For centuries, English law recognized a difference between the law courts (where juries would resolve disputes that sought a legal remedy—money damages, for instance—based on settled principles of common law) and the courts of equity or chancery courts (where chancellors in equity would, without a jury, resolve disputes that sought equitable relief—an injunction, for instance—based on flexible principles of general fairness). These two types of tribunals co-existed under English law, but evolved with separate sets of rules and procedures. The distinction between law and equity was imported into American jurisprudence during our colonial period, and then preserved in the U.S. Constitution.

One of the innovations ushered in by the Federal Rules of Civil Procedure in 1938 was the "merger" of law and equity for procedural purposes. Rule 2 accomplished that goal. Rule 2 did away with "law courts" and "equity courts," with "chancellors in equity," and with "legal procedures" and "equitable procedures." Instead, federal courts were now authorized to hear just one, unified "form of action"—called a "civil action"—and, in resolving that dispute, federal judges were authorized to award legal remedies, equitable remedies, or both in the same, unitary proceeding. *See Petrella v. Metro-Goldwyn-Mayer, Inc.,* 572 U.S. 663, 678–79 (2014).

THE ARCHITECTURE OF RULE 2

Rule 2 does not have much architecture (or many words, for that matter). The nine words of Rule 2 have just one principal goal—to merge together the authority of federal courts to hear, in one unitary proceeding, both legal claims and equitable claims.

HOW RULE 2 WORKS IN PRACTICE

Civil Action Defined

The term "civil action" means a federal civil lawsuit, regardless of how that lawsuit might be labeled or titled. The term encompasses all component "claims" and "cases" within that lawsuit. To qualify as a civil action, the proceeding must actually have been commenced.

Joinder of All Claims and Defenses

Without a separate "law-side" and "equity-side" to the federal courts, a party may now join all claims and defenses (legal and equitable) against all opposing parties in the same one action—assuming that the Rules and applicable statutes would permit such joinder.

The Distinction Between "Law" and "Equity" Still Matters

Although the federal courts no longer recognize a distinction in procedure between cases on the "law-side" and suits in "equity," this distinction still persists in some limited contexts where the federal courts may yet be called upon to discern the substantive "form" of the litigation (*i.e.,* legal or equitable). This inquiry may arise when, for instance, the court has to decide whether a litigant enjoys a right to a trial by jury, *see Wooddell v. Int'l Bhd. of Elec. Workers, Local 71,* 502 U.S. 93, 97 (1991), or when, in diversity cases, the controlling State law retains the law/equity distinction as to substantive issues (like the applicable statute of limitations). Although the Rules have fused law and equity into a single procedural framework, the federal courts still apply equity *principles* in appropriate cases. *See Petrella v. Metro-Goldwyn-Mayer, Inc.,* 572 U.S. 663, 678–79 (2014).

II. COMMENCING AN ACTION; SERVICE OF PROCESS, PLEADINGS, MOTIONS, AND ORDERS

RULE 3

COMMENCING AN ACTION

A civil action is commenced by filing a complaint with the court.

[Amended April 30, 2007, effective December 1, 2007.]

UNDERSTANDING RULE 3

HOW RULE 3 FITS IN

The date that a lawsuit begins can be very important. It may determine whether the lawsuit is timely filed, or instead barred as stale under a statute of limitations. It may resolve whether personal jurisdiction and subject-matter jurisdiction exist (both of which are ordinarily gauged by circumstances existing on the day the lawsuit begins). It may also be crucial for purposes under other Rules, such as the Rule for compulsory counterclaims which may excuse the need to file such claims if they are already the subject of another "pending" action. Rule 3 aids in resolving these sorts of issues by fixing a clear, unambiguous date for the beginning of every federal civil lawsuit.

THE ARCHITECTURE OF RULE 3

The single sentence of Rule 3 needs no architectural orientation. In plain language, the Rule installs an easy-to-apply approach for determining the date on which a federal action "commences."

HOW RULE 3 WORKS IN PRACTICE

Pre-"Commencement" Issues

Prior to the filing of the complaint, the federal district court lacks authority to act in the dispute (because the dispute has not yet been "commenced"). Filing a paper other than a complaint will not trigger commencement, unless the court can properly treat the filed paper as a complaint.

Service of Process Generally Not Required for "Commencement"

Service of process is generally not required for the lawsuit to "commence." So long as service is completed within 90 days after the complaint is filed with the court, the litigants become "plaintiff" and "defendant" when the complaint is filed, not when it is served.

(However, the date service of process is completed could become significant under a State's statute of limitations in diversity cases, as described below.)

"Commencement" Is Provisional—Without Service, Action Dismissible in 90 Days

Although an action becomes "pending" when the complaint is filed, Rule 4(m) authorizes the district court to dismiss the action, without prejudice, if service of both the summons and the complaint is not made within 90 days of commencement (unless good cause is shown why service was not accomplished during that period).

"Commencement" Is Provisional—Action Dismissible for Lack of Diligent Prosecution

Once a plaintiff files the complaint, the plaintiff must prosecute the action with diligence. Rule 3 does not relieve plaintiffs of their obligation to keep moving the case forward after filing. The court may dismiss any action for lack of due diligence in proceeding with the lawsuit. *See* Rule 41(b).

"Commencement" in Federal Question Cases

Ordinarily, in cases invoking the court's federal question jurisdiction, Rule 3 will act to toll the statute of limitations upon the filing of the complaint. *See Henderson v. United States,* 517 U.S. 654, 657 n.2 (1996). One exception exists—where the federal question is based on a statute that, itself, contains a special, separate "commencement" provision; in those cases, the terms of that statute will control. In neither event will State law ordinarily be used to determine the date of "commencement." Even where the federal law lacks a specific statute of limitations, and the applicable limitations period is "borrowed" either from another federal law or from State law, Rule 3's commencement function will govern, and the filing of the complaint will generally toll the applicable statute of limitations period.

"Commencement" in Diversity-of-Citizenship Cases

In cases invoking the court's diversity jurisdiction, the date of commencement will be used to assess uniquely federal issues, such as the presence of diverse citizenship and the running of time periods set by the Federal Rules. However, in diversity cases, Rule 3 will not always toll the applicable State law statute of limitations. The *Erie* doctrine and its progeny (discussed in Sections 2.18 to 2.23 of this text) compels that, where State law provides a contrary tolling requirement or tolling limitation, Rule 3 cannot be permitted to give the State law cause of action a longer life in a federal court than it would otherwise have in the State courts. *See Walker v. Armco Steel Corp.,* 446 U.S. 740 (1980); *Ragan v. Merchants Transfer & Warehouse Co.,* 337 U.S. 530 (1949). Thus, in a diversity lawsuit, if under State law the limitations period would not be considered tolled until service of process is accomplished or the filing fee is paid, Rule 3 will not act to toll the limitations period merely upon filing. *See Henderson v. United States,* 517 U.S. 654, 657 n.2 (1996).

"Commencement" in Supplemental Jurisdiction Cases

In cases invoking the court's supplemental jurisdiction over an otherwise non-qualifying State claim, those State law claims will likely be treated by federal courts in the same manner as the courts would in diversity cases.

Commencement and Removed Cases

Ordinarily, a case is not considered "re"-commenced if it is removed to federal court. Instead, the general federal approach holds that a lawsuit is deemed "commenced" at one discrete moment in time—typically, when the original lawsuit is filed in a court of competent jurisdiction. Nevertheless, if an applicable State law requires effective service as a prerequisite to "commencement," the lawsuit might be considered ineligible for removal until the defendant is successfully served.

Commencement and Amended Complaints

Amended complaints can sometimes require pre-filing permission from the court. *See* Rule 15. In such cases, many courts have ruled that the amended complaint is deemed filed, for "commencement" purposes, as of the date that a motion seeking the court's permission for leave to amend is filed.

Special Prerequisites for Commencement

Certain federal statutes contain special prerequisites for commencing a civil action, such as receiving a right-to-sue letter or exhausting available administrative remedies. Thus, merely filing a complaint pursuant to Rule 3 might not toll the statute of limitations if such prerequisites apply and are not met.

Filing Electronically

Legal papers must now be filed with a federal court electronically, unless the Rules, local procedures, or the court otherwise directs. *See* Rule 5(d)(3). When a complaint is filed through proper electronic means, "commencement" usually occurs when the filing process is complete, regardless of whether the filing system experiences an electronic glitch or the filing fee remains unpaid.

Filing by Mail

Service and filing rules are different. A paper is considered "served" when addressed to its recipient, proper postage is affixed, and it is placed in the possession of the U.S. Postal Service. This "mailbox" rule for service does not ordinarily suffice to "commence" a federal lawsuit. Instead, if original papers are mailed to the Clerk's Office for filing, filing is usually only considered complete—and the lawsuit only "commences"—upon the Clerk's receipt of the complaint.

Filing with the Court After Business Hours

Rule 77 prescribes that the District Courts are "always open." Accordingly, a complaint might be deemed filed as of the moment it was delivered to the Clerk's Office, even if delivered after the Clerk's regular business hours.

Filing Fees

Some (but not all) federal courts require that all filing fees be paid prior to a lawsuit being considered "commenced."

Pauper and Prisoner Plaintiffs

The federal courts have an *in forma pauperis* procedure which can allow a federal judge, upon request, to authorize the commencement of a lawsuit without a payment of filing fees. *See* 28 U.S.C. § 1915. Some courts will even consider a lawsuit to be conditionally commenced upon the simultaneous filing of a complaint and a motion to proceed *in forma pauperis* (provided that, if the motion is later denied, filing fees are promptly paid). That conditional commencement might also toll the applicable limitations period. In complaints prepared by *pro se* plaintiffs who are prisoners, the courts may follow a variation of the "mailbox" rule—but one that deems a lawsuit as "commenced" upon delivery of the complaint to appropriate prison officials.

RULE 4
SUMMONS

(a) Contents; Amendments.

(1) *Contents.* A summons must:

(A) name the court and the parties;

(B) be directed to the defendant;

(C) state the name and address of the plaintiff's attorney or—if unrepresented—of the plaintiff;

(D) state the time within which the defendant must appear and defend;

(E) notify the defendant that a failure to appear and defend will result in a default judgment against the defendant for the relief demanded in the complaint;

(F) be signed by the clerk; and

(G) bear the court's seal.

(2) *Amendments.* The court may permit a summons to be amended.

(b) Issuance. On or after filing the complaint, the plaintiff may present a summons to the clerk for signature and seal. If the summons is properly completed, the clerk must sign, seal, and issue it to the plaintiff for service on the defendant. A summons—or a copy of a summons that is addressed to multiple defendants—must be issued for each defendant to be served.

(c) Service.

(1) *In General.* A summons must be served with a copy of the complaint. The plaintiff is responsible for having the summons and complaint served within the time allowed by Rule 4(m) and must furnish the necessary copies to the person who makes service.

(2) *By Whom.* Any person who is at least 18 years old and not a party may serve a summons and complaint.

(3) *By a Marshal or Someone Specially Appointed.* At the plaintiff's request, the court may order that service be made by a United States marshal or deputy marshal or by a person specially appointed by the court. The court must so order if the plaintiff is authorized to proceed in forma pauperis under 28 U.S.C. § 1915 or as a seaman under 28 U.S.C. § 1916.

(d) Waiving Service.

(1) *Requesting a Waiver.* An individual, corporation, or association that is subject to service under Rule 4(e), (f), or (h) has a duty to avoid

unnecessary expenses of serving the summons. The plaintiff may notify such a defendant that an action has been commenced and request that the defendant waive service of a summons. The notice and request must:

(A) be in writing and be addressed:

(i) to the individual defendant; or

(ii) for a defendant subject to service under Rule 4(h), to an officer, a managing or general agent, or any other agent authorized by appointment or by law to receive service of process;

(B) name the court where the complaint was filed;

(C) be accompanied by a copy of the complaint, 2 copies of the waiver form appended to this Rule 4, and a prepaid means for returning the form;

(D) inform the defendant, using the form appended to this Rule 4, of the consequences of waiving and not waiving service;

(E) state the date when the request is sent;

(F) give the defendant a reasonable time of at least 30 days after the request was sent—or at least 60 days if sent to the defendant outside any judicial district of the United States—to return the waiver; and

(G) be sent by first-class mail or other reliable means.

(2) *Failure to Waive.* If a defendant located within the United States fails, without good cause, to sign and return a waiver requested by a plaintiff located within the United States, the court must impose on the defendant:

(A) the expenses later incurred in making service; and

(B) the reasonable expenses, including attorney's fees, of any motion required to collect those service expenses.

(3) *Time to Answer After a Waiver.* A defendant who, before being served with process, timely returns a waiver need not serve an answer to the complaint until 60 days after the request was sent—or until 90 days after it was sent to the defendant outside any judicial district of the United States.

(4) *Results of Filing a Waiver.* When the plaintiff files a waiver, proof of service is not required and these rules apply as if a summons and complaint had been served at the time of filing the waiver.

(5) *Jurisdiction and Venue Not Waived.* Waiving service of a summons does not waive any objection to personal jurisdiction or to venue.

(e) Serving an Individual Within a Judicial District of the United States. Unless federal law provides otherwise, an individual—other than a minor, an incompetent person, or a person whose waiver has been filed—may be served in a judicial district of the United States by:

(1) following State law for serving a summons in an action brought in courts of general jurisdiction in the State where the district court is located or where service is made; or

(2) doing any of the following:

(A) delivering a copy of the summons and of the complaint to the individual personally;

(B) leaving a copy of each at the individual's dwelling or usual place of abode with someone of suitable age and discretion who resides there; or

(C) delivering a copy of each to an agent authorized by appointment or by law to receive service of process.

(f) Serving an Individual in a Foreign Country. Unless federal law provides otherwise, an individual—other than a minor, an incompetent person, or a person whose waiver has been filed—may be served at a place not within any judicial district of the United States:

(1) by any internationally agreed means of service that is reasonably calculated to give notice, such as those authorized by the Hague Convention on the Service Abroad of Judicial and Extrajudicial Documents;

(2) if there is no internationally agreed means, or if an international agreement allows but does not specify other means, by a method that is reasonably calculated to give notice:

(A) as prescribed by the foreign country's law for service in that country in an action in its courts of general jurisdiction;

(B) as the foreign authority directs in response to a letter rogatory or letter of request; or

(C) unless prohibited by the foreign country's law, by:

(i) delivering a copy of the summons and of the complaint to the individual personally; or

(ii) using any form of mail that the clerk addresses and sends to the individual and that requires a signed receipt; or

(3) by other means not prohibited by international agreement, as the court orders.

(g) Serving a Minor or an Incompetent Person. A minor or an incompetent person in a judicial district of the United States must be served by following State law for serving a summons or like process on such a defendant in an action brought in the courts of general jurisdiction of the State where service is made. A minor or an incompetent person who is not within any judicial district of the United States must be served in the manner prescribed by Rule 4(f)(2)(A), (f)(2)(B), or (f)(3).

(h) Serving a Corporation, Partnership, or Association. Unless federal law provides otherwise or the defendant's waiver has been filed, a domestic or foreign corporation, or a partnership or other unincorporated association that is subject to suit under a common name, must be served:

(1) in a judicial district of the United States:

(A) in the manner prescribed by Rule 4(e)(1) for serving an individual; or

(B) by delivering a copy of the summons and of the complaint to an officer, a managing or general agent, or any other agent authorized by appointment or by law to receive service of process and—if the agent is one authorized by statute and the statute so requires—by also mailing a copy of each to the defendant; or

(2) at a place not within any judicial district of the United States, in any manner prescribed by Rule 4(f) for serving an individual, except personal delivery under (f)(2)(C)(i).

(i) Serving the United States and Its Agencies, Corporations, Officers, or Employees.

(1) *United States.* To serve the United States, a party must:

(A) (i) deliver a copy of the summons and of the complaint to the United States attorney for the district where the action is brought—or to an assistant United States attorney or clerical employee whom the United States attorney designates in a writing filed with the court clerk—or

(ii) send a copy of each by registered or certified mail to the civil-process clerk at the United States attorney's office;

(B) send a copy of each by registered or certified mail to the Attorney General of the United States at Washington, D.C.; and

(C) if the action challenges an order of a nonparty agency or officer of the United States, send a copy of each by registered or certified mail to the agency or officer.

(2) *Agency; Corporation; Officer or Employee Sued in an Official Capacity.* To serve a United States agency or corporation, or a United States officer

or employee sued only in an official capacity, a party must serve the United States and also send a copy of the summons and of the complaint by registered or certified mail to the agency, corporation, officer, or employee.

(3) *Officer or Employee Sued Individually.* To serve a United States officer or employee sued in an individual capacity for an act or omission occurring in connection with duties performed on the United States' behalf (whether or not the officer or employee is also sued in an official capacity), a party must serve the United States and also serve the officer or employee under Rule 4(e), (f), or (g).

(4) *Extending Time.* The court must allow a party a reasonable time to cure its failure to:

(A) serve a person required to be served under Rule 4(i)(2), if the party has served either the United States attorney or the Attorney General of the United States; or

(B) serve the United States under Rule 4(i)(3), if the party has served the United States officer or employee.

(j) Serving a Foreign, State, or Local Government.

(1) *Foreign State.* A foreign State or its political subdivision, agency, or instrumentality must be served in accordance with 28 U.S.C. § 1608.

(2) *State or Local Government.* A State, a municipal corporation, or any other State-created governmental organization that is subject to suit must be served by:

(A) delivering a copy of the summons and of the complaint to its chief executive officer; or

(B) serving a copy of each in the manner prescribed by that State's law for serving a summons or like process on such a defendant.

(k) Territorial Limits of Effective Service.

(1) *In General.* Serving a summons or filing a waiver of service establishes personal jurisdiction over a defendant:

(A) who is subject to the jurisdiction of a court of general jurisdiction in the State where the district court is located;

(B) who is a party joined under Rule 14 or 19 and is served within a judicial district of the United States and not more than 100 miles from where the summons was issued;

(C) when authorized by a federal statute.

(2) *Federal Claim Outside State-Court Jurisdiction.* For a claim that arises under federal law, serving a summons or filing a waiver of service establishes personal jurisdiction over a defendant if:

(A) the defendant is not subject to jurisdiction in any State's courts of general jurisdiction; and

(B) exercising jurisdiction is consistent with the United States Constitution and laws.

(*l*) Proving Service.

(1) *Affidavit Required.* Unless service is waived, proof of service must be made to the court. Except for service by a United States marshal or deputy marshal, proof must be by the server's affidavit.

(2) *Service Outside the United States.* Service not within any judicial district of the United States must be proved as follows:

(A) if made under Rule 4(f)(1), as provided in the applicable treaty or convention; or

(B) if made under Rule 4(f)(2) or (f)(3), by a receipt signed by the addressee, or by other evidence satisfying the court that the summons and complaint were delivered to the addressee.

(3) *Validity of Service; Amending Proof.* Failure to prove service does not affect the validity of service. The court may permit proof of service to be amended.

(m) Time Limit for Service. If a defendant is not served within 90 days after the complaint is filed, the court—on motion or on its own after notice to the plaintiff—must dismiss the action without prejudice against that defendant or order that service be made within a specified time. But if the plaintiff shows good cause for the failure, the court must extend the time for service for an appropriate period. This subdivision (m) does not apply to service in a foreign country under Rule 4(f), 4(h)(2), or 4(j)(1) or to service of a notice under Rule 71.1(d)(3)(A).

(n) Asserting Jurisdiction over Property or Assets.

(1) *Federal Law.* The court may assert jurisdiction over property if authorized by a federal statute. Notice to claimants of the property must be given as provided in the statute or by serving a summons under this rule.

(2) *State Law.* On a showing that personal jurisdiction over a defendant cannot be obtained in the district where the action is brought by reasonable efforts to serve a summons under this rule, the court may assert jurisdiction over the defendant's assets found in the district.

Jurisdiction is acquired by seizing the assets under the circumstances and in the manner provided by State law in that district.

Official Forms *for* Waiver of Service

Official Form #1: Rule 4 Notice of a Lawsuit and Request to Waive Service of Summons.

(Caption)

To (name the defendant or—if the defendant is a corporation, partnership, or association—name an officer or agent authorized to receive service):

Why are you getting this?

A lawsuit has been filed against you, or the entity you represent, in this court under the number shown above. A copy of the complaint is attached.

This is not a summons, or an official notice from the court. It is a request that, to avoid expenses, you waive formal service of a summons by signing and returning the enclosed waiver. To avoid these expenses, you must return the signed waiver within (give at least 30 days or at least 60 days if the defendant is outside any judicial district of the United States) from the date shown below, which is the date this notice was sent. Two copies of the waiver form are enclosed, along with a stamped, self-addressed envelope or other prepaid means for returning one copy. You may keep the other copy.

What happens next?

If you return the signed waiver, I will file it with the court. The action will then proceed as if you had been served on the date the waiver is filed, but no summons will be served on you and you will have 60 days from the date this notice is sent (see the date below) to answer the complaint (or 90 days if this notice is sent to you outside any judicial district of the United States).

If you do not return the signed waiver within the time indicated, I will arrange to have the summons and complaint served on you. And I will ask the court to require you, or the entity you represent, to pay the expenses of making service.

Please read the enclosed statement about the duty to avoid unnecessary expenses.

I certify that this request is being sent to you on the date below.

Date: __________

____

(Signature of the attorney or unrepresented party)

____

(Printed name)

____

(Address)

____

(E-mail address)

____

(Telephone number)

Official Form #2:
Rule 4 Waiver of the Service of Summons.

(Caption)

To (name the plaintiff's attorney or the unrepresented plaintiff):

I have received your request to waive service of a summons in this action along with a copy of the complaint, two copies of this waiver form, and a prepaid means of returning one signed copy of the form to you.

I, or the entity I represent, agree to save the expense of serving a summons and complaint in this case.

I understand that I, or the entity I represent, will keep all defenses or objections to the lawsuit, the court's jurisdiction, and the venue of the action, but that I waive any objections to the absence of a summons or of service.

I also understand that I, or the entity I represent, must file and serve an answer or a motion under Rule 12 within 60 days from ___________________, the date when this request was sent (or 90 days if it was sent outside the United States).

If I fail to do so, a default judgment will be entered against me or the entity I represent.

Date: __________

____

(Signature of the attorney or unrepresented party)

____

(Printed name)

____

(Address)

____

(E-mail address)

____

(Telephone number)

(Attach the following)

Duty to Avoid Unnecessary Expenses of Serving a Summons

Rule 4 of the Federal Rules of Civil Procedure requires certain defendants to cooperate in saving unnecessary expenses of serving a summons and complaint. A defendant who is located in the United States and who fails to return a signed waiver of service requested by a plaintiff located in the United States will be required to pay the expenses of service, unless the defendant shows good cause for the failure.

"Good cause" does not include a belief that the lawsuit is groundless, or that it has been brought in an improper venue, or that the court has no jurisdiction over this matter or over the defendant or the defendant's property.

If the waiver is signed and returned, you can still make these and all other defenses and objections, but you cannot object to the absence of a summons or of service.

If you waive service, then you must, within the time specified on the waiver form, serve an answer or a motion under Rule 12 on the plaintiff and file a copy with the court. By signing and returning the waiver form, you are allowed more time to respond than if a summons had been served.

[Amended January 21, 1963, effective July 1, 1963; February 28, 1966, effective July 1, 1966; April 29, 1980, effective August 1, 1980; amended by Pub.L. 97–462, § 2, January 12, 1983, 96 Stat. 2527, effective 45 days after January 12, 1983; amended March 2, 1987, effective August 1, 1987; April 22, 1993, effective December 1, 1993; April 17, 2000, effective December 1, 2000; April 30, 2007, effective December 1, 2007; April 29, 2015, effective December 1, 2015; April 28, 2016, effective December 1, 2016.]

UNDERSTANDING RULE 4

HOW RULE 4 FITS IN

Courts can only decide cases if they have the lawful authority to do so. That lawful authority requires jurisdiction over the parties (*personal jurisdiction*), jurisdiction over the type of the dispute (*subject-matter jurisdiction*), and proper venue. (These three requirements are discussed in detail in Sections 2.1 to 2.17 of this *Student's Guide.*)

Rule 4 implicates the first of these requirements—personal jurisdiction. It contains procedures a federal trial court will apply in acquiring personal jurisdiction over the parties. The Rule sets the approved methods for giving notice to defendants that a federal civil lawsuit has been filed against them ("service of process"), and also establishes the territorial reach of each federal court to act.

Although effective service of process is a critical ingredient for personal jurisdiction, it alone is not sufficient to confirm that the court's exercise of personal jurisdiction over a particular defendant is proper. It does not, for example, verify whether "minimum contacts" exist or if a defendant is "essentially-at-home" in the forum. Those constitutional questions must be resolved, instead, under the prevailing standards recognized in the case law. Nor will complying with Rule 4 automatically verify that the manner of delivering notice to the defendant is constitutionally adequate. That question, too, must be considered in view of the controlling case law on the issue.

Rule 4's purpose is supplemental to these constitutional standards. Rule 4 sets out the procedures that must be followed for serving the defendants with notice, *assuming* those defendants are constitutionally amenable to the court's personal jurisdiction, that venue is proper, and that the notice, in context, meets the constitutional prerequisites.

THE ARCHITECTURE OF RULE 4

The organization of Rule 4 can seem confusing. Its structure is not immediately clear on a quick reading. An easy way to master Rule 4 is to divide it into four groups of subparts, organized by function, and then learn the procedures of each group. Those groups are:

- *Logistics for Service of Process:* These subparts set the requirements for most every kind of service (e.g., what each summons must contain, who must perform the service, how formal service can be waived, how service is proven, and the time limits for service). These are Rules 4(a)–(d) & (*l*)–(m) and Forms #1 and #2.
- *Methods for Service of Process:* These subparts list the allowable manner for service particular types of defendants (e.g., people, children, incompetent persons, businesses and entities, governments and government actors). These are Rules 4(e)–(j).
- *Methods for Exercising In Rem Jurisdiction:* Rule 4(n) sets the procedures for exercising *in rem* jurisdiction—jurisdiction over property and things.
- *Territorial Reach:* Lastly, Rule 4(k) establishes the territorial reach of federal trial courts—how far their personal jurisdiction "reach" can extend.

Grouping Rule 4 this way will help you master its content. For ease of reference, however, the Commentary that follows tracks Rule 4's subparts in the order in which they appear in the Rule itself.

HOW RULE 4 WORKS IN PRACTICE

Before delving into the various subparts of Rule 4, a few preliminary concepts should be understood about federal service of process:

What It Means—"Service" of "Process"

The term "process" means the legal instrument through which a court acquires lawful authority to act upon a person or property in resolving a civil dispute—generally, "process" means a summons directing a person or entity to appear in court. "Service" means the formal delivery of that summons (and its necessary accompaniment, the lawsuit's complaint) upon a defending party. So, together, "service" of "process" means the formalized delivery of notice to a defendant that a federal court is asserting coercive authority over that defendant in order to resolve a civil dispute. The "service" of this "process" (or a defendant's waiver of his or her entitlement to that procedure) is considered a constitutional prerequisite for a court's exercise of personal jurisdiction. *See BNSF Ry. Co. v. Tyrrell*, 137 S. Ct. 1549, 1555–56 (2017); *Omni Capital Int'l, Ltd. v. Rudolf Wolff & Co.*, 484 U.S. 97, 104 (1987).

"Constitutional" Notice *vs.* "Rule 4" Notice

The U.S. Constitution's Due Process Clause requires that service be completed in a manner that is "reasonably calculated," under the circumstances, to apprise the defendant of the pending lawsuit and to afford a reasonable opportunity to make a defense. *See Jones v. Flowers*, 547 U.S. 220, 226 (2006); *Mullane v. Central Hanover Bank & Trust Co.*, 339 U.S. 306, 314 (1950). Meeting this constitutional standard is essential, but not sufficient. The manner of service must *also* comport with the procedural requirements set by Rule 4.

Actual Notice Is Not *Required*

The mere fact that a defendant did not receive actual notice of the lawsuit does not necessarily render service of process defective or personal jurisdiction improper. *See Jones v. Flowers,* 547 U.S. 220, 226 (2006); *Dusenbery v. United States,* 534 U.S. 161, 171 (2002). So long as the constitutional "reasonably calculated" standard established by *Mullane* is satisfied, lack of actual notice does not offend the Due Process Clause. *See Jones v. Flowers,* 547 U.S. 220, 226 (2006). One caveat: if a plaintiff comes to discover that the attempted service failed (for example, a notification from the post office that a mailing was undeliverable), due process requires that the plaintiff to undertake additional efforts to re-attempt service if it would be reasonable, under the circumstances, to do so. *See id.* at 226–39.

Actual Notice Alone Is Not *Enough*

Although the core goal of service is to ensure that the defendants are aware of the lawsuit pending against them, simply proving their actual, subjective awareness is unlikely to be sufficient. Actual receipt of notice likely will satisfy the Constitution's due process requirements, but formal compliance with Rule 4 is required as well. *See Freedom Watch, Inc. v. Organization of Petroleum Exporting Countries*, 766 F.3d 74, 81 (D.C. Cir. 2014). However, if actual notice occurred, Rule 4 will likely be given a liberal construction.

Distinguishing Service of Process from Jurisdiction and Venue

Service of the summons and complaint (or waiver of service) is a prerequisite to the district court's exercise of jurisdiction over a defendant. *See Omni Capital Int'l, Ltd. v. Rudolf Wolff & Co.,* 484 U.S. 97, 103 (1987). But complying with the federal service rules does not mean that proper jurisdiction and proper venue exists. *See* Rule 82. Though impacted by service, those concepts (jurisdiction and venue) are distinct from service and must be separately satisfied. *See Henderson v. United States,* 517 U.S. 654, 670 (1996). All of these requirements—proper service, proper jurisdiction, and proper venue—are required before federal judicial power may be exercised.

Service of process is the event by which a court asserts its judicial authority over parties in a lawsuit. *See Mississippi Pub. Corp. v. Murphree*, 326 U.S. 438, 444–45 (1946). Ordinarily, that formality is not required as to plaintiffs because plaintiffs are the ones invoking, and thus consenting to, the court's exercise of power of them. *See Adam v. Saenger*, 303 U.S. 59, 67–68 (1938). But the formality is required as to all those parties who are being haled involuntarily before the court (defendants). *See Int'l Shoe Co. v. Washington*, 326 U.S. 310, 316 (1945) (historically, exercising judicial authority was "grounded" on court's actual, physical, "de facto power" over a defendant's person or property); *Murphy Bros. v. Michetti Pipe Stringing, Inc.*, 526 U.S. 344, 350 (1999) (notice, via service of process, is "the contemporary counterpart" of that exercise of physical power). Service of process thus accomplishes two objectives: it asserts the court's exercise of its authority over nonconsenting parties to a lawsuit and it is the means by which those nonconsenting parties are notified of both the pendency of the lawsuit and their need to appear and mount a defense.

Immunity from Service

Defendants who might otherwise be properly served with process may sometimes be "immune" from service. Immunity from service is governed by federal case law, and exists where the due administration of justice demands it. *See Stewart v. Ramsay,* 242 U.S. 128, 129 (1916). Whether to confer the immunity is vested in the discretion of the district court; the purpose of the immunity is *not* primarily to protect the defendant who is seeking to avoid service, but instead to aid the court in its judicial administration. Persons are generally immune from service when they are present in the jurisdiction to attend court, to give a deposition, to conduct settlement discussions in connection with another, unrelated lawsuit, or to participate in a legislative or administrative hearing process. *See Lamb v. Schmitt,* 285

U.S. 222, 225 (1932); *Page Co. v. MacDonald,* 261 U.S. 446, 447–49 (1923). This immunity generally encompasses not only the time when the person is actually present and participating in such proceedings, but also typically extends for a reasonable period before and after the proceedings to allow the person to enter and then freely leave the jurisdiction.

Persons may also be immune from service when they are lured by fraud or trickery into the jurisdiction by the plaintiff who then attempts to serve them. *See Fitzgerald & Mallory Const. Co. v. Fitzgerald,* 137 U.S. 98, 104 (1890). Indeed, some courts have even adopted a bright-line rule for in-State negotiations, holding that when a plaintiff invites a defendant to enter the foreign jurisdiction for settlement discussions, the plaintiff may not, during those discussions, serve the defendant with process unless defendants are either cautioned that they may be served while present or, after having entered the jurisdiction, are first given an opportunity to depart immediately after the discussions fail.

This immunity can be waived. A defendant who fails to timely assert immunity may be deemed to have waived it. Likewise, a defendant who is immune for the purposes of attending court or a deposition may waive the immunity by arriving in the jurisdiction prematurely, by conducting other business while in the jurisdiction, or by failing to leave the jurisdiction promptly. Defendants may also lack immunity if they enter the forum to defend against criminal charges, to attend proceedings as a mere "spectator" with no obligation to be there, or when the service involves the same case or a case arising out of or involving the same subject matter as the one for which the defendants are already appearing.

Service in Removed Cases

Once a case has been removed from State court to federal court, service of process can be completed (or, if defective, new process can issue) as though the lawsuit had been filed originally in federal court. *See* 28 U.S.C. § 1448. Prior to removal, the applicable State laws will typically govern the propriety of service and process; following removal, the federal Rules will govern.

Service When "Federal Law Provides Otherwise"

Congress has, on occasion, written laws that contain their own, particular service of process provisions that may alter the requirements of Rule 4.

Burden of Proving Service of Process

The party attempting service generally bears the burden of establishing that the service is proper (though, ordinarily, that burden is not implicated until the service is contested). This burden may shift, however, if the opposing party does not promptly move to challenge the purported service. If a default judgment is entered against such a party, that party may bear the burden of proving that the purported service was defective.

RULE 4(a) Contents of and Amending Summons

What the law calls "original process" has two instruments, as noted above—the summons and the complaint. The roles played by these two instruments differ. The complaint informs defendants *why* they are being sued and for what; the summons alerts defendants that they *are* being sued and *cautions* them that they *need* to respond promptly and defend themselves. The form of a federal summons is now standardized for all federal civil cases. It is available for download from the federal courts' website. *See* Form AO 440, *Summons in a Civil Action* (https://www.uscourts.gov/forms/notice-lawsuit-summons-subpoena/summons-civil-action). That approved form of summons must:

- *Be Issued from the Clerk,* bearing the court's seal and the clerk's signature;

- *Identify the Case,* by listing the court, the parties, and the name and address of the plaintiff's attorney (or plaintiff, if unrepresented);
- *Be Directed to the Defendant,* specifically;
- *Note the Deadline to Appear and Defend;* and
- *Warn Against Default,* by cautioning the defendant that a failure to appear and defend will result in the entry of a default judgment for the relief requested in the complaint.

PRACTICING LAW UNDER THIS SUBPART

Invalid Content of Summons

A summons that has not been issued, signed, and sealed by the clerk of court is a nullity and cannot confer personal jurisdiction over the defendant; this defect is usually considered fundamental and, ordinarily, cannot be waived.

Otherwise, Form of Summons Is Liberally Examined; Amendments

In considering whether to dismiss due to a summons' defects, courts construe the summons requirements liberally, provided the recipient is given sufficient notice and is not otherwise prejudiced. Even still, a defendant has the right to receive a compliant summons. Thus, if the summons omits one of the technical requirements for proper form, but otherwise generally complies with the Rule's fundamental requirements, the court may choose not to dismiss the lawsuit but to instead permit an amendment to the summons or grant some other cure.

RULE 4(b) Issuance of Summons

Obtaining the summons is the responsibility of the plaintiff, who must see to it that the summons is prepared in an appropriate form and submitted to the court clerk for signing and sealing. If the plaintiff's summons is proper, the clerk will sign and seal the form, and hand it back it to the plaintiff for service. Copies of the summons must be issued for each defendant.

PRACTICING LAW UNDER THIS SUBPART

Issuance of Summons Liberally Examined

Courts will liberally construe the issuance requirements of Rule 4(b). If the summons is sufficiently accurate to provide proper notice, and any alleged defect in form has not prejudiced the defendant, a defect in the form of summons as issued might be discounted as harmless (and the plaintiff afforded an opportunity to amend the summons to cure whatever error there might be).

Photocopies of Summons in Multi-Defendant Cases

An original summons—with raised seal-of-the-court and a pen-signed signature of the clerk—may not be necessary in cases involving multiple defendants. It may be sufficient, in such cases, that each defendant receive the complaint and a photocopy of the summons.

RULE 4(c)	Service

For effective service, the two instruments of "original process"—the summons and the complaint—must be served together. Neglecting to serve either one (or including incomplete copies) can result in a dismissal of the lawsuit. The plaintiff is responsible for arranging for timely, proper service, and may select anyone to perform that task so long as the selected person is at least 18 years old and not a party. A U.S. Marshal can service process, but only if ordered to do so by the court.

PRACTICING LAW UNDER THIS SUBPART

Selecting the Right Process Server

Except in certain cases (such as those involving pauper plaintiffs or seamen plaintiffs), the plaintiff generally is responsible for selecting the person who will perform the act of serving process. Typically, the plaintiff hires a commercial process server who accomplishes the task for a fee. Plaintiffs cannot themselves serve process (because they are "parties" to the lawsuit). A party's attorney is not prohibited from being the process-server, although this practice is imprudent: disputes can arise over the adequacy of service, and having a disinterested, professional process server is often useful in those contests.

Service by Mail

Service by mail is not always authorized (as discussed in the various service method subparts below). But when it is permitted, the person performing the act of mailing must be at least 18 years of age and a non-party.

Service by Commercial Overnight Courier Service

When service of process is attempted by a commercial courier service (like FedEx, UPS, or DHL), it is unclear whether such a delivery qualifies as "mail" service, as delivery made "personally" or at a "dwelling house," or otherwise.

Service by U.S. Marshal or Others Specially Appointed

The court, upon a plaintiff's request, may direct that the U.S. Marshal or some other specially-appointed person serve process. Such court-appointed service is required in the cases of pauper plaintiffs and seamen plaintiffs. If such an appointment is made (and provided the plaintiff was entitled such service and cooperated with the U.S. Marshal in accomplishing it), the plaintiff is permitted to rely on the Marshal to complete service.

Service When a Complaint Has Been Amended

Formal service of process is usually required only for the original complaint; later pleadings (including amended complaints) are typically served under the less rigorous procedures of Rule 5. There are exceptions, however. If the original complaint is amended before formal service of process has been accomplished with the original (now superseded) complaint, proper service must deliver the revised pleading rather than the original one. Other circumstances may require formal service of the amended complaint, such as where the revised pleading asserts claims against new parties or materially alters the claims against existing parties, where service on the attorney is unlikely to ensure notice to the represented party, or where constitutional due process otherwise demands.

RULE 4(d) Waiving Service

Arranging for formal service of process is expensive and time-consuming; serving process can be embarrassing and, sometimes, even fraught with confrontation dangers. To help reduce the cost and delay of federal litigation, plaintiffs are permitted to invite defendants to "waive" (or forego) their right to formal delivery of process. When a plaintiff makes such an invitation properly, defendants are generally expected to agree to a waiver (with few exceptions) and, if they refuse, without good cause, they must reimburse the plaintiffs for the cost of accomplishing formal service.

PRACTICING LAW UNDER THIS SUBPART

Constitutionality

The constitutionality of the waiver-of-service rule has been addressed only cursorily (and upheld). *See United States v. Hafner,* 421 F.Supp.2d 1220, 1224 (D.N.D. 2006).

Who May Invoke the Waiver-of-Service Procedure

The waiver-of-service procedure applies only to individuals, corporations, and associations served under Rule 4(e), (f), or (h). The procedure may be used with those types of parties whether they are served in the United States or in a foreign country. The waiver-of-service procedure is usually not available for serving: (1) the United States Government; (2) agencies, corporations, or officers of the United States; (3) other governments and government-related entities; or (4) minors and incompetent persons. Note, however, that although federal officers are ineligible for waiver-of-service when sued in their official capacities, they are *not* exempt when sued in their capacity as individuals.

Plaintiff's Choice

A plaintiff is not required to use this waiver-of-service option. The plaintiff may always choose instead to proceed with traditional formal service of process.

Defendant's Response Options

The Rule does not *require* the defendant to waive, although the defendant will likely confront financial consequences for baselessly failing to do so (see below). In any event, if the defendant ignores the invitation or otherwise refuses to waive, the plaintiff must proceed with formal service under an appropriate provision of Rule 4.

Why Defendants Would Agree—Incentives for Waiving

By agreeing to waive formal service of process, a defendant's time for responding to the complaint is usually nearly tripled—from 21 days (following personal service) to 60 days (following request for waiver). For defendants who are served outside the United States, the extension is even longer—a waiving defendant served outside the United States has 90 days to respond to the complaint. Note: this 90-day period is triggered not by the defendant's foreign citizenship, but by the mailing of the waiver forms to an address outside the United States. Agreeing to waive also avoids the confrontation and embarrassment of formal service.

Why Defendants Would Agree—Consequences of Not Waiving

If the defendant lacks "good cause" for refusing to waive service, the court must order the defendant to reimburse plaintiff for the costs of service (a process known as "taxing costs). These costs include the expenses incurred in formally serving process on the defendant, as well as a reasonable attorney's fee for any motion practice required to collect those service costs. Before any costs and attorney's fees will be taxed, the prescribed time for the defendant to waive service must first have expired. Ordinarily, no expenses can be taxed against a non-waiving defendant located outside the United States.

- *What Is "Good Cause"?* The mere belief that the lawsuit is unjust or unmeritorious, or that the court lacks jurisdiction, does not qualify as "good cause." Nor does a refusal caused by counsel's busy schedule or by the presence of nonprejudicial defects in the waiver form. But "good cause" likely exists if the waiver request was never received, if the prerequisites of Rule 4(d) have not been satisfied or the waiver forms contain serious defects, if the recipient cannot read the request (due to illiteracy or otherwise), or if formal service of process had already been completed before the time for waiver expires.

Waiver Procedure

To use the waive-of-service procedure, claimants must formally and unequivocally request a defendant to waive service, and must do so by complying with the six requirements listed below. A failure to meet each requirement may result in a failed service and/or refusal by the court to impose any penalties for a defendant's failure to waive. The party invoking the waiver-of-service procedure bears the burden of proving compliance with the requirements. The mere fact that the defendants come to learn that a complaint has been filed against them will not excuse compliance with the requirements nor will an informally expressed willingness to waive which is then never formalized. (However, when the parties agree to a waiver independently of the provisions of Rule 4(d), the requirements need not be met.)

To qualify under Rule 4(d), the waiver request must:

- *Be in Writing;*
- *Be Addressed to the Individual Defendant or the Entity Defendant's Officer, Managing or General Agent, or Other Authorized Agent* (sending a "blind" mailing simply to a business address is insufficient, as is sending it to a party's attorney (unless that attorney has been given authority to accept the mailing));
- *Give the Defendant a Reasonable Time to Return the Signed Waiver* (at least 30 days, or 60 days if mailed to a foreign country);
- *List the Return Date, the Presiding Court, the Date the Request Is Sent, and the Consequences of Waiving (or Not Waiving) Service* (the official notice form is reprinted at the end of Rule 4's text);
- *Be Accompanied by:* (1) a copy of the complaint, (2) two copies of the official waiver form (which is also reprinted at the end of Rule 4's text), and (3) a prepaid means for returning the form; and
- *Actually Be Sent, by either first-class mail or "other reliable means"* (this may include private hand delivery or fax).

When a Waiver-of-Service Becomes Effective

Service is not considered waived merely because a plaintiff requests it. Rather, waivers-of-service are effective only if the receiving defendant actually signs and returns the waiver form and, then, only when the signed form is filed with the court. Oral waivers are not proper. This effective date becomes relevant for those States where limitations periods are tolled only upon service, and not mere commencement.

- *Impact on Defendant's Response Time:* This waiver-effective date does not set the time for defendant's response. Instead, that response period begins to run earlier, from the date the *request* for waiver was *sent*, and it then expires 60 days later (90 days if the waiver was mailed to a foreign country).

- *Impact on Rule 4(m) and Limitations Periods:* After a waiver request is sent and while the defendant ponders whether to waive or not, the 90-day window for completing service (Rule 4(m)) and, perhaps, the statute of limitations may continue to run. Neither is tolled simply because the plaintiff has requested a service waiver.

Motion to Recover Service Expenses

Where a waiver-eligible defendant refuses, without good cause, to waive formal service of process, a motion to collect the costs and expenses of actual service can be filed promptly after the actual, formal service is completed. The plaintiff need not wait until the bill of costs process at the litigation's end. A defendant's obligation to reimburse these costs is *not* affected by who eventually becomes the prevailing party in the litigation; rather, this obligation remains even if the defendant is otherwise entitled to its bill of costs at the end of the case. Reimbursable expenses may include a reasonable attorney's fee for prosecuting the motion to collect costs, but may *not* include any attorney's fee associated with arranging for formal service after the defendant's refusal to waive. Attorney's fees might not be reimbursed when the plaintiff proceeds *pro* se. The courts scrutinize carefully the requested fees and costs to guard against overreaching by counsel in their requests for reimbursement.

Venue and Jurisdiction Defenses Preserved

A defendant who waives formal service of process does not lose the right to contest venue and jurisdiction. The defendant does, however, waive any objection to the sufficiency of both a summons and the method of service, though objections to the timeliness of service might still be proper.

U.S. Marshal's Use of Waiver-of-Service Procedure

When the Rules authorize service by the U.S. Marshal, the Marshal may mail the waiver-of-service forms to the defendants, prior to attempting to serve process personally.

RULE 4(e) — Serving Individuals Within a Judicial District of the United States

Serving people (other than children or incompetent persons) who are served within the United States can be accomplished in any of six different ways:

- ***Specific Federal Law:*** By serving in any manner authorized by Congress for that particular type of lawsuit; or
- ***Waiver:*** By having the defendant "waive" formal service under Rule 4(d); or
- ***State Law:*** By serving in a manner authorized by the State in which the district court sits, or by the State in which the service is to be accomplished; or
- ***Personal Delivery:*** By personally delivering the summons and complaint to the individual being served; or
- ***Left at Dwelling:*** By leaving the summons and complaint at the individual's dwelling or usual place of abode with a person of suitable age and discretion who is residing there; or
- ***Agent:*** By delivering the summons and complaint to an agent appointed by the individual (or appointed by law) to receive service.

PRACTICING LAW UNDER THIS SUBPART

Service upon Individuals, Generally

This Rule applies whenever service is made within the United States upon a defendant who is a natural person. Accordingly, it encompasses service on a natural person who conducts his or her unincorporated business under a trade name.

Service Pursuant to Federal Statute

In addition to the procedures explicitly described in Rule 4(e) and discussed below, service is also proper in any manner "otherwise" authorized by Congress by statute.

State Law Service Option—Generally

The Rules permit service in any manner authorized by *either* the State in which the district court sits *or* the State in which the service is to be accomplished.

State Law Service Option—Service by Mail

Other than the waiver-of-service procedures set in Rule 4(d), the Rules do not expressly authorize service by mail. However, because many States have service procedures permitting service by mail (and because service there then permits the use of those State procedures by federal litigants), such service is often available in federal litigation.

State Law Service Option—Serving at Place of Business

The Rules do not expressly authorize serving individuals by leaving a copy of the summons and complaint at the individual's regular place of business. This type of service is, nevertheless, often still available to a plaintiff because many States authorize service at business addresses.

State Law Service—Serving by Publication

The Rules do not nationally authorize service by publication. But if the laws of either the federal district's host State or the State of delivery permit service by publication, serving in a manner that complies with either of those States' laws will be proper.

State Law Service—Serving by E-Mail and Social Media

The Rules do not nationally authorize service by e-mail or through social media portals. But if the laws of either the federal district's host State or the State of delivery permit such service, serving in a manner that complies with either of those States' laws will be proper.

Service by Personal Delivery

Personal delivery may not always require that the recipient walk away from the encounter clutching the summons and complaint. The service documents must be "tendered" to the recipient. If the recipient is physically confronted with service, and refuses to take personal possession of the service documents, service by personal delivery may sometimes still be accomplished by, for example, leaving the documents near the recipient (such as on a nearby table or on the floor near the person). Many courts have ruled that "personal delivery" cannot be accomplished through the mails, including certified mail.

Service at an Individual's Dwelling or Usual Abode

An individual can be served with process by delivering the summons and complaint to a "person of suitable age and discretion" residing at the defendant's dwelling or usual place of abode. In such cases, the process need not be handed directly to the actual defendant, but it still must be delivered personally to someone residing there. Moreover, the recipient need not necessarily be an adult, so long as the court reaches the case-by-case, fact-specific determination that the recipient was of "suitable age and discretion." Nevertheless, the recipient ordinarily must be "residing" at the home; service upon a non-resident maid will likely be ineffective. Serving permanent staff is less clear. Serving an apartment building's concierge might qualify as proper service on an apartment's resident, while serving the complex's security guard might not.

- *Transient Defendants:* Service at a "dwelling" or "usual place of abode" may not always be an available option. In certain circumstances, there may be no acceptable "dwelling" service location for transient defendants, such as those living aboard ships or those who are homeless, living on the streets or in shelters.
- *Traveling Defendants:* An individual engaged in prolonged travel (for example, a lengthy work assignment away from home) retains the same "usual place of abode" for service purposes, even though that person may be often away.
- *Hotels and Motels:* In certain circumstances, particularly during long, extended stays, service can be appropriate at a hotel or motel where the defendant is residing.
- *Multiple "Usual Abodes":* A person may have two or more "usual places of abode" (and may be properly served at any one of them), so long as each contains sufficient indicia of the permanence of the person's residence there.
- *Relatives, Family, and Friends:* Unless it is also the defendant's dwelling or usual place of abode, service on the home of the defendant's relatives, family, or friends is usually not sufficient.

Service on an Individual's Agent

An individual (including a non-resident person not otherwise present in the forum) may be served with process by serving that individual's in-forum agent for service. The recipient "agent," however, must be authorized to accept service either by appointment or by operation of law. This ordinarily requires appointment for the express purpose of receiving process. Some States have provided, by statute, that service on non-residents (who are otherwise amenable to jurisdiction within the State) may be accomplished by serving the secretary of state, the director of the department of motor vehicles, or some similar State law official.

Service on an Individual's Attorney

Service upon an individual is proper by serving the individual's attorney *only* when the attorney has been specifically authorized to accept service on the individual's behalf.

RULE 4(f) Serving Individuals in a Foreign Country

Serving people (other than children or incompetent persons) who are served outside the United States can be accomplished in any of five different ways:

- ***Specific Federal Law:*** By serving in any manner authorized by Congress for that particular type of lawsuit; or
- ***Waiver***: By having the defendant "waive" formal service under Rule 4(d), if not prohibited by the law of the foreign country of service; or
- ***International Agreement—4(f)(1):*** By serving in any manner that is internationally agreed upon and reasonably calculated to give notice, such as the *Hague Convention on the Service Abroad of Judicial and Extrajudicial Documents in Civil or Commercial Matters* (*Hague Service Convention*), unless Congress has established otherwise; or
- ***Other Reasonable Methods—4(f)(2):*** Where no international agreement exists (or, if one exists, it merely allows but does not specify the means of service), by serving through any

method that is reasonably calculated to give notice, as set out below (unless Congress has established otherwise); or

- o *Foreign Law:* In the manner prescribed by that country for local service in an action in its courts of general jurisdiction; or
- o *Letters Rogatory:* In the manner directed by that country in response to a letter rogatory or letter of request; or
- o *Personal Delivery/Mail Delivery:* Unless prohibited by that foreign country's law, by either (i) personally delivering the summons and complaint to the individual or (ii) using any form of mail that the clerk addresses and sends, and that requires a signed receipt.

- *Court Order—4(f)(3):* In any other manner directed by the court, so long as the chosen method is not prohibited by international agreement.

PRACTICING LAW UNDER THIS SUBPART

Applies to Foreign Service, Not Foreign Citizenship

Rule 4(f) is not triggered merely because the defendant is a citizen of a foreign country. Foreign nationals living, traveling, or conducting business within the United States generally may be served with process domestically under Rule 4(e), just as any other individual may. Instead, Rule 4(f) is triggered only when the defendant—whether an American national or a citizen of another country—is served outside the United States.

Service Pursuant to Federal Statute

In addition to the procedures explicitly described in Rule 4(f) and discussed below, service is also proper in any manner "otherwise" authorized by Congress by statute.

Domestic Service Inside the United States Might Still Be Possible

When serving an individual located in a foreign country, a plaintiff may invoke one of the foreign country service methods (set out in Rule 4(f)), but also, if the defendant has a presence in or authorized agent in the United States, service may also be proper on that agent, at a dwelling, or by following the applicable State's service laws, all as permitted by Rule 4(e).

Serving Minors / Incompetent Persons Abroad

By its terms, the service methods approved in this Rule 4(f) do not apply to serving minors and incompetent persons. Instead, that service is addressed in Rule 4(g).

International Agreement (Treaty)—Requirement of Hague Convention Service

The Supreme Court has ruled that service abroad in accordance with the *Hague Service Convention* is mandatory, wherever that Convention applies. *See Volkswagenwerk Aktiengesellschaft v. Schlunk,* 486 U.S. 694, 700 (1988). Some courts, however, have interpreted this precedent as still permitting court-ordered service, even when Convention service could be possible. The Convention obviously will not apply when the receiving Nation is not a signatory to that treaty, nor will it apply if the signatory Nation refuses to comply with the treaty's provisions, where the defendant's address is unknown, or where service can be effected inside the United States. Service under the Convention may require the federal court to issue a formal request for service directly to the receiving Nation's designated authority. Alternatively, service by mail under the Convention may be proper (see discussion below).

International Agreement—Local Service Details

Process served pursuant to an international agreement must comport with all specific, peculiar requirements imposed by the host country, such as the translation of process into the local language.

Other Reasonable Methods—Generally

When no international agreement exists, or when an existing agreement is merely permissive without specifying service methods, four means of service are expressly approved (so long as they are reasonably calculated to give notice). That one or more of these are potentially available to accomplish service does not necessarily preclude the judge's approval of a specially tailored method by court order instead. These four methods will often be, in application, very nation-specific:

- *Foreign Law:* The service method chosen must be "prescribed" by the local country's law for service in its general jurisdiction courts.
- *Letters Rogatory:* This service method is cast in terms of compliance with a case-specific directive from the local country's officials.
- *Personal Delivery/Mail Service:* Unlike the first service method here, service under these last two options does not require affirmative authorization from the local law, but merely the absence of an affirmative local law prohibition (as least under the majority view). This method of mailed service, when applicable, must be made by the clerk of court; if mailed by the parties or someone else, it will likely fail.

Court Order—Generally

So long as the method of service is not prohibited by international agreement, the plaintiff can request and the district court can order a means of service specifically tailored to achieve service upon individuals in a foreign country. This type of "court-ordered" service has been particularly useful to the courts when encountering elusive international defendants, especially those striving to evade service of process. This "court-ordered" service option has been applied by the courts to authorize service by publication, ordinary postal mail, facsimile transmission and telex, email, texting or messaging, social media, delivery to certain members of the defendant's family, delivery to an affiliated business address, delivery to the defendant's attorney or registered agent, and via private overnight courier.

Court Order—Service by E-Mail

Courts disagree as to whether the *Hague Service Convention* tolerates court-ordered e-mail service. Some courts, albeit cautiously, have ordered alternative service of process by e-mail in cases involving international defendants with a known e-mail address, who engaged in Internet activities, and who attempt to evade service by other means. Noting the many complications with e-mail service (*e.g.,* an inability to confirm actual receipt of an e-mail message, system compatibility issues, possible failure of attachments (such as exhibits) to transmit, be received, or be "opened" in comprehensible form, etc.), courts have granted e-mail service only on a case-by-case basis, upon a proper balancing of these limitations against the corresponding benefits of such service in particular circumstances. Among the conditions they may impose, courts that approve e-mail service will likely require that the e-mail address be shown to be an authentic means of reaching the recipient and that the e-mail, once transmitted, did not generate a return "bounce-back" or similar failed-delivery message. Recently, courts have shown an increasing willingness to consider permitting e-mail service.

Service Internationally Through Postal Mail

Serving original process via international postal delivery may be accomplished in several ways:

- *First,* many Nations are signatories to the *Hague Service Convention*, and service by international mail is permitted in *Convention*-signatory Nations so long as (a) they have not objected to service by mail and (b) mailed service is allowed in the American forum. *See Water Splash, Inc. v. Menon*, 137 S. Ct. 1504, 1508–13 (2017).
- *Second,* international mail service may be accomplished if the receiving Nation does not forbid it *so long as* it is dispatched by the American clerk of court with a signed receipt required *and* there is no applicable international agreement in place (*e.g.,* the receiving Nation is not a *Hague Service Convention* signatory) or, if in place, any agreement permits such service. Exacting compliance with these requirements is essential: such mailed service is *not* effective if it is performed by someone other than the court clerk or if the serving party fails to prove affirmatively that service by mail is not prohibited by the foreign country's law.
- *Third,* such service may be expressly ordered by the American court, provided, too, that it is not forbidden by the receiving Nation *and* there is no applicable international agreement or the applicable agreement permits such service.
- *Fourth,* the Rule broadly permitting service in a manner "prescribed by the law of the foreign country for service in that country" probably will not suffice to authorize international mail service.

Effect of Foreign Service

Foreign countries are (obviously) not parties to the U.S. Constitution's Full Faith and Credit Clause, and thus the enforcement abroad of a judgment entered by an American federal court is dependent on comity and international treaties. Moreover, in certain foreign countries, failure to adhere to the host nation's service regulations could even subject the unwary process server to criminal penalties.

RULE 4(g) Serving Minors and Incompetent Persons

Serving children or incompetent persons can be accomplished in any manner approved by the State where the service is to be made. If service would occur outside the United States, it may be made in any manner prescribed by the law of the country where the service would occur, as directed in response to a letter rogatory or request, or in such other manner as the court may direct. For obvious reasons, children and incompetent persons are not expected to "waive" formal service of process.

RULE 4(h) Serving Corporations, Partnerships, and Associations

Serving a corporation, a partnership, or an unincorporated association may be accomplished in several ways:

- ***Specific Federal Law:*** By serving in any manner authorized by Congress for that particular type of lawsuit; or
- ***Waiver:*** By having the defendant "waive" formal service under Rule 4(d); or
- ***State Law:*** By serving in any manner authorized either by the State in which the district court sits, or by the State in which the service is to be accomplished; or

- ***Officer, Managing Agent, or General Agent:*** By delivering the summons and complaint to an officer, managing agent, or general agent; or
- ***Other Authorized Agent:*** By delivering the summons and complaint to an agent appointed to receive service or authorized by law to receive service; and if required by statute, by also mailing the summons and complaint to the defendant; or
- ***Foreign Country:*** If service would occur outside the United States, by serving in any manner provided for service upon individuals in that foreign country, except personal service.

PRACTICING LAW UNDER THIS SUBPART

Service on Domestic Company's Officer, or Managing or General Agent

To effectively serve a corporation, partnership, or association through an officer, managing agent, or general agent, the summons and complaint must be directed and delivered to such a person. Simply addressing the mail to the company generally, or to its legal department, will generally not suffice. Whether the served individual qualifies as an officer, managing agent, or general agent is a highly fact-specific inquiry, often hinging on the person's authority within the organization. The burden of proving that status lies with the serving party. Persons qualifying for this status typically hold positions of executive responsibility. Thus, delivering service papers to just any employee or representative of the company will not constitute proper service, unless some other provision of federal or State law permits it. Accordingly, service on one of the company's owners, board members, office managers, attorneys, insurance reps, or receptionists or secretaries might not, without more, qualify as proper service. Service on a qualifying individual need not occur at the company's headquarters; service might be proper wherever the officer, managing agent, or general agent can be found.

Service on Authorized Agent

Corporations, partnerships, and associations can also be served by delivering the summons and complaint to any other agent specially authorized to receive service, either by appointment or by operation of law. Such person or entity must have been actually (or impliedly) appointed or authorized, and the serving party bears the burden of establishing that fact.

Service Pursuant to Federal Statute

In addition to the procedures explicitly described in Rule 4(h) and discussed here, service is also proper in any manner "otherwise" authorized by Congress by statute.

Service Pursuant to State Law

A corporation, partnership, or unincorporated association may also be served in any manner authorized by *either* the State in which the district court sits *or* the State in which the service is to be accomplished.

Service at Domestic Company Headquarters

The Rules do *not* specifically authorize service by leaving a copy of the summons and complaint at the company's headquarters. This type of service, however, might still be proper, if permitted by State law (which Rule 4(h) borrows).

Service Made Outside the United States

Service on either a foreign or domestic entity can be accomplished outside the United States by serving that corporation, partnership, or association in any manner authorized by Rule 4(f) for serving individuals outside the United States *except* personal service. Failure to comply with the provisions of that Rule will render the service ineffective. (Note: foreign corporations, partnerships, or associations may also be served inside the United States just like domestic corporations, if one of their officers, managing agents, general agents, or authorized agents can be properly served here.)

RULE 4(i) — Serving the United States, Its Agencies, Corporations, and Officers

Because a judgment against the United States of America (or one of its agencies, corporations, or officers) is, in truth, a judgment against the taxpayers, the requirements for effective service are imposing. A plaintiff suing a federal defendant must serve twice—once at the local federal attorney's office and once on the U.S. Attorney General in Washington, D.C. This obligation of serving twice is intended to ensure that the government realizes it is being sued and is afforded a clear opportunity to marshal an appropriate response.

PRACTICING LAW UNDER THIS SUBPART

Duplicate Service Is Mandatory, Not Optional

When serving the United States, its agencies, corporations, or officers, the multiple service requirements of Rule 4(i) are obligatory; failing to comply with these obligations will defeat proper service and prevent the court from acquiring jurisdiction over the federal defendants.

Applicability of the Waiver-of-Service Procedure

The Rule 4(d) waiver-of-service procedure is *not* authorized for serving the United States or its agencies or, courts seem to agree, for serving federal personnel sued in their official capacities. Courts are divided whether waiver-of-service can be used in lawsuits suing federal personnel in their individual capacities.

When the United States Is the Defendant

When the plaintiff's lawsuit names the federal government as the defendant, original process must be served as follows:

(1) ***First, United States Attorney:*** By *either* (a) personally delivering the summons and complaint to the United States Attorney for the judicial district in which the action is brought, or her/his designee, *or* (b) sending the summons and complaint by registered or certified mail to the civil process clerk at the office of that United States Attorney; *and*

(2) ***Second, Attorney General:*** By *also* sending a copy of the summons and complaint by registered or certified mail to the U.S. Attorney General in Washington, D.C.; *and*

(3) ***Then, Perhaps, Federal Officer or Agency:*** In lawsuits attacking the validity of an order of a non-party officer or agency of the United States, by *also* sending a copy of the summons and complaint by registered or certified mail to such officer or agency.

When Federal Officers, Agencies, or Corporations Are the Defendants

When the plaintiff's lawsuit names a federal officer, a federal agency, or a federal corporation as the defendant, original process must be served as follows:

(1) ***First, United States:*** By serving the United States (see above); *and*

(2) ***Second, Federal Officer, Agency, or Corporation:*** By *also* sending a copy of the summons and complaint by registered or certified mail to the federal officer, agency, or corporation named as a defendant.

When Federal Officers/Employees Are Sued in Their *Individual* Capacities

In certain instances, federal officers and employees may be sued in their individual—rather than official—capacities. *See Bivens v. Six Unknown Named Agents of Federal Bureau of Narcotics*, 403 U.S. 388, 396–97 (1971). In such cases, the type of service required will depend on the allegations of the pleading:

- *On-the-Job Claims:* If the federal officers or employees are sued in their individual capacities for acts or omissions occurring in connection with the performance of their federal duties, then proper service requires (1) service upon the United States *and* (2) service upon the officer or employee under Rule 4(e), (f), or (g).
- *Claims Unrelated to the Job:* If the federal officers or employees are sued in their individual capacities for any other acts or omissions (that is, for conduct unrelated to the performance of their federal duties), then proper service requires only service under Rule 4(e), (f), or (g). Service on the United States is not required.

These procedures apply to former federal officers and employees, as well as current personnel.

If the plaintiff intends to sue the federal officials in *both* their individual and official capacities, the plaintiff must: (1) individually serve the officials under Rule 4(e), (f), or (g); *and* (2) serve the United States as well under Rule 4(i). The plaintiff generally does not need to serve the official twice personally (*i.e.,* one service for each capacity).

To "Send" a "Copy" to Certain Defendants

The requirement to "send" a "copy" of service papers to certain federal defendants may possibly be met by photocopies of those originals, but the papers must be sent by either certified or registered mail with delivery confirmed.

Curing Incomplete Service on Federal Defendants

Because these multiple service obligations can prove difficult, Rule 4(i) permits a "cure" for incomplete service in cases requiring service on officers, agencies, or federal corporations. The court must allow a reasonable cure time: (a) if, in complaints against federal agencies, corporations, or officers/employees sued in their official capacities, the local U.S. Attorney or the Attorney General has been served but others have not yet been; and (b) if, in complaints against federal officers/employees sued in their individual capacities for on-the-job claims, those officers or employees have been served, but the United States has not yet been.

RULE 4(j) Serving Foreign, State, or Local Governments

Properly serving a foreign, State, or local government depends on the type of government served. Although somewhat less complex than serving federal defendants, the task of serving these governments is still a bit intricate.

PRACTICING LAW UNDER THIS SUBPART

Waiver-of-Service

The waiver-of-service procedure of Rule 4(d) is *not* authorized for serving foreign, State, or local governments. Whether the waiver procedure may be used to serve employees of a foreign, State, or local government in their official capacities is unclear.

The Foreign Entities Rule, Generally

Original process on foreign government defendants must be served in accordance with the federal Foreign Sovereign Immunities Act (FSIA), 28 U.S.C. § 1608. The FSIA permits four types of service, listed in order of required preference (*i.e.,* the plaintiff must use method one, unless it is unavailable, in which case the plaintiff must use method two, unless it is unavailable, and so on). The provisions of the Act demand "strict adherence."

Serving Foreign Governments

The four permitted methods for serving a foreign government, as prescribed by the FSIA, are, in descending order of preference:

(1) ***Agreed-Method:*** In any manner arranged between the plaintiff and the foreign State, but if not then:

(2) ***International Agreement:*** In accordance with an applicable international treaty or convention, such as the *Hague Convention on the Service Abroad of Judicial and Extrajudicial Documents in Civil or Commercial Matters*, but if not then:

(3) ***Ministry of Foreign Affairs:*** By the clerk of court mailing a copy of the summons and complaint and a notice of suit, along with any necessary translations, in a manner requiring a signed receipt, to the head of the ministry of foreign affairs, but if such service is not available within 30 days, then:

(4) ***Special Consular Services:*** By the clerk of court mailing a copy of the summons and complaint and a notice of suit, along with any necessary translations, in a manner requiring a signed receipt, to the United States Director of Special Consular Services, for transmittal to the foreign State through diplomatic channels.

Serving Foreign Agencies and Instrumentalities

The three permitted methods for serving foreign agencies and instrumentalities, as prescribed by the FSIA, are, in descending order of preference:

(1) ***Agreed-Method:*** By serving process in any manner arranged between the plaintiff and the foreign agency or instrumentality, but if not then:

(2) ***Agent or International Agreement:*** *Either* (a) by delivering process to an officer, managing agent, or general agent of the foreign agency or instrumentality, or to an agent appointed by the foreign agent or instrumentality to receive service of process or authorized by law to receive such service; *or* (b) by serving process in accordance with an applicable international treaty or convention, such as the *Hague Convention on the Service Abroad of Judicial and Extrajudicial Documents in Civil or Commercial Matters,* but if not then:

(3) ***Letter Rogatory, Clerk Mailing, or Court Order:*** In one of the following manners: (a) by delivering process (together with a translation thereof) as directed in response to a letter rogatory or letter of request; *or* (b) by the clerk of court mailing process (along with translations thereof) in a manner requiring a signed receipt, to the agency or instrumentality; *or* (c) by order of court consistent with the law of the place where service is to be accomplished.

Serving State and Local Governments, Generally

A State, municipal corporation, or other government organization may be served with original process in either of two ways, service under either of which is sufficient:

(1) ***Chief Executive Officer:*** By personally delivering the summons and complaint to the chief executive officer of the State, municipal corporation, or governmental organization (note that "delivery," in this provision, has been interpreted to exclude service by mail), but to include agents of the chief executive officer who represent themselves to be authorized recipients for service); or

(2) ***State Law:*** By serving the summons and complaint in the manner authorized by the State in which the service is to be accomplished (which may permit mailing). Some State laws require service on *multiple* officials in order to be proper. Personal service on an official while traveling outside the State or local territory is unlikely to confer jurisdiction on the official's government.

(3) ***Serving State/Local Government Individuals:*** A lawsuit against State or local government personnel in their official capacities is ordinarily considered a lawsuit against the government itself. *See Will v. Michigan Dep't of State Police*, 491 U.S. 58, 72 (1989). Accordingly, service should be proper upon serving that government. Individual capacity lawsuits, however, require service that complies with Rule 4(e).

Serving State and Local Governments, Eleventh Amendment Concerns

The Eleventh Amendment to the U.S. Constitution restricts the authority of the federal courts to hear lawsuits against States. *See Pennhurst State School & Hosp. v. Halderman*, 465 U.S. 89, 100 (1984). Additionally, individual State and municipal sovereign immunity laws limit the federal courts' ability to enter awards against States, municipalities, and governmental entities.

RULE 4(k) Territorial Limits of Effective Service

As discussed earlier (see Section 2.4), personal jurisdiction always involves a two-level inquiry: first, the ***legislative step***, asking whether the court has been granted the power by its legislature to hear disputes involving the category of actors that includes the defendant; and, second, the ***constitutional step*** (or "due process" inquiry), asking whether the court has exercised those powers in a manner that comports with the Due Process Clause of the U.S. Constitution. Rule 4(k) answers the first of these inquiries for the federal courts—what power did Congress legislatively grant the federal judiciary? How broad is their reach?

PRACTICING LAW UNDER THIS SUBPART

Exercise of Federal Personal Jurisdiction

Upon effective service of process or a filed waiver of formal service, the federal courts may exercise personal jurisdiction in four situations:

- ***State Statutes:*** Over defendants who are amenable to suit in the State where the district court is sitting in accordance with the provisions of that State's jurisdictional (often, "long-arm") statutes (in other words, the federal courts are authorized to "borrow" the jurisdictional reach of their host States); or

- ***100-Mile "Bulge" Rule:*** Over defendants joined as impleaded third-parties (under Rule 14) or necessary parties (under Rule 19) and who are served within 100 miles of the place where the summons issues; or
  - ♦ **NOTE:** The bulge rule does *not* apply to service on the original parties to the lawsuit, nor (when it applies) does it require forum-related minimum contacts on the part of the bulge party.
- ***Federal Statutes:*** Over defendants who are amenable to suit in the district court pursuant to the terms of some particular federal statute (such as, for example, the federal interpleader statute, 28 U.S.C. § 1335); or
- ***National-Contacts Jurisdiction:*** Over defendants who are amenable to "national-contacts" jurisdiction (discussed below).

Reminder—Exercise Must *Also* Be Constitutional

Satisfying one of the criteria in the Rule 4(k) schedule means that the federal court's exercise of jurisdiction comports with the Rules, not necessarily that it comports with the U.S. Constitution. That separate inquiry must be conducted as well. *See Daimler AG v. Bauman*, 134 S. Ct. 746, 753 (2014). Remember: personal jurisdiction is a two-step inquiry.

What Is "National-Contacts" Jurisdiction?

A federal court may have personal jurisdiction over nonresident defendants who, being sued under federal law, have sufficient contacts with the United States as a Nation to warrant the exercise of a federal court's jurisdiction, even though they lack the contacts with any particular State needed to satisfy a State long-arm statute. *See* Rule 4(k)(2); *Omni Capital Int'l, Ltd. v. Rudolf Wolff & Co.*, 484 U.S. 97, 111 (1987). This "national-contacts" option was created to fill a perceived gap in the reach of federal authority. Because of its exacting requirements, however, it is likely to apply only infrequently.

Requirements for "National-Contacts" Jurisdiction

To qualify for national-contacts jurisdiction, three conditions (in addition to proper service or waiver of service) are required:

(1) *Federal Claims:* Plaintiff's claims against the defendant must arise under federal law;

(2) *No Conventional Jurisdiction Possible:* The defendant must be beyond the jurisdictional reach of any individual State court and no situation-specific federal statute applies to confer jurisdiction; *and*

(3) *Exercise of Personal Jurisdiction Is Constitutional:* The exercise of personal jurisdiction over the defendant would not offend the Constitution or other federal law. This inquiry implicates the 5th Amendment (not the 14th Amendment) Due Process Clause. To date, neither the U.S. Supreme Court nor the majority of federal circuits has discerned a meaningful difference between those two clauses. However, in assessing whether a defendant's contacts are sufficient for "national-contacts" personal jurisdiction, courts examine all of the defendant's contacts with, and throughout, the United States. In doing so, courts may conduct the traditional general (*all-purpose*) jurisdiction and specific (*case-linked*) jurisdiction inquiries. General jurisdiction using this Rule 4(k)(2) is unlikely because that type of jurisdiction can only be exercised constitutionally in a forum where the defendant is "essentially at home" (and a foreign defendant meeting that standard in the United States will probably also be amenable to some State's long-arm statute). Specific jurisdiction using this Rule 4(k)(2) is more tenable as it may be exercised on the basis of contacts aimed purposefully towards the United States that give rise or relate to the pending lawsuit, without an unyielding obligation to show actual, physical contacts here.

Burden of Proof in "National-Contacts" Jurisdiction Cases

The plaintiff bears the burden of establishing the prerequisites for Rule 4(k)(2) national-contacts jurisdiction, and limited jurisdictional discovery may be granted to help with that burden. The courts are divided, however, on how that burden is discharged.

The majority approach requires the plaintiff to make three prima facia showings: (1) the claim arises under federal law; (2) no situation-specific federal statute confers jurisdiction; and (3) the defendant's contacts with the United States nationally satisfy due process concerns. *See Touchcom, Inc. v. Bereskin & Parr,* 574 F.3d 1403, 1414–15 (Fed.Cir. 2009) (joining Fifth, Seventh, Ninth, Eleventh, and D.C. Circuits). Once the plaintiff makes these showings, the burden then shifts to the defendant to show whether some specific State does indeed possess jurisdiction. If the defendant does so, the plaintiff may (a) seek a transfer to that State, (b) discontinue the lawsuit and re-file it, or (c) contest the defendant's assertions. This burden-shifting technique invests the defendant with the ability to "knock out" Rule 4(k)(2) by actually conceding personal jurisdiction in some other State. Conversely, failing to do so will permit the federal court to proceed with the Rule 4(k)(2) analysis without the accompanying burden of a tedious 50-State constitutional analysis.

The minority approach adds a further, more onerous requirement: that the plaintiff certify, based on information available to party and counsel, that the defendant is not subject to the jurisdiction of any U.S. State. *See Base Metal Trading, Ltd. v. OJSC "Novokuznetsky Aluminum Factory,"* 283 F.3d 208, 215 (4th Cir.2002) (joining First Circuit). This requires the type of 50-State constitutional analysis that the majority approach rejects.

RULE 4(*l*) Proving Service

The plaintiff confirms for the court that proper service of process has been accomplished by arranging for the filing of a proof-of-service. Usually, this verification is prepared by the person whom the plaintiff has enlisted to perform the service.

PRACTICING LAW UNDER THIS SUBPART

Effect of Proof of Service

A filed proof of service is recognized as prima facie evidence that service was properly accomplished. But, the presumption of validity is rebuttable. Accordingly, an affidavit from the recipient specifically denying his or her authority to accept service may be sufficient to rebut the presumption, though a mere denial of service, devoid of evidentiary support, will probably not suffice. If the presumption is rebutted, the burden of proving proper service of process returns to the plaintiff.

Nature of Proof

The proof of service should contain sufficient facts to confirm that valid service has been accomplished (*e.g.,* the specific place where process was left, the name of the recipient). Where service was made by someone other than a U.S. Marshal, an affidavit of service is required, although proof by other means may, under proper circumstances, be acceptable.

Service Outside the United States

If service is made under a treaty or other international agreement, proof of service must be in accordance with that treaty or agreement. If service is made in any other manner, proof of service must include a receipt signed by the addressee or other satisfactory evidence of delivery.

Failure to Present Proof of Service

The plaintiff "must" make a proof of service to the court. But a failure to perform that filing chore will not negate a service of process that had been otherwise properly accomplished. Thus, a defendant cannot claim a postponement of its duty to respond to a complaint merely because no proof of service has yet been filed or, if filed, is somehow flawed in form. This liberality in proving a successful service does not, of course, excuse the obligation to actually accomplish a proper, timely service of process. A failure to prove service may still have some consequences, however. Unless the court has other grounds for finding that service has been properly accomplished, the failure to file a proof of service will likely defeat the court's ability to enter a default judgment.

RULE 4(m) Time Limit for Service

Serving process is a task that must be performed expeditiously. Until the defendant is served, that defendant may not be aware it is being sued and, if it is not, obviously it will not have begun preparing to respond and defend itself. Thus, the plaintiff needs to move swiftly to complete this critical step in order for the lawsuit to move forward. Ordinarily, the summons and complaint must be served within 90 days after the complaint is filed, unless the plaintiff is able to show "good cause" why service could not be made within that time. If "good cause" is not shown, the district court must either dismiss the lawsuit without prejudice or, in its discretion, direct that service be accomplished within a new specified time.

PRACTICING LAW UNDER THIS SUBPART

Timely Service—The 90-Day Service Period

A federal lawsuit is "commenced" by filing the complaint (*see* Rule 3), and then remains pending for 90 days to enable the claimant to accomplish a valid service of process upon (or obtain a waiver from) each defendant. Failure to complete service within that 90-day window exposes the lawsuit to dismissal.

Dismissals for Failing to Serve Within 90 Days

Dismissals under this Rule for failure to timely serve process are made without prejudice. But such a dismissal could still have a prejudicial effect—if, by the time the plaintiff re-files the lawsuit, the applicable statute of limitations has expired, then the earlier dismissal will have had the effect of terminating the claim altogether. Moreover, a Rule 4(m) dismissal is generally considered an abandoned claim, and is accorded no interruptive effect on the running of the statute of limitations; thus, the dismissal is the equivalent (for these purposes) of the claim having never been filed at all.

Distinction: Mandatory *vs.* Permissive Extensions

When considering an extension requires, courts distinguish between justified delay ("good cause") and excusable neglect. As to the former (justified delay), the district court *must* grant a plaintiff an extension for "an appropriate period." When good cause is not shown, the district court has the option of either dismissing the lawsuit without prejudice or, in the exercise of its discretion, excusing the delay by issuing an order that directs that service be completed within a specified additional period of time.

"Good Cause" Extensions—Which Courts *Must* Grant

The plaintiff bears the burden of proving that "good cause" exists to excuse a delay in service of process. No fixed guidelines define "good cause," and it remains an exercise of discretion. But the burden of showing good cause is heavy. It typically requires a showing of both diligence on the server's part and a valid reason for the delay. In an appropriate circumstance, courts may also balance whether the delay has caused prejudice to the defendant. Accordingly, a service-evading defendant (or one who is difficult to locate or who refuses a request to waive formal service), a pending bankruptcy stay, a sudden illness or natural catastrophe, or some similarly intruding external factor may justify a finding of good cause. The good cause standard is applied narrowly to protect only those litigants who have exercised meticulous care in attempting to complete service. Inadvertence or negligence by counsel is not enough, nor is the mere absence of bad faith. As one court aptly warned: "The lesson to the federal plaintiff's lawyer is not to take any chances. Treat the [Rule 4(m) time limit] with the respect reserved for a time bomb." *See Braxton v. United States,* 817 F.2d 238, 241 (3d Cir. 1987) (quotation omitted).

Permissive Extensions—Which Courts *May* Grant

When "good cause" is not shown, the decision whether to dismiss or grant a further extension is committed to the district court's discretion (essentially, plaintiffs throw themselves "on the mercy of the district court"). Although Rule 4(m) lists no criteria for making this determination, the district court is nevertheless still obligated to consider whether circumstances exist to warrant an extension of the 90-day service period. (Although encouraged to do, the Rule does not require district judges to detail the reasoning for their rulings.) In making this evaluation, the court may examine, among other factors, the length of and reasons for the delay, good faith, whether the delay was within the plaintiff's control, prejudice to the defendants, whether the applicable statute of limitations would bar a re-filing, whether the failure to timely serve was due to a difficulty in serving government officials, whether the offending party is proceeding *pro se,* whether the unserved defendant has been evading service or concealing a defect in service, and whether service was eventually accomplished and, if so, how far beyond the 90-day period. Moreover, a defendant's admission of liability will prove an important factor tilting in favor of granting a permissive extension. The courts of appeals review such decisions under an abuse of discretion standard, and can be expected to often affirm any reasoned and principled decision by the trial court.

- *Note:* Although the effect of the statute of limitations may be considered by the court in evaluating whether to grant a permissive extension, this does not mean that a permissive extension is mandatory whenever a dismissal would result in a time-bar. Instead, the district court must assess all circumstances, including the litigants' behavior as time-bar approached, in deciding whether a permissive extension is warranted.

Defendants Can Waive the 90-Day Period

Although Rule 4(m) contains mandatory-sounding dismissal language, defendants may still waive the 90-day service period by (among other ways) failing to raise that objection in any Rule 12 motion that is filed.

Sua Sponte Dismissals and Extensions

When service has not been effected within the 90-day service period, the court need not wait for a party's motion to act. On its own initiative, the court may dismiss the action or may order that service be completed within some new, specified time. Either *sua sponte* action requires prior "notice to the plaintiff."

Foreign Service and the 90-Day Service Window

The 90-day service period does not apply to service that occurs in a foreign country, or to service on a foreign country and its political subdivisions, agencies, and instrumentalities. However, the time allowable for accomplishing foreign service is not necessarily unbounded; district courts retain the ability to control their dockets. Some courts have conditioned this "exemption" from the 90-day service period on a showing that good faith attempts were made to serve within the prescribed period; if no such attempts were made, these courts hold that the exemption will not apply and the passage of the prescribed time can justify a dismissal. Other courts have applied a more encompassing "flexible due diligence" standard to decide if a post-time-expiration day foreign service ought to be allowed.

New 90-Day Period for Newly Added Parties

When a complaint is amended to add new parties, the plaintiff is given 90 days from the date of amendment to serve the new defendants. Note, however, that this new 90-day clock will apply only to the newly-added parties; amendments will ordinarily not extend the time for serving parties who were named earlier.

Removed Cases and the 90-Day Period

In cases "removed" from State court to federal court, the 90-day service period runs from the date of removal as to all parties who have not yet been served at all, on whom service has not been perfected, or on whom an attempted service proves to be defective. *See* 28 U.S.C. § 1448. (The removal process is discussed in Section 2.13 to 2.15 of this text.)

RULE 4(n) Assisting Jurisdiction over Property or Assets

Federal courts may exercise *in rem* or *quasi in rem* jurisdiction (jurisdiction over property or assets) in only two situations: (1) when Congress authorizes them to do so, and (2) in a manner provided by State law, but only if the plaintiff first shows that acquiring *in personam* jurisdiction cannot be acquired through reasonable efforts. For a discussion of *in rem* and *quasi in rem* jurisdiction, see Sections 2.3, 2.6, and 2.7 of this *Student's Guide*.

PRACTICING LAW UNDER THIS SUBPART

Procedure for Property-Based Jurisdiction

A federal court may exercise *in-rem* or *quasi-in-rem* jurisdiction over tangible and intangible property located within its geographic district, but only in two circumstances:

- ***Federal Statute:*** when a federal statute permits it, 28 U.S.C. § 1655; in such cases, the required notice to claimants of the property must either conform to the statute's requirements or be accomplished by serving a summons under this Rule 4; or

- ***State Law:*** when a defendant's assets are found in the district, but only upon a showing that personal jurisdiction over the defendant cannot be obtained there by reasonable efforts to serve a summons under this Rule 4; in such cases, jurisdiction is acquired by seizing the assets under circumstances and in a manner provided by the local State law.

In addition to satisfying these Rule 4(n) requirements, the court's exercise of property-based jurisdiction must, of course, also meet constitutional due process standards.

Effect

A judgment in an *in rem* or *quasi in rem* lawsuit acts only upon the seized property; it has no *in personam* effect. Thus, a plaintiff cannot enforce an *in rem* or *quasi in rem* judgment against property of the defendant located outside the forum State. *See Shaffer v. Heitner*, 433 U.S. 186, 207 n.23 (1977) (liability of *in rem* defendant limited to value of property).

Amount in Controversy

An *in rem* or *quasi in rem* action only permits execution of the seized property; the courts, however, are divided on the proper method for computing the amount in controversy in federal diversity cases—either by the value of the seized property or the sum stated in the complaint's demand clause. (Note: If the plaintiff's claim exceeds the value of seized property, the plaintiff is free to sue elsewhere for the remaining, unrecovered amount of the claim.)

Due Process

Just as in the *in personam* jurisdiction context, a federal court can ordinarily hear an *in rem* or *quasi in rem* action only if the Due Process test is satisfied.

RULE 4.1

SERVING OTHER PROCESS

(a) In General. Process—other than a summons under Rule 4 or a subpoena under Rule 45—must be served by a United States marshal or deputy marshal or by a person specially appointed for that purpose. It may be served anywhere within the territorial limits of the State where the district court is located and, if authorized by a federal statute, beyond those limits. Proof of service must be made under Rule 4(*l*).

(b) Enforcing Orders: Committing for Civil Contempt. An order committing a person for civil contempt of a decree or injunction issued to enforce federal law may be served and enforced in any district. Any other order in a civil-contempt proceeding may be served only in the State where the issuing court is located or elsewhere in the United States within 100 miles from where the order was issued.

[Adopted April 22, 1993, effective December 1, 1993; April 30, 2007, effective December 1, 2007.]

UNDERSTANDING RULE 4.1

HOW RULE 4.1 FITS IN

Rule 4.1 fills a gap—Rule 4 sets the procedures for serving original process, Rule 45 sets the procedures for serving a subpoena, and then Rule 4.1 sets the procedures for serving all other sorts of "process." What is "other process"? That concept includes execution orders (to enforce the terms of a civil judgment), orders to show cause, orders of civil commitment (but not criminal commitment), and certain orders for injunctions, attachments, arrests, and judicial sales. (Note, however, that service of process is generally *not* required for decrees and injunctions issued upon existing parties (those who have already been served with original process).)

THE ARCHITECTURE OF RULE 4.1

The organization of this brief Rule is straightforward. The first subpart identifies those eligible to serve "other process," sets the territorial reach for such service, and adopts the standard method for proving effective service. The second subpart addresses service and enforcement of civil commitment decrees and orders.

HOW RULE 4.1 WORKS IN PRACTICE

Process Server

"Other process" must be served either by the U.S. Marshal, a deputy U.S. Marshal, or some other person specially appointed for the purpose by the court. (Whether to appoint a U.S. Marshal or some other person is left to the court's discretion, unless the plaintiff is a pauper or seaman.) Service performed by anyone else is defective.

Limits of Service

"Other process" may be served either within the State in which the district court is sitting or as otherwise provided by federal statute. Special procedures, however, guide serving and enforcing orders of civil commitment. Proper service and enforcement in those proceedings will depend on whether the law to be enforced is federal or State. If federal law, the order may be served and enforced in any federal district. If State law (as in diversity cases), the order may be served only within the State of the issuing court or elsewhere in the United States within 100 miles of where the order was issued.

Proof of Service

The process server—the U.S. Marshal, deputy U.S. Marshal, or specially appointed person—must file a proof of service with the court as provided in Rule 4(*l*).

RULE 5

SERVING AND FILING PLEADINGS AND OTHER PAPERS

(a) Service: When Required.

(1) *In General.* Unless these rules provide otherwise, each of the following papers must be served on every party:

(A) an order stating that service is required;

(B) a pleading filed after the original complaint, unless the court orders otherwise under Rule 5(c) because there are numerous defendants;

(C) a discovery paper required to be served on a party, unless the court orders otherwise;

(D) a written motion, except one that may be heard ex parte; and

(E) a written notice, appearance, demand, or offer of judgment, or any similar paper.

(2) *If a Party Fails to Appear.* No service is required on a party who is in default for failing to appear. But a pleading that asserts a new claim for relief against such a party must be served on that party under Rule 4.

(3) *Seizing Property.* If an action is begun by seizing property and no person is or need be named as a defendant, any service required before the filing of an appearance, answer, or claim must be made on the person who had custody or possession of the property when it was seized.

(b) Service: How Made.

(1) *Serving an Attorney.* If a party is represented by an attorney, service under this rule must be made on the attorney unless the court orders service on the party.

(2) *Service in General.* A paper is served under this rule by:

(A) handing it to the person;

(B) leaving it:

(i) at the person's office with a clerk or other person in charge or, if no one is in charge, in a conspicuous place in the office; or

(ii) if the person has no office or the office is closed, at the person's dwelling or usual place of abode with someone of suitable age and discretion who resides there;

(C) mailing it to the person's last known address—in which event service is complete upon mailing;

(D) leaving it with the court clerk if the person has no known address;

(E) sending it to a registered user by filing it with the court's electronic-filing system or sending it by other electronic means that the person consented to in writing—in either of which events service is complete upon filing or sending, but is not effective if the filer or sender learns that it did not reach the person to be served; or

(F) delivering it by any other means that the person consented to in writing—in which event service is complete when the person making service delivers it to the agency designated to make delivery.

(3) *Using Court Facilities.* [Abrogated effective Dec. 1, 2018.]

(c) Serving Numerous Defendants.

(1) *In General.* If an action involves an unusually large number of defendants, the court may, on motion or on its own, order that:

(A) defendants' pleadings and replies to them need not be served on other defendants;

(B) any crossclaim, counterclaim, avoidance, or affirmative defense in those pleadings and replies to them will be treated as denied or avoided by all other parties; and

(C) filing any such pleading and serving it on the plaintiff constitutes notice of the pleading to all parties.

(2) *Notifying Parties.* A copy of every such order must be served on the parties as the court directs.

(d) Filing.

(1) *Required Filings; Certificate of Service.*

(A) *Papers after the Complaint.* Any paper after the complaint that is required to be served must be filed no later than a reasonable time after service. But disclosures under Rule 26(a)(1) or (2) and the following discovery requests and responses must not be filed until they are used in the proceeding or the court orders filing: depositions, interrogatories, requests for documents or tangible things or to permit entry onto land, and requests for admission.

(B) *Certificate of Service.* No certificate of service is required when a paper is served by filing it with the court's electronic-filing system. When a paper that is required to be served is served by other means:

(i) if the paper is filed, a certificate of service must be filed with it or within a reasonable time after service; and

(ii) if the paper is not filed, a certificate of service need not be filed unless filing is required by court order or by local rule.

(2) *Nonelectronic Filing.* A paper not filed electronically is filed by delivering it:

(A) to the clerk; or

(B) to a judge who agrees to accept it for filing, and who must then note the filing date on the paper and promptly send it to the clerk.

(3) *Electronic Filing and Signing.*

(A) *By a Represented Person—Generally Required; Exceptions.* A person represented by an attorney must file electronically, unless nonelectronic filing is allowed by the court for good cause or is allowed or required by local rule.

(B) *By an Unrepresented Person—When Allowed or Required.* A person not represented by an attorney:

(i) may file electronically only if allowed by court order or by local rule; and

(ii) may be required to file electronically only by court order, or by a local rule that includes reasonable exceptions.

(C) *Signing.* A filing made through a person's electronic-filing account and authorized by that person, together with that person's name on a signature block, constitutes the person's signature.

(D) *Same as Written Paper.* A paper filed electronically is a written paper for purposes of these rules.

(4) *Acceptance by the Clerk.* The clerk must not refuse to file a paper solely because it is not in the form prescribed by these rules or by a local rule or practice.

[Amended January 21, 1963, effective July 1, 1963; March 30, 1970, effective July 1, 1970; April 29, 1980, effective August 1, 1980; March 2, 1987, effective August 1, 1987; April 30, 1991, effective December 1, 1991; April 22, 1993, effective December 1, 1993; April 23, 1996, effective December 1, 1996; April 17, 2000, effective December 1, 2000; April 23, 2001, effective December 1, 2001; April 12, 2006, effective December 1, 2006; April 30, 2007, effective December 1, 2007; April 26, 2018, effective December 1, 2018.]

UNDERSTANDING RULE 5

HOW RULE 5 FITS IN

Civil litigation is often very document-heavy. Each party is likely to produce many documents as a federal lawsuit runs its course. Who should receive copies of those various documents? When, and how? Which documents need to be filed with the court clerk in order to be included within the official case record? Rule 5 addresses each of these service and filing questions. This is a *general* rule only, however. It does not apply in those circumstances when some other Rule or a federal statute, or the presiding judge, sets a different service or filing obligation.

THE ARCHITECTURE OF RULE 5

This Rule has four subparts, and their organization is easy to discern. The first three subparts address when service is required for most legal documents, on whom, and how it is to be accomplished. The last subpart addresses the issue of filing documents with the court.

HOW RULE 5 WORKS IN PRACTICE

Each of the four subparts of Rule 5 is discussed, in order, below.

RULE 5(a) Service Required

The obligation to serve copies of legal documents on all fellow litigants is a broad duty. All parties are entitled to prompt knowledge of litigation developments. Accordingly, once a party has "appeared" in a lawsuit (that is, formally notified the court that he or she is actively participating in the case, either personally or through an attorney), that party is entitled to receive copies of: all pleadings in the case after the complaint (serving a complaint is addressed separately, by Rule 4); all discovery papers in the case; all written motions in the case; all court orders in the case that are required to be served; and most other legal papers in the case (such as notices, demands, offers of judgment, etc.).

PRACTICING LAW UNDER THIS SUBPART

Exceptions—When Rule 5 Does *Not* Apply

Rule 5 does not apply to original complaints (which must, instead, be served under the often more rigorous standards established in Rule 4), *ex parte* motions (when the filing party deliberately (and properly) does *not* want to notify the opposition), pleadings among numerous defendants (addressed separately by Rule 5(c)), and papers that are governed by other service rules or statutes.

Another Exception—Pleadings Asserting Claims Against New Parties

Pleadings asserting claims against new parties (*e.g.*, third-party claims) must always be served formally, as original process, pursuant to Rule 4, and not under this Rule 5.

Another Exception—Pleadings Modifying Claims Against Existing Parties

Pleadings modifying pending claims or asserting new claims against existing parties (*i.e.*, by amending an original pleading) are usually served under the less demanding methods of this Rule 5—provided, of course, original service of process has already been accomplished under Rule 4. Nevertheless, formal service under Rule 4 may still be required if:

- New claims are asserted against parties who have defaulted;
- The recipient's attorney has ceased to represent that party or other circumstances show that service on the attorney is unlikely to ensure notice to that party; or
- Fairness or due process concerns compel it (such as where the nature of the claims has changed so fundamentally that the original basis for exercising personal jurisdiction is now in doubt).

Serving Pleadings (and Other Papers) Against Defaulting Parties

Once proper service of original process is accomplished under Rule 4, it is expected that the served party will "appear" (by filing a "notice of appearance" or otherwise) and defend the case. If, instead, that party defaults, future pleadings and other papers in the lawsuit ordinarily do not need to be served on that party (which includes *amended* complaints). There is an exception. If a later pleading asserts a new claim for relief against the non-appearing party, that later pleading must be served upon the non-appearing party pursuant to Rule 4, *as original process*. This is intended to ensure that a party, once served, is enabled to make a prudent decision, informed of all consequences, of whether to answer or default. A claim is considered "new" when it differs substantially from the original pleading.

Effect of Unserved Pleadings and Other Papers

A pleading or other paper that must be served (either under Rule 4 or Rule 5) but is not served will ordinarily be given no legal effect. Thus, amended complaints that are filed but not served are ineffective (usually will not supersede the original), and exhibits to filed documents that are not served may not be relied upon in motion practice.

RULE 5(b) Method of Service

The rigorous service standards for "original process," set out in Rule 4, are generally *not* required for the service of other, subsequent documents in the lawsuit. Original process is performed with special formality in order to ensure that those served parties come to understand that they are being sued and must promptly defend themselves. Once that notice is accomplished, the rigor expected in serving other, later documents is relaxed.

PRACTICING LAW UNDER THIS SUBPART

Permitted Methods for Service Under Rule 5

If service is permitted under Rule 5 *and* if the to-be-served party is represented by counsel, service is accomplished by serving the party's lawyer (and not the party directly). However, service may be made on the party directly if a specific Rule so requires, if the party is unrepresented, or if the court so requires. Service may be accomplished in any of the following ways:

- By ***Hand Delivery:*** To either to the party's lawyer or, if unrepresented or if the court orders otherwise, to the party; *or*
- By ***Office Delivery:*** Left at the recipient's office with the person "in charge" of the office or, if no one is "in charge" of the office, in a conspicuous place there; *or*
- By ***Home Delivery:*** If hand delivery and office service are unavailable, left at the recipient's residence with a person of suitable age and discretion residing there; *or*
- By ***Mailing:*** To the recipient's "last known address," *or*
- By ***Leaving with the Court Clerk:*** If the recipient's address is unknown; *or*
- By ***Electronic Transmission:*** Through the court's electronic-filing system or other electronic means that the recipient has agreed to in writing; *or*
- By ***Other Means:*** That the parties have agreed to in writing.

Parties Represented by Multiple Attorneys

Service is complete upon serving one attorney for each represented party. If a party is represented by multiple counsel, multiple service is ordinarily not required.

Actual Notice Is Not Always Sufficient, or Even Necessary

The fact that a party received actual notice of a legal paper will not necessarily excuse a failure to properly serve under Rule 5. Nor will a failure to receive actual notice invalidate service, so long as Rule 5 is followed faithfully and the service, as attempted, was reasonably calculated, under the circumstances, to both impart notice and provide an opportunity to respond.

Service at an Office

Service may be completed at the served person's office, by "handing" it to the served person or by "leaving" it with "a clerk," with some "other person in charge," or if there is no one in charge, "in a conspicuous place in the office."

Service at Home

Service can be accomplished at the served person's home, if hand delivery or office service are unavailable. Presumably, this Rule will be interpreted by the courts in the same manner as Rule 4. Thus, the recipient of service need not necessarily be an adult, so long as the court reaches the case-by-case factual determination that the recipient is of "suitable age and discretion." Generally, service must be made on a person "residing" at the home; service on a maid or other non-resident might be ineffective.

Service by Mail

If service is made by mail, that service is deemed complete at the moment a properly posted envelope is deposited with the U.S. Post Office. The Post Office's failure to postmark the envelope on the day of deposit does not alter this effect. Non-receipt or non-acceptance usually does not affect the validity of service.

- ♦ **NOTE:** Rule 6(d) gives the recipient of *mailed* service 3 extra days to respond.

Service via the Clerk of Court

Though permitted, this option offers a very narrow service path. Delivery to the clerk of court can qualify as proper service only if (a) original service of process (or service waiver) has already been accomplished under Rule 4 and, then, (b) only if the current address of that once-served recipient is not known.

Service by Electronic Means

Two methods for electronic service are permitted. *First*, if the server and served party (or served party's attorney) are both registered users of the federal court's e-filing system, a document filed electronically can be served electronically through that system. No separate consent is required. *Second*, the parties can separately consent to electronic transmission through other means (like ordinary e-mail), so long as they do so in writing. However, such consent usually cannot be implied from conduct (*e.g.*, including an e-mail address on letterhead, routinely e-mailing one another, objector's own reliance on using e-mail, or failing to earlier object). Consenting parties should reach specific written agreement on the scope of their consent (*e.g.*, desired recipient, transmission address, format for attachments, duration of consent). Absent an agreement otherwise, and even when this consent has been obtained, parties may still serve traditionally through the mail. Service by electronic transmission is considered complete when: (a) a registered user files a paper with the court's e-filing system for transmission to another registered user; *or* (b) a sender transmits electronically to a recipient using an agreed upon method.

- *Failed Transmission:* If the serving party learns, after the electronic transmission is attempted, that the transmission failed and did not reach the intended recipient, the service is not considered effective and the server is required to take further actions to make effective service. (The court is not responsible for notifying users of a failed e-filing system transmission.) A failed transmission can be a mechanical one (*e.g.*, an "incomplete" or "failed" message) or one relating to a change in the recipient's profile (*e.g.*, original counsel consents to the court's electronic filing service, but a change in counsel renders this consent ineffective).

Service by "Other Means"

Service by some "other means" is also approved, provided that the recipient has consented, in writing, to the alternative method for service.

Private Overnight Courier Services

Private overnight courier services (such as FedEx, UPS, or DHL) are not the Post Office, and they do not provide "mail" service. Thus, service through a private courier might not constitute service by "mail" pursuant to Rule 5(b)(2)(C) and, therefore, service is unlikely considered completed upon the courier's taking possession of the document. Rather, service by a private courier service is more likely to be deemed a type of personal service, complete only upon the courier's delivery of the document to the ultimate recipient. If, however, service by private courier has been consented to, it may qualify as effective service by "other means." (Overnight courier services provided by the U.S. Post Office, however, are likely still considered "mail" service.)

Prisoner Plaintiffs

For documents served by *pro se* prisoners, the courts generally recognize a "mailbox" rule that deems documents as served upon delivery of those documents to the prison officials.

RULE 5(c) Serving Numerous Defendants

Where an unusually large number of defendants are sued, the court may order that the defendants need not serve every other defendant with pleadings and responses. The court may also order that crossclaims, counterclaims, and affirmative defenses are deemed automatically denied or avoided as among the numerous defendants. Note, however, that these provisions are only effective upon court order.

PRACTICING LAW UNDER THIS SUBPART

Plaintiff Must Always Serve and Be Served

Rule 5(c) does not excuse service *on the plaintiff* of all papers, nor does it excuse service *by the plaintiff* of all papers.

Only Defendants' Pleadings/Responses

This subpart applies only to defendants' pleadings and responses; all other papers must be served normally.

RULE 5(d) Filing with the Court

Filing documents with the court achieves two objectives. Filing ensures that there is an official record for the lawsuit, maintained by the court's clerk, where the parties and the general public can go to examine the progress of the litigation. Filing also ensures that the presiding judge has access to the core legal documents in the case.

PRACTICING LAW UNDER THIS SUBPART

What Must Be Filed, and When

Any paper that is required to be served must be filed with the court. Filing must occur within a "reasonable" time after service (though attorneys will usually file and serve simultaneously, or nearly so). Whether the time between service and filing is "reasonable" is left to the judge's discretion. Moreover, Rule 5(d) sets a general standard only. If the court sets a specific time for filing a document, that order must be obeyed.

Exception—Discovery Papers

To conserve the physical resources of the clerk's office and federal courthouses, discovery requests and discovery responses are *not* to be filed with the court unless and until (a) they are actually "used" in court proceedings or (b) the court so orders. This prohibition applies to requests, responses, and objections made under the Rules governing depositions, interrogatories, admissions, production demands, and entry upon land demands, as well as to deposition transcripts themselves. Inappropriately filed discovery materials will likely be stricken from the official court docket. There is no implied right of public access to this sort of unfiled discovery.

- *"Used in the Proceeding":* This phrase is interpreted broadly to include those discovery materials used in connection with motions, pretrial conferences, and otherwise. However, a party who "uses" discovery materials while interrogating witnesses during depositions need not file those materials with the court. Moreover, if a party "uses" only a portion of a voluminous discovery document, only the "used" portion need be filed with the court (although any other party would be free to file other relevant portions used).

Method of Filing—Electronically

Electronic filing is mandatory by parties who are represented by counsel, unless the court (upon a showing of good cause) or some local rule provides otherwise. Parties who are unrepresented by counsel (that is, parties who are representing themselves *pro se*) are *required* to file electronically only when ordered to do so by the court or by some local rule (which must contain reasonable exceptions). Unrepresented parties may, in their discretion, file electronically only if permitted to do so by the court or by some local rule.

- *Signing:* Filing electronically through the filer's electronic-filing account with the court, if authorized by the filer and includes the filer's name in a signature block, constitutes the filer's electronic "signature."
- *Just Like Paper:* Documents filed electronically are treated the same as written papers that are physically filed.

Method of Filing—By Other Means

When filing is permitted through nonelectronic means, such filing may be accomplished in either of two ways:

- *Delivery to Court Clerk:* But such filings are only deemed effective when they come into the possession of the clerk of court. Thus, leaving a document lying against or slipped underneath the clerk's office door will generally not be considered an effective filing until the time the clerk actually receives the document. Likewise, a document will not be deemed "filed" when it is mailed to the clerk (with certain prisoner plaintiff exceptions). Instead, such a document will only be deemed "filed" when the clerk receives the mail. A document placed in an after-hours depository box maintained by the clerk's office, however, should qualify as effective filing.
- *Delivery to a Judge:* But only if the judge agrees to accept the document for filing; if the judge so agrees, the judge must note the filing date on the document and promptly send it along to the court clerk.

Certificate of Service

Every document that is not filed electronically must be accompanied by a "certificate of service," which should identify the document served, the date of service, and the manner of delivery. The certificate can be filed separately, if filed within a reasonable time after service. A document filed electronically needs no separate certificate of service.

Enforcing the Rule

Ordinarily, in the absence of contumacious behavior, a failure to timely file a properly-served pleading will be remedied by an order compelling the filing, and not with a dismissal.

Effect of Unpaid Fees

Most courts accept a filing as effective, even if the required filing fees have not yet been paid (provided they are promptly paid thereafter).

Refusal by Clerk to Accept for Filing

A paper is considered "filed" upon the completion of the act of delivering it to the clerk of court; procedural flaws in the paper will not impede the "filing." Although neither the clerk of court (nor the clerk's electronic-filing system) may refuse to file a paper that does not conform to the Rules or to the district's local rules, the clerk may advise the filing party or attorney of the paper's deficiencies. A local rule may also instruct the clerk to inform the judge of the paper's defect (and the judge can then order the paper to be refused). The task of enforcing rules concerning procedure and form are reserved exclusively for the judge.

Prisoner Plaintiffs

As with service under Rule 5(b), a *pro se* prisoner's papers are usually deemed "filed" under Rule 5(d) upon delivery of those documents to appropriate prison officials.

Other Rules

Certain Rules and the district's local rules may prescribe specific other service and filing guidelines.

RULE 5.1

CONSTITUTIONAL CHALLENGE TO A STATUTE—NOTICE, CERTIFICATION, AND INTERVENTION

(a) Notice by a Party. A party that files a pleading, written motion, or other paper drawing into question the constitutionality of a federal or State statute must promptly:

(1) file a notice of constitutional question stating the question and identifying the paper that raises it, if:

(A) a federal statute is questioned and the parties do not include the United States, one of its agencies, or one of its officers or employees in an official capacity; or

(B) a State statute is questioned and the parties do not include the State, one of its agencies, or one of its officers or employees in an official capacity; and

(2) serve the notice and paper on the Attorney General of the United States if a federal statute is questioned—or on the State attorney general if a State statute is questioned—either by certified or registered mail or by sending it to an electronic address designated by the attorney general for this purpose.

(b) Certification by the Court. The court must, under 28 U.S.C. § 2403, certify to the appropriate attorney general that a statute has been questioned.

(c) Intervention; Final Decision on the Merits. Unless the court sets a later time, the attorney general may intervene within 60 days after the notice is filed or after the court certifies the challenge, whichever is earlier. Before the time to intervene expires, the court may reject the constitutional challenge, but may not enter a final judgment holding the statute unconstitutional.

(d) No Forfeiture. A party's failure to file and serve the notice, or the court's failure to certify, does not forfeit a constitutional claim or defense that is otherwise timely asserted.

[Adopted April 12, 2006, effective December 1, 2006; amended April 30, 2007, effective December 1, 2007.]

UNDERSTANDING RULE 5.1

HOW RULE 5.1 FITS IN

Intervention is the procedure by which a non-party to a civil litigation seeks to gain entry into a lawsuit as a newly-appearing party to either seek (as a fellow plaintiff) or oppose (as a new defendant) the relief being sought in the case. This procedure is governed by Rule 24, and is usually reserved for instances in which the non-party asserts some interest in the pending lawsuit that could be damaged if that non-party were to be kept out of the litigation. Rule 5.1 is intended to facilitate a certain type of intervention—intervention by the government (federal or State) into a lawsuit where one of its statutes is being challenged constitutionally. Because the result of such a lawsuit could be a judicial order declaring that federal or State statute unconstitutional (and, therefore, invalid), Rule 5.1 is designed to ensure that the potentially impacted government receives early notice of such a challenge and an opportunity to seek intervention to defend its law. *See generally Diamond v. Charles,* 476 U.S. 54, 62 (1986) (governments have standing to defend their laws).

THE ARCHITECTURE OF RULE 5.1

This Rule has four subparts, which perform essentially three functions. The first two subparts—Rules 5.1(a) and (b)—direct that both the contesting party and the judge notify the impacted government of the pending constitutional challenge to one its laws. The last subpart—Rule 5.1(d)—limits the consequence from a *failure* to make those notifications. The middle subpart—Rule 5.1(c)—sets the procedures should the notified government elect to intervene.

HOW RULE 5.1 WORKS IN PRACTICE

Each of the four subparts of Rule 5.1 is discussed, in order, below.

RULE 5.1(a) Notice by a Party

A party who is contesting (or "drawing into question") the constitutionality of a federal or State statute must perform two acts. First, that party must file a "notice" of the challenge with the federal court, setting out the nature of challenge and identifying the document where that challenge is raised. Second, that party must then serve both the "notice" and the challenge document on the federal or State attorney general (whomever is confronting the challenge).

PRACTICING LAW UNDER THIS SUBPART

Applies Only When Statutes Are Challenged Constitutionally

This obligation is triggered only when a *statute* is challenged, and only when that challenge is a *constitutional* one. A lawsuit that challenges some other non-statutory law or that merely contests whether a statute applies or how it ought to be interpreted does not implicate this Rule 5.1.

Method / Timing of Notice and Service

Service of the notice on the affected federal or State attorney general must be made via certified or registered mail, or by electronic service through any electronic address established by the attorney general for this purpose. Other that admonishing that notice be made "promptly," the Rule sets no specific time period for notice.

Exception to Notice and Service Requirement

If a federal or State statute is challenged in a lawsuit where the United States or the affected State is already a party (or where its agencies or officers are sued in an official capacity), there is obviously no need for separate notice under Rule 5.1(a).

No New Claim or Right

This Rule is not intended to create a new or independent cause of action or basis for relief; it is, instead, merely a vehicle to help ensure that notice to the affected federal or State attorney general will occur.

RULE 5.1(b) Certification by the Court

To better ensure that the impacted government learns of the pending challenge to its law, the federal judge is also assigned a notification duty—one that is independent of and in addition to the notification obligation imposed on the challenging party. The presiding judge must "certify" to the appropriate federal or State attorney general that the constitutional challenge is pending.

PRACTICING LAW UNDER THIS SUBPART

Court's Duty to Certify

This seemingly redundant certification obligation is imposed on the court for two reasons. First, if the constitutional challenge was not raised by a party, the court's certification could be the only means of assuring that the interested federal or State attorney general will receive notice of the challenge. Second, because Rule 5.1(d) prohibits a forfeiture of a properly asserted constitutional claim or defense for a party's failure to serve the required notice, the judicial certification requirement can backstop a party's uninspired motivation to give the notice.

Timing of Certification

The Rule establishes no specific time period for the court to perform its certification duty, beyond the prohibition that no final adjudication of unconstitutionality may be entered prior to certification or notice.

RULE 5.1(c) Intervention; Final Decision on the Merits

When a constitutional challenge to a federal or State statute is underway, the relevant federal or State attorney general enjoys a right of intervention and a rather flexible time limit within which to do so. While that attorney general is considering intervention, the court may proceed forward with a case, but may not, during this period, enter a final judgment holding a statute unconstitutional.

PRACTICING LAW UNDER THIS SUBPART

Time to Intervene

An impacted attorney general may intervene as of right within 60 days of filing of the notice of constitutional challenge or certification of the challenge, whichever is earlier. However, the court is authorized to extend the 60-day limit on motion or *sua sponte*.

Intervention Only Permitted, Not Required

The attorney general is not *required* to exercise the right to intervene; the decision whether to intervene or not is a matter left to the attorney general's discretion. Thus, an attorney general's choice not to intervene does not preclude his or her right to oppose a constitutional challenge raised in a later case.

Court Rulings While Intervention Periods Are Pending

Until the time for intervention expires, a court may not enter a final judgment declaring a federal or State law unconstitutional; it may, however, reject the constitutional challenge at any time. In practice, courts tend to either postpone a ruling on constitutionality until the government intervenes or, if obviously unmeritorious, deny the constitutional challenge with a right of reconsideration (should the government intervene to object).

RULE 5.1(d) No Forfeiture

A challenging party might neglect to file the required notice or the presiding judge might fail to file the requisite certification. Such oversights will *not* cause a party to forfeit any constitutional claim or defense that is otherwise asserted in a timely manner.

PRACTICING LAW UNDER THIS SUBPART

Consequences for a Failure to Notify or Certify

Although a forfeiture of a constitutional claim or defense is prohibited, the Rule is silent as to other possible consequences of a failure by a party to notify or a court to certify. Such failures are not a jurisdictional defect. But, to allow time for the executive branch's views to be aired and considered, courts have entered various orders to remedy such failures, including: directing parties to give belated notice, postponing a case's consideration (or ordering its rehearing), permitting post-argument notification with permission to intervene, and vacating orders to facilitate a trial-level opportunity to intervene.

RULE 5.2

PRIVACY PROTECTION FOR FILINGS MADE WITH THE COURT

(a) **Redacted Filings.** Unless the court orders otherwise, in an electronic or paper filing with the court that contains an individual's social-security number, taxpayer-identification number, or birth date, the name of an individual known to be a minor, or a financial-account number, a party or nonparty making the filing may include only:

(1) the last four digits of the social-security number and taxpayer-identification number;

(2) the year of the individual's birth;

(3) the minor's initials; and

(4) the last four digits of the financial-account number.

(b) **Exemptions from the Redaction Requirement.** The redaction requirement does not apply to the following:

(1) a financial-account number that identifies the property allegedly subject to forfeiture in a forfeiture proceeding;

(2) the record of an administrative or agency proceeding;

(3) the official record of a State-court proceeding;

(4) the record of a court or tribunal, if that record was not subject to the redaction requirement when originally filed;

(5) a filing covered by Rule 5.2(c) or (d); and

(6) a pro se filing in an action brought under 28 U.S.C. §§ 2241, 2254, or 2255.

(c) **Limitations on Remote Access to Electronic Files; Social-Security Appeals and Immigration Cases.** Unless the court orders otherwise, in an action for benefits under the Social Security Act, and in an action or proceeding relating to an order of removal, to relief from removal, or to immigration benefits or detention, access to an electronic file is authorized as follows:

(1) the parties and their attorneys may have remote electronic access to any part of the case file, including the administrative record;

(2) any other person may have electronic access to the full record at the courthouse, but may have remote electronic access only to:

(A) the docket maintained by the court; and

(B) an opinion, order, judgment, or other disposition of the court, but not any other part of the case file or the administrative record.

(d) Filings Made Under Seal. The court may order that a filing be made under seal without redaction. The court may later unseal the filing or order the person who made the filing to file a redacted version for the public record.

(e) Protective Orders. For good cause, the court may by order in a case:

(1) require redaction of additional information; or

(2) limit or prohibit a nonparty's remote electronic access to a document filed with the court.

(f) Option for Additional Unredacted Filing Under Seal. A person making a redacted filing may also file an unredacted copy under seal. The court must retain the unredacted copy as part of the record.

(g) Option for Filing a Reference List. A filing that contains redacted information may be filed together with a reference list that identifies each item of redacted information and specifies an appropriate identifier that uniquely corresponds to each item listed. The list must be filed under seal and may be amended as of right. Any reference in the case to a listed identifier will be construed to refer to the corresponding item of information.

(h) Waiver of Protection of Identifiers. A person waives the protection of Rule 5.2(a) as to the person's own information by filing it without redaction and not under seal.

[Adopted April 30, 2007, effective December 1, 2007.]

UNDERSTANDING RULE 5.2

HOW RULE 5.2 FITS IN

The Internet age poses danger to information security, especially for sensitive information relating to personal and financial privacy. The federal courts could be attractive targets for privacy and security mischief. Accordingly, Rule 5.2 was added in 2007 to address growing concerns about the vulnerability of information stored with the federal courts. Under the Rule, certain personal data identifiers (*i.e.,* social security numbers, taxpayer-ID numbers, financial account numbers, and the full names of children) are given heightened protection, with other safeguards for social security and immigration cases. Additional protections can be ordered by the court for good cause. Invoking these benefits is a burden placed on parties and their counsel.

THE ARCHITECTURE OF RULE 5.2

This Rule has eight subparts, which can be bundled into four groups. The first three subparts (Rules 5.2(a), (b), and (c)) create obligations and exemptions that apply unless the court orders otherwise. The next two subparts (Rules 5.2(d) and (e)) grant the court additional authority to modify or heighten the nature and extent of privacy protections. The two subparts that follow (Rules 5.2(f) and (g)) give the filing party options in making its filings. The last subpart (Rule 5.2(h)) confirms that filers waive the privacy protections of this Rule by failing to abide by its provisions.

HOW RULE 5.2 WORKS IN PRACTICE

From many categories of court filings, parties may "redact" (meaning to blacken-over or otherwise conceal) or "seal" (meaning to shield from public access) certain personal data identifiers that may appear in those filings. In social security and immigration cases (where such identifiers are likely to be both especially relevant and peculiarly vulnerable), the redaction right does not generally apply, but electronic access to those files is restricted. For good cause, parties may seek enhanced protections beyond those set forth in Rule 5.2. The right to claim these protections (and the duty of doing so) lies with parties and their counsel.

PRACTICING LAW UNDER THIS RULE

The Rule's Odd "May-Include-Only" Syntax

Rule 5.2(a) is oddly worded. It advises parties and nonparties that they "may include only" redacted versions of certain information. This ambiguous syntax supports two different interpretations: either the granting of a choice (*i.e.*, a filer has been given an non-obligatory option to redact)[1] or the imposing of a prohibition (*i.e.*, a filer has been forbidden from doing anything other than redacting).[2] To date, the courts resoundingly have assumed the latter, that Rule 5.2(a) establishes a mandatory redaction obligation (albeit one that can be waived).

The Redaction Right

Both parties and nonparties who are making a filing with the court must redact the following information from their court filings:

- *Social Security Number/Taxpayer ID Number:* In lieu thereof, the filer may include only the last four digits of those numbers;
- *Birth Month and Day:* The filer may include only birth years;
- *Minor's Name:* In lieu thereof, the filer may include only the minor's initials (and, potentially, the initials of the minor's parents); and
- *Financial Account Numbers:* In lieu thereof, the filer may include only the last four digits of those numbers.

---

[1] As in: In ordering my baseball ticket package for the year, I may order the full season's games, or I instead *may include only* those ten games I most want to watch.

[2] As in: In mailing in that ticket order, a fan *may include only* a check, and never cash or a credit card charge.

In order to facilitate the ready use of the redacted information, the filer may, if he or she wishes, choose among two alternatives. The filer may supplement the redacted version of the materials with an unredacted copy filed under seal. Or the filer may supplement the redacted version by filing, under seal, a "reference list" that decodes the redactions.

The Sealing Right

In addition to the sealing options to which a filer is entitled as a supplement to redacted filings, the court may withdraw the right of redaction in favor of a filing under seal (which the court may later unseal or order be replaced with a redaction).

Applies to Paper Filings (and Trial Exhibits), as Well as Electronic Filings

Rule 5.2 applies broadly to all filings, whether made electronically or in paper form. Many judicial districts scan materials filed in paper form into their electronic case files, thus rendering those materials electronically accessible to the public in much the same way as they would had they been filed electronically in the first instance. Trial exhibits, if filed with the court, fall similarly within the reach of Rule 5.2.

Exceptions to the Redaction Right

The right of redaction does *not* apply in the following circumstances: (a) when the court orders otherwise, (b) in a forfeiture proceeding, if the financial account number identifies property claimed to be subject to forfeiture, (c) to the record of an administrative or agency proceeding, (d) to the official record of a State court proceeding, (e) to the record of a court or tribunal where the record was not subject to the redaction requirement when originally filed, (f) to social security and immigration cases, (g) to cases where the court orders that filings be sealed and not redacted, and (h) to *pro se* filings in actions brought under 28 U.S.C. §§ 2241, 2254, or 2255. There is unlikely to be an exception to the redaction duty merely because the document or information might be otherwise publicly accessible.

The Burden of Redacting / Sealing

The burden of exercising this right of redaction or sealing rests with the filer of the materials, and not with the courts or otherwise. Consequently, if a party intends to take advantage of the privacy and security benefits of this right, either the party or counsel must remember to perform the redaction or seek the sealing. The drafters urged counsel to remind their clients that personal data identifiers that could have been, but were not, protected will be publicly accessible over the Internet. The court may, however, order a redaction or sealing *sua sponte.*

Intended (and Inadvertent) Waivers

Parties may intentionally (balancing costs against benefits) or inadvertently (oversight or carelessness) waive their entitlement to Rule 5.2's protection by filing their information without redaction and not under seal. A minor's guardian can waive the redaction protections on behalf of the represented child. An inadvertent failure to redact or seal may be remedied upon motion to the court.

Additional Privacy / Security Protections

Rule 5.2's listing of particular categories of personal data identifiers is not intended to create a negative implication that *only* those categories of data are entitled to protection or that the abbreviated identifiers (*e.g.,* last four digits, minor's initials) are not themselves entitled, in an appropriate case, to be shielded. For "good cause," the court may grant protective orders allowing the redaction of additional information, or either limiting or barring remote electronic access by a nonparty to a filed document. In doing so, the court must balance privacy concerns against the presumptive open-access-to-court-records.

Social Security and Immigration Cases

Citing the "prevalence of sensitive information and the volume of filings," the drafters singled out certain social security and immigration cases for special treatment. These cases are *not* entitled to the automatic right of redaction. Although parties and their counsel enjoy unrestricted access to such filings, nonparties are entitled to remote electronic access only to case docket numbers and court disposition documents; to gain full access to the files, nonparties must access them in-person at the courthouse (and may do so, at the courthouse, electronically).

No New Claim or Right

This Rule does not create a new or independent claim or right of action for its violation.

Enforcement and Sanctions

Courts enforce the redaction obligations by orders that direct parties (or the clerk's office) to perform a redaction; temporarily seal or withdraw unredacted filings pending substitution; strike or otherwise ignore unredacted filings; publicly admonish failed compliance; and, in appropriate cases, impose sanctions. In considering whether to impose sanctions, courts have been influenced by the degree of counsel's vigilance and whether the misstep was unintentional. A bargained-for agreement to further seal court documents is, alone, unlikely to defeat that presumption.

Privacy Protection and "Particularized" Pleading

Certain federal claims require enhanced detail in pleading (such as fraud, governed by Rule 9(b)), and the redaction/sealing procedures may be used to properly balance privacy with this command for additional pleading specificity.

RULE 6

COMPUTING AND EXTENDING TIME; TIME FOR MOTION PAPERS

(a) Computing Time. The following rules apply in computing any time period specified in these rules, in any local rule or court order, or in any statute that does not specify a method of computing time.

(1) *Period Stated in Days or a Longer Unit.* When the period is stated in days or a longer unit of time:

(A) exclude the day of the event that triggers the period;

(B) count every day, including intermediate Saturdays, Sundays, and legal holidays; and

(C) include the last day of the period, but if the last day is a Saturday, Sunday, or legal holiday, the period continues to run until the end of the next day that is not a Saturday, Sunday, or legal holiday.

(2) *Period Stated in Hours.* When the period is stated in hours:

(A) begin counting immediately on the occurrence of the event that triggers the period;

(B) count every hour, including hours during intermediate Saturdays, Sundays, and legal holidays; and

(C) if the period would end on a Saturday, Sunday, or legal holiday, the period continues to run until the same time on the next day that is not a Saturday, Sunday, or legal holiday.

(3) *Inaccessibility of the Clerk's Office.* Unless the court orders otherwise, if the clerk's office is inaccessible:

(A) on the last day for filing under Rule 6(a)(1), then the time for filing is extended to the first accessible day that is not a Saturday, Sunday, or legal holiday; or

(B) during the last hour for filing under Rule 6(a)(2), then the time for filing is extended to the same time on the first accessible day that is not a Saturday, Sunday, or legal holiday.

(4) *"Last Day" Defined.* Unless a different time is set by a statute, local rule, or court order, the last day ends:

(A) for electronic filing, at midnight in the court's time zone; and

(B) for filing by other means, when the clerk's office is scheduled to close.

(5) *"Next Day" Defined.* The "next day" is determined by continuing to count forward when the period is measured after an event and backward when measured before an event.

(6) *"Legal Holiday" Defined.* "Legal holiday" means:

(A) the day set aside by statute for observing New Year's Day, Martin Luther King Jr.'s Birthday, Washington's Birthday, Memorial Day, Independence Day, Labor Day, Columbus Day, Veterans' Day, Thanksgiving Day, or Christmas Day;

(B) any day declared a holiday by the President or Congress; and

(C) for periods that are measured after an event, any other day declared a holiday by the State where the district court is located.

(b) Extending Time.

(1) *In General.* When an act may or must be done within a specified time, the court may, for good cause, extend the time:

(A) with or without motion or notice if the court acts, or if a request is made, before the original time or its extension expires; or

(B) on motion made after the time has expired if the party failed to act because of excusable neglect.

(2) *Exceptions.* A court must not extend the time to act under Rules 50(b) and (d), 52(b), 59(b), (d), and (e), and 60(b).

(c) Motions, Notices of Hearing, and Affidavits.

(1) *In General.* A written motion and notice of the hearing must be served at least 14 days before the time specified for the hearing, with the following exceptions:

(A) when the motion may be heard ex parte;

(B) when these rules set a different time; or

(C) when a court order—which a party may, for good cause, apply for ex parte—sets a different time.

(2) *Supporting Affidavit.* Any affidavit supporting a motion must be served with the motion. Except as Rule 59(c) provides otherwise, any opposing affidavit must be served at least 7 days before the hearing, unless the court permits service at another time.

(d) Additional Time After Certain Kinds of Service. When a party may or must act within a specified time after being served and service is made under Rule 5(b)(2)(C) (mail), (D) (leaving with the clerk), or (F) (other means consented to), 3 days are added after the period would otherwise expire under Rule 6(a).

[Amended effective March 19, 1948; July 1, 1963; July 1, 1966; July 1, 1968; July 1, 1971; August 1, 1983; August 1, 1985; August 1, 1987; December 1, 1999; April 23, 2001, effective December 1, 2001; April 25, 2005, effective December 1, 2005; April 30, 2007, effective December 1, 2007; March 26, 2009, effective December 1, 2009; April 28, 2016, effective December 1, 2016.]

UNDERSTANDING RULE 6

HOW RULE 6 FITS IN

Time is important in the law. It can sometimes spell the difference between winning and losing. Consider a statute of limitations, for example. Filing a lawsuit even one day late can—all by itself—doom a litigant's ability to obtain a recovery. And that is only one example. Time periods and time deadlines abound in litigation: the time for serving process, the time for answering a complaint, the time for amending a pleading, the time for demanding a jury trial, the time for impleading a third-party, the time for responding to interrogatories, the time for correcting a deposition transcript, the time for seeking summary judgment, the time for moving for a new trial, and the list goes on.

Because of how important (and how numerous) time limitations are, counting the passage of time correctly is essential to competently practicing law. Is the day a time period begins to run counted in computing the deadline (*i.e.*, is that day #1, or does day #1 begin on the next day)? What happens if a time period ends on a Saturday? On Thanksgiving Day? On a day when the courthouse is snowed in or its e-filing system is down? When does the last day of a time period end, at 5pm, midnight, or some other time? Can a litigant obtain an extension of time? Under what circumstances? Rule 6's task is to supply answers to these questions.

THE ARCHITECTURE OF RULE 6

This Rule has four subparts, designed to achieve three goals. Rule 6(a) establishes the national time-computation procedures for federal courts (unless Congress provides otherwise for a particular statute)—how time is to be counted, how time periods begin and end, and what days are excluded from that computation.

Rules 6(b) and (d) concern extensions of those time periods. Rule 6(d) creates certain automatic extensions. Rule 6(b) sets the procedures for requesting other types of extensions.

Rule 6(c) sets standardized time periods for motions, notices of hearing, and affidavits.

HOW RULE 6 WORKS IN PRACTICE

Each of the four subparts of Rule 6 is discussed, in order, below.

RULE 6(a) | Computing Time

Rule 6(a) sets the procedures for counting the passage of time. All time periods established by the Rules, local rules, court orders, and federal statutes are governed by the Rule 6(a) procedures. Rule 6(a) will not apply when Congress, in a particular statute, sets a different counting procedure, nor will it apply when the court imposes a "date certain" or "time-certain" deadline (*e.g.*, "File by 1:30 p.m. on April 14"). Time periods governed by Rule 6(a) may not end on a weekend or legal holiday (or, with filing deadlines only, on a day when the courthouse is deemed "inaccessible"). In such instances, Rule 6(a) supplies a brief, automatic extension.

PRACTICING LAW UNDER THIS SUBPART

Periods Set in Units of Days or Longer

In counting periods stated in units of time measured in days, months, or years, the day that triggers the period is excluded and then every following day is counted. If the period ends on a weekend or a legal holiday, the period is extended to the end of the next day that is not a weekend or legal holiday. (For filing deadlines, the period is also extended past days that the courthouse is inaccessible.) Thus, for example, if a Rule period is due to expire on Saturday, February 21 (and assuming Monday, February 23 was Washington's Birthday), Rule 6(a) will extend that period so it expires at the day's end on Tuesday, February 24.

- *Triggering Event:* What starts a time period running will depend on the implicated statute, rule, regulation, or other law.
- *When a Day "Ends":* Unless otherwise specified, a day "ends" for electronic filing at midnight in the court's time zone, and for all nonelectronic filings when the clerk's office is scheduled to close.
- *Counting Months:* The length of our months varies. At least one court has chosen to count monthly periods as starting after the triggering day and then running to the eve of the same calendar date as the starting day in the next month. *See Stevens v. Jiffy Lube Int'l, Inc.*, 911 F.3d 1249, 1252 (9th Cir. 2018).
- *Courthouse Inaccessibility:* The Rules do not define "inaccessible," and its meaning has evolved through case law. Bad weather is not the only qualifying cause. Courts have found "inaccessibility" when the clerk's office is closed *officially* for any reason (including inclement weather), when local weather conditions near the courthouse make traveling to the clerk's office dangerous, difficult, or impossible, or when other circumstances make the courthouse unreachable as a practical matter. An individual's own, personal weather-related or other logistical difficulties, which do not also cause the clerk's office to close, close early, or be otherwise dangerous to reach, generally will not qualify for this extension.
    - ♦ *Inaccessibility and Electronic Filings:* If the clerk's office is *physically* inaccessible, at least one court has ruled that an inaccessibility extension is warranted *even if* the filing could have been accomplished electronically.

Periods Set in Units of Hours

In counting periods stated in units of time measured in hours, the period begins immediately upon the triggering event and includes every hour thereafter. If the period ends on a weekend or a legal holiday, the period is extended to the same time on the next day that is not a weekend or legal holiday. (For filing deadlines, the period is also similarly extended past days that the courthouse is inaccessible.)

- *Inaccessible Final "Hour":* No extensions are automatically provided on days when the clerk's office is inaccessible *unless* that inaccessibility continues into the final hour of the hourly time period.
- *No Rounding-Up:* There is no "rounding" of hourly time periods. They will expire at the precise minute that the computation method produces (*e.g.*, 2:17 p.m.), and not be "rounded-up" to the next whole hour.
- *Crossing Daylight Savings Time:* Because *every* hour is counted, an hourly time period that straddles the shift between daylight savings time and standard time will not produce an extra hour of time.

Legal Holidays—Federal

The term "legal holiday" includes any day so declared by the President or Congress. There are currently ten standing federal holidays:

(1) New Year's Day

(2) Dr. Martin Luther King, Jr.'s Birthday

(3) Washington's Birthday

(4) Memorial Day

(5) Independence Day

(6) Labor Day

(7) Columbus Day

(8) Veterans' Day

(9) Thanksgiving Day

(10) Christmas Day

Legal Holidays—State

A special procedure governs holidays that are declared by States. For "forward-looking" time periods (*i.e.*, acts to be taken within a time *after* a triggering event), State holidays are considered "legal holidays" under Rule 6(a). Time periods typically cannot end on such days. However, for "backward-looking" time periods (*i.e.*, acts to be taken no less than a certain time *before* an event), State holidays are *not* considered "legal holidays" under Rule 6(a). In such instances (like with Rule 26(f), which requires an attorney's meeting at least 21 days before a scheduling conference), the 21st day *can* fall on a State holiday and that day will *not* be excluded from the computation.

Legal Holidays—Identifying When There Is One

From time to time, special federal holidays have been recognized. Likewise, States are free to recognize their own holidays, even if the federal judiciary is otherwise open. *See, e.g., Yepremyan v. Holder,* 614 F.3d 1042, 1044 (9th Cir. 2010) (California: day after Thanksgiving); *Tamez v. Manthey,* 589 F.3d 764, 769 (5th Cir. 2009) (Texas: Texas Independence Day); *Seacor by Seacor v. Sec'y of Dep't of Health & Human Servs.,* 34 Fed. Cl. 141, 143–44 (1995) (Massachusetts: Patriot's Day).

Occasionally, identifying whether a particular day qualifies as a "legal holiday" under Rule 6(a) can prove difficult. On those occasions, courts note that the Rule provides "reasonable flexibility," and is intended to abate the "hardship" of permitting "days of rest to shorten already tight deadlines." *See Mashpee Wampanoag Tribal Council, Inc. v. Norton,* 336 F.3d 1094, 1098–99 (D.C. Cir. 2003). On days when the clerk's office is declared closed by the district's chief judge, the answer is less certain.

Effect on Time Periods Set by Private Contracts

The Rule 6(a) procedures do not generally apply to time periods set in private contracts.

Effect on State Statutes of Limitation

The Rule 6(a) procedures may govern State limitations periods, provided the applicable State statute of limitations contains no contrary computation method. *See Walker v. Armco Steel Corp.*, 446 U.S. 740, 748–49 (1980).

RULE 6(b) Extending Time

The district courts may extend many (but not all) of the time periods set by the Rules. Extensions sought before a time period expires may be granted for "good cause." Extensions sought after a time period expires may be granted only "on motion" and only if both "good cause" and "excusable neglect" are proven. Time periods for many post-trial motions may not be extended at all.

PRACTICING LAW UNDER THIS SUBPART

Automatic Extensions Addressed Elsewhere

Automatic extensions (those supplied without a court order) are addressed by other subparts of this Rule. *See* Rule 6(a)(1)(C) & Rule 6(a)(2)(C) (extensions when time periods would end on weekends or legal holidays); Rule 6(a)(3)(A)–(B) (extensions when time periods would end on day courthouse is inaccessible); Rule 6(d) (extensions after being served by mail, by special consent, or by delivery to clerk). This subpart only concerns extensions available upon court order.

No Stipulated Extensions

Ordinarily, parties may not extend the time periods set in the Rules by simply stipulating to the extension by agreement of the parties. Court approval is required. Sometimes, however, extensions can be pre-approved by these Rules or in a district's local rules. In all events, courts anticipate the civility and mutual respect among members of the bar that ought to encourage attorney consent to one another's reasonable, non-prejudicial, good faith extension requests.

Extensions *Before* the Time Period Expires

If the extension request is made *before* the time period expires, the district court, in its discretion, may grant an extension for "good cause." *See Lujan v. Nat'l Wildlife Fed'n,* 497 U.S. 871, 896 (1990). Neither notice to the adversary nor a formal motion is required by the Rule, although applicable local rules may establish a more specific extension procedure. "Good cause" is not an especially rigorous standard, and has been interpreted broadly and liberally. But "good cause" still requires at least a reasonable explanation why, despite the party's diligence, an approaching deadline cannot be met. When sought in good faith and without prejudicing the adversary, pre-expiration extensions are routinely granted. Nonetheless, the court's discretion in ruling remains broad. When useful, the district court may convene an evidentiary hearing to explore the issues of good faith and prejudice.

Extensions *After* the Time Period Expires

If the extension request is made *after* the time period expires, the district court's discretion is more restricted. The district court may grant such an extension if: (1) "good cause" is shown (discussed above), *and* (2) the failure to act was the result of "excusable neglect." The Supreme Court has described excusable neglect hurdle as the greater of these two obstacles to a post-expiration extension. *See Lujan v. National Wildlife Fed'n,* 497 U.S. 871, 897 (1990).

Excusable neglect is tested with care; general unfamiliarity with the Rules or a crowded professional schedule will not constitute excusable neglect, nor will a delay taken for strategic reasons. Demonstrating excusable neglect is not easy, nor was it intended to be. A formal request for an excusable neglect extension is required; trial courts abuse their discretion in granting such relief in the absence of a motion by the affected litigant.

The Supreme Court has noted that excusable neglect is a "somewhat elastic concept," grounded in equity, not limited exclusively to omissions caused by circumstances outside the moving party's control, but which must be assessed in view of all relevant circumstances surrounding the omission. *See Pioneer Inv. Servs. Co. v. Brunswick Assocs. Ltd. P'ship,* 507 U.S. 380, 390–95 (1993) (construing excusable neglect in bankruptcy context). For example, an attorney's inexplicable failure to read and apply "crystal clear" legal rules will not be deemed excusable neglect, but an attorney's "plausible misinterpretation" of an ambiguous legal rule may be. Likewise, an inadvertent, good faith, understandable, minimal, and nonprejudicial calendaring error may qualify, though unexceptional, ordinary calendaring missteps or a crowded work schedule likely will not. Malfunctioning of the court's electronic filing systems will likely qualify, but technical difficulties experienced in counsel's law office might not. The fact that the error lies with the attorney, and not with the attorney's client, is *not* dispositive on whether "excusable neglect" exists. Clients are held responsible for the omissions of their attorneys, even if the clients are not separately culpable for the error.

In testing whether the neglect was excusable, courts have been guided expressly or inferentially by the U.S. Supreme Court's decision in *Pioneer Inv. Servs. Co. v. Brunswick Assocs. Ltd. P'ship,* 507 U.S. 380, 390–95 (1993) (construing excusable neglect in bankruptcy context) and have considered the following factors:

(1) The prejudice to the opponent (which must encompass something more than just the chore of having to now respond to and litigate an otherwise untimely filing);

(2) The length of the delay and its potential impact on the course of the judicial proceedings;

(3) The causes for the delay, and whether those causes were within the reasonable control of the moving party; and

(4) The moving party's good faith.

On occasion, courts have also tested for other equitable criteria, such as;

(5) Whether the omission reflected professional incompetence, such as an ignorance of the procedural rules;

(6) Whether the omission reflected an easily manufactured excuse that the court could not verify;

(7) Whether the moving party had failed to provide for a consequence that was readily foreseeable; and

(8) Whether the omission constituted a complete lack of diligence.

Courts have often ranked reason-for-delay and delay length as especially important considerations. Thus, a party's failure to offer any explanation for a missed deadline is, alone, enough to doom most requests to extend an expired deadline. Likewise, a district court's ignoring of a material factor, weighing an improper factor, or committing a serious error while weighing correct factors all may merit reversal on appeal. Courts are unlikely to approve new extensions if prior extensions have been granted and ignored.

No Extensions for Most Post-Trial Motions

The end of a civil trial is often followed by the filing of post-trial motions. The deadlines for filing such motions "must not" be extended by the court. *See* Rule 6(b)(2). This prohibition is intended to help ensure that the finality of federal judgments (and, with it, appealability) is not inappropriately postponed. For years, the prohibition haunted practitioners, who were confronted by a dishearteningly brief 10-day period for filing post-trial motions. In 2009, those time periods were enlarged to their current, sensible length of 28 days. The prohibition on timing extensions remains unchanged, however. District judges may not extend the deadline for filing post-trial motions seeking:

(1) A judgment as a matter of law, under Rule 50(b);

(2) A new trial, under Rules 50(d), 59(b), or 59(d);

(3) An amendment or expansion of a court's findings in a non-jury (bench) trial, under Rule 52(b); or

(4) An alteration or amendment to, or relief from, a judgment, under Rules 59(e) or 60(b).

This prohibitory language notwithstanding, two nuances in the caselaw merit attention. First, the prohibition is viewed by many courts as a non-jurisdictional "claim-processing" rule, which means it can be forfeited if not timely invoked. Thus, while district judges are prohibited by Rule 6(b)(2) from doing so, if they inadvertently overlook the prohibition and grant a post-trial motion extension, adversaries must properly object to that misstep or their right to do so is lost. *See, e.g., Legg v. Ulster Cty.*, 820 F.3d 67, 78–79 (2d Cir. 2016). (Note one further trap for the unwary: such untimely-filed post-trial motions will *not* suspend the time for taking an appeal. *See* Fed. R. App. P. 4(a)(4)(A).) Second, an old case law exemption from the Seventh Circuit Court of Appeals held that in "unique circumstances" these periods could be extended, provided there was a genuine ambiguity in the Rule language to begin with and the district court took action that gave the parties the specific assurance (albeit improperly) that an extension had been granted. *See Eady v. Foerder,* 381 F.2d 980 (7th Cir. 1967). The validity of this exemption has been often questioned and always limited tightly, and the Supreme Court has now rejected its application in a related context. *See Bowles v. Russell,* 551 U.S. 205, 213–14 (2007).

Time Periods Set by Statute

The pre-2007 language was clear that extensions under Rule 6(b) could only be granted to time periods set by the Rules themselves or by court orders; statutory time periods could not be extended. Rule 6(b) was "restyled" in 2007, and as rewritten, now omits this limiting language. The effect of this restyling change remains uncertain. The few courts that have addressed the issue have ruled that restyled Rule 6(b), like its predecessor, does not authorize extensions to statutory time periods.

Scope of Extension

The language of a party's proposed extension order should be chosen with care. An order extending the time for a defendant to "answer" the complaint does not necessarily extend the time for "moving" to dismiss the complaint. Therefore, broad language is advised: *e.g.,* requesting an extension to "answer, move, or otherwise plead."

RULE 6(c) Motions, Notices of Hearing, Affidavits

A written motion and notice of hearing must be served on the non-moving party at least 14 days before a motion hearing date, unless the district court specifies otherwise. This 14-day notice procedure applies to those district courts with "motion days" or the equivalent (where motions are heard orally). The Rule provides that the non-moving party must be served with notice of all motions at least 14 days before the hearing day, unless the court directs otherwise.

PRACTICING LAW UNDER THIS SUBPART

Special Timing

This 14-day notice requirement is a default rule of general application. Any Rule that contains a specific, different time period supersedes this default rule, as does any court order fixing a different time period.

Motion Affidavits

When a motion is supported with affidavits, the supporting affidavits must be served simultaneously with the motion. When an opposition to a motion is supported with affidavits, the opposing affidavits must be served not less than 7 days before the hearing. Affidavits submitted in support of reply briefs are not addressed by the Rule (although courts are likely to accept them if they are filed along with the reply briefs and constitute proper rebuttal). The purpose of this Rule is to restrain a moving party from belatedly "springing new facts" on an opponent. The district court has discretion in enforcing this Rule (and may modify it). Untimely affidavits may be stricken.

Exception: Affidavits opposing a motion for new trial must be served within 14 days after service of the motion.

RULE 6(d) Additional Time After Certain Kinds of Service

If a party must perform an act within a specified period after *being served* with some prior document, that specified period is extended by 3 days if the party was served the document by mail, by specially pre-agreed electronic or non-electronic means, or by leaving it with the court clerk (if permitted).

PRACTICING LAW UNDER THIS SUBPART

Purpose

Other Rules permit service of certain legal papers to be made by mail, by special pre-agreed means, and by leaving the papers with the court clerk when the served party has no known address. These sorts of service options are ordinarily considered complete at the time of mailing, transmission, or delivery to the clerk; completed service does *not* await actual receipt. To compensate for time lapses caused by postal and similar delays, Rule 6(d) adds 3 extra days to several time periods.

- *No 3-Day Extension for Regular Electronic Service:* Maturing technologies and widespread user skills have reduced the risk of service delays caused by suspended or failed electronic transmissions. Thus, no automatic 3-day extensions follow electronic service (in circumstances where electronic service is permitted), though extensions could still be ordered when the electronic service prejudices the recipient.

Applies to "After-Service" Deadlines Only

This 3-day extension applies only to responses due within a certain time after "service" of a preceding document.

No 3-Day Extension to "After-Filing" Deadlines

There is *no* 3-day extension when responses are due within a prescribed time after the "filing" of a document, even if that document was served through the mails, by pre-agreed means, or left with the clerk. Nor is a 3-day extension self-acquired by the act of mailing a document that must otherwise be filed by a particular date.

No 3-Day Extension to "After-Receipt" Deadlines

There generally is also *no* 3-day extension where responses are due within a prescribed period after actual "receipt" of a document, even if the received document was served through the mails, special service,, or clerk's office delivery.

No 3-Day Extension to "Date-Certain" Deadlines

There is no 3-day extension for date-specific deadlines fixed by the court.

No 3-Day Extension to Most Statutes of Limitation

The prevailing view among the courts is that the 3-day extension period does not apply to extend statutes of limitation.

RULE 7

PLEADINGS ALLOWED; FORM OF MOTIONS AND OTHER PAPERS

(a) Pleadings. Only these pleadings are allowed:

(1) a complaint;

(2) an answer to a complaint;

(3) an answer to a counterclaim designated as a counterclaim;

(4) an answer to a crossclaim;

(5) a third-party complaint;

(6) an answer to a third-party complaint; and

(7) if the court orders one, a reply to an answer.

(b) Motions and Other Papers.

(1) *In General.* A request for a court order must be made by motion. The motion must:

(A) be in writing unless made during a hearing or trial;

(B) state with particularity the grounds for seeking the order; and

(C) state the relief sought.

(2) *Form.* The rules governing captions and other matters of form in pleadings apply to motions and other papers.

[Amended effective March 19, 1948; July 1, 1963; August 1, 1983; April 30, 2007, effective December 1, 2007.]

UNDERSTANDING RULE 7

HOW RULE 7 FITS IN

The process of pleading has changed dramatically over the years. A century ago, pleading was a highly-technical, specialized maze of ancient writs, heavily-detailed allegations, and an extended back-and-forth exchange of legal instruments. It was decried in many quarters as a wily lawyers' game, where an unintended, incidental misstep could doom a litigant's claim or defense. When the Federal Rules of Civil Procedure took effect in 1938, their design endeavored to reduce the number, complexity, and technical risks of pleadings. Today, the scores of ancient pleading options have been thinned down to just the seven pleading types listed in Rule 7 (and the last of those is rarely used). This small group represents the *only* pleadings federal courts expect or permit.

Rule 7 also concerns the general requirements for motions in federal court. A "motion" is a request to the court for the issuance of some sort of judicial order. Parties can "move" for an order, for example, to dismiss a pleading, to extend the time for filing an answer, to amend a complaint, to compel a delinquent party to answer discovery, to certify a class action, to obtain summary judgment, to seek various other types of relief from the judge, and for other purposes.

THE ARCHITECTURE OF RULE 7

This Rule is simple. The first subpart lists the seven pleadings allowed in federal court; the second subpart installs the general requirements for motions.

HOW RULE 7 WORKS IN PRACTICE

These two subparts of Rule 7 are discussed, in order, below.

RULE 7(a) Pleadings

Rule 7(a) lists the seven types of pleadings that may be filed in federal court: (1) a complaint; (2) an answer to a complaint; (3) a reply to a counterclaim, if the counterclaim is so designated; (4) an answer to a crossclaim; (5) a third-party complaint; and (6) a third-party answer. These six are commonly filed pleadings. A seventh pleading—a reply to an answer—is permitted, but only by court order.

PRACTICING LAW UNDER THIS SUBPART

Not Pleadings

The very short list in Rule 7(a) is exhaustive. Assuming no counterclaim or crossclaim is filed, the pleadings in a typical case are considered closed once a complaint and answer have been filed.

Consequently, the following documents—which do not appear in the Rule 7(a) list—are *not* "pleadings" in federal court: a petition or writ, a "freestanding" (or "stand-alone") counterclaim or crossclaim not pleaded in an answer, a notice of removal, a motion, a response to a motion, a "suggestion" of a lack of jurisdiction, a brief or memorandum, exhibits to briefs, affidavits, declarations, discovery papers, expert reports and testimony, certificates of merit, jury instructions and verdict forms, and notices of appeal.

Definitions Used in Rule 7

(1) *Complaint:* A complaint is the document that begins a lawsuit by setting out the initial plaintiff's claim for relief. There can be only one operative version of a complaint in a federal civil action; amended complaints supplant their predecessors.

(2) *Answer:* An answer is the document that sets out a party's defenses, objections, and responses (including counterclaims and crossclaims) to the complaint.

(3) *Counterclaim:* A counterclaim is that portion of an answer that sets out a party's offensive claims against the suing party. (Counterclaims, thus, are not themselves considered pleadings; instead, they are merely part of a pleading.)

(4) *Crossclaim:* A crossclaim is that portion of an answer that sets out a party's claims against a co-plaintiff or co-defendant (that is, someone aligned on the same side of the "v."), often seeking indemnification or contribution. (Crossclaims are also not considered pleadings for the same reason that counterclaims are not pleadings.)

(5) *Answers to Counterclaims/Crossclaims:* Answers to counterclaims and crossclaims are considered to be pleadings.

(6) *Reply:* A reply is the pleading by which a party responds to an answer, a counterclaim answer, a crossclaim answer, or a third-party answer. Pleading in response to an answer is unusual; such replies are not permitted as of right. A court order is required before a party may file a reply. New matter pleaded in an answer (to which a reply would respond) is deemed by the Rules to be automatically denied or avoided. *See* Rule 8(b)(6).

Motion to Permit or Compel a Reply

To be granted permission ("leave") to file a reply, or to compel such a filing by another litigant, the moving party must make a clear and convincing showing of substantial reasons or extraordinary circumstances that warrant a reply. Courts may permit or compel a reply to an answer for several reasons: when a type of new matter is pleaded in the answer that might affect the outcome of the trial or might otherwise greatly broaden the issues in the case, when the information sought through the reply cannot be acquired through discovery, when a misdesignated affirmative defense must be answered or clarified, or when the case otherwise should not proceed without a reply. A typical example of such court-ordered replies arises in federal civil rights cases, where a court often directs plaintiffs to file specific and particularized responses to a public official's immunity defense. *See Crawford-El v. Britton,* 523 U.S. 574, 597–98 (1998).

RULE 7(b) Motions and Other Papers

The surprisingly few national requirements for motions in federal court are set by Rule 7(b). But those national requirements are often supplemented by local procedures (such as local court rules or chambers rules issued by a particular judge).

PRACTICING LAW UNDER THIS SUBPART

Formal Requirements for Motions

All motions must be in writing, unless they are presented during a hearing or trial. A written "notice of hearing" on the motion will satisfy this requirement.

- *Form:* Written motions must comply with the requirements of Rule 10—they must include a caption listing the name of the court, the title of the action, the docket number, and the title of the motion.
- *Contents:* Written motions must set forth "with particularity" the grounds for seeking the order and the relief sought. This particularity requirement ensures that the court and the adversary receive ample notice of both the relief requested and the moving party's reasoning, so that the court fully understands the motion

and the adversary has a meaningful opportunity to respond. The Rule is given a liberal application; "ritualistic detail" is not required and supporting memoranda may be examined in testing a motion's adequacy (though courts will not consult materials submitted after the filing period, as that would defeat the Rule's notice goal). Nonetheless, courts expect reasonable particularity in motions. In making this assessment, the court will consider whether any party is prejudiced by the motion's form and whether it can rule fairly on the motion. Requests for relief made in a passing comment, a stray sentence to a brief, or a footnote are likely to fail the particularity test. A motion that fails that test may be dismissed or denied.

  - *Consequences:* The consequence of a non-compliant motion may be that the court discounts it as a nullity, with potentially devastating ramifications.
  - *Motions to Amend:* When a party submits a motion to amend, the particularity requirement may require the party to attach to the motion a copy of the proposed amended pleading, unless the motion sets forth the substance of or otherwise adequately describes the contemplated revision. Informal amendment requests—unaccompanied by the proposed amended pleading itself or a summary of its substance—do not conform to Rule 7(b) and may be refused for that reason.

- *Supporting Memorandum or Brief:* Rule 7 does not expressly require a party to submit a supporting memorandum or brief along with motions or oppositions to motions, although many districts impose that obligation by local or chambers rule.
- *Form of Order:* Many local rules obligate the moving party to attach a form of order to the motion which, if signed and entered, would grant the relief requested in the motion. Similarly, the party opposing a motion may be required to attach a form of order which would deny the requested relief.
- *Attaching Affidavits and Other Exhibits:* A party may support a motion with affidavits or other materials, but such attachments can trigger serious ramifications. *See* Rule 12(d).
- *Signing:* The written motion must be signed in accordance with Rule 11 by the party's counsel or, if unrepresented, by the party herself. If the motion is not signed after the omission is called to the attention of the party or the party's counsel, the court may strike the document. *See* Rule 11(a).
- *Service:* A signed copy of the motion or "notice of hearing" must be served upon counsel for represented parties or, if unrepresented, upon the party herself. Unless the court directs otherwise, service must be accomplished not later than 14 days prior to the hearing on the motion.
  - *Certificate of Service:* Unless filed electronically, the motion must contain a certificate of service verifying that it was served.
- *Filing:* If the motion is served before it is filed, it (or any "notice of hearing") must be filed no later than "a reasonable time" after service.

Rules Governing Pleading Forms Also Apply to Motions

The styling of captions and the form of pleadings also apply to motions.

Opposing Written Motions

Rule 7 contains no requirement that an opponent file an "answer" to any motion and, absent a local or chambers rule to the contrary, a motion can be opposed solely by filing a brief or memorandum. The form, signing, filing, and service requirements for motions are applicable to oppositions as well.

Hearings and Arguments on Written Motions

The court may, in its discretion, schedule a motion for a hearing or oral argument. Neither is expressly required under the Rules, although local rule provisions may specify additional hearing and argument requirements. Hearings held *ex parte* (without notice to the opponent) are generally discouraged and are permitted only in exceptional circumstances, such as applications for temporary restraining orders.

Oral Motions

Oral motions are permitted if made during a hearing or trial, so long as they are raised in open court. This presentation will satisfy the writing requirement of Rule 7 if the oral motion is transcribed or otherwise recorded. This "writing" requirement for oral motions functions to ensure that the motion is accurately memorialized. Oral motions must also meet the obligation of stating, with particularity, the moving party's grounds for the relief sought.

Amendments to Motions

Neither Rule 7 nor any other Rule expressly provides for amendments to motions. Because motions are not "pleadings," the amendment procedures of Rule 15 do not apply. Nonetheless, federal courts are vested with those inherent powers reasonably needed to manage their affairs and "achieve the orderly and expeditious disposition of cases," provided the exercise of such powers will not violate any express Rule or statute. *See Dietz v. Bouldin*, 579 U.S. ___, 136 S. Ct. 1885, 1891–92 (2016). Consequently, federal courts possess broad discretion to permit amendments and supplements to motions when doing so will enable the case to be resolved justly, fairly, and without prejudicing others. Practitioners choose to seek leave of court to amend a filed motion, rather than withdraw it and file a new motion, when, for example, a new filing would be out of time or otherwise improper.

Local Procedures Often Supplement the National Rules

Nearly every district has promulgated local rules governing motion practice before its courts and, in some instances, individual judges have issued "standing orders" (or "chambers orders") regulating such particulars as the time for and method of responding to motions, page limitations for motions and responses, the acceptability of "reply briefs," chambers' policies on courtesy copies for the presiding judge, and the scheduling of oral arguments.

RULE 7.1

DISCLOSURE STATEMENT

(a) Who Must File; Contents. A nongovernmental corporate party must file two copies of a disclosure statement that:

(1) identifies any parent corporation and any publicly held corporation owning 10% or more of its stock; or

(2) states that there is no such corporation.

(b) Time to File; Supplemental Filing. A party must:

(1) file the disclosure statement with its first appearance, pleading, petition, motion, response, or other request addressed to the court; and

(2) promptly file a supplemental statement if any required information changes.

[Added April 29, 2002, effective December 1, 2002; April 30, 2007, effective December 1, 2007.]

UNDERSTANDING RULE 7.1

HOW RULE 7.1 FITS IN

An obvious ingredient to any fair litigation is a presiding judge who is unbiased and impartial. When judges have some connection to the parties or to the lawsuit that reasonably could call into question their impartiality, they are expected to "recuse" (that is, to disqualify themselves and step aside) from presiding in that case. Rule 7.1 aids judges in making that recusal decision. But it addresses only one circumstance that could require a judge's recusal: when that judge may be financially interested in a party or in the outcome. The Rule requires any party that is a corporation (except for governmental corporations) to disclose the identity of its corporate parent(s) and its major corporate shareholders.

THE ARCHITECTURE OF RULE 7.1

This Rule is organized plainly. The first subpart identifies who must make these disclosures and what the disclosures must contain. The second subpart sets the time-frame for disclosing and imposes a further duty to supplement if the disclosed information changes.

HOW RULE 7.1 WORKS IN PRACTICE

Limited Purpose

This Rule is not designed to cover all circumstances that might call for a district judge's recusal. Rather, the Rule has a far narrower reach, targeting only certain information that would trigger a judge's automatic financial interest disqualification.

Automatic Financial Interest Recusals

Under the automatic financial interest disqualification canon, federal judges must recuse when they (individually, as fiduciaries, or their immediate household families) have a financial interest in the subject matter of the pending dispute or in one of the litigants, or any other interest that might be substantially affected by the litigation's outcome. *See* Code of Conduct for United States Judges at Canon 3C(1)(c).

Who Must Disclose

The disclosure obligation applies to non-governmental corporate litigants. Persons or entities that are not parties to the litigation, as well as parties that are not corporations, have no disclosure duty under this Rule.

What Must Be Disclosed

Disclosing parties must file with the court a written statement that either (1) identifies each parent corporation and publicly held corporation owning 10% or more of their stock, *or* (2) states that no such corporation exists. Two copies of the statement must be filed. The Rule imposes no further disclosure requirements

When Must Disclosure Occur

The disclosure is due when a party files its first appearance, pleading, petition, motion, response, or other request addressed to the court. Timeliness can sometimes be influenced by circumstances, however.

Serving Disclosures on Other Parties

The Rule is silent as to whether the statement must be served on other parties.

Supplementing the Statement

Parties are also obligated under the Rule to "promptly" file a supplemental statement when any change in the required information occurs.

More Extensive Disclosures Under Local Rules

Local rules may require additional disclosures.

Consequences of Delinquent or Non-Filing

The Rule prescribes no particular ramification for failing to file (or to file timely). The Rule 7.1 Statement has not been construed as an inflexible precondition for filing a motion or brief in a lawsuit, and courts have excused a failure to file (or timely file) if no prejudice occurs and the oversight is promptly corrected. A typical response by the courts has simply been an order directing the delinquent party to make its filing. When, however, the omission is persistent (especially after the court presses for the filing), the failure to file can result in contempt, monetary penalties, dismissal, striking appearances and jury demands, or other sanctions.

Collateral Uses of Statement

Both litigants and the courts have used disclosure statements and the information the statements contain for various collateral purposes, including ruling on motions (although other courts have been less willing to give disclosure statements such a broadened use).

Requirement of a Pleading: 7(A)

1. simple, concie, direct
2. can be in a single count or seperate if multiple claims
3. must be in numbered ¶'s, practizable
4. may say as many claims, regardless of inconsistency

How to satisfy a complaint:

1. plaintiff must allege citizenship of individual persons when they are parties to the action
2. plaintiff must allege the citizenship of all the members of parties that are unicorp. entitres (aka. sole practitioner or association)
3. plaintiff must allege the A.I.C. (exclusive of interest & costs) exceeds $75,001

Iqubal Case:

- court must identify allegation in the complaint that are not entitled to the assumption of truth (so need to seperate pleadings of fact & pleadings of conclusion)
- court must evaluate the factual assertions to determine whether "they plausible suggest an entitlement to relief"

Legal Conclusion v. Factual Allegation

1. legal conclusions are to be dismissed → "x is violating the equal protection clause"
2. factual allegations → are what you want → "x is discrimination on basis of race"

Denials 8(B) Answers

- admit or deny in short & plain terms
- 8(C) state any affirmative defenses in answer
- counterclaims: contain as many as you want to P's
- crossclaims: as many as you want to co-Def's
- general denial = all things (even jurisd.) // special denial = certain parts

RULE 8

GENERAL RULES OF PLEADING

(a) Claim for Relief. A pleading that states a claim for relief must contain:

(1) a short and plain statement of the grounds for the court's jurisdiction, unless the court already has jurisdiction and the claim needs no new jurisdictional support;

(2) a short and plain statement of the claim showing that the pleader is entitled to relief; and

(3) a demand for the relief sought, which may include relief in the alternative or different types of relief.

(b) Defenses; Admissions and Denials.

(1) *In General.* In responding to a pleading, a party must:

(A) state in short and plain terms its defenses to each claim asserted against it; and

(B) admit or deny the allegations asserted against it by an opposing party.

(2) *Denials—Responding to the Substance.* A denial must fairly respond to the substance of the allegation.

(3) *General and Specific Denials.* A party that intends in good faith to deny all the allegations of a pleading—including the jurisdictional grounds—may do so by a general denial. A party that does not intend to deny all the allegations must either specifically deny designated allegations or generally deny all except those specifically admitted.

(4) *Denying Part of an Allegation.* A party that intends in good faith to deny only part of an allegation must admit the part that is true and deny the rest.

(5) *Lacking Knowledge or Information.* A party that lacks knowledge or information sufficient to form a belief about the truth of an allegation must so state, and the statement has the effect of a denial.

(6) *Effect of Failing to Deny.* An allegation—other than one relating to the amount of damages—is admitted if a responsive pleading is required and the allegation is not denied. If a responsive pleading is not required, an allegation is considered denied or avoided.

(c) Affirmative Defenses.

(1) *In General.* In responding to a pleading, a party must affirmatively state any avoidance or affirmative defense, including:

- accord and satisfaction;
- arbitration and award;
- assumption of risk;
- contributory negligence;
- duress;
- estoppel;
- failure of consideration;
- fraud;
- illegality;
- injury by fellow servant;
- laches;
- license;
- payment;
- release;
- res judicata;
- statute of frauds;
- statute of limitations; and
- waiver.

(2) *Mistaken Designation.* If a party mistakenly designates a defense as a counterclaim, or a counterclaim as a defense, the court must, if justice requires, treat the pleading as though it were correctly designated, and may impose terms for doing so.

(d) Pleading to Be Concise and Direct; Alternative Statements; Inconsistency.

(1) *In General.* Each allegation must be simple, concise, and direct. No technical form is required.

(2) *Alternative Statements of a Claim or Defense.* A party may set out two or more statements of a claim or defense alternatively or hypothetically, either in a single count or defense or in separate ones. If a party makes alternative statements, the pleading is sufficient if any one of them is sufficient.

(3) *Inconsistent Claims or Defenses.* A party may state as many separate claims or defenses as it has, regardless of consistency.

(e) Construing Pleadings. Pleadings must be construed so as to do justice.

8(e) → gives direction on how court should construe pleadings: ① liberality has priority over a technicality, ② courts should do substantial justice, ③ court should not give pleadings unwarranted generous amounts of reading that it prejudices, ④ be less stringent to pleadings from lay-person → e.g. pro H.C. ↓ but it doesn't have to re-draft it for them

[Amended effective July 1, 1966; August 1, 1987; April 30, 2007, effective December 1, 2007; April 28, 2010 effective December 1, 2010.]

UNDERSTANDING RULE 8

HOW RULE 8 FITS IN

The term "pleadings" refers to the various formal written instruments (like a complaint and an answer) where the parties set out their respective claims and defenses. These documents are designed to give notice of claims and defenses to both the adversary and the court. The pleadings stage of civil litigation begins at the outset of the lawsuit. (Rule 3 instructs that a federal lawsuit "commences" with the filing of the first pleading, the complaint.)

Historically, the pleadings stage was marked by artful gamesmanship by skilled strategists. It was an age of writs, demurrers, rebutters, sur-rebutters, replies, and other legal jargon aplenty. A party's pleadings could be defeated merely for having been cast with the wrong title or label. The result was an intricate, lawyerly crafting contest, where even modest technical missteps could spell doom (where the true merits of the clients' actual claims and defenses might never be reached at all).

The Federal Rules of Civil Procedure were devised to avoid much of this. When they took effect in 1938, the shift was nothing short of a revolution in civil procedure. In place of technicalities, the Rules instructed that "[n]o technical form is required." In place of the buffeting array of circumstance-specific writs, the Rules limited pleadings to only 7 in number and commanded that they "be simple, concise, and direct." In place of copious details and legalese, the Rules looked only for "short and plain" statements. The Rules expected the pleadings stage only to impart "notice" of the parties' claims and defenses, with the evidentiary-level factual details to be supplied during the later discovery stage, and the testing of the factual and evidentiary adequacy of those arguments reserved until even later during the summary judgment stage. In short, the job of pleadings in federal court under the Rules was intended to be far more modest than it had been traditionally.

Still, many of the Rules are devoted to pleadings and the pleadings stage. Rule 7 lists the allowable pleadings. Rule 10 sets the form of pleadings. Rule 11 imposes ethical standards on pleaders. Rule 12 describes how to raise and press defenses to pleadings. Rules 13 and 14 permit new claims to be asserted in pleadings. Rules 17 through 25 concern joinder of parties in pleadings. Rule 15 establishes the process for amending pleadings. For all the Rules' emphasis on simplifying this stage of litigation, there remains a large swath of ground still to cover.

Among all those pleadings rules, two stand out as central to this process—Rules 8 and 9. These two are the core around which all the other pleading Rules revolve. Rule 8 explains the general approach for asserting and responding to claims, and installs the simplicity standard by which federal pleadings are to be judged. Rule 9 supplements the general requirements of Rule 8, by setting out a list of adjustments and enhancements to those general pleading norms.

THE ARCHITECTURE OF RULE 8

Rule 8 is separated into five subparts. Rule 8(a) addresses the manner for pleading claims that seek relief. Rules 8(b) and (c) prescribe the method for responding to such claims, including how to assert the responding party's general and affirmative defenses. Rules 8(d) and (e) emphasize the simplicity, conciseness, and lack of technicality expected from pleaders.

HOW RULE 8 WORKS IN PRACTICE

These five subparts of Rule 8 are discussed, in order, below.

RULE 8(a) Claim for Relief

To plead a claim that seeks relief in federal court, the pleader's obligations are three-fold. In "short" and "plain" language, that pleader must: (1) allege the grounds for the court's subject-matter jurisdiction; (2) show a claim that entitles the pleader to relief; and (3) state a demand for the relief the pleader is requesting. In 2007 and 2009, the U.S. Supreme Court decided two cases, *Bell Atlantic Corp. v. Twombly* and *Ashcroft v. Iqbal*, that introduced some new uncertainty into the pleader's task, and today the effect of those decisions is still being gauged. Both are discussed below.

PRACTICING LAW UNDER THIS SUBPART

Element 1: Grounds for Jurisdiction

A party filing a claim for relief in a complaint, counterclaim, crossclaim, or third-party complaint must state in short and plain terms the basis for the court's subject matter jurisdiction for each count. Subject-matter jurisdiction is discussed in detail in Sections 2.10 through 2.13 of this text.

- *When Jurisdiction Is Based on Diversity:* The pleader must allege: (1) the citizenship of each party (*e.g.*, for individuals, their State of citizenship; for corporations, their State of incorporation *and* their principal place of business; for unincorporated entities, the citizenship of all their members); and (2) that the amount in controversy—exclusive of interest and costs—exceeds $75,000.
    - *"Special" Diversity:* When jurisdiction is based on a special type of diversity, the pleader must properly allege those prerequisites. *See, e.g.*, 28 U.S.C. § 1332(d)(2) (Class Action Fairness Act diversity); 28 U.S.C. § 1335 (statutory interpleader diversity).
- *When Jurisdiction Is Based on a Federal Question:* The pleader must allege the specific constitutional provisions, laws, or treaties that permit such jurisdiction.
- *When Jurisdiction Is Based on Admiralty:* Parties intending to proceed under the rules governing admiralty or maritime claims must include a statement in their complaint declaring the action as an admiralty or maritime claim. *See* Rule 9(h).
- *When Jurisdiction Is Based on Supplemental Jurisdiction:* When diversity, federal question, or admiralty/maritime jurisdiction exists as to one or more claims in the complaint, the pleader may allege the right to litigate certain other State-law claims in the same case when those claims are so related to qualifying claims that they form part of the same "case or controversy." *See* 28 U.S.C. § 1367.

No allegations needed in a complaint

- *Exception—Jurisdiction Already Acquired:* No statement of jurisdictional grounds is required if subject-matter jurisdiction has already been acquired in the lawsuit (but careful practitioners often prefer to allege jurisdiction to be safe).
- *Remedy for Failure:* Omitting a statement of jurisdictional grounds can result in dismissal.
- *Pleading Personal Jurisdiction:* Ordinarily, plaintiffs need not allege personal jurisdiction in their complaint; Rule 8(a) requires only that subject-matter jurisdiction be alleged. (The obligation to *object* to personal jurisdiction is a task instead typically reserved for the defending party.)
- *"Plausibly" Pleading Jurisdiction:* Courts have often held that personal jurisdiction need not be alleged in a complaint (though electing to do so is not improper). Unlike personal jurisdiction, subject-matter jurisdiction is structural (not a convenience based defense), does not depend on being contested by a defendant (but can be raised by anyone at any time), and cannot be conferred by consent, waiver, or forfeiture (but must instead be confirmed independently by the court). Thus, there is sense in requiring a complaint to plead only subject-matter jurisdiction, while awaiting a motion or an answer to contest personal jurisdiction. Nonetheless, a minority of courts have rotely incanted that alleging personal jurisdiction is a pleader's obligation (language that might be explained as just an incautious expression of the burdens during a personal jurisdiction challenge).

Element 2: Short and Plain Statement of the Claim

The pleader must next state, in short and plain terms, a claim showing an entitlement to relief. This requires pleaders to give their opponents fair notice of their claim and the grounds upon which it rests. *See Tellabs, Inc. v. Makor Issues & Rights, Ltd.,* 551 U.S. 308, 319 (2007). Guided by this standard, the Rules generally impose a more lenient pleading obligation than do many State courts. There is no need, for example, for pleaders to incant "magical words" of the law. Intricately detailed factual allegations are not necessary. *See Ashcroft v. Iqbal,* 556 U.S. 662, 678 (2009). Nor need pleaders even identify their precise legal theory. *See Skinner v. Switzer,* 562 U.S. 521, 529 (2011). (Indeed, even asserting an incorrect legal theory might not always be fatal.) The Rules rely on discovery and summary judgment, rather than pleadings, to flesh out the disputed facts and cull unmeritorious cases. *See Swierkiewicz v. Sorema N. A.,* 534 U.S. 506, 512 (2002).

But, although encouraging brevity, the federal pleading duty is still far from trivial; the pleading must contain "enough" to give defendants fair notice of a complaint's claims and the grounds for them. The pleaded claim must be facially "plausible"—that is, it must allege sufficient factual content to permit the reasonable inference that the defendant is liable for unlawful conduct. *See Iqbal,* 556 U.S. at 678. Obviously, this implicates a highly context-specific inquiry. A "plausible" auto collision case may be very concisely pleaded, whereas a "plausible" antitrust or business fraud case may demand a more robust factual presentation.

The mandate, then, for pleaders is to allege "**sufficient facts**"—enough to move beyond the level of speculation, to "nudge[ ] their claims across the line from conceivable to plausible." *See Bell Atlantic Corp. v. Twombly,* 550 U.S. 544, 570 (2007). When will pleaded facts be "sufficient"? Zeroing in more exactly on that target has proven practically and conceptually elusive. Judicial direction from the lower courts has also not always been clear or uniform. Some courts have emphasized a distinction between pleading a "claim" (which is required) and pleading facts that correspond to each element of a legal theory (which, in their view, is not required). Other courts have cautioned that legal allegations do not "go unscrutinized;" and pleaders must still discharge their "responsibility for identifying the nature of [their] claim."

While doctrinal imprecision abounds, some useful guiding markers seem settled. The "plausibility" standard is an objective target, not a subjective one. It does not require that, as pleaded, the claims appear "likely" or "probably" true. *See Twombly*, 550 U.S. at 556. But pleading just the "sheer possibility" of a claim will not suffice. *See Iqbal,* 556 U.S. at 678. A mere "thread-bare" or "formulaic" recital of elements, naked legal conclusions, and unadorned, "the-defendant-unlawfully-harmed-me" accusations will also not be enough. *See id.*

Offering only equivocal factual allegations—ones equally consistent with either culpable or innocent conduct—fails to raise the required reasonable inference of "plausibility." *See id.* Instead, the pleaded allegations must be factual (not conclusory) and suggestive (not neutral). *See Twombly*, 550 U.S. at 557 n.5. Thus, proffering a conclusory inference without supporting facts will not do. In the end, a claim's allegations must "possess enough heft" to show an entitlement to relief (thus justifying that the costly process of litigation continue). *See id.* at 557.

- *"Plausibly" Pleading Claims:* In *Bell Atlantic Corp. v. Twombly,* the Supreme Court announced the "plausibility" pleading standard (discussed above). In so doing, the Court expressly overruled the oft-quoted, very forgiving pleading mantra from its 1957 decision in *Conley v. Gibson* (namely, that no complaint should be dismissed for failing to properly state a claim "unless it appears beyond doubt that the plaintiff can prove no set of facts in support of his claim which could entitle him to relief."). The *Conley* language, wrote the Court, "earned its retirement" because it might, incorrectly, preserve a conclusorily pleaded claim on the mere theoretical chance that it might later find support. *See Twombly,* 550 U.S. at 554–63 (2007) ("retiring" language in *Conley v. Gibson,* 355 U.S. 41, 45–46 (1957)).

  The Court later confirmed that *Twombly's* "plausibility" standard is not limited only to antitrust cases (the type of lawsuit *Twombly* was). *See Iqbal,* 556 U.S. at 684. But precisely how this "plausibility" line is to be drawn remains uncertain, and it can impose a foreboding burden on those pleaders who sue just on the basis of a suspicion or surmise (given that their access to discovery, of course, comes only if the complaint survives). It is clear that the standard lies somewhere between fact pleading and conclusory recitations of elements. As summarized by one court, plausibility requires that the pleader supply those case details necessary "to present a story that holds together," and courts will ask only "*could* these things have happened, not *did* they happen." *Swanson v. Citibank, N.A.,* 614 F.3d 400, 404 (7th Cir. 2010).

- *"Information-and-Belief" Pleading:* For many years, pleaders lacking certain knowledge have made allegations based on "information and belief" (sort of an educated guess resting on certain fact-based inferences). The viability of this sort of "information and belief" pleading remains unclear after *Twombly*.

- *"Short and Plain," and Pleading with Excessive Factual Detail:* Each statement of claim must be "short and plain" (*i.e.,* brief and clear). Nonetheless, practitioners have long debated the wisdom of pleading with more detail than the Rules require. Some believe that added detail helps educate the judge. Others reject that view as unrealistic. In any event, an unnecessarily detailed pleading is risky. It invites a pre-answer motion to dismiss premised on the very detail so gratuitously supplied. And in extreme circumstances, it may even warrant a dismissal for verbosity.

- *Sua Sponte Dismissals:* In those rare instances of complaints so confused, ambiguous, vague, or unintelligible as to defy comprehension, *sua sponte* dismissals may be proper.

- *Enhanced Pleading Exceptions:* In certain types of claims, the Rules or the underlying law itself impose on the pleader an enhanced obligation of additional claim detail. For example, claims must be alleged with particularity when: (1)

pleading fraud and mistake, under Rule 9(b); (2) pleading demand futility in a shareholder derivative action, under Rule 23.1; and (3) pleading scienter under the Private Securities Litigation Reform Act, 15 U.S.C. § 78U–4(b).

- *Case Law Exceptions:* Although courts occasionally have tried to impose more elaborate pleading standards in certain categories of cases, it now appears settled that the only permissible exceptions to the "notice" pleading standard of Rule 8(a) are those contained in other Rules themselves. *See Leatherman v. Tarrant Cty. Narcotics Intelligence & Coordination Unit,* 507 U.S. 163, 168 (1993).

Element 3: Demand for Relief

The pleader must also make a demand for judgment that identifies the remedies desired and the parties against whom relief is sought. This does not require enormous specificity. For example, most courts do not require complaints to contain a demand for a particular amount of damages (beyond the obligation, in diversity cases, to plead a qualifying amount in controversy), and demanding an improper remedy will not necessarily foreclose the recovery of a proper one. But this flexibility is not unbounded; the complaint must demand relief of some sort and what is demanded must be relief the law allows.

- *"Plausibly" Pleading Relief:* The courts are unsettled whether the "plausibility" pleading standard established in the *Twombly* decision should govern the pleading of a demand for relief, though the sounder view would reject such an application.
- *Pleading Damages:* Although pleaders are not required to do more than state "the relief sought," the Rules *do* require pleaders to identify the type of relief they seek. Thus, a pleading for equitable relief without any damages demand might foreclose the ability to press for damages later.
- *Pleading Unliquidated Damages:* By local rule, certain Districts expressly forbid a plaintiff to plead a specific sum of unliquidated damages (instead, such pleaders are permitted only to demand unliquidated damages generally).
- *Equitable and Declaratory Relief:* A party seeking equitable relief must plead the specific act to be prohibited or compelled; a party seeking declaratory relief must plead the specific declaration sought.
- *Special Damages:* A claimant must plead special damages with specificity, as dictated by Rule 9(g).
- *Remedy for Failure:* Some courts have ruled that omitting a proper demand for relief is not necessarily fatal to a claim's survival, while others hold that such an omission justifies dismissal.
- *Default Judgment:* In cases of default judgment, a claimant is limited to the specific amount of the demand, as provided by Rule 54(c).
- *Jury Demand:* A jury demand may be included as part of the original pleading. Rule 38 controls when and how a party may request (or waive) trial by jury.
- *Alternative, Hypothetical, and Inconsistent Demands:* A party may assert all demands for legal or equitable relief alternatively, hypothetically, and/or inconsistently. Rule 8(d) protects that right; under this Rule, portions of a pleading cannot be offered as admissions against other portions containing inconsistent or alternative averments.

Pleadings from *Pro Se* Litigants

Pleadings filed by *pro se* litigants are held to a less stringent standard than those prepared by attorneys. *See Erickson v. Pardus,* 551 U.S. 89, 94 (2007) (per curiam). Nevertheless, *pro se* pleadings are not relieved of the obligation to allege sufficient facts to support a proper, "plausible" legal claim.

RULE 8(b) Defenses; Admissions and Denials

In answering a federal pleading that states a claim for relief, pleaders are directed to respond in "short" and "plain" terms. Responding parties are expected to perform three tasks in their responses: (1) to admit or deny each allegation made against them; (2) to state their defenses to each claim asserted against them; and (3) to assert any counterclaim (against the claimant) or any crossclaim (against a fellow defendant) that they may wish to press. Responses must be crafted with care. A failure to deny (or to deny properly) results in an admission.

PRACTICING LAW UNDER THIS SUBPART

Responsive Pleading Options

When an allegation has been asserted against them, and a responsive pleading is required to that allegation, pleaders have only three options: (1) admit the allegation, (2) deny it, or (3) state a lack of knowledge or information necessary to admit or deny it. The Rules do not approve or permit other types of responses, and choosing to answer in other ways is a dangerous practice (as shown below).

Denials Must Fairly Respond to the Substance of Each Allegation

The purpose of a responsive pleading is to identify for both the opponent and the court those allegations which are contested, as distinct from those which are conceded. Thus, when responsively pleading, parties are obligated to "fairly" respond to the "substance" of an allegation. *See* Rule 8(b)(2). Each portion of each allegation must be addressed (any portion not denied may be considered admitted), and pleaders may not do so in a manner that equivocates or confuses the issues. Ergo, offering an antiquated reply that evades a fair and substantive response is improper. For this reason, refusing to substantively respond because the allegation is "a conclusion of law," or is a characterization of a document "that speaks for itself," or is a contention that fails to state a cognizable claim for relief, or is an averment that is neither admitted nor denied because the party "demands strict proof thereof" are all examples of evading, rather than fairly responding, to the substance of a pleaded allegation. Counter-pleading in this manner can have case-devastating consequences (though courts may sometimes overlook these evasive practices when they do not appear alone but instead are coupled with an unambiguous denial).

Types of Proper Denials

The Rules permit a party to deny an opponent's allegations in a pleading in several ways, provided the method chosen comports with Rule 11:

- *General Denials:* which deny all allegations of a pleading (including those asserting the court's jurisdiction). No magic language is required for a general denial, so long as that intent is clear. But because such absolute, categorical denials of everything alleged will rarely comport with Rule 11, they are uncommon.
- *Qualified General Denials:* deny all allegations of a pleading (or a grouped cluster of allegations) except for certain specific ones.
- *Specific Denials:* deny particular paragraphs, one at a time. It is the most common form of pleading denials.

- *Partial Denials:* deny a portion of particular allegation, with a companion concession that identifies other portions that are admitted (this may often be required in order to fairly meet an allegation's substance, as discussed above).

Failure to Deny Factual Allegations

A failure to deny the factual allegations of a complaint or amended complaint will deem them admitted. Use of unauthorized pleading options (discussed above) can have the same disastrous effect. However, courts are unlikely to deem as admitted those facts that were not well pleaded or statements that constitute mere conclusions of law. Nor will courts enter judgment against a defaulting party based on deemed-admitted facts without first testing whether those facts actually state a cognizable claim for relief.

Failure to Deny Amount of Damages

Although a failure to deny usually causes the allegation to be deemed admitted, this result does not occur with allegations relating to the amount of damages.

Denials Based upon Lack of Knowledge or Information

A party may also respond by pleading a lack of knowledge or information. But to do so, the party must plead *both* lack of knowledge *and* lack of information. In certain circumstances, lack of information may be asserted where the information at issue may exist but has proven to be difficult to uncover. A party pleading lack of knowledge and information is also bound by the obligation of honesty in pleading; an allegation that is obviously within the responding party's knowledge or information cannot be avoided, and averring lack of knowledge or information in such circumstances may have the unintended effect of *admitting* the allegation.

- *Duty of Investigation:* A party denying based upon a lack of knowledge and information has the duty to reasonably investigate whether the information exists and how difficult it would be to find.
- *Effect:* A response properly based upon a lack of knowledge and information eludes the effect of a deemed-admission, and thus operates like a denial.

Duty to Re-Assert Denials to Amended Pleadings

When a pleading is one to which a response is required, and it is later amended, the opponent is obligated to timely respond to the amended pleading with either a motion to dismiss or an answer. *See* Rule 15(a)(3). The safest path to do so is to respond by filing a new document (motion or answer) addressed specifically to the amended pleading, but if the amended allegations against the responding party have not materially changed and were previously addressed in a motion or answer to the original pleading, a court might, in an appropriate circumstance, treat the earlier motion or answer as an acceptable response.

No Duty to Respond to Answers, Generally

Unless it contains a counterclaim or crossclaim, or the court orders a reply, pleaders need not—and may not—respond to an answer. All new matter and affirmative defenses contained in an answer are considered denied or avoided automatically. *See* Rule 8(b)(6).

No Duty to Respond to Allegations Against Others

Pleaders need not responsively plead to allegations directed solely at someone else. If, however, the allegations directly or inferentially target the responsive pleader, a response is required.

Special Matters

Rule 9 requires that certain matters be denied more specifically, such as the capacity of a party to sue or be sued, the legal existence of a party, the authority of a party to sue or be sued in a representative capacity, the occurrence or performance of conditions precedent, the issuance of a judgment, or the legality of a document or act.

Fifth Amendment

Where an answer would subject a party to criminal charges or be used as evidence or a link in the evidence in a criminal proceeding, the pleader may refuse to answer by claiming the privilege to be free from self-incrimination, founded in the Fifth Amendment to the United States Constitution.

"Notice" Pleading of Defenses

Courts are divided on what effect *Twombly* and the Rule 8(a) "plausible" pleading mandate (discussed above) may have on defenses. Some courts have ruled that defenses (like claims) must be asserted with sufficient detail to be "plausible;" others reject that view.

RULE 8(c) Affirmative Defenses

In preparing an answer, responsive pleaders must include any "affirmative defenses" they wish to assert. An affirmative defense is a *fact* that is offered by the responding party that would, if proven true, avoid or reduce an opponent's claim for relief. Failing to plead such defenses risks waiving them.

PRACTICING LAW UNDER THIS SUBPART

Definition of Affirmative Defense

An affirmative defense (or "avoidance," an infrequently used common law term) is a defensive assertion of new facts or arguments that, if found to be true, would defeat or reduce the claim even if the claim's allegations are proven true. Consider the affirmative defense of statute of limitations, for example: a patient suing her doctor for medical malpractice could have all the evidence needed to persuade a jury that she was hurt by her doctor's negligence, yet still lose because she waited too long to file.

Burden of Proving Affirmative Defenses

The party raising an affirmative defense has the burden of proving it. *See Taylor v. Sturgell*, 553 U.S. 880, 907 (2008).

Burden of Pleading Affirmative Defenses

The party proposing to prove an affirmative defense also has the burden of pleading it by asserting it in response to the relevant pleading (if that pleading is one that allows a response). The goal of this requirement, consistent with federal pleading generally, is to provide notice to the opponent, avoid surprise and undue prejudice, and afford the opponent a chance to argue, if able, why the defense is unfounded. *See Blonder-Tongue Labs., Inc. v. University of Illinois Found.*, 402 U.S. 313, 350 (1971).

Properly Pleading Affirmative Defenses

The pleaders' duty is to "affirmatively state" their avoidances and affirmative defenses in their responsive pleading. Affirmative defenses should be labeled as such and pleaded in separate paragraphs. Unlike claims (which are governed by Rule 8(a)), Rule 8(c) does not require that affirmative defenses or avoidances make an entitlement "showing." Courts are divided on whether the *Twombly* "plausibility" standard (discussed above) governs the pleading of affirmative defenses. *See* William M. Janssen, *The Odd State of Twiqbal Plausibility in Pleading Affirmative Defenses*, 70 WASH. & LEE L. REV. 1573 (2013) (collecting and cataloguing cases). Courts that require "plausibly"-pleaded affirmative defenses have found that some affirmative defenses may be "plausibly" pleaded quite simply, while other affirmative defenses need a more detailed description. In any event, bald, laundry lists of affirmative defenses are always vulnerable to dismissal.

But No Duty to Respond to Affirmative Defenses

Although the party asserting them must plead affirmative defenses, there is no duty (absent a court order) on the party opposing affirmative defenses to answer or otherwise counter-plead to them. Instead, the Rules deem any affirmative defenses automatically denied or avoided.

Enumerated Affirmative Defenses

Rule 8(c) contains a *non-exhaustive* list of defenses that must be pleaded affirmatively. *See Jones v. Bock,* 549 U.S. 199, 212 (2007). That list includes: accord and satisfaction, arbitration and award, assumption of risk, contributory negligence, duress, estoppel, failure of consideration, fraud, illegality, injury by fellow servant, laches, license, payment, release, res judicata, statute of frauds, statute of limitations, and waiver.

Unenumerated Affirmative Defenses

A particular defense's absence from the Rule 8(c) list does not necessarily mean it will not be considered an affirmative defense for purposes of this Rule. In fact, whether a defense is an affirmative one or not can sometimes be quite unclear. Resolving that question involves a circumstance-dependent, fact-specific inquiry, for which the courts have developed several different tests: whether that defense would bar the right to relief even if the plaintiff's allegations were admitted or proven true (perhaps the most familiar, classical definition); whether the defendant would bear the burden of proving that defense; whether that defense involves an element necessary or extrinsic to plaintiff's cause of action or would merely controvert the plaintiff's proof; or whether a failure to plead it affirmatively would deprive the plaintiff of an opportunity to rebut the defense or adjust litigation strategy to meet it.

Waiver (Forfeiture)

An affirmative defense that is not timely pleaded may be deemed lost (or, as it is often phrased by the courts, "waived" or "forfeited"). *See Day v. McDonough*, 547 U.S. 198, 202 (2006). But waiver does not follow inexorably. Waiver may be excused where the unpleaded affirmative defense is later raised without bad faith, dilatory motive, or prejudice to any other party, where it comes to the timely notice of the other party through different means, or where it is actually tried with the parties' implied consent. Waiver may also be excused where the "interests of justice" so warrant and where the defense was raised at a "pragmatically sufficient time." Thus, for example, in an appropriate case, an affirmative defense asserted for the first time by motion for summary judgment may be treated by the court as a motion to amend the defendant's answer, which would prevent waiver. Notwithstanding this general liberality, trial courts enjoy broad discretion, and their decisions will not usually be disturbed unless they are unreasonable. In exercising their discretion, the courts remain vigilant to protect the plaintiff against being "ambushed" by an unpleaded affirmative defense. For this reason, waiver is likely to be found where a pleader unexplainably delays in asserting a known or knowable affirmative defense, or where the pleader relies on a contentless "failure-to-state-a-claim" placeholder to rescue some specific but unasserted affirmative defense. If waived, an affirmative defense ordinarily cannot be later revived by asserting it during subsequent motion practice. *See Wood v. Milyard*, 566 U.S. 463, 470 (2012) ("affirmative defense, once forfeited, is 'exclu[ded] from the case' ").

Raising Affirmative Defenses *Sua Sponte*

Some courts have held that certain defenses—such as *res judicata* and collateral estoppel—may, in certain instances, be raised by the court *sua sponte,* mindful of the strong public interest in conserving scarce judicial resources by avoiding improper relitigations. Otherwise, courts will usually resist raising affirmative defenses *sua sponte.*

RULE 8(d) Pleading to Be Concise and Direct; Alternative Statements; Inconsistency

This subpart, along with Rule 8(e), emphasizes just how liberally the Rules treat the pleading stage. Whether a pleader is stating a claim for relief or responding to one, the Rules expect all pleadings to be stated in a simple, direct, and concise manner. No technical pleading form is needed. Pleadings may include claims or defenses that are asserted alternatively, hypothetically, and even inconsistently (subject, of course, to the pleader's Rule 11 duty to plead honestly).

PRACTICING LAW UNDER THIS SUBPART

Simple, Concise, and Direct

All pleaded allegations must be short, concise, and direct. While mere verbosity or excessive length is unlikely, alone, to prompt a dismissal, a pleading may be dismissed (or an amendment required) if the pleading is so convoluted that a court cannot discern a meritorious claim or defense. If the convoluted pleading is not thereafter remedied, it can be dismissed with prejudice and without further right of re-pleading.

Alternative, Hypothetical, and Inconsistent Pleadings

Statements of claims or defenses may be asserted in the alternative, hypothetically, and even inconsistently. Such inconsistent pleading may occur when legitimate doubt exists as to the true facts (every pleading, including alternative, hypothetical, and inconsistent ones, must still abide by the obligations set in Rule 11). Thus, for example, a pleader often may allege an unjust enrichment claim as an alternative to a breach of contract claim, unless the existence of a valid, enforceable contract is uncontested or the equity claim is foreclosed for other reasons. Of course, at trial, the pleader cannot recover on both inconsistent theories. Moreover, the court must be able to readily identify claims or defenses that are pleaded alternatively, hypothetically, or inconsistently. Although no "magic words" are required, it must be reasonably obvious from the pleading itself that such claims or defenses are being asserted. While separate inconsistent *claims* and *defenses* are permitted under the Rules, the factual allegations *within* each claim or defense cannot be inconsistent with the alleged right of recovery, or else the claim or defense could defeat itself. Finally, although pleaders may plead in the alternative, they may not, in the pithy admonishment of one court, "plead in the ambiguous." *See Joe Hand Promotions, Inc. v. Creative Entm't, LLC,* 978 F.Supp.2d 1236, 1240 (M.D. Fla. 2013). At least one of the alternative allegations must meet the requisite pleading standards.

Inconsistent Pleadings as Admissions

Because Rule 8(d) protects a party's right to plead inconsistent claims and defenses, statements made in claims or defenses cannot generally be offered as admissions against other claims or defenses within the same pleading that contain inconsistent or alternative averments. However, unequivocal averments of fact, made *within* a particular claim or defense, may constitute judicial admissions that conclusively bind the pleader throughout the litigation. Additionally, if the positions taken by the pleader are accepted by the court, the pleader may be foreclosed by judicial estoppel from taking an inconsistent, contrary position in later proceedings.

RULE 8(e) | Construing Pleadings

This closing subpart highlights the commitment of the Rules to ensure that pleadings are construed liberally, provided of course that they provide the adverse party with proper notice of what is being alleged.

PRACTICING LAW UNDER THIS SUBPART

All Pleadings Construed Liberally

One fundamental tenor and philosophy of the Rules is liberality over technicality. Because Rule 8(e) requires the courts to construe pleadings "as to do justice," all pleadings are construed liberally. In federal practice, form is never exalted over substance, and courts are watchful that drafting mistakes alone do not deny a party justice. Each pleading is examined as a whole. In testing federal pleadings, the familiar contract law principle of construing documents against their drafters is not applied. Courts will not rely solely on the labels used by the pleader to describe claims or defenses, but may reach deeper and seek out the true substance of the allegations. Where those allegations, so construed, would state a cognizable claim or defense, the requirements of Rule 8 may be satisfied.

But No Unwarranted Constructions

Although pleadings are liberally construed, the court must still "do justice." A pleading will not be given so unwarrantedly generous a reading that it prejudices another party or denies a party fair notice of a claim or defense. Courts are, thus, not obligated to invent for the pleader a claim or defense not present on a fair reading of the pleading, nor need they grant a pleader a type of relief not fairly demanded within the pleading (especially when doing so will cause prejudice).

Pleadings Drafted by Laypersons

Courts generally apply less stringent standards to pleadings drafted by laypersons, such as *pro se* habeas corpus petitions and social security applications. *See Erickson v. Pardus,* 551 U.S. 89, 94 (2007) (per curiam). But nothing in this liberality obliges the court to redraft a *pro se* pleading.

9(a) Special Damages:

- Special Damages → damages that cover further costs & consequences from an action that must be specially pleaded or are thus waived (lost wages, value of any lost time, value of lost earning capacity)
  - * actually realized (so factually occurred)
  - * reasonable certainty (in being proven
- General Damages → just damages that flow from the wrongful act (pain & suffering is a natural consequence flowing)
  - * if predictable, it's general damages
  - * if not predictable = special damages

9(b) Fraud/Mistake/Mind Conditions: (malice, intent, knowledge)

- must be pled with particularity
- describe the circumstances constituting the mistake → who, what, when, where, how, precise nature
- if P does not plead w/ particularity, court should allow them to ammend the complaint, unless allowing the amendment would be futile or not cure the deficiency

↳ must say precisely the nature of the mistake, who made the mistake, and when

PARTICULARITY for fraud/mistake

RULE 9

PLEADING SPECIAL MATTERS

(a) Capacity or Authority to Sue; Legal Existence.

(1) *In General.* Except when required to show that the court has jurisdiction, a pleading need not allege:

(A) a party's capacity to sue or be sued;

(B) a party's authority to sue or be sued in a representative capacity; or

(C) the legal existence of an organized association of persons that is made a party.

(2) *Raising Those Issues.* To raise any of those issues, a party must do so by a specific denial, which must state any supporting facts that are peculiarly within the party's knowledge.

(b) Fraud or Mistake; Conditions of Mind. In alleging fraud or mistake, a party must state with particularity the circumstances constituting fraud or mistake. Malice, intent, knowledge, and other conditions of a person's mind may be alleged generally.

(c) Conditions Precedent. In pleading conditions precedent, it suffices to allege generally that all conditions precedent have occurred or been performed. But when denying that a condition precedent has occurred or been performed, a party must do so with particularity.

(d) Official Document or Act. In pleading an official document or official act, it suffices to allege that the document was legally issued or the act legally done.

(e) Judgment. In pleading a judgment or decision of a domestic or foreign court, a judicial or quasi-judicial tribunal, or a board or officer, it suffices to plead the judgment or decision without showing jurisdiction to render it.

(f) Time and Place. An allegation of time or place is material when testing the sufficiency of a pleading.

(g) Special Damages. If an item of special damage is claimed, it must be specifically stated.

(h) Admiralty or Maritime Claim.

(1) *How Designated.* If a claim for relief is within the admiralty or maritime jurisdiction and also within the court's subject-matter jurisdiction on some other ground, the pleading may designate the claim as an admiralty or maritime claim for purposes of Rules 14(c), 38(e), and 82 and the Supplemental Rules for Admiralty or Maritime Claims and Asset

Forfeiture Actions. A claim cognizable only in the admiralty or maritime jurisdiction is an admiralty or maritime claim for those purposes, whether or not so designated.

(2) *Designation for Appeal.* A case that includes an admiralty or maritime claim within this subdivision (h) is an admiralty case within 28 U.S.C. § 1292(a)(3).

[Amended effective July 1, 1966; July 1, 1968; July 1, 1970; August 1, 1987, April 11, 1997, effective December 1, 1997; April 12, 2006, effective December 1, 2006; April 30, 2007, effective December 1, 2007.]

UNDERSTANDING RULE 9

HOW RULE 9 FITS IN

Rule 9 is the companion to Rule 8, and those two Rules should be read together. Rule 8 sets out the general requirements for pleading claims and defenses. Rule 9 adjusts and supplements those general requirements for certain circumstances. So, in sum, the federal pleader's equation is this: follow the directions in Rule 8 *unless* Rule 9 (or some other Rule or statute) instructs otherwise.

The adjustments in Rule 9 are few in number but important. They reinforce how generally most facts can be pleaded (such as intent, knowledge, conditions precedent, official documents and acts, and judgments). Then, they isolate certain facts that must be pleaded with greater detail (like fraud, mistake, and special damages, or when contesting capacity to sue or conditions precedent). And they specify the manner for invoking the federal courts' admiralty or maritime jurisdiction.

THE ARCHITECTURE OF RULE 9

Rule 9 is separated into eight subparts. For ease of use, those subparts can be grouped into four functional categories. First, the Rule identifies those facts that must be pleaded with an enhanced level of specificity (Rules 9(a)(2), (b), (c), and (g)). Second, the Rule reconfirms those facts that are properly pleaded in a general manner (Rule 9(a)(1), (b), (c), (d), and (e)). Third, the Rule permits any allegation of time or place to be considered in testing a pleading's adequacy (Rule 9(f)). Fourth, the Rule explains the manner for invoking admiralty or maritime jurisdiction (Rule 9(h)).

HOW RULE 9 WORKS IN PRACTICE

These eight subparts of Rule 9 are discussed, in order, below.

RULE 9(a) Capacity or Authority to Sue; Legal Existence

Pleaders ordinarily do not need to allege a party's legally-recognized capacity or authority to sue or be sued, nor an association's legal existence. For example, a partnership need not allege that it is a lawful partnership which is permitted, under the governing law, to sue or be sued in its partnership name. Likewise, a pleader that is suing a limited liability corporation (LLC) need not allege that the LLC is capable of being sued in its organizational name. Importantly, an adversary can challenge both these premises (namely, that the partnership can sue and that the LLC can be sued), but if the adversary intends to do so, some additional pleading obligations apply.

PRACTICING LAW UNDER THIS SUBPART

Exception—When Necessary to Show Jurisdiction

Notwithstanding this general rule, a party's capacity or authority to sue, or an association's legal existence, *must* be pleaded if necessary to establish the subject-matter jurisdiction of the federal courts.

Procedure for *Challenging* Capacity

Ordinarily, a litigant seeking to challenge (a) a party's legal existence, (b) a party's capacity to sue or be sued, or (c) a party's authority to sue or be sued in a representative capacity must raise the issue by specific denial in a responsive pleading or pre-answer motion to dismiss. The required "specific denial" does not always obligate the pleader to spell out in detail why capacity is lacking; but the pleader must include all specific facts that are "peculiarly" within that party's knowledge. The purpose of this pleading duty is to place the adversary on appropriate notice of the capacity defense. Once pleaded, there is no further duty on the party challenging capacity to file an early dispositive motion on the issue.

Waiver of Challenges to Capacity

The defense of lack of capacity or authority to sue or be sued, or an association's legal existence, is usually waived if not timely and specifically pleaded. Waiver may be excused if the defense is tried by consent, affirmatively apparent from the face of the complaint and a specific denial is unnecessary, was raised at the pragmatically earliest time, or where the court finds a lack of prejudice under the circumstances of the delay. If, however, the defense affects the court's subject-matter jurisdiction, a party may assert that defense at any time or the court may raise it *sua sponte*.

RULE 9(b) Fraud or Mistake; Conditions of Mind

Pleaders alleging fraud (whether as a claim or defense) must do so "with particularity." The same is true for allegations of mistake. But all other "conditions of the mind"—such as malice, intent, or knowledge—need only be pleaded generally.

PRACTICING LAW UNDER THIS SUBPART

Why Require "Particularity"?

Some claims—like fraud—may have an *in terrorem* or stigmatizing effect on defendants and their reputations, and can be easily fabricated (because the evidence is frequently circumstantial). The courts expect pleaders to perform a greater pre-complaint investigation in such cases, to ensure that any such claim is responsibly supported and not defaming or extortionate. This practice also allows an early and informed response from the party defending against such accusations, and guards against lawsuits filed in the unsubstantiated hope of discovering an unknown wrong (*i.e.*, to disincentivize a "sue first, ask questions later" strategy). It helps to ensure that only viable claims of fraud or mistake are permitted to proceed to discovery. Thus, requiring that such claims be pleaded with particularity (1) ensures that the defendants have fair notice of the plaintiff's claim, (2) helps safeguard the defendants against spurious accusations and resulting reputational harm, (3) reduces the possibility that a meritless fraud claim can remain in the case, by ensuring that the full and complete factual allegation is not postponed until discovery, and (4) protects defendants against "strike" suits.

Amount of Particularity Required

The amount of particularity or specificity required for pleading fraud or mistake will differ from case to case, but generally depends upon the amount of access the pleader has to the specific facts, considering the complexity of the claim, the relationship of the parties, the context in which the alleged fraud or mistake occurs, and the amount of specificity necessary for the adverse party to prepare a responsive pleading.

The particularity requirement of Rule 9 is not, however, intended to abrogate or mute the Rule 8 "notice" pleading standard that applies in federal courts, and the two Rules must be read harmoniously. Plaintiffs are still obligated to plead only "notice" of a fraud or mistake claim (viewed, as are all claims, through the *Twombly* "plausibility" lens). Neither exhaustive particularity nor a showing of evidentiary proofs is needed. But Rule 9(b) plainly compels a higher degree of notice. Thus, in fraud and mistake claims, pleaders usually must supply the "newspaper-first-paragraph"—the "who, what, when, where, and how" of the alleged scheme or mistake. This "newspaper-paragraph" requirement, however, is not applied with great rigidity, so long as precision and substantiation are somehow injected into the pleading. Omniscience is not required, but nor is conclusory pleading acceptable. The particularity requirement must be met in the pleading itself; generally, courts will not consider after-the-fact elaborations in briefs and memoranda when testing particularity.

Fraud

Pleaders are obligated to place fraud defendants on notice of the "precise misconduct" with which they are accused. Each of the elements of the alleged fraud must be pleaded with particularity. More is required than mere conclusory allegations of plans or schemes, or a bald recitation of the technical elements of fraud or facts that show only that a fraud could have been possible. Thus, courts often require the pleader to allege (1) the time, place, and contents of the false representations or omissions, and explain how they were fraudulent, (2) the identity of the person making the misrepresentations, (3) how the misrepresentations misled the plaintiff, and (4) what the speaker gained from the fraud. In the end, the pleaded facts must give rise to a "strong inference" of fraud to comport with Rule 9(b). (Ordinarily, however, it is only the *circumstances* of the fraud that must be pleaded with particularity; as for all other facts, the less demanding standard of Rule 8 applies.) Any fraud averment that does not meet this standard is likely to be stricken or dismissed.

- *Claims "Grounded" in Fraud:* The "particularity" requirement of Rule 9(b) applies not only to claims expressly denominated as "fraud" allegations, but also to claims that are "grounded" in or "sound" in fraud, including misrepresentation (but only when it "sounds" in fraud), fraudulent inducement or concealment, forgery, breach of fiduciary duty involving fraud, aiding and abetting a fraud, and other claims involving deceptive conduct.

- *Federal Statutory Fraud Claims:* Generally, the "particularity" requirement of Rule 9(b) applies equally to both federal statutory fraud and common law fraud, and may be enhanced by Congress still further, as it has been with federal securities fraud claims.
- *State Law Fraud Claims:* The "particularity" requirement applies to State-law fraud claims as well.

Mistake

A party must also plead mistake with particularity. This obligates the pleader to plead with particularity the circumstances constituting the mistake—the "who, what, when, where, and how" of the mistake, which likely includes the precise nature of the mistake, who made the mistake, and when.

No Common Law Additions to Rule 9(b)'s List

Rule 9(b) requires that only fraud and mistake be pleaded with particularity. It is now quite clear that courts are not permitted to add to this list and require, through case-made edict, that other types of claims be pleaded with particularity. *See Leatherman v. Tarrant Cty. Narcotics Intelligence & Coordination Unit*, 507 U.S. 163, 168 (1993).

Malice, Intent, Knowledge, and Condition of Mind

A party may allege malice, intent, knowledge, and condition of mind generally, as with any ordinary allegation under Rule 8. But this concept of tolerable "generality" is a relative one. Although the enhanced pleading obligations of Rule 9(b) do not apply, the Rule 8 requirements of *Twombly* "plausibility" still do, and the pleaded allegations must give rise to an inference of the requisite state of mind.

Pleading Tensions Between Fraud and Intent

There is internal tension between Rule 9(b)'s requirement that fraud—which ordinarily requires an intent to deceive—be pleaded with particularity, and Rule 9(b)'s companion provision that intent itself may be pleaded generally. Courts usually resolve this apparent inconsistency by requiring that when the claim is based upon allegations of fraud, the party must plead the fraud with particularity, and then intent generally.

Group Pleading in Fraud Cases

The particularized pleading requirement is designed to notify each defendant of his, her, or its purported role in the alleged misconduct. Lumping multiple defendants together in a group pleading (*e.g.*, "defendants misled the plaintiff by stating that . . .") may defeat this notice objective and, thus, may be found to be improper under Rule 9(b). Although the courts might not require a pleader to always parse each fact and attribute every false statement to a particular defendant (especially in cases alleging conspiracy), the pleader will be obligated to notify each defendant as to how he or she is alleged to have participated in the fraud.

Fraud / Mistake in Counterclaims and Affirmative Defenses

When asserting fraud or mistake in counterclaims or affirmative defenses, the pleader must assert fraud or mistake there with particularity.

Non-Party Fraud or Mistake

Where fraud or mistake was committed by nonparties or when alleging that nonparties were defrauded, a party may plead that fraud or mistake more generally.

Opposing an Insufficiently Particularized Pleading

A party may challenge a pleading that fails to plead fraud or mistake with particularity by filing a Rule 12(e) motion for a more definite statement, a Rule 12(f) motion to strike, or a Rule 12(b) motion to dismiss. Often, parties assert all these motions in the alternative. The Rule 9(b) particularity requirement is ordinarily not testable later at the summary judgment stage, since by that time the requirement's goal (supplying the detail necessary for the opponent to frame an informed defense) has likely become mooted.

Granting Leave to Amend

Where a complaint is dismissed for failing to allege with particularity, leave to amend should generally be granted freely, unless an amendment is futile and would not cure the particularity deficiency.

Constitutionality of Enhanced Pleading

Any enhanced pleading duty necessarily carries with it the risk that, on occasion, it might cause the dismissal of a valid claim which, had the claim been permitted to reach discovery, could have found sound evidentiary support. The Supreme Court considered this possibility and, citing the authority of Congress and the Rules' drafters to adopt special pleading procedures, found no Seventh Amendment (jury right) impediment. *See Tellabs, Inc. v. Makor Issues & Rights, Ltd.*, 551 U.S. 308, 327 n.9 (2007).

RULE 9(c) Conditions Precedent

A "condition precedent" is an act or event that must occur before some legal consequence takes effect. For example, a condition precedent to a sale of real estate might be a satisfactory examination of the property performed by a licensed home inspector; a condition precedent to a contract for the sale of a car might be the delivery of that car in satisfactory condition to the buyer's home. Pleaders may be obligated, under the governing law, to allege that all conditions precedent have occurred before they are entitled to a remedy. Rule 9(c) permits pleaders to make these allegations generally. However, a *challenge* to the occurrence of a condition precedent must be set forth *specifically* and with particularity.

PRACTICING LAW UNDER THIS SUBPART

Applies to Both Contractual and Statutory Conditions

The pleading practice set forth in Rule 9(c) for conditions precedent applies whether the conditions precedent are contractual or statutory in nature.

Duty to Plead Conditions Precedent

Courts are divided on what pleading duty Rule 9(c) imposes. Some interpret Rule 9(c) as imposing no affirmative duty to allege the performance of conditions precedent at all. Those courts view Rule 9(c) as simply setting forth the procedure for alleging such performance if the pleader chooses to do so. Other courts read Rule 9(c) as affirmatively imposing a duty to plead such performance, albeit in a general fashion. When the pleading of the performance of conditions precedent is required (whether by so interpreting Rule 9(c) or by dictate of some other law), a failure to so plead may prompt a dismissal (usually without prejudice).

General Allegations Sufficient to *Plead* Conditions

When performance of conditions precedent is pleaded, that pleading need not allege in detail how each condition was performed; the allegations are usually sufficient if they aver generally that all conditions precedent have been performed. Such a pleading would be very brief, simply tracking the text of Rule 9(c). Other courts require more, such as pleading those facts from which an inference arises that all conditions precedent have been performed.

- *"Plausibility" Pleading:* Courts are divided on whether *Twombly* plausibility applies to Rule 9(c). Some courts accept only non-conclusory, factually-specific pleading of conditions precedent, while others allow very general averments to suffice.
- *Applies to All Claimants:* The "allege-generally" right seems to apply to all types of claimants, including counterclaim, crossclaim, and third-party claim pleaders.
- *Allegation Can Support a Dismissal:* If a pleader elects to do more than plead generally, the added specificity the pleader includes can be used, where appropriate, to justify the claim's dismissal.

Specific Allegations Necessary to *Deny* Conditions

Where a defendant seeks to challenge a plaintiff's allegation that a condition precedent has been fulfilled, the denial must be pleaded with specificity and particularity. A failure to so plead deems admitted the allegation that conditions precedent were satisfied. Courts may, however, construe a defendant's attempt at denial leniently, and accept an imperfect denial if it imparts fair notice and imposes no unfair prejudice. Once a condition precedent has been adequately contested by the pleading, the burden returns to the plaintiff to prove that the condition precedent contested by the defendant has been met.

RULE 9(d) Official Document or Act

A party asserting the existence or legality of an official document need only assert that the official document was issued legally or the official act was performed legally. Conversely, a party opposing the official document or act must specifically assert the defect in the official document or the illegality of the official act.

RULE 9(e) Judgment

When pleading the issuance of any judgment or decision, a pleader need not also set forth matter showing the jurisdictional authority of the tribunal issuing the judgment. Instead, the pleader should specifically identify the judicial body issuing the judgment, the date of the judgment, the parties participating in the proceeding, and the character or effect of the judgment. A party resisting such a judgment should do so specifically, not generally, by alleging the particular defect in the judgment.

RULE 9(f) Time and Place

Pleaders are not required under either Rule 8 or Rule 9 to specifically allege time or place (although the governing law for the particular type of claim or defense the pleader is asserting may impose such an obligation). Rule 9(f) has a different function. It confirms that, anytime time or place is pleaded, those averments are considered material, and, therefore, can be examined in testing the sufficiency of a pleading. Thus, for example, if the pleaded averments of time or place establish an obvious defense (such as time-bar), the inclusion of those averments can support a Rule 12(b)(6) dismissal.

RULE 9(g) Special Damages

The term "special damages" refers to a particular type of remedy. When the pleader is seeking "special damages," the allegation must be pleaded with particularity.

PRACTICING LAW UNDER THIS SUBPART

Purpose

The obligation to plead special damages with specificity is designed to alert the defending parties to the nature of those damages (thus avoiding trial surprise by the extent or character of the claim) and to ensure the court is advised of the claim.

What Are "Special Damages"?

Identifying special damages is not always clear. "General" damages are the usual, ordinary, natural, direct, and proximate consequences of a defendant's conduct, and thus are inferable from the conduct alleged. By contrast, "special" damages are those that, though perhaps natural and not unexpected, are not necessarily the predictable, inevitable consequences of a defendant's conduct, and thus are not obviously inferable. Special damages depend on the peculiar context of the dispute. For example, in a trespass action, general damages encompass injury to the land itself whereas special damages might include impacts on plaintiff's intended plans for that land. Because they are not obviously inferable, an intent to pursue special damages might not come to the defendant's attention unless pleaded with specificity. Emotional distress damages, defamation damages, business destruction and loss of good will, and damages flowing from trade disparagement often denominated as special damages, and, thus, must be pleaded with specificity. Attorney's fees have traditionally been categorized as special damages, although some recent authority distinguishes between fees recoverable as an element of the underlying substantive claim (likely to be special damages) and fees recoverable under a cost-shifting regimen (likely to not be). Liquidated damages typically are not special damages. In diversity cases, what constitutes special damages is determined by the pertinent State's law.

Pleading with "Specificity"

A party must plead special damages by alleging the claimed actual damages with particularity and by averring how those damages were the natural and direct result of the defendant's conduct. This obligation is not reducible to a precise formula, and will depend on the nature of the claim at issue, the alleged injury, and the causal connection between the two. Averments must be sufficiently specific to allow the opponent to meaningfully respond. Consequently, vague, conclusory catch-all allegations (such as broadly-grouping language like "including but not limited to") are unlikely to be sufficient under Rule 9(g), nor are rounded figures and general dollar amounts. An appropriate statement of special damages will generally also include an estimate of the total damages, along with a listing of the specific items that comprise that sum. Conversely, a conclusory declaration that a party was "damaged" and that "business" was "curtail[ed]" will generally be found inadequate.

Consequences of Failing to Plead Special Damages

A party's failure to plead special damages with specificity may bar that party's recovery of those damages. However, because there is no timing requirement in the Rule, a party can often seek leave from the court to amend to include items of special damages in a pleading. Moreover, because the goal is to protect against unfair surprise, the court may excuse (or at least liberally construe) a weakly pleaded special damages allegation if those damages were not an essential element of the underlying claim or where the opponent was not actually prejudiced by the absence of further specificity.

RULE 9(h) Admiralty and Maritime Claims

The U.S. Constitution confers federal subject-matter jurisdiction in "all Cases of admiralty and maritime Jurisdiction." U.S. Const. art. III. For many years, admiralty and maritime cases had their own rules of procedure. In 1966, those rules were merged into the Federal Rules of Civil Procedure, with seven special provisions preserved for admiralty and maritime cases. (The text of those seven provisions, the "Supplemental Rules for Admiralty or Maritime Claims and Asset Forfeiture Actions," is reprinted at the end of the Rules.) To be eligible to have admiralty or maritime rules apply, a pleader must designate the claim as one invoking the federal admiralty or maritime jurisdiction.

PRACTICING LAW UNDER THIS SUBPART

Election to Proceed in Admiralty/Maritime

In filing an admiralty or maritime claim, a plaintiff may have a choice to make—to proceed using the special admiralty procedures or not. When the only basis for federal jurisdiction is admiralty jurisdiction, there is no choice; admiralty procedures apply automatically. But when an admiralty dispute also has another basis for federal jurisdiction (*e.g.*, diversity), the claimant has a right to elect how to proceed. If a claimant invokes both admiralty and another basis for jurisdiction, the claim will likely proceed in admiralty. This right of election is determined claim-by-claim; non-admiralty claims are not converted into admiralty claims merely by being joined with admiralty claims, nor will a claim cognizable in both admiralty and diversity jurisdiction lose its ability to proceed in diversity merely by being joined with an admiralty-only claim (provided that claim has invoked only a non-admiralty basis for jurisdiction). This admiralty election is not necessarily irrevocable; a claimant can always request leave to amend (on such a motion, the court will consider whether the claimant took an unfair advantage of the original election or otherwise prejudiced the other parties).

Significance of Election: Admiralty Procedures

An announced intent to proceed in admiralty or maritime jurisdiction is not, of course, dispositive of the question whether such jurisdiction exists. *See Jerome B. Grubart, Inc. v. Great Lakes Dredge & Dock Co.*, 513 U.S. 527, 533–34 (1995). Nor does it necessarily determine whether admiralty or maritime law governs. Rather, choosing to proceed in admiralty is merely the means by which pleaders claim access to those special procedures that have, historically, attached to actions in admiralty.

Significance of Election: No Jury Trial

Ordinarily, choosing to proceed in admiralty means that the claims in the case are decided by the court, and not by a jury (it thus defeats any right by a defendant to demand a jury trial). Beyond these bright-line principles, the availability of a jury trial in admiralty proceedings is "unduly complex." The U.S. Supreme Court has ruled that while the Seventh Amendment does not compel jury trials in admiralty cases, neither does it (or any other constitutional provision) prohibit them. *See Fitzgerald v. U. S. Lines Co.*, 374 U.S. 16, 20 (1963). The ramifications of that conclusion can be far-reaching. For example, if a plaintiff demands a jury trial in a case that invoked jurisdiction both in admiralty and on a second basis, that jury demand will be honored (so long as the plaintiff is not found to have elected to proceed in admiralty). When a plaintiff joins two claims (an admiralty-only one with a non-admiralty one), convening a jury trial for the entire proceeding is not improper if the claims "arise out of one set of facts" and splitting them would prove "cumbersome, confusing, and time consuming." *See id.* When a counterclaim is asserted against an original claim that had invoked admiralty jurisdiction, the result is less certain: courts are divided on whether the plaintiff's admiralty election deprives the counterclaim of its right to a jury trial. If the counterclaim's jury demand is honored, it is also possible that the effect of that ruling could force even the original admiralty claim into a jury trial. Other joinder contexts invite still more uncertainties. It also seems that parties can, by agreement, consent to a jury trial that would not otherwise exist in an admiralty proceeding.

Type of Designation Required

The purpose of the designation requirement is to alert the court and fellow parties that the plaintiff intends to proceed under the admiralty rules. To do so, the plaintiff must include an affirmative statement in the pleadings expressing the intent to have the lawsuit proceed as an admiralty or maritime case. Obviously, merely announcing a Rule 9(h) election will not convert a non-admiralty claim into an admiralty claim, though *failing* to make the designation will mean that the claim is not proceeding in admiralty. A plaintiff need not specifically incant a citation to Rule 9(h), although that is certainly the preferred practice; instead, a simple statement invoking the right to proceed in admiralty is usually sufficient. The absence of a jury demand is one indication that the party intends to proceed in admiralty. When the plaintiff's intent is unclear (*e.g.*, affirmatively asserting both admiralty and another basis for jurisdiction), some courts will honor the admiralty designation notwithstanding the ambiguity.

RULE 10

FORM OF PLEADINGS

(a) Caption; Names of Parties. Every pleading must have a caption with the court's name, a title, a file number, and a Rule 7(a) designation. The title of the complaint must name all the parties; the title of other pleadings, after naming the first party on each side, may refer generally to other parties.

(b) Paragraphs; Separate Statements. A party must state its claims or defenses in numbered paragraphs, each limited as far as practicable to a single set of circumstances. A later pleading may refer by number to a paragraph in an earlier pleading. If doing so would promote clarity, each claim founded on a separate transaction or occurrence—and each defense other than a denial—must be stated in a separate count or defense.

(c) Adoption by Reference; Exhibits. A statement in a pleading may be adopted by reference elsewhere in the same pleading or in any other pleading or motion. A copy of a written instrument that is an exhibit to a pleading is a part of the pleading for all purposes.

[Amended April 30, 2007, effective December 1, 2007.]

UNDERSTANDING RULE 10

HOW RULE 10 FITS IN

This is another of the pleadings rules. The required substantive content for pleadings is addressed elsewhere (Rules 8 and 9). The types of permitted pleadings are set out in Rule 7. The obligation of pleading ethically is covered by Rule 11.

Rule 10 focuses more mundanely on form. It mandates that pleadings all must begin with a "caption" (or heading)—identifying the litigants' names, the court, the document's title, and a court docketing number. It directs that claims and defenses be set forth in numbered paragraphs, with each paragraph limited to a single set of circumstances. It permits the use of separate "counts" for claims or defenses premised on a separate transaction or occurrence, when doing so would promote clarity. Earlier paragraphs may be adopted by reference (*i.e.*, cross-referenced) to avoid repetition, and exhibits may be attached to pleadings.

THE ARCHITECTURE OF RULE 10

Rule 10 is brief, separated into three subparts that are organized simply. The first requires a caption. The second requires paragraphing of allegations and the possible use of separate counts. The third allows for the pleader to cross-reference back to earlier allegations without repeating them, and directs that any document attached to the pleading is a considered to be a part of the pleading.

HOW RULE 10 WORKS IN PRACTICE

These three subparts of Rule 10 are discussed, in order, below.

RULE 10(a) Captions; Names of Parties

The "caption" (or formal heading) must appear at the start of every pleading and motion.

PRACTICING LAW UNDER THIS SUBPART

Contents of Caption

Captions must contain: (a) the name of the court; (b) the title of the action (including all party names); (c) the file or docket number; and (d) the document's designation (*e.g.*, complaint, answer).

Party Names

The title of every lawsuit must list the names of the parties. In the complaint, the listing must be comprehensive: all parties must be included. Persons and entities not listed there usually are not considered parties to that lawsuit.

- *Actual Names:* The actual, true names of the parties must be supplied. Descriptive titles (without names) may be appropriate, but only when they clearly identify the party. "Alias" names are not permitted, and pleading with them can justify dismissal.
- *After the Complaint:* In all pleadings (and motions) subsequent to the complaint, the caption can be shortened to include only the names of the first plaintiff and first defendant, followed (where necessary) by an indication that others are parties to the case (*e.g.*, "et al.," an abbreviation of a Latin term often used in the law, meaning "and others").
- *Notices of Appeal:* All parties should be listed again in a notice of appeal. Omitting names (for example, with "et al.") may fail to perfect the appeal as to anyone whose intent to appeal is not objectively clear.
- *Errors in Caption:* Captioning errors may be overlooked (or cured by amendment) if the court determines they caused no prejudice and did not compromise the goal of adequate notice.

Fictitious Name and Pseudonym Litigation

Parties have an automatic right to omit "personal data identifiers." Minors, for example, are permitted by right to litigate using only their initials, instead of their full names. Parties may also seek protective orders to grant the redaction of additional personally identifying information when "good cause" exists. *See* Rule 5.2.

In unusual circumstances, courts may permit parties to identify themselves throughout the lawsuit by a fictitious name or pseudonym (*e.g.* "Jane Doe"). Such permission is extraordinary and conflicts with the public's right to open access to the judiciary, a concern of constitutional dimension, and with the right of private litigants to confront their accusers. In fact, some courts recognize a presumption against such pleading, and others have emphasized that parties in civil cases, bringing lawsuits of their own volition to vindicate their own interests, must be prepared to stand publicly behind their allegations. The practice is, therefore, often refused even in cases involving issues of great intimacy and sensitivity.

There are no "hard and fast" rules that courts follow in judging whether to permit pseudonym litigation. Instead, courts balance the plaintiff's interest in anonymity against the public's interest in disclosure and the prejudice that may befall the defendant. In performing this balance, courts have weighed various factors. Some courts have considered: (1) whether anonymity is genuinely based on a desire to preserve privacy in a sensitive, highly personal matter, or merely to avoid the annoyance and criticism that the litigation might trigger; (2) whether loss of anonymity poses a risk of retaliatory physical or mental harm to the litigant or to non-parties; (3) the ages of those seeking anonymity (and particularly whether a child is involved); (4) whether their opponent is a governmental or a private party; and (5) the risk of unfairness to that opponent if anonymity were permitted. Other courts have endorsed different criteria in addition to, or in place of, these factors. But, in any event, most lists seem non-exhaustive in nature, with trial judges discouraged from engaging in a mere mechanical exercise of checking items off a list. To proceed by pseudonym, the party must petition the court for permission. Permission, if granted, may be accompanied by a requirement that the true names of the parties be disclosed to the defendants and the court, but sealed to the general public.

Temporary Fictitious Naming

At the outset of litigation, a party may temporarily identify an opponent with a fictitious name so long as the identities of the opponents are clear and their actual names will be uncovered through discovery.

Alterations to the Caption

Beyond the shortening of party names in filings after the complaint, immaterial alterations to the caption, such as changes in capitalization, fonts, or typefaces, are generally not improper and will not require remedy by the court.

RULE 10(b) Paragraphs; Separate Statements

Pleadings must set out both claims and defenses in separate, numbered paragraphs, each of which, as far as practicable, should contain just a single set of circumstances. Pleadings should contain separate counts for claims arising from different transactions or occurrences, if doing so adds clarity. Defenses (other than denials) should be set forth in separately as well.

PRACTICING LAW UNDER THIS SUBPART

Paragraphing a Pleading's Allegations

The purpose of the requirement of separate, numbered paragraphs is to ensure a pleading that imparts fair notice, one that is easily understood by both the opponent and the court, and one that can be clearly answered. Later pleadings may refer back to an earlier pleading's allegations by their paragraph numbers.

Pleading in Separate Counts

A party may include in a single count all theories of recovery, so long as those theories are all premised on the same facts. The more common practice, however, is to plead distinct claims and theories in separate counts. In any event, where the claims and theories rest on different facts or where clarity otherwise requires it, distinct claims and theories must be pleaded in separate counts. Separate counts help to ensure that the pleadings achieve their goals of framing the issues, providing a platform for informed pretrial proceedings and discovery management, and facilitating evidentiary admissibility decisions at trial. The practice also enables a court to grant dispositive relief with respect to an entire count, and not just part of one. Thus, the dictates of Rule 10 are not intended to be exceptions to the federal practice against technical forms of pleading, but instead provide the guidelines that help ensure that pleadings are "simple, concise, and direct."

Violations and Remedy

Improper paragraph numbering or lack of conciseness will usually not defeat a pleading, unless the violations interfere with the ability to understand the claims or defenses or otherwise cause prejudice. However, when a party's pleading provides insufficient notice of the claims because of its confusing structure, the absence of numbered paragraphs, or the improper combination of multiple claims in a single count, the opposing party may move for a more definite statement, to strike the pleading, or for dismissal. Dismissals should be ordered only where it is virtually impossible to connect an allegation with the claim it is intended to support. All such motions should be made before counter-pleading. The typical initial remedy is an order to replead (or a dismissal with leave to amend).

RULE 10(c) Adoption by Reference; Exhibits

Pleaders sometimes find the need to refer back to allegations made earlier in the same pleading or to repeat facts, claims, or defenses. An obvious but cumbersome way for pleaders to do this would be by repeating the same allegations multiple times. To avoid this page-consuming, inefficient practice, pleaders are permitted to "adopt by reference" portions of their earlier allegations and, thus, to simply direct the reader back to consult earlier paragraphs. Additionally, pleaders may, on occasion, want to draw the judge's attention to a particular document, and may do so by attaching it to their pleading. This is permitted, but the practice has a consequence (one that might prove either helpful or harmful, or both): the attachment is considered to be a *part* of the pleading for all purposes.

PRACTICING LAW UNDER THIS SUBPART

Adopting Paragraphs by Reference

This practice must be used with care. Thoughtlessly adopting wholesale prior sections of a pleading, including portions not germane to the point at issue, violates this Rule.

Adopting Documents or Pleadings by Reference

A party may adopt documents or pleadings (in whole or in part) by reference so long as the adopted document or pleading is expressly named. Generally, this practice is limited to documents and pleadings that are already before the court. Documents or pleadings filed in another lawsuit usually cannot be adopted by reference, nor may parts of an abandoned pleading.

Attaching Exhibits

A party may (but is not required to) attach to a pleading copies of "written instruments," such as contracts, notes, legal documents, and other writings on which a claim or defense is based.

- *Unusual Attachments:* Exhibits that are especially lengthy or that contain evidentiary matter (such as deposition transcripts) may not quality for attachment. Similarly, newspaper articles, commentaries, and cartoons, cryptic memo notes, photographs and x-rays, investigative reports, expert reports, affidavits, and copies of superseded pleadings may also not qualify. However, emails, text messages, video recordings, briefs, and court rulings may be proper.
- *Attachments by Opponent:* If the pleader does *not* attach, but instead merely refers to, a written instrument in the pleading, the opponent may usually then attach that instrument to the responsive pleading, so long as the instrument is indisputably authentic and "central" to the original pleader's claim.

Effect of Attaching Exhibits

Exhibits attached to a pleading are made a part of that pleading for all purposes.

- *Ruling on Motions to Dismiss:* The court may consider a pleading's attachments in ruling on dismissal motions. If an inconsistency exists between the attachment and the pleaded allegations, the attachment will often control (unless the pleaded allegations are specific, well-pleaded, and contradict statements in the attachment that are merely conclusory). Similarly, where an attachment reveals a "built-in" defense that bars recovery as a matter of law (such as a statute of limitations bar), the court may grant a dismissal.
- *"Vouching" Risk:* By adopting by reference a portion of an attached document, the pleader does not necessarily "vouch" for the truth of all the contents of the document. The attached document will be read in conjunction with the pleading that adopts it. Thus, a defamation plaintiff may safely attach an allegedly libelous writing without being deemed to have admitted as true all the asserted libels contained in the writing, just as a commercial plaintiff, alleging the non-receipt of goods, may attach an allegedly forged receipt without admitting that the document truthfully recounts that the goods were received.

Adopting by Reference in Motions

Portions of pleadings may be adopted by reference in a motion, but nothing in the Rule expressly permits the adoption of motions (or portions of motions) into another motion.

RULE 11

SIGNING PLEADINGS, MOTIONS, AND OTHER PAPERS; REPRESENTATIONS TO THE COURT; SANCTIONS

(a) Signature. Every pleading, written motion, and other paper must be signed by at least one attorney of record in the attorney's name—or by a party personally if the party is unrepresented. The paper must state the signer's address, e-mail address, and telephone number. Unless a rule or statute specifically states otherwise, a pleading need not be verified or accompanied by an affidavit. The court must strike an unsigned paper unless the omission is promptly corrected after being called to the attorney's or party's attention.

(b) Representations to the Court. By presenting to the court a pleading, written motion, or other paper—whether by signing, filing, submitting, or later advocating it—an attorney or unrepresented party certifies that to the best of the person's knowledge, information, and belief, formed after an inquiry reasonable under the circumstances:

(1) it is not being presented for any improper purpose, such as to harass, cause unnecessary delay, or needlessly increase the cost of litigation;

(2) the claims, defenses, and other legal contentions are warranted by existing law or by a nonfrivolous argument for extending, modifying, or reversing existing law or for establishing new law;

(3) the factual contentions have evidentiary support or, if specifically so identified, will likely have evidentiary support after a reasonable opportunity for further investigation or discovery; and

(4) the denials of factual contentions are warranted on the evidence or, if specifically so identified, are reasonably based on belief or a lack of information.

(c) Sanctions.

(1) *In General.* If, after notice and a reasonable opportunity to respond, the court determines that Rule 11(b) has been violated, the court may impose an appropriate sanction on any attorney, law firm, or party that violated the rule or is responsible for the violation. Absent exceptional circumstances, a law firm must be held jointly responsible for a violation committed by its partner, associate, or employee.

(2) *Motion for Sanctions.* A motion for sanctions must be made separately from any other motion and must describe the specific conduct that allegedly violates Rule 11(b). The motion must be served under Rule 5,

but it must not be filed or be presented to the court if the challenged paper, claim, defense, contention, or denial is withdrawn or appropriately corrected within 21 days after service or within another time the court sets. If warranted, the court may award to the prevailing party the reasonable expenses, including attorney's fees, incurred for the motion.

(3) *On the Court's Initiative.* On its own, the court may order an attorney, law firm, or party to show cause why conduct specifically described in the order has not violated Rule 11(b).

(4) *Nature of a Sanction.* A sanction imposed under this rule must be limited to what suffices to deter repetition of the conduct or comparable conduct by others similarly situated. The sanction may include nonmonetary directives; an order to pay a penalty into court; or, if imposed on motion and warranted for effective deterrence, an order directing payment to the movant of part or all of the reasonable attorney's fees and other expenses directly resulting from the violation.

(5) *Limitations on Monetary Sanctions.* The court must not impose a monetary sanction:

(A) against a represented party for violating Rule 11(b)(2); or

(B) on its own, unless it issued the show-cause order under Rule 11(c)(3) before voluntary dismissal or settlement of the claims made by or against the party that is, or whose attorneys are, to be sanctioned.

(6) *Requirements for an Order.* An order imposing a sanction must describe the sanctioned conduct and explain the basis for the sanction.

(d) Inapplicability to Discovery. This rule does not apply to disclosures and discovery requests, responses, objections, and motions under Rules 26 through 37.

[Amended April 28, 1983, effective August 1, 1983; March 2, 1987, effective August 1, 1987; April 22, 1993, effective December 1, 1993; April 30, 2007, effective December 1, 2007.]

UNDERSTANDING RULE 11

HOW RULE 11 FITS IN

Great mischief could follow if pleaders—either in alleging a claim or defending against one—were free to make allegations without first having a proper basis for doing so. Lawsuits are serious business. They can have grave, sometimes devastating, personal and professional ramifications. Consider a businessperson who alleges (without any basis) that her partner is stealing money from the company, or a doctor who defends against a medical malpractice claim by alleging (without any basis) that the patient's illness is actually attributable to his random, indiscriminate sexual encounters, or a supermarket that accuses (without any basis) a fruit supplier of distributing apples contaminated with a deadly fungus caused by careless packing practices. The significant collateral reverberations from these *factually* baseless allegations are obvious.

Legally baseless claims also raise serious concerns. Consider, for example, a pleader who, having done a woefully poor job of pre-filing legal research, asserts a claim or defense without ever realizing that the courts had previously considered the very same argument and squarely rejected it. Worse still, consider the pleader who asserts such a legally baseless claim or defense in the hope that the other side will be hoodwinked, will fail to discover or perhaps overlook contradicting case law, and will propose an unmerited (extortionate) settlement.

Baseless lawsuits consume scarce judicial resources, impose needless costs and distraction to the victim, and result in often terrible collateral consequences. But, in policing such mischief, legitimate lawyering creativity must not be chilled or unfairly restricted. In the 1950s, formidable, existing case authority supported the legality of "separate but equal" racially segregated public schools. That was settled law. Yet courageous civil rights litigators argued that this existing law was unconstitutional, notwithstanding its precedential nature, and should be revisited and rejected. Certainly, constraints designed to ensure ethical pleading ought not to be applied in a manner that holds back the sound evolution of the law or punishes legitimate (often heroic) lawyering creativity.

Rule 11 is intended to establish a prudent ethical balance for pleadings, motions, and other papers served or filed with the federal courts. Factually baseless claims and defenses are improper, but sometimes factually under-developed allegations may be appropriate when the discovery stage is reasonably likely to yield the missing factual support. Legally baseless claims and defenses are improper, but sometimes thoughtful arguments can be framed that legal positions that are today unsupported by existing law should be modified or abandoned altogether. Always improper are filing legal documents with the goal of harassing, delaying, or otherwise punishing an opponent.

Rule 11 installs the ethical norms for pleadings, motions, and other filed or served papers, as well as the sanctions and sanctioning procedure for policing conduct that falls below those standards.

THE ARCHITECTURE OF RULE 11

Rule 11 has four subparts. Rules 11(a) and (b) install the ethical mandate for pleadings, motions, and other papers—they require that all such filings be signed and, further, pronounce that the act of signing constitutes a formal representation by the signer to the court that the pleading complies with the Rule's ethical standards. Rule 11(c) sets the limits and procedures for sanctioning non-compliant filings. Rule 11(d) instructs that this Rule's requirements do *not* apply to unethical behavior during the discovery stage of civil litigation.

HOW RULE 11 WORKS IN PRACTICE

These three subparts of Rule 11 are discussed, in order, below.

RULE 11(a) Signature

Rule 11 begins with a signing obligation. All federal pleadings, written motions, and other papers must be signed by an attorney or, if the litigant is not represented by counsel, by the litigant himself or herself. An unsigned filing "must" be stricken by the court unless that omission is corrected promptly. As Rule 11(b) makes clear, the signer's ethical obligations are triggered by this act of signing.

PRACTICING LAW UNDER THIS SUBPART

Purpose and Scope of Rule 11, Generally

The purposes of Rule 11 are to deter baseless filings and to "streamline the administration and procedure of the federal courts." *See Cooter & Gell v. Hartmarx Corp.*, 496 U.S. 384, 393 (1990). By its terms, Rule 11 applies to every pleading, written motion, or other paper filed or served in the course of litigation, as well as to advocacy of documents previously filed. It does not apply to misconduct unrelated to signed documents. It does not apply to misconduct unrelated to signed documents.

Signature of Attorney

If a party has retained counsel, at least one attorney must sign each document and provide his or her address, e-mail, and telephone number. A signature that purports to be made on behalf of an entire law firm does not satisfy the signature requirement of Rule 11. *See Pavelic & LeFlore v. Marvel Entm't Group,* 493 U.S. 120, 125–26 (1989). Use of an attorney's e-filing login and password to electronically file a document constitutes the signature of that attorney on that document for purposes of Rule 11.

Signature of Unrepresented Party

A party must sign the document if the party is not represented by counsel. The party must provide his or her own address, e-mail, and telephone number. Although courts may be more lenient with *pro se* litigants, such litigants are not immune from Rule 11's signing duty, the Rule's substantive obligations, or the Rule's sanctions. Some courts have interpreted Rule 11 to prohibit a represented party from acting on his own behalf unless the district court first enters an order of substitution.

Verification and Affidavits

Traditionally, court filings would be accompanied by verifications or affidavits, swearing to the truth of the material contained within them. This requirement is largely abolished in federal practice (except when expressly required by another rule or statute). Now, the simple signature of a party or counsel is the substitute, in federal court, for that traditional representation and assurance of truthfulness.

Failure to Sign

If a document subject to Rule 11 is not signed, the court "must" strike the document unless the omission is "promptly corrected" once its absence is called to the proponent's attention. *See Becker v. Montgomery*, 532 U.S. 757, 765 (2001) (Rule 11's signature requirement and cure "go hand in hand").

Rule 11 Is Broadly Applied

Rule 11 acts as a governor to protect the federal courts and adversaries from misconduct by lawyers and unrepresented parties. Consequently, the Rule applies even in cases where it is subsequently determined that the district court lacked subject-matter jurisdiction. *See Willy v. Coastal Corp.*, 503 U.S. 131, 138–39 (1992). It also applies when the federal judge retains jurisdiction to impose sanctions even after a case has been voluntarily dismissed without prejudice.

Not Applicable By Party Against Own Attorney

Ordinarily, Rule 11 cannot be invoked by represented parties against their own attorneys.

Not Applicable to Appellate Practice (*After* Filing Notice of Appeal)

Rule 11 applies in the federal district courts. The federal appellate rules contain their own sanctioning provision. However, Rule 11 does encompass notices of appeal, which begin the appeal process but are filed in the district court.

Not Applicable to Documents Filed in State Court

Rule 11 cannot be used to sanction the signer of the document filed in State court.

RULE 11(b) Representations to the Court

The act of "presenting" to the court any pleading, written motion, or other paper (which includes signing it, filing it, submitting it, or later advocating it) triggers a series of four "certifications" that the presenter is deemed to be making to the judge: namely, that the presentation has a proper purpose, that it has proper legal support, that is has proper factual support, and that any denials are factually justified.

PRACTICING LAW UNDER THIS SUBPART

Starting Point—The Obligation to Make a Reasonable Inquiry

All persons who sign, file, submit, or later advocate documents are deemed to be certifying to the court that the document or advocacy is: (a) based upon the person's best knowledge, information, or belief, which is in turn (b) based upon an inquiry that was reasonable under the circumstances of the particular case. An attorney operates under a "continuous obligation to make inquiries." *See Battles v. City of Ft. Myers,* 127 F.3d 1298, 1300 (11th Cir. 1997). While an attorney may rely on information provided by a client, such information must be the product of a reasonable inquiry. The duty of reasonable inquiry applies to both unrepresented parties as well as represented parties and their attorneys, and establishes an objective standard reasonable under the circumstances. *See Business Guides, Inc. v. Chromatic Commc'ns Enters., Inc.*, 498 U.S. 533, 551–54 (1991).

Representation #1—No Improper Purpose

By presenting a document or arguing on its behalf, the proponent certifies that the presentation has no improper purpose, such as harassment or undue delay or expense. This language is intended to regulate bad faith filings. How this improper purpose standard is applied may depend on whether the accused is an attorney or party, and whether the motion is instigated by a party or *sua sponte* by the court. The prevailing standard has been framed in different ways: whether the legal position at issue has "no chance of success" or is supported by "no reasonable argument;" whether the pleading or contention is culpably careless; whether a reasonable attorney in similar circumstances would not have believed his or her actions legally justified; whether the arguments are unequivocally frivolous or show objective unreasonableness; whether the actions "compromise standards of professional integrity and competence;" and whether the actions are "akin to contempt."

Note, however, that while bad faith or a mischievous purpose can indeed warrant the imposition of sanctions under this "improper purpose" standard, less malevolently culpable behavior (such as innocent but careless lawyering) can nonetheless still trigger sanctions under this and other Rules.

The filing of contradictory pleadings or making an isolated overstatement will not a necessarily violate Rule 11, unless the court also finds that bad faith was involved (such as filing frivolous pleadings after being warned by the court or repackaging unsuccessful prior claims in a new lawsuit under a different cause of action). A writing filed for any improper purpose may be sanctionable even if it factually and legally supported.

Representation #2—Proper Support in the Law

In addition to having a proper purpose, a person presenting a document or arguing on its behalf also certifies that the arguments in the presentation are *either* justified by existing law *or* are "nonfrivolous" arguments for altering existing law. Courts are careful to apply this standard with circumspection; Rule 11 sanctions are reserved only for correcting litigation abuse, not for "adventuresome, though responsible, lawyering which advocates creative legal theories." *See Mary Ann Pensiero, Inc. v. Lingle*, 847 F.2d 90, 94 (3d Cir. 1988).

Representation #3—Proper Support in the Facts

A person presenting a document or arguing on its behalf also certifies that the factual contentions being made have "evidentiary support" or, when specifically so stated, will likely have evidentiary support after a reasonable opportunity for further investigation or discovery. This sets a lesser standard than that the allegations be "well grounded" in fact. *See Rotella v. Wood,* 528 U.S. 549, 560–61 (2000). Sanctions generally may not be imposed against an attorney if there is evidence to support the lawyer's assertions; however, mere speculation and conclusory allegations coupled with general carelessness may rise to the level of a violation.

Representation #4—Foundation for Denials

Lastly, a person who denies factual contentions certifies that those denials are warranted by the evidence, unless the person specifically identifies the denial as one reasonably based upon belief or a lack of information.

Conduct That Is Not Considered a "Representation" to the Court

Conduct not involving a document submitted to the court, including the failure to submit a document, is not sanctionable under Rule 11. Thus, disregard of a court order, attorney misconduct during trial, and oral statements made during argument that are not included in written submissions to the court do not typically fall under Rule 11—though they may well justify the imposition of sanctions under other law.

Representations Apply to Portions of Presentations, as Well as the Whole

Portions of a document might be in violation of Rule 11, even though other portions of the same document are ethically compliant.

Simply Failing to Prevail Is Not a Violation

Obviously, to be sanctionable under Rule 11, something more than merely failing to win is required. Rule 11 is not a strict liability provision; a violation may be found only when some significant carelessness or misbehavior is identified. Thus, before finding a violation, the court must be satisfied that: (1) the document at issue is, objectively, either legally or factually baseless, and (2) the attorney did not perform a reasonable, competent pre-filing investigation.

Improper Rule 11 Motions Can, Themselves, Also Violate Rule 11

Attorneys (and unrepresented parties) may assert that an opponent has violated Rule 11 in a written—and signed—motion, which itself is subject to review under Rule 11 and can, itself, be subject to accusations of violations of Rule 11.

RULE 11(c) Sanctions

The "signing" obligation of Rule 11(a) and the presenter's "certifications" of Rule 11(b) are the foundations for the remedies that appear in Rule 11(c). An attorney or unrepresented party may be punished with sanctions for violating a certification made to the court through the act of signing, filing, submitting, or advocating a pleading, written motion, or other paper, and this subpart sets that procedure. An inquiry to assess whether behavior is sanctionable can be initiated by motion from a party or by the court itself. The goal of any sanction is deterrence.

PRACTICING LAW UNDER THIS SUBPART

The Goal of Rule 11 Sanctions—Deterrence

Sanctions for violations of Rule 11(b) are to be imposed primarily to deter similar violations by the offender and by others similarly situated. This current policy represents a change in practice from earlier versions of Rule 11, which had included a substantially stronger interest in compensating parties injured by Rule 11 violations. *See generally* Amendments to the Federal Rules of Civil Procedure, 1993, 146 F.R.D. 401, 508 (Apr. 22, 1993) (Scalia, J., dissenting) (opposing amendments' rejection of a compensation model for Rule 11: "As seen from the viewpoint of the victim of an abusive litigator, these revisions convert Rule 11 from a means of obtaining compensation to an invitation to throw good money after bad.").

Initiating a Sanctions Inquiry—Two Paths

An inquiry into whether Rule 11(b) has been violated and whether sanctions under Rule 11(c) are appropriate can be initiated in two ways: (1) by motions filed by a party and (2) by *sua sponte* orders of the judge. Each path is discussed below in turn.

Path #1: Sanction Motions—Who May Seek and When

Ordinarily, only persons who are parties to the litigation have standing to initiate a Rule 11 sanctions inquiry (non-parties generally may not do so, except in narrow circumstances where they are affected directly by the allegedly violative conduct). The time for filing such party-initiated motions is constrained by the "safe harbor" requirement (discussed below), but must occur before the case concludes—although the court can retain jurisdiction to render its ruling even after closing the case.

Path #1: Sanction Motions—"Safe Harbor"

Motions for Rule 11 sanctions cannot be filed instantly after an alleged violation. Instead, the adversary (the one alleged to have violated Rule 11) must be given an opportunity to retract or correct the offending paper, claim, defense, contention, or denial. This is the "safe harbor" rule. The rule requires that the alleged violator be served with an *un-filed* copy of the motion, and then be afforded 21 days to withdraw or correct the allegedly offending act. (Some courts hold that a letter specifying an intent to seek sanctions and the basis for them may satisfy this requirement.) If the challenged document is withdrawn or corrected within those 21 days (or such other time as the court may direct), the Rule 11 sanctions motion may *not* be filed with the court, and no sanctions will be imposed.

- *Waivability:* Although the "safe harbor" provision entitles the alleged violator to a 21-day cure period, that entitlement can be waived either expressly or impliedly, if the alleged violator does not object to the premature filing with the court.

Path #1: Sanction Motions—Separate and Specific

Rule 11 sanctions motions must, first, be filed separately from all other motions (they cannot, for example, be embedded in a motion to dismiss or appear as a closing point or footnote in some other filing). Second, Rule 11 motions must be specific, highlighting for the court the particular conduct the opponent claims has violated Rule 11(b).

Path #1: Sanction Motions—Service and Due Process

Motions seeking Rule 11 sanctions must be served as required by Rule 5. Any person or entity who may be subjected to Rule 11 sanctions has a constitutionally protected due process right to present a defense before any sanction is imposed. The quality and nature of that opportunity will vary with the circumstances.

Path #2: *Sua Sponte* Orders—"Show-Cause" Orders

If the judge believes there may have been a violation of Rule 11(b), the judge may independently initiate the sanction process without waiting for one of the parties to make a motion. In such a case, the judge will issue an order directing the attorney, law firm, or party to "show cause" why no violation has occurred (in order words, to come to court with an explanation justifying the behavior in question). In its "show-cause" order, the court must identify the potentially offending conduct with reasonable specificity. Normally, a "show-cause" order will be issued only in circumstances analogous to contempt of court. In considering whether to award sanctions, the court must ensure that the parties receive both notice and an opportunity to defend against the proposed sanction.

Path #2: *Sua Sponte* Orders—No Formal "Safe Harbor"

In court-initiated motions, the judge is bound by no express "safe harbor" obligation, like the one imposed on fellow parties seeking sanctions by motion; however, the court in its discretion may afford an offending party substantial leeway in responding.

Path #2: *Sua Sponte* Orders—Timing

Like sanction motions filed by a fellow party, a sanction proceeding initiated by the court must begin while the case is still "live" (and before a dismissal); however, such court-initiated proceedings may continue on, even after a litigation is voluntarily dismissed, so long as they were timely begun.

Nature of Possible Sanctions—The "Snapshot Rule"

Whether Rule 11 sanctions are appropriate and the date from which sanctions can be assessed is ordinarily determined as of the time a document is filed. However, Rule 11 also imposes a duty of continuing diligence, and can be violated when a party continues to maintain a position despite discovery, new evidence, or other information revealing that a certain litigating position has no merit.

Nature of Possible Sanctions—Types Available Generally

The types of sanctions available under Rule 11 can vary. A court may, for example, impose nonmonetary sanctions (like a public reprimand, a dismissal, or mandatory ethics retraining or pro bono service), may impose monetary sanctions that are paid into the treasury of the court, or may require reimbursement of some or all of an opposing party's attorney's fees and expenses (or any combination of these). The court may not award a payment to an opposing party unless it was sought by motion; such an award is unavailable when the court acts to sanction on its own initiative. Generally, any monetary sanction must flow directly from the conduct described in the Rule 11 motion.

Nature of Possible Sanctions—Limits on Attorney's Fees as Sanctions

Rule 11 envisions deterrence sanctions, not compensatory (fee-shifting) ones. Sanctions are not tied to the outcome of the litigation, and instead depend on whether a specific filing is well founded. Of course, Rule 11 monetary sanctions will usually shift the cost of only the offending portion of the litigation, not the cost of the litigation as a whole. But there are circumstances when a fee award is still proper to serve a deterrence objective. As noted above, the court may not award any Rule 11 monetary sanction (including attorney's fees) when sanctions are imposed *sua sponte*, though a court may award attorney's fees under its inherent powers if the party being sanctioned has acted in bad faith. When a sanction includes payment of an opposing party's attorney's fees or associated costs, courts may use a "lodestar" method of calculating the appropriate fee amount. Under this method, the awarded amount is computed by multiplying the number of lawyering hours worked by an appropriate hourly rate. The amount of awarded fees is limited to fees incurred as a direct consequence of the sanctioned misbehavior. Fees for government attorneys are calculated on the same basis as prevailing rates in the private sector.

Nature of Possible Sanctions—When Monetary Sanctions Are *Not* Available

Monetary sanctions (like attorney's fees or other financial penalties) may not be assessed against a client who is represented by counsel when the basis for the sanction is a violation of Rule 11(b)'s representation that the contested contention be warranted by existing law or a non-frivolous argument for changing the law. Conversely, monetary sanctions obviously remain available against attorneys or non-represented parties who violate this representation.

Other, Non-Rule 11 Remedies

Rule 11 is a powerful tool, but it does not displace remedies that the courts, litigants, and others may have to address litigating misbehavior. Such other remedies might include contempt, a censure or reprimand, disciplinary complaints to a bar, State civil claims (such as abuse of process lawsuits), and sanctioning authority granted by other rules (such as those to combat frivolous appeals) or statutes (such as sanctions for vexatious litigation, 28 U.S.C. § 1927; improper removal, 28 U.S.C. § 1447(c); and frivolous *in forma pauperis* filings, 28 U.S.C. § 1915). In addition, the courts have "inherent powers" to sanction lawyers for misconduct. *See Chambers v. NASCO, Inc.*, 501 U.S. 32 (1991).

The Sanctions Order—Generally

If the court imposes Rule 11 sanctions, it must describe the offending conduct and explain the basis for the sanction imposed. If the award includes attorney's fees, the court should explain the basis for the fee award and specify who, as between the parties and their lawyers, is to pay the award.

The Sanctions Order—Who May Be Sanctioned

In appropriate circumstances the court may sanction attorneys, law firms, and/or parties. In fact, the Rule's language creates a strong presumption in favor of imposing sanctions upon an entire law firm whenever one of its personnel is sanctioned. *See* Rule 11(c)(1) ("Absent exceptional circumstances, a law firm must be held jointly responsible for a violation committed by its partner, associate, or employee.").

The Sanctions Order—Judicial Discretion

The decision to grant or deny sanctions is vested in the district judge's discretion. *See Cooter & Gell v. Hartmarx Corp.*, 496 U.S. 384, 405 (1990). In close cases, the district court should provide an explanation of the reasons for its sanctions ruling; absent such an explanation, the ruling may, on appeal, be sent back to the judge for more explanation. Due to the highly deferential abuse-of-discretion standard of review, an appellate court which finds an abuse of discretion in a denial of Rule 11 sanctions will not generally impose the sanctions in the first instance, but will remand to the district court for further proceedings. Congress retains authority to reduce judicial discretion, and has occasionally done so. Rule 11 does not authorize a judge to impose sanctions in a case pending in another court unless the case merely originated there and was removed to the present court.

The Sanctions Order—Costs of Presenting or Opposing Sanctions Motion

The court has discretion to award costs, including attorney's fees, associated with presenting or opposing a sanctions motion.

The Sanctions Order—Inapplicability to Rule 11(a) Violations

By its terms, the sanctions procedure set in Rule 11(c) applies only to violations of the representations made by an attorney or an unrepresented party under Rule 11(b); the signing mandate contained in Rule 11(a) is policed under that Rule alone, which directs the court to strike unsigned papers if not later promptly signed.

The Sanctions Order—Appeals

A sanctioned attorney who desires to appeal the imposition of Rule 11 sanctions cannot rely on a client's notice of appeal from the underlying merits rulings. A district court's decision on a post-judgment Rule 11 motion is a separate judgment that requires the filing of a separate notice of appeal. Interlocutory appeals of Rule 11 sanctions are generally not permitted.

RULE 11(d) Inapplicable to Discovery

Rule 11 sanctions cannot be imposed for most unethical behavior committed during the discovery stage of litigation. This might seem odd (and regrettable), given the types of serious ethical misconduct that sometimes occurs in discovery. But the exemption is easily explained. Rule 11(d) exists because the discovery rules have their own, specially-tailored ethical mandates in Rule 26(g) and Rule 37.

12(c)
- 12b(6) can be raised in any pleading, motion, or trial

Waiver Of Rule 12 Defenses:

- rule 12 defenses are waived if omitted from a prelim. motion to dismiss under this rule

- 4 waivable defenses: ① lack of PJ, ② improper venue, ③ insufficient process, ④ insufficient service of process
  - ① → 12b2, ② → 12b3, ③ → 12b4, ④ → 12b5
  - if you do not include those rule 12 defenses in your prelim. motion, then you waived them

Anticipation of Defenses:

- a party to a claim is not required to anticipate defenses, but they are allowed to → p's just must make sure that if they do, they don't forget to comply w/ 12b
  - triggered by not asserting it in the responsive pleading

If you file a pre-answer motion for these 4, then you can't bring up again.

RULE 12

DEFENSES AND OBJECTIONS: WHEN AND HOW PRESENTED; MOTION FOR JUDGMENT ON THE PLEADINGS; CONSOLIDATING MOTIONS; WAIVING DEFENSES; PRETRIAL HEARING

(a) Time to Serve a Responsive Pleading.

(1) *In General.* Unless another time is specified by this rule or a federal statute, the time for serving a responsive pleading is as follows:

(A) A defendant must serve an answer:

(i) within 21 days after being served with the summons and complaint; or

(ii) if it has timely waived service under Rule 4(d), within 60 days after the request for a waiver was sent, or within 90 days after it was sent to the defendant outside any judicial district of the United States.

(B) A party must serve an answer to a counterclaim or crossclaim within 21 days after being served with the pleading that states the counterclaim or crossclaim.

(C) A party must serve a reply to an answer within 21 days after being served with an order to reply, unless the order specifies a different time.

(2) *United States and Its Agencies, Officers, or Employees Sued in an Official Capacity.* The United States, a United States agency, or a United States officer or employee sued only in an official capacity must serve an answer to a complaint, counterclaim, or crossclaim within 60 days after service on the United States attorney.

(3) *United States Officers or Employees Sued in an Individual Capacity.* A United States officer or employee sued in an individual capacity for an act or omission occurring in connection with duties performed on the United States' behalf must serve an answer to a complaint, counterclaim, or crossclaim within 60 days after service on the officer or employee or service on the United States attorney, whichever is later.

(4) *Effect of a Motion.* Unless the court sets a different time, serving a motion under this rule alters these periods as follows:

(A) if the court denies the motion or postpones its disposition until trial, the responsive pleading must be served within 14 days after notice of the court's action; or

(B) if the court grants a motion for a more definite statement, the responsive pleading must be served within 14 days after the more definite statement is served.

(b) How to Present Defenses. Every defense to a claim for relief in any pleading must be asserted in the responsive pleading if one is required. But a party may assert the following defenses by motion:

(1) lack of subject-matter jurisdiction;

(2) lack of personal jurisdiction;

(3) improper venue;

(4) insufficient process;

(5) insufficient service of process;

(6) failure to state a claim upon which relief can be granted; and

(7) failure to join a party under Rule 19.

A motion asserting any of these defenses must be made before pleading if a responsive pleading is allowed. If a pleading sets out a claim for relief that does not require a responsive pleading, an opposing party may assert at trial any defense to that claim. No defense or objection is waived by joining it with one or more other defenses or objections in a responsive pleading or in a motion.

(c) Motion for Judgment on the Pleadings. After the pleadings are closed—but early enough not to delay trial—a party may move for judgment on the pleadings.

(d) Result of Presenting Matters Outside the Pleadings. If, on a motion under Rule 12(b)(6) or 12(c), matters outside the pleadings are presented to and not excluded by the court, the motion must be treated as one for summary judgment under Rule 56. All parties must be given a reasonable opportunity to present all the material that is pertinent to the motion.

(e) Motion for a More Definite Statement. A party may move for a more definite statement of a pleading to which a responsive pleading is allowed but which is so vague or ambiguous that the party cannot reasonably prepare a response. The motion must be made before filing a responsive pleading and must point out the defects complained of and the details desired. If the court orders a more definite statement and the order is not obeyed within 14 days after notice of the order or within the time the court sets, the court may strike the pleading or issue any other appropriate order.

(f) Motion to Strike. The court may strike from a pleading an insufficient defense or any redundant, immaterial, impertinent, or scandalous matter. The court may act:

(1) on its own; or

(2) on motion made by a party either before responding to the pleading or, if a response is not allowed, within 21 days after being served with the pleading.

(g) Joining Motions.

(1) *Right to Join.* A motion under this rule may be joined with any other motion allowed by this rule.

(2) *Limitation on Further Motions.* Except as provided in Rule 12(h)(2) or (3), a party that makes a motion under this rule must not make another motion under this rule raising a defense or objection that was available to the party but omitted from its earlier motion.

(h) Waiving and Preserving Certain Defenses.

(1) *When Some Are Waived.* A party waives any defense listed in Rule 12(b)(2) to (5) by:

(A) omitting it from a motion in the circumstances described in Rule 12(g)(2); or

(B) failing to either:

(i) make it by motion under this rule; or

(ii) include it in a responsive pleading or in an amendment allowed by Rule 15(a)(1) as a matter of course.

(2) *When to Raise Others.* Failure to state a claim upon which relief can be granted, to join a person required by Rule 19(b), or to state a legal defense to a claim may be raised:

(A) in any pleading allowed or ordered under Rule 7(a);

(B) by a motion under Rule 12(c); or

(C) at trial.

(3) *Lack of Subject-Matter Jurisdiction.* If the court determines at any time that it lacks subject-matter jurisdiction, the court must dismiss the action.

(i) Hearing Before Trial. If a party so moves, any defense listed in Rule 12(b)(1) to (7)—whether made in a pleading or by motion—and a motion under Rule 12(c) must be heard and decided before trial unless the court orders a deferral until trial.

[Amended December 27, 1946, effective March 19, 1948; January 21, 1963, effective July 1, 1963; February 28, 1966, effective July 1, 1966; March 2, 1987, effective August 1, 1987; April 22, 1993, effective December 1, 1993; April 17, 2000, December 1, 2000; April 30, 2007, effective December 1, 2007; March 26, 2009, effective December 1, 2009.]

UNDERSTANDING RULE 12

HOW RULE 12 FITS IN

Without question, Rule 12 is among the most frequently used of the Federal Rules of Civil Procedure. Lawyers and judges know this Rule well. Law students must also.

The Rule sets procedures for defenses and objections. It begins by setting the time periods for responsive pleadings (that is, for pleadings that are responding to an earlier pleading). As Rule 7 makes clear, the allowable pleadings in federal court comprise a very short list. Not all pleadings command (or permit) a response—for example, a defendant must respond to a plaintiff's complaint, but a plaintiff often need not (and usually may not) respond to a defendant's answer. When responses are required, Rule 12 sets the time periods for them.

Rule 12 also offers a responding party a choice: that responding party may respond by filing a pleading (an answer) *or* may instead choose to file a pre-answer motion that raises one or more of the defenses or objections set out in the Rule. The effect of such a pre-answer motion is to suspend the time for filing an answer while the court ponders the merits of the motion. Most often, these pre-answer motions challenge fundamental, threshold issues in a case—whether jurisdiction exists to hear the dispute, whether venue is proper, whether the parties were properly served with original process, whether the asserted claim or defense can qualify for relief, whether all required parties have been joined to the action, and whether the pleading is clear enough to even permit the opponent to frame an intelligent response. As this list demonstrates, the Rule 12 defenses and objections raise critical, preliminary questions that often go the heart of the court's ability to continue on with the lawsuit. If those defenses or objections are meritorious, and if the court can make that assessment at the outset of a lawsuit, no further time need be wasted. The lawsuit (or certain claims or defenses within it) can be terminated speedily, with a minimum of effort and expense.

Rule 12 confirms that no responsive pleader is *required* to file a pre-answer motion. That choice lies with the responsive pleader's discretion. But *if* the responsive pleader elects to file such a motion (instead of just filing an answer), a few ramifications follow. First, the pleader is *permitted* to join into that one, single, omnibus pre-answer motion all of the Rule 12 defenses and objections the pleader then has. Second, the pleader is *obligated* to assert in the motion certain defenses and objections (*i.e.*, objections to personal jurisdiction, venue, and service of process) or will lose the right to assert them later. Third, the pleader can press the judge to render a pre-trial ruling on the motion.

Finally, Rule 12 permits either party to seek a judgment "on the pleadings" once all pleadings have been filed. The standard the court will use to examine such a request will vary depending on how that motion is supported.

The goal of all these procedures is quite simple. If there is a problem with the pleadings, it should be resolved quickly. If that problem dooms a claim or a defense, that claim or defense should be dispatched early so as not to waste the parties' or the court's time any longer.

THE ARCHITECTURE OF RULE 12

Rule 12 has nine subparts. Those subparts can be functionally grouped into six:

The first group sets the time for the responding pleader to react to another party's pleadings, and grants that responsive pleader the choice of filing either a counter-pleading or a pre-pleading motion (Rule 12(a)).

The second group lists those types of defenses and objections that may be asserted in a pre-pleading motion to dismiss (Rule 12(b)).

The third group authorizes two other types of motions—a motion to force a more definite statement from a pleader or a motion to strike a pleaded allegation—that might be filed with, or instead of, a motion to dismiss (Rules 12(e) and (f)).

The fourth group establishes procedures for all these pre-pleading motions: that they can be joined together in a single filing, that omitting certain defenses and objections from the filing will waive them, and that a party can ask the court for a pretrial ruling (Rules 12(g), (h), and (i)).

The fifth group authorizes a motion for judgment "on the pleadings" by either party once the pleadings stage has ended (Rule 12(c)).

The sixth and final group addresses the consequence of the court considering extrinsic matters—that is, matters separate from the pleadings themselves—in ruling on either a motion to dismiss or a motion for judgment on the pleadings (Rule 12(d)).

HOW RULE 12 WORKS IN PRACTICE

These nine subparts of Rule 12 are discussed, in order, below.

RULE 12(a) Time to Serve a Responsive Pleading

Rule 12 begins with timing. Answers to complaints must ordinarily be served within 21 days after service, except when service is waived (then 60 days if waived from the U.S. or 90 days if waived from abroad) or when serving the federal government, its agencies, or certain of its officers or employees (then 60 days). Answers to counterclaims and crossclaims, as well as court-ordered replies to an answer, must be served within 21 days from service.

PRACTICING LAW UNDER THIS SUBPART

Computing the Time to Respond

The time periods set by Rule 12(a) apply to pleadings that allow responses. (If no responsive pleading is required, defenses and objections can be asserted at trial.)

- *Calculated from Service:* By their terms, these time periods run from (and to) the dates of *service*, not the dates of *filing*.

- *Time for Pre-Answer Motions:* The Rules do not expressly set the time for filing pre-answer motions, but it is generally assumed that the deadlines mirror those governing the service of answers.

Special Time Period—When Formal Service of Process Is Waived

Waiving formal service of process is strongly incentivized through generous extensions of these response times. A defendant who agrees to waive formal service receives 60 days to respond (if the waiver request was mailed to a U.S. address) and 90 days to respond (if mailed to an address outside the U.S.). *See* Rule 4(d). These extensions apply only to service of original process. The time periods run from the date the waiver request was sent.

Special Time Period—Serving the United States, Its Officers and Agencies

Responsive pleadings must be served within 60 days by the United States, by its agencies, and by those federal officers and employees who are *either* sued in their "official" capacities or sued in their "individual" capacities for acts or omissions occurring in connection with the performance of their federal duties. In "individual" capacity, "on-the-job" claim lawsuits against federal personnel, this 60-day period begins to run when the individual is served or when the U.S. Attorney is served, whichever is later. In all other cases (lawsuits against the United States, a federal agency, or a federal officer or employee sued in an official capacity), the 60-day period begins to run when the U.S. Attorney is served. This pleading timetable applies to both current and former federal officers and employees.

♦ **NOTE:** When a pleading names as defendants both a governmental party and a non-governmental party, only the governmental party receives 60 days to serve a responsive pleading. The non-governmental party's time for serving a responsive pleading is unaffected.

Special Time Period—Extensions by the Court or the Parties

The time for serving responsive pleadings (like most other time periods set by the Rules) may be extended by court order and by a court-approved stipulation by the parties.

Special Time Period—Tolling Effect of Rule 12(b) Motions

Rule 12(b) motions to dismiss and Rule 12(e) motions for more definite statement must be filed before a responsive pleading (because, by their nature, the remedy they seek is pre-answer relief). The act of serving either motion ordinarily suspends the party's time for serving a responsive pleading, and that tolling will usually continue until the court has ruled on the pending motion. Thereafter, the time for filing the now-delayed responsive pleading is as follows:

- If the court's order on the motion denies relief or postpones resolving the motion until trial, the responsive pleading must be served within 14 days after "notice" of the court's action,
- If the court's order resolves a motion for more definite statement by requiring a clearer claim, the responsive pleading to the more definite statement must be served within 14 days after service of the more definite statement.
- The court may deviate from these time periods by establishing special schedules for a case, which then control.

The tolling effect of a pending Rule 12(b) motion may be altered (or eliminated completely) in the following circumstances:

- *Motion by Other Defendant:* The tolling effect of a pending Rule 12(b) motion does not inure to the benefit of all defendants; only those defendants who file a Rule 12(b) motion receive the tolling.

- *Motions Filed Against Amended Pleadings:* It is not clear whether a party who files a Rule 12(b) motion to an amended pleading is entitled automatically to a new Rule 12(a) tolling period.
- *Motions to Strike:* It is also not clear whether a motion to strike will toll the time for responsive pleading, although many scholars think a tolling is unlikely.
- *Summary Judgment Motions:* Rule 12(b) motions receive the tolling effect; Rule 56 motions might not. Thus, filing an early summary judgment in lieu of either a Rule 12 motion or an answer might *not* toll the running of the 21-day response period (and, thus, risks admitting all pleaded allegations).
- *Motions Converted to Summary Judgment Motions:* When materials outside the pleadings are presented with a Rule 12(b) motion (and not excluded by the court), the Rule 12(b) motion generally must be converted to a Rule 56 motion for summary judgment.
- *Partial Motions:* A party who files a Rule 12(b) motion to a portion, but not all, of a pending pleading (*e.g.,* motion to dismiss counts I, III, and VI) will likely toll its entire responsive pleading obligation. A strong majority of courts favor this approach, though a small minority and some practitioner commentary favor the view that the responding party must serve an interim, partial answer to all unchallenged portions of the pleading.
- *Appellate Remands:* It is not clear how much time a defendant has to responsively plead if an appellate court reverses a Rule 12(b) motion the trial court had granted.

RULE 12(b) How to Present Defenses

All legal and factual defenses to a claim for relief must be asserted in the responsive pleading to that claim. However, seven enumerated defenses may alternatively be asserted by motion served before the responsive pleading is due.

PRACTICING LAW UNDER THIS SUBPART

Obligation to Assert Defenses and Objections

All defenses to a claim for relief must be asserted in a responsive pleading (if a responsive pleading is required). If no responsive pleading is required, that party may ordinarily assert its defenses, for the first time, at trial. If a responsive pleading is required, the pleader is given a strategic choice: the following seven enumerated defenses and objections may be asserted *either* in the responding party's answer *or* by pre-answer motion:

- Lack of Subject-Matter Jurisdiction, Rule 12(b)(1).
- Lack of Personal Jurisdiction, Rule 12(b)(2).
- Improper Venue, Rule 12(b)(3).
- Insufficient Process, Rule 12(b)(4).
- Insufficient Service of Process, Rule 12(b)(5).
- Failure to State a Claim for which Relief Can Be Granted, Rule 12(b)(6).
- Failure to Join a Party Under Rule 19 (persons needed for just adjudication), Rule 12(b)(7).

Motion Permitted, Not Compelled

No pleader is *compelled* to file a pre-answer motion, even if one would be proper. Pleaders may instead proceed directly to a responsive pleading and raise their defenses and objections there.

Waiver Risks with Defenses and Objections

The act of asserting a particular defense or objection will not result in a waiver of other, perhaps inconsistent defenses or objections asserted along with it. But neglecting to assert it may: if a party chooses to file a Rule 12 motion which includes no objection to 12(b)(2) personal jurisdiction, 12(b)(3) venue, 12(b)(4) process, or 12(b)(5) service, those four omitted objections are deemed waived and ordinarily cannot be raised later in a responsive pleading, a motion, or at trial. *See* Rule 12(h).

Time for Making Motion

The Rules do not prescribe a fixed time for filing pre-answer motions (beyond requiring that they be made before responsively pleading). Some courts have ruled that the time periods set in Rule 12(a) for responsive pleadings do not necessarily set the time deadline for filing motions. Consequently, the safest filing windows for pre-answer motions are the responsive pleading deadlines set in Rule 12(a). Nonetheless, some courts, citing the absence of an explicit motions deadline, have allowed Rule 12(b) motions to be filed after the responsive pleading deadline so long as the filing occurs before an answer—though this liberality can carry serious risks. This view of motion timing might, in an appropriate case, permit an amendment to a pending motion to add a previously omitted defense.

Form of Motion

Rule 12 provides only sparse guidance on the form and procedure for federal motion practice. Other Rules provide some additional detail. For example, Rule 7 requires that motions generally be in writing, include a caption, state with particularity the basis for the motion, and request specific relief. Rule 11 mandates that all motions be signed and be presented for only proper, legally-warranted, factually-warranted purposes. Rule 5 requires that motions be served upon each party to the litigation and be filed with the court within a reasonable time after service. Rule 78 provides for the hearing and disposition of motions, and provides that the district court, by rule or order, may permit motions to be submitted and determined on the written submissions only, without oral argument.

Most other details of federal motion practice and procedure are governed by local court rules and chambers policies, and may vary greatly from court to court. For example, some local rules require that the moving party meet and confer with the adversary before filing any motion, or that motions be accompanied by a supporting brief (limited to a certain number of pages), or that a proposed court order be supplied, etc.

Time for / Form of Response to Motion

The Rules also provide very little guidance on the practice and procedure for responding to motions. This detail is also almost always governed by the district's local rules of practice, which may establish requirements regarding time for responding, forms of responses, and page limits for responsive briefs or memoranda.

Preliminary Motions Not Listed in Rule 12

Rule 12 does not provide an exhaustive list of all possible preliminary motions. For example, motions for extensions of time, to amend a pleading, to intervene, to substitute parties, or for the entering of a stay or an order commanding the posting of security may all be raised as preliminary motions. The court's broad discretion and the federal policy against unwarranted, dilatory motions are the principal limitations on such unenumerated motions.

Amended Pleadings

An amended complaint supersedes its predecessor. Although a responsive pleader cannot ordinarily use the filing of such an amendment to revive defenses or objections that could have been asserted to the original complaint earlier, but were not and are now waived, if the amended complaint adds new theories or alters the lawsuit's scope, the defendant is usually free to file a new answer (which could include new defenses and counterclaims).

RULE 12(b)(1) | Dismissal for Lack of Subject-Matter Jurisdiction

The first of the Rule 12(b) defenses and objections permits a challenge to the federal court's subject-matter jurisdiction. Subject-matter jurisdiction is the constitutional and statutory authority of the federal court to hear a dispute. Because it implicates the structural power of the tribunal, an objection to subject-matter jurisdiction cannot be waived or forfeited, and may be asserted at any time. Subject-matter jurisdiction is discussed in detail in Sections 2.9 through 2.12 of this *Student's Guide.*

PRACTICING LAW UNDER THIS SUBPART

Types of Subject-Matter Jurisdiction Challenges

A claim can be challenged under this provision either *facially* ("technically") or *substantively* ("factually"). On a *facial* challenge, the defendant contests the sufficiency of the pleader's allegations of subject-matter jurisdiction. A pleader is required to adequately aver the basis for the court's jurisdiction; if the pleader fails to do so, the lawsuit can be dismissed. *See Gibbs v. Buck,* 307 U.S. 66, 77 (1939). On a *substantive* challenge, the defendant disputes the underlying truth of the pleader's alleged jurisdictional facts. In such a challenge, the pleading itself may have adequately alleged the presence of federal subject-matter jurisdiction, but the actual facts and allegations before the court may belie that averment, confirming that federal jurisdiction is absent and, thus, compelling the case's dismissal. *See id.*

Legal Test

The existence of subject-matter jurisdiction is tested as of the date the lawsuit was filed. *See Grupo Dataflux v. Atlas Glob. Grp., L.P.*, 541 U.S. 567, 574 (2004). In removed cases, however, it is tested instead on the date of removal. *See Koenigsberger v. Richmond Silver Mining Co.,* 158 U.S. 41, 49–50 (1895). Some courts hold that removed case jurisdiction is tested as of *both* dates (date of filing and date of removal). In diversity cases, a post-filing dismissal of a non-diverse party may rescue a court's subject-matter jurisdiction, *see Newman-Green, Inc. v. Alfonzo-Larrain,* 490 U.S. 826, 832 (1989); though a post-filing change in a party's citizenship will not, *see Grupo Dataflux*, 541 U.S. at 575.

The legal test used to conduct the subject-matter jurisdiction assessment depends on the type of challenge:

- *Facial (or "Technical") Challenges:* In examining facial (or technical) challenges to federal subject-matter jurisdiction, the court will construe the complaint liberally, accept all uncontroverted, well-pleaded factual allegations as true, and view all reasonable inferences in plaintiff's favor. *See Scheuer v. Rhodes,* 416 U.S. 232, 234–37 (1974). But legal conclusions (even those couched as factual allegations) will not be assumed true. The court will view the allegations as a whole; if a conclusory averment of subject-matter jurisdiction is contradicted by other allegations in the pleading, the case may be dismissed. *See Gibbs v. Buck,* 307 U.S. 66 (1939). This approach mirrors the procedure (and safeguards for the nonmoving party) of Rule 12(b)(6). The adequacy of the pleading will be tested under the "short and plain" standard of Rule 8(a)(1), with some courts applying the "plausibility" lens established in *Twombly* to conduct the inquiry. (The *Twombly* standard is discussed with Rule 8.) Whether subject-matter jurisdiction exists is tested as of the date the lawsuit was filed.

- *Substantive (or "Factual") Challenges:* In substantive (or factual) subject-matter jurisdiction attacks, the court will *not* presume that plaintiff's controverted factual allegations are true, but may instead weigh the evidence and find the facts, so long as this factfinding does not involve the merits of the dispute. *See Arbaugh v. Y&H Corp.,* 546 U.S. 500, 514 (2006). In doing so, the court enjoys broad discretion. The court may rule on the basis of undisputed record facts, may receive and consider extrinsic evidence, or may convene an evidentiary hearing or plenary trial to resolve disputed jurisdictional facts. Whether to convene such a hearing will depend on whether the parties have requested one and on the circumstances (including whether the parties have received notice and a fair opportunity to be heard). If a material fact concerning jurisdiction is disputed, a plenary hearing may be necessary to resolve the contested issue.
- *"Intertwined" Merits:* If the merits are so intertwined with the jurisdiction issue that the two cannot be compartmentalized, the ultimate resolution of the court's subject-matter jurisdiction may need to await trial. *See Arbaugh v. Y&H Corp.*, 546 U.S. 500, 514 (2006). In such instances, several courts apply summary judgment principles, inquiring whether a genuine dispute exists over material jurisdiction facts; if so, the lawsuit must proceed to trial for the factfinder's determination of those facts. Other courts differ in their approach.

Burden of Proof

When challenged, the party invoking the court's subject-matter jurisdiction bears the burden of establishing it. *See Thomson v. Gaskill,* 315 U.S. 442, 446 (1942). On a facial challenge, the party bears only a pleading burden, not an evidentiary one. On a substantive challenge (and at trial), the party assumes a merits burden which must be carried by a preponderance of the evidence. In federal question cases, the party must demonstrate a nonfrivolous claim based on federal law (not an especially onerous burden), and must meet all other statutory prerequisites for litigating the federal claim (such as exhaustion of administrative remedies and compliance with all claims-filing limitations and requirements). *See Neitzke v. Williams,* 490 U.S. 319, 327 (1989). In diversity cases, the party must demonstrate complete diversity of citizenship, *see City of Indianapolis v. Chase Nat'l Bank of New York,* 314 U.S. 63, 69 (1941), and a claim that in good faith exceeds $75,000, exclusive of interest and costs, *see St. Paul Mercury Indem. Co. v. Red Cab Co.,* 303 U.S. 283, 289 (1938). In all cases, the party must demonstrate constitutional standing and a live "case or controversy" subject to the federal courts' judicial power under Article III of the Constitution. *See Spokeo, Inc. v. Robins*, 578 U.S. ___, 136 S. Ct. 1540, 1547 (2016).

Timing and Waiver

Verifying its subject-matter jurisdiction is a federal court's "first duty" in every case. Consequently, challenges to subject-matter jurisdiction may be raised at any time, by any party, or by the court. Such challenges can even be raised after final judgment is entered. A party cannot waive or forfeit the requirement of subject-matter jurisdiction, *see Arbaugh v. Y&H Corp.,* 546 U.S. 500, 514 (2006); nor can the parties consent to have a case heard in federal court where subject-matter jurisdiction is absent, *see Neirbo Co. v. Bethlehem Shipbuilding Corp.,* 308 U.S. 165, 173–74 (1939).

Extrinsic Materials

The appropriate role for extrinsic materials depends on the type of Rule 12(b)(1) challenge the parties make. In a facial (or technical) attack, the court is limited to considering the complaint alone (supplemented, perhaps, by its attached exhibits and any facts that are uncontested or subject to judicial notice). In a substantive (or factual) attack, the parties may produce affidavits and other materials to support their positions on subject-matter jurisdiction. The court may also consider matters of public record.

Allowing Pre-Ruling Jurisdictional Discovery

When a defendant moves to dismiss for lack of subject-matter jurisdiction, discovery of the factual issues implicated by the motion may be permitted. The party seeking the discovery bears the burden of showing its need.

Hearing on Motion

Although a court must afford the plaintiff an opportunity to be heard before dismissing under Rule 12(b)(1), an evidentiary or oral hearing is not always necessary.

Sua Sponte Dismissals

Because confirming its subject-matter jurisdiction is a court's first duty in every case, whether an objection is made by a party or not, *sua sponte* (court-initiated) dismissals are always possible; such dismissals may be ordered by the presiding trial court or a later appeals court. *See Arbaugh v. Y&H Corp.,* 546 U.S. 500, 506 (2006).

Ruling Deferred

Although the question of subject-matter jurisdiction is resolved by the court, not the jury, the court may defer ruling on the challenge until after further materials are presented, after discovery is conducted, or after evidence is received at trial. *See Land v. Dollar,* 330 U.S. 731, 735 (1947). The court may *not,* however, defer ruling upon a subject-matter jurisdictional challenge in order to rule instead upon a potentially simpler dispositive motion attacking the underlying merits of the lawsuit. *See Steel Co. v. Citizens for a Better Env't,* 523 U.S. 83 (1998).

Remedy

Generally, the court will permit a party to amend unless it is clear that subject-matter jurisdiction cannot be truthfully averred. When the court lacks subject-matter jurisdiction, it must dismiss the case in its entirety. *See Arbaugh v. Y&H Corp.,* 546 U.S. 500, 514 (2006).

Prejudice on Dismissal

A dismissal for lack of subject-matter jurisdiction is not a decision on the merits (nor could it be since the dismissal confirms the court's lack of authority to act on the merits); accordingly, such dismissals ordinarily will not preclude plaintiffs from re-filing their claims in courts that have the right to hear their disputes. However, where the requirements for pleading a claim overlap entirely with the requirements for pleading its subject-matter jurisdiction, a dismissal may qualify as a merits ruling. *See Brownback v. King,* ___ U.S. ___, 141 S. Ct. 740, 749–50 & n.8 (2021).

Dismissal's Effect on Supplemental Jurisdiction Claims

If a lawsuit's federal claims are dismissed for lack of subject-matter jurisdiction, then all supplemental jurisdiction claims must ordinarily be dismissed as well.

Appealability

A dismissal premised upon a lack of subject-matter jurisdiction is ordinarily considered an immediately appealable "final order," absent leave to amend. However, denying a motion to dismiss for lack of subject-matter jurisdiction generally is interlocutory and not immediately appealable.

RULE 12(b)(2) Dismissal for Lack of Personal Jurisdiction

The second of the Rule 12(b) defenses and objections permits a challenge to the court's exercise of personal jurisdiction (either *in personam* or *in rem*) over a party or property. Personal jurisdiction implicates both statutory and constitutional concerns, but unlike subject-matter jurisdiction, it is a protection afforded defendants that they may waive or consent to forego. Personal jurisdiction is discussed in detail in Sections 2.2 through 2.8 of this text.

PRACTICING LAW UNDER THIS SUBPART

In Personam and *In Rem* Actions

Motions under this Rule may be used to challenge any asserted personal jurisdiction by the court, whether *in personam, in rem,* or *quasi in rem.* To be proper, an exercise of personal jurisdiction by a federal court must satisfy both the Rules' limit on territorial reach (*i.e.,* Rule 4(k)) and the Constitution's due process requirements.

"Special" and "General" Appearances

Historically, a litigant who came to contest a court's personal jurisdiction would do so only by "special" (or "limited") appearance, so as to ensure that the very act of appearing in court to contest jurisdiction was not, in fact, an act by which the litigant submitted to the court's authority. The Rules have abandoned these different types of appearances. Now, a defendant can assert jurisdictional defenses, venue defenses, and even substantive defenses under Rule 12 without impliedly consenting to the court's personal jurisdiction.

Burden of Proof

The party inviting the court's exercise of personal jurisdiction, the party invoking that jurisdiction—ordinarily, the plaintiff or third-party plaintiff—bears the burden of demonstrating that it exists, and must do so as to each resisting opponent. *See, e.g., Bristol-Myers Squibb Co. v. Superior Ct.*, 582 U.S. ___, 137 S. Ct. 1773, 1783 (2017) (specific jurisdiction "must be met as to each defendant"). The *nature* of that burden changes (and may shift), depending on the type of personal jurisdiction being invoked. The *weight* of that burden changes as well, depending on the way the challenge is made. Precisely when this burden is triggered seems to now divide the courts. For some courts, the burden is triggered by the act of filing a claim for relief (under this view, alleging personal jurisdiction is a pleading obligation); for other courts, the burden is triggered once a resisting defendant contests the court's exercise of personal jurisdiction by filing a motion to dismiss. If properly raised and preserved, an objection to personal jurisdiction can obligate the invoking party to prove at trial, by a preponderance of the evidence, all salient jurisdictional facts.

Types of Challenges

A defendant can challenge personal jurisdiction theoretically or factually (or both). Theoretical challenges contest the plaintiff's theory of jurisdiction (*e.g.,* that the defendant subjected itself to jurisdiction in the forum by engaging in a particular set of actions). If the court determines that those facts, if proven to be true, would subject the defendant to personal jurisdiction in the forum, no hearing or factual resolution is required and the theoretical challenge fails. Alternatively (or additionally), the defendant may challenge personal jurisdiction factually by disputing jurisdictional facts the plaintiff has averred. When jurisdiction is challenged factually, the court or the factfinder must resolve the factual dispute.

Legal Test

How a court performs the Rule 12(b)(2) inquiry, and the weight borne by the party invoking the court's personal jurisdiction, hinges on whether the challenge is posed as a theoretical one or as a factual one:

- *Theoretical (Facial) Challenges:* If the motion rests on the pleadings and allegations alone, the plaintiff only has to present a *prima facie* showing of jurisdiction—namely, that those factual allegations, as set out in the complaint, motion papers, memoranda, and affidavits, are sufficient, if credited by the factfinder, to confer personal jurisdiction. No differential factfinding is performed; instead, the uncontroverted allegations in the complaint are accepted as true, and factual disputes are resolved in the pleader's favor. For all of these reasons, this burden on plaintiff is considered "relatively slight." Note, however, that neither legal conclusions and argumentative inferences nor allegations expressly contradicted by affidavit will be presumed true, and any uncontradicted facts offered by the defendant may also be considered. Moreover, the plaintiff's burden is also only a preliminary one; if the jurisdictional challenge is renewed, the plaintiff will later have to prove the jurisdictional facts at trial by a preponderance of the evidence.
- *Factual Challenges:* If the defendant goes beyond a theoretical challenge and contests the underlying truth of plaintiff's jurisdictional allegations (or when the court otherwise finds it unfair to make merely a preliminary ruling), the court may conduct an evidentiary hearing, from which it can find the jurisdictional facts. At the hearing (which may or may not involve live testimony), the court must allow the parties a fair opportunity to present their jurisdictional evidence and supporting legal arguments. Throughout the process, the plaintiff bears the full preponderance burden (and may no longer rest on mere allegations).
- *"Intertwined" Merits:* If such factfinding would be prove to be intertwined with the merits, courts may defer a final jurisdictional ruling until trial, allowing the jury to resolve the implicated factual dispute (for both jurisdictional and merits purposes). Other courts prefer an intermediate approach, permitting an evidentiary hearing with limited factfinding to predict the probable likelihood of personal jurisdiction which, if found, then allows the case to proceed but again postpones until trial the ultimate determination of jurisdiction.
- *A Middle Course:* Sometimes, a court might opt for a middle course. If the defendant submits affidavits or other evidence opposing jurisdiction but no evidentiary hearing is held, the plaintiff must respond with affirmative evidence of its own showing jurisdiction but its burden remains a *prima facie* one. In such instances, the court resolves any factual disputes revealed by the filings in plaintiff's favor.
- *No Implied "Companion" Motions:* Personal jurisdiction, venue, and service may each be challenged together, but only if done expressly; moving on one ground does not imply (or avoid waiver of) an unexpressed challenge on another ground.

Timing and Waiver

Challenges to personal jurisdiction are waived, unless raised by pre-answer motion (if there is one) or in the responsive pleading. *See* Rule 12(h). Even if properly raised, the defense may later be deemed forfeited if the defendant fails to seasonably press for a ruling on the objection, conducts itself as though jurisdiction exists, or misbehaves during jurisdictional discovery. But there usually is no waiver when a defendant, having properly preserved its objection to personal jurisdiction, also includes a responsive claim for affirmative relief (*e.g.*, counterclaim, crossclaim, third-party claim), nor is a party who consented to personal jurisdiction in an earlier case foreclosed from objecting to it in a later one.

Waiting for Default to Raise Personal Jurisdiction Objections

Ordinarily, defendants must raise objections to personal jurisdiction either in their Rule 12 motion or in their answer (if no Rule 12 motion is filed). But defendants have one further option: they may default and then resist the resulting judgment collaterally. But defendants choose this strategy at their peril; if their collateral attack on jurisdiction fails, they almost certainly will be held to have abandoned their right to defend on the merits. *See Ins. Corp. of Ireland, Ltd. v. Compagnie des Bauxites de Guinee,* 456 U.S. 694, 706 (1982); *Baldwin v. Iowa State Traveling Men's Ass'n*, 283 U.S. 522, 525 (1931).

"Renewed" Motion at Trial

A motion to dismiss for lack of personal jurisdiction is usually resolved before trial. *See* Rule 12(i). However, the court's ruling on the motion can be tentative and preliminary (especially when made under the predictive *prima facie* standard). At trial, the defendant can renew the motion and insist that the plaintiff affirmatively prove, by a preponderance of the evidence, all the alleged jurisdictional facts. The defendant must renew the motion to do so. Although the trial court may *sua sponte* return to the earlier jurisdictional objection, it is not required to do so, and in such cases is entitled to apply a mere reconsideration standard (essentially, revisiting the same forgiving *prima facie* analysis performed earlier).

Extrinsic Materials

The parties may submit—and the court, in ruling, may consider—affidavits, interrogatories, depositions, oral testimony (if an evidentiary hearing is convened), and other materials to support their positions on personal jurisdiction.

Allowing Pre-Ruling Jurisdictional Discovery

Access to jurisdictionally-targeted discovery may be made available to the parties. *See Oppenheimer Fund, Inc. v. Sanders,* 437 U.S. 340, 351 (1978). Consequently, courts may grant limited jurisdictional discovery before ruling on a Rule 12(b)(2) motion to dismiss for lack of personal jurisdiction. Whether, and under what constraints, to permit jurisdictional discovery are matters typically reserved for the trial judge's discretion. Jurisdictional discovery may be allowed where a "colorable" case for jurisdiction has been made, where the material facts that bear on jurisdiction are controverted, where a more satisfactory development of those facts is necessary, and where plaintiff has demonstrated that discovery will permit a supplementation of the jurisdictional allegations. Conversely, such discovery may be properly refused when it is untimely sought, where the request is improperly supported or based on mere hunches and conjecture, where the claim is "attenuated" and based on bare allegations that are specifically denied, where a colorable case for jurisdiction has not been made, where the plaintiff's claim is "clearly frivolous" or otherwise based on alleged facts that, even if true, would not support jurisdiction, or where the plaintiff lacks a good faith belief that such discovery could support the jurisdictional allegations. Jurisdictional discovery is often dependent on the specific circumstances presented.

- *Foreign Discovery:* Generally, a party may (but is not necessarily obligated to) pursue foreign discovery through the Hague Evidence Convention. *See Societe Nationale Industrielle Aerospatiale v. U.S. Dist. Court for So. Dist. of Iowa,* 482 U.S. 522, 533–36 (1987). When personal jurisdiction over the foreign party is contested, the courts are divided as to whether discovery can proceed simply under the Rules or whether Convention discovery is required until the question of jurisdiction is resolved.

Sua Sponte Dismissals

Several Circuits forbid *sua sponte* (judge-initiated) dismissals for lack of personal jurisdiction, reasoning that the objection is a waivable defense that must be properly asserted or else it is lost. Other Circuits permit *sua sponte* dismissals, provided plaintiffs are afforded an opportunity to contest the issue and to introduce new supporting evidence (sometimes as late as on appeal). Still others permit (or require) *sua sponte* examinations of personal jurisdiction when defendants have not appeared to defend and a default judgment against them is being sought.

Ruling Deferred

The court may defer ruling on the challenge until after further materials are presented or after jurisdictional discovery is conducted, or even, in appropriate cases, until trial. But a court generally must resolve personal jurisdiction issues before reaching merits issues. *Cf. Ruhrgas AG v. Marathon Oil Co.*, 526 U.S. 574, 578 (1999) (no "unyielding hierarchy" among jurisdictional requirements; courts are free to resolve simpler personal jurisdiction challenges before reaching more difficult questions of subject-matter jurisdiction). Functionally, then, a court has three options for resolving challenges to personal jurisdiction:

(1) Hear and resolve the motion before trial, by applying the preponderance-of-the-evidence standard;

(2) Defer the motion until time of trial, provided the plaintiff has offered a prima facie showing of jurisdiction; or

(3) Apply an intermediate scrutiny in circumstances where it would be unfair to require a defendant to incur the expenses and burden of a trial on the merits in view of a substantial jurisdictional question. In those instances, the court will defer the motion until trial only if the plaintiff first demonstrates a likelihood that personal jurisdiction exists over the defendant.

Remedy

If a court determines that it lacks the ability to exercise personal jurisdiction in a dispute, it may either dismiss the lawsuit or transfer it to any federal court where it could have been brought.

Prejudice on Dismissal

A dismissal for lack of personal jurisdiction generally does not preclude the plaintiff from refiling the lawsuit against the defendant in a forum where that defendant is amenable to jurisdiction. *See Ritzen Grp., Inc. v. Jackson Masonry, LLC*, 140 S. Ct. 582, 590 (2020).

Appealability

A dismissal as to all defendants for lack of personal jurisdiction is generally considered an appealable "final order." Conversely, a dismissal as to less than all defendants or a denial of the motion to dismiss is not a final order and ordinarily cannot be immediately appealed. If a court revisits an earlier personal jurisdiction following a "renewed" motion at or after trial, appealing the later ruling may be necessary to preserve the issue for appeal.

RULE 12(b)(3) Dismissal for Improper Venue

The third of the Rule 12(b) defenses and objections permits a challenge to the venue of the litigation. Like personal jurisdiction, venue is a protection afforded defendants against an inconvenient forum and, like personal jurisdiction, it can be waived. Venue is discussed in detail in Sections 2.14 and 2.15 of this text.

PRACTICING LAW UNDER THIS SUBPART

Proper Scope of Rule 12(b)(3)

Venue protects defendants against the risk that the plaintiff will select an unfair or unduly inconvenient place for trial. Rule 12(b)(3) is the proper vehicle for seeking dismissal only when venue in the chosen forum is *improper* under the federal venue statutes (though the court retains the discretion to transfer, rather than dismiss, were it to find venue improper). Rule 12(b)(3) is not the proper tool for seeking a convenience transfer or a dismissal or transfer pursuant to a forum selection clause or mandatory arbitration clause. *See Atlantic Marine Const. Co. v. U.S. Dist. Court for Western Dist. of Texas,* 571 U.S. 49, 55 (2013). However, if a mis-labeled motion's true intent is clear and no prejudice would result, a court might reframe the motion and rule on it using the appropriate analysis.

Burden of Proof

In its motion, a party opposing venue must first show why venue is improper. Courts are divided on who, then, must carry the ultimate burden in a Rule 12(b)(3) contest. Under the majority view, the party asserting venue (ordinarily, the plaintiff) must bear that burden. Under the minority view, the party opposing venue must demonstrate that it is improper. As with personal jurisdiction challenges, the weight of the burden changes, depending on the way the challenge is made.

Legal Test

The procedure for resolving a Rule 12(b)(3) motion is the same as the procedure used for testing challenges to personal jurisdiction. The court may resolve the motion on the basis of the written submissions alone, or may convene an evidentiary hearing.

With written submissions alone (without a hearing), a venue challenge is generally defeated if the plaintiff sets forth sufficient facts which, if proven true, would confer venue. Under this standard, plaintiff's well-pleaded factual allegations regarding venue are accepted as true; all reasonable inferences and factual conflicts are also resolved in plaintiff's favor. No such deference, however, will be given to unsupported inferences or legal conclusions. In ruling, the court may take judicial notice of appropriate public records.

Once the plaintiff's venue allegations are controverted by the opponent (by affidavit or otherwise), those allegations will no longer be presumed true, and the plaintiff must go beyond the pleadings by offering affirmative evidence in support of the forum's venue. Contested facts are resolved in the plaintiff's favor.

Finally, if the court convenes an evidentiary hearing, the allegations are not presumed true, the preponderance of the evidence standard applies, and the court may assess credibility and find the facts (though it ought to avoid factfinding that encroaches into the merits of the case).

- *No Implied "Companion" Motions:* Personal jurisdiction, venue, and service may each be challenged together, but only if done expressly; moving on one ground does not imply (or avoid waiver of) an unexpressed challenge on another ground.

Timing and Waiver

Venue challenges are waived unless raised by motion (if there is one) or in the responsive pleading. *See* Rule 12(h). Once the Rule 12 motion period and the responsive pleading time have passed, an otherwise "waived" venue defense cannot ordinarily be raised by the court on its own initiative; *sua sponte* venue dismissals are ordinarily improper. A defaulting defendant, thus, generally is deemed to have waived any objections to venue. When properly asserted and preserved, a venue objection is unlikely to be deemed waived merely because the objecting defendant also asserts a counterclaim.

Cases Involving Multiple Defendants or Claims

Where a case involves more than one defendant, or more than one claim against a defendant, venue must be proper as to each defendant and as to each claim.

Extrinsic Materials

The parties may submit affidavits and other materials to support their positions on improper venue.

Pre-Ruling Venue Discovery

The court may, in its discretion, permit limited discovery to aid in resolving the motion.

Remedy

Ordinarily, a court may either dismiss for improper venue or transfer to a forum where venue would be proper.

Sequence in Ruling

Although courts ordinarily resolve pending personal jurisdictional challenges first, they have discretion, in appropriate circumstances, to dismiss or transfer on venue grounds without sorting through a more nettlesome jurisdictional dispute. *See Leroy v. Great W. United Corp.*, 443 U.S. 173, 180 (1979). *See also Goldlawr, Inc. v. Heiman*, 369 U.S. 463, 466–67 (1962) (court lacking personal jurisdiction may still transfer to new venue).

Ruling Deferred

The court may defer ruling on a venue challenge pending further factual development.

Renewed Motion at Trial

Although rarely discussed, it is likely that a pretrial rejection of a venue challenge does not foreclose a renewed challenge at trial or relieve the plaintiff of its obligation to establish the requisite venue facts at trial by a preponderance of the evidence.

Prejudice on Dismissal

A dismissal for improper venue generally does not preclude the plaintiff from re-filing the claim in a forum where venue is proper.

Appealability

Ordinarily, a dismissal for improper venue is immediately appealable as a "final order." Conversely, a denial of a motion to dismiss for lack of venue is interlocutory and not immediately appealable.

RULE 12(b)(4)–12(b)(5) Dismissal for (or Quashing of) Insufficient Process or Service

The fourth and fifth of the Rule 12(b) defenses and objections relate to service of process. When there is a defect in the process itself (for example, the summons was unsigned or lacked the court's official seal), the lawsuit can be dismissed or, more likely, the attempted service can be "quashed" (meaning: voided) under Rule 12(b)(4). When the manner of the delivery of process was deficient (for example, the process was delivered to the wrong recipient or in an untimely or otherwise improper way), the lawsuit can also be dismissed or the service can be quashed under Rule 12(b)(5). The requirements for a proper service of process are addressed in Rule 4.

PRACTICING LAW UNDER THIS SUBPART

Insufficient Process—Rule 12(b)(4)

The process (summons and complaint) may be insufficient if the forms are technically deficient (*e.g.*, wrong name or not sealed by the clerk). Because dismissals for defects in the forms of summons are generally disfavored, courts often overlook minor technical defects (particularly where they can be cured), unless the complaining party is able to demonstrate actual prejudice.

Insufficient Service—Rule 12(b)(5)

Service of the process may be insufficient if, for example, the mode of delivery is invalid, service is made on an improper person, or delivery is either never accomplished or not accomplished within 90 days after commencement (*see* Rule 4(m)).

Distinguishing Between Rules 12(b)(4) and 12(b)(5)

Although they are distinct, the differences between motions under Rules 12(b)(4) and 12(b)(5) have not always been clear or observed in practice. A mislabeling of a Rule 12(b)(4) or 12(b)(5) motion, particularly if no one is prejudiced may be overlooked by the courts.

Relationship Between Service of Process and Personal Jurisdiction

Service of process is a prerequisite for personal jurisdiction. Courts generally cannot exercise adjudicating power over a defendant who has not properly been served with (or waived service of) original process. *See Murphy Bros. v. Michetti Pipe Stringing, Inc.*, 526 U.S. 344, 350 (1999).

Legal Test

A motion to dismiss under these two Rules must be made with specificity, by describing how the process or service failed and why that failure prejudiced the defendant. Once a proper motion is made, the plaintiff must make a *prima facie* demonstration of proper process and service through specific factual averments and other supporting materials; conclusory statements will usually not overcome a defendant's sworn representation controverting good service. (But, likewise, a defendant's motion comprised of only conclusory, unsworn assertions is unlikely to overcome a process server's affidavit.) The plaintiff will usually be given the benefit of any factual doubts in resolving a service challenge, and the requisites for Rule 4 service are liberally construed. Courts may resolve any disputed questions of fact by considering affidavits, depositions, and oral testimony. The adequacy of service accomplished after removal is tested under these Rules (and not State law). If properly raised and preserved, an objection to process or to service of process can obligate the serving party to prove at trial, by a preponderance of the evidence, all salient facts necessary to establish proper service.

- *No Implied "Companion" Motions:* Personal jurisdiction, venue, and service may each be challenged together, but only if done expressly; moving on one ground does not imply (or avoid waiver of) an unexpressed challenge on another ground.

Burden of Proof

Once a party resisting service raises a credible challenge, the burden then shifts, in the view of most courts, to the serving party must show that the court's personal jurisdiction is properly exercised. The process server's return is *prima facie* evidence of good service; but such proof is not conclusive, and can be overcome by strong and convincing evidence to the contrary. A conclusory representation of proper service will not overcome a defendant's sworn affidavit otherwise.

Timing and Waiver

Challenges to either the form of process or the adequacy of service are waived unless raised in the pre-answer motion (if there is one) or in the responsive pleading (if no motion is filed). *See* Rule 12(h). Consequently, a defendant generally may not move for a dismissal under these Rules *after* filing an answer that omitted that defense or *after* filing a pre-answer Rule 12 motion that omitted that defense. Waiver can also follow when a defendant makes a motion to transfer for improper venue (under 28 U.S.C. § 1406) which neglects to include that defendant's alternative challenge to process and/or service. Of course, defendants will not waive these defenses by appearing in court to assert them, or by not supplying plaintiffs with advance notice of an intent to raise them. But the defenses may still be forfeited—even if properly asserted originally—if the movant fails to timely press for a ruling or otherwise participates in the litigation in a manner that belies those defenses.

Waiting for Default to Raise Service Objections

Defendants do not waive process or service objections by failing to timely assert them if, due to the process or service failure, those defendants never learned about the attempted service in time to object. In such circumstances, the defendants should be permitted to raise their objections when the purported service comes to their attention or even by collateral attack on any ensuing judgment. *See generally Ins. Corp. of Ireland v. Compagnie des Bauxites de Guinee*, 456 U.S. 694, 706 (1982) ("A defendant is always free to ignore the judicial proceedings, risk a default judgment, and then challenge that judgment on jurisdictional grounds in a collateral proceeding."); *Baldwin v. Traveling Men's Assn.*, 283 U.S. 522, 525 (1931) (same). Less certain is whether defendants who actually know of the attempted service may properly withhold their objections to it and wait to assert them in a later collateral attack. In any collateral attack, defendants likely will bear the burden of proving the process or service deficiency.

Extrinsic Materials

The parties may produce affidavits and other materials to support their positions on insufficient process or service. The court may properly receive and consider such materials (as well as those of which it may take judicial notice) in deciding the motion, and may even convene an evidentiary hearing—all without converting the motion to dismiss into a motion for summary judgment.

Remedy

A party may request that the case be dismissed under these Rules or, alternatively, that service be quashed (invalidated) and reattempted. The court, too, has discretion. If process or service is found to be defective, the court may either quash or dismiss, but will likely choose to quash if there is a reasonable prospect that the defendant can be properly served with sufficient process. Although the dismissal option remains available to the courts, courts will typically dismiss only when the failure of process or service prejudices the defendant or where proper service is unlikely to be accomplished.

Ruling Deferred

It may be proper to sidestep a pending challenge to service of process, in order to dismiss on the merits on a separately pending Rule 12(b)(6) motion.

Prejudice on Dismissal

A dismissal for insufficient process or service is generally without prejudice and will not usually preclude the plaintiff from attempting to re-serve properly. Where, however, the applicable limitations period has expired, it likely is not error to grant an insufficient process or service dismissal with prejudice.

Appealability

Because dismissals for insufficient process or service are generally without prejudice and interlocutory, they are not immediately appealable as final orders unless the running of the applicable limitations period has caused a time-bar.

RULE 12(b)(6) — Dismissal for Failure to State a Claim upon Which Relief Can Be Granted

The sixth of the Rule 12(b) defenses and objections permits a challenge to the adequacy of a pleading. This Rule is the modern-day descendant of the common law "demurrer," a historical technique by which a defendant would "admit" the pleading's allegations and then argue to the court that, even as admitted, the allegations were still insufficient to allow the claim to move forward. The federal version of this tool is encompassed in Rule 12(b)(6), and allows courts to terminate lawsuits that are fatally flawed in order to spare the litigants the unnecessary burdens of further litigation. In essence, Rule 12(b)(6) is the remedy for a pleader's failure to satisfy the federal pleading obligations, including those imposed by Rules 8 and 9.

PRACTICING LAW UNDER THIS SUBPART

Legal Test

Rule 12(b)(6) motions test the sufficiency of a pleading. A claim will fail this inspection under Rule 12(b)(6) if it asserts a legal theory that is not cognizable as a matter of law, *see Neitzke v. Williams*, 490 U.S. 319, 326–27 (1989); or because the factual tale alleged is implausible, *see Bell Atlantic Corp. v. Twombly,* 550 U.S. 544, 555 & 570 (2007).

When a claim is challenged under this Rule, the court presumes that all well-pleaded allegations are true, resolves all reasonable doubts and inferences in the pleader's favor, and views the pleading in the light most favorable to the non-moving party. *See Twombly*, 550 U.S. at 555. No claim will be dismissed merely because the trial judge disbelieves the allegations or feels that recovery is remote or unlikely. *See id.* Neither detailed factual allegations nor evidentiary-level factual showings are required of pleaders. *See id.*

Yet, although encouraging brevity, the federal pleading duty is far from trivial. The pleading must contain "enough" information to give defendants fair notice of both the complaint's claims and the grounds on which they rest. *See Tellabs, Inc. v. Makor Issues & Rights, Ltd.*, 551 U.S. 308, 319 (2007). Specifically, federal pleaders must demonstrate that their allegations "possess enough heft" to *show* an *entitlement to relief* (and, thereby, are sufficient to allow the costly process of litigation to continue). *See Twombly,* 550 U.S. at 557. Pleaders must allege enough facts to raise their claims beyond the level of speculation, by "nudg[ing] their claims across the line from conceivable to plausible." *Id.* at 570. To cross into this "realm of plausible liability," a pleader's allegations must be factual (not conclusory) and suggestive (not neutral). *Id.* at 557 n.5. A successful pleader, therefore, is expected to do more than merely incant labels, conclusions, and the formulaic elements of a cause of action. *See Ashcroft v. Iqbal,* 556 U.S. 662, 678 (2009).

In testing for comportment with Rule 12(b)(6), courts perform a two-step inquiry—first, legal conclusions will be isolated, so as to uncover the pleading's purely factual allegations, and second, those factual allegations will be presumed true and then examined for plausibility. *Id.* at 678–79. Only a pleading's *facts* are presumed true at this stage; its speculation and conjecture is not, nor are its bald assertions, conclusions, or inferences, legal conclusions "couched" or "masquerading" as facts, unwarranted deductions of fact, or averments contradicted by its own exhibits or other materials of which the court may take proper notice. *See, e.g., id.* at 678–79; *Twombly*, 550 U.S. at 555.

A claim is facially "plausible" when it alleges sufficient factual content to permit the reasonable inference that the defendant is liable for unlawful conduct, thus giving rise to a "reasonably founded hope that the discovery process will reveal relevant evidence" to support the claims. *See Twombly,* 550 U.S. at 559. Determining whether a claim crosses the "plausibility" line is a "context-specific task" that draws on the deciding court's "judicial experience and common sense." *See Iqbal,* 556 U.S. at 679. To reach the "realm of plausible liability," a pleader's allegations must be factual (not conclusory) and suggestive (not neutral). *See Twombly*, 550 U.S. at 557 n.5. Pleaders must meet this pleading burden for each element required for a recovery under some actionable theory (although when tested, a pleading is not parsed, part by part, but is read as a whole). Pleadings that are unable to "show" the requisite plausible entitlement to relief are thereby exposed by Rule 12(b)(6) at an early stage in the litigation so as to minimize the costs of time and money by the litigants and the courts. *See Twombly,* 550 U.S. at 558.

How *Bell Atlantic v. Twombly* "Plausibility" Impacts Rule 12(b)(6)

The Supreme Court announced the "plausibility" pleading standard in *Bell Atlantic Corp. v. Twombly,* 550 U.S. 544 (2007), which was an antitrust case. In so doing, the Court expressly overruled the oft-quoted, very forgiving pleading mantra from its 1957 decision in *Conley v. Gibson*, 355 U.S. 41, 45–46 (1957) (namely, that no complaint should be dismissed for failing to state a claim "unless it appears beyond doubt that the plaintiff can prove no set of facts in support of his claim which could entitle him to relief"). The *Conley* language, wrote the Court in *Twombly*, "earned its retirement" because it might preserve an insufficient, conclusorily-pleaded claim on the mere theoretical chance that it might later find support. *See Twombly,* 550 U.S. at 562–63. Two years later, the Court in *Ashcroft v. Iqbal* confirmed that this "plausibility" standard was not reserved just for antitrust cases (like *Twombly* was). *See Iqbal,* 556 U.S. at 684.

The full import of *Twombly* is still being assessed, with courts reluctant to stake out broad predictions about *Twombly*'s application at the margins and other courts suggesting that *Twombly* might still not even apply in all contexts. But, for the most part, courts have generally read the decision as effecting a meaningful (though perhaps not seismic) change in direction in federal pleading (prompted principally, it is believed, by the burgeoning costs of discovery). Precisely how *Twombly* applies depends on the specific context. Much of the pre-*Twombly* federal pleading mandate survives. The basic "notice" pleading standard remains the rule in federal courts. The pleading of tediously detailed factual allegations is still not required, nor the pleading of every fact necessary to sustain the plaintiff's merits burden. Nor will a claim be dismissed because the factual allegations do not support the pleader's chosen legal theory, if those allegations would provide for relief under another viable theory. It is also still not the courts' role to weigh its subjective assessment of whether the pleader's ultimate success on the merits is probable or unlikely, or to choose between competing allegations that are both plausible. The requisite "plausibility," therefore, is *not* measured by a likelihood of success. But, though "plausibility" does not require a showing of "probability," it also is not satisfied upon a showing of mere "possibility." *See Iqbal,* 556 U.S. at 678. Thus, allegations that are "merely consistent" with (and not "plausibly suggestive" of) liability are not enough. *See id.*; *Twombly*, 550 U.S. at 557.

But the post-*Twombly* "notice" pleading standard is still markedly different from *Conley*'s (at least theoretically) forgiving directive that a complaint should not be dismissed unless a court is able, from that pleading, to positively confirm that the pleader has no possible claim for relief. In other words, under *Conley*, unless the pleader's allegations actually *denied* any possible avenue for recovery, the complaint might not have been dismissed. After *Twombly,* the required inquiry seems to invert the former one: now, a proper complaint must do more than merely *avoid foreclosing* all possible bases for recovery;

it must instead affirmatively *suggest* an actual *entitlement to relief* by supplying allegations that push the claim above the level of mere speculation. And this "plausibility" must now appear affirmatively, on the face of the pleading. In practice, the *Twombly* standard erects a flexible pleading benchmark that varies depending on the type of claim chosen and the type of allegations pleaded: a "plausible" auto accident case may be very concisely pleaded, whereas a "plausible" antitrust or RICO case (often built on inferences from facts that might be either innocent or culpable) may demand a fuller factual presentation.

Using Rule 12(b)(6) with Other Enhanced-Pleading Failures

Several Rules and some federal statutes obligate parties to plead certain claims or defenses with enhanced detail (*e.g.*, Rule 9(b)). A pleading that lacks that required additional detail constitutes a failure to state a cognizable claim, remedied through a Rule 12(b)(6) motion to dismiss.

Burden of Proof

The burden of proving that the pleader has failed to state a claim lies with the moving party. Accordingly, dismissal is not warranted merely because a non-moving party fails to oppose the motion; courts must independently assess the challenged pleading against the pleading standards.

Timing and Waiver

The defense of failure to state a claim may be asserted by motion filed before an answer. Courts disagree whether multiple such pre-answer challenges are technically proper and, if so, whether a later pre-answer motion may raise arguments that existed but were not asserted earlier (courts may tolerate successive motions when, under the circumstances, doing so will serve the interests of justice). The defense may also be asserted post-answer, in a Rule 12(c) motion for judgment on the pleadings or in a Rule 56 motion for summary judgment. A mislabeled post-answer Rule 12(b)(6) motion may be treated as a Rule 12(c) motion, if no prejudice results. Finally, the defense of failure-to-state-a-claim may also be raised during trial, but will be deemed waived if not asserted at least by that time. *See* Rule 12(h)(2).

Extrinsic Materials

In ruling on a Rule 12(b)(6) motion, the court focuses principally on the complaint itself, but often may also consider a small category of additional materials: exhibits attached to the complaint (unless their authenticity is questioned); documents that the complaint incorporates by reference; documents that, though not attached to the complaint, accompany the dismissal motion, are integral to and relied upon in the complaint, and are not contested as inauthentic; information subject to judicial notice; matters of public record (such as orders and other materials in the record of the case); concessions by plaintiffs made in their response to the motion; and any additional facts set out in briefs (so long as they are consistent with the pleadings). Albeit inadvertently, an exhibit that incontestably discredits verifiable factual allegations that are central to the pleading's claim can render that claim implausible and, thus, dismissible.

The parties *may* submit (and the court *may* consider) further materials, but with a consequence—the motion will be re-cast. If the court, in its discretion, considers such additional extrinsic evidence, the motion must be converted into a Rule 56 request for summary judgment. *See* Rule 12(d).

Dismissing "Built-In" Affirmative Defenses

The court will dismiss for failing to state a claim where the face of the complaint reveals patent, "built-in" affirmative defenses, such as statute of limitations, preclusion, preemption, exhaustion of administrative remedies, or statute of frauds. Parties can, in this manner, essentially "plead themselves out of court" in two ways. First, they can allege facts that establish (perhaps inadvertently) an affirmative defense or that success on the merits is not otherwise possible. Second, they can attach extrinsic materials to their pleadings that reveal the presence of the same sort of "built-in" defenses. "Built-in" defense dismissals are proper only were the damning facts are readily ascertainable from the complaint, the public record, or other allowable sources of judicial notice, *and* those facts conclusively demonstrate the defense.

Sua Sponte Motions

The trial court may, on its own initiative, and without an adversary's motion, dismiss a pleading for failing to state a claim upon which relief may be granted. Such dismissals should be granted sparingly. Generally, the trial court must first notify the pleader of its intention to grant a *sua sponte* dismissal and permit an opportunity to amend or otherwise respond.

Pro Se Litigants

Courts are particularly cautious while inspecting pleadings prepared by plaintiffs who lack counsel and are proceeding *pro se*. Often inartful, and rarely composed to the standards expected of practicing attorneys, *pro se* pleadings are viewed with considerable liberality and are held to less stringent standards than those expected of pleadings drafted by lawyers. *See Erickson v. Pardus,* 551 U.S. 89, 94 (2007) (per curiam). This relaxation persists after *Twombly*. Nevertheless, unrepresented plaintiffs are not relieved of their obligation to allege sufficient facts to support a cognizable legal claim. Moreover, courts may usually not give *pro se* litigants legal advice, lest the courts' impartiality be called into question. Dismissals of *pro se* pleaders are ordinarily accompanied by leave to replead (unless it is clear that the best possible case has been pleaded).

Oral Argument

The trial judge may, but is not obligated to, convene oral argument on a Rule 12(b)(6) motion to dismiss.

Postponing Discovery

Some courts suspend discovery after a Rule 12(b)(6) motion is filed, and then continuing for so long as it remains pending. Because such motions challenge pleading (and not evidentiary) sufficiency, pleaders are ordinarily not allowed to engage in discovery to rescue deficient allegations.

Voluntary Dismissals While Motion Is Pending

Plaintiffs may voluntarily dismiss a lawsuit at any time prior to the point where their adversaries serve an answer or a motion for summary judgment. Consequently, plaintiffs are generally permitted to voluntarily dismiss their lawsuits while a pre-answer motion to dismiss is pending (and that privilege likely persists even when the defendant attaches extrinsic materials to its motion, which would otherwise command a conversion to summary judgment procedures—provided the court has not yet converted the motion).

Manner of Ruling

Although no detailed written opinion is required, the practice preferred by the appellate courts is that a dismissal be accompanied by some explanation for the decision, so as to supply both the parties and any reviewing court with the benefit of the trial court's reasoning.

Ruling Deferred

Where circumstances persuade the court that claims should not be dismissed until further factual development is accomplished, the court may deny the Rule 12(b)(6) motion and revisit the merits of claims on a Rule 12(c) motion for judgment on the pleadings or a Rule 56 motion for summary judgment. But pre-ruling discovery is not, as a matter of course, necessarily available to all litigants resisting a motion to dismiss. *See Bell Atlantic Corp. v. Twombly*, 550 U.S. 544, 556–57 (2007).

Post-Ruling Amendments to the Pleadings

The court will generally permit the pleader one post-dismissal opportunity to amend, even when the court doubts that the pleading defects can be overcome, unless the court concludes that any amendment would be futile or inequitable.

- *Failing to Request Leave to Amend:* Although courts often grant leave to amend a dismissed complaint even when it is not requested, neglecting to seek such leave (even if in the alternative) is a very dangerous risk.
- *Duty to Explain Proposed Amendments:* When a repleading appears futile, courts may insist (prior to any amendment) that the plaintiffs first explain how a subsequent revision would cure their pleading deficiency.
- *Appealing, Rather than Amending:* A plaintiff who is otherwise entitled to file an amended complaint following a Rule 12(b)(6) dismissal may choose instead to stand on the original complaint and appeal the dismissal.
- *Amendments After Entry of Judgment:* The generous post-dismissal amendment practice changes once the trial court enters its judgment. At that point, post-judgment relief (under Rules 59 or 60) is necessary, though a timely submitted, credible post-dismissal amendment will likely be considered carefully.

Prejudice on Dismissal

Unless the ruling is premised on mere technical pleading defects or the court directs otherwise (or permits an amended pleading), a dismissal for failing to state a claim is deemed to be a ruling on the merits, and, once final, is accorded full res judicata effect. *See Federated Dept. Stores, Inc. v. Moitie,* 452 U.S. 394, 399 (1981). Conversely, an order denying dismissal under Rule 12(b)(6) does not conclusively resolve anything, nor does it somehow forecast who will prevail at trial (or even whether the case can survive summary judgment).

Appealability

Whether Rule 12(b)(6) rulings are appealable (immediately or otherwise) can be a challenging inquiry and merits careful study. A ruling that grants a Rule 12(b)(6) motion in its entirety and with prejudice, thus terminating the litigation, will almost certainly be a final order and immediately appealable. However, the ruling might not be immediately appealable if it grants the motion but allows repleading, or if it grants the motion only in part. If the ruling denies the motion, the ruling is likely not be immediately appealable, or, if the plaintiff has prevailed at trial, appealable at all. But exceptions exist. For example, a ruling that denies a dismissal on certain immunity grounds may be immediately appealed, as may denials that are "inextricably intertwined" with another order that is immediately appealable.

RULE 12(b)(7) Dismissal for Failure to Join a Rule 19 Party

The seventh and last of the Rule 12(b) defenses and objections permits a challenge to the absence from the lawsuit of a party whom Rule 19 would characterize as "required" for a fair adjudication. (Rule 19's purpose is to facilitate the joinder, into a single lawsuit, of all parties who are inseparably interested in a dispute, to protect their interests and the interests of the existing parties, as well as to shield the courts against a squandering of judicial resources.)

PRACTICING LAW UNDER THIS SUBPART

Legal Test

The courts are hesitant to dismiss for failure to join absent parties, and will not do so on a vague possibility that unjoined persons may have an interest affected by the litigation. The test is not mechanically formalistic, but hinges on the peculiar factual circumstances each case presents. *See Provident Tradesmens Bank & Trust Co. v. Patterson*, 390 U.S. 102, 118 (1968). When a Rule 12(b)(7) motion is filed, the court will conduct a three-step assessment. The court, first, will determine if someone absent from the lawsuit qualifies as a "required" party within the meaning of Rule 19(a). If so, the court, second, will require that the absent party be joined into the lawsuit if it is feasible to do so. If it is not, the court, third, will apply the Rule 19(b) criteria to assess whether to proceed in that party's absence or to dismiss the lawsuit. The court conducts this inquiry on the basis of the pleadings as they appear at the time the joinder is proposed. The court will accept all of the pleader's well-pleaded factual allegations as true, and will draw all reasonable inferences in the pleader's favor. However, legal conclusions and conclusorily-supported "threadbare recitals" of elements will not be accepted as true. The ultimate decision is committed to the trial court's sound discretion.

Timing and Waiver

An objection to the absence of a Rule 19 required party may be asserted by motion filed before a responsive pleading, in the responsive pleading itself, by motion for judgment on the pleadings, or during the trial on the merits. But the trial judge has the discretion to reject a motion as untimely if the motion is found to have been submitted intentionally late to serve a litigant's own strategic purposes, rather than to protect interests relating to an absent party.

Burden of Proof

The burden lies with the person seeking the dismissal. Some courts, however, shift the burden to the party opposing joinder once a *prima facie* case of required party status has been made.

Motions by Nonparties

It is unclear whether nonparties may move for a Rule 19 dismissal, though courts often treat such motions as mislabeled intervention requests or suggestions for *sua sponte* Rule 19 rulings.

Sua Sponte Motions

Although the absence of a Rule 19 party is not a jurisdictional defect, the court may, on its own initiative, raise the absence of a Rule 19 party. *See Republic of Philippines v. Pimentel*, 553 U.S. 851, 861 (2008).

Remedy

The court will, if possible, order that an absent Rule 19(a) required party be joined in the lawsuit. If joinder is not possible, the court will consider whether in equity and good conscience the lawsuit should continue without the absent party. *See* Rule 19(b). Dismissals are disfavored, however, and will be granted only when the defect cannot be cured.

Extrinsic Materials

The parties may produce affidavits and other materials to support their positions on the absence of a Rule 19 party. The courts differ on the legal effect of such extrinsic materials. Some courts hold that those materials can be considered freely without converting the motion into a summary judgment analysis (*see* Rule 12(d)), while others hold that a conversion is required.

Ruling Deferred

The court may defer ruling on the challenge until after discovery is conducted.

Prejudice on Dismissal

A dismissal for lack of a Rule 19 party is proper only when the defect cannot be cured. Moreover, such a dismissal generally does not preclude the plaintiff from re-instituting the claim in a court that can join the absent party.

Appealability

The district court's denial of a Rule 12(b)(7) motion is usually interlocutory and not immediately appealable.

RULE 12(c) Judgment on the Pleadings

When confronting a claim for relief, a defending party may file an answer (as prescribed by Rule 12(a)) or a pre-answer motion (as permitted by Rule 12(b)). Such pre-answer motions ask that the court rule on the defending party's Rule 12(b) defenses and objections before that party is obligated to file its answer. But early judicial rulings can be sought using another tool as well. The defending party can file its answer to the complaint and, once the pleadings stage is closed, file a motion with the court seeking a judgment on the pleadings under this Rule 12(c). A defending party may choose to wait and use Rule 12(c) for many strategic reasons, but most often because the party believes its chances of succeeding on its motion are improved by the court having the ability to read its answer.

PRACTICING LAW UNDER THIS SUBPART

Purpose

Rule 12(c) can be used to achieve either of two separate objectives. A Rule 12(c) motion can be used to seek a substantive, merits disposition of the underlying dispute on grounds that are exposed by an examination of the pleadings. Alternatively, a Rule 12(c) motion can be used to press, *post-answer*, three of the Rule 12 defenses—failure to state a claim, to state a legal defense, or to join a Rule 19 required party. Neither type of motion is ripe until the pleadings have formally closed. Regardless of the type of use, a Rule 12(c) motion remains a pleadings-based attack, with its inquiry limited principally to the pleadings themselves (unlike summary judgment motions, which permit consideration of extrinsic sources of evidence).

Legal Test

Because the motion represents a challenge at an embryonic stage in the litigation, the court will construe the pleadings liberally, and will not resolve contested facts. Instead, the court will accept all well-pleaded material allegations of the nonmoving party as true, and view all facts and inferences in a light most favorable to the pleader. But legal conclusions will not be presumed true, and no unwarranted factual inferences will be drawn to aid a pleader. In ruling, a court may consider whether claims have been undermined by pleaded allegations or by properly considered extrinsic facts or materials.

The courts have articulated different tests for deciding Rule 12(c) motions, depending on the motion's purpose. When the motion seeks a merits disposition of the dispute, the test tracks the summary judgment inquiry and asks whether—informed by the averments and responses in the pleadings—the movant is entitled to a judgment as a matter of law because no genuine dispute exists as to any material fact. Unlike summary judgment motions, however, this type of Rule 12(c) motion considers only the face of the pleadings and a few other modest categories of extrinsic materials. Alternatively, when the motion seeks only to press a Rule 12 defense, the test tracks the Rule 12(b)(6) inquiry and asks whether the contested pleading succeeded in alleging a "plausible" claim for relief or in stating a proper legal defense. (The *Twombly* "plausibility" standard is discussed with Rule 8(a).) A few courts apply a curious hybrid test that cites the Rule 12(b)(6) standard as controlling but adds the "no-material-factual-dispute" inquiry as well.

- *Post-Discovery Motions:* One court has suggested that the operative legal test might differ depending on whether the motion is filed during or after discovery.
- *No Implied Trial Admissions:* Although Rule 12(c) presumes the pleaders' facts as true for motion purposes, the moving party is free, if its motion is denied, to disprove or contradict those facts at trial.
- *Cross-Motions:* When both parties file motions for judgment on the pleadings, the court treats each motion as if the other had not been filed (*i.e.*, with each motion, accepting the non-movant's allegations of fact as true and drawing reasonable inferences in that party's favor).

Timing and Waiver

A motion for judgment on the pleadings is premature if filed before the pleadings have closed. Thus, the motion is not ripe if the complaint (and any counterclaims, crossclaims, or third-party claims) have not yet been answered. However, motions need not be postponed until the period for amendments as-of-right to the pleadings has passed or until discovery is completed. Courts may treat an out-of-time (post-answer) Rule 12(b)(6) motion to dismiss as though it were filed as a Rule 12(c) motion. Rule 12(c) contains no explicit outer time limit on filing, beyond the admonition that all such motions must be filed "early enough not to delay trial." Thus, the fact that discovery has already begun does not necessarily render the motion untimely. But this time window is not unbounded. Motions filed too long after the pleadings are closed may be refused as untimely. Rule 12(c) cannot be used to revive defenses and objections that a party waived by failing to assert in a pre-answer Rule 12(b) motion or responsive pleading, and waivable defenses not included in a party's Rule 12(c) motion are also likely lost (even though they may have been preserved in that party's answer). When Rule 12(c) and Rule 56 motions are both pending, the court need not necessarily rule on the Rule 12(c) motion first.

Dismissing "Built-In" Affirmative Defenses

As in Rule 12(b)(6) practice, the court may grant judgment on the pleadings when the allegations (or the content of properly-considered extrinsic materials) reveal an affirmative defense that defeats the pleader's claim. Indeed, some courts hold that "built-in" affirmative defenses are only properly raised by Rule 12(c) (or Rule 56) motions, and not by Rule 12(b)(6).

Civil Rights and *Pro Se* Cases

Several courts view Rule 12(c) motions as "disfavored" in civil rights cases, and hold that such motions should be applied with "particular strictness" and in a manner that tests pleadings under a "very lenient, even de minimis" standard. Likewise, complaints filed *pro se* are tested liberally, though a plausible claim for relief must nevertheless be stated.

Extrinsic Materials

In ruling on a Rule 12(c) motion, the court may consider the pleaded allegations, exhibits attached to the complaint, incorporated in it by reference, matters of public record, facts subject to judicial notice, and motion exhibits that are integral to the complaint and authentic. If the court, in its discretion, considers (or does not exclude) any other extrinsic evidence presented by the parties on a Rule 12(c) motion, the court must convert the motion into a request for summary judgment under Rule 56. Nonetheless, given the liberality of federal amendments, courts might allow extrinsic materials generated during pre-ruling discovery to fill gaps in a pleading, and may otherwise affirm the use of extrinsic materials in a Rule 12(c) context when doing so is harmless error.

Remedy

If the Rule 12(c) motion is granted, the prevailing parties obtain a final judgment in their favor.

Prejudice on Entry

Granting a Rule 12(c) motion for judgment on the pleadings will ordinarily terminate the case with prejudice, but a court may permit a post-ruling leave to amend (unless it is clear that no amendment could save the pleading).

Appealability

For the same reasons noted in Rule 12(b)(6)'s discussion of appealability, one must proceed with care in analyzing appeals from Rule 12(c) motions for judgment on the pleadings. Generally, a decision granting such a motion is considered a "final order," and is thus immediately appealable, but a decision denying such a motion is deemed "interlocutory" and must await a final disposition on the merits.

RULE 12(d) Presenting Matters Outside the Pleadings

Motions made under Rule 12(b)(6) and Rule 12(c) have a narrow litigation purpose: to test the adequacy of pleadings. Obviously, then, when ruling on these motions, courts may not (absent a few narrow exceptions) consider materials outside the pleadings when assessing whether those pleadings are adequate. Nonetheless, a court may decide that, under the circumstances, it needs to consider extrinsic materials. If it does so, the court must ordinarily then "convert" the pending motion into one seeking summary judgment. In ruling on such "converted" motions, courts must abide by the requirements of Rule 56.

PRACTICING LAW UNDER THIS SUBPART

Mechanics of "Conversion"

When, while considering a Rule 12(b)(6) or 12(c) motion, a court is presented with materials outside the pleadings, and does not exclude them, the court is obligated to "convert" the pleadings challenge into a summary judgment motion. To do so, the court must give all parties notice of the conversion and an opportunity to both be heard and to present further materials in support of their positions on the now-converted motion. Following conversion, and upon a proper request by the parties, the court typically ensures that the parties have a reasonable opportunity for discovery prior to ruling on the converted motion. (Ordinarily, conversion (and the consideration of extrinsic materials) is not appropriate when discovery has not yet occurred.) The court then proceeds to evaluate the motion as a request for summary judgment under Rule 56. Conversion ensures that the distinct policies of pleadings challenges (*i.e.*, testing the adequacy of the allegations) and factual challenges (*i.e.*, testing the availability of supporting facts) are respected.

Triggering "Conversion"

Although this conversion procedure is mandatory, not discretionary, conversion does not occur automatically. The court retains the discretion to *ignore* any extra-pleading materials that the parties may have submitted, in which case no conversion is necessary. In fact, even when the court fails to expressly exclude the extra-pleading materials, a conversion may not be necessary if the materials were, in fact, ignored by the court or otherwise irrelevant to the court's resolution of the motion.

Type of Required Notice of "Conversion"

The required notice of conversion may be either actual or constructive. The former is more obvious and transparent, and thus to be preferred. But actual, formal notice might not be necessary if the non-moving party should have reasonably anticipated the conversion, was not taken by surprise, and was not deprived of a reasonable opportunity to respond to the extra-pleading materials. Thus, a court's neglect in providing formal notice may be excused, for example, where the moving party dual-labeled its motion to dismiss as a motion for summary judgment "in the alternative," where the non-movants had submitted extra-pleading materials of their own, or where the non-movants failed to show that factual materials existed which controvert the moving party's contentions.

Exceptions to the "Conversion" Requirement

Various exceptions to the conversion procedure have been recognized. No conversion is required ordinarily when the court considers: exhibits attached to the complaint (unless their authenticity is questioned); documents the complaint incorporates by reference or which are otherwise integral to the claim (provided they are undisputed); information subject to judicial notice; and matters of public record. Note, however, parties cannot escape this conversion rule simply by attaching to their answer whatever extrinsic materials might be helpful to their later motion.

A few other exceptions are noteworthy. No conversion is usually required if only a portion of a document is attached as an exhibit to the complaint, and the moving party simply submits remaining portions with its motion. A party may waive any objection to a failure to properly convert by failing to timely contest it. And, even if not waived, a failure to properly convert may be deemed harmless if the non-moving party had an adequate opportunity to respond and was not otherwise prejudiced or when the court rules on the basis of some concession made by plaintiffs in their response to the motion.

Notifying *Pro Se* Litigants of Conversion

Because they are unlikely to appreciate the potentially dispositive consequence of a conversion to summary judgment procedures, *pro se* litigants will ordinarily be entitled to notice of that conversion and its meaning.

Reverse "Conversions"

At least one Circuit has rejected the possibility of *reverse* "conversions": treating a summary judgment motion as a Rule 12(b)(6) motion to dismiss in order to assess the pleading's adequacy under the *Twombly* "plausibility" standard.

RULE 12(e) Motion for More Definite Statement

On occasion (and those occasions are rare), a party might be unable to discharge its duty of responding to a pleading because that pleading is impenetrably vague or ambiguous. Obviously, pleaders cannot be expected to respond to something they cannot understand. Rule 12(e) permits parties to seek a court order directing that an incomprehensible pleading be replaced with an understandable one.

PRACTICING LAW UNDER THIS SUBPART

Distinct from Rule 12(b)(6) Motions

Motions to dismiss and motions for more definite statements are not interchangeable. A motion to dismiss under Rule 12(b)(6) attacks a pleading for failing to allege a cognizable claim eligible for some type of relief. In contrast, a Rule 12(e) motion for more definite statement attacks pleadings that may or may not be capable of stating cognizable legal claims, but are so unintelligibly unclear in their present form that drafting a response to them is impossible.

- *Mislabeled Motions:* A motion to dismiss under Rule 12(b)(6) that, more correctly, is a motion for a more definite statement may be so converted by the court in its discretion.
- *Filing Both Motions:* A party may file a motion to dismiss and a motion for more definite statement at the same time. In an appropriate case, the court may consider the motion for more definite statement first and hold the motion to dismiss in abeyance.

Disfavored Motion

The Rules require the pleader to serve only a short, plain statement showing an entitlement to relief. *See* Rule 8(a)(2). Due to these liberal pleading requirements in federal court, motions for a more definite statement are disfavored and granted only sparingly. They are not a substitute for discovery, and ordinarily will not be granted where the level and nature of the detail sought is a proper role for discovery.

Legal Test

Motions for a more definite statement target unintelligibility, not a mere lack of detail. They are proper only when a pleading is so hopelessly vague or ambiguous that a defendant cannot understand the allegations and, therefore, cannot fairly be expected to frame a response or denial, at least not without risking prejudice. Such motions are particularly ill-suited to situations where the information sought is already within the defendant's knowledge, and the motion merely seeks the formality of the recital of known facts. Nevertheless, courts continue to grant these motions, even though disfavored, when the federal notice pleading standards are not met. Just as Rule 12(e) motions are not legitimate substitutes for discovery, discovery is not a fair substitute for proper pleading. Courts and litigants are entitled to know, at the pleading stage, who is being sued, why, and for what. Whether to grant or deny a Rule 12(e) motion is committed to the district judge's sound discretion. Courts have found Rule 12(e) useful in various contexts, including:

- *Special Pleading Obligations:* To seek facts that must be specially pleaded, such as fraud, mistake, and special damages. *See* Rule 9.
- *Threshold Defenses:* To seek (in certain particular situations only) facts necessary to determine whether threshold defenses exist, such as immunity from suit (what motivated the conduct), statute of limitations (when claim arose), or statute of frauds (whether contract was written or oral, term for performance).
- *Rule 10 Violations:* To seek a repleading of a complaint or claim that is confusingly consolidated in a single count (when multiple counts would be proper), lacks numbered paragraphs, or otherwise violates the presentation dictates of Rule 10.

Burden of Proof

The burden lies with the moving party to demonstrate that the challenged pleading is too vague or ambiguous to permit a response. The moving party must identify the deficiencies in the pleading, list the details sought to be provided, and assert an inability to frame a response. The motion must be made formally and properly.

Timing and Waiver

Obviously, a motion for more definite statement must be filed before the party serves a response to the pleading that the party is claiming is so vague and ambiguous that responding is impossible. The moving party should appreciate the consequence of moving for Rule 12(e) relief—once any Rule 12 motion is made (which includes Rule 12(e)), any waivable defense that could have been joined in that motion—but was omitted—will be considered lost. *See* Rules 12(g)–(h). To abate the harshness of this result, the court may permit the moving party to withdraw the Rule 12(e) motion so as to permit a more complete Rule 12 filing.

Tolling Effect

While the motion is pending, the party's time for serving a response to the challenged pleading is postponed. If the motion is granted, the responsive pleading must be served within 14 days after service of the more definite statement (unless the court orders otherwise). *See* Rule 12(a)(4)(B). If the motion is denied, the responsive pleading must be served with 14 days after notice of the court's ruling (unless the court orders otherwise). *See* Rule 12(a)(4)(A).

Applies Only to Pleadings

By its terms, Rule 12(e) is available to compel more definite statements only in pleadings. It cannot be used to require added detail in motions.

Use by Claimants

When an answer pleads an unintelligible defense, some courts permit claimants to invoke Rule 12(e) to force a repleading of that defense. Other courts reject that use, reasoning that, because claimants are usually not required to counter-plead to an answer, Rule 12(e)—by its terms—is inapplicable.

Sua Sponte Motions

The district court may, on its own initiative, strike a deficient pleading and direct the pleader to file a more definite statement. This *sua sponte* option is especially valuable to resolve "shotgun pleading" deficiencies, or when a motion to dismiss is pending but the more appropriate relief is repleading with a more definite statement.

Remedy

To comply with a Rule 12(e) order, the pleader must amend its pleading to add sufficient detail to satisfy the court and meet the adversary's objections. If the pleader fails to serve a more definite statement, fails to serve it timely, or fails to include a meaningful enhancement to deficiently-pleaded allegations, the court may strike the pleading or make such other order as it deems just, including a dismissal with prejudice.

Appealability

Rulings on motions for a more definite statement are ordinarily considered interlocutory and not immediately appealable.

RULE 12(f) Motion to Strike

The courts are permitted to "strike" (or remove) from a pleading an allegation found to be redundant, immaterial, impertinent, or scandalous, and also may "strike" from an answer any defense found to be insufficient. This authority to strike, however, is sharply limited.

PRACTICING LAW UNDER THIS SUBPART

Purpose

Both insufficient defenses and redundant, immaterial, impertinent, or scandalous matter may be stricken from a pleading in order to avoid the time, effort, and expense necessary to litigate spurious issues. Such motions may be granted when necessary to clean up the pleadings, streamline the litigation, or sidestep unnecessary efforts on immaterial issues. But this remedy is considered a "drastic" one, and is never permitted for idle ends. The motion generally cannot be used to purposelessly cull pleadings of mere hyperbole, attempts at humor, or other poor drafting decisions.

General Test

Motions to strike are disfavored by the courts, and rarely granted, especially so when they delay the litigation with little corresponding benefit. In considering a motion to strike, courts will generally apply the same test used to determine a Rule 12(b)(6) motion—the courts will deem as admitted all of the nonmoving party's well-pleaded facts, draw all reasonable inferences in the pleader's favor, and resolve all doubts in favor of denying the motion to strike. But the court will not accept as true the non-moving party's conclusions of law. If disputed questions of fact or law remain as to the challenged material or defense, the motion to strike must be denied. Likewise, if any doubt remains as to the potential later relevance of the contested allegations, the motion will be denied. Beyond these legal constraints, the decision to strike or not is committed to the district judge's discretion.

Burden of Proof

The burden lies with the party moving to strike. Given the disfavored nature of the relief, the burden on the moving party is formidable. The moving party must state the basis for the motion with particularity and identify specifically the relief sought. The moving party must show at least that the allegations bear no possible relation to the controversy. Many courts require, also, a showing of prejudice were the allegations to remain unstricken. But this prejudice requirement remains a bit controversial. Rule 12(f) does not, by its terms, require any showing of prejudice, and for this reason some courts have refused to impose that obligation on the movant. The seeming majority of courts, however, test for prejudice, often citing, as support, the disfavor with which Rule 12(f) relief is viewed. If considered, the requisite prejudice will exist when the contested allegation would confuse the issues or, by its length and complexity, would place an undue burden on the respondent, inject the possibility of unnecessarily extensive and burdensome discovery, improperly increase the time, expense, and complexity of the trial, or otherwise unduly burden the moving party.

Test for Striking Defenses as "Insufficient"

A motion to strike is the claimant's parallel to a Rule 12(b)(6) motion to dismiss. The court may strike any defense that is legally insufficient either as a matter of pleading or as a matter of law. Defenses that are insufficiently pleaded are those that fail to impart the level of notice required by Rules 8 and 9.

Defenses that are insufficient as a matter of law if they are not recognized defenses to the pleaded claims, could otherwise not succeed under any circumstances (that is, no evidence in support of those defenses would be admissible at trial), might confuse the issues in the lawsuit, or are expressed inadequately (especially true for those courts that apply the *Twombly* "plausibility" standard to assess a defense's sufficiency; note that courts are divided on whether *Twombly* ought to govern this inquiry). The objective of such strikes is to eliminate irrelevant and frivolous defenses, the trial of which would otherwise unnecessarily waste time and money. Thus, to strike a defense, the moving party must generally show there is no question of fact or law which might allow the challenged defense to succeed (and, in some courts, prejudice if the defense remains in the case) In conducting this analysis, the court will construe the pleadings liberally in the favor of the defendant (the non-moving party). However, the court is not obligated to accept naked, conclusory defenses. Ordinarily, if the motion has merit, the court will strike the insufficient defense in its entirety, and will not attempt to carve the defense in portions. If the defense is stricken, the pleader will generally be granted leave to file an amended answer unless the amendment would be futile.

Test for Striking "Redundant, Immaterial, Impertinent, or Scandalous" Matter

Absent a good reason, courts will generally not tamper with pleadings. A court will not strike such matter unless it bears no possible relation to the parties' dispute or could confuse the issues. Thus, facts supplying important context and background, though not strictly relevant to a claim's elements, should not be stricken. Moreover, mere redundancy, immateriality, impertinence, or scandalousness is not sufficient to justify striking an allegation—the allegation must generally also be shown to be prejudicial to the moving party. (This prejudice requirement seems likely to dim any Rule 12(f) motion's chance for success if the trial is to proceed non-jury.) If any doubt exists whether the contested matter should be stricken, the motion should be denied. Consequently, to prevail on such a motion, the moving party must establish that: (1) no evidence in support of the contested allegations would be admissible at trial; (2) the allegations have no bearing on issues relevant to the case; and (3) denying the strike would prejudice the moving party.

If granted, the court's order will typically describe in detail the precise matter that must be stricken.

- *Redundant Matter:* A redundant allegation is a needless repetition of other averments.
- *Immaterial Matter:* Immaterial allegations are those that either bear no essential or important relationship to the pleader's claim for relief or contain a statement of unnecessary particulars, or when no evidence to support them would be admissible at trial.
- *Impertinent Matter:* An impertinent allegation is an averment that does not pertain to, or is unnecessary to, the issues in dispute. If the pleader would not be permitted to offer evidence at trial in support of the allegation, the allegation is likely impertinent.
- *Scandalous Matter:* Scandalous matter does not merely offend someone's sensibilities; it must cast a person or entity in an improperly derogatory light. Such matter will not be stricken if it describes acts or events relevant to the parties' dispute, unless the descriptions contain unnecessary detail.

Striking Improper Jury Demands

Rule 12(f) is also a proper vehicle for striking an improper demand for trial by jury.

Striking Class Action Allegations

Rule 12(f) is theoretically available to strike class action allegations, but only in the rare instance where it is obvious from the pleadings that class treatment would not be proper.

Striking Documents Other than Pleadings

As defined in Rule 12(f), motions to strike are directed to "pleadings" only. Consequently, these motions are technically not available to strike material contained in motions, briefs, affidavits, or other non-pleadings. Nonetheless, some courts have considered Rule 12(f) challenges to non-pleadings, or construed such challenges as mislabeled invitations to adjudicate the admissibility of the contested materials, often reasoning that Rule 12(f) offers the only viable vehicle for challenging the materiality and pertinence of the documents under attack. But, many other courts reject this view. Note, some federal districts have authorized a separate motion to "strike" for non-compliance with local rules (such as no sur-reply briefs without prior approval).

Timing and Waiver

A motion to strike must be made before a responsive pleading is served or, if no responsive pleading is required, within 21 days after service of the preceding pleading. In view of the court's authority to strike on its own initiative, this 21-day period is often not applied strictly when the proposal to strike has merit. Parties must appreciate the consequence of moving to strike under Rule 12(f)—only one, pre-answer Rule 12 motion is permitted, and if one is filed, any waivable defense that could have been joined with—but was omitted from—the Rule 12(f) motion will be considered lost. *See* Rules 12(g)–(h). Accordingly, movants must take care to ensure that all pre-answer motions they intend to make, and especially their waivable defenses, are asserted together with their Rule 12(f) motion to strike in an omnibus motion.

***Sua Sponte* Strikes**

The court may, on its own initiative, strike matter from a pleading. Thus, the court may properly consider a party's untimely motion or "suggestion" under Rule 12(f) to strike matter from the pleading.

Extrinsic Materials

Generally, the court will not consider extrinsic materials on a motion to strike. Instead, the grounds supporting the motion to strike must be readily apparent from the face of the pleadings at issue, from materials incorporated within them by reference, or from content of which the court may take judicial notice. If the court does consider extrinsic materials, the motion to strike must ordinarily be converted into a motion for summary judgment.

Mislabeled Rule 12(f) Motions

The appropriate vehicle for testing the factual sufficiency of a pleading is usually not a motion to strike, but a Rule 12(b)(6) motion to dismiss or a Rule 12(c) motion for judgment on the pleadings. Ordinarily, a mislabeled motion to strike that challenges factual sufficiency will simply be treated as a motion to dismiss.

Prejudice on Dismissal

Where an allegation or defense is stricken as technically deficient, the dismissal is generally without prejudice, thus allowing a refiling with a technically correct pleading.

Appealability

Although scant case law exists on the point, rulings on motions to strike are usually considered interlocutory and not immediately appealable.

RULE 12(g) Joining Motions

Defending parties are not required to file Rule 12 motions; they may, instead, simply file an answer to the complaint and proceed on to the next stage of litigation. But if they decide to file a Rule 12 motion, those defending parties are permitted (and *expected*) to join together—in one, omnibus motion—all Rule 12 defenses and objections they may then have.

PRACTICING LAW UNDER THIS SUBPART

Rule and Its Consequences

The operation of Rule 12 can be tricky and merits careful study. Any Rule 12 motion may be joined with any other Rule 12 motion. *See* Rule 12(g)(1). This consolidation mandate produces four consequences once a Rule 12 motion is made:

- *First,* a party is generally permitted to make only one Rule 12 motion; thus, a party who intends to have the court resolve *any* Rule 12 defense or objection at the pre-answer motion stage must also simultaneously present to the court *every* other Rule 12 defense or objection the party intends to then raise. *See* Rule 12(g)(2).
- *Second,* including all such Rule 12 defenses and objections together at once causes no forfeiture of those that are inconsistent with one another.
- *Third,* omitting from any Rule 12 pre-answer motion an objection to personal jurisdiction, venue, process, or service of process likely waives that objection. *See* Rule 12(h)(1).
- *Fourth,* omitting other, non-waivable Rule 12 defenses and objections (except subject-matter jurisdiction) still likely waives the party's right to have those matters considered at the pre-answer stage, thus relegating the party to having to wait until later in the case to assert them.

The intent behind these four consequences is to avoid piecemeal litigating tactics, where defendants seek dismissal on one ground, lose there, and then seek dismissal anew on a different ground.

Exception—Prohibition Applies If Defenses Were "Available"

A party is required to assert in an omnibus motion only those defenses and objections "available" to that party. For example, a party is obviously not obliged to assert an objection to untimely service while the time permitted for timely service has not yet expired. Thus, new defenses and objections may be later asserted if they are triggered by an alteration to the pleadings, by a change in the law occurring while the motion is pending, or by other interim developments. But parties must act promptly. An unnecessarily lengthy delay in asserting a latent Rule 12 objection may, itself, be deemed a waiver.

Exception—Objections to Subject-Matter Jurisdiction

Objections to subject-matter jurisdiction concern the court's authority to hear and decide the case and, as such, cannot be lost through waiver. *See* Rule 12(h)(3).

Exception—Successive Rule 12(b)(6) Motions to Dismiss

A pre-answer motion may challenge a complaint under Rule 12(b)(6) for failing to state a claim upon which relief can be granted. But Rule 12(b)(6) is accorded special treatment under Rule 12(g)'s consolidation mandate. The *defense* of failure-to-state-a-claim is not waived if omitted from a pre-answer Rule 12 motion; instead, that *defense* may be raised in a later pleading, a Rule 12(c) motion for judgment on the pleadings, or at trial. *See* Rule 12(g)(2). Less clear, however, is whether that *defense* can be raised in a second or subsequent *pre-answer* motion, or must it wait until later. Some courts have interpreted this Rule to tolerate successive pre-answer Rule 12(b)(6) motions (at least absent prejudice or adverse impact on judicial economy). Other courts disagree, reading the Rule as rendering improper the filing of successive pre-answer motions to dismiss (especially where they raise arguments that could have been asserted earlier). Those courts, however, then often forgive this technical misstep as harmless error.

"Amending" a Rule 12 Motion

To avoid waiving Rule 12 defenses that were omitted inadvertently from a Rule 12 motion, parties may seek leave of court to "amend" or supplement their Rule 12 motions to include the omitted defenses or objections. In considering such amendments, the court may examine whether the amendment request was filed before the Rule 12 motion was heard, the time interval between the original Rule 12 motion and the attempted correction, the moving party's good faith, and the likelihood that the omission was intentional and tactical, or merely inadvertent.

Applies Only to Same Moving Party

The consolidation obligation is only triggered when the same party attempts to make a later Rule 12 motion. Thus, a Rule 12 filing by one co-defendant does not foreclose a later Rule 12 filing by a different co-defendant, even when they share the same counsel.

Applies to All Rule 12 Motions

This omnibus consolidation requirement applies to all Rule 12 motions, including the Rule 12(b) defenses as well as Rule 12(e) motions for more definite statements and Rule 12(f) motions to strike. Thus, a motion seeking only a more definite statement will likely have the effect of waiving challenges to personal jurisdiction, venue, process, and service.

Applies Only to Rule 12 Motions

This consolidation provision applies only to Rule 12 motions and only to defenses that may be asserted under Rule 12. It does not apply to motions allowed under other Rules or laws, nor does it apply to affirmative defenses (which remain preserved, even after a Rule 12 motion, if timely asserted in the responsive pleading).

Later Rule 12(c) Motion on Same Grounds

A party enjoys the right to press a failure to state a claim defense in a post-answer Rule 12(c) motion for judgment on the pleadings. *See* Rule 12(g)(2). Most courts construe this right broadly, permitting its use even where the party could have, or actually did, press this same defense in its earlier pre-answer motion. Other courts, though permitting such motions, question whether such a use comports with Rule 12(g)'s "consolidation" policy.

RULE 12(h) Waiving and Preserving Certain Defenses

Rule 12(h) and the preceding Rule 12(g) must be understood together. Rule 12(g) authorizes the joining together—in one single, omnibus motion—of all defenses and objections permitted by Rule 12. Recall, that a responding party is *not* obligated to file a Rule 12 motion, but may instead simply file an answer to the complaint and proceed on in litigation. But *if* the responding party chooses to file a Rule 12 motion, and *if* that party decides to omit one or more of the allowable Rule 12 defenses and objections from that motion, Rule 12(h) sets out the consequences.

PRACTICING LAW UNDER THIS SUBPART

Early Waivable Defenses and Objections

Four defenses and objections—lack of personal jurisdiction (Rule 12(b)(2)), improper venue (Rule 12(b)(3)), insufficient process (Rule 12(b)(4)), and insufficient service (Rule 12(b)(5))—are waived unless they are:

- *Asserted by Pre-Answer Motion*, if a pre-answer Rule 12 motion is filed, or

- *Asserted in the Answer*, if no pre-answer Rule 12 motion is filed (though raising a waivable defense in the answer *after* omitting it from a pre-answer Rule 12 motion will not rescue it).

Purpose

Judicial economy underlies this early-waiver provision. It is designed to prevent the delaying effect of the piecemeal assertion of Rule 12 objections and defenses through multiple motions, and to permit the early dismissal of inappropriate claims before the court devotes unnecessary time and resources to adjudication.

Waiver Only If Defenses Were "Available"

The waiver provision of Rule 12(h) will apply only to bar unasserted defenses and objections that were "available" at the time of the party's Rule 12 motion or responsive pleading. *See* Rule 12(h)(1)(A).

Waiver Is Mandatory, Not Discretionary

The waiver provision of Rule 12(h) seems to impose a mandatory, not discretionary, obligation.

Waiver by Improper Assertion

A Rule 12(h) waivable defense may be lost by asserting it too obscurely or indirectly, by asserting it incompletely, or by asserting it in an untimely way.

Waiver (or "Forfeiture") by Implication

By the very act of suing, a plaintiff impliedly waives any personal jurisdiction and venue objections. *See Adam v. Saenger*, 303 U.S. 59, 67–68 (1938). Defendants, too, by their conduct, may impliedly relinquish objections to personal jurisdiction, venue, insufficient process, or insufficient service of process, even though those defenses were originally asserted properly. Such a forfeiture may follow when the contesting defendant fails to promptly press the court for a dispositive ruling on its objections, behaves during the litigation in a manner that effectively submits to the court's jurisdiction, or is sanctioned for noncompliance with court orders.

- *No Waiver by Early Filings:* A defendant who files documents during the pre-answer/pre-motion period will ordinarily not trigger this forfeiture-by-implication doctrine.
- *No Waiver by Asserting Affirmative Claims:* Although some contrary authority persists, many courts hold that a party does *not* waive a properly asserted objection to personal jurisdiction by pressing an affirmative claim for relief (like a counterclaim), or by filing ancillary motions (like a request for stay or injunction pending appeal) premised on the asserted jurisdictional defense. This view construes such affirmative claims for relief as simply contingent on the court's denial of the party's jurisdictional objections.
- *No Waiver After Motion Loss:* A defendant who properly asserts a waivable defense, presses for dismissal on that basis, but loses, will ordinary not waive the pressed defense by continuing to participate in defending the case.

Waiver by Post-Answer Rule 12(c) Motion Omission

A waivable defense that has been preserved in a party's answer may still yet be waived if that defense is omitted from a post-answer motion for judgment on the pleadings.

Waiver Not Avoided by Others' Motions

In a multi-party lawsuit, one defendant's preservation of a defense or objection will not necessarily preserve that same defense or objection for other parties.

Avoiding Waiver by Answering Only (No Motion)

Parties have the option of asserting their defenses *either* by motion *or* in their responsive pleading. Thus, unless a waiver (or "forfeiture") by implication later occurs (see above), parties who elect not to file a Rule 12 motion at all still dutifully preserve their defenses and objections by asserting them in their responsive pleading, and may thereafter challenge them on a Rule 12(c) motion for judgment on the pleadings.

Avoiding Waiver By Amending an Answer

A party who chooses not to file a pre-answer Rule 12 motion will lose any waivable defenses and objections which that party omits from its answer *or any amendment to its answer allowed "as a matter of course."* This "matter-of-course" amendment window is narrow, encompassing only one amendment and only if it is done either (a) within 21 days after service of the original answer or (b) if a response to that original answer was required, within 21 days after service of the responsive pleading or responsive Rule 12(b), (e), or (f) motion. Although amendments beyond this brief time window are "freely" given "when justice so requires," those are not "matter-of-course" amendments, but depend on leave of court, and they cannot rescue an omitted waivable defense or objection.

Avoiding Waiver By "Amending" / Supplementing a Motion

A party who chose to file a pre-answer Rule 12 motion but omitted from that filing a waivable defense may request the court to exercise its discretion to allow that party to amend or supplement its pending motion.

Preserved But Waivable Defenses and Objections

Defenses and objections to a failure to state a claim upon which relief can be granted (Rule 12(b)(6)), failure to join an indispensable party (Rule 12(b)(7)), and failure to state a legal defense (Rule 12(f)) are waived *only* if not asserted before the close of trial. These defenses, though generally preserved throughout the lawsuit, may not be raised for the first time in post-trial motions or on appeal.

- *Only One Pre-Answer Rule 12(b)(6) Motion:* Some (but not all) courts hold that successive, pre-answer Rule 12(b)(6) motions are prohibited by Rule 12(g)'s requirement that all Rule 12 defenses (including failure to state a claim) be raised in a single pre-answer motion—if the party chooses to file a motion at all.
- *Non-Waiver Applies to Rule 19(b) Parties Only:* Rule 12(h) preserves only the defense of dismissal for failing to join a required party whose joinder is not feasible. The failure to join a Rule 19(a) required party who could be feasibly joined is waived if omitted from a pre-answer Rule 12 motion, if one is filed, or from the responsive pleading, if one is not.

Objections to Subject-Matter Jurisdiction

Because objections to the court's subject-matter jurisdiction concern the court's structural authority to hear and decide the parties' dispute, no one can waive such an objection, be estopped from raising the objection, or cure such a problem by consenting to jurisdiction where none exists. *See Wachovia Bank v. Schmidt,* 546 U.S. 303, 316 (2006).

- *Asserted at Any Time:* Objections to subject-matter jurisdiction may be made in the omnibus Rule 12 motion, in the responsive pleading, in subsequent pretrial motions, in a motion for relief from final judgment, or on appeal. *See Arbaugh v. Y&H Corp.,* 546 U.S. 500, 506 (2006). However, once the lawsuit is no longer pending, a party who neglected to raise subject-matter jurisdiction objections is likely foreclosed from doing so collaterally. *See Ins. Corp. of Ireland v. Compagnie des Bauxites de Guinee,* 456 U.S. 694, 702 n.9 (1982); *Chicot County Drainage Dist. v. Baxter State Bank,* 308 U.S. 371, 374–78 (1940).

- *Styling of Post-Answer Motions:* Although a motion to dismiss for lack of subject-matter jurisdiction is technically untimely if filed after the pleadings are closed, the courts will typically treat such a belated filing as a Rule 12(c) motion, a Rule 12(h)(3) motion, or as a "suggestion" to the court that it lacks subject-matter jurisdiction, and will then apply the familiar Rule 12(b)(1) standards.
- *Raised by Court:* Both trial courts and appeals courts have the obligation to check subject-matter jurisdiction and, if they detect its absence, to raise that objection.

Waiting for Default, Then Collaterally Attacking

Although the Rules require defendants to raise their objections to process, service, and personal jurisdiction in either an omnibus Rule 12 motion or the answer (if no motion is filed), these defenses are not necessarily lost where the defendants neither appear nor defend, but default. In that instance, the constitutional protections of due process may permit those defendants to raise those objections in opposition to the motion for default or collaterally. *See Insurance Corp. of Ireland, Ltd. v. Compagnie des Bauxites de Guinee,* 456 U.S. 694, 706 (1982). But defendants act at their peril if they actually receive notice of the pending lawsuit and choose to ignore it, in reliance on their own, untested belief that process, service, or personal jurisdiction was faulty. Minimally, they must guess correctly. If they've guessed wrong, they likely forfeit their right to defend on the merits. Conversely, if they timely raise these objections (and thus avoid a default), they have assented to the forum's jurisdiction to determine its own jurisdiction, and are thereafter barred from attacking collaterally and must appeal.

- *Actual Notice:* Defendants who seek to object on service grounds, but who received actual notice of the lawsuit, may be found to have waived their service objections or to have had those objections otherwise materially limited.
- *Appearing to Defend Post Default:* Appearing to participate in proceedings following entry of default will likely waive service and personal jurisdiction objections, unless, upon appearing, the defaulting party promptly asserts them.
- *Appearing and Abandoning:* Likewise, those objections may also be waived if the defendant begins to assert them but then abandons them.
- *Burden of Proof:* In a direct challenge, the party invoking the court's jurisdiction bears the burden of proving it; in a collateral challenge, the party contesting the original court's jurisdiction has the burden of disproving it.

RULE 12(i) Hearing Before Trial

A party who asserts a Rule 12 defense or objection, whether by answer or by motion, may request that the court hear and rule on the matter before trial. The court, in turn, must schedule such a pretrial resolution for the motion, unless it instead orders the matter deferred until time of trial.

PRACTICING LAW UNDER THIS SUBPART

Rule 12(b) Defenses Asserted by Motion

When a Rule 12(b) defense or objection is asserted by motion, the moving papers themselves should include a "notice of hearing" or similar references following the practice dictated by the local rules. Ordinarily, courts resolve Rule 12(b) and Rule 12(c) motions by issuing a pretrial Memorandum and Order.

Rule 12(b) Defenses Asserted by Responsive Pleading

When a Rule 12(b) defense or objection is asserted only in the responsive pleading (*i.e.,* where no pre-answer Rule 12(b) motion for dismissal is filed), a Rule 12(i) application for preliminary hearing is the vehicle used to obtain a pretrial determination from the court on those defenses and objections.

When Pretrial Determinations Are Proper

Even in the presence of a genuine factual dispute, the court may nevertheless decide, *pretrial,* challenges affecting subject-matter jurisdiction, personal jurisdiction, standing, venue, and certain threshold defenses (like preclusion). In deciding whether these types of issues should be determined preliminarily (or should, instead, await resolution at trial), the court weighs the need to test these defenses and the litigants' interest in having the objections resolved promptly, against the expense and delay of a preliminary hearing, the court's difficulty in deciding the issues preliminarily, and the likelihood that the issues will become so interconnected with the merits that deferring them until trial would be preferable.

On Motion or *Sua Sponte*

A hearing may be ordered upon a party's request or by the court *sua sponte.*

Oral Argument and Hearing

The moving party is generally not *entitled* to oral argument or an evidentiary hearing on the motion; instead, the right of "hearing" conferred by this Rule is ordinarily satisfied upon affording a party the opportunity to, in some manner, present its views and arguments to the court. Moreover, the court enjoys discretion on what type of hearing to allow: a hearing only on briefs, an oral argument, or a full evidentiary hearing.

When Pretrial Determinations Are Properly Deferred

A district court's *pretrial* review and disposition of Rule 12(b) defenses and Rule 12(c) motions is discretionary, not mandatory. In appropriate cases, involving peculiarly complicated factual and legal issues, or where further factual development is necessary, the court may defer resolving Rule 12(b) defenses until time of trial.

How to know when counterclaim is compulsory:

(1) whether evidence is relevant to P's claim & D's counterclaim, OR
(2) whether the claim & counterclaim raise the same issue of law & fact

No matter how compulsory, it is not going to be compulsory if:

(a) already pled in another action pending at the time when the claim could be filed
(b) P brought suit by attachment or other process resulting only in rem or q-i-r. jurisdiction & def has not filed a counterclaim
(c) requires joining parties over whom the court lacks jurisdiction, or
(d) the def did not have it, the claim did not exsist yet — when D served its answer

Permissive: not mandatory, may bring up if wants to
→ no logical connection btw. claims

RULE 13

COUNTERCLAIM AND CROSSCLAIM

(a) Compulsory Counterclaim.

(1) In General. A pleading must state as a counterclaim any claim that—at the time of its service—the pleader has against an opposing party if the claim:

(A) arises out of the transaction or occurrence that is the subject matter of the opposing party's claim; and

(B) does not require adding another party over whom the court cannot acquire jurisdiction.

(2) Exceptions. The pleader need not state the claim if:

(A) when the action was commenced, the claim was the subject of another pending action; or

(B) the opposing party sued on its claim by attachment or other process that did not establish personal jurisdiction over the pleader on that claim, and the pleader does not assert any counterclaim under this rule.

(b) Permissive Counterclaim. A pleading may state as a counterclaim against an opposing party any claim that is not compulsory.

(c) Relief Sought in a Counterclaim. A counterclaim need not diminish or defeat the recovery sought by the opposing party. It may request relief that exceeds in amount or differs in kind from the relief sought by the opposing party.

(d) Counterclaim Against the United States. These rules do not expand the right to assert a counterclaim—or to claim a credit—against the United States or a United States officer or agency.

(e) Counterclaim Maturing or Acquired After Pleading. The court may permit a party to file a supplemental pleading asserting a counterclaim that matured or was acquired by the party after serving an earlier pleading.

(f) [Abrogated]

(g) Crossclaim Against a Coparty. A pleading may state as a crossclaim any claim by one party against a coparty if the claim arises out of the transaction or occurrence that is the subject matter of the original action or of a counterclaim, or if the claim relates to any property that is the subject matter of the original action. The crossclaim may include a claim that the coparty is or may be liable to the cross-claimant for all or part of a claim asserted in the action against the cross-claimant.

(h) Joining Additional Parties. Rules 19 and 20 govern the addition of a person as a party to a counterclaim or crossclaim.

(i) Separate Trials; Separate Judgments. If the court orders separate trials under Rule 42(b), it may enter judgment on a counterclaim or cross-claim under Rule 54(b) when it has jurisdiction to do so, even if the opposing party's claims have been dismissed or otherwise resolved.

[Amended effective March 19, 1948; July 1, 1963; July 1, 1966; August 1, 1987; April 30, 2007, effective December 1, 2007; March 26, 2009, effective December 1, 2009.]

UNDERSTANDING RULE 13

HOW RULE 13 FITS IN

The initial complaint contains the claims that the plaintiffs are asserting against the defendants. In order to facilitate the resolution of all of the related claims at one time, the Rules allow a variety of additional claims to be joined to the action after the plaintiffs commence it. Rule 13 governs two such claims.

Counterclaims are claims that the defendants have back against the plaintiffs. Some types of claims have limits on the nature of the claim or liability that the claiming party may assert, but not so for counterclaims—any claim that a defendant has against a plaintiff qualifies as a counterclaim. Counterclaims are divided into two categories, however: compulsory and permissive. Compulsory counterclaims are those that arise out of the same transaction or occurrence as the plaintiffs' claims against the defendants (and that do not require adding a party over whom the court cannot exercise jurisdiction, as described in Rule 19). A defendant must assert all compulsory counterclaims or they are waived. Any claim that a defendant has against a plaintiff that is not a compulsory counterclaim is a permissive counterclaim, which the defendant may assert or reserve for a later action without risking waiver.

The other type of claims covered by Rule 13 are crossclaims—claims by one defending party against a co-defendant. In contrast to the unrestricted nature of permissive counterclaims, Rule 13 requires that a crossclaim arise out of the same transaction or occurrence as the plaintiffs' claims against the defendants (or relates to the same property as the plaintiff's claim if that claim relates to property, such as a title dispute). However, Rule 18 allows a party asserting one qualifying crossclaim to assert any other claims that party has against the crossclaim defendant—related or unrelated. Thus, if a defending party wants to assert any claims against another defendant, it must assert one transactionally related crossclaim, and then may assert all other claims it has against that defendant. All crossclaims are permissive—they may be asserted in the action or reserved for a future action.

Historically, some courts did not allow a defendant to assert a contribution claim unless and until the defendant was held liable to the plaintiff. The reasoning for this restriction was that the defendant's contribution claim did not accrue—mature into a claim that could be presented in court—until the defendant had been held liable for more than its fair share of the liability; only then could the defendant seek to recoup the excess it paid above its fair share. This practice led to inefficiencies, so Rule 13 now clarifies that a defendant may seek contribution by crossclaim during the pendency of the plaintiff's claim against that defendant.

Rule 13 also contains two provisions applying generally to both counterclaims and crossclaims. It specifies that Rules 19 and 20 apply to adding additional parties for counterclaims and crossclaims. Thus, for example, Rule 20 allows a plaintiff to join two or more parties as defendants if the plaintiff is asserting transactionally related claims against the defendants and the claims share at least one common issue of fact or law. Accordingly, a defendant asserting a counterclaim against a plaintiff may join another party as an additional defendant to the counterclaim if authorized by Rule 20. Rule 13 also authorizes the court to conduct a separate trial and enter a separate judgment on a counterclaim or crossclaim, even if the primary claim has been dismissed or settled.

Keep in mind that authorization under these joinder rules to bring a claim as part of a lawsuit is only one part of the analysis; the party asserting the claim must also establish subject-matter jurisdiction, personal jurisdiction, and venue. Sometimes, these aspects of the court's authority are easy to establish. For example, if a defendant asserts a compulsory counterclaim, the court will likely find supplemental jurisdiction, personal jurisdiction, and venue without any difficulty. Conversely, a permissive counterclaim is unlikely to qualify for supplemental jurisdiction, and instead will need an independent basis for subject-matter jurisdiction. See the Getting Started section for a detailed discussion of these topics.

THE ARCHITECTURE OF RULE 13

Rule 13 contains five subsections addressing counterclaims, one subsection covering crossclaims, and two subsections that apply to both. Rules 13(a)–(e) contain the provisions governing counterclaims. Rule 13(a) defines compulsory counterclaims and establishes the exceptions to the general definition. Rule 13(b) defines all other claims as permissive counterclaims. Rule 13(c) clarifies that counterclaims may assert any type of liability, not just offsets to the plaintiff's claims. Rule 13(d) contains a narrow provision regarding counterclaims against the United States, and Rule 13(e) authorizes defendants to assert counterclaims by supplemental pleadings if the basis for the counterclaim arises after the initial pleadings.

The lone rule governing crossclaims is located in Rule 13(g), which contains both the limitation requiring that a crossclaim be transactionally related to the claim asserted against the crossclaim plaintiff and the clarification that a crossclaim may assert a claim for contribution. Rule 13(h) allows joinder of additional parties to crossclaims and counterclaims under the provisions of Rule 19 and Rule 20. Finally, Rule 13(i) contains the provisions authorizing the court to adjudicate counterclaims and crossclaims even if the original claim has terminated.

HOW RULE 13 WORKS IN PRACTICE

RULE 13(a) Compulsory Counterclaim

Subject to some exceptions discussed below, compulsory counterclaims are those counterclaims arising from the same transaction or occurrence that gave rise to the plaintiff's complaint. Such counterclaims are so closely related to claims already raised by a plaintiff that it would be inefficient to litigate them in separate actions. Consequently, compulsory counterclaims generally must be asserted in the pending litigation or they are waived.

PRACTICING LAW UNDER THIS SUBPART

Procedure

Compulsory counterclaims are typically asserted by pleading them in the answer to a complaint or other claim—a defendant might file an answer that includes counterclaims against the plaintiff.

Same Transaction or Occurrence

Counterclaims are compulsory if they arise out of the same transaction or occurrence that is the subject of the opposing party's claim. Some courts construe this standard liberally, finding a counterclaim compulsory when there is any significant logical relationship between the plaintiff's claim and the counterclaim. Other courts require substantial overlap in all elements of the claims before deeming a counterclaim compulsory.

Exceptions

There are a number of circumstances in which a counterclaim is exempted from being deemed compulsory even though it arises out of the same transaction or occurrence as a claim filed by an opposing party:

(1) *Rule 13(a) Inapplicable Until Service of Responsive Pleading:* Even if a counterclaim arises from the same transaction or occurrence as a plaintiff's claim, it does not become a compulsory counterclaim until the time when the party holding the counterclaim is required to file a responsive pleading. Thus, if a defendant initially filed a motion to dismiss under Rule 12(b) prior to answering the complaint and the court granted the motion to dismiss, the defendant never had an obligation to file a responsive pleading. In that circumstance, any claim the defendant had against the plaintiff would not be deemed a compulsory counterclaim, and would be preserved for assertion in subsequent litigation.

(2) *Lack of Jurisdiction over Third Parties:* If a counterclaim requires joinder of some additional person not subject to the court's jurisdiction, the counterclaim will not be deemed compulsory, irrespective of the amount of overlap it shares with the plaintiff's claim. See Rule 19 for a discussion of when a person is required to be joined as a party.

(3) *Pending Lawsuits:* A counterclaim is not compulsory if it has already been sued upon in other litigation. Thus, if one person filed suit in a State court, and the opponent of that claim then sued in federal court asserting a transactionally related claim, the original State claim would not be a compulsory counterclaim in the federal court action because it is already the subject of pending litigation. This makes sense—the party who first filed the action in State court should be permitted to litigate its claim in its court of choice, rather than being forced to litigate it as a counterclaim in the defendant's chosen court.

Subject-Matter Jurisdiction

Compulsory counterclaims must satisfy subject-matter jurisdiction. Because compulsory counterclaims must arise from the same transaction or occurrence as the plaintiff's claim, counterclaims almost always meet the requirements for supplemental jurisdiction. *See Baker v. Gold Seal Liquors, Inc.,* 417 U.S. 467, 470 (1974).

Personal Jurisdiction over Plaintiffs

Plaintiffs can rarely assert personal jurisdiction objections to compulsory counterclaims; by instituting an action in a particular court, a plaintiff is held to have consented to that court's jurisdiction to adjudicate related claims, and by definition, a compulsory counterclaim is closely related to the plaintiff's claim.

Venue

Most courts hold that venue is deemed proper for compulsory counterclaims.

Failure to Assert a Compulsory Counterclaim

Defendants who do not assert compulsory counterclaims are usually barred from raising the claims in subsequent litigation.

RULE 13(b) Permissive Counterclaim

Permissive counterclaims are all counterclaims that are not compulsory. Permissive counterclaims may be filed in the pending action, but they may also be asserted in a separate action.

PRACTICING LAW UNDER THIS SUBPART

Procedure

Permissive counterclaims are typically filed as part of the answer to the complaint.

Subject-Matter Jurisdiction

Permissive counterclaims must satisfy requirements for subject-matter jurisdiction, like all other claims. Unlike compulsory counterclaims, however, supplemental jurisdiction is unlikely to apply to permissive counterclaims because they generally do not arise out of the same case or controversy as the claims already in the case (or they would be compulsory). Thus, permissive counterclaims normally require a basis for original subject-matter jurisdiction.

Venue

It is unsettled whether permissive counterclaims must satisfy venue requirements.

Failure to Assert a Permissive Counterclaim

If a party holding a permissive counterclaim chooses not to assert it in the pending litigation, the party may assert it at a later date in a separate action.

RULE 13(c) Relief Sought in a Counterclaim

Counterclaims may be for any amount, irrespective of whether the amount sought in the counterclaim exceeds the amount sought in the other party's claim. Additionally, counterclaims may seek kinds of relief not sought in the opposing party's claim. For example, if the opposing party's claim sought money damages only, the counterclaim could seek either money damages, equitable relief, or both money damages and equitable relief.

RULE 13(d) Counterclaim Against the United States

As a general rule, the United States and its officers and agencies are immune from suits in federal courts unless the United States waives its sovereign immunity. Rule 13(d) clarifies that the counterclaim provisions of Rule 13(a) and (b) do not alter the law of sovereign immunity.

RULE 13(e) Counterclaim Maturing or Acquired After Pleading

If counterclaims mature or are acquired after a party has pleaded, the party may choose to assert them in a supplemental pleading, subject to the court's discretion.

PRACTICING LAW UNDER THIS SUBPART

Procedure

A party seeking to assert a Rule 13(e) counterclaim must file a motion and supporting materials explaining the circumstances in which the counterclaim matured or was acquired.

Party's Discretion

Rule 13(e) is permissive in nature, even if the counterclaim arises from the same transaction or occurrence as the opposing party's claim. Thus, a party holding a counterclaim of the kind controlled by Rule 13(e) may assert it, subject to the court's permission, but is under no obligation to do so.

Judicial Discretion

If a party seeks to raise a Rule 13(e) counterclaim, the court retains discretion to refuse to hear the counterclaim in the pending action. Generally, courts permit Rule 13(e) counterclaims where they will not confuse the trier of fact or where they will not unfairly prejudice other parties, particularly through excessively delaying the litigation. Rule 13(e) counterclaims that arise out of the same transaction or occurrence as the opposing party's claim are more likely to be heard in the pending litigation.

Jurisdiction and Venue

Just like regular counterclaims, Rule 13(e) counterclaims need subject-matter jurisdiction and venue.

RULE 13(f) Abrogated

RULE 13(g) Crossclaim Against Coparty

Persons who are already parties to a suit may bring crossclaims—claims against persons on the same side of the litigation—that are transactionally related to the claims asserted against them.

PRACTICING LAW UNDER THIS SUBPART

Procedure

Crossclaims are typically raised in a responsive pleading—a defendant might file an answer that includes crossclaims against a codefendant.

Crossclaims Are Always Permissive

Unlike compulsory counterclaims, all crossclaims are permissive and may be asserted in the pending litigation or in a separate action.

Same Transaction or Occurrence

A crossclaim must arise out of the same transaction or occurrence as the original action, or relate to the same property that is in dispute in the original action. In this important sense, crossclaims, though permissive, are fundamentally different from permissive counterclaims, which typically arise from a transaction or occurrence that is unrelated to the original action. See the discussion of compulsory counterclaim in Rule 13(a) for an explanation of the standard for "same transaction or occurrence."

Additional Rule 18 Claims

Once a party has asserted one crossclaim that qualifies under Rule 13(g)—a claim that is transactionally related—the party may assert any other claims it has against the crossclaim defendant, even if entirely unrelated, under Rule 18(a).

Subject-Matter Jurisdiction

Like all claims, the court must have subject-matter jurisdiction over crossclaims. *See McNutt v. General Motors Acceptance Corp. of Indiana,* 298 U.S. 178, 189 (1936). However, because crossclaims must arise out of the same transaction or occurrence as the original action, crossclaims usually will satisfy the requirements of supplemental jurisdiction. Additional claims joined pursuant to Rule 18(a) may not, though.

Personal Jurisdiction and Venue

Although crossclaims must meet the requirements of personal jurisdiction and venue, if the court has personal jurisdiction over the crossclaim defendant and venue for the original action, those doctrines will be satisfied for the crossclaim as well.

RULE 13(h) Joining Additional Parties

Occasionally, a counterclaim or crossclaim will require the joinder of persons who are not yet parties. Rule 13(h) authorizes the use of Rules 19 and 20, governing joinder of persons, to achieve that end.

PRACTICING LAW UNDER THIS SUBPART

Procedure

Although the law is not entirely settled, it appears that when counterclaimants or crossclaimants seek to join additional parties under Rule 13(h), they may simply make appropriate service on the parties to be joined and provide notice to those already parties. There appears to be no need to file a motion requesting leave to join the parties.

Prerequisite of One Party

Counterclaims and crossclaims cannot be brought unless at least one person being sued is already a party to the action. However, once one such person is sued on a counterclaim or crossclaim, other persons may be joined on that counterclaim or crossclaim, subject to the terms and conditions of Rules 19 and 20.

Comparison with Impleader

Both Rule 13(h) and Rule 14 authorize joinder of nonparties. A key difference between them is that Rule 13(h) requires that the claim against the nonparty be joined to a claim against an existing party. Rule 14, by contrast, allows a defending party to join a nonparty without the need to assert a claim against an existing party. Additionally, Rule 14 requires a claim asserting that the third-party defendant is liable, in whole or in part, for the liabilities asserted against the third-party plaintiff (sometimes called "derivative liability" or contribution). Rule 13(g) requires only that the crossclaim arise out of the same transaction or occurrence; the liability asserted need not be derivative, and Rule 13(a) does not impose any restrictions on the nature of counterclaims.

Subject-Matter Jurisdiction, Personal Jurisdiction, and Venue

Rule 13(h) claims must satisfy subject-matter jurisdiction, personal jurisdiction, and venue, like all other claims (although venue will be deemed satisfied). Since Rule 13(h) contemplates the addition of parties under Rules 19 and 20, be sure to consider the exception to supplemental jurisdiction under 28 U.S.C. § 1367(b) (discussed in the Getting Started section above).

RULE 13(i) Separate Trials; Separate Judgments

Because additional claims added to a case through Rules 13(a), (b), and (g) have substantial potential for confusing the trier of fact or delaying adjudication of the original claims, the court may hold separate hearings, as provided by Rule 42(b), and/or enter separate judgments, as provided by Rule 54(b). Courts have substantial discretion in these determinations.

RULE 14

THIRD-PARTY PRACTICE

(a) When a Defending Party May Bring in a Third-Party.

(1) *Timing of the Summons and Complaint.* A defending party may, as third-party plaintiff, serve a summons and complaint on a nonparty who is or may be liable to it for all or part of the claim against it. But the third-party plaintiff must, by motion, obtain the court's leave if it files the third-party complaint more than 14 days after serving its original answer.

(2) *Third-Party Defendant's Claims and Defenses.* The person served with the summons and third-party complaint-the "third-party defendant":

(A) must assert any defense against the third-party plaintiff's claim under Rule 12;

(B) must assert any counterclaim against the third-party plaintiff under Rule 13(a), and may assert any counterclaim against the third-party plaintiff under Rule 13(b) or any crossclaim against another third-party defendant under Rule 13(g);

(C) may assert against the plaintiff any defense that the third-party plaintiff has to the plaintiff's claim; and

(D) may also assert against the plaintiff any claim arising out of the transaction or occurrence that is the subject matter of the plaintiff's claim against the third-party plaintiff.

(3) *Plaintiff's Claims Against a Third-Party Defendant.* The plaintiff may assert against the third-party defendant any claim arising out of the transaction or occurrence that is the subject matter of the plaintiff's claim against the third-party plaintiff. The third-party defendant must then assert any defense under Rule 12 and any counterclaim under Rule 13(a), and may assert any counterclaim under Rule 13(b) or any crossclaim under Rule 13(g).

(4) *Motion to Strike, Sever, or Try Separately.* Any party may move to strike the third-party claim, to sever it, or to try it separately.

(5) *Third-Party Defendant's Claim Against a Nonparty.* A third-party defendant may proceed under this rule against a nonparty who is or may be liable to the third-party defendant for all or part of any claim against it.

(6) *Third-Party Complaint In Rem.* If it is within the admiralty or maritime jurisdiction, a third-party complaint may be in rem. In that event, a

reference in this rule to the "summons" includes the warrant of arrest, and a reference to the defendant or third-party plaintiff includes, when appropriate, a person who asserts a right under Supplemental Rule C(6)(a)(i) in the property arrested.

(b) When a Plaintiff May Bring in a Third-Party. When a claim is asserted against a plaintiff, the plaintiff may bring in a third-party if this rule would allow a defendant to do so.

(c) Admiralty or Maritime Claim.

(1) *Scope of Impleader.* If a plaintiff asserts an admiralty or maritime claim under Rule 9(h), the defendant or a person who asserts a right under Supplemental Rule C(6)(a)(i) may, as a third-party plaintiff, bring in a third-party defendant who may be wholly or partly liable—either to the plaintiff or to the third-party plaintiff-for remedy over, contribution, or otherwise on account of the same transaction, occurrence, or series of transactions or occurrences.

(2) *Defending Against a Demand for Judgment for the Plaintiff.* The third-party plaintiff may demand judgment in the plaintiff's favor against the third-party defendant. In that event, the third-party defendant must defend under Rule 12 against the plaintiff's claim as well as the third-party plaintiff's claim; and the action proceeds as if the plaintiff had sued both the third-party defendant and the third-party plaintiff.

[Amended effective March 19, 1948; July 1, 1963; July 1, 1966; August 1, 1987; April 17, 2000, effective December 1, 2000; April 12, 2006, effective December 1, 2006; April 30, 2007, effective December 1, 2007; March 26, 2009, effective December 1, 2009.]

UNDERSTANDING RULE 14

HOW RULE 14 FITS IN

Sometimes, the plaintiff chooses not to sue all of the potential defendants—the Rules do not place any obligation on a plaintiff to sue every possible defendant and plaintiffs often choose not to sue a potential defendant for strategic reasons. Particularly when the plaintiff is asserting joint and several liability—where the plaintiff can recover 100% of the damages from any defendant—a plaintiff might choose to sue only a defendant with "deep pockets" or a defendant with weaker defenses.

In such cases, the law does not permanently saddle that unlucky defendant with 100% of the liability. Rather, the targeted defendant may seek contribution from the other responsible persons. One avenue is to wait until the original action concludes, and then bring an entirely new lawsuit asserting contribution claims against those who were not named as defendants in the original action. Rule 14 provides another option, permitting parties who are defending against claims to "implead" or join other persons, not yet parties, as "third-party defendants."

Rule 14 requires that a third-party plaintiff assert a contribution claim in order to join new third-party defendants. This requirement that a defendant/third-party plaintiff assert a claim that the newly joined third-party defendant is liable for some or all of the defendant's liability to the plaintiff is narrower than the requirement that compulsory counterclaims and crossclaims be transactionally related. However, once a defendant has asserted one qualifying third-party claim, it may join any other claims it has against the third-party defendant—related or unrelated—under Rule 18(a).

Once a nonparty has been impleaded as a third-party defendant, further pleading proceeds much like normal pleading. The third-party defendant asserts defenses in a Rule 12 motion or an answer, and asserts counterclaims and crossclaims as provided by Rule 13. One wrinkle, however, is that the original plaintiff and the third-party defendant may assert transactionally related claims directly against each other. If the original plaintiff asserts such a claim against the third-party defendant, the third-party defendant may assert not only its own defenses but any defenses of the original defendant/third-party plaintiff. The idea behind this provision is that the third-party defendant was impleaded to contribute to the original defendant's liability, so is entitled to any defenses limiting that liability—if the plaintiff wanted to avoid that limitation, the plaintiff should have sued the third-party defendant in the original complaint.

Although less common than third-party complaints, a third-party defendant may implead a fourth party defendant, who may implead a fifth party defendant, and so on. Similarly, but even less common, a plaintiff who is the defendant to a counterclaim may implead a third-party defendant to the counterclaim.

THE ARCHITECTURE OF RULE 14

The primary content of Rule 14 is located in Rule 14(a), which authorizes the practice of impleading third-party defendants, describes the type of liability that a third-party plaintiff must assert, and sets forth the procedures for asserting all of the sequential claims and defenses flowing from the third-party claim.

Rule 14(b) authorizes plaintiffs who are defending counterclaims to implead third-party defendants. Rule 14(c) contains special provisions governing the application of Rule 14 to admiralty and maritime claims.

HOW RULE 14 WORKS IN PRACTICE

RULE 14(a) A Defending Party May Bring in a Third Party

A defending party may implead a nonparty as a third-party defendant by asserting a claim that the nonparty is liable for all or part of the liability asserted against the defending party. Once a nonparty has been impleaded, the parties to the action assert claims and defenses against each other in a manner similar to that used by the original plaintiffs and defendants.

PRACTICING LAW UNDER THIS SUBPART

Purpose

The purpose of Rule 14 is to allow the named defendants to seek contribution from nonparties without having to wait until the conclusion of the original action and then to commence an entirely new action against the nonparties.

Third-Party Plaintiff's Discretion

A party's right to implead under Rule 14 is optional; there is no obligation to implead nonparties.

Who May Be Impleaded

Only persons not already parties are impleaded. For existing parties, a crossclaim is the proper mechanism for seeking contribution.

Service on the Nonparty

A third-party defendant is joined by service of a summons and third-party complaint, as described in Rule 4(k).

Time; Leave of Court

Rule 14(a) permits service of a third-party complaint "at any time." However, a party may file a third-party complaint without obtaining leave of court only in the 14-day period following that party's service of an answer to a claim, or by a different deadline set by court order. Thereafter, a defending party must seek leave of court by motion to file a third-party complaint. Generally, courts permit assertion of impleader claims unless they are raised so late in a pending suit that they unreasonably prejudice persons who are already parties.

Contribution or Derivative Liability

Rule 14(a) explicitly provides that a third-party complaint must include a claim asserting that a third-party defendant is or may be liable for all or part of the claim asserted against the third-party plaintiff (in the nature of a contribution claim, sometimes called "derivative liability").

Additional Rule 18 Claims

Once a party is properly impleaded under Rule 14 by asserting a claim for contribution or derivative liability, Rule 18(a) authorizes the joinder or addition of any other claims, related or not, derivative or not, that the third-party plaintiff has against the third-party defendant. If the Rule 18 claims do not relate to the claims in the original complaint, however, they would not qualify for supplemental jurisdiction and would therefore need their own basis of federal subject-matter jurisdiction.

Counterclaims by Third-Party Defendants

Third-party defendants may file counterclaims against third-party plaintiffs, consistent with Rule 13. The requirements of Rule 13(a) apply, and compulsory counterclaims are waived if not filed in the pending action.

Crossclaims by Third-Party Defendants

If more than one third-party defendant has been impleaded, the third-party defendants may file crossclaims against one another under the terms of Rule 13(g).

Third-Party Defendants' Claims Against Plaintiffs

A third-party defendant may make claims against an original plaintiff that arise out of the same transaction or occurrence as the claims originally filed by the plaintiff. Such claims are permissive, in that they may either be raised or retained for subsequent litigation.

Plaintiffs' Claims Against Third-Party Defendants

A plaintiff may assert a claim against a third-party defendant, provided that the claim arises out of the same transaction or occurrence as the original claims against the defendants. The assertion of such a claim is discretionary, and a plaintiff may choose to retain the claim for subsequent litigation. If a plaintiff asserts a claim directly against a third-party defendant, the third-party defendant may assert both its own defenses and any defenses of the original defendant/third-party plaintiff.

Third-Party Defendants' Counterclaims Against Plaintiffs

If a plaintiff sues a third-party defendant, any counterclaims the third-party defendant may have are governed by Rule 13.

Severance; Separate Trials

Third-party practice has obvious potential for complexity and for confusing a trier of fact. Therefore, any party to the litigation may move to sever the claims.

Fourth-Party Practice

Rule 14(a) grants third-party defendants the same power to implead as is enjoyed by the defendants. Thus, third-party defendants may join persons not yet parties who may be liable to the third-party defendants for part or all of the liability the third-party defendants may have to the parties asserting claims against them.

Subject-Matter Jurisdiction, Personal Jurisdiction, and Venue

Every third-party claim must satisfy subject-matter jurisdiction, personal jurisdiction, and venue. Because third-party claims are generally closely related to the original claims between the plaintiff and defendant, subject-matter jurisdiction can usually be obtained under supplemental jurisdiction. However, keep in mind the exception to supplemental jurisdiction in 28 U.S.C. § 1367(b) when a plaintiff is asserting a claim against an impleaded party.

RULE 14(b) When a Plaintiff May Bring in Third Party

If a plaintiff is the subject of a counterclaim, the plaintiff may join third parties who may be liable for part or all of that counterclaim.

RULE 14(c) Admiralty or Maritime Claims

When the original cause of action arises under the court's admiralty jurisdiction, the defendant may join third persons by alleging either that: they are liable to reimburse the defendant for some or all of the defendant's liability; or that the third persons are liable directly to the plaintiff.

15(c) → Relation Back: for events b4 OG pleading was filed

- it relates back to date of OG pleading, if same conduct, transaction, or occurence set forth in original pleading
- means that the claim asserted in the amended pleading will be treated as tho it had been asserted in the OG pleading
- it allows a party to add a claim by amendment after S.O.L. have passed.

↳ ex. if you learn abt. fraud, you can add that fraud claim onto OG claim & treat it as if the fraud claim was always there.

☆ - pretty much it allows a party to add a claim by an amendment after limitations period has passed → allows them to come back after being barred!! ☆

- should be same conduct, transaction, or occurence set out in the OG pleading

Amended v. Supplemental

Amended - adding something before OG pleading was filed

Supplemental (1367) - adding something after OG pleading was filed

RULE 15

AMENDED AND SUPPLEMENTAL PLEADINGS

(a) Amendments Before Trial.

(1) *Amending as a Matter of Course.* A party may amend its pleading once as a matter of course within:

(A) 21 days after serving it, or

(B) if the pleading is one to which a responsive pleading is required, 21 days after service of a responsive pleading or 21 days after service of a motion under Rule 12(b), (e), or (f), whichever is earlier.

(2) *Other Amendments.* In all other cases, a party may amend its pleading only with the opposing party's written consent or the court's leave. The court should freely give leave when justice so requires.

(3) *Time to Respond.* Unless the court orders otherwise, any required response to an amended pleading must be made within the time remaining to respond to the original pleading or within 14 days after service of the amended pleading, whichever is later.

(b) Amendments During and After Trial.

(1) *Based on an Objection at Trial.* If, at trial, a party objects that evidence is not within the issues raised in the pleadings, the court may permit the pleadings to be amended. The court should freely permit an amendment when doing so will aid in presenting the merits and the objecting party fails to satisfy the court that the evidence would prejudice that party's action or defense on the merits. The court may grant a continuance to enable the objecting party to meet the evidence.

(2) *For Issues Tried by Consent.* When an issue not raised by the pleadings is tried by the parties' express or implied consent, it must be treated in all respects as if raised in the pleadings. A party may move—at any time, even after judgment—to amend the pleadings to conform them to the evidence and to raise an unpleaded issue. But failure to amend does not affect the result of the trial of that issue.

(c) Relation Back of Amendments.

(1) *When an Amendment Relates Back.* An amendment to a pleading relates back to the date of the original pleading when:

(A) the law that provides the applicable statute of limitations allows relation back;

(B) the amendment asserts a claim or defense that arose out of the conduct, transaction, or occurrence set out—or attempted to be set out—in the original pleading; or

(C) the amendment changes the party or the naming of the party against whom a claim is asserted, if Rule 15(c)(1)(B) is satisfied and if, within the period provided by Rule 4(m) for serving the summons and complaint, the party to be brought in by amendment:

(i) received such notice of the action that it will not be prejudiced in defending on the merits; and

(ii) knew or should have known that the action would have been brought against it, but for a mistake concerning the proper party's identity.

(2) *Notice to the United States.* When the United States or a United States officer or agency is added as a defendant by amendment, the notice requirements of Rule 15(c)(1)(C)(i) and (ii) are satisfied if, during the stated period, process was delivered or mailed to the United States attorney or the United States attorney's designee, to the Attorney General of the United States, or to the officer or agency.

(d) Supplemental Pleadings. On motion and reasonable notice, the court may, on just terms, permit a party to serve a supplemental pleading setting out any transaction, occurrence, or event that happened after the date of the pleading to be supplemented. The court may permit supplementation even though the original pleading is defective in stating a claim or defense. The court may order that the opposing party plead to the supplemental pleading within a specified time.

[Amended January 21, 1963, effective July 1, 1963; February 28, 1966, effective July 1, 1966; March 2, 1987, effective August 1, 1987; April 30, 1991, effective December 1, 1991; amended by Pub.L. 102–198, § 11, December 9, 1991, 105 Stat. 1626; amended April 22, 1993, effective December 1, 1993; April 30, 2007, effective December 1, 2007; March 26, 2009, effective December 1, 2009.]

UNDERSTANDING RULE 15

HOW RULE 15 FITS IN

Rule 15 governs the circumstances in which parties may amend their pleadings. Generally, parties have an automatic right to amend their pleadings one time within 21 days of serving the pleading or, if the pleading is one that requires an answer or other responsive pleading, within 21 days of receiving the answer or a Rule 12 motion. After the 21-day period expires, parties need consent from opposing parties or leave of court to amend. Rule 15 establishes a policy of liberal amendment, and the courts will grant motions to amend unless the amendment would prejudice another party. If an amended pleading requires an answer or other response, the answer will be due the later of 14 days after the amended pleading or the due date for the answer to the original pleading.

One of the issues occasionally implicated by an amended complaint is the date on which it is deemed filed for purposes of the statute of limitations. Statutes of limitations generally require that a complaint be *filed* within the specified period of time following the time the cause of action *accrues*. Thus, for example, if the statute of limitations is two years from the date of a tort, the plaintiff must file the complaint within that two-year period. If the plaintiff files the original complaint within the two-year period, then seeks to file an amended complaint after the end of the two-year period, any claim first asserted in the amended complaint will only be timely if it is deemed to have been filed on the date of the original complaint, known as "relating back."

Rule 15(c) controls when an amended complaint relates back to the original complaint, and has different tests depending on whether the amended complaint merely adds new claims or also adds new parties. It provides that a complaint adding new claims relates back if the new claims arise out of the same conduct, transaction, or occurrence as the original complaint. The test for relation back is more stringent, however, for an amended complaint adding new parties. Such a complaint will relate back only if it arises out of the same conduct, transaction, or occurrence as the original complaint and, within the time for service of the original complaint (generally 90 days), the newly added party received notice of the action and knew that it would have been named as a defendant in the original complaint if the plaintiff had not made a mistake about the defendant's identity.

The reason for this limitation is to balance the consequences of a mistake about the defendant's identity against the interests that statutes of limitations protect. Statutes of limitations recognize that it becomes more difficult to defend against claims with the passage of time—memories fade and evidence is lost. Accordingly, the relation back requirement in Rule 15 ensures that a defendant added by amendment has received notice of the action within the time contemplated by the statute of limitations—the statute of limitations period plus the service period.

Although most amendments occur near the beginning of an action, Rule 15 allows amendments during or even after trial. Normally, the evidence allowable at trial is limited to that relevant to the claims and defenses in the pleadings. If evidence outside that scope is introduced at trial without objection, however, the pleadings will be deemed amended to conform to the evidence. Conversely, if another party objects to evidence as outside the scope of the pleadings, the court can allow the offering party to amend the pleadings if doing so will not prejudice other parties, and may grant a continuance to cure any prejudice.

Rule 15 also authorizes supplemental pleadings, cousin to amended pleadings. A supplemental pleading is designed to address a transaction, occurrence, or event that happened after the date of the pleading to be supplemented—asserting facts, claims, or defenses that the party could not have asserted at the time of the original pleading. A supplemental pleading is appended to the end of the original pleading, which remains operative (in contrast to an amended pleading, which supplants the original pleading entirely). Parties do not have a right to file supplemental pleadings, and instead must file a motion requesting leave of court. If the supplemental pleading requires an answer, the court will set the date for the answer.

THE ARCHITECTURE OF RULE 15

Rule 15 is divided into four subsections. Rule 15(a) governs amendments before trial, specifying the procedures for amendment as of right, amendment with leave of court, and responses to amended pleadings. Rule 15(b) governs amendments during and after trial. Rule 15(c) contains the requirements for relation back. Finally, Rule 15(d) governs supplemental pleadings.

HOW RULE 15 WORKS IN PRACTICE

RULE 15(a) Amendments Before Trial

Parties have an automatic right to amend a pleading a single time within 21 days after serving it. Additionally, if the pleading is one that requires a responsive pleading, the pleading may be amended as of right once within 21 days after service of either a responsive pleading or a motion under Rule 12(b), (e), or (f), whichever is earlier. If a party's right to amend has lapsed, a party must seek leave to amend from either the opposing party or the court.

PRACTICING LAW UNDER THIS SUBPART

Amendment as of Right

A party may amend a pleading one time without leave of court or consent of opposing parties, under either of two circumstances. First, a pleading may be amended as of right if the amendment is filed within 21 days after serving it. Additionally, if the pleading to be amended requires a responsive pleading, it may be amended as of right within 21 days of service of a responsive pleading or 21 days after service of a motion under Rule 12(b), (e), or (f) (whichever is earlier).

Multiple Opposing Parties

If some opposing parties have filed responsive pleadings and the 21-day window for amendment as of right has ended, but other parties have not, courts generally hold that the original pleading may be amended as of right, at least as to those parties who have not yet pleaded.

Adverse Party's Consent

If a party's proposed amendment falls outside the time limits described above, the opposing party may consent to the amendment. When their duties to their own clients are not at issue, attorneys often cooperate in such matters as a matter of professional courtesy, and because they recognize that refusing to consent may lead to an expensive motion with the same outcome. If the opposing party consents to an amendment, there is no need to obtain court approval. Rule 15(a) requires that this consent be in writing.

Leave of Court

If a proposed amendment cannot be filed as of right and the opposing party will not consent, a party may file a motion seeking leave to amend. The proposed amendment must be an exhibit to the motion.

Standard of Discretion

Rule 15(a) directs the court to grant leave to amend "freely . . . when justice so requires," and in practice the burden is usually on the party opposing the amendment to demonstrate why the amendment should not be permitted. If leave to amend is denied, it will often occur because an amendment would create unfair prejudice to another party, such as when discovery is already complete or there has been substantial unjustified delay in moving to amend. *See Krupski v. Costa Crociere, S.p.A.,* 560 U.S. 536, 553 (2010). By contrast, no unfair prejudice exists simply because a party has to defend against new or better pleaded claims. Moreover, at least some courts hold that where a complaint's deficiency could be cured by an amendment, leave to amend must be given.

Futility

When a party has no right to amend and must obtain leave of court to do so, a court may deny leave if the amendment would be futile, *e.g.,* would still fail to state a claim.

Cases Removed from State Court

If, after a case is removed, a plaintiff seeks to amend the complaint to join non-diverse defendants whose joinder would destroy diversity, the district court may permit or deny joinder. If the court denies joinder, the court continues to have jurisdiction over the case. However, if the court permits joinder, diversity jurisdiction no longer exists and (in the absence of some other basis for subject-matter jurisdiction) the court must then remand the case to State court.

That situation gets more complicated if, after removal, a plaintiff exercises the right to amend a pleading as of right and joins a non-diverse defendant. If Rule 15(a) could be used in that manner, it would undermine the district court's discretion to retain the removed case by denying joinder. Courts have resolved this conflict by concluding that the courts have authority to deny joinder under Rule 15(a), notwithstanding the plaintiff's apparent right under that Rule.

Relation to Joinder Rules

When a party seeks to amend a complaint under Rule 15(a) to join additional claims or parties, the joinder will not be permitted simply because the requirements of Rule 15 have been met. In addition, the applicable joinder rules must also be satisfied. Thus, for example, if a defendant seeks to amend its answer to add a crossclaim, the defendant must satisfy the requirements for a crossclaim in Rule 13(g) as well as the requirements for an amendment under Rule 15.

Relation to Dismissal Under Rule 41(a)

If a plaintiff seeks to dismiss some, but not all, claims, the courts are divided as to whether the proper procedure is amendment under Rule 15(a) or dismissal under Rule 41(a). When a plaintiff seeks to dismiss all of its claims, the proper procedure is dismissal under Rule 41(a).

Rule 16 and Case Management

While, as a general rule, leave to amend is granted freely in the interest of justice, the likelihood of obtaining permission to amend diminishes drastically if the court has entered a scheduling order with a deadline for amending pleadings and that deadline has passed. In that situation, the "good cause" standard for changing a deadline in a Rule 16 order controls, not the liberal amendment standard under Rule 15.

Effect of Amendment

Once an amendment is properly filed, it displaces the earlier pleading which it amends. An amendment also nullifies pending motions; a party wishing to attack the amended pleading must file a new motion.

Responding to Amended Pleadings

If the amended pleading is one to which a responsive pleading is appropriate, the opposing party will have either the time remaining before a response to the unamended version was due or fourteen days—whichever is longer—to respond. *See Nelson v. Adams USA, Inc.,* 529 U.S. 460, 465 (2000).

RULE 15(b) Amendments During and After Trial

Rule 15(b) permits amendments to pleadings in two circumstances. The first situation arises when an issue not raised in the pleadings is tried by consent or without objection. The second occurs when an issue not raised in the pleadings is objected to, but the proposed amendment either will not create unfair prejudice or any such prejudice can be cured.

PRACTICING LAW UNDER THIS SUBPART

Timing

Although the title of Rule 15(b) suggests that its provisions are limited to amendments at the time of trial, motions to amend under Rule 15(b) may theoretically be made at any time, including in the context of a motion for summary judgment.

Failure to Object

Parties who fail to object to the introduction of evidence relating to matters not within the four corners of the pleadings have impliedly consented to adjudication of those matters, and courts will deem the pleadings accordingly amended.

Rule 15(b) Motion

If parties are found to have consented to litigation of issues outside the original pleadings, there is no requirement of a motion or formal amended pleading. However, if an opposing party objects to evidence going to a new claim or defense, the party seeking to introduce that evidence should seek leave to amend by motion.

Grounds for Denying Rule 15(b) Amendments

Courts deny Rule 15(b) amendments on any of four grounds: bad faith; undue delay; unfair prejudice to an opponent; or futility of a proposed amendment. Determinations of unfair prejudice are highly fact specific. The most likely circumstance in which such prejudice will be found occurs when the objecting party is surprised by the evidence and has not had a reasonable opportunity to prepare for it.

Curing Unfair Prejudice

If the source of unfair prejudice is surprise, courts may cure the problem by granting a continuance so that the objecting party can prepare for the new evidence. Such an order may include reopening discovery.

RULE 15(c) Relation Back of Amendments

Rule 15(c) governs the circumstances in which an amended pleading will be treated as though it was filed on the date of the original pleading. This determination is only relevant to the applicability of statutes of limitations to claims raised in amended pleadings.

PRACTICING LAW UNDER THIS SUBPART

Amendment Adding New Claim

When an amended pleading adds a new claim among the existing parties, it will relate back to the original pleading when the claim or defense in the amended pleading arises from the same conduct, transaction, or occurrence as that set forth—or attempted to be set forth—in the original pleading. Courts look to the degree of overlap of evidence between the events raised in the amended pleading and the original pleading to determine whether they arise out of the same conduct, transaction, or occurrence. This standard is measured by the facts pleaded; it does not depend on the legal theory offered. Thus, an amendment may relate back notwithstanding that the proffered amendment offers a new legal theory.

Amendment Adding a New Party

When an amended pleading adds a new party, it will relate back to the original pleading if: (1) the claim against the new party arises from the same conduct, transaction, or occurrence set forth in, or attempted to be set forth in, the original pleading; and (2) within the 90-day period after filing of the original pleading that Rule 4(m) provides for service of process, the new party named in the amended pleading both received sufficient notice of the pendency of the action so as not to be prejudiced in preparing a defense, and knew or should have known that but for a mistake of identity the party would have been named in the original pleading. The first element—same conduct, transaction, or occurrence—is the requirement relating to amendments adding a new claim. The other element has two parts—fair notice and awareness of a mistake in identity—that are explained immediately below.

(1) *Notice:* The notice does not need to be formal notice, but must, in the particular circumstances of the case, ensure that the party joined is not unfairly prejudiced by an amended pleading. For example, a parent or subsidiary corporation of an entity sued in the original complaint would probably be held to have notice of the original action. *See Krupski v. Costa Crociere, S.p.A.,* 560 U.S. 538, 545 (2010).

(2) *Knowledge of Mistaken Identity:* Before an amended pleading joining a new party may relate back, the proponent of the pleading must also establish that within the 90-day period provided by Rule 4(m), the person to be joined knew or should have known that the person would have been sued in the original pleading but for a mistake in identity. *See Krupski v. Costa Crociere, S.p.A.,* 560 U.S. 538, 548 (2010). Thus, if a subsidiary corporation was sued when the claim should have been against its parent, and the subsidiary was served within the period provided by Rule 4(m), the parent might be charged with timely knowledge of the fact that the proper defendant should have been the parent. *Id.* With natural persons, the requirement may be satisfied when the name of the proper defendant is similar to the name of the person originally designated as a defendant and the proper defendant knew of the mistake within the time limit established by Rule 4(m).

Relation Back Authorized by Statute of Limitations

Relation back is also authorized when the applicable statute of limitations provides for relation back.

Right to Amend Independent

Rule 15(c) deals only with whether an amendment will be treated as though it was filed at an earlier date rather than the actual date of filing—whether the amendment relates back to the date the original pleading was filed. The determination of the right to amend is controlled by Rules 15(a) and (b). Thus, these are two separate analyses—whether amendment is permitted and, if so, whether the amended complaint relates back. For example, if the plaintiff wants to amend the complaint within 21 days of receiving the answer, the plaintiff has an absolute right to do so under Rule 15(a). That right to amend, however, does not control whether the amended complaint will relate back—that question is answered by Rule 15(c).

Undue Delay and Relation Back

Under Rule 15(a), a court may properly deny leave to amend a pleading when a party has delayed excessively and without good cause in seeking leave. However, delay plays no role in an evaluation of relation back under Rule 15(c). *See Krupski v. Costa Crociere, S.p.A.*, 560 U.S. 538, 555 (2010).

Comparison to Real Party in Interest Under Rule 17

Rule 17(a), governing requirements to prosecute a case in the name of the real party in interest, expressly provides that joinder or substitution of the real party in interest automatically relates back to the original filing date, apparently without regard to the requirements of Rule 15.

"John Doe" Pleadings

Some courts hold that an amendment that substitutes the actual defendant for a "John Doe" designation cannot relate back because the plaintiff was openly unaware of the defendant's identity, not mistaken about it.

RULE 15(d) Supplemental Pleadings

Parties may seek leave to supplement previous pleadings to encompass events that have occurred since the earlier pleadings were filed.

PRACTICING LAW UNDER THIS SUBPART

Leave of Court

There is no unqualified right to file a supplemental pleading; authority to file a supplemental pleading is obtained by filing a motion. Decisions to grant or deny Rule 15(d) motions to supplement pleadings are generally based on the same factors of fairness courts weigh when considering motions to amend pleadings under Rule 15(a), focusing on prejudice to other parties.

Party's Discretion

Supplemental pleadings are optional. Thus, if a party acquires a claim as a result of facts arising after the original pleading was filed, and the requirements of Rule 15(d) are satisfied, the party has an opportunity, but not a duty, to file a supplemental claim.

Time to File

Rule 15(d) contains no restriction on the time in which a supplemental pleading may be filed. However, the court may consider inappropriate delay in attempting to assert supplemental claims as grounds for refusing to grant permission to file the supplemental pleading.

Only Factual Developments After the Initial Pleading

Supplemental pleadings are restricted to events occurring since initiation of the suit. If the issues raised predate the original pleadings, an amended, not supplemental, pleading is the appropriate mechanism for raising them. Intervening judicial decisions that change the applicable law are not the sort of "occurrences or events" that might implicate Rule 15(d)—the intervening new law may apply, but need not be set forth in a supplemental pleading.

Relationship to Original Pleadings

Unlike amended pleadings, supplemental pleadings add to, rather than displace, the original pleadings.

Responses to Supplemental Pleadings

Rule 15(d) does not create either a right or duty to respond to a supplemental pleading. Instead, the Rule vests the court with authority to order a response when appropriate in the circumstances of a case. Typically, an opportunity to respond will be permitted when the supplemental pleading asserts a new cause of action.

Relation Back of Supplemental Pleadings

Because supplemental pleadings address only events that have occurred since the original pleadings were filed, no question normally arises as to whether supplemental pleadings relate back to the date the original pleadings were filed. However, where relation back is important to the supplemental pleadings, courts tend to apply the standards of Rule 15(c) to determine whether relation back should be permitted.

RULE 16

PRETRIAL CONFERENCES; SCHEDULING; MANAGEMENT

(a) Purposes of a Pretrial Conference. In any action, the court may order the attorneys and any unrepresented parties to appear for one or more pretrial conferences for such purposes as:

(1) expediting disposition of the action;

(2) establishing early and continuing control so that the case will not be protracted because of lack of management;

(3) discouraging wasteful pretrial activities;

(4) improving the quality of the trial through more thorough preparation; and

(5) facilitating settlement.

(b) Scheduling.

(1) *Scheduling Order.* Except in categories of actions exempted by local rule, the district judge—or a magistrate judge when authorized by local rule—must issue a scheduling order:

(A) after receiving the parties' report under Rule 26(f); or

(B) after consulting with the parties' attorneys and any unrepresented parties at a scheduling conference.

(2) *Time to Issue.* The judge must issue the scheduling order as soon as practicable, but unless the judge finds good cause for delay, the judge must issue it within the earlier of 90 days after any defendant has been served with the complaint or 60 days after any defendant has appeared.

(3) *Contents of the Order.*

(A) *Required Contents.* The scheduling order must limit the time to join other parties, amend the pleadings, complete discovery, and file motions.

(B) *Permitted Contents.* The scheduling order may:

(i) modify the timing of disclosures under Rules 26(a) and 26(e)(1);

(ii) modify the extent of discovery;

(iii) provide for disclosure, discovery, or preservation of electronically stored information;

(iv) include any agreements the parties reach for asserting claims of privilege or of protection as trial-preparation material after information is produced, including agreements reached under Federal Rule of Evidence 502;

(v) direct that before moving for an order relating to discovery, the movant must request a conference with the court;

(vi) set dates for pretrial conferences and for trial; and

(vii) include other appropriate matters.

(4) *Modifying a Schedule.* A schedule may be modified only for good cause and with the judge's consent.

(c) Attendance and Matters for Consideration at a Pretrial Conference.

(1) *Attendance.* A represented party must authorize at least one of its attorneys to make stipulations and admissions about all matters that can reasonably be anticipated for discussion at a pretrial conference. If appropriate, the court may require that a party or its representative be present or reasonably available by other means to consider possible settlement.

(2) *Matters for Consideration.* At any pretrial conference, the court may consider and take appropriate action on the following matters:

(A) formulating and simplifying the issues, and eliminating frivolous claims or defenses;

(B) amending the pleadings if necessary or desirable;

(C) obtaining admissions and stipulations about facts and documents to avoid unnecessary proof, and ruling in advance on the admissibility of evidence;

(D) avoiding unnecessary proof and cumulative evidence, and limiting the use of testimony under Federal Rule of Evidence 702;

(E) determining the appropriateness and timing of summary adjudication under Rule 56;

(F) controlling and scheduling discovery, including orders affecting disclosures and discovery under Rule 26 and Rules 29 through 37;

(G) identifying witnesses and documents, scheduling the filing and exchange of any pretrial briefs, and setting dates for further conferences and for trial;

(H) referring matters to a magistrate judge or a master;

(I) settling the case and using special procedures to assist in resolving the dispute when authorized by statute or local rule;

(J) determining the form and content of the pretrial order;

(K) disposing of pending motions;

(L) adopting special procedures for managing potentially difficult or protracted actions that may involve complex issues, multiple parties, difficult legal questions, or unusual proof problems;

(M) ordering a separate trial under Rule 42(b) of a claim, counterclaim, crossclaim, third-party claim, or particular issue;

(N) ordering the presentation of evidence early in the trial on a manageable issue that might, on the evidence, be the basis for a judgment as a matter of law under Rule 50(a) or a judgment on partial findings under Rule 52(c);

(O) establishing a reasonable limit on the time allowed to present evidence; and

(P) facilitating in other ways the just, speedy, and inexpensive disposition of the action.

(d) Pretrial Orders. After any conference under this rule, the court should issue an order reciting the action taken. This order controls the course of the action unless the court modifies it.

(e) Final Pretrial Conference and Orders. The court may hold a final pretrial conference to formulate a trial plan, including a plan to facilitate the admission of evidence. The conference must be held as close to the start of trial as is reasonable, and must be attended by at least one attorney who will conduct the trial for each party and by any unrepresented party. The court may modify the order issued after a final pretrial conference only to prevent manifest injustice.

(f) Sanctions.

(1) *In General.* On motion or on its own, the court may issue any just orders, including those authorized by Rule 37(b)(2)(A)(ii)–(vii), if a party or its attorney:

(A) fails to appear at a scheduling or other pretrial conference;

(B) is substantially unprepared to participate—or does not participate in good faith—in the conference; or

(C) fails to obey a scheduling or other pretrial order.

(2) *Imposing Fees and Costs.* Instead of or in addition to any other sanction, the court must order the party, its attorney, or both to pay the reasonable expenses—including attorney's fees—incurred because of any noncompliance with this rule, unless the noncompliance was

substantially justified or other circumstances make an award of expenses unjust.

[Amended April 28, 1983, effective August 1, 1983; March 2, 1987, effective August 1, 1987; April 22, 1993, effective December 1, 1993; April 12, 2006, effective December 1, 2006; April 30, 2007, effective December 1, 2007; April 29, 2015, effective December 1, 2015.]

UNDERSTANDING RULE 16

HOW RULE 16 FITS IN

Rule 16 provides the primary mechanisms for the district court to schedule and oversee the cases on its docket and to expedite disposition, avoid waste, and promote settlement. In most cases, Rule 16 *requires* the court to issue a scheduling order near the start of the case setting deadlines and procedures for a variety of topics like amending the pleadings, joining third parties, discovery, motion practice, and trial. Rule 16 authorizes the court to convene an initial pretrial conference before it issues the scheduling order, and to convene additional pretrial conferences for a variety of purposes throughout the course of the action. Whenever the court chooses to hold a pretrial conference, the court must issue an order detailing the actions taken at the conference and establishing the course of action to be followed. Such orders are binding unless subsequently modified by the court. If a party fails to comply with a Rule 16 order or fails to appear for a Rule 16 conference, the court may sanction the party.

Although Rule 16 provides substantial detail about the matters that the judge should or may address at pretrial conferences and in pretrial orders, many courts provide even greater detail in their local rules. Thus, lawyers should consult both Rule 16 and the applicable local rules regarding case management issues.

THE ARCHITECTURE OF RULE 16

Rule 16 covers a broad swath of case management activities, and uses six subparts to organize its material. Rule 16(a) provides the judge with broad authority to schedule pretrial conferences and contains a nonexclusive list of the types of topics the court might address at a pretrial conference.

Rule 16(b) obligates the court to issue the initial scheduling order—sometimes called the Case Management Order or CMO—and contains a variety of related procedures. It provides two options to the judge: the judge can base the scheduling order solely on the parties' discovery plan prepared and submitted under Rule 26(f); or the court may hold a pretrial conference to discuss the parties' discovery plan and other aspects of the case, and then issue the scheduling order informed by both the parties' discovery plan and the discussion at the pretrial conference. Rule 16(b) sets the time within which the judge must issue the CMO, and lists the topics the CMO *must* address and additional topics the CMO *may* address. Finally, Rule 16(b) provides that the CMO may be modified only on a showing of "good cause." Thus, once the dates for various activities are set in the CMO, they become more difficult to move (although most judges are pretty lenient about reasonable extensions of time).

Rule 16(c) addresses subsequent pretrial conferences. It contains the requirements for attendance at such conferences, and a list of the topics the court may address. Rule 16(d) then requires the court to memorialize such pretrial conferences with a pretrial order. Rule 16(e) authorizes the court to hold a final pretrial conference "as close to the trial date as reasonable" and to issue a final pretrial order memorializing the actions at that final pretrial conference.

Finally, Rule 16(f) provides for sanctions if a party either violates a pretrial order or fails to attend, or fails to be properly prepared for, a pretrial conference.

HOW RULE 16 WORKS IN PRACTICE

RULE 16(a) Pretrial Conferences

Rule 16(a) outlines the general parameters and objectives for the court's pretrial conferences with the parties. It promotes case management by the court to make cases operate more efficiently and expeditiously, and to facilitate settlement.

RULE 16(b) Scheduling

After receiving the discovery report required under Rule 26(f) or after conducting a scheduling conference under Rule 16(a), the court must issue a scheduling order setting timetables for pretrial matters. This scheduling order must be issued within the earlier of 60 days after the appearance of a defendant and 90 days after the service of the complaint.

PRACTICING LAW UNDER THIS SUBPART

Mandatory Topics

The court's order must include time limits for: joining parties; amending pleadings; filing motions; and completing discovery.

Optional Topics

At the court's discretion, the scheduling order may also include: modifications of time limits for disclosures under Rule 26(a) and supplements under Rule 26(e)(1) and modifications of the extent of discovery; the disclosure, discovery, or preservation of electronically stored information; provisions for recalling inadvertently produced privileged documents; a requirement that parties request a conference with the court before filing a discovery motion; dates for pretrial conferences and for trial; and other matters the court deems appropriate.

Modification of Scheduling Order Deadlines

For good cause shown, the court may grant a motion modifying the deadlines in the scheduling order. Good cause is shown when the schedule cannot reasonably be met despite the diligence of the party seeking the extension. Note that this good cause standard replaces any other standard that might apply in the absence of the Rule 16 order. Thus, for example, the liberal standard for amending pleadings in Rule 15 is replaced by the good cause standard in Rule 16 once the date for amending pleadings in a pretrial order has passed.

RULE 16(c) — Attendance and Matters for Consideration at Pretrial Conferences

Rule 16(c) contains a general list of topics that the court may consider at Rule 16 conferences. Rule 16(c) also allows for the consideration of any other matters that may facilitate the "just, speedy, and inexpensive disposition of the action."

PRACTICING LAW UNDER THIS SUBPART

Topics for Conferences

During a pretrial conference, the court may seek to: define and simplify the contested facts, theories, and issues; eliminate frivolous claims or defenses; determine whether an amendment of the pleadings is necessary; address disclosure and discovery issues; seek the admission or denial of facts or documents; make advance rulings on the admissibility of evidence and the appropriateness of expert witnesses; require parties to file lists identifying witnesses and documents; entertain requests to limit witnesses; govern the order of proof at trial; and discuss pretrial narrative statements, pending motions, stipulations limiting the issues for trial, and scheduling matters. The court may consider stays, consolidations, or separate trials. The court may also require parties to schedule presentation of evidence so that, if judgment as a matter of law or judgment on partial findings is appropriate, the court may reach those questions early in the trial. The court will also likely explore the potential for settlement.

Representatives at Conferences

An attorney or party representative with the authority to enter stipulations and make admissions must be present at Rule 16 conferences. Rule 16(c) authorizes the court to allow an attorney or party representative to be available by other means, such as by telephone.

Memorializing Pretrial Conferences

A court reporter generally will be present at pretrial conferences. In unusual circumstances and at the discretion of the court, parties may bring their own stenographers if the court does not order a court reporter.

Settlement

The court may order parties to attend a conference where settlement will be discussed but may not coerce parties into settlement. Some judges take a very gentle approach to settlement discussions, others more actively explore or encourage settlement, and some apply considerable pressure on the parties to settle cases.

RULE 16(d) — Pretrial Orders

The court must issue a pretrial order memorializing the actions taken at any pretrial conference. These are sometimes "minute orders," descriptions of the actions taken at a pretrial conference that are simply entered onto the docket.

RULE 16(e) | Final Pretrial Conference and Orders

The court will usually conduct the final pretrial conference as close to trial as possible. At the final pretrial conference, the court will set the schedule for any remaining motions and set a trial date. An attorney who will conduct the trial or an unrepresented party must attend the conference with the authority to enter stipulations and make admissions.

PRACTICING LAW UNDER THIS SUBPART

Pretrial Memorandum or Narrative Statement

(1) *Time:* The court will usually provide a date on which the parties must file a pretrial memorandum or pretrial narrative statement. The court usually orders the plaintiff's pretrial narrative statement to be filed first and the defendant's pretrial narrative statement several weeks later.

(2) *Contents:* Local rule or court order will typically define the information parties are required to include in their pretrial narrative statements. Ordinarily, the parties must state their legal theories or defenses, provide a list of witnesses and documents to be presented at trial, detail the intended use of expert witnesses, and describe any exceptional legal or evidentiary questions that will be asserted at trial.

Final Pretrial Order

The court will incorporate the information provided by the parties in their pretrial narrative statements and other submissions into its final pretrial order. Once a final pretrial order has been entered, it supersedes all pleadings and controls the subsequent course of the case. *See Rockwell Intern. Corp. v. United States,* 549 U.S. 457, 465 (2007).

Modification of Final Pretrial Order

In contrast to other Rule 16 orders which may be modified for good cause, the final pretrial order may be modified only to prevent manifest injustice.

RULE 16(f) | Sanctions

Upon motion or on the court's own initiative, the court may impose sanctions against a party who fails to comply with a pretrial order. Sanctions may also attach to incorrect or incomplete pretrial statements or the failure to participate in a pretrial conference in good faith.

PRACTICING LAW UNDER THIS SUBPART

Sanctions Imposed on Party's Motion

A party may file a motion for sanctions when another party or attorney: does not obey a scheduling or pretrial order; does not appear at a pretrial conference; is unprepared at a pretrial conference; or does not act in good faith at a pretrial conference.

Sanctions Imposed *Sua Sponte*

The court may impose sanctions on its own initiative. Before imposing sanctions *sua sponte*, the court must provide notice and an opportunity to be heard to the party to be sanctioned.

Nature of Sanctions

Sanctions may be assessed to punish for improper conduct, for purposes of deterrence, or to compensate the party injured by the improper conduct. The court can impose any sanctions it deems appropriate, including but not limited to the following:

(1) *Discovery Sanctions:* Rule 16(f) incorporates the discovery sanctions found in Rule 37(b)(2)(B), (C), and (D), such as refusing to allow a party to support or oppose designated claims or defenses, striking pleadings in whole or in part, precluding witnesses not properly disclosed, or treating the conduct as contempt of court.

(2) *Reasonable Expenses:* The court must require the sanctioned person to pay reasonable expenses, including costs and attorney's fees, caused by noncompliance with Rule 16 unless the court finds that the noncompliance was "substantially justified" or that an award of expenses would be "unjust." These expenses may be the only sanctions ordered or may be in addition to other sanctions.

(3) *Dismissal:* The court may even dismiss a case or enter default judgment for failure to obey pretrial orders. However, a trial court must apply lesser sanctions, rather than case-dispositive sanctions, except in an extreme situation where there is a clear record of delay or disobedience.

Who May Be Sanctioned

The court may impose sanctions against a party and/or an attorney of a party. Where a represented party has no knowledge of the sanctionable activity, the court may order sanctions against the attorney alone and preclude reimbursement from the client.

Capacity to Sue or be Sued:
(1) real party in interest → so the party which the substantive law governs
(2) P must have the capacity to sue & every D must have the capacity to be sued

How to Raise it?
- raise the objection that P is not real party in interest as an affirmative defense in the def's answer or motion to dismiss → w/ specific denial.

Must be "Timely Raised":
should be: ① when D knew or should have known about these facts, ② timing should allow P a reasonable time to prove its status, ③ whether it allows time for real party to join the action, & ④ case-specific considerations

Can you be anonymous?
- only if (a) highly sensitive & personal, (b) real danger of physical harm, as would be incurred as result of disclosure (c) when injury litigated against
- Factors considered: (1) is it to avoid criticism, or legit, (2) is there risk of harm, (3) ages, (4) is it against government, (5) risks unfairness to opposing party

IV. PARTIES

RULE 17

PLAINTIFF AND DEFENDANT; CAPACITY; PUBLIC OFFICERS

(a) Real Party in Interest.

(1) *Designation in General.* An action must be prosecuted in the name of the real party in interest. The following may sue in their own names without joining the person for whose benefit the action is brought:

(A) an executor;

(B) an administrator;

(C) a guardian;

(D) a bailee;

(E) a trustee of an express trust;

(F) a party with whom or in whose name a contract has been made for another's benefit; and

(G) a party authorized by statute.

(2) *Action in the Name of the United States for Another's Use or Benefit.* When a federal statute so provides, an action for another's use or benefit must be brought in the name of the United States.

(3) *Joinder of the Real Party in Interest.* The court may not dismiss an action for failure to prosecute in the name of the real party in interest until, after an objection, a reasonable time has been allowed for the real party in interest to ratify, join, or be substituted into the action. After ratification, joinder, or substitution, the action proceeds as if it had been originally commenced by the real party in interest.

(b) Capacity to Sue or Be Sued. Capacity to sue or be sued is determined as follows:

(1) for an individual who is not acting in a representative capacity, by the law of the individual's domicile;

(2) for a corporation, by the law under which it was organized; and

(3) for all other parties, by the law of the State where the court is located, except that:

(A) a partnership or other unincorporated association with no such capacity under that State's law may sue or be sued in its common name to enforce a substantive right existing under the United States Constitution or laws; and

(B) 28 U.S.C. §§ 754 and 959(a) govern the capacity of a receiver appointed by a United States court to sue or be sued in a United States court.

(c) Minor or Incompetent Person.

(1) *With a Representative.* The following representatives may sue or defend on behalf of a minor or an incompetent person:

(A) a general guardian;

(B) a committee;

(C) a conservator; or

(D) a like fiduciary.

(2) *Without a Representative.* A minor or an incompetent person who does not have a duly appointed representative may sue by a next friend or by a guardian ad litem. The court must appoint a guardian ad litem—or issue another appropriate order—to protect a minor or incompetent person who is unrepresented in an action.

(d) Public Officer's Title and Name. A public officer who sues or is sued in an official capacity may be designated by official title rather than by name, but the court may order that the officer's name be added.

[Amended effective March 19, 1948; October 20, 1949; July 1, 1966; August 1, 1987; August 1, 1988; November 18, 1988; April 30, 2007, effective December 1, 2007.]

UNDERSTANDING RULE 17

HOW RULE 17 FITS IN

Rule 17 determines who may prosecute or defend an action in federal court. The Rule starts by requiring that the named plaintiff generally be the "real party in interest." The primary purpose of this requirement is to protect the defendant against a subsequent action by the party actually entitled to recover, thereby ensuring that a defendant will not be subject to multiple lawsuits. Rule 17 does not define "real party in interest," but it normally means that the plaintiff must actually possess, under the applicable substantive law, the right sought to be enforced—someone whose interests will be materially affected by the outcome of the litigation. There are exceptions, however, such that representatives of the real party in interest like executors, guardians, and administrators may be the named party. If a complaint is challenged as not naming the real party in interest, the court must give the real party in interest an opportunity to ratify, join, or be substituted into the action, in which case the action proceeds as if it had originally been commenced by the real party in interest.

Rule 17 also specifies the source of the law for determining the "capacity to sue or be sued." This phrase refers to the legal ability to appear as a party in a lawsuit. For example, minors generally cannot be named parties in lawsuits, and are typically represented in lawsuits by their guardians. The determination of whether an individual, business, or other entity has the capacity to sue or be sued is generally based on the applicable State laws of capacity.

For individuals, Rule 17 directs that their capacity is determined by the law of their State of domicile. The capacity of a corporation is determined by the law of its State of incorporation. The capacity rules for partnerships and other unincorporated associations are more complex. If the cause of action arises under federal law, Rule 17 accords the partnership the capacity to sue or be sued. If the cause of action arises under State law, the capacity laws of that State determine the partnership's capacity. Aside from receivers appointed by a federal court (whose capacity is set by federal statute), the capacity of all other parties is determined by the law of the State where the action is pending.

In the event that litigation implicates the rights of a minor or incompetent person, Rule 17 authorizes appointed representatives like guardians to represent the person. If the minor or incompetent person does not have a duly appointed representative, the court must appoint a "guardian ad litem" or guardian for purposes of the litigation.

Rule 17 also addresses suits by or against a public officer. It allows the officer to be designated by title rather than by name, and authorizes the court to order that the officer's name be added.

THE ARCHITECTURE OF RULE 17

Rule 17 is divided into four subsections. Rule 17(a) contains the general rule requiring actions to be prosecuted and defended by the real parties in interest, and lists the exceptions to that general rule. It also provides for joinder of the real party in interest if not included in the original complaint. Rule 17(b) describes which law governs the capacity of the parties to sue and be sued. Rule 17(c) explains the options when the interests of a minor or other incompetent person are at issue in the litigation. Finally, Rule 17(d) addresses the naming of a public officer in a lawsuit.

HOW RULE 17 WORKS IN PRACTICE

RULE 17(a) Real Party in Interest

The only parties on whose behalf suits may be initiated are those persons whose interests will be materially affected by the outcome and who are entitled to enforce the right asserted under the governing substantive law. Such persons should be the named plaintiffs, with certain exceptions. This requirement is imposed on plaintiffs so that defendants will only have to face one suit over the same interest.

PRACTICING LAW UNDER THIS SUBPART

Naming the Interested Party

Subject to exceptions discussed below, the real party in interest must be the party named in the caption as a plaintiff. *See Lincoln Property Co. v. Roche,* 546 U.S. 81, 90–93 (2005). Rule 17 does not define the "real party in interest," but the term generally means that the plaintiff must actually possess the right sought to be enforced—someone whose interests will be materially affected by the outcome of the litigation.

No Mandatory Joinder of All Plaintiffs: Rule 19

The plaintiff (or claimant) must generally be *a* real party in interest. However, Rule 17 does not require the joinder of *all* real parties in interest. Rule 19's provisions regarding required parties, however, may mandate such nonparties' participation.

Rule 17(a) and Defendants

Rule 17(a) governs circumstances in which *plaintiffs* (or persons asserting claims) must be added; it does not address whether *defendants* must be joined—Rule 19 addresses required defendants. *See Lincoln Property Co. v. Roche,* 546 U.S. 81, 90 (2005).

Raising a Rule 17 Defense

The manner in which a party may invoke Rule 17(a) is not settled. Some courts indicate that the appropriate way to raise Rule 17 is through the answer, while other authority indicates it might be the appropriate subject of a motion.

Timing; Waiver

Rule 17(a) does not provide a time limit for asserting a Rule 17 defense. However, if the defense is not asserted with reasonable promptness, it is waived.

Exceptions to Naming Interested Party

The following categories of persons are exempted from the general principle that the named party be the real party in interest: executors; administrators; guardians; bailees; trustees; persons who have made contracts on behalf of third parties; and representative parties authorized by statute.

Diversity Jurisdiction

In the circumstances where Rule 17(a) allows a representative to sue on behalf of the real parties in interest, as discussed above, it is important to determine whether diversity jurisdiction will depend on the citizenship of the representative or the real party in interest. This requires context-specific research. *See, e.g., Americold Realty Trust v. Conagra Foods, Inc.,* 577 U.S. 378, 382–84 (2016) (nature of the action determines whether diversity jurisdiction turns on citizenship of trustee or trust members).

Remedy for Improper Plaintiff

If the real party in interest is not a named plaintiff, the preferred remedy is to provide an opportunity to amend so that the action can be prosecuted by the real party in interest. Before a court grants a motion to dismiss, it must allow a real party in interest a reasonable opportunity to join the action, or, if permitted as an exception to Rule 17(a), to ratify continuation of the action in the name of the original plaintiff.

RULE 17(b) Capacity to Sue or Be Sued

Rule 17(b) chooses the law that will govern the capacity of a person to prosecute or defend a suit.

PRACTICING LAW UNDER THIS SUBPART

Natural Persons

For individuals, the law which determines their capacity to sue or be sued is the law of their domicile. Domicile is generally defined as the jurisdiction where a person has established a physical presence and has the intent to remain for an indefinite period.

Corporations

The capacity of a corporation to sue or be sued is governed by the law of the jurisdiction in which the corporation is incorporated.

Unincorporated Associations

The capacity of an unincorporated association to sue or be sued is governed by the law of the State where the court is located. However, if that State law does not provide such capacity for the association, then Rule 17(b) authorizes suits by an unincorporated association when the cause of action arises under the Constitution or a federal statute.

Capacity for All Other Parties

For circumstances not addressed by the specific provisions in Rule 17(b), the law governing capacity is that of the State in which the court sits.

Capacity Distinguished from Real Party in Interest

Capacity and real party in interest advance two different concepts. Capacity addresses the capability of the party to participate in litigation. For example, an adult individual of "sound mind" may have the capacity to sue or be sued. Unless the individual also has a material interest in the outcome of a cause of action, however, the individual may not bring a suit because the individual is not the real party in interest. Thus, to bring a suit, a party must have both "capacity" under the applicable law chosen by Rule 17(b) and a real stake in the outcome as defined by Rule 17(a). In contrast, a defendant need only satisfy the law of capacity selected by Rule 17(b).

RULE 17(c) Minor or Incompetent Persons

Rule 17(c) controls the manner in which infants and other persons unable to represent their own interests will be represented in federal court. The provisions apply irrespective of whether the infant or incompetent person is participating as a plaintiff or defendant.

PRACTICING LAW UNDER THIS SUBPART

Infants and Incompetents Already Represented

Where persons unable to protect their own interests already have representatives legally charged with the duty to care for them outside of litigation, such as guardians, these representatives have authority to sue or defend on behalf of the persons in their care.

Infants and Incompetents Not Already Represented

Where persons unable to protect their own interests are not already within the legal care of others, they may be represented in litigation by persons chosen to protect their interests. The court has power to appoint such guardians *ad litem* (persons who will represent the interest of others in litigation), and to make other orders consistent with the best interests of infants and incompetents in litigation.

Determination of Incompetence

There is no prerequisite that a State authority determine incompetence before a district court appoints a guardian *ad litem*. However, if it has been determined that an unrepresented party is incompetent, the district court has an affirmative duty to appoint a guardian *ad litem* or to take other appropriate action. If a district court receives "verifiable evidence of incompetence," it is required to make a *sua sponte* determination of competence.

Other Orders

The district court may issue other orders necessary to protect infants and incompetents. This authority includes the power to determine rates of compensation for guardians *ad litem* and to determine which party shall bear the cost of such expenses.

RULE 17(d) Public Officer's Title and Name

Rule 17(d) allows suit by or against a public officer under either that person's official title or personal name. The court may add the individual's name in cases where the official title alone has been used. The primary advantage of suing a public officer by title, rather than individual name, is that departure of the person from office does not require a substitution of names under Rule 25.

---

18 → Joinder:
- may assert as many as you want → there is no requirement of being related to be joined. Thus, can be totally unrelated
- not compelled to bring all permissive claims, but they can or cannot... it's up to them.
  ↳ BUT if compulsory, you have to or else you are barred

Rule 13(a)
- compulsory counterclaim requirements of 13(a) apply to any party who has a related claim against an OPPOSING PARTY
- 13(g) applies to related claims of co-party, irrespective of if they are Ps, D's, or 3rd party D's

RULE 18

JOINDER OF CLAIMS

(a) In General. A party asserting a claim, counterclaim, crossclaim, or third-party claim may join, as independent or alternative claims, as many claims as it has against an opposing party. as many as you want!!

(b) Joinder of Contingent Claims. A party may join two claims even though one of them is contingent on the disposition of the other; but the court may grant relief only in accordance with the parties' relative substantive rights. In particular, a plaintiff may state a claim for money and a claim to set aside a conveyance that is fraudulent as to that plaintiff, without first obtaining a judgment for the money.

[Amended effective July 1, 1966; August 1, 1987; April 30, 2007, effective December 1, 2007.]

UNDERSTANDING RULE 18

HOW RULE 18 FITS IN

Although Rule 18 is short, it serves an extremely important purpose. It is one of the linchpins of the scheme of joinder rules designed to foster efficient use of the courts. These joinder rules allow parties and claims to be joined in a single action when they are sufficiently related that it would be more effective and efficient for the court and the parties to resolve them in one proceeding. Conversely, if the claims and parties in a single action become too disconnected, some of the parties may have to endure costly and time-consuming proceedings that have no bearing on their claims or defenses. Rule 18 provides an important piece of the Rules' balancing apparatus.

Rule 18 provides that, if one party has already asserted a claim, counterclaim, crossclaim, or third-party claim against another party, the claiming party may also assert any other claims it has against that defending party, whether or not they are related in any way to the first claim. Thus, for example, Rule 13(g) provides that a defendant may assert a crossclaim against a codefendant if the crossclaim is transactionally related to the plaintiff's claim against the defendant. Once the defendant has asserted one such transactionally related crossclaim, Rule 18 authorizes the defendant to assert any other claims against the codefendant, even if not transactionally related. This rule thus promotes efficiency—once two parties are in court on one claim, they might as well have the option to litigate all of their disputes. Of course, as with all claims, the court must have subject-matter jurisdiction over claims brought under Rule 18, and any unrelated Rule 18 claims will not qualify for supplemental jurisdiction and will need their own original subject-matter jurisdiction.

Rule 18 also authorizes a party to assert claims that are contingent on resolution of other claims in the same action. For example, a plaintiff may bring a personal injury claim and also include a claim alleging that the defendant fraudulently transferred assets to the defendant's spouse to shield the assets from any judgment ensuing on the personal injury claim. The second claim is only potentially relevant if the plaintiff succeeds on the first claim, but the plaintiff may maintain both claims in the same action.

THE ARCHITECTURE OF RULE 18

The broad authorization for a party to assert all the claims it has against another party is found in Rule 18(a). Rule 18(b) contains the provision authorizing a claim that is contingent on resolution of another claim.

HOW RULE 18 WORKS IN PRACTICE

RULE 18(a) In General

Rule 18(a) broadly authorizes a party who has already asserted one proper claim against a defending party to assert any other claims the party has against that defending party, regardless of the nature and relatedness of the claims and regardless of the nature of the remedies sought.

PRACTICING LAW UNDER THIS SUBPART

Parties Who May Join Claims

The right to join claims is not limited to the original plaintiff, but is also available to defending parties asserting counterclaims, crossclaims, or third-party claims.

Rule 18(a) Is Permissive, Not Compulsory

Rule 18 does not impose any obligation on parties to bring all of their claims. Other rules, however, may impose such obligations, such as Rule 13(a) addressing compulsory counterclaims.

Crossclaims and Third-Party Claims

Whereas Rule 13(g) and Rule 14 contain restrictions on the type of claim that a defendant may assert as a crossclaim or third-party claim, once a defendant has asserted a proper crossclaim or third-party claim, Rule 18(a) authorizes the defendant to add additional claims that are outside these restrictions.

Jurisdiction and Venue

Claims joined under Rule 18(a) must still satisfy the requirements of subject-matter jurisdiction, personal jurisdiction, and venue.

Joinder of Additional Parties

Rule 18 only governs joinder of claims, not joinder of parties. If multiple claims are to be asserted by or against multiple parties, Rule 20 governs the requirements to be met for the inclusion of the various parties.

RULE 18(b) Joinder of Contingent Claims

A claimant may join two claims in a single action even if the outcome of one of the claims is contingent on the outcome of the other.

Rule 19 - Required Joinder of Parties

- Supplemental jurisdiction <u>only</u> exists if the second plaintiff is diverse from each defendant on their own. → so each P has to be at $75,001 on their own

- supplemental jurisdiction statute <u>only</u> used where there is NO FQ jurisdiction → only if there is complete diversity of citizenship

- Absent complete diversity, there is <u>NO</u> OG jurisdiction due to "contamination"

- ex: if party is <u>necessary</u> under rule 19, it is just regular div., NOT under 1367

☆ - <u>must</u> join the P bc in their absence, <u>complete relief cannot be granted</u>, <u>OR</u> they have interest in subj. matter, <u>AND</u> nonjoinder will impact the parties. ☆

→ needed to be joined for outcome reasons.

↳ no div. needed

<u>Key</u>:
- both Rule 19 & 20 are from same case or controversy.
- thus, both could be joinder in §1367

- FQ is always in §1367 sup. juris.
- Div. cannot be in §1367 if it contaminates jurisdiction

- FQ = ALWAYS in §1367

- D's always get in thru §1367, never P's. Rule 19 is for P's. [illegible]
- if no FQ & joined by Rule 19, claim is <u>excluded</u> from §1367 bc in 19 it's from a Plaintiff [illegible] ~~courts want to settle the related matters~~

RULE 19

REQUIRED JOINDER OF PARTIES

(a) Persons Required to Be Joined if Feasible.

(1) *Required Party.* A person who is subject to service of process and whose joinder will not deprive the court of subject-matter jurisdiction must be joined as a party if:

(A) in that person's absence, the court cannot accord complete relief among existing parties; or

(B) that person claims an interest relating to the subject of the action and is so situated that disposing of the action in the person's absence may:

(i) as a practical matter impair or impede the person's ability to protect the interest; or

(ii) leave an existing party subject to a substantial risk of incurring double, multiple, or otherwise inconsistent obligations because of the interest.

(2) *Joinder by Court Order.* If a person has not been joined as required, the court must order that the person be made a party. A person who refuses to join as a plaintiff may be made either a defendant or, in a proper case, an involuntary plaintiff.

(3) *Venue.* If a joined party objects to venue and the joinder would make venue improper, the court must dismiss that party.

(b) When Joinder Is Not Feasible. If a person who is required to be joined if feasible cannot be joined, the court must determine whether, in equity and good conscience, the action should proceed among the existing parties or should be dismissed. The factors for the court to consider include:

(1) the extent to which a judgment rendered in the person's absence might prejudice that person or the existing parties;

(2) the extent to which any prejudice could be lessened or avoided by:

(A) protective provisions in the judgment;

(B) shaping the relief; or

(C) other measures;

(3) whether a judgment rendered in the person's absence would be adequate; and

(4) whether the plaintiff would have an adequate remedy if the action were dismissed for nonjoinder.

(c) Pleading the Reasons for Nonjoinder. When asserting a claim for relief, a party must state:

(1) the name, if known, of any person who is required to be joined if feasible but is not joined; and

(2) the reasons for not joining that person.

(d) Exception for Class Actions. This rule is subject to Rule 23.

[Amended effective July 1, 1966; August 1, 1987; April 30, 2007, effective December 1, 2007.]

UNDERSTANDING RULE 19

HOW RULE 19 FITS IN

The general rule for civil actions in federal courts is that the plaintiff may choose who to sue and who not to sue. Thus, for example, if a plaintiff believes he was injured by a lawnmower containing a defectively manufactured blade, the plaintiff may sue the lawnmower manufacturer, blade manufacturer, or both, depending on practical and strategic considerations. If the plaintiff chooses only to sue the lawnmower manufacturer, neither defendant is unfairly disadvantaged; the blade manufacturer is happy to be left off the caption, and the lawnmower manufacturer has the option to implead the blade manufacturer as a third-party defendant (under Rule 14) or to defend by itself, then bring a contribution claim in a separate action against the blade manufacturer if the plaintiff succeeds.

Sometimes, however, the plaintiff's decision to omit a potential defendant creates problems. For example, if a plaintiff seeks to recover from a limited fund that the defendant controls and a nonparty also has a claim against that fund, the rights of the defendant or the nonparty might be impaired by a ruling in favor of the plaintiff if the case proceeds without the nonparty. If the plaintiff's claim exhausts the fund, and the nonparty subsequently establishes a claim against the fund as well, either the nonparty will be harmed because the fund has been depleted or the defendant will be exposed to liabilities exceeding the fund.

Rule 19 addresses situations when a person with an interest in the outcome of an action is not named as a party. It requires joinder, when feasible, of nonparties if proceeding in their absence would either materially reduce the likelihood that the court can provide justice for the existing parties or protect the existing parties from double exposure, or would impair the ability of the nonparties to protect their interests. Such a nonparty is referred to as a "required party."

Rule 19 also directs the court as to how to proceed if a required party cannot be joined for reasons of jurisdiction or venue. It provides the court with discretion to dismiss the case or to proceed without the required party, and provides factors for exercising that discretion.

Thus, analysis under Rule 19 entails three steps. First, the court will determine whether a nonparty is a required party. If so, the court will determine whether the party can be joined, from a jurisdictional and venue perspective. If so, the court will order the required party's joinder. If not, the court must determine whether to dismiss the case or proceed without the required party.

In order to facilitate consideration of required parties, Rule 19 imposes an obligation on the plaintiff to identify potentially interested parties in the complaint. Based on this information, or based on any other information, a defendant may file a motion to dismiss for failure to include a required party under Rule 12(b)(7).

THE ARCHITECTURE OF RULE 19

The language identifying required parties is located in Rule 19(a). If a required party cannot be joined, Rule 19(b) addresses whether the court should dismiss the case or continue without that person. Rule 19(c) imposes the obligation on parties asserting claims to identify potentially interested persons who they have not included in their claim. Rule 19(d) simply clarifies that, for class actions, Rule 19 yields to Rule 23.

HOW RULE 19 WORKS IN PRACTICE

RULE 19(a) Persons Required to Be Joined if Feasible

When feasible, persons should be joined in a lawsuit when their absence will either materially reduce the likelihood that the court can provide justice for those already parties or be detrimental to the nonparties themselves.

PRACTICING LAW UNDER THIS SUBPART

Joinder of Required Parties

The court may order that required parties be joined in the following circumstances:

(1) The court identifies a person in whose absence complete relief cannot be granted to those already parties to the case;

(2) The court identifies a party whose interest may be impaired either practically or legally. *See Samantar v. Yousuf,* 560 U.S. 305, 324 (2010). By contrast, when the interests of an absent party are adequately represented by existing parties, the absent party is not a required party; and

(3) Where several persons have overlapping interests in a defendant's property and there is a possibility of inconsistent obligations. For example, if a tenant seeks an injunction to enforce a lease against a landlord, and another person holds a potentially conflicting lease, joinder of the second tenant will prevent the risk that the landlord will be subject to inconsistent duties to the two tenants.

Procedure

A party may make a Rule 19(a) motion to join a required party. Additionally, the court may raise the issue *sua sponte. Republic of Philippines v. Pimentel,* 553 U.S. 851, 860 (2008). A nonparty may seek to participate by motion to intervene under Rule 24.

Service on Nonparties

If the court determines that a person should be joined, it will direct that service be made upon that person. Such service may employ the "bulge" provision of Rule 4(k), permitting service within 100 miles of the court.

Joinder of Plaintiffs

When a person should join as a plaintiff but refuses to do so, the court may order the joinder of the person as an involuntary plaintiff or as a defendant. *See Independent Wireless Telegraph Co. v. Radio Corporation of America*, 269 U.S. 459 (1926).

Joinder in Diversity Cases

In diversity cases, joining an additional party may adversely affect subject-matter jurisdiction. Courts have limited ability to avoid the problem, depending on whether the person to be joined should be joined as a plaintiff or a defendant. If the person to be joined could be made either an involuntary plaintiff or a defendant, the court may preserve jurisdiction simply by aligning the joined person in a way that maintains diversity. However, if the person can only be joined as a defendant and that joinder would destroy diversity, the court must apply Rule 19(b) to determine whether to proceed without the non-joined party.

Venue

Joined persons retain the right to object to venue. When joinder of the nonparty would destroy venue, the court must deny the motion to join. In that circumstance, the court must consult Rule 19(b) to determine whether to proceed without the non-joined party.

RULE 19(b) When Joinder Is Not Feasible

Rule 19(b) governs whether the court should proceed without persons who should be joined under the provisions of Rule 19(a), but who cannot be joined because their joinder would defeat jurisdiction or venue. The court has substantial discretion to determine, under the considerations listed in Rule 19(b), whether to continue the litigation without the person or to dismiss the action. Thus, in essence, the court must determine whether the participation of the nonparty who is a "necessary person" but who cannot be joined is so essential to the fairness of the proceeding that the case should not move forward without that person.

PRACTICING LAW UNDER THIS SUBPART

Factors

Rule 19(b) lists factors for the court to consider in deciding whether to dismiss a case or proceed in the event of a required party who cannot be joined. The court balances these factors—each one does not need to be satisfied—and may also consider additional factors not on the list. The analysis is very fact-specific. *See Republic of Philippines v. Pimentel*, 553 U.S. 851, 862 (2008).

(1) *Adverse Consequences of Proceeding Without a Person:* The court will examine whether adverse consequences such as legal or practical damage may result by proceeding without a party. For example, persons already parties may be damaged if the suit creates the potential for inconsistent judgments discussed in Rule 19(a). Similarly, a person not joined may be harmed if the suit proceeds to judgment and exhausts a fund from which compensation might otherwise have been anticipated. By contrast, if a potential party shows no interest in a case, the court might conclude that its interests are not significantly affected by the outcome of the case.

(2) *Avoiding Adverse Consequences:* The court will determine if means are available to the court for minimizing potential damage to the interests that are at risk without the participation of the person at issue. For example, if a tenant sought injunctive relief against a landlord but did not include another person also claiming to have rights as a tenant, and the tenant agreed to a damage remedy rather than an injunction, the risk to the landlord of mutually inconsistent injunctions is minimized, and the case may be allowed to proceed.

(3) *Adequacy of a Judgment:* The court will consider "adequacy" primarily from the point of view of the public interest in efficient and final disposition of legal disputes. Thus, a judgment in a person's absence that will leave related claims by or against that person undecided may be deemed an "inadequate" judgment.

(4) *Availability of Another Forum:* The court will examine whether another forum is available in which the claimant may sue existing defendants as well as the person who cannot be joined. When another forum is not available to the claimant, the court in most cases will proceed with the action.

Comparison with Rule 20

Rule 20 governs circumstances in which a plaintiff has ***authority*** to join other persons as parties when they share an interest in a lawsuit. Rule 19, by contrast, ***requires*** joinder when a person's presence is central to the administration of justice in the case.

Effect of Dismissal

A dismissal under Rule 19(b) is without prejudice to refiling unless the order of dismissal provides otherwise (see Rule 41).

RULE 19(c) Pleading the Reasons for Nonjoinder

Parties seeking relief must identify in their pleadings potentially interested persons who have not been joined and explain why they are not included in the action. A court may use such information to notify these persons, so that they may seek to intervene on their own initiative. The defendant may use the names provided by the plaintiff as a basis for a motion to dismiss the action for failure to join required parties under Rule 12(b)(7).

RULE 19(d) Exception for Class Actions

When Rule 19 and Rule 23 (governing class actions) both apply to a case and they are in conflict, Rule 23 controls.

Rule ~~[illegible]~~ 20 → P can be joined if it asserts a claim from the same case or controversy that is against D & assert joint, several, or alternative liability.

- they can be joined if they want that relief

- FQ = always in §1367
- ~~If we FQ and there is in div, then~~
~~If a P is joined under Rule 20,~~
~~then the claim is [illegible] excluded~~
~~be [illegible] the diversity is not necessary~~
~~destroyed & their joinder~~

☆ - D's joined are allowed sup. jurisd. under 1367; P's are not. ☆

~~FQ~~ → **Fed Rule 20: Gap**:

→ ability to join parties!! & ability to sever parties ←

- parties rely on Rule 20 when:
  1. joining non-parties to a suit (like interpleaders)
  2. severing parties from a lawsuit bc the claims asserted by or against them don't meet req. of rule 20

- some courts require ~~[illegible]~~ non-parties to join under FRCP 24 → and only allow parties already joined to move to join someone

RULE 20

PERMISSIVE JOINDER OF PARTIES

(a) Persons Who May Join or Be Joined.

(1) *Plaintiffs.* Persons may join in one action as plaintiffs if:

(A) they assert any right to relief jointly, severally, or in the alternative with respect to or arising out of the same transaction, occurrence, or series of transactions or occurrences; and

(B) any question of law or fact common to all plaintiffs will arise in the action.

(2) *Defendants.* Persons—as well as a vessel, cargo, or other property subject to admiralty process in rem—may be joined in one action as defendants if:

(A) any right to relief is asserted against them jointly, severally, or in the alternative with respect to or arising out of the same transaction, occurrence, or series of transactions or occurrences; and

(B) any question of law or fact common to all defendants will arise in the action.

(3) *Extent of Relief.* Neither a plaintiff nor a defendant need be interested in obtaining or defending against all the relief demanded. The court may grant judgment to one or more plaintiffs according to their rights, and against one or more defendants according to their liabilities.

(b) Protective Measures. The court may issue orders—including an order for separate trials—to protect a party against embarrassment, delay, expense, or other prejudice that arises from including a person against whom the party asserts no claim and who asserts no claim against the party.

[Amended effective July 1, 1966; August 1, 1987; April 30, 2007, effective December 1, 2007.]

UNDERSTANDING RULE 20

HOW RULE 20 FITS IN

Rule 20 describes the circumstances in which a plaintiff may join with other plaintiffs in a single complaint, and controls when multiple defendants may be joined together in a single complaint. The provisions for multiple plaintiffs and multiple defendants are parallel—both require claims that arise out of the same transaction or occurrence or series of transactions or occurrences, and both require at least one issue of law or fact common to each plaintiff or each defendant.

These requirements are part of the Rules' balancing of competing interests in the joinder rules. If multiple parties—plaintiffs or defendants—are involved in claims arising out of the same events and involving common issues of law or fact, it is efficient to include them in one lawsuit. For example, the pertinent documents and witnesses are likely to be relevant to these multiple parties, so it is more efficient for them all to participate in one set of discovery, rather than repeating the same discovery in multiple separate cases. In contrast, if parties do not share at least one common issue of law or fact, including them in one lawsuit will likely cause the parties to have to sit through multiple procedures that have no bearing on them.

Rule 20 specifies that every plaintiff and every defendant does not need to be interested in every claim in the case—they just each need to participate in at least one transactionally related claim with a common issue of law or fact. It also authorizes the court to issues orders, including an order for separate trials, to avoid prejudicing parties from proceedings or evidence that does not bear on them.

THE ARCHITECTURE OF RULE 20

Rule 20 is divided into two subsections. Rule 20(a) contains the tests for multiple plaintiffs joining together in one action and for multiple defendants being joined in one action. Rule 20(b) authorizes the court to issue orders to protect parties from prejudice caused by the multiplicity of claims and parties authorized by the Rules.

HOW RULE 20 WORKS IN PRACTICE

RULE 20(a) Persons Who May Join or Be Joined

There are two requirements for parties to join together as plaintiffs in one action: 1) the persons who are joining as plaintiffs must assert claims that arise out of the same transaction or occurrence, or series of transactions or occurrences; and 2) all the plaintiffs must share in common at least one question of law or fact. The test for joining multiple persons as defendants is the same.

PRACTICING LAW UNDER THIS SUBPART

Joinder Explained

Although "joinder" sounds like it might entail joining or adding new parties to an existing action, it actually also encompasses including parties in the initial action. Thus, if two plaintiffs want to sue two defendants, Rule 20(a) will control whether a single complaint may include all of those parties.

Same Transaction or Occurrence

Parties may join together as plaintiffs, or be joined as defendants, so long as the claims involving them arise out of the same transaction or occurrence, or the same series of transactions or occurrences. The courts have adopted various standards for determining whether two claims arise out of the same transaction or occurrence. In general, this requirement is satisfied if there is a substantial logical relationship between the transactions or occurrences at issue. The phrase "series of transactions or occurrences" is an important one, significantly broadening the reach of Rule 20(a).

Common Question of Fact or Law

Rule 20(a) requires only that the joined parties share a single common question of fact or law; there is no requirement that the actions involving various parties overlap with one another to any greater degree. Thus, for example, defendants who are allegedly jointly liable will almost invariably be subject to Rule 20 joinder.

Permissive Joinder

Rule 20(a) is permissive only, allowing joinder but not requiring it.

Right to Relief Still Judged Separately

Notwithstanding joinder, parties still receive judgment according to the respective merits of their individual claims or defenses.

Jurisdiction and Venue

For each claim between parties joined under Rule 20(a), subject-matter jurisdiction must be satisfied. Likewise, the court will need personal jurisdiction over every defendant joined under Rule 20(a). Finally, venue must be proper in the court for the parties and claims joined in the action. These concepts are discussed at greater length in the Getting Started section of this text.

Relation to Rule 18

Rule 18 governs joinder of *claims* by a single plaintiff against a single defendant. Rule 20 governs joinder of *parties* in a single action.

RULE 20(b) Protective Measures

Although Rule 20(a) may permit plaintiffs to join together, or to join multiple defendants together, the court retains discretion to order separate trials or other procedures in the interest of justice. Primary factors considered by the court in determining whether to order separate trials are unreasonable embarrassment, delay, expense, or other prejudice.

§1367: We are here bc we have these joined parties from rule 19 & 20, & we want to see if Fed. Ct. has sup. jurisdiction over these claims from the same case or controversy. (Pretty much → anchor claim has OG jurisd, can the other claims thru sup. jurisd, also have OG jurisd.?)

STEP 1: Is the additional claim part of same case or controversy as the ANCHOR CLAIM?

- courts will have sup. jurisd whenever they had OG jurisd. if no div. is contaminated.
- if FQ (ex. anti-trust), but is non-diverse, this IS OKAY & will have sup. jurisd bc:
  - if FQ = always has sup. jurid.
  - if DIV = then be careful bc cannot contaminate, so make sure they're from dif. states & that AIC is met for each party.
- why do courts allow this?
  - traditional old reason: "common nucleus of operative fact"
  - new modern common law = "bc same case or controversey"
- if thru Div & the added party does not meet AIC on own, then the OG anchor claim is contaminated, and now no sup. jurisd. can exist
- if all elements are met for sup. jurisd, court <u>cannot deny</u> it's entry in 1367(a) → so FQ!!
  - ↳ court has no discretion to deny its exercise of sup. jurisd. over a claim which has deemed to have OG jurisdic like its anchor claim.

STEP 2:

not ex.
- if one FQ → you always satisfy req. for sup. jurisd.
- if by a defendant wanting to join as a D → you always satisfy req. for sup. jurisd. and can be joined
- if P adding a claim = OKAY!! (just can't add a P).

excluded
- issues = if you are a Plaintiff!
  - ↳ P's are excluded from sup. jurisd if:
    - is a P joined by 3rd party practice
    - is a P joined by Rule 19 or 20 (required or permissive joinder)
    - is a P from intervention / applicant wanting to intervene

not ex.
- P's can <u>always</u> add <u>claims</u>, whether they are compuls / permissive, if it's to that same D. They just cannot add a <u>Plaintiff</u>.
  - ↳ 1367 does not exclude claims.

RECAP for DIV. → P can add claims, just not P's, D's can always join] DIV.
→ if FQ and not Div, then all can join.] FQ

RULE 21

MISJOINDER AND NONJOINDER OF PARTIES

Misjoinder of parties is not a ground for dismissing an action. On motion or on its own, the court may at any time, on just terms, add or drop a party. The court may also sever any claim against a party.

[April 30, 2007, effective December 1, 2007.]

UNDERSTANDING RULE 21

HOW RULE 21 FITS IN

One of the driving principles behind the Federal Rules of Civil Procedure was to eliminate many of the technical traps of some of the historical procedural regimes and to foster resolution of disputes on the merits. Toward that end, Rule 21 clarifies that misjoinder or nonjoinder that violates other Rules or principles governing multiparty litigation does not, on its own, warrant dismissal of the entire case. It also provides the court with discretion to add or drop parties and to sever claims against a party for separate trials.

THE ARCHITECTURE OF RULE 21

Addressing one contained topic, Rule 21 consists of a single section.

HOW RULE 21 WORKS IN PRACTICE

What Constitutes Misjoinder

Joinder may be improper for a variety of reasons, including joinder that does not meet the requirements of the joinder rules, such as Rule 20(a) or Rule 14, and situations in which a party defeats jurisdiction or venue.

Consequence of Misjoinder

The consequence of misjoinder depends on the nature of the misjoinder. If a party's inclusion in an action does not comply with the rules governing joinder of parties, the court will order the inappropriately joined party dismissed so that the remainder of the action may continue—Rule 21 explicitly states that misjoinder is not a basis for dismissal of an entire action. If the joinder of a party produces defects in jurisdiction or venue—such as the inclusion of a non-diverse defendant in a diversity jurisdiction case—then the proper remedy turns on an analysis of whether the party is a required party under Rule 19. If not, the court again may simply dismiss the party who creates the defect. If so, then the court will conduct a Rule 19(b) analysis of whether to dismiss the entire action or just the party. *See Newman-Green, Inc. v. Alfonzo-Larrain,* 490 U.S. 826, 832 (1989).

Failure to Join

If a party should have been joined but was not—for example a required party under Rule 19—the court will simply order joinder of the missing party.

Timing

The court may order dismissal or the addition of a party at any time in the action, even on appeal, subject only to the need to protect all parties from unfair prejudice. *See Newman-Green, Inc. v. Alfonzo-Larrain,* 490 U.S. 826, 832 (1989).

Motion

Adding or dropping a party may be done upon motion of someone already a party or upon the court's own initiative.

Severance of Claims or Parties

Even if parties or claims have been appropriately joined, the court may use Rule 21 to order separate trials in the interest of justice.

Relation to Rule 42(b)

When a claim is severed under Rule 21, it ceases to be part of the same suit. By contrast, if an issue is separated under Rule 42(b), it will be tried separately but remain part of the same lawsuit. The most important result of this distinction is that severed proceedings under Rule 21 become final as each proceeding goes to judgment, and may be appealed individually. Separate trials under Rule 42(b), by contrast, are typically not ready for appeal until all claims and issues are decided.

Stakeholder = has no interest in it.

Interpleader: A person posesses NO interest ~~in land (land~~ for example), wants to settle a claim bc 2 other ppl think they own the land.
→ allows a person that is posession of property, a stakeholder, to settle the competing claims in one lawsuit by forcing the people who claim to own the property to litigate the question of ownership

2 Types of Interpleader: Rule interpleader (R.22) & Statutory interpleader (§1335)

→ similarities of the two:
1. there must be a single & identifiable property, fund, or right
2. stakeholder must not claim an interest in the property, fund, or right
3. more than one claimant claims an interest in the prop. fund, or right
4. stakeholder must demonstrate a real, reasonable fear of double litigation
5. stakeholder must act timely to file the interpleader action (11 month delay after recieving notice of claims was untimely)

→ after interpleader action, the 2 claimants who claim interest, now will litigate for the property. stakeholder now out of it.

stat. interpleader (reference pg. 811)
1. 500+ AND at least 2 are diverse for SMJ. Stakeholder need not be div.
2. venue = proper where 1 citizen resides
3. use S.O.P. of nationwide rules
4. stakeholder must deposit the property with the court here only

Statutory interpleader → notes on pg. 811
§1335

RULE 22

INTERPLEADER

(a) Grounds.

(1) *By a Plaintiff.* Persons with claims that may expose a plaintiff to double or multiple liability may be joined as defendants and required to interplead. Joinder for interpleader is proper even though:

(A) the claims of the several claimants, or the titles on which their claims depend, lack a common origin or are adverse and independent rather than identical; or

(B) the plaintiff denies liability in whole or in part to any or all of the claimants.

(2) *By a Defendant.* A defendant exposed to similar liability may seek interpleader through a crossclaim or counterclaim.

(b) Relation to Other Rules and Statutes. This rule supplements—and does not limit—the joinder of parties allowed by Rule 20. The remedy this rule provides is in addition to—and does not supersede or limit—the remedy provided by 28 U.S.C. §§ 1335, 1397, and 2361. An action under those statutes must be conducted under these rules.

[Amended effective October 20, 1949; August 1, 1987; April 30, 2007, effective December 1, 2007.]

UNDERSTANDING RULE 22

HOW RULE 22 FITS IN

When one party holds an asset and multiple other parties claim some right to or interest in the asset, the party holding the asset potentially faces considerable risk. Say, for example, the administrator of a fund is aware of claims against the fund that exceed the total value of the fund. If the administrator starts paying out claims in the order they arrive, or in any other order, there may come a time when the fund is exhausted but some of the claims remain unsatisfied. Alternatively, the administrator might start prorating the payments and later discover that some of the claims were not valid. In either event, the unhappy claimants might bring actions against the administrator.

Federal procedure provides two options for the holder of an asset or "stake" subject to competing claims. Both of these options are referred to as "interpleader," where the stakeholder interpleads or deposits the stake into the court to let the claimants vie for the asset through judicial proceeding, thereby mitigating the stakeholder's risk of being sued by the unsatisfied claimants. One of these options is Rule 22 interpleader and the other is "statutory interpleader" under 28 U.S.C. §§ 1335, 1397, and 2361. These forms of interpleader have some differences that make one or the other more advantageous in a given situation, and are concurrent, such that the stakeholder may choose either if both are available. This section will explain both options.

THE ARCHITECTURE OF RULE 22

The provisions governing Rule 22 interpleader are located in Rule 22(a). Rule 22(b) clarifies that statutory interpleader is also available in federal court. Statutory interpleader is housed in three sections of title 28: Sections 1335, 1397, and 2361. Section 1335 provides the federal courts with subject-matter jurisdiction over statutory interpleader actions. Section 1397 provides venue in the judicial districts where any of the claimants resides. Section 2361 contains the procedures for statutory interpleader.

HOW RULE 22 WORKS IN PRACTICE

RULE 22(a) Grounds

Interpleader allows a party holding an asset or stake to join multiple parties who have mutually inconsistent claims to the stake, so that the court can determine the parties' rights in the stake in a single proceeding.

PRACTICING LAW UNDER THIS SUBPART

Claims Against the Stake

The only requirement under Rule 22 is that the interpleader plaintiff plead that the competing claims are at least partly inconsistent with one another, *e.g.*, where the claims against a fund exceed the value of the fund.

Plaintiff as Claimant

Although the interpleader plaintiff does not need to have a claim to or interest in the stake, it may assert such a claim. For example, where a limited insurance fund is subject to claims exceeding the value of the fund, the insurance company may initiate the interpleader action and then contend that none of the claims against the insurance fund has merit.

Defendants May Employ Interpleader

Sometimes a stakeholder will already have been sued by a claimant, but other claimants are not parties to the action. In such circumstances the stakeholder defendant is entitled to initiate the interpleader action through a counterclaim or crossclaim, and then join the other claimants in the action. *See Grubbs v. General Elec. Credit Corp.,* 405 U.S. 699, 705, n.2 (1972).

Subject-Matter Jurisdiction

Rule 22 does not create subject-matter jurisdiction in interpleader actions; an independent basis for federal subject-matter jurisdiction is required. Statutory interpleader under 28 U.S.C. § 1335, discussed below, creates subject-matter jurisdiction for qualifying statutory interpleader actions.

Personal Jurisdiction

Interpleader actions are actions against individuals, not against the asset, and so must satisfy requirements of personal jurisdiction. This means that service of process on claimants must satisfy Rule 4 service requirements as well as constitutional Due Process protections discussed in the Getting Started section.

Venue Requirements

Rule 22 interpleader actions are subject to the general venue requirements contained in 28 U.S.C. § 1391. In contrast, statutory interpleader actions have a special venue section, 28 U.S.C. § 1397.

Payment into Court: Relation to Rule 67

Rule 22 does not require that the stakeholder turn the asset in dispute over to the custody of the court. However, in practice, payment into court occurs in many Rule 22 cases. Rule 67, authorizing a party to pay a sum of money in dispute into court pending the outcome of the case, is sometimes the mechanism for payment of the stake into court in Rule 22 cases.

RULE 22(b) Relation to Other Rules and Statutes

Rule 22 explicitly states that interpleader under the Rule exists alongside and complements, rather than supersedes, statutory interpleader, discussed below.

HOW STATUTORY INTERPLEADER WORKS IN PRACTICE

28 U.S.C. § 1335 Interpleader

As with all claims, a federal court must have subject matter-jurisdiction before it can hear statutory interpleader claims. However, the requirements for diversity jurisdiction in statutory interpleader are considerably more relaxed than those which Rule 22 actions must satisfy. Statutory interpleader actions satisfy diversity jurisdiction if the stake at issue is worth $500 or more and if the citizenship of one of the claimants is diverse from that of any other claimant (not including the stakeholder). Statutory interpleader cases may also proceed in federal court if they satisfy federal question jurisdiction.

28 U.S.C. § 1397 — Interpleader

Venue in a statutory interpleader action may be found in any judicial district in which one of the claimants resides. This requirement differs from the traditional federal court venue requirements which apply to Rule 22 interpleader.

28 U.S.C. § 2361 — Process and Procedure

Section 2361 sets forth a variety of procedures for statutory interpleader. It provides substantially expanded personal jurisdiction over the claimants, often providing the plaintiff with a major advantage over analogous provisions governing Rule 22 actions. Section 2361 also authorizes the district court to enter orders enjoining claimants from pursuing other proceedings relating to the stake and to enter final judgment discharging the stakeholder from further liability.

PRACTICING LAW UNDER THIS SUBPART

Process and Personal Jurisdiction

Statutory interpleader provides for nationwide personal jurisdiction and service of process. Rule 22 actions, by contrast, must satisfy standard requirements for personal jurisdiction and service of process.

Inconsistent Claims

Like Rule 22, the federal interpleader statute requires that the interpleader plaintiff plead that the claims are independent of, and at least partly inconsistent with, one another, *e.g.*, where the claims against a fund exceed the value of the fund.

Stakeholder as Claimant

The statutory interpleader plaintiff may also be a claimant, as is the case with Rule 22 interpleader. *See State Farm Fire & Cas. Co. v. Tashire,* 386 U.S. 523, 533 (1967).

Defendants May Employ Interpleader

Unlike Rule 22, the federal interpleader statute contains no *explicit* authority for defendants to initiate interpleader actions through a counterclaim or crossclaim. However, defendants may employ the interpleader statute in a manner parallel to that explicitly authorized by Rule 22.

Payment into Court

The interpleader statute *requires* that the plaintiff deposit the asset at issue with the court. *See Republic of Philippines v. Pimentel,* 553 U.S. 851, 871 (2008). This requirement is relaxed only if the plaintiff provides a bond in an amount subject to the court's discretion. There is no similar explicit requirement for a bond in a Rule 22 action, but courts often require similar performance by plaintiffs in Rule 22 cases anyway.

Final Relief for Disinterested Stakeholders

Section 2361 authorizes the district court to discharge a disinterested stakeholder from further liability relating to the stake.

Enjoining Other Claims

In statutory interpleader cases, the federal court may enjoin other federal or State proceedings that may affect the assets that are the subject of the interpleader action. No comparable authority exists in Rule 22 actions.

All Appropriate Orders

Section 2361 also authorizes the court to "make all appropriate orders to enforce its judgment." This provision authorizes awards of costs and attorney's fees.

RULE 23

CLASS ACTIONS

(a) Prerequisites. One or more members of a class may sue or be sued as representative parties on behalf of all members only if:

(1) the class is so numerous that joinder of all members is impracticable;

(2) there are questions of law or fact common to the class;

(3) the claims or defenses of the representative parties are typical of the claims or defenses of the class; and

(4) the representative parties will fairly and adequately protect the interests of the class.

(b) Types of Class Actions. A class action may be maintained if Rule 23(a) is satisfied and if:

(1) prosecuting separate actions by or against individual class members would create a risk of:

(A) inconsistent or varying adjudications with respect to individual class members that would establish incompatible standards of conduct for the party opposing the class; or

(B) adjudications with respect to individual class members that, as a practical matter, would be dispositive of the interests of the other members not parties to the individual adjudications or would substantially impair or impede their ability to protect their interests;

(2) the party opposing the class has acted or refused to act on grounds that apply generally to the class, so that final injunctive relief or corresponding declaratory relief is appropriate respecting the class as a whole; or

(3) the court finds that the questions of law or fact common to class members predominate over any questions affecting only individual members, and that a class action is superior to other available methods for fairly and efficiently adjudicating the controversy. The matters pertinent to these findings include:

(A) the class members' interests in individually controlling the prosecution or defense of separate actions;

(B) the extent and nature of any litigation concerning the controversy already begun by or against class members;

(C) the desirability or undesirability of concentrating the litigation of the claims in the particular forum; and

(D) the likely difficulties in managing a class action.

(c) Certification Order; Notice to Class Members; Judgment; Issues Classes; Subclasses.

(1) *Certification Order.*

(A) *Time to Issue.* At an early practicable time after a person sues or is sued as a class representative, the court must determine by order whether to certify the action as a class action.

(B) *Defining the Class; Appointing Class Counsel.* An order that certifies a class action must define the class and the class claims, issues, or defenses, and must appoint class counsel under Rule 23(g).

(C) *Altering or Amending the Order.* An order that grants or denies class certification may be altered or amended before final judgment.

(2) *Notice.*

(A) *For (b)(1) or (b)(2) Classes.* For any class certified under Rule 23(b)(1) or (b)(2), the court may direct appropriate notice to the class.

(B) *For (b)(3) Classes.* For any class certified under Rule 23(b)(3)—or upon ordering notice under Rule 23(e)(1) to a class proposed to be certified for purposes of settlement under Rule 23(b)(3)—the court must direct to class members the best notice that is practicable under the circumstances, including individual notice to all members who can be identified through reasonable effort. The notice may be by one or more of the following: United States mail, electronic means, or other appropriate means. The notice must clearly and concisely state in plain, easily understood language:

(i) the nature of the action;

(ii) the definition of the class certified;

(iii) the class claims, issues, or defenses;

(iv) that a class member may enter an appearance through an attorney if the member so desires;

(v) that the court will exclude from the class any member who requests exclusion;

(vi) the time and manner for requesting exclusion; and

(vii) the binding effect of a class judgment on members under Rule 23(c)(3).

(3) *Judgment.* Whether or not favorable to the class, the judgment in a class action must:

(A) for any class certified under Rule 23(b)(1) or (b)(2), include and describe those whom the court finds to be class members; and

(B) for any class certified under Rule 23(b)(3), include and specify or describe those to whom the Rule 23(c)(2) notice was directed, who have not requested exclusion, and whom the court finds to be class members.

(4) *Particular Issues.* When appropriate, an action may be brought or maintained as a class action with respect to particular issues.

(5) *Subclasses.* When appropriate, a class may be divided into subclasses that are each treated as a class under this rule.

(d) Conducting the Action.

(1) *In General.* In conducting an action under this rule, the court may issue orders that:

(A) determine the course of proceedings or prescribe measures to prevent undue repetition or complication in presenting evidence or argument;

(B) require—to protect class members and fairly conduct the action—giving appropriate notice to some or all class members of:

(i) any step in the action;

(ii) the proposed extent of the judgment; or

(iii) the members' opportunity to signify whether they consider the representation fair and adequate, to intervene and present claims or defenses, or to otherwise come into the action;

(C) impose conditions on the representative parties or on intervenors;

(D) require that the pleadings be amended to eliminate allegations about representation of absent persons and that the action proceed accordingly; or

(E) deal with similar procedural matters.

(2) *Combining and Amending Orders.* An order under Rule 23(d)(1) may be altered or amended from time to time and may be combined with an order under Rule 16.

(e) Settlement, Voluntary Dismissal, or Compromise. The claims, issues, or defenses of a certified class—or a class proposed to be certified for purposes of settlement—may be settled, voluntarily dismissed, or compromised only with the court's approval. The following procedures apply to a proposed settlement, voluntary dismissal, or compromise:

(1) *Notice to the Class.*

(A) *Information that Parties Must Provide to the Court.* The parties must provide the court with information sufficient to enable it to determine whether to give notice of the proposal to the class.

(B) *Grounds for a Decision to Give Notice.* The court must direct notice in a reasonable manner to all class members who would be bound by the proposal if giving notice is justified by the parties' showing that the court will likely be able to:

(i) approve the proposal under Rule 23(e)(2); and

(ii) certify the class for purposes of judgment on the proposal.

(2) *Approval of the Proposal.* If the proposal would bind class members, the court may approve it only after a hearing and only on finding that it is fair, reasonable, and adequate after considering whether:

(A) the class representatives and class counsel have adequately represented the class;

(B) the proposal was negotiated at arm's length;

(C) the relief provided for the class is adequate, taking into account:

(i) the costs, risks, and delay of trial and appeal;

(ii) the effectiveness of any proposed method of distributing relief to the class, including the method of processing class-member claims;

(iii) the terms of any proposed award of attorney's fees, including timing of payment; and

(iv) any agreement required to be identified under Rule 23(e)(3); and

(D) the proposal treats class members equitably relative to each other.

(3) *Identifying Agreements.* The parties seeking approval must file a statement identifying any agreement made in connection with the proposal.

(4) *New Opportunity to Be Excluded.* If the class action was previously certified under Rule 23(b)(3), the court may refuse to approve a settlement unless it affords a new opportunity to request exclusion to individual class members who had an earlier opportunity to request exclusion but did not do so.

(5) *Class-Member Objections.*

(A) *In General.* Any class member may object to the proposal if it requires court approval under this subdivision (e). The objection must state whether it applies only to the objector, to a specific subset of the class, or to the entire class, and also state with specificity the grounds for the objection.

(B) *Court Approval Required for Payment in Connection with an Objection.* Unless approved by the court after a hearing, no payment or other consideration may be provided in connection with:

(i) forgoing or withdrawing an objection, or

(ii) forgoing, dismissing, or abandoning an appeal from a judgment approving the proposal.

(C) *Procedure for Approval After an Appeal.* If approval under Rule 23(e)(5)(B) has not been obtained before an appeal is docketed in the court of appeals, the procedure of Rule 62.1 applies while the appeal remains pending.

(f) Appeals. A court of appeals may permit an appeal from an order granting or denying class-action certification under this rule, but not from an order under Rule 23(e)(1). A party must file a petition for permission to appeal with the circuit clerk within 14 days after the order is entered, or within 45 days after the order is entered if any party is the United States, a United States agency, or a United States officer or employee sued for an act or omission occurring in connection with duties performed on the United States' behalf. An appeal does not stay proceedings in the district court unless the district judge or the court of appeals so orders.

(g) Class Counsel.

(1) *Appointing Class Counsel.* Unless a statute provides otherwise, a court that certifies a class must appoint class counsel. In appointing class counsel, the court:

(A) must consider:

(i) the work counsel has done in identifying or investigating potential claims in the action;

(ii) counsel's experience in handling class actions, other complex litigation, and the types of claims asserted in the action;

(iii) counsel's knowledge of the applicable law; and

(iv) the resources that counsel will commit to representing the class;

(B) may consider any other matter pertinent to counsel's ability to fairly and adequately represent the interests of the class;

(C) may order potential class counsel to provide information on any subject pertinent to the appointment and to propose terms for attorney's fees and nontaxable costs;

(D) may include in the appointing order provisions about the award of attorney's fees or nontaxable costs under Rule 23(h); and

(E) may make further orders in connection with the appointment.

(2) *Standard for Appointing Class Counsel.* When one applicant seeks appointment as class counsel, the court may appoint that applicant only if the applicant is adequate under Rule 23(g)(1) and (4). If more than one adequate applicant seeks appointment, the court must appoint the applicant best able to represent the interests of the class.

(3) *Interim Counsel.* The court may designate interim counsel to act on behalf of a putative class before determining whether to certify the action as a class action.

(4) *Duty of Class Counsel.* Class counsel must fairly and adequately represent the interests of the class.

(h) Attorney's Fees and Nontaxable Costs. In a certified class action, the court may award reasonable attorney's fees and nontaxable costs that are authorized by law or by the parties' agreement. The following procedures apply:

(1) A claim for an award must be made by motion under Rule 54(d)(2), subject to the provisions of this subdivision (h), at a time the court sets. Notice of the motion must be served on all parties and, for motions by class counsel, directed to class members in a reasonable manner.

(2) A class member, or a party from whom payment is sought, may object to the motion.

(3) The court may hold a hearing and must find the facts and state its legal conclusions under Rule 52(a).

(4) The court may refer issues related to the amount of the award to a special master or a magistrate judge, as provided in Rule 54(d)(2)(D).

[Amended effective July 1, 1966; August 1, 1987; April 24, 1998, effective December 1, 1998; March 27, 2003, effective December 1, 2003; April 30, 2007, effective December 1, 2007; March 26, 2009, effective December 1, 2009; April 26, 2018, effective December 1, 2018.]

UNDERSTANDING RULE 23

HOW RULE 23 FITS IN

In the typical lawsuit, the parties named as plaintiffs in the complaint assert claims against the parties named as defendants in the complaint. These parties may assert further claims against each other, and may even bring in nonparties and third-party defendants. In the end, however, the only claims that are litigated are claims between the named parties.

Sometimes, that typical process is impractical. For example, if a company engages in conduct that is unlawful or actionable, and as a result harms a lot of people in a relatively small way, the typical process is problematic. For one thing, if each individual claim is small, it may not be worth pursuing the claims in light of the costs of litigation. Furthermore, if the number of injured claimants is large—say 10,000—it may be impractical to bring each claim as a separate action but also impractical to combine them in one traditional action.

The solution to this problem is class actions, governed by Rule 23. In a class action, a law suit is maintained on behalf of (or, rarely, against) a large number of people, but only a few "class representatives" are specifically named in the complaint. These named representatives are class members who make many decisions for the entire class.

Rule 23 establishes four criteria for maintaining a class action. The first is numerosity—the members of the class must be so numerous as to make individual actions impracticable. The second is commonality—there must be common issues of law or fact among the class members. The third is typicality—the claims of the class representatives must be typical of the claims of the other class members. The fourth is adequacy of representation—requiring that the class representatives will fairly protect the interests of the class. Every class action must meet all four of these criteria.

In addition, every class action must fit within at least one of the four approved categories of class action, designed to ensure that a class action is a sensible way to proceed. The first category authorizes classes where the class opponent would be subject to incompatible duties if the actions were to proceed separately (for example, individual employee benefits actions might result in similarly situated employees being accorded different employment status). The second category authorizes classes where there is a risk of impairment to the nonparties' rights if the actions were to proceed separately (by, for example, depletion of a limited fund by the parties asserting claims). The third category authorizes classes where the action involves injunctive or declaratory relief (to protect the class opponent from, for example, conflicting injunctions from individual proceedings). The final category is a more general catch-all, authorizing classes where the court determines that the questions of law or fact common to the members of the class predominate over other questions and a class action is a superior procedure for resolving the claims.

Class actions do not occur at the whim of the class representatives. Rather, the court must "certify" that the "putative class" is appropriate to proceed as a class action. The class certification process is an important landmark in class action litigation—the granting or denial of class certification often leads to settlement favorable to one side or the other.

Because there is potential for enriching the representatives at the expense of the class members who are not representatives and who therefore do not participate fully in many decisions, the court is charged with the obligation to monitor carefully important steps in the litigation process, such as approval of settlements and of attorney's fees. Class actions also present special problems of case management for the courts, so the trial judge has substantial additional authority to supervise progress in a class action.

THE ARCHITECTURE OF RULE 23

Rule 23 covers a wide range of issues related to class actions, and has a correspondingly robust structure in eight subparts. The base criteria for maintaining a class action are located in Rules 23(a) and (b). Rule 23(a) contains the four criteria that all class actions must satisfy. The four classifications of class action—into one of which each class action must fit—are found in Rule 23(b).

Many of the procedures for class actions reside in Rules 23(c)–(f). Rule 23(c) covers matters such as: the timing and contents of the court order certifying the class; notices to the class members of many of the details of the class action (including details about opting out of the class); the requirements for judgments in class actions; and subclasses or classes related to individual issues. Rule 23(d) describes the orders that a court may enter during a class action. Rule 23(e) contains the provisions for settling or compromising a class action, requiring the court to order notice to the class members and to ensure that the settlement is "fair, reasonable, and adequate." Rule 23(f) authorizes immediate appeal of class certification orders, but provides that the appeal does not necessarily stay the proceeding.

Special provisions regarding class counsel are located in Rules 23(g) and (h). Rule 23(g) contains the provisions regarding selecting class counsel. It requires the court's involvement in appointing class counsel and describes class counsel's obligations. Rule 23(h) requires the court to approve attorney's fees for class counsel.

HOW RULE 23 WORKS IN PRACTICE

RULE 23(a) Prerequisites

The specialized purpose of class actions—handling large numbers of litigants through class representatives—makes necessary a series of requirements intended to ensure that the opportunity to bring a class action is not misused or abused. *See Taylor v. Sturgell,* 553 U.S. 880, 900–01 (2008). Rule 23(a) sets forth four requirements, all of which must be satisfied before the court will certify a class action. *See Wal-Mart Stores, Inc. v. Dukes,* 564 U.S. 338, 345 (2011).

Satisfying all four criteria does not guarantee that the case will proceed as a class action. In addition to the requirements of Rule 23(a), a court will not certify a class action unless it fits within one of the categories of class action in Rule 23(b) as well. Class actions must also meet the requirements of personal jurisdiction, federal subject-matter jurisdiction, and venue, although these requirements apply somewhat differently to class actions. Additionally, even if a proposed class meets all the requirements mentioned above, the district court may still decide not to certify the class action.

PRACTICING LAW UNDER THIS SUBPART

Rule 23(a) Requirements for a Class

Every class action in federal court must meet all four prerequisites set forth in Rule 23(a).

(1) *Numerosity:* Rule 23(a)(1) requires that the class membership be so large that the alternative of joinder is "impracticable." There is no threshold number of class members required to satisfy the numerosity requirement. A class comprising many hundreds or thousands of members will almost surely meet this test. Classes of fifteen litigants or fewer will almost certainly not meet this test, and will instead be consigned to joinder of parties under Rule 20. *See General Tel. Co. of the Northwest, Inc. v. Equal Employment Opportunity Commission*, 446 U.S. 318, 330 (1980). Several circuits apply a rebuttable presumption that 40 members satisfies the numerosity threshold.

(2) *Commonality:* Rule 23(a)(2) requires the existence of common questions of law or fact among the class members before the case will be certified as a class action. *See Wal-Mart Stores, Inc. v. Dukes,* 564 U.S. 338, 345–46 (2011). To satisfy this requirement, the common questions need not predominate.

(3) *Typicality:* Rule 23(a)(3) requires that the claims of class representatives be typical of the class as a whole. Generally, the class representatives need not have claims identical in all respects with those of other members of the class. Substantial commonality appears to be sufficient, even if differences exist among the claims, such as different issues of damages. This requirement is intended to ensure that class representatives will represent the best interests of class members who are not playing an active part in managing the litigation. It also overlaps considerably with the case law requirement that class representatives be members of the class.

(4) *Representatives Must Fairly Protect the Class:* Because class actions vest authority over the interests of passive members of the class in the hands of class representatives, Rule 23(a)(4) requires the court to ensure that class representatives will meet those responsibilities fully and capably. There is no "bright line" establishing when Rule 23(a)(4) is satisfied, but courts tend to be particularly sensitive to this requirement. Potential conflicts of interest may disqualify applicants, as can a suggestion that the proposed class representative lacks integrity. *See Amchem Prod., Inc. v. Windsor,* 521 U.S. 591, 625 (1997). If, in the course of litigation, the trial court finds that class representatives previously approved have become inadequate, the court retains authority to order appointment of new representatives.

Diversity Jurisdiction

In most plaintiff class actions, federal subject-matter jurisdiction based on diversity of citizenship is governed by 28 U.S.C. § 1332(d) (but note that § 1332(d) does not apply to defendant classes). Subject to a few exceptions, § 1332(d)(2) provides that the amount in controversy for class actions must exceed $5,000,000, exclusive of interest and costs. Section 1332(d)(6) allows aggregation of the class claims to satisfy this requirement, in contrast to the non-class context in which aggregation of claims by multiple plaintiffs is greatly limited.

Section 1332(d)(2) contains relaxed standards for diversity of citizenship as well, permitting the diversity of citizenship requirement to be met in any of three ways: (a) a single member of the class may be a citizen of an American State that is different from the citizenship of any defendant; (b) a single member of the class may be a citizen or subject of a foreign State and any defendant is a citizen of an American State; or (c) a single member of a class may be a citizen of an American State and any defendant is either a foreign State or a citizen or subject of a foreign State. This standard is sometimes referred to as "minimal diversity," in contrast to "complete diversity" for non-class actions.

Section 1332(d) also contains exceptions to the special jurisdictional standards for class actions. Together, however, these exceptions probably constitute a relatively small proportion of the total number of class actions that are now otherwise jurisdictionally eligible to be filed in federal district court. The first exception arises when more than one-third, but less than two-thirds, of the class members as well as the primary defendants are citizens of the same State in which the action was originally filed. In that circumstance, § 1332(d) affords the district court *discretion to decline* to exercise its jurisdiction, in the interest of justice and considering the totality of the circumstances, after considering six factors: (1) whether the claims involve matters of national or interstate interest; (2) whether the claims will be subject to the law of the forum State or the laws of other States; (3) whether the original pleading in the class action was pleaded in a manner intended to avoid federal jurisdiction; (4) whether the action was filed in a forum with a "distinct" nexus with the class, the alleged wrong, or the defendants; (5) whether the forum is the place of citizenship of a disproportionate number of class members, and the remaining class members are dispersed among a substantial number of other States; and (6) whether, during the previous three years, other class actions asserting similar claims were filed on behalf of the same persons.

Another exception *requires* the district court to decline jurisdiction if more than two-thirds of the class members are citizens of the forum State and either: (1) the primary defendants are also citizens of the forum State; or (2) at least one significant defendant is a citizen of the forum State, principal injuries giving rise to the cause of action occurred in the forum State, and during the previous three years, no similar class action involving essentially the same parties has been filed.

Additionally, the more generous jurisdictional standards of § 1332(d) do not apply if the primary defendants are States, State agencies, or State officials, or if the membership of the proposed class is less than one hundred. Finally, these jurisdictional standards do not apply to three distinct categories of class actions: lawsuits arising under designated federal securities laws; lawsuits relating to the internal affairs of corporations arising under the laws of the States where such corporations are incorporated; and lawsuits relating to the rights, duties, and obligations pursuant to a security as defined by federal law.

For purposes of § 1332(d), the citizenship of an unincorporated association such as a partnership is the same as for a corporation—it will be deemed a citizen of the State in which its principal place of business is located and the State in which it was organized.

Where § 1332(d) does not apply, diversity of citizenship is satisfied if the class representatives are diverse from the party opposing the class and the normal standard for amount in controversy requirement is satisfied. *See Supreme Tribe of Ben Hur v. Cauble,* 255 U.S. 356, 364–67 (1921).

Federal Question and Supplemental Jurisdiction

Federal courts may exercise federal question or supplemental jurisdiction over class actions in the same manner as conventional litigation.

Personal Jurisdiction

Jurisdiction over a defendant in a class action is obtained in the same manner, and subject to the same requirements, as jurisdiction over any defendant in conventional litigation. The same is true for personal jurisdiction over a class of defendants, *i.e.,* each individual must be subject to the jurisdiction of the court before that individual is subject to the judgment.

Venue

Venue in class actions does not generally differ from venue in conventional litigation, with one potential exception. If venue is based on the residence of the class, the residences of the class representatives are examined, not those of the entire class.

Removal

Removal of a class action is governed by 28 U.S.C. § 1453. It generally provides that removal of class actions is similar to removal of other claims, as provided in § 1446, with a few exceptions. First, the one-year limitation on removal based on after-acquired diversity jurisdiction does not apply. Second, the limitation on removal by a defendant who is a resident of the forum State does not apply. Finally, the requirement that all parties join in or consent to the removal does not apply.

Defendant Classes

Most class action cases are suits in which the class members are the plaintiffs. However, it is possible that the class members may be the defendants, such as when a plaintiff claims a broad class of defendants is violating its copyright by selling products that infringe the copyrighted design. In that unusual circumstance, the provisions of Rule 23 apply in much the same fashion as they apply to plaintiff classes, with only a few differences. One difference is that members of a defendant class are entitled to constitutional protections regarding notice, in addition to the protections provided by Rule 23. This difference tends to have little practical impact, however, because class representatives are obligated to protect the interests of passive class members, including providing appropriate notice, as provided in Rule 23(c). A more significant potential distinction between a plaintiff class and a defendant class is a heightened need with a defendant class to ensure that the representatives adequately represent the interests of the class. The concern is greater with defendant classes because, at least initially, the representatives of a defendant class are chosen by the plaintiff who is suing the class.

Class Representatives Must Be Class Members

At the time of commencement of the action, the class representatives must be members of the class. *See East Texas Motor Freight System Inc. v. Rodriguez,* 431 U.S. 395, 403 (1977). If a class representative was once a member but subsequently ceases to be a member of the class, the proper remedy is to select a new, suitable member of the class as a replacement representative.

Contractual Waivers

In general, a contractual provision precluding class arbitration or class litigation is enforceable in federal court. *See AT&T Mobility LLC v. Concepcion,* 563 U.S. 333, 351 (2011).

Rule 23 Controls in Diversity Cases

Rule 23's procedures regarding class actions are procedural law, not substantive law, and thus apply in diversity cases even if a State law would bar class action treatment under the circumstances of the case. *See Shady Grove Orthopedic Associates, P.A. v. Allstate Insurance Co.,* 559 U.S. 393, 402 (2010).

Offers of Judgment

Offers of judgment under Rule 68 cause two potential problems in the context of a class action. An offer of judgment is a procedure where the defendant offers to allow the plaintiff to enter judgment against the defendant in an amount specified in the offer. If the plaintiff declines and then subsequently recovers less than the offer, the plaintiff bears the defendant's costs from that point forward even if successful.

Defendants attempted to take advantage of the offer of judgment provision by making an offer of judgment for the full amount of the claims of the named representatives, trying to moot their claims. Courts recognized this potential problem, and have held that a Rule 68 offer of judgment to an individual plaintiff cannot be used to render a putative class action moot.

The second problem arises because Rule 68 provides that if a proper offer of judgment is made and accepted, the court has no discretion and must enter judgment. Rule 23, by contrast, affords the court substantial authority to review and approve (or veto) a proposed settlement of a class action. Courts have resolved this conflict by treating the authority of a district court under Rule 23 as an exception to the otherwise mandatory nature of Rule 68.

Statutes of Limitation: Equitable Tolling

In a case based on federal question jurisdiction, institution of a class action tolls applicable statutes of limitations for the class. *See American Pipe & Const. Co. v. Utah,* 414 U.S. 538, 550–51 (1974). This doctrine of equitable tolling applies to class actions arising from State law claims only when State law also provides for equitable tolling.

RULE 23(b) Types of Class Actions

In addition to the four prerequisites for every class action in Rule 23(a), a class must fit within at least one of the categories of class described in Rule 23(b).

PRACTICING LAW UNDER THIS SUBPART

Category 1: Risk of Incompatible Duties for Class Opponent

A class may be certified if the opposing party would otherwise be at risk of being subjected to incompatible duties. For example, a class of employees could sue an employer who, if faced with separate lawsuits by individual employees, might end up owing inconsistent benefit obligations to similarly situated employees.

Category 2: Risk of Practical Impairment of Nonparties' Interests

A class may be certified if piecemeal litigation involving individual class members may produce injustice for class members who are not parties to the individual litigation. One common application of this category of class occurs when numerous claimants may seek relief from a limited fund and, in the absence of class certification, individual lawsuits might deplete the fund before all worthy claimants had a chance to obtain some share of the fund. *See Ortiz v. Fibreboard Corp.,* 527 U.S. 815, 834 (1999).

"Incompatible Duties" Contrasted with "Risk of Practical Impairment"

The "incompatible duties" standard protects the opponent of the class from the possibility of inconsistent obligations. The "risk of practical impairment" standard protects the individual class members, who otherwise would not be able to share recovery in limited resources in a proportional manner, fair to all.

Category 3: Classes Seeking Injunctive or Declaratory Relief

A class may be certified where the primary relief sought is injunctive or declaratory in nature. There are two elements to satisfy before a class may be certified under this category: the class must share a general claim against the non-class party; and the class must seek final injunctive or declaratory relief. Race and gender discrimination class actions, seeking an alteration in the future behavior of the opponent of the class, are typical of the class actions certified under this category. *See Wal-Mart Stores, Inc. v. Dukes,* 564 U.S. 338, 360 (2011).

Category 4: Predominance of Common Legal or Factual Questions

A class may be certified if questions of law or fact common to the members of the class predominate over other questions. This "catch-all" certification is often a last resort for litigants who cannot be certified under any other portion of Rule 23(b). Two special requirements exist for this category of class, both of which must be satisfied.

Predominance

First, the common questions must *predominate* over individual interests. *See Tyson Foods, Inc. v. Bouaphakeo*, 577 U.S. 442, 453–54 (2016). Individual damages issues are a potential complication when the district court addresses the question of predominance, but the court has some flexibility in considering ways to address this point. *See Comcast Corp v. Behrend*, 569 U.S. 27, 34–38 (2013).

Superior Means

Second, the court must find that a class action is the superior means of adjudicating the controversy. In reaching the "superiority" determination, a court is required to make four findings described below. While the court is required to make findings on the four points listed, there is no requirement that all four findings must be resolved in favor of certification. Instead, the court has discretion to weigh its findings in determining whether class certification is the superior method of litigating the controversy. The court may also address other considerations in addition to the four listed factors.

(1) *Individual Interests in Separate Actions:* The court will evaluate the desire of individual litigants to pursue their own separate actions, and the net balance of interests between such individuals and the class as a whole. Because individual litigants who feel the need to control their own cases may exercise their right under Rule 23(c) to "opt out" of a Rule 23(b)(3) class, it is usually possible to certify the class and still accommodate most of the needs of such individuals.

(2) *Pending Litigation:* The court will also consider the effects of any other pending litigation on the proposed class action. If individual class members have already begun to pursue their own cases, it may be difficult to justify certification of a Rule 23(b)(3) class on grounds of judicial economy.

(3) *Geography:* If the case is being heard in an area of the country where the class or the evidence is concentrated, this factor would weigh in favor of continuing as a class action in the chosen forum.

(4) *Difficulties in Managing a Class Action:* Courts can refuse to certify if too many administrative difficulties exist in a class action. In exercising this discretion, courts consider a wide variety of factors affecting ease of administration of a case. Examples of problems in managing a class include internal disputes within a class, problems of notification of class members, and the impact that State law variations can have on management in a multi-state case.

RULE 23(c) Certification Order; Notice to Class Members; Judgment; Issues Classes; Subclasses

Rule 23(c) establishes the procedure and timing of motions to certify the case as a class action and the process to be followed once a class is certified.

PRACTICING LAW UNDER THIS SUBPART

Class Certification by Motion or Court Initiative

A party may seek class certification by motion. If the class representatives do not make a motion to certify, the court may make the certification decision on its own initiative.

Timing

There is no rigid timetable for resolving the certification issue, but courts are directed to make the decision "at an early practicable time."

Defining Claims, Issues, or Defenses

If a class is certified, the district court must include in the certification order a clear and complete summary of the claims, issues, and defenses subject to class treatment.

Notice to Rule 23(b)(1) and (2) Classes

For classes certified pursuant to Rule 23(b)(1) or (2) (addressing the risk of incompatible obligations to the defendant, impairment of claimants' rights, or requests for injunctive relief), the district court may, but is not required to, order notice to class members. This authority supplements the court's power under Rule 23(d)(2) to issue notice to class members. Courts will be cautious in their use of notice to Rule 23(b)(1) and (2) classes so as not to burden the class representatives with unnecessary costs of notice.

Notice to Rule 23(b)(3) Classes

Individual members of Rule 23(b)(3) classes (the catch-all provision) must receive the "best notice practicable." Notice may be by U.S. mail, electronic means, or "other appropriate means," and will often include mail service on all class members whose identities and addresses are known. *See generally Eisen v. Carlisle and Jacquelin,* 417 U.S. 156 (1974). The financial burden of this notice is generally borne by the class representatives. *See Oppenheimer Fund, Inc. v. Sanders,* 437 U.S. 340, 356–59 (1978). The provisions regarding notice for Rule 23(b)(3) classes also apply to the Rule 23(e)(1) notice requirement in connection with settlements of classes that are proposed to be certified under Rule 23(b)(3). Thus, in some cases, class representatives should be selected with an eye to their financial resources as well as their dedication to the litigation.

Opting out of the Class

Notice to class members of a Rule 23(b)(3) class must contain instructions for opting out of the class. For Rule 23(b)(1) and (2) classes, a district court has discretion to permit opting out.

No Requirement to "Opt In"

There is no provision requiring class members to "opt in" or be excluded from a class. *Phillips Petroleum Co. v. Shutts,* 472 U.S. 797, 798 (1985).

Parties Bound by Judgment

Class actions certified under either Rule 23(b)(1) or (b)(2) have binding effect on whomever the court finds to be within the membership of the class. Rule 23(b)(3) actions bind class members who did not opt out and whom the court defines as members. *See generally Taylor v. Sturgell,* 553 U.S. 880, 894 (2008).

Subclasses

The court may create classes only as to particular issues or subclasses within an action. If subclasses are certified, each subclass is treated as an independent class for purposes of the action. *See Ortiz v. Fibreboard Corp.,* 527 U.S. 815, 831 (1999).

RULE 23(d) Conducting the Action

The court may craft orders governing class actions. Central to class actions is a need to protect the interests of the class members who are not the active class representatives. At the same time, the potential administrative complexity of class actions requires that the court have tools to ensure that the litigation remains manageable.

PRACTICING LAW UNDER THIS SUBPART

Undue Repetition of Evidence

The court has broad discretion to issue orders prescribing measures designed to limit cumulative or repetitive evidence.

Additional Notice to Class Members

The court may order additional notice to class members to ensure fair treatment of passive members of the class. The court's authority under this provision is broad, and encompasses discretion to order notice to the class of almost any important event in the litigation. The court may use its power for a variety of purposes, including: notice to a class of pending litigation; notification of proposed judgments; identification of class representatives to the whole class; and informing the class of key decision points.

Supervision of Class Representatives and Intervenors

The court may issue orders imposing conditions on class representatives and intervenors to advance both fair representation for the class and expeditious processing of the entire case.

RULE 23(e) Settlement, Voluntary Dismissal, or Compromise

The court must approve voluntary dismissal or compromise of actions already certified as class actions or proposed to be certified, and proposals to settle the case must be submitted to the entire class for approval. This requirement of court supervision recognizes the fact that class actions are especially vulnerable to the possibility that the class representatives or the class attorneys may be placed in circumstances where their personal interests conflict with the interests of passive class members. The risk of inappropriate collaboration between class representatives or class counsel and the class opponent is probably greatest when questions of settlement or voluntary dismissal are at issue. Rule 23(e) attempts to suppress such collaboration by imposing a series of obligations on both the court and the parties seeking approval of the proposed settlement.

PRACTICING LAW UNDER THIS SUBPART

Judicial Approval of Settlements

Class representatives have authority to settle claims, issues, or defenses as appropriate. However, the district court must approve or veto settlement, and must solicit the views of class members before making its decision. *See Devin v. Scardelletti,* 536 U.S. 1, 14 (2002). Judicial approval is required even if the court has not yet certified the class.

No Court Protection of Class Opponents

The duty of the district court to protect the interests of class members does not extend to parties (usually defendants) who are not members of the class.

Notice of Proposed Settlement or Voluntary Dismissal

The parties must provide the court with sufficient information to enable the court to determine whether to give notice of the proposed settlement to the class. This information should generally describe: the extent and type of benefits the settlement will confer on the class; details about the claim process and anticipated rate of claims, including disposition of unclaimed funds; the likely range of litigation outcomes and the risks of full litigation; the extent of discovery completed; and the handling of attorney's fees. The court must direct notice in a "reasonable manner" to all class members who will be bound by the settlement or voluntary dismissal if the court will likely: (1) approve the settlement; and (2) certify the class for purposes of judgment on the proposal (if the class has not been previously certified).

Objections to Settlement

Any member of a class has standing to object to a proposed settlement or voluntary dismissal of a kind that requires judicial approval under Rule 23(e). The objection may be on behalf of the individual class member, a subset of the class, or the entire class, and must state the objection with sufficient specificity such that the parties can respond to them and the court can evaluate them. Objectors may seek compensation for their efforts in asserting their objections under Rule 23(h). To avoid improper conduct with regard to objections—either objectors asserting objections simply to extract a payment or the parties buying the silence of legitimate objectors—court approval is required to provide a payment or other consideration in connection with the withdrawal of an objection or the dismissal or abandonment of an appeal of a judgment approving a settlement.

Disclosure of Side Agreements

The proponents of a proposed settlement or voluntary dismissal must disclose any agreements that have been made that relate to the proposal.

Standard for Approving Settlement

Courts evaluating the fairness of a proposed settlement consider whether: (1) the class representatives and class counsel have adequately represented the class; (2) the proposal was negotiated at arm's length; (3) the relief provided for the class is adequate, taking into account: the costs, risks, and delay of trial and appeal; the effectiveness of any proposed method of distributing relief to the class, including the method of processing class-member claims; the terms of any proposed award of attorney's fees, including timing of payment; and any agreement required to be identified under Rule 23(e)(3); and (4) the proposal treats class members equitably relative to each other. The power to approve settlement of a class action lies within the court's discretion, and such decisions are rarely disturbed on appeal. However, some important considerations may restrict judicial discretion. First, while the court is authorized to determine whether the settlement is fair to passive members of the class, the court must still give substantial deference to a consensus of class members on the wisdom of the settlement. Second, while the court must pass on the fairness of the proposal, it may not rewrite the settlement to make it conform to the court's view of a satisfactory settlement. Third, the court's duty is primarily to the members of the class. If persons have previously opted out of the class, the court has no power or duty to use the settlement process to address their interests. *See generally Evans v. Jeff D.,* 475 U.S. 717, 726–28 (1986).

Hearing and Findings re Settlement

The district court must hold a hearing and make findings before approving a class settlement or voluntary dismissal.

Additional Opportunity to Opt Out of Class

Members of classes previously certified under Rule 23(b)(3) are entitled to an additional opportunity to opt out of a proposed settlement or voluntary dismissal.

Special Provisions for "Coupon" Settlements

Congress has enacted a number of provisions that are effective in class actions in which some or all members of the class will receive their award in the form of coupons. In such cases, the court must hold a hearing and determine, in a written finding, that the settlement is fair, reasonable, and adequate to class members. The court has authority, upon motion, to obtain expert testimony on the issue of the actual value to class members of the coupons that are redeemed.

Class Settlements and *Cy Pres*

Cy Pres is a doctrine that originated in the context of charitable trusts and distributions. Historically, it has been applied when the terms of a charitable gift cannot be fulfilled. In that situation, rather than treating the gift as having failed, courts sometimes apply *cy pres* to re-direct the gift to a deserving third party to achieve a purpose similar to the original intent of the gift. In the context of class action settlements, *cy pres* has sometimes been applied to re-distribute excess settlement funds when, *e.g.*, the identity of class members is unknown or some other reason prevents distribution to class members.

Notice of Settlement to Government Officials

Within ten days of the filing of a proposed settlement with the district court, each defendant participating in the proposed settlement must serve notice of the proposed settlement, along with a variety of the underlying documents, to the Attorney General of the United States and the appropriate State official of each State where any of the class members resides, as set forth in 28 U.S.C. § 1715.

RULE 23(f) Appeals

Parties may seek immediate interlocutory appeal of a district court's decision granting or denying class certification. Consequently, the parties might not have to wait until the end of the litigation in the district court to learn whether the decision to certify (or not) would be upheld.

PRACTICING LAW UNDER THIS SUBPART

Appellate Discretion

Appellate courts have discretion to permit or deny an appeal of an order granting or denying class certification. Several situations arise where a circuit court is more likely to permit interlocutory appellate review of a class certification decision. First, if a denial of class certification would probably preclude any realistic chance that individual claims could be prosecuted and the district court's decision was questionable, circuits are inclined to grant review. Second, if a district court's grant of class certification puts substantial pressure on a defendant to settle without regard to the merits of a case and the certification grant was questionable, interlocutory review is appropriate. Third, interlocutory review is appropriate if it will help develop law regarding class actions.

Time

Any application for an interlocutory appeal of a certification order must be made to the circuit court within 14 days after the district court has entered its order. This time limit is extended to 45 days if the United States or one of its agencies, officers, or employees is a party.

Stay of District Court Proceedings

If the circuit court allows an appeal under Rule 23(f), the appeal does not automatically stay proceedings in the district court. Instead, a party seeking such a stay must apply to either the district court or the court of appeals.

RULE 23(g) Class Counsel

Rule 23(g) governs the manner in which a court will supervise the appointment of counsel to represent the class. Rule 23(g) identifies four factors the court must evaluate in appointing class counsel: the work an attorney has already done on the case; the attorney's experience in other class actions and complex litigation; the attorney's familiarity with law applicable to the case; and the attorney's resources. At the end of its evaluation, the court should be able to satisfy itself that the potential class counsel will "fairly and adequately represent the interests of the class." Ultimately, the court has a duty to select from among the potential attorneys the lawyer(s) who will best represent the class.

RULE 23(h) Attorney's Fees and Nontaxable Costs

Rule 23(h) establishes a procedure for seeking and objecting to attorney's fees.

PRACTICING LAW UNDER THIS SUBPART

Methods of Calculation

The appropriate amount of a fee is usually determined through one of two methods. If a fund is available, courts award the lawyers a percentage of the fund. *See Blum v. Stenson,* 465 U.S. 886, 900 (1984). If the court believes another approach is appropriate or where no fund is available, *e.g.,* where the class sought injunctive relief, courts typically measure the appropriate fee through a "lodestar" approach. This calculation begins by determining appropriate hourly rates for individual lawyers, which are then multiplied by the number of hours actually and reasonably expended on the project.

Motion

An application for attorney's fees is made by motion, served on all parties. If the motion is made by class counsel, as it typically will be, it must also be directed to class members in a reasonable manner.

Objections, Hearing, and Findings

Both class members and the party who may have to pay the fees have standing to object to the motion. The court has discretion—not an obligation—to hold a hearing on the motion.

Independent Assessment

A court's duty to assess the reasonableness of an award of fees is an independent obligation, even where parties have reached agreement on a dollar amount.

RULE 23.1

DERIVATIVE ACTIONS BY SHAREHOLDERS

(a) Prerequisites. This rule applies when one or more shareholders or members of a corporation or an unincorporated association bring a derivative action to enforce a right that the corporation or association may properly assert but has failed to enforce. The derivative action may not be maintained if it appears that the plaintiff does not fairly and adequately represent the interests of shareholders or members who are similarly situated in enforcing the right of the corporation or association.

(b) Pleading Requirements. The complaint must be verified and must:

(1) allege that the plaintiff was a shareholder or member at the time of the transaction complained of, or that the plaintiffs share or membership later devolved on it by operation of law;

(2) allege that the action is not a collusive one to confer jurisdiction that the court would otherwise lack; and

(3) state with particularity:

(A) any effort by the plaintiff to obtain the desired action from the directors or comparable authority and, if necessary, from the shareholders or members; and

(B) the reasons for not obtaining the action or not making the effort.

(c) Settlement, Dismissal, and Compromise. A derivative action may be settled, voluntarily dismissed, or compromised only with the court's approval. Notice of a proposed settlement, voluntary dismissal, or compromise must be given to shareholders or members in the manner that the court orders.

[Added effective July 1, 1966; amended effective August 1, 1987; April 30, 2007, effective December 1, 2007.]

UNDERSTANDING RULE 23.1

HOW RULE 23.1 FITS IN

A shareholder derivative lawsuit is a special type of litigation reserved for a particular factual circumstance. It is a civil action filed by a shareholder (or member) of a corporation or unincorporated association. It alleges that the shareholder's (or member's) company has been injured or possesses some other right that the company's leadership is failing to pursue. In effect, the shareholder (or member) is suing to protect the company from harm due to the inaction of its officers, directors, or comparable leaders. Often, the shareholder derivative lawsuit is aimed at the officers, directors, or other leaders for alleged misbehavior or inattention. These types of lawsuits can help vindicate a company's rights for the best interests of all shareholders. But these lawsuits also risk disrupting and distracting the company's leadership, diverting energy, talent, and resources to wasteful concerns, and potentially harassing the company's leaders into an unmeritorious settlement that degrades the company's assets (and thus harms the very shareholders whose interests the lawsuit should be protecting). Rule 23.1 imposes a series of procedural requirements—not normally present in other civil actions—to help preserve the benefit of shareholder derivative lawsuits while containing their risks.

THE ARCHITECTURE OF RULE 23.1

Rule 23.1 has three subparts, none of which is lengthy. The first subpart sets the threshold requirements for filing a shareholder derivative lawsuit. The second subpart imposes additional pleading requirements for such lawsuits. The third subpart installs safeguards for settling, dismissing, and otherwise compromising lawsuits once they are filed.

HOW RULE 23.1 WORKS IN PRACTICE

These three subparts of Rule 23.1 are discussed, in order, below.

RULE 23.1(a) Prerequisites

Shareholders of a corporation (or members of an unincorporated association) may bring, on their company's behalf, a civil action that the company has not asserted. Those company rights may be enforced derivatively only by persons who will fairly and adequately represent the interests of other similarly situated shareholders or members.

PRACTICING LAW UNDER THIS SUBPART

Who Can File

To use Rule 23.1, a plaintiff must be a "shareholder" or "member" seeking to enforce a right of a corporation or unincorporated association.

Subject-Matter Jurisdiction

The company is the intended beneficiary of shareholder derivative lawsuits. *See Koster v. Lumbermens Mut. Cas. Co.*, 330 U.S. 518, 522–23 (1947). As such, the company is normally treated as a required party needed for just adjudication. *See* Rule 19(a). In diversity-based lawsuits, the decision of how to align the company—as a fellow plaintiff or a fellow defendant—may significantly impact a federal court's ability to continue to hear the case. Often, courts will try to align the company in a manner that avoids defeating diversity, but courts are under no firm obligation to do so and, on occasion, have ruled that the most appropriate alignment is one that defeats diversity.

Personal Jurisdiction

Personal jurisdiction over defendants who are natural persons is acquired in the same manner as in other litigation. For corporations aligned as defendants, however, Congress enacted a special service of process provision for shareholder derivative suits, which allows plaintiffs to serve process on those corporate defendants "in any district where [they are] organized or licensed to do business or . . . [are] doing business." *See* 28 U.S.C. § 1695.

Venue

A special venue statute for shareholder derivative actions provides that the plaintiff may sue in any judicial district where the corporation itself might have sued the same defendants. *See* 28 U.S.C. § 1401.

RULE 23.1(b) Pleading Requirements

Shareholder derivative action complaints must meet the pleading standards established in Rules 8, 9, 10, and 11, but must also contain the additional content described in Rule 23.1(b).

PRACTICING LAW UNDER THIS SUBPART

Verification of Complaint

Unlike the general practice in federal civil procedure, complaints that initiate shareholder derivative actions must be sworn and notarized. This swearing requirement will not usually prevent laypersons from filing in reliance on competent information they develop during their own personal investigation or obtain through advice from qualified others. *See Surowitz v. Hilton Hotels Corp.*, 383 U.S. 363, 371–73 (1966).

Pleading Continuous Ownership

A shareholder derivative complaint must allege that the action is being initiated by someone who:

(1) was a shareholder at the time the cause of action arose, or who became a shareholder by operation of law from someone who had been a shareholder at that time; *and*

(2) remained a shareholder at the time the suit was filed.

If the plaintiff is divested of ownership while the lawsuit is pending, the lawsuit will usually be dismissed.

Pleading Absence of Collusion

The plaintiff must also affirm that the shareholder derivative procedure was not invoked to manufacture federal jurisdiction that would otherwise be lacking. This manipulation possibility could arise in diversity cases with the citizenship of the company. The company is likely to be aligned as a fellow plaintiff in a shareholder's derivative action, and if the company is not diverse from the defendants, an obvious jurisdictional problem arises. This diversity-defeating dilemma could be rectified if the company were repositioned as a defendant, rather than a plaintiff. Such a realignment is permitted in shareholder derivative actions when the court finds, for example, that the corporation is controlled by persons antagonistic to the interests of the stockholder plaintiffs. *See Smith v. Sperling,* 354 U.S. 91, 95–96 n.3 (1957).

Antagonism of this nature may be found where the corporate managers are simply opposed to the lawsuit. *See Swanson v. Traer,* 354 U.S. 114, 116 (1957).

Pleading Demand or Demand-Futility with Particularity

Before filing the claim, a shareholder derivative plaintiff must first make a demand on the corporate officers to pursue the lawsuit themselves ("demand"), or demonstrate why it is clear on the facts that such a demand ought to be excused ("demand futility"). The facts of this demand, or the facts demonstrating its futility, must be pleaded with particularity. The standard by which the facts are evaluated is a matter of State law. *See Kamen v. Kemper Fin. Servs., Inc.,* 500 U.S. 90, 98–99 (1991). Consequently, the plaintiff must allege in the complaint, with particularity, the following facts:

(1) the efforts plaintiff made, if any, to encourage those who control the company (officers, directors, or other comparable leaders) to take action; *and*

(2) the reasons why the efforts were unsuccessful, or reasons why no effort was made.

This enhanced pleading obligation is usually satisfied by explaining the facts behind the allegation. Plaintiffs, however, are not ordinarily entitled to conduct discovery to establish the particular facts underlying an allegation of futility.

Special Litigation Committees

When officers of a company are faced with a Rule 23.1 demand to pursue a lawsuit on their company's behalf, a typical response has been to appoint a "special litigation committee" to investigate the matter. In that circumstance, courts will usually grant a request to postpone proceedings in the derivative action until the committee can complete its work and make a report recommending a course of action (*e.g.,* terminate the litigation, assume control of it, or authorize the original plaintiff to continue it). The court has authority to accept or reject the recommendation.

Adequacy of Representation

The plaintiff in a shareholder derivative suit must be a person who will adequately represent the best interests of those—the company and other shareholders—on whose behalf the lawsuit is prosecuted.

RULE 23.1(c) Settlement, Dismissal, and Compromise

Most types of federal civil lawsuits can be settled privately, without judicial approval of the settlement's terms and provisions. That is not true in shareholder derivative actions. Because shareholder derivative actions are litigated on behalf of others (the company and its shareholders), a settlement, voluntary dismissal, or other compromise of the action is permitted only upon the court's approval and only after proper notice to shareholders.

PRACTICING LAW UNDER THIS SUBPART

Settlement Subject to Court Approval

Shareholder derivative actions may not be voluntarily dismissed or settled without prior judicial approval. *See Burks v. Lasker,* 441 U.S. 471, 485 n.16 (1979). The district court enjoys broad discretion to evaluate a proposed settlement. In determining whether to approve a settlement, the court may consider the views of persons who will be affected by the outcome of the case (such as shareholders). In theory, the court is not to re-write a proposed settlement, but should limit itself to approving or disapproving the deal that was proposed. In practice, though, courts have the ability to influence the contents of a settlement by indicating what they consider a satisfactory compromise. Persons who wish to oppose a proposed settlement or appeal a settlement must generally first intervene in the case.

Notice of Settlement

The court must order notice of voluntary dismissals or proposed settlements to interested persons. Subject to the constraints of due process, the court enjoys substantial discretion to determine the manner in which notification will occur.

Bond Requirements

Many States require that plaintiffs in shareholder derivative actions post bonds, from which the defendants will be compensated for litigation expenses if the defendants prevail. Rule 23.1 contains no such requirement. In diversity lawsuits, however, it is settled that federal courts will enforce requirements established by State law.

Numerosity Requirements

Unlike in class actions, shareholder derivative plaintiffs ordinarily need not show that they represent any particular number of similarly interested persons.

RULE 23.2

ACTIONS RELATING TO UNINCORPORATED ASSOCIATIONS

This rule applies to an action brought by or against the members of an unincorporated association as a class by naming certain members as representative parties. The action may be maintained only if it appears that those parties will fairly and adequately protect the interests of the association and its members. In conducting the action, the court may issue any appropriate orders corresponding with those in Rule 23(d), and the procedure for settlement, voluntary dismissal, or compromise must correspond with the procedure in Rule 23(e).

[Added effective July 1, 1966; April 30, 2007, effective December 1, 2007.]

UNDERSTANDING RULE 23.2

HOW RULE 23.2 FITS IN

Both class actions (under Rule 23) and shareholder derivative actions (under Rule 23.1) permit plaintiffs to litigate in a representative capacity, seeking a remedy that could benefit both them and others who are similarly interested in the case's outcome but are not present before the court as parties. Because such actions could significantly impact the rights and obligations of *absent* persons, courts must be more vigilant in overseeing the litigation. Rule 23.2 extends some of the procedural protections of class actions and shareholder derivative lawsuits to members of *unincorporated* associations who are sued through representatives, or on whose behalf representatives have initiated suit. Rule 23.2 is devoted to ensuring that representatives of the *unincorporated* association adequately represent the interest of the entire membership of that association.

THE ARCHITECTURE OF RULE 23.2

Rule 23.2 has no subparts, and the architecture of its brief content is plain.

HOW RULE 23.2 WORKS IN PRACTICE

No New Substantive Right-to-Sue Created

This Rule does not *create* a right for representatives of an unincorporated association to sue or be sued. Rather, it only governs when the applicable State or federal law provides a cause of action by or against the unincorporated association.

Requirement of Membership in Unincorporated Association

Before a plaintiff may represent the interests of an unincorporated association, the plaintiff must prove that the association exists and the plaintiff is a member. Whether the association has a separate, legal existence is determined by the forum State's law. *See* Rule 17(b).

Fair and Adequate Representation

The court must ascertain whether the interests of the proposed plaintiff conflicts with those of the association itself or its membership. Some courts require that the association's representatives meet the standards developed for adequate representation in class actions.

Orders Regulating Proceedings

Rule 23.2 explicitly incorporates Rule 23(d), governing the court's power to issue orders in the course of class action litigation. Because the court's authority under Rule 23(d) is broad, the effect is to give the trial court wide discretion to issue orders ensuring both the efficient processing of the case and substantial protection for passive members of the unincorporated association.

Approval of Settlement

Rule 23.2 also explicitly incorporates Rule 23(e), which vests the courts with substantial authority to approve or disapprove settlements in class actions. As a practical matter, the effect is to require not only consultation of Rule 23(e), but also consideration of keeping the judge abreast of the progress of settlement discussions.

Numerosity

Rule 23.2 imposes no requirement that the membership of the unincorporated association rise above some minimum number.

Citizenship for Diversity Jurisdiction

Where an unincorporated association may sue or be sued through representatives, an established practice is to determine diversity by examining the citizenship of the representatives. Thus, an unincorporated association often can create diversity jurisdiction by selecting a representative who is a citizen of a different State from the defendants (provided that the amount in controversy exceeds the jurisdictional limit of $75,000, exclusive of interest and costs).

Testing for Amount in Controversy in Diversity Cases

A prevailing practice used by federal courts is to test the amount in controversy by examining the individual claims of the association's members. This approach may create a serious jurisdictional hurdle. If, for example, the association has a claim for $1,000,000, but has 10,000 members, with each member having an equal share in the $1,000,000 claim, the value of the lawsuit to each member is only $100—well short of the diversity threshold.

RULE 24
INTERVENTION

(a) Intervention of Right. On timely motion, the court must permit anyone to intervene who:

(1) is given an unconditional right to intervene by a federal statute; or

(2) claims an interest relating to the property or transaction that is the subject of the action, and is so situated that disposing of the action may as a practical matter impair or impede the movant's ability to protect its interest, unless existing parties adequately represent that interest.

(b) Permissive Intervention.

(1) *In General.* On timely motion, the court may permit anyone to intervene who:

(A) is given a conditional right to intervene by a federal statute; or

(B) has a claim or defense that shares with the main action a common question of law or fact.

(2) *By a Government Officer or Agency.* On timely motion, the court may permit a federal or State governmental officer or agency to intervene if a party's claim or defense is based on:

(A) a statute or executive order administered by the officer or agency; or

(B) any regulation, order, requirement, or agreement issued or made under the statute or executive order.

(3) *Delay or Prejudice.* In exercising its discretion, the court must consider whether the intervention will unduly delay or prejudice the adjudication of the original parties' rights.

(c) Notice and Pleading Required. A motion to intervene must be served on the parties as provided in Rule 5. The motion must state the grounds for intervention and be accompanied by a pleading that sets out the claim or defense for which intervention is sought.

[Amended effective March 19, 1948; October 20, 1949; July 1, 1963; July 1, 1966; August 1, 1987; December 1, 1991; April 12, 2006, effective December 1, 2006; April 30, 2007, effective December 1, 2007.]

UNDERSTANDING RULE 24

HOW RULE 24 FITS IN

Plaintiffs are generally considered the "masters" of their lawsuits: which parties are in those lawsuits are generally a claimant's prerogative. For example, Rule 18 allows plaintiffs wide discretion in determining which claims to assert in the same lawsuit, and Rule 20 affords plaintiffs broad in whom (if anyone) to name as a fellow plaintiff and whom to sue as a defendant. But Rule 24 can impact those choices. It permits persons and entities who have *not* been named as parties to try to force their way into a lawsuit. The Rule is not obligatory—it does not compel such persons to try to enter (or "intervene") in a lawsuit. Instead, those nonparties ordinarily retain a choice—try to enter this pending lawsuit or wait to pursue their interests in some other way. But if such persons or entities decide to try to intervene into the lawsuit, Rule 24 establishes the procedures for doing so.

THE ARCHITECTURE OF RULE 24

Rule 24 has three subparts. The first sets the procedure for "intervention of right." Here, the courts' discretion is quite narrow. It *must* allow a person or entity to intervene into the lawsuit if the application is timely made and satisfies the prerequisites of Rule 24(a).

The second subpart sets the procedure for "permissive intervention." Here, the courts' discretion is broader, since the applicant is not seeking (or is unable to meet the prerequisites for) intervention of right. When an applicant seeks permissive intervention, the court *may* allow the person or entity to intervene into the lawsuit if the application is timely made, if the requirements of Rule 24(b) are satisfied, and only after first considering whether intervention would unduly delay or prejudice the resolution of the original parties' rights.

The third and final subpart imposes notice and pleading requirements for intervention. An applicant's motion to intervene must be served on all parties to the lawsuit, must state the grounds for intervening, and must be accompanied by a pleading that contains the applicant's proposed claim or defense.

HOW RULE 24 WORKS IN PRACTICE

These three subparts of Rule 24 are discussed, in order, below.

RULE 24(a) Intervention of Right

Interventions of right must be permitted by the court, subject to narrow exceptions. A party may intervene as of right under two circumstances: where a federal statute confers an unconditional right to intervene; or where the intervenor, in a timely manner, shows a legally protectable interest that is not adequately represented by the existing parties and which, unless intervention is granted, could be impaired or impeded.

PRACTICING LAW UNDER THIS SUBPART

Intervenor's Choice

There is no obligation to intervene. A person or entity who might well be able to satisfy the prerequisites for intervention is not *required* to pursue intervention. *See Martin v. Wilks*, 490 U.S. 755, 763 (1989). To the contrary, that person or entity can usually pass on intervention and pursue a remedy through other means, if they so choose.

Option 1—Intervention by Unconditional Statutory Right

The first basis for intervention of right—Rule 24(a)(1)—depends on the applicability of some federal statute that confers on the prospective intervenor an unconditional right to intervene in the pending litigation. Applicants who satisfy this statutory intervention right do not need to show an interest-impairment, as required of intervenors under Rule 24(a)(2); the two intervention paths operate independently. But statutory intervention rights are construed narrowly. As a practical result, and to enhance their intervention chances, persons seeking to intervene under Rule 24(a) often supplement their application with an argument under the interest-impairment test of Rule 24(a)(2).

Option 2—Intervention by Showing Interest Is Impaired or Impeded

The right to intervene under Rule 24(a)(2) exists when the court finds that the applicant had met three prerequisites: (1) an interest in the subject matter of the pending litigation; (2) a substantial risk that the pending litigation will, as a practical matter, impair or impede that interest; and (3) the existing litigants do not adequately represent that interest. By the terms of the Rule, a final element—timeliness—must also be shown. If intervention is granted, the intervening party must continue to meet these requirements throughout the duration of the litigation, or be subject to being dismissed from the case.

- *Showing #1—Interest in the Subject Matter:* The type of "interest" that will satisfy Rule 24(a)(2) is always fact-dependent. A person who has an interest that, by itself, could constitute an independent case or controversy will likely meet the requirement. However, that level of interest might not always be necessary. An actual economic or property interest in the subject matter of the litigation will likely satisfy this element, but the absence of such an interest is not always fatal. A substantial privacy interest, for example, may be sufficient. But a mere desire to add to the factual record of the lawsuit or to advance a general ideological viewpoint will probably prove insufficient. In testing for a qualifying interest, the courts may examine the extent to which the intervening party will be legally bound by the judgment in the pending litigation.
- *Showing #2—Impairing (or Impeding) of That Interest:* To show an "impairment" or "impeding" of an interest, an applicant may endeavor to show that principles of preclusion or stare decisis may apply to foreclose or compromise the applicant's ability to sue elsewhere or later. But other practical consequences of litigation (short of preclusion or stare decisis) may also satisfy this element. For example, even though a party may not, through preclusion principles, be legally bound by the judgment, a substantial risk of practical impairments on that person's ability to litigate later can sometimes constitute sufficient risk. A provable *certainty* that the interest will be impaired or impeded is generally unnecessary.
- *Showing #3—Adequate Representation by Existing Parties:* Even if the person seeking intervention demonstrates the elements of "interest" and "impair/impede," intervention under Rule 24(a)(2) will still be denied if the interest at risk is

represented adequately by the existing parties to the action. The intervenor bears this burden, but it is minimal. *See Trbovich v. United Mine Workers of Am.,* 404 U.S. 528, 538 n.10 (1972). Typically, the burden is easily carried unless the intervenor and an existing party share truly identical objectives. Lack of adequate representation is most easily demonstrated if the interest is not currently represented at all, or if the existing parties have positions clearly adverse to those of the proposed intervenor. A mere difference in tactics is often not enough. Adequate representation is generally presumed where a State represents its citizens, citizens seek to intervene as of right, and the State shares the same interest as those citizens. There must continue to be a lack of adequate representation by other parties throughout the litigation or the intervenor risks being dismissed from the case.

- *Showing #4—Timeliness:* Unlike timing elements in some other Rules, the actual time limits for intervening are not set out in Rule 24(a). Here, courts confronting an intervention of right application possess their broadest discretion. Generally, courts weigh four factors in determining the timeliness of an intervention request: (1) length of delay in seeking intervention; (2) prejudicial impact of such delay on existing parties; (3) prejudice to intervenor if intervention is denied; and (4) other factors affecting fairness in an individual case. Requests for intervention made post-judgment or post-settlement are less likely to be granted (but not impossible). The timeliness of a motion to intervene is frequently measured from the time the applicant should have known his interest was not adequately represented. An initial decision to reject intervention on grounds of lack of timeliness is rarely disturbed on appeal.

Burden of Proof

While an applicant seeking to intervene as of right has the burden to show that requirements for intervention are met, those requirements are often broadly interpreted in favor of intervention.

Conditions on Intervention

If a court permits intervention as of right, it may impose conditions on such intervention.

Subject-Matter Jurisdiction

When a person seeks to intervene as of right, subject-matter jurisdiction may be established either through an independent basis of original jurisdiction (such as diversity of citizenship or federal question jurisdiction) or, if available, through supplemental jurisdiction. (Subject-matter jurisdiction is discussed in detail in Sections 2.9 through 2.12 of this *Student's Guide.*) Supplemental jurisdiction's use with intervenors is complicated, however. Congress has foreclosed supplemental jurisdiction's use, in diversity-only cases, with non-diverse intervenors seeking to be aligned as new plaintiffs as well with claims by plaintiffs against non-diverse intervenors. *See* 28 U.S.C. § 1367(b). In federal question cases, the supplemental jurisdiction question for intervenors is clearer: there is no congressional prohibition and, thus, supplemental jurisdiction is routinely available in such cases whether the intervenor-as-of-right is aligned as new plaintiff or new defendant. Also, an intervenor's arrival into a lawsuit cannot ordinarily be used to supply subject-matter jurisdiction in a lawsuit that otherwise would lack it.

Standing Requirement and Intervenors

The courts are divided on whether the intervenor, like a party, must always satisfy the requirement of independent standing. One point is certain, though: if the intervenor is seeking relief beyond what the original plaintiff is pursuing, the intervenor must demonstrate standing to do so. *See Town of Chester v. Laroe Estates, Inc.*, 581 U.S. ___, 137 S. Ct. 1645 (2017).

Personal Jurisdiction

When a person or entity moves to intervene, that applicant ordinarily submits to the jurisdiction of the court; thus, personal jurisdiction generally exists by consent.

Class Actions

An absent (non-named) class member seeking intervention as of right must satisfy the same requirements as other intervenors. But the class nature of the lawsuit does have some unique impacts. The clock for timely intervention does not begin to run on an absent class member until that person knows that the named class representatives will not represent his or her interest. The filing of a class action also tolls the running of the applicable statute of limitations for prospective intervenors; if class treatment is denied by the court, the statute then resumes running so as to allow members of the (former) class action to seek intervention into the lawsuit as named parties. See *Am. Pipe & Const. Co. v. Utah*, 414 U.S. 538, 553 (1974). Also, a non-named class member who objects in a timely manner to a proposed classwide settlement need not intervene in order to appeal the settlement. *See Devlin v. Scardelletti,* 536 U.S. 1, 14 (2002).

Amicus Curiae Are Not Intervenors

Amicus curiae are non-parties who offer to share their views or information with the tribunal as "friends of the court." Courts do not equate amicus status with the rights and responsibilities of a party joined through intervention.

RULE 24(b) Permissive Intervention

Permissive intervention is not intervention that the court *must* allow, but instead that the court *may* allow in its discretion. Consequently, the requirements for seeking it are less demanding. It does not require the applicant to demonstrate the sort of interest required for intervention of right. Instead, a court may grant permissive intervention when a timely motion shows that intervention is conditionally authorized by statute or when the applicant has a claim or defense that shares a common question of law or fact with the pending action. The court's discretion to grant or reject such intervention applications is (obviously) far broader than with intervention of right.

PRACTICING LAW UNDER THIS SUBPART

Permissive Intervention by Conditional Statutory Right

Congress can create a statutory right of intervention conditioned on the fulfillment of certain requirements. Intervention under such a statute would be permissive.

Permissive Intervention by Showing a Common Question of Law or Fact

More often, permissive intervention is granted where the person seeking it demonstrates a common question of law or fact between that applicant's claim or defense and the pending litigation. In satisfying this requirement, applicants need not show that they share a direct personal or economic "interest" in the pending litigation; only a shared common question of law or fact is necessary.

Permissive Intervention for Public Officials

Permissive intervention is also authorized for officers or agencies if the pending litigation raises: (a) questions of law administered by the officer or agency; or (b) questions of regulations issued by the officer or agency.

Timing

Applications to intervene under Rule 24(b) must be "timely". The determination of what constitutes a timely application rests within the court's discretion and hinges, unsurprisingly, on the facts and circumstances in a particular case. Because Rule 24(b) intervention questions do not typically affect the interests of nonparties as consequentially as in Rule 24(a) intervention of right cases, courts tend to hold motions for permissive intervention to a more rigorous standard of timeliness than would be applied to motions for intervention of right.

Delay or Prejudice

Permissive intervention may be denied if it would unduly delay or prejudice the pending litigation. That might occur if the complexity added by an intervenor would prolong the litigation excessively. Similarly, unacceptable prejudice to existing parties might occur if the presence of the intervenor might shift the focus of the litigation from the pending issues to those newly introduced by the intervenor. To the extent that the intervenor's claim is duplicative or weak on its merits, courts may be inclined to give greater weight to concerns about delay or prejudice.

Standing for Non-Statutory Permissive Intervention

Although an "interest" is not required, an applicant seeking permissive intervention may still be required to have a sufficient stake in the litigation to satisfy ordinary requirements for standing.

Independent Basis for Subject-Matter Jurisdiction

Applicants attempting to intervene permissively must establish an independent basis for subject-matter jurisdiction. Supplemental jurisdiction is not usually available to those proposing to intervene permissively as fellow plaintiffs, and may not be available for those proposing to enter permissively as fellow defendants. *See* 28 U.S.C. § 1367(b).

Conditional Permissive Intervention

If permissive intervention is granted, the court has substantial authority to impose conditions on the intervention.

RULE 24(c) Notice and Pleading Required

Applicants seeking to intervene must serve their motions on all existing parties, state the grounds for intervening, and accompany their motions with a pleading that identifies their claim or defense.

PRACTICING LAW UNDER THIS SUBPART

Contents, Service, and Filing

An applicant's motion to intervene must state the grounds for the intervention, must be served on all existing parties, and must be filed with the court. *See* Rule 5.

An Accompanying Proposed Pleading

Accompanying the as-filed and as-served motion must be a proposed pleading by the applicant that sets out the claim or defense for which intervention is being sought.

RULE 25
SUBSTITUTION OF PARTIES

(a) Death.

(1) *Substitution if the Claim Is Not Extinguished.* If a party dies and the claim is not extinguished, the court may order substitution of the proper party. A motion for substitution may be made by any party or by the decedent's successor or representative. If the motion is not made within 90 days after service of a statement noting the death, the action by or against the decedent must be dismissed.

(2) *Continuation Among the Remaining Parties.* After a party's death, if the right sought to be enforced survives only to or against the remaining parties, the action does not abate, but proceeds in favor of or against the remaining parties. The death should be noted on the record.

(3) *Service.* A motion to substitute, together with a notice of hearing, must be served on the parties as provided in Rule 5 and on nonparties as provided in Rule 4. A statement noting death must be served in the same manner. Service may be made in any judicial district.

(b) Incompetency. If a party becomes incompetent, the court may, on motion, permit the action to be continued by or against the party's representative. The motion must be served as provided in Rule 25(a)(3).

(c) Transfer of Interest. If an interest is transferred, the action may be continued by or against the original party unless the court, on motion, orders the transferee to be substituted in the action or joined with the original party. The motion must be served as provided in Rule 25(a)(3).

(d) Public Officers; Death or Separation from Office. An action does not abate when a public officer who is a party in an official capacity dies, resigns, or otherwise ceases to hold office while the action is pending. The officer's successor is automatically substituted as a party. Later proceedings should be in the substituted party's name, but any misnomer not affecting the parties' substantial rights must be disregarded. The court may order substitution at any time, but the absence of such an order does not affect the substitution.

[Amended effective October 20, 1949; July 19, 1961; July 1, 1963; August 1, 1987; April 30, 2007, effective December 1, 2007.]

UNDERSTANDING RULE 25

HOW RULE 25 FITS IN

Dismissal of federal lawsuits on the basis of a curable technicality is heavily disfavored under the Rules. Rule 25 is designed to address four of those curable defect categories. This Rule must be read in conjunction with Rule 17(a), which instructs that federal civil lawsuits must be prosecuted only in the names of, and for the benefit of, the "real parties in interest." Nonetheless, there are times when the real parties in interest are unable to continue on as litigants—when they die, become incompetent, or depart from public office. In such circumstances, Rule 25 allows for the substitution into the lawsuit of successor parties who may then continue the task of prosecuting or defending those lawsuits.

THE ARCHITECTURE OF RULE 25

Rule 25 has four subparts, each addressing a separate type of allowable substitution. The first subpart addresses substitution following death. The second subpart concerns substitution upon incompetency. The third subpart sets out substitution rights following a transfer of interest. The fourth subpart provides for substitution by public office holders.

HOW RULE 25 WORKS IN PRACTICE

These four subparts of Rule 25 are discussed, in order, below.

RULE 25(a) Death

Substitution is permitted when a party dies during the lawsuit, provided the applicable substantive law permits the claim in litigation to survive.

PRACTICING LAW UNDER THIS SUBPART

When Substitution Is Permitted

This substitution procedure is available only if the decedent was alive at the time the lawsuit commenced. Additionally, substitution upon death also requires that the claim in litigation be capable of surviving the party's death, a matter resolved by reference to the controlling federal or State law. If, under that controlling law, the claim does not survive the death of the party, there can be no substitution.

Suggestion of Death Filed and Served

The fact that a party has died is brought to the court's attention by a written "suggestion of death," filed and served on all parties pursuant to Rule 5. Nonparty representatives of the deceased should be served pursuant to Rule 4.

Procedure for Substitution—Motion for Substitution

Any party, or persons affiliated with the deceased party, may make a motion for substitution. The motion (along with a notice of hearing) must be filed and served on all parties in accordance with Rule 5 and on any nonparties in accordance with Rule 4. Service may be made in any federal judicial district. Until a motion for substitution has been made and granted, the court has no authority to proceed with the deceased party's case.

Procedure for Substitution—Timing

Motions for substitution must be made within 90 days after the "suggestion of death" is served. Although a party may have been deceased for a substantial period before a formal "suggestion of death" is made, the 90-day limitation is not usually triggered until that filing occurs. If, however, the movant delays more than 90 days after the "suggestion of death" is made, the action by or against the deceased "must" be dismissed. Notwithstanding this apparently mandatory language, courts have exercised discretion to extend the time in which a party may move for substitution.

Hearing

If there is a dispute as to the appropriateness of the proposed substituted party, the court has a duty to resolve the issue and may hold a hearing before ruling on the motion. The notice of hearing should be filed and served on all parties.

Status of Successor

A party who replaces a deceased party receives the status the deceased party possessed at the time of death. For example, if the deceased party had already consented to trial by a magistrate judge, the successor is bound by that consent.

RULE 25(b) Incompetency

Substitution is permitted when a party becomes incompetent during the course of the litigation.

PRACTICING LAW UNDER THIS SUBPART

Survival of the Action

Incompetency will not ordinarily extinguish a cause of action.

Procedure for Substitution—Motion for Substitution

The incompetent party's representative must file a motion with the court for substitution. The motion along with a notice of hearing must be filed and served on all parties (in accordance with Rule 5) and any nonparties (in accordance with Rule 4), and service may be made in any federal judicial district.

Procedure for Substitution—Timing

The Rule contains no express reference to time limitations for motions to substitute incompetent parties, though some courts have imposed a "reasonable" time filing obligation.

RULE 25(c) Transfer of Interest

When the holder of an interest in litigation transfers that interest to another, the lawsuit may be continued by (or against) the *original* party. However, the transferee may, upon motion to the court, seek permission to join in the lawsuit or to substitute in place of the original party.

PRACTICING LAW UNDER THIS SUBPART

Option to Substitute Parties

As this subpart makes clear, the new holder of the interest is not required to be substituted for the transferor party. Instead, the action will continue in the name of the transferor unless the court chooses to order the joinder or substitution of the transferee. Thus, the case may go to judgment without any substitution of parties having occurred, and the absence of a formal substitution will have no consequence.

Procedure for Substitution—Motion for Substitution

A transferee who seeks to join or substitute must file a motion with the court. The motion, along with a notice of hearing, must be filed and served on all parties (in accordance with Rule 5) and any nonparties (in accordance with Rule 4). Service may be made in any federal judicial district.

Procedure for Substitution—Timing

The Rule contains no express reference to time limitations for motions by transferees to join or substitute.

Procedure for Substitution—Evidentiary Hearing

Courts often conduct an evidentiary hearing when considering a Rule 25(c) motion, though there is no express requirement that the court do so.

Subject-Matter Jurisdiction

Joinder of a nondiverse transferee under this subpart usually does not destroy diversity jurisdiction. *See Freeport-McMoRan, Inc. v. K N Energy, Inc.*, 498 U.S. 426, 428 (1991). However, if the nondiverse transferee was someone who would have been indispensable under Rule 19 at the time the case was filed, joinder will destroy diversity jurisdiction. *See id.*

Personal Jurisdiction

When successors in interest are joined under Rule 25(c), they are usually subject to the personal jurisdiction of the court simply because they are successors-in-interest, whether or not their forum activities would separately satisfy, for example, the minimum contacts test or other basis for personal jurisdiction.

Status of Successor

A party who enters a case as the legal successor of a corporation receives the status which the predecessor corporation possessed at the time the successor entered the case. For example, if the predecessor corporation had already consented to trial by a magistrate judge, the successor is bound by that consent.

When the Transferee Is Bound

For this subpart to bind a transferee to the same obligations that burdened the transferor, an "interest" must be transferred between the parties. The Rule does not define an interest, but the mere purchase of assets by a successor entity does not usually bind the successor to the obligations of the transferor.

Extinguishing Corporate Causes of Action

This subpart follows the substantive law on the issue of survival of a cause of action after corporate reorganizations. Thus, if substantive law directs that dissolution of a corporation also extinguishes the corporation's causes of action, Rule 25(c) will not preserve the cause of action.

RULE 25(d) Public Officers; Death or Separation from Office

Public office holders (*e.g.*, the President, the Director of EPA or FDA, a governor, or a mayor) often sue or are sued in their official capacities. In other words, the lawsuit may be captioned with the officeholder's name ("U.S. Department of Agriculture Secretary Sally Jones, plaintiff" or "Governor Robert Smith, defendant"), even though the lawsuit is actually asserting a claim by or against the office that person occupies. In such official capacity lawsuits, when the named public officer dies, resigns, or otherwise ceases to hold that office, the successor office holder is substituted automatically into the lawsuit and the case continues.

PRACTICING LAW UNDER THIS SUBPART

Applies in Official Capacity Lawsuits Only

This automatic substitution procedure applies only when public officers are named as parties in their official capacities. It does not apply where those persons (who happen to be public officers) are suing or being sued personally. Thus, for example, if Agriculture Secretary Jones struck a passerby with her miss-hit golf ball or if Governor Smith caused a wreck when he drove his car through a red light after a family dinner, both will be sued personally (not officially) and this subpart will have no application.

Procedure for Substitution—No Motion Necessary

Because the substitution of public officers occurs automatically, there is no need to file or serve any motion for substitution.

Procedure for Substitution—Timing

Because this subpart directs that substitution occurs "automatically," there is no time requirement (nor any need for one).

Order of Substitution

The court has discretion to issue a formal order that a new public officer be substituted for a predecessor, but need not do so. Whether the court does so or not, the automatic substitution will have already occurred.

Substitutions in the Caption of the Case

After substitution, proceedings should be styled in the name of the substituted party. However, this directive is usually no more than a formality, for no consequence follows to the continued use of the name of the departed officer—unless such error somehow has an adverse effect on the case.

Effect of Automatic Substitution—Survival of the Action

An action by or against a public officer does not abate when the incumbent officer leaves his or her post.

Events Prior to Substitution: Stipulations, Admissions, etc.

Substitution of an official for a predecessor in office ordinarily binds the successor to the results of previous events in the case as if no substitution had been made.

RULE 26

DUTY TO DISCLOSE; GENERAL PROVISIONS GOVERNING DISCOVERY

(a) Required Disclosures.

(1) *Initial Disclosure.*

(A) *In General.* Except as exempted by Rule 26(a)(1)(B) or as otherwise stipulated or ordered by the court, a party must, without awaiting a discovery request, provide to the other parties:

(i) the name and, if known, the address and telephone number of each individual likely to have discoverable information—along with the subjects of that information—that the disclosing party may use to support its claims or defenses, unless the use would be solely for impeachment;

(ii) a copy—or a description by category and location—of all documents, electronically stored information, and tangible things that the disclosing party has in its possession, custody, or control and may use to support its claims or defenses, unless the use would be solely for impeachment;

(iii) a computation of each category of damages claimed by the disclosing party—who must also make available for inspection and copying as under Rule 34 the documents or other evidentiary material, unless privileged or protected from disclosure, on which each computation is based, including materials bearing on the nature and extent of injuries suffered; and

(iv) for inspection and copying as under Rule 34, any insurance agreement under which an insurance business may be liable to satisfy all or part of a possible judgment in the action or to indemnify or reimburse for payments made to satisfy the judgment.

(B) *Proceedings Exempt from Initial Disclosure.* The following proceedings are exempt from initial disclosure:

(i) an action for review on an administrative record;

(ii) a forfeiture action in rem arising from a federal statute;

(iii) a petition for habeas corpus or any other proceeding to challenge a criminal conviction or sentence;

(iv) an action brought without an attorney by a person in the custody of the United States, a State, or a State subdivision;

(v) an action to enforce or quash an administrative summons or subpoena;

(vi) an action by the United States to recover benefit payments;

(vii) an action by the United States to collect on a student loan guaranteed by the United States;

(viii) a proceeding ancillary to a proceeding in another court; and

(ix) an action to enforce an arbitration award.

(C) *Time for Initial Disclosures—In General.* A party must make the initial disclosures at or within 14 days after the parties' Rule 26(f) conference unless a different time is set by stipulation or court order, or unless a party objects during the conference that initial disclosures are not appropriate in this action and states the objection in the proposed discovery plan. In ruling on the objection, the court must determine what disclosures, if any, are to be made and must set the time for disclosure.

(D) *Time for Initial Disclosures—For Parties Served or Joined Later.* A party that is first served or otherwise joined after the Rule 26(f) conference must make the initial disclosures within 30 days after being served or joined, unless a different time is set by stipulation or court order.

(E) *Basis for Initial Disclosure; Unacceptable Excuses.* A party must make its initial disclosures based on the information then reasonably available to it. A party is not excused from making its disclosures because it has not fully investigated the case or because it challenges the sufficiency of another party's disclosures or because another party has not made its disclosures.

(2) *Disclosure of Expert Testimony.*

(A) *In General.* In addition to the disclosures required by Rule 26(a)(1), a party must disclose to the other parties the identity of any witness it may use at trial to present evidence under Federal Rule of Evidence 702, 703, or 705.

(B) *Witnesses Who Must Provide a Written Report.* Unless otherwise stipulated or ordered by the court, this disclosure must be accompanied by a written report—prepared and signed by the witness—if the witness is one retained or specially employed to provide expert testimony in the case or one whose duties as the party's employee regularly involve giving expert testimony. The report must contain:

(i) a complete statement of all opinions the witness will express and the basis and reasons for them;

(ii) the facts or data considered by the witness in forming them;

(iii) any exhibits that will be used to summarize or support them;

(iv) the witness's qualifications, including a list of all publications authored in the previous 10 years;

(v) a list of all other cases in which, during the previous 4 years, the witness testified as an expert at trial or by deposition; and

(vi) a statement of the compensation to be paid for the study and testimony in the case.

(C) *Witnesses Who Do Not Provide a Written Report.* Unless otherwise stipulated or ordered by the court, if the witness is not required to provide a written report, this disclosure must state:

(i) the subject matter on which the witness is expected to present evidence under Federal Rule of Evidence 702, 703, or 705; and

(ii) a summary of the facts and opinions to which the witness is expected to testify.

(D) *Time to Disclose Expert Testimony.* A party must make these disclosures at the times and in the sequence that the court orders. Absent a stipulation or a court order, the disclosures must be made:

(i) at least 90 days before the date set for trial or for the case to be ready for trial; or

(ii) if the evidence is intended solely to contradict or rebut evidence on the same subject matter identified by another party under Rule 26(a)(2)(B) or (C), within 30 days after the other party's disclosure.

(E) *Supplementing the Disclosure.* The parties must supplement these disclosures when required under Rule 26(e).

(3) *Pretrial Disclosures.*

(A) In General. In addition to the disclosures required by Rule 26(a)(1) and (2), a party must provide to the other parties and promptly file the following information about the evidence that it may present at trial other than solely for impeachment:

(i) the name and, if not previously provided, the address and telephone number of each witness—separately identifying those the party expects to present and those it may call if the need arises;

(ii) the designation of those witnesses whose testimony the party expects to present by deposition and, if not taken stenographically, a transcript of the pertinent parts of the deposition; and

(iii) an identification of each document or other exhibit, including summaries of other evidence—separately identifying those items the party expects to offer and those it may offer if the need arises.

(B) *Time for Pretrial Disclosures; Objections.* Unless the court orders otherwise, these disclosures must be made at least 30 days before trial. Within 14 days after they are made, unless the court sets a different time, a party may serve and promptly file a list of the following objections: any objections to the use under Rule 32(a) of a deposition designated by another party under Rule 26(a)(3)(A)(ii); and any objection, together with the grounds for it, that may be made to the admissibility of materials identified under Rule 26(a)(3)(A)(iii). An objection not so made—except for one under Federal Rule of Evidence 402 or 403—is waived unless excused by the court for good cause.

(4) *Form of Disclosures.* Unless the court orders otherwise, all disclosures under Rule 26(a) must be in writing, signed, and served.

(b) Discovery Scope and Limits.

(1) *Scope in General.* Unless otherwise limited by court order, the scope of discovery is as follows: Parties may obtain discovery regarding any nonprivileged matter that is relevant to any party's claim or defense and proportional to the needs of the case, considering the importance of the issues at stake in the action, the amount in controversy, the parties' relative access to relevant information, the parties' resources, the importance of the discovery in resolving the issues, and whether the burden or expense of the proposed discovery outweighs its likely benefit. Information within this scope of discovery need not be admissible in evidence to be discoverable.

(2) *Limitations on Frequency and Extent.*

(A) *When Permitted.* By order, the court may alter the limits in these rules on the number of depositions and interrogatories or on the length of depositions under Rule 30. By order or local rule, the court may also limit the number of requests under Rule 36.

(B) *Specific Limitations on Electronically Stored Information.* A party need not provide discovery of electronically stored information from sources that the party identifies as not reasonably accessible because of undue burden or cost. On motion to compel discovery or for a protective order, the party from whom discovery is sought must show that the information is not reasonably accessible because of undue burden or cost. If that showing is made, the court may nonetheless order discovery from such sources if the requesting party shows good cause, considering the limitations of Rule 26(b)(2)(C). The court may specify conditions for the discovery.

(C) *When Required.* On motion or on its own, the court must limit the frequency or extent of discovery otherwise allowed by these rules or by local rule if it determines that:

(i) the discovery sought is unreasonably cumulative or duplicative, or can be obtained from some other source that is more convenient, less burdensome, or less expensive;

(ii) the party seeking discovery has had ample opportunity to obtain the information by discovery in the action; or

(iii) the proposed discovery is outside the scope permitted by Rule 26(b)(1).

(3) *Trial Preparation: Materials.*

(A) *Documents and Tangible Things.* Ordinarily, a party may not discover documents and tangible things that are prepared in anticipation of litigation or for trial by or for another party or its representative (including the other party's attorney, consultant, surety, indemnitor, insurer, or agent). But, subject to Rule 26(b)(4), those materials may be discovered if:

(i) they are otherwise discoverable under Rule 26(b)(1); and

(ii) the party shows that it has substantial need for the materials to prepare its case and cannot, without undue hardship, obtain their substantial equivalent by other means.

(B) *Protection Against Disclosure.* If the court orders discovery of those materials, it must protect against disclosure of the mental impressions, conclusions, opinions, or legal theories of a party's attorney or other representative concerning the litigation.

(C) *Previous Statement.* Any party or other person may, on request and without the required showing, obtain the person's own previous statement about the action or its subject matter. If the request is refused, the person may move for a court order, and Rule 37(a)(5) applies to the award of expenses. A previous statement is either:

(i) a written statement that the person has signed or otherwise adopted or approved; or

(ii) a contemporaneous stenographic, mechanical, electrical, or other recording—or a transcription of it—that recites substantially verbatim the person's oral statement.

(4) *Trial Preparation: Experts.*

(A) *Deposition of an Expert Who May Testify.* A party may depose any person who has been identified as an expert whose opinions may be presented at trial. If Rule 26(a)(2)(B) requires a report from the expert, the deposition may be conducted only after the report is provided.

(B) *Trial-Preparation Protection for Draft Reports or Disclosures.* Rules 26(b)(3)(A) and (B) protect drafts of any report or disclosure required under Rule 26(a)(2), regardless of the form in which the draft is recorded.

(C) *Trial-Preparation Protection for Communications Between a Party's Attorney and Expert Witnesses.* Rules 26(b)(3)(A) and (B) protect communications between the party's attorney and any witness required to provide a report under Rule 26(a)(2)(B), regardless of the form of the communications, except to the extent that the communications:

(i) relate to compensation for the expert's study or testimony;

(ii) identify facts or data that the party's attorney provided and that the expert considered in forming the opinions to be expressed; or

(iii) identify assumptions that the party's attorney provided and that the expert relied on in forming the opinions to be expressed.

(D) *Expert Employed Only for Trial Preparation.* Ordinarily, a party may not, by interrogatories or deposition, discover facts known or opinions held by an expert who has been retained or specially employed by another party in anticipation of litigation or to prepare for trial and who is not expected to be called as a witness at trial. But a party may do so only:

(i) as provided in Rule 35(b); or

(ii) on showing exceptional circumstances under which it is impracticable for the party to obtain facts or opinions on the same subject by other means.

(E) *Payment.* Unless manifest injustice would result, the court must require that the party seeking discovery:

(i) pay the expert a reasonable fee for time spent in responding to discovery under Rule 26(b)(4)(A) or (D); and

(ii) for discovery under (D), also pay the other party a fair portion of the fees and expenses it reasonably incurred in obtaining the expert's facts and opinions.

(5) *Claiming Privilege or Protecting Trial-Preparation Materials.*

(A) *Information Withheld.* When a party withholds information otherwise discoverable by claiming that the information is privileged or subject to protection as trial-preparation material, the party must:

(i) expressly make the claim; and

(ii) describe the nature of the documents, communications, or tangible things not produced or disclosed—and do so in a manner that, without revealing information itself privileged or protected, will enable other parties to assess the claim.

(B) *Information Produced.* If information produced in discovery is subject to a claim of privilege or of protection as trial-preparation material, the party making the claim may notify any party that received the information of the claim and the basis for it. After being notified, a party must promptly return, sequester, or destroy the specified information and any copies it has; must not use or disclose the information until the claim is resolved; must take reasonable steps to retrieve the information if the party disclosed it before being notified; and may promptly present the information to the court under seal for a determination of the claim. The producing party must preserve the information until the claim is resolved.

(c) Protective Orders.

(1) *In General.* A party or any person from whom discovery is sought may move for a protective order in the court where the action is pending—or as an alternative on matters relating to a deposition, in the court for the district where the deposition will be taken. The motion must include a certification that the movant has in good faith conferred or attempted to confer with other affected parties in an effort to resolve the dispute without court action. The court may, for good cause, issue an order to protect a party or person from annoyance, embarrassment, oppression, or undue burden or expense, including one or more of the following:

(A) forbidding the disclosure or discovery;

(B) specifying terms, including time and place or the allocation of expenses, for the disclosure or discovery;

(C) prescribing a discovery method other than the one selected by the party seeking discovery;

(D) forbidding inquiry into certain matters, or limiting the scope of disclosure or discovery to certain matters;

(E) designating the persons who may be present while the discovery is conducted;

(F) requiring that a deposition be sealed and opened only on court order;

(G) requiring that a trade secret or other confidential research, development, or commercial information not be revealed or be revealed only in a specified way; and

(H) requiring that the parties simultaneously file specified documents or information in sealed envelopes, to be opened as the court directs.

(2) *Ordering Discovery.* If a motion for a protective order is wholly or partly denied, the court may, on just terms, order that any party or person provide or permit discovery.

(3) *Awarding Expenses.* Rule 37(a)(5) applies to the award of expenses.

(d) Timing and Sequence of Discovery.

(1) *Timing.* A party may not seek discovery from any source before the parties have conferred as required by Rule 26(f), except in a proceeding exempted from initial disclosure under Rule 26(a)(1)(B), or when authorized by these rules, by stipulation, or by court order.

(2) *Early Rule 34 Requests.*

(A) *Time to Deliver.* More than 21 days after the summons and complaint are served on a party, a request under Rule 34 may be delivered:

(i) to that party by any other party, and

(ii) by that party to any plaintiff or to any other party that has been served.

(B) *When Considered Served.* The request is considered to have been served at the first Rule 26(f) conference.

(3) *Sequence.* Unless the parties stipulate or the court orders otherwise for the parties' and witnesses' convenience and in the interests of justice:

(A) methods of discovery may be used in any sequence; and

(B) discovery by one party does not require any other party to delay its discovery.

(e) Supplementing Disclosures and Responses.

(1) *In General.* A party who has made a disclosure under Rule 26(a)—or who has responded to an interrogatory, request for production, or request for admission—must supplement or correct its disclosure or response:

(A) in a timely manner if the party learns that in some material respect the disclosure or response is incomplete or incorrect, and if the additional or corrective information has not otherwise been made known to the other parties during the discovery process or in writing; or

(B) as ordered by the court.

(2) *Expert Witness.* For an expert whose report must be disclosed under Rule 26(a)(2)(B), the party's duty to supplement extends both to information included in the report and to information given during the expert's deposition. Any additions or changes to this information must be disclosed by the time the party's pretrial disclosures under Rule 26(a)(3) are due.

(f) Conference of the Parties; Planning for Discovery.

(1) *Conference Timing.* Except in a proceeding exempted from initial disclosure under Rule 26(a)(1)(B) or when the court orders otherwise, the parties must confer as soon as practicable—and in any event at least 21 days before a scheduling conference is to be held or a scheduling order is due under Rule 16(b).

(2) *Conference Content; Parties' Responsibilities.* In conferring, the parties must consider the nature and basis of their claims and defenses and the possibilities for promptly settling or resolving the case; make or arrange for the disclosures required by Rule 26(a)(1); discuss any issues about preserving discoverable information; and develop a proposed discovery plan. The attorneys of record and all unrepresented parties that have appeared in the case are jointly responsible for arranging the conference, for attempting in good faith to agree on the proposed discovery plan, and for submitting to the court within 14 days after the conference a written report outlining the plan. The court may order the parties or attorneys to attend the conference in person.

(3) *Discovery Plan.* A discovery plan must state the parties' views and proposals on:

(A) what changes should be made in the timing, form, or requirement for disclosures under Rule 26(a), including a statement of when initial disclosures were made or will be made;

(B) the subjects on which discovery may be needed, when discovery should be completed, and whether discovery should be conducted in phases or be limited to or focused on particular issues;

(C) any issues about disclosure, discovery, or preservation of electronically stored information, including the form or forms in which it should be produced;

(D) any issues about claims of privilege or of protection as trial-preparation materials, including—if the parties agree on a procedure to assert these claims after production—whether to ask the court to include their agreement in an order under Federal Rule of Evidence 502;

(E) what changes should be made in the limitations on discovery imposed under these rules or by local rule, and what other limitations should be imposed; and

(F) any other orders that the court should issue under Rule 26(c) or under Rule 16(b) and (c).

(4) *Expedited Schedule.* If necessary to comply with its expedited schedule for Rule 16(b) conferences, a court may by local rule:

(A) require the parties' conference to occur less than 21 days before the scheduling conference is held or a scheduling order is due under Rule 16(b); and

(B) require the written report outlining the discovery plan to be filed less than 14 days after the parties' conference, or excuse the parties from submitting a written report and permit them to report orally on their discovery plan at the Rule 16(b) conference.

(g) Signing Disclosures and Discovery Requests, Responses, and Objections.

(1) *Signature Required; Effect of Signature.* Every disclosure under Rule 26(a)(1) or (a)(3) and every discovery request, response, or objection must be signed by at least one attorney of record in the attorney's own name—or by the party personally, if unrepresented—and must state the signer's address, e-mail address, and telephone number. By signing, an attorney or party certifies that to the best of the person's knowledge, information, and belief formed after a reasonable inquiry:

(A) with respect to a disclosure, it is complete and correct as of the time it is made; and

(B) with respect to a discovery request, response, or objection, it is:

(i) consistent with these rules and warranted by existing law or by a nonfrivolous argument for extending, modifying, or reversing existing law, or for establishing new law;

(ii) not interposed for any improper purpose, such as to harass, cause unnecessary delay, or needlessly increase the cost of litigation; and

(iii) neither unreasonable nor unduly burdensome or expensive, considering the needs of the case, prior discovery in the case, the amount in controversy, and the importance of the issues at stake in the action.

(2) *Failure to Sign.* Other parties have no duty to act on an unsigned disclosure, request, response, or objection until it is signed, and the court must strike it unless a signature is promptly supplied after the omission is called to the attorney's or party's attention.

(3) *Sanction for Improper Certification.* If a certification violates this rule without substantial justification, the court, on motion or on its own, must impose an appropriate sanction on the signer, the party on whose behalf the signer was acting, or both. The sanction may include an order to pay the reasonable expenses, including attorney's fees, caused by the violation.

[Amended December 27, 1946, effective March 19, 1948; January 21, 1963, effective July 1, 1963; February 28, 1966, effective July 1, 1966; March 30, 1970, effective July 1, 1970; April 29, 1980, effective August 1, 1980; April 28, 1983, effective August 1, 1983; March 2, 1987, effective August 1, 1987; April 22, 1993, effective December 1, 1993; April 17, 2000, effective December 1, 2000; April 12, 2006, effective December 1, 2006; April 30, 2007, effective December 1, 2007; April 28, 2010, effective December 1, 2010; April 29, 2015, effective December 1, 2015.]

UNDERSTANDING RULE 26

HOW RULE 26 FITS IN

Discovery is the term used for the process in litigation where the parties obtain information from each other. Although the most obvious goal in the discovery process is to gather the evidence relevant to the claims and defenses in the case held by the opposing parties, there are many other potential objectives as well. Discovery can yield admissions as to certain facts, obviating the need to prove those facts at trial. Discovery can also garner ammunition for impeachment—evidence that a party can use to cast doubt about the credibility of opposing witnesses. Likewise, discovery may reveal information about an opponent's positions, strategy, and version of the events so that the discovering party can plan its strategy accordingly.

Discovery is not always the most exciting phase of a lawsuit, but it is often the most important. In complex cases, discovery can account for a significant portion of the time and money incurred in the litigation process. The discovery of electronically stored information, or ESI, has become particularly pivotal in many actions. Young lawyers often perform the bulk of the discovery tasks in complex cases, and they can make themselves more valuable by embracing discovery and learning its intricacies.

Commensurate with its importance in the civil litigation process, discovery occupies its own section of the Rules, Section V titled Depositions and Discovery. Section V spans from Rule 26 through Rule 37 (and although Rule 45, pertaining to subpoenas, is located in the Trial section of the Rules, it actually has greater application in the discovery process than it does in the trial process). Section V is bookended by two of the broad general Rules that apply to all of the discovery activities authorized by the Rules. Rule 26 defines the scope of discovery and sets forth the general procedures and protections. At the back end, Rule 37 contains the procedures for enforcing the discovery rules and sanctioning parties who transgress those rules. In between are the individual Rules that govern interrogatories (Rule 33), production requests (Rule 34), requests for admission (Rule 36), depositions (Rules 27, 28, 30, 31, and 32), and medical or mental examinations (Rule 35).

Of all the discovery rules, Rule 26 is the most important—it is the omnibus rule that controls the parameters for all of the discovery devices set forth in the discovery section of the Rules. And maybe the most important provision in Rule 26 is Rule 26(b)(1), which defines the scope of discovery for all of the discovery procedures as "any nonprivileged matter that is relevant to any party's claim or defense and proportional to the needs of the case." That one clause clarifies that privileged matter like attorney-client communications are exempt from discovery, requires that matter be relevant to a claim or defense already in the case to be discoverable, and introduces the concept of proportionality—balancing the benefits and burdens of discovery.

In addition to this balancing, Rule 26 establishes a variety of limitations and protections for the participants in discovery. Rule 26 limits discovery that is unreasonably cumulative or duplicative, or that can be obtained from another source that is more convenient or less burdensome or expensive. If the matter sought is ESI, the responding party may object that accessing the information would be unduly burdensome or costly.

Rule 26 also houses a number of provisions relating to information shielded by privilege or related doctrine. Although a party need not provide privileged matter during discovery, the party asserting the privilege must advise the opposing party of the privilege assertion, and must describe the circumstances justifying the privilege assertion. This information is typically provided in a "privilege log" that describes details like the author of the privileged document, the recipients, the date of its creation, and the subject matter. These privileges typically come from the applicable body of law governing the claims in the action, but Rule 26 also creates a nationally-uniform protection for "trial preparation materials" that is derived from the common law "work product" doctrine and functions much like a privilege. The trial preparation materials protection shields from discovery documents that are prepared in anticipation of litigation, certain witness statements, and certain communications with experts. It applies to all cases proceeding in federal court, regardless of whether they are governed by federal or State substantive law.

The protections for privileged communications and trial preparation materials are automatic, but Rule 26 also contains provisions that authorize the court, in its discretion, to impose other limitations. These discretionary limitations are issued in "protective orders." On motion, and for "good cause," the court may issue a protective order forbidding or limiting the specified discovery, protecting the manner in which sensitive trade secret or confidential information is handled, or shielding a party from the burdens of discovery in a whole host of other manners.

In order to make the discovery process flow more smoothly, Rule 26 requires the parties to conduct a discovery conference before they commence discovery. At this conference, the parties discuss a list of topics related to the discovery process, such as the amount of time they will need for discovery, adjustments to the limits on the number of interrogatories and depositions, and potential issues that they anticipate in connection with the discovery of ESI. The parties then prepare a report of their conference and send it to the judge, who uses the report to frame the initial case management order setting the dates and parameters for discovery.

In general, the parties may not commence discovery until they have conducted their discovery conference. After the conference, though, they may conduct discovery in any sequence they choose, and one party is not constrained by the discovery conducted by the other party—meaning that, just because Party A chooses to conduct written discovery first before proceeding to depositions, Party B is not prohibited from starting with depositions right from the outset.

Most discovery occurs pursuant to affirmative request by one party to another. For example, a party wanting a category of documents sends a production request to another party requesting all documents within that category. Rule 26 contains three exceptions to this party-triggered process—stages at which parties must make disclosures automatically, without waiting for a request from another party. These categories of information are deemed so routine and necessary that it is more efficient to impose the obligation to disclose them as a matter of course, rather than burdening the parties with a request and response process.

The first automatic disclosure occurs at the beginning of a case, when each party must disclose the documents and witnesses the party intends to use to support its own claims or defenses. The second occurs in the middle of the case, when the parties must disclose expert reports describing the opinions their experts will offer. The final automatic disclosure occurs shortly before trial, when the parties disclose information related to the trial like the witnesses and exhibits they intend to offer.

In recognition that all of the information may not be immediately available at the outset of the lawsuit, Rule 26 imposes an ongoing obligation to supplement these disclosures and the other discovery responses. This duty to supplement applies to disclosures and responses that the party learns were incomplete or inaccurate when made and also extends to responses that were originally accurate but that have become inaccurate or incomplete over time.

Finally, Rule 26 contains a parallel provision to Rule 11 (which requires that each pleading, motion, brief, and other non-discovery document submitted to the court be signed, certifying that the document is supported by fact and law and is not being filed for an improper purpose). Rule 26 requires that each discovery document be signed. It provides that the signature constitutes a certification that: disclosures and discovery responses are complete and correct; that objections are based on existing law or a nonfrivolous argument for modifying the law; that the discovery or response is not intended to harass, delay, or drive up the cost of litigation; and that the discovery is not unreasonable or unduly burdensome or expensive.

THE ARCHITECTURE OF RULE 26

Rule 26 is one of the longest rules in the Federal Rules of Civil Procedure, and it has a multi-part structure to organize its various components. Rule 26(a) sets forth the provisions regarding the automatic disclosures. Rule 23(a)(1) addresses the initial disclosure, describing the contents and timing of the disclosure. It also lists some narrow categories of cases that are exempt from the requirement. Rule 23(a)(2) addresses the expert disclosure. It sets forth the requirements for disclosing a typical hired expert—an "expert report" that lists the expert's opinions and the bases for the opinions, as well as background information about the expert's qualifications and prior experience. For an unretained expert, such as a treating physician who will offer expert opinion testimony but who is not being paid as an expert, Rule 23(a)(2) imposes a lesser disclosure obligation—a summary of the expert's opinions and the bases for the opinions. Rule 23(a)(3) describes the final automatic disclosure, the pretrial disclosure, which requires disclosure of information related to the evidence to be presented at the trial.

Rule 26(b) sets the scope of discovery. Rule 26(b)(1) is the starting point, defining the scope. The balance of Rule 26(b) contains various limitations and protections. These provisions include protections for burdensome discovery of ESI, trial preparation materials, witness statements, and communications with expert witnesses. Rule 26(b) also contains the requirements for describing matter withheld on the basis of privilege—typically in a privilege log. Rule 26(c) authorizes the court to enter protective orders designed to protect responding parties from problematic discovery.

Rule 26(d) speaks to the timing and sequencing of discovery. It sets the starting point for discovery—the end point is typically set by the judge in the initial case management order. Once discovery commences, Rule 26(d) specifies that each party may conduct discovery in any sequence it chooses, without regard for the sequence chosen by other parties.

Rule 26(e) establishes the obligations to supplement discovery. It addresses supplementation of both the automatic disclosures and the affirmative discovery techniques.

Rule 26(f) obligates the parties to conduct a discovery conference where they discuss, and attempt to agree on, many of the parameters for discovery. They then jointly prepare a discovery plan for submission to the court. Rule 26(f)(3) contains a list of topics the plan must address. The judge then typically uses this discovery plan as the starting point for the initial case management order.

Finally, Rule 26(g) imposes the signature requirement on all discovery papers. It describes the certifications that an attorney makes by signing a discovery document, and establishes the sanctions for an improper certification.

HOW RULE 26 WORKS IN PRACTICE

RULE 26(a) — Required Disclosures

Rule 26(a) requires that parties disclose certain information automatically, without the need for discovery requests, at three points during the litigation. First, all parties must make broad initial disclosures at or shortly after they conduct the discovery meeting under Rule 26(f). Second, all parties must make disclosures about expert testimony 90 days before trial. Third, all parties must make the pretrial disclosures 30 days before trial. These disclosure deadlines are often modified by court order.

RULE 26(a)(1) — Initial Disclosure

At the commencement of discovery, each party must disclose: 1) the identity of individuals with discoverable information that the party may use *to support its own claims or defenses*; 2) a copy of the documents that the party may use *to support its own claims or defenses* or a description of those documents by category and location; 3) a computation of each category of damages and the documents upon which that computation is based; and 4) certain insurance information.

PRACTICING LAW UNDER THIS SUBPART

Time for Initial Disclosure

Parties must make their initial disclosures at or within 14 days after the discovery meeting required by Rule 26(f), unless a different time is set by court order or stipulation. Thus, Rule 26 establishes the following typical sequence for the early discovery events:

- First, the court may schedule an initial scheduling conference and must issue an initial scheduling order;
- Second, the parties conduct their Rule 26(f) discovery meeting at least 21 days before the court's initial scheduling conference or the due date for the scheduling order;
- Third, the parties make their voluntary disclosures by, at the latest, 14 days after their Rule 26(f) discovery meeting;
- Fourth, in cases where the court conducts an initial scheduling conference, the parties meet with the judge to set the timetable for the balance of the discovery events; and
- Finally, the court issues its initial scheduling order.

Content of Initial Disclosure

Rule 26(a)(1) requires automatic initial disclosure of four categories of information:

(i) *Potential Witnesses:* Parties must disclose the name, and if known the address and telephone number, of each individual likely to have discoverable information that the disclosing party may use to support its own claims or defenses. Parties must also identify the subjects of such information.

(ii) *Documents:* Parties must provide a copy of, or a description by category and location of, all documents, electronically stored information, and tangible things that the disclosing party may use to support its own claims or defenses. Except in cases with very few documents, parties will often disclose categories and locations rather than producing all the documents. Opposing parties who want copies of documents disclosed by description must request them in discovery. Parties must provide or describe all disclosable documents in their "possession, custody, or control." This is an important concept in discovery, and is explained in more detail in the discussion of Rule 34.

(iii) *Damages Computations:* Each party must provide a computation—not just the totals or an estimate—of any category of damages claimed by that party. This requirement typically applies to plaintiffs, but also applies to defendants seeking damages in a counterclaim or crossclaim. It only applies to damages that are capable of calculation, not to subjective damages like emotional distress or pain and suffering. Each party must also produce the non-privileged documents supporting the computation, including documents bearing on the nature and extent of injuries suffered.

(iv) *Insurance:* Each party must provide all insurance policies that may provide coverage for part or all of any judgment that might be entered in the action. You might wonder why insurance information is part of this initial disclosure—it is potentially important information in evaluating settlement prospects.

Only Information to Support the Disclosing Party's Claims or Defenses

Rule 26(a)(1) requires disclosure only of information and documents that the disclosing party may use to support its own claims or defenses. This provision dovetails with the exclusionary sanction of Rule 37(c)(1), so that a party may not use information or documents not disclosed initially or by supplement. That does not mean that information that undermines a party's claims or defenses is not discoverable, of course. Rather, to obtain information or documents that do not support a party's claims or defenses, opposing parties must serve affirmative discovery like interrogatories or document requests.

Impeachment

Information and documents that a party may use solely for impeachment need not be disclosed.

Excluded Proceedings

Rule 26(a)(1)(B) excludes 9 categories of proceedings from the initial disclosures: (1) appeals from administrative proceedings; (2) a forfeiture action *in rem* arising from a federal statute; (3) petitions for habeas corpus or like challenges to criminal convictions or sentences; (4) *pro se* prisoner actions; (5) actions to enforce or quash an administrative summons or subpoena; (6) actions by the United States to recover benefit payments; (7) actions by the United States to collect on student loans guaranteed by the United States; (8) proceedings ancillary to proceedings in other courts; and (9) actions to enforce arbitration awards.

Disclose Information "Reasonably Available"

The parties must make their initial disclosures based on the information then "reasonably available." A party may not avoid the initial disclosure requirements by claiming that its investigation is not yet complete; the Rules envision that the initial disclosure will often be incomplete, and account for this through the duty to supplement as additional information is encountered.

Failure to Disclose

Failure to make the initial disclosures required by Rule 26(a)(1) may preclude the party from using the undisclosed witness or information as evidence on a motion, at a hearing, or at trial, unless the party failing to make the disclosure can demonstrate that the failure was harmless or there was substantial justification. Generally, providing the identity of a witness or producing the documents in discovery will not excuse failure to disclose under Rule 26(a)(1), because that does not put the other party on notice that the producing party may use that witness or those documents to support its claims or defenses. For example, a party may produce a great volume documents in discovery that it does not intend to offer affirmatively to support its positions, so merely producing a document is not the equivalent of identifying it as a document the party intends to offer. However, if the full substance of the required disclosure is conveyed in discovery, the matter will not be excluded.

Disclosures Automatic

The initial disclosures are automatically required, without any need for a request or demand.

Stipulations Not to Disclose

The parties may stipulate to the elimination or modification of the initial disclosures unless precluded from doing so by local rule or court order.

RULE 26(a)(2) Disclosure of Expert Testimony

Each party must disclose the identity of its testifying expert witnesses and some information about their testimony. For typical retained experts, parties must disclose a detailed expert report. For non-retained experts such as treating physicians, parties must disclose a summary of the opinions to be offered by the experts.

PRACTICING LAW UNDER THIS SUBPART

Which Experts

Rule 26(b)(2) divides experts into three categories. The first category includes the typical expert witness who is engaged to provide expert testimony for purposes of the litigation. It also includes employees of the party who are "specially employed to provide expert testimony in the case" or "whose duties as the party's employee regularly involve giving expert testimony." The second category includes experts who will testify but have not been engaged (and are not being paid). Treating physicians frequently fall into this category. It also includes other employees of the party who will offer expert testimony, but do not qualify under the first category. The final category includes experts who will not testify, such as consulting experts. Parties are generally not required to make disclosures for these non-testifying experts. For the other two categories, the nature of the disclosure varies, as described below.

Content of Disclosure

The disclosure must contain the identity of any witness who may provide expert testimony under the Federal Rules of Evidence governing expert testimony (primarily rules 701–705). For the typical expert witnesses who was retained or specially employed to provide expert testimony in the lawsuit, the disclosure must include an expert report as described below. For experts who were not retained, such as a treating physician who will offer expert opinions, the disclosure must contain the subject matter on which the expert is expected to present evidence and a summary of the facts and opinions to which the witness is expected to testify.

Expert Report

Each expert report must be in writing and signed by the expert (but the lawyers sometimes play a heavy role in the drafting process). The report must contain: a complete statement of all the expert's opinions and the basis and reasons for each opinion; the facts or data considered by the expert, including documents provided by counsel; any exhibits to be used as support for or as a summary of the opinions; the qualifications of the expert and all publications authored by the expert in the past 10 years; the expert's compensation for the review and testimony; and a list of all other cases in which the expert has testified at trial or at deposition in the past four years.

Failure to Disclose Report

The failure to disclose a timely report meeting the requirements of Rule 26(a)(2)(B) may preclude the party from introducing the testimony as evidence on a motion, at a hearing, or at trial, either altogether or as to specific opinions not disclosed in the report. Such sanctions are "automatic and mandatory" unless the party failing to disclose can show the failure was justified or harmless. At the same time, a party who believes that an opposing party has disclosed an inadequate expert report should file a motion to compel a more complete report or a motion to exclude the expert promptly, because waiting until trial to raise the issue may result in waiver.

Treating Physicians

An expert report is generally not required for a treating physician to testify regarding the treatment if the party has not retained the physician as an expert, although a number of courts require an expert report when the treating physician will offer testimony beyond the scope of the treatment rendered. However, parties must disclose the subject matter and a summary of the facts and opinions as to which a treating physician is expected to testify under F.R.E. 702 (pertaining to expert testimony). It is unsettled whether a treating physician's testimony about the treatment constitutes F.R.E. 702 expert testimony or percipient fact testimony.

Disclosures Automatic

The expert disclosures are automatically required, without any need for a request or demand.

Time for Expert Disclosure

In the absence of a court order or stipulation, the expert disclosures must be made 90 days before the trial date.

Rebuttal Testimony

Parties must disclose rebuttal expert testimony. The court usually sets the time for disclosure of rebuttal testimony, which is often 30 days after disclosure of the testimony it is rebutting. Rebuttal testimony must explain, repel, counteract, or disprove evidence of the adverse party; courts will not allow parties to use rebuttal expert testimony to advance new arguments or new evidence.

RULE 26(a)(3) Pretrial Disclosures

Prior to trial, the parties must disclose the witnesses that they may call at trial, the deposition testimony that they may offer at trial, and the exhibits that they may offer at trial.

PRACTICING LAW UNDER THIS SUBPART

Time for Pretrial Disclosure

The time for pretrial disclosures is often set by the court. In the absence of a court deadline, the expert disclosures must be made 30 days before the trial date.

Content of Pretrial Disclosure

Rule 26(a)(3) requires a pretrial disclosure of the following information:

(i) *Witnesses:* The parties must disclose the name and, unless already disclosed, the address and phone number of each witness that they may call at trial. The disclosure should separately indicate those witnesses the parties expect to testify and those the parties may call if needed (the purpose of this distinction is to give the court and the parties a realistic list of the likely witnesses while also allowing parties to protect their right to call other less likely witnesses (by listing them as "may call if needed" witnesses, avoiding the sanction of exclusion of undisclosed witnesses));

(ii) *Depositions:* The parties must designate the deposition testimony that they intend to introduce. If the deposition was recorded other than stenographically, then the parties must provide a transcript of the parts of the testimony they intend to introduce; and

(iii) *Exhibits:* The parties must identify all exhibits, including demonstrative or summary exhibits, that they may use at trial. The disclosure should separately indicate those exhibits that the parties expect to introduce and those that they may introduce if needed.

Impeachment

The pretrial disclosure is not required to include documents or testimony to be introduced solely for impeachment.

Failure to Disclose

Any witnesses, deposition testimony, or exhibits not properly disclosed under Rule 26(a)(3) will be excluded from use at trial unless the failure was substantially justified or harmless.

Discovery Seeking Rule 26(a)(3) Information

Parties will not be required to respond to discovery requests seeking the information covered by Rule 26(a)(3) at an earlier stage in the litigation. Thus, a party does not need to respond substantively to an interrogatory seeking witness names or a document request seeking trial exhibits and can instead respond that the information will be provided by Rule 26(a)(3) disclosure.

Objections to Deposition Testimony or Exhibits

As explained in the discussion of Rule 30, many objections to deposition testimony are preserved until a party seeks to offer the testimony into the record. The pretrial disclosure triggers this process. A party who objects to the use of any portion of a deposition or to a deposition exhibit must serve and file a written objection within 14 days of the disclosure of the intent to use the deposition or exhibit. The statement of the objection should specify the grounds for the objection. Failure to state an objection is a waiver of the objection, except for objections to relevancy under Rules 402 and 403 of the Federal Rules of Evidence (because relevance objections depend on the context in which the testimony is offered).

Disclosures Automatic

The pretrial disclosures are automatically required, without any need for a request or demand.

RULE 26(a)(4) — Form of Disclosure

The automatic disclosures under Rule 26(a) should be in writing, signed, and served on other parties, unless otherwise directed by local rule or court order. Only the pretrial disclosure under Rule 26(a)(3) must be filed with the court; the other disclosures are not filed unless they are used in a motion or the court orders filing. The signature constitutes a certification that the disclosure is complete and accurate under Rule 26(g)(1).

RULE 26(b)(1) — Discovery Scope and Limits—Scope in General

In general, any matter that is relevant to the claim or defense of any party in the pending action and is proportional to the needs of the case is discoverable unless it is privileged.

PRACTICING LAW UNDER THIS SUBPART

Covered Actions

The discovery rules apply to all civil actions in federal court, except for the narrow exceptions listed in Rule 81 (such as certain admiralty matters and matters in arbitration pursuant to federal statute).

"Relevant" Defined

The term "relevant" is not defined by the Rules, but is extremely broad. Courts have defined "relevant" to encompass "any matter that bears on, or that reasonably could lead to other matters that could bear on, any issue that is or may be in the case." Courts also have defined "relevant" as "germane." *See Oppenheimer Fund, Inc. v. Sanders,* 437 U.S. 340, 351 (1978).

Relevant to "Any Party's Claim or Defense"

A party may discover any matter that is relevant to any claim or defense that is pleaded in the case, regardless of which party raises the claim or defense. Conversely, discovery is not permitted to develop potential additional claims or defenses, to identify additional parties, or to gather information for use in another proceeding. If a claim has been dismissed, further discovery that is relevant only to that claim will not be allowed. *See Oppenheimer Fund, Inc. v. Sanders,* 437 U.S. 340, 351 (1978).

Relevant vs. Admissible

Evidence need not be admissible to be relevant, and thus discoverable. For example, a settlement agreement between the plaintiff and one defendant might not be admissible at trial but might be relevant to determining another defendant's right to a set-off, and would therefore be discoverable. Conversely, admissible evidence is almost always discoverable. *See Seattle Times Co. v. Rhinehart,* 467 U.S. 20, 29–30 (1984).

Proportionality

Discovery must be "proportional to the needs of the case"—essentially the expected benefits of the discovery must be in line with the cost and burden of the discovery and the value of the case. Rule 26(b)(1) contains a list of factors for evaluating proportionality: the importance of the issues at stake in the action, the amount in controversy, the parties' relative access to relevant information, the parties' resources, the importance of the discovery in resolving the issues, and whether the burden or expense of the proposed discovery outweighs its likely benefit. Under Rule 26(b)(2), the court must limit discovery that it determines is not proportional to the needs of the case, but has broad discretion in considering and weighing the factors. Some courts hold that they have an affirmative duty to assess proportionality, even if the parties do not raise it. The ultimate burden is on the party seeking to resist the discovery to demonstrate that the discovery is not proportional to the needs of the case—typically using evidence—but the practical effect of the rule is that both parties often must submit evidence supporting their positions on proportionality. Parties may, and in some situations must, submit affidavits or other evidence regarding the proportionality factors.

Limitations on Discovery

The broad scope of discovery authorized by Rule 26(b)(1) is curtailed by the limitations in the balance of Rule 26(b) relating to discovery that is cumulative or unduly burdensome and to trial preparation materials.

Jurisdictional Issues

Discovery is allowed with respect to jurisdictional issues. *See Oppenheimer Fund, Inc. v. Sanders,* 437 U.S. 340, 351 (1978). Thus, parties may conduct discovery pertaining to other parties' citizenship, the amount in controversy, or a party's contacts with the forum State.

Location of Evidence

Parties may take discovery about the location and existence of documents and other evidence and about the identity and location of persons having knowledge of discoverable matters.

Impeachment

Discovery is generally allowed of matters that would be used to impeach other parties' witnesses. Thus, one normally may ask whether the responding party has any criminal convictions and may inquire as to prior statements.

Privileges

Privileged matters are protected from discovery. Privileges in federal court depend upon whether the action involves a State law issue or a federal cause of action. If a State's substantive laws are being applied, that State's laws of privilege also apply, except as to the trial preparation materials (work product) protection, which is governed by Rule 26(b)(3) and federal common law. If the action is governed by federal law, then Rule 501 of the Federal Rules of Evidence applies. Essentially, Rule 501 instructs the federal courts to develop a body of federal common law privileges.

Raising Claim of Privilege

The normal manner for raising a privilege is by objecting to a particular request or inquiry. For example, at a deposition, a party may orally raise an objection to an individual question, then refuse to provide the privileged information (by counsel instructing the witness not to answer). In response to interrogatories, document requests, or requests for admission, a party may make a written objection to individual questions or requests and withhold the privileged information. The objection must include sufficient information so that the court and opposing counsel can assess the applicability of the privilege.

Waiver of Privilege

Privileges generally are waived by voluntary disclosure, including disclosure during discovery. Thus, caution should be exercised in discussing or responding to discovery requests pertaining to privileged matters.

Documents Containing Privileged and Non-Privileged Matters

If part of a document contains privileged matters and part does not, a party must provide the non-privileged matter, but may redact the privileged matter.

Particular Privileges

A detailed analysis of every potential privilege is beyond the scope of this book. The following is an overview of the most commonly asserted privileges:

- *Attorney-Client:* The attorney-client privilege applies to all confidential communications between a client and the client's attorney that occur in connection with legal representation or in the process of obtaining legal representation. It applies to communications to an in-house attorney if the attorney is providing legal services. It does not protect documents or other physical evidence provided to the attorney (other than written communications to the attorney), the underlying facts, or information or evidence gathered by the attorney from other sources.
- *Self-Incrimination:* The Fifth Amendment to the United States Constitution provides all persons (whether or not parties to a litigation) with a privilege against testifying in a manner that would tend to incriminate them. The privilege applies at depositions, interrogatories, requests for admission, and production of documents, as well as at trial. Corporations may not assert the privilege, but corporate representatives may assert it if their testimony would incriminate them personally, regardless of whether they are testifying in their individual or representative capacities. *See United States v. Kordel,* 397 U.S. 1, 8 (1970).
- *Governmental Privileges:* The United States has some extra privileges:
    - *Governmental Informer Privilege:* The United States has a qualified privilege to refuse to reveal the identity of an informer. *See Roviaro v. United States,* 353 U.S. 53, 59 (1957).
    - *Government's Privilege for Military or State Secrets:* The United States has a qualified privilege for matters that involve military or State secrets. *See General Dynamics Corp. v. United States,* 563 U.S. 478, 484 (2011).

- o *Government's Statutory Privilege:* Some statutes require governmental agencies and other entities to file certain documents or reports, and designate the submissions as confidential. A common example is income tax returns, which the United States receives and keeps, but is not required to produce to private litigants.
- o *Executive Privilege:* The Executive branch of the United States government has a general qualified privilege, grounded in the need for the executive branch to gather information. *See United States v. Nixon,* 418 U.S. 683, 707–08 (1974).

- *Other Privileges:* In some States, communications with spouses, physicians, clergy, journalists, accountants, and social workers are privileged.

RULE 26(b)(2) Limitations on Frequency and Extent

Rule 26(b)(2) requires the court, "on motion or on its own," to limit the frequency or extent of discovery if: the discovery is unreasonably cumulative or duplicative; the discovery is obtainable from another source more convenient, less burdensome, or less expensive; or the discovery is outside the scope of discovery as set forth in Rule 26(b)(1) (*i.e.*, not nonprivileged, relevant to a claim or defense, and proportional to the needs of the case). The court must also limit discovery if the party seeking the discovery has had "ample opportunity" to obtain the information during prior discovery. Rule 26(b)(2)(B) also establishes a procedure for limiting the need to search for and produce electronically stored information if it would be unreasonably burdensome or costly to do so.

PRACTICING LAW UNDER THIS SUBPART

Objections to Specific Requests

One method of asserting the limitations in Rule 26(b)(2) is by making an objection to a discovery request, such as objecting to an interrogatory or request for production as cumulative or overly burdensome.

Required Limitations

The court must limit discovery in 3 circumstances:

(i) if the discovery is unreasonably cumulative or duplicative, or can be obtained from another source that is more convenient, less burdensome, or less expensive;

(ii) if the party seeking the discovery has already had ample opportunity to obtain the information in discovery; or

(iii) if the discovery is outside the scope permitted by Rule 26(b)(1), *i.e.*, is not relevant to a party's claim or defense and is not proportional.

Alteration of Limits Established by Other Rules

Other rules place limits on discovery, such as the duration of depositions and the number of interrogatories and depositions, which may be altered by court order. These limits may also be altered by stipulation under Rule 29.

Electronically Stored Information

Rule 26(b)(2)(B) limits discovery of electronically stored information from sources that are not "reasonably accessible" because of undue burden or cost, and establishes a procedure for invoking the limitation. The party invoking the protection must identify the sources of information that it is neither searching nor producing with sufficient particularity that the requesting party can evaluate the burden and cost of producing the information. If the requesting party still believes that the information should be produced, the parties must confer to see if they can resolve the issue without court intervention. If the informal conference does not resolve the issue, the requesting party may file a motion to compel or the responding party may file a motion for a protective order. In either type of motion, the responding party bears the burden of showing that the information is not reasonably accessible, in terms of undue burden or cost. Even following such a showing, the court may require production of the information upon good cause shown.

RULE 26(b)(3) Trial Preparation: Materials

Rule 26(b)(3) provides limited protection to otherwise discoverable documents and tangible things that a party or its representative prepared in anticipation of litigation. Such materials must be produced in discovery *only* when the information contained there is not reasonably available from any other source. The protection for "trial preparation materials" in Rule 26(b)(3) is essentially the codification of the "work product" doctrine first announced by the Supreme Court in *Hickman v. Taylor*, 329 U.S. 495 (1947), and both the courts and this section will use both terms.

PRACTICING LAW UNDER THIS SUBPART

Documents and Tangible Things Only (and Intangible Mental Impressions)

The trial preparation materials protection applies only to documents and tangible things. Some courts also allow a party to assert the work product protection—the common law doctrine established in *Hickman v. Taylor*—in response to discovery inquires that seek the party's trial strategy, counsel's mental impressions, or "intangible work product." It does not apply to facts known or gathered relating to the litigation, which generally are discoverable, although it may apply to documents that describe the facts.

Prepared in Anticipation of Litigation

The trial preparation materials protection applies only to documents prepared in anticipation of litigation. The focus of the analysis is whether the *purpose* for the creation of the document was the anticipation of litigation. Most courts apply the protection to documents prepared when litigation is expected but has not yet been commenced; the timing of the preparation of the documents is not critical, as long as they were primarily concerned with the litigation. Conversely, the protection does not apply to documents prepared in the regular course of business while litigation is pending. The trend seems to be to apply the protection to documents prepared in anticipation of any litigation, not just the pending action. *See F.T.C. v. Grolier, Inc.,* 462 U.S. 19, 26 (1983).

Prepared by Parties and Their Agents

The trial preparation materials protection applies to documents prepared by parties and their agents. Thus, the trial preparation materials protection applies to reports prepared by investigators on behalf of a party. Unlike the attorney-client privilege, the trial preparation materials protection does not require any involvement by an attorney, so long as the document is prepared by a party or a party's agent in anticipation of litigation.

Obtaining Trial Preparation Materials

Trial preparation materials are discoverable if the requesting party makes a sufficient showing of two requirements:

1) that the attorney has a *substantial* need for the information; and

2) that the party cannot, without undue hardship, obtain the same or substantially equivalent information.

For example, a party may obtain a written witness statement in opposing counsel's files if the witness is no longer available. Similarly, there may be no substitute for photographs taken or records created shortly after an incident. As discussed immediately below, however, opinion work product is shielded from discovery even if the opposing party makes the two showings required to obtain fact work product.

Mental and Legal Impressions

The mental impressions and legal evaluations of an attorney, investigator, or claims agent (sometimes referred to as "core" or "opinion" work product) enjoy an almost absolute privilege from disclosure. Thus, an attorney may redact statements reflecting mental and legal impressions from trial preparation materials that must be disclosed under Rule 26(b)(3).

Statements

A party may always obtain a copy of the party's own statement or a statement by the party's agent or representative—an opposing party may not contend that the statement is work product. To obtain a copy of a party's statement, the party does not need to use the document request procedures in Rule 34, but instead may simply make a request under Rule 26(b)(3). A statement can either be a written statement that the party has signed or otherwise adopted or approved, or a contemporaneous verbatim recording of the party's oral statement. A nonparty witness has a right to a copy of the witness's own statement. Parties, in contrast, do not have an absolute right to a copy of a nonparty witness's statement.

Burden of Proof

The party asserting the trial preparation materials doctrine has the burden of demonstrating that the subject documents are trial preparation materials. The party seeking an opponent's trial preparation materials then has the burden of showing the necessity of obtaining the trial preparation materials and the lack of substantially equivalent evidence elsewhere or that the protection has been waived.

Waiver

Evaluating waiver of the trial preparation materials doctrine entails an evaluation of F.R.E. 502 as well as Rule 26(b)(3). Generally, disclosure of documents to an adverse party, or in a manner such that an adverse party may see the documents, constitutes a waiver of the trial preparation materials protection with respect to those documents. Disclosure of documents to someone not adverse, such as a co-defendant or a consultant, may not constitute a waiver of the trial preparation materials protection. This differs from most privileges, which are waived by disclosure to anyone, not just parties. Some courts hold that, in contrast to the attorney-client privilege, waiver of the trial preparation materials protection applies only to the documents disclosed, not to the entire subject matter.

Discovery Stage Only

Trial preparation materials may be withheld as privileged during discovery, then used at trial. Note the contrast with most other privileges, which cannot be asserted during discovery then waived at trial.

RULE 26(b)(4) Trial Preparation: Experts

Discovery of the typical engaged expert who will testify at trial normally consists of the expert disclosure under Rule 26(a)(2) and a deposition of the expert, and may also include interrogatories or production requests for documents outside the protections in Rule 26(b)(4), which shield draft expert reports and most communications with testifying experts. Only very limited discovery is permitted with respect to non-testifying experts.

PRACTICING LAW UNDER THIS SUBPART

Depositions of Testifying Experts

Parties may take the deposition of any expert witness who may testify at trial. Expert depositions occur after the expert disclosures under Rule 26(a)(2).

Experts Specially Retained but Not Expected to Testify

A party may not, by interrogatory or deposition, discover facts known by, or opinions held by, experts who are not expected to testify, including their identity, unless the party makes a showing of exceptional circumstances rendering it impracticable to obtain facts or opinions on the same subject by other means. Such further discovery might be allowed when the particular consulting expert was the only expert to examine evidence that is no longer available (such as a blood sample or accident scene).

Discovery of Treating Physician

There is a split of authority as to whether a treating physician is a fact witness or an expert witness for purposes of the provisions of Rule 26(b)(4).

Experts Informally Consulted

No discovery is permitted of experts informally consulted but not retained.

Experts Employed or Generally Retained by a Party

Full discovery is permitted regarding an expert who is a full-time employee of a party or who was retained generally, rather than in connection with pending or anticipated litigation. No expert fees are awarded in connection with such discovery.

Experts Who Witnessed or Participated in Events

Discovery pertaining to an expert who acquired her knowledge through witnessing or participating in the events that form the basis for the complaint is not covered by Rule 26(b)(4), which is limited to information acquired or developed in anticipation of litigation. Thus, full fact discovery is allowed regarding such experts, and no expert fees are awarded.

Party Who Is an Expert

A party cannot avoid discovery or obtain expert fees by claiming to be an expert witness.

Drafts of Expert Reports

Drafts of expert reports or expert disclosures for testifying experts are not discoverable. In contrast, draft reports prepared by non-retained experts are not shielded from discovery.

Communications with Experts

Communications between counsel and experts who are required to provide an expert report (*i.e.,* those retained or specially employed to testify) are protected as trial preparation materials unless they pertain to: (i) compensation for the expert; (ii) the facts or data that counsel provided and the expert considered in forming the opinions to be expressed; or (iii) the assumptions that counsel provided and the expert relied on in forming the opinions to be expressed. Communications with experts who are not required to provide expert reports (*i.e.*, treating physicians and other experts not retained or specially employed) are not protected under Rule 26(b)(4)—but they may be protected under other doctrines or privileges.

Ex Parte Communications with Experts for Another Party

A party should not have *ex parte* communications with an expert for another party.

Testifying Expert Discovery Fees

The court must impose the reasonable expert fees incurred in responding to discovery on the party taking discovery of an expert who may testify at trial unless manifest injustice would result. For a deposition, the fee normally includes compensation for time testifying and may or may not include preparation time.

RULE 26(b)(5) Claiming Privilige or Protecting Trial-Preparation Materials

A party who withholds information based on a claim of privilege or work product/trial preparation materials protection must state the claim expressly and describe the nature of the documents or information so withheld in a manner that will enable other parties to assess the claim of privilege or protection. If privileged information is inadvertently produced in discovery, the producing party may so notify the parties that received the information. The receiving parties must then either return, sequester, or destroy the information, but may present the issue to the court for a ruling on the validity of the privilege assertion.

PRACTICING LAW UNDER THIS SUBPART

Manner of Asserting Privilege

Many courts require a party asserting a privilege as to documents to produce a privilege log describing the documents withheld. The Rules do not specify the time for production of a privilege log, and the case law varies. Some courts hold that the log must be produced at the same time the response to the document request is due—within 30 days of the request—and some allow a "reasonable" time. Privileges may be waived broadly for failure to produce a privilege log or to produce a sufficiently detailed log, or specifically for any documents omitted from the privilege log. At a deposition, a party may orally raise an objection to an individual question, then refuse to provide the privileged information (by counsel instructing the witness not to answer). In response to interrogatories or requests for admission, a party may make a written objection to individual questions or requests and withhold the privileged information.

Failure to State Claim of Privilege with Sufficient Specificity

If a party withholds information without properly disclosing the basis, the party may have waived the privilege, and may be subject to sanctions under Rule 37(b)(2).

Challenging Privilege Assertions

A party may challenge the privilege assertion for documents listed on a privilege log by filing a motion to compel, which places the burden on the party asserting the privilege to establish an evidentiary basis, by affidavit, deposition transcript, or other evidence, for each element of the privilege. The court may also review the challenged documents *in camera* and make its own determinations.

Recalling Privileged Information

A party believing that it has produced privileged information may provide a notification to the parties who have received the information. The notification should be in writing (unless circumstances do not allow, such as in a deposition) and should be sufficiently detailed to allow the receiving parties to evaluate the claim of privilege. After receiving such a notification, the receiving party must return, sequester, or destroy the specified information and all copies (including taking reasonable steps to retrieve any information that the receiving party had already disclosed to other persons). If it does not agree with the privilege assertion, it can present the information to the court under seal for a determination of the privilege claim. During the court's review of the privilege claim, the receiving party is prohibited from using the information and the producing party must preserve it. Alternatively, the parties can propose their own procedures for privileged information that has inadvertently been produced or disclosed.

Waiver of the Privilege for Recalled Information

Rule 26(b)(5)(B) does not address whether the privilege or protection is preserved or waived for information that was disclosed and then recalled. In other words, the accidental production might or might not have resulted in waiver of the privilege, and the Rule 26(b)(5)(B) recall procedure does not affect that analysis, which instead is controlled by the applicable law on privilege waiver.

RULE 26(c) — Protective Orders

The court may enter orders designed to protect the parties and witnesses during the discovery process.

PRACTICING LAW UNDER THIS SUBPART

Which Court

Protective orders are obtained by motion filed in the district where the action is pending. In the case of a deposition that is to occur in a different district, a motion may also be filed where the deposition is to occur.

Certificate of Conference

A motion for protective order must include a certification that the movant has in good faith conferred or attempted to confer with the other party in an effort to resolve the dispute without court action. Courts will frequently deny motions for protective orders that do not include the meet and confer certificate.

Timing

There is no set period for filing a motion for a protective order. Normally, the motion must be filed before the discovery is to occur, unless there is no opportunity to do so.

Who May File

A motion may be brought by the person whose interests are affected by the subject discovery, which may be a party or a nonparty from whom discovery is sought (typically by subpoena). A party may not move for a protective order to protect the interests of a nonparty, but may move to protect the party's own interests when discovery is sought from the nonparty.

Purpose of Protective Order

Rule 26(c) specifically instructs the court to limit the frequency or extent of discovery if justice so requires to protect someone from annoyance, embarrassment, oppression, or undue burden or expense. *See Seattle Times Co. v. Rhinehart,* 467 U.S. 20, 35 n.21 (1984). Protective orders are also frequently used to limit the frequency or extent of discovery if: (i) the discovery sought is unreasonably cumulative or is obtainable from a more convenient or less burdensome or expensive source; (ii) the party seeking the discovery has had ample opportunity to obtain the information; or (iii) the discovery is outside the scope of discovery set forth in Rule 26(b)(1). Protective orders generally apply to formal discovery, and it is not settled whether courts may limit informal investigations.

Good Cause

Protective orders are entered for "good cause." The court has almost complete discretion in determining what constitutes good cause. *See Seattle Times Co. v. Rhinehart,* 467 U.S. 20, 36 (1984). The proportionality principles from Rule 26(b)(1) will govern the good cause analysis; the court will balance the need of the party seeking the discovery against the burden on the party responding. The party seeking the protective order has the burden of showing that good cause exists by stating particular and specific facts. *See Gulf Oil Co. v. Bernard,* 452 U.S. 89, 102 (1981).

Depositions vs. Written Discovery

Motions for protective orders are most common in connection with depositions because such motions are the only mechanism for asserting a concern about a deposition issue in advance of the deposition. With written discovery, a party can make objections to individual requests without providing a substantive response (and without the expense and burden of filing a motion). The onus then shifts to the party seeking the discovery to move to compel an answer under Rule 37(a).

Types of Protective Order

Rule 26(c)(1) authorizes the court to protect a person from "annoyance, embarrassment, oppression, or undue burden or expense." The Rule then lists eight kinds of protective orders, which are discussed immediately below. The list is not exclusive, however, and the court has broad discretion to make any type of protective order required by justice. The specifically enumerated categories are below.

(1) *Order That Disclosure or Discovery Not Be Had:* The court may order that the automatic disclosure or requested discovery not occur.

(2) *Specified Terms and Conditions:* The court can impose terms and conditions on the automatic disclosure or the taking of discovery. The court may designate the time, location, or conditions of a deposition, or the time to respond to discovery requests. The court may order the party seeking discovery to pay the responding party's resulting expenses or may allocate the costs of responding among the parties. The court may set deadlines for the completion of various phases of discovery or order that discovery be conducted in a particular sequence. The court may delay or stay of discovery—for example, while a dispositive motion is pending.

(3) *Method of Discovery:* The court may direct that discovery, either generally or as to an individual witness or topic, be taken by a particular method (such as by written discovery only, not by oral deposition). The general principle is that the parties may select their own discovery methods without unnecessary interference from the court. Thus, most motions to restrict the discovery methods are denied unless the moving party shows special circumstances.

(4) *Limit of Scope or Time:* The court may limit the scope of the automatic disclosures or discovery to specific areas of inquiry or to a specific time period. The court may also limit discovery to a critical or threshold issue. If a jurisdictional dispute exists, the court may restrict discovery to the jurisdictional issues, then permit broad discovery if jurisdiction is found to exist. Similarly, if liability and damages are to be tried separately, the court may restrict discovery to liability issues until the first phase of the case is complete.

(5) *Persons Present:* The court may exclude (or "sequester") the public, the press, other witnesses, or other nonparties from a deposition or access to documents produced in discovery. The court generally will not exclude the parties or their attorneys.

(6) *Sealed Transcript:* In general, discovery produced by private litigants is private until it is filed, at which point it becomes public. A party wanting to avoid disclosure of the information it provides may move for an order that documents, discovery responses, or deposition transcripts be sealed, and thus not part of the public record. Once a sealing order has been entered, parties are prohibited from disclosing to third persons information obtained pursuant to the court order. Courts are generally reluctant to seal discovery materials.

(7) *Confidential Information:* The court may enter an order restricting disclosure of private personal information, trade secrets, and confidential research, development, or commercial information obtained during discovery. *See Seattle Times Co. v. Rhinehart,* 467 U.S. 20, 24–29 (1984). There is no absolute privilege or protection with respect to such matters. *See Federal Open Market Committee of Federal Reserve System v. Merrill,* 443 U.S. 340, 362 (1979). The normal procedure is for the parties to negotiate an agreement as to the handling of confidential information, which is often memorialized in a stipulated confidentiality order signed by the court—this procedure gives the court the ability to enforce the parties' agreement. If the parties cannot agree to a confidentiality stipulation, the responding party can move for a protective order or the party seeking the discovery can move to compel under Rule 37(a).

(8) *Simultaneous Exchange:* The court may order the parties to simultaneously file designated documents or information in sealed envelopes, to be opened as directed by the court. This procedure is most common in patent cases, where it can be an advantage to know an opponent's contentions.

Order Compelling Discovery

If the court denies a motion for a protective order, it may at the same time issue an order compelling the discovery. Such an order can facilitate obtaining sanctions under Rule 37.

Expenses and Attorney's Fees

The court must require the party losing a motion for protective order to pay the expenses the opposing party incurred in connection with the motion, including reasonable attorney's fees, unless the losing party's position was "substantially justified," or other circumstances make such an award unjust.

RULE 26(d) Timing and Sequence of Discovery

With one exception, parties may not conduct discovery prior to their discovery conference under Rule 26(f). The exception is that parties may serve Rule 34 document requests prior to the Rule 26(f) conference to facilitate discussion of document production issues, but for purposes of calculating the response date, they are deemed served as of the time of the Rule 26(f) conference. After the Rule 26(f) conference, each party may conduct whatever discovery that party chooses, in any sequence, regardless of the discovery undertaken by other parties. The various discovery devices may be used in any order or simultaneously.

PRACTICING LAW UNDER THIS SUBPART

Commencement of Discovery

Normally, parties may not conduct discovery, other than document requests as discussed immediately below, prior to their discovery conference under Rule 26(f). Expedited discovery may be conducted by court order for good cause shown or by stipulation.

Early Service of Document Requests

A party may serve or be served with document requests 21 days after the party has been served with the summons and complaint (except that a defendant cannot serve document requests on a codefendant who has not yet been served with the summons and complaint). The purpose is not to accelerate the response time, but rather to allow the parties to discuss document production issues at their Rule 26(f) conference and to raise them with the court at an early stage of the proceedings. Accordingly, the requests will be deemed served as of the time of the Rule 26(f) conference and the response will not be due until 30 days later.

No Set Discovery Sequence

Although interrogatories and document production typically precede depositions, each party may conduct discovery in any sequence it chooses. Likewise, the parties may conduct discovery simultaneously; there is no obligation for any party to wait until others have completed their discovery. A party believing a particular sequence or schedule is important may move for a protective order under Rule 26(c). Additionally, the parties can stipulate to a particular discovery sequence.

Failure to Respond by Another Party Not an Excuse

A party is not excused from responding to discovery because another party has failed to respond to discovery. The proper remedy if another party fails to answer discovery is a motion to compel under Rule 37(a), not a refusal to comply with valid discovery requests.

RULE 26(e) Supplementing Disclosures and Responses

Parties have a duty to supplement automatic disclosures and discovery responses if they were incomplete or incorrect at the time they were made or have become so with the passage of time. This duty is automatic, and does not require a request.

PRACTICING LAW UNDER THIS SUBPART

Conditions Requiring Supplemental Responses

The following three conditions require supplemental disclosures or responses:

(1) *Automatic Disclosures:* A party must at reasonable intervals supplement its initial, expert, and pretrial disclosures if the party or its attorney learns that the information disclosed was incomplete or incorrect and the information has not otherwise been made known to the other parties;

(2) *Incorrect Response:* A party must supplement a response to an interrogatory, request for inspection, or request for admission that the party or its attorney learns was incorrect or incomplete if the information has not otherwise been made known to the other parties; and

(3) *Court Order:* The duty to supplement may also arise by court order.

After-Acquired Information

The duty to supplement is triggered by information or documents acquired after serving the original disclosure or response—it is not an excuse that the disclosure or response was accurate when made.

Timing of Supplemental Responses

No specific time period is established for the duty to supplement. Instead, supplements are to be made "in a timely manner." The duty to supplement is ongoing and does not end when discovery ends. Supplements made after the close of discovery, however, may not satisfy the Rules, particularly when the party had the documents or information in its possession, custody, or control prior to the close of discovery.

No Request to Supplement Needed

The obligations to supplement are self-effectuating; there is no need to serve a request to supplement or motion to compel. Nonetheless, a party will sometimes serve a request to supplement or a motion to compel if it is concerned that another party has new information that it has not yet disclosed or produced.

Sanctions

Failure to supplement a disclosure or discovery response is the equivalent of providing incorrect information in the initial disclosure or response. The court may exclude evidence or claims, may order a continuance and further discovery, or take any other action it deems appropriate (*see* Rule 37 for a more detailed analysis of the available sanctions).

RULE 26(f) Conference of the Parties; Planning for Discovery

The parties must confer and develop a proposed discovery plan to be submitted to the court addressing a variety of discovery issues, including the discovery schedule and any modifications to the limits or scope of discovery.

PRACTICING LAW UNDER THIS SUBPART

Time for Conference

The parties must confer "as soon as practicable and in any event at least 21 days before a scheduling conference is held or a scheduling order is due under Rule 16(b)."

Agenda for Discovery Conference

At the discovery conference, the parties must discuss all of the topics that the discovery plan addresses (listed below). In addition, the parties should discuss the nature and basis of their claims and defenses, the possibilities of prompt settlement or resolution of the case, and issues relating to preserving discoverable information. They must also either make or arrange for the initial automatic disclosures required by Rule 26(a)(1).

Content of Discovery Plan

The discovery plan should indicate the parties' positions or proposals concerning:

(1) *Automatic Disclosures:* Any changes to the timing, form, or requirement for disclosures under Rule 26(a). The plan must explicitly state when the initial disclosures were or are to be made;

(2) *Discovery Scope and Schedule:* The likely subjects of discovery, the completion date for discovery, and any discovery that should be conducted in phases or limited to or focused on particular issues;

(3) *Electronically Stored Information:* Issues relating to the disclosure, production, or preservation of electronically stored information, including the sources of such information, the form in which it should be produced, and the costs of such production;

(4) *Privilege Issues:* Issues relating to claims of privilege or work product protection, including any procedures to be used in the event of the inadvertent production of privileged information (to the extent that they differ from the procedures in Rule 26(b)(2)(B));

(5) *Discovery Limits:* Any changes to the discovery limits established by the Rules or by local rule, plus any additional limits; and

(6) *Other Orders:* Any other case management or protective orders proposed for the court's consideration.

Submission of Plan

The parties should submit to the court a written report of the plan within 14 days of the discovery meeting. Many local rules contain a report template.

Good Faith Participation

The attorneys (and unrepresented parties) have a good faith obligation to schedule the discovery conference and to attempt to agree on a proposed discovery plan and report.

RULE 26(g) — Signing Disclosures and Discovery Requests, Responses, and Objections

Rule 26(g) requires that parties and lawyers conduct the discovery process in good faith. It requires that every disclosure, request for discovery, and response or objection must be signed by at least one attorney of record (or by the party, if unrepresented). The signature constitutes a certification that to the best of the signer's knowledge, information, and belief, the document is complete and correct, and is being served for proper purposes within the Rules.

PRACTICING LAW UNDER THIS SUBPART

Certification for the Initial and Pretrial Disclosures

For the initial disclosures and the pretrial disclosures, the signature constitutes a certification to the best of the signer's knowledge, information, and belief formed after "reasonable inquiry" that the disclosure is complete and correct. Expert disclosures, typically in the form of expert reports, are signed by the expert, and thus not covered by this Rule.

Certification for Other Discovery Documents

For discovery requests, responses, and objections, the signature constitutes a certification to the best of the signer's knowledge, information, and belief formed after "reasonable inquiry" that:

(A) The document is consistent with the Rules and existing law, or with a nonfrivolous argument for extension, modification, or reversal of existing law, or for establishing new law;

(B) The document is not imposed for any improper purpose, such as to harass, delay, or cause needless expense for an opponent; and

(C) The discovery is not unreasonably or unduly burdensome or expensive, given the nature of the case, the discovery already conducted, the amount in controversy, and the importance of the issues at stake in the litigation.

Unsigned Discovery Documents

If without substantial justification a discovery disclosure, request, response, or objection is unsigned, other parties should advise the party making the disclosure, request, response, or objection. If counsel for that party fails to sign the document promptly, the unsigned document will be stricken, no party will be obligated to respond to the unsigned document, and the attorney serving the unsigned discovery document may be subject to sanctions.

Sanctions

If a certification is made in violation of Rule 26(g) without substantial justification, the court must impose an appropriate sanction on the party, the attorney, or both. The sanction may include expenses incurred because of the violation, including attorney's fees, and may also include substantive sanctions like dismissal.

RULE 27

DEPOSITIONS TO PERPETUATE TESTIMONY

(a) Before an Action Is Filed.

(1) *Petition.* A person who wants to perpetuate testimony about any matter cognizable in a United States court may file a verified petition in the district court for the district where any expected adverse party resides. The petition must ask for an order authorizing the petitioner to depose the named persons in order to perpetuate their testimony. The petition must be titled in the petitioner's name and must show:

(A) that the petitioner expects to be a party to an action cognizable in a United States court but cannot presently bring it or cause it to be brought;

(B) the subject matter of the expected action and the petitioner's interest;

(C) the facts that the petitioner wants to establish by the proposed testimony and the reasons to perpetuate it;

(D) the names or a description of the persons whom the petitioner expects to be adverse parties and their addresses, so far as known; and

(E) the name, address, and expected substance of the testimony of each deponent.

(2) *Notice and Service.* At least 21 days before the hearing date, the petitioner must serve each expected adverse party with a copy of the petition and a notice stating the time and place of the hearing. The notice may be served either inside or outside the district or State in the manner provided in Rule 4. If that service cannot be made with reasonable diligence on an expected adverse party, the court may order service by publication or otherwise. The court must appoint an attorney to represent persons not served in the manner provided in Rule 4 and to cross-examine the deponent if an unserved person is not otherwise represented. If any expected adverse party is a minor or is incompetent, Rule 17(c) applies.

(3) *Order and Examination.* If satisfied that perpetuating the testimony may prevent a failure or delay of justice, the court must issue an order that designates or describes the persons whose depositions may be taken, specifies the subject matter of the examinations, and states whether the depositions will be taken orally or by written interrogatories. The depositions may then be taken under these rules, and the court may issue

orders like those authorized by Rules 34 and 35. A reference in these rules to the court where an action is pending means, for purposes of this rule, the court where the petition for the deposition was filed.

(4) *Using the Deposition.* A deposition to perpetuate testimony may be used under Rule 32(a) in any later-filed district-court action involving the same subject matter if the deposition either was taken under these rules or, although not so taken, would be admissible in evidence in the courts of the State where it was taken.

(b) Pending Appeal.

(1) *In General.* The court where a judgment has been rendered may, if an appeal has been taken or may still be taken, permit a party to depose witnesses to perpetuate their testimony for use in the event of further proceedings in that court.

(2) *Motion.* The party who wants to perpetuate testimony may move for leave to take the depositions, on the same notice and service as if the action were pending in the district court. The motion must show:

(A) the name, address, and expected substance of the testimony of each deponent; and

(B) the reasons for perpetuating the testimony.

(3) *Court Order.* If the court finds that perpetuating the testimony may prevent a failure or delay of justice, the court may permit the depositions to be taken and may issue orders like those authorized by Rules 34 and 35. The depositions may be taken and used as any other deposition taken in a pending district-court action.

(c) Perpetuation by an Action. This rule does not limit a court's power to entertain an action to perpetuate testimony.

[Amended effective March 19, 1948; October 20, 1949; July 1, 1971; August 1, 1987; April 25, 2005, effective December 1, 2005; April 30, 2007, effective December 1, 2007; March 26, 2009, effective December 1, 2009.]

UNDERSTANDING RULE 27

HOW RULE 27 FITS IN

Almost all discovery in federal court occurs after the case has been commenced, under timing constraints established generally in Rule 26 and specifically in the rules governing each specific discovery device. Rule 27 is an exception to this general rule. It addresses the situation where someone needs to preserve testimony that is at risk of becoming unavailable (such as by death of the witness), yet the person cannot preserve the testimony in the ordinary way by simply taking a deposition because litigation has not yet been commenced and, for some reason, cannot be commenced, or while an appeal is pending.

Under these circumstances, Rule 27 allows a person to take a deposition to preserve the testimony (see Rule 30 for a description of what a deposition is). However, because these depositions are such a departure from the normal course, Rule 27 imposes significant restrictions on them. In order to obtain a Rule 27 deposition to preserve testimony, the person seeking the deposition must submit a verified petition—a petition accompanied by a statement signed by the petitioner stating that the facts in the petition are accurate. As explained in more detail below, in this petition, the person seeking the deposition must persuade the court that there is a need to preserve the testimony for a case that will, in the future, proceed in federal court but that the person cannot presently commence.

THE ARCHITECTURE OF RULE 27

Rule 27 contemplates depositions to preserve testimony in two circumstances: prior to commencement of the action and while an appeal is pending. Rule 27(a) addresses depositions to preserve testimony prior to the commencement of the action, and Rule 27(b) addresses depositions to preserve testimony while an appeal is pending. Rule 27(c) preserves the right to preserve testimony by methods other than Rule 27—it is not the exclusive method of preserving testimony.

HOW RULE 27 WORKS IN PRACTICE

RULE 27(a) Before an Action Is Filed

A person who anticipates becoming a party to a federal lawsuit, but who is not yet able to commence the lawsuit, may seek leave to take a deposition to preserve testimony that is in danger of being lost.

PRACTICING LAW UNDER THIS SUBPART

Petition

A request to take a Rule 27 deposition is made by petition containing the following:

(1) A statement that the petitioner expects to be a party to an action in federal court, but is presently unable to bring the action (remember, subject-matter jurisdiction is a Constitutional limitation on the powers of federal courts. In a normal lawsuit, the complaint must set forth the basis for federal subject-matter jurisdiction. Here, the court does not have a complaint so must use the information in the petition to satisfy itself that it has the Constitutional power to rule on the petition);

(2) A description of the subject matter of the anticipated action and the petitioner's relationship to the action;

(3) The facts that the petitioner intends to establish by the testimony, and the petitioner's need for perpetuating the testimony;

(4) The identities and addresses of the persons expected to be adverse parties in the action; and

(5) The identity of the deponent(s) and a detailed description of the substance of their testimony.

The petition must be verified (*i.e.*, accompanied by a statement signed by the petitioner that the factual averments are accurate) and must include a proposed order describing the procedure and scope of the deposition.

Preservation of Documents

On its face, Rule 27 only authorizes depositions, not document requests. However, some courts will allow parties to use Rule 27 to preserve documentary evidence that might be lost.

Certainty of Litigation Unnecessary

A party does not need to demonstrate that litigation is absolutely certain in order to prevail on a motion to perpetuate; instead, the court must find the party to be acting in anticipation of litigation.

Certainty of Loss of Testimony Unnecessary

A party does not need to demonstrate certainty that the testimony will be lost, such as when the deponents are on their death beds. Rather, a party must show that there is a danger of the testimony or evidence being lost, which might be satisfied when circumstances indicate that memories may fade. In making this determination, the deponent's age alone can present a sufficient risk the deponent will be unable to testify in the future.

Inability to Bring Suit

One requirement for petitions to perpetuate testimony under Rule 27(a) is that the movant not be able to bring a lawsuit. One basis for such inability is a lack of sufficient information to draft the complaint under the constraints of Rule 11. However, Rule 27 may not be used to uncover or discover testimony necessary to file suit, and applies only where known testimony is to be preserved.

Standard for Ruling

The court will order the deposition if it is satisfied that the perpetuation of the testimony may prevent a future failure or delay of justice.

Conduct of the Deposition

The court must designate the deponent(s), the subject matter of the examination, and whether the deposition will be oral or written. The deposition is then taken in accordance with the terms of the court order and Rules 30 and 31 (governing oral and written depositions).

Scope of Deposition

The scope of a deposition under Rule 27 is often narrower than a typical discovery deposition, and generally will be governed by the court's order. In general, courts have required that the evidence to be preserved be material and competent, not merely discoverable under general discovery provisions.

Subject-Matter Jurisdiction

A proceeding to perpetuate testimony is not a separate civil action, and does not require its own basis for jurisdiction. However, the petition must demonstrate that the anticipated legal action is eligible to proceed in federal court.

RULE 27(b) Pending Appeal

Rule 27 may be used while a case is on appeal, or while the period to appeal is running, to preserve testimony in the event that further proceedings are needed. A request for a deposition pending an appeal is made by motion (not petition, in contrast to Rule 27(a)) to the district court where the action proceeded. The motion must include the names and addresses of the deponents, the substance of their testimony, and the reasons for perpetuating their testimony.

RULE 27(c) Perpetuation by an Action

Rule 27 is not the exclusive method of perpetuating testimony. Thus, for example, a deposition that would be admissible in a subsequent proceeding in State court will also be admissible in federal court, even though the offering party may not have complied with Rule 27. Likewise, a party may preserve testimony under a method authorized by statute.

RULE 28

PERSONS BEFORE WHOM DEPOSITIONS MAY BE TAKEN

(a) Within the United States.

(1) *In General.* Within the United States or a territory or insular possession subject to United States jurisdiction, a deposition must be taken before:

(A) an officer authorized to administer oaths either by federal law or by the law in the place of examination; or

(B) a person appointed by the court where the action is pending to administer oaths and take testimony.

(2) *Definition of "Officer."* The term "officer" in Rules 30, 31, and 32 includes a person appointed by the court under this rule or designated by the parties under Rule 29(a).

(b) In a Foreign Country.

(1) *In General.* A deposition may be taken in a foreign country:

(A) under an applicable treaty or convention;

(B) under a letter of request, whether or not captioned a "letter rogatory";

(C) on notice, before a person authorized to administer oaths either by federal law or by the law in the place of examination; or

(D) before a person commissioned by the court to administer any necessary oath and take testimony.

(2) *Issuing a Letter of Request or a Commission.* A letter of request, a commission, or both may be issued:

(A) on appropriate terms after an application and notice of it; and

(B) without a showing that taking the deposition in another manner is impracticable or inconvenient.

(3) *Form of a Request, Notice, or Commission.* When a letter of request or any other device is used according to a treaty or convention, it must be captioned in the form prescribed by that treaty or convention. A letter of request may be addressed "To the Appropriate Authority in [name of country]." A deposition notice or a commission must designate by name or descriptive title the person before whom the deposition is to be taken.

(4) *Letter of Request—Admitting Evidence.* Evidence obtained in response to a letter of request need not be excluded merely because it is not a verbatim transcript, because the testimony was not taken under oath, or

because of any similar departure from the requirements for depositions taken within the United States.

(c) Disqualification. A deposition must not be taken before a person who is any party's relative, employee, or attorney; who is related to or employed by any party's attorney; or who is financially interested in the action.

[Amended December 27, 1946, effective March 19, 1948; January 21, 1963, effective July 1, 1963; April 29, 1980, effective August 1, 1980; March 2, 1987, effective August 1, 1987; April 22, 1993, effective December 1, 1993; April 30, 2007, effective December 1, 2007.]

UNDERSTANDING RULE 28

HOW RULE 28 FITS IN

Rule 28 is a largely technical, and relatively minor, rule that governs who may serve as the neutral "officer" who administers a deposition. There is a more detailed discussion of depositions in Rule 30, but in general depositions are discovery procedures where a witness appears and answers questions under oath posed by the lawyers in the case. The testimony is typically recorded, often by a stenographer who also serves as the "officer" for the deposition, administering the oath and retaining the exhibits as well as recording the testimony.

Rule 28 does not actually set criteria for serving as an officer, and instead allows anyone authorized by State or federal law or appointed by the court to administer depositions. It also controls taking a deposition in a foreign country for use in a case proceeding in a U.S. federal court. Finally, it lists criteria that disqualify candidates from consideration, such as being related to a party.

THE ARCHITECTURE OF RULE 28

Rule 28(a) contains the core provisions governing who may administer a deposition within the U.S., and Rule 28(b) contains the corresponding rules for taking a deposition in a foreign country. The circumstances that disqualify someone from administering a deposition are set forth in Rule 28(c).

HOW RULE 28 WORKS IN PRACTICE

RULE 28(a) Within the United States

In the United States, or a territory or insular possession, depositions may be taken before an officer authorized to administer oaths under federal or State law. Typically, a stenographer is such an officer. A deposition may also be taken before someone appointed by the court, or before a person designated by the parties by stipulation pursuant to Rule 29.

RULE 28(b) In a Foreign Country

Depending upon the laws of the foreign country, a deposition in a foreign country may be taken:

(1) Pursuant to any applicable treaty or convention (such as the Hague Convention);

(2) Pursuant to a letter request (or "letter rogatory"), which is a formal communication between the court in which an action is proceeding and another court requesting that the testimony of a foreign witness be taken under the direction of the foreign court;

(3) Upon a notice of deposition by any person authorized to administer oaths either by the laws of the foreign country or the United States; or

(4) Before persons commissioned by the court, who will have power to administer an oath and hear testimony by virtue of their oaths.

In some countries, the taking of evidence under unauthorized procedures may subject the interrogator to severe—even criminal—sanctions. Before taking such evidence, a lawyer should consult the Hague Convention and all treaties.

RULE 28(c) Disqualification

The officer at a deposition may not be a relative, employee, or attorney of any of the parties, or an employee or relative of an attorney for a party, or anyone with a financial interest in the action.

PRACTICING LAW UNDER THIS SUBPART

Objections

Objections to the officer must be raised before the deposition starts or as soon thereafter as the interest of the officer becomes known or should have become known with due diligence. Otherwise, the objection is waived.

RULE 29

STIPULATIONS ABOUT DISCOVERY PROCEDURE

Unless the court orders otherwise, the parties may stipulate that:

(a) a deposition may be taken before any person, at any time or place, on any notice, and in the manner specified—in which event it may be used in the same way as any other deposition; and

(b) other procedures governing or limiting discovery be modified—but a stipulation extending the time for any form of discovery must have court approval if it would interfere with the time set for completing discovery, for hearing a motion, or for trial.

[Amended March 30, 1970, effective July 1, 1970; April 22, 1993, effective December 1, 1993; April 30, 2007, effective December 1, 2007.]

UNDERSTANDING RULE 29

HOW RULE 29 FITS IN

The discovery rules set various time limitations, numeric limitations, and other restrictions on discovery. These are just defaults, however, and the parties are free to stipulate to modified discovery procedures. The primary restraint on this ability to modify the discovery procedures is that the parties may not enter into a stipulation extending the time for any discovery if the extension would interfere with a hearing or trial date or the court's overall discovery deadline. Thus, the judge controls the overall schedule, but within the framework the judge has established, the parties may agree to their own set of discovery procedures.

THE ARCHITECTURE OF RULE 29

Rule 29 has two clauses. The first is limited to depositions, and provides that the parties may stipulate to all of the procedures to be used, such as the officer who administers the deposition, the time and place of the deposition, and the manner for taking the testimony. The second broadly allows the parties to modify any of the other discovery procedures, so long as the parties do not agree to an extension of time that interferes with a date the court has set for a hearing, for trial, or for completing discovery.

HOW RULE 29 WORKS IN PRACTICE

Form of Stipulation

Stipulations under Rule 29 may be written or oral. They are self-effectuating, and do not need to receive court approval or even be filed with the court (unless they would affect the court's schedule as discussed below).

Court Deadlines for Discovery, a Hearing, or Trial

The parties need court approval to modify a discovery date or deadline if the extension would interfere with the court's discovery deadline or with a hearing or trial date. Thus, for example, a court might not enforce a stipulation to conduct a deposition after the court's discovery deadline.

Court Override

The court can order that parties perform under the Rules as written, vitiating any stipulations.

RULE 30

DEPOSITIONS BY ORAL EXAMINATION

(a) When a Deposition May Be Taken.

(1) *Without Leave.* A party may, by oral questions, depose any person, including a party, without leave of court except as provided in Rule 30(a)(2). The deponent's attendance may be compelled by subpoena under Rule 45.

(2) *With Leave.* A party must obtain leave of court, and the court must grant leave to the extent consistent with Rule 26(b)(1) and (2):

(A) if the parties have not stipulated to the deposition and:

(i) the deposition would result in more than 10 depositions being taken under this rule or Rule 31 by the plaintiffs, or by the defendants, or by the third-party defendants;

(ii) the deponent has already been deposed in the case; or

(iii) the party seeks to take the deposition before the time specified in Rule 26(d), unless the party certifies in the notice, with supporting facts, that the deponent is expected to leave the United States and be unavailable for examination in this country after that time; or

(B) if the deponent is confined in prison.

(b) Notice of the Deposition; Other Formal Requirements.

(1) *Notice in General.* A party who wants to depose a person by oral questions must give reasonable written notice to every other party. The notice must state the time and place of the deposition and, if known, the deponent's name and address. If the name is unknown, the notice must provide a general description sufficient to identify the person or the particular class or group to which the person belongs.

(2) *Producing Documents.* If a subpoena duces tecum is to be served on the deponent, the materials designated for production, as set out in the subpoena, must be listed in the notice or in an attachment. The notice to a party deponent may be accompanied by a request under Rule 34 to produce documents and tangible things at the deposition.

(3) *Method of Recording.*

(A) *Method Stated in the Notice.* The party who notices the deposition must state in the notice the method for recording the testimony. Unless the court orders otherwise, testimony may be recorded by audio, audiovisual, or stenographic means. The noticing party bears the recording costs. Any party may arrange to transcribe a deposition.

(B) *Additional Method.* With prior notice to the deponent and other parties, any party may designate another method for recording the testimony in addition to that specified in the original notice. That party bears the expense of the additional record or transcript unless the court orders otherwise.

(4) *By Remote Means.* The parties may stipulate—or the court may on motion order—that a deposition be taken by telephone or other remote means. For the purpose of this rule and Rules 28(a), 37(a)(2), and 37(b)(1), the deposition takes place where the deponent answers the questions.

(5) *Officer's Duties.*

(A) *Before the Deposition.* Unless the parties stipulate otherwise, a deposition must be conducted before an officer appointed or designated under Rule 28. The officer must begin the deposition with an on-the-record statement that includes:

(i) the officer's name and business address;

(ii) the date, time, and place of the deposition;

(iii) the deponent's name;

(iv) the officer's administration of the oath or affirmation to the deponent; and

(v) the identity of all persons present.

(B) *Conducting the Deposition; Avoiding Distortion.* If the deposition is recorded nonstenographically, the officer must repeat the items in Rule 30(b)(5)(A)(i)–(iii) at the beginning of each unit of the recording medium. The deponent's and attorneys' appearance or demeanor must not be distorted through recording techniques.

(C) *After the Deposition.* At the end of a deposition, the officer must state on the record that the deposition is complete and must set out any stipulations made by the attorneys about custody of the transcript or recording and of the exhibits, or about any other pertinent matters.

(6) *Notice or Subpoena Directed to an Organization.* In its notice or subpoena, a party may name as the deponent a public or private corporation, a partnership, an association, a governmental agency, or other entity and must describe with reasonable particularity the matters for examination. The named organization must designate one or more

officers, directors, or managing agents, or designate other persons who consent to testify on its behalf; and it may set out the matters on which each person designated will testify. Before or promptly after the notice or subpoena is served, the serving party and the organization must confer in good faith about the matters for examination. A subpoena must advise a nonparty organization of its duty to confer with the serving party and to designate each person who will testify. The persons designated must testify about information known or reasonably available to the organization. This paragraph (6) does not preclude a deposition by any other procedure allowed by these rules.

(c) Examination and Cross-Examination; Record of the Examination; Objections; Written Questions.

(1) *Examination and Cross-Examination.* The examination and cross-examination of a deponent proceed as they would at trial under the Federal Rules of Evidence, except Rules 103 and 615. After putting the deponent under oath or affirmation, the officer must record the testimony by the method designated under Rule 30(b)(3)(A). The testimony must be recorded by the officer personally or by a person acting in the presence and under the direction of the officer.

(2) *Objections.* An objection at the time of the examination—whether to evidence, to a party's conduct, to the officer's qualifications, to the manner of taking the deposition, or to any other aspect of the deposition—must be noted on the record, but the examination still proceeds; the testimony is taken subject to any objection. An objection must be stated concisely in a nonargumentative and nonsuggestive manner. A person may instruct a deponent not to answer only when necessary to preserve a privilege, to enforce a limitation ordered by the court, or to present a motion under Rule 30(d)(3).

(3) *Participating Through Written Questions.* Instead of participating in the oral examination, a party may serve written questions in a sealed envelope on the party noticing the deposition, who must deliver them to the officer. The officer must ask the deponent those questions and record the answers verbatim.

(d) Duration; Sanction; Motion to Terminate or Limit.

(1) *Duration.* Unless otherwise stipulated or ordered by the court, a deposition is limited to 1 day of 7 hours. The court must allow additional time consistent with Rule 26(b)(1) and (2) if needed to fairly examine the deponent or if the deponent, another person, or any other circumstance impedes or delays the examination.

(2) *Sanction.* The court may impose an appropriate sanction—including the reasonable expenses and attorney's fees incurred by any party—on a person who impedes, delays, or frustrates the fair examination of the deponent.

(3) *Motion to Terminate or Limit.*

(A) *Grounds.* At any time during a deposition, the deponent or a party may move to terminate or limit it on the ground that it is being conducted in bad faith or in a manner that unreasonably annoys, embarrasses, or oppresses the deponent or party. The motion may be filed in the court where the action is pending or the deposition is being taken. If the objecting deponent or party so demands, the deposition must be suspended for the time necessary to obtain an order.

(B) *Order.* The court may order that the deposition be terminated or may limit its scope and manner as provided in Rule 26(c). If terminated, the deposition may be resumed only by order of the court where the action is pending.

(C) *Award of Expenses.* Rule 37(a)(5) applies to the award of expenses.

(e) Review by the Witness; Changes.

(1) *Review; Statement of Changes.* On request by the deponent or a party before the deposition is completed, the deponent must be allowed 30 days after being notified by the officer that the transcript or recording is available in which:

(A) to review the transcript or recording; and

(B) if there are changes in form or substance, to sign a statement listing the changes and the reasons for making them.

(2) *Changes Indicated in the Officer's Certificate.* The officer must note in the certificate prescribed by Rule 30(f)(1) whether a review was requested and, if so, must attach any changes the deponent makes during the 30-day period.

(f) Certification and Delivery; Exhibits; Copies of the Transcript or Recording; Filing.

(1) *Certification and Delivery.* The officer must certify in writing that the witness was duly sworn and that the deposition accurately records the witness's testimony. The certificate must accompany the record of the deposition. Unless the court orders otherwise, the officer must seal the deposition in an envelope or package bearing the title of the action and marked "Deposition of [witness's name]" and must promptly send it to the attorney who arranged for the transcript or recording. The attorney

must store it under conditions that will protect it against loss, destruction, tampering, or deterioration.

(2) *Documents and Tangible Things.*

(A) *Originals and Copies.* Documents and tangible things produced for inspection during a deposition must, on a party's request, be marked for identification and attached to the deposition. Any party may inspect and copy them. But if the person who produced them wants to keep the originals, the person may:

(i) offer copies to be marked, attached to the deposition, and then used as originals—after giving all parties a fair opportunity to verify the copies by comparing them with the originals; or

(ii) give all parties a fair opportunity to inspect and copy the originals after they are marked-in which event the originals may be used as if attached to the deposition.

(B) *Order Regarding the Originals.* Any party may move for an order that the originals be attached to the deposition pending final disposition of the case.

(3) *Copies of the Transcript or Recording.* Unless otherwise stipulated or ordered by the court, the officer must retain the stenographic notes of a deposition taken stenographically or a copy of the recording of a deposition taken by another method. When paid reasonable charges, the officer must furnish a copy of the transcript or recording to any party or the deponent.

(4) *Notice of Filing.* A party who files the deposition must promptly notify all other parties of the filing.

(g) Failure to Attend a Deposition or Serve a Subpoena; Expenses. A party who, expecting a deposition to be taken, attends in person or by an attorney may recover reasonable expenses for attending, including attorney's fees, if the noticing party failed to:

(1) attend and proceed with the deposition; or

(2) serve a subpoena on a nonparty deponent, who consequently did not attend.

[Amended January 21, 1963, effective July 1, 1963; March 30, 1970, effective July 1, 1970; March 1, 1971, effective July 1, 1971; November 20, 1972, effective July 1, 1975; April 29, 1980, effective August 1, 1980; March 2, 1987, effective August 1, 1987; April 22, 1993, effective December 1, 1993; April 17, 2000, effective December 1, 2000; April 30, 2007, effective December 1, 2007; April 29, 2015, effective December 1, 2015; April 27, 2020, effective December 1, 2020.]

UNDERSTANDING RULE 30

HOW RULE 30 FITS IN

A deposition is a procedure in which a witness—party or nonparty—appears in a conference room or similar location, is placed under oath, and then answers questions posed by the lawyers involved in the proceeding. Purposes for depositions can include gathering relevant information, exploring areas for potential cross-examination or impeachment at trial, and pinning down the witness's story. The testimony is transcribed or recorded in some fashion, and may subsequently be used to refresh the witness's recollection or impeach the witness if the witness changes the testimony, and in some circumstances can be used to prove elements of a claim or defense. Depositions can be extremely powerful tools, as they are often the only opportunity that a lawyer has to speak to an opposing party directly, without filtering by that party's lawyer.

Rule 30 is one of four rules that specifically govern depositions: Rules 28, 30, 31, and 32. Rules 30 and Rule 31 address the procedures for and conduct at the actual deposition, with Rule 30 covering oral examination and Rule 31 covering written questions (a procedure that is rarely used). Rule 32 then specifies how parties may use a deposition transcript or recording in subsequent stages of the lawsuit. Rule 28 controls who may be the neutral officer who administers a deposition, typically a stenographer or videographer.

Although the rules authorize depositions by both oral and written questions, the vast majority of depositions are by oral examination, and Rule 30 sets forth the rules governing the conduct at such depositions. It covers a broad range of topics relating to the mechanics of depositions, including: limits on the number and duration of depositions; the procedures for "noticing" or scheduling depositions; technical requirements for recording depositions; taking depositions of designated representatives of corporations; the conduct of direct and cross-examination and the manner of interposing objections; the process for witnesses to review the transcript and make changes; and sanctions for failing to attend a properly-noticed deposition.

In addition to the four rules specifically focused on depositions, the general rules governing all discovery also apply to depositions. For example, the scope of inquiry in a deposition is the general scope of discovery in Rule 26(b)(1). A party wishing to limit the duration of a deposition or prevent inquiry into certain topics would file a motion for a protective order under Rule 26(c). And a party believing that an opponent has acted improperly at a deposition would file a motion to compel or for sanctions under Rule 37.

THE ARCHITECTURE OF RULE 30

Rule 30 contains seven subparts governing a myriad of details about depositions. Roughly speaking, the subsections track the course of the deposition process, starting with noticing and recording the deposition, moving through the conduct at the deposition to review of the transcript, and concluding with sanctions for misconduct.

Rule 30(a) addresses when a party may schedule a deposition on its own and when it needs leave of court. It authorizes a party to schedule a deposition on its own unless one of three limitations exists: the deposition would exceed the limit on the number of depositions; the witness has already been deposed; or the parties have not yet conducted their Rule 26(f) discovery conference.

Rule 30(b) sets forth the procedures for scheduling a deposition. Depositions of parties are scheduled by simply sending a notice, while depositions of nonparties also require a subpoena under Rule 45. The notice must contain the date, time, and location of the deposition and the manner in which it will be recorded. The notice may also require the deponent to bring specified documents to the deposition. Rule 30(b) also contains provisions regarding the officer for the deposition—typically a stenographer or videographer who conducts the recording and administers the oath. Finally, Rule 30(b) contains a very important subsection—Rule 30(b)(6)—which allows a party to require a corporation or other entity to designate a representative to provide the corporation's collective knowledge about specified topics.

Rule 30(c) controls the manner of examination during the deposition, essentially providing that examination proceeds in the manner it would at trial, with direct and cross-examination. It specifies which objections are raised during the deposition and which may be asserted if another party seeks to use the deposition testimony in a subsequent stage of the action. It generally requires that lawyers make objections that can be cured by rephrasing, and preserves all other objections. For example, if a question is compound, other lawyers must object to give the questioning lawyer the opportunity to break the compound question into two separate, unobjectionable questions. Conversely, if the question seeks irrelevant information, rephrasing it will not cure the relevance objection, so Rule 30 does not require other lawyers to object during the deposition—those objections are asserted at the time a party attempts to use the deposition testimony at a hearing or trial. Rule 30(c) also requires objections to be stated in a non-suggestive manner, so that a lawyer cannot use objections to coach the witness as to how to respond. Finally, Rule 30(c)(2) contains an important limitation on when a lawyer may instruct a witness not to answer a question.

Rule 30(d) establishes a default length of a deposition at one day of seven hours. It authorizes sanctions against an attorney or witness who impedes or delays the examination (such as an attorney who excessively objects or interrupts the questioning or who makes "speaking objections" that coach the witness). Finally, it authorizes a party or the witness to suspend the deposition to make a motion to terminate the deposition or limit its scope on the grounds that the deposition is being conducted in bad faith or to unreasonably annoy, embarrass, or oppress the party or witness.

Rules 30(e) and (f) both address the deposition transcript or recording. First, the witness is entitled to review the transcript and make any corrections on an "errata sheet." Then, the deposition officer certifies and distributes copies.

Lastly, Rule 30(g) authorizes a party who appears for a deposition that does not occur to recover the party's resulting expenses, including attorney's fees, if the party noticing the deposition either failed to appear to conduct the deposition or failed to properly subpoena a nonparty witness who failed to appear.

HOW RULE 30 WORKS IN PRACTICE

RULE 30(a) When a Deposition May Be Taken

In general, a party may take the deposition of up to 10 witnesses, party or otherwise, at any time after the parties have conducted the discovery conference under Rule 26(f) and before the discovery deadline (typically set in the court's Case Management Order). A party may only depose each witness one time, absent a stipulation or court order otherwise.

PRACTICING LAW UNDER THIS SUBPART

Persons Subject to Deposition

Rule 30 authorizes any party to take the deposition of any person, party or not, without leave of court. A party may even take the party's own deposition—which ordinarily would not make sense (there's no real benefit to having a party's lawyer ask the party questions on the record, they can do that privately), but would be warranted if, for example, the party will be unable to attend trial. One limitation on this broad right is called the "Apex Doctrine," under which some courts hold that high-ranking governmental officials or corporate officers cannot be deposed unless the "apex" individual has firsthand knowledge of relevant facts and those facts cannot be obtained through less intrusive forms of discovery (to prevent harassment of those "apex" individuals for leverage purposes).

Number of Depositions

The plaintiffs as a group are limited to 10 depositions total, as are the defendants and third-party defendants. This number may be increased or decreased by stipulation or by order of court. A deposition of a company representative under Rule 30(b)(6) generally counts as only one deposition, regardless of how many representatives the company designates.

Repeat Depositions

Leave of court or a stipulation of the parties is required to depose someone a second time. Leave of court is not required to reconvene and continue a deposition that was suspended or not completed the first day.

Time for Conducting Depositions

Depositions generally may be taken at any time after the Rule 26(f) discovery conference and before the cut-off date for discovery established by the court. Leave of court is generally required to depose someone outside these time limits.

RULE 30(b)(1) Notice of the Deposition; Other Formal Requirements: Notice In General

A party intending to take a deposition must serve a written notice upon all other parties identifying the deponent and time and location of the deposition. Depositions are only admissible against parties properly noticed or actually represented at the deposition.

PRACTICING LAW UNDER THIS SUBPART

Content of Notice

A deposition notice must state the date, time, and place of the deposition, and the manner of recording the deposition. It must also state the name and address of the deponent, if known, or a general description sufficient to identify the deponent. The deposition notice does not need to describe the topics to be covered in the deposition (except for a notice to take the deposition of a designated representative of a corporation, discussed below in Rule 30(b)(6)). If a subpoena *duces tecum* (seeking documents) is to be served under Rule 45, then the notice must include a description of the documents sought.

Service and Filing of Notice

Deposition notices are served on all parties, but are not filed.

Failure to Serve Notice

If a party does not receive a notice of a deposition and does not appear or is not represented at the deposition, the testimony cannot be used against that party, even if the party had actual knowledge that the deposition was to occur.

Timing of Notice

Rule 30(b)(1) states that a party must give "reasonable" notice. There is no bright line as to what is reasonable notice, and the determination is extremely discretionary.

Deposition of a Party

A deposition notice compels parties to attend a deposition, without the need for a subpoena. A corporate party is required to produce directors, officers, and managing agents pursuant to a notice of deposition; a subpoena is required for other employees.

Deposition of a Nonparty

A notice of deposition is not binding on a nonparty. Instead, a subpoena must be issued pursuant to Rule 45 to force a nonparty to attend a deposition. However, the party taking the deposition must still serve a deposition notice upon the other parties.

Place of Examination

Although the party noticing the deposition sets the location, the witness or other parties may challenge the location by motion for protective order. For a nonparty witness, the witness may not be required to travel more than 100 miles from the place where the witness resides, is employed, or regularly transacts business. For a party deponent, the court has discretion to control the location of a deposition, but in general, plaintiffs will be required to travel to the district where the suit is pending for their depositions, whereas defendants can have their depositions taken where they work or live.

RULE 30(b)(2) Producing Documents

A witness may be compelled to bring documents to a deposition by including a description of the documents in the notice of deposition (for a party witness) or by issuing a subpoena *duces tecum* under Rule 45(a)(1)(A)(iii) and including a description in the notice (for a nonparty witness). However, if the witness is a party, then the party must be accorded 30 days to interpose objections to the document request (the rationale being that one should not be able to circumvent the 30-day period in the document request rule by issuing a notice of deposition).

RULE 30(b)(3) Method of Recording

The party taking the deposition may have it recorded by audio, audiovisual, or stenographic means, and must specify the means of recording in the deposition notice. Other parties may arrange for additional methods of recording.

PRACTICING LAW UNDER THIS SUBPART

Cost of Recording

The party taking the deposition bears the cost of the party's chosen method(s) of recording. If another party arranges for an additional method of recording, that party bears the cost of that additional method.

Use of Nonstenographic Depositions

In order to use a nonstenographically recorded deposition at trial or in connection with a dispositive motion, a party must submit a transcript of the portions to be introduced for the court's use.

RULE 30(b)(4) By Remote Means

The parties may stipulate, or move the court for an order, that a deposition be taken by telephone, videoconference, or other remote means. Generally, leave to take depositions by remote means will be granted liberally. Such depositions are deemed to occur in the district where the deponent is located when answering the questions, and the court reporter/officer should be in the presence of the witness, not the attorneys.

RULE 30(b)(5) Officer's Duties

Unless the parties stipulate otherwise, a deposition must be conducted before an officer qualified under Rule 28. At the beginning of a deposition, the officer places on the record administrative details identifying and describing the deposition. During the deposition, the officer must accurately and neutrally depict the witness's demeanor and appearance in the recording. The camera angle and focus should remain constant, and may not be manipulated to emphasize or de-emphasize certain testimony or otherwise influence viewer perceptions.

RULE 30(b)(6) Notice or Subpoena Directed to an Organization

Rule 30(b)(6) allows a party to notice the deposition of a corporation, partnership, association, governmental agency, or other organization and to specify the areas of inquiry. The named organization must then designate one or more representatives to testify as to the organization's collective information regarding the designated areas of inquiry. Designated witnesses' testimony is not limited to their firsthand knowledge, and they must prepare for the deposition so that they can present the entire entity's information. This is an extremely powerful and useful tool when an attorney does not know the best witness to examine regarding a particular topic or wants to efficiently gather all of the organization's information on the designated topics in one deposition.

PRACTICING LAW UNDER THIS SUBPART

Content of Notice

The notice (and the subpoena, for a nonparty) must state that the organization has the duty to designate a representative and must specify the areas of inquiry with reasonable particularity.

Selection of Representatives

The representative does not have to be an officer or director of the organization, does not need to be the most knowledgeable person about the listed topics, and in fact does not even need to be employed by the organization. Instead, the company has a duty to make a conscientious, good-faith effort to designate a representative capable of testifying regarding the designated topics. Regardless of the status of the representative, however, the representative's testimony will be admissible against the organization and the organization must prepare the representative to testify as to the organization's collective knowledge and information. If no single individual can provide the corporation's testimony as to all the designated topics, the corporation must name more than one representative.

Duty to Confer

The 2020 amendment to Rule 30(b)(6) imposed a requirement that the party serving the deposition notice or subpoena and the organization to be deposed by designated representative confer about the topics for the deposition before or promptly after service. The objective of this conference is to make the deposition more effective and efficient and to minimize disputes. Ideally, the discussion will lead to clarity and focus for the topics and better selection and preparation of the designated representative(s).

Deposition of Specific High-Ranking Individual

To depose a specific officer, director, or managing agent of an organization, a party should not use Rule 30(b)(6), which allows the recipient to pick the deponent; rather, a party should serve a notice of deposition indicating that the individual's testimony is sought in the individual's official capacity.

Sanctions Against Organization

If the designated representative fails to appear for the deposition, the corporation or organization is subject to sanctions. Likewise, if a designated representative cannot answer questions squarely within the topics listed in the notice of deposition, then the corporation has failed to comply with its obligations under the rule and may be subject to sanctions. The organization can also be sanctioned for failing to designate a representative.

Scope of Testimony

The scope of testimony in a Rule 30(b)(6) deposition is controlled by two considerations. Like any discovery, the testimony is limited by the scope of discovery considerations in Rule 26(b)(1), such as privilege, relevance to a claim or defense in the case, and proportionality, and the limitations in the remaining subsections of Rule 26(b). Additionally, the scope of testimony is affected by the topics listed in the deposition notice. As to those topics, the representative(s) must testify to all matters known or reasonably available to the organization regarding the designated topics, which may necessitate gathering documents and interviewing witnesses and having the individual(s) review and become familiar with the documents and information. Thus, the representative will often testify to matters outside the representative's personal knowledge.

Duty to Prepare

The organization has a duty to gather the information and prepare the representative(s) so that the representatives can give complete, knowledgeable, and binding testimony

Effect of Testimony

Testimony by a Rule 30(b)(6) representative regarding the designated topics is the testimony of the organization and has the effect of an evidentiary admission that may be controverted or explained by the party.

RULE 30(c) Examination and Cross-Examination; Record of the Examination; Objections; Written Questions

In general, the examination of witnesses at a deposition proceeds much like at trial, except that many objections are reserved until the testimony is offered into evidence. Objections to questions must be stated in a non-suggestive and nonargumentative manner.

PRACTICING LAW UNDER THIS SUBPART

Oath or Affirmation

The officer will put the witness under oath or affirmation at the beginning of the deposition.

Examination

Examination proceeds as at trial and subject to the Federal Rules of Evidence, with direct examination and cross-examination, except that examination proceeds irrespective of objections. Unlike trial, cross-examination is not limited to matters raised on direct, although the admission at trial of the deposition transcript may be limited on that basis. Because no judge is present to rule on objections, the witness answers each question even if there is an objection unless instructed not to answer by counsel (which is only authorized in very narrow circumstances, as described below).

Objections to Questions

Some objections to questions must be raised at the time of the deposition or they are waived, others are reserved until trial. The way to determine whether an objection must be made is to determine whether the examiner could rephrase the question to cure the objection. Thus, parties must object to leading questions in order to give the examiner an opportunity to ask the question in a non-leading fashion. Conversely, parties do not need to raise objections such as relevancy or competency that cannot be cured.

Stating Objections

Objections must be stated in a non-suggestive manner. Attorneys should not use an objection to instruct the witnesses how to answer (or not answer) a question. However, the specific nature of the objection should be stated so that the court later can rule on the objection (*e.g.,* "objection, leading" or "objection, lack of foundation").

Answering After Objections to Questions

After an objection to the nature of a question, the witness answers the question subject to the objection. The court then rules on any objections at the time the testimony is offered into evidence or otherwise proffered to the court. The only exception to this procedure is if an attorney gives an instruction not to answer a question, as discussed below.

Instruction Not to Answer

An instruction to a witness not to answer a question is only allowed in three narrow circumstances: to claim a privilege (*e.g.*, attorney-client communication); to enforce a court order limiting the scope or length of the deposition; or to suspend the deposition for purposes of filing a motion under Rule 30(d)(3) relating to improper conduct. Thus, it is inappropriate for counsel to instruct a witness not to answer a question on the basis of relevance, or on the basis that the question has been asked and answered, is harassing, or is outside the areas of inquiry identified in the notice of deposition for a Rule 30(b)(6) deposition of a party representative. If an attorney improperly instructs a witness not to respond to a question, sanctions are available under Rule 30(d)(2).

RULE 30(d) Duration; Sanction; Motion to Terminate or Limit

A deposition is limited to 7 hours during 1 day, absent a stipulation or court order. If a witness or lawyer engages in unreasonable or vexatious conduct during a deposition, the court may impose appropriate sanctions including the expenses caused by such conduct, including attorney's fees.

PRACTICING LAW UNDER THIS SUBPART

Motion to Extend Time

A party may file a motion to extend or reduce the 1-day, 7-hour limitation for specified depositions or for the case in general. The court must allow additional time if needed for a "fair examination" of the witness or if the examination has been impeded or delayed by another person or by circumstances.

Motion to Terminate or Limit Deposition

A party may move to limit the time of or terminate a deposition. In order to prevail, the moving party must demonstrate that the examination was being conducted in bad faith or in an unreasonably annoying, embarrassing, or oppressive manner.

Sanctions for Impediment or Delay

If a party, attorney, or witness engages in conduct that unreasonably impedes, delays, or otherwise frustrates a deposition, the court may, upon motion or *sua sponte*, impose an "appropriate sanction" on the person engaging in the obstructive behavior. A common sanction is a second deposition of the witness, but the court has broad discretion and may even dismiss the case. The court may also impose the reasonable expenses and attorney's fees caused by the behavior on the offending person.

Suspension of Deposition

A party desiring to make a motion to terminate or limit the deposition may suspend the deposition for the period of time necessary to make the motion.

RULE 30(e) Review by the Witness; Changes

The opportunity to review and correct the transcript is available upon timely request. Typically, at the end of the deposition, the officer will ask the witness whether the witness wants to read and review the transcript or waive that right.

PRACTICING LAW UNDER THIS SUBPART

Submission of Changes

If a review is requested, the court reporter will make the deposition transcript available to the witness, typically by sending a copy to the witness to review. The witness must submit an errata statement describing any changes within 30 days. The statement should state the reasons for the changes and be signed by the witness.

Changes in Form

Changes in form, such as typographic errors, are entered into the transcript with an explanation as to the reason for the change.

Changes in Substance

The courts vary as to whether and when they will allow a witness to make changes in the substance of the testimony, which are also entered into the transcript with an explanation as to the reason for the change. With changes in substance, the deposition can be reconvened to explore the basis for the substantive change. A deponent who changes the answers may be impeached with the former answers. Some courts do not allow substantive changes when they view the changes as an attempt to create issues of fact to prevent summary judgment, sometimes referred to as the "sham affidavit" rule.

RULE 30(f) Certification and Delivery; Exhibits; Copies of the Transcript or Recording; Filing

The officer must certify that the witness was duly sworn and that the deposition transcript was a true record of the testimony given by the deponent.

PRACTICING LAW UNDER THIS SUBPART

Filing of Transcript

Ordinarily, deposition transcripts should not be filed. However, under Rule 5(d), once a deposition is used in a proceeding, the attorney must file it.

Copies of the Transcript

Any party or the deponent can purchase a copy of the recording of the deposition.

Exhibits

Upon the request of a party, a document produced or used at a deposition may be marked for identification and annexed to the deposition transcript.

RULE 30(g) Failure to Attend a Deposition or Serve a Subpoena; Expenses

The court may award expenses, including attorney's fees, to a party that appears for a deposition that does not occur because either: (1) the party noticing the deposition does not attend; or (2) the party fails to subpoena a witness and that witness does not appear.

RULE 31

DEPOSITIONS BY WRITTEN QUESTIONS

(a) When a Deposition May Be Taken.

(1) *Without Leave.* A party may, by written questions, depose any person, including a party, without leave of court except as provided in Rule 31(a)(2). The deponent's attendance may be compelled by subpoena under Rule 45.

(2) *With Leave.* A party must obtain leave of court, and the court must grant leave to the extent consistent with Rule 26(b)(1) and (2):

(A) if the parties have not stipulated to the deposition and:

(i) the deposition would result in more than 10 depositions being taken under this rule or Rule 30 by the plaintiffs, or by the defendants, or by the third-party defendants;

(ii) the deponent has already been deposed in the case; or (iii) the party seeks to take a deposition before the time specified in Rule 26(d); or

(B) if the deponent is confined in prison.

(3) *Service; Required Notice.* A party who wants to depose a person by written questions must serve them on every other party, with a notice stating, if known, the deponent's name and address. If the name is unknown, the notice must provide a general description sufficient to identify the person or the particular class or group to which the person belongs. The notice must also state the name or descriptive title and the address of the officer before whom the deposition will be taken.

(4) *Questions Directed to an Organization.* A public or private corporation, a partnership, an association, or a governmental agency may be deposed by written questions in accordance with Rule 30(b)(6).

(5) *Questions from Other Parties.* Any questions to the deponent from other parties must be served on all parties as follows: cross-questions, within 14 days after being served with the notice and direct questions; redirect questions, within 7 days after being served with cross-questions; and recross-questions, within 7 days after being served with redirect questions. The court may, for good cause, extend or shorten these times.

(b) Delivery to the Officer; Officer's Duties. The party who noticed the deposition must deliver to the officer a copy of all the questions served and of the notice. The officer must promptly proceed in the manner provided in Rule 30(c), (e), and (f) to:

(1) take the deponent's testimony in response to the questions;

(2) prepare and certify the deposition; and

(3) send it to the party, attaching a copy of the questions and of the notice.

(c) Notice of Completion or Filing.

(1) *Completion.* The party who noticed the deposition must notify all other parties when it is completed.

(2) *Filing.* A party who files the deposition must promptly notify all other parties of the filing.

[Amended March 30, 1970, effective July 1, 1970; March 2, 1987, effective August 1, 1987; April 22, 1993, effective December 1, 1993; April 30, 2007, effective December 1, 2007; April 29, 2015, effective December 1, 2015.]

UNDERSTANDING RULE 31

HOW RULE 31 FITS IN

A deposition is a procedure in which a witness—party or nonparty—appears in a conference room or similar location, is placed under oath, and then answers questions posed by the lawyers involved in the proceeding. The lawyers typically pose their questions orally under Rule 30, but may also pose their questions in writing under Rule 31.

Depositions by written questions are rarely used, and their only advantage seems to be that they may be less expensive and burdensome than depositions by oral question. The most common use of depositions by written question may be as a court-ordered alternative for a deposition by oral questions when there is an objection to the oral deposition. Because depositions by written question under Rule 31 are so infrequent, whereas depositions by oral question under Rule 30 are routine, please see the discussion of Rule 30 for a fuller explanation of depositions generally.

THE ARCHITECTURE OF RULE 31

Rule 31 contains three subparts. Rule 31(a) addresses when a party may schedule a deposition on its own and when it needs leave of court. Rule 31(a) also sets forth the requirements for a deposition notice, and authorizes parties to take the deposition by written questions of a designated representative of a corporation or other organization under the provisions of Rule 30(b)(6). Finally, Rule 31(a)(5) authorizes other parties to submit their own written questions and establishes the schedule for doing so.

Rule 31(b) requires the parties to submit their written questions to the officer who will be present at the deposition, and specifies the duties of that officer to take the witness's testimony and to prepare, certify, and distribute the transcript. Lastly, Rule 31(c) obligates the party who noticed the deposition to notify all other parties of the completion of the deposition, and obligates any party who files the deposition to notify all other parties.

HOW RULE 31 WORKS IN PRACTICE

RULE 31(a) When a Deposition May Be Taken

In general, a party may take the deposition (by oral or written questions) of up to 10 witnesses, party or otherwise, at any time after the parties have conducted the discovery conference under Rule 26(f) and before the discovery deadline (typically set in the court's Case Management Order). A party may only depose each witness one time, absent a stipulation or court order otherwise. Depositions by written questions are commenced by sending the questions and a deposition notice to the witness (with a copy to all parties). If the witness is a non-party, the noticing party must also serve a subpoena on the witness under Rule 45. Parties may also take the depositions by written question of a designated representative of a corporation, and the provisions of Rule 30(b)(6) apply.

Once one party has noticed a deposition by written questions, other parties may submit additional "cross-questions" within 14 days. The noticing party may then submit "redirect questions" within 7 days of receiving the cross-questions, and other parties may serve "recross-questions" within 7 days of receiving the redirect questions.

PRACTICING LAW UNDER THIS SUBPART

Notice

A party seeking to take a deposition by written questions must serve a notice on all other parties stating the name and address of the deponent, if known, or a general description sufficient to identify the deponent and providing the name or title and address of the stenographer or officer before whom the deposition will be taken.

Timing of Notice

The notice of written deposition may be served at any time after the parties have conducted the discovery conference under Rule 26(f), or earlier with leave of court. The latest time to conduct a deposition upon written questions will be governed by the court's scheduling order.

Number of Depositions

The plaintiffs as a group are limited to 10 depositions total, without distinction between written and oral examination, as are the defendants and the third-party defendants. This number may be increased or decreased by stipulation or by order of court.

Scope of Questions

The scope of the written deposition questions is the same as oral questions, and is controlled by Rule 26.

Corporate Representative

A party may require a corporation or organization to designate a representative to respond to the questions, as described in detail above under Rule 30(b)(6).

Objections

Objections to the form of a written question (*e.g.*, because it is leading) must be served in writing upon the party serving the question within the time for serving succeeding questions and within 7 days of the last questions authorized.

RULE 31(b) Delivery to the Officer; Officer's Duties

Once all the questions have been served, the party initiating the deposition provides all the questions to the deposition officer. The officer then promptly takes the deposition by reading the questions and recording the answers. A transcript is then prepared and submitted to the witness as provided in Rule 30 governing oral depositions.

RULE 31(c) Notice of Completion or Filing

When the deposition has been completed, the party who noticed the deposition must provide notice to all other parties. Local rules usually determine whether the officer files a sealed transcript with the court. If so, the party noticing the deposition must promptly give notice of the filing of the transcript to all other parties.

RULE 32

USING DEPOSITIONS IN COURT PROCEEDINGS

(a) Using Depositions.

(1) *In General.* At a hearing or trial, all or part of a deposition may be used against a party on these conditions:

(A) the party was present or represented at the taking of the deposition or had reasonable notice of it;

(B) it is used to the extent it would be admissible under the Federal Rules of Evidence if the deponent were present and testifying; and

(C) the use is allowed by Rule 32(a)(2) through (8).

(2) *Impeachment and Other Uses.* Any party may use a deposition to contradict or impeach the testimony given by the deponent as a witness, or for any other purpose allowed by the Federal Rules of Evidence.

(3) *Deposition of Party, Agent, or Designee.* An adverse party may use for any purpose the deposition of a party or anyone who, when deposed, was the party's officer, director, managing agent, or designee under Rule 30(b)(6) or 31(a)(4).

(4) *Unavailable Witness.* A party may use for any purpose the deposition of a witness, whether or not a party, if the court finds:

(A) that the witness is dead;

(B) that the witness is more than 100 miles from the place of hearing or trial or is outside the United States, unless it appears that the witness's absence was procured by the party offering the deposition;

(C) that the witness cannot attend or testify because of age, illness, infirmity, or imprisonment;

(D) that the party offering the deposition could not procure the witness's attendance by subpoena; or

(E) on motion and notice, that exceptional circumstances make it desirable—in the interest of justice and with due regard to the importance of live testimony in open court—to permit the deposition to be used.

(5) *Limitations on Use.*

(A) *Deposition Taken on Short Notice.* A deposition must not be used against a party who, having received less than 14 days' notice of the deposition, promptly moved for a protective order under Rule 26(c)(1)(B) requesting that it not be taken or be taken at a different time or place—and this motion was still pending when the deposition was taken.

(B) *Unavailable Deponent; Party Could Not Obtain an Attorney.* A deposition taken without leave of court under the unavailability provision of Rule 30(a)(2)(A)(iii) must not be used against a party who shows that, when served with the notice, it could not, despite diligent efforts, obtain an attorney to represent it at the deposition.

(6) *Using Part of a Deposition.* If a party offers in evidence only part of a deposition, an adverse party may require the offeror to introduce other parts that in fairness should be considered with the part introduced, and any party may itself introduce any other parts.

(7) *Substituting a Party.* Substituting a party under Rule 25 does not affect the right to use a deposition previously taken.

(8) *Deposition Taken in an Earlier Action.* A deposition lawfully taken and, if required, filed in any federal- or State-court action may be used in a later action involving the same subject matter between the same parties, or their representatives or successors in interest, to the same extent as if taken in the later action. A deposition previously taken may also be used as allowed by the Federal Rules of Evidence.

(b) Objections to Admissibility. Subject to Rules 28(b) and 32(d)(3), an objection may be made at a hearing or trial to the admission of any deposition testimony that would be inadmissible if the witness were present and testifying.

(c) Form of Presentation. Unless the court orders otherwise, a party must provide a transcript of any deposition testimony the party offers, but may provide the court with the testimony in nontranscript form as well. On any party's request, deposition testimony offered in a jury trial for any purpose other than impeachment must be presented in nontranscript form, if available, unless the court for good cause orders otherwise.

(d) Waiver of Objections.

(1) *To the Notice.* An objection to an error or irregularity in a deposition notice is waived unless promptly served in writing on the party giving the notice.

(2) *To the Officer's Qualification.* An objection based on disqualification of the officer before whom a deposition is to be taken is waived if not made:

(A) before the deposition begins; or

(B) promptly after the basis for disqualification becomes known or, with reasonable diligence, could have been known.

(3) *To the Taking of the Deposition.*

(A) *Objection to Competence, Relevance, or Materiality.* An objection to a deponent's competence—or to the competence, relevance, or materiality of testimony—is not waived by a failure to make the objection before or during the deposition, unless the ground for it might have been corrected at that time.

(B) *Objection to an Error or Irregularity.* An objection to an error or irregularity at an oral examination is waived if:

(i) it relates to the manner of taking the deposition, the form of a question or answer, the oath or affirmation, a party's conduct, or other matters that might have been corrected at that time; and

(ii) it is not timely made during the deposition.

(C) *Objection to a Written Question.* An objection to the form of a written question under Rule 31 is waived if not served in writing on the party submitting the question within the time for serving responsive questions or, if the question is a recross-question, within 7 days after being served with it.

(4) *To Completing and Returning the Deposition.* An objection to how the officer transcribed the testimony—or prepared, signed, certified, sealed, endorsed, sent, or otherwise dealt with the deposition—is waived unless a motion to suppress is made promptly after the error or irregularity becomes known or, with reasonable diligence, could have been known.

[Amended March 30, 1970, effective July 1, 1970; November 20, 1972, effective July 1, 1975; April 29, 1980, effective August 1, 1980; March 2, 1987, effective August 1, 1987; April 22, 1993, effective December 1, 1993; April 30, 2007, effective December 1, 2007; March 26, 2009, effective December 1, 2009.]

UNDERSTANDING RULE 32

HOW RULE 32 FITS IN

Rules 27, 28, 30, and 31 control the way you arrange for and conduct a deposition. Once the deposition is over and has been transcribed or recorded, what can you do with it? Rule 32 answers that question. The Rules generally favor live testimony—where the witness appears in court and testifies. With that policy in mind, Rule 32 makes a distinction between two types of use: use of the deposition to "impeach" a witness; and use of the deposition for other purposes, such as to prove the facts that are disputed in the lawsuit.

Impeaching a witness, in this context, means attacking the witness's credibility by demonstrating that the witness testified differently at the deposition from how the witness is testifying at the trial. For example, if a witness testifies at a deposition that the light was red at the time of an accident, then testifies at trial that the light was green, the attorney for another party can introduce the prior inconsistent deposition testimony. Although the witness likely would have an opportunity to explain the inconsistency, it potentially makes the witness seem uncertain or untruthful. Because the witness who is being impeached is testifying live at trial, Rule 32 generally allows use of a deposition for impeachment as long as the deposition was properly noticed and conducted.

If a party wants to use a deposition for purposes other than impeachment—generally as a substitute for live testimony—Rule 32 imposes additional restrictions. A deposition may be used for any purpose—not just impeachment—in two circumstances: 1) if the witness was a party and the person seeking to use the deposition is an adverse party; or 2) if the witness is "unavailable," such as dead, incapacitated, or so far away that the witness cannot be subpoenaed to testify live. Using the above example, if a party wanted to use the deposition transcript, not to impeach a witness but to prove the light was red, the party could only do so if the deposition witness was a party or was unavailable.

Note that the requirements and restrictions in Rule 32 are in addition to those in the Federal Rules of Evidence. Thus, the use deposition testimony must comply with both Rule 32 and the applicable Federal Rules of Evidence.

Rule 32 also contains a provision protecting against the use of a misleading excerpt of a deposition. If one party introduces only part of a deposition, other parties may compel the offering party to also introduce other parts that, in fairness, should be considered along with the part that was introduced. Returning to our example, if the witness testified at the deposition that, "When I looked, the light was red. However, I only looked after I heard the accident." and one party only offered the first sentence, another party could require that the second sentence be introduced into evidence at the same time. Note that the timing is significant—normally, the other party would have to wait until its turn to question that witness, after the first party was finished, to introduce portions of the deposition it wanted the jury to hear, perhaps after the jury had formed initial impressions that might be difficult to change. Rule 32 prevents that prejudice by allowing the jury to hear the entire context at one time.

Remember from Rule 30 that some objections are raised at the time of the deposition and others are reserved. Rule 32 addresses the manner in which parties may present, and the court will rule on, objections to deposition testimony. It also provides that certain objections are waived if not properly presented.

THE ARCHITECTURE OF RULE 32

The core content of Rule 32—the provisions controlling the manner in which a party may use deposition testimony—is found in Rule 32(a). Rule 32(a) is chock full of content, and contains eight subparts. Rule 32(a)(1) covers general rules applying to any use of a deposition, such as the recognition that the deposition must also be admissible under the Federal Rules of Evidence. Rules 32(a)(2)–(4) set forth the conditions under which a party may use a deposition for impeachment and for other purposes. Rule 32(a)(5) contains protections limiting use of depositions taken with short notice. Rule 32(a)(6) authorizes other parties to require introduction of other, related portions of a deposition to provide context and ensure fairness. Rule 32(a)(7) ensures that substitution of parties does not prevent use of a deposition. Finally, Rule 32(a)(8) sets forth the conditions under which a party may use a deposition from a prior action.

Rules 32(b) and (d) address objections to the use of deposition testimony. Rule 32(b) clarifies that a party may make any objections to the admission of deposition testimony that the party could make if the witness were present and testifying live. Rule 32(d) governs waiver of objections to the deposition, including objections to the notice, to the officer's qualifications, and to the manner in which the deposition testimony was taken. It works hand-in-hand with Rule 30(c), which requires certain objections to be asserted during the deposition, and allows others to be raised at the time a party attempts to use the deposition under Rule 32.

Lastly, Rule 32(c) controls the form in which parties may, or must, present deposition testimony when they are attempting to use it. It requires parties to provide the court with a transcript of the deposition testimony they are introducing, even if they intend to introduce it in another form, such as a videorecording. This provision, among other things, facilitates the court's ruling on objections and other uses of the testimony.

HOW RULE 32 WORKS IN PRACTICE

RULE 32(a) Using Depositions

Although one purpose of a deposition is to gather facts and learn about the case, another purpose is to create a transcript and, sometimes, a videorecording, to be used at later stages of the litigation. Deposition testimony can be used to support a motion, at a hearing, or at trial, and Rule 32(a) establishes the rules for such use.

PRACTICING LAW UNDER THIS SUBPART

General Requirements for Using a Deposition

Rule 32 establishes a three-part test for admissibility of deposition testimony that the party seeking to introduce the testimony must satisfy:

(1) The party against whom the testimony is offered was present at, represented at, or had reasonable notice of, the deposition;

(2) The testimony is otherwise admissible under the Federal Rules of Evidence; and

(3) The testimony is admissible under the provisions in Rule 32(a)(2)–(8), which allows testimony for impeachment, testimony of an adverse party, and testimony of an unavailable witness.

Use for Impeachment

A deposition may always be used to impeach or contradict a witness (if the three general requirements above are met). A party may use a deposition to impeach the party's own witness, if permitted by the applicable rules of evidence.

Use for Substantive Purposes

The deposition of an adverse party may be used as substantive evidence (to prove or disprove a fact). This principle applies to a party organization's officers, directors, and managing agents, and to representatives designated under Rule 30(b)(6). The deposition of an unavailable nonparty witness may be used as substantive, non-impeachment evidence if the party seeking to introduce the testimony establishes one of the following five conditions:

(A) The witness is dead;

(B) The witness is more than 100 miles from the courthouse (measured "as the crow flies") or outside the United States, unless it appears that the party offering the testimony procured the absence of the witness;

(C) The deponent is unable to attend trial because of age, sickness, infirmity, or imprisonment;

(D) The party offering the deposition was unable to procure the deponent's attendance at trial by subpoena despite the use of reasonable diligence; or

(E) Exceptional other circumstances. For example, a court might admit the deposition testimony of a witness who refused to testify at trial by invoking a privilege. Note, however, that the general policy favoring live testimony leads to a restrictive reading of this "catchall" clause.

Must Comply with Rules of Evidence

Even if the criteria in Rule 32 for use of a deposition have been satisfied, the deposition must still be admissible under the Federal Rules of Evidence. The rules of evidence are applied as though the deponent were present and testifying. Thus, the effect of Rule 32 is to negate the hearsay objection.

Use of Part of a Deposition

If a party introduces only part of a deposition, any adverse party may require the offering party to introduce additional parts necessary to clarify the offered text. Such adverse parties have the right to have the additional text introduced immediately following the admission of the offered testimony.

Deposition Taken in Another Matter

A party may use a deposition transcript from another matter if the other matter involves the same subject matter between the same parties (or persons in privity with the parties), or if the use is otherwise authorized by the Federal Rules of Evidence. The proposed use of the transcript still must comply with the other provisions of Rule 32 and with the Federal Rules of Evidence. Thus, for example, a party may only use the deposition of a nonparty witness taken from another matter if the witness is unavailable.

Against Whom/Reasonable Notice

The deposition may be used against any party who was present or represented at, or had reasonable notice of, the deposition. A deposition cannot be used against a party who received less than 14 days' notice and who had filed a motion for a protective order that was pending at the time of the deposition.

Discovery Depositions vs. Depositions for Use at Trial

Rule 32 does not draw any distinctions between depositions taken for discovery purposes and those taken "for use at trial."

RULE 32(b) Objections to Admissibility

Deposition testimony may not be introduced if the testimony would not be admissible if the witness were present and testifying live.

RULE 32(c) Form of Presentation

A party offering nonstenographic forms of deposition testimony—such as videorecorded testimony—must also provide a transcript to the court. Note that the party must also have provided a transcript to all other parties in advance of trial under Rule 26. In a jury trial, any party may require that depositions be offered in nonstenographic form if available, unless the deposition is being used for impeachment or the court orders otherwise for good cause shown.

RULE 32(d) Waiver of Objections

Objections to the procedures at a deposition must be asserted as soon as practicable or they are waived. Objections to questions are governed by the provisions in Rules 30 and 31, such that objections that may be cured by rephrasing the question must be asserted at the time of the deposition, and all other objections are reserved until a party seeks to use the deposition.

PRACTICING LAW UNDER THIS SUBPART

Defects in Procedures

Objections to the notice must be made in writing to the party issuing the notice, unless there was no opportunity to object. Objections as to the manner of the oath or affirmation administered must be made at the time of the deposition or they are waived. Objections to the qualifications of the officer must be made before the start of the deposition or they are waived. Objections as to the manner of transcription or as to the procedures used in correcting and signing the transcript must be made in the form of a motion to suppress, which must be made with "reasonable promptness" after the defect is discovered or should have been discovered with due diligence.

Objections to Questions

Objections that can be cured by rephrasing the question, such as leading question objections, must be raised at the deposition (or served in writing, for depositions by written questions under Rule 31) or they are waived. All other objections, such as relevance, hearsay, capacity, competence, etc., are reserved until the testimony is offered.

RULE 33

INTERROGATORIES TO PARTIES

(a) In General.

(1) *Number.* Unless otherwise stipulated or ordered by the court, a party may serve on any other party no more than 25 written interrogatories, including all discrete subparts. Leave to serve additional interrogatories may be granted to the extent consistent with Rule 26(b)(1) and (2).

(2) *Scope.* An interrogatory may relate to any matter that may be inquired into under Rule 26(b). An interrogatory is not objectionable merely because it asks for an opinion or contention that relates to fact or the application of law to fact, but the court may order that the interrogatory need not be answered until designated discovery is complete, or until a pretrial conference or some other time.

(b) Answers and Objections.

(1) *Responding Party.* The interrogatories must be answered:

(A) by the party to whom they are directed; or

(B) if that party is a public or private corporation, a partnership, an association, or a governmental agency, by any officer or agent, who must furnish the information available to the party.

(2) *Time to Respond.* The responding party must serve its answers and any objections within 30 days after being served with the interrogatories. A shorter or longer time may be stipulated to under Rule 29 or be ordered by the court.

(3) *Answering Each Interrogatory.* Each interrogatory must, to the extent it is not objected to, be answered separately and fully in writing under oath.

(4) *Objections.* The grounds for objecting to an interrogatory must be stated with specificity. Any ground not stated in a timely objection is waived unless the court, for good cause, excuses the failure.

(5) *Signature.* The person who makes the answers must sign them, and the attorney who objects must sign any objections.

(c) Use. An answer to an interrogatory may be used to the extent allowed by the Federal Rules of Evidence.

(d) Option to Produce Business Records. If the answer to an interrogatory may be determined by examining, auditing, compiling, abstracting, or summarizing a party's business records (including electronically stored information), and if the burden of deriving or ascertaining the answer will be substantially the same for either party, the responding party may answer by:

(1) specifying the records that must be reviewed, in sufficient detail to enable the interrogating party to locate and identify them as readily as the responding party could; and

(2) giving the interrogating party a reasonable opportunity to examine and audit the records and to make copies, compilations, abstracts, or summaries.

[Amended December 27, 1946, effective March 19, 1948; March 30, 1970, effective July 1, 1970; April 29, 1980, effective August 1, 1980; April 22, 1993, effective December 1, 1993; April 12, 2006, effective December 1, 2006; April 30, 2007, effective December 1, 2007; April 29, 2015, effective December 1, 2015.]

UNDERSTANDING RULE 33

HOW RULE 33 FITS IN

An interrogatory is a written question that one party may send to another during the discovery process. Each party is limited to 25 interrogatories, unless the parties or court agree to a different limit. Interrogatories may pose purely factual questions or may ask questions that blend fact and law (sometimes called "contention interrogatories"). Parties have a right to send interrogatories, and do not need to ask for permission from the court.

The recipient must respond within 30 days, although stipulated extensions are common. The response often consists of a mixture of objections and substantive responses. The attorney is responsible for the objections, and the attorney's signature certifies under Rule 26(g) that the objections are made in good faith. The party must sign a verification attesting to the accuracy of the factual responses—this is one of the few places where the federal rules require such a verification.

Rule 33 does not contain any details about how other parties may use interrogatory responses. Rather, the use of the interrogatory responses is controlled by the Federal Rules of Evidence. In general, though, an interrogatory response may be used against the party that made the response, but is not a binding admission; if the party testifies inconsistently with the interrogatory response, opposing parties may use the response for impeachment but the party may attempt to explain the inconsistency.

Sometimes, interrogatories request detailed information that is located in documents held by the responding party. If that is the case, the responding party may refer the requesting party to the documents instead of drafting a substantive response. However, the responding party may only take advantage of this option if the information is actually located in the documents and the burden would be substantially the same for either party to analyze the documents and extract the information.

THE ARCHITECTURE OF RULE 33

Rule 33 has a straightforward structure, with four subsections. Rules 33(a) and (b) contain the general provisions for propounding and responding to interrogatories. Rule 33(a) provides the details for drafting and sending interrogatories. It sets the limit on the number of interrogatories and defines the permissible scope of the interrogatories. Rule 33(b) contains the corresponding obligations of the responding party. It establishes who must respond, sets the time for responding, contains provisions regarding objections, and describes who must sign the responses. Rule 33(c) directs lawyers to the Federal Rules of Evidence to determine permissible uses of interrogatory responses. Finally, Rule 33(d) establishes the option to produce documents in lieu of drafting a response.

HOW RULE 33 WORKS IN PRACTICE

RULE 33(a) In General

Any party may serve up to 25 interrogatories or questions on any other party. The scope of interrogatories is the broad discovery available under Rule 26.

PRACTICING LAW UNDER THIS SUBPART

Who May Be Served

Interrogatories are limited to parties to the action, although the party need not be an adverse party. If the party is a corporation, interrogatories should be addressed to the corporation, not to a corporate officer or the attorney. In class actions, the courts are split as to whether only the named representatives can be served.

Time for Service

Interrogatories can be served after the parties have conducted the discovery conference under Rule 26(f), or earlier with leave of court. The Rules do not set an outer limit on how late in the case interrogatories may be served, but many local rules or case management orders will set such a limit. Usually, when such a deadline exists, interrogatories must be served so that the answers are due before the deadline.

Number

Each party may serve up to 25 interrogatories on each other party. This limit may be adjusted pursuant to a court order or stipulation. Note that parties may coordinate to maximize their allowable interrogatories. For example, in a case with multiple plaintiffs, they may divide up topics, effectively expanding the number of interrogatories that may be served on each defendant. If an interrogatory has subparts, each subpart may count as a separate interrogatory if it is really a discrete question.

Scope of Questions

The scope of interrogatories is controlled by Rule 26(b). The information sought must be relevant to the claims or defenses in the case and proportional to the needs of the case, but need not be admissible evidence. Privileged information is not discoverable, and discovery is limited with respect to expert witnesses and trial preparation materials as discussed in Rule 26(b).

Opinions or Contentions

Rule 33 authorizes interrogatories that seek an opinion or contention that relates to fact or the application of law to fact. However, the court may order that a contention interrogatory not be answered until discovery is complete or until after the pre-trial conference is held. An interrogatory that asks for a pure legal conclusion, without application to the facts, is improper.

Form

Parties have a great deal of latitude in framing interrogatories, as long as the responding party can reasonably determine the information to include in the answer. Only rarely will a question be so ambiguous that it does not require an answer, although the responding party can limit the scope of its answer.

RULE 33(b) Answers and Objections

The responding party must answer interrogatories separately and in writing within 30 days after service. Objections must be stated with specificity, and objections are waived if not made timely. The responding party must sign the answers and the attorney must sign any objections.

PRACTICING LAW UNDER THIS SUBPART

Answers

Each interrogatory must be answered separately and fully in writing unless an objection is interposed in lieu of an answer. The answer must include all information within the party's possession, custody, or control or known by the party's agents. This includes *facts* in an attorney's possession and information supplied to the party by others. At the same time, a party does not have to obtain publicly available information not in its possession, custody, or control. If the party has no such information within its possession, custody, or control, the answer may so state. If only some information is available, that information must be provided, and may be prefaced with a statement placing the answer in context. The responding party must serve the answers on all other parties.

Time to Answer

Answers and objections are due within 30 days of service. Extensions of this deadline are quite common, typically by an informal email exchange, and may also be extended by order of court. Failure to serve a response in a timely manner may constitute a waiver of all objections.

Who Answers

Technically, the party must answer the interrogatories, not the party's attorney (although it is common practice for the attorney to draft the answers). The attorney interposes the objections. If the party is a corporation or organization, an officer or agent will answer for the corporation. The answering officer or agent need not have first-hand knowledge of the information being provided. However, the responding agent's answers must provide the composite knowledge available to the party.

Verification

Interrogatory answers must include a signed verification or affidavit attesting to the accuracy of the answers. When the party is an individual, the party, not the attorney, must sign the verification. This is one of the few exceptions to the general principle under the Federal Rules of Civil Procedure that the attorney may sign all pleadings and papers. A representative of a corporate party may verify interrogatory answers without personal knowledge of every response by furnishing the information available to the corporation. The courts generally allow an attorney to verify interrogatory answers for a corporation. If the responding party makes objections, the attorney must sign the response.

Objections

If the responding party believes that a particular interrogatory is outside the scope of discovery or otherwise improper, the party may object to the question in lieu of answering it or in conjunction with an answer that takes the objection into account. The objection must be made in writing, must state the grounds of the objection with specificity, and must be signed by the attorney for the responding party. Many courts hold that general or boilerplate objections are ineffective. Some common objections are:

- *Overly broad, unduly vague, and ambiguous:* When a question is written so broadly that it extends to information not relevant to the claims or defenses in the matter (such as a question not limited in time to the events relevant to the complaint), the question may be overly broad. When a question is susceptible to numerous meanings, it may be unduly vague and ambiguous. In general, these objections are probably not justification for refusing to answer a question altogether, but the responding party can raise the objection, then expressly limit the scope of the response.
- *Burdensome and oppressive:* In general, the responding party must produce the information available without *undue* effort or expense (recognizing that all discovery responses require *some* effort and expense). Thus, questions that require extensive research, compilation of data, or evaluation of data may be objectionable. The responding party is not required to prepare the adverse party's case. Likewise, an interrogatory that seeks a high level of detail may be overly burdensome.
- *Privileged information:* Questions that seek information protected by the attorney-client privilege or by another privilege are objectionable. When privileged information is withheld, the responding party must explicitly state the objection and describe the nature of the information not provided sufficiently to enable other parties to assess the applicability of the privilege. Care should be exercised in responding to such interrogatories, because the privilege may be waived by revealing part or all of the privileged communication.
- *Non-discoverable expert information:* Rule 26(b)(4) limits the scope of discovery directed towards experts. It generally requires the responding party to provide an expert report for each expert it may call as a witness, and thereafter allows other parties to depose such experts. Further discovery with respect to such witnesses is available only upon motion. Rule 26(b)(4)(B) does not allow any discovery with respect to experts not intended to be called as witnesses, absent "exceptional circumstances."
- *Not proportional to the needs of the case:* A party may object that an interrogatory seeks information that is not proportional to the needs of the case, in light of the factors listed in Rule 26(b)(1).

Failure to Object Is Waiver

All grounds for objection must be specifically stated in a timely response or they are waived, unless excused by the court for good cause shown.

Objection to Part of Interrogatory

If only part of an interrogatory is objectionable, the responding party must answer the interrogatory to the extent that it is not objectionable. Thus, if an interrogatory is overly broad, the responding party should provide information responsive to the interrogatory as if narrowed so as not to be overly broad.

Insufficient Answer or Improper Objection

If the responding party fails to answer sufficiently or objects to an interrogatory, the propounding party may file a motion to compel under Rule 37(a).

Failure to Answer

If a party files no response to an interrogatory (as opposed to an insufficient response as discussed above), the court may impose the sanctions specified in Rule 37(b)(2), such as deeming certain facts established or refusing to allow the party to oppose or support certain claims.

Sanctions for Untrue Answers

If an answer is untrue, either at the time it was made or subsequently, and is not corrected by supplementation, the court may exclude certain evidence related to the topic or make whatever order justice requires. The person signing the verification may also be subject to sanctions for making a false verification.

Requests for Documents

Interrogatories may not be used to obtain documents. Rather, a document request must be made under Rule 34. However, interrogatories may inquire about the existence of documents and the facts contained in documents. Furthermore, the responding party may, under certain circumstances, produce documents in lieu of answering an interrogatory, as discussed below under Rule 33(d).

RULE 33(c) Use

Answers to interrogatories may be used at trial or in support of a motion. They are treated like any other evidence and may be offered and admitted into evidence as allowed by the Federal Rules of Evidence. Interrogatory answers are generally not hearsay with respect to the party making the answer because they are party admissions. However, they may be hearsay if offered against another party. Interrogatory answers may be objected to on any other grounds, such as relevance. Interrogatory answers are not binding admissions. Thus, a party can supplement or amend its answers, and even absent an amendment, a party may take a different position at trial unless it would prejudice another party. Opposing parties may then impeach by questioning the reason for the changed answer.

RULE 33(d) Option to Produce Business Records

A party may produce business records in lieu of answering an interrogatory when requested information is located in documents and the burden of extracting the requested information would be substantially equal for either party.

PRACTICING LAW UNDER THIS SUBPART

Business Records Only

Only business records of the responding party may be used in lieu of interrogatory answers. Thus, a party cannot produce pleadings or deposition transcripts or refer to public sources of information instead of answering an interrogatory.

Records Must Contain the Information

In order to respond to an interrogatory by producing business records, a party must affirmatively state that the records contain the requested information; it is not sufficient to state that the records *may* contain the information.

Identify Specific Records

A party responding to an interrogatory by producing business records must provide sufficient detail so that the propounding party can identify which individual documents contain the information requested.

Equal Burden to Derive the Answer

In order to respond to interrogatories by producing business records, the burden of deriving or ascertaining the answer must be substantially equal for the requesting party and the producing party.

RULE 34

PRODUCING DOCUMENTS, ELECTRONICALLY STORED INFORMATION, AND TANGIBLE THINGS, OR ENTERING ONTO LAND, FOR INSPECTION AND OTHER PURPOSES

(a) In General. A party may serve on any other party a request within the scope of Rule 26(b):

(1) to produce and permit the requesting party or its representative to inspect, copy, test, or sample the following items in the responding party's possession, custody, or control:

(A) any designated documents or electronically stored information—including writings, drawings, graphs, charts, photographs, sound recordings, images, and other data or data compilations—stored in any medium from which information can be obtained either directly or, if necessary, after translation by the responding party into a reasonably usable form; or

(B) any designated tangible things; or

(2) to permit entry onto designated land or other property possessed or controlled by the responding party, so that the requesting party may inspect, measure, survey, photograph, test, or sample the property or any designated object or operation on it.

(b) Procedure.

(1) *Contents of the Request.* The request:

(A) must describe with reasonable particularity each item or category of items to be inspected;

(B) must specify a reasonable time, place, and manner for the inspection and for performing the related acts; and

(C) may specify the form or forms in which electronically stored information is to be produced.

(2) *Responses and Objections.*

(A) *Time to Respond.* The party to whom the request is directed must respond in writing within 30 days after being served or—if the request was delivered under Rule 26(d)(2)—within 30 days after the parties' first Rule 26(f) conference. A shorter or longer time may be stipulated to under Rule 29 or be ordered by the court.

(B) *Responding to Each Item.* For each item or category, the response must either state that inspection and related activities will be permitted as requested or state with specificity the grounds for objecting to the request, including the reasons. The responding party may state that it will produce copies of documents or of electronically stored information instead of permitting inspection. The production must then be completed no later than the time for inspection specified in the request or another reasonable time specified in the response.

(C) *Objections.* An objection must state whether any responsive materials are being withheld on the basis of that objection. An objection to part of a request must specify the part and permit inspection of the rest.

(D) *Responding to a Request for Production of Electronically Stored Information.* The response may state an objection to a requested form for producing electronically stored information. If the responding party objects to a requested form—or if no form was specified in the request—the party must state the form or forms it intends to use.

(E) *Producing the Documents or Electronically Stored Information.* Unless otherwise stipulated or ordered by the court, these procedures apply to producing documents or electronically stored information:

(i) A party must produce documents as they are kept in the usual course of business or must organize and label them to correspond to the categories in the request;

(ii) If a request does not specify a form for producing electronically stored information, a party must produce it in a form or forms in which it is ordinarily maintained or in a reasonably usable form or forms; and

(iii) A party need not produce the same electronically stored information in more than one form.

(c) Nonparties. As provided in Rule 45, a nonparty may be compelled to produce documents and tangible things or to permit an inspection.

[Amended December 27, 1946, effective March 19, 1948; March 30, 1970, effective July 1, 1970; April 29, 1980, effective August 1, 1980; March 2, 1987, effective August 1, 1987; April 30, 1991, effective December 1, 1991; April 22, 1993, effective December 1, 1993; April 12, 2006, effective December 1, 2006; April 30, 2007, effective December 1, 2007; April 29, 2015, effective December 1, 2015.]

UNDERSTANDING RULE 34

HOW RULE 34 FITS IN

Along with depositions, requests to inspect (often called "document requests" or "production requests") are one of the most important discovery tools. In fact, making the relevant documents available to all parties is deemed so fundamental to the litigation process that, unlike most discovery devices, the Rules place no limit on the number of requests to inspect a party may serve (and, as with interrogatories, parties do not need to ask for permission from the court to serve requests to inspect). Although requests to inspect documents are by far the most common application of Rule 34, a party may use the rule to inspect tangible things—like the product in a products liability case—or land.

The scope of document requests, like all discovery generally, is controlled by Rule 26(b)(1), and extends to any nonprivileged matter relevant to a party's claim or defense and proportional to the needs of the case. However, Rule 34 contains another important scope concept; it extends to all documents in the responding party's "possession, custody, or control." This phrase is broadly framed to ensure full access to relevant documents. It essentially means that parties cannot refuse to produce documents in their files by arguing that the documents actually belong to someone else, nor can they shield documents by turning them over to someone else; if the party retains control over the documents (*i.e.*, can get them back by asking), then the party must produce them.

Recognizing the importance of electronic media in modern society, Rule 34 contains a number of provisions addressing the production of "electronically stored information," commonly referred to as "ESI." The Rules are drafted both broadly and in general terms to encompass all forms of electronically stored information in a world where methods of electronic communication emerge so rapidly that the Rules could not be amended quickly enough to describe them specifically.

Not only is the discovery of ESI important, however, it adds cost and complexity to the process. ESI is typically gathered using computers to search for and select responsive documents, either through search terms or more "intelligent" algorithms. Parties often use computer programs to organize the documents that are relevant to the litigation, and the format in which documents are produced becomes important—a program may work better with pdfs, jpegs, or documents in their native format. In some cases, "metadata"—the hidden data that many programs store about files, such as the author, date of creation, date of last modification, etc.—is important, and the manner of producing ESI may affect whether metadata is preserved and produced.

Rule 34 contains a number of provisions to address these ESI complications. It authorizes early service of document requests so that the parties may identify and address ESI problems or disputes in their Rule 26(f) discovery conference or in an early conference with the judge. It also authorizes the requesting party to specify the format in which the responding party should produce the ESI, and allows the responding party to object to that format. Other more general protections relating to ESI are found in Rule 26.

The recipient must respond to document requests within 30 days, although stipulated extensions are common. The response often consists of a mixture of objections and statements regarding whether the responding party has responsive documents. Unlike interrogatory responses, only the attorney signs the response to document requests; the responding party does not sign a verification for responses to document requests. If the responding party objects to a document request, the response must both: 1) state the objection with specificity; and 2) state whether the responding party is withholding any documents on the basis of the objection. These requirements allow the requesting party to evaluate whether to challenge the response with a motion to compel under Rule 37(a).

In addition to the written response, the responding party must provide the responsive documents. Rule 34 establishes two options. First, the party may make the documents available for the requesting party to inspect. The requesting party may then arrange for copies as it sees fit. Alternatively, the responding party may simply make copies of the responsive documents and provide them to the requesting party.

Rule 34 also establishes two options for organizing the responsive documents. First, the party may "label them to correspond to the categories in the request." Typically, parties put unique identifying numbers on each page of each document they are producing to create a record of what they have produced. They then use these numbers to inform the requesting party which documents were responsive to each document request. Alternatively, parties may produce documents "as they are kept in the ordinary course of business." Under this approach, a party might allow an opponent to access the party's files to conduct its own search for responsive documents. This approach may be cheaper and easier for the responding party, but potentially raises privilege concerns and gives the opponent unfettered access to the files.

Document requests routinely implicate privileged documents. Although Rule 34 does not explicitly reference "privilege logs," they have become the accepted manner for handling privileged documents. A privilege log is a listing of each privileged document that the responding party is withholding. It must contain enough information about the circumstances supporting the privilege that the requesting party and the judge can assess the privilege assertion. At the same time, the log should not disclose the content of the privileged communication or the privilege may be waived.

Rule 34 only authorizes document requests to parties. A subpoena under Rule 45 is required to obtain documents from a nonparty.

THE ARCHITECTURE OF RULE 34

Rule 34 packs a lot of content into three subsections, with most of the detail in Rule 34(b). Rule 34(a) generally authorizes the service of request to inspect documents, tangible things, and land. Rule 34(b) contains the procedures for such requests. It describes the content of the requests, sets the time for and content of the written response, contains provisions regarding ESI, and describes the manner for producing responsive documents. Rule 34(c) directs the use of subpoenas under Rule 45 to obtain documents from nonparties.

HOW RULE 34 WORKS IN PRACTICE

RULE 34(a) In General

The scope of document requests and other discovery under Rule 34 is the broad discovery available under Rule 26. Generally, any nonprivileged document that is relevant to any party's claim or defense within the party's "possession, custody, or control" is discoverable unless it was prepared in anticipation of litigation, it pertains to expert witnesses, or producing it would be disproportionate to the needs of the case or unreasonably burdensome to produce.

PRACTICING LAW UNDER THIS SUBPART

Documents

"Documents" is broadly defined to include all forms of recorded information. Rule 34(a) specifically lists writings, drawings, graphs, charts, photographs, phonorecords, and other data compilations.

Electronically Stored Information

Rule 34(a) specifically includes "electronically stored information" (commonly referred to as "ESI") among the categories of documents and things that must be produced. ESI is intended to be a broad and flexible term encompassing email and information "stored in any medium." For more information about the discovery of ESI, see the Sedona Principles, Third Edition: Best Practices, Recommendations & Principles for Addressing Electronic Document Production,[1] upon which the courts have come to rely.

Metadata

One particular form of electronically stored information that has drawn considerable attention in litigation is metadata (data about data), which describes the data that many programs store about the documents created in the program, such as the identity of the author, when the document was created, the identity of those editing the document, and when those edits occurred. Metadata raises a host of issues (including preservation or destruction of metadata and potential attorney-client privilege issues), and should be discussed during the Rule 26(f) conference. A party seeking metadata should specifically request it.

No Duty to Create Documents

Generally, a party is not required to create documents meeting the document requests, only to produce documents already in existence. However, a party may be required to query an existing database for relevant information.

Tangible Things

Rule 34 allows a party to inspect and copy, test, or sample tangible things relevant to the action (*e.g.*, the allegedly defective product in a product liability case).

Property

A party has the right to enter onto another party's land to inspect, measure, survey, photograph, test, or sample property or a designated object or operation thereon if relevant to the pending action

Documents Within a Party's Possession, Custody, or Control

A party must produce all discoverable documents or things responsive to a request that are in the party's possession, custody, or control. Control means the legal or practical right to obtain the documents on demand. Documents held by the party's attorney, expert, insurance company, healthcare provider, accountant, bank, spouse, contractor, officer, or agent are deemed to be within the party's control. Likewise, documents held by a subsidiary, affiliated corporation, or branch office in another State may be within a party's control. Documents owned by a third person but possessed by a party are within the party's custody. Electronic documents on the server of a third-party provider, such as text messages or emails, are within the control of the party. The courts are divided as to whether a party will be deemed to have possession, custody, or control of documents which the party may release by authorization, such as medical records. A party must produce all documents in its

---

[1] Available at https://thesedonaconference.org/sites/default/files/publications/The%20Sedona%20Principles%20Third%20Edition.19TSCJ1.pdf.

possession, custody, or control even if it believes that the requesting party already has the documents.

Duty to Search for Documents

A responding party must make a reasonable search of all sources reasonably likely to contain responsive documents.

Documents Available from Another Source

The fact that copies of documents are available from another source, such as public records, is not, by itself, a valid basis for objecting or refusing to produce such documents if they are within the possession, custody, or control of the responding party. Depending on the circumstances, however, the availability of alternative sources for the requested documents may support an objection on the basis of undue burden. A party that does not have the requested records in its possession, custody, or control will not be required to obtain those documents from public sources or third parties.

Motion for a Protective Order

As an alternative to making objections to individual document requests, the responding party may make a motion for a protective order under Rule 26(c). A motion for a protective order is appropriate when most or all of a set of document requests is too burdensome or cumulative.

RULE 34(b) Procedure

Rule 34(b) contains a variety of details about serving and responding to requests to inspect.

PRACTICING LAW UNDER THIS SUBPART

Who May Serve

Any party may serve document requests.

Who May Be Served

Document requests are limited to parties to the action, although the recipient need not be an adverse party (documents are obtained from nonparties by a subpoena under Rule 45). If the recipient is a corporation, document requests should be addressed to the corporation, not to a corporate officer or the attorney.

Service and Filing of Document Requests

The party propounding the document requests must serve them on all other parties. Document requests are not filed unless they are the subject of a motion, in which case they can be attached as an exhibit. Responses are similarly served but not filed.

Time for Service

Most discovery cannot commence until the parties have conducted their discovery conference under Rule 26(f). Rule 34 creates an exception for document requests. Starting 21 days after a defendant has been served with the summons and complaint, production requests may be served on that party or by that party on a plaintiff or any other defendant who has also been served. The Rules do not set an outer limit on how late in the case document requests may be served, but many local rules or case management orders will set such a limit. Usually, when such a deadline exists, document requests must be served so that the response is due before the deadline.

Number

The Rule contains no limitation on the number of document requests. Some districts have local rules limiting the number of document requests.

Form of Requests

A request for inspection should be a formal document setting forth the items or categories of items to be inspected with "reasonable particularity." What constitutes "reasonable particularity" depends on the particular situation; essentially, the test is whether the responding party can determine what documents to produce. The request should also specify a reasonable time, place, and manner for the inspection. The time designated should be after the time to respond has elapsed (30 days). If the request seeks electronically stored information, the request may, but is not required to, specify the form in which the information is to be produced.

Response

A party served with a document request must serve a written response. The response should fairly respond to each request. It may state that the request will be complied with in the manner requested. It may also specify some other reasonable time or place, or manner for the production or inspection. The response may also raise objections to some or all of the requests. If the request does not specify the form for production of electronically stored information, or if the responding party has objected to the form specified in the request, then the response must specify the form in which electronically stored information will be produced. Finally, the response may advise that the party has no such documents in its possession, custody, or control. The response is signed by the attorney, but is not required to be verified or under oath, in contrast to interrogatory answers. The response must be served upon all parties.

Time to Respond

A written response is due within 30 days of service, except that, for document requests served before the parties' Rule 26(f) conference, the responses are due 30 days after the Rule 26(f) conference. The time to respond may be modified by informal agreement or stipulation under Rule 29. If the responding party intends to object to some of the document requests, a stipulation for an extension should specify that the time is extended to answer and serve objections. The period for responding may also be shortened or lengthened by the court, typically upon motion by one of the parties.

Objections

If the responding party determines that a particular document request is outside the scope of discovery or otherwise problematic, the party may object to the request in lieu of or in addition to making the documents available for inspection. The objection must be made in writing and must state the grounds of the objection with specificity, and a number of courts hold that general or boilerplate objections are ineffective. Some common objections are:

- *Overly broad, unduly vague, and/or ambiguous:* When a document request is written so broadly that it extends to documents not relevant to the claims or defenses in the matter (such as a request not limited in time to the events relevant to the complaint), the request may be overly broad. When a request is susceptible to numerous meanings, it may be unduly vague and ambiguous. In general, these objections are probably not justification for refusing to provide documents altogether, but the responding party can raise the objection, then expressly limit the scope of the response.

- *Burdensome and oppressive:* In general, the responding party must produce the documents available without undue effort or expense (recognizing that all discovery responses require effort and expense). Thus, requests that require extensive research, compilation, or evaluation of documents may be objectionable. The responding party is not required to prepare the adverse party's case. The reasonableness of a request is within the court's discretion.

- *Privileged information:* Requests that seek documents protected by the attorney-client privilege or by another privilege are objectionable. When privileged documents are withheld, the responding party must explicitly state the objection and describe the nature of the documents not produced sufficiently to enable other parties to assess the applicability of the privilege. A log of the documents withheld on the basis of privilege should be provided to the requesting party, either at the time of the responses or at a mutually agreeable time. Care should be exercised in responding to such requests, because the privilege may be waived by revealing part or all of the privileged documents.
- *Trial preparation materials (work product):* Rule 26(b)(3) provides that trial preparation materials may be discovered only upon a showing that the party is unable to obtain the equivalent information through other means without undue hardship. Documents withheld as trial preparation materials are typically listed on the privilege log.
- *Non-discoverable expert information:* Rule 26(b)(4) limits the scope of discovery directed towards experts. It generally requires the responding party to provide an expert report for each expert the party may call as a witness, and thereafter allows other parties to depose such experts. Further discovery with respect to such witnesses is available only upon motion. Rule 26(b)(4)(B) does not allow any discovery with respect to experts not intended to be called as witnesses, absent "exceptional circumstances."
- *Not proportional to the needs of the case:* A party may object that a document request seeks information that is not proportional to the needs of the case, in light of the factors listed in Rule 26(b)(1).
- *Form of electronically stored information:* If the requesting party specifies a form for the production of electronically stored information that the responding party believes is burdensome or otherwise objectionable, Rule 34(b) specifically provides for objections to the request.

Court Rulings on Objections

The district court has extremely broad discretion in ruling on objections to document requests. The court will balance the need for the documents and the burden of producing them, but will generally require production unless the administration of justice would be impeded. The court may allow inspection under specified conditions, and may restrict further disclosure of sensitive documents. The court may also conduct an "*in camera*" inspection—privately inspect the documents—before ruling.

Statement Regarding Objections and Withheld Documents

A party making an objection to a Rule 34 request must state whether any responsive materials are being withheld on the basis of that objection. The responding party does not need to make a detailed log of each document withheld, and only needs to alert other parties to the fact that documents have been withheld so they can make a more informed decision as to whether to challenge the objection and can conduct an "informed discussion" about what was withheld. An objection that explains the scope of the response will be deemed to satisfy this requirement. For example, if the response objects that the request is overly broad in terms of the time covered by the request, then states that the responding party will produce all responsive documents within the last five years, other parties will be on notice that the responding party has withheld documents more than five years old.

Objection to Part of Request

If any part of a request is objectionable, the responding party must specify the objectionable part and respond to the remaining parts. A number of courts have held that the common practice of objecting, then answering "subject to and without waiving" the objections is improper and waives the objections unless the response describes in particularity the documents not being provided.

Production of Documents

The responding party has the option of allowing the serving party to inspect, copy, test, or sample the documents or of providing copies of the responsive documents. If the responding party chooses to allow the requesting party to inspect the documents, the responding party may allow access to the documents as they are normally kept (*i.e.*, "There is our file room."). If the responding party provides copies of or access to selected responsive documents, the party must organize and label them to correspond to the categories requested. Some courts do not require a party to organize and label ESI, recognizing that parties use electronic searching techniques for ESI.

Time for Production

The responding party must produce the responsive documents at the time specified in the request or at another "reasonable time" specified in the response. Neither the Rule nor the advisory committee notes give any guidance as to what would be considered a reasonable time.

Cost of Gathering and Copying

In general, the producing party bears the cost of searching for and gathering responsive documents. If the responding party makes documents available for inspection, the requesting party must pay for copies of the documents it chooses to have copied. The rules are silent about who pays for copies if the responding party chooses to produce copies of the responsive documents instead of making them available for inspection, and the courts have not yet addressed this issue. The court has the authority to shift some or all of the costs of collecting and producing documents to the requesting party. Cost shifting has become increasingly common with ESI.

Production of Electronically Stored Information

The preservation and production of electronically stored information raises a host of issues, many of which are discussed in the Sedona Principles: Best Practices, Recommendations & Principles for Addressing Electronic Document Production.[2]

- *Format for Production:* Rule 34(b) allows, but does not require, the requesting party to specify the form in which it is requesting electronically stored information (such as pdf, jpeg, tiff, or native format). If the requesting party wants the electronically stored information in a particular format (such as one that is compatible with a particular software application or one that includes metadata), the requesting party should so specify in the request. The responding party can then produce it in that form or object and specify the form in which it will produce the electronically stored information. If the requesting party does not specify the form, then the responding party must produce it in the form in which it is ordinarily maintained or in a form that is reasonably usable. Unless the responding party is producing the electronically stored information in the form specified by the requesting party, the responding party must specify the form it intends to use for production in its written response to the document request.

[2] The Sedona Principles, Third Edition: Best Practices, Recommendations & Principles for Addressing Electronic Document Production, 19 Sedona Conf. J. 1 (2019), available at https://thesedonaconference.org/sites/default/files/publications/The%20Sedona%20Principles%20Third%20Edition.19TSCJ1.pdf.

Under any of these scenarios, a party need not produce electronically stored information in more than one form unless ordered to do so by the court.

- *Access to Servers and Hard Drives:* Sometimes, the requesting party will seek access to the producing party's servers or hard drives or to have those devices imaged so that the requesting party can conduct its own searches or forensic analysis, but the courts will require that only when the specific situation warrants.

Procedures for Inspection, Testing, or Sampling

Procedures for inspection, testing, or sampling, such as who will be present and protocols for the testing or sampling, are set by agreement of the parties or by the court. Requests to perform destructive testing or invasive sampling are more likely to draw objection or require court intervention.

Sanctions for Failure to Respond

If a party files no response to a set of document requests, the court may impose sanctions under Rule 37(b)(2), such as deeming certain facts established or refusing to allow the party to oppose or support certain claims. The court may also deem objections to the document requests waived by the failure to file a timely response. Furthermore, the court must award reasonable expenses, including attorney's fees, caused by the responding party's failure to answer, unless the court finds that the failure to answer was justified.

RULE 34(c) Nonparties

Although document requests or requests for inspection cannot be served on a nonparty, documents or inspections can be obtained from a nonparty by a subpoena under Rule 45. Furthermore, Rule 34 does not preclude an independent action for production of documents or things or for permission to enter onto land (but such actions may be unnecessary under the expanded subpoena powers in Rule 45).

RULE 35

PHYSICAL AND MENTAL EXAMINATIONS

(a) Order for an Examination.

(1) *In General.* The court where the action is pending may order a party whose mental or physical condition—including blood group—is in controversy to submit to a physical or mental examination by a suitably licensed or certified examiner. The court has the same authority to order a party to produce for examination a person who is in its custody or under its legal control.

(2) *Motion and Notice; Contents of the Order.* The order:

(A) may be made only on motion for good cause and on notice to all parties and the person to be examined; and

(B) must specify the time, place, manner, conditions, and scope of the examination, as well as the person or persons who will perform it.

(b) Examiner's Report.

(1) *Request by the Party or Person Examined.* The party who moved for the examination must, on request, deliver to the requester a copy of the examiner's report, together with like reports of all earlier examinations of the same condition. The request may be made by the party against whom the examination order was issued or by the person examined.

(2) *Contents.* The examiner's report must be in writing and must set out in detail the examiner's findings, including diagnoses, conclusions, and the results of any tests.

(3) *Request by the Moving Party.* After delivering the reports, the party who moved for the examination may request—and is entitled to receive—from the party against whom the examination order was issued like reports of all earlier or later examinations of the same condition. But those reports need not be delivered by the party with custody or control of the person examined if the party shows that it could not obtain them.

(4) *Waiver of Privilege.* By requesting and obtaining the examiner's report, or by deposing the examiner, the party examined waives any privilege it may have—in that action or any other action involving the same controversy—concerning testimony about all examinations of the same condition.

(5) *Failure to Deliver a Report.* The court on motion may order—on just terms—that a party deliver the report of an examination. If the report is not provided, the court may exclude the examiner's testimony at trial.

(6) *Scope.* This subdivision (b) applies also to an examination made by the parties' agreement, unless the agreement states otherwise. This subdivision does not preclude obtaining an examiner's report or deposing an examiner under other rules.

[Amended effective July 1, 1970; August 1, 1987; November 18, 1988; December 1, 1991; April 30, 2007, effective December 1, 2007.]

UNDERSTANDING RULE 35

HOW RULE 35 FITS IN

Rule 35 authorizes a party to request a physical or mental examination of another party if that party's physical or mental condition has been placed "in controversy." Thus, for example, if a plaintiff brought a lawsuit claiming that the defendant's negligence caused an injury to the plaintiff's leg, the defendant could request that a doctor examine the plaintiff's leg to assess the nature and extent of the injury. A Rule 35 examination is a discretionary discovery tool that a party may choose to employ, like interrogatories, document requests, and depositions, but with a twist; a party does not have a right to a Rule 35 examination, and instead must file a motion and obtain a court order or a stipulation from the party to be examined. Furthermore, the burden on the moving party is not the ordinary burden of persuasion, but instead is the heightened "good cause" standard. When a party's physical condition is plainly in controversy, however, stipulations for Rule 35 examinations are common.

Rule 35 also contains provisions requiring the examiner to prepare a written report setting out the examiner's findings. The Rule allows the examined party to request a copy of the report, but invoking that right obligates the examined party to produce copies of any reports it has from examinations for the same condition.

THE ARCHITECTURE OF RULE 35

Rule 35 has only two subsections. Rule 35(a) describes the circumstances that warrant an examination and contains the procedures for obtaining the examination. Rule 35(b) contains the requirement to prepare a report of the examination and the rules for exchanging copies of the report and of similar reports.

HOW RULE 35 WORKS IN PRACTICE

RULE 35(a) Order for an Examination

Rule 35 requires a party to submit to a mental or physical examination when the party's mental or physical condition is at issue in the action. In contrast to most other discovery procedures, mental or physical examinations are available only by stipulation or motion for "good cause," which will generally exist in every case in which the plaintiff is claiming personal injuries.

PRACTICING LAW UNDER THIS SUBPART

Consent

In many cases, the circumstances justifying a Rule 35 examination are apparent, and the party to be examined consents to the examination. For example, in a tort action where the plaintiff seeks to recover for personal injuries, many plaintiffs will consent to an examination of the alleged injuries. The consent can be by formal stipulation under Rule 29 or by informal agreement.

Motion

Absent consent, a request for examination must be made by motion, with a proposed order attached, served upon the person to be examined and all parties. The motion should specify the time, place, manner, conditions, and scope of the examination and the person or persons by whom it is to be made, as well as the grounds supporting the motion.

Order

If the court grants a motion for a Rule 35 examination, it must issue an order that specifies the examiner and the time, place, manner, conditions, and scope of the examination. The order may also include protective measures deemed appropriate by the court.

Persons Subject to Examination

In general, only parties are subject to Rule 35 examination. Additionally, a person who is within the control of a party may be subject to examination. Thus, a parent suing on behalf of an injured child may have to produce the child for examination.

Condition in Controversy

Examinations for a particular condition are allowed only when that condition is in controversy. The plaintiff's condition is typically placed at issue by the claims in the complaint, but can also be placed at issue by representations made during the litigation or by a defense.

Good Cause

The court will order an examination "for good cause shown." *See Schlagenhauf v. Holder,* 379 U.S. 104 (1964) (describing "good cause" as a determination that must be made on a case-by-case basis). The burden of demonstrating good cause rests with the moving party. The requirement of good cause is not a formality; the court must genuinely balance the need for the information with the right to privacy and safety of the party. *Id.* at 118. In a tort action where the plaintiff seeks to recover for personal injuries, good cause will almost always be found to exist. It becomes less clear when the party has not put the party's own mental or physical condition at issue.

Time for Filing Motion

There is no time limit on the filing of a motion for an examination, although the court can take the timing of the motion into account in considering the motion.

Who Conducts Examination

The examination may be conducted by any suitably licensed or certified examiner or examiners. In general, the court will allow the movant to select the examiner unless the person to be examined raises a valid objection. The court may reject a particular examiner upon a showing of bias or, under certain circumstances, if the examiner is a different gender from the person to be examined. Some local rules have provisions regarding the selection of a neutral examiner.

Testimony of Examiner

The party conducting the examination may call the examiner to testify as an expert witness (assuming the criteria for expert testimony are satisfied). The courts are split as to whether the party who was examined may call the examiner as an expert.

Scope of Examination

The type of examination allowable depends on the circumstances of the case. Examinations can include blood tests, DNA tests, x-rays, electrocardiograms, fingerprint analysis, and other safe, medically accepted tests indicated by the condition at issue. Vocational examinations are also permissible. The burden on the movant to show good cause will be greater if the tests are more invasive, painful, or burdensome, or if repeated examinations are sought. However, a party that objects to a particular test as too painful or invasive may be precluded from offering evidence of the type that would result from the test. The courts are divided as to whether the motion must identify each test to be administered.

Mental Examinations

Mental examinations are allowable if a person's mental condition is at issue. The examination may be conducted by a psychiatrist or psychologist. Many courts are reluctant to order a mental examination based solely on a "garden variety" emotional distress allegation.

Time and Location

The court will designate the time and location of the examination in the order.

Cost of Examination

The moving party must pay the medical or professional expenses of the examination. The person to be examined is not compensated, however, for transportation costs and lost time.

Who Is Present at the Examination

The court has discretion to determine who may be present at the examination. Some courts allow persons being examined by a doctor to bring their own physicians, others do not. It is also unsettled whether attorneys have a right to be present.

RULE 35(b) Examiner's Report

Upon request by the party or person examined, the party who moved for the examination must provide a copy of a detailed written report by the examiner, together with any reports of earlier examinations for the same condition. Following the delivery of such a copy, the examined party must provide copies of reports of any other examinations for the same condition, whether conducted before or after the Rule 35 examination.

PRACTICING LAW UNDER THIS SUBPART

Report

The examiner must prepare a written report that sets out in detail the examiner's findings, including diagnoses, conclusions, and the results of any tests.

The Report Limits Testimony by the Examiner

Testimony by the examiner will be limited to the opinions disclosed in the report.

Obtaining Reports by Other Discovery Procedures

The parties may use other discovery procedures in lieu of or in addition to the report exchange procedures in Rule 35, such as document requests or deposition of the examiner.

Failure to Draft Report

If the examiner fails to prepare or provide a report, the court may exclude the examiner's testimony.

RULE 36

REQUESTS FOR ADMISSION

(a) Scope and Procedure.

(1) *Scope.* A party may serve on any other party a written request to admit, for purposes of the pending action only, the truth of any matters within the scope of Rule 26(b)(1) relating to:

(A) Facts, The Application Of Law To Fact, Or Opinions about either; and

(B) the genuineness of any described documents.

(2) *Form; Copy of a Document.* Each matter must be separately stated. A request to admit the genuineness of a document must be accompanied by a copy of the document unless it is, or has been, otherwise furnished or made available for inspection and copying.

(3) *Time to Respond; Effect of Not Responding. A* matter is admitted unless, within 30 days after being served, the party to whom the request is directed serves on the requesting party a written answer or objection addressed to the matter and signed by the party or its attorney. A shorter or longer time for responding may be stipulated to under Rule 29 or be ordered by the court.

(4) *Answer.* If a matter is not admitted, the answer must specifically deny it or state in detail why the answering party cannot truthfully admit or deny it. A denial must fairly respond to the substance of the matter; and when good faith requires that a party qualify an answer or deny only a part of a matter, the answer must specify the part admitted and qualify or deny the rest. The answering party may assert lack of knowledge or information as a reason for failing to admit or deny only if the party states that it has made reasonable inquiry and that the information it knows or can readily obtain is insufficient to enable it to admit or deny.

(5) *Objections.* The grounds for objecting to a request must be stated. A party must not object solely on the ground that the request presents a genuine issue for trial.

(6) *Motion Regarding the Sufficiency of an Answer or Objection.* The requesting party may move to determine the sufficiency of an answer or objection. Unless the court finds an objection justified, it must order that an answer be served. On finding that an answer does not comply with this rule, the court may order either that the matter is admitted or that an amended answer be served. The court may defer its final decision until

a pretrial conference or a specified time before trial. Rule 37(a)(5) applies to an award of expenses.

(b) Effect of an Admission; Withdrawing or Amending It. A matter admitted under this rule is conclusively established unless the court, on motion, permits the admission to be withdrawn or amended. Subject to Rule 16(e), the court may permit withdrawal or amendment if it would promote the presentation of the merits of the action and if the court is not persuaded that it would prejudice the requesting party in maintaining or defending the action on the merits. An admission under this rule is not an admission for any other purpose and cannot be used against the party in any other proceeding.

[Amended December 27, 1946, effective March 19, 1948; March 30, 1970, effective July 1, 1970; March 2, 1987, effective August 1, 1987; April 22, 1993, effective December 1, 1993; April 30, 2007, effective December 1, 2007.]

UNDERSTANDING RULE 36

HOW RULE 36 FITS IN

Most discovery responses can be shown to the jury or judge as evidence, but they are not really binding. For example, if a party acknowledges at a deposition that the light was red, the party may testify at trial that the light was really green. The party may be cross-examined about the prior testimony, and may present an explanation as to the change (*e.g.*, "I misunderstood the question" or "I thought you meant red in the other direction"). The jury or judge may or may not believe the explanation, but at least the party has the opportunity to try. Rule 36 provides a mechanism to obtain an admission that cannot be avoided so easily. If a party admits a request for admission under Rule 36, that matter is conclusively established, and cannot be controverted at trial. Thus, if a party has admitted a request to admit that the light was red, the party cannot attempt to explain away that admission at trial.

Rule 36 authorizes a party to serve another party with requests to admit in two categories: 1) requests to admit facts, the application of law to facts (similar to contention interrogatories), or opinions about either; and 2) the genuineness or authenticity of any documents (to avoid the need to have a record custodian appear and testify about the documents' authenticity). Requests for admission are a discretionary discovery device—any party may choose to serve them without leave of court. Rule 36 does not limit the number of requests for admission, although some local rules establish a limit.

The recipient of requests for admission must serve a response within 30 days. Rule 36 attempts to avoid dodging the request by requiring that, if the response does not admit the request, it must specifically deny it or state in detail what the answering party cannot admit or deny it. The response may include objections as well.

Rule 36 (in conjunction with Rule 37) establishes a number of sanctions associated with requests for admission. The first is self-implementing; if a party does not timely respond to a request, the request is deemed admitted. This point bears repeating—if a party fails to respond to a request for admission, it is deemed admitted; calendaring the response date for requests for admission is a really good idea. Second, if a responding party denies a request and the requesting party subsequently proves that the matter was true or the document was genuine, then the requesting party may file a motion seeking its attorney's fees in proving the matter true or the document authentic, and the court must grant the motion unless it finds that the responding party had a reasonable basis to believe it would prevail on the matter.

So, what happens if a party inadvertently fails to respond timely or admits something the party later regrets? Upon motion, the court may allow a party to modify or withdraw an admission, but only if the court is persuaded that the modification or withdrawal would not prejudice the other party. Thus, if a party realizes two days late that it forgot to respond, a court would likely find that the two-day delay did not prejudice the other party. Conversely, if discovery is completed, a withdrawal might prejudice the requesting party, who will no longer be able to conduct discovery about the topic of the admission.

THE ARCHITECTURE OF RULE 36

Rule 36 has only two subsections. Rule 36(a) describes the permissible topics for requests for admission and contains the procedures for serving and responding to requests for admission. Rule 36(b) establishes the effect of an admission and provides procedures for withdrawing or amending admissions.

HOW RULE 36 WORKS IN PRACTICE

RULE 36(a) Scope and Procedure

Rule 36 establishes a procedure whereby one party serves requests for admission on another party, who must investigate and either admit, deny with specificity, justify an inability to admit or deny, or object to each requested admission. Any request that is not denied in a timely fashion is admitted.

Rule 36 requests may address two topics: 1) facts or the application of law to facts; and 2) the authenticity of documents (to avoid having a records custodian appear to lay a foundation). Rule 36 admissions are particularly valuable in that any matter admitted is conclusively established—and thus may not be countered or explained away at trial. This quality is unique to requests for admission; admissions made in response to interrogatories or at depositions are generally admissible at trial, but are not conclusively established.

PRACTICING LAW UNDER THIS SUBPART

Who May Be Served

Requests for admission are limited to parties to the action, although the party need not be an adverse party.

Time for Service

Requests for admission can be served after the parties have conducted the discovery conference under Rule 26(f). The Rules do not set an outer limit on how late in the case requests for admission may be served, and courts are split as to whether requests for admission are discovery devices subject to a general discovery cutoff. However, many local rules or case management orders will set a time limit for requests for admission. Usually, when such a time limit exists, requests for admission must be served so that the response is due before the specified deadline.

Contents and Format of Request

Each fact or matter for which admission is requested should be set forth in a separate paragraph. All facts that are part of the request should be set forth in the request; it is improper to incorporate facts by reference to other text. Requests for admission should be simple, direct, and concise so they may be admitted or denied with little or no explanation or qualification.

Scope and Topics

The scope of requests for admission is the broad discovery available under Rule 26. Within that scope, Rule 36 authorizes requests for admission in two categories:

- *Facts, the Application of Law to Fact, or Opinions About Either:* Requests for admission may pertain to any issue in the case, including the ultimate facts at issue, the application of law to fact, or jurisdictional issues, but may not seek an admission as to a pure conclusion of law.
- *Authenticity of Documents:* A request may ask that the genuineness or authenticity of a document be admitted. Each request should be limited to a single document and a copy of the document should be attached, unless it has already been provided.

Number

Rule 36 contains no limitation on the number of requests for admission. Some districts have local rules limiting the number of requests.

Who Must Receive Copies

All parties must be served with a copy of the requests for admissions.

Time to Answer

A written response is due within 30 days of service. The time to answer may be extended by stipulation under Rule 29. Additionally, the court has discretion to lengthen or shorten the time in which a party must respond.

Service and Filing of Requests and Responses

All parties must be served with a copy of the requests for admissions and the response. The requests and response are not filed at the time of service, but may be filed as an exhibit to a motion.

Form of Response

The response should be in writing and signed by the attorney, or by the party if unrepresented.

Responses

The responding party essentially has four possible responses to a request for admission: the party can admit the request (in part or in full); deny the request (in part or in full); set forth reasons why the party cannot admit or deny the request; or object to the request (by a specific objection or by a motion for a protective order).

Denials

A denial must specifically address the substance of the requested admission. The denial may be as simple as the single word "denied," or may be a longer sentence, but may not sidestep the request or be evasive.

Partial Denials

If the responding party believes that part of a requested admission is accurate and part is not, the proper response is to admit the accurate portion and deny the balance.

Inability to Admit or Deny

If the responding party is genuinely unable to admit or deny the requested admission, the party can so state, but must describe in detail why, after reasonable inquiry the party cannot admit or deny. Some courts hold that a general statement that the responding party has insufficient information to respond will be treated as an insufficient answer, and upon motion the court will treat the answer as an admission or will order a further answer. Other courts hold that a statement that the responding party has made reasonable inquiry is sufficient, without detail about the nature of the inquiry.

Objections

Objections must be made in writing within the time allowed for answering. Typical grounds for objections to requests for admission are:

- *Privilege:* If a response requires the disclosure of privileged matters, it is objectionable. *See* Rule 26(b)(5) (discussing commonly asserted privileges).
- *Vague or Ambiguous:* A request may be objectionable if it is so vague or ambiguous that the responding party cannot answer it.
- *Seeking a Pure Legal Conclusion:* A request may be objectionable if it seeks a pure legal conclusion, although it may properly seek the application of law to fact. Thus, "admit that negligence has the following four elements under the law applicable to this case . . ." would be objectionable as seeking a pure legal conclusion.

Improper Objections

A party cannot refuse to answer a request on the basis that the serving party already knows the answer, that the request calls for an opinion or contention, that the subject matter is within the other party's own knowledge, that it invades the province of the jury, that it addresses a subject for expert testimony, that it presents a genuine issue for trial, that it pertains to the "ultimate facts," that the document at issue speaks for itself, that the responding party is not the custodian of the document, or that it is more properly directed to another party. Likewise, it is irrelevant who has the ultimate burden of proof with respect to the matter for which admission is requested.

Opinions and Conclusions

A request for admission is not objectionable because it involves an opinion or contention that relates to fact or the application of law to fact. A request may not seek a pure legal conclusion, with no application to the facts.

Failure to Respond

Failure to respond in a timely fashion is deemed an admission. The court has discretion to allow a party to submit responses after the allowed time for a response.

Motion to Determine Sufficiency

If a party believes that a response is insufficient or that an objection is improper, the party can move the court to determine the sufficiency of the answer or objection. "Insufficient" refers to the specificity of the response, not whether the response is correct or in good faith. The burden will be on the party raising an objection to show that the objection was proper. If the court determines that the answer was insufficient, it can deem the answer an admission or can order a more complete answer. The court may also defer ruling until later in the pretrial proceedings.

Sanctions

The sanctions available depend upon the conduct of the responding party. The sanction for failure to respond is that the requests are deemed admitted. The sanction for improperly denying a request is that the responding party will be required to pay the costs of the other party incurred in proving the matter, including attorney's fees, under Rule 37(c). The sanction for an insufficient answer or improper objection is that the response may be deemed an admission, plus, if the requesting party filed a motion to compel, the responding party will be liable for the requesting party's expenses in bringing the motion, including a reasonable attorney's fee.

RULE 36(b) Effect of an Admission; Withdrawing or Amending It

An admission is deemed conclusively established unless the court permits withdrawal or amendment of the admission.

PRACTICING LAW UNDER THIS SUBPART

Binding Nature of Formal Admissions

A matter formally admitted under Rule 36 is conclusively established and may not be contradicted. In contrast, a statement at a deposition or in an interrogatory answer may be controverted or explained away at trial (*e.g.*, "I misspoke when I said that. Here's what I meant . . ."). Likewise, an informal, extrajudicial admission is admissible evidence, but not conclusive.

Admissions Binding Only in Pending Proceeding

An admission is only binding within the action in which the request was served.

Use of Admissions at Trial or in Motion Practice

An admission may be introduced at trial or in the context of a motion, such as a motion for summary judgment.

Use by Party Making Admission

The party making the admission may not introduce it at trial.

Coparties Not Bound

An admission will only be binding on the admitting party and will not be binding on any coparties.

Withdrawal

A party may file a motion to withdraw or amend an admission. The court may allow withdrawal or amendment when doing so will aid in the resolution of the matter on the merits and when the party who obtained the admission will not be prejudiced by the amendment or withdrawal. Notably absent from this test is any mention of the responding party's conduct or reason for seeking the amendment or withdrawal.

RULE 37

FAILURE TO MAKE DISCLOSURES OR TO COOPERATE IN DISCOVERY; SANCTIONS

(a) Motion for an Order Compelling Disclosure or Discovery.

(1) *In General.* On notice to other parties and all affected persons, a party may move for an order compelling disclosure or discovery. The motion must include a certification that the movant has in good faith conferred or attempted to confer with the person or party failing to make disclosure or discovery in an effort to obtain it without court action.

(2) *Appropriate Court.* A motion for an order to a party must be made in the court where the action is pending. A motion for an order to a nonparty must be made in the court where the discovery is or will be taken.

(3) *Specific Motions.*

(A) *To Compel Disclosure.* If a party fails to make a disclosure required by Rule 26(a), any other party may move to compel disclosure and for appropriate sanctions.

(B) *To Compel a Discovery Response.* A party seeking discovery may move for an order compelling an answer, designation, production, or inspection. This motion may be made if:

(i) a deponent fails to answer a question asked under Rule 30 or 31;

(ii) a corporation or other entity fails to make a designation under Rule 30(b)(6) or 31(a)(4);

(iii) a party fails to answer an interrogatory submitted under Rule 33; or

(iv) a party fails to produce documents or fails to respond that inspection will be permitted—or fails to permit inspection—as requested under Rule 34.

(C) *Related to a Deposition.* When taking an oral deposition, the party asking a question may complete or adjourn the examination before moving for an order.

(4) *Evasive or Incomplete Disclosure, Answer, or Response.* For purposes of this subdivision (a), an evasive or incomplete disclosure, answer, or response must be treated as a failure to disclose, answer, or respond.

(5) *Payment of Expenses; Protective Orders.*

(A) *If the Motion Is Granted (or Disclosure or Discovery Is Provided After Filing).* If the motion is granted—or if the disclosure or requested discovery is provided after the motion was filed—the court must, after giving an opportunity to be heard, require the party or deponent whose conduct necessitated the motion, the party or attorney advising that conduct, or both to pay the movant's reasonable expenses incurred in making the motion, including attorney's fees. But the court must not order this payment if:

(i) the movant filed the motion before attempting in good faith to obtain the disclosure or discovery without court action;

(ii) the opposing party's nondisclosure, response, or objection was substantially justified; or

(iii) other circumstances make an award of expenses unjust.

(B) *If the Motion Is Denied.* If the motion is denied, the court may issue any protective order authorized under Rule 26(c) and must, after giving an opportunity to be heard, require the movant, the attorney filing the motion, or both to pay the party or deponent who opposed the motion its reasonable expenses incurred in opposing the motion, including attorney's fees. But the court must not order this payment if the motion was substantially justified or other circumstances make an award of expenses unjust.

(C) *If the Motion Is Granted in Part and Denied in Part.* If the motion is granted in part and denied in part, the court may issue any protective order authorized under Rule 26(c) and may, after giving an opportunity to be heard, apportion the reasonable expenses for the motion.

(b) Failure to Comply with a Court Order.

(1) *Sanctions in the District Where the Deposition Is Taken.* If the court where the discovery is taken orders a deponent to be sworn or to answer a question and the deponent fails to obey, the failure may be treated as contempt of court. If a deposition-related motion is transferred to the court where the action is pending, and that court orders a deponent to be sworn or to answer a question and the deponent fails to obey, the failure may be treated as contempt of either the court where the discovery is taken or the court where the action is pending.

(2) *Sanctions Sought in the District Where the Action Is Pending.*

(A) *For Not Obeying a Discovery Order.* If a party or a party's officer, director, or managing agent—or a witness designated under Rule

30(b)(6) or 31(a)(4)—fails to obey an order to provide or permit discovery, including an order under Rule 26(f), 35, or 37(a), the court where the action is pending may issue further just orders. They may include the following:

(i) directing that the matters embraced in the order or other designated facts be taken as established for purposes of the action, as the prevailing party claims;

(ii) prohibiting the disobedient party from supporting or opposing designated claims or defenses, or from introducing designated matters in evidence;

(iii) striking pleadings in whole or in part;

(iv) staying further proceedings until the order is obeyed;

(v) dismissing the action or proceeding in whole or in part;

(vi) rendering a default judgment against the disobedient party; or

(vii) treating as contempt of court the failure to obey any order except an order to submit to a physical or mental examination.

(B) *For Not Producing a Person for Examination.* If a party fails to comply with an order under Rule 35(a) requiring it to produce another person for examination, the court may issue any of the orders listed in Rule 37(b)(2)(A)(i)(vi), unless the disobedient party shows that it cannot produce the other person.

(C) *Payment of Expenses.* Instead of or in addition to the orders above, the court must order the disobedient party, the attorney advising that party, or both to pay the reasonable expenses, including attorney's fees, caused by the failure, unless the failure was substantially justified or other circumstances make an award of expenses unjust.

(c) Failure to Disclose, to Supplement an Earlier Response, or to Admit.

(1) *Failure to Disclose or Supplement.* If a party fails to provide information or identify a witness as required by Rule 26(a) or (e), the party is not allowed to use that information or witness to supply evidence on a motion, at a hearing, or at a trial, unless the failure was substantially justified or is harmless. In addition to or instead of this sanction, the court, on motion and after giving an opportunity to be heard:

(A) may order payment of the reasonable expenses, including attorney's fees, caused by the failure;

(B) may inform the jury of the party's failure; and

(C) may impose other appropriate sanctions, including any of the orders listed in Rule 37(b)(2)(A)(i)–(vi).

(2) *Failure to Admit.* If a party fails to admit what is requested under Rule 36 and if the requesting party later proves a document to be genuine or the matter true, the requesting party may move that the party who failed to admit pay the reasonable expenses, including attorney's fees, incurred in making that proof. The court must so order unless:

(A) the request was held objectionable under Rule 36(a);

(B) the admission sought was of no substantial importance;

(C) the party failing to admit had a reasonable ground to believe that it might prevail on the matter; or

(D) there was other good reason for the failure to admit.

(d) Party's Failure to Attend Its Own Deposition, Serve Answers to Interrogatories, or Respond to a Request for Inspection.

(1) *In General.*

(A) *Motion; Grounds for Sanctions.* The court where the action is pending may, on motion, order sanctions if:

(i) a party or a party's officer, director, or managing agent—or a person designated under Rule 30(b)(6) or 31(a)(4)—fails, after being served with proper notice, to appear for that person's deposition; or

(ii) a party, after being properly served with interrogatories under Rule 33 or a request for inspection under Rule 34, fails to serve its answers, objections, or written response.

(B) *Certification.* A motion for sanctions for failing to answer or respond must include a certification that the movant has in good faith conferred or attempted to confer with the party failing to act in an effort to obtain the answer or response without court action.

(2) *Unacceptable Excuse for Failing to Act.* A failure described in Rule 37(d)(1)(A) is not excused on the ground that the discovery sought was objectionable, unless the party failing to act has a pending motion for a protective order under Rule 26(c).

(3) *Types of Sanctions.* Sanctions may include any of the orders listed in Rule 37(b)(2)(A)(i)–(vi). Instead of or in addition to these sanctions, the court must require the party failing to act, the attorney advising that party, or both to pay the reasonable expenses, including attorney's fees, caused by the failure, unless the failure was substantially justified or other circumstances make an award of expenses unjust.

(e) Failure to Preserve Electronically Stored Information. If electronically stored information that should have been preserved in the anticipation or conduct of litigation is lost because a party failed to take reasonable steps to preserve it, and it cannot be restored or replaced through additional discovery, the court:

(1) upon finding prejudice to another party from loss of the information, may order measures no greater than necessary to cure the prejudice; or

(2) only upon finding that the party acted with the intent to deprive another party of the information's use in the litigation may:

(A) presume that the lost information was unfavorable to the party;

(B) instruct the jury that it may or must presume the information was unfavorable to the party; or

(C) dismiss the action or enter a default judgment.

(f) Failure to Participate in Framing a Discovery Plan. If a party or its attorney fails to participate in good faith in developing and submitting a proposed discovery plan as required by Rule 26(f), the court may, after giving an opportunity to be heard, require that party or attorney to pay to any other party the reasonable expenses, including attorney's fees, caused by the failure.

[Amended December 29, 1948, effective October 20, 1949; March 30, 1970, effective July 1, 1970; April 29, 1980, effective August 1, 1980; amended by Pub.L. 96–481, Title II, § 205(a), October 21, 1980, 94 Stat. 2330, effective October 1, 1981; amended March 2, 1987, effective August 1, 1987; April 22, 1993, effective December 1, 1993; April 17, 2000, effective December 1, 2000; April 12, 2006, effective December 1, 2006; April 30, 2007, effective December 1, 2007; April 16, 2013, effective December 1, 2013; April 29, 2015, effective December 1, 2015.]

UNDERSTANDING RULE 37

HOW RULE 37 FITS IN

Rules 26 through 36 govern the ways in which parties may obtain information, admissions, and other assistance through discovery. But what happens when the discovery process breaks down or when opposing parties do not fulfill their discovery obligations? That's where Rule 37 fits in. It provides the policing mechanisms for the discovery process. It addresses two primary functions in that regard: compelling parties to perform as the Rules require and sanctioning parties who fail to do so.

The process for compelling other parties to perform their obligations under the discovery rules is relatively straightforward. A party who believes that another party has not properly performed—such as by failing to submit responses to discovery requests or by submitting discovery responses that are inadequate—may file a "motion to compel." The court then has broad discretion to grant or deny the motion, as with almost all discovery issues. In connection with the order granting or denying the motion, the court must award attorney's fees to the prevailing party (unless each side wins some of the issues, the losing party's position was "substantially justified," or the court finds circumstances that make an award of attorney's fees "unjust").

The process for sanctions is substantially more complicated because the potential need for sanctions can arise in a multitude of circumstances. Rule 37(b) authorizes a wide variety of sanctions. Some of them relate to the evidence, such as precluding evidence not properly provided during discovery or deeming certain facts established without the need for evidence. Other sanctions involve advising the jury of discovery misconduct. The court may even impose case-concluding sanctions like dismissal or judgment in extreme circumstances. Finally, as with the motion to compel, the court will ordinarily award attorney's fees to the prevailing party.

The procedural pathway and the available sanctions depend, in part, on the particular issue before the court. Virtually all of the array of sanctions are available when a party fails to comply with an order compelling discovery, fails to respond to interrogatories or document requests, or fails to appear for a properly noticed deposition. Some transgressions, however, trigger special sanctions. For example, failure to respond to requests for admission results in the requests being deemed admitted without the need for a motion or any other pretrial action by the party who sent the requests. Likewise, failure to disclose a document required by any of the automatic disclosure in Rule 26(a) results in the exclusion of that document from evidence, again without any pretrial action by an opposing party.

Failure to preserve—or "spoliation" of—electronically stored evidence (ESI) has its own set of sanctioning procedures. Rule 37(e) establishes prerequisites that must be satisfied before any sanction is permissible, then sets two tiers of sanctions. The most severe sanctions—case-concluding sanctions or an "adverse inference" instruction to the jury that it may or must presume that the lost ESI would have been harmful to the party failing to preserve it—are available only if the court finds a party acted with the specific intent to affect the litigation when it failed to preserve the ESI. Lesser sanctions are available if the court finds that another party was prejudiced by the spoliation of the ESI, and are limited to the sanctions necessary to cure the prejudice.

The duty to first "meet and confer" with the other party to attempt to resolve discovery disputes informally is a theme throughout the discovery enforcement process. A party must meet and confer before filing a motion to compel or a motion for sanctions for failure to respond to interrogatories or document requests. There are certain situations, however, where Rule 37 allows a party to seek sanctions immediately, without meeting and conferring. When a party has failed to comply with an order compelling it to fulfill its discovery obligations, the aggrieved party does not have to conduct a second meet and confer (having already done so as a prerequisite to filing the motion to compel). Likewise, the self-implementing sanctions for undisclosed documents and unanswered requests for admission do not require a meet and confer.

Discovery disputes are not the most enjoyable aspect of litigation—most judges and lawyers strongly prefer to avoid them, and they can drive up the cost of litigation. For those reasons, lawyers should participate in the discovery process both in good faith and with an open mind to compromise. Having said that, discovery disputes are part of the litigation process, and understanding and applying Rule 37 properly can be critical to being a successful lawyer.

THE ARCHITECTURE OF RULE 37

Rule 37 is one of the longer and more complex rules in the Federal Rules of Civil Procedure, and it has an accordingly complex structure. Rule 37(a) contains the procedures for motions to compel, and Rules 37(b) through (f) contain the various sanctions provisions.

Rule 37(a) authorizes motions to compel in a variety of circumstances: when a party fails to make the disclosures under Rule 26(a); when a party fails to answer an interrogatory or document request or provides an evasive or incomplete answer; when a party fails to produce the responsive documents pursuant to a document request; when a deponent fails to answer a question at a deposition; or when a party fails to designate a representative for a deposition under Rule 30(b)(6). Rule 37(a) also contains the requirement to meet and confer prior to filing a motion to compel, and specifies that the motion should be made in the court where the case is pending (not, for example, where the performance of the discovery obligation should have occurred, unless the person not performing is a nonparty). If the court denies a motion to compel, Rule 37(a) authorizes the court to enter a protective order under Rule 26(c) protecting the responding party from similar discovery in the future. Finally, Rule 37(a) contains provisions regarding the award of attorney's fees to the prevailing party.

Rule 37(b) provides the next step after a successful motion to compel. If the opposing party still fails to comply, the requesting party may file a motion for sanctions under Rule 37(b) (again in the court where the action is pending). Rule 37(b) then provides a long, nonexclusive list of the available sanctions. It clarifies that contempt is available as a sanction in most situations, but not for a violation of the obligations in Rule 35 relating to a mental or physical examination. Like Rule 37(a), it also imposes attorney's fees on the losing party.

Rules 37(c) and (d) contain special sanctions provisions for a variety of circumstances. Rule 37(c) provides for exclusion of information or witnesses not properly disclosed during the automatic disclosures under Rule 26(a) or by supplement under Rule 26(e). Rule 37(c) also sets the sanction for an improper denial of a request for admission. Rule 37(d) provides the sanctioning authority for failure to attend the party's own deposition or to respond to written discovery.

Rule 37(e) establishes a framework for sanctions for failure to preserve ESI. It starts with some prerequisites for any sanctions, then sets the criteria for lesser sanctions if the spoliation causes prejudice to another party, and more severe sanctions if the spoliation was intended to affect the litigation.

Finally, Rule 37(f) controls sanctions for failing to participate in good faith in the discovery planning process mandated by Rule 26(f).

HOW RULE 37 WORKS IN PRACTICE

RULE 37(a) — Motion for an Order Compelling Disclosure or Discovery

If an opponent fails to perform its obligations under the discovery rules, the first step—after trying to resolve the dispute informally—is to make a motion for an order compelling the discovery sought. Specific situations warranting a motion to compel include when a party: fails to make any of the disclosures required under Rule 26(a); fails to respond or to respond properly to duly served discovery requests; disagrees with the objections interposed by the other party and wants to compel more complete answers; fails to appear for a properly noticed deposition; believes a witness has improperly refused to answer a deposition question; fails to designate a representative to testify at a deposition under Rule 30(b)(6); or fails to exercise good faith efforts to produce its expert for a deposition.

PRACTICING LAW UNDER THIS SUBPART

Procedures

Motions to compel should include the disputed discovery requests and any responses as exhibits, and should contain the meet and confer certification (discussed below). They are served on all parties and filed with the court. There is no set time limit for filing a motion to compel, and the court will consider delay in filing the motion and the procedural posture of the case in deciding whether a motion to compel is timely. The court has broad discretion in ruling on a motion to compel.

Meet and Confer Certification

The motion to compel must be accompanied by a certification that the movant has in good faith conferred or attempted to confer with the other party or person in an effort to resolve the dispute without court action. The certification can simply be a statement in the motion. If the moving party attempted unsuccessfully to meet and confer, the certification should describe the party's efforts to meet with the opposing party. In general, courts will deny motions to compel that do not have a meet and confer certificate.

Which Court

The proper court in which to file a motion to compel depends on the location and status of the person or entity that is the subject of the motion. If the person or entity is a party, then a motion to compel must be filed in the court where the action is pending. If the motion to compel pertains to a subpoena for deposition or to produce documents issued to a nonparty witness, then a motion to compel should be filed in the district where performance was to occur. That court can adjudicate the motion or transfer it to the court where the action is pending.

Expenses

In general, the victorious party in a motion to compel is entitled to recover its expenses in preparing the motion, including reasonable attorney's fees, from the losing party, its attorney, or both. The movant is also entitled to expenses if the respondent provides a disclosure or discovery response after the motion was filed. The award of expenses by the court is mandatory unless: the movant failed to confer with the respondent in good faith prior to filing the motion; the losing party demonstrates that its conduct was "substantially justified;" or if other circumstances render an award of expenses "unjust." The award of sanctions does not depend on a finding of bad faith or willful misconduct by the sanctioned party. As a practical matter, though, many judges are reluctant to award attorney's fees and frequently find a basis to avoid imposing sanctions.

- *Substantially Justified:* To demonstrate substantial justification, the losing party must demonstrate some unsettled issue of law or like circumstance; good faith generally does not equate to substantial justification. *See Pierce v. Underwood,* 487 U.S. 552, 565 (1988).
- *Circumstances Rendering an Award Unjust:* Determining whether an award of sanctions would be unjust is a flexible analysis that entails consideration of the nature of the offending party's conduct and the harm or prejudice to the opposing party.
- *Opportunity to be Heard:* The court must provide the non-moving party with an opportunity to be heard, either orally or in writing, before imposing sanctions.
- *Motion Granted in Part:* If a motion to compel is granted in part and denied in part, the court may apportion the expenses as it sees fit.
- *Nonparties:* The expense provisions apply only to certain motions involving nonparties. Fees will be awarded in connection with a nonparty making a motion

to obtain a copy of the nonparty's statement. A nonparty may be required to pay expenses incurred because of the nonparty's failure to attend a deposition if a court order had already been entered compelling the nonparty's attendance.

- *Reasonableness of Fees:* The court will typically examine the claimed fees and award only the fees it determines to be reasonable.

Evasive or Incomplete Answer

An evasive or incomplete answer or disclosure is treated as a failure to answer or disclose.

Motion Denied—Protective Order

If the court denies a motion to compel, it can at the same time enter a protective order under Rule 26(c).

RULE 37(b) Failure to Comply with a Court Order

Rule 37(b) contains a list of sanctions that become available if a party or deponent fails to obey a court order compelling discovery under Rule 37(a). Other portions of Rule 37 incorporate the list of sanctions in Rule 37(b), such as Rules 37(c) and (d), which impose sanctions if a party fails altogether to perform certain discovery obligations. The court generally has broad discretion to impose one or more of the listed sanctions or any other sanction it deems appropriate.

PRACTICING LAW UNDER THIS SUBPART

Violation of Order Prerequisite

Rule 37(b) does not authorize sanctions unless the court has already issued a discovery order with which a party or deponent has failed to comply. Any discovery order may satisfy this prerequisite, such as a motion to compel under Rule 37(a), an order issued in a conference under Rule 16, or an order requiring an examination under Rule 35. Some courts authorize sanctions under Rule 37(b) for violations of protective orders issued under Rule 26(c). Although Rule 37(b) is limited to violations of court orders, Rules 37(c) and 37(d) authorize the court to impose the sanctions listed under Rule 37(b) for conduct other than the violation of a discovery order, as discussed below.

- *Exception to Order Prerequisite:* Courts occasionally impose the sanctions listed in Rule 37(b) in the absence of a violation of an order compelling discovery, using the courts' inherent power to manage cases on their dockets.

Sanctions by Court Where Action Pending

Rule 37(b)(2) lists specific categories of sanctions that the court where the action is pending may impose on a party (or an officer, director, or managing agent of a party) and/or an attorney who fails to obey a discovery order. The court has broad discretion to impose any sanction or combination of sanctions it deems appropriate, as long as the sanction is "just" and there is a nexus between the sanction and the discovery violation. The listed sanctions authorize a court to:

- *Deem Facts Established:* The court may deem as established the facts that the moving party was seeking to establish. *See Insurance Corp. of Ireland, Ltd. v. Compagnie des Bauxites de Guinee,* 456 U.S. 694, 705 (1982).
- *Adverse Inference Instruction:* Although Rule 37(b) does not specifically refer to it, courts sometimes issue an adverse inference instruction to the jury, allowing or

requiring them to presume that lost evidence would have been adverse to the party failing to preserve it.

- *Prohibit Evidence:* The court may refuse to allow the disobedient party to introduce certain matters into evidence, or to support or oppose certain claims.
- *Strike Pleadings:* The court may strike any pleading or portion of a pleading.
- *Issue Stay:* The court may stay further proceedings until the order is obeyed.
- *Dispositive Ruling:* In extreme situations, typically for repeat offenders where lesser sanctions have proved unsuccessful, the court may dismiss an action or portions of the action or may enter judgment against the disobedient party.
- *Contempt:* The court may treat the failure to obey its order as a contempt of court, with the exception of a failure to submit to a mental or physical examination (which is punishable by other sanctions, but not as contempt).

List Not Exclusive

The court is not limited to the sanctions listed in Rule 37(b)(2), and may make any order that is "just." In practice, however, courts generally have imposed only those sanctions listed.

Sanctions by Court Where Deposition to Occur

If a nonparty witness fails to comply with an order to appear and be sworn in for a deposition or an order to answer a question at a deposition, the court issuing the order—typically the court where the deposition was to occur—may treat the failure as a contempt of court.

No Meet and Confer Requirement

In contrast to many of the sanctions provisions, a party does not need to meet and confer with the opposing party before filing a motion for sanctions under Rule 37(b). The rationale for this exception is that the parties would have already met and conferred before obtaining the first discovery order—which the opposing party has violated—and that a second meet and confer is therefore not warranted.

Expenses

In addition to, or instead of, the listed sanctions, the court will also require the party not complying with the court order and/or the party's attorney to pay all expenses, including reasonable attorney's fees, incurred by the moving party as a result of the failure to comply. This includes expenses incurred in the motion for sanctions, but not expenses incurred in obtaining the order compelling the discovery (although those expenses may be recoverable under Rule 37(a) as discussed above). The court must award such expenses unless it finds that the failure was "substantially justified" or that other circumstances exist that would make the award "unjust."

Preservation Order

The importance of discovery of electronically stored information has led parties to seek orders requiring opposing parties to preserve evidence. If a party violates a preservation order by failing to preserve ESI, sanctions are available under Rule 37(e), which controls sanctions for spoliation of ESI. If a party violates a preservation order by failing to preserve evidence other than ESI, sanctions are available under Rule 37(b). If a party violates a preservation order by failing to preserve ESI, sanctions may be available under both Rules 37(b) and 37(e).

Failure to Comply by Corporate Representative

The court may also impose sanctions on a party that is a corporation or organization if its officer, director, managing agent, or designated representative fails to obey an order.

RULE 37(c) — Failure to Disclose, to Supplement an Earlier Response, or to Admit

If a party improperly fails to make the automatic disclosures under Rule 26(a) or makes false or misleading disclosures, or if a party fails to supplement a prior discovery response as required by Rule 26(e)(1), the party generally will not be permitted to use the information or documents not properly provided, and may be subject to a variety of additional sanctions. If a party improperly fails to admit a matter, that party must pay the cost the other party incurred in proving the matter.

PRACTICING LAW UNDER THIS SUBPART

Exclusion of Matter Not Disclosed

If a party fails to make the automatic disclosures under Rule 26(a) in a timely manner or makes false, incomplete, or misleading disclosures, the party will not be permitted to use at trial or in a motion the documents, information, expert testimony, or witnesses not properly disclosed, unless the party demonstrates that the failure was "substantially justified" or harmless. The exclusion of evidence or witnesses not properly disclosed is automatic, and there is no need to meet and confer or file a motion for sanctions.

Exclusion of Matter Not Properly Provided by Supplement

If a party fails to supplement its automatic disclosures or to supplement a prior discovery response as required under Rule 26(e)(1), the party will not be permitted to use at trial the documents, information, opinions, damages, or witnesses not properly disclosed, unless the party can demonstrate that it had "substantial justification" or the failure was harmless.

Additional Sanctions

In addition to or in lieu of precluding the evidence, upon motion and after an opportunity to be heard, the court may inform the jury of the party's failure to disclose or supplement or impose additional sanctions, including the sanctions listed above under Rule 37(b). The court has broad discretion in awarding sanctions under Rule 37(c).

Failure to Admit

If a party fails to admit a matter that another party subsequently proves, the other party can move for its reasonable expenses, including attorney's fees, incurred in proving the matter. The court must then award expenses unless one of the following four conditions exists:

(1) The request was objectionable;

(2) The admission sought was of no substantial importance, such as when the proof of the matter was trivial;

(3) The party refusing to admit had reasonable grounds to believe that it would be successful on the matter; or

(4) Other good reasons exist for the failure to admit, such as a genuine inability to determine the truth of the matter.

Party Only

Expenses and fees under Rule 37(c) may be awarded against the party only, not against the attorney, in contrast to other provisions of Rule 37.

Explanation of Sanctions

The court order must state the basis for its decision to impose sanctions so that the sanctioned party may obtain meaningful appellate review.

RULE 37(d) Party's Failure to Attend Its Own Deposition, Serve Answers to Interrogatories, or Respond to a Request for Inspection

Rule 37(d) provides that upon motion, sanctions are immediately available against a party who fails to appear for the party's deposition after being served with proper notice, fails to answer or object to properly-served interrogatories, or fails to serve a written response to a properly-served request to inspect documents or things. Thus, a court order is not a prerequisite to sanctions under Rule 37(d).

PRACTICING LAW UNDER THIS SUBPART

Parties Only

Rule 37(d) applies only to parties; a nonparty's failure to attend a deposition may result in contempt sanctions, but does not result in automatic sanctions under Rule 37(d).

Failures of a Party's Rule 30(b)(6) Representative

A corporation or organization that is a party is subject to the sanctions in Rule 37(d) if its officer, director, managing agent, or person designated to testify under Rule 30(b)(6) fails to appear for a deposition after being properly noticed. Likewise, if a party refuses to designate a representative under Rule 30(b)(6), the party will be subject to sanctions under Rule 37(d).

Certification of Conference

A motion for sanctions under Rule 37(d) for failure to respond to interrogatories or requests for inspection must include a certification that the movant has in good faith conferred or attempted to confer with the other party or person in an effort to obtain a response without court action. This requirement does not apply to the failure to appear for a deposition (because the harm already occurred when the noticing party showed up for the deposition and the deponent did not appear, so an agreement during a meet and confer to appear at another date does not cure the harm).

Available Sanctions

Rule 37(d) states that the court may impose whatever sanctions are "just," including those listed in Rule 37(b) except for contempt of court sanctions (because the party has not violated a court order). The court has broad discretion in deciding what sanction to impose. The court can consider all the circumstances, such as whether the failure was accidental or in bad faith in determining the sanctions to impose.

Expenses

The court must require that the party failing to participate in discovery and/or the party's attorney pay the resulting expenses of the other party, including reasonable attorney's fees, unless it finds that the failure was "substantially justified" or that other circumstances exist that would make the award "unjust." The award of expenses can be in addition to or instead of other sanctions.

Incomplete Response to Interrogatories or Document Requests

Rule 37(d) only applies if the party fails altogether to serve a response to interrogatories or document requests. If the party serves an incomplete or evasive response, the proper procedure is a motion to compel under Rule 37(a), then a motion for sanctions under Rule 37(b) if the party does not comply with the court order. Some courts allow sanctions under Rule 37(d) when the response to the discovery requests is so deficient as to be tantamount to no response at all.

Compliance After Motion

Once a motion for sanctions has been filed, the non-participating party cannot avoid sanctions by responding to the discovery request. However, the court can consider that conduct in deciding what sanctions to impose.

RULE 37(e) Failure to Preserve Electronically Stored Information

Rule 37(e) contains the provisions for sanctioning a party who fails to take reasonable steps to preserve electronically stored information that it was required to preserve. It does not authorize any sanctions unless there was a duty to preserve the lost information, the information was lost because a party failed to take reasonable steps to preserve it, and the information cannot be restored or replaced through additional discovery. If the court finds prejudice to another party from the loss of the information, it may impose only measures no greater than necessary to cure the prejudice. If the court finds that the spoliating party acted with the intent to deprive another party of the information's use in the litigation, the court may impose the more severe sanctions of presuming that the information was unfavorable to the spoliating party, instructing the jury that it may or must presume that the information was unfavorable to the spoliating party, dismissing the action, or entering a default judgment.

PRACTICING LAW UNDER THIS SUBPART

Prerequisites for Sanctions

Rule 37(e) authorizes sanctions for failure to preserve ESI only if three prerequisites are met:

(1) There must have been a duty to preserve the ESI at the time the ESI was lost. Rule 37 does not create a duty to preserve; that duty is found in common law or statutes and typically arises when litigation has been commenced or is reasonably anticipated and the ESI is reasonably likely to be relevant to a party's claim or defense;

(2) The ESI was lost because a party failed to take reasonable steps to preserve it. ESI lost despite reasonable measures to preserve it, such as through the routine operation of a computer system or as a result of damage to a computer system, will not support sanctions; and

(3) The ESI cannot be restored or replaced through additional discovery. ESI often exists in multiple locations, so loss from one location will not support sanctions if the ESI also exists in another location. ESI that might have been deemed inaccessible, such as ESI located on backup tapes, might become discoverable if the accessible versions have been lost.

Sanctions to Cure Prejudice to Another Party

If the court finds the three prerequisites satisfied and finds prejudice to another party from the loss of the information, the court may impose sanctions, but may only impose measures no greater than necessary to cure the prejudice. The court has wide discretion in fashioning an appropriate sanction to cure the prejudice, and the measures need not cure every conceivable prejudicial effect. The measures may not include the more severe sanctions in Rule 37(e)(2), however. Examples of appropriate sanctions include forbidding the spoliating party from introducing certain evidence at trial, permitting parties to present evidence and arguments to the jury about the loss of the ESI, and giving instructions to the jury to assist it in evaluating such evidence and argument, and monetary penalties.

Sanctions for Intent to Affect the Litigation

If the court finds the above prerequisites satisfied and finds that the party acted with the intent to deprive another party of the information's use in the litigation, the court may impose more severe sanctions. In a bench trial, the court may presume that the lost ESI was unfavorable to the party failing to preserve it. In a jury trial, the court may make an adverse inference instruction to the jury that it may or must presume the information was unfavorable to the party failing to preserve it. The court may also impose dispositive sanctions, dismissing the action or entering default judgment for the plaintiff.

RULE 37(f) Failure to Participate in Framing a Discovery Plan

If a party fails to participate in developing a proposed discovery plan as required by Rule 26(f), the court may, after opportunity for a hearing, require the party failing to participate to pay the expenses of the other party, including reasonable attorney's fees, caused by the failure.

VI. TRIALS

RULE 38

RIGHT TO A JURY TRIAL; DEMAND

(a) Right Preserved. The right of trial by jury as declared by the Seventh Amendment to the Constitution—or as provided by a federal statute—is preserved to the parties inviolate.

(b) Demand. On any issue triable of right by a jury, a party may demand a jury trial by:

(1) serving the other parties with a written demand—which may be included in a pleading—no later than 14 days after the last pleading directed to the issue is served; and

(2) filing the demand in accordance with Rule 5(d).

(c) Specifying Issues. In its demand, a party may specify the issues that it wishes to have tried by a jury; otherwise, it is considered to have demanded a jury trial on all the issues so triable. If the party has demanded a jury trial on only some issues, any other party may—within 14 days after being served with the demand or within a shorter time ordered by the court—serve a demand for a jury trial on any other or all factual issues triable by jury.

(d) Waiver; Withdrawal. A party waives a jury trial unless its demand is properly served and filed. A proper demand may be withdrawn only if the parties consent.

(e) Admiralty and Maritime Claims. These rules do not create a right to a jury trial on issues in a claim that is an admiralty or maritime claim under Rule 9(h).

[Amended February 28, 1966, effective July 1, 1966; March 2, 1987, effective August 1, 1987; April 22, 1993, effective December 1, 1993; April 30, 2007, effective December 1, 2007; March 26, 2009, effective December 1, 2009.]

UNDERSTANDING RULE 38

HOW RULE 38 FITS IN

Rule 38 starts the "Trials" section of the Rules. Rules 38 and 39 contain the provisions for obtaining a jury trial, with Rule 38 setting forth the procedures for requesting, or "demanding," a jury trial and Rule 39 controlling whether an action will be tried before a jury or will be tried before a judge in a "bench trial." Recognize at the outset, though, that these Rules do not create the right to a jury trial or define the extent of the right—the Seventh Amendment to the Constitution defines the right to a jury trial. Accordingly, Rule 38 states that it "preserves" the rights in the Seventh Amendment. To understand the parameters of the right to a jury trial, then, lawyers must turn to Supreme Court precedent, not to the text of the Rules.

Although the Seventh Amendment creates the right to a jury trial in certain circumstances, those rights are waivable and require affirmative action. Specifically, Rule 38 provides that a party must file and serve a jury trial "demand," and that failure to make a timely demand results in waiver of the right to a jury trial. It also sets forth the procedures for making a demand and for seeking to withdraw a demand, should the party change its mind.

THE ARCHITECTURE OF RULE 38

Rule 38 is relatively short, but still has five subsections. Rule 38(a) is simply a declaration that the Seventh Amendment right to a jury trial is preserved. Rule 38(b) contains the procedures for making a demand for a jury trial. Rule 38(c) allows parties to demand a jury trial for individual issues or claims, rather than for the entire case. Rule 38(d) contains two separate provisions, one that deems the right to a jury trial waived if no demand is served timely, and one that prevents withdrawal of a jury trial demand unless all parties consent. Finally, Rule 38(e) excludes Admiralty and Maritime claims from the jury trial provisions in the Rules.

HOW RULE 38 WORKS IN PRACTICE

RULE 38(a) — Right Preserved

Rule 38 essentially codifies the Constitution's Seventh Amendment, which provides that the parties have a right to trial by jury for all suits at common law with more than $20 in controversy. In general, a suit "at common law" refers to a legal claim—typically seeking money damages—not an equitable claim such as a claim for injunctive relief.

PRACTICING LAW UNDER THIS SUBPART

Jury Right Preserved, Not Created

Rule 38 does not create a right to a jury trial; that right arises under the Seventh Amendment to the Constitution or under federal statute. Rule 38(a) recognizes that the Federal Rules of Civil Procedure are designed to "preserve" the constitutional right to a jury.

"At Common Law"—Law vs. Equity

Under the Seventh Amendment and Rule 38, the parties have a right to a jury in all actions that, in 1791 at the time of the enactment of the Seventh Amendment, would have been tried "at common law," such as tort or breach of contract actions for money damages, but no right to a jury in actions that historically would have been tried in the courts of equity, such as actions for injunctive relief of specific performance. *See Tull v. United States,* 481 U.S. 412, 417 (1987) ("Prior to the Amendment's adoption, a jury trial was customary in suits brought in the English *law* courts. In contrast, those actions that are analogous to 18th-century cases tried in courts of equity or admiralty do not require a jury trial."). Although there are no longer separate courts of law and equity in the federal court system, the historical distinction remains critical for determining the right to a jury trial.

Jury Right Provided by Statute

The right to a jury trial may be provided by statute. In such cases, the procedures for invoking or demanding the right to a jury trial may be governed by the statute, not Rule 38.

Counterclaims

The right to a jury trial extends to counterclaims (permissive or compulsory), even if the complaint only contains equitable claims. *See Beacon Theatres, Inc. v. Westover,* 359 U.S. 500, 508 (1959).

Declaratory Judgment Actions

The right to a jury trial is preserved in declaratory judgment actions—actions that seek a declaration of the parties' rights rather than affirmative relief like money damages or an injunction. If an issue would have been triable by a jury if brought as an affirmative claim, it will also be triable to a jury in a declaratory judgment action. *See Beacon Theatres, Inc. v. Westover,* 359 U.S. 500, 509–10 (1959).

Newly Created/Statutory Claims

For claims that did not exist in 1791 at the time of the Seventh Amendment, such as statutory claims or new common law claims, the Supreme Court developed a two-pronged analysis to evaluate the right to a jury trial for such claims. The court will try to determine the cause of action in existence in 1791 most analogous to the new claim and see whether that claim enjoyed the right to a jury trial, and will consider whether the relief sought is more akin to a legal or equitable remedy, with the latter factor having a greater impact on the outcome. *See Chauffeurs, Teamsters and Helpers, Local No. 391 v. Terry,* 494 U.S. 558, 565 (1990); *Granfinanciera v. Nordberg*, 492 U.S. 33, 42 (1989).

Right Depends on Facts

The court bases its rulings on the issues raised by the *facts and relief alleged in the pleadings*, not on the labels used by the parties. *See Dairy Queen, Inc. v. Wood,* 369 U.S. 469, 478–79 (1962).

Jury Issues First

When there are jury and nonjury issues or claims present, the jury should first determine the jury trial issues, then the court should resolve any remaining issues, so that the right to a jury trial on the legal claims is not infringed through the judge's prior determination of the equitable claims. *See Beacon Theatres, Inc. v. Westover,* 359 U.S. 500, 510–11 (1959). Any factual findings made by the jury are then binding on the judge when trying the nonjury issues.

RULE 38(b) Demand

Any party may assert its right to a jury trial by making a jury trial "demand." The demand then applies to all parties for the duration of the case.

PRACTICING LAW UNDER THIS SUBPART

Form of Demand

The jury trial demand should be in writing, and can be part of a pleading or a separate signed document. Rule 38 does not require any particular language or placement, so long as the intent to demand a jury is clear. To avoid timing problems, many lawyers include the jury trial demand on the complaint or answer.

Timing of Service and Filing

A party wishing a jury trial for an issue must *serve* a jury trial demand within 14 days after service of the last pleading raising or responding to that issue. Normally, the last pleading is the answer to the pleading raising the issue. The party must also *file* the jury trial demand within a reasonable time, as provided in Rule 5(d). If a jury trial demand is served after the 14th day, the court has discretion to consider the demand. A party waives its right to a jury trial unless it properly serves and files a demand.

No Need for Other Parties to Make Additional Demands

Once one party has made a jury demand, the other parties may rely on that demand and do not need to file jury demands of their own.

Amendments

An amended pleading does not restart the jury trial demand clock for issues raised in the original pleading, but would create the right to make a jury trial demand for an altogether new claim.

Removal

The removing party or the plaintiff may make a jury trial demand within 14 days of filing the removal petition. Others may make demands within 14 days of service of the petition. If a pleading directed to the issue on which a jury is sought is filed after the petition, then all parties have 14 days from service of the pleading to file a jury trial demand. If, prior to removal, a party has made a jury demand in accordance with State procedures or has made a jury demand that would satisfy federal requirements, or if State procedures do not require a demand, then no jury trial demand is necessary following removal.

Objections to Jury Trial Demand

A party objecting to a jury trial demand may challenge it by filing a motion to strike. The Rules do not specify a time limit for moving to strike a jury trial demand.

RULE 38(c) Specifying Issues

A party may limit a jury trial demand to specific issues. Other parties then have 14 days to make a jury trial demand for remaining issues. A jury trial demand that does not specify individual issues is deemed a demand for a jury trial on all issues that are properly triable to a jury.

RULE 38(d) Waiver; Withdrawal

Failure to serve and file a timely jury trial demand is a waiver of the right, even if the failure was inadvertent. Likewise, a party waives the right to a jury trial if the party participates in a nonjury trial without objecting. Once a jury trial demand has been made, it cannot be withdrawn except with the consent of all parties. However, if the case develops such that the right to a jury trial no longer exists, the court can designate the case as nonjury without the consent of the parties.

RULE 38(e) Admiralty and Maritime Claims

Rule 38 does not create a right to a jury trial for admiralty or maritime claims.

RULE 39

TRIAL BY JURY OR BY THE COURT

(a) When a Demand Is Made. When a jury trial has been demanded under Rule 38, the action must be designated on the docket as a jury action. The trial on all issues so demanded must be by jury unless:

(1) the parties or their attorneys file a stipulation to a nonjury trial or so stipulate on the record; or

(2) the court, on motion or on its own, finds that on some or all of those issues there is no federal right to a jury trial.

(b) When No Demand Is Made. Issues on which a jury trial is not properly demanded are to be tried by the court. But the court may, on motion, order a jury trial on any issue for which a jury might have been demanded.

(c) Advisory Jury; Jury Trial by Consent. In an action not triable of right by a jury, the court, on motion or on its own:

(1) may try any issue with an advisory jury; or

(2) may, with the parties' consent, try any issue by a jury whose verdict has the same effect as if a jury trial had been a matter of right, unless the action is against the United States and a federal statute provides for a nonjury trial.

[Amended April 30, 2007, effective December 1, 2007.]

UNDERSTANDING RULE 39

HOW RULE 39 FITS IN

Rule 39 contains the provisions controlling which actions are tried before a jury and which actions are tried before a judge. Its provisions are triggered by a jury trial demand under Rule 38, following which the court will designate the case as a jury action on the docket. The court must then conduct a jury trial unless the parties stipulate to a nonjury trial or the court determines that the parties did not have a right to a jury trial under the Seventh Amendment or a federal statute. Even if no party makes a proper demand for a jury trial under Rule 38, however, Rule 39 authorizes the parties to file a motion seeking a jury trial on any issue for which the party could have demanded a jury trial.

For actions where no right to a jury trial exists, Rule 39 provides two options for empaneling a jury. First, the court may empanel an advisory jury. An advisory jury is a jury that participates in a trial just like a regular jury, but whose verdict is not binding on the court—the judge takes the advisory jury verdict into consideration, but has the authority to issue a judgment that differs from the verdict.

Second, if the parties consent, the court may conduct a binding jury trial even for issues where no right to a jury trial exists.

THE ARCHITECTURE OF RULE 39

Rule 39 contains three subsections. Rule 39(a) obligates the court, following a proper jury trial demand, to designate the case as a jury action on the docket and to conduct a jury trial unless the parties stipulate to a bench trial or the court determines that no right to a jury trial exists. Rule 39(b) authorizes the court, on motion, to conduct a jury trial in the absence of a proper jury trial demand for issues where the right to a jury trial exists. Rule 39(c) contains the court's options to conduct a trial before a binding or advisory jury for actions where the right to a jury trial does not exist.

HOW RULE 39 WORKS IN PRACTICE

RULE 39(a) — When a Demand Is Made

Once a jury trial has been demanded for a claim, the docket will be so designated and the claim must be tried to a jury unless the parties stipulate otherwise or the court determines that no right to a jury trial exists.

PRACTICING LAW UNDER THIS SUBPART

Stipulations

The parties may stipulate to a nonjury trial, even if a timely jury trial demand has been filed. The stipulation should be clear and unambiguous, and must be made either:

- in writing and filed with the court; or
- orally in open court and entered in the record.

Striking Improper Jury Demand

When a party has filed a jury trial demand for a claim where no jury rights exists, such as an equity claim, the court should order a nonjury trial, either *sua sponte* or upon motion to strike.

Jury Verdict Following Demand Binding

If a trial occurs before a jury following a jury trial demand, the verdict is binding and may not be treated as advisory.

Waiver by Participation in Bench Trial

Participating in a bench trial without objection may constitute a waiver of the right to a jury trial, even if a timely demand was filed.

RULE 39(b) — When No Demand Is Made

When no party has filed a timely jury trial demand, the court will hear the trial unless, upon motion and in its discretion, the court orders a jury trial of claims for which a jury trial could properly have been made.

RULE 39(c) — Advisory Jury; Jury Trial by Consent

The judge may empanel an advisory jury if the case will not be tried to a binding jury, and may conduct a binding jury trial of any claim—legal or equitable—if all parties consent.

PRACTICING LAW UNDER THIS SUBPART

Broad Discretion to Empanel Advisory Jury

The court may empanel an advisory jury on motion or *sua sponte*. The court has broad discretion as to whether to empanel an advisory jury even if the parties do not consent.

Advisory Verdict Non-Binding

The judge is the ultimate trier of fact with an advisory jury and has complete discretion to adopt or reject the verdict of the advisory jury.

Binding Jury with Consent

If no claims at law are present, the judge still may empanel a normal, binding jury with the consent (either express or by failure to object) of *all* parties. Consent of the parties does not require the judge to empanel a jury, it merely gives the court the discretion to do so. An exception to this rule is that certain statutes prohibit jury trials in specified actions against the United States.

RULE 40
SCHEDULING CASES FOR TRIAL

Each court must provide by rule for scheduling trials. The court must give priority to actions entitled to priority by a federal statute.

[Amended April 30, 2007, effective December 1, 2007.]

UNDERSTANDING RULE 40

HOW RULE 40 FITS IN

Rule 40 delegates the trial scheduling function to individual district courts, who are directed to formulate their own rules for placing cases on the trial calendar.

THE ARCHITECTURE OF RULE 40

Rule 40 sets forth its relatively simple terms in two short sentences.

HOW RULE 40 WORKS IN PRACTICE

Individual Judges' Broad Discretion

Individual judges have broad discretion regarding scheduling of cases on their dockets. They may give precedence to cases of public importance or cases in which delay will cause hardship. *But see Clinton v. Jones,* 520 U.S. 681, 707–708 (1997) (the court abused its discretion in deferring trial until after president left office).

Precedence by Statute

Rule 40 recognizes that some statutes provide for precedence for actions brought under the statute's provisions.

Motion for Continuance

The trial judge has great discretion in ruling on motions to continue a trial date.

RULE 41

DISMISSAL OF ACTIONS

(a) Voluntary Dismissal.

(1) By the Plaintiff.

(A) Without a Court Order. Subject to Rules 23(e), 23.1(c), 23.2, and 66 and any applicable federal statute, the plaintiff may dismiss an action without a court order by filing:

(i) a notice of dismissal before the opposing party serves either an answer or a motion for summary judgment; or

(ii) a stipulation of dismissal signed by all parties who have appeared.

(B) Effect. Unless the notice or stipulation states otherwise, the dismissal is without prejudice. But if the plaintiff previously dismissed any federal- or State-court action based on or including the same claim, a notice of dismissal operates as an adjudication on the merits.

(2) By Court Order; Effect. Except as provided in Rule 41(a)(1), an action may be dismissed at the plaintiff's request only by court order, on terms that the court considers proper. If a defendant has pleaded a counterclaim before being served with the plaintiff's motion to dismiss, the action may be dismissed over the defendant's objection only if the counterclaim can remain pending for independent adjudication. Unless the order states otherwise, a dismissal under this paragraph (2) is without prejudice.

(b) Involuntary Dismissal; Effect. If the plaintiff fails to prosecute or to comply with these rules or a court order, a defendant may move to dismiss the action or any claim against it. Unless the dismissal order states otherwise, a dismissal under this subdivision (b) and any dismissal not under this rule—except one for lack of jurisdiction, improper venue, or failure to join a party under Rule 19—operates as an adjudication on the merits.

(c) Dismissing a Counterclaim, Crossclaim, or Third-Party Claim. This rule applies to a dismissal of any counterclaim, crossclaim, or third-party claim. A claimant's voluntary dismissal under Rule 41(a)(1)(A)(i) must be made:

(1) before a responsive pleading is served; or

(2) if there is no responsive pleading, before evidence is introduced at a hearing or trial.

(d) Costs of a Previously Dismissed Action. If a plaintiff who previously dismissed an action in any court files an action based on or including the same claim against the same defendant, the court:

(1) may order the plaintiff to pay all or part of the costs of that previous action; and

(2) may stay the proceedings until the plaintiff has complied.

[Amended effective March 19, 1948; July 1, 1963; July 1, 1966; July 1, 1968; August 1, 1987; December 1, 1991; April 30, 2007, effective December 1, 2007.]

UNDERSTANDING RULE 41

HOW RULE 41 FITS IN

The Rules contain a number of mechanisms for terminating cases. For example, if a defendant does not answer, the plaintiff may seek a default judgment under Rule 55. Defects in the complaint or in due process related to the complaint might result in dismissal under Rule 12. Lack of factual support for claims or defenses might lead to summary judgment under Rule 56. Rule 41 provides another avenue for terminating a case, and it establishes three procedural mechanisms for obtaining a dismissal under its terms: by filing a notice; by stipulation; or by motion.

One of the most common situations for using Rule 41 is to obtain a dismissal of a case that the parties have settled. A large percentage of cases end in settlement, and Rule 41 is frequently employed in the form of a stipulated order submitted to the court. Rule 41 also authorizes a plaintiff to dismiss a case unilaterally, without consent from the defendant or court permission, so long as the plaintiff dismisses the case early in the proceeding, before the defendant has answered or filed a motion for summary judgment. Note that a Rule 12 motion to dismiss does not terminate the right to voluntary dismissal—if the defendant identifies a flaw in the complaint in an early motion to dismiss, the plaintiff may elect to walk away by dismissing the complaint. Thus, if the defendant files a Rule 12(b)(2) motion to dismiss for lack of personal jurisdiction, the plaintiff can simply file a notice of dismissal and then refile in another State.

If the defendant has already answered or filed a motion for summary judgment and the defendant will not stipulate to dismissal, the plaintiff may still seek dismissal of the action, but needs court permission. The rationale for this requirement is that the defendant incurs costs as a case proceeds, and therefore the likelihood that the defendant will suffer prejudice from the plaintiff's dismissal increases as the case proceeds—the defendant will have incurred attorney's fees and other costs for no real purpose, so the court involvement is designed to protect the defendant.

All of the above types of dismissal are "voluntary dismissals"—dismissals where the *plaintiff* is *voluntarily* dismissing the case. Rule 41 also authorizes a *defendant* to seek "*involuntary* dismissal." Rule 41 lists three types of conduct by a plaintiff that will potentially support a defendant's motion for involuntary dismissal: failure to prosecute the case (letting it languish); failure to comply with the Federal Rules of Civil Procedure (typically repeated, systematic failure); or failure to comply with the court's orders. Involuntary dismissal must be sought by motion, and the defendant will have the burden of persuasion.

With any dismissal under Rule 41, it is important to understand the rules regarding whether the dismissal is "with prejudice"—meaning that the plaintiff cannot file another action with the same claim again—or "without prejudice" (see the Getting Started section of this book for a more detailed discussion of these concepts). A voluntary dismissal is presumed to be without prejudice unless it specifies otherwise. Often, though, a stipulated dismissal following settlement will specify that the dismissal is with prejudice. Conversely, an involuntary dismissal is presumed to be with prejudice unless it specifies otherwise.

The "Two-Dismissal Rule" provides an exception to these general presumptions. If a plaintiff has already dismissed a claim once, the second dismissal of the same claim is deemed to be "on the merits," resulting in a dismissal with prejudice. The Two-Dismissal Rule is designed to prevent a plaintiff from harassing a defendant by repeatedly filing and dismissing the same claim.

THE ARCHITECTURE OF RULE 41

The two primary subsections of Rule 41 address voluntary dismissals (Rule 41(a)) and involuntary dismissals (Rule 41(b)). Rule 41(a) is further divided into two important subsections, one for voluntary dismissals that do not require court action and one for voluntary dismissals by motion. Rule 41(c) extends the provisions for dismissal of the plaintiff's claims in Rules 41(a) and (b) to joined claims—counterclaims, crossclaims, and third-party claims—providing parallel provisions to the provisions for dismissing the plaintiff's claims. Finally, Rule 41(d) authorizes the court to award costs to a defendant if the plaintiff commences an action after previously having dismissed the same claim against the same defendant, and authorizes the court to stay the second action until the plaintiff has complied with the cost order.

HOW RULE 41 WORKS IN PRACTICE

RULE 41(a)(1) Voluntary Dismissal; By the Plaintiff

The plaintiff may dismiss an action without consent of the court either by stipulation of all parties or unilaterally if the defendant has not yet filed an answer or motion for summary judgment.

PRACTICING LAW UNDER THIS SUBPART

Notice of Dismissal

Dismissal under Rule 41(a)(1) is achieved by filing a "notice of dismissal," no motion or court order is required.

Timing of Notice

Unless stipulated to by all parties, a plaintiff may only file a notice of dismissal under Rule 41(a)(1) if the defendant has not yet served an answer or motion for summary judgment. Otherwise, a plaintiff must file a motion under Rule 41(a)(2), which does not contain a time limitation.

Notice Must Be Unconditional

A notice of dismissal must be unconditional and unequivocal.

Stipulation by All Parties

A stipulation for dismissal of the entire action must be signed by all parties who have appeared in the action or it is not effective. If the dismissal is only as to select parties, only those parties must sign the stipulation.

Effect of Voluntary Dismissal

A voluntary dismissal leaves the situation as if the lawsuit had never been filed, unless the dismissal is specified as with prejudice. A voluntary dismissal that is specified as with prejudice is given the same res judicata/claim preclusion effect as any other judgment. In general, a dismissal under Rule 41(a) deprives the court of any further jurisdiction. If parties want the court to retain jurisdiction (such as to enforce a settlement agreement), they need to ask the court to enter an order to that effect before the dismissal is filed.

Prejudice; Two-Dismissal Rule

Dismissals by notice or stipulation are presumed without prejudice unless they specify otherwise. Voluntary dismissals under Rule 41(a)(1) by the plaintiff are governed by the Two-Dismissal Rule: although the first voluntary dismissal of a given claim is presumed to be without prejudice, the second dismissal acts as a final adjudication on the merits and will preclude a third action asserting a claim that was or could have been asserted in the earlier actions.

Two-Dismissal Rule for Actions in State Court

The Two-Dismissal Rule applies to actions filed in State court on the first occasion. However, if the second action is filed and dismissed in State court, it will not trigger the Two-Dismissal Rule unless the State has a similar rule. Once an action is barred in federal court by the Two-Dismissal Rule, it will also be barred in State court.

Rules and Statutes Requiring Court Approval of Dismissals

Rule 41 is expressly subject to the provisions of Rule 23(e) (requiring court approval for the dismissal of a class action) and Rule 66 (governing cases in which a receiver has been appointed). Voluntary dismissal under Rule 41(a)(1), without court approval, may not apply in claims under statutes that require court approval of settlements, such as *qui tam* actions, actions under the Fair Labor Standards Act, and shareholders' derivative actions.

Dismissal Following Rule 12(b) Motions to Dismiss

In general, a motion to dismiss pursuant to Rule 12(b) for failure to state a claim or for lack of jurisdiction, proper service of process, or venue does not terminate the plaintiff's unilateral right to dismiss.

Dismissal of Part of Action

Courts differ as to the proper procedural mechanism for voluntarily dismissing part of an action. Some courts allow voluntary dismissal of part of an action by notice pursuant to Rule 41. Other courts only allow voluntary dismissal of an entire action and require dismissal of part of an action to be accomplished by a motion to amend pursuant to Rule 15(a).

RULE 41(a)(2) — By Court Order; Effect

Except as provided in Rule 41(a)(1) above (authorizing dismissal by stipulation or before an answer or motion for summary judgment has been filed), voluntary dismissal of an action must be by court order.

PRACTICING LAW UNDER THIS SUBPART

Discretion of Court

The decision whether to grant or deny the plaintiff's motion for voluntary dismissal is within the sound discretion of the court, although some courts hold that the court has no discretion to deny a motion to dismiss *with prejudice* (reasoning that it is unfair to force an unwilling plaintiff to go to trial). A court should grant a motion for voluntary dismissal unless a defendant can show that it will suffer some plain legal prejudice as a result. In general, courts are more likely to grant motions for voluntary dismissal at earlier stages of the litigation.

Conditions

The court may include terms and conditions in its order granting voluntary dismissal in order to prevent prejudice to the defendant. Examples of such conditions include the payment of costs and/or attorney's fees, the payment of costs and fees in the future if the plaintiff subsequently chooses to refile the action, the production of specified documents, making the dismissal with prejudice, requiring that any subsequent action be filed in the same court, providing that discovery from the pending action would carry over to any subsequent actions, and an agreement not to assert specified claims in another action. If the plaintiff is unhappy with the conditions imposed by the court, the plaintiff may decline the dismissal.

Prejudice

A court order granting voluntary dismissal is presumed to be without prejudice unless it explicitly specifies otherwise. The Two Dismissal Rule, described above, does not apply to voluntary dismissals by court order.

Counterclaims

If the defendant has filed a counterclaim, then the plaintiff cannot dismiss the action against the defendant's objections unless the counterclaim can remain pending for adjudication.

Dismissal of Part of Action

The plaintiff may dismiss some, but not all, of the defendants, but courts differ as to the proper procedural mechanism for voluntarily dismissing part of an action. Some courts allow voluntary dismissal by court order pursuant to Rule 41(a)(2). Some courts require a motion to amend pursuant to Rule 15(a).

Enforcement of Settlement Agreement

Normally, a federal court does not retain jurisdiction over an action to enforce the terms of a settlement and stipulated dismissal. In order to vest the district court with such jurisdiction, parties often include in their motion for voluntary dismissal or in their attached proposed order a provision that the court will continue to have jurisdiction to enforce the parties' settlement agreement.

RULE 41(b) Involuntary Dismissal; Effect

Involuntary dismissal is a remedy that a defendant may seek by motion. Rule 41(b) governs two types of involuntary dismissals: dismissal for failure to prosecute; and dismissal for failure to comply with other Rules or with a court order.

PRACTICING LAW UNDER THIS SUBPART

Disfavored

Involuntary dismissal is within the discretion of the court, but is disfavored and is granted sparingly.

Failure to Prosecute

The court may dismiss for failure to prosecute *sua sponte* or upon motion. Local Rules may specify the conditions for dismissal for failure to prosecute (for example, lack of activity for a period of one year).

Failure to Comply with Order

The court may dismiss an action based on the plaintiff's failure to comply with a court order *sua sponte* or upon motion.

Failure to Comply with Rules

The court may dismiss an action for failure to comply with the Rules (although most courts would not dismiss for failure to comply with the Rules unless the conduct was egregious and ongoing). For example, the plaintiff may risk involuntary dismissal by persistently refusing to file a pretrial statement. In contrast, if a party fails to comply with the discovery rules, sanctions—including dismissal—are appropriate under the discovery rules, not Rule 41. To determine whether Rule 41 dismissal is an appropriate sanction for violation of a particular Rule, also review the author commentary and case law discussing that Rule.

Presumed With Prejudice

Involuntary dismissals under Rule 41 are presumed to be with prejudice unless the court specifies otherwise.

RULE 41(c) Dismissing a Counterclaim, Crossclaim, or Third-Party Claim

The provisions of Rule 41 apply to counterclaims, crossclaims, and third-party claims with equal force.

RULE 41(d) Costs of a Previously Dismissed Action

If a plaintiff who has already *voluntarily* dismissed an action commences another action on the same claim, the court, in its discretion, can stay the second action until the plaintiff pays such costs of the first action as the court deems appropriate. The courts are split as to whether an award of costs under Rule 41(d) may include attorney's fees.

RULE 42

CONSOLIDATION; SEPARATE TRIALS

(a) Consolidation. If actions before the court involve a common question of law or fact, the court may:

(1) join for hearing or trial any or all matters at issue in the actions;

(2) consolidate the actions; or

(3) issue any other orders to avoid unnecessary cost or delay.

(b) Separate Trials. For convenience, to avoid prejudice, or to expedite and economize, the court may order a separate trial of one or more separate issues, claims, crossclaims, counterclaims, or third-party claims. When ordering a separate trial, the court must preserve any federal right to a jury trial.

[Amended effective July 1, 1966; April 30, 2007, effective December 1, 2007.]

UNDERSTANDING RULE 42

HOW RULE 42 FITS IN

Rule 42 allows the court to control the manner in which the cases on its docket are organized; the court may consolidate several separate actions into a single proceeding—either entirely or for specific phases or purposes—or may conduct separate trials of various claims or issues that were joined in a single action. The Rule fosters efficiency and fairness. It establishes a threshold requirement for consolidation that the actions have at least one common issue of law or fact—it would be too confusing and wasteful to try two or more completely unrelated cases at the same time. It establishes convenience, prejudice-avoidance, time, and cost as the considerations for ordering separate trials for issues or claims joined in a single action. In general, the trial court has broad discretion regarding consolidation or conducting separate trials.

THE ARCHITECTURE OF RULE 42

Rule 42 addresses two topics—consolidation and separate trials—and has a short section to address each topic. Rule 42(a) establishes the conditions for consolidation and Rule 42(b) contains the criteria for ordering separate trials.

HOW RULE 42 WORKS IN PRACTICE

RULE 42(a) Consolidation

When multiple actions pending before one court share common issues of law or fact, the court can consolidate the actions, either completely or for limited proceedings or stages.

PRACTICING LAW UNDER THIS SUBPART

Procedures

Consolidation is achieved by motion of any party or by the court *sua sponte*. Local rules may determine to which judge a motion to consolidate should be presented if the matters are pending before different judges. In appropriate circumstances, the court may appoint one counsel as lead or liaison counsel.

Court's Discretion

In deciding whether to consolidate actions, the court should balance the savings to the judicial system against the possible inconvenience, delay, or prejudice to the parties. The court has broad discretion in this balancing process, and does not need the parties' consent.

Common Issues Necessary

Although the court has broad discretion, it may not consolidate actions that do not share at least one common issue of law or fact. It may consolidate actions that do not have the same parties or claims, however.

Limited Consolidation

The court may consolidate actions for all purposes, for pretrial proceedings only, for specified hearings or issues, or for trial.

Actions in Different Districts

Actions in different districts may not be consolidated. However, if actions are pending in different districts that ought to be consolidated, the actions may be transferred to a single district, then consolidated, as provided in the Multidistrict Litigation, or MDL, procedures.

Actions Remain Separate

In general, consolidated actions retain their separate identity. *See Hall v. Hall*, 138 S. Ct. 1118, 1125 (2018). Thus, the pleadings will remain separate and the court will enter separate judgments in each action.

RULE 42(b) Separate Trials

The court may conduct separate trials of any claim or issue.

PRACTICING LAW UNDER THIS SUBPART

Procedure

The court may order separate trials *sua sponte* or by motion of any party.

Court's Discretion

Rule 42(b) lists three circumstances supporting bifurcation—for convenience, to avoid prejudice, or to expedite and economize—and any one of these may support bifurcation. In deciding whether to order separate trials, the court will balance the savings to the judicial system against the possible inconvenience, delay, or prejudice to the parties. The court has broad discretion in this balancing process and may bifurcate over a party's objection. Many courts hold that bifurcation should be the exception, not a routine procedure. Even in situations where bifurcation is more common, like the separation of the liability phase from the damages phase, courts will scrutinize requests for bifurcation.

Single Action

A separation under Rule 42 separates aspects of the action for trial, but the aspects remain part of a single action, and result in a single judgment. This contrasts with claims that are severed pursuant to Rule 21.

Common Circumstances for Separate Trials

The most common instance of separate trials is when the court first conducts a trial as to liability, then as to damages if necessary. Punitive damages are also sometimes bifurcated. Bifurcation may also be appropriate when trial of one issue may obviate the need to try another.

Jury Trials

The procedures the court employs for separate trials may not affect the parties' rights to a jury trial. Separate trials may be conducted before one jury or different juries. If there are jury and nonjury claims present, the jury claims may have to be tried first, so that the court does not make factual findings that should properly have been made by the jury. See *Dairy Queen, Inc. v. Wood*, 369 U.S. 469, 479 (1962); *Beacon Theatres, Inc. v. Westover*, 359 U.S. 500, 510–11 (1959).

RULE 43

TAKING TESTIMONY

(a) In Open Court. At trial, the witnesses' testimony must be taken in open court unless a federal statute, the Federal Rules of Evidence, these rules, or other rules adopted by the Supreme Court provide otherwise. For good cause in compelling circumstances and with appropriate safeguards, the court may permit testimony in open court by contemporaneous transmission from a different location.

(b) Affirmation Instead of an Oath. When these rules require an oath, a solemn affirmation suffices.

(c) Evidence on a Motion. When a motion relies on facts outside the record, the court may hear the matter on affidavits or may hear it wholly or partly on oral testimony or on depositions.

(d) Interpreter. The court may appoint an interpreter of its choosing; fix reasonable compensation to be paid from funds provided by law or by one or more parties; and tax the compensation as costs.

[Amended effective July 1, 1966; July 1, 1975; August 1, 1987, December 1, 1996; April 30, 2007, effective December 1, 2007.]

UNDERSTANDING RULE 43

HOW RULE 43 FITS IN

Prior to the enactment of the Federal Rules of Evidence, Rule 43 was entitled "Evidence" and contained evidence provisions that functioned as a very general set of evidence rules. However, in conjunction with the enactment of the Federal Rules of Evidence in 1975, Rule 43 was dramatically scaled back. Today, it contains a grab-bag of minor provisions relating to the taking of testimony. It establishes a preference for live testimony in open court, but authorizes testimony by videoconference or other form of "contemporaneous transmission." Courts have regularly found the issues surrounding COVID-19 to constitute good cause for remote testimony. Rule 43 accords a witness the option of making a "solemn affirmation" to testify truthfully instead of taking an oath (which typically contains a religious reference). It speaks to the manner of submitting evidence to support a motion, allowing submission of affidavits, deposition testimony, or live testimony. Finally, Rule 43 authorizes the court to appoint an interpreter and to determine how the interpreter is paid.

THE ARCHITECTURE OF RULE 43

Rule 43 distributes these four loosely-related topics into four subsections. Rule 43(a) contains the provisions relating to live testimony in open court. Rule 43(b) authorizes witnesses to make a solemn affirmation in lieu of an oath. Rule 43(c) contains the options for supporting a motion with evidence, and Rule 43(d) contains the provisions regarding interpreters.

HOW RULE 43 WORKS IN PRACTICE

RULE 43(a) In Open Court

There is a preference in federal court for testimony taken in open court. All testimony must be in that form unless otherwise authorized by the Federal Rules of Evidence, federal statute, or stipulation by the parties. Rule 43(a) also allows the transmitting of testimony from a different location. However, transmitted testimony is permitted only for good cause shown in compelling circumstances. Transmitted testimony might be allowed when unexpected circumstances, such as an accident or illness, render a witness unable to appear in court. In cases where remote testimony is to be used, the court must employ appropriate safeguards to protect the procedure and the parties' interests.

RULE 43(b) Affirmation Instead of an Oath

A party who, for religious reasons or otherwise, chooses not to take an oath, may make a "solemn affirmation" instead.

RULE 43(c) Evidence on a Motion

A party may submit affidavits and documentary evidence in support of or in opposition to a motion; an evidentiary hearing is not required. The court, in its discretion, may order oral evidence taken or may request deposition transcripts when a motion is based on facts not of record. The court may also consider a motion solely on the parties' written submissions.

RULE 43(d) Interpreter

The court may, in its discretion, appoint an interpreter, who then should take an oath or affirmation that the translation will be accurate. If an interpreter is appointed, the court may determine the interpreter's fees. The court may apportion the fees among the parties, and may award the fees as costs after the conclusion of the trial.

RULE 44

PROVING AN OFFICIAL RECORD

(a) Means of Proving.

(1) *Domestic Record.* Each of the following evidences an official record—or an entry in it—that is otherwise admissible and is kept within the United States, any State, district, or commonwealth, or any territory subject to the administrative or judicial jurisdiction of the United States:

(A) an official publication of the record; or

(B) a copy attested by the officer with legal custody of the record—or by the officer's deputy—and accompanied by a certificate that the officer has custody. The certificate must be made under seal:

(i) by a judge of a court of record in the district or political subdivision where the record is kept; or

(ii) by any public officer with a seal of office and with official duties in the district or political subdivision where the record is kept.

(2) *Foreign Record.*

(A) *In General.* Each of the following evidences a foreign official record—or an entry in it—that is otherwise admissible:

(i) an official publication of the record; or

(ii) the record—or a copy—that is attested by an authorized person and is accompanied either by a final certification of genuineness or by a certification under a treaty or convention to which the United States and the country where the record is located are parties.

(B) *Final Certification of Genuineness.* A final certification must certify the genuineness of the signature and official position of the attester or of any foreign official whose certificate of genuineness relates to the attestation or is in a chain of certificates of genuineness relating to the attestation. A final certification may be made by a secretary of a United States embassy or legation; by a consul general, vice consul, or consular agent of the United States; or by a diplomatic or consular official of the foreign country assigned or accredited to the United States.

(C) *Other Means of Proof.* If all parties have had a reasonable opportunity to investigate a foreign record's authenticity and accuracy, the court may, for good cause, either:

(i) admit an attested copy without final certification; or

(ii) permit the record to be evidenced by an attested summary with or without a final certification.

(b) Lack of a Record. A written statement that a diligent search of designated records revealed no record or entry of a specified tenor is admissible as evidence that the records contain no such record or entry. For domestic records, the statement must be authenticated under Rule 44(a)(1). For foreign records, the statement must comply with (a)(2)(C)(ii).

(c) Other Proof. A party may prove an official record—or an entry or lack of an entry in it—by any other method authorized by law.

[Amended effective July 1, 1966; August 1, 1987; December 1, 1991; April 30, 2007, effective December 1, 2007.]

UNDERSTANDING RULE 44

HOW RULE 44 FITS IN

In general, all evidence needs to be authenticated in some fashion. Typically, such authentication is accomplished by having a witness testify that the record is what it purports to be. For example, a picture is typically authenticated by having a witness testify that the picture is an accurate depiction of what it portrays. Likewise, business records are typically authenticated by having witnesses testify that they are the custodians of the records and that the records came from the company's files where the custodians maintain them.

If a party wants to prove the existence or contents of an official record, such as a weather bureau record, a record of conviction, a tax return, or a marriage or birth certificate, Rule 44 establishes options for authenticating the record. A party may prove an official record by introducing an official publication of the record or by submitting a copy of the record accompanied by a certificate from the officer who has custody of the record. A party may prove lack of an official record—*e.g.*, no tax return exists—by introducing a written statement that a diligent search uncovered no record, accompanied by a certificate of the officer who would have custody of the record. Rule 44 is not the only mechanism for proving an official record, and Rule 44 explicitly authorizes proof by another method authorized by law.

THE ARCHITECTURE OF RULE 44

Rule 44(a) contains the procedures for proving an official record and Rule 44(b) describes how to prove the absence of an official record. Rule 44(a) is further divided into two subsections, one for United States records and one for foreign records. Finally, Rule 44(c) is a "savings clause," expressly allowing proof of any official record by any other means authorized by law.

HOW RULE 44 WORKS IN PRACTICE

RULE 44(a)(1) Means of Proving; Domestic Record

An official record kept within the United States is authenticated if it is an official publication or if it is a copy of an official record which is attested to by the legal custodian and accompanied by a certificate made by a judge or public officer with a seal of office.

PRACTICING LAW UNDER THIS SUBPART

Official Record

"Official record" is not a defined term, but includes such documents as weather bureau records, records of conviction, tax returns, marriage and birth certificates, and selective service files. "Official" does not mean "public"; the public need not have access to "official records."

Authentication Only, Not Admissibility

Rule 44 only *authenticates* records. It does not render the records admissible or immune from other objections such as relevance or hearsay (but see the exception to the hearsay rule for official records).

Official Publication

When a document has been printed by government authority, its authenticity is established.

Attested Copy

A copy of an official record may be attested to by the officer having legal custody of the record or by the officer's deputy.

- *Certificate:* The attested copy must be accompanied by a certificate that the attesting individual has custody of the record. The certificate may be made by a judge in the district or political subdivision in which the document is kept or by a public official with duties in the district or political subdivision in which the document is kept, provided that the official has a seal of office and authenticates the certificate with that seal.

RULE 44(a)(2) Means of Proving; Foreign Record

A foreign official record may be authenticated in essentially the same manner as a domestic record (described immediately above), with some minor variations.

PRACTICING LAW UNDER THIS SUBPART

Official Publication

As with a domestic official record, official publications of foreign official records are self-authenticating. Under this rule, a document that, on its face, appears to be an official publication will be admissible unless another party can demonstrate that it is not an official publication. Official publications from a foreign government website will be accepted by the court as self-authenticating.

Attested Copy with Certificate

A foreign official record may be attested to by any person authorized by the laws of that country to attest records if the signature is certified by a secretary of embassy or legation, consul general, consul, vice consul or consular agent of the United States, or a diplomatic or consular official of the foreign country assigned or accredited to the United States.

Attested Copy Without Certificate

The court has discretion to admit an attested copy of a foreign official record without a certificate if all parties have had a reasonable opportunity to investigate the authenticity and accuracy of the record or for good cause.

RULE 44(b) Lack of a Record

A party may prove the absence of a particular record with a written statement that after diligent search, no record or entry of the specified nature exists. The statement must be authenticated in the same manner as for an official record.

RULE 44(c) Other Proof

The methods in Rule 44 are not exclusive. Quite often, an official will testify as to the authenticity of an official record. Similarly, certain documents are self-authenticating under Rules 901 and 902 of the Federal Rules of Evidence. Additionally Rule 902 allows the court to relax the Rule 44 authentication requirements if the party so requesting shows that it was unable to satisfy the Rule's requirements for authentication despite reasonable efforts.

RULE 44.1
DETERMINING FOREIGN LAW

A party who intends to raise an issue about a foreign country's law must give notice by a pleading or other writing. In determining foreign law, the court may consider any relevant material or source, including testimony, whether or not submitted by a party or admissible under the Federal Rules of Evidence. The court's determination must be treated as a ruling on a question of law.

[Added effective July 1, 1966; amended effective July 1, 1975; August 1, 1987; April 30, 2007, effective December 1, 2007.]

UNDERSTANDING RULE 44.1

HOW RULE 44.1 FITS IN

When a claim, defense, or other issue that arises under a foreign country's laws is before the court, the judge must determine the contents of that foreign law. Rule 44.1 establishes procedures when a party intends to raise such an issue of foreign law. It requires the party to provide notice of its intent to rely on foreign law, then authorizes the judge to rely on any relevant source of information to determine the foreign law, even if the information would otherwise be inadmissible under the Federal Rules of Evidence. Common methods of proving foreign law include treatises and testimony from lawyers familiar with the foreign law.

THE ARCHITECTURE OF RULE 44.1

Rule 44.1 addresses this single topic in a single section.

HOW RULE 44.1 WORKS IN PRACTICE

Notice of Foreign Law Issue

A party must give written notice to the court and all other parties of its intent to raise an issue concerning foreign law. The notice should specify the issues or claims purportedly governed by foreign law, but need not state the specific provisions of the foreign law.

Form of Notice

The notice may be included in a pleading or may be a separate document.

Timing for Notice

Rule 44.1 does not set a specific time for filing the notice. If the notice is a separate document, it should be served as soon as possible to give a reasonable opportunity to all parties to prepare. If not already raised, issues of foreign law are sometimes raised at the pretrial conference.

Party Giving Notice

Notice is normally given by the party whose claim or defense is based on foreign law, but may be raised by any party. If one party has given notice, other parties can rely on that notice and do not need to provide their own notices. If parties believe that a different foreign law applies from the law raised by another party, they should issue separate notices.

Court Determines Foreign Law

The determination of foreign law is a matter of law, not a matter of fact, and is therefore made by the court. *Animal Sci. Prod., Inc. v. Hebei Welcome Pharm. Co.*, 138 S. Ct. 1865, 1868 (2018).

Materials Used by the Court

The court may consider any relevant material or source to determine foreign law, regardless of whether it is admissible. *Animal Sci. Prod., Inc. v. Hebei Welcome Pharm. Co.*, 138 S. Ct. 1865, 1868 (2018). Common methods of proving foreign law are through expert testimony or declarations, affidavits from lawyers practicing in the foreign country, and treatises. The court may also do its own research or seek the aid of an expert witness to help in the interpretation of foreign law, but is under no obligation to do so.

Burden of Proof

The party seeking application of foreign law has the burden of proving the applicability and content of the foreign law. In the absence of proof of foreign law, the court may presume that the foreign law would be the same as local law.

Choice of Law

Rule 44.1 is implicated only after the court has determined that a foreign country's laws apply using the forum State's choice of law provisions in diversity actions and federal common law choice of law rules for claims arising under federal statutes.

RULE 45

SUBPOENA

(a) In General.

(1) *Form and Contents.*

(A) *Requirements—In General.* Every subpoena must:

(i) state the court from which it issued;

(ii) state the title of the action and its civil-action number;

(iii) command each person to whom it is directed to do the following at a specified time and place: attend and testify; produce designated documents, electronically stored information, or tangible things in that person's possession, custody, or control; or permit the inspection of premises; and

(iv) set out the text of Rule 45(d) and (e).

(B) *Command to Attend a Deposition—Notice of the Recording Method.* A subpoena commanding attendance at a deposition must state the method for recording the testimony.

(C) *Combining or Separating a Command to Produce or to Permit Inspection; Specifying the Form for Electronically Stored Information.* A command to produce documents, electronically stored information, or tangible things or to permit the inspection of premises may be included in a subpoena commanding attendance at a deposition, hearing, or trial, or may be set out in a separate subpoena. A subpoena may specify the form or forms in which electronically stored information is to be produced.

(D) *Command to Produce; Included Obligations.* A command in a subpoena to produce documents, electronically stored information, or tangible things requires the responding person to permit inspection, copying, testing, or sampling of the materials.

(2) *Issuing Court.* A subpoena must issue from the court where the action is pending.

(3) *Issued by Whom.* The clerk must issue a subpoena, signed but otherwise in blank, to a party who requests it. That party must complete it before service. An attorney also may issue and sign a subpoena if the attorney is authorized to practice in the issuing court.

(4) *Notice to Other Parties Before Service.* If the subpoena commands the production of documents, electronically stored information, or tangible

things or the inspection of premises before trial, then before it is served on the person to whom it is directed, a notice and a copy of the subpoena must be served on each party.

(b) Service.

(1) *By Whom and How; Tendering Fees.* Any person who is at least 18 years old and not a party may serve a subpoena. Serving a subpoena requires delivering a copy to the named person and, if the subpoena requires that person's attendance, tendering the fees for 1 day's attendance and the mileage allowed by law. Fees and mileage need not be tendered when the subpoena issues on behalf of the United States or any of its officers or agencies.

(2) *Service in the United States.* A subpoena may be served at any place within the United States.

(3) *Service in a Foreign Country.* 28 U.S.C. § 1783 governs issuing and serving a subpoena directed to a United States national or resident who is in a foreign country.

(4) *Proof of Service.* Proving service, when necessary, requires filing with the issuing court a statement showing the date and manner of service and the names of the persons served. The statement must be certified by the server.

(c) Place of Compliance.

(1) *For a Trial, Hearing, or Deposition.* A subpoena may command a person to attend a trial, hearing, or deposition only as follows:

(A) within 100 miles of where the person resides, is employed, or regularly transacts business in person; or

(B) within the State where the person resides, is employed, or regularly transacts business in person, if the person

(i) is a party or a party's officer; or

(ii) is commanded to attend a trial and would not incur substantial expense.

(2) *For Other Discovery.* A subpoena may command:

(A) production of documents, electronically stored information, or tangible things at a place within 100 miles of where the person resides, is employed, or regularly transacts business in person; and

(B) inspection of premises at the premises to be inspected.

(d) Protecting a Person Subject to a Subpoena; Enforcement.

(1) *Avoiding Undue Burden or Expense; Sanctions.* A party or attorney responsible for issuing and serving a subpoena must take reasonable steps to avoid imposing undue burden or expense on a person subject to the subpoena. The court for the district where compliance is required must enforce this duty and impose an appropriate sanction—which may include lost earnings and reasonable attorney's fees—on a party or attorney who fails to comply.

(2) *Command to Produce Materials or Permit Inspection.*

(A) *Appearance Not Required.* A person commanded to produce documents, electronically stored information, or tangible things, or to permit the inspection of premises, need not appear in person at the place of production or inspection unless also commanded to appear for a deposition, hearing, or trial.

(B) *Objections.* A person commanded to produce documents or tangible things or to permit inspection may serve on the party or attorney designated in the subpoena a written objection to inspecting, copying, testing, or sampling any or all of the materials or to inspecting the premises—or to producing electronically stored information in the form or forms requested. The objection must be served before the earlier of the time specified for compliance or 14 days after the subpoena is served. If an objection is made, the following rules apply:

(i) At any time, on notice to the commanded person, the serving party may move the court for the district where compliance is required for an order compelling production or inspection.

(ii) These acts may be required only as directed in the order, and the order must protect a person who is neither a party nor a party's officer from significant expense resulting from compliance.

(3) *Quashing or Modifying a Subpoena.*

(A) *When Required.* On timely motion, the court for the district where compliance is required must quash or modify a subpoena that:

(i) fails to allow a reasonable time to comply;

(ii) requires a person to comply beyond the geographical limits specified in Rule 45(c);

(iii) requires disclosure of privileged or other protected matter, if no exception or waiver applies; or

(iv) subjects a person to undue burden.

(B) *When Permitted.* To protect a person subject to or affected by a subpoena, the court for the district where compliance is required may, on motion, quash or modify the subpoena if it requires:

(i) disclosing a trade secret or other confidential research, development, or commercial information; or

(ii) disclosing an unretained expert's opinion or information that does not describe specific occurrences in dispute and results from the expert's study that was not requested by a party.

(C) *Specifying Conditions as an Alternative.* In the circumstances described in Rule 45(d)(3)(B), the court may, instead of quashing or modifying a subpoena, order appearance or production under specified conditions if the serving party:

(i) shows a substantial need for the testimony or material that cannot be otherwise met without undue hardship; and

(ii) ensures that the subpoenaed person will be reasonably compensated.

(e) Duties in Responding to a Subpoena.

(1) *Producing Documents or Electronically Stored Information.* These procedures apply to producing documents or electronically stored information:

(A) *Documents.* A person responding to a subpoena to produce documents must produce them as they are kept in the ordinary course of business or must organize and label them to correspond to the categories in the demand.

(B) *Form for Producing Electronically Stored Information Not Specified.* If a subpoena does not specify a form for producing electronically stored information, the person responding must produce it in a form or forms in which it is ordinarily maintained or in a reasonably usable form or forms.

(C) *Electronically Stored Information Produced in Only One Form.* The person responding need not produce the same electronically stored information in more than one form.

(D) *Inaccessible Electronically Stored Information.* The person responding need not provide discovery of electronically stored information from sources that the person identifies as not reasonably accessible because of undue burden or cost. On motion to compel discovery or for a protective order, the person responding must show that the information is not reasonably accessible because of undue burden or cost. If that showing is made, the court may nonetheless order discovery from such sources if the requesting party shows good cause, considering the limitations of Rule 26(b)(2)(C). The court may specify conditions for the discovery.

(2) *Claiming Privilege or Protection.*

(A) *Information Withheld.* A person withholding subpoenaed information under a claim that it is privileged or subject to protection as trial-preparation material must:

(i) expressly make the claim; and

(ii) describe the nature of the withheld documents, communications, or tangible things in a manner that, without revealing information itself privileged or protected, will enable the parties to assess the claim.

(B) *Information Produced.* If information produced in response to a subpoena is subject to a claim of privilege or of protection as trial-preparation material, the person making the claim may notify any party that received the information of the claim and the basis for it. After being notified, a party must promptly return, sequester, or destroy the specified information and any copies it has; must not use or disclose the information until the claim is resolved; must take reasonable steps to retrieve the information if the party disclosed it before being notified; and may promptly present the information under seal to the court for the district where compliance is required for a determination of the claim. The person who produced the information must preserve the information until the claim is resolved.

(f) Transferring a Subpoena-Related Motion. When the court where compliance is required did not issue the subpoena, it may transfer a motion under this rule to the issuing court if the person subject to the subpoena consents or if the court finds exceptional circumstances. Then, if the attorney for a person subject to a subpoena is authorized to practice in the court where the motion was made, the attorney may file papers and appear on the motion as an officer of the issuing court. To enforce its order, the issuing court may transfer the order to the court where the motion was made.

(g) Contempt. The court for the district where compliance is required—and also, after a motion is transferred, the issuing court—may hold in contempt a person who, having been served, fails without adequate excuse to obey the subpoena or an order related to it.

[Amended December 27, 1946, effective March 19, 1948; December 29, 1948, effective October 20, 1949; March 30, 1970, effective July 1, 1970; April 29, 1980, effective August 1, 1980; April 29, 1985, effective August 1, 1985; March 2, 1987, effective August 1, 1987; April 30, 1991, effective December 1, 1991; April 25, 2005, effective December 1, 2005; April 12, 2006, effective December 1, 2006; April 30, 2007, effective December 1, 2007; April 16, 2013, effective December 1, 2013.]

UNDERSTANDING RULE 45

HOW RULE 45 FITS IN

The vast majority of the provisions in the Rules only apply to parties. This is particularly true in the discovery context. Thus, a party may only serve interrogatories, production requests, requests for admission, and deposition notices on another *party*. Rule 45 provides the mechanism for obtaining documents or testimony from a *nonparty*. Because Rule 45 imposes obligations on a nonparty, who typically has no stake or other involvement in the outcome of the action, it includes a variety of protections for nonparty recipients of subpoenas.

Recall that, in order to provide proper notice to a defendant and obligate the defendant to appear and defend against the plaintiff's claims, the plaintiff must serve both the complaint *and a summons* on the defendant, in accordance with Rule 4. In fact, when commencing an action, the "process" in the phrase "service of process" is the summons, not the complaint. It is the summons that "attaches" the defendant and makes the defendant bound by the outcome of the proceeding. A subpoena is also a form of process, and once properly served, obligates the recipient to perform the tasks described in the subpoena.

Issuing a subpoena does not require the judge's involvement, or even permission. Nor does it require assistance from the clerk's office or the U.S. Marshals. Rather, attorneys are authorized to issue subpoenas as they see fit (subject to the limitations discussed below). A subpoena issues from the court where an action is pending, even if performance of the subpoena is to occur outside that district. Form subpoenas are generally available from court websites, with blanks to be filled in with the pertinent information. They are then served by any nonparty who is over 18 years old. If the subpoena requires attendance (such as at a deposition or hearing), the service must also include one day's attendance fee and mileage (but the attendance fee is set by statute and is woefully inadequate to compensate a witness for the burdens imposed by a subpoena).

There are limits, of course, on both the nature and location of the tasks that may be compelled by subpoena. Starting with the nature of the tasks, a subpoena may only compel the recipient to produce documents or to appear to testify; a subpoena cannot compel the recipient to answer interrogatories or requests for admission. The testimony may come in the form of a deposition or at a hearing or trial.

The limits on the location of the tasks are designed to protect the recipient from undue burden. Every subpoena subjects the recipient to burden, so Rule 45 only attempts to minimize that burden, not eliminate it. Accordingly, a subpoena may only compel performance by a nonparty within 100 miles of where the nonparty resides, is employed, or regularly transacts business in person.

In addition to these limitations on the location and nature of the performance required by a subpoena, Rule 45 imposes an obligation on a party serving a subpoena to avoid imposing undue burden or expense on the recipient. Rules 45(d) and (e) set forth a variety of protections for subpoena recipients in language that must be included in the subpoena (thus alerting subpoena recipients to their duties and rights).

One particularly powerful protection for recipients of a subpoena to produce documents or permit an inspection is the right to send a written objection to the party serving the subpoena. An objection relieves the recipient of the duty to perform the tasks in the subpoena and shifts the burden to the issuing party to obtain a court order compelling compliance. This objection right is not available to the recipient of a subpoena to testify—to avoid the obligation to appear, the recipient would need to file a motion to quash or modify the subpoena or a motion for a protective order.

Performance of the tasks in the subpoena proceed much like the equivalent discovery tasks. If the subpoena is for a deposition, the deposition proceeds like any other deposition except that, typically, the attorneys for the parties do not represent the witness, and thus generally may not instruct the witness not to answer questions. Sometimes, the nonparty recipient will bring counsel to the deposition, and the witness's counsel may instruct the witness not to answer a question in accordance with the limitations in Rule 30.

If the subpoena requires production of documents, it will include a list of the documents to be produced. The rules for document production in Rule 34 generally apply, such that the subpoena will apply to documents in the recipient's possession, custody, or control that are responsive and within the scope of discovery in Rule 26(b)(1)—nonprivileged matter relevant to any party's claim or defense and proportional to the needs of the case.

THE ARCHITECTURE OF RULE 45

Rule 45 is one of the longest rules in the Federal Rules of Civil Procedure, and it has an accordingly complex structure. It is located in the chapter of trial rules—Rules 38–53—but could just as easily be situated in the discovery rules chapter. It has two main blocks: Rules 45(a) and 45(b) contain the provisions authorizing the issuance and service of subpoenas; and Rules 45(c), 45(d), and 45(e) contain protections for the subpoena recipient. Rule 45(f) contains procedures for transferring a motion related to a subpoena from the court where the action is pending to the court where performance is to occur. Rule 45(g) clarifies that the court may use its contempt powers to enforce subpoenas.

Drilling down, Rule 45(a) contains a variety of procedural provisions regarding subpoenas. It describes the content of a subpoena (including the required language from Rules 45(d) and 45(e) notifying the recipient of Rule 45's protections), and identifies the tasks a subpoena may require of the recipient. It specifies how an attorney issues a subpoena and serves it on other parties, and from which court it issues. Rule 45(b) contains the procedures for serving a subpoena, both within and outside the United States.

Turning to the protections for the recipient, Rule 45(c) limits how far the recipient must travel in performing the tasks required by the subpoena. Rule 45(d) creates a duty for the person issuing the subpoena to avoid undue burden on the recipient, and describes the recipient's options to object or file a motion to quash when it believes a subpoena is excessively burdensome. For motions to quash, Rule 45(d) identifies circumstances when the court *must* quash the subpoena and other circumstances when it has discretion to grant or deny the motion. It further authorizes the court to modify the subpoena or specify the conditions under which the recipient must perform.

Rule 45(e) describes the recipient's duties in responding to a subpoena. It contains provisions similar to Rule 34 governing ESI and privileged documents.

HOW RULE 45 WORKS IN PRACTICE

RULE 45(a) In General

Parties to legal proceedings have the power to issue a subpoena compelling a nonparty to appear and testify at a deposition, hearing, or trial at a designated time and location, produce documents or things, or permit the inspection of premises.

PRACTICING LAW UNDER THIS SUBPART

Issuance

Typically, a subpoena is issued by an attorney, acting as an officer of the court. To be effective, the subpoena must be signed by the issuing attorney. An attorney may issue a subpoena on behalf of any court before which the attorney is authorized to practice. This applies equally to attorneys admitted *pro hac vice* (for one matter only).

Contents

Every subpoena should:

(1) state the name of the court issuing the subpoena;

(2) contain the caption and civil action number of the case;

(3) command the recipient to appear and give testimony (describing the method of recording if the testimony is to be given at a deposition), to produce for inspection the documents, electronically stored information, or things described in the subpoena or in an attachment thereto, and/or to permit inspection of premises, at a designated time and location; and

(4) recite the language in subsections (c) and (d) of Rule 45.

♦ **NOTE:** Blank subpoenas generally are available on the uscourts.gov website or at the clerk's office and will include the requisite language.

Scope

Subpoenas are limited to two functions: compelling a witness to testify (in the old days, sometimes called a subpoena *ad testificandum*) and compelling a nonparty to permit the inspection of documents, tangible things, or property (sometimes called a subpoena *duces tecum*). Thus, a party cannot, by subpoena, compel a nonparty to answer interrogatories, answer requests for admission, preserve documents, or submit to a medical examination under Rule 35. The scope of documents or information that can be obtained by subpoena is the same as the scope of discovery generally under Rule 26.

Which Court

All subpoenas are issued from the court where the action is pending (even for a deposition occurring outside the district or state where the action is pending).

Number

There is no limit on the number of subpoenas in a civil action (but the limits on the number and duration of depositions in Rule 30 will apply to depositions taken pursuant to subpoena).

Time

Subpoenas for trial testimony may be served at any time. The majority of the courts treat subpoenas to testify at depositions or for production of documents as discovery activities that must be issued within the discovery deadlines.

Subpoenas to Produce Documents

Nonparties may be compelled to produce documents in their possession, custody, or control pursuant to a subpoena *duces tecum*. The provisions from Rule 34(a) governing documents in the responding party's "possession, custody, or control" and for handling privileged documents apply to subpoenas *duces tecum*. Prior to serving a subpoena for the production of documents, the issuing party must provide notice and a copy of the subpoena to all other parties, so that they may object to or challenge the subpoena before production occurs. A subpoena for documents may be a stand-alone document or may be combined with a subpoena to testify.

Subpoena to Inspect Property

A subpoena may be used to obtain inspection, testing, or sampling of the real or personal property of a nonparty.

Subpoena for Testimony

A subpoena may be used to compel a witness—party or nonparty—to appear and testify at a hearing or trial. A subpoena may also be used to compel a nonparty to testify at a deposition (parties are compelled to testify at depositions by deposition notice under Rule 30, without the need for a subpoena).

Subpoena Unnecessary for Parties for Discovery Purposes

A subpoena is not necessary to take the deposition of a party or an officer, director, or managing agent of a party, or to compel a party to produce documents; a notice of deposition pursuant to Rule 30(b) or Rule 31(a) or a document request under Rule 34 is sufficient. A subpoena is necessary for all other employees of corporations or other entities and to compel parties to appear and testify at hearings or trials.

RULE 45(b) Service

Subpoenas may be served at any place within the United States (nationwide service) by any nonparty at least 18 years old.

PRACTICING LAW UNDER THIS SUBPART

Manner of Service

Service is accomplished by "delivery" to the named person. The courts are divided as to whether that delivery must be personal, in-hand service or can be accomplished by delivery to the recipient's residence or place of business (which seems to be the trend).

Proof of Service

If necessary, service can be proved by filing a statement of the date and manner of service, certified by the person making service.

Service on Corporate Agents

Service on the agent of a corporation constitutes service on the corporation.

Tender of Expenses

If the recipient's attendance is commanded, service must be accompanied by the tender of the fees and expenses for a one-day appearance, unless the issuing party is the United States or a United States officer or agency. There is no requirement to tender witness fees and expenses when the subpoena is only for the production of documents. The amount of fees and expenses is controlled by 28 U.S.C. § 1821.

Service in a Foreign Country

Under certain circumstances, a witness subject to the jurisdiction of the court may be in a foreign country. The procedure for issuing a subpoena to such a witness is governed by 28 U.S.C. § 1783 (the Walsh Act), which provides for the issuance of such a subpoena if the court finds that the witness's testimony or documents are "necessary in the interest of justice," and it is not possible to obtain the testimony or documents by other means.

♦ **NOTE:** The Walsh Act only governs issuing a subpoena to a trial witness. Rule 30 discusses how and when foreign witnesses may be deposed.

Notice to Other Parties

If the subpoena is for a deposition, a notice of deposition and the subpoena must be served on all parties pursuant to Rule 30 or Rule 31. If the subpoena requires the production of documents or inspection of premises, notice must be served upon all parties prior to service on the recipient so that the other parties may assert any privileges or objections and may obtain the same or additional documents.

RULE 45(c) Place of Compliance

The recipient of a subpoena generally will not be required to travel more than 100 miles from where the recipient resides, works, or regularly transacts business to perform the functions required by the subpoena (*e.g.*, testify and/or produce documents). A recipient may be required to travel anywhere within the State where the person resides, works, or regularly transacts business to give testimony if the person is a party, an officer of a party, or is commanded to testify at trial.

PRACTICING LAW UNDER THIS SUBPART

Testimony at Deposition or Hearing

A subpoena to testify at a deposition or hearing may require the recipient to travel at most 100 miles from where the recipient resides, is employed, or regularly transacts business in person. If the recipient is a party or officer of a party, the recipient may be required to travel anywhere with the State where the recipient resides, is employed, or regularly transacts business in person.

Testimony at Trial

A subpoena to testify at trial may require the recipient to travel up to 100 miles from, or anywhere within the State, where the recipient resides, is employed, or regularly transacts business in person, unless a nonparty witness would incur substantial expense if required to travel from a location that is within the State but more than 100 miles. If a nonparty recipient would incur substantial expense to travel within the State but more than 100 miles, the issuing party can reimburse the recipient for the travel expenses, thereby requiring the recipient to travel within the State.

Production of Documents, ESI, and Tangible Things

A subpoena to produce documents, ESI, or tangible things may require the recipient to travel at most 100 miles from where the recipient resides, is employed, or regularly transacts business in person. ESI is typically exchanged electronically, rendering these limitations inapplicable.

RULE 45(d) Protecting a Person Subject to a Subpoena; Enforcement

An attorney has a duty not to issue a subpoena for improper purposes or to impose undue burden on the recipient of the subpoena. Rule 45(d) provides mechanisms to challenge subpoenas that violate these duties.

PRACTICING LAW UNDER THIS SUBPART

Duty to Avoid Undue Burden

An attorney issuing a subpoena has a duty to avoid causing undue burden or expense to the recipient or any other person. Some courts use the proportionality concepts from Rule 26(b)(1) to analyze whether expense or burden is "undue." Many courts also recognize that nonparties, who typically do not have any stake in the outcome of the litigation, should not be subjected to the same burdens as parties. The court *must* enforce this duty and *must* impose an appropriate sanction, which may include attorney's fees and lost wages, on a party or attorney who fails to comply with this duty.

Attendance by Person Producing Documents

A person subpoenaed to produce documents or things or to permit an inspection need not actually appear at the designated time, as long as the person complies with the subpoena.

Objection to Subpoena to Produce Documents

A person subpoenaed to produce documents or things or to permit an inspection may serve an objection to all or part of the subpoena within 14 days after service of the subpoena (or before the time designated in the subpoena, if sooner). Objections to subpoenas are customarily made by letter. Once an objection has been served on the party issuing the subpoena, the subpoena recipient is not obligated to comply with the subpoena. Failure to serve timely objections may constitute a waiver of objections to the subpoena other than objections relating to service, and grounds omitted from the objections are also waived. Only nonparties may serve objections; parties must contest a subpoena by a motion to quash or modify. Additionally, the objection procedure is optional; a recipient may file a motion to quash or modify (discussed below) instead.

- *Nonparties Only:* Only nonparties may serve objections; parties must contest a subpoena by a motion to quash or modify the subpoena or a motion for protective order.

- *Objection Procedure Not Applicable to Subpoena to Testify*: The objection procedure does not apply to testimonial subpoenas; those may only be challenged by a motion to quash or modify the subpoena, as discussed below.
- *Motion to Compel following Objection*: If a subpoena recipient serves an objection to the subpoena or fails to respond, the serving party may file a motion to compel under Rule 37(a) in the court for the district where compliance is required. The motion must be served on the subpoena recipient as well as all other parties.
- *Significant Expense/Compensation for Respondent:* If the recipient of a subpoena to produce documents or permit inspection serves an objection and the issuing party files a motion to compel, the court must, if it grants the motion, protect the responding person from significant expense resulting from compliance. The compensation may include lost wages and attorney's fees.

Motion to Quash or Modify; Mandatory Relief

A subpoena recipient, or another person asserting privilege, may move to quash a subpoena in the court for the district where compliance is required. The motion must be "timely" filed—the recipient should file the motion before the subpoena date for performance and a party should file the motion before the subpoena is served. Rule 45(d)(3) lists situations in which a subpoena *must* be quashed or modified:

(1) *Time to Comply:* the subpoena does not provide reasonable time to comply;

(2) *Distance to Travel:* the subpoena requires a person not a party or officer of a party to travel beyond the limits specified in Rule 45(c) (generally, 100 miles from where the recipient resides, is employed, or regularly transacts business in person);

(3) *Privileged Matters:* the subpoena requires the disclosure of privileged or other protected matters. Some courts require a subpoena recipient to provide the serving party with a privilege log when objecting on the basis of privilege; or

(4) *Undue Burden:* the subpoena subjects the recipient to undue burden. One of the factors that affects undue burden is whether the requested information can be obtained from the parties. This provision is sometimes used as justification for imposing the nonparty's expenses on the party issuing the subpoena to cure the undue burden on the nonparty.

Motion to Quash or Modify; Permissive Relief upon Demonstration of Substantial Need

Rule 45(d)(3)(B) lists circumstances in which the court has discretion to quash or modify a subpoena. The court also has the option of imposing conditions on the recipient's compliance, if the serving party shows a "substantial need" for the testimony, documents, or inspection and ensures that the recipient will be reasonably compensated. These circumstances are:

(1) *Trade Secrets:* the subpoena requires disclosure of trade secrets or other confidential research, development, or commercial information; or

(2) *Unretained Experts:* the subpoena seeks opinions from experts who have not been retained (so that other parties cannot obtain the experts' testimony by subpoena without paying their fees).

RULE 45(e) Duties in Responding to a Subpoena

Although Rule 45(e) is broadly titled "duties in responding to a subpoena," its provisions only address the recipient's duties when responding to a subpoena to produce documents. It requires that documents may be produced as they are normally kept or may be separated, organized, and labeled to correspond to the requests. When privileges are asserted, the recipient must expressly describe the privilege assertions with enough detail that other parties and the court can assess the privilege assertion.

PRACTICING LAW UNDER THIS SUBPART

Production of Documents

The scope of production under a subpoena is the same as the scope for discovery generally under Rule 26—essentially nonprivileged matter relevant to any party's claim or defense and proportional to the needs of the case. The responding party has the option of allowing the serving party to inspect and copy the documents where they are normally kept, or may collect the responsive documents and organize and label them to correspond to the categories requested.

Electronically Stored Information

Rule 45 expressly allows for the party issuing the subpoena to request to inspect, copy, sample, or test electronically stored information.

- *Form of Electronically Stored Information:* Rule 45(e)(1)(B) allows, but does not require, the requesting party to specify the form in which it is requesting electronically stored information (*i.e.*, PDF, JPG, TIFF, native format, etc.). If the requesting party does not specify the form, then the responding person must produce the electronically stored information in the form in which it is ordinarily maintained or in a form that is reasonably usable. In any event, a person need not produce electronically stored information in more than one form.
- *Undue Burden or Cost:* If the responding person believes that the production of electronically stored information from certain sources will cause undue burden or cost, the person can, in lieu of producing the information, identify those sources. In such cases, the court may specify conditions for the production, such as requiring the requesting party to pay the expenses of the production.

Asserting a Privilege

When the subpoena recipient seeks to withhold information that is privileged, the recipient must expressly claim the privilege and describe the nature of the documents, communications, or things not produced in sufficient detail that the court and parties can assess the privilege. The party asserting the privilege should provide a detailed privilege log at the time of asserting the privilege or within a reasonable time thereafter.

Recalling Privileged Information

Rule 45(e)(2)(B) establishes a procedure to recall privileged information that has already been produced. Anyone believing that a person has produced privileged information in response to a subpoena may provide a notification to the parties who have received the information. After receiving such a notification, the receiving party must return, sequester, or destroy the specified information and all copies (including taking reasonable steps to retrieve any information that the receiving party had already disclosed to other persons). If the receiving party does not agree with the privilege assertion, it can present the information to the court for the district where compliance is required for a determination of the privilege claim. During the pendency of the court's review of the privilege claim, the receiving party is prohibited from using the information and the producing party must preserve it.

RULE 45(f) Transferring a Subpoena—Related Motion

Motions regarding the scope or validity of a subpoena are filed in the district where performance of the subpoena is to occur, and that court can transfer such motions to the court where the action is pending if the person subject to the subpoena consents or the court finds "exceptional circumstances." Such circumstances are rare, and the person seeking transfer bears the burden of establishing appropriate grounds. Generally, a court will transfer a motion only when the potential for disrupting the underlying litigation outweighs the interests of the nonparty subpoena recipient in obtaining local resolution of the motion. The court where the action is pending then transfers its order back to the original court for enforcement.

RULE 45(g) Contempt

Failure to obey a properly served, valid subpoena or subpoena-related order without adequate excuse is a contempt of the court for the district where compliance is required. Contempt is the only sanction for a nonparty failing to comply with a subpoena.

PRACTICING LAW UNDER THIS SUBPART

Proper Challenge to Improper Subpoena

If a party believes that a subpoena is not valid, the proper response is to file a motion to quash or for a protective order, not to ignore the subpoena.

Holding Subpoena Recipient in Contempt

Before sanctions may be imposed on a person charged with contempt under Rule 45, due process requires that the person receive notice and an opportunity to be heard and that the court have personal jurisdiction over the person to be sanctioned. The court will impose contempt sanctions if the moving party establishes by clear and convincing evidence that: (1) a subpoena set forth an unambiguous command; (2) the alleged contemnor violated that command; (3) the violation was significant, meaning the alleged contemnor did not substantially comply with the subpoena; and (4) the alleged contemnor failed to make a reasonable and diligent effort to comply.

RULE 46

OBJECTING TO A RULING OR ORDER

A formal exception to a ruling or order is unnecessary. When the ruling or order is requested or made, a party need only state the action that it wants the court to take or objects to, along with the grounds for the request or objection. Failing to object does not prejudice a party who had no opportunity to do so when the ruling or order was made.

[Amended effective August 1, 1987; April 30, 2007, effective December 1, 2007.]

UNDERSTANDING RULE 46

HOW RULE 46 FITS IN

Historically, preserving an objection for appeal was a two-step process. First, the party had to object. If the judge overruled the objection, the party then had to note its "exception" to the ruling. Failure to follow this process resulted in waiver of the objection. Rule 46 eliminates this duplicative process, declaring formal exceptions unnecessary. It also preserves a party's right to appeal a ruling even in the absence of an objection if the party had no opportunity to object.

THE ARCHITECTURE OF RULE 46

Rule 46 sets forth these related provisions in one relatively short section.

HOW RULE 46 WORKS IN PRACTICE

Applies to All Stages

Rule 46 applies to all stages of a trial, from voir dire through jury instructions.

Form of Objection

In order to preserve an issue for appeal, an objection must state the particular grounds upon which the objection rests; it is not sufficient to state simply, "objection," or to make a general objection. The primary purpose of the specificity requirement is to apprise the court of the litigant's position so that the court can correct its ruling if appropriate. Consequently, if the grounds are obvious to the trial judge, an appellate court may overlook a lack of specificity.

Formal Exceptions Unnecessary

It is not necessary to note an "exception" or take any other action to preserve a properly raised but overruled objection.

Failure to Object—Waiver

In general, failure to object to a ruling or issue constitutes a waiver of the ruling or issue, but an attorney need not object if there is no opportunity to do so. Additionally, the appeals court may consider on appeal an issue to which no objection was asserted when the basis was so clear that no objection was necessary, such as when the attorney has already objected to the same evidence. Also, the appellate court may overlook the lack of an objection if the error was so fundamental that it caused a miscarriage of justice.

RULE 47
SELECTING JURORS

(a) Examining Jurors. The court may permit the parties or their attorneys to examine prospective jurors or may itself do so. If the court examines the jurors, it must permit the parties or their attorneys to make any further inquiry it considers proper, or must itself ask any of their additional questions it considers proper.

(b) Peremptory Challenges. The court must allow the number of peremptory challenges provided by 28 U.S.C. § 1870.

(c) Excusing a Juror. During trial or deliberation, the court may excuse a juror for good cause.

[Amended effective July 1, 1966; December 1, 1991; April 30, 2007, effective December 1, 2007.]

UNDERSTANDING RULE 47

HOW RULE 47 FITS IN

Although many aspects of the jury selection process vary considerably from court to court, there are some consistent components. In general, the clerk's office gathers a large panel of potential jurors, from which the actual jurors are selected. There is usually a process for collecting information from the panel members, often by combination of written questionnaires and oral questioning (often called "voir dire"). This information includes demographic information like age, address, educational background, and occupation, as well as information bearing on potential bias, like relationship or familiarity with the parties or lawyers. In some courts, the lawyers make brief statements and ask questions, and in others the judge or a clerk asks the questions.

Once this information is solicited, the lawyers have an opportunity to strike jurors from the pool. There are two types of strikes—for cause and peremptory. With strikes for cause, a party typically challenges the juror and the judge then decides whether the juror should remain on the panel (sometimes after asking the juror if he or she can issue a verdict based on the evidence or would be swayed by the grounds identified in the challenge). In contrast, lawyers have almost unfettered discretion in exercising peremptory strikes—the only recognized improper grounds for a peremptory strike are race and gender.

Because many of the details of the jury selection process are controlled by local rules or even chambers rules, Rule 47 is very general. It authorizes the court to oversee the examination of jurors to gather information about them and provides the court with broad discretion in how it structures this examination. It also generally describes the processes for striking potential jurors.

THE ARCHITECTURE OF RULE 47

Rule 47(a) authorizes the court to manage the questioning of jurors. Rules 47(b) and (c) address peremptory and for cause strikes of potential jurors.

HOW RULE 47 WORKS IN PRACTICE

RULE 47(a) Examining of Jurors

The court and/or the parties may ask prospective jurors questions in order to determine bias and to enable the parties to exercise their peremptory challenges in a meaningful manner.

PRACTICING LAW UNDER THIS SUBPART

Scope of Examinations

The court has broad discretion with respect to the scope of voir dire. It may conduct the examination itself or allow the parties to do so. If the court conducts the examination, the parties may submit proposed questions, which the court may ask if it deems them appropriate.

Qualifications for Jurors

The qualifications for jurors are governed by the Jury Selection and Service Act of 1968, 28 U.S.C. § 1861 *et seq.* Essentially, jurors must be United States citizens, have resided in the district for at least one year, meet minimum literacy requirements and be fluent in English, be mentally and physically capable of service, and be free from pending charges or past convictions of crimes punishable by imprisonment for more than 2 years.

Excluded Groups

The Jury Selection and Service Act of 1968 provides for the establishment of certain groups who are precluded or excused from serving. Generally, these include: persons providing vital services (such as members of the armed services and policemen); persons for whom service would be a particular hardship (such as sole proprietors, mothers with young children, persons with gravely ill family members); and those excluded by the court for partiality or because they are likely to be disruptive.

RULE 47(b) Peremptory Challenges

Peremptory challenges are challenges that a party makes unilaterally, without the need for court permission or approval. Peremptory challenges are governed by 28 U.S.C. § 1870, which provides that each party has three peremptory challenges, and generally need not give any explanation for using those challenges. When there are multiple plaintiffs or defendants, the court may require them to exercise the challenges collectively or may allow additional challenges. Although parties have almost unfettered discretion in exercising peremptory strikes, it is improper to use a peremptory challenge to exclude a juror on the basis of race or gender. *See Edmonson v. Leesville Concrete Co., Inc.*, 500 U.S. 614, 616 (1991) (race); *J.E.B. v. Alabama ex rel. T.B.*, 511 U.S. 127, 129 (1994) (gender).

RULE 47(c) Excusing a Juror

The court may excuse a juror for reasons of sickness, family emergency, juror misconduct, or for other "good cause." In deciding whether to excuse a juror, a judge may consider not only the juror's spoken words, but also gestures and other behaviors. A juror's refusal to join the majority is not grounds for excuse.

RULE 48
NUMBER OF JURORS; VERDICT

(a) Number of Jurors. A jury must begin with at least 6 and no more than 12 members, and each juror must participate in the verdict unless excused under Rule 47(c).

(b) Verdict. Unless the parties stipulate otherwise, the verdict must be unanimous and must be returned by a jury of at least 6 members.

(c) Polling. After a verdict is returned but before the jury is discharged, the court must on a party's request, or may on its own, poll the jurors individually. If the poll reveals a lack of unanimity or lack of assent by the number of jurors that the parties stipulated to, the court may direct the jury to deliberate further or may order a new trial.

[Amended effective December 1, 1991; April 30, 2007, effective December 1, 2007; March 26, 2009, effective December 1, 2009.]

UNDERSTANDING RULE 48

HOW RULE 48 FITS IN

Rule 48 controls the makeup and decisions of a jury. It provides that a jury must consist of six to 12 jurors. It provides that the jury's verdict must be unanimous, and gives the parties the right to demand that the jury be polled to verify that the verdict was in fact unanimous. These provisions may be altered by stipulation, such that the parties may agree to a jury smaller than six or to a decision by less than a unanimous verdict.

THE ARCHITECTURE OF RULE 48

The three aspects of juries controlled by Rule 48—jury size, jury unanimity, and jury polling—are divided among Rule 48's three subsections. Rule 48(a) controls the size of a jury, Rule 48(b) discusses jury unanimity, and Rule 48(c) provides for jury polling.

HOW RULE 48 WORKS IN PRACTICE

RULE 48(a) Number of Jurors

The court may select any number of jurors from six to 12. The parties may also stipulate to fewer than six jurors. For longer or more controversial trials, with a greater risk of jurors being excused during the trial, courts will tend to empanel a jury of greater than six.

RULE 48(b) Verdict

Absent a stipulation, verdicts must be unanimous. Verdicts are considered unanimous even if one or more jurors reluctantly joins just to reach a verdict.

PRACTICING LAW UNDER THIS SUBPART

Excused Jurors

If a juror is excused for illness or other reason, a unanimous verdict among the remaining jurors will be valid if at least six jurors remain. If fewer than six remain, the parties may consent to allow the trial or deliberations to continue and then will be bound by the verdict. Otherwise, the court will declare a mistrial.

Stipulations

By stipulation, the parties can agree that a unanimous decision is not necessary, and that the decision of a specified majority will be taken as the decision of the jury. The parties may also stipulate to a jury of fewer than six members.

Further Deliberations Following Deadlock—Allen Charges

If a jury reports being unable to reach a unanimous verdict, the majority of the courts allow an "Allen charge," an instruction to the jury to deliberate further to attempt to break the deadlock. *See Allen v. United States*, 164 U.S. 492 (1896).

RULE 48(c) Polling

After the verdict is read and before the jury is discharged, a party may demand that the jury be polled to verify that the verdict is unanimous and that no juror was coerced into signing the verdict. The court may also poll the jury *sua sponte*. If one or more jurors dissents, the court may require the jury to deliberate further or may declare a mistrial. Polling must occur before the verdict is recorded and the jury is discharged.

RULE 49

SPECIAL VERDICT; GENERAL VERDICT AND QUESTIONS

(a) Special Verdict.

(1) *In General.* The court may require a jury to return only a special verdict in the form of a special written finding on each issue of fact. The court may do so by:

(A) submitting written questions susceptible of a categorical or other brief answer;

(B) submitting written forms of the special findings that might properly be made under the pleadings and evidence; or

(C) using any other method that the court considers appropriate.

(2) *Instructions.* The court must give the instructions and explanations necessary to enable the jury to make its findings on each submitted issue.

(3) *Issues Not Submitted.* A party waives the right to a jury trial on any issue of fact raised by the pleadings or evidence but not submitted to the jury unless, before the jury retires, the party demands its submission to the jury. If the party does not demand submission, the court may make a finding on the issue. If the court makes no finding, it is considered to have made a finding consistent with its judgment on the special verdict.

(b) General Verdict with Answers to Written Questions.

(1) *In General.* The court may submit to the jury forms for a general verdict, together with written questions on one or more issues of fact that the jury must decide. The court must give the instructions and explanations necessary to enable the jury to render a general verdict and answer the questions in writing, and must direct the jury to do both.

(2) *Verdict and Answers Consistent.* When the general verdict and the answers are consistent, the court must approve, for entry under Rule 58, an appropriate judgment on the verdict and answers.

(3) *Answers Inconsistent with the Verdict.* When the answers are consistent with each other but one or more is inconsistent with the general verdict, the court may:

(A) approve, for entry under Rule 58, an appropriate judgment according to the answers, notwithstanding the general verdict;

(B) direct the jury to further consider its answers and verdict; or

(C) order a new trial.

(4) *Answers Inconsistent with Each Other and the Verdict.* When the answers are inconsistent with each other and one or more is also inconsistent with the general verdict, judgment must not be entered; instead, the court must direct the jury to further consider its answers and verdict, or must order a new trial.

[Amended effective July 1, 1963; August 1, 1987; April 30, 2007, effective December 1, 2007.]

UNDERSTANDING RULE 49

HOW RULE 49 FITS IN

At the conclusion of a jury trial, the jury renders its decision in a "verdict." There are a number of different forms the verdict can take, the simplest of which is a "general verdict." With a general verdict, the verdict slip gives the jury the option of designating that they find for the defendant or designating that they find for the plaintiff and writing down the amount they award to the plaintiff.

One of the limitations with a general verdict is that, if an appellate court finds a legal error by the trial court, no one knows the basis of the jury's ruling; everyone just knows the bottom-line result. Thus, the legal error identified by the appellate court might have been fundamental to the outcome or might have been irrelevant, and that uncertainty often necessitates a new trial.

Rule 49 establishes two alternatives to a general verdict designed to minimize the likelihood that the court will need to conduct a new trial if the verdict is subsequently vacated on appeal. The court may submit a "special verdict" to the jury, which requires the jury to make a separate finding as to each issue of material fact. Alternatively, the court may submit both a general verdict and written questions which obtain the jury's factual findings on the pivotal issues framed by the questions. With sufficient information gathered through a special verdict or written questions, the court may be able to mold the verdict to be consistent with both the jury's factual findings and the law as instructed by the court of appeals, avoiding the need for a new trial.

One of the risks with these alternative approaches is that the jury might return a verdict form that contains inconsistencies—after all, jurors are lay people and the legal process can be confusing. Rule 49 provides the court with options to resolve these inconsistencies.

THE ARCHITECTURE OF RULE 49

Rule 49(a) contains the procedures for special verdicts, requiring the court to submit each factual issue to the jury and to instruct the jury as to how to make its findings. It also provides that failure to object to an issue's omission from the special verdict constitutes waiver of the right to a jury trial on that issue—placing the onus of making sure every issue is addressed in the special interrogatories on the parties.

Rule 49(b) contains the procedures for general verdicts with written questions. It authorizes the practice, requires the court to instruct the jury as to how to perform its duties, and provides the court with options when the answers to the questions are either internally inconsistent or are inconsistent with the general verdict.

HOW RULE 49 WORKS IN PRACTICE

RULE 49(a) Special Verdict

The court may require the jury to return special verdicts as to each issue of material fact, instead of a general verdict in favor of one party.

PRACTICING LAW UNDER THIS SUBPART

Comparison with General Verdict

A general verdict is a single statement disposing of the entire case (*e.g.,* "We find in favor of the defendant."). Special verdicts ask the jury to decide specific factual questions (*e.g.,* "At the time of the accident, was the vehicle proceeding at an excessive rate of speed?").

Roles of the Court and the Jury with Special Verdicts

With special verdicts, the jury is not asked to apply the law to the facts of the case and announce the ultimate outcome. Rather, after the jury returns its special verdict responses making factual findings, the court applies the relevant law and determines the final result.

Court's Discretion as to the Use of Special Verdicts

The court has virtually absolute discretion as to the use of special verdicts. This discretion extends to determining the content and layout of the verdict form, provided that the questions asked are reasonably capable of an interpretation that would allow the jury to address all factual issues essential to judgment. Generally, special verdicts are more appropriate in complex cases. Special verdicts are also valuable when the status of the law is uncertain, because if the trial court is reversed on the law, sufficient special verdicts may render a new trial unnecessary.

Scope of Questions

The special verdicts should fairly present the case, and should cover all factual issues.

Instructions to Jury

The court must give the jury sufficient instructions so that they can determine each issue before them.

Omission of Issues

If the court submits special verdicts to the jury and omits a question of material fact raised by the pleadings or evidence, a party must object to the omission before the jury retires or that party waives the right to a jury trial on that issue. As to issues not submitted to the jury and not objected to, the court may make the finding.

Consistency of Special Verdicts

If there is a construction of the special verdicts that renders them consistent, the court will adopt it. Otherwise, the court may require the jury to deliberate further or may declare a mistrial. The court may not, however, enter judgment contrary to the jury's special verdicts.

Objections

Objections to the special verdicts should be made before the jury retires. Objections to the jury's responses or to the judgment to be entered based on the jury's responses should be made, if possible, before the jury is discharged. Courts disagree as to whether failure to do so results in a waiver of the objections.

RULE 49(b) General Verdict with Answers to Written Questions

The court may submit to the jury a general verdict and written questions or interrogatories about specific factual issues. Written questions can focus the jury's attention on important factual issues and provide a mechanism to ensure that the general verdict is consistent with the factual findings. Additionally, if the court is subsequently reversed on a legal issue, a new trial may be avoided if the questions contain sufficient findings such that the court can determine the proper outcome based on the appellate court's legal rulings and the jury's factual findings.

PRACTICING LAW UNDER THIS SUBPART

Court's Discretion to the Use of Written Questions

As with special verdicts, the court has virtually absolute discretion with respect to the use of written questions to the jury and with respect to the format of the questions.

Scope of Questions

Because the jury also returns a general verdict, the scope of the questions is not as critical as with special verdicts—every issue need not be covered.

Answers and Verdict Consistent

If the general verdict is consistent with the answers to the questions, then the court will enter judgment accordingly. Ambiguity usually will be resolved in favor of consistency.

Answers and Verdict Not Consistent

If the answers to the questions are internally consistent but not consistent with the general verdict, the court has three options: it can order the jury to deliberate further; it can enter judgment based on the answers if they are sufficient; or it can declare a mistrial. The court may not enter judgment based on the general verdict in the face of inconsistent answers. If the answers are internally inconsistent and inconsistent with the general verdict, the court can order further deliberations or declare a mistrial, but cannot enter judgment.

Inconsistent Answers

When the answers to the questions are internally inconsistent, the court may order the jury to deliberate further or may order a new trial.

Inconsistent General Verdicts

When general verdicts on different claims are inconsistent, a court may not simply mold one of the two verdicts to be consistent with the other. Rather, the court may: (1) allow the verdicts to stand; (2) attempt to read the verdicts in a manner that will resolve the inconsistencies; (3) resubmit the question to the jury; or (4) order a new trial.

RULE 50

JUDGMENT AS A MATTER OF LAW IN A JURY TRIAL; RELATED MOTION FOR A NEW TRIAL; CONDITIONAL RULING

(a) Judgment as a Matter of Law.

(1) *In General.* If a party has been fully heard on an issue during a jury trial and the court finds that a reasonable jury would not have a legally sufficient evidentiary basis to find for the party on that issue, the court may:

(A) resolve the issue against the party; and

(B) grant a motion for judgment as a matter of law against the party on a claim or defense that, under the controlling law, can be maintained or defeated only with a favorable finding on that issue.

(2) *Motion.* A motion for judgment as a matter of law may be made at any time before the case is submitted to the jury. The motion must specify the judgment sought and the law and facts that entitle the movant to the judgment.

(b) Renewing the Motion After Trial; Alternative Motion for a New Trial. If the court does not grant a motion for judgment as a matter of law made under Rule 50(a), the court is considered to have submitted the action to the jury subject to the court's later deciding the legal questions raised by the motion. No later than 28 days after the entry of judgment—or if the motion addresses a jury issue not decided by a verdict, no later than 28 days after the jury was discharged—the movant may file a renewed motion for judgment as a matter of law and may include an alternative or joint request for a new trial under Rule 59. In ruling on the renewed motion, the court may:

(1) allow judgment on the verdict, if the jury returned a verdict;

(2) order a new trial; or

(3) direct the entry of judgment as a matter of law.

(c) Granting the Renewed Motion; Conditional Ruling on a Motion for a New Trial.

(1) *In General.* If the court grants a renewed motion for judgment as a matter of law, it must also conditionally rule on any motion for a new trial by determining whether a new trial should be granted if the judgment is

later vacated or reversed. The court must state the grounds for conditionally granting or denying the motion for a new trial.

(2) *Effect of a Conditional Ruling.* Conditionally granting the motion for a new trial does not affect the judgment's finality; if the judgment is reversed, the new trial must proceed unless the appellate court orders otherwise. If the motion for a new trial is conditionally denied, the appellee may assert error in that denial; if the judgment is reversed, the case must proceed as the appellate court orders.

(d) Time for a Losing Party's New-Trial Motion. Any motion for a new trial under Rule 59 by a party against whom judgment as a matter of law is rendered must be filed no later than 28 days after the entry of the judgment.

(e) Denying the Motion for Judgment as a Matter of Law; Reversal on Appeal. If the court denies the motion for judgment as a matter of law, the prevailing party may, as appellee, assert grounds entitling it to a new trial should the appellate court conclude that the trial court erred in denying the motion. If the appellate court reverses the judgment, it may order a new trial, direct the trial court to determine whether a new trial should be granted, or direct the entry of judgment.

[Amended January 21, 1963, effective July 1, 1963; March 2, 1987, effective August 1, 1987; April 30, 1991, effective December 1, 1991; April 22, 1993, effective December 1, 1993; April 27, 1995, effective December 1, 1995; April 12, 2006, effective December 1, 2006; April 30, 2007, effective December 1, 2007; March 26, 2009, effective December 1, 2009.]

UNDERSTANDING RULE 50

HOW RULE 50 FITS IN

The purpose of a trial is to resolve *factual* disputes—generally issues where the fact finder must assess witness credibility and decide who to believe. In contrast, legal disputes are resolved by the judge based on legal analysis and precedent, without the need for credibility determinations. Recognizing this function of trials, the Rules establish two junctures when courts assess whether there are genuine disputes regarding the material facts, and will declare no further need for a trial if they find no such factual disputes.

The most common and well-known of these junctures is the motion for summary judgment stage. Parties generally file motions for summary judgment under Rule 56 after the completion of discovery, asserting that, with all the evidence out in the open, there are no genuine disputes regarding the material facts, and that they are entitled to win as a matter of law under those undisputed facts.

Rule 50 provides the second juncture for asserting that no further trial is necessary—motions for judgment as a matter of law. Rule 50 motions occur in the first instance at a jury trial, once one side has offered all of its evidence on a particular claim, defense, or issue. The other side may then file a motion for judgment as a matter of law, arguing that even if the jury believes every piece of evidence offered by the opposing party, that evidence would not support a ruling in the opposing party's favor.

A party bringing an unsuccessful Rule 50 motion for judgment as a matter of law must renew the motion again at the conclusion of the trial—failure to follow this two-step process may result in waiver of the grounds that could have been asserted in a Rule 50 motion.

Motions for judgment as a matter of law are adjudicated under the same standard as motions for summary judgment, discussed in detail below in the coverage for Rule 56, with one nuanced difference; a court is more likely to conditionally deny a motion for judgment as a matter of law and let the jury reach a verdict. Then, the judge might grant a renewed motion if the judge believes the jury's verdict is not supported by the evidence. This approach both accords greater respect to the parties' Seventh Amendment right to a jury trial and reduces the likelihood of needing to conduct a new trial if it turns out on appeal that the judge was wrong in overturning the jury's verdict—the verdict can simply be reinstated. In fact, to foster this approach, Rule 50 provides that, if the court denies a motion for judgment as a matter law during trial, it is presumed to have done so subject to the right to revisit the decision following trial in a renewed motion.

Renewed Rule 50 motions are often accompanied by motions for a new trial under Rule 59. Rule 50 addresses the complex relationship between these two options for providing relief from an improper jury verdict. The proper choice usually depends on whether the jury's verdict contains enough information—through a special verdict or written questions as covered by Rule 49—that the court can determine the proper outcome without infringing the constitutional right to a jury trial.

THE ARCHITECTURE OF RULE 50

Rule 50 has five subparts, two of which address Rule 50 motions and three of which address the interplay between Rule 50 and Rule 59. Rules 50(a) and (b) set forth the provisions for filing the original and renewed motion for judgment as a matter of law. Rule 50(b) also authorizes parties to join motions for a new trial with their renewed motions for judgment as a matter of law.

Rules 50(c), (d), and (e) all work together to specify how a renewed motion for judgment as a matter of law under Rule 50(b) interrelates to a motion for a new trial under Rule 59. Rule 50(c) requires a court granting a Rule 50(b) motion for judgment on the pleadings also to make a conditional ruling on the motion for a new trial, so that an appellate court has the benefit of the trial court's ruling should it reverse the trial court's ruling under Rule 50(b). Rule 50(d) sets a 28-day time period for a party losing a Rule 50(b) motion to file a motion for a new trial under Rule 59. Finally, Rule 50(e) contains the provisions authorizing a party who successfully opposes a Rule 50 motion to advance grounds for a new trial on appeal, in the event the moving party appeals the denial and the court of appeals reverses the ruling on the Rule 50 motion.

HOW RULE 50 WORKS IN PRACTICE

RULE 50(a) Judgment as a Matter of Law

Rule 50(a) allows the court to take a case away from the jury by entering a judgment as a matter of law if there is not sufficient evidence in the record to raise a genuine factual dispute.

PRACTICING LAW UNDER THIS SUBPART

Who May Make a Rule 50(a) Motion

Although motions for judgment as a matter of law are most commonly made by defendants, plaintiffs may also make Rule 50(a) motions. Thus, if the plaintiff enters evidence sufficient to support each element of the plaintiff's case and that evidence is not contradicted during the defendant's case, the plaintiff will be entitled to a judgment as a matter of law. Some courts hold that a judge may also enter judgment as a matter of law *sua sponte,* although other courts hold that judgment as a matter of law may only be made on grounds properly raised by the parties in a Rule 50(a) motion, calling into question the court's ability to issue judgment as a matter of law *sua sponte.*

Form and Timing of Motion

A motion for judgment as a matter of law may be made orally or in writing, but must be made explicitly and on the record. A motion for judgment as a matter of law must specify the judgment sought (*i.e.,* the counts or issues upon which judgment is sought) and the law and facts supporting the judgment. Any issue not clearly articulated in the Rule 50(a) motion may be waived. The motion may be made after the opposing party has been fully heard on an issue, at any time before submission of the case to the jury. Such motions are typically made at the close of the plaintiff's case (by the defendant) or at the close of the record.

Entire Claims or Individual Issues

A motion for judgment as a matter of law may seek judgment on entire claims or defenses or on specific issues that are not wholly dispositive of a claim or defense.

Standard

The standard for a motion for judgment as a matter of law is the same as for a motion for summary judgment (making that substantial body of case law applicable). Judgment as a matter of law is appropriate when the evidence in the record could not properly support a particular verdict. *See Anderson v. Liberty Lobby, Inc.*, 477 U.S. 242, 250–51 (1986). The court must view all evidence and draw all inferences in the light most favorable to the party opposing the motion; it may not make credibility determinations or weigh the evidence. *See Reeves v. Sanderson Plumbing Prods., Inc.*, 530 U.S. 133, 150 (2000). However, the court may disregard testimony that is opposed to undisputed physical facts. Moreover, a "mere scintilla" of evidence is not sufficient to avoid judgment as a matter of law. *See A.B. Small Co. v. Lamborn & Co.*, 267 U.S. 248, 254 (1925). Given the sanctity of the jury process, however, many courts are reluctant to take a case away from a jury.

Binding Jury Trials Only

Rule 50 applies only to binding jury cases. The appropriate motion in non-jury trials and trials with an advisory jury is a motion for judgment on partial findings under Rule 52(c).

Opportunity to Cure

A major purpose of the motion is to provide the opposing party with an opportunity to cure the deficiency in the evidence.

Motion Held Under Consideration

The court is under no obligation to grant a motion for judgment as a matter of law even if the record supports the motion. Courts often defer ruling on a Rule 50(a) motion, allowing the jury to reach a verdict in order to minimize the likelihood of needing a new trial. If the jury reaches the same conclusion as the judge, then the judge will take no action. If the jury reaches the opposite conclusion, the judge can enter judgment as a matter of law. Then, if the case is appealed and the appellate court disagrees with the judge, there is no need for a new trial as the court can simply reinstate the jury verdict.

Motion Granted

If the court grants a motion for judgment as a matter of law, it will enter the appropriate judgment without involvement of the jury.

Motion Denied—Conditional Submission to the Jury

If the court does not grant the motion for judgment as a matter of law, the court is considered to have submitted the action to the jury subject to the court later deciding the questions raised by the motion. If it was the defendant's motion that the court denied, the defendant may put on evidence. However, if the plaintiff's case lacked evidence supporting a certain element and that evidence is brought out during the defendant's case, the deficiency will be cured.

Failure to Make a Rule 50(a) Motion—Prerequisite to Appeal

A motion for judgment as a matter of law before the close of the record is a prerequisite to challenging the sufficiency of the evidence on appeal. *See Unitherm Food Systems, Inc. v. Swift-Eckrich, Inc.*, 546 U.S. 394, 399 (2006). The courts are divided as to whether appellate issues other than those relating to the sufficiency of the evidence, such as pure issues of law, are affected (see the Summary Judgment Motions bullet below). An exception to this principle occurs if the verdict constitutes plain error on the face of the record and a miscarriage of justice would result if the verdict remained in effect.

Issues Previously Raised in Unsuccessful Summary Judgment Motions

The courts differ as to the extent to which a party must raise issues from an unsuccessful motion for summary judgment as a motion for judgment as a matter of law. Some courts do not require presentation of pure legal issues in the form of a Rule 50 motion. Others require all issues raised in a summary judgment motion to be presented in a Rule 50 motion in order to preserve the issues for appeal.

RULE 50(b) — Renewing the Motion After Trial; Alternative Motion for a New Trial

After trial, parties must renew their unsuccessful Rule 50(a) motions for judgment as a matter of law, and the court can enter a judgment that is inconsistent with the jury's verdict if it determines that the verdict was not supported by the evidence.

PRACTICING LAW UNDER THIS SUBPART

Content of Motion

A renewed motion for judgment after trial must state the grounds for relief, and may include only those grounds raised in the original motion for judgment as a matter of law.

Timing

The motion must be filed not later than 28 days after the *entry* of the judgment (not the notice of entry of the judgment). If the jury does not return a verdict, such as with a mistrial, or if the subject of the motion for judgment as a matter of law was an issue not decided by the verdict, the parties have 28 days from the discharge of the jury.

Failure to File is Waiver of Appeal

Failure to file a renewed motion under Rule 50(b) limits a party's right to appeal. *See generally Ortiz v. Jordan*, 562 U.S. 180, 189 (2011). Likewise, parties waive individual arguments by failing to assert them in support of or in opposition to the Rule 50(b) motion.

Same Standard as Rule 50(a)

A renewed motion for judgment as a matter of law under Rule 50(b) is evaluated under the same standard as the initial motion under Rule 50(a); the motion will be denied if the evidence in the record could properly support the verdict, viewing the evidence and all inferences in the light most favorable to the non-moving party.

Motion During Trial a Prerequisite

A party cannot make a motion for judgment after trial unless it filed a motion for judgment as a matter of law before the case was submitted to the jury, and may not assert grounds that were not raised in the Rule 50(a) motion (unless the grounds were not available at that time). If there was no motion for judgment as a matter of law but the evidence does not support the verdict, the court can order a new trial under Rule 59. *See Johnson v. New York, N.H. & H.R. Co.*, 344 U.S. 48, 54 (1952).

Motion for a New Trial

A party may join a motion for a new trial with a motion for judgment after trial, or request a new trial in the alternative. A new trial is favored over a judgment contrary to the verdict when it appears that the party could present sufficient evidence to support the verdict at a future date.

Court's Options in Ruling on a Rule 50(b) Motion and a Motion for New Trial

If the jury returned a verdict, the court may allow the verdict to stand, order a new trial, or direct entry of judgment as a matter of law. If no verdict was returned, the court may order a new trial or direct the entry of judgment as a matter of law. When a motion for new trial is joined with a motion for judgment after trial, Rule 50 specifically requires that the court rule on both motions.

RULE 50(c) Granting the Renewed Motion; Conditional Ruling on a Motion for a New Trial

If the court grants a motion for judgment as a matter of law after trial and a motion for a new trial was also filed, the court must also make a conditional ruling on the motion for a new trial setting forth the reasons for its conditional ruling.

PRACTICING LAW UNDER THIS SUBPART

New Trial Ruling Conditional on Appellate Reversal

The trial court's rulings on the motion for a new trial are applicable if the appeals court reverses the granting of the judgment as a matter of law. In that case, the appeals court will generally enter the original verdict or order a new trial, depending on the trial court's conditional ruling.

Failure to Issue a Conditional Ruling

If a court fails to issue a conditional ruling on the motion for a new trial, the appellate court has the authority to either remand to the trial court to decide the motion for a new trial or decide the motion itself.

RULE 50(d) Time for a Losing Party's New-Trial Motion

If the court grants a motion for judgment as a matter of law, the party against whom judgment was entered may file a Rule 59 motion for a new trial no later than 28 days after the entry of judgment.

RULE 50(e) Denying the Motion for Judgment as a Matter of Law; Reversal on Appeal

If the losing party appeals the denial of a motion for judgment as a matter of law, the prevailing party may on appeal assert grounds for a new trial in the event that the court reverses the denial of the motion for judgment as a matter of law. If the appellate court does reverse, it may order the entry of judgment, order a new trial, or remand to the trial court to determine whether a new trial is warranted.

RULE 51

INSTRUCTIONS TO THE JURY; OBJECTIONS; PRESERVING A CLAIM OF ERROR

(a) Requests.

(1) *Before or at the Close of the Evidence.* At the close of the evidence or at any earlier reasonable time that the court orders, a party may file and furnish to every other party written requests for the jury instructions it wants the court to give.

(2) *After the Close of the Evidence.* After the close of the evidence, a party may:

(A) file requests for instructions on issues that could not reasonably have been anticipated by an earlier time that the court set for requests; and

(B) with the court's permission, file untimely requests for instructions on any issue.

(b) Instructions. The court:

(1) must inform the parties of its proposed instructions and proposed action on the requests before instructing the jury and before final jury arguments;

(2) must give the parties an opportunity to object on the record and out of the jury's hearing before the instructions and arguments are delivered; and

(3) may instruct the jury at any time before the jury is discharged.

(c) Objections.

(1) *How to Make.* A party who objects to an instruction or the failure to give an instruction must do so on the record, stating distinctly the matter objected to and the grounds for the objection.

(2) *When to Make.* An objection is timely if:

(A) a party objects at the opportunity provided under Rule 51(b)(2); or

(B) a party was not informed of an instruction or action on a request before that opportunity to object, and the party objects promptly after learning that the instruction or request will be, or has been, given or refused.

(d) Assigning Error; Plain Error.

(1) *Assigning Error.* A party may assign as error:

(A) an error in an instruction actually given, if that party properly objected; or

(B) a failure to give an instruction, if that party properly requested it and—unless the court rejected the request in a definitive ruling on the record—also properly objected.

(2) *Plain Error.* A court may consider a plain error in the instructions that has not been preserved as required by Rule 51(d)(1) if the error affects substantial rights.

[Amended effective August 1, 1987; March 27, 2003, effective December 1, 2003; April 30, 2007, effective December 1, 2007.]

UNDERSTANDING RULE 51

HOW RULE 51 FITS IN

In cases tried before a jury, the jury renders a verdict (discussed above in Rule 49) declaring which party wins and which party loses. Before they render their verdict, the jurors will have listened to the evidence and will have decided what they think really happened, based on the testimony they believed. But how do they know what the law says about those events? The judge explains the law to the jury in what are referred to as "jury instructions," the reading of which is sometimes called "charging" the jury. The judge typically reads a set of written instructions to the jurors before they deliberate. The instructions cover the substantive law applicable to the case—the elements of the claims and defenses—as well as instructions applicable to jurors more generally, such as instructions about picking a foreperson, deliberating, making credibility determinations, weighing the evidence, etc. Although the jury is fully instructed before they deliberate, the judge may give further instructions during the deliberations if the jury asks questions or the need for further instructions otherwise arises.

Rule 51 contains procedures relating to the jury instructions. The process starts with an opportunity for the parties to propose jury instructions. These are often based on sets of model jury instructions or on applicable case law. The judge typically sets a date for submission of proposed jury instructions sometime shortly before or during trial, and may allow the parties to submit supplemental proposed instructions after the close of evidence. After reviewing the parties' proposed instructions, the judge determines which instructions to give to the jury. Judges are not limited to the parties' proposed instructions, and frequently include instructions that neither party has proposed.

Before the parties give their closing arguments to the jury, the judge must advise them of the jury instructions to be delivered. This process allows the lawyers to take the final instructions into account in framing their closing arguments. The judge must also give the parties an opportunity—on the record but outside the jury's presence—to object to the instructions (both those to be provided and those the judge refuses to provide). The judge must provide this opportunity before the judge instructs the jury, although parties may also object if the judge misstates or omits an instruction when charging the jury. Failure to properly object to the instructions can result in waiver of the right to appeal based on the content of the instructions.

THE ARCHITECTURE OF RULE 51

Rule 51's organization tracks the jury instruction process sequentially. Rule 51(a) contains the procedures for parties to submit proposed instructions to the judge. Rule 51(b) sets forth the requirements for the judge to instruct the jury. Rule 51(c) requires the judge to give the parties the opportunity to object to the instructions, and Rule 51(d) warns of waiver for failure to object.

HOW RULE 51 WORKS IN PRACTICE

RULE 51(a) Requests

The parties may submit proposed jury instructions to the court.

PRACTICING LAW UNDER THIS SUBPART

Timing of Requests

Requests for jury instructions are normally made at the close of the evidence, or earlier if the court so directs. If the court has set a time before the close of evidence for submission of requests for instructions, a party may submit additional requests for instructions after the close of evidence on issues that the party could not have anticipated when it first submitted its requests. The court, in its discretion, may consider untimely requests.

Form and Content of Requests

Requests normally should be reasonably neutral statements of the law governing the case, and not overly argumentative. Requests should be in writing.

RULE 51(b) Instructions

The court must inform the parties of its proposed instructions before instructing the jury and before the parties' closing arguments to the jury, and must give the parties an opportunity to object on the record and out of the jury's hearing.

PRACTICING LAW UNDER THIS SUBPART

Informing Parties of Proposed Instructions

The court is required to inform the parties of its proposed jury instructions and its rulings on the parties' requests before the closing arguments and before it instructs the jury, so that the counsel may adjust their closings accordingly.

Form and Procedure for Instructions

Instructions are given to the jury in open court at any time after trial begins and before the jury is discharged. The judge may repeat portions of the charge or give a supplemental charge at the jury's request, and may instruct them to keep trying if they claim to be deadlocked. The judge may submit a written copy of the instructions to the jury, although it is not commonly done in federal court.

Content of Instructions

If the court is going to use a general verdict, the court should give an instruction on every material legal issue in the case. The instruction should clearly and understandably convey the status of the applicable law. There is no particular wording or order mandated, and the judge need not use the language requested by the parties. If the court is using a special verdict addressing factual questions to the jury, the jury instructions need not address issues of substantive law, but may still address issues like the burden of proof.

Opportunity to Object

The court must give the parties an opportunity to raise objections to the instructions on the record and out of the hearing of the jury before the instructions and closing arguments are delivered. If the court fails to give the parties an opportunity to raise the objections, parties with objections should request an opportunity.

RULE 51(c) Objections

Objections to the instructions must be made on the record with a statement of the grounds.

PRACTICING LAW UNDER THIS SUBPART

Content of Objection

An objection must distinctly state the matter objected to and the grounds for the objection. Parties must state their objections with sufficient clarity and specificity that the judge can understand the nature of the objection and remedy the problem if the judge agrees. Any issue not so raised in an objection is waived, subject only to plain error review under Rule 51(d). See generally *Microsoft Corp. v. i4i Ltd. P'ship*, 564 U.S. 91, 112 (2011); *Connick v. Thompson*, 563 U.S. 51, 75 (2011).

Time of Objections

A party must object to the content of the instructions at the opportunity provided by the court before the instructions and closing arguments are delivered, even if the party has previously raised and attempted to preserve the same objection. If a party was not informed of an instruction or action on a request for an instruction prior to the opportunity to object provided by the court, the party may object promptly upon learning that the instruction was or would be given or refused.

Objection on the Record

Objections to jury instructions must be on the record; objections made off the record in chambers are not effective. It is not sufficient to have proposed an instruction that the court does not give.

RULE 51(d) Assigning Error; Plain Error

A party may base an appeal on an instruction if the party made a proper objection or upon plain error.

PRACTICING LAW UNDER THIS SUBPART

Appeal of Issues Preserved by Objection

In general, a party may only raise on appeal issues regarding the instructions that the party properly raised as objections before the trial court. A party may only raise on appeal an issue regarding an instruction not given if the party made a proper request for the instruction and either the court made a definitive ruling on the record rejecting the request or the party made a proper objection regarding the omitted instruction.

Appeal of Issues Not Preserved by Objection

The appeals court may, under extreme circumstances when justice demands, reverse even if no objections were made when an instruction contains plain error.

RULE 52

FINDINGS AND CONCLUSIONS BY THE COURT; JUDGMENT ON PARTIAL FINDINGS

(a) Findings and Conclusions.

(1) *In General.* In an action tried on the facts without a jury or with an advisory jury, the court must find the facts specially and state its conclusions of law separately. The findings and conclusions may be stated on the record after the close of the evidence or may appear in an opinion or a memorandum of decision filed by the court. Judgment must be entered under Rule 58.

(2) *For an Interlocutory Injunction.* In granting or refusing an interlocutory injunction, the court must similarly state the findings and conclusions that support its action.

(3) *For a Motion.* The court is not required to state findings or conclusions when ruling on a motion under Rule 12 or 56 or, unless these rules provide otherwise, on any other motion.

(4) *Effect of a Master's Findings.* A master's findings, to the extent adopted by the court, must be considered the court's findings.

(5) *Questioning the Evidentiary Support.* A party may later question the sufficiency of the evidence supporting the findings, whether or not the party requested findings, objected to them, moved to amend them, or moved for partial findings.

(6) *Setting Aside the Findings.* Findings of fact, whether based on oral or other evidence, must not be set aside unless clearly erroneous, and the reviewing court must give due regard to the trial court's opportunity to judge the witnesses' credibility.

(b) Amended or Additional Findings. On a party's motion filed no later than 28 days after the entry of judgment, the court may amend its findings—or make additional findings—and may amend the judgment accordingly. The motion may accompany a motion for a new trial under Rule 59.

(c) Judgment on Partial Findings. If a party has been fully heard on an issue during a nonjury trial and the court finds against the party on that issue, the court may enter judgment against the party on a claim or defense that, under the controlling law, can be maintained or defeated only with a favorable finding on that issue. The court may, however, decline to render any judgment until the close of the evidence. A judgment on partial findings must be supported by findings of fact and conclusions of law as required by Rule 52(a).

[Amended December 27, 1946, effective March 19, 1948; January 21, 1963, effective July 1, 1963; April 28, 1983, effective August 1, 1983; April 29, 1985, effective August 1, 1985; April 30, 1991, effective December 1, 1991; April 22, 1993, effective December 1, 1993; April 27, 1995, effective December 1, 1995; April 30, 2007, effective December 1, 2007; March 26, 2009, effective December 1, 2009.]

UNDERSTANDING RULE 52

HOW RULE 52 FITS IN

In cases tried before a jury, Rules 47 through 51 dictate many of the procedures, such as selecting the jury, instructing the jury, and jury verdicts. Nonjury trials, or "bench trials," where the judge hears the evidence and makes the factual findings, are significantly less cumbersome procedurally. Rule 52 provides all of the procedures for bench trials analogous to those in Rules 47–51 for jury trials.

Instead of a verdict reached by the jury at the end of the trial process, in a bench trial the judge makes written findings of fact and conclusions of law. The judge may issue these immediately following trial, but much more often, the judge solicits proposed findings of fact and conclusions of law from the parties, then issues the court's findings and conclusions after reviewing the parties' submissions. These can occur months—and sometimes many months—after the end of the trial. The judge also issues findings of fact and conclusions of law following proceedings relating to temporary restraining orders or preliminary injunctions, but is not required to do so when ruling on motions.

Rule 52(c) establishes the bench-trial equivalent of a Rule 50 motion for judgment as a matter of law. It authorizes the judge to rule against a party on a claim, defense, or issue if the party has already introduced all its evidence on that issue and the court finds the evidence insufficient to support the party's position. The fundamental difference between these two types of motion is that in a Rule 52(c) motion, the judge—as the ultimate fact finder in a bench trial—may make credibility determinations and neither party enjoys any presumptions in its favor.

After the court enters its findings of fact and conclusions of law, the parties have 28 days to point out errors to the court and ask the court to alter or supplement its findings and conclusions. After they are finalized, the court will enter judgment based on the findings and conclusions. If the judgment is appealed, the court of appeals will give great deference to the trial court's findings of fact, and will not disturb them unless they are "clearly erroneous." The trial court's conclusions of law, in contrast, are reviewed "*de novo*"—without deference—by the appellate courts.

THE ARCHITECTURE OF RULE 52

Rule 52 has three subparts. Rule 52(a) contains the bulk of Rule 52's substance, setting forth the general provisions obligating the court to make findings of fact and conclusions of law. Rule 52(b) addresses requests to the court to make additional or modified findings, and Rule 52(c) contains the provisions for partial findings once a party has been fully heard on an issue.

HOW RULE 52 WORKS IN PRACTICE

RULE 52(a) Findings and Conclusions

Following a non-jury trial, the trial judge must explicitly state findings of fact and conclusions of law upon which the judge bases the judgment.

PRACTICING LAW UNDER THIS SUBPART

Findings and Conclusions Mandatory

The requirement that the judge make findings of fact and conclusions of law is mandatory and automatic; the parties do not need to request findings.

Content of Findings and Conclusions

The findings must be sufficient to indicate the factual basis for the ultimate judgment and permit meaningful appellate review, but need not address all the evidence presented at trial. The court should make separate findings of fact and conclusions of law.

Credibility Determinations and Inferences

When making findings of fact, the court makes creditability determinations, accepting or rejecting the testimony of witnesses and drawing any inferences it deems appropriate.

Proposed Findings and Conclusions

The court may require the parties to submit proposed findings of fact and conclusions of law, although the court's wholesale adoption of the prevailing party's submission is discouraged.

Proceedings Covered by Rule 52

The court must make findings of fact and conclusions of law in non-jury trials, proceedings for preliminary or permanent injunctions, and when the court grants a motion for judgment after the plaintiff has presented evidence pursuant to Rule 52(c). Rule 52 does not apply to motions.

Findings in Jury Trials

In jury trials, Rule 52 applies to any issues decided by the court instead of the jury. The court must also make findings of fact and conclusions of law in a case tried before an advisory jury.

Form

The findings of fact and conclusions of law must be on the record. They may be a separate document or may be included in an order or opinion. The court may also make its findings orally on the record. The court should make separate findings of fact and conclusions of law.

Appeals of Findings

Rule 52(a)(6) sets the standard for appellate review of the trial court's findings, and provides that they will not be set aside unless clearly erroneous. *Ohio v. Am. Express Co.*,

138 S. Ct. 2274, 2294 (2018). It also requires appellate courts to give "due regard" to the trial court's credibility determinations. In contrast, the trial court's conclusions of law are reviewed *de novo*.

RULE 52(b) Amended or Additional Findings

Upon motion, the court may amend or supplement its findings and/or judgment.

PRACTICING LAW UNDER THIS SUBPART

Timing

Motions to amend the findings must be filed no later than 28 days after entry of final judgment. This time period is absolute, and cannot be enlarged by the court.

Grounds

Proper grounds for a motion to amend include newly discovered evidence, a change in the law, or a manifest error of fact or law by the trial court. A motion to amend should not merely relitigate old issues, reargue the merits of the case, or raise arguments that could have been raised prior to the issuance of judgment.

RULE 52(c) Judgment on Partial Findings

At any time in a non-jury trial after a party has presented all its evidence with respect to a particular issue, the court may enter judgment against that party on that issue if the evidence failed to persuade the judge.

PRACTICING LAW UNDER THIS SUBPART

Timing of Motion

A Rule 52(c) motion may be made at any time after all the evidence has been presented on a particular topic; although motions for judgment on partial findings are typically made at the close of the opposing party's case, the movant technically does not need to wait until the opposing party has rested.

Standard for Granting

The trial judge rules on motions for judgment on partial findings as a final factfinder, reviewing all evidence presented thus far without presumptions in favor of either party. The judge grants the motion if, upon the evidence already presented, the judge would find in favor of the moving party.

Findings of Fact and Conclusions of Law

If the judge grants a motion for judgment on partial findings, the judge must make findings of fact and conclusions of law pursuant to Rule 52(a).

Deferred Ruling

The judge has discretion to defer ruling until all evidence has been presented. If the judge defers ruling on a motion for judgment on partial findings and either party enters additional evidence regarding the subject of the motion, the judge will consider all the evidence when ultimately ruling.

RULE 53
MASTERS

(a) Appointment.

(1) *Scope.* Unless a statute provides otherwise, a court may appoint a master only to:

(A) perform duties consented to by the parties;

(B) hold trial proceedings and make or recommend findings of fact on issues to be decided without a jury if appointment is warranted by:

(i) some exceptional condition; or

(ii) the need to perform an accounting or resolve a difficult computation of damages; or

(C) address pretrial and posttrial matters that cannot be effectively and timely addressed by an available district judge or magistrate judge of the district.

(2) *Disqualification.* A master must not have a relationship to the parties, attorneys, action, or court that would require disqualification of a judge under 28 U.S.C. § 455, unless the parties, with the court's approval, consent to the appointment after the master discloses any potential grounds for disqualification.

(3) *Possible Expense or Delay.* In appointing a master, the court must consider the fairness of imposing the likely expenses on the parties and must protect against unreasonable expense or delay.

(b) Order Appointing a Master.

(1) *Notice.* Before appointing a master, the court must give the parties notice and an opportunity to be heard. Any party may suggest candidates for appointment.

(2) *Contents.* The appointing order must direct the master to proceed with all reasonable diligence and must state:

(A) the master's duties, including any investigation or enforcement duties, and any limits on the master's authority under Rule 53(c);

(B) the circumstances, if any, in which the master may communicate ex parte with the court or a party;

(C) the nature of the materials to be preserved and filed as the record of the master's activities;

(D) the time limits, method of filing the record, other procedures, and standards for reviewing the master's orders, findings, and recommendations; and

(E) the basis, terms, and procedure for fixing the master's compensation under Rule 53(g).

(3) *Issuing.* The court may issue the order only after:

(A) the master files an affidavit disclosing whether there is any ground for disqualification under 28 U.S.C. § 455; and

(B) if a ground is disclosed, the parties, with the court's approval, waive the disqualification.

(4) *Amending.* The order may be amended at any time after notice to the parties and an opportunity to be heard.

(c) Master's Authority.

(1) *In General.* Unless the appointing order directs otherwise, a master may:

(A) regulate all proceedings;

(B) take all appropriate measures to perform the assigned duties fairly and efficiently; and

(C) if conducting an evidentiary hearing, exercise the appointing court's power to compel, take, and record evidence.

(2) *Sanctions.* The master may by order impose on a party any noncontempt sanction provided by Rule 37 or 45, and may recommend a contempt sanction against a party and sanctions against a nonparty.

(d) Master's Orders. A master who issues an order must file it and promptly serve a copy on each party. The clerk must enter the order on the docket.

(e) Master's Reports. A master must report to the court as required by the appointing order. The master must file the report and promptly serve a copy on each party, unless the court orders otherwise.

(f) Action on the Master's Order, Report, or Recommendations.

(1) *Opportunity for a Hearing; Action in General.* In acting on a master's order, report, or recommendations, the court must give the parties notice and an opportunity to be heard; may receive evidence; and may adopt or affirm, modify, wholly or partly reject or reverse, or resubmit to the master with instructions.

(2) *Time to Object or Move to Adopt or Modify.* A party may file objections to—or a motion to adopt or modify—the master's order, report, or recommendations no later than 21 days after a copy is served, unless the court sets a different time.

(3) *Reviewing Factual Findings.* The court must decide de novo all objections to findings of fact made or recommended by a master, unless the parties, with the court's approval, stipulate that:

(A) the findings will be reviewed for clear error; or

(B) the findings of a master appointed under Rule 53(a)(1)(A) or (C) will be final.

(4) *Reviewing Legal Conclusions.* The court must decide de novo all objections to conclusions of law made or recommended by a master.

(5) *Reviewing Procedural Matters.* Unless the appointing order establishes a different standard of review, the court may set aside a master's ruling on a procedural matter only for an abuse of discretion.

(g) Compensation.

(1) *Fixing Compensation.* Before or after judgment, the court must fix the master's compensation on the basis and terms stated in the appointing order, but the court may set a new basis and terms after giving notice and an opportunity to be heard.

(2) *Payment.* The compensation must be paid either:

(A) by a party or parties; or

(B) from a fund or subject matter of the action within the court's control.

(3) *Allocating Payment.* The court must allocate payment among the parties after considering the nature and amount of the controversy, the parties' means, and the extent to which any party is more responsible than other parties for the reference to a master. An interim allocation may be amended to reflect a decision on the merits.

(h) Appointing a Magistrate Judge. A magistrate judge is subject to this rule only when the order referring a matter to the magistrate judge states that the reference is made under this rule.

[Amended February 28, 1966, effective July 1, 1966; April 28, 1983, effective August 1, 1983; March 2, 1987, effective August 1, 1987; April 30, 1991, effective December 1, 1991; April 22, 1993, effective December 1, 1993; March 27, 2003, effective December 1, 2003; April 30, 2007, effective December 1, 2007; March 26, 2009, effective December 1, 2009.]

UNDERSTANDING RULE 53

HOW RULE 53 FITS IN

Sometimes, a judge is faced with an issue that would be unusually burdensome or time consuming to handle or that requires an expertise that the judge lacks. In such situations, the judge may appoint a "master" to assist the judge.

For example, if a case requires an accounting of the finances of a business or otherwise involves a complicated damages calculation, the judge might appoint an accountant as a master to perform the accounting or damages calculation. Likewise, some courts have a panel of masters who are experienced in e-discovery, and appoint them to oversee the e-discovery process in particularly complex or challenging cases.

Rule 53 generally affords the court broad discretion in the appointment of masters, but it requires the judge to consider both the imposition of the expense of the master on the parties and the likely delay when deciding whether to appoint a master. Similarly, Rule 53 places few restrictions on who the judge may select as a master, so long as the master does not have a close relationship to the parties, lawyers, or cause of action. The judge may appoint a magistrate judge to serve as a master, although actions by a magistrate judge do not come under the ambit of Rule 53 unless the district judge so specifies.

The procedure for the use of a master starts with notice to the parties, providing them an opportunity to express their positions on the use of a master and to propose candidates. If the judge decides to appoint a master, the judge issues an order describing the master's duties, setting any limits on the master's authority, and specifying the manner in which the master may communicate with the parties. The order also establishes the time limits for the master's tasks and submissions to the judge, describing any materials the master should preserve and include. Finally, the order addresses the master's rate of compensation and the allocation of the compensation among the parties.

Once appointed, a master has most—but not all—of the powers of the trial judge. The master may issue orders, hold evidentiary hearings with witness testimony and documentary evidence, and may impose sanctions on misbehaving parties. A master does not have contempt powers, though, and instead may recommend that the judge hold a party in contempt.

Typically, a master submits a "report" or "report and recommendation" to the court at the end of the process. The parties then have 21 days to file written objections. Normally, the court then reviews the master's procedures, factual determinations, and conclusions of law de novo—with no deference—unless the parties stipulate to be bound by the master's factual findings. The judge may then adopt, modify, or reject the master's report—it is ultimately the judge who decides the case.

THE ARCHITECTURE OF RULE 53

Rule 53 covers a lot of ground in regulating the master process, and accordingly is broken into eight subparts. Rule 53(a) contains the general provisions authorizing appointment of a master, describing the appropriate circumstances for an appointment and the rules for disqualification. Rule 53(b) sets forth the required content for the court's order appointing a master, and Rule 53(c) describes the powers that masters may exercise. Rules 53(d) and (e) contain short provisions describing how masters file and serve their orders and reports. Rule 53(f) directs the court as to how to review and use masters' orders and reports. Rule 53(g) addresses the master's compensation, and Rule 53(h) clarifies that a magistrate judge who performs activities in an action is not considered a master unless specifically appointed as a master by order under Rule 53.

HOW RULE 53 WORKS IN PRACTICE

RULE 53(a) Appointment

The court may appoint a special master to conduct trials in limited circumstances to conduct certain pretrial and post-trial functions.

PRACTICING LAW UNDER THIS SUBPART

Functions Performed by Master

Rule 53 authorizes a master to:

- Perform duties consented to by the parties;
- Hold trial proceedings and make recommended findings of fact on non-jury issues if the appointment is warranted by an exceptional condition or by the need to perform an accounting or resolve a difficult computation of damages; and
- Address pretrial or post-trial matters if they cannot be addressed effectively and timely by the court.

Ineligible Persons

A person cannot be a master if related to the parties, the action, or the court under the same standards that govern disqualification of a judge set forth in 28 U.S.C. § 455. The clerk of court and the clerk's deputies are also ineligible. The parties can waive this restriction with the court's approval.

Court's Discretion—Expense and Delay

The court has discretion as to whether to refer a matter to a master, but reference should be the exception, not the rule. In determining whether to appoint a master, the court must consider the fairness of imposing the cost of the master's compensation on the parties and the effects of delay, and the court has discretion to refuse to appoint a master even if the parties have consented.

Common References

References are most common in patent, trademark, and copyright actions. They are also used occasionally to supervise discovery (and increasingly frequently e-discovery), to determine damages when the damages are difficult to calculate, and to oversee compliance with injunctions or other court orders.

RULE 53(b) Order Appointing a Master

A master is appointed by an order setting forth the duties and parameters of the reference.

PRACTICING LAW UNDER THIS SUBPART

Notice and Opportunity to Be Heard

The court must give notice of the proposed appointment of a master to the parties and provide an opportunity to be heard before appointing the master.

Contents of Order

The order appointing a master must:

- Direct the master to proceed with all reasonable diligence;
- State the master's duties and any limits on the master's authority;
- State the circumstances, if any, in which the master may communicate *ex parte* with the court or a party;
- State the nature of the materials to be preserved and filed as the record of the master's activities;
- State the time limits, methods of filing the record, other procedures, and standards for reviewing the master's orders, findings, and recommendations; and
- State the basis, terms, and procedures for determining the master's compensation under Rule 53(g).

Affidavit re Grounds for Disqualification

Before the court can enter the order appointing the master, the master must file an affidavit disclosing whether there is any ground for disqualification under 28 U.S.C. § 455. If a ground for disqualification is disclosed, the court may not enter the order unless the parties consent to waive the disqualification.

RULE 53(c) Master's Authority

Absent specific limitations in the order appointing the master, the master has all powers necessary to perform the referred matters, including regulating the proceedings, ruling on evidentiary issues, placing witnesses under oath, examining witnesses, and sanctioning parties. The court has the duty to oversee the special master's performance of the master's duties to ensure that they are appropriately discharged.

RULE 53(d) Master's Orders

A master who makes an order must file the order with the clerk and promptly serve a copy on each party. The clerk must enter the order on the docket.

RULE 53(e) — Master's Reports

A master must prepare reports as directed by the order of appointment. The master must file all reports with the clerk and promptly serve a copy upon each party unless the court directs otherwise. The master should provide the court with all portions of the record that the master deems relevant to a report. The parties may seek to designate additional materials from the record, and may seek to supplement the record. The court may require that additional materials from the record be filed.

RULE 53(f) — Action on the Master's Order, Report, or Recommendations

Rule 53(f) sets forth the procedures for the court to act on the master's report and the standards by which the court should review the report.

PRACTICING LAW UNDER THIS SUBPART

Actions by the Parties

A party may file objections to the master's order, report, or recommendation no later than 21 days from the time the order, report, or recommendation is served, unless the court sets a different time. A party may also file a motion to adopt or modify the order, report, or recommendations in the same timeframe.

Actions by the Court

When considering an order, report, or recommendation from a master, the court may adopt or affirm, modify, reject or reverse in whole or in part, or resubmit to the master with instructions. The court has discretion to consider additional evidence in connection with its review of the master's report, but is not required to do so.

Opportunity to Be Heard

Before acting on an order, report, or recommendation from a master, the court must provide the parties with an opportunity to be heard (which may consist of written submissions).

Time for Objections

A party may file objections to the master's order, report, or recommendation no later than 21 days from the time the order, report, or recommendation is served, unless the court sets a different time.

Review of Master's Findings of Fact

Absent a stipulation otherwise, the court must decide de novo all objections to findings of fact made or recommended by a master. The parties may stipulate, with the court's consent, that the master's findings of fact will only be reviewed for clear error. The parties may also stipulate, with the court's consent, that the master's findings of fact will be final if the master was appointed by consent or was appointed to address pretrial or post-trial matters.

Review of Master's Conclusions of Law

The court must decide de novo all objections to conclusions of law made or recommended by a master.

RULE 53(g) Compensation

The court sets the compensation for a master. The master's compensation will be allocated among the parties or taken from the subject matter of the litigation.

PRACTICING LAW UNDER THIS SUBPART

Amount of Compensation

The court establishes the compensation for a master in the order of appointment. The court may also require the posting of a bond to secure payment of the fee or require the payment of the fee into escrow.

Who Pays the Master's Compensation

The court may impose the master's fee upon any party or may apportion it among the parties. In assigning responsibility for the master's fee, the court should consider the nature and amount of the controversy, the parties' financial means, and the extent to which any party is more responsible for the reference to the master. The court may make interim allocations and may adjust the interim allocation later to reflect the decision on the merits. The court may also direct that the fee be paid from any fund or subject matter of the action in the custody of the court.

RULE 53(h) Appointing a Magistrate Judge

The provisions of Rule 53 do not pertain to matters referred to magistrate judges unless the order of reference specifically states that it is made pursuant to Rule 53.

VII. JUDGMENT

RULE 54

JUDGMENT; COSTS

(a) Definition; Form. "Judgment" as used in these rules includes a decree and any order from which an appeal lies. A judgment should not include recitals of pleadings, a master's report, or a record of prior proceedings.

(b) Judgment on Multiple Claims or Involving Multiple Parties. When an action presents more than one claim for relief—whether as a claim, counterclaim, crossclaim, or third-party claim—or when multiple parties are involved, the court may direct entry of a final judgment as to one or more, but fewer than all, claims or parties only if the court expressly determines that there is no just reason for delay. Otherwise, any order or other decision, however designated, that adjudicates fewer than all the claims or the rights and liabilities of fewer than all the parties does not end the action as to any of the claims or parties and may be revised at any time before the entry of a judgment adjudicating all the claims and all the parties' rights and liabilities.

(c) Demand for Judgment; Relief to Be Granted. A default judgment must not differ in kind from, or exceed in amount, what is demanded in the pleadings. Every other final judgment should grant the relief to which each party is entitled, even if the party has not demanded that relief in its pleadings.

(d) Costs; Attorney's Fees.

(1) *Costs Other Than Attorney's Fees.* Unless a federal statute, these rules, or a court order provides otherwise, costs—other than attorney's fees—should be allowed to the prevailing party. But costs against the United States, its officers, and its agencies may be imposed only to the extent allowed by law. The clerk may tax costs on 14 days' notice. On motion served within the next 7 days, the court may review the clerk's action.

(2) *Attorney's Fees.*

(A) *Claim to Be by Motion.* A claim for attorney's fees and related nontaxable expenses must be made by motion unless the substantive law requires those fees to be proved at trial as an element of damages.

(B) *Timing and Contents of the Motion.* Unless a statute or a court order provides otherwise, the motion must:

(i) be filed no later than 14 days after the entry of judgment;

(ii) specify the judgment and the statute, rule, or other grounds entitling the movant to the award;

(iii) state the amount sought or provide a fair estimate of it; and

(iv) disclose, if the court so orders, the terms of any agreement about fees for the services for which the claim is made.

(C) *Proceedings.* Subject to Rule 23(h), the court must, on a party's request, give an opportunity for adversary submissions on the motion in accordance with Rule 43(c) or 78. The court may decide issues of liability for fees before receiving submissions on the value of services. The court must find the facts and state its conclusions of law as provided in Rule 52(a).

(D) *Special Procedures by Local Rule; Reference to a Master or a Magistrate Judge.* By local rule, the court may establish special procedures to resolve fee-related issues without extensive evidentiary hearings. Also, the court may refer issues concerning the value of services to a special master under Rule 53 without regard to the limitations of Rule 53(a)(1), and may refer a motion for attorney's fees to a magistrate judge under Rule 72(b) as if it were a dispositive pretrial matter.

(E) *Exceptions.* Subparagraphs (A)–(D) do not apply to claims for fees and expenses as sanctions for violating these rules or as sanctions under 28 U.S.C. § 1927.

[Amended December 27, 1946, effective March 19, 1948; April 17, 1961, effective July 19, 1961; March 2, 1987, effective August 1, 1987; April 22, 1993, effective December 1, 1993; amended April 29, 2002, effective December 1, 2002; March 27, 2003, effective December 1, 2003; April 30, 2007, effective December 1, 2007; March 26, 2009, effective December 1, 2009.]

UNDERSTANDING RULE 54

HOW RULE 54 FITS IN

A "judgment" is a particular type of court order. Usually, it is the order by which a federal judge closes out proceedings in a civil lawsuit. For example, after a jury returns its verdict, the court will likely issue a "judgment" that converts the jury's decision into the case's final, official result. Obviously, not all court rulings are "judgments". Indeed, most of the rulings a judge will make during the life of a civil lawsuit—*e.g.*, orders to amend pleadings, to permit special service of process, to allow additional depositions, to resolve a challenge to a proposed expert witness, to extend times for filing briefs—will not qualify as "judgments." Determining whether a court order qualifies as a "judgment" is important for two reasons. First, a "judgment" is an order from which an appeal can be taken (most other trial court orders cannot be appealed until the end of the case). Second, a "judgment" is enforceable; it permits the victorious party to enforce the remedy it won (*e.g.*, money, an injunction, or other relief) nationally.

Rule 54 is the first of several Rules that concern "judgments." Collectively, this series of Rules define "judgments," approve their types and form, set the manner, timing, and prerequisites of their entry, and establish various procedures for relieving parties of their effects.

THE ARCHITECTURE OF RULE 54

Rule 54 has four subparts. The first subpart sets the definition of a federal judgment. The second subpart authorizes judges to enter some partial, federal judgments early—before a case is completely finished—when that portion of the litigation relating to one of several claims or one of several parties is fully concluded. The third subpart establishes what relief can be granted in a default and a non-default judgment. The fourth subpart directs that judgments be increased by an award of costs under certain conditions, and then establishes the procedure for an award of attorney's fees, when those fees are properly awardable.

HOW RULE 54 WORKS IN PRACTICE

These four subparts of Rule 54 are discussed, in order, below.

RULE 54(a) Definition; Form

Broadly defined, a "judgment" is any federal order or judicial decree from which an appeal may be taken. The "judgment" should be austere; it should not include extraneous materials like recitations of the pleadings, a report by a master, or a record of prior proceedings.

PRACTICING LAW UNDER THIS SUBPART

Definition

To be a "judgment" within the meaning of this subpart, the court's order or decree must be a ruling from which an appeal can be taken. In the federal courts, appeals may be taken from *final decisions* by district courts and from a limited category of other, non-final, interlocutory rulings. Although no particular wording or form is prescribed, *see United States v. Hark*, 320 U.S. 531, 534 (1944); a ruling qualifies as a "final decision" (and, thus, a "judgment") if it clearly shows the district judge's intention that the order serve as his or her final act in the case. *See United States v. F. & M. Schaefer Brewing Co.*, 356 U.S. 227, 232–34 (1958). Conversely, most non-final, interim orders do not qualify as "judgments" and are not appealable unless another Rule or statute provides otherwise.

Should Appear Alone

To avoid confusion and uncertainty about what is (and is not) a "judgment," it should appear alone. A judgment should not include recitals of the pleadings, a report from a master, or a record of prior proceedings.

RULE 54(b)	Judgment on Multiple Claims or Involving Multiple Parties

A "judgment" will ordinarily end the lawsuit in its entirety. Thus, courts usually will not enter a "judgment" as to less than all claims in a case or as to less than all parties. The standard procedure is to wait until all claims involving all parties have been adjudicated, and then issue a final "judgment." On occasion, however, deviating from this norm may be necessary. This subpart provides for such a deviation—it permits a judge to make a ruling that adjudicates less-than-all claims or less-than-all parties "final," and thus immediately appealable.

PRACTICING LAW UNDER THIS SUBPART

Purpose

When they were adopted, the Federal Rules of Civil Procedure liberalized the possibilities for joining multiple claims and multiple parties into a single lawsuit. *See Sears, Roebuck & Co. v. Mackey*, 351 U.S. 427, 432–33 (1956). But routinely permitting separate, piecemeal appeals from rulings that were incrementally resolving various parts of a multi-claim, multi-party lawsuit would be inefficient and contrary to the historic federal policy favoring one appeal on all issues at the conclusion of the lawsuit. *See Curtiss-Wright Corp. v. General Elec. Co.*, 446 U.S. 1, 8 (1980). Nonetheless, compelling litigants to wait out the disposition of all parts of such a lawsuit could, occasionally, prove unduly harsh or unjust; for those instances, Rule 54(b) supplied a possible remedy—partial final judgments. *See Gelboim v. Bank of America Corp.*, 574 U.S. 405, 409–10 (2015); *Dickinson v. Petroleum Conversion Corp.*, 338 U.S. 507, 511 (1950).

The Ordinary Practice (No Immediate Appeal)

Absent a Rule 54(b) determination, interim rulings that do not end the litigation in its entirety are interlocutory, not immediately appealable, and subject to revision by the district judge. *See Dietz v. Bouldin*, 136 S. Ct. 1885, 1892 (2016). This right of revision is broad, but not limitless; it is cabined in by other doctrines (such as law-of-the-case).

Three Prerequisites to Rule 54(b) Partial Judgments

In evaluating whether to grant a Rule 54(b) determination, the district courts function somewhat like a "dispatcher." *See Curtiss-Wright Corp. v. General Elec. Co.*, 446 U.S. 1, 8 (1980). They may "dispatch" a portion of the lawsuit for immediate appeal, but only if: (1) at least one claim or the rights and liabilities of at least one party have become fully resolved; (2) there is no just reason to delay the appeal; *and* (3) the court directs that a partial final judgment be entered on the docket.

Prerequisite #1: Claim or Party Fully Resolved

An adjudication must either (a) finally resolve at least one claim or (b) finally resolve the rights and liabilities of at least one party, such that nothing more is left to do on that claim or with that party but await the conclusion of the remaining portions of the litigation. *See Curtiss-Wright Corp. v. General Elec. Co.*, 446 U.S. 1, 7 (1980). This limitation is a pivotal one. Rule 54(b) does not alter the normal rules of appellate finality for individual claims, and no appeal may be taken from district court rulings on any particular claim until the court finally resolves that claim. *See Sears, Roebuck & Co. v. Mackey*, 351 U.S. 427, 437 (1956). Rule 54(b) has no application where the lawsuit involves either a single claim only or multiple claims that have already been resolved to finality. See *Gelboim v. Bank of America Corp.*, 574 U.S. 405, 416 (2015). Thus, for example, where a portion of a claim is resolved, but the amount of damages, the question of insurance coverage, or affirmative defenses remain still to be decided, that claim has not been finally resolved (even if all other issues are completely adjudicated), and an immediate appeal is improper.

- *Multiple Claims:* An appeal from one dismissed claim (when other claims still remain) is possible only when that claim is resolved entirely and as to all parties. Thus, Rule 54(b) is inapplicable where the lawsuit involves either a single claim only or multiple claims that have already been resolved to finality.
- *"Claim" Defined:* The term "claim" is not defined in the Rule nor well explained in Supreme Court precedent; as a result, the concept proves sometimes elusive in application. No universal, bright-line rules aid in the defining task. A "claim" is, at base, an enforceable right arising from a set of facts. Beyond that generality, the law-drawing becomes more opaque. A simple variation in legal theory alone will not suffice to create a separate "claim," nor will the mere fact that the allegations were pleaded separately. Rather, this assessment implicates practical concerns. Multiple claims might exist where each claim is factually independent, where each claim could be enforced separately, where each claim seeks to vindicate a different legal right, where there is more than one potential recovery, or where different types of relief are requested. If, however, only one recovery is possible (even though several legal theories are offered to support that recovery) or if alternative recoveries either substantially overlap or are mutually exclusive, the partial adjudication cannot be immediately appealed under Rule 54(b). One test of a claim's separability asks whether that claim so overlaps the claims that remain for trial that an appeal at the end of the case on the retained claims would compel the court to retrace the same ground it would have addressed had the first claim received a Rule 54(b) determination; if so, the Rule 54(b) determination will likely be denied. But this "overlap" inquiry is performed with care; the mere existence of some factual overlap will not, alone, defeat the possibility of multiple claims. Counterclaims and claims in consolidated cases are assessed using this same inquiry.
- *Multiple Parties:* An appeal by one dismissed party (when claims by other parties still remain) is possible only when that party's rights and interests are resolved entirely and the district court so signifies. Rule 54(b) is not just limited to defendants. If the criteria for Rule 54(b) is satisfied, the dismissal of any party (plaintiff or defendant) may be appealed. A named, but unserved, defendant will not be considered a "party" for the purpose of applying this Rule unless the court contemplates further action as to that defendant.

Prerequisite #2: No Just Reason For Delay

The district court must state, in clear and unmistakable language, that there is no just cause to delay the appeal of the adjudicated claim or the adjudicated rights and liabilities of a party. This determination requires a weighing of both the equities in the case and the judicial administrative interests (especially the interest in avoiding piecemeal appeals). Ordinarily, this weighing will favor an immediate appeal only where delay in appealing presents some risk of hardship or injustice that would be avoided by an immediate review, where a plaintiff could be prejudiced by a delay in recovering a monetary judgment, or where an expensive, duplicative trial could be avoided by reviewing a dismissed claim promptly before the remaining claims reach trial. Conversely, where multiple claims, even if separate, could again be subject to yet another review in a later appeal, or where the claims—though discrete—are so interrelated as to form a single factual unit, an immediate appeal would be improper. Whether "just cause" exists is a determination made on a case-by-case basis. See Sears, Roebuck & Co. v. Mackey, 351 U.S. 427, 436 (1956). Certain nonexhaustive criteria guide the court's consideration:

- The relationship between adjudicated and unadjudicated claims;
- The possibility that the need for appellate review might be mooted by future developments in the district court;
- The possibility that the district court might be obligated to consider the same issue on a later occasion;
- The presence (or absence) of a claim or counterclaim that could result in a set-off against the judgment now sought to be made final and appealed; and
- Other factors, including delay, economic and solvency concerns, shortening of trial time, frivolity of competing claims, and expense.

A Rule 54(b) determination is likely to be improper where the litigation itself, and the contested claim's resolution, is routine and would inevitably return to the trial court on essentially the same set of facts.

Prerequisite #3: Entry of Partial Judgment Directed

In clear and unmistakable language, the district court must also direct that judgment is entered as to at least one claim or one party.

Use of "Magic Language"

Immediate appealability hinges on the district court "expressly" determining that there is no just reason for delay and then directing entry of a partial final judgment. A court's failure to incant this exact language may be overlooked in some cases, if the trial judge's intent to proceed under Rule 54(b) is otherwise unmistakably clear. But not all courts follow this approach. In any event, however it is communicated, the determination must always be made "expressly" and the intent "unmistakable."

- *Abandoned Claims:* A district court's judgment that resolves some open claims, but leaves others unaddressed, may still be deemed to be final (even without the inclusion of the "magic language"), if the unaddressed claims were abandoned or otherwise terminated by subsequent events.
- *Subsequent Determination:* An order lacking the Rule 54(b) specifics may be cured by a supplemental order, including one issued upon remand from the courts of appeals.

Explanation by the District Court

Detailed statements of reasons are not necessary. But in its order entering a Rule 54(b) judgment, the district court must clearly and cogently explain why it has concluded that an immediate appellate review of the order is advisable, or those reasons must be readily apparent from the record. The district court should not simply reprint, in boilerplate, the formula of the Rule or autograph a defendant's Rule 54(b) request. The court of appeals may, in the absence of a written explanation, dismiss the appeal as inappropriately allowed under Rule 54(b), or subject the determination to special scrutiny. Although dismissal of the appeal is permitted (and perhaps even likely) without a corresponding explanation from the trial court, dismissal is not compulsory; the failure to offer a written explanation is *not* a jurisdictional defect that *compels* the appeal's dismissal.

Duty of Counsel in Explanation Requirement

In moving for a Rule 54(b) determination, the courts expect counsel, as officers of the court and advocates for an immediate appeal, to assist the district judge by making appropriate submissions that express the reasons for and basis of a Rule 54(b) determination. In fact, if the trial judge fails to offer a detailed explanation for the Rule 54(b) determination, the reasons offered by counsel can assume special significance. But counsel cannot, by agreement that they exist, create the Rule 54(b) prerequisites if they are absent.

Burden of Proof

The moving party bears the burden of establishing that a partial judgment should be entered under Rule 54(b).

Procedure and Timing for Rule 54(b) Determinations

The Rule establishes no fixed procedure for obtaining a Rule 54(b) determination. Case law tends to confirm that trial judges may make such determinations either *sua sponte* or upon motion of a party. Some courts have set a narrow time window for Rule 54(b) motions. *See King v. Newbold*, 845 F.3d 866, 868 (7th Cir. 2017) (absent "extreme hardship," determination cannot be made beyond 30 days from entry of contested order). Other courts refuse to endorse any rigid, judicially-crafted deadline. *See Bank of N.Y. v. Hoyt*, 108 F.R.D. 184, 185 (D.R.I. 1985) (eschewing any "inflexible criterion").

Discretion of District Judge

The court is not *required* to enter a final judgment in an action involving multiple claims or parties where the court resolves claims involving less than all parties or less than all claims. To the contrary, whether to enter a judgment under Rule 54(b) is reserved for the sound discretion of the district judge. *See Curtiss-Wright Corp. v. General Elec. Co.*, 446 U.S. 1, 8 (1980). Because such judgments are contrary to the historic federal policy against piecemeal appeals, Rule 54(b) orders are not granted routinely, or merely with the hope of avoiding a trial, or as an accommodation to counsel. Instead, the district court must carefully balance the needs of the parties for an immediate appeal against the interest of efficient management of the litigation. Rule 54(d) determinations are the exceptions, not the rule.

- *No "Tag-Along" Partial Appeals:* A decision to permit an immediate appeal of one ruling is not, alone, sufficient justification to grant Rule 54(b) relief for other rulings.

Effect of Rule 54(b) Judgments

Once a Rule 54(b) judgment is entered, the time for appeal on that judgment begins to run (as does the accrual of post-judgment interest). Consequently, failing to file an appeal promptly after entry of the Rule 54(b) judgment may forever forfeit the right of appeal.

Effect of Non-Rule 54(b) Partial Rulings

Unless the court enters a separate judgment under Rule 54(b), litigants in a multi-party case who are dismissed may technically remain in the case until the final resolution of all claims as to all parties. Dismissed litigants are, however, entitled to rely on the dismissal. Thus, unless and until notified otherwise, dismissed litigants need not participate in discovery, in pretrial proceedings, or in the trial itself.

"Certification" Nomenclature

Often in the case law, the Rule 54(b) determination procedure is described as a "certification." This is a misnomer. The term "certification" describes the procedure for seeking immediate appellate review of interlocutory orders under 28 U.S.C. § 1292(b). Conversely, a Rule 54(b) determination, if granted, effectively severs what becomes a *final* judgment (albeit as to one or more but fewer than all claims or parties) from the remaining claims and parties in the case.

Appealability of Denials of Rule 54(b) Requests

Rule 54(b) operates to create an exception to the settled federal policy disfavoring piecemeal appeals. Unsurprisingly, courts have rebuffed attempts to immediately challenge denials of Rule 54(b) determinations as premature and unappealable until a final ruling is entered on the merits.

Appeals—Improper Rule 54(b) Determinations

A district judge's Rule 54(b) determination is examined on appeal. The court of appeals will assess the appealed-from order's eligibility under Rule 54(b), even if the propriety of the Rule 54(b) determination is uncontested (the appeals court in such an instance will consider the matter *sua sponte*). If the appeals court finds that the district court's Rule 54(b) determination was given or prepared improperly, appellate jurisdiction is lost and the appeal will be dismissed.

Appeals—Prematurely Filed

If an appeal is taken prior to the district court issuing a Rule 54(b) determination, many Circuits have ruled that the belated determination "ripens" the otherwise premature appeal, so long as the Rule 54(b) determination issues prior to the date the court of appeals considers the appeal.

Appeals—Scope of "Determination"

On appeal following a Rule 54(b) determination, the court of appeals will confine its review only to those specific claims or parties regarding which the determination was granted (including all merged interlocutory orders). Other aspects of the still-ongoing lawsuit will not be examined during the appeal.

RULE 54(c) Demand for Judgment; Relief to Be Granted

The district court generally must grant all the relief to which the prevailing party is entitled, whether or not such relief was formally requested in the pleadings. Pleadings serve as "guides" to the nature of the case, but the lawsuit is ultimately measured by what is pleaded and proven, not merely by what was demanded. Default judgments are different, however; the district court may not award relief in a default judgment beyond that sought in the complaint.

PRACTICING LAW UNDER THIS SUBPART

Default Judgments

Defendants don't always default by accident or neglect. Sometimes, defendants default deliberately, perhaps reasoning that the relief the claimant's pleading seeks is not worth the fight to resist. Consequently, because a litigant may be relying on the as-pleaded demand in choosing to default, a claimant may not receive a default judgment that differs either in "kind" or in "amount" from what was sought in the pleadings. Among the sparse exceptions to this rule are where the defendant originally appeared in the action and was placed on proper notice of the possible expanded relief and where the complaint fairly identified the nature of the claimed loss and placed the defendant on notice that the value of that loss would continue to accrue during the litigation.

- *"Defaulting" Party:* A party defaults within the meaning of Rule 54(c) by either failing to appear at all or defaulting following an appearance.
- *Differing in "Kind":* Whether relief on default differs in "kind" hinges on whether the pleadings afforded adequate notice of that relief.
- *Boilerplate Language:* In determining (for default purposes) what remedies have been pleaded, courts are disinclined to expand the available remedies on the basis of vague, boilerplate, catch-all language in a pleading.

Non-Default Judgments

Where the defendant has answered or otherwise appeared to defend the lawsuit, a plaintiff may receive a judgment for an amount greater than that sought in the complaint, as well as types of relief not mentioned in the complaint's demand clause. It is generally the court's duty to grant all appropriate relief. Defendants, likewise, may benefit from Rule 54(c)'s liberality.

Limitations on Awarding Additional Relief

The Rule's liberality is intended to protect against the risk that clumsy drafting or technical missteps could deprive the pleader of a deserved recovery. But the courts' ability to award unpleaded relief is not unbounded. The courts' remedy-awarding authority remains tethered to the lawsuit. While the demand clause does not rigidly constrain the relief options available to a court, a fair reading of the entire pleading does. The Rule does not countenance "trial-by-ambush." Thus, the Rule will not permit a recovery on issues or claims that were not actually litigated, nor will it revive relief lost in the pleadings or through a failure of proof. It will not allow relief against a defendant from whom no relief has been sought, or force upon the litigants a remedy none of them desires. Litigants will be held bound to representations made during a pretrial conference or in a pretrial order that outlined the claims and relief in the case. In short, this Rule will not permit an additional award that would be unfairly prejudicial or unjust. Thus, pleaders may not manipulatively "cap" their claims to achieve some tactical advantage, and then receive under this Rule the very relief they earlier shunned.

- *Types of Unpleaded Relief Permitted:* Courts have sometimes permitted litigants to recover punitive damages, nominal damages, attorney's fees, prejudgment interest, accruing ERISA damages, and even declaratory and injunctive relief where those remedies were not expressly sought in the complaints, in appropriate cases.

RULE 54(d) Costs and Attorney's Fees

The United States follows the "American Rule," where each party to a lawsuit ordinarily pays its own litigation expenses (as contrasted with the "English Rule," where the loser is often ordered to pay its adversary's litigation expenses). This subpart marks a modest exception to that prevailing general approach. Federal courts typically award (or "tax") "costs" to the prevailing party in a lawsuit; the clerk may tax such "costs" on 14 days' notice—subject to later judicial review upon timely motion. This category of taxable "costs" is a narrow one, limited to those items set by statute. Attorney's fees are not "costs" and are ordinarily not taxable as such. However, when some other law permits an award of attorney's fees, this subpart sets the procedures for seeking and awarding them.

PRACTICING LAW UNDER THIS SUBPART

Governing Law

Federal law governs the availability and scope of allowable costs, even in diversity cases and even if State law would dictate a different result.

For Whom Costs May Be Taxed (*Prevailing Party* Defined)

Costs should ordinarily be taxed in favor of the prevailing party, unless a Rule or federal statute directs otherwise. A prevailing plaintiff is one who succeeds on some significant issue in the litigation and thereby achieves some of the benefit sought in filing the lawsuit. A plaintiff, thus, "prevails" by obtaining a judgment on the merits or a court-order consent decree, by obtaining an award of monetary damages (even nominal damages), or by obtaining some other relief that materially alters the parties' legal relationship by modifying the behavior of the defendant in a way that directly benefits the plaintiff. *See Buckhannon Bd. & Care Home, Inc. v. West Virginia Dept. of Health & Human Resources*, 532 U.S. 598, 605 (2001). Conversely, a plaintiff who loses the judgment, but whose litigation nonetheless prompts the opponent to *voluntarily* change its behavior in some way or can otherwise cite to some "moral victory" is likely *not* a prevailing party. Similarly, a settlement, even one brokered by the court or prompted by a court's comments on the case's merits, will likely produce a "prevailing party" only if it results in a consent decree.

A prevailing defendant is one who defeats the litigation and obtains a denial of relief. Thus, a dismissal, with prejudice and on the merits, of all claims against a defendant will generally make that defendant a prevailing party as well dismissals that include without-prejudice dismissals of companion State law claims over which the court has declined to exercise supplemental jurisdiction.

A litigant need not succeed on all issues to qualify as a prevailing party. For example, a counterclaiming defendant may be deemed a prevailing party by defeating the larger primary claim even if losing on the smaller counterclaim. Some courts hold that there can be only one prevailing party, though, in mixed judgment outcomes, that status might be assigned claim-by-claim.

Generally, there are no prevailing parties if the case is dismissed for lack of jurisdiction or *forum non conveniens*. Similarly, if certain parties prevail originally, but later lose under a subsequent ruling at the trial court or on appeal, their status (and their entitlement to costs) has changed.

Against Whom May Costs Be Taxed

Under Rule 54(d), costs may be taxed only against the nonprevailing party; costs may not be taxed under this Rule against counsel for a litigant. When taxed in a multiple-lawsuit proceeding, costs should be allocated among the various cases.

Types of Taxable Costs

Litigation expenses fall broadly into three categories—taxable "costs", nontaxable expenses, and attorney's fees. Congress set the categories of taxable "costs" by statute, and they are deliberately modest, usually representing only a fraction of total litigation expenses (though parties may, by contract, alter this standard). *See* 28 U.S.C. § 1920; *Taniguchi v. Kan Pacific Saipan, Ltd.*, 566 U.S. 560, 573 (2012). Though limited, those costs can nevertheless still be substantial and often may constitute a substantial measure of discovery costs. These statutorily permitted taxable costs are:

1. **Clerk and U.S. Marshal fees**, which might even include *pro hac vice* admission fees;

2. **Transcript fees**, for *both* printed or electronically recorded transcripts, so long as they were "necessarily obtained for use in the case" (including transcripts received into evidence or otherwise "necessary" for trial preparation, but not for transcripts taken solely for discovery purposes, as a mere convenience to counsel or the court, or of witnesses withdrawn or precluded); court reporter attendance fees, and real-time transcript feeds, videotape depositions and perhaps even the stenographic transcription of those videotapes.

3a. **Printing fees**;

3b. **Witness fees and witnesses' travel and subsistence expenses**, where the witnesses' testimony was material, relevant, and reasonably necessary to the case (including officers/directors of a corporate party, provided they are not personally also parties);

4a. **Fees to "exemplify" materials** (which may include reimbursement for many methods of illustration, including models, charts, graphs, and perhaps computerized presentation systems, but likely not electronically-stored information processing expenses or ancillary document gathering or other preparatory costs);

4b. **Fees to print copies of any materials** if necessary for use in the case (which likely includes copying documents for discovery, and also likely encompasses, in an electronic data environment, the "functional equivalent" of making copies (*e.g.*, scanning, format conversion, and maybe imaging) but likely excludes other preparatory ESI expenses (*e.g.*, searching, gathering, culling)); in seeking reimbursement, a copy-by-copy tracking or itemization may not be necessary, so long as a reasonably accurate calculation is supplied; to recover costs, a copy-by-copy tracking might not be required, but a bill of costs showing a reasonably accurate calculation will be);

5. **Certain docket fees**; and

6. **Fees for court-appointed experts** (which often include guardians and special masters) and interpreters (though limited to oral interpreters, not translators of written work).

Litigation Expenses That Ordinarily Cannot Be Taxed

Litigation-related expenses that fall outside the scope of "costs" may not be taxed under Rule 54(d) unless authorized by agreement, other statute, or court rule. *See Arlington Cent. School Dist. Bd. of Educ. v. Murphy*, 548 U.S. 291, 301 (2006). Thus, courts ordinarily will not tax as "costs" the fees and expenses of expert witnesses (beyond the modest travel and subsistence expenses noted above for witnesses generally); computer-assisted legal research; trial consultants who prepared computer animations, videos, powerpoint slides, and graphic illustrations; postage, overnight courier, and similar messenger or delivery services; telephone calls; facsimile transmissions; paralegals; travel, lodging, transportation, and parking; mediation; or post-trial/pre-appeal costs (like supersedeas bond premiums). Courts are divided on whether the costs of private process servers are taxable.

Attorney's Fees as Costs

In the absence of a federal statute or Rule providing otherwise, attorney's fees may not be taxed as costs beyond the modest provisions set forth in 28 U.S.C. § 1923. *See Arlington Cent. School Dist. Bd. of Educ. v. Murphy*, 548 U.S. 291, 301 (2006).

Burden of Proof

The burden of proving the amount of compensable costs lies with the party seeking those costs. Once the prevailing party demonstrates the amount of its costs and that they fall within an allowable category of taxable costs, the prevailing party enjoys the strong presumption that its costs will be awarded in full measure. The party opposing the award of costs bears the burden of demonstrating that the award would be improper.

Discretion of District Court

Rule 54(d) provides that costs "should" be taxed. The courts have interpreted this mandate to create a presumption in favor of the award of costs to the prevailing party, but reserves for the district judge the discretion to deny costs in appropriate circumstances. *See Marx v. General Revenue Corp.*, 568 U.S. 371, 377 (2013). A "sound basis" is needed to overcome this presumption, since denying costs is viewed as a "penalty" that deprives a litigant of an entitlement. If the court chooses not to award costs to a prevailing party, the court must explain its good reasons for not doing so (although a formal written opinion is not required when costs are awarded or denied entirely). An implicit justification will ordinarily be insufficient to sustain the denial on appeal, unless the reasons for denying costs are clear.

Mandatory Reasons for Denying Costs

The district court must deny costs if another Rule or federal statute so commands. *See Marx v. General Revenue Corp.*, 568 U.S. 371, 377 (2013). Statutory displacement can occur when Congress imposes certain conditions on or installs an alternative standard for awarding costs (regardless of whether the statute recites an actual intent to displace Rule 54(d)). *See id.* at 377–78. But statutory silence usually leaves the ordinary Rule 54(d) approach in place. *See id.* at 377–88.

Discretionary Reasons for Denying Costs

The proper exercise of a trial court's discretion to deny costs may hinge on whether the costs pay for materials necessarily obtained for use in the case. Additionally, costs may be denied, for example, where both parties partially prevail in the litigation, where the prevailing party's recovery was only nominal or substantially less than what was sought (or where costs would be disproportionate to the litigation's results), where a party prevailed only after the opponent had first obtained a modicum of relief, where the prevailing party needlessly prolonged the litigation or otherwise behaved in bad faith, where the losing party is indigent or would become indigent by paying, or where there is some other injustice in taxing costs. Other discretionary criteria leave the courts divided. Some courts have rested a refusal to tax costs of a plaintiff's good faith in litigating, financial disparity, the case's complexity, difficulty, or closeness, its public interest, and whether taxing costs might chill future litigation. Other courts reject such additional grounds for denying costs.

Taxing Costs For or Against the United States

The United States may be awarded costs in the same manner as any prevailing party. Costs may be taxed against the United States in accordance with the list set forth in 28 U.S.C. § 1920, except that in non-tort actions, the district court may refuse to tax costs upon a finding that the United States' position was substantially justified or where special circumstances make an award of costs unjust. *See* 28 U.S.C. § 2412.

Procedure and Timing: Non-Attorney's Fee Costs

To obtain an award of costs, the prevailing party must file a "Bill of Costs" with the clerk (the district court may have a preprinted form for this purpose). The Bill of Costs must be verified by affidavit. The clerk may tax costs on 14-days' notice. Within 7 days thereafter, a disappointed party may seek court review of the clerk's assessment. A failure to seek review within this period may waive the losing party's right to challenge the award. Other courts disagree. In any event, a party is not usually expected to file a Bill of Costs until that party has "prevailed." The district court is authorized to conduct a *de novo* review of the clerk's assessments. Costs may be taxed against multiple losing parties either in allocated amounts or jointly and severally. The time for filing a Bill of Costs is typically regulated by local court rule, but usually is set after the court has rendered its decision in the case.

Procedure and Timing: Attorney's Fees & Nontaxable Expenses

Where an award of attorney's fees and related non-taxable expenses is appropriate, Rule 54(d)(2) fixes the procedure for obtaining an award of such fees and related non-taxable expenses. This procedure does *not* apply to attorney's fees recoverable as an element of damages (*e.g.*, under terms of a contract) or to fees and expenses awarded as sanctions. Courts are cautioned against permitting fees requests to spur a "second major litigation." *See Hensley v. Eckerhart*, 461 U.S. 424, 437 (1983). Typically, such motions are decided on affidavits alone, without additional discovery or evidentiary hearings. The procedure follows:

(1) *Motion Required:* The prevailing party must apply by motion for such an award. The motion must: (a) specify the judgment; (b) identify the legal source authorizing such an award of fees or expenses; and (c) state the amount, or a fair estimate of the amount, of the requested award.

(2) *Time for Filing:* Unless provided otherwise by statute, court order, or local court rule, motions must be filed with the court "no later" than 14 days after entry of judgment. This time trigger assumes a qualifying judgment (which encompasses preliminary injunctions and, also, will usually require compliance with the separate document rule). Failure to file within this allotted time constitutes a waiver of a party's right to recover such fees or expenses. This deadline helps both to ensure that the opponent receives proper notice of the fees claim and to promote a prompt fees ruling from the district court, thus permitting simultaneous appellate review of both the merits and the fees award. The deadline also forecloses the revival of disputes that adversaries reasonably thought were closed. Most courts agree that this 14-day period does not begin to run until post-trial motions under Rules 50(b), 52(b), or 59 are resolved.

(3) *Time for Serving:* Motions for attorney's fees and nontaxable costs must be served in accordance with Rule 5(a).

(4) *Opponent's Response:* Upon request, the court must provide the opponent with the opportunity to present evidence in opposition to the requested award.

(5) *Hearings:* Neither an evidentiary hearing nor an oral argument is required; instead, motions are typically resolved on affidavits alone.

(6) *Court's Delegation:* The court may enlist the help of a Special Master for setting the proper value to be awarded for the attorney services provided. The court may also refer the entire motion to a magistrate judge for a Report & Recommendation.

(7) *Court's Ruling:* In ruling on a Rule 54(d)(2) motion, the court must issue findings of fact and conclusions of law as required under Rule 52(a) and must issue a separate judgment as required under Rule 58. The court may, at its option, bifurcate its consideration of the motion to resolve liability issues first, before considering the amount of an appropriate award.

(8) *Additional Procedures by Local Rule:* Rule 54(d)(2) permits the district courts to promulgate local rules to govern procedures for claims without the need for extensive evidentiary hearings.

Procedure: Costs Bonds

Collateral to the authority to award costs, courts also have the authority to require litigants to post a bond to safeguard against dissipation of funds needed to reasonably cover anticipated taxable costs. Cost bonds are not sanctions and may not be imposed upon indigent parties in a manner that functionally denies them access to the federal courts.

Effect of an Attorney's Fees Motion on "Finality"

The filing of a Rule 54(d)(2) motion for an award of attorney's fees does not ordinarily affect the finality of the underlying judgment (which means, the time for taking an appeal begins to run from entry of the judgment, even though a motion for fees might still be pending). However, when a *timely* motion for fees is made, and so long as no notice of appeal has yet been filed (or become effective), the district court may enter an order directing that the fees motion be deemed to have the same effect as a timely Rule 59 motion and, thereby, toll the time for taking an appeal until after the motion is resolved. In such an instance, a single appeal is thereafter permitted (to challenge the merits ruling, the fees award, or both). This tolling option applies only to fees motions, not to the taxation of costs. If, however, the district court does not issue a tolling order, the time for taking an appeal from the fees ruling runs separately from the time for appealing the merits judgment, and usually does not begin until the district court has entirely completed its work in resolving the fees issues.

RULE 55

DEFAULT; DEFAULT JUDGMENT

(a) Entering a Default. When a party against whom a judgment for affirmative relief is sought has failed to plead or otherwise defend, and that failure is shown by affidavit or otherwise, the clerk must enter the party's default.

(b) Entering a Default Judgment.

(1) *By the Clerk.* If the plaintiff's claim is for a sum certain or a sum that can be made certain by computation, the clerk—on the plaintiff's request, with an affidavit showing the amount due—must enter judgment for that amount and costs against a defendant who has been defaulted for not appearing and who is neither a minor nor an incompetent person.

(2) *By the Court.* In all other cases, the party must apply to the court for a default judgment. A default judgment may be entered against a minor or incompetent person only if represented by a general guardian, conservator, or other like fiduciary who has appeared. If the party against whom a default judgment is sought has appeared personally or by a representative, that party or its representative must be served with written notice of the application at least 7 days before the hearing. The court may conduct hearings or make referrals—preserving any federal statutory right to a jury trial—when, to enter or effectuate judgment, it needs to:

(A) conduct an accounting;

(B) determine the amount of damages;

(C) establish the truth of any allegation by evidence; or

(D) investigate any other matter.

(c) Setting Aside a Default or a Default Judgment. The court may set aside an entry of default for good cause, and it may set aside a final default judgment under Rule 60(b).

(d) Judgment Against the United States. A default judgment may be entered against the United States, its officers, or its agencies only if the claimant establishes a claim or right to relief by evidence that satisfies the court.

[Amended effective August 1, 1987; April 30, 2007, effective December 1, 2007; March 26, 2009, effective December 1, 2009; April 29, 2015, effective December 1, 2015.]

UNDERSTANDING RULE 55

HOW RULE 55 FITS IN

Time matters in civil litigation. When a claim seeking affirmative relief is asserted against a party in federal court, the Rules require that party to respond to the claim in a timely way. The time for responding is set by Rule 12. The manner for responding is set by Rule 8 (if the response is an answer) or by Rule 12 (if the response is a motion). If, however, the party fails to file any timely response to the pending claim, a "default" (and, later, a "default judgment") can be entered against that delinquent party. This defaulting process can result in an abrupt and final end to the litigation, with the claimant declared the winner in the dispute and with a conclusive, enforceable judgment against the delinquent party, the loser.

The courts do not favor this defaulting process; they would much prefer to have every defending party come to court and explain their side of the dispute. But when defending parties fail to timely do so, the courts must ensure that litigation moves forward, that justice not be needlessly delayed for the nondelinquent parties, and that the court system be cleared of stalled cases so that the active claims and defenses of other parties, waiting patiently behind that case, can be heard.

Sometimes parties default deliberately—because, for example, those parties have no genuine defense and, rather than engage a lawyer to mount a costly fight, are content to have a final judgment entered against them. Sometimes parties have a good excuse for missing a response deadline, and should be relieved of any default that has been entered against them. Both situations require protective measures that Rule 55 and Rule 54(c) install so that the defaulting process is as fair as it can be. (Rule 54(c) forbids the granting of a default judgment that differs "in kind" or exceeds "in amount" what was requested in the pleadings. *See* Rule 54(c).)

THE ARCHITECTURE OF RULE 55

Rule 55 has four subparts. The first two set the general process for federal defaults. The first subpart sets the procedure for entering a "default," the first step in the two-step defaulting process. The second subpart sets the procedure for entering a "default judgment," the second and final step in the defaulting process. The third subpart creates a process for relieving a delinquent party of a default when proper grounds exist to do so. The fourth subpart establishes a special process for defaulting the United States government, federal officers, and federal agencies.

HOW RULE 55 WORKS IN PRACTICE

These four subparts of Rule 55 are discussed, in order, below.

RULE 55(a) — Entering a Default

Entering "default" is the first of the two steps in the defaulting process. The court clerk enters the "default." It is a formal notation on the official court record that marks the fact that the adversary was obligated under the Rules to defend against a claim and has failed to do so in the time allowed.

PRACTICING LAW UNDER THIS SUBPART

Distinguished from Default Judgment

The clerk's entry of a party's default is a *prerequisite* for the entry of judgment upon that default. It is, in effect, akin to a finding of liability with the entry of final judgment yet to come.

Prerequisites to an Entry of a Default

A motion for entry of default must be made promptly and properly. The party against whom default is being sought must be subject to the court's jurisdiction. Additionally, the clerk of court must be satisfied, by the movant's affidavit or otherwise, that the delinquent party was properly served with process and has thereafter failed to plead or otherwise defend. Courts have interpreted the phrase "otherwise defend" broadly, permitting entries of default for persistent lack of pretrial diligence or discovery misbehavior, failure to appear at an adjourned trial's resumption, dismissing counsel without an appointed replacement, and abandonment of an active defense. Conversely, where a party has failed to properly plead but is unquestionably "otherwise" defending, a pleading failure might be excused.

Entry Against *Any* Defending Party

Although most often used against a delinquent defendant, the default procedure can be applied against any defending party having an unmet obligation to counter-plead (such as a plaintiff on a counterclaim, a fellow defendant on a crossclaim, or a third-party defendant on an impleader).

Entry of Default Is Mandatory

If a defending party is found to have failed to plead or otherwise defend, entry of default is mandatory, not discretionary. Indeed, a delinquent party is considered already to be default, even if the formal entry of default has not yet been made.

Entry by Clerk or Court

Although entry of default is typically a ministerial act undertaken by the clerk, the district judges possess the power to enter default as well.

Contested Motions for Entry of Default

Where a motion for entry of default is opposed by a party who has entered an appearance, the courts may, in considering the contested motion, apply the criteria guiding motions to set aside a default.

Effect of Entry of Default

The entry of default provides formal notice to litigants that they are in default (that is, delinquent on the obligation to "plead or otherwise defend"). Upon entry, a defaulting party is deemed to have admitted all well-pleaded allegations of the complaint (except for the amount of damages); allegations that are not well-pleaded, as well as conclusions of law, are not deemed admitted. This greatly limits that party's ability to defend the lawsuit. A defaulting party is ordinarily foreclosed from raising any defenses other than a challenge to the legal sufficiency of the pleading to support a cognizable judgment, the adequacy of service of process, and the propriety of the court's jurisdiction. Default is not, however, an absolute confession of liability and of the opponent's right to recover, and the court may examine the pleaded allegations to confirm that they do, in fact, state a cognizable cause of action.

Appealability

Entry of default is an interlocutory order, from which an immediate appeal ordinarily cannot be taken. However, in an appeal from entry of a default judgment, the appeals court may review both the entry of default as well as the ensuing entry of default judgment.

RULE 55(b) Entering a Default Judgment

Where a defending party has been defaulted for failing to appear and the moving party has submitted evidence by affidavit establishing damages in a sum certain or in a sum that can be made certain by computation, the clerk of court may enter a default judgment upon motion. In all other cases, the *court* (and *not* the clerk of court) may enter a default judgment.

PRACTICING LAW UNDER THIS SUBPART

Effect of a Default Judgment

A default judgment transforms a defending party's admissions (which occur upon entry of the default) into a final judgment; it usually terminates the litigation by producing an enforceable, final award in favor of the pleader.

Prerequisites to a Default Judgment

Before a default judgment may be granted, a "default" under Rule 55(a) must first have been entered. The request for a default judgment must be made promptly. The entering court must confirm that it has subject-matter jurisdiction over the dispute, and also may (some Circuits hold "must") confirm that it possesses personal jurisdiction over the defaulting defendant. The court must then determine whether the now-admitted facts constitute a proper cause of action and a legitimate basis for entry of a judgment. (Although defaulting parties are precluded from contesting facts now deemed admitted, they may always challenge whether those admitted facts establish a cognizable claim for relief. *See Ohio Cent. R. Co. v. Central Trust Co.*, 133 U.S. 83, 91 (1890)). Some courts have characterized this inquiry as akin to a "reverse" motion to dismiss—confirming judicially that the pleaded allegations plausibly suggest an entitlement to the default remedy sought. If damages are awarded, their amount must be fixed. The court must respect the due process rights of the defaulting party, which requires minimally the 7-day notice to appearing defendants (see below) and the opportunity to be heard on the details and nature of the resulting default judgment.

The "Appearance" 7-Day Rule

If a default judgment is being sought against a party who has "appeared" (as that term is used in Rule 55(b)), that party must be served with *written* notice of the application for a default judgment at least 7 days before the hearing. Such an appearance, obviously, must have occurred *before* the default judgment is entered in order to trigger the entitlement to written notice. The entitlement to notice can be waived if an objection is not timely raised.

Defining a Party's "Appearance"

A defending party "appears" in the action by making some presentation or submission to the court (*e.g.*, filing an entry of appearance, serving a responsive pleading, serving a Rule 12 motion to dismiss, or having counsel attend a conference on the client's behalf). Some courts have taken an even wider view, ruling that "appearing" within the meaning of Rule 55(b) is not necessarily limited to a formal event in court. For example, informal acts such as correspondence or telephone calls between counsel might constitute the requisite appearance, as can engaging in settlement negotiations. Given the judiciary's disfavor of default judgments, courts may search to find that an appearance has occurred. Nevertheless, merely accepting or waiving service of process will not qualify as "appearing" within the meaning of this Rule.

Entry of Default Judgment by Clerk

The clerk may only enter a default judgment where the following three prerequisites are met:

(1) A defendant was defaulted because of a failure to appear; *and*

(2) The defendant is not a minor or incompetent person; *and*

(3) The moving party submits an affidavit establishing that the amount due is either a sum certain or a sum that can be made certain by computation.

- *"Sum Certain" Defined:* A claim is not a "sum certain" under Rule 55 unless there is no doubt as to the amount that must be awarded, that the amount due is beyond question (such as actions on money judgments or negotiable instruments). This standard is not met where some portion of damages, such as "reasonable" attorney's fees or punitive damages, still needs to be determined.

Entry of Default Judgment by Court

In all other circumstances, the court may enter the default judgment:

(1) Where the defaulting party has "appeared", in which case that party must be served with written notice of the application for default judgment at least 7 days before any hearing on the application; or

(2) Where the defaulting party is a minor or incompetent person, in which case a default judgment may be entered only if the minor or incompetent is represented; or

(3) Where the amount due is not certain or the relief sought is noneconomic; or

(4) Where the defaulting party has been defaulted for a reason other than a failure to appear. For example, in appropriate circumstances, a default judgment can be entered as a sanction against a misbehaving litigant.

Fashioning the Default Judgment

When the damages amount is not a sum certain, the court may convene an evidentiary hearing or simply rely on affidavits or other documentary evidence. Convening an evidentiary hearing may not be mandatory in all cases; so long as a proper factual basis supports the court's award, whether (and how) to conduct hearings is often left to the trial judge's discretion. The Rule expressly approves of hearings when needed for an accounting or a determination of damage amounts, to receive evidence on allegations, or to otherwise investigate. Although the entry of default deprives the defaulting party of the right to contest most of the complaint's factual allegations (unless the default is set aside), that party may contest the amount of damages. Thus, all the well-pleaded facts in the complaint are presumed true, except those factual allegations relating to the amount of damages, which the moving party must prove with reasonable certainty and which the court must independently determine. Moreover, although proximate cause (when properly pleaded) is irrefutably established upon the defendant's default, the moving party must still show that the compensation requested relates to damages flowing naturally from the loss alleged. An evidentiary basis must support the damages sought. However, all doubts and reasonable inferences from the damages evidence are drawn in the moving party's favor.

Default in Multiple Defendant Cases

Where the plaintiff alleges joint liability against multiple defendants or the defendants have closely related defenses, the default of one defendant usually will not result in a judgment against another defendant. Instead, the court will allow the lawsuit to proceed as to the other, non-defaulting defendants. The result in the litigation (*e.g.,* judgment for plaintiff or judgment for defendants) will then simply be entered as to the defaulting defendant as well. *See Frow v. De La Vega,* 82 U.S. 552, 554 (1872).

Defaulting Defendants in the Military

The federal Soldiers' and Sailors' Civil Relief Act of 1940, 50 U.S.C. App. § 3931, prohibits the entry of any federal or State judgment by default against absent military defendants, unless the court first appoints counsel to represent the absent defendants' interests. Often, the court may simply stay a lawsuit against the absent military defendants until their return.

Limitation on Default Judgments

No judgment by default can be greater in amount or different in kind from the demand contained in the complaint. *See* Rule 54(c).

Discretion of District Court

Judgments by default are disfavored and are never granted as a matter of right. Whether to enter a judgment by default is a decision entrusted to the sound discretion of the district court. Thus, a party's default does not entitle the plaintiff to an automatic default judgment, nor need the judge presume that the pleader's allegations constitute a valid cause of action. Before exercising their discretion and entering a default judgment, courts may examine the standards for setting aside a default; whether a responsive pleading has since (though belatedly) been received; and a myriad of other factors, such as the federal policy favoring decisions on the merits, the presence of excusable neglect, the clarity of the grounds for default, the adequacy of notice, the size of the claim, the facts in dispute, and prejudice to either party. Nevertheless, and notwithstanding the preference for decisions on the merits, where the inquiry satisfies the court that a default judgment is proper, it will be entered. Unresponsive litigants should not be allowed to halt the adversary process, and diligent parties should be protected against undue delay and uncertainty.

Appealability

An entry of judgment by default constitutes a final order, provided it is not conditional and does not contemplate any further proceedings. Whether it is appealable can be less clear. Some courts require, as a prerequisite to appealability, that the losing party first file a motion with the district judge requesting that the default judgment be vacated; others do not so require. A refusal to enter judgment by default is considered interlocutory, generally appealable only when the case's final order is entered.

RULE 55(c) Setting Aside Default or a Default Judgment

In appropriate circumstances, the court may set aside (or "lift", "vacate") either a default or a default judgment. Defaults may be set aside for good cause. Default judgments may be set aside in accordance with the standards prescribed in Rule 60(b) (which governs the grounds upon which a party may seek relief from a judgment).

PRACTICING LAW UNDER THIS SUBPART

Policy and Liberality

Defaults and default judgments are disfavored, since they are inconsistent with the federal courts' preference for resolving disputes on their merits. This preference is reflected in the two-step default process (default first, default judgment later), which affords two opportunities to appear and seek to avoid the effects of default. Motions for relief from both defaults and default judgments are considered liberally and are often granted. Where only a default has been entered (without an ensuing default judgment), the standard for lifting the default is especially generous.

Setting Aside a Default

Rule 55(c) authorizes the district courts, "for good cause," to set aside the entry of a default. Not susceptible to a precise definition, "good cause" has been labeled a liberal and "mutable" standard, one anchored in equity that varies from situation to situation. It is a standard applied generously since a judgment has not yet been entered upon the default. Doubts in "close cases" will likely favor a finding of good cause. Ergo, entries of default are often set aside. The requisite "good cause," however, is not "good cause" for the defendant's mistake, but rather "good cause" justifying the court's intervention to set the default aside. An absence of jurisdiction will obviously qualify.

Otherwise, in testing for "good cause," the courts generally consider the following three factors: (1) proof that the default was not willful or culpable (which typically requires more than mere inaction or negligence); (2) existence of a meritorious defense (which usually is not a very heavy burden but requires only the alleging of sufficient facts that, if true, would constitute a defense); and (3) whether the opponent would be prejudiced were the default lifted (which means not merely delay or the chore of having to prove the merits, but some loss of evidence, unavailability of witnesses, or other impairment of the ability to prove the merits). Some courts also include, as a leading factor, an inquiry into the swiftness of the action taken to remedy the default.

In addition to these leading factors, courts have often considered other equitable criteria as well, including: (a) whether the default resulted from a good faith mistake in following a rule of procedure; (b) the nature of the defendant's explanation for defaulting; (c) any history of dilatory conduct; (d) the amount in controversy; (e) the availability of effective alternative sanctions; (f) whether entry of a default would produce a harsh or unfair result; and (g) various other factors.

For many courts, each particular consideration need not be satisfied, and the list of criteria is seen as a non-exhaustive list of mere indicators. For those courts, motions to set aside default are made in a commonsense way, and without adhering rigidly on mechanical formulas. Other courts take a more unyielding approach, treating the leading factors as mandatory, with a failure to meet any one sufficient, alone, to justify denying the motion.

Vacating a Judgment by Default

Once a judgment is entered upon a party's default, the task of vacating it becomes more difficult. The court may vacate a default judgment if the defaulting party satisfies one of the Rule 60(b) reasons for vacating a judgment (*i.e.,* mistake, inadvertence, surprise, excusable neglect, newly discovered evidence, misconduct by an adverse party, void judgment, or satisfied or discharged judgment). Default judgments are "the biggest weapon in the district court's armory." *See Mommaerts v. Hartford Life and Acc. Ins. Co.,* 472 F.3d 967, 967–69 (7th Cir. 2007). They may be useful in reining in recalcitrant parties or penalizing prejudicial tactics. Such judgments generally are not appropriate where the misstep does not prejudice the adversary or costs the erring party an otherwise certain victory. Rather, this is an equitable inquiry that considers all relevant circumstances. The time for filing such motions is set forth in Rule 60(b).

Burden of Proof

The burden of demonstrating that either a default or default judgment should be lifted lies with the moving party.

Discretion of District Court

Because they clash with the federal courts' preference for decisions on the merits, defaulting a party is viewed as a drastic step and extreme sanction, and ought to be reserved for only rare occasions. Accordingly, at least the "good cause" criteria are applied forgivingly, with doubts resolved in favor of lifting the default. Whether to set aside the entry of default or vacate a default judgment is left to the discretion of the district judge. Where it did not explain its reasoning, a district court's decision to vacate may nevertheless be upheld where the basis for the ruling is apparent.

Sua Sponte Set Asides

Although defaults and default judgments are set aside usually upon motion of a party, the district courts may do so *sua sponte.*

RULE 55(d) Judgment Against the United States

The entry of default judgments against the United States is especially disfavored. Federal taxpayers (on whom the burden of paying the default judgment would ultimately fall) should not be called upon to pay a penalty imposed as the consequence of the neglect of some government official, if to do so would cause an unmerited windfall to a litigant. Thus, default judgments against the United States or against any federal agency or officer cannot be entered unless and until the plaintiff establishes, by evidence satisfactory to the court, a claim or right to relief.

PRACTICING LAW UNDER THIS SUBPART

Applies Only to Default Judgments, Not Defaults

Although default judgments may not be entered summarily against the United States, the default itself may be.

Plaintiff's Burden

To obtain a default judgment against the United States or federal officers or agencies, plaintiffs must carry the heavy burden of establishing a claim or right-to-relief. They must do so by evidence that is satisfactory to the court. This inquiry does not necessarily require a hearing, or either more or different evidence than might otherwise be received. (However, at least one court has ruled that the burden for default against the United States requires a demonstration of an evidentiary basis that is legally sufficient for a reasonable jury to find for the plaintiff.) Instead, the courts assume a flexible approach in determining the procedures necessary to conduct this inquiry. If uncontroverted, a plaintiff's *evidence* may be accepted as true, but if the government comes forward with a meritorious defense and a willingness to litigate, the default judgment will likely be denied.

Foreign Governments

By statute, Congress requires that this same "satisfies-the-court" standard be applied in actions against foreign governments, foreign political subdivisions, and foreign agencies and instrumentalities. *See* 28 U.S.C. § 1608(e).

RULE 56

SUMMARY JUDGMENT

(a) Motion for Summary Judgment or Partial Summary Judgment. A party may move for summary judgment, identifying each claim or defense—or the part of each claim or defense—on which summary judgment is sought. The court shall grant summary judgment if the movant shows that there is no genuine dispute as to any material fact and the movant is entitled to judgment as a matter of law. The court should state on the record the reasons for granting or denying the motion.

(b) Time to File a Motion. Unless a different time is set by local rule or the court orders otherwise, a party may file a motion for summary judgment at any time until 30 days after the close of all discovery.

(c) Procedures.

(1) *Supporting Factual Positions.* A party asserting that a fact cannot be or is genuinely disputed must support the assertion by:

(A) citing to particular parts of materials in the record, including depositions, documents, electronically stored information, affidavits or declarations, stipulations (including those made for purposes of the motion only), admissions, interrogatory answers, or other materials; or

(B) showing that the materials cited do not establish the absence or presence of a genuine dispute, or that an adverse party cannot produce admissible evidence to support the fact.

(2) *Objection That a Fact Is Not Supported by Admissible Evidence.* A party may object that the material cited to support or dispute a fact cannot be presented in a form that would be admissible in evidence.

(3) *Materials Not Cited.* The court need consider only the cited materials, but it may consider other materials in the record.

(4) *Affidavits or Declarations.* An affidavit or declaration used to support or oppose a motion must be made on personal knowledge, set out facts that would be admissible in evidence, and show that the affiant or declarant is competent to testify on the matters stated.

(d) When Facts Are Unavailable to the Nonmovant. If a nonmovant shows by affidavit or declaration that, for specified reasons, it cannot present facts essential to justify its opposition, the court may:

(1) defer considering the motion or deny it;

(2) allow time to obtain affidavits or declarations or to take discovery; or

(3) issue any other appropriate order.

(e) Failing to Properly Support or Address a Fact. If a party fails to properly support an assertion of fact or fails to properly address another party's assertion of fact as required by Rule 56(c), the court may:

(1) give an opportunity to properly support or address the fact;

(2) consider the fact undisputed for purposes of the motion;

(3) grant summary judgment if the motion and supporting materials—including the facts considered undisputed—show that the movant is entitled to it; or

(4) issue any other appropriate order.

(f) Judgment Independent of the Motion. After giving notice and a reasonable time to respond, the court may:

(1) grant summary judgment for a nonmovant;

(2) grant the motion on grounds not raised by a party; or

(3) consider summary judgment on its own after identifying for the parties material facts that may not be genuinely in dispute.

(g) Failing to Grant All the Requested Relief. If the court does not grant all the relief requested by the motion, it may enter an order stating any material fact—including an item of damages or other relief—that is not genuinely in dispute and treating the fact as established in the case.

(h) Affidavit or Declaration Submitted in Bad Faith. If satisfied that an affidavit or declaration under this rule is submitted in bad faith or solely for delay, the court—after notice and a reasonable time to respond—may order the submitting party to pay the other party the reasonable expenses, including attorney's fees, it incurred as a result. An offending party or attorney may also be held in contempt or subjected to other appropriate sanctions.

[Amended effective March 19, 1948; July 1, 1963; August 1, 1987; April 30, 2007, effective December 1, 2007; March 26, 2009, effective December 1, 2009; April 28, 2010, effective December 1, 2010.]

—The 2010 Summary Judgment Amendments—

The federal summary judgment rule—Rule 56—was extensively revised effective December 2010. The current text of the Rule appears above. However, because many important cases in your study of summary judgment refer to the Rule's pre-amended language, that earlier version is reprinted below for your reference:

[Rule 56—Summary Judgment: as it appeared prior to December 2010:]

(a) By a Claiming Party. A party claiming relief may move, with or without supporting affidavits, for summary judgment on all or part of the claim.

(b) By a Defending Party. A party against whom relief is sought may move, with or without supporting affidavits, for summary judgment on all or part of the claim.

(c) Time for a Motion, Response, and Reply; Proceedings.

(1) These times apply unless a different time is set by local rule or the court orders otherwise:

(A) a party may move for summary judgment at any time until 30 days after the close of all discovery;

(B) a party opposing the motion must file a response within 21 days after the motion is served or a responsive pleading is due, whichever is later; and

(C) the movant may file a reply within 14 days after the response is served.

(2) The judgment sought should be rendered if the pleadings, the discovery and disclosure materials on file, and any affidavits show that there is no genuine issue as to any material fact and that the movant is entitled to judgment as a matter of law.

(d) Case Not Fully Adjudicated on the Motion.

(1) *Establishing Facts.* If summary judgment is not rendered on the whole action, the court should, to the extent practicable, determine what material facts are not genuinely at issue. The court should so determine by examining the pleadings and evidence before it and by interrogating the attorneys. It should then issue an order specifying what facts—including items of damages or other relief—are not genuinely at issue. The facts so specified must be treated as established in the action.

(2) *Establishing Liability.* An interlocutory summary judgment may be rendered on liability alone, even if there is a genuine issue on the amount of damages.

(e) Affidavits; Further Testimony.

(1) *In General.* A supporting or opposing affidavit must be made on personal knowledge, set out facts that would be admissible in evidence, and show that the affiant is competent to testify on the matters stated. If a paper or part of a paper is referred to in an affidavit, a sworn or certified copy must be attached to or served with the affidavit. The court may permit an affidavit to be supplemented or opposed by depositions, answers to interrogatories, or additional affidavits.

(2) *Opposing Party's Obligation to Respond.* When a motion for summary judgment is properly made and supported, an opposing party may not rely merely on allegations or denials in its own pleading; rather, its response must by affidavits or as otherwise provided in this rule—set out specific facts showing a genuine issue for trial. If the opposing party does not so respond, summary judgment should, if appropriate, be entered against that party.

(f) When Affidavits Are Unavailable. If a party opposing the motion shows by affidavit that, for specified reasons, it cannot present facts essential to justify its opposition, the court may:

(1) deny the motion;

(2) order a continuance to enable affidavits to be obtained, depositions to be taken, or other discovery to be undertaken; or

(3) issue any other just order.

(g) Affidavit Submitted in Bad Faith. If satisfied that an affidavit under this rule is submitted in bad faith or solely for delay, the court must order the submitting party to pay the other party the reasonable expenses, including attorney's fees, it incurred as a result. An offending party or attorney may also be held in contempt.

UNDERSTANDING RULE 56

HOW RULE 56 FITS IN

If a federal case is properly pleaded and timely defended, does that mean that it will necessarily reach a courtroom to be tried? The answer is "no." Many cases are settled before they reach trial, with the parties agreeing to a negotiated resolution of the dispute. That usually results in a voluntary dismissal of the lawsuit (*see* Rule 41(a)). Cases can also be terminated before trial on a motion for summary judgment, the subject of this Rule.

Motions for summary judgment examine whether some (or all) of the claims and/or defenses in the lawsuit have the necessary evidentiary support. If they do not (or if the evidence is so one-sided that no reasonable person could possibly rule in the opponent's favor), there is no need to convene a trial on that claim or defense. After all, if there is no true factual dispute to sort out, there is no need for a factfinder. In that instance, judgment on that claim or defense can be entered "summarily." *See Murray v. Kindred Nursing Ctrs. West LLC*, 789 F.3d 20, 24–25 (1st Cir. 2015) (summary judgment avoids "full-dress trials in unwinnable cases").

Motions for summary judgment are usually (but not always) filed after the pleadings stage of the case is closed and after discovery (or most discovery) has been finished. Those motions bring with them, as one court has written, " 'put up or shut up' time for the non-moving party." *See Harney v. Speedway Super-America, LLC*, 526 F.3d 1099, 1104 (7th Cir. 2008). They require the party who seeks to avoid the entry of "summary" judgment to come forward and show the court why there is a genuine, materially-disputed contest for a factfinder to resolve.

Motions for summary judgment differ significantly from Rule 12(b) dismissals and Rule 12(c) judgments on the pleadings. Unlike those sorts of motions, summary judgment considers the provable facts, not just the pleaded allegations. A party may have adequately *alleged* a claim or defense; summary judgment tests whether that party now has the evidence needed to *prove* that claim or defense.

Motions for summary judgment also differ from Rule 50 judgments as a matter of law (JMOL), but the difference there is largely one of timing. The controlling legal standard (is there a triable issue for the factfinder?) is the same. *See Anderson v. Liberty Lobby, Inc.*, 477 U.S. 242, 250–51 (1986). But that inquiry is conducted pre-trial in the summary judgment context, and is examined on the basis of the pleadings, discovery, affidavits, and other "cold" evidence. Conversely, JMOL assessments are made during or after trial, with the judge having listened to the actual, live testimony and evidentiary presentation. In other words, Rule 50 motions for JMOL ask whether there is any need for the trial—then underway—to continue on to the jury deliberation stage; Rule 56 motions for summary judgment ask, often much earlier, whether there is any need to convene a trial in the first place.

THE ARCHITECTURE OF RULE 56

Rule 56 appears to have a complex structure but, on closer examination, it is easily understood. Consider organizing the Rule into four groups.

The first group—subparts (a) and (b)—sets the test for summary judgment and the time for filing motions seeking such judgments.

The second group—subparts (c) and (d)—establishes the procedures the parties may use to show the presence or the absence of a genuine, triable dispute, and supplies the non-moving party with a procedure for asking the court to postpone a ruling on the motion until more discovery can be finished.

The third group—subparts (e), (f), and (g)—creates options the court may use in ruling on the motion. It addresses how the court may rule when a party has failed to adequately support or respond to the motion, when the court believes a different type of ruling is proper than the one the motion seeks, or when the court agrees that only some of the relief the motion seeks is proper.

The final group—subpart (h)—addresses what action the court may take if it finds that an affidavit or declaration from one of the parties was submitted during the summary judgment motion process in bad faith or solely to delay the litigation.

HOW RULE 56 WORKS IN PRACTICE

These eight subparts of Rule 56 are discussed, in order, below.

RULE 56(a) Motion for Summary Judgment or Partial Summary Judgment

The test for summary judgment is set out concisely in this sub-part. A court may terminate by summary judgment any claim, defense, or lawsuit when there is no true dispute as to any fact of consequence and one of the parties is entitled to judgment as a matter of law.

PRACTICING LAW UNDER THIS SUBPART

Motions by Claiming Parties

Summary judgment is not only a defensive tool; claimants can move for summary judgment on their own claims as well. They bear a heavier burden when doing so, however.

Motions by Defending Parties

Defending parties may move for summary judgment. Courts are divided on whether filing a pre-answer summary judgment motion will have the effect of tolling the time for filing a responsive pleading (as a pre-answer Rule 12(b) motion would). In any event, it is clear that filing an answer is not a prerequisite for filing a summary judgment motion.

Motions by Both Parties (Cross-Motions)

Both parties may seek summary judgment in the same action, with "cross-motions" under Rule 56, discussed below.

Motions by Others

Summary judgment is available only when one party is formally asserting a claim against, or defending against a claim formally asserted by, another party. The rights of parties can only be resolved by summary judgment if claims or defenses are already pending.

Partial Motions

Motions may seek summary judgment as to the entire claim or defense, or just parts of a claim or defense.

Purpose of Summary Judgment

The purpose of summary judgment is to isolate, and then terminate, claims and defenses that are factually unsupported. *See Celotex Corp. v. Catrett,* 477 U.S. 317, 323–24 (1986). It is not a disfavored technical shortcut, but rather an integral component of the Rules. *See id.* at 327. Summary judgment motions must be resolved with regard not only for the rights of those asserting claims and defenses to have their positions heard by a factfinder, but also for the rights of persons opposing such claims and defenses to demonstrate, under this Rule and *before* trial, that the claims and defenses have no factual basis. *See id.* Thus, a party moving for summary judgment forces the opponent to come forward with at least one sworn averment of fact essential to the contested portion(s) of that opponent's claims or defenses, before the time-consuming process of litigation will continue. *See Lujan v. National Wildlife Fed'n,* 497 U.S. 871, 888–89 (1990).

Legal Test

Summary judgment shall be granted if the summary judgment record shows that: (1) there is no genuine dispute, (2) as to any material fact, and (3) the moving party is entitled to judgment. *See Beard v. Banks,* 548 U.S. 521, 529 (2006).

- *Genuine Dispute:* A "genuine dispute" exists when a rational factfinder, considering the evidence in the summary judgment record, could find in favor of the non-moving party. *See Anderson v. Liberty Lobby, Inc.,* 477 U.S. 242, 247–52 (1986). Ergo, a dispute is "genuine" if it has a real basis in the evidentiary record. A "genuine dispute" is not created by a mere "scintilla" of favorable evidence, or by evidence that is only "colorable" or insufficiently probative. *See id.* at 252. It is also not created by positing a factual scenario that is definitively contradicted by incontestable evidence in the summary judgment record. *See Scott v. Harris,* 550 U.S. 372, 380 (2007). When a claim or defense is factually improbable, a more persuasive record may be needed to show a "genuine dispute." *See Matsushita Elec. Indus. Co., Ltd. v. Zenith Radio Corp.,* 475 U.S. 574, 587 (1986). The court will test for a "genuine dispute" through the lens of the quantum of proof applicable to the substantive claim or defense at issue (*e.g.,* if the claim or defense must be established by clear and convincing proof, the court will assess whether the proffered evidence could lead a reasonable factfinder to conclude that such a quantum of evidence is present). *See Anderson,* 477 U.S. at 254.
- *Material Fact:* A fact is "material" if it might affect the outcome of the case. *See Anderson,* 477 U.S. at 248. Whether a fact qualifies as "material" hinges on the substantive law at issue. Disputes (even if "genuine") over irrelevant or unnecessary facts will not defeat a motion for summary judgment. *See Scott,* 550 U.S. at 380.
- *Appropriate as a Matter of Law:* Judgment is appropriate "as a matter of law" when the moving party should prevail because the non-moving party has failed to make an adequate showing on an essential element of its case, as to which that party has the burden of proof. *See Celotex Corp. v. Catrett,* 477 U.S. 317, 323 (1986). Thus, the mere fact that the moving party's summary judgment record is uncontested, *see Edwards v. Aguillard,* 482 U.S. 578, 595 (1987), or even unresponded to, is not enough. Even then, the Rule 56 prerequisites must be present before summary judgment may be entered.

Burdens of Proof

The party moving for summary judgment bears the initial burden of showing the absence of a genuine, material dispute and an entitlement to judgment. *See Celotex Corp. v. Catrett,* 477 U.S. 317, 323 (1986). This showing does not necessarily require the moving party to disprove the opponent's claims or defenses. *See id.* Instead, this burden may often be discharged simply by pointing out for the court an absence of evidence in support of the non-moving party's claims or defenses. *See id.* Although a modest threshold, this burden remains a real one; it requires more than an empty, unparticularized assertion that the opponent has produced no evidence. This prima facie burden is heavier when the moving party is the one having the ultimate burden of persuasion at trial, requiring that party to show not only that it can carry its burden of proving all essential elements of its claim or defense, but also that no reasonable jury would disbelieve that evidence. *See Hunt v. Cromartie,* 526 U.S. 541, 553 (1999).

If the moving party meets its prima facie burden, then the burden of going forward shifts to the non-moving party to show, by affidavit or otherwise, that a genuine dispute of material fact remains for the factfinder to resolve. *See Celotex Corp.,* 477 U.S. at 323. The non-moving party's burden is not especially onerous, but nor is it trifling. Indeed, once this stage arrives, the non-moving party is not saved by mere allegations or denials, assertions in legal memoranda or argument, speculation, conclusory statements, empty rhetoric, characterizations of disputed facts, mere suspicion, or simply recounting the generous notice-pleading standards of the federal courts. Nor will an earnest hope to discover evidence suffice, or a promise to come forward later with proof, a hope to discredit the opponent's evidence at trial, or the possibility that a jury could disbelieve the moving party's evidence. While circumstantial evidence may properly be considered, it must lead to more than speculation to ward off summary judgment. In sum, "hope" and brash conjecture are not enough. Evidence, not contentions, avoids summary judgment." *See Al-Zubaidy v. TEK Indus., Inc.,* 406 F.3d 1030, 1036 (8th Cir. 2005). And non-moving parties must arrive brandishing more than "a cardboard sword." *See Calvi v. Knox Cty.,* 470 F.3d 422, 426 (1st Cir. 2006).

Accordingly, a non-moving party must "go beyond the pleadings," *see id.* at 324, and show adequately probative evidence creating a triable controversy. A party does not meet this burden by offering evidence which is merely colorable or which implies some metaphysical factual doubt, or by simply theorizing a "plausible scenario" in support of the party's claims, especially when that proffered scenario conflicts with direct, contrary evidence. Rather, the non-moving party must identify specific record evidence and explain how that material defeats summary judgment. (And if the non-moving party has the ultimate burden of persuasion (*e.g.*, as a claimant), it must do so as to each essential element on which it bears that burden.)

Ruling on the Motion, Generally

If the moving party fails to carry its initial prima facie burden of showing the absence of a genuine, material dispute or its entitlement to judgment, the court will deny the motion. If, however, the moving party carries its initial burden, the court "shall" grant summary judgment for that party if the non-moving party's response fails to show a genuine, material dispute. *See Beard v. Banks,* 548 U.S. 521, 529 (2006). Conversely, if the non-moving party succeeds in showing a genuine, material dispute (or otherwise demonstrates why the moving party is not entitled to a judgment), the court must deny the motion. *See Ortiz v. Jordan,* 562 U.S. 180, 188 (2011). In sum, the Rule imposes a "relatively lenient standard" to survive the motion and continue on to trial. *See Amgen Inc. v. Connecticut Ret. Plans & Trust Funds,* 568 U.S. 455, 479–80 (2013). If, on the evidence presented, a fair-minded jury could return a verdict for the nonmoving party, summary judgment will be denied. *See Anderson v. Liberty Lobby, Inc.,* 477 U.S. 242, 248 (1986).

"Shall"—Discretion in Ruling

There is some controversy over Rule 56(a)'s use of the verb "shall." A court has no discretion to decide motions on the basis of clearly erroneous findings of fact, an erroneous legal standard, or an improper application of the law. Nor is there discretion to grant summary judgment where a genuine, material dispute remains. *See Ortiz v. Jordan,* 562 U.S. 180, 188 (2011).

In all other contexts, however, the proper measure of a court's discretion is less clear. Some case precedent suggests that very little discretion exists. *See Beard v. Banks,* 548 U.S. 521, 529 (2006) ("the law requires entry of judgment" if non-moving party fails to show genuine issue of material fact). But other precedent suggests differently. *See Kennedy v. Silas Mason Co.*, 334 U.S. 249, 256–57 (1948). For example, some courts hold that summary judgment may be denied where the factual records are thin or contain gaps that could be resolved by readily obtainable evidence, where the court concludes that a fuller factual development is necessary, or where there is some particular reason to believe that the wiser course would be to proceed to trial. *See Anderson v. Liberty Lobby, Inc.,* 477 U.S. 242, 254 (1986); *Kennedy v. Silas Mason Co.,* 334 U.S. 249, 256–57 (1948). In a non-jury/bench trial, the district judge may have more discretion still.

Ruling on the Motion, Doubts and Inferences

In ruling on a motion for summary judgment, the court will never weigh the evidence or find the facts. *See Anderson v. Liberty Lobby, Inc.,* 477 U.S. 242, 255 (1986). Instead, the court's role under Rule 56 is narrowly limited to assessing the threshold issue of whether a genuine dispute exists as to material facts requiring a trial. *See id.* at 249. Thus, the evidence of the non-moving party will be believed as true, all doubts will be resolved against the moving party, all evidence will be construed in the light most favorable to the non-moving party, and all reasonable doubts and inferences will be drawn in the non-moving party's favor. *See id.* at 255. Of course, this generous treatment applies only to the non-moving party's *evidence*; as noted above, unsupported contentions or speculation cannot ward off summary judgment. The court also may credit those portions of the moving party's evidence, from disinterested sources, that are uncontradicted and unimpeached. *See Reeves v. Sanderson Plumbing Prods., Inc.,* 530 U.S. 133, 151 (2000).

The boundary dividing reasonable inferences from impermissible speculation is frequently thin, though certainly consequential. "Reasonable" inferences are those reasonably drawn from all the facts then before the court, after sifting through the universe of all possible inferences the facts could support. "Reasonable" inferences need not be necessarily more probable or likely than other inferences that might tilt in the moving party's favor. Instead, so long as more than one reasonable inference can be drawn, and one inference creates a genuine dispute of material fact, the trier of fact is entitled to decide which inference to believe and summary judgment on that ground is not appropriate. *See Hunt v. Cromartie,* 526 U.S. 541, 552 (1999).

Conversely, an inference is an unreasonable one if it is strained, supported only by acrimonious invective or speculation and conjecture, posits vacantly that something had to have happened, or rests only on barebones and conclusory assertions.

Ruling on the Motion, Credibility Questions

The proper inquiry in a summary judgment motion is not which side has the most evidence, but merely whether enough evidence favors the nonmoving party to support a decision for that party. For this reason, courts will not decide the credibility of witnesses or other evidence in ruling on a motion for summary judgment. *See Anderson v. Liberty Lobby, Inc.,* 477 U.S. 242, 255 (1986). Evaluating credibility, weighing evidence, and drawing factual inferences are all functions reserved for the jury. *See id.* However, simply lobbing broad, conclusory attacks on a witness's credibility is not enough to defeat summary judgment.

Ruling on the Motion, State of Mind Questions

Summary judgment is not automatically foreclosed merely because a person's state of mind (such as motive, knowledge, intent, good faith or bad faith, malice, fraud, conspiracy, or consent) is at issue. But such cases will seldom lend themselves to a summary disposition because questions of credibility will ordinarily abound. *See Hutchinson v. Proxmire,* 443 U.S. 111, 122 (1979). Thus, summary judgment is seldom granted, or at least applied sparingly, in cases involving peculiarly intensive state of mind questions such as employment discrimination actions, antitrust cases, and certain intellectual property disputes.

Ruling on the Motion, Predominantly Legal Disputes

Summary judgment is often appropriate in cases where the disputes are primarily legal, rather than factual in nature.

Stipulated Facts

If the parties stipulate to the facts, obviously no genuine dispute as to material facts then exists for a factfinder to resolve. Nevertheless, the summary judgment standard remains the same. The court must draw inferences from the stipulated facts, and resolve those inferences in favor of the non-moving party.

Cross-Motions

Cross-motions for summary judgment are also examined under the usual Rule 56 standards. Each cross-motion must be evaluated on its own merits, with the court viewing all facts and reasonable inferences in the light most favorable to the nonmoving party. Thus, the mere fact that cross-motions have been filed does not, by itself, necessarily justify the entry of a summary judgment, nor will the denial of one cross-motion compel the grant of the other cross-motion.

Trial Court's Duty to Explain

Trial judges are advised to set forth, on the record, the reasons for their disposition of summary judgment motions, although the particular form and content of that explanation is left to the court's discretion. *See* Rule 56(a) advisory committee note to 2010 amendments. This requirement facilitates both subsequent trial-level proceedings and appeals. But trial courts are ordinarily not expected to pen "elaborate essays using talismanic phrases," unless doing so is necessary to dispel appellate concerns that material facts were overlooked or a wrong legal standard was applied. *See Jackson v. Federal Exp.*, 766 F.3d 189, 196–97 (2d Cir. 2014).

Effect of a Summary Judgment Ruling—"Law of the Case"

The "law of the case" doctrine holds that when a court decides upon a rule of law, that decision should generally control the same issues throughout the subsequent stages in the same case. *See Arizona v. California,* 460 U.S. 605, 618 (1983). The doctrine is based on the sound, salutary policy of judicial finality—that all litigation should come to an end. But this is a prudential doctrine; it guides and influences the court's exercise of discretion, but it does not limit the court's jurisdiction or power. *See id.* It may not apply where intervening controlling authority warrants a revisiting of an earlier decision. Because *denials* of summary judgment generally do nothing more than acknowledge that a genuine issue of material fact remains for trial, such denials are typically not accorded any preclusive effect nor do they become "law of the case". *See Switzerland Cheese Ass'n, Inc. v. E. Horne's Market, Inc.,* 385 U.S. 23, 25 (1966). The same is true for other interlocutory rulings that preceded the entry of summary judgment.

Constitutionality of Summary Judgment

Only once has the Supreme Court examined the constitutionality of summary judgment, on a claim that the procedure deprives defeated claimants of their Seventh Amendment rights to a trial by jury. The Court rejected this argument, reasoning that any time summary judgment is granted, it is only because there *is* no triable issue for the jury. *See Fidelity & Deposit Co. v. United States,* 187 U.S. 315, 319–21 (1902). No lower federal court has ever declared summary judgment unconstitutional. *But see* Suja A. Thomas, *Why Summary Judgment is Unconstitutional,* 93 VA. L. REV. 139 (2007) (arguing why Rule 56 violates the Seventh Amendment).

Appealability

The general rule is that an order granting summary judgment is appealable when it constitutes the "final order" in the case (*i.e.*, the ruling wraps up everything) or, if non-final (such as partial summary judgments), if the district court permits a proper interlocutory appeal under Rule 54(b) or 28 U.S.C. § 1292(b).

The appealability of an order denying summary judgment is less simple. If the denial is based on the presence of genuinely disputed facts, that order decides merely that the case must continue; it neither finally settles nor tentatively resolves anything else about the merits. *See Switzerland Cheese Ass'n, Inc. v. E. Horne's Market, Inc.,* 385 U.S. 23, 25 (1966). For this reason, it is ordinarily not immediately appealable. *See Ortiz v. Jordan,* 562 U.S. 180, 188. In fact, several courts hold that, once a trial on the merits occurs, the denial order can never be reviewed on appeal, because the "prediction" that denial represented has been rendered moot by the actual introduction of evidence at trial. Other courts recognize an exception to this general prohibition, and permit a summary judgment denial to be reviewed on appeal if the denial was based on the interpretation of a pure question of law. *See New York Marine & General Ins. Co. v. Continental Cement Co., LLC,* 761 F.3d 830, 838 (8th Cir. 2014) (surveying divided case law). Other courts narrow that exception still further, permitting review when the denial was based on a pure question of law and the judge was the factfinder (non-jury, bench trial). Other courts hold that, although such review is generally denied, an appeal might be tolerated were "extraordinary circumstances" to exist.

- *Exceptions:* It is important to note that exceptions exist. For example, if the motion asserts questions of immunity from suit, a denial of summary judgment may be immediately appealable.

RULE 56(b) Time to File a Motion

Parties may move for summary judgment at any time until 30 days after the close of all discovery, absent a local rule or court order directing otherwise. The time for responding to motions is left undefined, to be set by local rule or court order.

PRACTICING LAW UNDER THIS SUBPART

Time for Filing

A national timing procedure governs summary judgment motions, permitting their filing at any time "until 30 days after the close of discovery." This procedure is only a "default" provision, however, and can be modified freely by local rule or court order. Indeed, because a time deadline specially tailored to the needs of the particular case will often "work better," this national default timeframe is likely to be replaced in most cases by case-specific scheduling orders, periods proposed by the parties, case staging regimes, or local rules. Unless local rules or scheduling orders provide otherwise, motions for summary judgment are timely even if filed before an answer or dismissal motion.

Quick Motions (Filed Before / During Discovery)

Early summary judgment motions (those filed at the time the lawsuit is commenced or otherwise before, or during, discovery) are clearly permitted, unless foreclosed by local rules or scheduling orders. Such early filings, though consistent with some prior case law, seemed at odds with the Supreme Court's admonition in 1986 that summary judgment should be granted only after the nonmoving party has had an "adequate time for discovery." *See Celotex Corp. v. Catrett,* 477 U.S. 317, 322 (1986). Recent opinions continue to incant this assurance.

Seeking a deferral of a ruling pending further discovery always remains an option for the nonmoving party. *See* Rule 56(d). In any event, in practice, pre-discovery summary judgment motions are the exception, not the norm.

Time for Responding

The Rules set no national time period for responding to summary judgment motions. Following longstanding practice, this response period is instead addressed by local rule in the applicable District or by chambers order.

RULE 56(c) Procedures

This subpart establishes several nationally-uniform summary judgment procedures: the way to factually supporting motions and oppositions; the method for objecting to improper support for motions or oppositions; the content of the summary judgment record; and the proper content for supporting or opposing affidavits and declarations. Certain other summary judgment procedures developed through case law over time.

PRACTICING LAW UNDER THIS SUBPART

Procedure #1: How to Support Factual Positions

The burdens on parties moving for, and resisting, summary judgment are discussed with Rule 56(a) above.

The summary judgment procedure begins when the moving parties "identify" each claim, defense, or part thereof on which they seek summary judgment. They thus isolate the battleground for the summary judgment contest (consequently, the nonmoving parties generally need not offer contesting evidence on issues and points not raised by the moving papers).

Once the contours of the contest are set, parties moving for, and those resisting, summary judgment must factually support their positions. In a procedure that essentially codifies the burden-shifting summary judgment approach described by the Supreme Court in *Celotex Corp. v. Catrett,* 477 U.S. 317 (1986), the parties must discharge that obligation of factual support in either of two ways:

- *Option A:* The parties may cite the court to certain parts of the summary judgment record (which may contain depositions, documents, electronically stored information, affidavits or declarations, stipulations, admissions, interrogatory answers, and other materials). In doing so, their citation must be specific and to "particular parts" of the record materials. *See Clapper v. Amnesty Int'l USA,* 568 U.S. 398, 411–12 (2013).
- *Option B:* The parties may show either (a) that the materials cited by their opponent do not establish the absence or presence of a genuine dispute or (b) that the opponent cannot produce admissible evidence to support a claimed fact. Note, however, that where the party moving for summary judgment is the one bearing the ultimate burden of proof (*e.g.,* the claimant), the road to summary judgment is steeper and *Option B* has less relevance: such a movant may not merely point to an absence of support for the non-movant's positions but must also come forward with such affirmative support on each issue material to its case that no reasonable factfinder could rule otherwise.

Because summary judgment, when entered, obviates the need for a trial, facts forming the basis for such a ruling must be (1) material, (2) undisputed, and (3) admissible in evidence. In addition to the parties' submissions, the court may, in an appropriate circumstance, also consider evidence of which it may take judicial notice, even court filings and discovery in another lawsuit, so long as those materials are made part of the summary judgment record.

In addition to the direction provided by Rule 56(c)(1), many districts have promulgated local rules imposing additional submission obligations on the parties. For example, some districts require parties moving for summary judgment to file a listing of material facts claimed to be undisputed, which the court, then, may treat as admitted unless the non-moving party responds with specific evidence to the contrary.

Procedure #2: How to Object When the Support Offered Is Improper

Materials offered to support or oppose a fact during summary judgment briefing must be capable of being offered at trial in an admissible form. (Ordinarily, this does not mean that, at the motion briefing stage, the submitted facts be presented in an admissible form then, only that an admissible form exists by which those facts may be later introduced at trial). *See generally Celotex Corp. v. Catrett,* 477 U.S. 317 (1986).

A party may object that the opponent has supported a position (either seeking or opposing summary judgment) by material that cannot be presented *at trial* in a form that would be admissible as evidence. The objections must specifically explain what particular exhibit is improper and why (for example, demonstrating that the proffered evidence would be inadmissible as hearsay). Once made, the objection shifts the burden to the opponent to defend the contested material as admissible in its current form or to explain some other anticipated form by which it may be later admitted. Failure to make an objection under this Rule does not forfeit a later objection to admissibility at time of trial, though the absence of an objection invites the court to accept the evidence's admissibility as uncontested for the limited purpose of ruling on the summary judgment motion. In considering objections under this Rule, the trial judge may rule explicitly, or implicitly so long as the record clearly supports the apparent determination. In either event, in ruling, the judge may consider objected-to materials only after determining that their facts would be admissible at trial.

Other procedures appeared in case law, though the vitality of those common law requirement is not clear today. Formerly, for example, a party objecting to summary judgment materials *(e.g.,* that an affiant lacked personal knowledge or was incompetent) was *compelled* to object in a timely fashion or risk forfeiting the objection entirely. This procedure developed, examined one court, to avoid the objecting party playing the game of "dog-in-the-manger"—fighting the summary judgment motion on its merits and only later, if unsuccessful, unveiling technical objections as a hidden "ace". *See Desrosiers v. Hartford Life & Acc. Co.,* 515 F.3d 87, 91–92 (1st Cir. 2008). Also, some courts allowed improper affidavits to be attacked on a motion to strike (a controversy now resolved with the arrival of the Rule 56(c)(2) procedure).

Procedure #3: Content of Summary Judgment Record

The summary judgment record is generally understood as comprised of those materials filed with the judge—via briefs, exhibits, and appendices—in support of or in opposition to a pending summary judgment motion. Although tasked to consider the summary judgment record as a "whole," judges are only obliged to consider those particular materials *cited* by the parties in support of or in opposition to their respective positions. Judges are not required to "scour the record" independently, beyond those specific portions cited by the parties, in search of record material pertinent to the pending summary judgment motion. Such a separate, judicial canvass of the full record, though not forbidden, is not required, and judges are admonished, if they do canvass, to do so warily, mindful of their roles as neutral arbiters, not partisan advocates. Some courts had engrafted a caselaw-based caveat, directing trial judges to perform an independent record search in First Amendment and other sensitive case types (whether this mandate survives the 2010 arrival of Rule 56(c)(3) remains unresolved).

Procedure #4: Content of Affidavits / Declarations

Affidavits or declarations may be used to support or oppose a motion for summary judgment if they meet four prerequisites: (1) sworn or otherwise subscribed as true under a risk of perjury; (2) made on personal knowledge; (3) set out facts that would be admissible in evidence; and (4) show that the maker is competent to testify on the matters expressed. A court generally will not consider affidavits and declarations failing these prerequisites, though a submission may be received in part if a portion is inadmissible even if other portions are not.

- *Sworn:* An affidavit must be sworn and a declaration must be made under penalty of perjury to qualify. *See Adickes v. S. H. Kress & Co.,* 398 U.S. 144, 158 n.17 (1970). Thus, verified complaints (ordinarily not required under the Rules) likely suffice, while a party's unsworn statements and emails and an attorney's representations at oral argument generally will not.
- *Personal Knowledge:* The affidavit or declaration must be made upon personal knowledge, though the basis for that personal knowledge need not be stated if it is clear from the context. Statements based on "information and belief"—facts the maker *believes* are true, but does not *know* are true—are not proper. *See Automatic Radio Mfg. Co. v. Hazeltine Research,* 339 U.S. 827, 831 (1950). Likewise, inferences and opinions must be premised on first-hand observations or personal experience. A statement will not be rejected merely because it is a self-serving recitation by the party or one uncorroborated by other evidence (indeed, it would make little sense for a party to submit one that was not self-serving). But the self-serving affirmations must be more than mere conclusions or unsupported inferences; in other words, such statements must aver specific facts and otherwise satisfy the requirements of this Rule.
- *Specific Admissible Facts:* The affidavit or declaration must also contain specific facts which, in turn, must be admissible in evidence at time of trial. It is not necessary that the evidence be submitted in a *form* that would be admissible at trial (indeed, most summary judgment motions are supported and opposed by affidavit evidence), so long as the offered evidence may ultimately be presented at trial in an admissible form. *See generally Celotex Corp. v. Catrett*, 477 U.S. 317, 324 (1986) (parties need not depose their own witnesses). Thus, hearsay statements, conclusory averments, unfounded self-serving declarations, ambiguous statements, speculation or conjecture, or inadmissible expert opinions are generally improper in summary judgment affidavits and declarations. A party's promise that he or she has certain unidentified "additional evidence", which will be produced at trial, is insufficient to avoid summary judgment. *See Geske & Sons, Inc. v. N.L.R.B.,* 103 F.3d 1366, 1376 (7th Cir. 1997). Nor will the hope of a devastating cross-examination of the affiant suffice, at least not without specific, credibility-undermining evidence. But the specific-facts obligation does not require an affiant to prove a negative; a summary denial that an event occurred, made by an affiant with personal knowledge, can be proper.
- *Competence:* The affidavit or declaration must demonstrate that the maker is competent to testify as to the facts contained in the document. Competence to testify may be inferred from the documents themselves. Ordinarily, statements of counsel in a memorandum of law are not competent to support or oppose that litigant's own summary judgment position.

- *"Acquired" Competence:* In appropriate circumstances, the makers of affidavits and declarations can "acquire" competence and personal knowledge they otherwise lack by research and a proper review of records.
- *Impact of Rule 26(a)(2) Expert Disclosures:* Some courts have ruled that an expert may not be "competent" (nor the expert's affidavit "admissible") within the meaning of Rule 56(c)(4) if the proffering party had a duty of pretrial disclosure regarding the expert which that party failed to discharge.

Affidavits / Declarations to Authenticate Summary Judgment Documents and Exhibits

Documents (even documents obtained through discovery) might not automatically become part of a summary judgment record merely because they are cited in a supporting memorandum. Many courts have required that every document used to support or oppose a summary judgment motion be authenticated through an affidavit or declaration, which must be made upon personal knowledge and must both identify and authenticate the offered document. Documents that failed to satisfy this authentication requirement could be disregarded by the court in resolving the pending motion.

"Vouching" Risk with Summary Judgment Affidavits

A party offering a summary judgment affidavit or declaration effectively concedes that it qualifies for consideration (that is, that the statements made are sworn, made upon personal knowledge, factually specific and admissible, and competent). The court may properly deny a party's later, pretrial *in limine* motion to strike testimony that the same party had earlier itself offered in support of a summary judgment brief.

Contradictory Sworn Evidence from Same Party

Most courts have embraced the "sham affidavit" rule, which ordinarily prevents a party from defeating summary judgment by simply denying, in an affidavit or declaration, a statement that the party had earlier admitted in a sworn statement. To create a genuine dispute for trial sufficient to defeat summary judgment, such a party must, in addition to the denial itself, offer an explanation for the inconsistency that the district court finds adequate to allow a reasonable juror to *both* accept the current denial and yet still assume either the truth of, or the party's good faith belief in, the earlier sworn statement. *See Cleveland v. Policy Mgmt. Sys. Corp.,* 526 U.S. 795, 804 (1999). Thus, courts may allow subsequent, contradicting affidavits where the original statement was demonstrably mistaken (or genuinely ambiguous and the later affidavit supplies a mere clarification or supplementation) or where the affidavit contains newly discovered evidence.

Form of Motion / Local Rule Requirements

Motions for summary judgment generally must be in writing. Local rules may prescribe the briefing requirements for summary judgment motions, and such requirements have been enforced strictly. In some judicial districts, for example, the local rules require the moving parties to compile a list of all material facts they believe are not in dispute, and require nonmoving parties to submit a counterstatement listing material facts they believe to be disputed. A failure to contest the moving party's facts, in the manner prescribed by local rule, could constitute a concession accepting those facts as true.

Miscellaneous Other Procedures

Over time, federal courts have embraced various other local procedures for summary judgment practice, some local rule-based and some purely common law. Several follow:

- *Party Admissions:* Admissions by a party—whether express (intentional acknowledgment) or through default *(e.g.,* where a party fails to deny Rule 36 requests for admission)—are considered conclusive as to the matters admitted, cannot be contradicted by affidavit or otherwise, and can support a grant of summary judgment.

- *Live Oral Testimony:* Entertaining live oral testimony in conjunction with a summary judgment motion is rare and problematic. Because the summary judgment procedure is intended to offer a speedy resolution when the material facts are undisputed, and because the court may not resolve facts that remain disputed, oral testimony in summary judgment proceedings will only be granted "sparingly" and "with great care".
- *Briefs:* The court may consider concessions in a party's brief or during oral argument in gauging whether a genuine issue of material fact exists; otherwise, however, the parties' briefs are not evidence.

Submitting New Evidence in the Reply

If the moving party introduces new evidence in a reply brief or memoranda, the trial court should not accept and consider the new evidence without first affording the non-moving party an opportunity to respond.

Hearings and Oral Argument

Although the district court may, in its discretion, convene a hearing or oral argument on the Rule 56 motion, hearings and oral argument are not obligatory. *See* Rule 78(b).

Multiple Summary Judgment Motions

The district court may permit a second motion for summary judgment, especially where there has been an intervening change in the controlling law, where new evidence has become available or the factual record has otherwise expanded through discovery, or where a clear need arises to correct a manifest injustice.

RULE 56(d) When Facts Are Unavailable to the Nonmovant

Once a motion for summary judgment is filed, the non-moving party who hopes to defeat summary judgment must show to the court that a genuine and material factual dispute exists. If the non-moving party is still conducting essential and productive discovery or for some other reason is not yet ready or able to make that showing, the party may file an affidavit or declaration explaining why a ruling on summary judgment should be postponed. The court, in its discretion, may then grant a temporary reprieve if the reasons offered are persuasive.

PRACTICING LAW UNDER THIS SUBPART

Purpose

Rule 56(d) affords diligent litigants a "safety valve" designed to abate a premature swing of the "summary judgment axe." *See Rivera-Torres v. Rey-Hernandez,* 502 F.3d 7, 10–11 (1st Cir. 2007). The procedure it establishes as a condition for granting relief helps to ensure both that the Rule's protections are being invoked in good faith and that the district judge is afforded the showing needed to assess the merits of the request for a delay.

Formal Request Requirement

A party seeking Rule 56(d) relief must make that request specifically, for example by plainly asking the trial court to deny the pending motion or to defer it until discovery is completed. But the denial/deferral request need not necessarily be made by motion; indeed, the submission of an affidavit or some other sworn declaration alone may be sufficient. However, neglecting to seek relief at all, or making passing mention in a footnote to a brief, will not trigger the protection of this Rule.

Affidavit Requirement

Some courts will not consider a Rule 56(d) request unless it is accompanied by a sworn affidavit or proper declaration. Other courts accept representations of counsel (as officers of the court) as sufficient, or, in appropriate circumstances, may excuse the failure to submit a formal affidavit where all necessary information has been otherwise supplied.

Showing-of-Reasons Requirement

Although relief under this Rule is often and liberally granted, it does not come automatically. Before the courts will postpone a summary judgment ruling pending further discovery, the courts will generally require a Rule 56(d) movant to make three showings: (1) what particular discovery the movant intends to seek; (2) how that discovery would preclude the entry of summary judgment; and (3) why this discovery had not been or could not have been obtained earlier. Some courts require a further showing of a plausible basis for believing that the sought-after facts exist. In assessing the adequacy of the nonmovant's opportunity for discovery, the court will consider the time spanning through the date of its *ruling* on the summary judgment motion, not merely the time that elapsed before the filing of that motion.

Although the affidavit or declaration need not contain evidentiary facts, the showings made must be specific—vague or baldly conclusory statements will not suffice. Nor will a vacant hope that discovery will yield helpful evidence, or the mere assertion that critical evidence could lie in the opponent's possession. Moreover, the affidavit or declaration containing these showings must be authoritative (that is, it must be taken by someone with first-hand knowledge of the statements made).

A fulsome showing of all requirements raises a strong presumption in favor of relief. Conversely, a court is unlikely to grant relief where, for example, the moving party has not been diligent in beginning and pursuing discovery. (This includes pressing timely to challenge any improper discovery delays or other mischief.) "Rule 56(d) is meant to minister to the vigilant, not to those who sleep upon perceptible rights." *See Pina v. Children's Place*, 740 F.3d 785, 794–95 (1st Cir. 2014). If the moving party fails to adequately make these showings, the court may deny the requested postponement and rule upon the pending summary judgment motion.

When Rule 56(d) Requirements Might Be Relaxed

A failure to satisfy the ordinary Rule 56(d) requirements—a formal request, an affidavit, and a showing of reasons—may sometimes be relaxed or excused if summary judgment is sought before the nonmoving parties (through no fault of their own) have had an opportunity for discovery. *Pro se* litigants, too, might be forgiven for irregularities in the formality of a postponement request.

Postponing Very Early Filed Motions for Summary Judgment

When a summary judgment motion is filed very early in the litigation, before a realistic opportunity for discovery, courts generally grant Rule 56(d) postponements freely. Courts disagree whether parties are *entitled* to an opportunity for discovery prior to a ruling on summary judgment. In any event, summary judgment is often refused on early motions. *See Anderson v. Liberty Lobby, Inc.*, 477 U.S. 242, 250 n.5 (1986). With such early filed motions, the courts recognize that the Rule 56(d) affiant or declarant may not be capable of framing a postponement request with great specificity. Nevertheless, even with very early motions, Rule 56(d) relief may still be denied where the supporting affidavit or declaration is especially vague or conclusory or where additional discovery could not make a factual or legal difference to the outcome.

Timing

A Rule 56(d) motion to postpone a summary judgment ruling must be made in a timely fashion, which at least generally means before the party files a response to the pending motion or, in any event, prior to any scheduled oral argument on the motion. A party may not wait until after the court rules on the main Rule 56 motion. In other words, a party cannot oppose the motion on its merits, with the hope of unfurling a later Rule 56(d) request if that opposition fails.

Burden on the Movant

The party moving to postpone the summary judgment ruling bears the burden of demonstrating the requisite basis for relief under Rule 56(d).

District Court's Discretion / Options in Ruling

Whether to grant or deny a Rule 56(d) postponement is committed to the district court's wide discretion. In ruling, the district court must balance the moving party's need for the requested discovery against the burden the discovery and delay will place on the opposing party. Ordinarily, such requests are construed and granted liberally; denying properly made and supported motions is disfavored, especially following a showing that much of the sought-after information lies within the control of an adversary (particularly a recalcitrant one). If, however, the moving party fails to make a properly-supported motion (typically, a formal request, affidavit, and showing of specific reasons), the court may deny the requested postponement and proceed to rule on the pending summary judgment motion.

On the basis of a party's meritorious Rule 56(d) showings, the district court may: (1) deny the motion for summary judgment; (2) grant a continuance to allow affidavits to be prepared and submitted; (3) permit discovery; or (4) make any other order as is just. Conversely, if the court denies the Rule 56(d) motion, an explicit explanation is not necessary unless the evidence sought is relevant to a summary judgment ruling. The court should rule promptly on Rule 56(d) motions (for obvious fairness and efficiency reasons), and ordinarily should resolve any pending Rule 56(d) motion before proceeding on to decide the underlying summary judgment motion itself.

Appealability

Rules 56(d) rulings implicate the typical constraints governing the appealability of interlocutory rulings. An added wrinkle is introduced if the Rule 56(d) motion was referred to a magistrate judge for disposition: in such cases, the disappointed party's ability to appeal that ruling will also depend on whether that party first properly objected to the magistrate judge's disposition at the district court level

RULE 56(e) Failing to Properly Support or Address a Fact

When a party fails to properly support or oppose a motion for summary judgment, the court has several options. It may grant summary judgment (but only when such an order is proper and never merely because a party has procedurally defaulted). It may grant the delinquent party a further opportunity to show its support or opposition. It may consider the unaddressed fact to be undisputed for the purpose of the motion. Or it may issue some other appropriate order.

PRACTICING LAW UNDER THIS SUBPART

No Summary Judgments by "Default"

Summary judgment may not be entered automatically, upon the non-moving party's failure to respond at all or to respond properly. Likewise, summary judgment may not be denied automatically simply because the moving party failed to reply properly to the opponent's response. Instead, summary judgment should be granted if, but only if, it is appropriate to do so. Consequently, although it is treacherously unwise to fail to oppose a summary judgment motion, even entirely uncontested motions must still be examined carefully by the district court to determine whether a genuine dispute of material fact remains and whether judgment is appropriate as a matter of law (which includes confirming that the proffered legal theory is sound).

District Court's Options if Support Is Improper

When confronting an improperly supported motion or opposition, the court has several choices in how to respond:

- *Another Chance:* The court may (or may not to, in its discretion) permit the delinquent party a further opportunity to file a proper motion or response, with Rule 56(c)-qualifying support. It is presumed that this choice will likely be a court's "preferred first step." *See* Rule 56(e)(1) advisory committee note to 2010 amendments.
- *"Deemed" Undisputed:* A fact improperly supported or improperly contested may be treated by the court as undisputed. The court is not compelled to do so, however, and should not do so if the summary judgment record reveals the fact at issue to be genuinely disputed. (This does not compel the court to canvass the full record, but to at least review those materials cited in the motion papers.) If the court does treat the fact as undisputed, that consequence is limited to the summary judgment motion only; if the delinquent party survives summary judgment, he or she is not barred from contesting the fact in later proceedings.
- *Grant Summary Judgment:* Because a party's delinquent response cannot, alone, compel summary judgment, summary judgment is properly granted following a delinquent response only if the standards for summary judgment are otherwise satisfied. The same is true when a court treats improperly supported or improperly contested facts as undisputed.
- *Other Appropriate Order:* The court may also enter some other appropriate order, designed to prompt a proper presentation of the record. Nudging *pro se* litigants forward, refusing to consider unsupported assertions, striking (or ordering a supplementation of) a deficient submission, striking off improper portions of affidavits, deferring a ruling pending certain further analysis, and denying summary judgment but inviting a new motion later are examples.

Motions Involving *Pro Se* Litigants

Before summary judgment may be entered against unrepresented litigants, some courts have required that the unrepresented party first be expressly informed of the consequences of failing to come forward with contradicting evidence (*e.g.*, the party must be told he or she cannot rely merely on the allegations of the pleadings, and risks dismissal in doing so). Other courts adopt this special warning duty only in the context of incarcerated unrepresented parties; as to nonprisoner unrepresented parties, those courts would require no special warning.

RULE 56(f) Judgment Independent of the Motion

In ruling on a motion for summary judgment, the court has three obvious options: grant the motion, deny the motion, or grant in part and deny in part. This subpart supplies the court with three additional options: (1) it may grant summary judgment in favor of a party who has not sought it; (2) it may grant summary judgment on different grounds than those requested by the litigants; and (3) it may grant summary judgment *sua sponte.*

PRACTICING LAW UNDER THIS SUBPART

Summary Judgment for Non-Moving Parties

In resolving a pending motion for summary judgment, the court may grant summary judgment in favor of a party who has not requested it. Before doing so, the court must give the parties notice and reasonable time to respond (with a failure to do so excused only if the omission was harmless error). This type of summary judgment grant might be invoked in at least two contexts. First, in a multi-defendant case where one co-defendant obtains summary judgment on motion, the court may enter a similar summary judgment in favor of other similarly situated but non-moving co-defendants. Second, a court that denies a moving party's request for summary judgment may enter an unrequested summary judgment *against* that party and in favor of the non-moving party. Such judgments are generally only entered if the court is convinced that the factual record is fully developed, that the non-moving party is "clearly" entitled to judgment, and that entry of the judgment would not result in procedural prejudice to the losing party. Before granting such relief, the court must find that entering summary judgment is both proper and procedurally sound (that its entry does not offend fundamental fairness).

Summary Judgment on Unrequested Grounds

In resolving a pending motion for summary judgment, the court may grant summary judgment on grounds not advocated by the parties. Before doing so, the court must give the parties notice and reasonable time to respond. Even without proper notice, such summary judgments are permitted where that notice oversight proves to be harmless or any objection to the absent notice was waived.

Summary Judgment *Sua Sponte*

The court may enter summary judgment *sua sponte. See Celotex Corp. v. Catrett,* 477 U.S. 317, 326 (1986). In doing so, the court will apply the usual summary judgment standards, resolving all ambiguities and drawing all factual inferences in the target party's favor. But the case law cautions great care in the grant of *sua sponte* summary judgments, with some case law declaring them disfavored or even unnecessary (because the court can always invite a party to file the motion). Before granting summary judgment *sua sponte,* the court must provide advance notice of its intention and allow a reasonable time for response. Litigants must appreciate that they are targets of a summary judgment inquiry, and possess that motivation when preparing the response. The court's notice must identify for the parties those material facts that the court believes might not be genuinely disputed. The court must also ensure that the opponent's opportunity to respond is full and fair. Before entering summary judgment against a defending party, the court must allow a proper opportunity for that party to assert any affirmative defenses it may have. Failure to provide these procedural safeguards is reversible error, unless that error is harmless.

Earlier, some courts had held that discovery must either be completed or clearly be of no further benefit, before *sua sponte* summary judgments could be granted. Whether that view still represents good law today is unclear.

RULE 56(g) Failing to Grant All of the Requested Relief

After considering the standards for summary judgment, the court may conclude that summary judgment is not appropriate at all or not appropriate as to every claim or defense for which it was sought. Nevertheless, the inquiry might have revealed that certain material facts are not genuinely disputed. The court may (but is not required to) declare those facts as "established" for purposes of the case.

PRACTICING LAW UNDER THIS SUBPART

Purpose of the "Declaring-as-Established" Procedure

The goal of this procedure is to allow trial courts to salvage some constructive result from their efforts in ruling upon otherwise denied (or partially denied) summary judgment motions. Where the summary judgment inquiry demonstrates that certain material facts are not genuinely disputed, the court may declare them established for trial, even though summary judgment itself is being fully or partially denied. Such declared-facts may accelerate litigations by winnowing down the number of issues that must be tried.

Which Facts May Be Declared as Established

Provided the fact is a *material* one, any fact may be declared as undisputed by the court, including liability and damages facts (and even particular items of damages).

Standard for Declaring Facts as Established

Because this procedure is in the nature of a collateral byproduct of the summary judgment inquiry itself, the standard for declaring facts to be established is the same standard used in granting summary judgment. The parties need not *agree* on which material facts are undisputed (or that any of them are). Rather, the burden of demonstrating that a material fact is genuinely undisputed lies with the moving party, employing the same burden-of-going-forward shift used with summary judgment motions generally.

District Court's Discretion

The trial judge is not required to use this procedure. Instead, the decision lies entirely within the trial judge's discretion. Thus, for example, the court may decide that the exercise of declaring facts to be established will be more burdensome than addressing those facts through other means (like trial), or may conclude that a full trial may better illuminate those facts. Nor is the court necessarily required, if it grants relief under this Rule, to set out the declared facts in a *separate* order (or even in writing).

No Interference with Opposing Party's Strategy

Parties opposing summary judgment may choose strategically to concede (or to not affirmatively dispute) a certain fact, and to do so for summary judgment motion purposes only. The court must take care to ensure that such strategic, procedural concessions are not used to declare a fact as established when, at trial, it will be contested.

Making a Motion to Declare-as-Established

Courts are divided whether parties can file an independent motion seeking to have certain facts declared as established. Some courts hold that litigants could only seek full (or partial) summary judgments and not "declared-as-established" facts, or alternatively, that any such independent motion be made only "in the wake" of such an unsuccessful full motion. Other courts rejected this reasoning, and permitted the filing of distinct motions seeking "declared-as-established" rulings.

Timing

This Rule sets no timing parameters for Rule 56(g) relief, beyond the obvious constraint that the court must first have determined that full or partial summary judgment will not be granted.

Effect of Declared-as-Established Rulings

If the court chooses to grant them, "declared-as-established" rulings are not "judgments" and do not become "final orders" until the district court enters a final judgment. Such declarations are not immutable, and they have no *res judicata* effect. Nevertheless, such declarations are still rulings on a "dispositive motion", and will be treated as "law of the case". Thus, the parties are entitled to rely on the conclusiveness of the declaration and, absent good reason for doing so, the district court will not generally revisit or alter facts adjudicated under thus subpart. If the court later decides that good reasons exist to alter a "declared-as-established" ruling, the court must so inform the parties and permit them an opportunity to present evidence concerning any of the revisited issues.

RULE 56(h) Affidavit or Declaration Submitted in Bad Faith

If the district court concludes that an affidavit or declaration submitted in the course of a summary judgment proceeding was presented in bad faith or solely for purposes of delay, the court may order the offending party to pay reasonable expenses incurred by the party's adversary (including attorney's fees) as a result of the improper affidavits or declarations.

PRACTICING LAW UNDER THIS SUBPART

Purpose

The submission of bad faith affidavits and declarations derails, in an illegitimate way, the summary judgment process by creating the false impression of a genuine, material factual dispute that must await trial. Because the impression is not real, but simulated dishonestly, the maneuver forces the parties and the court to incur the time and costs of an unnecessary trial. This subpart is intended to combat that abuse. The Rule's protections, however, are not frequently invoked (or granted).

Express Requirements: Bad Faith or Delay

Courts may compensate a party who confronts summary judgment affidavits or declarations submitted either in bad faith or solely for purposes of delay. One of those two situations must be proven (or both may, because the bad faith motivation may be delay). Accordingly, the mere fact that a summary judgment affidavit proved to be unconvincing is not sufficient to trigger this Rule, nor is the opponent's disbelief in the affidavit's veracity or its conflict with other evidence. Misinformation included negligently is also not sanctionable. Instead, the circumstances must be "egregious": a deliberate or knowing act for an improper purpose, such as perjurious or blatantly false allegations or facts, a contradiction without a bona fide explanation, or a statement made without color, with dishonesty of belief or motive, or asserted wantonly or to harass, delay, or for some other improper purpose. The district courts have wide discretion in conducting this analysis.

Express Requirements: Notice and Time to Respond

No sanctions may be imposed until the offending party is first afforded notice and a reasonable time to respond.

Implied Requirements: Prejudice and Causation

This subpart's language seems austere, yet some courts have implied additional prerequisites for relief under the Rule. Some courts require the moving party to show prejudice before sanctions are awarded, and some courts will not award sanctions unless the offending document was actually considered by judge in resolving a summary judgment motion.

District Court's Discretion

Sanctions for violating this Rule are discretionary, not mandatory, and the breadth of the court's discretion is wide.

Available Sanctions

The district court enjoys an array of choices to address bad faith affidavits or declarations in summary judgment practice. The courts may strike the offending affidavits, compel the offenders to reimburse their adversaries for reasonable expenses (including attorney's fees) incurred by the submission, hold the offenders or their counsel in contempt, and impose "other appropriate sanctions." Moreover, false swearing could also expose the offending party to criminal prosecution.

Submissions Made in Any Summary Judgment Setting

The Rule applies to all affidavits and declarations made in a summary judgment context, including those made by both the moving and non-moving parties under Rule 56(c), as well as affidavits and declarations under Rule 56(d) seeking to postpone a summary judgment ruling.

Submissions Made in Non-Summary Judgment Settings

By its terms, this Rule applies only to affidavits and declarations presented in the summary judgment context. Affidavits and declarations submitted for other purposes, or in support of relief under other Rules, are not subject to Rule 56(h).

RULE 57

DECLARATORY JUDGMENT

These rules govern the procedure for obtaining a declaratory judgment under 28 U.S.C. § 2201. Rules 38 and 39 govern a demand for a jury trial. The existence of another adequate remedy does not preclude a declaratory judgment that is otherwise appropriate. The court may order a speedy hearing of a declaratory-judgment action.

[Amended effective October 20, 1949; April 30, 2007, effective December 1, 2007.]

UNDERSTANDING RULE 57

HOW RULE 57 FITS IN

Most civil judgments award the winner some measure of coercive relief—such as money, title to land or to some other property, or an injunctive order directing that the losing party do something or refrain from doing something. Declaratory judgments are different. They simply "declare" the rights and obligations of litigants, often without any accompanying coercive relief.

The purpose of declaratory judgments is to afford litigants an early opportunity to resolve their federal disputes so as to avoid the threat of impending litigation, as well as to obtain clarity in their legal relationships and the ability to make responsible decisions about their future. *See Medtronic, Inc. v. Mirowski Family Ventures, LLC*, 571 U.S. 191, 200–01 (2014). Lacking an ultimately coercive effect capable of being enforced through contempt, they are considered a somewhat "milder" form of legal relief. *See Steffel v. Thompson*, 415 U.S. 452, 471 (1974). Nevertheless, declaratory judgments often provide a very practical litigation solution: they can settle controversies before those disagreements ripen into full-fledged violations of law or breaches of duty.

Consider, for example, a patent infringement fight. Inventor designed an invention and had it patented. Second Inventor designed a competing invention, but is worried a court might rule that the competing invention "infringes" on the original invention. If Second Inventor markets the competing invention and is found to be infringing on the original Inventor's design, serious financial consequences might follow. So, Second Inventor might file a declaratory judgment action seeking a "declaration" that the original Inventor's patent is invalid (and, thus, unenforceable). If that lawsuit is successful, Second Inventor will be able to market the competing invention confident that it is non-infringing.

Declaratory judgments also enable probable-defendants to resolve a non-litigation standstill where the very delay in filing the lawsuit is a litigant's strategy (such as, in the above example, if the original Inventor *refuses* to sue immediately for patent infringement, waiting instead until Second Inventor has sold thousands of the competing invention—thereby maximizing the potential financial penalties). *See Medtronic, Inc.*, 571 U.S. at 201. Declaratory judgments also permit defendants who are confronting multiple claims to pursue an adequate, expedient, and comparably inexpensive declaration of rights that may avoid a multiplicity of actions.

In each of these ways, and others, declaratory judgments provide an effective procedural vehicle for "clearing the air".

THE ARCHITECTURE OF RULE 57

Rule 57 spans a brief three sentences; its organization is plain.

HOW RULE 57 WORKS IN PRACTICE

Relationship Between Rule 57 and the Declaratory Judgment Act

Independent of Rule 57, Congress has enacted the federal Declaratory Judgment Act, 28 U.S.C. §§ 2201 to 02. Courts have ruled that this Act is "mirrored by" and "functionally equivalent to" Rule 57.

Constitutional Requirements for Declaratory Judgments

Subject-Matter Jurisdiction. A plaintiff seeking declaratory relief must establish an independent basis for the district court's subject-matter jurisdiction *(e.g.,* diversity of citizenship or federal question). Subject-matter jurisdiction is discussed in detail in Sections 2.10 through 2.13 of this text. Neither the Act nor Rule 57 creates an independent, substantive right to litigate in federal court or expands the court's jurisdiction; instead, these provisions merely authorize a declaratory *remedy* in cases otherwise properly brought in federal court. *See Medtronic, Inc. v. Mirowski Family Ventures, LLC*, 571 U.S. 191, 197 (2014).

- ***Diversity Cases:*** In declaratory judgment cases founded on diversity, the amount in controversy is measured by the value of the object of the litigation. *See Hunt v. Wash. State Apple Adver. Comm'n,* 432 U.S. 333, 347 (1977).
- ***Federal Question Cases:*** In declaratory judgment cases founded on the presence of a federal question, the district courts will apply the "well-pleaded complaint" rule to assess whether the plaintiff's action arises under federal law. Ergo, if the federal nature of plaintiff's lawsuit comes only from plaintiff's anticipation that the defendant will assert a federal defense, the claim likely lacks subject-matter jurisdiction. *See Public Serv. Comm'n of Utah v. Wycoff Co.,* 344 U.S. 237, 249–49 (1952). When the declaratory judgment action is filed as an "inverted" lawsuit (*i.e.*, the expected defendant is filing preemptively against the party from whom a coercive claim for relief is anticipated), it is the underlying merits claim, and not the face of the declaratory judgment complaint, that will determine whether federal question jurisdiction lies. *See Medtronic, Inc.*, 571 U.S. at 197.

Actual Controversy. The district court may only enter a declaratory judgment where the dispute between the parties is definite and concrete, affecting the parties' adverse legal interests with sufficient immediacy as to justify relief. *See MedImmune, Inc. v. Genentech, Inc.,* 549 U.S. 118, 127 (2007). No declaratory judgment may be entered where the parties' dispute is hypothetical, abstract, or academic. *See id.* In other words, the dispute must be capable of being resolved by specific relief entered through a conclusive judicial decree; the ruling sought must be more than merely an opinion advising how the law would operate on a hypothetical set of facts. *See California v. Texas,* ___ U.S. ___, 141 S. Ct. 2104, 2115–16 (2021). Whether an actual controversy exists will be measured as of the time the complaint was filed; post-filing events are not sufficient.

Standing. The actual controversy requirement also requires a plaintiff with constitutional standing—that is, a "personal stake" in the controversy, something more than a "generalized grievance" shared equally by many others. *See Warth v. Seldin*, 422 U.S. 490, 498–99 (1975). Accordingly, a plaintiff must allege a personal injury-in-fact, "fairly traceable" to unlawful conduct by the defendant, and likely to be redressed by the relief that plaintiff is seeking. *See Steel Co. v. Citizens for a Better Env't*, 523 U.S. 83, 102–04 (1998); *Lujan v. Defs. of Wildlife*, 504 U.S. 555, 560–61 (1992). Declaratory relief does not operate "on legal rules in the abstract," but instead only with respect to specific parties. *See California v. Texas*, ___ U.S. ___, 141 S. Ct. 2104, 2115 (2021). For this reason, a party lacking a qualifying standing injury cannot seek a declaratory judgment simply to have a court declare a law unconstitutional. *See id.* at 2113–16. Note: apart from constitutional standing is the concept of "statutory" standing, which inquires whether a particular statute, invoked by the plaintiff, allows the cause of action and relief the lawsuit seeks. *See Bank of Am. Corp. v. City of Miami*, 581 U.S. ___, 137 S. Ct. 1296, 1302–03 (2017).

Ripeness / Mootness. The actual controversy requirement obligates the court to determine that the case is "ripe" for adjudication. This "ripeness" must remain throughout the lawsuit. Thus, the district court must decide at the time it is about to enter judgment whether an actual controversy still exists between the parties. Thus, even if an actual controversy existed at the time the lawsuit was filed, the court will not enter a declaratory judgment if later events ended the controversy and the dispute has become moot. *See Preiser v. Newkirk*, 422 U.S. 395, 401 (1975).

♦ **NOTE:** This mootness requirement may be excused where the plaintiff is able to show a substantial likelihood that the same controversy will recur in the future and would, then, still be evading review under normal mootness principles. *See Super Tire Eng'g Co. v. McCorkle*, 416 U.S. 115, 125–26 (1974).

The Prudential (Non-Constitutional) Concerns: Exercise of Discretion

Declaratory relief is never automatic or obligatory. *See Wilton v. Seven Falls Co.*, 515 U.S. 277, 288 (1995). The courts have no "unflagging duty" to hear declaratory judgment cases. Whether to grant or deny declaratory relief is vested in the sound discretion of the district court. *See id.* at 281. Likewise, the court has discretion in fashioning the relief and its extent. This discretion, though wide, is not boundless; the district court may not refuse on "whim or personal disinclination" to hear a declaratory judgment action, but must instead base its refusal on good reason (such as when the declaration would serve no useful purpose). *See Public Affairs Assocs., Inc. v. Rickover*, 369 U.S. 111, 112 (1962). If the court decides not to entertain the declaratory proceeding, it may either stay or dismiss the federal action, and may enter such an order before trial or after all arguments come to a close. *See Wilton v. Seven Falls Co.*, 515 U.S. 277, 287 (1995).

Factors for Court's Consideration

To decide whether to entertain a declaratory judgment action, courts generally assess three concerns: efficiency, fairness, and federalism. To do so, courts may weigh various factors, including: (1) the likelihood that a federal declaration will resolve the uncertainty of obligation which gave rise to the controversy; (2) the parties' convenience; (3) the public interest in settling the uncertainty; (4) the availability and relative convenience of other remedies; (5) the restraint favored when the same issues are pending in a State court; (6) avoidance of duplicative litigation; (7) preventing the declaratory action's use as a method of procedural fencing or a race for *res judicata;* and (8) (in insurance contexts) the inherent conflict of interest between an insurer's duty to defend and its attempt to characterize the action as falling within the scope of a policy exclusion. (The fact that a declaratory judgment action was commenced before a later-filed coercive lawsuit is unlikely to carry dispositive weight.) This list of factors in not exhaustive.

- *Effect of Parallel Pending State Lawsuits:* When another lawsuit is pending in State court raising the same issues and involving the same parties, the federal court may choose to abstain from exercising jurisdiction to hear a related federal declaratory judgment action, and is likely to do so unless, after rigorous examination, it is assured that other factors justify proceeding. *See Wilton v. Seven Falls Co.,* 515 U.S. 277, 282 (1995). (Such abstention will, however, be rare if the federal action seeks both declaratory and nondeclaratory relief.) Conversely, when no such parallel lawsuits are pending elsewhere, the federal court retains the discretion to decline to hear the federal case, though the absence of parallel State proceedings militates heavily in favor of exercising federal jurisdiction.

Statement of Circumstances Supporting Declaratory Jurisdiction

If a party contests the prudence of the district court's exercise of discretion to hear a declaratory judgment claim, the court must articulate the factual circumstances supporting the award of declaratory relief, unless the underlying claims are viable independently, apart from the declaratory relief.

Realignment of the Parties

In determining whether to grant a declaratory judgment, the courts may realign the parties in order to reflect the nature of the actual, underlying controversy. In making this determination, the courts may consider the underlying purposes of declaratory relief, the parties' respective burdens of proof, and the best, clearest method for presenting evidence to the jury. Where both sides will carry proof burdens at trial, realignment may be refused.

Burden of Proof

A party seeking a declaratory judgment bears the burden of proving the existence of an actual case or controversy. *See Cardinal Chemical Co. v. Morton Int'l Inc.,* 508 U.S. 83, 94 (1993). But assigning the ultimate merits burden of persuasion in declaratory judgment cases can prove to be nuanced. The burden of proof is considered a substantive aspect of the underlying claim. *See Medtronic, Inc. v. Mirowski Fam. Ventures, LLC,* 571 U.S. 191, 199 (2014). Consequently, in an action seeking a declaration that the named defendant lacks some sort of right as to which that defendant would bear the burden of proof were it to file a coercive lawsuit, that defendant may well bear the burden of proof in a declaratory judgment suit as well. *See id.* at 193–203.

Nature of Declaratory Relief

A declaratory judgment pronounces rights and relations, but by itself neither provides for nor orders any enforcement. But the Declaratory Judgment Act allows the award of other, further (non-declaratory) remedies after reasonable notice and hearing. *See* 28 U.S.C.A. § 2202. Indeed, this is typical; although the parties may hope that the sought-after declaration will prompt a negotiated resolution to their dispute, declaratory relief is often a prelude to a request for further remedies. Where appropriate, courts possess broad power to grant damage awards and injunctive relief in declaratory judgment actions. This includes attorney's fees, if those would be available in similar non-declaratory judgment settings.

The Existence of Other Possible Remedies

Declaratory relief is usually not foreclosed merely by showing that an adequate remedy other than a declaratory judgment exists. A declaratory judgment may be entered whether or not further relief is sought or could have been awarded. *See Powell v. McCormack,* 395 U.S. 486, 498–99 (1969). However, the existence of another, adequate remedy may convince the district court to exercise its discretion to deny declaratory relief in favor of some better or more effective remedy. *See National Private Truck Council, Inc. v. Oklahoma Tax Com'n,* 515 U.S. 582, 589 (1995). Moreover, where declaratory relief will not terminate the controversy, but further remedies will be sought in a different or subsequent proceeding, the declaratory judgment can be refused.

Exception: Where a special statutory proceeding has been provided to adjudicate a special type of case, declaratory relief may not be awarded. *See Katzenbach v. McClung,* 379 U.S. 294, 296 (1964).

Partial Remedy

If it exercises its discretion to hear a declaratory judgment case, the trial court is not obligated to rule on every issue presented. The court may, instead, properly choose to decide some of the issues raised and decline to decide others.

Declaratory vs. Injunctive Remedies

As between a declaratory or injunctive remedy, the district court enjoys discretion. Although a declaratory judgment cannot be enforced in contempt, it is "a real judgment, not just a bit of friendly advice"; it fixes the litigants' legal rights. *See Badger Catholic, Inc. v. Walsh,* 620 F.3d 775, 782 (7th Cir. 2010). It is also likely to be a more simple and less elaborate order than an injunction.

Any Party May Seek a Declaratory Judgment

Any party who has an interest in an actual controversy has standing to seek a declaratory judgment.

Rules of Procedure

All federal rules of procedure applicable generally to civil lawsuits apply in a declaratory judgment action. Thus, for example, no declaratory request is properly before the court until it is pleaded in a complaint for declaratory judgment, and the *Twombly* plausibility standard governs the adequacy of such a pleading. (*Twombly* is discussed with Rule 8(a).)

Expedited Treatment

The district court may order a speedy hearing in declaratory judgment cases, and may move such cases to the top of the court's calendar.

Timing

Because declaratory judgments supply only a remedy, not a claim, the applicable statute of limitations will typically be the same that governs the underlying claim.

Jury Trial

The right to a jury trial is preserved in declaratory judgment actions. If the issues would have been triable by a jury had something other than declaratory relief been sought, a right to a jury trial exists. *See Beacon Theatres, Inc. v. Westover,* 359 U.S. 500, 504 (1959). In such a case, refusing a party's proper jury trial demand may violate the Seventh Amendment.

Common Uses

Classically, declaratory judgments have proved useful in intellectual property cases, to resolve questions of validity and infringement, as the example that begins this discussion of Rule 57 illustrates. Declaratory judgments are also especially useful in insurance cases, to resolve policy coverage and interpretation disputes. *See Aetna Life Ins. Co. v. Haworth,* 300 U.S. 227, 242 (1937). But declaratory judgments have a far broader range than just these. For example, they may be useful in deciding the constitutionality of government laws, immunity questions, land title and property rights, competition and trade claims, scope of entitlements to beneficiaries, and prisoner rights.

Cautious Uses

The district courts frequently will refrain from invoking declaratory relief in cases involving important public issues, where the concreteness of a monetary or injunctive dispute is more advisable. *See Public Affairs Assocs., Inc. v. Rickover,* 369 U.S. 111, 112

(1962). Courts will also often deny declaratory relief that would act to interfere with a State criminal prosecution. *See Samuels v. Mackell,* 401 U.S. 66, 71–72 (1971).

Improper Uses

Declaratory relief is generally not available to merely adjudicate past conduct or to proclaim that one litigant is liable to another. It is also not available where a special statutory proceeding has been provided to adjudicate a special type of case.

Effect of a Declaratory Judgment

A declaratory judgment inures directly to the benefit of the plaintiff who received it, though the relief may, as a practical matter, have far broader ramifications. Declaratory judgments enjoy an exception to claim preclusion principles, permitting a victorious plaintiff to file a second lawsuit to pursue injunctive relief or damages. Issue preclusion principles apply normally; parties who have had their rights or obligations declared are ordinarily bound by that resolution in later proceedings.

Appealability

Whether a declaratory judgment order is immediately appealable depends upon the nature of the court's ruling. Once the court disposes of all the issues presented in the declaratory judgment action (either by ruling or by declining to rule), the declaratory judgment becomes final and appealable. Conversely, if the court enters an order resolving certain of the issues presented, but expressly leaves open other issues in the case, the order is interlocutory and, therefore, not immediately appealable.

RULE 58

ENTERING JUDGMENT

(a) Separate Document. Every judgment and amended judgment must be set out in a separate document, but a separate document is not required for an order disposing of a motion:

(1) for judgment under Rule 50(b);

(2) to amend or make additional findings under Rule 52(b);

(3) for attorney's fees under Rule 54;

(4) for a new trial, or to alter or amend the judgment, under Rule 59; or

(5) for relief under Rule 60.

(b) Entering Judgment.

(1) *Without the Court's Direction.* Subject to Rule 54(b) and unless the court orders otherwise, the clerk must, without awaiting the court's direction, promptly prepare, sign, and enter the judgment when:

(A) the jury returns a general verdict;

(B) the court awards only costs or a sum certain; or

(C) the court denies all relief.

(2) *Court's Approval Required.* Subject to Rule 54(b), the court must promptly approve the form of the judgment, which the clerk must promptly enter, when:

(A) the jury returns a special verdict or a general verdict with answers to written questions; or

(B) the court grants other relief not described in this subdivision (b).

(c) Time of Entry. For purposes of these rules, judgment is entered at the following times:

(1) if a separate document is not required, when the judgment is entered in the civil docket under Rule 79(a); or

(2) if a separate document is required, when the judgment is entered in the civil docket under Rule 79(a) and the earlier of these events occurs:

(A) it is set out in a separate document; or

(B) 150 days have run from the entry in the civil docket.

(d) Request for Entry. A party may request that judgment be set out in a separate document as required by Rule 58(a).

(e) Cost or Fee Awards. Ordinarily, the entry of judgment may not be delayed, nor the time for appeal extended, in order to tax costs or award fees. But if a timely motion for attorney's fees is made under Rule 54(d)(2), the court may act before a notice of appeal has been filed and become effective to order that the motion have the same effect under Federal Rule of Appellate Procedure 4(a)(4) as a timely motion under Rule 59.

[Amended December 27, 1946, effective March 19, 1948; January 21, 1963, effective July 1, 1963; April 22, 1993, effective December 1, 1993; April 29, 2002, effective December 1, 2002; April 30, 2007, effective December 1, 2007.]

UNDERSTANDING RULE 58

HOW RULE 58 FITS IN

A "judgment" is a substantive merits order by the trial judge from which an appeal may be taken. *See "How Rule 54 Fits In", supra.* It is usually the final order entered in a federal lawsuit. The effective date of judgments is crucial in civil litigation: that date triggers the time for filing timely post-trial motions, for taking a timely appeal, and for enforcing the court's decision. Accordingly, knowing when and how a judgment takes effect is essential. Rule 58 sets out the timing of and procedure for making judgments effective: that process is accomplished by "entering" (or, making a formal note of) the judgment on the official court record of the case.

THE ARCHITECTURE OF RULE 58

Rule 58 contains five subparts, each of which addresses one component of the process of judgment-entry. Subpart (a) sets out a threshold requirement for judgments—they must appear all by themselves in a separate document. Subparts (b) and (c) prescribe who may "enter" the judgment on the official court record (either the court clerk or the judge) and the timing of that "entry." Subpart (d) allows litigants to request an entry from the judge. Subpart (e) addresses the effect on the judgment if the question of court costs and attorney's fees (either or both of which may be added to the judgment) has yet to be decided by the court.

HOW RULE 58 WORKS IN PRACTICE

These five subparts of Rule 58 are discussed, in order, below.

RULE 58(a) | Separate Document

Because of the importance of judgments, the courts and the litigants need to know unambiguously that an order a judge has filed qualifies as a "judgment." To better do so, federal district judges are required under this subpart to set out judgments in a separate document—separate from and independent of any written opinion or other judicial notation. In this way, the likelihood of overlooking a judgment or of misunderstanding its effect is reduced.

PRACTICING LAW UNDER THIS SUBPART

The "Separate Document" Rule

Federal judgments must be set forth in writing in a separate document. This requirement was intended to create a bright-line for litigants and the courts, to help ensure that everyone is alerted to the entry of judgment and to the starting of the clock for filing post-verdict motions or for taking an appeal. *See Bankers Trust Co. v. Mallis,* 435 U.S. 381, 384 (1978). The Rule is designed to fix the long-haunting question of "when is a judgment a judgment." The Rule achieves this goal by insisting on a clear boundary between a judgment and a judge's opinion or memorandum explaining the reasons for that judgment.

The Rule mandates an extraordinarily austere approach to drafting judgments: the body of a proper judgment should state the relief granted and little else. This austerity should make clear for the parties that the time for filing post-trial motions or taking an appeal has begun. The separate document requirement applies to many categories of judgments, including summary judgments, declaratory judgments, preliminary injunctions, forfeiture orders, and orders on habeas motions.

When a "Separate Document" Is *Not* Required

A separate document is not required for an order "disposing" of a Rule 50(b) renewed motion for judgment after trial, a Rule 52(b) motion to amend or make additional findings of fact, a Rule 54(d) motion for attorney's fees, a Rule 59 motion for new trial or to alter or amend a judgment, or a Rule 60 motion for relief from a judgment or order. These exceptions create risks for the unwary—because a separate document is not required for these dispositions, the time for taking an appeal *will begin to run immediately*.

- *Amended Judgments:* It is unclear whether *amended* judgments require a "separate document" (the Rule's use of the phrase "disposing of" suggests possibly not). Some courts navigate this uncertainty by requiring a separate document when an amended judgment is granted, but not when one is denied.

What Qualifies as a "Separate Document"?

Except for the five exempted instances set out in the Rule's text, every judgment (as well as partial dispositions under Rule 54(b)) must be labeled "judgment" and must be set forth on a separate document. Thus, a judgment that is encumbered with extraneous text, such as an "extensive" recitation of legal reasoning, analysis, facts, or procedural history, fails the separateness requirement. (A very cursory explanation, however, devoid of legal analysis, may survive this examination.) Ergo, neither a judicial memorandum or opinion, nor marginal entry orders, nor minute orders, nor automated court e-mails of docketing text nor settlement decrees satisfy this requirement; indeed, even an otherwise qualifying judgment order that includes footnotes explaining its reasoning or that is mistakenly stapled to the end of a memorandum opinion will fail this separateness requirement. Thus, to qualify as a "separate document," the judgment must generally (1) be a self-contained, separate document, (2) state the relief granted, and (3) omit the reasoning used by the district court to reach that disposition.

- *Where Does the Court's Reasoning Go?:* Often times, a judgment can follow from a trial court's ruling on a dispositive motion (*e.g.*, a motion to dismiss or a motion for summary judgment). The trial court will typically prepare a written opinion explaining its decision that results in the judgment; that opinion may accompany—but must be a separate document from—the judgment itself.
- *Always Two Documents?:* The majority view holds that the separate document requirement can, in appropriate circumstances, be met even if there is only one document (such as when the court's reasoning and analysis was conveyed orally, during oral argument or a hearing).
- *Multi-Tasking Documents:* A judgment that recites, in a single document, the disposition of multiple motions may satisfy the Rule.
- *Electronic Docket Notations:* Such entries *can* qualify as a separate document, but only if they are more than merely ministerial, clerical notations and instead are self-contained, list the relief awarded, and have the signature (pen or electronic) of the judge.
- *Actual or Implied Clarity:* The fact that the litigants knew, or should have known, that the contested order was intended to serve as a final judgment will not excuse a failure to meet the separateness requirement. Debating over a "known-or-should-have-known" standard is precisely what Rule 58 is designed to avoid.
- *Using the "Order" Label:* The Circuits are divided as to whether a document marked "Order" can ever qualify under this Rule as a judgment, even if the "separate document" requirements are otherwise met.
- *Using the "Judgment" Label:* Although Rule 58 ordinarily requires that a qualifying judgment be labeled "Judgment", the inverse is not necessarily true. If a court's order does not qualify as a judgment under Rule 58, labeling it that way will not make it one. *See Riley v. Kennedy,* 553 U.S. 406, 419 (2008).
- *Using "Order and Judgment" Label:* At least one court has found that the use of this label did not defeat the separate document requirement.
- *Curing the Defect:* An intended judgment that violates the separate document requirement can be remedied by the court's entry of an amended judgment that avoids the defect.

Waiving the "Separate Document" Requirement

The "separate document" requirement is designed to create protection, not traps. *See Bankers Trust Co. v. Mallis,* 435 U.S. 381, 386 (1978) (per curiam). Accordingly, parties are free to wait to appeal until either the judgment is placed in a "separate document" (unless, of course, that judgment is exempt from the requirement) or the capped outside time period set by Rule 58(c) expires. But parties can also waive their entitlement to a "separate document" and file an early appeal from a judgment that is not set out in a proper "separate document." Choosing not to wait will not affect the validity of the appeal.

- *Appellee Cannot Stop Appeal:* An appellee cannot oppose an appellant's early appeal in order to insist that the appellant first return to the district court to demand compliance with the ministerial act of preparing a separate document judgment. If the appellant elects to waive the right to a separate document and immediately appeal, the appellee cannot stop it.

- *Waiver via Filing Post-Trial Motions:* Whether a party can *impliedly* waive a judgment's violation of the separate document requirement by the act of filing post-trial motions to the improper judgment is unclear.
- *Practitioners' Safe Harbor:* Because these early appeals are permitted, the effect grants the appellant a safe harbor. Consequently, when in doubt whether a separate document has been filed or not, the practitioner may always file an appeal.

RULE 58(b) Entering Judgment

Judgments may be entered by the court clerk following a jury's general verdict, for sums-certain or costs, or that deny relief. All other judgments must be entered by the judge.

PRACTICING LAW UNDER THIS SUBPART

Manner of Entering the Judgment

Unless it is a "partial" final judgment under Rule 54(b), all federal judgments are entered either by the clerk or by the court:

- *By the Clerk:* Unless the court otherwise orders, the clerk of court must, without awaiting any further direction from the court, promptly prepare, sign, and enter judgment when (i) the jury returns a general verdict, (ii) the court awards only costs or a sum certain, or (iii) the court denies all relief.
- *By the Court:* The court must review and promptly approve the form of judgment (which the clerk then must promptly enter) when (i) the jury returns a special verdict or a general verdict accompanied by interrogatories or (ii) the court grants other relief not described above. The district court's obligation to personally "approve" the judgment may be critical. The text of judgments are often drafted by clerks and, while often satisfactory in form, they can prove troublesome when the case's disposition is complicated and a non-attorney clerk is left "at sea" without judicial guidance.

Contents of Judgment

The judgment document must clearly state which parties are entitled to what relief.

Transferring Judgments to Another Judicial District

A judgment for money or property entered by one federal district court may be transferred to, and executed in, another district court. Such transfers are accomplished by filing a certified copy of the judgment in the new district court *after* the judgment has become final after appeal, by the expiration of time for appeal, or when, still pending appeal, the court so orders for good cause. The transferred judgment will have the same effect as any other judgment entered in the new district.

RULE 58(c) Time of Entry

Judgments are deemed to be entered the moment they are placed on the civil docket—unless a separate document is required. If a separate document is required, judgments are deemed entered the moment they are placed on the civil docket *if* the separate document requirement is met; otherwise, such judgments are deemed entered 150 days after they were recorded on the civil docket. Clarity and finality are the reasons for this 150-day window. If the judgment *should* have been set out in a separate document, but never was, the time for post-trial motions and appeals might never start running. Ergo, without the 150-day window, an appeal might be possible months, even years after the defective judgment was filed. The 150-day window places an outside cap on this uncertainty. If a separate document was required, the judge may correct a defective judgment but, if the judge fails to do so, the post-trial motion and appeals clock will at least begin to run no later than 150 days after docketing.

PRACTICING LAW UNDER THIS SUBPART

Significance of Time of "Entry of Judgment"

The time for a disappointed civil litigant to take an appeal runs from the time of "entry" of the appealed-from judgment. *See* Fed. R. App. P. 4(a)(1)(A). Because that time period is jurisdictional, cannot often be extended, and is appeal-dooming if not honored, knowing the date of a judgment's "entry" is critical in federal practice.

Triggering "Entry of Judgment" Date

The date the clerk enters the judgment "in the civil docket" is the trigger for calculating time under Rule 58(c). The clerk is obligated by Rule 79(a) to make this entry. This ministerial, administrative duty is distinct from the Rule 58(b)(2) duty of the court to approve a separate document judgment before it is deemed a true Rule 58 judgment.

Though ministerial, this docket "entering" act is still vulnerable to a surprising amount of confusion. *First,* there may be a flurry of docketing dates associated with any given order *(e.g.,* date listed on the document, date of signing, date of filing, date of entry); only the date of entry controls for Rule 58(c) purposes. *Second,* the clerk may, properly, record a "judgment" in the civil docket, even though the document so recorded fails the separate document requirement; in such cases, the time for appeal will usually not begin ticking until the 150-day cap expires. *Third,* the syntax used by the clerk in making the entry may be ambiguous, such as a local clerk's office practice to omit the term "ENTERED" when the entry date is the same as the filed date; in those instances, the date of actual entry—albeit identified with uncertainty—controls. *Fourth,* the clerk may defectively enter the judgment; in which case, the time for appeal again tolls until the 150-day cap expires. *Fifth*, the clerk may neglect to give notice of entry, or the notice given may fail to reach the litigants; because counsel are under an affirmative duty to monitor the official dockets, failure to discover such judgment entries may have calamitous consequences on post-trial motions and appeals.

Computing "Entry of Judgment" Date

A judgment must always be entered on the docket. To avoid the possibility that months or years could pass before the appeals clock might begin to run), this subpart imposes an outside time limit for triggering the appeal period:

- *When Separate Document Required:* If a separate document is required, the judgment is deemed to be entered on the date when:

  (1) it is actually entered in the civil docket, if it meet the separate document requirement *or*

  (2) 150 days elapses after entry in the civil docket, if it does not meet the separate document requirement.

  Thus, the time for a civil appeal is either 30 days (the normal appeal period, assuming a Rule 58-qualifying judgment has been entered) or 180 days (the normal appeal period plus 150 days, if no Rule 58-qualifying judgment was entered). Of course, at any point during the first 150 days, if the judge were to discover that he or she had entered a deficient order, and then correct it with a proper Rule 58-qualifying judgment, presumably a normal 30-day appeal period would begin to run from that entry.

- *When Separate Document Not Required:* If a separate document is not required (*i.e.,* involving a Rule 50(b), 52(b), 54(d), 59, or 60 motion), the judgment is deemed to be entered when it is entered in the civil docket.

Inapplicability of the 150-Day Cap

The 150-day outside time limit is only implicated when the order in question is a final one; absent a Rule 54(b) determination, an order disposing of less than all claims or less than all parties will not become a judgment merely because 150 days has passed since its entry.

Disregarding the 150-Day Cap

The 150-day outside time limit should be disregarded where it serves no purpose to apply it. Thus, for example, assessing the propriety of an appeal from a collateral order should *not* be complicated by the separate document requirement. To the contrary, appeal periods for collateral orders should start to run when the collateral order is entered, and should not await either the creation of a separate document or the passing of 150 days.

RULE 58(d) Request for Entry

Because a proper entry of judgment has serious procedural consequences (for, among other things, the time for appealing), a party may request the court to prepare and enter one.

PRACTICING LAW UNDER THIS SUBPART

Party's Request to Prompt a "Separate Document"

A party may request the district court to enter a "separate document" judgment. Allowing such requests helps protect a party's need to ensure that timing periods are promptly triggered for motions, appeals, and enforcement procedures. Thus, a party may make such a request in order to cure a "separate document" deficiency with an existing judgment, to seek a Rule 54(b) determination that would permit an immediate partial judgment appeal, or to quicken the pace for enforcement. Such a request can also be made by a party who suffers a dismissal *without prejudice,* and who wishes to appeal that dismissal rather than attempt to re-plead.

RULE 58(e) Cost or Fee Awards

To facilitate a single, consolidated appeal from both a lawsuit's merits ruling and a ruling on an award of attorney's fees, the district court may allow a pending attorney's fees motion to postpone the time for the case's finality until the court resolves that fees motion.

PRACTICING LAW UNDER THIS SUBPART

Purpose

Usually, the entry of final judgment is not postponed (nor is the time for taking an appeal extended) while the district court considers requests to tax costs or award attorney's fees. Concerns about resulting piecemeal litigation are considered outweighed by the need to promptly, clearly determine whether a merits appeal will be taken. *See Ray Haluch Gravel Co. v. Central Pension Fund of Int'l Union of Operating Eng'rs & Participating Employers*, 571 U.S. 177, 186–87 (2014). A Rule 58(e) motion offers an exception to this practice, which enhances judicial efficiency by allowing the appeals court to review a fees award appeal at the same time as it reviews the merits.

Effect of a Rule 58(e) Order

In order to allow a consolidated appeal of both its merits judgment and its ruling on attorney's fees, the district court may, in its discretion, enter an order under this subpart that treats a pending motion for an award of attorney's fees as the equivalent of a Rule 59 motion. If the court enters such an order, the time for appealing will not begin to run until the court decides the pending fees motion. *See id.* The court must, however, actually enter the Rule 58(e) order; the mere fact that a litigant has asked the court to enter such an order is not sufficient to toll. Nor does tolling occur merely by the filing of some other (non-Rule 58) post-trial motion seeking an award of attorney's fees. If the district court elects not to grant the order, it retains jurisdiction over the fee motion even while the merits appeal is pending, which in turn deprives the appeals court of jurisdiction over that issue pending the district court's ruling. A litigant who is then dissatisfied with the district court's fees decision must take a new appeal from that ruling.

Prerequisites for a Rule 58(e) Order

The court may enter a Rule 58(e) order only if: (1) the motion for fees is pending and has been timely made (*i.e.,* within 14 days after entry of judgment, unless provided otherwise by statute or court order), (2) no effective notice of appeal has yet been made, and (3) a timely notice of appeal is still possible (*i.e.,* the time for appealing has not already expired). *See Ray Haluch Gravel Co. v. Central Pension Fund of Int'l Union of Operating Eng'rs & Participating Employers*, 571 U.S. 177, 187 (2014).

Time for Entering a Rule 58(e) Order

While it is clear that the trial court may enter a Rule 58(e) order for a *pending* fees motion, courts are divided on whether such an order may be properly entered in anticipation of a *future* fees motion.

When the Order Is *Not* Proper

The practical effect of a Rule 58(e) motion is to delay the arrival of finality and, with it, the time for taking an appeal from the court's order. The reason why district courts are authorized to grant this postponement is efficiency: to permit one, consolidated appeal from both the trial court's judgment on the merits and its ruling on attorney's fees. If that goal cannot be attained, no Rule 58(e) postponement order is proper. Thus, if an appeal has already been taken from the merits ruling, if the attorney's fees motion has already been ruled upon, or if the merits judgment has already become unappealable (*e.g.,* if the appeal time has already expired), the district court has no reason or authority to issue such a postponement order. Nor may a Rule 58(e) order be used with interim fee awards (fees awarded before the court decides the merits of the case).

Order Applies Only to Fees, Not Costs

A postponement of finality under Rule 58(e) is, by its terms, only applicable to attorney's fee awards; finality cannot be suspended while costs are being taxed.

When Fees Are an Element of the Claim Itself

This subpart applies only to extend time for resolving Rule 54(d)(2) motions. In turn, Rule 54(d)(2) sets the fee-seeking motion procedure "*unless* the substantive law requires those fees to be proved at trial as an element of damages." Thus, a Rule 58(e) time extension seems unavailable for fee requests that, under applicable substantive law, cannot be pursued through Rule 54(d)(2). But this distinction can prove to be nuanced and uncertain; in such cases, practitioners are wise to appeal the merits ruling at once.

RULE 59

NEW TRIAL; ALTERING OR AMENDING A JUDGMENT

(a) In General.

(1) *Grounds for New Trial.* The court may, on motion, grant a new trial on all or some of the issues—and to any party—as follows:

(A) after a jury trial, for any reason for which a new trial has heretofore been granted in an action at law in federal court; or

(B) after a nonjury trial, for any reason for which a rehearing has heretofore been granted in a suit in equity in federal court.

(2) *Further Action After a Nonjury Trial.* After a nonjury trial, the court may, on motion for a new trial, open the judgment if one has been entered, take additional testimony, amend findings of fact and conclusions of law or make new ones, and direct the entry of a new judgment.

(b) Time to File a Motion for a New Trial. A motion for a new trial must be filed no later than 28 days after the entry of judgment.

(c) Time to Serve Affidavits. When a motion for a new trial is based on affidavits, they must be filed with the motion. The opposing party has 14 days after being served to file opposing affidavits. The court may permit reply affidavits.

(d) New Trial on the Court's Initiative or for Reasons Not in the Motion. No later than 28 days after the entry of judgment, the court, on its own, may order a new trial for any reason that would justify granting one on a party's motion. After giving the parties notice and an opportunity to be heard, the court may grant a timely motion for a new trial for a reason not stated in the motion. In either event, the court must specify the reasons in its order.

(e) Motion to Alter or Amend a Judgment. A motion to alter or amend a judgment must be filed no later than 28 days after the entry of the judgment.

[Amended effective March 19, 1948; July 1, 1966; April 27, 1995, effective December 1, 1995; April 30, 2007, effective December 1, 2007; March 26, 2009, effective December 1, 2009.]

UNDERSTANDING RULE 59

HOW RULE 59 FITS IN

Rule 59 is one of the post-trial motions authorized under the federal rules. In that respect, it joins Rule 50 (which permits judgments as a matter of law, or "JMOL"s, in jury trials), Rule 52 (which permits revisions to findings and judgments in bench trials), and Rule 60 (which permits relief from judgments or orders) in giving disappointed litigants a path to overturn a trial court ruling. Each of those motions is directed to the *trial court* that presided over the lawsuit. These are not "appeals." (Appeals are requests to a different tribunal, higher in the judicial hierarchy, to review what occurred in the trial court). Instead, these are *post-trial motions* which invite the *trial judge* to review and adjust the trial's outcome.

Rule 59 permits the grant of a new trial or, in the case of a bench trial, permits the trial judge to reopen the case, receive new testimony, and amend findings and conclusions. Rule 59 also permits motions for "reconsideration"—invitations to alter or amend a judgment the court has entered. Together, these provisions constitute a formidable armory of options to allow trial judges to reform the result of a civil trial when a correction is found to be needed.

In practice, parties often file two post-trial motions simultaneously: one seeking a JMOL or, if the court is not persuaded to grant that, a companion motion seeking a new trial. That practice highlights an important distinction between the two motions. A JMOL motion usually seeks an outright victory; it requests that the trial court declare the moving party the winner in the dispute. A new trial motion, in contrast, usually seeks only a "do-over"; it requests that the result in the trial be thrown out and a new trial be convened to hear the case anew. By combining the two motions as alternative requests for relief in the same filing, practitioners are able to press boldly for a complete victory (JMOL) but, hedging their bets if the judge is unconvinced, also propose the alternative, fall-back option of seeking the opportunity to try the case over again.

THE ARCHITECTURE OF RULE 59

Rule 59 has five subparts. Subpart (a) sets out the grounds for granting a new trial. It does this oddly; the subpart does not actually list the acceptable grounds for granting a new trial, but instead adopts as the standard those grounds for which new trials have "heretofore been granted" in federal court. Subpart (b) prescribes the time for filing a new trial motion. Subpart (c) establishes the time for filing affidavits in support of and in opposition to new trial motions. Subpart (d) permits the court to grant new trials *sua sponte* or for reasons not sought in the moving party's papers. Subpart (e) permits motions to alter or amend judgments.

HOW RULE 59 WORKS IN PRACTICE

These five subparts of Rule 59 are discussed, in order, below.

RULE 59(a) In General

The grounds for allowing a new trial are, oddly, not listed in the Rule. Instead, in both jury and bench trials, the court may grant a new trial for any reason for which new trials (jury trials) or rehearings (bench trials) were formerly granted in federal court. Case law confirms that those grounds include: where the verdict is against the weight of the evidence or is either excessive or inadequate; where probative evidence is newly discovered; or where conduct by the court, counsel, or the jury improperly influenced the deliberative process.

PRACTICING LAW UNDER THIS SUBPART

Procedure

Motions for new trial are usually made in writing and must state with particularity the grounds for relief.

Discretion of District Court

Whether the circumstances justify the granting of a new trial is a decision left to the sound discretion of the trial judge, and this discretion is far greater than the court's authority to grant a motion for judgment as a matter of law. *See Gasperini v. Center for Humanities, Inc.*, 518 U.S. 415, 433 (1996). So broad is this discretion in certain contexts, that one court has described it as "virtually unassailable on appeal." *See Michigan Millers Mut. Ins. Co. v. Asoyia, Inc.*, 793 F.3d 872, 878 (8th Cir. 2015). Although there is some dispute on the point, the majority view prescribes that, in considering such motions, trial judges are not bound to view the evidence in the light most favorable to the verdict winner. *See Allied Chem. Corp. v. Daiflon, Inc.*, 449 U.S. 33, 36 (1980). Instead, it may reweigh the evidence, accepting or rejecting evidence, witnesses, and other proof that the jury considered. But courts must proceed carefully, and avoid merely substituting their views for the jury's without good reason. The task of assessing whether to grant a new trial is, obviously, a highly fact-dependent one.

Grounds for New Trials

Rule 59(a) provides no list of proper reasons for which new trials may be granted, and relies instead upon historical practice. What historically justified a new trial in an action at law in the federal courts, today warrants a new trial following a jury verdict; what historically justified a rehearing in a suit in equity in the federal courts, today warrants a new trial following a bench decision. Understood broadly, new trials are proper when necessary to prevent a miscarriage of justice. The courts have recognized that new trials may be granted in at least the following circumstances:

- *Verdict Against the Weight of Evidence:* when the district court concludes that the factfinder's verdict is against the "clear" or "great" weight of the evidence, and a new trial is therefore necessary to prevent a miscarriage of justice. *See Byrd v. Blue Ridge Rural Elec. Co-op., Inc.*, 356 U.S. 525, 540 (1958). New trials on this ground—typically premised on the trial judge's disagreement with a jury's credibility assessments—must be granted cautiously, so as not to overstep the rightful province of the jury. Thus, because the jury's verdict should ordinarily be respected unless it constitutes a serious miscarriage of justice, new trials on this basis should be a rare occurrence, ordered with great restraint.
- *Verdict Is Excessive or Inadequate:* when the district court determines that the amount of the verdict is so unreasonable that it shocks the conscience;

- *"Remittitur":* If the court decides that the verdict is excessive, the court may offer the verdict winner a reduction—called a "remittitur"—in exchange for the court's denial of a motion for a new trial. *See Linn v. United Plant Guard Workers of America, Local 114,* 383 U.S. 53, 65–66 (1966). If the verdict winner accepts the court's offer, the verdict winner waives the right of appeal. *See Donovan v. Penn Shipping Co., Inc.,* 429 U.S. 648, 650 (1977) (per curiam). If remitted, the jury's verdict will usually be reduced to the maximum amount the jury could have awarded without being excessive. A trial court's decision on remittitur is accorded wide discretion, given that judge's ability to hear the testimony and assess the demeanor of the witnesses; a trial court's ruling that denies remittitur will be overturned on appeal only where the verdict is found to be so grossly excessive that the outcome is "monstrous or shocking." Noneconomic damages (such as pain and suffering) are usually remitted in only extraordinary circumstances. Properly done, remittitur will generally not offend the Seventh Amendment's entitlement to a jury trial. *See Gasperini v. Center for Humanities, Inc.,* 518 U.S. 415, 433 (1996). Remittitur may serve the laudable ends of avoiding delay and expense and limiting judicial intrusion into the jury's domain.
- *"Additur":* If the court finds that the verdict is inadequate, a federal court usually may *not* offer the verdict winner an increase in verdict size—called an "additur"—in exchange for the court's denial of a motion for new trial, due to Seventh Amendment concerns. *See Dimick v. Schiedt,* 293 U.S. 474, 486–87 (1935). Where the verdict is inadequate, the court's only option is ordering a new trial.

- *Newly Discovered Evidence:* when the district court learns of a party's newly discovered evidence. To entitle the moving party to a new trial, the newly discovered evidence generally: (1) must have existed as of the time of trial; (2) must have been excusably overlooked by the moving party, notwithstanding the moving party's diligence in attempting to discover it; (3) must be admissible; and (4) must be likely to alter the trial's outcome.
- *Improper Conduct by Counsel or the Court:* when improper conduct by either an attorney or the court unfairly influenced the verdict. A frequently asserted basis is error by the court in admitting or excluding evidence, though to receive a new trial on that ground requires that the error affect the moving party's substantial rights.
- *Improper Conduct Affecting the Jury:* when the jury verdict was not unanimous or was facially inconsistent, or when the jury was improperly influenced or improperly addressed by counsel, or when an erroneous jury instruction likely misled or confused the jury. Note, however, that after the verdict is returned, jurors usually may not impeach or alter their verdict except to testify as to improper, extrinsic influences.

Prejudice (Harmless Error)

Trial errors may only justify a new trial if they affect the substantive rights of the parties and are not cured by the trial judge's cautionary instructions to the jury. *See* Rule 61.

Burden of Proof

The burden of proving the necessity of a new trial is a heavy one, borne by the party seeking the relief.

Preservation and Waiver

A party may not seek a new trial on grounds not brought contemporaneously to the trial judge's attention. The courts recognize a narrow exception to this waiver rule where a trial error is so fundamental that gross injustice would result were it not corrected. Beyond this obligation of general preservation, motions for new trials (unlike Rule 50 motions for judgment as a matter of law) do not require a further pre-verdict motion, nor is a new trial motion at the district court level essential to preserving a right of appeal (although when the motion attacks sufficiency of the trial evidence, this point has been cast into some doubt).

Bench Trials

If a new trial is awarded following a bench trial, the district court may, upon retrial, open a judgment already entered, hear additional testimony, revise or add findings of fact and conclusions of law, and direct the entry of a new judgment. But such motions are usually not proper platforms for new evidence which could have been offered earlier, new theories, or a rehearing on the merits. Moreover, trial courts may refuse a reopening upon examining the probative value of the evidence at issue, the justification for the failure to offer it earlier, and the likelihood that the reopening will inflict undue prejudice.

Partial New Trials

The court may grant a partial new trial limited only to certain issues, provided the error justifying the new trial did not affect the determination of the remaining issues, and provided that the singular issue for retrial is so clearly distinct and separate from all other issues that a retrial of it alone will not be unjust. *See Gasoline Products Co. v. Champlin Refining Co.,* 283 U.S. 494, 500 (1931). When a partial new trial is granted, those portions of the original judgment that were not set aside by the court become part of the single, ultimate judgment following the new trial. Most commonly, courts have granted partial new trials on damages, following an error-free trial on liability issues, but partial new trials can be granted as to any "separable matter." If, however, the trial court concludes that passion influenced the jury, a partial new trial on the issue of damages alone is ordinarily improper; the court must instead order a new trial on all issues.

Comparing Rule 59 and Rule 60

Both Rule 59 and Rule 60 permit courts to grant relief from entered judgments. Beyond the timing differences between the two Rules, the standards for granting relief also differ. The showing for relief under Rule 60 is considered greater than that needed for Rule 59.

District Court Findings and Conclusions

In granting a new trial, the district court is ordinarily under no obligation to set out supporting findings of fact and conclusions of law.

Appealability

An order granting a new trial is generally interlocutory and not immediately appealable, absent a showing that the court lacked authority to enter the order. *See Allied Chemical Corp. v. Daiflon, Inc.,* 449 U.S. 33, 34 (1980). An order denying a new trial is also usually not immediately appealable, and perhaps not appealable at all: some courts disallow nearly all appeals from orders denying a new trial (relegating parties solely to an appeal from the underlying final judgment instead), while other courts refuse appeals when the basis for the new trial motion was that the verdict was against the weight of the evidence.

RULE 59(b) Time to File a Motion for a New Trial

The deadline for filing a motion for a new trial is 28 days after entry of judgment. (The process of "entering" a "judgment" is discussed in Rules 54 and 58.) To be timely, the motion must be *filed* within that 28-day time window, not just served on opposing counsel.

PRACTICING LAW UNDER THIS SUBPART

Each Party Seeking Relief Must File

In a multi-party case, a motion by one litigant under Rule 59 will not excuse the non-filing by another litigant; each party seeking relief under this Rule must move for it. Likewise, a party whose post-trial motion period has run cannot belatedly "join" a co-party's pending motion to resuscitate an otherwise expired Rule 59 filing opportunity.

Timely Motion Tolls Appeal Period

A timely-filed motion for a new trial delays the finality of the underlying judgment and tolls the time for appeal until the district judge rules on the new trial motion.

- *Tolling Applies to All Parties:* A timely filed Rule 59 motion tolls the time for appeal for all parties.

No Extensions

The 28-day filing window may not be extended under Rule 6 by court order. Over the years, two common law exceptions were recognized to this prohibition, though only one persists. If an out-of-time Rule 59 motion is filed, but not objected to, the court may, in its discretion, consider the untimely motion (though it now seems clear that the untimely motion will not toll the time for taking an appeal, *see* Fed. R. App. P. 4(a)(4)(A)). In any event, courts may treat an untimely Rule 59 motion as one made under Rule 60 and assess it under that Rule.

3-Day Service Extension Does *Not* Apply

Because Rule 59(b) requires *filing* (not service) no later than 28 days after entry of judgment, the 3-day extension after service by mail does not apply. *See* Rule 6(d).

Motion Filed After Notice of Appeal

The filing of a notice of appeal is jurisdictional and, once filed, will ordinarily divest the district court of its jurisdiction. But, if a timely Rule 59 motion is thereafter made, the earlier-filed notice of appeal lies dormant until the district court resolves the pending motion. *See Griggs v. Provident Consumer Discount Co.,* 459 U.S. 56, 58 (1982) (per curiam).

Appeals Filed During Pendency of Motion

A prematurely filed appeal is treated as filed as of the date the trial court ultimately disposes of the pending Rule 59 motion (although the notice of appeal may well need to be amended to reflect the appealed-from order).

Amended Judgments

Where an amended judgment is filed which alters the legal rights or obligations of the parties, a new time period for filing Rule 59 motions might be triggered.

RULE 59(c) — Time to Serve Affidavits

A party may support a motion for new trial with affidavits. To do so, the supporting affidavits must be filed with the motion. Opposing affidavits may be filed 14 days thereafter.

RULE 59(d) — New Trial on the Court's Initiative or for Other Reasons Not in the Motion

The court may grant a new trial *sua sponte* (on its own initiative and without a party's request). The court may also grant a new trial for reasons different from those set out in a moving party's motion papers.

PRACTICING LAW UNDER THIS SUBPART

Grounds

The court may grant a new trial for any reason that a party could have permissibly requested by motion. *See* Rule 59(a).

Timing

A court that intends to grant a new trial on its own initiative must do so within 28 days after the entry of judgment. When a court receives a motion, but decides to grant a new trial for reasons not specified in the motion, the timing is less clear.

Granting on Different Grounds

When a court decides to grant a new trial for reasons different from those set forth in the moving party's papers, the court must give the parties notice of this intention and an opportunity to be heard.

Specifying Grounds for New Trial

When the court grants a motion for a new trial on its own initiative or on grounds different from those stated in a party's motion papers, the order must specify the grounds for the court's decision.

RULE 59(e) — Motion to Alter or Amend a Judgment

The court may alter or amend its judgment, provided it does so within the 28-day window. Motions under this subpart are often labeled as motions for "reconsideration".

PRACTICING LAW UNDER THIS SUBPART

Purpose

The purpose of Rule 59(e) is to provide the district court with a means for correcting errors that may have "crept into the proceeding" while that court still holds jurisdiction over the case. *See Sosebee v. Astrue*, 494 F.3d 583, 589 (7th Cir. 2007). It thus gives the trial court the opportunity to cure its own mistakes (if it believes it made any) or to re-examine matters encompassed within its decision on the merits. *See White v. New Hampshire Dept. of Employment Sec.*, 455 U.S. 445, 451 (1982). Should an error be found, use of this Rule to permit self-correction by the rendering court might even eliminate the need for an appeal.

Grounds

No listing of allowable grounds for altering or amending a judgment is included in the language of Rule 59(e). Federal case law has been left to fill in that void. That case law recognizes four grounds that justify such relief:

- *Intervening Change in the Law:* To qualify, the change must be to controlling law.
- *Newly Discovered Evidence:* To qualify, such evidence must usually have been discovered only after trial, notwithstanding the party's diligence, be material and not merely cumulative or impeaching, and be likely to cause a new result.
- *Correcting Legal Error:* To qualify, the error must be "manifest" or "clear."
- *Prevent Manifest Injustice:* This is a "catch-all" factor, as well as an attribute implicit in any grant of Rule 59(e) relief, and generally requires a showing of prejudice that is clear, certain, and fundamentally unfair.

Typically, a Rule 59(e) motion is proper, for example, where the court misunderstood the facts, a party's arguments, or the controlling law, where the original judgment failed to provide that relief which the court found a party entitled to receive, or where the party seeks a post-judgment award of prejudgment interest. But the motion is improper if it seeks no substantive change of the court's mind, presents long possessed "new" information, or advances positions that could have and should have been advanced prior to judgment. *See Banister v. Davis*, 590 U.S. ___, 140 S. Ct. 1698, 1703 (2020). Nor, as the case law familiarly incants, should the motion be used to merely rehash previously considered and rejected arguments, though this prohibition is bounded by the court's privilege to correct an earlier mistake if convinced it made one.

Burden of Proof

The burden of proving that Rule 59(e) warrants the requested relief lies with the moving party.

District Court's Discretion

The decision whether to alter or amend a judgment is generally committed to the discretion of the trial judge, absent an error of law. Exercising this discretion calls upon the court to balance two competing interests—the need to bring litigation to a close and the need to render just rulings based on all the facts. Relief under Rule 59(e) is an extraordinary remedy, reserved for exceptional circumstances, and granted only sparingly;[FN] it is considered quite difficult to obtain.

Explanations for Rulings

Often, denials of Rule 59(e) motions are not accompanied by explanation, and none is usually required.

28-Day Period to *File* Motion to Alter or Amend

A motion to alter or amend a judgment must be filed within 28 days after the district court enters that judgment (note: this time period runs from the date of *filing*, not service or receipt). An out-of-time Rule 59 motion may be treated as a Rule 60(b) motion, if the grounds asserted would support relief under that Rule. If the court later amends its judgment, the timeliness of a Rule 59(e) motion is dated from that amendment only if the motion relates to content that the court altered.

No Extensions

The court may not grant a party any extensions to this time period. *See* Rule 6(b). An untimely Rule 59(e) motion may be deemed a nullity, or, in an appropriate case, treated as a Rule 60(b) motion for relief from a judgment. However, a technical, electronic filing error may be excused, provided the clerk's office received the filing timely. Moreover, when an untimely Rule 59(e) motion is filed, but not objected to by the non-moving party, the timeliness objection may be deemed forfeited through waiver. This can prove to be a shallow comfort, though; if the trial court grants the motion, the aggrieved party might receive meaningful relief, but if the trial court denies the motion, the aggrieved party's time for taking an appeal will almost certainly be already lost.

3-Day Service Extension Does Not Apply

Because Rule 59(e) requires *filing* (not service) no later than 28 days after entry of judgment, the 3-day extension after service by mail does not apply.

Motion Suspends Appeal Period

Like Rule 59 motions for new trial, a timely-filed Rule 59(e) motion to alter or amend the judgment suspends the time for appeal. In multi-party cases, a timely-filed Rule 59 motion by any party suspends the appeal time for everyone. A prematurely filed appeal during the pendency of a Rule 59(e) motion is held in abeyance until the date the district court resolves the pending motion. An untimely Rule 59(e) motion generally will not suspend the time for appeal, nor, generally, will a second or later Rule 59(e) motion. However, the trial court's ruling on a Rule 59(e) motion may change "matters of substance" or resolve a "genuine ambiguity" in the court's original order and, in those infrequent cases, a new judgment is recognized, from which a new Rule 59(e) motion (with appeal-period suspension effect) may be filed.

- *Appealing Correctly:* The filing of a timely, proper Rule 59(e) motion will suspend the time for filing an appeal from the original underlying *merits* ruling, and not just from the court's disposition of the Rule 59(e) motion itself (but only if the appealing parties make that intent clear).

"Particularity" Requirement for Motion

All Rule 59(e) motions must satisfy the "particularity" requirement of Rule 7(b)(1). Failure to do so may have dire consequences, including a loss of appeal-period suspension. Thus, a "skeleton" motion that fails to alert the court or the other litigants of the grounds for which an alteration or amendment is sought may be deemed improper and, thus, ineffective in suspending the appeal period. In any event, a motion that idly asks that an earlier judgment be reconsidered (without more) is almost certainly to be denied.

Motions for "Reconsideration"

The Rules do not expressly recognize motions for "reconsideration" (although individual local Districts may).

When "reconsideration" is sought from an interlocutory order *(e.g.,* a denial of a motion to dismiss or for summary judgment), that motion is not properly considered under Rule 59(e) but, instead, as simply a request for the district court to revisit its earlier ruling.

When "reconsideration" is sought from a true judgment or other final order, such a motion will be treated *either* as one under Rule 59(e) *or* as one under Rule 60(b), a classification typically dependent on the date the motion is filed. If filed within the 28-day period set for Rule 59(e) motions, the "reconsideration" will generally be treated under Rule 59(e). Otherwise, the courts will likely examine the motion under Rule 60(b). In either case, the applicable legal analysis will depend on the grounds asserted for the relief requested.

The standards governing motions for "reconsideration" usually track the Rule 59(e) criteria. Thus, such motions will not be granted absent "highly unusual circumstances." These motions do not provide litigants with an opportunity for a "second bite at the apple," *Sequa Corp. v. GBJ Corp.*, 156 F.3d 136, 144 (2d Cir.1998); or allow them, like Emperor Nero, to "fiddle as Rome burns," *Vasapolli v. Rostoff*, 39 F.3d 27, 36 (1st Cir. 1994); or to "ante up and play a new hand," *Markel Am. Ins. Co. v. Diaz-Santiago*, 674 F.3d 21, 33 (1st Cir. 2012); or license a litigation "game of hopscotch" in which parties switch from one legal theory to a new one "like a bee in search of honey," *Cochran v. Quest Software, Inc.*, 328 F.3d 1, 11 (1st Cir. 2003); or "to turn back the clock, erase the record, and try to reinvent [the] case," *Perez v. Lorraine Enters., Inc.*, 769 F.3d 23, 32 (1st Cir. 2014). In other words, motions for reconsideration are not vehicles for relitigating old issues. But nor are they motions for "initial consideration." Courts properly decline to consider new arguments or new evidence on reconsideration where those arguments or evidence were available earlier.

Mislabeled Motions

A motion made under Rule 59(e) but which is, in substance, a Rule 50(b) motion for judgment as a matter of law, a Rule 54(b) motion to reconsider an interlocutory order, or a Rule 58(e) fees award motion, will be treated as such.

Appealability

An order granting a timely-filed motion to alter or amend a judgment is immediately appealable only if it ends the litigation at the trial level. An order denying such a motion likely will be immediately appealable because it usually has that litigation-ending effect at the trial level.

RULE 60

RELIEF FROM A JUDGMENT OR ORDER

(a) Corrections Based on Clerical Mistakes; Oversights and Omissions. The court may correct a clerical mistake or a mistake arising from oversight or omission whenever one is found in a judgment, order, or other part of the record. The court may do so on motion or on its own, with or without notice. But after an appeal has been docketed in the appellate court and while it is pending, such a mistake may be corrected only with the appellate court's leave.

(b) Grounds for Relief from a Final Judgment, Order, or Proceeding. On motion and just terms, the court may relieve a party or its legal representative from a final judgment, order, or proceeding for the following reasons:

(1) mistake, inadvertence, surprise, or excusable neglect;

(2) newly discovered evidence that, with reasonable diligence, could not have been discovered in time to move for a new trial under Rule 59(b);

(3) fraud (whether previously called intrinsic or extrinsic), misrepresentation, or misconduct by an opposing party;

(4) the judgment is void;

(5) the judgment has been satisfied, released or discharged; it is based on an earlier judgment that has been reversed or vacated; or applying it prospectively is no longer equitable; or

(6) any other reason that justifies relief.

(c) Timing and Effect of the Motion.

(1) *Timing.* A motion under Rule 60(b) must be made within a reasonable time—and for reasons (1), (2), and (3) no more than a year after the entry of the judgment or order or the date of the proceeding.

(2) *Effect on Finality.* The motion does not affect the judgment's finality or suspend its operation.

(d) Other Powers to Grant Relief. This rule does not limit a court's power to:

(1) entertain an independent action to relieve a party from a judgment, order, or proceeding;

(2) grant relief under 28 U.S.C. § 1655 to a defendant who was not personally notified of the action; or

(3) set aside a judgment for fraud on the court.

(e) Bills and Writs Abolished. The following are abolished: bills of review, bills in the nature of bills of review, and writs of coram nobis, coram vobis, and audita querela.

[Amended effective March 19, 1948; October 20, 1949; August 1, 1987; April 30, 2007, effective December 1, 2007.]

UNDERSTANDING RULE 60

HOW RULE 60 FITS IN

Rule 60 is one of the post-trial motions authorized under the federal rules. In that respect, it joins Rule 50 (which permits judgments as a matter of law, or "JMOL"s, in jury trials), Rule 52 (which permits revisions to findings and judgments in bench trials), and Rule 59 (which permits new trials) in giving disappointed litigants a path to overturn a trial court ruling. Each of those motions is directed to the *trial court* that presided over the lawsuit. These are not "appeals." (Appeals are requests to a different tribunal, higher in the judicial hierarchy, to review what occurred in the trial court). Instead, these are *post-trial motions* which invite the *trial judge* to review and adjust the trial's outcome.

Rule 60 allows judges to reopen a judgment for two types of reasons: either to correct some incidental, ministerial mistake (like, for example, mistyping the amount of the jury's verdict) or, substantively, to relieve a party from the effects of the court's earlier order (because, for example, there had been a fraud committed by opposing party or the court lacked jurisdiction to hear the case). Obviously, granting this sort of relief interferes with the judiciary's commitment to see litigations come to an end, for winners to rest easy in the knowledge that old disputes will not be exhumed and revisited, and for losers to move past the dispute and on with their lives. Thus, settled judgments are not lightly reopened, and the standard for doing so is demanding. This Rule endeavors to balance this important need for litigation finality against the also important goal of ensuring that justice is done.

THE ARCHITECTURE OF RULE 60

Rule 60 has five subparts. Subpart (a) permits the correction of clerical errors. Subpart (b) addresses substantive grounds for reopening a judgment, listing six different reasons that might support that relief. Subpart (c) imposes a timing requirement on certain types of these motions. Subpart (d) preserves for the federal courts certain other bases for reopening judgments that are not enumerated in this Rule. Subpart (e) abolishes certain historic devices for reopening judgments.

HOW RULE 60 WORKS IN PRACTICE

These five subparts of Rule 60 are discussed, in order, below.

RULE 60(a) — Corrections Based on Clerical Mistakes; Oversights and Omissions

Cleaning up technical missteps is the aim of this subpart. When some error has prevented the judgment—as entered—from accurately reflecting the judgment the court intended, this subpart can be invoked to correct it. This subpart is not used when the deciding court is rethinking its intended outcome and wishes to change its mind (those types of revisions are assessed under the next subpart, Rule 60(b)). Rather, this subpart is invoked when the court still intends to rule as it originally did, but the manner in which that ruling was reduced to writing contains a mistake that needs correction.

PRACTICING LAW UNDER THIS SUBPART

Procedure

Motions to correct clerical errors are made to the district court that rendered the judgment sought to be corrected.

Sua Sponte Corrections

The court *sua sponte* may raise clerical errors for correction. Before doing so, however, the court must provide the parties with fair notice of its intention, allow them the opportunity to present their positions, and assure itself that no significant prejudice would follow from correcting the errors. *See Day v. McDonough,* 547 U.S. 198, 210 (2006).

Types of Correctable Errors

Rule 60(a) is reserved for correcting "blunders in execution," but not for "a change of mind." *See Harman v. Harper,* 7 F.3d 1455, 1457 (9th Cir. 1993). Given the broad discretion the courts enjoy with Rule 60(a), this distinction is pivotal. An error qualifying for correction under Rule 60(a) is quintessentially a minor and ministerial one, never a substantively factual or legal one. The distinction lies with the court's intent. Where the judgment, as entered, fails to reflect the original intention of the court (due to some inaccurate transcription, inadvertent omission, math error, or similar flaw in recitation), the error can be corrected with Rule 60(a). Conversely, where the judgment accurately captures an intention that the court is now rethinking, Rule 60(a) does not apply. The "touchstone" is "fidelity to the intent" of the original judgment. *See Tattersalls, Ltd. v. DeHaven*, 745 F.3d 1294, 1298 (9th Cir. 2014).

But Rule 60(a) is not limited to mere typos. The Rule may be used to clarify the original order by inserting its "necessary implications" (to ensure full implementation and enforcement) or by resolving an ambiguity to better reflect contemporaneous intent.

Whose Errors

Relief under Rule 60(a) is available to remedy clerical mistakes committed by the court clerk, the judge, the parties, and the jury. *See Day v. McDonough,* 547 U.S. 198, 210–11 (2006).

Mislabeled "Substantive" Motions

An incorrectly labeled Rule 60(a) motion that actually seeks substantive alterations of a judgment may, in the court's discretion, be treated as a request for Rule 59(e) or Rule 60(b) relief.

Time for Correction

The district court may correct a Rule 60(a) error whenever it is found. Even after an appeal is taken, such mistakes can still be corrected by the district judge (though, if the correction is not made pursuant to a Rule 60(a) motion filed within 28 days of judgment entry, the district court will need to seek leave from the appeals court to make the correction). *See* Rule 62.1 Corrections after the appeal is concluded may be made upon leave of the appeals court, or without leave if the corrections would not alter any appellate ruling.

Implications for Appeal

A Rule 60(a) motion filed within 28 days of judgment entry suspends the time for taking an appeal. An appeal from a Rule 60(a) motion filed beyond that period will likely be limited solely to correctness of the Rule 60(a) ruling and not to the underlying merits.

RULE 60(b) Other Ground for Relief

This subpart is reserved for substantive errors, where a party is inviting the court to change its mind and undo its prior judgment. There are six reasons for which such a reopening might be proper: (1) mistake, inadvertence, surprise, or excusable neglect; (2) newly discovered evidence; (3) fraud; (4) the judgment is void; (5) the judgment is satisfied, released, discharged, based on an earlier overturned judgment, or cannot be equitably applied any longer; and (6) exceptional circumstances.

PRACTICING LAW UNDER THIS SUBPART

Purpose

Tracing back to the original appearance of the federal civil rules, Rule 60(b) codifies the courts' inherent, discretionary power—recognized for centuries in English practice—to set aside judgments where enforcement would produce an inequity. This procedure endeavors to strike a balance between two sometimes conflicting principles—that litigation be drawn to its final close and that justice be done. *See United Student Aid Funds, Inc. v. Espinosa*, 559 U.S. 260, 276 (2010). Because upsetting a settled judgment clashes with finality, *see Gonzalez v. Crosby*, 545 U.S. 524, 529 (2005); such relief is considered extraordinary, is never given lightly, but awarded sparingly and only when exceptional circumstances prevented acting sooner. Rule 60(b) relief is not available to remedy deliberate litigation choices in strategy later shown to be unwise ones or to serve as a substitute for an appeal.

Threshold Procedural Requirement—Final Judgment

Rule 60(b) relief is available only from *final* judgments, orders, and proceedings. Consequently, it usually may not be used with interlocutory orders, voluntary dismissals, and consent decrees.

Reasons for Granting Substantive Relief

Rule 60(b) provides five specified reasons for which substantive (non-clerical) relief may be granted, and adds a sixth catch-all category for reasons not otherwise specifically listed. Ordinarily, proper post-judgment relief under Rule 60(b) will not be denied simply because the moving party failed to invoke the proper reason or Rule sub-part—provided, of course, that the substantive argument for relief is apparent. But, the moving party must usually make five showings: (1) a timely-filed motion; (2) a meritorious defense; (3) an absence of unfair prejudice to the opponent; (4) exceptional circumstances; and (5) satisfying at least one of the six subsections of this Rule.

Reason 1—Mistake, Inadvertence, Surprise, or Excusable Neglect

Relief from a judgment or order may be granted for mistakes by any person, not just a party, and even legal errors by the court. This category may permit relief where the order or judgment results from such circumstances as an inability to consult with counsel, a misunderstanding regarding a duty to appear, a failure to receive service, or, in some circumstances, an attorney's negligent failure to meet a deadline or other professional misstep. (Note, however, that not all courts recognize attorney negligence as capable of qualifying under this category, and those that do impose a heavy standard.) This category also permits relief when the district court made a substantive error of law or fact in its judgment or order.

The standard for relief under this category is a demanding one. Whether relief is appropriate is assessed case by case: not every error or omission in the course of litigation will qualify as "excusable neglect", nor will routine carelessness, a lack of diligence, preventable technology vulnerabilities, a confusion concerning the Rules or the law, or a party's misunderstanding of the consequences of her actions (even after advice of counsel) qualify for relief. Relief cannot be invoked merely to evade consequences of legal positions and litigation strategies undertaken. Moreover, otherwise careful clients can be penalized for omissions of their careless attorneys.

As a threshold showing, the moving party must demonstrate that the error made did not result from his or her own culpable conduct, and instead that the party has behaved with appropriate diligence. To qualify as "excusable neglect", the conduct is tested against an equitable standard, one that weighs the totality of the circumstances; among the factors the courts consider in this analysis are: (1) prejudice to the opponent; (2) length of delay and impact on the proceedings; (3) reason for the delay; and (4) the moving party's good faith. The "reason-for-delay" factor is characterized as the "key" factor for this analysis, although the analysis is ordinarily not *per se* or mechanical.

- *Default Judgments:* When invoked to seek relief from a default judgment, Rule 60(b) typically obligates the moving party to show good cause, quick action in correcting the default, absence of prejudice to the non-movant, and the existence of a meritorious defense. *See* Rule 55(c). Courts may also consider whether the case implicates the public interest or would impose an especially significant financial loss on the defendant.

Reason 2—Newly Discovered Evidence

Relief from an order or judgment may also be granted on the basis of new evidence where: (1) the evidence has been newly discovered since trial, (2) the moving party was diligent in discovering the new evidence, (3) the new evidence is not merely cumulative or impeaching, (4) the new evidence is material, and (5) in view of the new evidence, a new trial would probably produce a different result. Implicit in these elements is the recognition that the evidence must be of facts that, though in existence at the time of trial, were not discovered until after trial. Relief is not necessarily foreclosed, though, merely because the party was aware of the evidence earlier (if that evidence remained inaccessible), nor merely because it relates to an issue that had been earlier litigated). Moreover (and implicitly), the newly discovered evidence must be both admissible and credible.

These requirements are strictly enforced (in fact, one court has even required that they be proved by clear and convincing evidence, *see Luna v. Bell*, 887 F.3d 290, 294 (6th Cir. 2018)). If the movant fails to meet *any* of these prerequisites, the Rule 60(b)(2) motion may be denied.

Reason 3—Fraud, Misrepresentation, Other Adversary Misconduct

Relief from a judgment or order may be permitted on the basis of misconduct where: (1) the moving party possessed a meritorious claim at trial, (2) the adverse party engaged in fraud, misrepresentation, or other misconduct, and (3) that mischief prevented the moving party from fully and fairly presenting its case during trial. (Courts are divided on whether the moving party must also show that the misconduct likely altered the case's outcome; in courts requiring such a showing, proving knowing or deliberate misbehavior may allow that requirement to be inferred.)

This category is the "lineal descendant" of the rule in equity that a court, finding fraud or undue influence, may alter or negate a written instrument. Relief is reserved for judgments that were unfairly obtained, not at those that are claimed to be just factually in error. Indeed, an actual factual error in the judgment may not even be required. This provision is remedial, and is liberally construed. It authorizes relief not only for fraud, but for misrepresentations and misconduct as well. Thus, such relief may be granted to remedy belatedly uncovered misbehavior during discovery, provided it interfered substantially with the moving party's ability to fully and fairly try the case.

The Rule does not define "fraud," but a typical understanding of fraud is: "the knowing misrepresentation of a material fact, or concealment of the same when there is a duty to disclose, done to induce another to act to his or her detriment." *See Info-Hold, Inc. v. Sound Merch., Inc.,* 538 F.3d 448, 455–56 (6th Cir. 2008). In appropriate cases, relief under this category may be granted to remedy belatedly uncovered misconduct during discovery, but only where the challenged behavior substantially interfered with the moving party's ability to fully and fairly try the case. Ordinarily, relief under this category is reserved for instances where the fraud was committed by the adversary (and not by the party's own counsel or other non-adversaries). Further, the fraud must generally have been perpetrated in the course of litigation, and not, for example, during an underlying commercial transaction. A party's entitlement to relief must be proven by clear and convincing evidence.

Reason 4—Void Judgment

Relief may also be granted where the judgment or order is void. This Rule's definition of a "void" judgment is quite narrow, however. A ruling that is alleged to be simply incorrect is not "void." *See United Student Aid Funds, Inc. v. Espinosa,* 559 U.S. 260, 270 (2010). Nor is a judgment "void" if it is merely "voidable" (based on the existence of a particular defense or objection). The remedy for those failings is a timely appeal, for which Rule 60(b)(4) is no substitute. *See id.* at 271. Instead, a judgment is "void" only if it is a "legal nullity"—premised on a fundamental jurisdictional flaw or due process error. *See id.* A "void" judgment is one that the rendering court was powerless to enter or that contravened due process. Even then, to trigger relief, the judgment must represent a clear usurpation of judicial power (or, as many courts have written, the judgment must lack even an "arguable basis" for jurisdiction.) Thus, a judgment entered without subject-matter or personal jurisdiction, or which in some other manner transgressed constitutional due process or exceeded proper judicial authority, is likely "void." *See id.* at 270–71.

Very little discretion is accorded the district court in making this ruling; either the judgment is "void", in which case relief must be granted, or it is not. Courts are divided on which party bears the burden of proof in Rule 60(b)(4) challenges: some courts impose the burden on the party who invoked the court's jurisdiction originally, while others vest the burden with the movant.

Reason 5—Changed Circumstances

Relief from a judgment or order may also be granted where the circumstances justifying the ruling have changed, such as (1) where the judgment is satisfied, released, or discharged, (2) where a prior judgment on which the present judgment is based has been reversed or otherwise vacated, or (3) in any other circumstance where the continued enforcement of the judgment would be inequitable (*e.g.,* a change in legislative or decisional law, or a change in critical facts). *See Agostini v. Felton,* 521 U.S. 203, 215–16 (1997).

These three grounds are disjunctive; any one is sufficient to justify relief. *See Horne v. Flores,* 557 U.S. 433, 454 (2009). This encompasses the traditional power invested in a court of equity to modify its decree when appropriate in view of changed circumstances. *See Frew ex rel. Frew v. Hawkins,* 540 U.S. 431, 441–42 (2004). The courts are divided whether such relief may be granted *sua sponte.*

The "satisfied, released, or discharged" clause is often invoked by parties seeking to have a judgment satisfied by the court, due to an ongoing dispute with the judgment holder over the judgment. That alternative is also available in consent decree cases upon a showing of substantial compliance, although the movant's burden is considered heavy.

The "based-on-earlier-judgment" alternative usually requires that the prior judgment have a preclusionary (res judicata or collateral estoppel) effect, and not a mere precedential impact.

Relief under the "changed circumstances" category is only available where there is a prospective effect to the challenged judgment; the mere fact that the law has changed since the judgment was entered or that a ruling will have future collateral estoppel effect (something obviously common to many rulings) or otherwise causes some reverberations into the future does not provide the requisite "prospective" effect necessary for relief under this provision. *See generally Rufo v. Inmates of Suffolk Cty. Jail*, 502 U.S. 367, 383 (1992). Ordinarily, orders or judgments that dismiss or otherwise deny injunctive relief will not possess the necessary "prospective" effect, nor will money judgments because the set nature of the monetary outlay provides the finality. In evaluating such motions, the courts consider whether a substantial change in circumstances or law has occurred since the contested order was entered, whether complying with the contested order would cause extreme and unexpected hardship, and whether a good reason for modification exists. *See Horne,* 557 U.S. at 447. The party seeking relief bears the burden of proving changed circumstances warranting relief, but once that entitlement is shown, the court must modify the order. *See id.* The proposed modification must be "suitably tailored" to meet the new legal or factual circumstances.

> ♦ **NOTE:** Lower courts may not apply Rule 60(b)(5) in *anticipation* of the Supreme Court's overruling of an earlier precedent. To the contrary, the Supreme Court instructs that where one of its precedents applies directly to the circumstances at hand, even though the precedent's reasoning has been undermined by other opinions, the lower courts should follow the precedent and leave to the Supreme Court the prerogative of overruling its own decisions. *See Agostini v. Felton,* 521 U.S. 203, 236 (1997).

Reason 6—In the Interests of Justice

Finally, relief from a judgment or order may be permitted to further the interests of justice. This "catch-all" category is reserved for extraordinary circumstances causing unexpected, extreme hardship. *See Gonzalez v. Crosby,* 545 U.S. 524, 535 (2005). The reach of Rule 60(b)(6) is broad, described as a "grand reservoir of equitable power to do justice in a particular case." *See Kile v. United States*, 915 F.3d 682, 687 (10th Cir. 2019). But while its reach is broad, its application in practice is tightly constrained.

Relief under this Rule is rare, and rests on a case-by-case, highly fact-intensive balancing of finality and doing justice. It does not offer an unsuccessful litigant an opportunity "to take a mulligan." *See Kramer v. Gates,* 481 F.3d 788, 792 (D.C. Cir. 2007). It is never a substitute for direct appeal. Seeking relief under this Rule generally requires a showing of actual injury and the presence of circumstances beyond the movant's control that prevented timely action to protect her interests. In considering such motions, courts may assess the risk of injustice to the parties and the risk that public confidence in the judicial process might be undermined. *See Buck v. Davis*, 580 U.S. ___, 137 S. Ct. 759, 777–78 (2017). There is some authority for the conclusion that this Rule is limited to setting aside a judgment or order, and may not be used to grant affirmative relief. Relief on the basis of a change in decisional law is unlikely. *See Agostini v. Felton*, 521 U.S. 203, 239 (1997).

This "catch-all" category and the preceding five specific Rule 60(b) categories are mutually exclusive. Thus, if the reason for which catch-all relief is sought fits topically within one of the five specific categories, an inability to satisfy that category's prerequisites does not make the movant eligible for relief under the catch-all category. *See Pioneer Inv. Servs. Co. v. Brunswick Assocs. Ltd. P'ship,* 507 U.S. 380, 393 (1993). (But an inability to satisfy one of the five specific categories also does not necessarily foreclose the possibility of catch-all relief on other, different grounds.) "Something more" is required, and, given the breadth of the reasons captured by Rule 60(b)(1) through (b)(5), there is an understandably thin volume of cases explaining when that "something more" will be present to warrant relief under Rule 60(b)(6). Note, however, that some cases have ruled that Rule 60(b)(6) may be proper where a defaulted client seeks relief from judgment on the basis of an extremely gross negligence of, or abandonment by, counsel. But it is never available to remedy deliberate strategic choices in litigation that later prove to be unwise.

Burden of Proof

Except as noted above in a sub-rule specific discussion, the party seeking relief from a judgment or order bears the burden of demonstrating that the prerequisites for such relief are satisfied. Because this relief is not intended to be a substitute for appeal, some courts have elevated the level of proof required for recovery. Because the relief is fundamentally equitable, equitable defenses against the moving party (*e.g.,* unclean hands) may foreclose it.

Discretion of District Judge

Whether to grant relief under Rule 60(b) is left to the broad discretion of the trial court, absent legal error. *See Buck v. Davis*, 580 U.S. ___, 137 S. Ct. 759, 777–78 (2017). In the case of "void" judgments attacked under Rule 60(b)(4), however, the district court's discretion is almost illusory, if it exists at all. True "void" judgments are "legal nullities," and the court's refusal to vacate such judgments is a *per se* abuse of discretion.

Jurisdiction

No new independent basis for the court's jurisdiction is necessary to support a Rule 60(b) motion or ruling. Rather, such a proceeding is deemed to be a continuation of the original action, and jurisdiction to consider a later Rule 60(b) motion is not divested by subsequent events.

Procedure

Motions under this Rule should be made to the court that rendered the judgment. Absent a local rule dictating otherwise, the court is not required to convene a hearing on Rule 60(b) motions, but may choose to do so in its discretion. The court generally does not need to enter findings of fact and conclusions of law to grant Rule 60(b) relief, although a careful articulation of its analysis is advised as "helpful" and aiding appellate review.

Vacating Judgments Entered by Other Courts

One court should attempt to vacate a judgment entered by a different court under Rule 60(b) only in extraordinary circumstances, yet courts seem to possess the authority to do so in an appropriate case.

Who May Seek Relief

Relief under this Rule may be requested by a party, a party's legal representative, or one in privity with a party. Absent unusual circumstances, non-parties cannot seek Rule 60(b) relief.

Sua Sponte Motions

The Circuits are divided on whether a district court may, on its own initiative, grant relief from a judgment or order under Rule 60(b). When such *sua sponte* relief is permitted, the courts generally demand that the parties receive notice and an opportunity to be heard before the relief is ordered.

Appealability

Orders granting relief under Rule 60(b) are generally interlocutory and not immediately appealable (unless their effect ends the litigation). Appeals can be taken from orders denying Rule 60(b) relief, but such appeals ordinarily implicate only the propriety of that denial, and not the underlying judgment's merits (which ordinarily are reviewed only through a direct appeal of that judgment itself). *See Browder v. Director, Dep't of Corrections of Illinois,* 434 U.S. 257, 263 (1978).

RULE 60(c) Timing and Effect of Motion

Relief under Rule 60(b)—that is, relief from a judgment for *substantive* reasons—must be sought within a "reasonable" time after entry of the challenged judgment or order. However, a fixed, outside deadline of 1 year is imposed when relief is sought under the first three Rule 60(b) grounds (mistake, newly discovered evidence, and fraud). The mere act of filing a Rule 60(b) motion does *not* affect the challenged judgment's finality or suspend its effect.

PRACTICING LAW UNDER THIS SUBPART

Timing for Rule 60(b) Motions Only

This subpart sets the timing requirements for Rule 60(b) motions only. Motions under Rule 60(a)—to correct clerical errors (as discussed above)—are not controlled by this subpart.

Burden of Proof

The burden of proving that a Rule 60(b) motion was timely filed lies with the moving party.

The "Void" Judgment Ground

Relief from a "void" judgment or order can be sought at any time. Laches and similar finality principles generally have no effect on void judgments; the courts have held that the mere passage of time will not convert a void judgment into a proper one. However, if a party attacks the court's jurisdiction and loses on that issue, the question of jurisdiction becomes *res judicata* and, accordingly, the judgment is no longer vulnerable to being voided under this Rule; instead, such a party's recourse is a direct, timely merits appeal. *See Durfee v. Duke,* 375 U.S. 106, 109 (1963).

The Uncapped "Reasonable" Time Grounds

Relief from a judgment or order that is sought under either Reason 5 ("changed circumstances") or Reason 6 ("interests of justice") must be made "within a reasonable time" after entry of the judgment or order being challenged. The courts determine whether the time of filing is "reasonable" on a case-by-case basis, dependent on the circumstances. It is not assessed merely by the length of time that passes between discovery and filing (though the greater that time, the less likely it is to be reasonable), and the period is not necessarily *more* than a year (but might be less than one). Rather, the courts consider the length of delay along with its explanation, any resulting prejudice, any circumstances favoring relief, the nature of the dispute, and whether the public interest is implicated. For some courts, prejudice is a pivotal inquiry.

The 1-Year Capped "Reasonable" Time Grounds

Seeking relief from a judgment or order under any of the first three Rule 60(b) grounds must also be done within a reasonable time, but in no event later than 1 year from the entry of the challenged ruling. *See Pioneer Inv. Servs. Co. v. Brunswick Assocs. Ltd. P'ship,* 507 U.S. 380, 393 (1993). Thus, this 1-year time limit applies to Reason 1 ("mistake, inadvertence, surprise"), Reason 2 ("newly discovered evidence"), and Reason 3 ("fraud, misrepresentation, other adversary misconduct").

No Extensions

Where the 1-year time limit is specified in Rule 60(c), the period is "absolute" and the district court lacks the authority to extend the time for bringing a motion. However, there is developing case law that when an untimely Rule 60(b) motion is filed, but not objected to by the non-moving party, the timeliness objection may be deemed forfeited.

Effect on Finality or a Judgment's Operation

The act of filing a motion for relief under Rule 60 does not affect the finality of the underlying judgment, nor does it suspend that judgment's operation.

Effect on Appeals

A Rule 60 motion that is filed quickly—within the 28-day post-trial motions period—suspends the time for taking an appeal until the motion is resolved by the trial judge (and, similarly, any appeal filed during such a motion's pendency lies dormant until the motion is resolved). *See* Fed. R. App. P. 4(a)(4). But only the first such motion has this suspension effect; second or later post-judgment motions will usually not suspend. Rule 60 motions filed outside the 28-day period do not suspend the appeal time (even if the opponent fails to object). *See* Fed. R. App. P. 4(a)(4)(A). If the motion is filed beyond 28 days and while an appeal is then pending, the district judge is able to grant the motion only upon remand from the appeals court (although denials of the motion may be proper). *See* Rule 62.1.

RULE 60(d) Other Powers to Grant Relief

Although Rule 60 vests the trial court with authority to grant relief from a judgment or order, this grant of authority is not exclusive. The court enjoys other powers to grant relief that are not enumerated expressly in subparts (a) or (b).

PRACTICING LAW UNDER THIS SUBPART

Relief by an Independent Action

Litigants may seek relief from a judgment or order by filing an "independent action", a proceeding that sounds in equity. *See United States v. Beggerly,* 524 U.S. 38, 43–44 (1998). Independent actions are distinct from a motion under Rule 60. They are permitted in only exceptional cases to prevent grave miscarriages of justice. *See id.* at 46. An independent action may be maintained where:

(1) the judgment should not, in good conscience, be enforced;

(2) a good defense exists to the plaintiff's lawsuit;

(3) fraud, accident, or mistake prevented the defendant from obtaining the benefit of the good defense;

(4) the defendant is free of fault and negligence; *and*

(5) there is no adequate remedy at law.

The Rule 60(c) time limits do not apply to independent actions in equity (although courts are wary—but not necessarily prohibitive—of litigants using independent actions to evade timeliness problems in what could otherwise be a Rule 60(b) motion). If the independent action is filed in the same court that granted the judgment, supplemental jurisdiction exists—regardless of diversity or federal question jurisdiction. *See Beggerly,* 524 U.S. at 46. Absent prejudice, a mislabeled independent action may be treated as a Rule 60(b) motion, and vice versa.

Relief by Section 1655 of the Judiciary Code

Congress has, by statute, created a procedure for the enforcement and the removal of liens, incumbrances, and clouds upon the title to real or personal property. *See* 28 U.S.C. § 1655. This statute provides a means for notifying the affected defendant of the pending proceeding. Defendants who do not receive prior notification may act within 1 year to have the judgment lifted and appear to defend (provided they pay any costs assessed by the court).

Relief Due to Fraud on the Court

Finally, the district court also possesses the inherent power, grounded in equity, to grant relief where the judgment or order is obtained through a fraud on the court. *See Hazel-Atlas Glass Co. v. Hartford-Empire Co.,* 322 U.S. 238, 248–49 (1944). Since a ruling procured through fraud is not a true ruling at all, no time limits apply, provided relief is sought within a reasonable time. The court may grant the relief on its own initiative or on motion. (Relief from this type of fraud requires a level of severity "several notches" above what is needed under Rule 60(b)(3)). Movants bear the demanding burden of showing extraordinary circumstances. Such fraud must be proven by clear and convincing evidence.

To constitute a fraud on the court, the alleged misconduct must be something more than fraud among the litigants. Instead, the misconduct must be an assault on the integrity of the judicial process, which defiles the court itself or is perpetrated by officers of the court in such a manner that the impartial system of justice fails to function. *See Hazel-Atlas Glass Co.,* 322 U.S. at 245–46. The misconduct must also have been unknown at the time the court acted and must cause such prejudice to the moving party, affecting the outcome of the case, that it would be manifestly unconscionable to permit the judgment to remain. Thus, the moving party must generally show (1) an officer of the court (2) committing an intentional fraud (3) directed against the court itself (4) which, in fact, succeeds in deceiving that court. Fraud in the discovery process, to the extent it meets this standard, can support relief.

RULE 60(e) Bills and Writs Abolished

Certain old common law writs that traditionally authorized relief from a judgment—the writs of coram nobis, coram vobis, audita querela, and bills of review—are abolished in federal civil proceedings. Filings under these ancient writs may be treated by the courts as motions for relief under Rule 60(b). Note, however, that although abolished by the Rules for civil cases, many such writs exist in criminal proceedings.

RULE 61

HARMLESS ERROR

Unless justice requires otherwise, no error in admitting or excluding evidence—or any other error by the court or a party—is ground for granting a new trial, for setting aside a verdict, or for vacating, modifying, or otherwise disturbing a judgment or order. At every stage of the proceeding, the court must disregard all errors and defects that do not affect any party's substantial rights.

[Amended April 30, 2007, effective December 1, 2007.]

UNDERSTANDING RULE 61

HOW RULE 61 FITS IN

No matter how careful and conscientious the district judge might be, how attentive he or she is to every small detail in a case, errors can sometimes still creep in during the conduct of civil litigation. A judge may, for example, decide on reflection that he or she improperly allowed or denied a witness's testimony, wrongly admitted or excluded trial exhibits, misspoke while instructing jurors on the law, erred in drafting a jury's verdict sheet, or made some other mistake during the case. Does the fact that such an error occurred during a federal civil case entitle litigants to have the verdict overturned, the judgment vacated, or a new trial granted? Rule 61 answers that question definitively. Not every error requires correction. Instead, errors that are found to be legally "harmless"—that is, mistakes that "do not affect any party's substantial rights"—must be disregarded by the judge.

THE ARCHITECTURE OF RULE 61

Rule 61 spans a brief two sentences. Its structure is clear.

HOW RULE 61 WORKS IN PRACTICE

Standard for "Harmlessness"

Rule 61 directs that errors, at all stages of the case, "must" be disregarded if they do not affect the parties' substantial rights (*i.e.*, if they are "harmless"). The Rule does not further define harmlessness, and the Supreme Court has cautioned against invoking "mandatory presumptions and rigid rules" to detect it. *See Shinseki v. Sanders*, 556 U.S. 396, 407 (2009). Instead, the Court prefers "case-specific application of judgment." *See id.* Over the years, judges have largely been guided by a discussion of harmlessness from the criminal, statutory context, where the Court once perceived the "very plain admonition" of harmlessness as this: "Do not be technical, where technicality does not really hurt the party whose rights in the trial and in its outcome the technicality affects." *See Kotteakos v. United States*, 328 U.S. 750, 759–60 (1946) (explaining that principle developed in era where trials had become "a game for sowing reversible error"). Cautious about over-defining the term, the Court offered two guides: if there is a sure conviction that the error did not influence, or "had but very slight effect" on, the jury, the error is harmless; but harmlessness is absent "if one cannot say, with fair assurance, after pondering all that happened without stripping the erroneous action from the whole, that the judgment was not substantially swayed by the error." *See id.* at 764–65. A more exacting definition is probably impossible, just as it is impossible to ignore the subjectivity inherent in the inquiry itself. In testing for harmlessness, courts consider the entire record and assess on a case-by-case basis. Every reasonable possibility of prejudice need not be disproved, but harmlessness cannot be founded merely on a belief that the trial ended in a correct result. At its core, the harmless error inquiry examines whether the trial error could (or did) affect "the outcome of a case to the substantial disadvantage of the losing party." *See United States v. O'Keefe,* 169 F.3d 281, 287 n.5 (5th Cir. 1999). Unsurprisingly, this risk of prejudice is considered greater in close cases, than in more one-sided cases.

Burden of Proof

The party moving for relief bears the burden of establishing that a trial error affected that party's substantial rights and, thus, was not harmless. *See Palmer v. Hoffman,* 318 U.S. 109, 116 (1943). (In conducting their assessment, some courts, however, seem to suppose that harm is presumed, rather than proved.)

Federal Law Controls

Under *Erie* principles, the federal (not State) construction of the harmless error rule usually controls where the federal and State standards are inconsistent. (The *Erie* doctrine and its progeny is discussed in Sections 2.18 to 2.23 of this text.)

Applies to All Errors

The harmless error rule applies to all types of errors, including most constitutional errors. The courts of appeals review rulings of the district courts under this standard as well. *See* 28 U.S.C. § 2111 (fixing harmlessness standard for appeals).

Errors in Rulings on Pleadings

Technical errors in pleadings will generally be discounted as harmless.

Errors in Ruling on Motions

The same "substantial rights" standard applies to errors in ruling upon motions. Thus, for example, an improper striking of an amended complaint is harmless if the proposed amendment would not have prevented a dismissal, an improper dismissal of a claim is harmless if it would not have (in light of later discovery) survived summary judgment, an improper dismissal of counterclaims is harmless when those claims could be asserted in another proceeding, and an improper scope of a summary judgment ruling or improper consideration (or exclusion) of summary judgment affidavits and exhibits is harmless where, in context, the effect could not have been prejudicial, and a reliance on clearly erroneous facts in denying a motion to decertify a class action or in making a fees award is harmless when other, properly found facts justify those rulings.

Errors in Admitting or Excluding Evidence

The district court enjoys broad discretion to admit or exclude evidence, including expert and rebuttal evidence. Errors in such rulings are harmless if the party raises no objection, or "invited" the error through earlier questioning of a witness, if the evidence wrongfully admitted or excluded was cumulative, if other, uncontested evidence was sufficiently robust to support the judgment, if adequate curative instructions are given, or if the rulings are otherwise determined not to have caused substantial prejudice or to have substantially influenced the jury. However, evidentiary rulings that affected the substantial rights of a party are *not* harmless, and the rulings must be reversed.

In making this "harmlessness" evaluation, the court views the error in light of the entire record. The court considers the centrality of the evidence and the prejudicial effect of the inclusion or exclusion of the evidence. The court also examines whether other evidence is "sufficiently strong" to support a conclusion that the evidentiary error had no effect on the outcome. If the properly admitted evidence is not sufficient to support the verdict, the wrongful admission of evidence is not harmless. Some courts begin with a "presumption of prejudice"—thus, only if the court can say with fair assurance that the judgment was not substantially affected by the wrongfully admitted or excluded evidence, will the error be considered harmless. Other courts seem to adopt the opposite approach. The courts are particularly careful in discounting an error as harmless in close cases, or where the evidence was "substantively important, inflammatory, repeated, emphasized, or unfairly self-serving." *See Doty v. Sewall*, 908 F.2d 1053, 1057 (1st Cir. 1990).

- *Cumulative Effect of Multiple Errors:* Although each individual evidentiary error might not, standing alone, have affected a party's substantial rights, the court may find that the collective effect of multiple evidentiary errors deprived the moving party of a fair trial.
- *Manner of Presentation:* The harmlessness standard also applies to rulings on the manner in which evidence is presented or displayed to the jury.

Errors in Seating Jurors

Errors in striking or refusing to strike prospective jurors are also measured under the harmless error standard.

Errors in Jury Instructions

Jury instructions must be considered in their entirety. If the charging errors would not have changed the trial result, or if the parties waived the errors by failing to timely object, challenges to jury instructions will be rejected as harmless. Conversely, if the jury may have based their verdict on an erroneous instruction, or if the instruction was otherwise prejudicially misleading, confusing, or legally incorrect, or affected a party's substantial rights, a new trial is warranted.

Errors in Jury Verdict Form Interrogatories

Whether mistakes in crafting jury interrogatories on the verdict form is deemed reversible error will also be measured under the harmless error standard.

Errors During/After Jury Deliberations

Mistakes in permitting juror examination of exhibits or in recalling a discharged jury for further deliberations are tested under the harmless error standard. *See Dietz v. Bouldin*, 579 U.S. ___, 136 S. Ct. 1885, 1891–97 (2016).

Errors in Ruling on Counsel's Conduct During Trial

Misconduct by counsel during trial will be deemed harmless unless the court determines that the misconduct affected the verdict, as will errors in permitting inappropriate counsel invitations for jury participation in a trial demonstration. In testing errors occurring during argument by counsel, the court will assess (1) the argument's nature and seriousness, (2) if the opponent invited the argument, (3) if the argument could be rebutted effectively, (4) effective curative instructions, and (5) the weight of the evidence.

Errors in Bench Judgments

In bench trials, errors are harmless if the record shows that the district judge would have reached the same judgment regardless of the error. Thus, a judge's mistaken application of a certain method of damages valuation (one to which there was no testimony or other record basis) will be deemed harmless if the effect of the error caused no prejudice.

Error in Granting or Denying Jury Trial

The court's mistaken decision to grant a jury trial is generally harmless error, but an improper denial of a jury trial is usually grounds for reversal.

RULE 62

STAY OF PROCEEDINGS TO ENFORCE A JUDGMENT

(a) Automatic Stay. Except as provided in Rule 62(c) and (d), execution on a judgment and proceedings to enforce it are stayed for 30 days after its entry, unless the court orders otherwise.

(b) Stay by Bond or Other Security. At any time after judgment is entered, a party may obtain a stay by providing a bond or other security. The stay takes effect when the court approves the bond or other security and remains in effect for the time specified in the bond or other security.

(c) Stay of an Injunction, Receivership, or Patent Accounting Order. Unless the court orders otherwise, the following are not stayed after being entered, even if an appeal is taken:

(1) an interlocutory or final judgment in an action for an injunction or receivership; or

(2) a judgment or order that directs an accounting in an action for patent infringement.

(d) Injunction Pending an Appeal. While an appeal is pending from an interlocutory order or final judgment that grants, continues, modifies, refuses, dissolves, or refuses to dissolve or modify an injunction, the court may suspend, modify, restore, or grant an injunction on terms for bond or other terms that secure the opposing party's rights. If the judgment appealed from is rendered by a statutory three-judge district court, the order must be made either:

(1) by that court sitting in open session; or

(2) by the assent of all its judges, as evidenced by their signatures.

(e) Stay Without Bond on an Appeal by the United States, Its Officers, or Its Agencies. The court must not require a bond, obligation, or other security from the appellant when granting a stay on an appeal by the United States, its officers, or its agencies or on an appeal directed by a department of the federal government.

(f) Stay in Favor of a Judgment Debtor Under State Law. If a judgment is a lien on the judgment debtor's property under the law of the State where the court is located, the judgment debtor is entitled to the same stay of execution the State court would give.

(g) Appellate Court's Power Not Limited. This rule does not limit the power of the appellate court or one of its judges or justices:

(1) to stay proceedings—or suspend, modify, restore, or grant an injunction—while an appeal is pending; or

(2) to issue an order to preserve the status quo or the effectiveness of the judgment to be entered.

(h) Stay with Multiple Claims or Parties. A court may stay the enforcement of a final judgment entered under Rule 54(b) until it enters a later judgment or judgments, and may prescribe terms necessary to secure the benefit of the stayed judgment for the party in whose favor it was entered.

[Amended effective March 19, 1948; October 20, 1949; July 19, 1961; August 1, 1987; April 30, 2007, effective December 1, 2007; March 26, 2009, effective December 1, 2009; April 26, 2018, effective December 1, 2018.]

UNDERSTANDING RULE 62

HOW RULE 62 FITS IN

A final judgment in a federal civil case determines the litigants' rights and obligations. Whether by jury verdict, bench trial ruling, or otherwise, the judgment in the case declares the winners and losers on the issues litigated. Not unexpectedly, the winners would generally like to move speedily forward to obtain the benefits of their victory (money, injunction, or some other relief). Conversely, the defeated parties will want to consider how next to proceed. Those defeated parties could allow the judgment to remain undisturbed, or they could file post-trial motions or an appeal (or both, in sequence) in an effort to have the judgment undone. What happens to the winners in that latter circumstance? Can the winners proceed nevertheless to collect on a money judgment or have an injunction enforced, or must they wait out the defeated parties' post-judgment challenges? The general rule is that a federal court's judgment normally takes effect regardless of whether an appeal is intended or even filed—unless that judgment has been "stayed". *See Coleman v. Tollefson*, 575 U.S. 532, 539 (2015). Rule 62 provides the procedure for issuing those suspensions (or "stays") of a judgment's execution and enforcement activity following the judgment's entry.

THE ARCHITECTURE OF RULE 62

Rule 62 has eight subparts that, at first glance, seem confusing. But those subparts can be easily understood in six groups. Subpart (a) establishes the 30-day automatic stay that most every federal judgment receives. Subpart (b) permits the court to grant additional stays (beyond the automatic stay). Subpart (c) lists three types of orders that are not stayed, absent a contrary court order. Subparts (d), (e), and (g) concern stays while appeals are pending. Subpart (f) borrows State law to determine certain stays when the judgment involves a State law lien on a debtor's property. Subpart (h) grants the court flexibility in stays when partial judgments (permitted under Rule 54(b)) are involved.

HOW RULE 62 WORKS IN PRACTICE

These eight subparts of Rule 62 are discussed, in order, below.

RULE 62(a) Automatic Stay

Federal civil judgments cannot be executed upon or enforced for 30 days following their entry, unless the court or another Rule provides otherwise (this period was expanded in 2018 from its former 14-day duration). This 30-day stay occurs automatically, without court order or motion by any party.

PRACTICING LAW UNDER THIS SUBPART

Postponement Effect

The 30-day automatic stay postpones the execution or enforcement of the judgment (in other words, during this stay period, a money judgment cannot be executed upon, nor an injunction decree enforced). But the automatic stay does not affect the appealability of the judgment or the running of the time for taking an appeal. Nor does the stay impact the judgment's *res judicata* effect.

Exceptions to the Automatic Stay

The automatic stay period will not apply if another Rule or a court order directs otherwise.

Expiration of Automatic Stay Period

Once the 30-day automatic stay period expires, a party may seek execution or enforcement of the judgment unless another subpart of Rule 62 provides otherwise.

Armed Services Personnel

The Soldiers and Sailors Civil Relief Act of 1940, 50 U.S.C. §§ 203–04, App. §§ 523 to 24, provides that a court may stay the execution of any judgment, or vacate or stay an attachment or garnishment, entered against a person in the military service.

RULE 62(b) Stay by Bond or Other Security

The filing of post-trial motions or an appeal does not suspend the execution and enforcement of the contested judgment (beyond, of course, the automatic stay of Rule 62(a)). Nevertheless, a party can suspend execution and enforcement of most judgments by posting a bond or other type of security to protect the victor during post-trial motions and/or the appeal, provided the bond or other security is first approved by the district court.

PRACTICING LAW UNDER THIS SUBPART

Stay Opportunity as of Right

Parties generally have the ability to obtain a further stay, beyond that granted automatically by Rule 62(a)—provided those parties post a bond or other security with the court.

Timing

The stay authorized by this subpart takes effect when the court approves the bond or other security, and then remains in effect for the time specified in the bond or other security. Because the mere act of filing post-trial motions or filing an appeal does not stay execution or enforcement, litigants typically file their motion for a stay by bond or other security before the end of the 30-day automatic stay period.

The Bond / Other Security Requirement

A bond posted to stay the execution or enforcement of a judgment is usually known as a "supersedeas bond," the name of a traditional writ that was used to stay the execution of a legal judgment. The bond's amount will usually be set at a sum sufficient to satisfy the judgment plus interest, although the court may also require that the bond include costs and damages for delay. The court has the discretion to order a lesser amount, or other type, of security. Additionally, the court may order the movant to provide written notice to the opposing parties of any material disposition of the movant's assets. Failure to post a bond under this subpart will not affect a party's right to appeal, but, absent a stay, execution and enforcement can begin.

District Court Discretion

Once the motion for stay is made, the court has discretion to stay execution or enforcement of the judgment, subject to the exceptions contained in Rule 62(c) and (d). The court also has discretion to establish conditions for the security of the adverse party during the pendency of the stay. Stays pending appeal constitute "extraordinary relief" for which the movant bears a heavy burden.

Effect of Denial

When the court denies a stay, the judgment is binding (and may be enforced) until vacated by the court or reversed on appeal.

RULE 62(c) Stay of an Injunction, Receivership, or Patent Accounting Order

Three categories of orders are exempted from being stayed, absent a further court order: (1) interlocutory or final judgments in actions for an injunction; (2) interlocutory or final judgment in actions for a receivership; and (3) judgments or orders directing an accounting in actions for infringement of patents.

RULE 62(d) Injunction Pending an Appeal

As noted in Rule 62(c), there are no automatic stays in judgments in injunction actions (unless the court orders otherwise). Instead, a judgment that grants, continues, modifies, refuses, dissolves, or refuses to dissolve or modify an injunction ordinarily takes effect immediately. However, when an appeal is pending that challenges such a judgment, the court may suspend, modify, restore, or grant an injunction as an interim measure, awaiting the disposition of the appeal.

PRACTICING LAW UNDER THIS SUBPART

Permissible Scope of Interim Order

This subpart applies to both final judgments and interlocutory judgments in injunction actions, and applies whether the judgment grants, continues, modifies, refuses, dissolves, or refuses to dissolve or modify an injunction. However, this subpart only allows the court to modify its injunction as an *interim* measure (in order, for example, to preserve a status quo).

Time for Filing

A party may make a motion under this subpart after the notice of appeal has been filed and at any time while the appeal is pending.

Place of Filing

A motion under this subpart should be made in the judgment-rendering district court. If, however, the district court denies relief or provides only inadequate relief, the party may press the motion in the appropriate court of appeals or, in extraordinary circumstances, at the U.S. Supreme Court. *See* Rule 62(g).

Motion Prerequisites

A motion under this subpart requires the moving party to show: (a) a strong likelihood of success on the merits of the appeal; (b) the movant's irreparable injury, unless the stay is granted; (c) the absence of substantial harm to other interested parties; and (d) that a grant of the motion will not harm the public interest. *See Hilton v. Braunskill,* 481 U.S. 770, 776 (1987).

Requirements of the Order

An order issued under this subpart must set forth the reasons for its issuance and be specific in its terms. The court will usually order the moving party to post a bond or other security during the period of the stay or the injunction on terms that "secure the opposing party's rights."

Three-Judge District Court

When a district court of three judges, sitting by statute, renders judgment in an injunction case, a motion to stay that judgment should be addressed to all three judges. Such a court may only issue a stay pending an appeal in open court or by signature of all three judges.

RULE 62(e) — Stay Without Bond on an Appeal by the United States, Its Officers, or Its Agencies

When the party seeking the stay-pending-appeal is the United States as a party, or its officers or agencies (or when the appeal is directed by a federal department), the district court may not condition the granting of such a stay on the posting of a bond, obligation, or other security. *See* 28 U.S.C. § 2408.

RULE 62(f) Stay in Favor of a Judgment Debtor Under State Law

If the district court's judgment creates a lien upon the debtor's property on the basis of a State law of the same State where the district court is located, a special requirement is imposed. That debtor is entitled to the same stay of execution that would have been given in State court. The court has no discretion to otherwise deny such a stay.

RULE 62(g) Appellate Court's Power Not Limited

The federal appeals courts are not limited by Rule 62 from issuing stays-pending-appeals; from suspending, modifying, restoring, or granting injunction pending an appeal; or from preserving the status quo or a judgment's effectiveness pending an appeal.

RULE 62(h) Stay with Multiple Claims or Parties

A court may, under Rule 54(b), issue a partial final judgment, thereby permitting an immediate appeal from that ruling. *See* Rule 54(b). When a court does so, it may stay enforcement of the partial final judgment until it enters some or all of the remaining judgments in the case, and may also set terms to secure the effect of the partial final judgment for the victors.

PRACTICING LAW UNDER THIS SUBPART

Discretion / Standards for Granting a Stay with Rule 54(b) Judgments

The court has discretion to decide a motion for stay in partial final judgment cases, balancing the equities of the parties and considering the administration of the case.

Posting of Security

When staying the enforcement or execution of a partial final judgment, the court may condition its stay on the posting of security to help ensure performance on that part of the judgment. *See Curtiss-Wright Corp. v. General Elec. Co.,* 446 U.S. 1, 13 (1980).

RULE 62.1

INDICATIVE RULING ON A MOTION FOR RELIEF THAT IS BARRED BY A PENDING APPEAL

(a) Relief Pending Appeal. If a timely motion is made for relief that the court lacks authority to grant because of an appeal that has been docketed and is pending, the court may:

(1) defer considering the motion;

(2) deny the motion; or

(3) state either that it would grant the motion if the court of appeals remands for that purpose or that the motion raises a substantial issue.

(b) Notice to the Court of Appeals. The movant must promptly notify the circuit clerk under Federal Rule of Appellate Procedure 12.1 if the district court states that it would grant the motion or that the motion raises a substantial issue.

(c) Remand. The district court may decide the motion if the court of appeals remands for that purpose.

[Added March 26, 2009, effective December 1, 2009.]

UNDERSTANDING RULE 62.1

HOW RULE 62.1 FITS IN

Traditionally, it was understood that once an appeal was taken, the district court was thereupon divested of jurisdiction. This understanding was anchored in the principle that two courts could not both possess jurisdiction over a case at the same time. But the principle created practical challenges. The time for filing post-trial motions is 28 days from entry of the contested judgment; the time for taking an appeal from that contested judgment is (usually) 30 days from its entry. Consequently, it was not uncommon for an appeal to be taken by one party either before another party filed its post-trial motions or while that party's post-trial motions were still pending. Divesting the district court of jurisdiction in such a circumstance was an obviously unsatisfying, inefficient outcome. It eliminated the opportunity for the district court to consider granting the very relief an appellant was seeking (and thereby possibly obviating the need for any appeal at all).

Amendments to the Federal Rules of Appellate Procedure have relaxed, to a degree, the severity of this jurisdiction-divesting principle. Now, the timely filing of many post-trial motions results in the district court retaining its jurisdiction to rule on those motions—even if an appeal has been filed. *See* Fed. R. App. P. 4(a)(4).

But there still remains the possibility that some post-trial motions (like, for example, a Rule 60(b)(2) motion to reopen a judgment because of newly-discovered evidence) could be timely-filed yet also outside the ordinary 28-day post-trial motion period and, thus, ineligible to preserve the district court's jurisdiction to rule. Rule 62.1 addresses that circumstance. If a timely motion is filed in the district court which that court (due to the jurisdiction-divesting principle) lacks authority to grant, the trial judge is given three options: (1) it may defer its consideration of the motion; (2) it may deny the motion; or (3) it may inform the court of appeals either that it is inclined to grant the motion (were its jurisdiction to be restored) or that it considers the motion as raising a substantial issue that would merit further study. If the third of these options were selected, the court of appeals is authorized to respond by remanding the case back to the district court for its further consideration of the pending motion. *See* Fed. R. App. P. 12.1.

THE ARCHITECTURE OF RULE 62.1

Rule 62.1 consists of three subparts, all brief and easily understood. Subpart (a) grants the district court its three options. Subpart (b) directs the moving party to notify the court of appeals if the district judge advises that it is inclined either to grant the motion or consider it seriously. Subpart (c) authorizes the district judge to rule, should the court of appeals remand the case.

HOW RULE 62.1 WORKS IN PRACTICE

These three subparts of Rule 62.1 are discussed, in order, below.

RULE 62.1(a) Relief Pending Appeal

When, due to the filing of an appeal, a district court lacks the authority to rule on a timely post-trial motion, it is empowered to defer the motion, deny the motion, or notify the court of appeals of its intent to grant the motion or to consider it carefully because it raises a "substantial issue."

PRACTICING LAW UNDER THIS SUBPART

Motion Must Be Timely

The district court has these three options only if the pending motion is timely filed.

Procedure Not Needed

The procedure established in Rule 62.1 is unnecessary if the pending post-trial motion is timely-filed under: (1) Rule 50, for a judgment as a matter of law; (2) Rule 52(b), for an amending or supplementing of factual findings; (3) Rule 54, for attorney's fees (if time is extended under Rule 58); (4) Rule 59, for an alteration or amendment to a judgment; (5) Rule 59, for a new trial; or (6) Rule 60, for relief from a judgment or order (but only if the motion is filed within 28 days). In those six instances, the district court's right to proceed is granted automatically by the Federal Rules of Appellate Procedure. *See* Fed. R. App. P. 4(a)(4)(A).

RULE 62.1(b) Notice to the Court of Appeals

If the district court "indicates" that it would grant the pending motion filed or that it considers the motion as raising a "substantial issue," the moving party must promptly so notify the appellate court.

RULE 62.1(c) Remand

If, following the district court's "indication" of its intent, the court of appeals remands the case, the district court may then rule on the pending motion.

RULE 63

JUDGE'S INABILITY TO PROCEED

If a judge conducting a hearing or trial is unable to proceed, any other judge may proceed upon certifying familiarity with the record and determining that the case may be completed without prejudice to the parties. In a hearing or a nonjury trial, the successor judge must, at a party's request, recall any witness whose testimony is material and disputed and who is available to testify again without undue burden. The successor judge may also recall any other witness.

[Amended effective August 1, 1987; December 1, 1991; April 30, 2007, effective December 1, 2007.]

UNDERSTANDING RULE 63

HOW RULE 63 FITS IN

A judge who begins a trial or hearing might be unable to continue presiding due to that judge's death, sickness, injury, other disability, recusal, disqualification, or retirement. Historically, such a departure by the presiding judge during a judicial proceeding often required that the matter be stopped and then begun anew before a second judge. Given the increasing length of trials in federal court and the expected concomitant increase in the number of trials interrupted by a judge's departure, this outcome was deemed unacceptable.

Rule 63 creates another option. Following a departure, any other judge of the court may now proceed with the case if that judge reads the pertinent portions of the record, certifies familiarity with that record, and decides that he or she may proceed in the case without causing prejudice to the parties. In a non-jury hearing or trial, if the successor judge proceeds with the case, he or she must recall any witnesses requested by the parties, if their testimony is material and disputed and if the witnesses are available to return to testify without undue burden. The successor judge may also recall any witnesses to become better familiar with the record.

THE ARCHITECTURE OF RULE 63

Rule 63 has three sentences, and its structure is plain.

HOW RULE 63 WORKS IN PRACTICE

Conditions for Inability to Proceed

A judge's departure must rest on compelling reasons (such as sickness, death, disability, retirement, recusal, or disqualification). A judge may not withdraw for mere personal convenience.

Statement of Grounds for Withdrawal

A withdrawing judge must state on the record the reasons for his or her withdrawal.

Only Applicable *After* Hearing or Trial Begins

The certification obligation of Rule 63 is only triggered if the substitution is made *after* a hearing or trial has begun; before that time, a substitution may be made without any requirement of certification by the substituting judge.

Certifying Familiarity with the Record

Once a trial or hearing has begun, no substitute judge can replace a departing judge without first "certifying familiarity with the record." It is this certification procedure that ensures that Due Process is not violated when the case resumes. Although an express "certification" is plainly preferred, the court of appeals will likely not reverse in the absence of an express certification so long as the successor judge's statements confirm compliance with the record familiarity requirement. Nor will the appeals court likely reverse for unfortunate, though nonprejudicial, misstatements in the certification. This certification requirement obligates the substitute judge to read and consider all relevant portions of the record. What portions of the record the successor judge is required to learn depends upon the nature of the successor judge's role in the case. For example, if the successor judge inherits a jury trial before the evidence has closed, the judge must become familiar with the entire record so as to properly rule upon relevance-based evidentiary objections; but if the successor judge inherits the case after the entry of verdict or judgment, the judge need only review those portions of the record relevant to the particular issues challenged by post-trial motions. *See Mergentime Corp. v. Washington Metropolitan Area Transit Auth.,* 166 F.3d 1257 (D.C. Cir. 1999).

Prerequisite for Substitution

In order for a judge to be substituted, there must be an available transcript or a recording to permit the replacement judge to become familiar with the proceedings that occurred prior to the substitution.

Jury Trials

In a jury trial, the parties are not reflexively entitled to a new trial merely because the judge is unable to continue to preside, even when that occurs after the jury's verdict but before post-trial motions. Nor, in such circumstances, do the parties have the right to insist that a witness be recalled. Instead, if the successor judge can certify familiarity with the record and can determine that the proceedings are able to be completed without prejudice to the parties, nothing more is required. Should the judge choose to do so, however, the successor judge has the discretion to recall a witness.

Bench Trials

In a non-jury trial, the parties have the ability to insist that certain witnesses be recalled and reheard by the successor judge:

(1) *Testimony of Available Witness:* When a witness is available, the successor judge *must* honor a party's recall request if the witness's testimony is material, disputed, and obtainable without undue burden. Even without such a request, the successor judge *may* recall any other witness discretionarily and *must* recall any witness whose credibility is in question but undeterminable from the record if that witness's testimony is material, disputed, and obtainable without undue burden.

(2) *Testimony of Unavailable Witness:* If a witness has become unavailable, such that a subpoena to compel testimony at trial is not possible, the successor judge can consider the testimony recorded at trial or, if the testimony was not material or not disputed, may choose not to hear the testimony at all.

(3) *Evidence Heard by the Original Judge:* In appropriate circumstances, the successor judge may base a factual finding on evidence actually heard by the original (now-unavailable) judge.

(4) *Entire New Trial:* If the issues in the case are especially complex, if new findings are required, and if many witnesses must be recalled, the successor judge may grant a new trial.

(5) *Factfinding Deference:* The involvement of a successor judge does not alter the ordinary deference that trial court factfinding enjoys on appeal, even when that factfinding is based entirely on a documentary record.

Previously Litigated Issues

Unless the controlling law has changed, the successor judge will not ordinarily revisit rulings made by the withdrawing judge. However, the successor judge is required to consider and rule upon allegations of trial error properly raised in post-trial motions. *See Mergentime Corp. v. Washington Metropolitan Area Transit Auth.,* 166 F.3d 1257, 1263 (D.C. Cir. 1999).

Option to Enter Summary Judgment

If, after reviewing the trial transcript, the successor judge decides that no credibility determinations are required and that one party is entitled to a judgment as a matter of law, summary judgment can be entered as an alternative to the successor judge "stepping into the shoes" of the original judge.

Waiver of Right to Object to the Successor Judge

Following the departure of the original judge, the litigants may be deemed to have waived any objection to the case's reassignment to a new judge if the litigants fail either to timely seek a new trial or timely object to a reassignment, or fail to timely insist upon the recall of witnesses. Minimally, a failure to object will likely relegate the appellate court to the very forgiving "plain error" standard of review.

VIII. PROVISIONAL AND FINAL REMEDIES

RULE 64

SEIZING A PERSON OR PROPERTY

(a) Remedies Under State Law—In General. At the commencement of and throughout an action, every remedy is available that, under the law of the State where the court is located, provides for seizing a person or property to secure satisfaction of the potential judgment. But a federal statute governs to the extent it applies.

(b) Specific Kinds of Remedies. The remedies available under this rule include the following—however designated and regardless of whether State procedure requires an independent action:

- arrest;
- attachment;
- garnishment;
- replevin;
- sequestration; and
- other corresponding or equivalent remedies.

[Amended April 30, 2007, effective December 1, 2007.]

UNDERSTANDING RULE 64

HOW RULE 64 FITS IN

Rule 64 concerns "provisional remedies"—the seizure of a person or property, occurring *before* any final judgment is entered, designed to secure the satisfaction of any judgment that might be later entered in the lawsuit. Provisional remedies may prove important in exigent circumstances (such as when assets are at risk of slipping out of the forum or a potential debtor is threatening to decamp to locations beyond the court's reach). This sort of preliminary, anticipatory, prophylactic relief is authorized in two circumstances: where Congress approves it by federal statute or where the law of the State where the district court sits permits it.

THE ARCHITECTURE OF RULE 64

Rule 64 has two subparts. Subpart (a) authorizes the seizure of persons or property to secure satisfaction of a potential judgment. Subpart (b) lists the kinds of remedies available for this purpose.

HOW RULE 64 WORKS IN PRACTICE

The two subparts of Rule 64 are discussed, in order, below.

RULE 64(a) Remedies Under State Law—In General

The pre-judgment seizure of persons and property is permitted to secure the satisfaction of a federal civil judgment if authorized by Congress or by local State law.

PRACTICING LAW UNDER THIS SUBPART

Time for Seeking a Seizure Order

A party may move the court for a seizure order under Rule 64 at any time after the federal action is commenced and, then, up until the time of judgment. *Post*-judgment remedies to satisfy a judgment are available under other Rules. *See* Rules 69–70.

Source of the Seizure Remedy

If seizure is permitted by federal statute, those provisions apply in place of any otherwise applicable State law remedy. If no federal statute applies, the pre-judgment seizure remedies available (if any) are those approved under the law of the State where the district court sits.

RULE 64(b) Specific Kinds of Remedies

The types of pre-judgment seizure remedies available in a federal trial court include: arrest, attachment, garnishment, replevin, sequestration, and other "corresponding or equivalent" remedies. Those types are available *if* permitted by Congress or by applicable State law, regardless of how they might be labeled and even if, under State law, a separate, independent action would usually be needed.

PRACTICING LAW UNDER THIS SUBPART

Subject-Matter Jurisdiction

The type of seizure authorized by Rule 64 does not require its own separate, independent basis for federal subject-matter jurisdiction.

Constitutional Limitations

Any seizure of persons or property accomplished under this Rule must also comport with the U.S. Constitution's requirement of due process. *See Connecticut v. Doehr*, 501 U.S. 1, 18 (1991) (finding failure of notice and opportunity to be heard).

Armed Services Personnel

Relief under Rule 64 is subject to the Soldiers' and Sailors' Civil Relief Act of 1940, 50 U.S.C. §§ 203, 204, App. §§ 523, 524, which prohibits seizure of the assets of absent military personnel in many circumstances.

Execution

A plaintiff who obtains in the lawsuit a final judgment is ordinarily entitled to execute on the previously-seized property to satisfy that judgment.

RULE 65

INJUNCTIONS AND RESTRAINING ORDERS

(a) Preliminary Injunction.

(1) *Notice.* The court may issue a preliminary injunction only on notice to the adverse party.

(2) *Consolidating the Hearing with the Trial on the Merits.* Before or after beginning the hearing on a motion for a preliminary injunction, the court may advance the trial on the merits and consolidate it with the hearing. Even when consolidation is not ordered, evidence that is received on the motion and that would be admissible at trial becomes part of the trial record and need not be repeated at trial. But the court must preserve any party's right to a jury trial.

(b) Temporary Restraining Order.

(1) *Issuing Without Notice.* The court may issue a temporary restraining order without written or oral notice to the adverse party or its attorney only if:

(A) specific facts in an affidavit or a verified complaint clearly show that immediate and irreparable injury, loss, or damage will result to the movant before the adverse party can be heard in opposition; and

(B) the movant's attorney certifies in writing any efforts made to give notice and the reasons why it should not be required.

(2) *Contents; Expiration.* Every temporary restraining order issued without notice must state the date and hour it was issued; describe the injury and state why it is irreparable; state why the order was issued without notice; and be promptly filed in the clerk's office and entered in the record. The order expires at the time after entry—not to exceed 14 days—that the court sets, unless before that time the court, for good cause, extends it for a like period or the adverse party consents to a longer extension. The reasons for an extension must be entered in the record.

(3) *Expediting the Preliminary-Injunction Hearing.* If the order is issued without notice, the motion for a preliminary injunction must be set for hearing at the earliest possible time, taking precedence over all other matters except hearings on older matters of the same character. At the hearing, the party who obtained the order must proceed with the motion; if the party does not, the court must dissolve the order.

(4) *Motion to Dissolve.* On 2 days' notice to the party who obtained the order without notice—or on shorter notice set by the court—the adverse party may appear and move to dissolve or modify the order. The court must then hear and decide the motion as promptly as justice requires.

(c) Security. The court may issue a preliminary injunction or a temporary restraining order only if the movant gives security in an amount that the court considers proper to pay the costs and damages sustained by any party found to have been wrongfully enjoined or restrained. The United States, its officers, and its agencies are not required to give security.

(d) Contents and Scope of Every Injunction and Restraining Order.

(1) *Contents.* Every order granting an injunction and every restraining order must:

(A) state the reasons why it issued;

(B) state its terms specifically; and

(C) describe in reasonable detail—and not by referring to the complaint or other document—the act or acts restrained or required.

(2) *Persons Bound.* The order binds only the following who receive actual notice of it by personal service or otherwise:

(A) the parties;

(B) the parties' officers, agents, servants, employees, and attorneys; and

(C) other persons who are in active concert or participation with anyone described in Rule 65(d)(2)(A) or (B).

(e) Other Laws Not Modified. These rules do not modify the following:

(1) any federal statute relating to temporary restraining orders or preliminary injunctions in actions affecting employer and employee;

(2) 28 U.S.C. § 2361, which relates to preliminary injunctions in actions of interpleader or in the nature of interpleader; or

(3) 28 U.S.C. § 2284, which relates to actions that must be heard and decided by a three-judge district court.

(f) Copyright Impoundment. This rule applies to copyright-impoundment proceedings.

[Amended effective March 19, 1948; October 20, 1949; July 1, 1966; August 1, 1987; April 23, 2001, effective December 1, 2001; April 30, 2007, effective December 1, 2007; March 26, 2009, effective December 1, 2009.]

UNDERSTANDING RULE 65

HOW RULE 65 FITS IN

Federal courts are authorized to issue preliminary injunctions and temporary restraining orders ("TRO"s). Neither is a final judgment. Instead, these are "provisional remedies," designed to achieve a particular, pretrial objective.

On occasion, a dispute may arise that simply cannot wait until trial. Indeed, if waiting until trial were required, the harm that would result in the meantime could be irreparable, such that no later court ruling could provide the injured party meaningful relief. Preliminary injunctions and TROs are crafted to reduce the risk of such irreparable harm as a dispute waits its turn in court. These provisional remedies are intended to "freeze" the parties' pre-dispute positions (that is, to maintain the "*status quo ante*") in a way that preserves the court's ability to render meaningful relief if the allegations of the claimant are proven true and actionable at trial.

Consider an example. An employee is hired by a company engaged in technical, highly confidential work. Suppose that company requires new employees to sign an agreement on the date of hiring. Suppose the terms of that agreement require new employees to agree that information they learn in the course of their employment is confidential and will not be shared with third parties. Suppose our employee signed this agreement, then later resigned, took confidential information belonging to the company, accepted a job with a competitor, and began sharing with that competitor his former company's secrets. It seems that employee may have breached the promise made to the company. But if the company files a lawsuit against the employee for theft or conversion and has to wait until the case finally is called for trial (months or maybe years later), the damage the lawsuit feared very well may have already been done. The employee could have already divulged the company's secret information, allowing the competitor to gain a crucial marketplace advantage. In fact, by the time the case ultimately comes to trial, the employee's behavior might have devastated the company or destroyed it entirely. At that point, a court would be hard-pressed to fashion a remedy that would do the company much good. That's where preliminary injunctions and TROs come in. They might, for example, forbid the employee from beginning work with, or even dealing with, the competitor until the court could convene the trial and hear evidence on whether the employee's behavior was proper. *See Basicomputer Corp. v. Scott*, 973 F.2d 507, 511–12 (6th Cir. 1992).

Although preliminary injunctions and TROs both act to "freeze" the parties to their pre-dispute positions, the two procedures differ. Preliminary injunctions may only be granted by the court after notice is given to the adverse party (and, hopefully, after that party has been heard). Temporary restraining orders are often issued more quickly, and may be granted—in certain circumstances—*without* giving notice to the adverse party. But the duration of TROs is very brief: they usually cannot exceed 14 days. In practice, where extreme exigency exists, a claimant (like the employer in the example above) could come to court seeking a TRO first, give the adversary notice *after* the TRO is issued, and then the court could schedule a preliminary injunction hearing for the coming week. There, the employee would be afforded the opportunity to be heard in defense, and might argue to the court why his behavior is not improper. If the court agrees with the employee, the TRO would be "dissolved." If the court agrees with the former employer, the TRO might be replaced with a preliminary injunction which could remain in place until the dispute came up for a full trial on the merits. If, at trial, the former employer prevails, the preliminary injunction could be converted into a *permanent* injunction in the court's final judgment.

THE ARCHITECTURE OF RULE 65

Rule 65 has six subparts, but its organization is easily understood. Subpart (a) sets the procedure for preliminary injunctions. Subpart (b) does the same for temporary restraining orders. Subparts (c), (d), and (f) establishes uniform practices for both types of orders—namely, the court may condition such orders on the moving party first posting security (to protect the adversaries from costs and damages they might suffer during the life of the preliminary injunction or TRO); the court must carefully set out the terms of its order; and the court may issue these orders in copyright impoundment proceedings. Subpart (e) provides that this Rule is not intended to modify other laws set by Congress for the granting of preliminary injunctions or TROs.

HOW RULE 65 WORKS IN PRACTICE

These six subparts of Rule 65 are discussed, in order, below.

RULE 65(a) Preliminary Injunction

The elements a party needs to prove in order to obtain a preliminary injunction are not established in the text of this subpart, but in case law. This subpart authorizes the court to issue preliminary injunctions only on notice to the opponent, and to accelerate and consolidate the trial on the merits of the dispute while it is hearing a preliminary injunction motion (so that the preliminary injunction motion and the merits trial can be considered together).

PRACTICING LAW UNDER THIS SUBPART

Substantive Case Law Requirements for Granting a Preliminary Injunction

The substantive requirements for a preliminary injunction are separate from, and in addition to, the modest procedures set out in this Rule subpart. They are found, instead, in case law, and must be satisfied before a preliminary injunction may issue. *See Grupo Mexicano de Desarrollo S.A. v. Alliance Bond Fund, Inc.*, 527 U.S. 308, 319 (1999). Although the requirements can vary by jurisdiction and type of case, courts generally consider the following factors in deciding whether to grant or deny a motion for a preliminary injunction:

(1) whether the potential harm to the moving party is irreparable (that is, whether the potential harm could be cured through a later award of money damages);

(2) the nature of the harm the opponent would face were the injunction granted;

(3) how others would be affected by the grant or denial of the injunction, including the impact on the public interest; and

(4) whether, in view of its position and evidence, the moving party is likely to succeed on the merits of the claim once the case comes to a full trial.

See Winter v. Natural Resources Defense Council, Inc., 555 U.S. 7, 20 (2008). Applicants for preliminary injunctive relief are generally expected to act with reasonable diligence. *See*

Benisek v. Lamone, 585 U.S. ___, 138 S. Ct. 1942, 1944 (2018). Preliminary injunctions are considered extraordinary remedies; they are not lightly or routinely granted. *See Winter*, 555 U.S. at 22. They are never granted as of right, but are vested in the district judge's equitable discretion. *See Benisek*, 138 S. Ct. at 1943–44. The pertinent inquiry is a highly fact-dependent one, and courts are counseled to mold any injunctive relief they order to meet the necessities of each case. *See Rondeau v. Mosinee Paper Corp.*, 422 U.S. 49, 61–62 (1975).

Applies to *Preliminary* Injunctions Only

By its terms, Rule 65 applies principally to requests for preliminary relief and, with the exception of subpart (d), has no application to grants or denials of *permanent* injunctions.

Notice and Hearing Requirements

The court may not issue a preliminary injunction without notice to the opposing party. The court must also hold a hearing before granting or refusing a preliminary injunction. The scope of the hearing is subject to the discretion of the court.

Consolidation with Trial on the Merits

The court has discretion to consolidate the preliminary injunction hearing with the trial on the merits by accelerating the trial on the court's calendar. If, however, the case on the merits is not yet ripe for trial (such as when discovery is not yet complete), courts will not consolidate the trial with the preliminary injunction hearing.

- *Timing of Order to Consolidate:* The court may order consolidation before or after commencement of the hearing on the preliminary injunction. Courts will not order consolidation unless all parties have adequate warning of the possibility of consolidation and a reasonable opportunity to prepare their positions on the merits. *See University of Texas v. Camenisch,* 451 U.S. 390, 395 (1981).
- *Non-Consolidation and Repetition of Evidence:* If the court does not consolidate the preliminary injunction hearing with the trial on the merits, evidence presented at the preliminary hearing is deemed preserved as part of the record. That evidence need not necessarily be repeated for trial.
- *Preservation of Jury Right:* Consolidation and/or preservation of evidence for trial may not interfere with a party's right to a jury trial. Thus, if the court decides a motion for a preliminary injunction by ruling on issues of fact, evidence presented on those issues of fact is preserved for trial. However, a jury will not be bound by the previous findings of fact made by the judge in the preliminary injunction hearing. *See Camenisch,* 451 U.S. at 395.

Modifying or Dissolving a Preliminary Injunction

A preliminary injunction granted in a case will dissolve upon the entry of a final judgment in that case. Before that time, a preliminary injunction can be modified or dissolved on motion of a party who demonstrates that changed circumstances warrant a change to or end of the injunctive relief. *See United States v. United Shoe Machinery Corp.,* 391 U.S. 244, 248 (1968).

Overlap with Rule 64 (Seizure of Persons or Property)

A preliminary injunction under Rule 65 is usually not available to seize persons or property in order to prevent a dissipation of assets. Instead, such relief must be sought under other laws, such as Rule 64. *See Grupo Mexicano de Desarrollo S.A. v. Alliance Bond Fund, Inc.,* 527 U.S. 308, 330–31 (1999). However, if the lawsuit also seeks equitable relief, the district court may grant a prejudgment injunction that freezes specific assets that are the subject of a restitution or rescission claim or that preserve the power of the court to grant final injunctive relief. *See Deckert v. Independence Shares Corp.,* 311 U.S. 282, 289 (1940).

Appealing an Injunction Order

A court's decision to grant, deny, dissolve, continue, or modify a preliminary injunction (or to refuse to dissolve or modify a preliminary injunction) is immediately appealable of right. *See* 28 U.S.C. § 1292(a)(1).

RULE 65(b) Temporary Restraining Order

Like a preliminary injunction, a temporary restraining order (TRO) is intended to "freeze" circumstances in place until further action can be taken. But these two tools are distinct. TROs may be issued without notice to the opponent, but only after a special showing and only if an expedited preliminary injunction hearing quickly follows. TROs can last only for 14 days (absent consent or good cause for a modest extension), and may be dissolved or modified on motion by the opponent.

PRACTICING LAW UNDER THIS SUBPART

Purpose of a Temporary Restraining Order

When irreparable injury may occur even during the brief period between the filing of the lawsuit and the convening of a preliminary injunction hearing, a TRO may be issued. The purpose of a TRO is to "freeze" the parties in their pre-dispute position until the court has an opportunity to hear a request for a preliminary injunction.

TRO on Notice to Opposing Party

This subpart is concerned principally with TROs issued *without* notice to an adversary, but a with-notice option is available in federal court. Written notice on formal service is the preferred method of giving notice. However, the court has substantial discretion to approve lesser notice. If written notice is impractical, a party seeking a TRO may attempt to notify the adversary orally.

TRO Without Notice to Opposing Party

A TRO issued without first notifying the opponent is permitted but disfavored. Before granting such relief, the court will search the record carefully to satisfy itself that there is a genuine need for such an *ex parte* remedy, and will generally require that the party seeking such relief satisfy all the requirements in this subpart, as well as all substantive case law prerequisites for a preliminary injunction. Thus, to obtain a TRO without providing notice to opposing parties, the moving party must provide proof of irreparable injury and a statement of the efforts made to notify the opposing party or why such notice ought not to be required.

- *Irreparable Injury:* By affidavit or verified complaint, the moving party must demonstrate the irreparable injury that will occur if the TRO is not issued without notice and an opportunity for the opponent to be heard.

  (1) *Affidavit or Verified Complaint:* The quality and detail required in an affidavit or complaint may vary, but the explanation should be sufficient for the court to assess the risk of irreparable injury and the need for prompt action.

  (2) *What Constitutes "Irreparable Injury":* This concept is a flexible, sometimes elusive one. It may exist when the potential loss will be difficult or impossible to calculate (possibly, lost future profits or business reputation). It may also exist when the loss is of a type normally considered incompensable by money (possibly, damage to unique property or land).

- *Statement Concerning Notice to Opponent:* The moving party must also explain in writing the efforts made (if any) to notify the opponent of the TRO hearing and the reasons why the court should not require further notification. The court may treat failure to make reasonable efforts as a ground for denying the motion for a TRO.
- *Contents of a TRO Order Issued Without Notice:* A TRO that is issued without notice must state the date and hour it was issued, must describe the injury found to be irreparable and why it is so, must state why the order was issued without notice to the opponent, and must be promptly filed in the clerk's office and entered on the official court record.

Duration of the TRO

A TRO issued without notice to the opponent must expire no later than 14 days after issuance, unless an extension is allowed by consent from the opponent or, upon good cause, the court extends it for a further period not to exceed an additional 14 days. *See Sampson v. Murray,* 415 U.S. 61, 86–87 (1974). If the court issues such an extension, its reasons for doing so must be memorialized on the record. The court may, of course, set the TRO to expire in a period *less* than 14 days.

Timing of Hearing on Preliminary Injunction Following a TRO

If the court grants a TRO without prior notice to opposing parties, the court must hold a hearing on an ensuing motion for a preliminary injunction "at the earliest possible time." That preliminary injunction hearing must move to the head of the court's docket, second only to other preliminary injunction matters that are already pending.

Failure to Press for a Preliminary Injunction Following a TRO

If, at the scheduled preliminary injunction hearing, a party who obtained a TRO without notice fails to come forward to press for preliminary relief, the court must dissolve the TRO it issued.

Motion to Modify or Dissolve a TRO

Like preliminary injunctions, TROs may be modified or dissolved on motion of a party. A party subject to a TRO issued without notice may move to dissolve or modify the order by providing at least 2 days' notice of a hearing on that motion, unless the court permits less notice. No specific time is prescribed for convening a hearing on a motion to modify or dissolve, though courts are directed to schedule such hearings "as expeditiously as the ends of justice require."

Appealing a TRO

Given its very brief life, a court's decision to grant, deny, modify, continue, or dissolve a temporary restraining order is generally not appealable.

RULE 65(c) Security

Before it may grant a preliminary injunction or temporary restraining order, the court usually must require that the moving party post a bond or other security. That bond or other security would then be available to reimburse the opponent for costs or damages the opponent might incur if it is later determined that the injunction or TRO was wrongfully issued. The amount of the required security lies with the court's discretion. No security may be required from the United States, federal officers, or federal agencies if they are the parties obtaining the injunction or TRO.

PRACTICING LAW UNDER THIS SUBPART

Mandatory (or Optional?) Security

The language of this subpart seems to suggest that the posting of a bond or other security is always required before a federal preliminary injunction or TRO may issue. Courts, however, often tend to treat the security requirement as a matter vested in the issuing court's discretion.

Time for Posting

If a bond or other security is required, it need be posted only when the preliminary injunction or TRO takes effect. Ordinarily, a party need not post security at the time it files its motion seeking such relief.

Amount of Security

The amount of security required is that sum needed (in the court's estimate) to compensate the opponent for that opponent's costs and damages if it is determined that the injunction or TRO was wrongfully issued (and, thus, the opponent wrongfully enjoined). The court has discretion to require posting of a lesser or even nominal amount, if the court finds that a smaller sum would better serve the interests of justice.

- *Increase in Amount of Security:* A party may seek the court to increase the amount of posted security, if that party believes the amount posted will prove insufficient to cover costs and damages. Such a motion may be made at any time the injunction or TRO is in effect (or may be re-imposed).

Definition of "Wrongfully Enjoined or Restrained"

An injunction or TRO may be found "wrongfully" issued if it is later determined that the enjoined party had, at all times, the lawful right to behave as it did.

Costs and Damages Recoverable

A wrongfully enjoined party's maximum recovery is generally limited to the amount of the posted security. *See W.R. Grace & Co. v. Local Union 759, Int'l Union of United Rubber, Cork, Linoleum & Plastic Workers of America,* 461 U.S. 757, 770 (1983). That party may, however, pursue an independent action for malicious prosecution in the unusual cases where the elements of that tort are satisfied. *See Meyers v. Block,* 120 U.S. 206, 211 (1887).

- *Procedure to Obtain Reimbursement:* The process for recovering against posted security is set out in Rule 65.1.

Actions Involving the United States

The United States, its officers, and agencies may not be directed to post security as a condition of receiving a preliminary injunction or TRO. *See* 28 U.S.C. § 2408.

A "*Non*-Injunction" Bond

One prerequisite for a preliminary injunction or TRO is that the harm facing the moving party must be "irreparable." *See* Commentary to Rule 65(a). "Irreparability" might be shown by demonstrating that the opponent would be unable to pay money damages to the moving party and, thus, that the only real, practical available remedy is an injunctive one. Some courts permit the opponent to defeat this argument (and, thus, avoid being enjoined) by posting a "non-injunction" bond that could demonstrate—to both the moving party and the court—that the opponent does indeed have adequate resources to pay any resulting judgment (and, thus, that no "irreparability" exists). *See Lakeview Tech., Inc. v. Robinson,* 446 F.3d 655, 658 (7th Cir. 2006).

RULE 65(d) Contents and Scope of Every Injunction and Restraining Order

Injunctions and restraining orders compel a party to behave in a certain manner, to do something or to refrain from doing something. Because such orders are intended to modify a party's behavior over that party's objections, the crafting and precision of the language of the injunction or restraining order becomes especially important. This subpart prescribes the required content of every injunction or restraining order, and identifies those whom it will bind.

PRACTICING LAW UNDER THIS SUBPART

Required Content—Reasons for Issuance

The injunction or restraining order must contain an explanation of the reasons why it was issued (though a failure to provide such an explanation might not, alone, compel a reversal). Elaborate detail is not necessary. Instead, an adequate explanation is one that states specifically the facts found by the court and the conclusions of law it reached.

- *Findings and Conclusions:* Alongside the requirements of this subpart, district courts must make findings of fact and conclusions of law when granting or denying a request for an interlocutory injunction. *See* Rule 52(a).

Required Content—Specific Terms

The injunction or restraining order must also be framed in specific terms, a requirement intended to ensure that court's mandate is readily understood, easily obeyed, and effectively enforced. *See Schmidt v. Lessard,* 414 U.S. 473, 476 (1974).

Required Content—Reasonably Detailed Description of Acts Restrained or Required

The court's injunction or restraining order must describe the required or prohibited acts with sufficient detail and clarity that a layperson who is bound by the order can tell what is allowed and what is forbidden. Courts will ordinarily not use highly technical language unless there is no other way to describe the impacted acts (and only then if the parties affected are likely to understand that jargon). The court's order also must be written, not oral.

- *Incorporation By Reference:* The required or prohibited acts may not be described by referring the reader to the complaint or other document (though some courts permit such cross-referencing if the referred-to document is physically attached to the court's order).
- *Request for Clarification:* A party who is uncertain as to the scope or directive of the court's order may petition the issuing court for clarification. Whether to issue such a clarification lies within the court's discretion. *See Regal Knitwear Co. v. NLRB,* 324 U.S. 9, 15 (1945).

Persons Bound by Order

Only the following persons are bound by the terms of an injunction or restraining order: (1) the parties; (2) the parties' officers, agents, servants, employees, and attorneys; and (3) other persons "in active concert or participation" with parties. *See Regal Knitwear Co. v. N.L.R.B.,* 324 U.S. 9, 15–16 (1945).

- *Notice Required:* No one is bound by an injunction or TRO unless and until that person receives fair notice of the order. However, formal notice in the form of service of process is not necessarily required to bind a party or those in privity with a party. A party or a person in a close relationship with a party may be bound if they simply have actual knowledge of the order. *See Spallone v. United States,* 493 U.S. 265, 276 (1990).

- *Personal Jurisdiction Needed:* Persons outside the jurisdiction of the court might not be subject to its order.
- *Persons in "Active Concert or Participation":* The court's order binds not only the parties themselves but also those who are in privity with those parties, who are "identified with them in interest," who are represented by them, and who are subject to their control. *See Golden State Bottling Co. v. NLRB,* 414 U.S. 168, 169 (1973). Thus, the objective of this "active concert or participation" language is to ensure that the bound parties do not undermine the order's mandate by having others carry out the prohibited acts on their behalf. *See Regal Knitwear Co. v. N.L.R.B.,* 324 U.S. 9, 14 (1945). The court's order can bind any unnamed member of a group that is subject to an injunction or TRO, provided that the group is sufficiently identified. Ordinarily, non-parties will not be bound by such an order unless they are given *actual* notice of that order and unless the prerequisites for constitutional standing (including traceability and redressability) are present.
- *Successors In Office:* An injunction against a public official also binds successors in office. *See also* Rule 25(d).

Disobeying the Injunction or TRO

Persons bound by an injunction or TRO who disobey its command are subject to the court's power of contempt. *See Gunn v. University Committee to End War in Viet Nam,* 399 U.S. 383, 389 (1970).

Applicability to *Permanent* Injunctions

Unlike other provisions of Rule 65, the provisions of this subpart ordinarily apply with equal force to permanent injunctions.

RULE 65(e) Other Laws Not Modified

Congress has enacted other federal laws that authorize injunctions and restraining orders. Those other, context-specific statutes (and the requirements they set) are not modified by the provisions of Rule 65.

RULE 65(f) Copyright Impoundment

Preliminary injunctions and TROs under this Rule 65 may be used in copyright impoundment proceedings, where the court orders the seizure and impounding of alleging infringing materials.

RULE 65.1

PROCEEDINGS AGAINST A SECURITY PROVIDER

Whenever these rules (including the Supplemental Rules for Admiralty or Maritime Claims and Asset Forfeiture Actions) require or allow a party to give security, and security is given with one or more security providers, each provider submits to the court's jurisdiction and irrevocably appoints the court clerk as its agent for receiving service of any papers that affect its liability on the security. The security provider's liability may be enforced on motion without an independent action. The motion and any notice that the court orders may be served on the court clerk, who must promptly send a copy of each to every security provider whose address is known.

[Added effective July 1, 1966; amended effective August 1, 1987; April 12, 2006, effective December 1, 2006; April 30, 2007, effective December 1, 2007; April 26, 2018, effective December 1, 2018.]

UNDERSTANDING RULE 65.1

HOW RULE 65.1 FITS IN

A security provider is a person or entity (often, a bonding company) who agrees to pay money or perform some other act if the client (the principal) fails to do so. For example, a security provider may issue a bond on behalf of a losing litigant to suspend execution and enforcement proceedings while that litigant's post-trial motions are being decided or while its appeal is pending (*see* Rule 62). Or a security provider may issue a bond on behalf of a litigant who has sought and obtained a preliminary injunction or temporary restraining order (*see* Rule 65(c)). These sorts of bonds act as protection for opponents. The bond amounts are there to ensure that assets are available against which opponents will collect on a judgment if post-trial motions or appeals are denied (and the losing litigant then fails to pay its obligation), or to supply reimbursement to opponents who suffer a loss due to a preliminary injunction or TRO that was wrongfully issued.

This Rule establishes an accelerated procedure for enforcing a principal's obligation against the posted bond or other security. The Rule thus hastens the opponent's access to the monies posted as security.

THE ARCHITECTURE OF RULE 65.1

Rule 65.1 is a single paragraph long. It commits security providers to the jurisdiction of the court, appoints the court's clerk as their agent for service of process, and permits enforcement against their bonds or other security without the need for the filing of an independent action.

HOW RULE 65.1 WORKS IN PRACTICE

Right to Collect Against a Security Provider

This Rule does not determine whether a party is entitled to enforce an obligation against a security provider's bond or other security; instead, that right is determined by the particular law that created the need for the security. For example, a party who was wrongfully enjoined under Rule 65 by a preliminary injunction or temporary restraining order often enjoys a rebuttal presumption in favor of recovering provable damages caused by that wrongful restraint, and that recovery can be accomplished against the bond or other security.

Alternative Procedures

Enforcement under this Rule is not the only means by which a party can seek to collect against a bond or other security. A party may instead file an independent action against the security provider in a State or federal court.

Motion for Judgment on the Bond or Other Security

The method for seeking to enforce an obligation against the security provider's bond or other security is a motion for judgment on the bond (or other security).

- *Time for Filing:* Generally, a party may seek recovery under this Rule once the court has adjudicated or altered the relief that the bond or other security secured (such as, for example, ruling that an injunction was wrongfully issued).
- *Consent to Personal Jurisdiction:* A security provider who posts a bond or other security is deemed as having submitted to the personal jurisdiction of the court for the purposes of litigating liability under that bond or other security.
- *Notice:* The security provider also is deemed as having appointed the clerk of court as its agent to receive service of process in matters relating to liability on the bond. The clerk will mail (or otherwise transmit, as the court may order) copies of the documents to all affected security providers whose addresses are known.
- *Subject-Matter Jurisdiction:* If a party seeks in the original action to collect against a bond or other security under this Rule, subject-matter jurisdiction will exist. Alternatively, if the party seeks to enforce against a bond or other security by filing an independent action, the court will have subject-matter jurisdiction under 28 U.S.C. § 1352.

Injunction Staying Enforcement

If a court enjoins proceedings against the bond or other security, that prohibition must be obeyed until it is modified or revoked. *See Celotex Corp. v. Edwards,* 514 U.S. 300, 306–07 (1995).

Collecting from the Principals

Although this Rule addresses the means by which a party may seek enforcement against a security provider's bond or other security, courts also permit use of this Rule for motions seeking similar relief against the provider's principal.

RULE 66

RECEIVERS

These rules govern an action in which the appointment of a receiver is sought or a receiver sues or is sued. But the practice in administering an estate by a receiver or a similar court-appointed officer must accord with the historical practice in federal courts or with a local rule. An action in which a receiver has been appointed may be dismissed only by court order.

[Amended effective March 19, 1948; October 20, 1949; April 30, 2007, effective December 1, 2007.]

UNDERSTANDING RULE 66

HOW RULE 66 FITS IN

A "receiver" is someone appointed by the court to take temporary custody of, and then work to preserve, property or other assets pending the outcome of some court proceeding. Typically, a receiver is appointed by the court when property or some other asset is being contested in litigation and the court is persuaded that the property or asset is in imminent danger of being lost, concealed, removed, diminished, or otherwise damaged. The purpose of a receivership—like preliminary injunctions and temporary restraining orders—is to preserve the parties' pre-dispute positions (the "*status quo ante*") while the court ponders the merits of an underlying fight.

Consider, for example, an automobile dealership that is owned by a family partnership. The family disagrees on what to do with their shared business. Some of the family partners (those who live nearby and operate it daily) want to close the business and sell all its assets. Other family partners (those who live faraway and play no role in its day-to-day operations) want to keep the business open and have it continue to operate. The local partners begin to sell all the automobiles that the dealership owns at drastically-reduced prices to quickly clear the lot. If this tactic is not interrupted, the faraway partners could have no meaningful remedy later—the business and its assets will have already been lost. To avoid that risk, the faraway partners might sue in federal court and request the appointment of a receiver, who would take custody of the business's assets and protect them while the court sorts through how best to resolve the family's squabble.

A receivership is not an end in itself. Rather, it is an ancillary or auxiliary remedy (like preliminary injunctions and TROs) designed to help ensure that the court is able to render meaningful relief on the underlying merits of the dispute. *See Gordon v. Washington,* 295 U.S. 30, 37 n.4 (1935).

THE ARCHITECTURE OF RULE 66

Rule 66 contains only three sentences. The first sentence confirms that the Federal Rules of Civil Procedure apply in lawsuits seeking the appointment of a receiver and in lawsuits where that appointed receiver sues or is sued. The second sentence directs that the receiver's work must comport with "the historical practice in federal courts" or with any locally-applicable rule. The third sentence requires a court order before receivership actions may be dismissed.

HOW RULE 66 WORKS IN PRACTICE

Role of Federal Equity Receivers

Receivership is justified only in extreme circumstances. It is not a substantive entitlement, but an ancillary remedy used to facilitate the primary relief sought in a lawsuit. Acting as equity tribunals, federal courts have broad discretion and powers to determine relief in an equity receivership. They appoint equity receivers to assume custody, control, and management of property that either is presently involved or is likely to become involved in litigation. The receiver is charged to preserve the property, and any rents or profits the property earns, until a final disposition by the court. Although typically appointed only to care for property, a federal equity receiver may be appointed where other, extraordinary circumstances compel intimate judicial supervision. *See Gordon v. Washington*, 295 U.S. 30, 37 (1935). *See also Morgan v. McDonough,* 540 F.2d 527, 534 (1st Cir. 1976) (appointment of federal receiver for public high school to implement desegregation orders).

- *Officer of the Court:* An equity receiver is deemed to be an officer of the court, not the agent of any litigant.

Controlling Law—Federal Rules for Appointment and Lawsuits

The Rules govern all actions in which a party seeks the appointment of a federal equity receiver, as well as all actions brought by or against the receiver once appointed.

Controlling Law—Historical Practice / Local Rules for Administration

Traditional federal practice and, where promulgated, local court rules guide a federal equity receiver in administering the receivership property. Although broad, the receiver's power is not unbridled; it does not necessarily extend to every conceivable claim relating to the receivership property. The substantive law of the State in which the receivership property is located dictates the manner in which the receiver must manage and operate the receivership property.

- *Federal Bankruptcy Principles:* Because bankruptcy and equity receivers share a common purpose and legal heritage, courts often consult bankruptcy principles in receivership contexts.

Appointing Receivers

Rule 66 does not create a substantive right to the appointment of a receiver; a statute or general principle of equity must first justify the appointment. Federal law controls whether an equity receiver should be appointed, even in a diversity case. Absent explicit consent from the defendant, the plaintiff ordinarily bears the burden of showing that a receiver should be appointed.

- *Judge's Discretion:* Whether to appoint a receiver lies within the district judge's discretion.
- *Who May Seek That A Receiver Be Appointed:* The appointment of a receiver may be requested by any person having a legally recognized right to the property—a mere interest or claim to the property will not be sufficient. Receivers are appointed frequently at the request of secured creditors, mortgagees, judgment creditors, and plaintiffs in shareholder derivative actions.

- *Who May Be Appointed As The Receiver:* The court may appoint as the receiver any person deemed capable of serving in that capacity. Ordinarily, this requires the appointment of someone who is indifferent between the parties. Federal law prevents the judge from appointing as a receiver any person related to the judge by consanguinity within the fourth degree, a clerk or deputy of the court (absent special circumstances), or a federal employee or person employed by the appointing judge.
- *Prerequisites for Appointment:* The appointment of a receiver is an extraordinary remedy, available only upon a clear showing that no remedy at law is available or adequate, and that a receivership is essential to protect the property from some threatened loss or injury pending a final disposition by the court. *See Gordon v. Washington,* 295 U.S. 30, 39 (1935). Although no precise formula exists for assessing whether a receiver ought to be appointed, the courts consider various factors, including:
    - the existence of a valid claim by the party seeking the appointment;
    - the imminent nature of any danger to the property, to its concealment or removal, or to its value;
    - the adequacy of other legal remedies;
    - the lack of a less drastic equitable remedy;
    - the plaintiff's probable success in the lawsuit and the risk of irreparable injury to the property;
    - whether the defendant has engaged, or may engage, in any fraudulent actions with respect to the property;
    - the likelihood that appointing the receiver will do more good than harm; *and*
    - whether the potential harm to the plaintiff outweighs the injury to others.

Generally, each factor need not be satisfied, so long as the court determines that its review favors the receiver's appointment.

Consent to Appointment

The court may appoint a receiver where the defendant both admits liability for the claim asserted in the litigation and consents to the appointment of a receiver—provided that there has been no improper attempt by the parties to collusively manufacture federal jurisdiction. *See In re Reisenberg,* 208 U.S. 90, 110 (1908).

Place of Appointment

Because the appointment of a receiver is a type of *in rem* proceeding, the appointing court must enjoy a strong relationship to the contemplated receivership: a substantial portion of the defendant's business must be conducted in the host district, or a substantial portion of the anticipated receivership property must be located within the host district.

Notice of Appointment

Generally, the court gives notice to all parties before appointing an equity receiver. But where notice is impractical or self-defeating, or where the appointment must be made immediately, the court enjoys the power to appoint a receiver *ex parte.*

Effect of Appointment

Once a receiver is appointed and gives the bond required by the court, the court and the receiver obtain exclusive jurisdiction of all of the defendant's property, no matter where it is kept. To obtain such jurisdiction over property outside the appointing district, the receiver must first file a copy of the complaint and appointment order in that foreign district. The fees and expenses of receivership are normally a charge against the administered property.

Actions by Receivers

A federal equity receiver is authorized to commence and prosecute any action necessary to accomplish the objectives of the receivership. The receiver may be directed to bring suit on specific instructions from the court, or the receiver may independently institute lawsuits pursuant to the receiver's general duties of receiving, controlling, and managing the receivership property. But a receiver's standing to sue is limited to redressing injuries to the entity in receivership.

- *May Sue in Any Jurisdiction:* The receiver may bring suit in any federal district, including those districts outside the court in which the receiver was formally appointed. *See* 28 U.S.C. § 754.

Actions Against Receivers

A person may often sue an equity receiver, without leave of court, for any of the receiver's actions taken after the receiver was appointed and during the receiver's management and operation of the receivership property. *See* 28 U.S.C. § 959(a). The receiver also has discretion to settle contested claims against receivership assets, provided those settlements are fair, equitable, and in the estate's best interest. Ordinarily, receivers cannot be held personally liable for their obligations, liabilities, and missteps. *See McNulta v. Lochridge*, 141 U.S. 327, 332 (1891).

- *Leave of Court Needed:* Leave of court is required before the receiver may be sued for claims that arise from the property owner's actions or for claims that do not challenge the receiver's actions since appointment. *See Barton v. Barbour,* 104 U.S. 126, 128 (1881). To protect the assets (and to avoid their diminution by the costs of defending lawsuits), the receivership court may issue a blanket injunction staying all litigation against the receiver and entities under the receiver's control. Although claimants are entitled to have their claims heard, the court enjoys broad control over the time and manner of those proceedings. Intentionally interfering with a receivership in violation of such an injunction is punishable as contempt.
- *Subject to Court's General Equity Power:* Suits against receivers remain subject to the court's general equity powers, which the court may exercise to achieve the ends of justice.

Subject-Matter Jurisdiction in Actions Involving Receivers

Receivers may only sue or be sued when the district court would enjoy subject-matter jurisdiction over the dispute.

- *Diversity Cases:* In diversity jurisdiction cases, the citizenship of the appointed receiver is examined to determine whether complete diversity exists.
- *Federal Question Cases:* The district court's act of appointing a federal receiver probably will suffice to vest that district court with subject-matter jurisdiction over actions brought by or against the receiver in that district. *See Gay v. Ruff,* 292 U.S. 25, 35 (1934). Thus, when instituted in the appointing district, suits by the receiver intended to accomplish the objectives of the receivership are deemed ancillary to the appointing court's subject-matter jurisdiction. *See Pope v. Louisville, N.A. & C. Ry. Co.,* 173 U.S. 573, 577 (1899). Likewise, suits may be maintained against the receiver in the receiver's appointing district even though no independent basis for subject-matter jurisdiction is present. *See Rouse v. Hornsby,* 161 U.S. 588, 590 (1896).

- *Outside Appointing District:* Suits by or against receivers instituted outside the appointing district will generally require an independent basis for federal subject-matter jurisdiction.

Dismissal of Actions Involving Receivers

After the court appoints a receiver in a litigation, the parties may not thereafter dismiss the litigation without first obtaining the court's approval. This requirement protects against a waste of the court's time in unnecessarily establishing a receivership.

Vacating or Terminating the Receivership

The district court may vacate the order appointing the receiver or terminate the receivership when the objectives of the receivership have been obtained or the need for the receiver has abated, or when the receiver was found to be improper in the first place.

Appeals

The district court's decision to appoint a receiver may be immediately appealed. *See* 28 U.S.C. § 1292(a)(2). The court of appeals will review the appointment under the lenient abuse of discretion standard. If the appointment is found to have been improvident, the court of appeals may reverse and tax the costs and expenses incurred in the receivership on the persons who procured the receivership.

Orders refusing to wind up the receivership or that otherwise have the effect of either ousting persons from their property or injuring the property may also be immediately appealed.

All other orders involving receivers may only be appealed after entry of a final order.

RULE 67

DEPOSIT INTO COURT

(a) Depositing Property. If any part of the relief sought is a money judgment or the disposition of a sum of money or some other deliverable thing, a party—on notice to every other party and by leave of court—may deposit with the court all or part of the money or thing, whether or not that party claims any of it. The depositing party must deliver to the clerk a copy of the order permitting deposit.

(b) Investing and Withdrawing Funds. Money paid into court under this rule must be deposited and withdrawn in accordance with 28 U.S.C. §§ 2041 and 2042 and any like statute. The money must be deposited in an interest-bearing account or invested in a court-approved, interest-bearing instrument.

[Amended effective October 20, 1949; August 1, 1983; April 30, 2007, effective December 1, 2007.]

UNDERSTANDING RULE 67

HOW RULE 67 FITS IN

Parties may sometimes want to (or be obligated to) deposit money or property with the court. For example, they may do so when a lawsuit contests title to certain money or other property, and the deposit is made to keep the asset safe during the litigation. They might do so to limit their exposure to interest on claims while the lawsuit is proceeding. Or they may be required to do so by law, such as where stakeholders are obligated to deposit their "stake" with the court as a precondition for seeking statutory interpleader. *See* 28 U.S.C. § 1335(a)(1). In any event, Rule 67 sets the procedure for making such a deposit into the court and establishes the requirements for investing and withdrawing funds following such a court deposit.

THE ARCHITECTURE OF RULE 67

Rule 67 has just two subparts. The first subpart sets the procedure for making the deposit into court. The second subpart sets the requirements for investing and withdrawing those funds.

HOW RULE 67 WORKS IN PRACTICE

These two subparts of Rule 67 are discussed, in order, below.

RULE 67(a) Depositing Property

A deposit of money or other property under Rule 67 is proper only if the underlying lawsuit (a) seeks money as at least part of the requested relief or (b) seeks title to money or "some other deliverable thing."

PRACTICING LAW UNDER THIS SUBPART

Court Order and Notice Required

Deposits may only be made with leave of court, on motion, and with notice to all other parties.

Motion to Seek Right to Make a Deposit

In a motion seeking permission to make a deposit under this Rule, the moving party must establish for the court (a) that the ownership of the asset to be deposited is contested and (b) that the amount of the disputed asset is a sum-certain. Thus, the court must be persuaded that the asset is subject to inconsistent claims; if there is only a single claim, this Rule is not applicable. The motion should also state the particular reasons for making the deposit (such as, for example, to avoid further responsibility for the deposited asset).

- *Motion by Holder:* This Rule authorizes holders of an asset to seek to make a court deposit. It does not, however, authorize others to seek an order compelling such a deposit from someone else.
- *Time for Making the Motion:* Such a motion may be made at any time during the life of the lawsuit.
- *Serving Clerk with Order:* If the court grants the motion, the moving party must serve the order on the clerk of court at the time of making the deposit.

Effect of Deposit

This Rule creates a place of safekeeping for money or other property; it does not, however, provide a forum for adjudicating the parties' legal rights or duties.

RULE 67(b) Investing and Withdrawing Funds

Court deposits are made with the Treasurer of the United States, and are placed in an interest-bearing account or a court-approved, interest-bearing instrument. Withdrawals may be made only upon court order.

PRACTICING LAW UNDER THIS SUBPART

Interest-Bearing Account

The clerk of court must invest any money paid into the court in an interest-bearing account or in an interest-bearing instrument approved by the court in the name and to the credit of the court. *See* 28 U.S.C. § 2041.

Withdrawal of Deposit

A withdrawal from the deposit may be made by one upon motion to the court and notice to the U.S. Attorney, along with "full proof of the right thereto." *See* 28 U.S.C. § 2042. The court may, thereupon, issue an order permitting the withdrawal. No money deposited with the court may be withdrawn without such a court order.

Unclaimed Deposits

Once the right to withdraw the deposit has been adjudicated or is no longer in dispute, the withdrawal must occur within 5 years. If no withdrawal is made during that period, the deposited asset will be deemed forfeited and credited to the United States. *See* 28 U.S.C. § 2042.

RULE 68

OFFER OF JUDGMENT

(a) Making an Offer; Judgment on an Accepted Offer. At least 14 days before the date set for trial, a party defending against a claim may serve on an opposing party an offer to allow judgment on specified terms, with the costs then accrued. If, within 14 days after being served, the opposing party serves written notice accepting the offer, either party may then file the offer and notice of acceptance, plus proof of service. The clerk must then enter judgment.

(b) Unaccepted Offer. An unaccepted offer is considered withdrawn, but it does not preclude a later offer. Evidence of an unaccepted offer is not admissible except in a proceeding to determine costs.

(c) Offer After Liability Is Determined. When one party's liability to another has been determined but the extent of liability remains to be determined by further proceedings, the party held liable may make an offer of judgment. It must be served within a reasonable time—but at least 14 days—before the date set for a hearing to determine the extent of liability.

(d) Paying Costs After an Unaccepted Offer. If the judgment that the offeree finally obtains is not more favorable than the unaccepted offer, the offeree must pay the costs incurred after the offer was made.

[Amended effective March 19, 1948; July 1, 1966; August 1, 1987; April 30, 2007, effective December 1, 2007; March 26, 2009, effective December 1, 2009.]

UNDERSTANDING RULE 68

HOW RULE 68 FITS IN

Rule 68 was intended to encourage settlements. *See Marek v. Chesny*, 473 U.S. 1, 5 (1985); *Delta Air Lines, Inc. v. August*, 450 U.S. 346, 352 (1981). It permits a defending party to make a proposal to the claimant to resolve a federal civil lawsuit on certain specified terms. The claimant then has 14 days to accept the offer. If the claimant fails to do so, and if, later, that claimant obtains a judgment equal to or less than the offer that was declined, the claimant must pay the costs the defending party incurred from the day the offer was made onward. For purposes of this Rule, "costs" generally do not include attorney's fees or damages (but, instead, usually only a narrower range of recoverable expenses set by Congress). Certain statutes may define "costs" more expansively. But, in most cases, practitioners find that the laudable goal of encouraging settlements is not frequently achieved by Rule 68's operation. The threat of a Rule 68 cost-shift is often not especially settlement-enticing because the size of the shiftable costs is often not that imposing.

One important clarification is necessary in understanding Rule 68 practice. Ordinary offers to settle a lawsuit do not fall within the scope of Rule 68. Settlements of lawsuits can occur in many ways, and often result in the lawsuit being voluntarily dismissed (without any finding of liability or any resulting, enforceable judgment). Rule 68 is different. It is a proposal by a defending party that it—the defending party—will actually *agree* to the *entry of judgment against it*, in accordance with the terms proposed. If accepted, the claimant will have obtained a judgment against the defending party. If it is not accepted, the claimant may suffer the financial consequences described above. In these ways, Rule 68 is quite distinct from a routine litigation settlement proposal.

THE ARCHITECTURE OF RULE 68

Rule 68 has four subparts. Subpart (a) sets the procedures for making and accepting an offer of judgment. Subpart (b) allows for offers to be declined (expressly or impliedly), permits multiple offers, and precludes (in most settings) the admission at trial of evidence that an offer was made. Subpart (c) approves the use of this procedure in bifurcated trials, where the issue of liability will be tried first, followed later by a hearing on damages or other extent of liability. Subpart (d) sets the consequence of an unaccepted offer.

HOW RULE 68 WORKS IN PRACTICE

These four subparts of Rule 68 are discussed, in order, below.

RULE 68(a) Making an Offer; Judgment on an Accepted Offer

Only *defending* parties may make a Rule 68 offer. Such offers must be made no later than 14 days before trial. The offer must propose specific terms on which defending parties will consent to allow a judgment to be entered against them. If the claimant accepts, then the offer, the acceptance, and proof-of-service are all filed with the court. The clerk will then enter judgment.

PRACTICING LAW UNDER THIS SUBPART

Offering a Judgment

The appropriate method of offering a Rule 68 judgment is to serve upon the claimant a written offer.

- *Offer to Multiple Claimants:* If an offer is made to multiple claimants, it must specify the proposed payment to each. If it fails to do so, it might not qualify for a cost-shift under this Rule.
- *Offer from Multiple Defendants:* If multiple defending parties collaborate in making an offer, the respective apportionment of the offered sum should be clear. Otherwise, if one or more of the offering parties is excused from the case, it may be difficult for the remaining offerors to prove that *their* offer was sufficient to trigger a cost-shift under this Rule.

- *Offers by Plaintiff:* Unless they are a defending party on a counterclaim, a crossclaim, or otherwise (*see* Rule 13 & 14), plaintiffs cannot make a Rule 68 offer of judgment. *See Delta Air Lines, Inc. v. August,* 450 U.S. 346, 350 & n.5 (1981).
- *Non-Rule 68 Offers:* As noted earlier, Rule 68 authorizes a special *type* of settlement offer. Parties are always permitted to propose to one another a resolution of their dispute outside the context of Rule 68.

Contents of Offer

A proper Rule 68 offer must propose to accept entry of judgment for a certain amount (or specific property) along with "the costs then accrued." In construing the terms of an offer, ordinary rules of contract law (such as ambiguities construed against the drafter) will apply.

- *Non-Money Claims:* Although it is used principally for claims seeking money or specific property, Rule 68 might be available in equity cases.
- *What Are "Costs"?* The term "costs" is generally understood to mean only those certain categories of expenses that Congress has enumerated as "taxable" under 28 U.S.C. § 1920, unless the substantive law applicable to the claims in the lawsuit prescribe further items of "costs." *See Scottsdale Ins. Co. v. Tolliver*, 636 F.3d 1273, 1278 n.7 (10th Cir. 2011).
- *Including Costs:* An offer can meet the requirement of including costs by itemizing them specifically or with a general recital that costs are included.
- *Attorney's Fees/Other Expenses as "Costs":* If the substantive law underlying the cause of action includes attorney's fees (or other items of expenses) as "costs," then those categories may be considered "costs" for Rule 68 purposes. *See Marek v. Chesny,* 473 U.S. 1, 8–9 (1985).

Timing of Offer

To be effective, a Rule 68 offer of judgment must be served on the party prosecuting a claim at least 14 days before the date set for the beginning of a trial. (If the trial is bifurcated, the time for offering may be governed by subpart (c) of this Rule.)

Revoking an Offer Once Made

Except in exceptional circumstances, a Rule 68 offer cannot be revoked during the 14-day acceptance period.

Time for Accepting an Offer

The claimant has 14 days to accept the offer. Failure to do so will result in the offer being deemed withdrawn. *See* Rule 68(b).

Method of Accepting an Offer

The appropriate method for accepting an offer of judgment is by written notice of acceptance delivered to the party who made the offer. The offer must be accepted in its entirety, or it is deemed rejected.

Entering Final Judgment on an Accepted Offer

If the claimant accepts the offer of judgment, either party may file the offer and notice of acceptance, along with proof of service, with the clerk of court. (Offers are not filed unless and until they are accepted.) The clerk then will enter judgment consistent with the offer and acceptance.

RULE 68(b) Unaccepted Offer

A Rule 68 offer of judgment that is not accepted is deemed withdrawn (though the defending party may make a subsequent offer at some later time). Unaccepted offers are not admissible in court, except to determine costs or to challenge subject-matter jurisdiction.

PRACTICING LAW UNDER THIS SUBPART

Timely Acceptance, or Deemed Withdrawal

As noted above, a claimant has 14 days after receipt of service of the written offer to accept the offer of judgment. If the offer is not accepted within that period, the offer is treated as withdrawn.

New Offers Following a Deemed Withdrawal (or Rejection)

Following a deemed-withdrawal of the offer (with the passing of 14 days) or an outright rejection of the offer, the offering party may renew the offer, or make a different offer, in which event a fresh 14-day period for acceptance begins to run.

When the Claimant Refuses to Accept an Offer for the *Full Amount* of a Claim

It may seem unusual, but a claimant might reject (or fail to accept) an offer of judgment proposing to resolve the dispute for precisely what the pleader seeks—the full value of the claim. The effect of such a non-acceptance had, for many years, been unclear. In 2016, the U.S. Supreme Court resolved the uncertainty: an unaccepted Rule 68 offer "has no force," no matter how good the offer is. *See Campbell-Ewald Co. v. Gomez*, 577 U.S. 153, 156 (2016) ("Like other unaccepted contract offers, it creates no lasting right or obligation. With the offer off the table, and the defendant's continuing denial of liability, adversity between the parties persists."). *But cf. id.* at 166 ("We need not . . . now decide whether the result would be different if a defendant deposits the full amount of the plaintiff's individual claim in an account payable to the plaintiff, and the court then enters judgment for the plaintiff in that amount.").

Admissibility of Evidence of an Offer of Judgment

If an offer of judgment is not accepted, the offer may not be used as evidence at trial. The only use to which a nonaccepted offer of judgment may be put is to determine costs, in the event that costs are shifted under subpart (d) of this Rule.

RULE 68(c) Offer After Liability Is Determined

Subpart (a) instructs that offers of judgment must be made at least 14 days before trial. When the trial is bifurcated, such that liability issues are determined first and, if needed, damages (or other extent of liability) resolved in a separate, subsequent proceeding, a "later" Rule 68 offer can be made. In such a circumstance, an offer is timely if made no less than 14 days before the damages (or extent of liability) phase of the trial is set to start.

RULE 68(d) Paying Costs After an Unaccepted Offer

A claimant need not accept an offer of judgment made by the defending party. However, if the claimant obtains a later judgment that is "not more favorable" than the declined offer—that is, if it is equal to or less than what was offered—the claimant must pay the recoverable costs the defending party incurred during the period after the offer was made.

PRACTICING LAW UNDER THIS SUBPART

Consequences of Nonacceptance

The consequences of not accepting a Rule 68 offer will depend on the outcome of the litigation:

- *Claimant Wins More than Amount Offered:* If the nonaccepting claimant won a judgment greater than the amount in the offer of judgment, the unaccepted offer has no consequence. Costs are awarded normally.
- *Claimant Wins an Amount Equal to or Lesser than Amount Offered:* If the nonaccepting claimant won a favorable final judgment, but one only equal to or less than the amount in the offer of judgment, the nonaccepting claimant party must pay the costs the offering party incurred after it made the offer. (Thus, a party that made an offer of judgment, and still lost the case, could still recover costs from the prevailing party.) The category of recoverable costs is discussed above. *See* Rule 68(a) ("*What Are 'Costs'?*").
- *Claimant Loses:* If the nonaccepting claimant loses the case, Rule 68 oddly has no effect. By its terms, the cost-shift granted by this subpart is triggered only when the claimant wins a judgment, but an equal or less favorable one. *See Delta Air Lines, Inc. v. August,* 450 U.S. 346, 352 (1981).

Attorney's Fees

Some federal laws (such as federal civil rights laws) provide for prevailing parties (*i.e.,* two-way cost shifting) or just prevailing plaintiffs (*i.e.,* one-way cost shifting) to recover their attorney's fees as part of recoverable costs. *See* 42 U.S.C. § 1988. With two-way cost-shifting statutes, the cost provisions for offers of judgment will apply in full to attorney's fees. *See Marek v. Chesny,* 473 U.S. 1, 8–9 (1985). With one-way cost-shifting statutes, the cost-shifting provisions for offers of judgment do not entitle a defendant to recover its attorney's fees after an unaccepted offer, but they do end the plaintiff's right to recover attorney's fees.

Determining Whether Judgment Is "More Favorable"

In cases involving only money damages, it is usually not difficult to calculate whether the judgment a party won is more favorable than an earlier offer of judgment. However, where a party obtains an injunction as part of a favorable judgment, the value of an injunction should be included in the calculation in determining whether a judgment is more favorable than an earlier offer of judgment.

RULE 69

EXECUTION

(a) In General.

(1) *Money Judgment; Applicable Procedure.* A money judgment is enforced by a writ of execution, unless the court directs otherwise. The procedure on execution—and in proceedings supplementary to and in aid of judgment or execution—must accord with the procedure of the State where the court is located, but a federal statute governs to the extent it applies.

(2) *Obtaining Discovery.* In aid of the judgment or execution, the judgment creditor or a successor in interest whose interest appears of record may obtain discovery from any person—including the judgment debtor—as provided in these rules or by the procedure of the State where the court is located.

(b) Against Certain Public Officers. When a judgment has been entered against a revenue officer in the circumstances stated in 28 U.S.C. § 2006, or against an officer of Congress in the circumstances stated in 2 U.S.C. § 118, the judgment must be satisfied as those statutes provide.

[Amended effective October 20, 1949; July 1, 1970; August 1, 1987; April 30, 2007, effective December 1, 2007.]

UNDERSTANDING RULE 69

HOW RULE 69 FITS IN

Civil "execution" is the process of enforcing a judgment that awards money to a party. Often, formal execution is unnecessary; the defeated party will simply just pay the judgment voluntarily. Execution procedures are needed when a voluntary payment is not forthcoming and the judgment winner has to collect his or her victory against a non-cooperating defeated party's assets. The chores of finding those assets, seizing them, and transforming them into the money necessary to satisfy the judgment are the roles of Rule 69. The process can prove very frustrating and time-consuming. The court's assistance in this process is accomplished through its issuance of a "writ of execution." (The procedure for enforcing a non-money judgment—such as an injunction—is addressed by Rule 70.)

THE ARCHITECTURE OF RULE 69

Rule 69 has two subparts. Subpart (a) establishes the procedures for execution and authorizes the re-opening of discovery to aid in the process of execution. Subpart (b) sets special requirements for execution against an Internal Revenue Service officer or an officer of Congress.

HOW RULE 69 WORKS IN PRACTICE

These two subparts of Rule 69 are discussed, in order, below.

RULE 69(a) In General

Federal execution of a money judgment must be by "writ of execution," unless the court directs otherwise. Execution procedures must follow the federal instructions set statutorily by Congress, if any; if none, the procedures must follow the instructions established by State law in the State where the district court is sitting. Discovery in aid of execution is permitted.

PRACTICING LAW UNDER THIS SUBPART

Writ of Execution

A writ of execution is a legal instrument that enforces the terms of a money judgment by formally authorizing the seizure and sale of assets belonging to the defeated party in order to satisfy the judgment. (The process of enforcing an *equitable* judgment is established in Rule 70.)

Subject-Matter Jurisdiction

Legal proceedings to collect judgments under Rule 69 are not considered actions independent of the original lawsuit, but merely a process used to enforce the court's judgment. *See Bank Markazi v. Peterson*, 578 U.S. 212, 232–33 (2016). *See also Kokkonen v. Guardian Life Ins. Co. of America,* 511 U.S. 375, 379–80 (1994) (federal courts' "ancillary" jurisdiction extends "to enable a court . . . to manage its proceedings, vindicate its authority, and effectuate its decrees").

Execution Procedures

Upon obtaining a writ of execution, the judgment winner may serve the writ on the U.S. Marshal or State officer, who will then execute—by attachment or otherwise—the property of the judgment loser. Execution can occur against property of the judgment loser that lies in the possession of third parties (such as, for example, a bank or investment company). The judgment loser's property can be sold at an execution or sheriff's sale, thereby raising the cash used to satisfy the judgment.

- *Applicability:* This Rule and its procedures only applies to money judgments (Rule 70 addresses enforcement of equitable decrees), and only to money judgments entered by a federal court; it has no application to State court judgments or other types of judgments.

- *Federal Procedures:* If a federal statute sets the type or manner of execution at issue, it governs. Federal remedies for executions in aid of judgments appear in 28 U.S.C. § 2001 *et seq.*
- *State Procedures:* In the absence of a governing federal statutory procedure, the execution process adopted by the State where the federal court is located will govern. *See Peacock v. Thomas,* 516 U.S. 349, 359 (1996). The available State law remedies vary from jurisdiction to jurisdiction, but often include garnishment, arrest, mandamus, contempt, or the appointment of a receiver.
- *Supplementing (or Even Supplanting) State Procedures:* Although district courts are directed to use State procedure to enforce money judgments (in the absence of a governing federal statute), they are also permitted to "direct otherwise." Federal courts have authority to supplement such procedures with federal practice when necessary. Indeed, if State law poses an obstacle to execution, federal courts might even be able to disregard State practice entirely.
- *Property Subject to the Writ of Execution:* Generally, State law will designate property of the judgment loser that may be taken to satisfy a civil judgment. State law usually also shields other property (for instance, retirement accounts, trade tools, medicines, etc.) as exempt from execution in that State.
- *Fees and Costs:* Fees for writs, subpoenas, keeping attached property, and for seizing, levying on, and selling property may be taxed as costs. *See* 28 U.S.C. § 1921.

Time for Execution

The time for execution, and the duration of the writ of execution and other execution instruments, is generally established by State law.

- *Stay of Execution:* An automatic suspension of execution on federal judgments runs for 30 days after entry. *See* Rule 62(a). Thereafter, further suspensions of execution (for example, while post-trial motions are under consideration or an appeal is pending) are permitted. *See* Rule 62.

Immunities from Execution

The Foreign Sovereign Immunities Act provides substantial immunity for foreign sovereigns from the jurisdiction of American courts. *See* 28 U.S.C. § 1604. The Act also immunizes the property of foreign States from attachment and execution. *See* 28 U.S.C. § 1609. The Eleventh Amendment to the U.S. Constitution generally bars execution against State property.

Registering a Judgment in District Outside Forum State

A judgment for money or property entered by any district court may be registered in any other district court by filing a certified copy of such judgment in the other district after the judgment has become final. *See* 28 U.S.C. § 1963. A judgment that has been registered has the same effect as the original judgment and may be enforced as would any other judgment. A consequence, however, of registering a judgment in federal court that was previously awarded in a different federal court in a different State is that the law of the enforcing State—not the judgment State—will normally control.

Discovery in Aid of Execution

One of the most frustrating challenges during formal execution procedures is locating assets of the defeated party to seize and sell. This subpart assists in that challenging process by permitting a re-opening of discovery for that asset-seeking purpose. A party trying to enforce a judgment may use either the federal or State discovery rules to uncover information concerning assets of the debtor and to aid in executing on the judgment. This subpart expressly provides that such discovery may be directed toward "any person," including persons not parties to the lawsuit (like banks). *See generally Republic of Argentina v. NML Cap., Ltd.*, 573 U.S. 134, 138 (2014) (commenting that rules permitting post-judgment execution discovery "are quite permissive," even with foreign nations as parties). Although construed "liberally" and given a "very broad" scope so as to provide an efficient, effective path to execute on judgments, post-judgment execution discovery remains bounded by relevance and proportionality constraints.

RULE 69(b) Against Certain Public Officers

A judgment that has been entered against a collector of the Internal Revenue Service or an officer of Congress can be converted from a *personal* obligation of that defeated party into an obligation borne solely by the United States Government.

PRACTICING LAW UNDER THIS SUBPART

Obtaining a "Certificate of Probable Cause"

An internal revenue officer (28 U.S.C. § 2006) or an officer of Congress (2 U.S.C. § 118) who has suffered an entry of an adverse judgment may apply to the court for a certificate of probable cause. Through that application, the court will determine whether the federal judgment debtor acted with probable and reasonable cause in performing his or her governmental duties. If the court so finds, the court will issue a certificate of probable cause.

Effect of the Certificate

The certificate of probable cause converts the action to one against the United States, thereby extinguishing the personal liability of the individual federal official. Subsequently, the judgment creditor may serve the certificate of probable cause, along with the judgment, on the United States Treasury. The Treasury will then be obligated to pay the amount of the judgment.

RULE 70

ENFORCING A JUDGMENT FOR A SPECIFIC ACT

(a) Party's Failure to Act; Ordering Another to Act. If a judgment requires a party to convey land, to deliver a deed or other document, or to perform any other specific act and the party fails to comply within the time specified, the court may order the act to be done—at the disobedient party's expense—by another person appointed by the court. When done, the act has the same effect as if done by the party.

(b) Vesting Title. If the real or personal property is within the district, the court—instead of ordering a conveyance—may enter a judgment divesting any party's title and vesting it in others. That judgment has the effect of a legally executed conveyance.

(c) Obtaining a Writ of Attachment or Sequestration. On application by a party entitled to performance of an act, the clerk must issue a writ of attachment or sequestration against the disobedient party's property to compel obedience.

(d) Obtaining a Writ of Execution or Assistance. On application by a party who obtains a judgment or order for possession, the clerk must issue a writ of execution or assistance.

(e) Holding in Contempt. The court may also hold the disobedient party in contempt.

[April 30, 2007, effective December 1, 2007.]

UNDERSTANDING RULE 70

HOW RULE 70 FITS IN

Civil "enforcement" is the process of obtaining performance of a judgment that awards non-monetary relief—such as the conveyance of land, the delivery of a deed or other document, or the performance of some other act. Often, formal enforcement proceedings are unnecessary; the defeated party could simply voluntarily comply with the judgment's mandate. Enforcement procedures are needed when voluntary performance is not forthcoming and the judgment winner has to have the judgment loser coerced into complying. The task of obtaining compliance with a non-money judgment is the role of Rule 70. (The process of executing upon a judgment for money is addressed by Rule 69.)

THE ARCHITECTURE OF RULE 70

Rule 70 has five subparts, each of which imparts separate types of enforcement authority. Subpart (a) permits the court to appoint someone else to perform the act the judgment loser is refusing to do. Subpart (b) allows the court to order that one party's title to property has been divested and that title has instead been vested in someone else. Subparts (c) and (d) authorize the clerk of court to issue writs of attachment, sequestration, execution, or assistance to aid in enforcement. Subpart (e) allows the court to hold the disobeying party in contempt.

HOW RULE 70 WORKS IN PRACTICE

These five subparts of Rule 70 are discussed, in order, below.

RULE 70(a) Party's Failure to Act; Ordering Another to Act

When a judgment is entered that requires a party to transfer property, to deliver a document or deed, or to perform some other act, but that party refuses to do so, the court may appoint someone else to perform that act in the disobeying person's stead. Such appointment will be at the expense of the non-performing party and will carry the same legal effect as if the act had been performed by the party himself or herself.

RULE 70(b) Vesting Title

When a judgment directs a party to give to another person title to certain real or personal property, the court is given a simple option—so long as the property is within the judicial district where the court is sitting. In such a circumstance, the court may enter a judgment that divests the party of title and then vests title in someone else. Such a judgment has the effect of a legally-executed conveyance.

PRACTICING LAW UNDER THIS SUBPART

When Property Is *Outside* the Judicial District

If the real or personal property is not located within the district in which the court sits, the court may appoint someone to convey the property as permitted in subpart (a).

RULE 70(c) Obtaining a Writ of Attachment or Sequestration

When a judgment directs a party to perform some act but that party refuses to do so, the judgment winner can attempt to coax the disobeying party into performing by having the clerk of court issue a writ of attachment (which permits the seizure of the disobedient party's property) or a writ of sequestration (which permits the placing of the disobedient party's property in the possession of the court or its designee). The goal of such writs is to induce the disobeying party—on pain of such attachment or sequestration—to do what the judgment has ordered that party to do.

RULE 70(d) Obtaining a Writ of Execution or Assistance

When a judgment or order directs a party to transfer possession of property to someone else, the judgment winner can have the clerk of court issue a writ of execution (which permits execution upon the property) or a writ of assistance (which allows others to cooperate in acquiring possession).

RULE 70(e) Holding in Contempt

In addition to all other remedies permitted by Rule 70, the court is also authorized to hold disobeying parties in contempt.

RULE 71

ENFORCING RELIEF FOR OR AGAINST A NONPARTY

When an order grants relief for a nonparty or may be enforced against a nonparty, the procedure for enforcing the order is the same as for a party.

[Amended effective August 1, 1987; April 30, 2007, effective December 1, 2007.]

UNDERSTANDING RULE 71

HOW RULE 71 FITS IN

Execution and enforcement of civil judgments are addressed in Rules 69 and 70. This Rule permits those same procedures to be used for or against *non-parties* when a judgment or order grants relief for a non-party or permits enforcement against a non-party. This Rule does not identify when such non-party grants or enforcements are proper. Instead, it merely supplies the procedures to be used when they are.

THE ARCHITECTURE OF RULE 71

Rule 71 spans a single sentence; its meaning is plain.

HOW RULE 71 WORKS IN PRACTICE

Enforcement *In Favor* of a Non-party

Orders can be enforced in favor of non-parties in the same manner as they might be in favor of parties. For example, a non-party might purchase property at a sheriff's sale that formerly belonged to a judgment loser and that was being sold at the court's behest to satisfy that judgment. That non-party purchaser may enforce against the judgment loser the obligation to transfer title in the same way as a party would.

Enforcement *Against* a Non-party

Orders can be enforced against non-parties in the same manner as they might be against parties (provided, of course, it is lawful and constitutional to allow enforcement against that non-party). For example, a non-party agent of a judgment loser (who possesses property on the judgment loser's behalf) may be compelled to deliver a deed to that property to the judgment winner in the same way as the judgment loser would.

IX. SPECIAL PROCEEDINGS

RULE 71.1

CONDEMNING REAL OR PERSONAL PROPERTY

(a) Applicability of Other Rules. These rules govern proceedings to condemn real and personal property by eminent domain, except as this rule provides otherwise.

(b) Joinder of Properties. The plaintiff may join separate pieces of property in a single action, no matter whether they are owned by the same persons or sought for the same use.

(c) Complaint.

(1) *Caption.* The complaint must contain a caption as provided in Rule 10(a). The plaintiff must, however, name as defendants both the property—designated generally by kind, quantity, and location—and at least one owner of some part of or interest in the property.

(2) *Contents.* The complaint must contain a short and plain statement of the following:

(A) the authority for the taking;

(B) the uses for which the property is to be taken;

(C) a description sufficient to identify the property;

(D) the interests to be acquired; and

(E) for each piece of property, a designation of each defendant who has been joined as an owner or owner of an interest in it.

(3) *Parties.* When the action commences, the plaintiff need join as defendants only those persons who have or claim an interest in the property and whose names are then known. But before any hearing on compensation, the plaintiff must add as defendants all those persons who have or claim an interest and whose names have become known or can be found by a reasonably diligent search of the records, considering both the property's character and value and the interests to be acquired. All others may be made defendants under the designation "Unknown Owners."

(4) *Procedure.* Notice must be served on all defendants as provided in Rule 71.1(d), whether they were named as defendants when the action commenced or were added later. A defendant may answer as provided in

Rule 71.1(e). The court, meanwhile, may order any distribution of a deposit that the facts warrant.

(5) *Filing; Additional Copies.* In addition to filing the complaint, the plaintiff must give the clerk at least one copy for the defendants' use and additional copies at the request of the clerk or a defendant.

(d) Process.

(1) *Delivering Notice to the Clerk.* On filing a complaint, the plaintiff must promptly deliver to the clerk joint or several notices directed to the named defendants. When adding defendants, the plaintiff must deliver to the clerk additional notices directed to the new defendants.

(2) *Contents of the Notice.*

(A) *Main Contents.* Each notice must name the court, the title of the action, and the defendant to whom it is directed. It must describe the property sufficiently to identify it, but need not describe any property other than that to be taken from the named defendant. The notice must also state:

(i) that the action is to condemn property;

(ii) the interest to be taken;

(iii) the authority for the taking;

(iv) the uses for which the property is to be taken;

(v) that the defendant may serve an answer on the plaintiff's attorney within 21 days after being served with the notice;

(vi) that the failure to so serve an answer constitutes consent to the taking and to the court's authority to proceed with the action and fix the compensation; and

(vii) that a defendant who does not serve an answer may file a notice of appearance.

(B) *Conclusion.* The notice must conclude with the name, telephone number, and e-mail address of the plaintiff's attorney and an address within the district in which the action is brought where the attorney may be served.

(3) *Serving the Notice.*

(A) *Personal Service.* When a defendant whose address is known resides within the United States or a territory subject to the administrative or judicial jurisdiction of the United States, personal service of the notice (without a copy of the complaint) must be made in accordance with Rule 4.

(B) *Service by Publication.*

(i) A defendant may be served by publication only when the plaintiff's attorney files a certificate stating that the attorney believes the defendant cannot be personally served, because after diligent inquiry within the State where the complaint is filed, the defendant's place of residence is still unknown or, if known, that it is beyond the territorial limits of personal service. Service is then made by publishing the notice—once a week for at least three successive weeks—in a newspaper published in the county where the property is located or, if there is no such newspaper, in a newspaper with general circulation where the property is located. Before the last publication, a copy of the notice must also be mailed to every defendant who cannot be personally served but whose place of residence is then known. Unknown owners may be served by publication in the same manner by a notice addressed to "Unknown Owners."

(ii) Service by publication is complete on the date of the last publication. The plaintiff's attorney must prove publication and mailing by a certificate, attach a printed copy of the published notice, and mark on the copy the newspaper's name and the dates of publication.

(4) *Effect of Delivery and Service.* Delivering the notice to the clerk and serving it have the same effect as serving a summons under Rule 4.

(5) *Proof of Service; Amending the Proof or Notice.* Rule 4(*l*) governs proof of service. The court may permit the proof or the notice to be amended.

(e) Appearance or Answer.

(1) *Notice of Appearance.* A defendant that has no objection or defense to the taking of its property may serve a notice of appearance designating the property in which it claims an interest. The defendant must then be given notice of all later proceedings affecting the defendant.

(2) *Answer.* A defendant that has an objection or defense to the taking must serve an answer within 21 days after being served with the notice. The answer must:

(A) identify the property in which the defendant claims an interest;

(B) state the nature and extent of the interest; and

(C) state all the defendant's objections and defenses to the taking.

(3) *Waiver of Other Objections and Defenses; Evidence on Compensation.* A defendant waives all objections and defenses not stated in its answer. No other pleading or motion asserting an additional objection or defense is

allowed. But at the trial on compensation, a defendant—whether or not it has previously appeared or answered—may present evidence on the amount of compensation to be paid and may share in the award.

(f) Amending Pleadings. Without leave of court, the plaintiff may—as often as it wants—amend the complaint at any time before the trial on compensation. But no amendment may be made if it would result in a dismissal inconsistent with Rule 71.1(i)(1) or (2). The plaintiff need not serve a copy of an amendment, but must serve notice of the filing, as provided in Rule 5(b), on every affected party who has appeared and, as provided in Rule 71.1(d), on every affected party who has not appeared. In addition, the plaintiff must give the clerk at least one copy of each amendment for the defendants' use, and additional copies at the request of the clerk or a defendant. A defendant may appear or answer in the time and manner and with the same effect as provided in Rule 71.1(e).

(g) Substituting Parties. If a defendant dies, becomes incompetent, or transfers an interest after being joined, the court may, on motion and notice of hearing, order that the proper party be substituted. Service of the motion and notice on a nonparty must be made as provided in Rule 71.1(d)(3).

(h) Trial of the Issues.

(1) *Issues Other Than Compensation; Compensation.* In an action involving eminent domain under federal law, the court tries all issues, including compensation, except when compensation must be determined:

(A) by any tribunal specially constituted by a federal statute to determine compensation; or

(B) if there is no such tribunal, by a jury when a party demands one within the time to answer or within any additional time the court sets, unless the court appoints a commission.

(2) *Appointing a Commission; Commission's Powers and Report.*

(A) *Reasons for Appointing.* If a party has demanded a jury, the court may instead appoint a three-person commission to determine compensation because of the character, location, or quantity of the property to be condemned or for other just reasons.

(B) *Alternate Commissioners.* The court may appoint up to two additional persons to serve as alternate commissioners to hear the case and replace commissioners who, before a decision is filed, the court finds unable or disqualified to perform their duties. Once the commission renders its final decision, the court must discharge any alternate who has not replaced a commissioner.

(C) *Examining the Prospective Commissioners.* Before making its appointments, the court must advise the parties of the identity and qualifications of each prospective commissioner and alternate, and may permit the parties to examine them. The parties may not suggest appointees, but for good cause may object to a prospective commissioner or alternate.

(D) *Commission's Powers and Report.* A commission has the powers of a master under Rule 53(c). Its action and report are determined by a majority. Rule 53(d), (e), and (f) apply to its action and report.

(i) Dismissal of the Action or a Defendant.

(1) *Dismissing the Action.*

(A) *By the Plaintiff.* If no compensation hearing on a piece of property has begun, and if the plaintiff has not acquired title or a lesser interest or taken possession, the plaintiff may, without a court order, dismiss the action as to that property by filing a notice of dismissal briefly describing the property.

(B) *By Stipulation.* Before a judgment is entered vesting the plaintiff with title or a lesser interest in or possession of property, the plaintiff and affected defendants may, without a court order, dismiss the action in whole or in part by filing a stipulation of dismissal. And if the parties so stipulate, the court may vacate a judgment already entered.

(C) *By Court Order.* At any time before compensation has been determined and paid, the court may, after a motion and hearing, dismiss the action as to a piece of property. But if the plaintiff has already taken title, a lesser interest, or possession as to any part of it, the court must award compensation for the title, lesser interest, or possession taken.

(2) *Dismissing a Defendant.* The court may at any time dismiss a defendant who was unnecessarily or improperly joined.

(3) *Effect.* A dismissal is without prejudice unless otherwise stated in the notice, stipulation, or court order.

(j) Deposit and Its Distribution.

(1) *Deposit.* The plaintiff must deposit with the court any money required by law as a condition to the exercise of eminent domain and may make a deposit when allowed by statute.

(2) *Distribution; Adjusting Distribution.* After a deposit, the court and attorneys must expedite the proceedings so as to distribute the deposit and to determine and pay compensation. If the compensation finally

awarded to a defendant exceeds the amount distributed to that defendant, the court must enter judgment against the plaintiff for the deficiency. If the compensation awarded to a defendant is less than the amount distributed to that defendant, the court must enter judgment against that defendant for the overpayment.

(k) Condemnation Under a State's Power of Eminent Domain. This rule governs an action involving eminent domain under State law. But if State law provides for trying an issue by jury—or for trying the issue of compensation by jury or commission or both—that law governs.

(*l*) Costs. Costs are not subject to Rule 54(d).

[Adopted April 30, 1951, effective August 1, 1951; amended January 21, 1963, effective July 1, 1963; April 29, 1985, effective August 1, 1985; March 2, 1987, effective August 1, 1987; April 25, 1988, effective August 1, 1988; amended by Pub.L. 100–690, Title VII, § 7050, November 18, 1988, 102 Stat. 4401 (although amendment by Pub.L. 100–690 could not be executed due to prior amendment by Court order which made the same change effective August 1, 1988); amended April 22, 1993, effective December 1, 1993; March 27, 2003, effective December 1, 2003; April 30, 2007, effective December 1, 2007; March 26, 2009, effective December 1, 2009.]

UNDERSTANDING RULE 71.1

HOW RULE 71.1 FITS IN

Federal and State governments have "eminent domain" power—the authority to take private property for public use. The "taking" (also called "condemning") of property for public use can occur, for example, when private land is needed to build a highway, a railroad spur, or an airport. The exercise of this authority of the sovereign is conditioned on fairly compensating the landowner for the taking. *See* U.S. Const. amend. V ("nor shall private property be taken for public use, without just compensation"). For many years, the process and procedures for this sort of property acquisition by the government were mired in a confusing morass of different laws. Rule 71.1 was the controversial solution to that challenge. Amended many times since it first took effect in 1951, this Rule 71.1 (formerly labeled "Rule 71A") now sets the procedures for condemning property under federal or State eminent domain authority.

THE ARCHITECTURE OF RULE 71.1

Rule 71.1 is complex, with twelve subparts. However, each subpart is well labeled, and the organization—though lengthy—is easy to follow. Subparts (a) and (k) provide that the Federal Rules of Civil Procedure govern all federal and State eminent domain condemnation proceedings, unless the text of Rule 71.1 itself directs otherwise or when State law alters jury trial procedures. Subpart (b) permits the joinder of multiple parcels of property into a single action (for example, to support the condemning of land for a single roadway). Subparts (c), (d), (e), (f), and (g) set the procedures for pleadings, parties, and service in eminent domain condemnation cases. Subpart (h) establishes procedures for trial. Subpart (i) permits dismissals of the entire action or of certain defendants. Subpart (j) allows for depositing into court the monies needed to compensate landowners for the taking of their property, and authorizes post-deposit distributions. Subpart (*l*) instructs that costs in these actions are not subject to the requirements set in Rule 54(d).

HOW RULE 71.1 WORKS IN PRACTICE

These twelve subparts of Rule 71.1 are discussed, in order, below.

RULE 71.1(a) Applicability of Other Rules

The Federal Rules of Civil Procedure govern eminent domain condemnation proceedings, unless the text of Rule 71.1 alters the general civil approach. (Many litigation procedures, like discovery and provisional remedies, are not addressed by Rule 71.1; accordingly, the procedures set by the Rules and used generally in federal civil actions will govern there.)

PRACTICING LAW UNDER THIS SUBPART

When Rule 71.1 Applies

Rule 71.1 applies to the condemnation of both real and personal property. It does not, however, alter supplementary condemnation statutes (such as the Declaration of Taking Act, 40 U.S.C. § 3114 *et seq.*, which permits the federal government to condemn property).

When Rule 71.1 Does Not Apply

Rule 71.1 does not ordinarily apply to "inverse condemnation" proceedings (that is, where a private landowner seeks just compensation for a government taking of property when no government-condemnation proceeding has been instituted).

Federal or State Law

Federal condemnation procedures are governed by federal law and precedent. State law only defines the nature of the real or personal property interest, such as the meaning of property, defining what is taken, or determining the ownership of land. The federal court may hear State law based condemnation proceedings, as permitted by Rule 71.1(k).

Jurisdiction and Venue

The district courts have original subject-matter jurisdiction over proceedings to condemn real property for the use of the United States, its agencies, or departments. *See* 28 U.S.C. § 1358. Venue will lie with the district court of the district in which the real property is located or, if located in different districts in the same State, in any such districts. *See* 28 U.S.C. § 1403.

RULE 71.1(b) Joinder of Properties

Condemnation in a single case is permitted over separate properties, even when they belong to different owners or are to be acquired for different public uses. Only in exceptional circumstances is the court required to conduct separate trials. To eliminate jury confusion over the relative value of properties, the court may separate the evidence concerning the damages sustained by (and compensation owed to) each property owner.

RULE 71.1(c) Complaint

A complaint in a condemnation action must follow a prescribed standard, one that differs in several respects from those required of plaintiffs in an ordinary federal civil action. The caption, contents, service, and filing process are each set by this subpart.

PRACTICING LAW UNDER THIS SUBPART

Caption

A condemnation complaint's caption must include the name of the court, the title of the action, the docket number, and the name of the type of pleading being presented. The caption must name as defendants both the property and at least one of the owners. Naming the property obligates the plaintiff to state the kind, quantity, and location of the property.

Contents of Complaint

The complaint must contain a short and plain statement of:

(1) the authority for the taking;

(2) the use for which the property is to be taken;

(3) a description of the property sufficient for identification;

(4) the interests to be acquired; and

(5) for each separate piece of property, the defendants who have been joined as owners or owners of an interest in the property.

Filing of Complaint and Notice

The plaintiff must file the complaint with the clerk and provide the clerk with at least one copy for the defendants. Upon the request of the clerk or the defendants, the plaintiff must furnish additional copies.

Joining Parties at Commencement

Although this subpart provides that the caption need include only one owner of the property, the condemnor must later join as defendants all persons or entities of title record having or claiming an interest in the property whose names are then known.

Joining of Parties Prior to Hearing on Compensation

Prior to a hearing involving compensation, the condemnor must add as defendants all persons who have an interest whose identities have been learned or can be ascertained by a reasonably diligent search of the records. "Reasonably diligent" search means the type of search a title searcher would undertake, but the extent of the search required will depend upon the character and value of the property involved and the interests to be acquired. Property owners joined after the commencement of the action must be served with notice by the clerk and allowed to file an answer. If there are owners whose identity is not known, they may be designated as "Unknown Owners."

Failure to Join a Party

There are no indispensable parties in a condemnation action. Therefore, the failure to join a party will not defeat the condemnor's title to the land because a condemnation action is an action *in rem*. If the condemnor fails to join a party, the omitted party may have the right to sue for compensation in the U.S. Claims Court after the condemnation is completed.

RULE 71.1(d) Process

Notice of the filing of a condemnation complaint must be delivered to the clerk of court, and service thereafter must be made on the named defendants. The contents of the required notice, the manner of serving the notice, the effect of the service, and proof of service are each prescribed by this subpart.

PRACTICING LAW UNDER THIS SUBPART

Preparing and Filing the Notice

The notices required of this subpart must be prepared by the plaintiff, who then must deliver the notice(s) (along with the condemnation complaint) to the court clerk. The clerk will file and enter the complaint in the record and deliver the notice (but not a copy of the complaint itself) to the U.S. Marshal or other specially-appointed person for service.

Content of the Notice

The plaintiff may prepare joint notices or individual ones, tailored to each property owner and parcel. Each notice must state:

(1) the court;

(2) the title of the action;

(3) the name of the defendant to whom it is directed;

(4) the nature of the action (condemning property);

(5) a description of the property sufficient for its identification;

(6) the interest to be taken;

(7) the authority for the taking;

(8) the uses for which the property is being taken;

(9) the time for answering the complaint (the defendant may serve an answer upon the plaintiff's attorney within 21 days after the service of the notice);

(10) the penalty for failing to answer (a consent to the taking, permitting the court to proceed to hear the action and fix compensation); and

(11) that any defendant who chooses not to file an answer may nevertheless file a notice of appearance.

The notice must also include the name, telephone number, and e-mail address of the plaintiff's attorney, as well as an address within the district in which the lawsuit is brought where that attorney may be served.

Persons Requiring Notice

At the commencement of the case, the clerk only provides notice to persons whose names appear in the complaint. One notice must be delivered to each named defendant, and it need contain only a description of the property to be taken from that defendant. Property owners joined after the filing of the complaint must be served with notice and allowed to answer.

Personal Service on U.S. Residents

For defendants who reside within the United States (including in its territories or insular possessions) and whose residences are known, personal service must be made in accordance with Rule 4.

Service by Publication

(1) *Persons Served by Publication:* A plaintiff may make service by publication on three types of defendants:

  (a) owners who do not reside in the United States, its territories, or insular possessions, and who, therefore, are beyond the territorial limits of personal service;

  (b) owners within the State in which the complaint is filed whose place of residence is unknown after a diligent search of the records; and

  (c) unknown owners.

(2) *Publication:* The plaintiff must publish the notice in a newspaper in the county where the land is located. When no newspaper exists in the county where the land is located, the plaintiff must publish the notice in a newspaper having a circulation in the area where the land is located. The plaintiff must publish the notice once a week for at least three successive weeks.

(3) *Proof of Publication:* When a plaintiff wishes to make proof of service by publication, the plaintiff's attorney must file with the court a certificate stating that the defendant cannot be served personally because the defendant's residence is beyond the personal service limits or, after diligent inquiry, defendant's residence is unknown. The plaintiff's attorney must attach to the certificate a printed copy of the published notice marked with the name of the newspaper and the dates of publication.

(4) *Defendants Who Cannot Be Served but Whose Residences Are Known:* In addition to publication, the plaintiff must mail a copy of the notice to each defendant who cannot be personally served but whose place of residence is known prior to the date of the last publication. Service is complete on the date of the last publication.

RULE 71.1(e) Appearance or Answer

Defendant property owners may respond to a condemnation complaint in two ways: by filing an answer or by serving a notice of an appearance.

PRACTICING LAW UNDER THIS SUBPART

Appearance

When the defendant intends to assert no defense or objection to the taking or to the complaint, the defendant may serve a notice of appearance. The notice of appearance should designate the property in which the defendant claims an interest. A defendant who serves such an appearance is entitled to receive notice of all subsequent proceedings that affect that defendant's interest.

Answer

To assert defenses or objections, the defendant must file an answer. Unlike most answers to complaints in ordinary federal civil actions, the defendant must make specific allegations. In the answer the defendant must identify the property, the defendant's interest in the property, and the asserted defenses/objections to the taking.

- *Time for Answering:* An answer to a condemnation complaint is due within 21 days of service of the notice. This response period may be extended on motion.
- *Counterclaims and Crossclaims:* A condemnation action answer may not contain a counterclaim or crossclaim. Such a claim must be brought in a separate action in the district court or the U.S. Court of Claims.

RULE 71.1(f) Amending Pleadings

A plaintiff may amend the condemnation action complaint multiple times without leave of court before the trial on compensation occurs. However, except as provided in subpart (i), the plaintiff may not amend the complaint to remove the names of defendants or claims. Within 21 days of the notice of each amended complaint, the defendant is entitled to file one amended answer as of right.

PRACTICING LAW UNDER THIS SUBPART

Procedure for Amending Complaint

The plaintiff may amend by filing with the clerk the amended pleading and by serving notice of the amended pleading on each defendant. The plaintiff need not serve a copy of the amended pleading itself on defendants. Instead, if a defendant or the clerk requests copies of the amended complaint, the plaintiff must supply them.

RULE 71.1(g) Substituting Parties

Upon proper motion and notice of hearing, the court may order the substitution of parties when a defendant dies or becomes incompetent, or transfers an interest after the defendant's joinder. If a new party is substituted, the plaintiff must serve a copy of the motion and notice of hearing on the new party, as provided by subpart (d). Rule 25, governing substitution of parties in most civil actions, does not apply in condemnation actions.

RULE 71.1(h) Trial of the Issues

In eminent domain condemnation actions instituted by the federal or State government, all issues (other than the issue of just compensation) will be decided by the court. The issue of compensation will be decided by either a special tribunal, a commission, a jury, or the court. Federal law may require the issue of compensation to be decided by a tribunal specially constituted by Congress. When any party demands a trial by jury, the court will decide whether to conduct a jury trial or to appoint a commission to decide the issue of compensation.

PRACTICING LAW UNDER THIS SUBPART

Trial by Jury

When any party demands a trial by jury, the court may conduct a jury trial or may instead appoint a commission to decide the issue of compensation. There is no constitutional right to a trial by jury in condemnation cases. *See United States v. Reynolds,* 397 U.S. 14, 18 (1970). If empaneled, a jury may decide only the issue of compensation.

(1) *Time for Demand:* Within the time allowed for the answer to the condemnation complaint (21 days of service of the notice of the complaint) or a further time fixed by the court, any party may demand a trial by jury.

(2) *Procedure for Trial by Jury:* The trial of a condemnation action proceeds similarly to any other civil proceeding involving a trial by jury. However, the judge will determine all issues other than the amount of compensation.

Trial by Commission

(1) *Appointment of Commission:* When a party demands a trial by jury, the court has discretion to refuse the demand and to, instead, appoint a commission to decide the issue of compensation. Although the court is not required to make findings of fact to support its determination to appoint a commission, for purposes of appellate review the court will often state in writing its reasons for appointing a commission.

- *Reasons for Appointing a Commission:* Courts have appointed commissions because, among other reasons, of local preference or habit, the preference of the U.S. Justice Department, the distance of the property from the courthouse, the complexity of the issues, the character of the land, the nature of the interest or the number of tracts taken, the need for numerous jury trials, the desirability of uniform awards, and to prevent discrimination.

(2) *Number of Commissioners:* A commission is generally composed of three persons (although the court may appoint two alternates to attend the hearing).

(3) *Appointment of Commissioners:* Usually, the court will appoint commissioners and alternate commissioners. Often, the court will appoint a lawyer or ex-judge as chair of the commission and one real estate person as a member. After appointing the commissioners, the court will advise the parties of the identity and qualifications of each prospective commissioner and alternate commissioner. The parties may examine the commissioners and may, for valid cause, object to the appointment of any commissioner.

(4) *Reformation and Revocation of Commission:* When the court believes the judgment of the commission has been affected by bias, the court may reform the commission

by replacing some or all of the commissioners. When justice so requires, such as instances of undue delay, the court may vacate the reference to the commission.

(5) *Procedure for Trial by Commission:*

(a) *Powers:* The commission will only try the issue of compensation; all other issues will be decided by the court. The commission has the same powers as a master in a non-jury trial. Proceedings before the commission are governed by Rule 53(c). The commission may regulate its proceedings, require the production of documents, rule on the admissibility of evidence, call and examine witnesses, and permit witnesses to be examined by the parties. These powers will be regulated indirectly by the court through its instructions to the commission in the order of reference.

(b) *Instructions:* In its order of reference, the trial judge will instruct the commissioners as to such issues as: the qualifications of expert witnesses, the weight to be given to other opinions of evidence, competent evidence of value, the best evidence of value, the manner of the hearing and the method of conducting it, the right to view the property, the limited purpose of viewing, and the kind of evidence which is inadmissible and the manner of ruling on the admissibility of evidence.

(c) *Admission of Evidence:* Although the court will control the kind of evidence which is admissible, the commission will apply the Federal Rules of Evidence when ruling on the admissibility of the evidence.

(i) *View of Property:* When necessary or conducive to a proper determination of compensation and when not inconvenient or the cause of undue delay or expense, the commission may view the property.

(6) *Findings and Report of Commission:* A majority of the commissioners will decide the amount of compensation to award, and the commission will submit a report. The findings and the report of the commission will follow the provisions of Rule 53(e)(2). In its report, the commission must show a clear factual basis for its finding, but need not make detailed findings. A proper commission report will state what evidence and what measure of damages the commission accepted and why it made the award it did. *See United States v. Merz,* 376 U.S. 192, 198 (1964).

(7) *Objection to Commission Report:* Within 21 days after service of the commission's report, a party must make and file with the court and serve on all other parties objections to the report. *See* Rule 53(f)(2). The party objecting to the report has the burden of demonstrating any claimed error in the report.

(8) *Trial Court Review of Commission Report:* The trial court must adopt the report of the commission unless it finds the report to be clearly erroneous. *See United States v. Merz,* 376 U.S. 192, 198 (1964). A trial court may find the report clearly erroneous when there was a substantial error in the proceedings, when the report was unsupported by substantial evidence or against the clear weight of the evidence, or when the report involved a misapplication of law. Courts have also found commission reports clearly erroneous when the award was grossly inadequate. When the trial court finds the report clearly erroneous, the court may examine the testimony and make its own judgment or it may recommit the matter to the commission with instructions.

(9) *Commissioners' Compensation:* Commissioners are compensated in reasonable relation to the services rendered. That compensation will be charged to the condemnor and may be included in the damage award, not taxed as costs against the award.

(10) *Appellate Court Review of Commission or Court Decision:* An appellate court reviews the judgment of a trial court under a clearly erroneous standard.

RULE 71.1(i) Dismissal of the Action or a Defendant

The procedures for dismissal depend on the posture of the proceedings. Prior to a hearing or declaration of taking, the action may be dismissed as of right. Where the government files a declaration of taking, acquires an interest, acquires title, or takes possession of the property before the entry of judgment, neither the plaintiff nor the court may dismiss an action, except by stipulation of the parties. *See Kirby Forest Indus., Inc. v. United States,* 467 U.S. 1, 12 n.18 (1984).

PRACTICING LAW UNDER THIS SUBPART

Dismissal Mechanics

(1) *As of Right:* The plaintiff may dismiss the action by filing a notice of dismissal with a brief description of the property at any time before a hearing on compensation has begun and before the plaintiff has either filed a declaration of taking as provided by statute, acquired title, acquired an interest, or taken possession of the property.

(2) *By Stipulation:* Before the entry of a judgment vesting plaintiff with title, an interest, or possession of the property, the parties may stipulate to a dismissal in whole or in part without an order of the court. After judgment, the parties may stipulate to a dismissal and the court may vacate the judgment and revest title in the defendant.

(3) *By Court Order:* If compensation has not yet been determined and paid, the court will decide whether to grant a voluntary dismissal after motion and hearing. However, if the plaintiff has taken title, acquired an interest, or taken possession of any part of the property, the court must award just compensation for the possession, title, or the interest taken.

Dismissal of Improperly and Unnecessarily Joined Parties

At any time, upon a motion or *sua sponte,* the court may dismiss a defendant who has no interest but has been unnecessarily or improperly joined.

Dismissal Without Prejudice

Unless stated in the order or the stipulation, a dismissal of a condemnation proceeding is without prejudice.

RULE 71.1(j) Deposit and Its Distribution

Money may be deposited with the court in condemnation actions, when required or permitted by statute. State substantive law will determine the amount to be deposited in State eminent domain actions; federal substantive law will determine the amount to be deposited in federal eminent domain actions.

PRACTICING LAW UNDER THIS SUBPART

Applicability

This subpart applies only to deposits made before judgment. The government-condemnor bears the burden and expenses of calculating and distributing the compensation owed.

The Declaration of Taking Act

The Declaration of Taking Act, 40 U.S.C. § 3114, supplements the procedure under this subpart. Under the Act, upon the filing of a declaration of taking and a deposit of the estimated compensation with the court, title immediately vests in the federal government.

(1) *Time for Filing:* A declaration of taking may be brought at the commencement of the condemnation action and at any time before a judgment.

(2) *Certification:* The chief of the government department or bureau acquiring the land will certify that the land is within the value prescribed by Congress.

(3) *Surrender of Possession/Encumbrances:* Upon the filing of a declaration of taking, the court will fix the time and the terms upon which the parties in possession will surrender possession of the property to the plaintiff. The court may also make orders concerning encumbrances, liens, rents, taxes, assessments, insurance, etc.

(4) *Amount of Award:* The judgment will include interest from the date of the taking to the date of the award, at the rate set by 40 U.S.C. § 3116. However, no interest will be ordered on money paid into the court. When the court or the jury awards an amount greater than the deposit, the court will enter judgment against the plaintiff and in favor of the defendant for the difference plus interest. When the deposit exceeds the award, the plaintiff will obtain the excess deposit from the clerk or will obtain judgment against the landowner if the deposit was already distributed.

(5) *Deposit and Distribution:* At the time of the taking and the deposit into the court, the court may order distribution of the deposit to the known defendants.

(6) *Appellate Review:* A transfer of title is not a final appealable judgment until a final judgment on compensation has been entered. *See Catlin v. United States,* 324 U.S. 229, 233 (1945).

Deposit and Distribution Under Other Statutes

When the Declaration of Taking Act is inapplicable, the process functions similarly. The plaintiff must deposit with the court any money required by law, and may deposit any money allowed by statute. After deposit, the court and parties expedite the proceedings to distribute the deposit and to determine compensation. At the conclusion, proper payment is made to the parties.

RULE 71.1(k) Condemnation Under a State's Power of Eminent Domain

A State may institute an eminent domain action in a federal district court when diversity jurisdiction exists. Similarly, a defendant (landowner) may remove a State eminent domain action to federal court when diversity jurisdiction exists. Such State eminent domain actions must be brought in the federal district court for the district in which the land is situated. In State eminent domain cases, the court will follow State law provisions regarding the right to trial by jury or a commission.

RULE 71.1(*l*) Costs

Condemnation proceedings are exempt from the cost provisions of Rule 54(d). Instead, the normal expenses of the proceeding will be charged to the condemnor. Expenses incurred in the distribution of the award are charged to the condemnee.

PRACTICING LAW UNDER THIS SUBPART

Expenses Paid by Condemnor

The condemnor pays the normal expenses for publication of notice, commissioners' fees, the costs of transporting commissioners/jurors for a view, witness fees, and the commissioner's expenses in recording the deed and executing the conveyance.

Expenses of Distribution

Expenses incurred in the distribution of the award (such as ascertaining the proper distributees and resolving conflicting claims) are chargeable against the award.

RULE 72

MAGISTRATE JUDGES: PRETRIAL ORDER

(a) Nondispositive Matters. When a pretrial matter not dispositive of a party's claim or defense is referred to a magistrate judge to hear and decide, the magistrate judge must promptly conduct the required proceedings and, when appropriate, issue a written order stating the decision. A party may serve and file objections to the order within 14 days after being served with a copy. A party may not assign as error a defect in the order not timely objected to. The district judge in the case must consider timely objections and modify or set aside any part of the order that is clearly erroneous or is contrary to law.

(b) Dispositive Motions and Prisoner Petitions.

(1) *Findings and Recommendations.* A magistrate judge must promptly conduct the required proceedings when assigned, without the parties' consent, to hear a pretrial matter dispositive of a claim or defense or a prisoner petition challenging the conditions of confinement. A record must be made of all evidentiary proceedings and may, at the magistrate judge's discretion, be made of any other proceedings. The magistrate judge must enter a recommended disposition, including, if appropriate, proposed findings of fact. The clerk must promptly mail a copy to each party.

(2) *Objections.* Within 14 days after being served with a copy of the recommended disposition, a party may serve and file specific written objections to the proposed findings and recommendations. A party may respond to another party's objections within 14 days after being served with a copy. Unless the district judge orders otherwise, the objecting party must promptly arrange for transcribing the record, or whatever portions of it the parties agree to or the magistrate judge considers sufficient.

(3) *Resolving Objections.* The district judge must determine de novo any part of the magistrate judge's disposition that has been properly objected to. The district judge may accept, reject, or modify the recommended disposition; receive further evidence; or return the matter to the magistrate judge with instructions.

[Former Rule 72 abrogated December 4, 1967, effective July 1, 1968; new Rule 72 adopted April 28, 1983, effective August 1, 1983; amended April 30, 1991, effective December 1, 1991; April 22, 1993, effective December 1, 1993; April 30, 2007, effective December 1, 2007; March 26, 2009, effective December 1, 2009.]

UNDERSTANDING RULE 72

HOW RULE 72 FITS IN

In civil cases, United States Magistrate Judges are assistants to federal trial judges.

Justices of the U.S. Supreme Court, Judges of the U.S. Courts of Appeals, and Judges of the U.S. District Courts are all nominated by the President and confirmed by the Senate. They are "Article III judges," because their authority derives from Article III of the U.S. Constitution. Once they assume their posts, they serve for life. U.S. Magistrate Judges are different. They do not serve for life (but for a set term of years) and are neither nominated by the President nor confirmed by the Senate (instead, they are selected and appointed by the U.S. District Court judges for whom they work). The position of U.S. Magistrate Judge was created by Congress in 1968. *See* 28 U.S.C. §§ 631–39. Thus, the position is a statutory one, not a constitutional one. The principal role of U.S. Magistrate Judges in civil litigation is to assist the district judges. (Their roles in criminal prosecutions are more expansive.)

Rules 72 and 73 address the civil litigation work that magistrate judges may perform. Rule 72 establishes the authority for magistrate judges to assume certain pretrial tasks in civil cases, when assigned those tasks by a district judge. Rule 73 sets the authority for magistrate judges to preside over both federal jury trials and federal bench trials, but only when the litigants consent.

THE ARCHITECTURE OF RULE 72

Rule 72 has two subparts. Subpart (a) sets the procedures (and division of responsibilities) when a district judge refers a *non-dispositive* pretrial matter to a magistrate judge. Subpart (b) establishes the procedures (and division of responsibilities) when a magistrate judge hears a *dispositive* pretrial matter or a prisoner petition challenging conditions of confinement.

HOW RULE 72 WORKS IN PRACTICE

These two subparts of Rule 72 are discussed, in order, below.

RULE 72(a) Nondispositive Matters

A district judge may refer *nondispositive* pretrial matters to a magistrate judge for decision. District judges can do so, or not do so, in their discretion. (The district judge does not need the parties' consent to make a referral of a nondispositive pretrial matter.) If such a referral is made, the magistrate judge must promptly hear and rule on the matter. Objections to such rulings may be taken to the district court.

PRACTICING LAW UNDER THIS SUBPART

"Nondispositive" Pretrial Matters

Nondispositive pretrial matters are those motions and matters that can arise during the preliminary processing of a federal civil case that do not "dispose" of a party's claim or defense. (A list of matters considered "dispositive" was enacted by Congress, and is discussed in subpart (b) below.) Most motions to amend, to voluntarily dismiss a claim or lawsuit, to join claims or parties, to resolve discovery disputes, to seal or unseal documents, to extend time, and the like qualify as nondispositive pretrial motions. But the labeling alone might not always resolve the question of whether a matter is dispositive or nondispositive. Courts instead consider the actual effect of a matter, beyond just its label, in making this assessment. *See Ocelot Oil Corp. v. Sparrow Indus.*, 847 F.2d 1458, 1465 (10th Cir. 1988).

Authority to Rule in Nondispositive Pretrial Matters

If a district judge refers a nondispositive pretrial matter to a magistrate judge, the magistrate judge is authorized to make a binding ruling on that nondispositive matter. The magistrate judge may do so by entering a written order (when doing so would be appropriate and an aid to further proceedings). The magistrate judge's ruling becomes effective when made, and requires no further action by the district judge—subject, of course, to a disappointed litigant's right to object and the district judge's right of review.

Objections to and Review of Nondispositive Pretrial Rulings

A party may object to a magistrate judge's nondispositive pretrial ruling by filing written objections within 14 days after being served with a copy of the order. Failure to make a timely objection may constitute a waiver of appellate review of the magistrate judge's order. Even if no objections are presented, the district judge may rehear or reconsider the matter *sua sponte.*

Review by Court of Appeals

A party may not appeal directly to the court of appeals from a magistrate judge's nondispositive pretrial order.

RULE 72(b) Dispositive Motions and Prisoner Petitions

A district judge may also refer *dispositive* pretrial matters to a magistrate judge, but only for a recommendation (not a ruling). In reaching such a recommendation, the magistrate judge may conduct evidentiary hearings and submit proposed findings of fact as appropriate. If a party makes a timely written objection to the recommendation of the magistrate judge, the district judge must make a *de novo* review of the record.

PRACTICING LAW UNDER THIS SUBPART

"Dispositive" Pretrial Matters

New concerns arise when the referred matter is a dispositive one. Because delegating adjudicative authority to a non-Article III judge may raise constitutional concerns, a different approach is required. Congress has listed by statute those pretrial matters it considers dispositive: (1) a motion for injunctive relief; (2) a motion for judgment on the pleadings; (3) a motion for summary judgment; (4) a motion to dismiss or permit maintenance of a class action; (5) a motion to dismiss for failure to state a claim upon which relief may be granted; and (6) a motion for involuntary dismissal. *See* 28 U.S.C. § 636(b)(1)(A).

In addition to this statutory list, courts have sometimes ruled that the following can, depend on the circumstances, be considered dispositive pretrial matters: (1) an application to proceed *in forma pauperis;* (2) certain motions to amend a pleading; (3) a motion for attorney's fees; (4) an order remanding a removed case back to State court; and (5) possibly a Rule 11 sanctions ruling.

Procedure for Magistrate Judge Consideration of Dispositive Pretrial Matters

Unlike with nondispositive pretrial motions (discussed in subpart (a) above), a magistrate judge who has been referred a *dispositive* pretrial matter may not rule on the dispute. Instead, magistrate judges are directed to prepare a "report and recommendation" for the district judge's consideration. In coming to that recommendation, magistrate judges enjoy substantial discretion. They may conduct hearings. They must make a record of all evidentiary proceedings, but have discretion whether to make a record of non-evidentiary proceedings. Once their assessment is concluded, magistrate judges must submit to the referring district judge their recommendation on how the matter ought to be resolved. When appropriate, the magistrate judge shall accompany that recommendation with proposed findings of fact. The clerk of the court is required to mail copies of the magistrate judge's report and recommendation to all parties.

Objecting to a Magistrate Judge's Report and Recommendation

A disappointed party may object to the magistrate judge's recommendation by filing specific, written objections within 14 days after being served with a copy of the report and recommendation. The opposing party may respond to those objections within 14 days after service.

- *Waiver of Right to a Review:* A party's failure to timely object constitutes a waiver by that party of its right to have the magistrate judge's report and recommendation reviewed by the district judge, as well as a waiver of that party's right to appeal the issue to the court of appeals.
- *Obligation to Order Transcript:* A party who properly objects to a magistrate judge's recommendation will promptly arrange for a transcription of the record or portions of the record agreed upon by the parties or as directed by the magistrate judge, unless directed otherwise by the district judge.

Review by District Judge of a Report and Recommendation

The district judge who referred a dispositive matter to a magistrate judge must conduct a *de novo* review of any portion of the report and recommendation to which a proper, timely objection has been made. In doing so, the district judge may accept, reject, or modify the recommended disposition or may re-commit the matter to the magistrate judge with instructions for further consideration. A district judge, under this *de novo* review standard, is not required to convene a new hearing, but is required to examine the issues upon which specific, written objections were based, either on the record or by receiving additional testimony. The courts are divided on whether and to what extent a district judge is obligated to review a magistrate judge's recommendation absent a timely objection.

Habeas Corpus

This subpart does not extend to habeas corpus petitions. Habeas corpus petitions are governed by specific statutes. *See* 28 U.S.C. §§ 2254–2255.

RULE 73

MAGISTRATE JUDGES: TRIAL BY CONSENT; APPEAL

(a) Trial by Consent. When authorized under 28 U.S.C. § 636(c), a magistrate judge may, if all parties consent, conduct a civil action or proceeding, including a jury or nonjury trial. A record must be made in accordance with 28 U.S.C. § 636(c)(5).

(b) Consent Procedure.

(1) *In General.* When a magistrate judge has been designated to conduct civil actions or proceedings, the clerk must give the parties written notice of their opportunity to consent under 28 U.S.C. § 636(c). To signify their consent, the parties must jointly or separately file a statement consenting to the referral. A district judge or magistrate judge may be informed of a party's response to the clerk's notice only if all parties have consented to the referral.

(2) *Reminding the Parties About Consenting.* A district judge, magistrate judge, or other court official may remind the parties of the magistrate judge's availability, but must also advise them that they are free to withhold consent without adverse substantive consequences.

(3) *Vacating a Referral.* On its own for good cause—or when a party shows extraordinary circumstances—the district judge may vacate a referral to a magistrate judge under this rule.

(c) Appealing a Judgment. In accordance with 28 U.S.C. § 636(c)(3), an appeal from a judgment entered at a magistrate judge's direction may be taken to the court of appeals as would any other appeal from a district-court judgment.

[Former Rule 73 abrogated December 4, 1967, effective July 1, 1968; new Rule 73 adopted April 28, 1983, effective August 1, 1983; amended March 2, 1987, effective August 1, 1987; April 22, 1993, effective December 1, 1993, April 11, 1997, effective December 1, 1997; April 30, 2007, effective December 1, 2007.]

UNDERSTANDING RULE 73

HOW RULE 73 FITS IN

This is the second of the two Rules concerning the use of U.S. Magistrate Judges in federal civil cases. (For a general description of U.S. Magistrate Judges and their roles, see Rule 72.) This Rule authorizes U.S. Magistrate Judges to hear full federal civil trials, either as factfinder in a bench trial or as presiding jurist in a jury trial. In effect, this Rule allows U.S. Magistrate Judges to assume the same trial role as Article III district court judges. But U.S. Magistrate Judges can only do so with the consent of the litigants. In the absence of such consent, such delegated authority would likely pose insurmountable constitutional problems. *See Northern Pipeline Const. Co. v. Marathon Pipe Line Co.*, 458 U.S. 50, 58–59 (1982) (plurality) (Constitution's "inexorable command" is that "[t]he judicial power of the United States must be exercised by courts having the attributes prescribed" in Article III).

THE ARCHITECTURE OF RULE 73

Rule 73 has three subparts. Subpart (a) authorizes trials before magistrate judges when the parties consent. Subpart (b) establishes both the consent procedure and the right of a district judge to revoke a referral. Subpart (c) permits direct appeals from these consented-to trials to the courts of appeals.

HOW RULE 73 WORKS IN PRACTICE

These three subparts of Rule 73 are discussed, in order, below.

RULE 73(a) Trial by Consent

Magistrate judges may exercise case-dispositive, final adjudicative authority in federal civil cases, but only upon the consent of the parties. Such consent from the parties must be free, voluntary, and unanimous. *See Holt-Orsted v. City of Dickson,* 641 F.3d 230, 233 (6th Cir. 2011). Upon the parties' consent, the district judge—by court order or standing local rule—may specially designate the magistrate judge to assume that authority and conduct the trial. *See* 28 U.S.C. § 636(c)(1). In such circumstances, the magistrate judge has the powers of a district judge (except the power of contempt).

PRACTICING LAW UNDER THIS SUBPART

Preserving the Record

Following such special designation, the magistrate judge must decide by what means the record should be preserved, such as verbatim by a court reporter or by electronic sound recording. *See* 28 U.S.C. § 636(c)(5). When deciding the means of preservation of the record, the magistrate judge may consider the complexity of the case, the likelihood of appeal, the costs of recording, and time constraints.

Contempt

Magistrate judges may not hold contempt hearings. Instead, a magistrate judge may certify the facts of the potential contempt to the district judge and serve an order to show cause why the disobedient party should not be held in contempt. The district judge will then make the contempt determination and impose any sanction. *See* 28 U.S.C. § 636(e).

RULE 73(b) Consent Procedure

Because the authority for magistrate judges to conduct civil trials hinges on the consent of the litigants, the consent process is handled with special care. The litigants may be advised of their ability to consent to a magistrate judge trial, but must also be advised that they are free to withhold that consent. The consent-confirming process is conducted by the clerk of court, without involving the district judge. Only if all parties consent will the clerk advise the district judge of the outcome of the consent-confirming process. For good cause or when a party shows exceptional circumstances, the district judge can reclaim the case.

PRACTICING LAW UNDER THIS SUBPART

Clerk-Conducted Consent Procedure

At the time the action is filed, the clerk of court notifies the parties in writing of their option to proceed before a magistrate judge. *See* 28 U.S.C. § 636(c)(2). To prevent the district judge from influencing the parties in their consent decision and to shield the district judge from knowing who may have refused consent, the clerk of court administers the complete consent procedure.

Time and Manner for Consent

The time for indicating a party's consent or lack of consent is set generally by local rule or court order. Parties generally indicate their consent by submitting completed consent forms supplied by the clerk for this purpose. Local rules establish procedures to ensure the voluntariness and willingness of consent, such as preventing the clerk of court from notifying litigants that their case will be heard sooner by a magistrate judge or that they will receive an experienced magistrate judge. Neither the district judge, the magistrate judge, nor the clerk of court may attempt to persuade the parties to consent to a trial before a magistrate judge.

- *Consent by New Parties:* In general, local rules will control the time within which new parties must exercise their right to consent to trial before a magistrate judge. The clerk of court will notify new parties of their right to consent in the same manner as the original parties. When an additional party is joined who does not consent to the participation of the magistrate judge, the district judge must hear the case.
- *Participation Without Objection As Consent:* If a party participates in a trial before a magistrate judge without objection, the court may infer that party's consent. *See Roell v. Withrow,* 538 U.S. 580, 581 (2003).

Vacating the Special Designation of a Magistrate Judge

Once consent has been given and the magistrate judge has been specially designated to preside over the trial, the parties generally cannot change their minds and withdraw their consent. *See Dixon v. Ylst*, 990 F.2d 478, 480 (9th Cir. 1993). However, a party can petition the district court to vacate its referral to the magistrate judge by showing extraordinary circumstances, or the district court may order the referral vacated on its own motion for good cause. *See* 28 U.S.C. § 636(c)(6). Such authority is rarely used, never exercised routinely, and reserved for truly exceptional circumstances.

RULE 73(c) Appealing a Judgment

A party who is dissatisfied with the judgment entered by a magistrate judge (following a trial by consent under this Rule) may appeal that judgment directly to the court of appeals in the same manner as any judgment entered by a district judge would be appealed.

RULES 74, 75, AND 76*

[ABROGATED (APR. 11, 1997, EFF. DEC. 1, 1997).]

* Rule 73(d) and Rules 74, 75, and 76 had formerly provided that when a magistrate judge hears a case, the parties could choose to appeal to either the district court or the court of appeals. In 1997 the so-called "optional appeal route" to the district court was abolished by Congress. Accordingly, the Supreme Court abrogated Rule 73(d) and Rules 74, 75, and 76 effective in December 1997. Henceforth, appeals from trials conducted by magistrate judges were made only to the appropriate court of appeals.

RULE 77

CONDUCTING BUSINESS; CLERK'S AUTHORITY; NOTICE OF AN ORDER OR JUDGMENT

(a) When Court Is Open. Every district court is considered always open for filing any paper, issuing and returning process, making a motion, or entering an order.

(b) Place for Trial and Other Proceedings. Every trial on the merits must be conducted in open court and, so far as convenient, in a regular courtroom. Any other act or proceeding may be done or conducted by a judge in chambers, without the attendance of the clerk or other court official, and anywhere inside or outside the district. But no hearing—other than one ex parte—may be conducted outside the district unless all the affected parties consent.

(c) Clerk's Office Hours; Clerk's Orders.

(1) *Hours.* The clerk's office—with a clerk or deputy on duty—must be open during business hours every day except Saturdays, Sundays, and legal holidays. But a court may, by local rule or order, require that the office be open for specified hours on Saturday or a particular legal holiday other than one listed in Rule 6(a)(4)(A).

(2) *Orders.* Subject to the court's power to suspend, alter, or rescind the clerk's action for good cause, the clerk may:

(A) issue process;

(B) enter a default;

(C) enter a default judgment under Rule 55(b)(1); and

(D) act on any other matter that does not require the court's action.

(d) Serving Notice of an Order or Judgment.

(1) *Service.* Immediately after entering an order or judgment, the clerk must serve notice of the entry, as provided in Rule 5(b), on each party who is not in default for failing to appear. The clerk must record the service on the docket. A party also may serve notice of the entry as provided in Rule 5(b).

(2) *Time to Appeal Not Affected by Lack of Notice.* Lack of notice of the entry does not affect the time for appeal or relieve—or authorize the court to

relieve—a party for failing to appeal within the time allowed, except as allowed by Federal Rule of Appellate Procedure (4)(a).

[Amended effective March 19, 1948; July 1, 1963; July 1, 1968; July 1, 1971; August 1, 1987; December 1, 1991; April 23, 2001, effective December 1, 2001; April 30, 2007, effective December 1, 2007.]

UNDERSTANDING RULE 77

HOW RULE 77 FITS IN

Rule 77 contains a variety of provisions pertaining to the operations of the district court and the clerk's office. It provides that the court is always "open," and requires that the clerk's physical office be open during "business hours." It also states that trials and hearings shall be conducted in a courtroom. Finally, Rule 77 controls notice of judgments and orders.

THE ARCHITECTURE OF RULE 77

Rule 77 contains four loosely related provisions in four subsections. Rule 77(a) directs that the courts are always open for filings. Rule 77(b) specifies where various types of proceedings may occur—whether in open court or in chambers. Rule 77(c) addresses the hours when the clerk's office must be open. Finally, Rule 77(d) obligates the clerk to serve the orders and judgments that the judge issues, but clarifies that the time for appeal is not affected by such service.

HOW RULE 77 WORKS IN PRACTICE

RULE 77(a) When Court Is Open

The district courts are deemed open at all times for purposes like filing papers and issuing process. This does not mean that the courthouse will be manned and physically open at all times. Rather, papers may be filed after hours by filing them on the court's electronic filing system, delivering them to the clerk or a deputy clerk, depositing them in a designated receptacle provided by the clerk and authorized by local rule, or even—under exceptional circumstances—leaving them with a judge.

RULE 77(b) Place for Trial and Other Proceedings

All trials must be conducted in open court and in a regular courtroom to the extent "convenient." Other proceedings, such as pretrial conferences, may be conducted in chambers or some other location. In general, no hearing may be held outside the district without consent of all parties.

RULE 77(c) Clerk's Office Hours; Clerk's Orders

At a minimum, the clerk's office must be open during business hours on all days except weekends and holidays. The hours may be expanded by local rule. The clerk's office has the power to take certain acts, such as entering default judgments and process to execute judgments. Such actions by the clerk's office are reviewable by the court and may be suspended, altered, or rescinded upon cause shown.

RULE 77(d) Serving Notice of an Order or Judgment

The clerk's office must serve notice of the entry of judgment on all parties who have entered appearances. Typically, the notice is automatically served on all parties of record by the court's electronic filing system, which is sufficient. However, the failure of the clerk to do so does not necessarily increase the time for appeal (but, the appellate courts may extend the time for appeal and may consider the failure of the clerk to send notice, and the district court may reopen and extend the time for appeal). A party who wants to ensure that all other parties have notice of the judgment (and thus that the time for appeal has begun to run) may serve the notice.

RULE 78

HEARING MOTIONS; SUBMISSION ON BRIEFS

(a) Providing a Regular Schedule for Oral Hearings. A court may establish regular times and places for oral hearings on motions.

(b) Providing for Submission on Briefs. By rule or order, the court may provide for submitting and determining motions on briefs, without oral hearings.

[Amended effective August 1, 1987; April 30, 2007, effective December 1, 2007.]

UNDERSTANDING RULE 78

HOW RULE 78 FITS IN

The manner in which each district, or even each individual judge, handles motions varies considerably. Some judges primarily rule on motions based on the parties' written submissions, only conducting oral argument upon request. Other judges routinely conduct oral argument, and some courts have regular motion days scheduled for such oral arguments.

Rule 78 codifies this flexibility. It allows each district to enact local rules establishing regular motion days for the presentation of motions requiring a hearing. However, judges may conduct oral arguments on motions at other times. Furthermore, the districts or individual judges may also provide that motions are to be determined on briefs only, without oral argument.

THE ARCHITECTURE OF RULE 78

Rule 78 has two short subsections. Rule 78(a) allows courts to establish motion days, or regular times and places for oral argument on motions. Rule 78(b) authorizes courts to decide motions based on the parties' written submissions, without oral argument.

HOW RULE 78 WORKS IN PRACTICE

RULE 78(a) Providing a Regular Schedule for Oral Hearings

The court may establish regular times for hearing arguments, but may also hear arguments at any time or place on notice that the court considers reasonable.

RULE 78(b) Providing for Submission on Briefs

The court may decide motions on the papers, without oral argument.

RULE 79

RECORDS KEPT BY THE CLERK

(a) Civil Docket.

(1) *In General.* The clerk must keep a record known as the "civil docket" in the form and manner prescribed by the Director of the Administrative Office of the United States Courts with the approval of the Judicial Conference of the United States. The clerk must enter each civil action in the docket. Actions must be assigned consecutive file numbers, which must be noted in the docket where the first entry of the action is made.

(2) *Items to be Entered.* The following items must be marked with the file number and entered chronologically in the docket:

(A) papers filed with the clerk;

(B) process issued, and proofs of service or other returns showing execution; and

(C) appearances, orders, verdicts, and judgments.

(3) *Contents of Entries; Jury Trial Demanded.* Each entry must briefly show the nature of the paper filed or writ issued, the substance of each proof of service or other return, and the substance and date of entry of each order and judgment. When a jury trial has been properly demanded or ordered, the clerk must enter the word "jury" in the docket.

(b) Civil Judgments and Orders. The clerk must keep a copy of every final judgment and appealable order; of every order affecting title to or a lien on real or personal property; and of any other order that the court directs to be kept. The clerk must keep these in the form and manner prescribed by the Director of the Administrative Office of the United States Courts with the approval of the Judicial Conference of the United States.

(c) Indexes; Calendars. Under the court's direction, the clerk must:

(1) keep indexes of the docket and of the judgments and orders described in Rule 79(b); and

(2) prepare calendars of all actions ready for trial, distinguishing jury trials from nonjury trials.

(d) Other Records. The clerk must keep any other records required by the Director of the Administrative Office of the United States Courts with the approval of the Judicial Conference of the United States.

[Amended effective March 19, 1948; October 20, 1949; July 1, 1963; April 30, 2007, effective December 1, 2007.]

UNDERSTANDING RULE 79

HOW RULE 79 FITS IN

Rule 79 establishes the record keeping duties of the district court clerk's office. It requires the clerk's office to maintain a "docket," a list that includes each case—identified by a unique number. The docket must contain a designation if any party has demanded a jury trial (as described in Rule 38), and must list by date and description each document the parties file or the judge issues.

The clerk must also keep a copy of every final judgment and appealable order that the court issues, as well as every order affecting title to or a lien on real or personal property, any other order that the court directs the clerk to keep, and any other records the clerk's offices are ordered to maintain by the Administrative Office of the United States Courts. In addition to maintaining the docket and the final judgments, orders, and other documents, the clerk's office must maintain an index of the docket and the other documents the clerk's office is required to maintain.

THE ARCHITECTURE OF RULE 79

Rule 79 divides the clerk's office's record-keeping duties into four subparts. Rule 79(a) contains the provisions regarding the docket. Rule 79(b) obligates the clerk to maintain copies of final judgments, appealable orders, and other documents. Rule 79(d) adds records designated by the Administrative Office to the list that the clerk must maintain. Finally, Rule 79(c) imposes the obligation to index the docket and the other documents the clerk maintains under Rule 79.

HOW RULE 79 WORKS IN PRACTICE

RULE 79(a) Civil Docket

The clerk must keep a civil docket, which is a chronological listing of each pleading, motion, brief, order, etc., filed in the case. The docket may be maintained electronically.

PRACTICING LAW UNDER THIS SUBPART

Description

The docket should contain a brief description of each entry. Entries should be listed chronologically and should show the date on which each document is entered.

Jury vs. Non-Jury

The docket should indicate if the case is to be tried before a jury.

Judgments

Judgments are not effective until entered on the docket.

Briefs

Although for some purposes, briefs are not considered part of the official record, briefs are generally filed and entered on the docket.

RULE 79(b) Civil Judgments and Orders

The clerk's office must retain a copy of every final judgment, appealable order, order creating a lien on property, and any other order as directed by the court. In practice, most courts now maintain electronic copies of all documents filed in the court, which can be accessed through the PACER system.

RULE 79(c) Indexes; Calendars

The clerk's office must maintain an index of the civil docket and of every civil judgment, appealable order, order creating a lien on property, and other order as directed by the court. The clerk's office must also maintain a calendar of all actions ready for trial, distinguishing jury and non-jury trials.

RULE 79(d) Other Records

The Administrative Office of the United States may direct that the clerk's offices maintain other books and records.

RULE 80

STENOGRAPHIC TRANSCRIPT AS EVIDENCE

If stenographically reported testimony at a hearing or trial is admissible in evidence at a later trial, the testimony may be proved by a transcript certified by the person who reported it.

[Amended effective March 19, 1948; April 30, 2007, effective December 1, 2007.]

UNDERSTANDING RULE 80

HOW RULE 80 FITS IN

Rule 80 pertains to the use of testimony at one hearing or trial as evidence at a subsequent hearing or trial. The Rule provides that a transcript certified by an official court reporter is proof of the prior testimony.

XI. GENERAL PROVISIONS

RULE 81

APPLICABILITY OF THE RULES IN GENERAL; REMOVED ACTIONS

(a) Applicability to Particular Proceedings.

(1) *Prize Proceedings.* These rules do not apply to prize proceedings in admiralty governed by 10 U.S.C. §§ 7651 to 7681.

(2) *Bankruptcy.* These rules apply to bankruptcy proceedings to the extent provided by the Federal Rules of Bankruptcy Procedure.

(3) *Citizenship.* These rules apply to proceedings for admission to citizenship to the extent that the practice in those proceedings is not specified in federal statutes and has previously conformed to the practice in civil actions. The provisions of 8 U.S.C. § 1451 for service by publication and for answer apply in proceedings to cancel citizenship certificates.

(4) *Special Writs.* These rules apply to proceedings for habeas corpus and for quo warranto to the extent that the practice in those proceedings:

(A) is not specified in a federal statute, the Rules Governing Section 2254 Cases, or the Rules Governing Section 2255 Cases; and

(B) has previously conformed to the practice in civil actions.

(5) *Proceedings Involving a Subpoena.* These rules apply to proceedings to compel testimony or the production of documents through a subpoena issued by a United States officer or agency under a federal statute, except as otherwise provided by statute, by local rule, or by court order in the proceedings.

(6) *Other Proceedings.* These rules, to the extent applicable, govern proceedings under the following laws, except as these laws provide other procedures:

(A) 7 U.S.C. §§ 292, 499g(c), for reviewing an order of the Secretary of Agriculture;

(B) 9 U.S.C., relating to arbitration;

(C) 15 U.S.C. § 522, for reviewing an order of the Secretary of the Interior;

(D) 15 U.S.C. § 715d(c), for reviewing an order denying a certificate of clearance;

(E) 29 U.S.C. §§ 159, 160, for enforcing an order of the National Labor Relations Board;

(F) 33 U.S.C. §§ 918, 921, for enforcing or reviewing a compensation order under the Longshore and Harbor Workers' Compensation Act; and

(G) 45 U.S.C. § 159, for reviewing an arbitration award in a railway-labor dispute.

(b) Scire Facias and Mandamus. The writs of scire facias and mandamus are abolished. Relief previously available through them may be obtained by appropriate action or motion under these rules.

(c) Removed Actions.

(1) *Applicability.* These rules apply to a civil action after it is removed from a State court.

(2) *Further Pleading.* After removal, repleading is unnecessary unless the court orders it. A defendant who did not answer before removal must answer or present other defenses or objections under these rules within the longest of these periods:

(A) 21 days after receiving—through service or otherwise—a copy of the initial pleading stating the claim for relief;

(B) 21 days after being served with the summons for an initial pleading on file at the time of service; or

(C) 7 days after the notice of removal is filed.

(3) *Demand for a Jury Trial.*

(A) *As Affected by State Law.* A party who, before removal, expressly demanded a jury trial in accordance with State law need not renew the demand after removal. If the State law did not require an express demand for a jury trial, a party need not make one after removal unless the court orders the parties to do so within a specified time. The court must so order at a party's request and may so order on its own. A party who fails to make a demand when so ordered waives a jury trial.

(B) *Under* Rule 38. If all necessary pleadings have been served at the time of removal, a party entitled to a jury trial under Rule 38 must be given one if the party serves a demand within 14 days after:

(i) it files a notice of removal; or

(ii) it is served with a notice of removal filed by another party.

(d) Law Applicable.

(1) *"State Law" Defined.* When these rules refer to State law, the term "law" includes the State's statutes and the State's judicial decisions.

(2) *"State" Defined.* The term "State" includes, where appropriate, the District of Columbia and any United States commonwealth or territory.

(3) *"Federal Statute" Defined in the District of Columbia.* In the United States District Court for the District of Columbia, the term "federal statute" includes any Act of Congress that applies locally to the District.

[Amended effective December 28, 1939; March 19, 1948; October 20, 1949; August 1, 1951; July 1, 1963; July 1, 1966; July 1, 1968; July 1, 1971; August 1, 1987; April 23, 2001, effective December 1, 2001; April 29, 2002, effective December 1, 2002; April 30, 2007, effective December 1, 2007; March 26, 2009, effective December 1, 2009.]

UNDERSTANDING RULE 81

HOW RULE 81 FITS IN

Tucked way in the back of the Rules in the General Provisions section, Rule 81 performs some important functions. As its title suggests, it controls the extent to which the Federal Rules of Civil Procedure apply in an assortment of contexts. It provides that the Rules do not apply to prize proceedings in admiralty and lists categories of proceedings where the Rules do apply, such as admission to citizenship proceedings.

Relatedly, Rule 81 controls the manner in which the Rules apply to proceedings that are commenced in State court, then removed to federal court (see the discussion of removal in the Getting Started section above). Because such proceedings are initiated under one set of rules—the State rules of procedure—and then shift to a court employing a different set of rules—the Federal Rules of Civil Procedure—opportunity for confusion abounds. Rule 81(c) specifies when the federal court will require compliance with the federal procedures and when parties may rely on their satisfaction of the State procedures.

Rule 81 also abolishes two old-fashioned writs, the writ of scire facias (a writ with a variety of functions such as reviving a judgment or effecting execution) and the writ of mandamus (a writ compelling an official to take an action). Rule 81 only abolishes these writs at the trial court level, however, and courts of appeal periodically issue writs of mandamus to the district courts ordering them to take a certain action or conduct proceedings in a specified manner.

Lastly, Rule 81 defines three terms: "State law;" "State;" and "federal statute." The Rules do not contain a general definition section, so the Supreme Court housed these definitions in Rule 81.

THE ARCHITECTURE OF RULE 81

Rule 81's architecture is somewhat jumbled, as it is the repository for two provisions that seem outside the scope suggested by the title. Nominally, Rule 81 describes when the Federal Rules of Civil

Procedure do and do not apply. To that end, the lists of procedures covered by and exempt from the Federal Rules of Civil Procedure are situated in Rule 81(a), and Rule 81(c) contains the provisions explaining when the Rules do and do not apply in removed actions.

Rules 81(b) and 81(d) depart somewhat from this focus. Rule 81(b) contains the provision abolishing the writs of scire facias and mandamus, and Rule 81(d) contains the definitions of "State law," "State," and "federal statute."

HOW RULE 81 WORKS IN PRACTICE

RULE 81(a) Applicability to Particular Proceedings

Rule 81(a) provides that the Rules do not apply to admiralty proceedings and lists categories of proceedings where the Rules provide default or supplemental procedures to be used as dictated by the specific statutes controlling those proceedings.

PRACTICING LAW UNDER THIS SUBPART

Not Applicable to Prize Proceedings in Admiralty

The Rules do not apply to prize proceedings in admiralty (essentially, proceedings relating to vessels, equipment, and cargo seized during armed conflict).

Applicable to Supplement Statutory Procedures

The Rules supplement the statutory procedures for the following:

- Bankruptcy Proceedings, to the extent provided by the Bankruptcy Rules;
- Admission to citizenship proceedings;
- Habeas Corpus Proceedings (*see Mayle v. Felix,* 545 U.S. 644, 654 (2005));
- Quo Warranto Proceedings;
- Proceedings to enforce subpoenas to testify or to produce documents issued by agencies of the United States;
- Proceedings to review orders of the Secretary of Agriculture;
- Proceedings arbitrated under the Federal Arbitration Act;
- Proceedings to review orders of the Secretary of the Interior;
- Proceedings to review orders of the Petroleum Control Boards;
- Proceedings to enforce orders of the National Labor Relations Board;
- Proceedings for enforcement or review of compensation orders under the Longshoremen's and Harbor Workers' Compensation Act; and
- Proceedings to review arbitration awards in railway-labor disputes.

Arbitrations

In proceedings arbitrated under federal statute, the Rules generally act as default provisions, applying when no arbitration rule addresses a procedural issue.

RULE 81(b) Scire Facias and Mandamus

Rule 81(b) abolishes the Writ of Scire Facias (a writ with a variety of functions such as reviving a judgment or effecting execution) and the Writ of Mandamus (a writ compelling an official to take an action) at the district court level.

RULE 81(c) Removed Actions

The Rules apply to actions commenced in State court and removed to federal court. Rule 81(c) contains procedures governing removed actions.

PRACTICING LAW UNDER THIS SUBPART

Rules Apply After Removal

When an action is commenced in state court, then removed to federal court, the Rules apply to pleadings or motions filed after the removal. Thus, Rules governing the form or service of pleadings would not apply to pleadings filed and served in State court prior to removal.

Time for Service of Complaint

For a defendant served with the complaint before removal, State law controls the timeliness of service. Rule 4(m) applies for defendants not served with the complaint prior to removal, and the 90-day deadline for service is calculated from the date of removal.

Time to Answer

If the defendant has not yet answered at the time of removal, the defendant may file an answer or responsive motion by the later of 7 days from the date of removal or 21 days from receipt of the original pleading (through proper service or otherwise) or service of the summons for a complaint that has been filed.

Jury Demand

Rule 81(c) contains a number of provisions explaining how jury trial demands work in cases filed in state court then removed to federal court. If a jury trial demand has been properly made in State court, no new demand is necessary. If no jury trial demand was made in State court and if all pleadings were filed in State court, the parties may make a jury trial demand within 14 days of removal to federal court. If no express jury trial demand is required under State law, none will be required in the removed action unless the court so directs.

RULE 81(d) Law Applicable

In general, when the Rules refer to "States," they include the District of Columbia. Thus, when the Rules refer to the law of the State in which the court sits, the United States District Court for the District of Columbia uses the law applied in the District of Columbia. The phrase "law of a State" includes State statutes and judicial decisions.

RULE 82

JURISDICTION AND VENUE UNAFFECTED

These rules do not extend or limit the jurisdiction of the district courts or the venue of actions in those courts. An admiralty or maritime claim under Rule 9(h) is governed by 28 U.S.C. § 1390.

[Amended effective October 20, 1949; July 1, 1966; April 23, 2001, effective December 1, 2001; April 30, 2007, effective December 1, 2007; April 28, 2016, effective December 1, 2016.]

UNDERSTANDING RULE 82

HOW RULE 82 FITS IN

Rule 82 serves a limited, but important, function. Federal courts are courts of limited subject-matter jurisdiction, meaning that they are only empowered to hear the categories of cases set forth in the Constitution and the implementing statutes enacted by Congress, as discussed in more detail in the Getting Started section above. Federal question jurisdiction and diversity jurisdiction are two examples of these categories. Rule 82 clarifies that the contours of the federal courts' jurisdiction is not altered by anything in the Federal Rules of Civil Procedure.

Rule 82 also provides that the Federal Rules of Civil Procedure do not affect venue in federal courts, which is controlled by federal statute. Relatedly, Rule 82 acknowledges that venue for admiralty and maritime actions is governed by 28 U.S.C. § 1390.

THE ARCHITECTURE OF RULE 82

Rule 82 provides clarification on three closely related topics, and the framers of Rule 82 did not see the need to separate these topics into any subsections; Rule 82 comprises two sentences in a single section.

HOW RULE 82 WORKS IN PRACTICE

As a general matter, the Rules do not extend or restrict the court's subject-matter jurisdiction. *See Henderson v. United States,* 517 U.S. 654 (1996). This principle is limited to *subject-matter* jurisdiction (*i.e.,* the type of case a district court can hear), not *personal* jurisdiction (*i.e.,* which parties must appear and defend themselves). Likewise, the Rules contain timing requirements that are often described as "jurisdictional" but do not affect the court's subject-matter jurisdiction. *See Kontrick v. Ryan,* 540 U.S. 443, 453–54 (2004).

RULE 83

RULES BY DISTRICT COURTS; JUDGE'S DIRECTIVES

(a) Local Rules.

(1) *In General.* After giving public notice and an opportunity for comment, a district court, acting by a majority of its district judges, may adopt and amend rules governing its practice. A local rule must be consistent with—but not duplicate—federal statutes and rules adopted under 28 U.S.C. §§ 2072 and 2075, and must conform to any uniform numbering system prescribed by the Judicial Conference of the United States. A local rule takes effect on the date specified by the district court and remains in effect unless amended by the court or abrogated by the judicial council of the circuit. Copies of rules and amendments must, on their adoption, be furnished to the judicial council and the Administrative Office of the United States Courts and be made available to the public.

(2) *Requirement of Form.* A local rule imposing a requirement of form must not be enforced in a way that causes a party to lose any right because of a nonwillful failure to comply.

(b) Procedure When There Is No Controlling Law. A judge may regulate practice in any manner consistent with federal law, rules adopted under 28 U.S.C. §§ 2072 and 2075, and the district's local rules. No sanction or other disadvantage may be imposed for noncompliance with any requirement not in federal law, federal rules, or the local rules unless the alleged violator has been furnished in the particular case with actual notice of the requirement.

[Amended effective August 1, 1985; April 27, 1995, effective December 1, 1995; April 30, 2007, effective December 1, 2007.]

UNDERSTANDING RULE 83

HOW RULE 83 FITS IN

The rules of procedure governing actions proceeding in federal court are found in a variety of repositories. The Federal Rules of Civil Procedure contain a significant portion of these procedural provisions, but certainly not all of them. Many procedures are housed in statutes, such as the statutes governing subject-matter jurisdiction, removal, and venue. These two sources of procedure generally apply to all the federal courts across the country.

Rule 83 pertains to the more localized sets of procedure. It authorizes each district to enact "local rules" that only apply to actions proceeding in that district. These local rules must be published for public comment, then approved by a majority of the district judges in the district. They must be consistent with, but not duplicative of, the Federal Rules of Civil Procedure.

For issues that are not controlled by either federal statute, the Federal Rules of Civil Procedure, or the district's local rules, a district court judge may regulate proceedings in any manner consistent with those sources of procedure.

Rule 83 also imposes two limitations on the permissible consequences for failure to comply with a local rule or an individual judge's procedures. First, a local rule addressing an issue of *form* must not be enforced in a way that causes a party to lose a *substantive right* because of a nonwillful failure to comply with the local rule. Second, no sanction or other disadvantage may be imposed for noncompliance with an individual judge's procedures unless the alleged violator has been furnished in the particular case with actual notice of the requirement. This rule protects lawyers—and particularly out-of-town lawyers—from being sanctioned for violating chambers rules they were not even aware of.

THE ARCHITECTURE OF RULE 83

Rule 83 is divided into two subsections, addressing local rules and individual judge's rules. Rule 83(a) authorizes local rules, provides the procedures for enacting local rules, limits the scope of local rules to supplementing federal statutes and the Federal Rules of Civil Procedure, and limits the consequences of a nonwillful failure to comply with a local rule. Rule 83(b) authorizes individual judges to fill gaps in the other sources of procedure with their own procedural rules, but requires the judges to provide copies of their rules to a party before imposing sanctions for violating those rules.

HOW RULE 83 WORKS IN PRACTICE

RULE 83(a) — Local Rules

Each district court may develop local rules. *See Hollingsworth v. Perry,* 558 U.S. 183, 191 (2010).

PRACTICING LAW UNDER THIS SUBPART

Consistent with Federal Rules

Local rules must be consistent with, but not duplicative of, Acts of Congress and the federal Rules. Additionally, numbering must be consistent with the federal Rules.

Typical Local Rules

Local rules can cover a wide variety of topics, and vary greatly in number and scope from district to district. Some typical local rules address:

- Admission to practice before the district courts;
- Admission *Pro Hac Vice;*

- Procedures for the recovery of court costs;
- Creation of divisions within the district;
- Form and number of copies of pleadings and briefs;
- Manner for presentation of motions;
- Continuances;
- Discovery procedures;
- Pretrial and status conferences, including pretrial statements;
- Courtroom rules and regulations, including the use of cameras and recording equipment;
- Size, selection, and instruction of the jury; and
- Handling and marking of exhibits.

Effect of Local Rule

A valid local rule has the effect of law, and must be obeyed. *Hollingsworth v. Perry,* 558 U.S. 183, 191 (2010). The court may impose sanctions when a party violates the court's local rules. However, a local rule imposing a requirement of form (as opposed to substance) may not be enforced in a manner that causes a party to lose rights for a "nonwillful" violation. Thus, a party may not be deprived of a right to a jury trial because it is unaware of or forgets a local rule requiring jury demands to be noted in the caption of pleadings.

Obtaining Copies

Local rules are often available on the court's website. A copy of the local rules can also be obtained from the clerk's office for a nominal fee.

RULE 83(b) Procedure When There Is No Controlling Law

In the absence of a federal or local rule of procedure, judges may regulate proceedings before them as they see fit, so long as the judge's procedures are consistent with federal law, the federal Rules, and local Rules. *See Dietz v. Bouldin*, 136 S. Ct. 1885, 1892 (2016).

PRACTICING LAW UNDER THIS SUBPART

Parties Must Have Actual Notice of Court Requirements

The court may not sanction or disadvantage a party for noncompliance with one of the court's chamber rules unless that party has been furnished in the particular case with actual notice of the rule. Actual notice can be achieved by providing parties with a copy of the judge's rules, by an order referencing the judge's standing order and indicating how copies can be obtained, or by oral notice at a Rule 16 conference.

RULE 84
FORMS
[ABROGATED]

[Amended effective March 19, 1948; April 30, 2007, effective December 1, 2007; abrogated April 29, 2015, effective December 1, 2015.]

UNDERSTANDING RULE 84

HOW RULE 84 FITS IN

Rule 84 used to authorize a set of federal forms that was appended to the Rules. It also provided that a pleading or other paper that was consistent with one of the official forms was deemed sufficient under the Rules. Rule 84 was abrogated on December 1, 2015. Although the forms no longer carry the official imprimatur of Rule 84, they are still available online at http://www.uscourts.gov/forms/civil-forms.

RULE 85

TITLE

These rules may be cited as the Federal Rules of Civil Procedure.

[Amended April 30, 2007, effective December 1, 2007.]

UNDERSTANDING RULE 85

HOW RULE 85 FITS IN

Rule 85 performs a single function—explaining the manner for citing to the Rules.

THE ARCHITECTURE OF RULE 85

Rule 85's single sentence does not warrant any complex structure, nor does it receive any.

HOW RULE 85 WORKS IN PRACTICE

The full title of the Rules is the "Federal Rules of Civil Procedure." The Rules should be cited as "Fed. R. Civ. P. ___."

RULE 86
EFFECTIVE DATES

(a) In General. These rules and any amendments take effect at the time specified by the Supreme Court, subject to 28 U.S.C. § 2074. They govern:

(1) proceedings in an action commenced after their effective date; and

(2) proceedings after that date in an action then pending unless:

(A) the Supreme Court specifies otherwise; or

(B) the court determines that applying them in a particular action would be infeasible or work an injustice.

(b) December 1, 2007 Amendments. If any provision in Rules 1–5.1, 6–73, or 77–86 conflicts with another law, priority in time for the purpose of 28 U.S.C. § 2072(b) is not affected by the amendments taking effect on December 1, 2007.

[Amended effective March 19, 1948; October 20, 1949; July 19, 1961; July 1, 1963; April 30, 2007, effective December 1, 2007.]

UNDERSTANDING RULE 86

HOW RULE 86 FITS IN

On a regular basis, the Supreme Court proposes amendments to the Federal Rules of Civil Procedure to Congress, under a process described in the Judicial Rulemaking section of this book. Those amendments go into effect on December 1 of the year in which they are proposed, unless Congress acts to prevent their effectiveness. Not surprisingly, such amendments apply to all cases commenced after the effective date of the amendments. It is less intuitive how amended provisions should apply to already pending cases, and the answer lies in Rule 86.

Rule 86 confirms that amended provisions in the Federal Rules of Civil Procedure apply to actions commenced before the effective date of the amendments unless: a) the Supreme Court specifies otherwise; or b) the district court determines that applying them in a particular action would be infeasible or work an injustice.

Rule 86 also contains one subsection devoted exclusively to a quirk in the 2007 amendment process. In 2007, the Rules were edited from top to bottom to make the language consistent, to improve the organization, and otherwise to clean up the language of the Rules. These "restyling" amendments were expressly nonsubstantive. In addition, the Supreme Court proposed a second separate of substantive amendments to a handful of rules the same year. Rule 86 harmonizes the effectiveness of these two simultaneous sets of amendments.

THE ARCHITECTURE OF RULE 86

The provisions governing the general applicability of amendments to pending and newly filed cases are located in Rule 86(a). Rule 86(b) contains the narrow provision governing the interaction of the two sets of amendments in 2007.

HOW RULE 86 WORKS IN PRACTICE

RULE 86(a) In General

In general, amendments to the Rules will apply to all actions filed after the effective date of the amendments, and to proceedings in actions filed before the effective date unless the Supreme Court has specified otherwise or the court determines that application of an amended provision would not be feasible or would work an injustice.

RULE 86(b) December 1, 2007 Amendments

Rule 86(b) addresses the interplay between the 2007 amendments to the Rules and the supersession clause in 28 U.S.C. § 2072(b). The supersession clause says that laws in conflict with one or more of the Rules shall have no further force and effect after such Rules have taken effect. In essence, the Rules are deemed to have superseded existing inconsistent laws. Because the supersession clause focuses on the sequence in time between the Rules and other laws, Rule 86(b) provides that the non-substantive changes to every Rule in the 2007 amendments do not affect the priority-in-time analysis.

SUPPLEMENTAL RULES FOR ADMIRALTY OR MARITIME CLAIMS AND ASSET FORFEITURE ACTIONS

Adopted February 28, 1966, effective July 1, 1966

The former Rules of Practice in Admiralty and Maritime Cases, promulgated by the Supreme Court on December 6, 1920, effective March 7, 1921, as revised, amended and supplemented, were rescinded, effective July 1, 1966.

Including Amendments effective December 1, 2009

RULE A

SCOPE OF RULES

(1) These Supplemental Rules apply to:

(A) the procedure in admiralty and maritime claims within the meaning of Rule 9(h) with respect to the following remedies:

(i) maritime attachment and garnishment,

(ii) actions in rem,

(iii) possessory, petitory, and partition actions, and

(iv) actions for exoneration from or limitation of liability;

(B) forfeiture actions in rem arising from a federal statute; and

(C) the procedure in statutory condemnation proceedings analogous to maritime actions in rem, whether within the admiralty and maritime jurisdiction or not. Except as otherwise provided, references in these Supplemental Rules to actions in rem include such analogous statutory condemnation proceedings.

(2) The Federal Rules of Civil Procedure also apply to the foregoing proceedings except to the extent that they are inconsistent with these Supplemental Rules.

[Added Feb. 28, 1966, eff. July 1, 1966; April 12, 2006, effective December 1, 2006.]

RULE B

IN PERSONAM ACTIONS: ATTACHMENT AND GARNISHMENT

(1) **When Available; Complaint, Affidavit, Judicial Authorization, and Process.** In an in personam action:

(a) If a defendant is not found within the district when a verified complaint praying for attachment and the affidavit required by Rule B(1)(b) are filed, a verified complaint may contain a prayer for process to attach the defendant's tangible or intangible personal property—up to the amount sued for—in the hands of garnishees named in the process.

(b) The plaintiff or the plaintiff's attorney must sign and file with the complaint an affidavit stating that, to the affiant's knowledge, or on information and belief, the defendant cannot be found within the district. The court must review the complaint and affidavit and, if the conditions of this Rule B appear to exist, enter an order so stating and authorizing process of attachment and garnishment. The clerk may issue supplemental process enforcing the court's order upon application without further court order.

(c) If the plaintiff or the plaintiff's attorney certifies that exigent circumstances make court review impracticable, the clerk must issue the summons and process of attachment and garnishment. The plaintiff has the burden in any post-attachment hearing under Rule E(4)(f) to show that exigent circumstances existed.

(d) (i) If the property is a vessel or tangible property on board a vessel, the summons, process, and any supplemental process must be delivered to the marshal for service.

(ii) If the property is other tangible or intangible property, the summons, process, and any supplemental process must be delivered to a person or organization authorized to serve it, who may be (A) a marshal; (B) someone under contract with the United States; (C) someone specially appointed by the court for that purpose; or, (D) in an action brought by the United States, any officer or employee of the United States.

(e) The plaintiff may invoke State-law remedies under Rule 64 for seizure of person or property for the purpose of securing satisfaction of the judgment.

(2) Notice to Defendant. No default judgment may be entered except upon proof—which may be by affidavit—that:

(a) the complaint, summons, and process of attachment or garnishment have been served on the defendant in a manner authorized by Rule 4;

(b) the plaintiff or the garnishee has mailed to the defendant the complaint, summons, and process of attachment or garnishment, using any form of mail requiring a return receipt; or

(c) the plaintiff or the garnishee has tried diligently to give notice of the action to the defendant but could not do so.

(3) Answer.

(a) By Garnishee. The garnishee shall serve an answer, together with answers to any interrogatories served with the complaint, within 21 days after service of process upon the garnishee. Interrogatories to the garnishee may be served with the complaint without leave of court. If the garnishee refuses or neglects to answer on oath as to the debts, credits, or effects of the defendant in the garnishee's hands, or any interrogatories concerning such debts, credits, and effects that may be propounded by the plaintiff, the court may award compulsory process against the garnishee. If the garnishee admits any debts, credits, or effects, they shall be held in the garnishee's hands or paid into the registry of the court, and shall be held in either case subject to the further order of the court.

(b) By Defendant. The defendant shall serve an answer within 30 days after process has been executed, whether by attachment of property or service on the garnishee.

[Added Feb. 28, 1966, eff. July 1, 1966, and amended Apr. 29, 1985, effective Aug. 1, 1985; Mar. 2, 1987, effective Aug. 1, 1987; April 17, 2000, effective December 1, 2000; April 25, 2005, effective December 1, 2005; amended March 26, 2009, effective December 1, 2009.]

RULE C

IN REM ACTIONS: SPECIAL PROVISIONS

(1) When Available. An action in rem may be brought:

(a) To enforce any maritime lien;

(b) Whenever a statute of the United States provides for a maritime action in rem or a proceeding analogous thereto.

Except as otherwise provided by law a party who may proceed in rem may also, or in the alternative, proceed in personam against any person who may be liable.

Statutory provisions exempting vessels or other property owned or possessed by or operated by or for the United States from arrest or seizure are not affected by this rule. When a statute so provides, an action against the United States or an instrumentality thereof may proceed on in rem principles.

(2) Complaint. In an action in rem the complaint must:

(a) be verified;

(b) describe with reasonable particularity the property that is the subject of the action; and

(c) state that the property is within the district or will be within the district while the action is pending.

(3) Judicial Authorization and Process.

(a) Arrest Warrant.

(i) The court must review the complaint and any supporting papers. If the conditions for an in rem action appear to exist, the court must issue an order directing the clerk to issue a warrant for the arrest of the vessel or other property that is the subject of the action.

(ii) If the plaintiff or the plaintiff's attorney certifies that exigent circumstances make court review impracticable, the clerk must promptly issue a summons and a warrant for the arrest of the vessel or other property that is the subject of the action. The plaintiff has the burden in any post-arrest hearing under Rule E(4)(f) to show that exigent circumstances existed.

(b) Service.

(i) If the property that is the subject of the action is a vessel or tangible property on board a vessel, the warrant and any supplemental process must be delivered to the marshal for service.

(ii) If the property that is the subject of the action is other property, tangible or intangible, the warrant and any supplemental process must be delivered to a person or organization authorized to enforce it, who may be: (A) a marshal; (B) someone under contract with the United States; (C) someone specially appointed by the court for that purpose; or, (D) in an action brought by the United States, any officer or employee of the United States.

(c) Deposit in Court. If the property that is the subject of the action consists in whole or in part of freight, the proceeds of property sold, or other intangible property, the clerk must issue—in addition to the warrant—a summons directing any person controlling the property to show cause why it should not be deposited in court to abide the judgment.

(d) Supplemental Process. The clerk may upon application issue supplemental process to enforce the court's order without further court order.

(4) Notice. No notice other than execution of process is required when the property that is the subject of the action has been released under Rule E(5). If the property is not released within 14 days after execution, the plaintiff must promptly—or within the time that the court allows—give public notice of the action and arrest in a newspaper designated by court order and having general circulation in the district, but publication may be terminated if the property is released before publication is completed. The notice must specify the time under Rule C(6) to file a statement of interest in or right against the seized property and to answer. This rule does not affect the notice requirements in an action to foreclose a preferred ship mortgage under 46 U.S.C. §§ 31301 et seq., as amended.

(5) Ancillary Process. In any action in rem in which process has been served as provided by this rule, if any part of the property that is the subject of the action has not been brought within the control of the court because it has been removed or sold, or because it is intangible property in the hands of a person who has not been served with process, the court may, on motion, order any person having possession or control of such property or its proceeds to show cause why it should not be delivered into the custody of the marshal or other person or organization having a warrant for the arrest of the property, or paid into court to abide the judgment; and, after hearing, the court may enter such judgment as law and justice may require.

(6) Responsive Pleading; Interrogatories.

(a) Statement of Interest; answer. In an action in rem:

(i) a person who asserts a right of possession or any ownership interest in the property that is the subject of the action must file a verified statement of right or interest:

(A) within 14 days after the execution of process, or

(B) within the time that the court allows;

(ii) the statement of right or interest must describe the interest in the property that supports the person's demand for its restitution or right to defend the action;

(iii) an agent, bailee, or attorney must state the authority to file a statement of right or interest on behalf of another; and

(iv) a person who asserts a right of possession or any ownership interest must serve an answer within 21 days after filing the statement of interest or right.

(b) Interrogatories. Interrogatories may be served with the complaint in an in rem action without leave of court. Answers to the interrogatories must be served with the answer to the complaint.

[Added Feb. 28, 1966, eff. Jul. 1, 1966, and amended Apr. 29, 1985, effective Aug. 1, 1985; Mar. 2, 1987, effective Aug. 1, 1987; Apr. 30, 1991, effective Dec. 1, 1991; April 17, 2000, effective December 1, 2000; April 29, 2002, effective December 1, 2002; April 25, 2005, effective December 1, 2005; April 12, 2006, effective December 1, 2006; amended March 26, 2009, effective December 1, 2009.]

RULE D

POSSESSORY, PETITORY, AND PARTITION ACTIONS

In all actions for possession, partition, and to try title maintainable according to the course of the admiralty practice with respect to a vessel, in all actions so maintainable with respect to the possession of cargo or other maritime property, and in all actions by one or more part owners against the others to obtain security for the return of the vessel from any voyage undertaken without their consent, or by one or more part owners against the others to obtain possession of the vessel for any voyage on giving security for its safe return, the process shall be by a warrant of arrest of the vessel, cargo, or other property, and by notice in the manner provided by Rule B(2) to the adverse party or parties.

[Added Feb. 28, 1966, eff. Jul. 1, 1966.]

RULE E

ACTIONS IN REM AND QUASI IN REM: GENERAL PROVISIONS

(1) Applicability. Except as otherwise provided, this rule applies to actions in personam with process of maritime attachment and garnishment, actions in rem, and petitory, possessory, and partition actions, supplementing Rules B, C, and D.

(2) Complaint; Security.

(a) *Complaint.* In actions to which this rule is applicable the complaint shall state the circumstances from which the claim arises with such particularity that the defendant or claimant will be able, without moving for a more definite statement, to commence an investigation of the facts and to frame a responsive pleading.

(b) *Security for Costs.* Subject to the provisions of Rule 54(d) and of relevant statutes, the court may, on the filing of the complaint or on the appearance of any defendant, claimant, or any other party, or at any later time, require the plaintiff, defendant, claimant, or other party to give security, or additional security, in such sum as the court shall direct to pay all costs and expenses that shall be awarded against the party by any interlocutory order or by the final judgment, or on appeal by any appellate court.

(3) Process.

(a) In admiralty and maritime proceedings process in rem or of maritime attachment and garnishment may be served only within the district.

(b) *Issuance and Delivery.* Issuance and delivery of process in rem, or of maritime attachment and garnishment, shall be held in abeyance if the plaintiff so requests.

(4) Execution of Process; Marshal's Return; Custody of Property; Procedures for Release.

(a) *In General.* Upon issuance and delivery of the process, or, in the case of summons with process of attachment and garnishment, when it appears that the defendant cannot be found within the district, the marshal or other person or organization having a warrant shall forthwith execute the process in accordance with this subdivision (4), making due and prompt return.

(b) *Tangible Property.* If tangible property is to be attached or arrested, the marshal or other person or organization having the warrant shall take it into the marshal's possession for safe custody. If the character or situation of the property is such that the taking of actual possession is impracticable, the marshal or other person executing the process shall affix a copy thereof to the property in a conspicuous place and leave a copy of the complaint and process with the person having possession or the person's agent. In furtherance of the marshal's custody of any vessel the marshal is authorized to make a written request to the collector of customs not to grant clearance to such vessel until notified by the marshal or deputy marshal or by the clerk that the vessel has been released in accordance with these rules.

(c) *Intangible Property.* If intangible property is to be attached or arrested the marshal or other person or organization having the warrant shall execute the process by leaving with the garnishee or other obligor a copy of the complaint and process requiring the garnishee or other obligor to answer as provided in Rules B(3)(a) and C(6); or the marshal may accept for payment into the registry of the court the amount owed to the extent of the amount claimed by the plaintiff with interest and costs, in which event the garnishee or other obligor shall not be required to answer unless alias process shall be served.

(d) *Directions With Respect to Property in Custody.* The marshal or other person or organization having the warrant may at any time apply to the court for directions with respect to property that has been attached or arrested, and shall give notice of such application to any or all of the parties as the court may direct.

(e) *Expenses of Seizing and Keeping Property; Deposit.* These rules do not alter the provisions of Title 28, U.S.C., § 1921, as amended, relative to the expenses of seizing and keeping property attached or arrested and to the requirement of deposits to cover such expenses.

(f) *Procedure for Release From Arrest or Attachment.* Whenever property is arrested or attached, any person claiming an interest in it shall be entitled to a prompt hearing at which the plaintiff shall be required to show why the arrest or attachment should not be vacated or other relief granted consistent with these rules. This subdivision shall have no application to suits for seamen's wages when process is issued upon a certification of sufficient cause filed pursuant to Title 46, U.S.C. §§ 603 and 604 or to actions by the United States for forfeitures for violation of any statute of the United States.

(5) Release of Property.

(a) *Special Bond.* Whenever process of maritime attachment and garnishment or process in rem is issued the execution of such process shall be stayed, or the property released, on the giving of security, to be approved by the court or clerk, or by stipulation of the parties, conditioned to answer the judgment of the court or of any appellate court. The parties may stipulate the amount and nature of such security. In the event of the inability or refusal of the parties so to stipulate the court shall fix the principal sum of the bond or stipulation at an amount sufficient to cover the amount of the plaintiff's claim fairly stated with accrued interest and costs; but the principal sum shall in no event exceed (i) twice the amount of the plaintiff's claim or (ii) the value of the property on due appraisement, whichever is smaller. The bond or stipulation shall be conditioned for the payment of the principal sum and interest thereon at 6 per cent per annum.

(b) *General Bond.* The owner of any vessel may file a general bond or stipulation, with sufficient surety, to be approved by the court, conditioned to answer the judgment of such court in all or any actions that may be brought thereafter in such court in which the vessel is attached or arrested. Thereupon the execution of all such process against such vessel shall be stayed so long as the amount secured by such bond or stipulation is at least double the aggregate amount claimed by plaintiffs in all actions begun and pending in which such vessel has been attached or arrested. Judgments and remedies may be had on such bond or stipulation as if a special bond or stipulation had been filed in each of such actions. The district court may make necessary orders to carry this rule into effect, particularly as to the giving of proper notice of any action against or attachment of a vessel for which a general bond has been filed. Such bond or stipulation shall be indorsed by the clerk with a minute of the actions wherein process is so stayed. Further security may be required by the court at any time.

If a special bond or stipulation is given in a particular case, the liability on the general bond or stipulation shall cease as to that case.

(c) *Release by Consent or Stipulation; Order of Court or Clerk; Costs.* Any vessel, cargo, or other property in the custody of the marshal or other person or organization having the warrant may be released forthwith upon the marshal's acceptance and approval of a stipulation, bond, or other security, signed by the party on whose behalf the property is detained or the party's attorney and expressly authorizing such release, if all costs and charges of the court and its officers shall have first been paid. Otherwise no property in the custody of the marshal, other person or organization having the warrant, or other officer of the court shall be released without an order of the court; but such order may be entered as of course by the clerk, upon the giving of approved security as provided by law and these rules, or upon the dismissal or discontinuance of the action; but the marshal or other person or organization having the warrant shall not deliver any property so released until the costs and charges of the officers of the court shall first have been paid.

(d) *Possessory, Petitory, and Partition Actions.* The foregoing provisions of this subdivision (5) do not apply to petitory, possessory, and partition actions. In such cases the property arrested shall be released only by order of the court, on such terms and conditions and on the giving of such security as the court may require.

(6) Reduction or Impairment of Security. Whenever security is taken the court may, on motion and hearing, for good cause shown, reduce the amount of security given; and if the surety shall be or become insufficient, new or additional sureties may be required on motion and hearing.

(7) Security on Counterclaim.

(a) When a person who has given security for damages in the original action asserts a counterclaim that arises from the transaction or occurrence that is the subject of the original action, a plaintiff for whose benefit the security has been given must give security for damages demanded in the counterclaim unless the court for cause shown, directs otherwise. Proceedings on the original claim must be stayed until this security is given unless the court directs otherwise.

(b) The plaintiff is required to give security under Rule E(7)(a) when the United States or its corporate instrumentality counterclaims and would have been required to give security to respond in damages if a private party but is relieved by law from giving security.

(8) Restricted Appearance. An appearance to defend against an admiralty and maritime claim with respect to which there has issued process in rem, or process of attachment and garnishment, may be expressly restricted to the defense of such claim, and in that event is not an appearance for the purposes of any other claim with respect to which such process is not available or has not been served.

(9) Disposition of Property; Sales.

(a) *Interlocutory Sales; Delivery.*

(i) On application of a party, the marshal, or other person having custody of the property, the court may order all or part of the property sold—with the sales proceeds, or as much of them as will satisfy the judgment, paid into court to await further orders of the court—if:

(A) the attached or arrested property is perishable, or liable to deterioration, decay, or injury by being detained in custody pending the action;

(B) the expense of keeping the property is excessive or disproportionate; or

(C) there is an unreasonable delay in securing release of the property.

(ii) In the circumstances described in Rule E(9)(a)(i), the court, on motion by a defendant or a person filing a statement of interest or right under Rule C(6), may order that the property, rather than being sold, be delivered to the movant upon giving security under these rules.

(b) *Sales; Proceeds.* All sales of property shall be made by the marshal or a deputy marshal, or by other person or organization having the warrant, or by any other person assigned by the court where the marshal or other person or organization having the warrant is a party in interest; and the proceeds of sale shall be forthwith paid into the registry of the court to be disposed of according to law.

(10) Preservation of Property. When the owner or another person remains in possession of property attached or arrested under the provisions of Rule E(4)(b) that permit execution of process without taking actual possession, the court, on a party's motion or on its own, may enter any order necessary to preserve the property and to prevent its removal.

[Added Feb. 28, 1966, eff. Jul. 1, 1966, and amended Apr. 29, 1985, effective Aug. 1, 1985; Mar. 2, 1987, effective Aug. 1, 1987; Apr. 30, 1991, effective Dec. 1, 1991; April 17, 2000, effective December 1, 2000; April 12, 2006, effective December 1, 2006.]

RULE F
LIMITATION OF LIABILITY

(1) Time for Filing Complaint; Security. Not later than six months after receipt of a claim in writing, any vessel owner may file a complaint in the appropriate district court, as provided in subdivision (9) of this rule, for limitation of liability pursuant to statute. The owner (a) shall deposit with the court, for the benefit of claimants, a sum equal to the amount or value of the owner's interest in the vessel and pending freight, or approved security therefor, and in addition such sums, or approved security therefor, as the court may from time to time fix as necessary to carry out the provisions of the statutes as amended; or (b) at the owner's option shall transfer to a trustee to be appointed by the court, for the benefit of claimants, the owner's interest in the vessel and pending freight, together with such sums, or approved security therefor, as the court may from time to time fix as necessary to carry out the provisions of the statutes as amended. The plaintiff shall also give security for costs and, if the plaintiff elects to give security, for interest at the rate of 6 percent per annum from the date of the security.

(2) Complaint. The complaint shall set forth the facts on the basis of which the right to limit liability is asserted and all facts necessary to enable the court to determine the amount to which the owner's liability shall be limited. The complaint may demand exoneration from as well as limitation of liability. It shall state the voyage if any, on which the demands sought to be limited arose, with the date and place of its termination; the amount of all demands including all unsatisfied liens or claims of lien, in contract or in tort or otherwise, arising on that voyage, so far as known to the plaintiff, and what actions and proceedings, if any, are pending thereon; whether the vessel was damaged, lost, or abandoned, and, if so, when and where; the value of the vessel at the close of the voyage or, in case of wreck, the value of her wreckage, strippings, or proceeds, if any, and where and in whose possession they are; and the amount of any pending freight recovered or recoverable. If the plaintiff elects to transfer the plaintiff's interest in the vessel to a trustee, the complaint must further show any prior paramount liens thereon, and what voyages or trips, if any, she has made since the voyage or trip on which the claims sought to be limited arose, and any existing liens arising upon any such subsequent voyage or trip, with the amounts and causes thereof, and the names and addresses of the lienors, so far as known; and whether the vessel sustained any injury upon or by reason of such subsequent voyage or trip.

(3) Claims Against Owner; Injunction. Upon compliance by the owner with the requirements of subdivision (1) of this rule all claims and proceedings against the owner or the owner's property with respect to the matter in question shall cease. On application of the plaintiff the court shall enjoin the further prosecution of any action or proceeding against the plaintiff or the plaintiff's property with respect to any claim subject to limitation in the action.

(4) Notice to Claimants. Upon the owner's compliance with subdivision (1) of this rule the court shall issue a notice to all persons asserting claims with respect to which the complaint seeks limitation, admonishing them to file their respective claims with the clerk of the court and to serve on the attorneys for the plaintiff a copy thereof on or before a date to be named in the notice. The date so fixed shall not be less than 30 days after issuance of the notice. For cause shown, the court may enlarge the time within which claims may be filed. The notice shall be published in such newspaper or newspapers as the court may direct once a week for four successive weeks prior to the date fixed for the filing of claims. The plaintiff not later than the day of second publication shall also mail a copy of the notice to every person known to have made any claim against the vessel or the plaintiff arising out of the voyage or trip on which the claims sought to be limited arose. In cases involving death a copy of such notice shall be mailed to the decedent at the decedent's last known address, and also to any person who shall be known to have made any claim on account of such death.

(5) Claims and Answer. Claims shall be filed and served on or before the date specified in the notice provided for in subdivision (4) of this rule. Each claim shall specify the facts upon which the claimant relies in support of the claim, the items thereof, and the dates on which the same accrued. If a claimant desires to contest either the right to exoneration from or the right to limitation of liability the claimant shall file and serve an answer to the complaint unless the claim has included an answer.

(6) Information to Be Given Claimants. Within 30 days after the date specified in the notice for filing claims, or within such time as the court thereafter may allow, the plaintiff shall mail to the attorney for each claimant (or if the claimant has no attorney to the claimant) a list setting forth (a) the name of each claimant, (b) the name and address of the claimant's attorney (if the claimant is known to have one), (c) the nature of the claim, i.e., whether property loss, property damage, death, personal injury etc., and (d) the amount thereof.

(7) Insufficiency of Fund or Security. Any claimant may by motion demand that the funds deposited in court or the security given by the plaintiff be increased on the ground that they are less than the value of the plaintiff's interest in the vessel and pending freight. Thereupon the court shall cause due appraisement to be made of the value of the plaintiff's interest in the vessel and pending freight; and if the court finds that the deposit or security is either insufficient or excessive it shall order its increase or reduction. In like manner any claimant may demand that the deposit or security be increased on the ground that it is insufficient to carry out the provisions of the statutes relating to claims in respect of loss of life or bodily injury; and, after notice and hearing, the court may similarly order that the deposit or security be increased or reduced.

(8) Objections to Claims: Distribution of Fund. Any interested party may question or controvert any claim without filing an objection thereto. Upon determination of liability the fund deposited or secured, or the proceeds of the vessel and pending freight, shall be divided pro rata, subject to all relevant provisions of law, among the several claimants in proportion to the amounts of their respective claims, duly proved, saving, however, to all parties any priority to which they may be legally entitled.

(9) Venue; Transfer. The complaint shall be filed in any district in which the vessel has been attached or arrested to answer for any claim with respect to which the plaintiff seeks to limit liability; or, if the vessel has not been attached or arrested, then in any district in which the owner has been sued with respect to any such claim. When the vessel has not been attached or arrested to answer the matters aforesaid, and suit has not been commenced against the owner, the proceedings may be had in the district in which the vessel may be, but if the vessel is not within any district and no suit has been commenced in any district, then the complaint may be filed in any district. For the convenience of parties and witnesses, in the interest of justice, the court may transfer the action to any district; if venue is wrongly laid the court shall dismiss or, if it be in the interest of justice, transfer the action to any district in which it could have been brought. If the vessel shall have been sold, the proceeds shall represent the vessel for the purposes of these rules.

[Added Feb. 28, 1966, eff. Jul. 1, 1966, and amended Mar. 2, 1987, effective Aug. 1, 1987.]

RULE G

FORFEITURE ACTIONS IN REM

(1) Scope. This rule governs a forfeiture action in rem arising from a federal statute. To the extent that this rule does not address an issue, Supplemental Rules C and E and the Federal Rules of Civil Procedure also apply.

(2) Complaint. The complaint must:

(a) be verified;

(b) state the grounds for subject—matter jurisdiction, in rem jurisdiction over the defendant property, and venue;

(c) describe the property with reasonable particularity;

(d) if the property is tangible, state its location when any seizure occurred and—if different—its location when the action is filed;

(e) identify the statute under which the forfeiture action is brought; and

(f) state sufficiently detailed facts to support a reasonable belief that the government will be able to meet its burden of proof at trial.

(3) Judicial Authorization and Process.

(a) Real Property. If the defendant is real property, the government must proceed under 18 U.S.C. § 985.

(b) Other Property; Arrest Warrant. If the defendant is not real property:

(i) the clerk must issue a warrant to arrest the property if it is in the government's possession, custody, or control;

(ii) the court—on finding probable cause—must issue a warrant to arrest the property if it is not in the government's possession, custody, or control and is not subject to a judicial restraining order; and

(iii) a warrant is not necessary if the property is subject to a judicial restraining order.

(c) Execution of Process.

(i) The warrant and any supplemental process must be delivered to a person or organization authorized to execute it, who may be: (A) a marshal or any other United States officer or employee; (B) someone under contract with the United States; or (C) someone specially appointed by the court for that purpose.

(ii) The authorized person or organization must execute the warrant and any supplemental process on property in the United States as soon as practicable unless:

(A) the property is in the government's possession, custody, or control; or

(B) the court orders a different time when the complaint is under seal, the action is stayed before the warrant and supplemental process are executed, or the court finds other good cause.

(iii) The warrant and any supplemental process may be executed within the district or, when authorized by statute, outside the district.

(iv) If executing a warrant on property outside the United States is required, the warrant may be transmitted to an appropriate authority for serving process where the property is located.

(4) Notice.

(a) Notice by Publication.

(i) When Publication Is Required. A judgment of forfeiture may be entered only if the government has published notice of the action within a reasonable time after filing the complaint or at a time the court orders. But notice need not be published if:

(A) the defendant property is worth less than $1,000 and direct notice is sent under Rule G(4)(b) to every person the government can reasonably identify as a potential claimant; or

(B) the court finds that the cost of publication exceeds the property's value and that other means of notice would satisfy due process.

(ii) Content of the Notice. Unless the court orders otherwise, the notice must:

(A) describe the property with reasonable particularity;

(B) state the times under Rule G(5) to file a claim and to answer; and

(C) name the government attorney to be served with the claim and answer.

(iii) Frequency of Publication. Published notice must appear:

(A) once a week for three consecutive weeks; or

(B) only once if, before the action was filed, notice of nonjudicial forfeiture of the same property was published on an official internet government forfeiture site for at least 30 consecutive days, or in a newspaper of general circulation for three consecutive weeks in a district where publication is authorized under Rule G(4)(a)(iv).

(iv) Means of Publication. The government should select from the following options a means of publication reasonably calculated to notify potential claimants of the action:

(A) if the property is in the United States, publication in a newspaper generally circulated in the district where the action is filed, where the property was seized, or where property that was not seized is located;

(B) if the property is outside the United States, publication in a newspaper generally circulated in a district where the action is filed, in a newspaper generally circulated in the country where the property is located, or in legal notices published and generally circulated in the country where the property is located; or

(C) instead of (A) or (B), posting a notice on an official internet government forfeiture site for at least 30 consecutive days.

(b) Notice to Known Potential Claimants.

(i) Direct Notice Required. The government must send notice of the action and a copy of the complaint to any person who reasonably appears to be a potential claimant on the facts known to the government before the end of the time for filing a claim under Rule G(5)(a)(ii)(B).

(ii) Content of the Notice. The notice must state:

(A) the date when the notice is sent;

(B) a deadline for filing a claim, at least 35 days after the notice is sent;

(C) that an answer or a motion under Rule 12 must be filed no later than 21 days after filing the claim; and

(D) the name of the government attorney to be served with the claim and answer.

(iii) Sending Notice.

(A) The notice must be sent by means reasonably calculated to reach the potential claimant.

(B) Notice may be sent to the potential claimant or to the attorney representing the potential claimant with respect to the seizure of the property or in a related investigation, administrative forfeiture proceeding, or criminal case.

(C) Notice sent to a potential claimant who is incarcerated must be sent to the place of incarceration.

(D) Notice to a person arrested in connection with an offense giving rise to the forfeiture who is not incarcerated when notice is sent may be sent to the address that person last gave to the agency that arrested or released the person.

(E) Notice to a person from whom the property was seized who is not incarcerated when notice is sent may be sent to the last address that person gave to the agency that seized the property.

(iv) **When Notice Is Sent.** Notice by the following means is sent on the date when it is placed in the mail, delivered to a commercial carrier, or sent by electronic mail.

(v) **Actual Notice.** A potential claimant who had actual notice of a forfeiture action may not oppose or seek relief from forfeiture because of the government's failure to send the required notice.

(5) Responsive Pleadings.

(a) Filing a Claim.

(i) A person who asserts an interest in the defendant property may contest the forfeiture by filing a claim in the court where the action is pending. The claim must:

(A) identify the specific property claimed;

(B) identify the claimant and state the claimant's interest in the property;

(C) be signed by the claimant under penalty of perjury; and

(D) be served on the government attorney designated under Rule G(4)(a)(ii)(C) or (b)(ii)(D).

(ii) Unless the court for good cause sets a different time, the claim must be filed:

(A) by the time stated in a direct notice sent under Rule G(4)(b);

(B) if notice was published but direct notice was not sent to the claimant or the claimant's attorney, no later than 30 days after final publication of newspaper notice or legal notice under Rule G(4)(a) or no later than 60 days after the first day of publication on an official internet government forfeiture site; or

(C) if notice was not published and direct notice was not sent to the claimant or the claimant's attorney:

(1) if the property was in the government's possession, custody, or control when the complaint was filed, no later than 60 days after the filing, not counting any time when the complaint was under seal or when the action was stayed before execution of a warrant issued under Rule G(3)(b); or

(2) if the property was not in the government's possession, custody, or control when the complaint was filed, no later than 60 days after the government complied with 18 U.S.C. § 985(c) as to real property, or 60 days after process was executed on the property under Rule G(3).

(iii) A claim filed by a person asserting an interest as a bailee must identify the bailor, and if filed on the bailor's behalf must state the authority to do so.

(b) Answer. A claimant must serve and file an answer to the complaint or a motion under Rule 12 within 21 days after filing the claim. A claimant waives an objection to in rem jurisdiction or to venue if the objection is not made by motion or stated in the answer.

(6) Special Interrogatories.

(a) Time and Scope. The government may serve special interrogatories limited to the claimant's identity and relationship to the defendant property without the court's leave at any time after the claim is filed and before discovery is closed. But if the claimant serves a motion to dismiss the action, the government must serve the interrogatories within 21 days after the motion is served.

(b) Answers or Objections. Answers or objections to these interrogatories must be served within 21 days after the interrogatories are served.

(c) Government's Response Deferred. The government need not respond to a claimant's motion to dismiss the action under Rule G(8)(b) until 21 days after the claimant has answered these interrogatories.

(7) Preserving, Preventing Criminal Use, and Disposing of Property; Sales.

(a) Preserving and Preventing Criminal Use of Property. When the government does not have actual possession of the defendant property the court, on motion or on its own, may enter any order necessary to preserve the property, to prevent its removal or encumbrance, or to prevent its use in a criminal offense.

(b) Interlocutory Sale or Delivery.

(i) **Order to Sell.** On motion by a party or a person having custody of the property, the court may order all or part of the property sold if:

(A) the property is perishable or at risk of deterioration, decay, or injury by being detained in custody pending the action;

(B) the expense of keeping the property is excessive or is disproportionate to its fair market value;

(C) the property is subject to a mortgage or to taxes on which the owner is in default; or

(D) the court finds other good cause.

(ii) Who Makes the Sale. A sale must be made by a United States agency that has authority to sell the property, by the agency's contractor, or by any person the court designates.

(iii) Sale Procedures. The sale is governed by 28 U.S.C. §§ 2001, 2002, and 2004, unless all parties, with the court's approval, agree to the sale, aspects of the sale, or different procedures.

(iv) Sale Proceeds. Sale proceeds are a substitute res subject to forfeiture in place of the property that was sold. The proceeds must be held in an interest-bearing account maintained by the United States pending the conclusion of the forfeiture action.

(v) Delivery on a Claimant's Motion. The court may order that the property be delivered to the claimant pending the conclusion of the action if the claimant shows circumstances that would permit sale under Rule G(7)(b)(i) and gives security under these rules.

(c) Disposing of Forfeited Property. Upon entry of a forfeiture judgment, the property or proceeds from selling the property must be disposed of as provided by law.

(8) Motions.

(a) Motion To Suppress Use of the Property as Evidence. If the defendant property was seized, a party with standing to contest the lawfulness of the seizure may move to suppress use of the property as evidence. Suppression does not affect forfeiture of the property based on independently derived evidence.

(b) Motion To Dismiss the Action.

(i) A claimant who establishes standing to contest forfeiture may move to dismiss the action under Rule 12(b).

(ii) In an action governed by 18 U.S.C. § 983(a)(3)(D) the complaint may not be dismissed on the ground that the government did not have adequate evidence at the time the complaint was filed to establish the forfeitability of the property. The sufficiency of the complaint is governed by Rule G(2).

(c) Motion To Strike a Claim or Answer.

(i) At any time before trial, the government may move to strike a claim or answer:

(A) for failing to comply with Rule G(5) or (6), or

(B) because the claimant lacks standing.

(ii) The motion:

(A) must be decided before any motion by the claimant to dismiss the action; and

(B) may be presented as a motion for judgment on the pleadings or as a motion to determine after a hearing or by summary judgment whether the claimant can carry the burden of establishing standing by a preponderance of the evidence.

(d) Petition To Release Property.

(i) If a United States agency or an agency's contractor holds property for judicial or nonjudicial forfeiture under a statute governed by 18 U.S.C. § 983(f), a person who has filed a claim to the property may petition for its release under § 983(f).

(ii) If a petition for release is filed before a judicial forfeiture action is filed against the property, the petition may be filed either in the district where the property was seized or in the district where a warrant to seize the property issued. If a judicial forfeiture action against the property is later filed in another district—or if the government shows that the action will be filed in another district—the petition may be transferred to that district under 28 U.S.C. § 1404.

(e) Excessive Fines. A claimant may seek to mitigate a forfeiture under the Excessive Fines Clause of the Eighth Amendment by motion for summary judgment or by motion made after entry of a forfeiture judgment if:

(i) the claimant has pleaded the defense under Rule 8; and

(ii) the parties have had the opportunity to conduct civil discovery on the defense

(9) Trial. Trial is to the court unless any party demands trial by jury under Rule 38.

[Added Apr. 12, 2006, eff. Dec. 1, 2006; amended March 26, 2009, effective December 1, 2009.]

PART V

APPENDIX OF FORMS

ABROGATION OF THE ORIGINAL CIVIL FORMS

Since the day they first took effect in 1938, the Federal Rules of Civil Procedure have been accompanied by an "Appendix of Forms". They were unveiled with great pride by the lead crafter of the Rules, Dean Charles E. Clark, who pronounced them a "most important part of the rules" because, he explained, "when you can't define you can at least draw pictures to show your meaning."[1] Originally, there were 34 official federal forms, a number that grew by two in 1993, and nearly all of which were substantially reworked during the 2007 "restyling" project.

Those official forms were abrogated effective December 2015. The Advisory Committee Notes accompanying the abrogation opined that the Forms' purpose in 1938, while useful then, had since "been fulfilled."[2] The Committee noted the availability of various alternative sources of federal civil forms (prepared by, among others, the Administrate Office of the United States Courts, the websites of various federal district courts, and private commercial suppliers), which it concluded rendered the official set "no longer necessary."[3] The Forms, however, have not left the scene without a fitting eulogy. *See* A. Benjamin Spencer, *The Forms Had A Function*, 15 NEV. L. REV. 1113 (2015).

CURRENT SOURCES OF FEDERAL CIVIL FORMS FOR USE TODAY

Not all federal forms were abrogated. Two survived—both for use in seeking and granting a waiver of formal service of process in accordance with the authority granted in Rule 4(d). This *Student's Guide* reprints both of these surviving official forms at the end of the text of Rule 4.

In addition, the Administration Office of the United States Courts maintains a small but valuable set of downloadable forms available at: http://www.uscourts.gov/forms/civil-forms. This same source also facilitates the process of locating forms preferred for use in the various local federal courts.

Private organizations also prepare sample forms that can be used, upon purchase or license, by practitioners

---

1 *See* Charles E. Clark, *Pleading Under the Federal Rules*, 12 WYO. L.J. 177, 181 (1958).

2 *See* Rule 84 advisory committee note 2015.

3 *See id.* The abrogation may have been hastened by discomfort with the official pleading forms and their perceived misalignment with the U.S. Supreme Court's recent pleading decisions in *Bell Atlantic Corp. v. Twombly* and *Ashcroft v. Iqbal*. *See supra* Rule 8(a). The advisory committee note endeavored to sidestep any intimation that its abrogation of the Forms was intended to adjust those pleading standards. *See* Rule 84 advisory committee note 2015 ("The abrogation of Rule 84 does not alter existing pleading standards or otherwise change the requirements of Civil Rule 8.").

PART VI

MULTIDISTRICT LITIGATION

Table of Sections

§ 5.1 Introduction

Congress created the Judicial Panel on Multidistrict Litigation in the late 1960's in response to the challenge of efficiently and effectively managing related, protracted, and complex civil cases that were being filed in various federal courts throughout the Nation. *See* 28 U.S.C. § 1407. At that time, nearly 2,000 separate but related electrical equipment antitrust cases were pending in 36 different federal judicial districts. *See* Robert A. Cahn, *A Look at the Judicial Panel on Multidistrict Litigation,* 72 F.R.D. 211 (1976). To manage these numerous distinct but related antitrust cases, Chief Justice Earl Warren appointed an advisory "Coordinating Committee for Multiple Litigation" which invited counsel and district court judges to attend hearings on how to economically supervise these electrical equipment litigations.

The Committee prepared and recommended more than 40 "national pretrial orders" for the cases, which were then entered voluntarily and collaboratively by the judges in most of the districts where these antitrust cases were pending. The orders established a coordinated system of national pretrial discovery, including a central document depository available to all parties and the conduct of depositions on a coordinated, nationwide schedule.

This voluntary, advisory procedure was so successful that Congress established a statutory, national multidistrict litigation court in 1968 with affirmative authority to direct the transfer of multidistrict civil cases that involve one or more common questions of fact to a single federal district for the purpose of consolidated or coordinated nationwide pretrial proceedings. *See* 28 U.S.C. § 1407(a). *See generally Gelboim v. Bank of America Corp.*, 574 U.S. 405, 410 (2015). This specialized court, the "Judicial Panel on Multidistrict Litigation", comprises 7 circuit and district court judges, designated from time to time by the Chief Justice, no 2 of whom may come from the same Circuit. *See* 28 U.S.C. § 1407(d).

The Judicial Panel is authorized to transfer cases for pretrial multidistrict litigation (or "MDL") treatment upon three findings: (a) that civil cases, then pending in different federal judicial districts, involve one or more common questions of fact, and that coordinated or consolidated pretrial proceedings, centralized before a single district court will (b) serve the convenience of parties and witnesses and (c) will promote the just and efficient conduct of the lawsuits. *See* 28 U.S.C. § 1407(a). If these prerequisites are met, MDL transfer to a central judicial district is appropriate, even if federal diversity jurisdiction, personal jurisdiction, or venue would otherwise be improper there over the transferred cases. The resulting post-transfer authority extends only to the parties and disputes subject to the transfer; jurisdiction does not extend to those parties or disputes not brought before the transferee court.

MDL treatment may be initiated by the Judicial Panel on its own initiative or upon motion by a party in any action believed to qualify for this type of coordination or consolidation. *See* 28 U.S.C. § 1407(c). A consolidation order by the Judicial Panel will ordinarily not be overturned unless it is "outlandish". *See Bennett v. Bayer Healthcare Pharms., Inc.*, 577 Fed.Appx. 616, 617–18 (7th Cir. 2014).

If MDL treatment is granted by the Judicial Panel, the ordinary procedure follows: a single judicial district and federal judge is selected by the Judicial Panel as the MDL court for all the cases; all qualifying federal lawsuits are then transferred to that federal judge for pretrial purposes; the MDL judge presides over and manages a nationwide, coordinated discovery and pretrial procedures program; and, in the event the cases are not disposed of or settled by the MDL judge by the close of the pretrial stage, the lawsuits are each transferred back to their districts of origin for trial. *See* 28 U.S.C. § 1407(a). Though consolidated in the MDL, individual cases ordinarily do not lose their discrete, separate legal character or morph into a new, single, monolithic "action" (at least not without deliberate action by the court and the parties to do so). *See Gelboim*, 574 U.S. at 413.

During consolidation, the MDL judge may rule on case-dispositive motions (though always mindful of each claimant's right to develop his or her unique facts separately), and consequently may grant motions to dismiss both on substantive grounds and for failures to abide by court scheduling orders and procedures. The MDL judge may also, when circumstances warrant, resolve the consolidated cases by summary judgment. Such orders—fully disposing of one or more cases, though leaving others still pending in the MDL—are usually final orders, subject to immediate appeal. *See Gelboim*, 574 U.S. at 413–16. The MDL judge may also rule on other, non-dispositive pretrial motions (such as motions to file omnibus pleadings, to amend or otherwise adjust the pleadings, to enforce venue requirements, and to resolve discovery disputes) and may order attendance at settlement conferences. The MDL judge may supervise the use of "master" complaints either for substantive, consolidated treatment or as legally inert administrative summaries of pleadings. The MDL judge may also impose litigation costs, but will usually allocate those costs ratably among the impacted cases. The law the MDL judge will apply during diversity-based proceedings will, ordinarily, follow the conflicts rules of the various originating transferor jurisdictions.

Remands are made by the Judicial Panel (not by the transferee judge), although the transferee judge retains a vital role of notifying the Judicial Panel (typically through a *"Suggestion to Remand"*) that the coordinated or consolidated proceedings have been concluded. Such a *Suggestion* by the transferee judge is afforded great weight. The parties do not need to assert their intention to seek remand in order to preserve it; rather, a remand at the close of all pretrial proceedings is presumed. But parties may request remand during the proceedings, though without the transferee judge's assent, such requests carry with them a heavy burden of persuasion. The Judicial Panel *must* remand when the coordinated or consolidated proceedings have concluded. *See Lexecon Inc. v. Milberg Weiss Bershad Hynes & Lerach*, 523 U.S. 26, 41 (1998). But it *may,* in its "unusually broad discretion", remand when all that remains to be accomplished is case-specific. The transferee judge may not self-assign the case in lieu of remand, at least absent a relinquishment by the parties to their entitlement to such a remand. *See id.* at 32–41. Thus, this MDL treatment is usually reserved as a vehicle for pretrial-and only pretrial-coordination and consolidation.

The extent to which a transferor court, following remand, may overrule the MDL transferee judge remains unsettled; but because routine revisitations of the MDL judge's rulings would deal MDL litigants a "Return To Go" card and thereby frustrate the intended goals of the MDL process, the courts tend to affix law-of-the-case deference to the MDL judge's orders.

The MDL procedure endeavors to achieve the economical use of the federal judiciary and the resolution of similar complex civil cases with the least cost and disruption to the parties and witnesses. *See Gelboim*, 574 U.S. at 410. During the coordinated or consolidated pretrial MDL proceedings, the MDL judge will typically look to the Federal Judicial Center's *Manual for Complex Litigation* as a primary resource for guiding the nationwide proceedings. Documents are generally produced only once for hundreds or thousands of cases, with responsive documents made available to all parties at a centralized document depository. Interrogatories and requests for admissions are served on behalf of a series of related cases. Witnesses and parties, whose testimony is relevant to many cases, are deposed only once (or at least far less often than otherwise) by a select group of lead or liaison counsel. Throughout the MDL process, the transferee judge generally possesses the power to act not only on behalf of the transferee district, but also with the powers of a district judge in every district from which the consolidated cases have been transferred.

The MDL judge's discretion is broad and commensurate with the enormous task of managing a large litigation involving numerous litigants from across the country and posing substantial legal questions implicating pleading, discovery, expert, timeliness, choice of law, cognizable claim, and causation issues. This authority encompasses the power to rule on motions relating to subpoenas issued from other judicial districts, including motions to quash and even to dismiss cases (for noncompliance with the MDL procedures). But, although broad, the MDL judge's discretion is not unbounded; the judge may not, in the cause of efficiency and docketing progress, engage in "assembly-line justice", disregard federal law or the civil rules, or retain post-pretrial authority over the case through self-reassignment or otherwise (absent authority to do so).

Appeals from the MDL judge's pretrial orders are often (but not always) heard by the Court of Appeals for the Circuit that encompasses the MDL judge's district. Sometimes, for instance, the Judicial Panel on Multidistrict Litigation may, in its discretion, elect not to permit Rule 54(b) immediate appeals (to the MDL judge's Court of Appeals) but, instead, to remand back to the originating transferor courts (with appeals, if any, to be taken to those various Courts of Appeals). Likewise, when the MDL judge's order implicates a ruling compelling or sanctioning a nonparty located outside the MDL judge's district, the appeal is generally taken to the Court of Appeals for the Circuit embracing the district of the foreign discovery event. The preclusive effects of MDL litigation can be complicated. For example, the decision to appeal an MDL ruling as to some consolidated defendants (and not all) will likely be preclusive once a final judgment is entered on the appeal, but perhaps not before.

Over the years, MDL pretrial treatment has been granted in many different types of lawsuits, including national products liability cases, personal injury cases, airplane disaster and other large calamity cases, antitrust cases, securities fraud cases, trade practices and consumer fraud cases, intellectual property cases, and a variety of other cases. In its first 27 years of use, the statutory multidistrict litigation procedure had been applied to more than 39,000 federal civil cases, of which more than 90% were resolved in the MDL and prior to trial. All told, well over two thousand MDL's have occurred, involving some of the most challenging litigations in the history of the federal judiciary. Today, a large percentage of the federal civil docket is conducted with MDL consolidations. Indeed, some recent scholarship suggests MDL treatment has "supplemented and perhaps displaced the class action device as a procedural mechanism for large settlements." *See Sullivan v. DB Invs., Inc.,* 667 F.3d 273, 334 (3d Cir. 2011) (Scirica, J., concurring) (citing Thomas E. Willging & Emery G. Lee III, *From Class Actions to Multidistrict Consolidations: Aggregate Mass-Tort Litigation after Ortiz,* 58 U. KAN. L. REV 775, 801 (2010)).

- For a more extensive treatment of MDL practice, see David F. Herr, *Multidistrict Litigation Manual: Practice Before The Judicial Panel On Multidistrict Litigation* (Thompson-West, revised annually).

§ 5.2 The Federal Multidistrict Litigation Statute, 28 U.S.C. § 1407

1407. Multidistrict Litigation

(a) When civil actions involving one or more common questions of fact are pending in different districts, such actions may be transferred to any district for coordinated or consolidated pretrial proceedings. Such transfers shall be made by the judicial panel on multidistrict litigation authorized by this section upon its determination that transfers for such proceedings will be for the convenience of parties and witnesses and will promote the just and efficient conduct of such actions. Each action so transferred shall be remanded by the panel at or before the conclusion of such pretrial proceedings to the district from which it was transferred unless it shall have been previously terminated: *Provided, however,* That the panel may separate any claim, crossclaim, counter-claim, or third-party claim and remand any of such claims before the remainder of the action is remanded.

(b) Such coordinated or consolidated pretrial proceedings shall be conducted by a judge or judges to whom such actions are assigned by the judicial panel on multidistrict litigation. For this purpose, upon request of the panel, a circuit judge or a district judge may be designated and assigned temporarily for service in the transferee district by the Chief Justice of the United States or the chief judge of the circuit, as may be required, in accordance with the provisions of chapter 13 of this title. With the consent of the transferee district court, such actions may be assigned by the panel to a judge or judges of such district. The judge or judges to whom such actions are assigned, the members of the judicial panel on multidistrict litigation, and other circuit and district judges designated when needed by the panel may exercise the powers of a district judge in any district for the purpose of conducting pretrial depositions in such coordinated or consolidated pretrial proceedings.

(c) Proceedings for the transfer of an action under this section may be initiated by—

(i) the judicial panel on multidistrict litigation upon its own initiative, or

(ii) motion filed with the panel by a party in any action in which transfer for coordinated or consolidated pretrial proceedings under this section may be appropriate. A copy of such motion shall be filed in the district court in which the moving party's action is pending.

The panel shall give notice to the parties in all actions in which transfers for coordinated or consolidated pretrial proceedings are contemplated, and such notice shall specify the time and place of any hearing to determine whether such transfer shall be made. Orders of the panel to set a hearing and other orders of the panel issued prior to the order either directing or denying transfer shall be filed in the office of the clerk of the district court in which a transfer hearing is to be or has been held. The panel's order of transfer shall be based upon a record of such hearing at which material evidence may be offered by any party to an action pending in any district that would be affected by the proceedings under this section, and shall be supported by findings of fact and conclusions of law based upon such record. Orders of transfer and such other orders as the panel may make thereafter shall be filed in the office of the clerk of the district court of the transferee district and shall be effective when thus filed. The clerk of the transferee district court shall forthwith transmit a certified copy of the panel's order to transfer to the clerk of the district court from which the action is being transferred. An order denying transfer shall be filed in each district wherein there is a case pending in which the motion for transfer has been made.

(d) The judicial panel on multidistrict litigation shall consist of seven circuit and district judges designated from time to time by the Chief Justice of the United States, no two of whom shall be from the same circuit. The concurrence of four members shall be necessary to any action by the panel.

(e) No proceedings for review of any order of the panel may be permitted except by extraordinary writ pursuant to the provisions of title 28, section 1651, United States Code. Petitions for an extraordinary writ to review an order of the panel to set a transfer hearing and other orders of the panel issued prior to the order either directing or denying transfer shall be filed only in the court of appeals having jurisdiction over the district in which a hearing is to be or has been held. Petitions for an extraordinary writ to review an order to transfer or orders subsequent to transfer shall be filed only in the court of appeals having jurisdiction over the transferee district. There shall be no appeal or review of an order of the panel denying a motion to transfer for consolidated or coordinated proceedings.

(f) The panel may prescribe rules for the conduct of its business not inconsistent with Acts of Congress and the Federal Rules of Civil Procedure.

(g) Nothing in this section shall apply to any action in which the United States is a complainant arising under the antitrust laws. "Antitrust laws" as used herein include those acts referred to in the Act of October 15, 1914, as amended (38 Stat. 730; 15 U.S.C. 12), and also include the Act of June 19, 1936 (49 Stat. 1526; 15 U.S.C. 13, 13a, and 13b) and the Act of September 26, 1914, as added March 21, 1938 (52 Stat. 116, 117; 15 U.S.C. 56); but shall not include section 4A of the Act of October 15, 1914, as added July 7, 1955 (69 Stat. 282; 15 U.S.C. 15a).

(h) Notwithstanding the provisions of section 1404 or subsection (f) of this section, the judicial panel on multidistrict litigation may consolidate and transfer with or without the consent of the parties, for both pretrial purposes and for trial, any action brought under section 4C of the Clayton Act.

[Added Pub.L. 90–296, § 1, Apr. 29, 1968, 82 Stat. 109, and amended Pub.L. 94–435, Title III, § 303, Sept. 30, 1976, 90 Stat. 1396.]

PART VII

FEDERAL APPELLATE PROCEDURE: AN OVERVIEW

Table of Sections

§ 6.1 Introduction

For many years, the rules and procedures governing federal appeals were contained within the Federal Rules of Civil Procedure. They were removed in 1968 when the new, freestanding *Federal Rules of Appellate Procedure* were promulgated. Although in-depth, rule-by-rule commentary of the federal appellate rules is beyond the scope of this *Student's Guide*, the bird's-eye summary below offers a general orientation to a few prominent features of federal appellate practice.

- **"RULE" versus "FED. R. APP. P.":** To avoid any confusion in the following discussion of appellate practice, this text will refer to the Federal Rules of Appellate Procedure with the abbreviation "Fed. R. App. P." As the *Student's Guide* has done throughout, references to the Federal Rules of Civil Procedure will be to "Rule."

§ 6.2 Step One: Appealability

Ordinarily, litigants may not appeal each time a district court enters an unfavorable ruling against them. Instead, disgruntled litigants are typically allowed only a single appeal at the end of the case, during which all claims of trial error are bundled together for an omnibus review. But there are exceptions. Litigants must be vigilant in remembering that once a ruling becomes appealable, the time for taking that appeal has come. Delaying can be irremediable.

♦ **NOTE:** This finality principle demands great attention. When an order becomes "final," it also usually becomes appealable. A delay thereafter in taking the appeal may forever foreclose the right of appeal. When an order is not immediately appealable, the premature filing of an appeal may be dismissed summarily.

PRACTICING LAW WITH THIS PRINCIPLE

Who May Appeal

Only the parties (or those who become parties) to a federal lawsuit may appeal a judgment entered in that lawsuit. *See Marino v. Ortiz*, 484 U.S. 301, 304 (1988) (per curiam).

Federal Appealability—An Overview

The right to a federal appeal is a "creature of statute", and exists only to that extent granted by Congress. *See Abney v. United States,* 431 U.S. 651, 656 (1977). Much like the district courts' subject-matter jurisdiction, federal appellate jurisdiction is not assumed, nor can it be conferred by waiver or consent. *See New York ex rel. Bryant v. Zimmerman,* 278 U.S. 63, 66 (1928). Every appellant bears the burden of showing that it exists. Moreover, federal appellate courts have an independent obligation to confirm the presence of their jurisdiction, even where the parties to the appeal are prepared to concede it. *See Bender v. Williamsport Area Sch. Dist.,* 475 U.S. 534, 541 (1986). If the appellate court determines that the trial court lacked subject-matter jurisdiction over the dispute, appellate jurisdiction will exist only for the limited purpose of rectifying that error. *See id.*

Final Decisions ("Final Orders")

Congress has vested the courts of appeals with jurisdiction to hear appeals from "final decisions" (often called "final orders") of the district courts. *See* 28 U.S.C. § 1291.

A final order is a ruling that "ends the litigation on the merits and leaves nothing for the court to do but execute the judgment" (and, perhaps, rule on post-trial motions, if any are later filed). *See Van Cauwenberghe v. Biard,* 486 U.S. 517, 521–22 (1988). It is, usually, the ruling by which the trial court "disassociates" itself from the case. *See Mohawk Indus., Inc. v. Carpenter,* 558 U.S. 100, 106 (2009). Typically, that order arrives at the completion of the entire case, *see Ritzen Grp., Inc. v. Jackson Masonry, LLC,* 589 U.S. ___, 140 S. Ct. 582, 586 (2020); with an entry of a final judgment, *see Hall v. Hall,* 584 U.S. ___, 138 S. Ct. 1118, 1124 (2018). This final order requirement supplies clear guidance to the parties: final orders normally confer upon the defeated litigant an immediate right to seek review in the appropriate court of appeals. *See id.* at 1131. The requirement is also intended to limit litigants to a single appellate opportunity, *see Microsoft Corp. v. Baker,* 137 S. Ct. 1702, 1712 (2017). This, in turn, reduces the expense, delay, burden, and inefficiency of piecemeal, successive appeals, *see Firestone Tire & Rubber Co. v. Risjord,* 449 U.S. 368, 374 (1981); and curbs the degree of encroachment on the special roles played by federal trial judges in managing civil litigation, *see Bullard v. Blue Hills Bank,* 575 U.S. 496, 501 (2015).

Nonetheless, the final order rule has been described as pragmatic not rigid, *see Microsoft Corp.,* 137 S. Ct. at 1712; and practical not technical. *See Gelboim v. Bank of America Corp.,* 574 U.S. 405, 409 (2015). Appealability will not hinge merely on whether the trial court labeled its order as "final." *See Riley v. Kennedy,* 553 U.S. 406, 419–20 (2008); *Sullivan v. Finkelstein,* 496 U.S. 617, 628 n.7 (1990). A district court's dismissal of a lawsuit with prejudice is always likely to be final. But a district court's dismissal that is technically denominated as "without prejudice" may yet qualify as a final order if, in the particular circumstances, the trial judge is "finished" with the case or imposes certain conditions that legally prejudices the litigant's ability to proceed in the trial court or the dismissed party decides not to amend. This "without-prejudice" setting is ripe with nuance and unpredictability. Even less clear is whether a party's own, voluntary, without-prejudice dismissal of portions of a lawsuit can produce the finality needed to appeal an adverse court ruling on other portions—an inquiry that may depend, in part, on whether that voluntary dismissal was acquired *before* an adverse, partially-dispositive order was entered or *after* (done with the goal of manufacturing a finality that would not otherwise exist). *Cf. Microsoft Corp.,* 137 S. Ct. at 1712–15 (rejecting "voluntary-dismissal tactic" in class action context). Almost all interim ("interlocutory") orders by the trial court (*e.g.,* denials of dispositive motions, discovery motions) are not considered final orders. *See Mohawk Indus., Inc.,* 558 U.S. at 108. Once finality arrives, only "judgments, not statements in opinions," are appealable. *See Black v. Cutter Labs.,* 351 U.S. 292, 297 (1956). *See generally Sexual Minorities Uganda v. Lively,* 899 F.3d 24, 29–32 (1st Cir. 2018) (prevailing party who objects to language in court's opinion generally cannot appeal).

Partial Final Orders (Rule 54(b))

Ordinarily, when the district court enters a judgment that disposes of less than all claims or all parties in a lawsuit, that case is not yet final (and appealable) and will not become so until all other claims affecting all other parties are finally resolved. However, the district court may, in the exercise of its discretion, convert such "partial" judgments into immediately appealable final orders by (a) finally resolving at least one claim or the rights and liabilities of at least one party, (b) expressly declaring that no just cause exists to delay the appeal from such a ruling, and (c) directing the entry of judgment on the ruling. *See* Rule 54(b).

Interlocutory Orders

Interlocutory orders are all other interim rulings by the district courts; such rulings do not purport to end the litigation, and further action in the case by the trial court is contemplated. *See Liberty Mut. Ins. Co. v. Wetzel*, 424 U.S. 737, 744 (1976). Because they are not "final orders," interlocutory rulings are generally not immediately appealable to the courts of appeals. *See Ashcroft v. Iqbal*, 556 U.S. 662, 672 (2009) (interlocutory appeals "are the exception, not the rule"). Review of interlocutory orders must ordinarily wait until the district court enters its final order on the merits of the litigation. Under well-settled appellate tenets, litigants may, in the course of appealing a final order, challenge many of the preceding interlocutory rulings previously entered by the trial court. *See Firestone Tire & Rubber Co. v. Risjord*, 449 U.S. 368, 374 (1981) (raise all errors in single appeal after final judgment on merits).

Permitted Interlocutory Appeals—Injunctions

Though they may not qualify as "final orders," interlocutory rulings that grant, continue, modify, refuse, or dissolve injunctions, or that refuse to dissolve or modify injunctions, are appealable immediately (provided, of course, the injunction has not already expired by its terms). *See* 28 U.S.C. § 1292(a)(1). This creates an exception to the general policy disfavoring piecemeal appeals. *See Gardner v. Westinghouse Broad. Co.,* 437 U.S. 478, 480 (1978). The exception is construed strictly and applied narrowly to allow effective challenges to "orders of serious, perhaps irreparable, consequence." *See Gardner v. Westinghouse Broad. Co.*, 437 U.S. 478, 480 (1978). Accordingly, an order that *specifically* grants, denies, or modifies an injunction will fall within this exception and be immediately appealable. An order that merely has the *practical effect* of granting, denying, or modifying an injunctive remedy may also be immediately appealable (regardless of how it was labeled or whether the parties even sought "injunctive" relief), but only when it has a serious, possibly irreparable consequence and can be effectively challenged only by immediate appellate review. *See generally Abbott v. Perez*, 138 S. Ct. 2305, 2319–20 (2018); *Carson v. American Brands, Inc.*, 450 U.S. 79, 83–84 (1981). "Modifying" an injunction is different than "interpreting" one; only the former is immediately appealable. And temporary restraining orders (TROs) are not (usually) immediately appealable, given their brief duration.

Permitted Interlocutory Appeals—Receivers

Though they may not qualify as "final orders," interlocutory rulings that appoint receivers, or refuse orders to wind up receiverships or take steps to accomplish those purposes (*i.e.*, directing disposals of property) are appealable immediately. *See* 28 U.S.C. § 1292(a)(2). This exception, too, is construed narrowly.

Permitted Interlocutory Appeals—Admiralty

Though they may not qualify as "final orders," interlocutory decrees that determine the rights and liabilities of parties to admiralty cases in which appeals from final decrees are allowed, are appealable immediately. *See* 28 U.S.C. § 1292(a)(3). This exception encompasses orders that decide the *merits* of admiralty cases—a determination made by assessing financial realities and other practical matters—and is construed narrowly but still in a manner faithful to the statute's plain meaning.

Discretionary Interlocutory Appeals

The district court may, in the exercise of its discretion, choose to certify certain non-final, interlocutory orders as eligible for immediate appellate review. *See* 28 U.S.C. § 1292(b).

Such certification by the district court does not require the court of appeals to hear the immediate appeal; rather, the courts of appeals also have discretion to reject it, and may do so for almost any reason (including docket congestion). *See Coopers & Lybrand v. Livesay,* 437 U.S. 463, 475 (1978).

Certification by the district judge is not routinely granted, and is reserved for "exceptional" cases. *See Caterpillar Inc. v. Lewis,* 519 U.S. 61, 74 (1996). It is not intended for ordinary error correction. Liberally granting such certifications is considered bad policy, as it undermines the appropriate division of responsibility between federal trial and appellate courts. Thus, the procedure exists to allow prompt resolution of "knotty" legal issues and to facilitate appellate review on "ephemeral" questions of law that might otherwise disappear as the record completes and finalizes.

Thus, litigants seeking certification bear a heavy burden. They must persuade the district judge to state in writing:

(1) That the order in question involves a "**controlling question of law**" (which generally means a question of "pure law", which can be resolved "quickly and cleanly" without laboring over the record—such as the meaning of a regulatory, statutory, or constitutional provision or common law doctrine, the resolution of which is *likely* (although not necessarily certain) to affect the future course of the litigation); and

(2) There is "**substantial ground for difference of opinion**" on the legal issue the order resolves (which generally means either that there is conflicting legal authority on the disputed issue or that the issue is a particularly difficult or uncertain one of first impression); and

(3) An immediate appeal from the interlocutory order may "**materially advance the ultimate termination of the litigation**" (which generally means that immediate appeal may avoid expensive and protracted litigation, not that it must have a final, dispositive effect).

All three criteria are required; failing to satisfy any one denies the district court the ability to grant a Rule 1292(b) certification. If certification is granted, the court generally should specify what question of law it finds to be "controlling"—although a failure to do so is not necessarily dispositive. Certification is jurisdictional; if certification is not granted, the court of appeals lacks authority to hear the appeal under Section 1292(b). If certification is granted, but then revoked by the trial judge before the court of appeals acquires jurisdiction, there likewise is no authority to hear the appeal.

There is no express time limit for asking the trial judge to grant a Section 1292(b) certification, although unreasonably dilatory requests may be denied by the trial judge or refused by the courts of appeals. If granted by the district judge, the party may petition the court of appeals within 10 days thereafter for permission to immediately appeal the certified question. *See* 28 U.S.C. § 1292(b). (An untimely petition defeats jurisdiction, though courts are divided on whether a district judge can rescue a belated petition by issuing a second Section 1292(b) certification.) The scope of the appellate review is limited to the certified order. The court may not reach beyond that order to consider other, uncertified rulings by the trial judge. *See Yamaha Motor Corp., U.S.A. v. Calhoun,* 516 U.S. 199, 205 (1996). But the court of appeals may, in its discretion, address any issue that is "fairly included" within the certified order itself; review is limited by the order that is certified, not by the precise question found to be controlling. *See id.* Other issues that are "inextricably intertwined" with the certified issue may be reached as well.

Collateral Order Doctrine

In addition to Rule-based and statutory exceptions to the final order limitation, the Supreme Court has developed a common law "collateral order" doctrine, which recognizes that certain legal rulings—collateral to the litigation's underlying merits—may nevertheless be deemed "final" and eligible for immediate appellate review. To qualify under the collateral order doctrine, the district court's order must:

(1) Conclusively resolve

(2) An "important question" that is separate from the underlying merits

(3) Which would be effectively unreviewable if the appeal had to await a final order on the merits.

See Coopers & Lybrand v. Livesay, 437 U.S. 463, 468–69 (1978). A failure to satisfy even one of these three requirements defeats the use of the collateral order doctrine. *See Gulfstream Aerospace Corp. v. Mayacamas Corp.,* 485 U.S. 271, 276 (1988).

The collateral order exception represents a narrow, common law construction of the final order doctrine. It is applied stringently and is never permitted to "swallow" the general prohibition against piecemeal appeals. *See Mohawk Indus., Inc. v. Carpenter,* 558 U.S. 100, 106 (2009). Although collateral orders typically involve a claimed right to "avoid" trial (a right which would be lost and effectively unappealable later), the Supreme Court has rejected the notion that this characteristic alone justifies collateral order treatment. *See Will v. Hallock,* 546 U.S. 345, 350–51 (2006). Instead, the Court has ruled that true collateral orders are those that would, if not immediately reviewed, imperil "a substantial public interest" or some high order value. *See Mohawk Indus.,* 558 U.S. at 106–10. Examples of rulings that may qualify include denials of litigation immunity, of leave to litigate anonymously, and to judicially seal or unseal documents.

Other Exceptions

Various other exceptions to the general final order principle exist, though an exhaustive discussion of those nuances is beyond the scope of this text.

---

§ 6.3 Step Two: Time for Taking an Appeal

In civil cases, an appeal generally must be taken within 30 days after the entry of the disputed judgment or order, although if the United States is a party this period is extended to 60 days. Except for a few narrow exceptions, this time period may not be waived or extended. A failure to file a timely appeal will forfeit that party's right of appeal.

PRACTICING LAW WITH THIS PRINCIPLE

Appeal Time Is Mandatory and Jurisdictional

The applicable time periods for taking an appeal are mandatory and jurisdictional. *See Bowles v. Russell,* 551 U.S. 205, 214 (2007). They cannot be waived, even for good cause shown. They also may not be extended, absent the few narrow exceptions discussed below.

Appeal Time When United States Is a Party

When the United States or a federal officer, employee, or agency is a party to the litigation, the parties have 60 days after the entry of the disputed judgment or order in which to take an appeal. *See* Fed. R. App. P. 4(a)(1)(B). This 60-day period applies to current and former federal officers and employees, and in both official-capacity lawsuits and those individual-capacity lawsuits that concern behavior that occurred in connection with that person's duties performed on behalf of the United States. *See* 28 U.S.C.A. § 2107(b)(4). The extended 60-day period applies to all parties in the case—the federal parties as well as all others. However, the federal entity must be an actual party for this 60-day longer period to apply. *See U.S. ex rel. Eisenstein v. City of New York,* 556 U.S. 928, 931 (2009).

Appeal Time When United States Is *Not* a Party

In all other cases, the parties have 30 days after the entry of the disputed judgment or order in which to take an appeal. *See* Fed. R. App. P.4(a)(1)(A).

When Opponent Appeals

Once one party takes an appeal, all other parties to the litigation have at least 14 days thereafter in which to take their own appeals. *See* Fed. R. App. P.4(a)(3). The parties receive the benefit of this 14-day "extension" period even if the original notice of appeal is defective or otherwise is dismissed. But that benefit only follows from an appeal by *another* party (and cannot be used to bootstrap a second, corrective appeal by the same party).

Some courts of appeals have ruled that this 14-day period is mandatory and jurisdictional—if the time period lapses, the right to cross-appeal is irretrievably lost. Other courts of appeals view the 14-day period as "proper procedure", but not jurisdictional; if appellate jurisdiction was already properly invoked with the filing of the *original* notice of appeal (*i.e.,* the one to which the cross-notice would be filed) the court may permit the 14-day period to be excused in a proper circumstance.

Appeal Time Begins to Run from Date of "Entry"

For purposes of timeliness on appeal, the appeal period begins to run when the order is "entered" on the docket, after being filed by the district judge (and not when the court issues, or the parties or their attorneys receive, a copy). *See* Fed. R. App. P. 4(a)(7). When the "separate document" requirement of Rule 58 applies, the time to appeal does not begin to run until the "separate document" prerequisite is met or the 150-day period expires, whichever comes first (although parties need not wait that long to file). *See* Rule 58; *Shalala v. Schaefer*, 509 U.S. 292, 303 (1993).

- *Interlocutory Order Caution:* When an appealable interlocutory order is entered—such as an injunction, a Rule 54(b) partial final judgment, a denial of intervention as of right, or a ruling qualifying under the collateral order doctrine—the appeal time runs from the entry of that order.

Computing Time for Taking Appeal

The period within which an appeal must be taken is calculated according to the counting method set in the federal appellate rules, and those rules will apply unless a different method for computing time is specified. *See* Fed. R. App. P. 26(a). In counting periods stated in units of time measured in days or longer (e.g., days, months, or years), the day that triggers the period is excluded and then every other day is included. If the period ends on a weekend or legal holiday, the period is extended to the end of the next day that is not a weekend or legal holiday. Unless otherwise specified, a day "ends" for electronic filing at midnight in the time zone of the court's principal office, and for most other filings when the clerk's office is scheduled to close. Also now expressly addressed are time periods set in hours, as well as the proper adjustments for federal and State holidays and courthouse inaccessibility.

- *Electronic Filing Caution:* Electronic filings might not be effective instantly; some courts hold that electronic filings are not complete (nor an electronically transmitted appeal deemed "filed") until certain confirming events first occur.

Extensions—By Filing Post-Trial Motions

The timely filing of certain post-trial motions will suspend the time for appeal (because their filing causes an otherwise final order of the district court to lose its finality). *See* Fed. R. App. P. 4(a)(4)(A); *Banister v. Davis*, 590 U.S. ___, 140 S. Ct. 1698, 1703 (2020). The post-trial motions that qualify for this suspension effect are:

- Motions for judgment as a matter of law, under Federal Rule of Civil Procedure 50(b);
- Motions to alter or supplement findings of fact, under Federal Rule of Civil Procedure 52(b);
- Motions for attorney's fees, under Federal Rule of Civil Procedure 54(d), but only if the district court extends the time for appeal in accordance with Federal Rule of Civil Procedure 58;
- Motions to alter or amend the judgment, under Federal Rule of Civil Procedure 59;
- Motions for a new trial, under Federal Rule of Civil Procedure 59; and
- Motions for relief from a judgment or order, under Federal Rule of Civil Procedure 60, but only if such motion is served within 28 days after entry of judgment.

These motions need not be successful (or, perhaps, even rule-compliant) to extend the appeal period. But the motions must be filed timely; an untimely filed post-trial motion will *not* suspend the appeal time (nor may a court manufacture timeliness for parties by vacating a final judgment already entered so as to provide them with a new 28-day filing window). Nonetheless, because post-trial timeliness is not jurisdictional, the district court may still hear an untimely post-trial motion if the non-moving party waives its timeliness objection, though doing so carries an important consequence: untimely-filed post-trial motions remain untimely for purposes of federal appeals and, thus, have no suspending effect on the time for taking an appeal (a time period which *is* jurisdictional). Thus, if the district court grants an untimely post-trial motion, the aggrieved party could receive meaningful relief, but if the court denies that motion, the aggrieved party's time for taking an appeal will almost certainly be already lost.

Once the district court grants or denies the last still-pending, timely post-trial motion, the original judgment's finality is restored and the appeals clock begins to tick (assuming, of course, that the district judge's ruling results in a final order). *See generally Banister v. Davis*, 590 U.S. ___, 140 S. Ct. 1698, 1703 (2020).

Triggering the Appeals Clock After Post-Trial Motions

The courts of appeals are divided on whether the district court must *expressly* rule on all pending post-trial motions before the appeal clock begins ticking. The majority rule holds that the appeal time remains suspended until the trial court explicitly grants or denies the pending post-trial motions. The minority view holds that the appeal period can begin to run as soon as the district court enters the judgment (interpreting such entry as an implicit denial of the post-trial motions).

Successive Post-Trial Motions

Most courts of appeals have ruled that after the time for appeal has been *once* extended by the filing of a tolling post-trial motion, the appeal period cannot be suspended *again* by the filing of a *subsequent* post-trial motion.

Abandoned Post-Trial Motions

If a party files timely post-trial motions, but then abandons them, the filing of those motions can be ignored; if the appeal period lapsed while those now-withdrawn motions were pending, appellate jurisdiction will likely be deemed lost.

Extensions—By District Court (Neglect or Good Cause)

Upon a showing of either excusable neglect or good cause, the district court may briefly extend the time for appeal. *See* Fed. R. App. P. 4(a)(5). To obtain such an extension, the movant *must* seek the extension within the original appeal period itself or within 30 days after the original appeal period expires. The district court may only extend the time for appeal for 30 days after the original appeal period expires, or for 14 days after the order granting the motion for extension is granted, whichever is later. (This timing regime is non-jurisdictional and may, in appropriate circumstances, be waived. *See Hamer v. Neighborhood Hous. Servs. of Chicago*, 138 S. Ct. 13, 18 (2017).) To request such an extension, an actual motion is required (merely filing a notice of appeal is not enough). Motions filed before the appeal time expires may be made *ex parte* (unless the court directs otherwise); motions filed after the appeal time expires must be made on proper notice to all other parties.

The moving party must prove *either* excusable neglect or good cause. Note, however, that the interpretation of these terms in this appellate context differs markedly from the far more forgiving interpretation given nearly identical terms in the context of Rule 6(b) of the Federal Rules of Civil Procedure.

- *Excusable Neglect Defined:* Excusable neglect applies in circumstances involving fault, and seeks an extension typically made necessary by something that should have been within the movant's control. *See* Fed. R. App. P. 4(a)(5)(A) advisory committee notes to 2002 amendments. It is neither a "toothless" standard nor a merciless one—equitable considerations drive the inquiry. In assessing whether the neglect is "excusable," a determination vested to the district court's discretion, the courts will assess the risk of prejudice to the non-moving party, the length of the delay, the delay's potential impact on the proceedings, the reason for the delay and (especially whether that reason was within the reasonable control of the moving party), and the moving party's good faith. *See Pioneer Inv. Servs. Co. v. Brunswick Assocs. Ltd. P'ship,* 507 U.S. 380, 395 (1993) (assessing "excusable neglect" in bankruptcy rules context). These factors (and others) are not mechanically given equal weight, and the actual balance may depend on the circumstances. "Excusable neglect" generally requires something more than an attorney's busy caseload or an oversight in consulting or reading the procedural rules, or a clerk's failure to notify parties of a ruling they could have discovered by periodically checking the docket.

- *Good Cause Defined:* Good cause applies in circumstances where there is no fault (excusable or otherwise), and seeks an extension typically made necessary by something that was not within the movant's control. *See* Fed. R. App. P. 4(a)(5)(A) advisory committee notes to 2002 amendments. Like excusable neglect, the good-cause determination is committed to the district court's discretion.

Extensions—By District Court (Non-Receipt)

If the district court determines that a party entitled to notice of the entry of a judgment or order did not timely receive that notice, the court may extend the time for appeal, but only under the following conditions:

- *Party's non-receipt within 21 days:* The court must first find that the party did not receive formal Rule 77(d) notice within 21 days after entry of the judgment or order (note, "receipt" is different than mere "service"), *see* Fed. R. App. P. 4(a)(6)(A); *and*

- *Party promptly moved to reopen the appeal period:* The non-noticed party must promptly move the district court to reopen the appeal period within 14 days after receiving or observing written notice of the entry from any source, *see* Fed. R. App. P. 4(a)(6)(B); *and*

- *Party moved no later than 180 days after entry:* The maximum window for seeking for an appeal extension can never last longer than 180 days (thus obligating practitioners to routinely check the court dockets, even when no formal notice has been received), *see id.; and*

- *No party is prejudiced by the extension:* The court must find that no party would be prejudiced by granting an appeal period extension, *see* Fed. R. App. P. 4(a)(6)(C); *and*
- *Actual extension may last only 14 days:* If an extension is granted, the non-noticed party can be given no more than an additional 14 days to file the appeal. *See* Fed. R. App. P. 4(a)(6).

The burden of demonstrating non-receipt rests with the moving party. Evidence that the order was properly mailed or transmitted over a court's official electronic filing system creates a presumption of receipt; if contested, the district court will, as factfinder, assess the evidence and determine the question of receipt or non-receipt. This Rule is triggered only by non-receipt; receiving but not opening or reading the notice does not qualify for relief. Motions for extensions due to non-receipt are committed to the district court's discretion. The district court may deny this extension even where the litigant otherwise satisfies the technical elements of the extension rule (provided, of course, that the basis for the court's denial is something other than the district court's own assessment of the merits of the appeal or that the party failed to learn of the entry of judgment independently through its own means). The moving party is ordinarily not required to demonstrate "excusable neglect" in order to justify such relief.

♦ **NOTE:** Seeking relief from orders under other rules, such as Rule 60(b), usually cannot be used to circumvent this 180-day limitation. Although this inflexible 180-day time boundary sometimes may sometimes work a misfortune, it is designed to finality the interests of finality in judgments against inequity to parties.

Extensions—By District Court (Fee Motions)

When a party makes a timely attorneys' fees motion under Rule 54(d), the district court may suspend the time for taking an appeal until the fees motion is resolved. *See* Rule 58(e).

Extensions—By Court of Appeals

The courts of appeals may not grant litigants an extension of the time for appeal under any circumstances. *See* Fed. R. App. P. 26(b)(1).

Premature Appeals

A notice of appeal filed after the district court announces its decision, but before the judgment or order is formally entered, will be deemed "filed" on the day the district court formally enters the judgment or order. *See* Fed. R. App. P. 4(a)(2); *FirsTier Mortg. Co. v. Investors Mortg. Ins. Co.*, 498 U.S. 269, 276 (1991). This rule will not apply to notices of appeal filed before a ruling is even announced or to appeals filed from orders that are plainly interlocutory and would not be immediately appealable upon entry (absent a Rule 54(b) determination).

A notice of appeal filed after the district court formally enters the judgment or order, but before the district court rules upon those types of post-trial motions that suspend the time for appeal, is deemed to lie dormant. The notice will become effective when the trial court rules on the outstanding post-trial motions. *See* Fed. R. App. P. 4(a)(4)(B). If the appellant intends to challenge not just the original judgment but the post-trial motion ruling as well, a new or amended notice of appeal will be necessary.

---

§ 6.4 Step Three: Procedure for Taking an Appeal

The procedure for taking a federal civil appeal is straightforward. The appealing parties must give proper "notice" of their intent to appeal, and must do so timely and to the proper court.

PRACTICING LAW UNDER THIS PRINCIPLE

Contents of Notice of Appeal, Generally

A "notice of appeal" is an easily-prepared, one-page form, the filing of which is generally considered "a simple, nonsubstantive act." *See Garza v. Idaho*, 586 U.S. ___, 139 S. Ct. 738, 746 (2019). In addition to typical formalities (like case caption and filer's signature block), a proper notice of appeal contains three further items: (1) the identity of the appealing parties; (2) the judgment or appealable interlocutory order being appealed; and (3) the name of the court to which the appeal is being taken. *See* Fed. R. App. P. 3(c)(1). These requirements are considered mandatory and jurisdictional. *See Gonzalez v. Thaler*, 132 S. Ct. 641, 651–52 (2012). The notice of appeal need not (and should not) set out the appealing parties' legal arguments.

- *Naming All Parties:* The parties to the appeal should each be individually named. The appealing parties are deemed to be only those whose names appear on the notice of appeal itself (or whose intent to appeal is otherwise "objectively clear" from the notice). *See* Fed. R. App. P. 3(c)(4). Although shorthand descriptions (like *et al.*) may, under certain circumstances, supply the requisite clarity, an express designation is always the safer course. Where clarity is missing, the appeal may be lost.
- *Naming the Ruling Being Appealed:* The judgment or order (or part thereof) that is being appealed must be designated. *See* Fed. R. App. P. 3(c)(1)(B). Typically, notices of appeal will designate the final judgment entered in the lawsuit, which ordinarily permits the appeal to encompass both that judgment and most earlier interlocutory orders entered in the case. An alternate (and more perilous) course is to designate in the notice of appeal a particular ruling (*e.g.*, "the April 10 order dismissing count four in the complaint"). Such a designation will likely be understood as appealing the specified ruling (and *only* that ruling). But this constraint is construed liberally and, in determining what has been appealed, the courts of appeals will "probe" the notice itself and may examine other information supplied by the appealing parties to supplement (and, perhaps, rescue) an otherwise deficient notice. *See Sanabria v. United States*, 437 U.S. 54, 67 n.21 (1978). Ergo, trial rulings not expressly listed in the notice of appeal may be reviewed if they bear a connection with rulings listed in the notice of appeal, the intent to appeal them is clear, and the opponent suffers no prejudice.
- *Naming Court of Appeals:* The notice of appeal must identify the specific court to which the appeal is being taken (unless only one proper court is possible).

Requirement #1: Naming the Appellants

An appeal is considered taken only by those parties named as appellants in the caption or body of the notice of appeal, unless a party's intent to appeal is otherwise "objectively clear" from the notice. Although shorthand descriptions (including "*et al.*") can, on occasion, supply that requisite clarity, an express designation is by far the safer course. Where clarity of a party's intent to appeal is missing, that party's right to appeal may be lost. *See generally Torres v. Oakland Scavenger Co.*, 487 U.S. 312, 314 (1988) (failure to name party in notice of appeal "constitutes a failure of that party to appeal"). The goal is notice—to opponents and to the court—and the avoidance of gamesmanship. *See Gonzalez v. Thaler*, 565 U.S. 134, 148 (2012) (otherwise, parties "could sit on the fence, await the outcome, and opt to participate only if it was favorable"). As for appellees, they need not be separately listed in the notice of appeal.

Requirement #2: Naming the Ruling Being Appealed

The notice of appeal must also designate the judgment or order that is being appealed. Typically, notices of appeal will designate the final judgment entered in the lawsuit, which ordinarily permits the appeal to encompass both that judgment and most earlier interlocutory orders entered in the case that have "merged" into the final judgment, even if each earlier order is not separately listed. An alternate (and more "perilous") course is to designate a particular ruling (*e.g.*, the April 10 order dismissing count four in the complaint). Such designations have often been understood as appealing the specified ruling (and *only* that ruling). But this constraint is construed liberally and, in determining what is being appealed, the appellate court will "probe" the notice itself and may examine other information supplied by the appealing parties to supplement (and, perhaps, rescue) an otherwise deficient notice. Ergo, trial rulings not expressly listed in the notice of appeal have been found reviewable if they bear a connection with rulings listed in the notice of appeal, the intent to appeal them is clear, and the opponent suffers no prejudice.

- *2021 Amendments:* In late 2021, the appeals rules were amended to simplify this ruling-identification chore and to reduce traps for the unwary:
  - prior rulings that merge into the designated judgment or appealable interlocutory order no longer need to be separately designated but, instead, are deemed automatically encompassed in the appeal; and
  - all appeals now automatically encompass the lawsuit's final judgment if the notice of appeal designates (i) a listed post-trial motion ruling, (ii) an order that adjudicates all remaining claims and the rights and liabilities of all remaining parties, or (iii) an unappealable interlocutory order and final judgment is thereafter entered, *unless* the appellant expressly states that the appeal is limited to only a specific, designated part of a judgment or appealable order.

Requirement #3: Naming the Appeals Court

The notice of appeal must identify the specific court to which the appeal is being taken (unless only one proper destination is possible).

Errors in the Notice of Appeal

The federal appeals rules are jurisdictional in nature. *See Smith v. Barry,* 502 U.S. 244, 248 (1992). But the rules prescribing the proper contents of a notice of appeal are construed liberally, and not hyper-technically. A "technical variance" from the rules may be excused, if the rule requirements are "functionally" satisfied. *See id.* That function is notice, both to the court and the adversaries, of the appealing parties and the rulings to be reviewed. *See id.* If the appellant's intent is clear (or fairly inferred) and the appellee is not prejudiced by a technical error (generally, through ensuring a full opportunity to brief the issue), such mistakes may be overlooked. This liberality may even permit a party's brief to substitute for an unfiled notice of appeal, where it provides all the requisite notice. *Pro se* appeals will be assessed with special liberality. Nevertheless, an appellant's subjective intentions are not enough, and if the notice demanded by the rules is not satisfied either literally or functionally, the appeal will fail. *See id.*

Privacy Protection for Personal Data Identifiers

The vulnerability of electronically-accessible court files to privacy and security mischief prompted the adoption of special redaction and sealing privileges for certain civil cases. *See* Rule 5.2. In cases where these privileges applied at the district court level, the privileges will extend to the appeal as well. *See* Fed. R. App. P. 25(a)(5).

Notice Must Be *Filed* Timely

The notice of appeal must be actually *filed* with the clerk of court within the time allotted for taking an appeal. *See* Fed. R. App. P. 3(a)(1) & 4(a)(1). When permitted, nonelectronic mailing or "serving" the notice on or before the deadline is not sufficient. For prisoners, a notice of appeal is deemed to be timely if the prisoner complies with the appeals rules' inmate filing procedures. *See* Fed. R. App. P. 4(c).

Place of Filing

A notice of appeal is filed with the clerk of the district court from which the appeal is taken. *See* Fed. R. App. P. 3(a). However, mistakenly filing the notice with the court of appeals will *not* defeat the appeal. If the notice is filed timely, albeit with the court of appeals, the appeals court clerk will note the date of filing and send the notice to the clerk of the district court. *See* Fed. R. App. P. 4(d). Filing in other, mistaken locations may doom the appeal.

Electronic Filing

Electronic filing is now the norm in federal court. *See* Rule 5(d); Fed. R. App. P. 25(a)(2)(B). It is required of all filers who are represented by counsel (unless, the court, upon a showing of good cause, or a local rule, by its terms, permits otherwise). Filers who are unrepresented may file electronically if permitted by court order or local rule.

Service Not Required

The appealing party need not serve the notice of appeal on all other parties; this service is made by the clerk of court. *See* Fed. R. App. P. 3(d)(1). The clerk's failure to serve the notice, however, does not defeat the appeal. *See* Fed. R. App. P. 3(d)(3).

- *Service Copies to the Court:* Although the appellant does not actually serve the notice of appeal on the other parties, the appellant is required to provide the clerk's office with sufficient copies of the notice for service. *See* Fed. R. App. P. 3(a)(1).

Joint Appeals

Joint appeals may be taken by two or more parties whose similar interests make such joinder practicable. *See* Fed. R. App. P. 3(b)(1). Each plaintiff, however, must file a timely notice of appeal. The fact that some similarly situated plaintiff's timely appealed is immaterial; the appeal of each plaintiff must be appropriately made.

Consolidated Appeals

Upon its own motion or by motion of a party, the court of appeals may consolidate the appeals of different parties. *See* Fed. R. App. P. 3(b)(2).

Fees

The appealing party must pay to the district court both the district court fee for appeal and the court of appeals' docket fee. Fed. R. App. P. 3(e). Failure to pay fees should not affect the docketing of an appeal. *See* Fed. R. App. P. 3(a)(2). *See also Parissi v. Telechron, Inc.*, 349 U.S. 46, 47 (1955). But continued nonpayment following docketing will invite dismissal for want of prosecution.

§ 6.5 Step Four: Stays Pending Appeal

A party may seek a stay of judgment by filing such an application with the district court. In applications *not* involving stays of injunctions, receiverships, or accountings in patent infringement actions, a party may request a stay pending appeal by filing a supersedeas bond or other security. Stay applications must be filed timely and, generally, initially in the district court.

PRACTICING LAW UNDER THIS PRINCIPLE

30-Day "Automatic" Stay

For a period of 30 days after a judgment is entered, the parties are barred from executing upon the judgment or pursuing further proceedings for its enforcement. *See* Rule 62(a). This automatic stay does *not* apply to judgments involving injunctions, judgments in receivership actions, or judgments or orders directing accountings in patent infringement actions.

Time to Apply for Stay

Applications for stay generally should be filed at the earliest possible opportunity. Because the automatic stay generally does not apply in certain injunction, receivership, and patent infringement circumstances, appellants in those cases do not enjoy the automatic 30-day stay period and the time for execution and enforcement will immediately arrive. An appeal bond or other security must first be approved by the court before any stay is effective. *See* Rule 62(b). Consequently, a delay in seeking a stay will expose the defeated party to execution and enforcement of the judgment.

Where to Apply for Stay

Ordinarily, stays pending appeal must be filed first with the district court. *See* Fed. R. App. P. 8(a)(1). Only in circumstances where applying in the district court is not practicable, or where the district court has denied the request or failed to grant all the relief requested, may a party request a stay in the court of appeals. *See* Fed. R. App. P. 8(a)(2).

Procedure for Stay Applications in the District Court

In cases that do not involve injunctions, receivers, or accountings in patent infringement cases, the posting of an appeal bond or other security-after it has been approved by the court-will stay execution and enforcement of the judgment. *See* Rule 62(d).

In cases involving injunctions, the district court may, in its discretion, grant a stay of the injunction pending appeal. *See* Rule 62(c). To obtain such a stay, the moving party must generally make the traditional showing required for any injunction: strong likelihood of success on the merits, irreparable injury, no substantial harm to others, and no damage to the public interest. The court may condition such a stay upon the posting of a bond or other appropriate security.

Procedure for Stay Applications in the Court of Appeals

In applying for a stay in the court of appeals, the moving party must make several showings in the motion papers (*see* Fed. R. App. P. 8(a)(2)(A) to (2)(E)):

(a) *Proceedings Before Trial Court:* The motion must show why a stay application cannot be practicably directed to the district judge, or that the district judge has denied a stay or failed to grant all the relief requested (the district court's reasons must be set forth); *and*

(b) *Reasons for Relief:* The motion must show the reasons for the relief requested, and set forth the facts relied upon in support of that showing. Relevant parts of the record must be included and, where the facts relied upon are subject to dispute, supporting affidavits or other sworn statements must also be included; *and*

(c) *Reasonable Notice:* Reasonable notice of the motion must be given to the non-moving party; *and*

(d) *Disposition:* The motion will ordinarily be resolved by a panel or division of the court, unless exceptional circumstances justify submitting the motion to a single judge; *and*

(e) *Bond or Security:* If the motion is granted, the court of appeals can condition the stay upon the filing in the district court of a bond or other appropriate security.

---

§ 6.6 Step Five: The Appeal Process

Once the appeal is timely filed, the court of appeals will send to each party a briefing notice that will schedule the filing of an Appellant's Brief, an Appellee's Brief, and an Appellant's Reply Brief. Thereafter, the court of appeals may schedule oral argument, the case will be submitted, and a written disposition on appeal will be filed.

PRACTICING LAW WITH THIS PRINCIPLE

Effect of Appeal

Once the appeal is taken, jurisdiction over the case generally passes from the district court to the court of appeals. *See Griggs v. Provident Consumer Discount Co.,* 459 U.S. 56, 58 (1982). The district court thereafter usually enjoys only the narrow power to preform ministerial functions, issue stays and injunctions pending appeal, and, in certain instances, award counsel fees. However, under the "indicative ruling" procedure, if the district court (after being divested of jurisdiction by an appeal) states that it would grant a trial-level motion or considers such a motion to raise a "substantial issue", the court of appeals may remand back to the district judge for further proceedings. *See* Fed. R. App. P. 12.1.

Compliance with Schedule and Procedures

Failure to comply with the court of appeals' schedule and procedures is ground for such action as the court of appeals deems appropriate, including denial of the right to participate in oral argument or even dismissal of the appeal itself. *See* Fed. R. App. P. 3(a)(2).

Designation of the Record and Statement of Issues

The "record" on appeal consists of (1) the original papers and exhibits filed in the trial court, (2) the transcript, and (3) a certified copy of docket entries. The "record" encompasses not just those exhibits admitted into evidence, but may include items presented for admission and denied by the district court. Within 14 days after filing the notice of appeal, the appealing party must order those portions of the transcript that are necessary for the appeal (or file a certificate stating that no transcript will be ordered). Unless the appellant orders the entire transcript, the appellant must, during this same 14-day period, file a statement of the issues for appeal and a list of the intended contents of the Appendix. The appellee may thereafter serve a counter-designation of additional portions of the transcript to be included. *See* Fed. R. App. P. 10, 11, & 30.

Briefing Procedures

Briefing procedures (including content, format, and length) are prescribed by the Appellate Rules. *See* Fed. R. App. P. 25, 28, 28,1, 30, 31, 32. Remember, as noted above, electronic filing is the norm in federal court. *See* Fed. R. App. P. 25(a)(2)(B). Additionally, local rules—which often vary by Circuit—almost always supplement these national procedures.

Briefing Privacy

Special redaction and sealing privileges are applied to certain civil cases in the district court (*e.g.,* social security numbers, taxpayer identification numbers, financial account numbers, birth years, and full names of minors may be presented in an abbreviated form). *See* Rule 5.2. In cases where these privileges applied at the district court level, the privileges will extend to the appeal as well. *See* Fed. R. App. P. 25(a)(5).

Briefing Reminders

The "Do's" and "Don't's" of effective appellate briefing could fill volumes. Several common oversights, however, are worth special mention:

- ***Disclosure Statement:*** The Appellate Rules require each non-governmental corporate party in every civil case to file a statement identifying each of its parent corporations and all publicly-held companies that own 10% or more of the party's stock, and to supplement that statement whenever the necessary information changes. *See* Fed. R. App. P. 26.1.
- ***Footnote Restrictions:*** Some courts of appeals have adopted local rules that limit the use of footnotes in appellate briefs.
- ***Citing "Unpublished" Decisions:*** For years, many courts of appeals forbade the citation of "unpublished", "nonprecedential", "not-for-publication", or similarly labeled decisions. In 2007, the Appellate Rules invalidated this local practice. *See* Fed. R. App. P. 32.1. Courts of appeals may no longer prohibit or discourage the citation of such decisions (although litigants citing opinions that are not publicly accessible through a commercial, legal research service, or court database must file and serve copies). Courts of appeals may, however, continue to issue opinions bearing those designations, and the rules do not prescribe what effect the court must give to such decisions. The amendment merely addresses the question of citation.

Oral Argument

Oral argument is permitted generally unless the appeal is frivolous, the dispositive issues were authoritatively decided, or the decisional process would not be significantly aided by argument because the facts and legal arguments are adequately set forth in the briefs. *See* Fed. R. App. P. 34(a)(2). The length, scheduling, and location of argument is set by the particular court of appeals.

---

§ 6.7 Step Six: Appeals to the United States Supreme Court

A party enjoys an appeal as of right to the United States Supreme Court in only very few circumstances. In all other cases, the Supreme Court has the discretion whether to permit or refuse appeals to that Court. In practice, only a small handful of the many thousands of requests for Supreme Court review are granted each year.

PRACTICING LAW WITH THIS PRINCIPLE

Appeals as of Right; Time to File

Whenever a specially convened three-judge district court panel declares any Act of Congress to be unconstitutional, a direct appeal may be taken to the Supreme Court. *See* 28 U.S.C. § 1253. Such appeals must be filed within 30 days of the date the district court's order is entered. *See* 28 U.S.C. § 2102(a). Congress may permit other direct appeals from the district courts, and such appeals must also be filed within 30 days of the district court's action. *See id.*

Discretionary Appeals; Time to File

The Supreme Court may, in its discretion, grant a party appellate review from other federal and State court rulings. Supreme Court review of federal appellate court decisions may be sought by petitioning for a Writ of Certiorari or by seeking a certification from the court of appeals. *See* 28 U.S.C. § 1254(1)–(2). (In Latin, "certiorari" means "to be informed of"; such writs of certiorari are of common law origin, and were (and are) issued by a higher court to a lower court requiring that the certified record in a case be delivered for review. *See Black's Law Dictionary* 207 (5th ed. 1979).) The Supreme Court may, in its discretion, also grant a Writ of Certiorari to review of decisions from the highest court of any State, but only where (a) a federal treaty or statute is drawn into question, (b) a State statute is drawn into question on federal grounds, or (c) any title, right, privilege, or immunity is specially set up or claimed under federal law. *See* 28 U.S.C. § 1257.

Petitions for Writs of Certiorari usually must be filed with the Supreme Court within 90 days after the entry of the disputed judgment or decree. *See* 28 U.S.C. § 2101.

Considerations in Granting Writs of Certiorari

The Supreme Court Rules provide a non-controlling, non-exhaustive list of the types of "compelling reasons" that may prompt the Court to grant a Writ of Certiorari. *See* U.S. S. Ct. R. 10(a) to (c). They are:

(1) A conflict among the federal Circuits on an "important matter";

(2) A conflict between a federal court of appeals and the highest court of a State on an "important federal question";

(3) A ruling by a court of appeals that "so far departed from the accepted and usual course of judicial proceedings" (or that sanctions such a departure by a lower court) that the Supreme Court's "supervisory power" is called for;

(4) A ruling by the highest court of a State that conflicts with the decision of another State's highest court or a federal court of appeals on an "important federal question"; or

(5) A ruling by a State court or a federal court of appeals that decides "an important question of federal law that has not been, but should be," settled by the Supreme Court, or that decides "an important federal question in a way that conflicts with relevant decisions" of the Supreme Court.

PART VIII

TITLE 28, JUDICIARY AND JUDICIAL PROCEDURE—SELECTED PROVISIONS

Including Amendments Current as of April 1, 2021

Table of Sections

---

§ 144. Bias or Prejudice of Judge

Whenever a party to any proceeding in a district court makes and files a timely and sufficient affidavit that the judge before whom the matter is pending has a personal bias or prejudice either against him or in favor of any adverse party, such judge shall proceed no further therein, but another judge shall be assigned to hear such proceeding.

The affidavit shall state the facts and the reasons for the belief that bias or prejudice exists, and shall be filed not less than ten days before the beginning of the term at which the proceeding is to be heard, or good cause shall be shown for failure to file it within such time. A party may file only one such affidavit in any case. It shall be accompanied by a certificate of counsel of record stating that it is made in good faith.

§ 451. Definitions

As used in this title:

The term "court of the United States" includes the Supreme Court of the United States, courts of appeals, district courts constituted by chapter 5 of this title, including the Court of International Trade and any court created by Act of Congress the judges of which are entitled to hold office during good behavior.

The terms "district court" and "district court of the United States" mean the courts constituted by chapter 5 of this title.

The term "judge of the United States" includes judges of the courts of appeals, district courts, Court of International Trade and any court created by Act of Congress, the judges of which are entitled to hold office during good behavior.

The term "justice of the United States" includes the Chief Justice of the United States and the associate justices of the Supreme Court.

The term "district" and "judicial district" mean the districts enumerated in Chapter 5 of this title.

The term "department" means one of the executive departments enumerated in section 1 of Title 5, unless the context shows that such term was intended to describe the executive, legislative, or judicial branches of the government.

The term "agency" includes any department, independent establishment, commission, administration, authority, board or bureau of the United States or any corporation in which the United States has a proprietary interest, unless the context shows that such term was intended to be used in a more limited sense.

§ 452. Courts Always Open; Powers Unrestricted by Expiration of Sessions

All courts of the United States shall be deemed always open for the purpose of filing proper papers, issuing and returning process, and making motions and orders.

The continued existence or expiration of a session of court in no way affects the power of the court to do any act or take any proceeding.

§ 455. Disqualification of Justice, Judge, or Magistrate

(a) Any justice, judge, or magistrate of the United States shall disqualify himself in any proceeding in which his impartiality might reasonably be questioned.

(b) He shall also disqualify himself in the following circumstances:

(1) Where he has a personal bias or prejudice concerning a party, or personal knowledge of disputed evidentiary facts concerning the proceeding;

(2) Where in private practice he served as lawyer in the matter in controversy, or a lawyer with whom he previously practiced law served during such association as a lawyer concerning the matter, or the judge or such lawyer has been a material witness concerning it;

(3) Where he has served in governmental employment and in such capacity participated as counsel, adviser or material witness concerning the proceeding or expressed an opinion concerning the merits of the particular case in controversy;

(4) He knows that he, individually or as a fiduciary, or his spouse or minor child residing in his household, has a financial interest in the subject matter in controversy or in a party to the proceeding, or any other interest that could be substantially affected by the outcome of the proceeding;

(5) He or his spouse, or a person within the third degree of relationship to either of them, or the spouse of such a person:

(i) Is a party to the proceeding, or an officer, director, or trustee of a party;

(ii) Is acting as a lawyer in the proceeding;

(iii) Is known by the judge to have an interest that could be substantially affected by the outcome of the proceeding;

(iv) Is to the judge's knowledge likely to be a material witness in the proceeding.

(c) A judge should inform himself about his personal and fiduciary financial interests, and make a reasonable effort to inform himself about the personal financial interests of his spouse and minor children residing in his household.

(d) For the purposes of this section the following words or phrases shall have the meaning indicated:

(1) "proceeding" includes pretrial, trial, appellate review, or other stages of litigation;

(2) the degree of relationship is calculated according to the civil law system;

(3) "fiduciary" includes such relationships as executor, administrator, trustee, and guardian;

(4) "financial interest" means ownership of a legal or equitable interest, however small, or a relationship as director, adviser, or other active participant in the affairs of a party, except that:

(i) Ownership in a mutual or common investment fund that holds securities is not a "financial interest" in such securities unless the judge participates in the management of the fund;

(ii) An office in an educational, religious, charitable, fraternal, or civic organization is not a "financial interest" in securities held by the organization;

(iii) The proprietary interest of a policyholder in a mutual insurance company, of a depositor in a mutual savings association, or a similar proprietary interest, is a "financial interest" in the organization only if the outcome of the proceeding could substantially affect the value of the interest;

(iv) Ownership of government securities is a "financial interest" in the issuer only if the outcome of the proceeding could substantially affect the value of the securities.

(e) No justice, judge, or magistrate shall accept from the parties to the proceeding a waiver of any ground for disqualification enumerated in subsection (b). Where the ground for disqualification arises only under subsection (a), waiver may be accepted provided it is preceded by a full disclosure on the record of the basis for disqualification.

(f) Notwithstanding the preceding provisions of this section, if any justice, judge, magistrate, or bankruptcy judge to whom a matter has been assigned would be disqualified, after substantial judicial time has been devoted to the matter, because of the appearance or discovery, after the matter was assigned to him or her, that he or she individually or as a fiduciary, or his or her spouse or minor child residing in his or her household, has a financial interest in a party (other than an interest that could be substantially affected by the outcome), disqualification is not required if the justice, judge, magistrate judge, bankruptcy judge, spouse or minor child, as the case may be, divests himself or herself of the interest that provides the grounds for the disqualification.

§ 636. Jurisdiction, Powers, and Temporary Assignment

(a) Each United States magistrate judge serving under this chapter shall have within the district in which sessions are held by the court that appointed the magistrate judge, at other places where that court may function, and elsewhere as authorized by law—

(1) all powers and duties conferred or imposed upon United States commissioners by law or by the Rules of Criminal Procedure for the United States District Courts;

(2) the power to administer oaths and affirmations, issue orders pursuant to section 3142 of title 18 concerning release or detention of persons pending trial, and take acknowledgements, affidavits, and depositions;

(3) the power to conduct trials under section 3401, title 18, United States Code, in conformity with and subject to the limitations of that section;

(4) the power to enter a sentence for a petty offense; and

(5) the power to enter a sentence for a class A misdemeanor in a case in which the parties have consented.

(b) **(1)** Notwithstanding any provision of law to the contrary—

(A) a judge may designate a magistrate judge to hear and determine any pretrial matter pending before the court, except a motion for injunctive relief, for judgment on the pleadings, for summary judgment, to dismiss or quash an indictment or information made by the defendant, to suppress evidence in a criminal case, to dismiss or to permit maintenance of a class action, to dismiss for failure to state a claim upon which relief can be granted, and to involuntarily dismiss an action. A judge of the court may reconsider any pretrial matter under this subparagraph (A) where it has been shown that the magistrate judge's order is clearly erroneous or contrary to law.

(B) a judge may also designate a magistrate judge to conduct hearings, including evidentiary hearings, and to submit to a judge of the court proposed findings of fact and recommendations for the disposition, by a judge of the court, of any motion excepted in subparagraph (A), of applications for posttrial[1] relief made by individuals convicted of criminal offenses and of prisoner petitions challenging conditions of confinement.

(C) the magistrate judge shall file his proposed findings and recommendations under subparagraph (B) with the court and a copy shall forthwith be mailed to all parties.

Within fourteen days after being served with a copy, any party may serve and file written objections to such proposed findings and recommendations as provided by rules of court. A judge of the court shall make a de novo determination of those portions of the report or specified proposed findings or recommendations to which objection is made. A judge of the court may accept, reject, or modify, in whole or in part, the findings or recommendations made by the magistrate judge. The judge may also receive further evidence or recommit the matter to the magistrate judge with instructions.

(2) A judge may designate a magistrate judge to serve as a special master pursuant to the applicable provisions of this title and the Federal Rules of Civil Procedure for the United States district courts. A judge may designate a magistrate judge to serve as a special master in any civil case, upon consent of the parties, without regard to the provisions of rule 53(b) of the Federal Rules of Civil Procedure for the United States district courts.

(3) A magistrate judge may be assigned such additional duties as are not inconsistent with the Constitution and laws of the United States.

(4) Each district court shall establish rules pursuant to which the magistrate judges shall discharge their duties.

(c) Notwithstanding any provision of law to the contrary—

(1) Upon the consent of the parties, a full-time United States magistrate judge or a part-time United States magistrate judge who serves as a full-time judicial officer may conduct any or all proceedings in a jury or nonjury civil matter and order the entry of judgment in the case, when specially designated to exercise such jurisdiction by the district court or courts he serves. Upon the consent of the parties, pursuant to their specific written request, any other part-time magistrate judge may exercise such jurisdiction, if such magistrate judge meets the bar membership requirements set forth in section 631(b)(1) and the chief judge of the district court certifies that a full-time magistrate judge is not reasonably available in accordance with guidelines established by the judicial council of the circuit. When there is more than one judge of a district court, designation under this paragraph shall be by the concurrence of a majority of all the judges of such district court, and when there is no such concurrence, then by the chief judge.

(2) If a magistrate judge is designated to exercise civil jurisdiction under paragraph (1) of this subsection, the clerk of court shall, at the time the action is filed, notify the parties of the availability of a magistrate judge to exercise such jurisdiction. The decision of the parties shall be communicated to the clerk of court. Thereafter, either the district court judge or the magistrate judge may again advise the parties of the availability of the magistrate judge, but in so doing, shall also advise the parties that they are free to withhold consent without adverse substantive consequences. Rules of court for the reference of civil matters to magistrate judges shall include procedures to protect the voluntariness of the parties' consent.

(3) Upon entry of judgment in any case referred under paragraph (1) of this subsection, an aggrieved party may appeal directly to the appropriate United States court of appeals from the judgment of the magistrate judge in the same manner as an appeal from any other judgment of a district court. The consent of the parties allows a magistrate judge designated to exercise civil jurisdiction under paragraph (1) of this subsection to direct the entry of a judgment of the district

1 So in original. Probably should be "post-trial".

court in accordance with the Federal Rules of Civil Procedure. Nothing in this paragraph shall be construed as a limitation of any party's right to seek review by the Supreme Court of the United States.

(4) The court may, for good cause shown on its own motion, or under extraordinary circumstances shown by any party, vacate a reference of a civil matter to a magistrate judge under this subsection.

(5) The magistrate judge shall, subject to guidelines of the Judicial Conference, determine whether the record taken pursuant to this section shall be taken by electronic sound recording, by a court reporter, or by other means.

(d) The practice and procedure for the trial of cases before officers serving under this chapter shall conform to rules promulgated by the Supreme Court pursuant to section 2072 of this title.

(e) Contempt authority.—

(1) In general.—A United States magistrate judge serving under this chapter shall have within the territorial jurisdiction prescribed by the appointment of such magistrate judge the power to exercise contempt authority as set forth in this subsection.

(2) Summary criminal contempt authority.—A magistrate judge shall have the power to punish summarily by fine or imprisonment, or both, such contempt of the authority of such magistrate judge constituting misbehavior of any person in the magistrate judge's presence so as to obstruct the administration of justice. The order of contempt shall be issued under the Federal Rules of Criminal Procedure.

(3) Additional criminal contempt authority in civil consent and misdemeanor cases.—In any case in which a United States magistrate judge presides with the consent of the parties under subsection (c) of this section, and in any misdemeanor case proceeding before a magistrate judge under section 3401 of title 18, the magistrate judge shall have the power to punish, by fine or imprisonment, or both, criminal contempt constituting disobedience or resistance to the magistrate judge's lawful writ, process, order, rule, decree, or command. Disposition of such contempt shall be conducted upon notice and hearing under the Federal Rules of Criminal Procedure.

(4) Civil contempt authority in civil consent and misdemeanor cases.—In any case in which a United States magistrate judge presides with the consent of the parties under subsection (c) of this section, and in any misdemeanor case proceeding before a magistrate judge under section 3401 of title 18, the magistrate judge may exercise the civil contempt authority of the district court. This paragraph shall not be construed to limit the authority of a magistrate judge to order sanctions under any other statute, the Federal Rules of Civil Procedure, or the Federal Rules of Criminal Procedure.

(5) Criminal contempt penalties.—The sentence imposed by a magistrate judge for any criminal contempt provided for in paragraphs (2) and (3) shall not exceed the penalties for a Class C misdemeanor as set forth in sections 3581(b)(8) and 3571(b)(6) of title 18.

(6) Certification of other contempts to the district court. Upon the commission of any such act—

(A) in any case in which a United States magistrate judge presides with the consent of the parties under subsection (c) of this section, or in any misdemeanor case proceeding before a magistrate judge under section 3401 of title 18, that may, in the opinion of the magistrate judge, constitute a serious criminal contempt punishable by penalties exceeding those set forth in paragraph (5) of this subsection, or

(B) in any other case or proceeding under subsection (a) or (b) of this section, or any other statute, where—

(i) the act committed in the magistrate judge's presence may, in the opinion of the magistrate judge, constitute a serious criminal contempt punishable by penalties exceeding those set forth in paragraph (5) of this subsection,

(ii) the act that constitutes a criminal contempt occurs outside the presence of the magistrate judge, or

(iii) the act constitutes a civil contempt,

the magistrate judge shall forthwith certify the facts to a district judge and may serve or cause to be served, upon any person whose behavior is brought into question under this paragraph, an order requiring such person to appear before a district judge upon a day certain to show cause why that person should not be adjudged in contempt by reason of the facts so certified. The district judge shall thereupon hear the evidence as to the act or conduct complained of and, if it is such as to warrant punishment, punish such person in the same manner and to the same extent as for a contempt committed before a district judge.

(7) Appeals of magistrate judge contempt orders.—The appeal of an order of contempt under this subsection shall be made to the court of appeals in cases proceeding under subsection (c) of this section. The appeal of any other order of contempt issued under this section shall be made to the district court.

(f) In an emergency and upon the concurrence of the chief judges of the districts involved, a United States magistrate judge may be temporarily assigned to perform any of the duties specified in subsection (a), (b), or (c) of this section in a judicial district other than the judicial district for which he has been appointed. No magistrate judge shall perform any of such duties in a district to which he has been temporarily assigned until an order has been issued by the chief judge of such district specifying (1) the emergency by reason of which he has been transferred, (2) the duration of his assignment, and (3) the duties which he is authorized to perform. A magistrate judge so assigned shall not be entitled to additional compensation but shall be reimbursed for actual and necessary expenses incurred in the performance of his duties in accordance with section 635.

(g) A United States magistrate judge may perform the verification function required by section 4107 of title 18, United States Code. A magistrate judge may be assigned by a judge of any United States district court to perform the verification required by section 4108 and the appointment of counsel authorized by section 4109 of title 18, United States Code, and may perform such functions beyond the territorial limits of the United States. A magistrate judge assigned such functions shall have no authority to perform any other function within the territory of a foreign country.

(h) A United States magistrate judge who has retired may, upon the consent of the chief judge of the district involved, be recalled to serve as a magistrate judge in any judicial district by the judicial council of the circuit within which such district is located. Upon recall, a magistrate judge may receive a salary for such service in accordance with regulations promulgated by the Judicial Conference, subject to the restrictions on the payment of an annuity set forth in section 377 of this title or in subchapter III of chapter 83, and chapter 84, of title 5 which are applicable to such magistrate judge. The requirements set forth in subsections (a), (b)(3), and (d) of section 631, and paragraph (1) of subsection (b) of such section to the extent such paragraph requires membership of the bar of the location in which an individual is to serve as a magistrate judge, shall not apply to the recall of a retired magistrate judge under this subsection or section 375 of this title. Any other requirement set forth in section 631(b) shall apply to the recall of a retired magistrate judge under this subsection or section 375 of this title unless such retired magistrate judge met such requirement upon appointment or reappointment as a magistrate judge under section 361.

§ 1251. Original Jurisdiction

(a) The Supreme Court shall have original and exclusive jurisdiction of all controversies between two or more States.

(b) The Supreme Court shall have original but not exclusive jurisdiction of:

(1) All actions or proceedings to which ambassadors, other public ministers, consuls, or vice consuls of foreign States are parties;

(2) All controversies between the United States and a State;

(3) All actions or proceedings by a State against the citizens of another State or against aliens.

§ 1253. Direct Appeals from Decisions of Three-Judge Courts

Except as otherwise provided by law, any party may appeal to the Supreme Court from an order granting or denying, after notice and hearing, an interlocutory or permanent injunction in any civil action, suit or proceeding required by any Act of Congress to be heard and determined by a district court of three judges.

§ 1254. Courts of Appeals; Certiorari; Certified Questions

Cases in the courts of appeals may be reviewed by the Supreme Court by the following methods:

(1) By writ of certiorari granted upon the petition of any party to any civil or criminal case, before or after rendition of judgment or decree;

(2) By certification at any time by a court of appeals of any question of law in any civil or criminal case as to which instructions are desired, and upon such certification the Supreme Court may give binding instructions or require the entire record to be sent up for decision of the entire matter in controversy.

§ 1257. State Courts; Certiorari

(a) Final judgments or decrees rendered by the highest court of a State in which a decision could be had, may be reviewed by the Supreme Court by writ of certiorari where the validity of a treaty or statute of the United States is drawn in question or where the validity of a statute of any State is drawn in question on the ground of its being repugnant to the Constitution, treaties, or laws of the United States, or where any title, right, privilege, or immunity is specially set up or claimed under the Constitution or the treaties or statutes of, or any commission held or authority exercised under, the United States.

(b) For the purposes of this section, the term "highest court of a State" includes the District of Columbia Court of Appeals.

§ 1291. Final Decisions of District Courts

The courts of appeals (other than the United States Court of Appeals for the Federal Circuit) shall have jurisdiction of appeals from all final decisions of the district courts of the United States, the United States District Court for the District of the Canal Zone, the District Court of Guam, and the District Court of the Virgin Islands, except where a direct review may be had in the Supreme Court. The jurisdiction of the United States Court of Appeals for the Federal Circuit shall be limited to the jurisdiction described in sections 1292(c) and (d) and 1295 of this title.

§ 1292. Interlocutory Decisions

(a) Except as provided in subsections (c) and (d) of this section, the courts of appeals shall have jurisdiction of appeals from:

(1) Interlocutory orders of the district courts of the United States, the United States District Court for the District of the Canal Zone, the District Court of Guam, and the District Court of the Virgin Islands, or of the judges thereof, granting, continuing, modifying, refusing or dissolving injunctions, or refusing to dissolve or modify injunctions, except where a direct review may be had in the Supreme Court;

(2) Interlocutory orders appointing receivers, or refusing orders to wind up receiverships or to take steps to accomplish the purposes thereof, such as directing sales or other disposals of property;

(3) Interlocutory decrees of such district courts or the judges thereof determining the rights and liabilities of the parties to admiralty cases in which appeals from final decrees are allowed.

(b) When a district judge, in making in a civil action an order not otherwise appealable under this section, shall be of the opinion that such order involves a controlling question of law as to which there is substantial ground for difference of opinion and that an immediate appeal from the order may materially advance the ultimate termination of the litigation, he shall so state in writing in such order. The Court of Appeals which would have jurisdiction of an appeal of such action may thereupon, in its discretion, permit an appeal to be taken from such order, if application is made to it within ten days after the entry of the order: *Provided, however,* that application for an appeal hereunder shall not stay proceedings in the district court unless the district judge or the Court of Appeals or a judge thereof shall so order.

(c) The United States Court of Appeals for the Federal Circuit shall have exclusive jurisdiction—

(1) of an appeal from an interlocutory order or decree described in subsection (a) or (b) of this section in any case over which the court would have jurisdiction of an appeal under section 1295 of this title; and

(2) of an appeal from a judgment in a civil action for patent infringement which would otherwise be appealable to the United States Court of Appeals for the Federal Circuit and is final except for an accounting.

(d) **(1)** When the chief judge of the Court of International Trade issues an order under the provisions of section 256(b) of this title, or when any judge of the Court of International Trade, in issuing any other interlocutory order, includes in the order a statement that a controlling question of law is involved with respect to which there is a substantial ground for difference of opinion and that an immediate appeal from that order may materially advance the ultimate termination of the litigation, the United States Court of Appeals for the Federal Circuit may, in its discretion, permit an appeal to be taken from such order, if application is made to that Court within ten days after the entry of such order.

(2) When the chief judge of the United States Court of Federal Claims issues an order under section 798(b) of this title, or when any judge of the United States Court of Federal Claims, in issuing an interlocutory order, includes in the order a statement that a controlling question of law is involved with respect to which there is a substantial ground for difference of opinion and that an immediate appeal from that order may materially advance the ultimate termination of the litigation, the United States Court of Appeals for the Federal Circuit may, in its discretion, permit an appeal to be taken from such order, if application is made to that Court within ten days after the entry of such order.

(3) Neither the application for nor the granting of an appeal under this subsection shall stay proceedings in the Court of International Trade or in the Court of Federal Claims, as the case may be, unless a stay is ordered by a judge of the Court of International Trade or of the Court of Federal Claims or by the United States Court of Appeals for the Federal Circuit or a judge of that court.

(4) **(A)** The United States Court of Appeals for the Federal Circuit shall have exclusive jurisdiction of an appeal from an interlocutory order of a district court of the United States, the District Court of Guam, the District Court of the Virgin Islands, or the District Court for the

Northern Mariana Islands, granting or denying, in whole or in part, a motion to transfer an action to the United States Court of Federal Claims under section 1631 of this title.

(B) When a motion to transfer an action to the Court of Federal Claims is filed in a district court, no further proceedings shall be taken in the district court until 60 days after the court has ruled upon the motion. If an appeal is taken from the district court's grant or denial of the motion, proceedings shall be further stayed until the appeal has been decided by the Court of Appeals for the Federal Circuit. The stay of proceedings in the district court shall not bar the granting of preliminary or injunctive relief, where appropriate and where expedition is reasonably necessary. However, during the period in which proceedings are stayed as provided in this subparagraph, no transfer to the Court of Federal Claims pursuant to the motion shall be carried out.

(e) The Supreme Court may prescribe rules, in accordance with section 2072 of this title, to provide for an appeal of an interlocutory decision to the courts of appeals that is not otherwise provided for under subsection (a), (b), (c), or (d).

§ 1331. Federal Question

The district courts shall have original jurisdiction of all civil actions arising under the Constitution, laws, or treaties of the United States.

§ 1332. Diversity of Citizenship; Amount in Controversy; Costs

(a) The district courts shall have original jurisdiction of all civil actions where the matter in controversy exceeds the sum or value of $75,000, exclusive of interest and costs, and is between—

(1) citizens of different States;

(2) citizens of a State and citizens or subjects of a foreign State, except that the district courts shall not have original jurisdiction under this subsection of an action between citizens of a State and citizens or subjects of a foreign State who are lawfully admitted for permanent residence in the United States and are domiciled in the same State;

(3) citizens of different States and in which citizens or subjects of a foreign State are additional parties; and

(4) a foreign State, defined in section 1603(a) of this title, as plaintiff and citizens of a State or of different States.

(b) Except when express provision therefor is otherwise made in a statute of the United States, where the plaintiff who files the case originally in the Federal courts is finally adjudged to be entitled to recover less than the sum or value of $75,000, computed without regard to any setoff or counterclaim to which the defendant may be adjudged to be entitled, and exclusive of interest and costs, the district court may deny costs to the plaintiff and, in addition, may impose costs on the plaintiff.

(c) For the purposes of this section and section 1441 of this title—

(1) a corporation shall be deemed to be a citizen of every State and foreign State by which it has been incorporated and of the State or foreign State where it has its principal place of business, except that in any direct action against the insurer of a policy or contract of liability insurance, whether incorporated or unincorporated, to which action the insured is not joined as a party-defendant, such insurer shall be deemed a citizen of—

(A) every State and foreign State of which the insured is a citizen;

(B) every State and foreign State by which the insurer has been incorporated; and

(C) the State or foreign State where the insurer has its principal place of business; and

(2) the legal representative of the estate of a decedent shall be deemed to be a citizen only of the same State as the decedent, and the legal representative of an infant or incompetent shall be deemed to be a citizen only of the same State as the infant or incompetent.

(d) **(1)** In this subsection—

(A) the term "class" means all of the class members in a class action;

(B) the term "class action" means any civil action filed under rule 23 of the Federal Rules of Civil Procedure or similar State statute or rule of judicial procedure authorizing an action to be brought by 1 or more representative persons as a class action;

(C) the term "class certification order" means an order issued by a court approving the treatment of some or all aspects of a civil action as a class action; and

(D) the term "class members" means the persons (named or unnamed) who fall within the definition of the proposed or certified class in a class action.

(2) The district courts shall have original jurisdiction of any civil action in which the matter in controversy exceeds the sum or value of $5,000,000, exclusive of interest and costs, and is a class action in which—

(A) any member of a class of plaintiffs is a citizen of a State different from any defendant;

(B) any member of a class of plaintiffs is a foreign State or a citizen or subject of a foreign State and any defendant is a citizen of a State; or

(C) any member of a class of plaintiffs is a citizen of a State and any defendant is a foreign State or a citizen or subject of a foreign State.

(3) A district court may, in the interests of justice and looking at the totality of the circumstances, decline to exercise jurisdiction under paragraph (2) over a class action in which greater than one-third but less than two-thirds of the members of all proposed plaintiff classes in the aggregate and the primary defendants are citizens of the State in which the action was originally filed based on consideration of—

(A) whether the claims asserted involve matters of national or interstate interest;

(B) whether the claims asserted will be governed by laws of the State in which the action was originally filed or by the laws of other States;

(C) whether the class action has been pleaded in a manner that seeks to avoid Federal jurisdiction;

(D) whether the action was brought in a forum with a distinct nexus with the class members, the alleged harm, or the defendants;

(E) whether the number of citizens of the State in which the action was originally filed in all proposed plaintiff classes in the aggregate is substantially larger than the number of citizens from any other State, and the citizenship of the other members of the proposed class is dispersed among a substantial number of States; and

(F) whether, during the 3-year period preceding the filing of that class action, 1 or more other class actions asserting the same or similar claims on behalf of the same or other persons have been filed.

(4) A district court shall decline to exercise jurisdiction under paragraph (2)—

(A) **(i)** over a class action in which—

(I) greater than two-thirds of the members of all proposed plaintiff classes in the aggregate are citizens of the State in which the action was originally filed;

(II) at least 1 defendant is a defendant—

(aa) from whom significant relief is sought by members of the plaintiff class;

(bb) whose alleged conduct forms a significant basis for the claims asserted by the proposed plaintiff class; and

(cc) who is a citizen of the State in which the action was originally filed; and

(III) principal injuries resulting from the alleged conduct or any related conduct of each defendant were incurred in the State in which the action was originally filed; and

(ii) during the 3-year period preceding the filing of that class action, no other class action has been filed asserting the same or similar factual allegations against any of the defendants on behalf of the same or other persons; or

(B) two-thirds or more of the members of all proposed plaintiff classes in the aggregate, and the primary defendants, are citizens of the State in which the action was originally filed.

(5) Paragraphs (2) through (4) shall not apply to any class action in which—

(A) the primary defendants are States, State officials, or other governmental entities against whom the district court may be foreclosed from ordering relief; or

(B) the number of members of all proposed plaintiff classes in the aggregate is less than 100.

(6) In any class action, the claims of the individual class members shall be aggregated to determine whether the matter in controversy exceeds the sum or value of $5,000,000, exclusive of interest and costs.

(7) Citizenship of the members of the proposed plaintiff classes shall be determined for purposes of paragraphs (2) through (6) as of the date of filing of the complaint or amended complaint, or, if the case stated by the initial pleading is not subject to Federal jurisdiction, as of the date of service by plaintiffs of an amended pleading, motion, or other paper, indicating the existence of Federal jurisdiction.

(8) This subsection shall apply to any class action before or after the entry of a class certification order by the court with respect to that action.

(9) Paragraph (2) shall not apply to any class action that solely involves a claim

(A) concerning a covered security as defined under 16(f)(3)[2] of the Securities Act of 1933 (15 U.S.C. 78p(f)(3)) and section 28(f)(5)(E) of the Securities Exchange Act of 1934 (15 U.S.C. 78bb(f)(5)(E));

(B) that relates to the internal affairs or governance of a corporation or other form of business enterprise and that arises under or by virtue of the laws of the State in which such corporation or business enterprise is incorporated or organized; or

(C) that relates to the rights, duties (including fiduciary duties), and obligations relating to or created by or pursuant to any security (as defined under section 2(a)(1) of the Securities Act of 1933 (15 U.S.C. 77b(a)(1)) and the regulations issued thereunder).

(10) For purposes of this subsection and section 1453, an unincorporated association shall be deemed to be a citizen of the State where it has its principal place of business and the State under whose laws it is organized.

---

[2] So in original. Reference to "16(f)(3)" probably should be preceded by "section".

(11) (A) For purposes of this subsection and section 1453, a mass action shall be deemed to be a class action removable under paragraphs (2) through (10) if it otherwise meets the provisions of those paragraphs.

(B) (i) As used in subparagraph (A), the term "mass action" means any civil action (except a civil action within the scope of section 1711(2)) in which monetary relief claims of 100 or more persons are proposed to be tried jointly on the ground that the plaintiffs' claims involve common questions of law or fact, except that jurisdiction shall exist only over those plaintiffs whose claims in a mass action satisfy the jurisdictional amount requirements under subsection (a).

(ii) As used in subparagraph (A), the term "mass action" shall not include any civil action in which—

(I) all of the claims in the action arise from an event or occurrence in the State in which the action was filed, and that allegedly resulted in injuries in that State or in States contiguous to that State;

(II) the claims are joined upon motion of a defendant;

(III) all of the claims in the action are asserted on behalf of the general public (and not on behalf of individual claimants or members of a purported class) pursuant to a State statute specifically authorizing such action; or

(IV) the claims have been consolidated or coordinated solely for pretrial proceedings.

(C) (i) Any action(s) removed to Federal court pursuant to this subsection shall not thereafter be transferred to any other court pursuant to section 1407, or the rules promulgated thereunder, unless a majority of the plaintiffs in the action request transfer pursuant to section 1407.

(ii) This subparagraph will not apply—

(I) to cases certified pursuant to rule 23 of the Federal Rules of Civil Procedure; or

(II) if plaintiffs propose that the action proceed as a class action pursuant to rule 23 of the Federal Rules of Civil Procedure.

(D) The limitations periods on any claims asserted in a mass action that is removed to Federal court pursuant to this subsection shall be deemed tolled during the period that the action is pending in Federal court.

(e) The word "States", as used in this section, includes the Territories, the District of Columbia, and the Commonwealth of Puerto Rico.

§ 1333. Admiralty, Maritime and Prize Cases

The district courts shall have original jurisdiction, exclusive of the courts of the States, of:

(1) Any civil case of admiralty or maritime jurisdiction, saving to suitors in all cases all other remedies to which they are otherwise entitled.

(2) Any prize brought into the United States and all proceedings for the condemnation of property taken as prize.

§ 1334. Bankruptcy Cases and Proceedings

(a) Except as provided in subsection (b) of this section, the district courts shall have original and exclusive jurisdiction of all cases under title 11.

(b) Except as provided in subsection (e)(2), and notwithstanding any Act of Congress that confers exclusive jurisdiction on a court or courts other than the district courts, the district courts shall have original but not exclusive jurisdiction of all civil proceedings arising under title 11, or arising in or related to cases under title 11.

(c) **(1)** Except with respect to a case under chapter 15 of title 11, nothing in this section prevents a district court in the interest of justice, or in the interest of comity with State courts or respect for State law, from abstaining from hearing a particular proceeding arising under title 11 or arising in or related to a case under title 11.

(2) Upon timely motion of a party in a proceeding based upon a State law claim or State law cause of action, related to a case under title 11 but not arising under title 11 or arising in a case under title 11, with respect to which an action could not have been commenced in a court of the United States absent jurisdiction under this section, the district court shall abstain from hearing such proceeding if an action is commenced, and can be timely adjudicated, in a State forum of appropriate jurisdiction.

(d) Any decision to abstain or not to abstain made under subsection (c) (other than a decision not to abstain in a proceeding described in subsection (c)(2)) is not reviewable by appeal or otherwise by the court of appeals under section 158(d), 1291, or 1292 of this title or by the Supreme Court of the United States under section 1254 of this title. Subsection (c) and this subsection shall not be construed to limit the applicability of the stay provided for by section 362 of title 11, United States Code, as such section applies to an action affecting the property of the estate in bankruptcy.

(e) The district court in which a case under title 11 is commenced or is pending shall have exclusive jurisdiction—

(1) of all the property, wherever located, of the debtor as of the commencement of such case, and of property of the estate; and

(2) over all claims or causes of action that involve construction of section 327 of title 11, United States Code, or rules relating to disclosure requirements under section 327.

§ 1335. Interpleader

(a) The district courts shall have original jurisdiction of any civil action of interpleader or in the nature of interpleader filed by any person, firm, or corporation, association, or society having in his or its custody or possession money or property of the value of $500 or more, or having issued a note, bond, certificate, policy of insurance, or other instrument of value or amount of $500 or more, or providing for the delivery or payment or the loan of money or property of such amount or value, or being under any obligation written or unwritten to the amount of $500 or more, if

(1) Two or more adverse claimants, of diverse citizenship as defined in subsection (a) or (d) of section 1332 of this title, are claiming or may claim to be entitled to such money or property, or to any one or more of the benefits arising by virtue of any note, bond, certificate, policy or other instrument, or arising by virtue of any such obligation; and if (2) the plaintiff has deposited such money or property or has paid the amount of or the loan or other value of such instrument or the amount due under such obligation into the registry of the court, there to abide the judgment of the court, or has given bond payable to the clerk of the court in such amount and with such surety as the court or judge may deem proper, conditioned upon the compliance by the plaintiff with the future order or judgment of the court with respect to the subject matter of the controversy.

(b) Such an action may be entertained although the titles or claims of the conflicting claimants do not have a common origin, or are not identical, but are adverse to and independent of one another.

§ 1337. Commerce and Antitrust Regulations; Amount in Controversy, Costs

(a) The district courts shall have original jurisdiction of any civil action or proceeding arising under any Act of Congress regulating commerce or protecting trade and commerce against restraints and monopolies: Provided, however, That the district courts shall have original jurisdiction of an action brought under section 11706 or 14706 of title 49, only if the matter in controversy for each receipt or bill of lading exceeds $10,000, exclusive of interest and costs.

(b) Except when express provision therefor is otherwise made in a statute of the United States, where a plaintiff who files the case under section 11706 or 14706 of title 49, originally in the Federal courts is finally adjudged to be entitled to recover less than the sum or value of $10,000, computed without regard to any setoff or counterclaim to which the defendant may be adjudged to be entitled, and exclusive of any interest and costs, the district court may deny costs to the plaintiff and, in addition, may impose costs on the plaintiff.

(c) The district courts shall not have jurisdiction under this section of any matter within the exclusive jurisdiction of the Court of International Trade under chapter 95 of this title.

§ 1338. Patents, Plant Variety Protection, Copyrights, Mask Works, Designs, Trademarks, and Unfair Competition

(a) The district courts shall have original jurisdiction of any civil action arising under any Act of Congress relating to patents, plant variety protection, copyrights and trademarks. No State court shall have jurisdiction over any claim for relief arising under any Act of Congress relating to patents, plant variety protection, or copyrights. For purposes of this subsection, the term "State" includes any State of the United States, the District of Columbia, the Commonwealth of Puerto Rico, the United States Virgin Islands, American Samoa, Guam, and the Northern Mariana Islands.

(b) The district courts shall have original jurisdiction of any civil action asserting a claim of unfair competition when joined with a substantial and related claim under the copyright, patent, plant variety protection or trademark laws.

(c) Subsections (a) and (b) apply to exclusive rights in mask works under chapter 9 of title 17, and to exclusive rights in designs under chapter 13 of title 17, to the same extent as such subsections apply to copyrights.

§ 1339. Postal Matters

The district courts shall have original jurisdiction of any civil action arising under any Act of Congress relating to the postal service.

§ 1340. Internal Revenue; Customs Duties

The district courts shall have original jurisdiction of any civil action arising under any Act of Congress providing for internal revenue, or revenue from imports or tonnage except matters within the jurisdiction of the Court of International Trade.

§ 1343. Civil Rights and Elective Franchise

(a) The district courts shall have original jurisdiction of any civil action authorized by law to be commenced by any person:

(1) To recover damages for injury to his person or property, or because of the deprivation of any right or privilege of a citizen of the United States, by any act done in furtherance of any conspiracy mentioned in section 1985 of Title 42;

(2) To recover damages from any person who fails to prevent or to aid in preventing any wrongs mentioned in section 1985 of Title 42 which he had knowledge were about to occur and power to prevent;

(3) To redress the deprivation, under color of any State law, statute, ordinance, regulation, custom or usage, of any right, privilege or immunity secured by the Constitution of the United States or by any Act of Congress providing for equal rights of citizens or of all persons within the jurisdiction of the United States;

(4) To recover damages or to secure equitable or other relief under any Act of Congress providing for the protection of civil rights, including the right to vote.

(b) For purposes of this section—

(1) the District of Columbia shall be considered to be a State; and

(2) any Act of Congress applicable exclusively to the District of Columbia shall be considered to be a statute of the District of Columbia.

§ 1345. United States As Plaintiff

Except as otherwise provided by Act of Congress, the district courts shall have original jurisdiction of all civil actions, suits or proceedings commenced by the United States, or by any agency or officer thereof expressly authorized to sue by Act of Congress.

§ 1346. United States As Defendant

(a) The district courts shall have original jurisdiction, concurrent with the United States Court of Federal Claims, of:

(1) Any civil action against the United States for the recovery of any internal-revenue tax alleged to have been erroneously or illegally assessed or collected, or any penalty claimed to have been collected without authority or any sum alleged to have been excessive or in any manner wrongfully collected under the internal-revenue laws;

(2) Any other civil action or claim against the United States, not exceeding $10,000 in amount, founded either upon the Constitution, or any Act of Congress, or any regulation of an executive department, or upon any express or implied contract with the United States, or for liquidated or unliquidated damages in cases not sounding in tort, except that the district courts shall not have jurisdiction of any civil action or claim against the United States founded upon any express or implied contract with the United States or for liquidated or unliquidated damages in cases not sounding in tort which are subject to sections 7104(b)(1) and 7107(a)(1) of title 41. For the purpose of this paragraph, an express or implied contract with the Army and Air Force Exchange Service, Navy Exchanges, Marine Corps Exchanges, Coast Guard Exchanges, or Exchange Councils of the National Aeronautics and Space Administration shall be considered an express or implied contract with the United States.

(b) (1) Subject to the provisions of chapter 171 of this title, the district courts, together with the United States District Court for the District of the Canal Zone and the District Court of the Virgin Islands, shall have exclusive jurisdiction of civil actions on claims against the United States, for money damages, accruing on and after January 1, 1945, for injury or loss of property, or personal injury or death caused by the negligent or wrongful act or omission of any employee of the Government while acting within the scope of his office or employment, under circumstances where the United States, if a private person, would be liable to the claimant in accordance with the law of the place where the act or omission occurred.

(2) No person convicted of a felony who is incarcerated while awaiting sentencing or while serving a sentence may bring a civil action against the United States or an agency, officer, or employee of the Government, for mental or emotional injury suffered while in custody without a

prior showing of physical injury or the commission of a sexual act (as defined in section 2246 of title 18).

(c) The jurisdiction conferred by this section includes jurisdiction of any set-off, counterclaim, or other claim or demand whatever on the part of the United States against any plaintiff commencing an action under this section.

(d) The district courts shall not have jurisdiction under this section of any civil action or claim for a pension.

(e) The district courts shall have original jurisdiction of any civil action against the United States provided in section 6226, 6228(a), 7426, or 7428 (in the case of the United States district court for the District of Columbia) or section 7429 of the Internal Revenue Code of 1986.

(f) The district courts shall have exclusive original jurisdiction of civil actions under section 2409a to quiet title to an estate or interest in real property in which an interest is claimed by the United States.

(g) Subject to the provisions of chapter 179, the district courts of the United States shall have exclusive jurisdiction over any civil action commenced under section 453(2) of title 3, by a covered employee under chapter 5 of such title.

§ 1349. Corporation Organized under Federal Law As Party

The district courts shall not have jurisdiction of any civil action by or against any corporation upon the ground that it was incorporated by or under an Act of Congress, unless the United States is the owner of more than one-half of its capital stock.

§ 1357. Injuries under Federal Laws

The district courts shall have original jurisdiction of any civil action commenced by any person to recover damages for any injury to his person or property on account of any act done by him, under any Act of Congress, for the protection or collection of any of the revenues, or to enforce the right of citizens of the United States to vote in any State.

§ 1359. Parties Collusively Joined or Made

A district court shall not have jurisdiction of a civil action in which any party, by assignment or otherwise, has been improperly or collusively made or joined to invoke the jurisdiction of such court.

§ 1361. Action to Compel an Officer of the United States to Perform His Duty

The district courts shall have original jurisdiction of any action in the nature of mandamus to compel an officer or employee of the United States or any agency thereof to perform a duty owed to the plaintiff.

§ 1367. Supplemental Jurisdiction

(a) Except as provided in subsections (b) and (c) or as expressly provided otherwise by Federal statute, in any civil action of which the district courts have original jurisdiction, the district courts shall have supplemental jurisdiction over all other claims that are so related to claims in the action within such original jurisdiction that they form part of the same case or controversy under Article III of the United States Constitution. Such supplemental jurisdiction shall include claims that involve the joinder or intervention of additional parties.

(b) In any civil action of which the district courts have original jurisdiction founded solely on section 1332 of this title, the district courts shall not have supplemental jurisdiction under subsection (a) over claims by plaintiffs against persons made parties under Rule 14, 19, 20, or 24 of the Federal Rules of Civil Procedure, or over claims by persons proposed to be joined as plaintiffs under Rule 19 of such rules, or seeking to intervene as plaintiffs under Rule 24 of such rules, when exercising supplemental jurisdiction over such claims would be inconsistent with the jurisdictional requirements of section 1332.

(c) The district courts may decline to exercise supplemental jurisdiction over a claim under subsection (a) if—

(1) the claim raises a novel or complex issue of State law,

(2) the claim substantially predominates over the claim or claims over which the district court has original jurisdiction,

(3) the district court has dismissed all claims over which it has original jurisdiction, or

(4) in exceptional circumstances, there are other compelling reasons for declining jurisdiction.

(d) The period of limitations for any claim asserted under subsection (a), and for any other claim in the same action that is voluntarily dismissed at the same time as or after the dismissal of the claim under subsection (a), shall be tolled while the claim is pending and for a period of 30 days after it is dismissed unless State law provides for a longer tolling period.

(e) As used in this section, the term "State" includes the District of Columbia, the Commonwealth of Puerto Rico, and any territory or possession of the United States.

§ 1369. Multiparty, Multiforum Jurisdiction

(a) In general.—The district courts shall have original jurisdiction of any civil action involving minimal diversity between adverse parties that arises from a single accident, where at least 75 natural persons have died in the accident at a discrete location, if—

(1) a defendant resides in a State and a substantial part of the accident took place in another State or other location, regardless of whether that defendant is also a resident of the State where a substantial part of the accident took place;

(2) any two defendants reside in different States, regardless of whether such defendants are also residents of the same State or States; or

(3) substantial parts of the accident took place in different States.

(b) Limitation of jurisdiction of district courts.—The district court shall abstain from hearing any civil action described in subsection (a) in which—

(1) the substantial majority of all plaintiffs are citizens of a single State of which the primary defendants are also citizens; and

(2) the claims asserted will be governed primarily by the laws of that State.

(c) Special rules and definitions.—For purposes of this section—

(1) minimal diversity exists between adverse parties if any party is a citizen of a State and any adverse party is a citizen of another State, a citizen or subject of a foreign State, or a foreign State as defined in section 1603(a) of this title;

(2) a corporation is deemed to be a citizen of any State, and a citizen or subject of any foreign State, in which it is incorporated or has its principal place of business, and is deemed to be a resident of any State in which it is incorporated or licensed to do business or is doing business;

(3) the term "injury" means—

(A) physical harm to a natural person; and

(B) physical damage to or destruction of tangible property, but only if physical harm described in subparagraph (A) exists;

(4) the term "accident" means a sudden accident, or a natural event culminating in an accident, that results in death incurred at a discrete location by at least 75 natural persons; and

(5) the term "State" includes the District of Columbia, the Commonwealth of Puerto Rico, and any territory or possession of the United States.

(d) Intervening parties.—In any action in a district court which is or could have been brought, in whole or in part, under this section, any person with a claim arising from the accident described in subsection (a) shall be permitted to intervene as a party plaintiff in the action, even if that person could not have brought an action in a district court as an original matter.

(e) Notification of judicial panel on multidistrict litigation.—A district court in which an action under this section is pending shall promptly notify the judicial panel on multidistrict litigation of the pendency of the action.

§ 1390. Scope

(a) Venue defined.—As used in this chapter, the term "venue" refers to the geographic specification of the proper court or courts for the litigation of a civil action that is within the subject-matter jurisdiction of the district courts in general, and does not refer to any grant or restriction of subject-matter jurisdiction providing for a civil action to be adjudicated only by the district court for a particular district or districts.

(b) Exclusion of certain cases.—Except as otherwise provided by law, this chapter shall not govern the venue of a civil action in which the district court exercises the jurisdiction conferred by section 1333, except that such civil actions may be transferred between district courts as provided in this chapter.

(c) Clarification regarding cases removed from State courts.—This chapter shall not determine the district court to which a civil action pending in a State court may be removed, but shall govern the transfer of an action so removed as between districts and divisions of the United States district courts.

§ 1391. Venue Generally

(a) Applicability of section.—Except as otherwise provided by law—

(1) this section shall govern the venue of all civil actions brought in district courts of the United States; and

(2) the proper venue for a civil action shall be determined without regard to whether the action is local or transitory in nature.

(b) Venue in general.—A civil action may be brought in—

(1) a judicial district in which any defendant resides, if all defendants are residents of the State in which the district is located;

(2) a judicial district in which a substantial part of the events or omissions giving rise to the claim occurred, or a substantial part of property that is the subject of the action is situated; or

(3) if there is no district in which an action may otherwise be brought as provided in this section, any judicial district in which any defendant is subject to the court's personal jurisdiction with respect to such action.

(c) Residency.—For all venue purposes—

(1) a natural person, including an alien lawfully admitted for permanent residence in the United States, shall be deemed to reside in the judicial district in which that person is domiciled;

(2) an entity with the capacity to sue and be sued in its common name under applicable law, whether or not incorporated, shall be deemed to reside, if a defendant, in any judicial district in which such defendant is subject to the court's personal jurisdiction with respect to the civil action in question and, if a plaintiff, only in the judicial district in which it maintains its principal place of business; and

(3) a defendant not resident in the United States may be sued in any judicial district, and the joinder of such a defendant shall be disregarded in determining where the action may be brought with respect to other defendants.

(d) Residency of corporations in States with multiple districts.—For purposes of venue under this chapter, in a State which has more than one judicial district and in which a defendant that is a corporation is subject to personal jurisdiction at the time an action is commenced, such corporation shall be deemed to reside in any district in that State within which its contacts would be sufficient to subject it to personal jurisdiction if that district were a separate State, and, if there is no such district, the corporation shall be deemed to reside in the district within which it has the most significant contacts.

(e) Actions where defendant is officer or employee of the United States.—(1) In general.—A civil action in which a defendant is an officer or employee of the United States or any agency thereof acting in his official capacity or under color of legal authority, or an agency of the United States, or the United States, may, except as otherwise provided by law, be brought in any judicial district in which (A) a defendant in the action resides, (B) a substantial part of the events or omissions giving rise to the claim occurred, or a substantial part of property that is the subject of the action is situated, or (C) the plaintiff resides if no real property is involved in the action. Additional persons may be joined as parties to any such action in accordance with the Federal Rules of Civil Procedure and with such other venue requirements as would be applicable if the United States or one of its officers, employees, or agencies were not a party.

(2) Service.—The summons and complaint in such an action shall be served as provided by the Federal Rules of Civil Procedure except that the delivery of the summons and complaint to the officer or agency as required by the rules may be made by certified mail beyond the territorial limits of the district in which the action is brought.

(f) Civil actions against a foreign State.—A civil action against a foreign State as defined in section 1603(a) of this title may be brought—

(1) in any judicial district in which a substantial part of the events or omissions giving rise to the claim occurred, or a substantial part of property that is the subject of the action is situated;

(2) in any judicial district in which the vessel or cargo of a foreign State is situated, if the claim is asserted under section 1605(b) of this title;

(3) in any judicial district in which the agency or instrumentality is licensed to do business or is doing business, if the action is brought against an agency or instrumentality of a foreign State as defined in section 1603(b) of this title; or

(4) in the United States District Court for the District of Columbia if the action is brought against a foreign State or political subdivision thereof.

(g) Multiparty, multiforum litigation.—A civil action in which jurisdiction of the district court is based upon section 1369 of this title may be brought in any district in which any defendant resides or in which a substantial part of the accident giving rise to the action took place.

§ 1397. Interpleader

Any civil action of interpleader or in the nature of interpleader under section 1335 of this title may be brought in the judicial district in which one or more of the claimants reside.

§ 1400. Patents and Copyrights, Mask Works, and Designs

(a) Civil actions, suits, or proceedings arising under any Act of Congress relating to copyrights or exclusive rights in mask works or designs may be instituted in the district in which the defendant or his agent resides or may be found.

(b) Any civil action for patent infringement may be brought in the judicial district where the defendant resides, or where the defendant has committed acts of infringement and has a regular and established place of business.

§ 1401. Stockholder's Derivative Action

Any civil action by a stockholder on behalf of his corporation may be prosecuted in any judicial district where the corporation might have sued the same defendants.

§ 1402. United States As Defendant

(a) Any civil action in a district court against the United States under subsection (a) of section 1346 of this title may be prosecuted only:

> **(1)** Except as provided in paragraph (2), in the judicial district where the plaintiff resides;
>
> **(2)** In the case of a civil action in a district court by a corporation under paragraph (1) of subsection (a) of section 1346, in the judicial district in which is located the principal place of business or principal office or agency of the corporation; or if it has no principal place of business or principal office or agency in any judicial district (A) in the judicial district in which is located the office to which was made the return of the tax in respect of which the claim is made, or (B) if no return was made, in the judicial district in which lies the District of Columbia. Notwithstanding the foregoing provisions of this paragraph a district court, for the convenience of the parties and witnesses, in the interest of justice, may transfer any such action to any other district or division.

(b) Any civil action on a tort claim against the United States under subsection (b) of section 1346 of this title may be prosecuted only in the judicial district where the plaintiff resides or wherein the act or omission complained of occurred.

(c) Any civil action against the United States under subsection of section 1346 of this title may be prosecuted only in the judicial district where the property is situated at the time of levy, or if no levy is made, in the judicial district in which the event occurred which gave rise to the cause of action.

(d) Any civil action under section 2409a to quiet title to an estate or interest in real property in which an interest is claimed by the United States shall be brought in the district court of the district where the property is located or, if located in different districts, in any of such districts.

§ 1404. Change of Venue

(a) For the convenience of parties and witnesses, in the interest of justice, a district court may transfer any civil action to any other district or division where it might have been brought or to any district or division to which all parties have consented.

(b) Upon motion, consent or stipulation of all parties, any action, suit or proceeding of a civil nature or any motion or hearing thereof, may be transferred, in the discretion of the court, from the division in which pending to any other division in the same district. Transfer of proceedings in rem brought by or on behalf of the United States may be transferred under this section without the consent of the United States where all other parties request transfer.

(c) A district court may order any civil action to be tried at any place within the division in which it is pending.

(d) Transfers from a district court of the United States to the District Court of Guam, the District Court for the Northern Mariana Islands, or the District Court of the Virgin Islands shall not be permitted under this section. As otherwise used in this section, "district court" includes the District Court of Guam, the District Court for the Northern Mariana Islands, and the District Court of the Virgin Islands, and the term "district" includes the territorial jurisdiction of that court.

§ 1406. Cure or Waiver of Defects

(a) The district court of a district in which is filed a case laying venue in the wrong division or district shall dismiss, or if it be in the interest of justice, transfer such case to any district or division in which it could have been brought.

(b) Nothing in this chapter shall impair the jurisdiction of a district court of any matter involving a party who does not interpose timely and sufficient objection to the venue.

(c) As used in this section, "district court" includes the District Court of Guam, the District Court for the Northern Mariana Islands, and the District Court of the Virgin Islands, and the term "district" includes the territorial jurisdiction of that court.

§ 1407. Multidistrict Litigation

[Note to Reader: See Part V of this text.]

§ 1412. Change of Venue

A district court may transfer a case or proceeding under title 11 to a district court for another district, in the interest of justice or for the convenience of the parties.

§ 1441. Removal of Civil Actions

(a) Generally.—Except as otherwise expressly provided by Act of Congress, any civil action brought in a State court of which the district courts of the United States have original jurisdiction, may be removed by the defendant or the defendants, to the district court of the United States for the district and division embracing the place where such action is pending.

(b) Removal based on diversity of citizenship.—(1) In determining whether a civil action is removable on the basis of the jurisdiction under section 1332(a) of this title, the citizenship of defendants sued under fictitious names shall be disregarded.

(2) A civil action otherwise removable solely on the basis of the jurisdiction under section 1332(a) of this title may not be removed if any of the parties in interest properly joined and served as defendants is a citizen of the State in which such action is brought.

(c) Joinder of federal law claims and State law claims.—(1) If a civil action includes

(A) a claim arising under the Constitution, laws, or treaties of the United States (within the meaning of section 1331 of this title), and

(B) a claim not within the original or supplemental jurisdiction of the district court or a claim that has been made nonremovable by statute,

the entire action may be removed if the action would be removable without the inclusion of the claim described in subparagraph (B).

(2) Upon removal of an action described in paragraph (1), the district court shall sever from the action all claims described in paragraph (1)(B) and shall remand the severed claims to the State court from which the action was removed. Only defendants against whom a claim described in paragraph (1)(A) has been asserted are required to join in or consent to the removal under paragraph (1).

(d) Actions against foreign States.—Any civil action brought in a State court against a foreign State as defined in section 1603(a) of this title may be removed by the foreign State to the district court of the United States for the district and division embracing the place where such action is pending. Upon removal the action shall be tried by the court without jury. Where removal is based upon this subsection, the time limitations of section 1446(b) of this chapter may be enlarged at any time for cause shown.

(e) Multiparty, multiforum jurisdiction.—(1) Notwithstanding the provisions of subsection (b) of this section, a defendant in a civil action in a State court may remove the action to the district court of the United States for the district and division embracing the place where the action is pending if—

(A) the action could have been brought in a United States district court under section 1369 of this title; or

(B) the defendant is a party to an action which is or could have been brought, in whole or in part, under section 1369 in a United States district court and arises from the same accident as the action in State court, even if the action to be removed could not have been brought in a district court as an original matter.

The removal of an action under this subsection shall be made in accordance with section 1446 of this title, except that a notice of removal may also be filed before trial of the action in State court within 30 days after the date on which the defendant first becomes a party to an action under section 1369 in a United States district court that arises from the same accident as the action in State court, or at a later time with leave of the district court.

(2) Whenever an action is removed under this subsection and the district court to which it is removed or transferred under section 1407(j) has made a liability determination requiring further proceedings as to damages, the district court shall remand the action to the State court from which it had been removed for the determination of damages, unless the court finds that, for the convenience of parties and witnesses and in the interest of justice, the action should be retained for the determination of damages.

(3) Any remand under paragraph (2) shall not be effective until 60 days after the district court has issued an order determining liability and has certified its intention to remand the removed action for the determination of damages. An appeal with respect to the liability determination of the district court may be taken during that 60-day period to the court of appeals with appellate jurisdiction over the district court. In the event a party files such an appeal, the remand shall not be effective until the appeal has been finally disposed of. Once the remand has become effective, the liability determination shall not be subject to further review by appeal or otherwise.

(4) Any decision under this subsection concerning remand for the determination of damages shall not be reviewable by appeal or otherwise.

(5) An action removed under this subsection shall be deemed to be an action under section 1369 and an action in which jurisdiction is based on section 1369 of this title for purposes of this section and sections 1407, 1697, and 1785 of this title.

(6) Nothing in this subsection shall restrict the authority of the district court to transfer or dismiss an action on the ground of inconvenient forum.

(f) Derivative removal jurisdiction.—The court to which a civil action is removed under this section is not precluded from hearing and determining any claim in such civil action because the State court from which such civil action is removed did not have jurisdiction over that claim.

§ 1442. Federal Officers or Agencies Sued or Prosecuted

(a) A civil action or criminal prosecution that is commenced in a State court and that is against or directed to any of the following may be removed by them to the district court of the United States for the district and division embracing the place wherein it is pending:

(1) The United States or any agency thereof or any officer (or any person acting under that officer) of the United States or of any agency thereof, in an official or individual capacity, for or relating to any act under color of such office or on account of any right, title or authority claimed under any Act of Congress for the apprehension or punishment of criminals or the collection of the revenue.

(2) A property holder whose title is derived from any such officer, where such action or prosecution affects the validity of any law of the United States.

(3) Any officer of the courts of the United States, for or relating to any act under color of office or in the performance of his duties;

(4) Any officer of either House of Congress, for or relating to any act in the discharge of his official duty under an order of such House.

(b) A personal action commenced in any State court by an alien against any citizen of a State who is, or at the time the alleged action accrued was, a civil officer of the United States and is a nonresident of such State, wherein jurisdiction is obtained by the State court by personal service of process, may be removed by the defendant to the district court of the United States for the district and division in which the defendant was served with process.

(c) Solely for purposes of determining the propriety of removal under subsection (a), a law enforcement officer, who is the defendant in a criminal prosecution, shall be deemed to have been acting under the color of his office if the officer—

(1) protected an individual in the presence of the officer from a crime of violence;

(2) provided immediate assistance to an individual who suffered, or who was threatened with, bodily harm; or

(3) prevented the escape of any individual who the officer reasonably believed to have committed, or was about to commit, in the presence of the officer, a crime of violence that resulted in, or was likely to result in, death or serious bodily injury.

(d) In this section, the following definitions apply:

(1) The terms "civil action" and "criminal prosecution" include any proceeding (whether or not ancillary to another proceeding) to the extent that in such proceeding a judicial order, including a subpoena for testimony or documents, is sought or issued. If removal is sought for a proceeding described in the previous sentence, and there is no other basis for removal, only that proceeding may be removed to the district court.

(2) The term "crime of violence" has the meaning given that term in section 16 of title 18.

(3) The term "law enforcement officer" means any employee described in subparagraph (A), (B), or (C) of section 8401(17) of title 5 and any special agent in the Diplomatic Security Service of the Department of State.

(4) The term "serious bodily injury" has the meaning given that term in section 1365 of title 18.

(5) The term "State" includes the District of Columbia, United States territories and insular possessions, and Indian country (as defined in section 1151 of title 18).

(6) The term "State court" includes the Superior Court of the District of Columbia, a court of a United States territory or insular possession, and a tribal court.

§ 1442a. Members of Armed Forces Sued or Prosecuted

A civil or criminal prosecution in a court of a State of the United States against a member of the armed forces of the United States on account of an act done under color of his office or status, or in respect to which he claims any right, title, or authority under a law of the United States respecting the armed forces thereof, or under the law of war, may at any time before the trial or final hearing thereof be removed for trial into the district court of the United States for the district where it is pending in the manner prescribed by law, and it shall thereupon be entered on the docket of the district court, which shall proceed as if the cause had been originally commenced therein and shall have full power to hear and determine the cause.

§ 1443. Civil Rights Cases

Any of the following civil actions or criminal prosecutions, commenced in a State court may be removed by the defendant to the district court of the United States for the district and division embracing the place wherein it is pending:

(1) Against any person who is denied or cannot enforce in the courts of such State a right under any law providing for the equal civil rights of citizens of the United States, or of all persons within the jurisdiction thereof;

(2) For any act under color of authority derived from any law providing for equal rights, or for refusing to do any act on the ground that it would be inconsistent with such law.

§ 1445. Nonremovable Actions

(a) A civil action in any State court against a railroad or its receivers or trustees, arising under sections 1–4 and 5–10 of the Act of April 22, 1908 (45 U.S.C. 51 to 54, 55 to 60), may not be removed to any district court of the United States.

(b) A civil action in any State court against a carrier or its receivers or trustees to recover damages for delay, loss, or injury of shipments, arising under section 11706 or 14706 of title 49, may not be removed to any district court of the United States unless the matter in controversy exceeds $10,000, exclusive of interest and costs.

(c) A civil action in any State court arising under the workmen's compensation laws of such State may not be removed to any district court of the United States.

(d) A civil action in any State court arising under section 40302 of the Violence Against Women Act of 1994 may not be removed to any district court of the United States.

§ 1446. Procedure for Removal of Civil Actions

(a) Generally.—A defendant or defendants desiring to remove any civil action from a State court shall file in the district court of the United States for the district and division within which such action is pending a notice of removal signed pursuant to Rule 11 of the Federal Rules of Civil Procedure and containing a short and plain statement of the grounds for removal, together with a copy of all process, pleadings, and orders served upon such defendant or defendants in such action.

(b) Requirements; generally.—(1) The notice of removal of a civil action or proceeding shall be filed within 30 days after the receipt by the defendant, through service or otherwise, of a copy of the initial pleading setting forth the claim for relief upon which such action or proceeding is based, or within 30 days after the service of summons upon the defendant if such initial pleading has then been filed in court and is not required to be served on the defendant, whichever period is shorter.

(2) (A) When a civil action is removed solely under section 1441(a), all defendants who have been properly joined and served must join in or consent to the removal of the action.

(B) Each defendant shall have 30 days after receipt by or service on that defendant of the initial pleading or summons described in paragraph (1) to file the notice of removal.

(C) If defendants are served at different times, and a later served defendant files a notice of removal, any earlier-served defendant may consent to the removal even though that earlier-served defendant did not previously initiate or consent to removal.

(3) Except as provided in subsection (c), if the case stated by the initial pleading is not removable, a notice of removal may be filed within thirty days after receipt by the defendant, through service or otherwise, of a copy of an amended pleading, motion, order or other paper from which it may first be ascertained that the case is one which is or has become removable.

(c) Requirements; removal based on diversity of citizenship.—(1) A case may not be removed under subsection (b)(3) on the basis of jurisdiction conferred by section 1332 more than 1 year after commencement of the action, unless the district court finds that the plaintiff has acted in bad faith in order to prevent a defendant from removing the action.

(2) If removal of a civil action is sought on the basis of the jurisdiction conferred by section 1332(a), the sum demanded in good faith in the initial pleading shall be deemed to be the amount in controversy, except that—

(A) the notice of removal may assert the amount in controversy if the initial pleading seeks—

(i) nonmonetary relief; or

(ii) a money judgment, but the State practice either does not permit demand for a specific sum or permits recovery of damages in excess of the amount demanded; and

(B) removal of the action is proper on the basis of an amount in controversy asserted under subparagraph (A) if the district court finds, by the preponderance of the evidence, that the amount in controversy exceeds the amount specified in section 1332(a).

(3) (A) If the case stated by the initial pleading is not removable solely because the amount in controversy does not exceed the amount specified in section 1332(a), information relating to the amount in controversy in the record of the State proceeding, or in responses to discovery, shall be treated as an "other paper" under subsection (b)(3).

(B) If the notice of removal is filed more than 1 year after commencement of the action and the district court finds that the plaintiff deliberately failed to disclose the actual amount in controversy to prevent removal, that finding shall be deemed bad faith under paragraph (1).

(d) Notice to adverse parties and State court.—Promptly after the filing of such notice of removal of a civil action the defendant or defendants shall give written notice thereof to all adverse parties and shall file a copy of the notice with the clerk of such State court, which shall effect the removal and the State court shall proceed no further unless and until the case is remanded.

(e) Counterclaim in 337 proceeding.—With respect to any counterclaim removed to a district court pursuant to section 337(c) of the Tariff Act of 1930, the district court shall resolve such counterclaim in the same manner as an original complaint under the Federal Rules of Civil Procedure, except that the payment of a filing fee shall not be required in such cases and the counterclaim shall relate back to the date of the original complaint in the proceeding before the International Trade Commission under section 337 of that Act.

(g)[3] **(1)** Where the civil action or criminal prosecution that is removable under section 1442(a) is a proceeding in which a judicial order for testimony or documents is sought or issued or sought to be enforced, the 30-day requirement of subsection (b) of this section and paragraph (1) of section 1455(b) is satisfied if the person or entity desiring to remove the proceeding files the notice of removal not later than 30 days after receiving, through service, notice of any such proceeding.

§ 1447. Procedure after Removal Generally

(a) In any case removed from a State court, the district court may issue all necessary orders and process to bring before it all proper parties whether served by process issued by the State court or otherwise.

[3] ED Note: In 2012, revisions to Section 1446 repositioned subpart 1446(f), leaving that subpart empty in the current statute.

(b) It may require the removing party to file with its clerk copies of all records and proceedings in such State court or may cause the same to be brought before it by writ of certiorari issued to such State court.

(c) A motion to remand the case on the basis of any defect other than lack of subject matter jurisdiction must be made within 30 days after the filing of the notice of removal under section 1446(a). If at any time before final judgment it appears that the district court lacks subject matter jurisdiction, the case shall be remanded. An order remanding the case may require payment of just costs and any actual expenses, including attorney fees, incurred as a result of the removal. A certified copy of the order of remand shall be mailed by the clerk to the clerk of the State court. The State court may thereupon proceed with such case.

(d) An order remanding a case to the State court from which it was removed is not reviewable on appeal or otherwise, except that an order remanding a case to the State court from which it was removed pursuant to section 1442 or 1443 of this title shall be reviewable by appeal or otherwise.

(e) If after removal the plaintiff seeks to join additional defendants whose joinder would destroy subject matter jurisdiction, the court may deny joinder, or permit joinder and remand the action to the State court.

§ 1448. Process after Removal

In all cases removed from any State court to any district court of the United States in which any one or more of the defendants has not been served with process or in which the service has not been perfected prior to removal, or in which process served proves to be defective, such process or service may be completed or new process issued in the same manner as in cases originally filed in such district court.

This section shall not deprive any defendant upon whom process is served after removal of his right to move to remand the case.

§ 1449. State Court Record Supplied

Where a party is entitled to copies of the records and proceedings in any suit or prosecution in a State court, to be used in any district court of the United States, and the clerk of such State court, upon demand, and the payment or tender of the legal fees, fails to deliver certified copies, the district court may, on affidavit reciting such facts, direct such record to be supplied by affidavit or otherwise. Thereupon such proceedings, trial, and judgment may be had in such district court, and all such process awarded, as if certified copies had been filed in the district court.

§ 1451. Definitions

For purposes of this chapter—

(1) The term "State court" includes the Superior Court of the District of Columbia.

(2) The term "State" includes the District of Columbia.

§ 1453. Removal of Class Actions

(a) Definitions.—In this section, the terms "class", "class action", "class certification order", and "class member" shall have the meanings given such terms under section 1332(d)(1).

(b) In general.—A class action may be removed to a district court of the United States in accordance with section 1446 (except that the 1-year limitation under section 1446(c)(1) shall not apply), without regard to whether any defendant is a citizen of the State in which the action is brought, except that such action may be removed by any defendant without the consent of all defendants.

(c) **Review of remand orders.**—

(1) In general.—Section 1447 shall apply to any removal of a case under this section, except that notwithstanding section 1447(d), a court of appeals may accept an appeal from an order of a district court granting or denying a motion to remand a class action to the State court from which it was removed if application is made to the court of appeals not more than 10 days after entry of the order.

(2) Time period for judgment.—If the court of appeals accepts an appeal under paragraph (1), the court shall complete all action on such appeal, including rendering judgment, not later than 60 days after the date on which such appeal was filed, unless an extension is granted under paragraph (3).

(3) Extension of time period.—The court of appeals may grant an extension of the 60-day period described in paragraph (2) if—

(A) all parties to the proceeding agree to such extension, for any period of time; or

(B) such extension is for good cause shown and in the interests of justice, for a period not to exceed 10 days.

(4) Denial of appeal.—If a final judgment on the appeal under paragraph (1) is not issued before the end of the period described in paragraph (2), including any extension under paragraph (3), the appeal shall be denied.

(d) **Exception.**—This section shall not apply to any class action that solely involves—

(1) a claim concerning a covered security as defined under section 16(f) (3) of the Securities Act of 1933 (15 U.S.C. 78p(f) (3)) and section 28(f)(5)(E) of the Securities Exchange Act of 1934 (15 U.S.C. 78bb(f)(5)(E));

(2) a claim that relates to the internal affairs or governance of a corporation or other form of business enterprise and arises under or by virtue of the laws of the State in which such corporation or business enterprise is incorporated or organized; or

(3) a claim that relates to the rights, duties (including fiduciary duties), and obligations relating to or created by or pursuant to any security (as defined under section 2(a)(1) of the Securities Act of 1933 (15 U.S.C. 77b(a)(1)) and the regulations issued thereunder).

§ 1631. Transfer to Cure Want of Jurisdiction

Whenever a civil action is filed in a court as defined in section 610 of this title or an appeal, including a petition for review of administrative action, is noticed for or filed with such a court and that court finds that there is a want of jurisdiction, the court shall, if it is in the interest of justice, transfer such action or appeal to any other such court (or, for cases within the jurisdiction of the United States Tax Court, to that court) in which the action or appeal could have been brought at the time it was filed or noticed, and the action or appeal shall proceed as if it had been filed in or noticed for the court to which it is transferred on the date upon which it was actually filed in or noticed for the court from which it is transferred.

§ 1651. Writs

(a) The Supreme Court and all courts established by Act of Congress may issue all writs necessary or appropriate in aid of their respective jurisdictions and agreeable to the usages and principles of law.

(b) An alternative writ or rule nisi may be issued by a justice or judge of a court which has jurisdiction.

§ 1652. State Laws As Rules of Decision

The laws of the several States, except where the Constitution or treaties of the United States or Acts of Congress otherwise require or provide, shall be regarded as rules of decision in civil actions in the courts of the United States, in cases where they apply.

§ 1653. Amendment of Pleadings to Show Jurisdiction

Defective allegations of jurisdiction may be amended, upon terms, in the trial or appellate courts.

§ 1654. Appearance Personally or by Counsel

In all courts of the United States the parties may plead and conduct their own cases personally or by counsel as, by the rules of such courts, respectively, are permitted to manage and conduct causes therein.

§ 1657. Priority of Civil Actions

(a) Notwithstanding any other provision of law, each court of the United States shall determine the order in which civil actions are heard and determined, except that the court shall expedite the consideration of any action brought under chapter 153 or section 1826 of this title, any action for temporary or preliminary injunctive relief, or any other action if good cause therefor is shown. For purposes of this subsection, "good cause" is shown if a right under the Constitution of the United States or a Federal Statute (including rights under section 552 of title 5) would be maintained in a factual context that indicates that a request for expedited consideration has merit.

(b) The Judicial Conference of the United States may modify the rules adopted by the courts to determine the order in which civil actions are heard and determined, in order to establish consistency among the judicial circuits.

§ 1658. Time Limitations on the Commencement of Civil Actions Arising under Acts of Congress

(a) Except as otherwise provided by law, a civil action arising under an Act of Congress enacted after the date of the enactment of this section may not be commenced later than 4 years after the cause of action accrues.

(b) Notwithstanding subsection (a), a private right of action that involves a claim of fraud, deceit, manipulation, or contrivance in contravention of a regulatory requirement concerning the securities laws, as defined in section 3(a)(47) of the Securities Exchange Act of 1934 (15 U.S.C. 78c(a)(47)), may be brought not later than the earlier of—

(1) 2 years after the discovery of the facts constituting the violation; or

(2) 5 years after such violation.

§ 1691. Seal and Teste of Process

All writs and process issuing from a court of the United States shall be under the seal of the court and signed by the clerk thereof.

§ 1692. Process and Orders Affecting Property in Different Districts

In proceedings in a district court where a receiver is appointed for property, real, personal, or mixed, situated in different districts, process may issue and be executed in any such district as if the property lay wholly within one district, but orders affecting the property shall be entered of record in each of such districts.

§ 1695. Stockholder's Derivative Action

Process in a stockholder's action in behalf of his corporation may be served upon such corporation in any district where it is organized or licensed to do business or is doing business.

§ 1696. Service in Foreign and International Litigation

(a) The district court of the district in which a person resides or is found may order service upon him of any document issued in connection with a proceeding in a foreign or international tribunal. The order may be made pursuant to a letter rogatory issued, or request made, by a foreign or international tribunal or upon application of any interested person and shall direct the manner of service. Service pursuant to this subsection does not, of itself, require the recognition or enforcement in the United States of a judgment, decree, or order rendered by a foreign or international tribunal.

(b) This section does not preclude service of such a document without an order of court.

§ 1697. Service in Multiparty, Multiforum Actions

When the jurisdiction of the district court is based in whole or in part upon section 1369 of this title, process, other than subpoenas, may be served at any place within the United States, or anywhere outside the United States if otherwise permitted by law.

§ 1731. Handwriting

The admitted or proved handwriting of any person shall be admissible, for purposes of comparison, to determine genuineness of other handwriting attributed to such person.

§ 1732. Record Made in Regular Course of Business; Photographic Copies

If any business, institution, member of a profession or calling, or any department or agency of government, in the regular course of business or activity has kept or recorded any memorandum, writing, entry, print, representation or combination thereof, of any act, transaction, occurrence, or event, and in the regular course of business has caused any or all of the same to be recorded, copied, or reproduced by any photographic, photostatic, microfilm, micro-card, miniature photographic, or other process which accurately reproduces or forms a durable medium for so reproducing the original, the original may be destroyed in the regular course of business unless its preservation is required by law. Such reproduction, when satisfactorily identified, is as admissible in evidence as the original itself in any judicial or administrative proceeding whether the original is in existence or not and an enlargement or facsimile of such reproduction is likewise admissible in evidence if the original reproduction is in existence and available for inspection under direction of court. The introduction of a reproduced record, enlargement, or facsimile does not preclude admission of the original. This subsection shall not be construed to exclude from evidence any document or copy thereof which is otherwise admissible under the rules of evidence.

§ 1733. Government Records and Papers; Copies

(a) Books or records of account or minutes of proceedings of any department or agency of the United States shall be admissible to prove the act, transaction or occurrence as a memorandum of which the same were made or kept.

(b) Properly authenticated copies or transcripts of any books, records, papers or documents of any department or agency of the United States shall be admitted in evidence equally with the originals thereof.

(c) This section does not apply to cases, actions, and proceedings to which the Federal Rules of Evidence apply.

§ 1734. Court Record Lost or Destroyed, Generally

(a) A lost or destroyed record of any proceeding in any court of the United States may be supplied on application of any interested party not at fault, by substituting a copy certified by the clerk of any court in which an authentic copy is lodged.

(b) Where a certified copy is not available, any interested person not at fault may file in such court a verified application for an order establishing the lost or destroyed record. Every other interested person shall be served personally with a copy of the application and with notice of hearing on a day stated, not less than sixty days after service. Service may be made on any nonresident of the district anywhere within the jurisdiction of the United States or in any foreign country.

Proof of service in a foreign country shall be certified by a minister or consul of the United States in such country, under his official seal.

If, after the hearing, the court is satisfied that the statements contained in the application are true, it shall enter an order reciting the substance and effect of the lost or destroyed record. Such order, subject to intervening rights of third persons, shall have the same effect as the original record.

§ 1735. Court Record Lost or Destroyed Where United States Interested

(a) When the record of any case or matter in any court of the United States to which the United States is a party, is lost or destroyed, a certified copy of any official paper of a United States attorney, United States marshal or clerk or other certifying or recording officer of any such court, made pursuant to law, on file in any department or agency of the United States and relating to such case or matter, shall, on being filed in the court to which it relates, have the same effect as an original paper filed in such court. If the copy so filed discloses the date and amount of a judgment or decree and the names of the parties thereto, the court may enforce the judgment or decree as though the original record had not been lost or destroyed.

(b) Whenever the United States is interested in any lost or destroyed records or files of a court of the United States, the clerk of such court and the United States attorney for the district shall take the steps necessary to restore such records or files, under the direction of the judges of such court.

§ 1738. State and Territorial Statutes and Judicial Proceedings; Full Faith and Credit

The Acts of the legislature of any State, Territory, or Possession of the United States, or copies thereof, shall be authenticated by affixing the seal of such State, Territory or Possession thereto.

The records and judicial proceedings of any court of any such State, Territory or Possession, or copies thereof, shall be proved or admitted in other courts within the United States and its Territories and Possessions by the attestation of the clerk and seal of the court annexed, if a seal exists, together with a certificate of a judge of the court that the said attestation is in proper form.

Such Acts, records and judicial proceedings or copies thereof, so authenticated, shall have the same full faith and credit in every court within the United States and its Territories and Possessions as they have by law or usage in the courts of such State, Territory or Possession from which they are taken.

§ 1739. State and Territorial Nonjudicial Records; Full Faith and Credit

All nonjudicial records or books kept in any public office of any State, Territory, or Possession of the United States, or copies thereof, shall be proved or admitted in any court or office in any other State, Territory, or Possession by the attestation of the custodian of such records or books, and the seal of his office annexed, if there be a seal, together with a certificate of a judge of a court of record of the county, parish, or district in which such office may be kept, or of the Governor, or secretary of State, the chancellor or keeper of the great seal, of the State, Territory, or Possession that the said attestation is in due form and by the proper officers.

If the certificate is given by a judge, it shall be further authenticated by the clerk or prothonotary of the court, who shall certify, under his hand and the seal of his office, that such judge is duly commissioned and qualified; or, if given by such Governor, secretary, chancellor, or keeper of the great seal, it shall be under the great seal of the State, Territory, or Possession in which it is made.

Such records or books, or copies thereof, so authenticated, shall have the same full faith and credit in every court and office within the United States and its Territories and Possessions as they have by law or usage in the courts or offices of the State, Territory, or Possession from which they are taken.

§ 1746. Unsworn Declarations under Penalty of Perjury

Wherever, under any law of the United States or under any rule, regulation, order, or requirement made pursuant to law, any matter is required or permitted to be supported, evidenced, established, or proved by the sworn declaration, verification, certificate, statement, oath, or affidavit, in writing of the person making the same (other than a deposition, or an oath of office, or an oath required to be taken before a specified official other than a notary public), such matter may, with like force and effect, be supported, evidenced, established, or proved by the unsworn declaration, certificate, verification, or statement, in writing of such person which is subscribed by him, as true under penalty of perjury, and dated, in substantially the following form:

(1) If executed without the United States: "I declare *(or certify, verify, or state)* under penalty of perjury under the laws of the United States of America that the foregoing is true and correct. Executed on *(date)*.

(Signature)".

(2) If executed within the United States, its territories, possessions, or commonwealths: "I declare *(or certify, verify, or state)* under penalty of perjury that the foregoing is true and correct. Executed on *(date)*.

(Signature)".

§ 1781. Transmittal of Letter Rogatory or Request

(a) The Department of State has power, directly, or through suitable channels—

(1) to receive a letter rogatory issued, or request made, by a foreign or international tribunal, to transmit it to the tribunal, officer, or agency in the United States to whom it is addressed, and to receive and return it after execution; and

(2) to receive a letter rogatory issued, or request made, by a tribunal in the United States, to transmit it to the foreign or international tribunal, officer, or agency to whom it is addressed, and to receive and return it after execution.

(b) This section does not preclude—

(1) the transmittal of a letter rogatory or request directly from a foreign or international tribunal to the tribunal, officer, or agency in the United States to whom it is addressed and its return in the same manner; or

(2) the transmittal of a letter rogatory or request directly from a tribunal in the United States to the foreign or international tribunal, officer, or agency to whom it is addressed and its return in the same manner.

§ 1782. Assistance to Foreign and International Tribunals and to Litigants before Such Tribunals

(a) The district court of the district in which a person resides or is found may order him to give his testimony or statement or to produce a document or other thing for use in a proceeding in a foreign or international tribunal, including criminal investigations conducted before formal accusation. The order may be made pursuant to a letter rogatory issued, or request made, by a foreign or international tribunal or upon the application of any interested person and may direct that the testimony or statement be given, or the document or other thing be produced, before a person appointed by the court. By virtue of his appointment, the person appointed has power to administer any necessary oath and take the testimony or statement. The order may prescribe the practice and procedure, which may be in whole or part the practice and procedure of the foreign country or the international tribunal, for taking the testimony or statement or producing the document or other thing. To the extent that the order does not prescribe otherwise, the testimony or statement shall be taken, and the document or other thing produced, in accordance with the Federal Rules of Civil Procedure.

A person may not be compelled to give his testimony or statement or to produce a document or other thing in violation of any legally applicable privilege.

(b) This chapter does not preclude a person within the United States from voluntarily giving his testimony or statement, or producing a document or other thing, for use in a proceeding in a foreign or international tribunal before any person and in any manner acceptable to him.

§ 1783. Subpoena of Person in Foreign Country

(a) A court of the United States may order the issuance of a subpoena requiring the appearance as a witness before it, or before a person or body designated by it, of a national or resident of the United States who is in a foreign country, or requiring the production of a specified document or other thing by him, if the court finds that particular testimony or the production of the document or other thing by him is necessary in the interest of justice, and, in other than a criminal action or proceeding, if the court finds, in addition, that it is not possible to obtain his testimony in admissible form without his personal appearance or to obtain the production of the document or other thing in any other manner.

(b) The subpoena shall designate the time and place for the appearance or for the production of the document or other thing. Service of the subpoena and any order to show cause, rule, judgment, or decree authorized by this section or by section 1784 of this title shall be effected in accordance with the provisions of the Federal Rules of Civil Procedure relating to service of process on a person in a foreign country. The person serving the subpoena shall tender to the person to whom the subpoena is addressed his estimated necessary travel and attendance expenses, the amount of which shall be determined by the court and stated in the order directing the issuance of the subpoena.

§ 1784. Contempt

(a) The court of the United States which has issued a subpoena served in a foreign country may order the person who has failed to appear or who has failed to produce a document or other thing as directed therein to show cause before it at a designated time why he should not be punished for contempt.

(b) The court, in the order to show cause, may direct that any of the person's property within the United States be levied upon or seized, in the manner provided by law or court rules governing levy or seizure under execution, and held to satisfy any judgment that may be rendered against him pursuant to subsection (d) of this section if adequate security, in such amount as the court may direct in the order, be given for any damage that he might suffer should he not be found in contempt. Security under this subsection may not be required of the United States.

(c) A copy of the order to show cause shall be served on the person in accordance with section 1783(b) of this title.

(d) On the return day of the order to show cause or any later day to which the hearing may be continued, proof shall be taken. If the person is found in contempt, the court, notwithstanding any limitation upon its power generally to punish for contempt, may fine him not more than $100,000 and direct that the fine and costs of the proceedings be satisfied by a sale of the property levied upon or seized, conducted upon the notice required and in the manner provided for sales upon execution.

§ 1785. Subpoenas in Multiparty, Multiforum Actions

When the jurisdiction of the district court is based in whole or in part upon section 1369 of this title, a subpoena for attendance at a hearing or trial may, if authorized by the court upon motion for good cause shown, and upon such terms and conditions as the court may impose, be served at any place within the United States, or anywhere outside the United States if otherwise permitted by law.

§ 1821. Per Diem and Mileage Generally; Subsistence

(a) **(1)** Except as otherwise provided by law, a witness in attendance at any court of the United States, or before a United States Magistrate, or before any person authorized to take his deposition pursuant to any rule or order of a court of the United States, shall be paid the fees and allowances provided by this section.

(2) As used in this section, the term "court of the United States" includes, in addition to the courts listed in section 451 of this title, any court created by Act of Congress in a territory which is invested with any jurisdiction of a district court of the United States.

(b) A witness shall be paid an attendance fee of $40 per day for each day's attendance. A witness shall also be paid the attendance fee for the time necessarily occupied in going to and returning from the place of attendance at the beginning and end of such attendance or at any time during such attendance.

(c) **(1)** A witness who travels by common carrier shall be paid for the actual expenses of travel on the basis of the means of transportation reasonably utilized and the distance necessarily traveled to and from such witness's residence by the shortest practical route in going to and returning from the place of attendance. Such a witness shall utilize a common carrier at the most economical rate reasonably available. A receipt or other evidence of actual cost shall be furnished.

(2) A travel allowance equal to the mileage allowance which the Administrator of General Services has prescribed, pursuant to section 5704 of title 5, for official travel of employees of the Federal Government shall be paid to each witness who travels by privately owned vehicle. Computation of mileage under this paragraph shall be made on the basis of a uniformed table of distances adopted by the Administrator of General Services.

(3) Toll charges for toll roads, bridges, tunnels, and ferries, taxicab fares between places of lodging and carrier terminals, and parking fees (upon presentation of a valid parking receipt), shall be paid in full to a witness incurring such expenses.

(4) All normal travel expenses within and outside the judicial district shall be taxable as costs pursuant to section 1920 of this title.

(d) **(1)** A subsistence allowance shall be paid to a witness when an overnight stay is required at the place of attendance because such place is so far removed from the residence of such witness as to prohibit return thereto from day to day.

(2) A subsistence allowance for a witness shall be paid in an amount not to exceed the maximum per diem allowance prescribed by the Administrator of General Services, pursuant to section 5702(a) of title 5, for official travel in the area of attendance by employees of the Federal Government.

(3) A subsistence allowance for a witness attending in an area designated by the Administrator of General Services as a high-cost area shall be paid in an amount not to exceed the maximum actual subsistence allowance prescribed by the Administrator, pursuant to section 5702(c)(B) of title 5, for official travel in such area by employees of the Federal Government.

(4) When a witness is detained pursuant to section 3144 of title 18 for want of security for his appearance, he shall be entitled for each day of detention when not in attendance at court, in addition to his subsistence, to the daily attendance fee provided by subsection (b) of this section.

(e) An alien who has been paroled into the United States for prosecution, pursuant to section 212(d)(5) of the Immigration and Nationality Act (8 U.S.C. 1182(d)(5)), or an alien who either has admitted belonging to a class of aliens who are deportable or has been determined pursuant to section 240 of such Act (8 U.S.C. 1252(b)) to be deportable, shall be ineligible to receive the fees or allowances provided by this section.

(f) Any witness who is incarcerated at the time that his or her testimony is given (except for a witness to whom the provisions of section 3144 of title 18 apply) may not receive fees or allowances under this section, regardless of whether such a witness is incarcerated at the time he or she makes a claim for fees or allowances under this section.

§ 1826. Recalcitrant Witnesses

(a) Whenever a witness in any proceeding before or ancillary to any court or grand jury of the United States refuses without just cause shown to comply with an order of the court to testify or provide other information, including any book, paper, document, record, recording or other material, the court, upon such refusal, or when such refusal is duly brought to its attention, may summarily order his confinement at a suitable place until such time as the witness is willing to give such testimony or provide such information. No period of such confinement shall exceed the life of—

(1) the court proceeding, or

(2) the term of the grand jury, including extensions, before which such refusal to comply with the court order occurred, but in no event shall such confinement exceed eighteen months.

(b) No person confined pursuant to subsection (a) of this section shall be admitted to bail pending the determination of an appeal taken by him from the order for his confinement if it appears that the appeal is frivolous or taken for delay. Any appeal from an order of confinement under this section shall be disposed of as soon as practicable, but not later than thirty days from the filing of such appeal.

(c) Whoever escapes or attempts to escape from the custody of any facility or from any place in which or to which he is confined pursuant to this section or section 4243 of title 18, or whoever rescues or attempts to rescue or instigates, aids, or assists the escape or attempt to escape of such a person, shall be subject to imprisonment for not more than three years, or a fine of not more than $10,000, or both.

§ 1914. District Court; Filing and Miscellaneous Fees; Rules of Court

(a) The clerk of each district court shall require the parties instituting any civil action, suit or proceeding in such court, whether by original process, removal or otherwise, to pay a filing fee of $350, except that on application for a writ of habeas corpus the filing fee shall be $5.

(b) The clerk shall collect from the parties such additional fees only as are prescribed by the Judicial Conference of the United States.

(c) Each district court by rule or standing order may require advance payment of fees.

§ 1915. Proceedings in Forma Pauperis

(a) **(1)** Subject to subsection (b), any court of the United States may authorize the commencement, prosecution or defense of any suit, action or proceeding, civil or criminal, or appeal therein, without prepayment of fees or security therefor, by a person who submits an affidavit that includes a statement of all assets such prisoner possesses that the person is unable to pay such fees or give security therefor. Such affidavit shall state the nature of the action, defense or appeal and affiant's belief that the person is entitled to redress.

(2) A prisoner seeking to bring a civil action or appeal a judgment in a civil action or proceeding without prepayment of fees or security therefor, in addition to filing the affidavit filed under paragraph (1), shall submit a certified copy of the trust fund account statement (or institutional equivalent) for the prisoner for the 6-month period immediately preceding the filing of the complaint or notice of appeal, obtained from the appropriate official of each prison at which the prisoner is or was confined.

(3) An appeal may not be taken in forma pauperis if the trial court certifies in writing that it is not taken in good faith.

(b) **(1)** Notwithstanding subsection (a), if a prisoner brings a civil action or files an appeal in forma pauperis, the prisoner shall be required to pay the full amount of a filing fee. The court shall assess and, when funds exist, collect, as a partial payment of any court fees required by law, an initial partial filing fee of 20 percent of the greater of—

(A) the average monthly deposits to the prisoner's account; or

(B) the average monthly balance in the prisoner's account for the 6-month period immediately preceding the filing of the complaint or notice of appeal.

(2) After payment of the initial partial filing fee, the prisoner shall be required to make monthly payments of 20 percent of the preceding month's income credited to the prisoner's account. The agency having custody of the prisoner shall forward payments from the prisoner's account to the clerk of the court each time the amount in the account exceeds $10 until the filing fees are paid.

(3) In no event shall the filing fee collected exceed the amount of fees permitted by statute for the commencement of a civil action or an appeal of a civil action or criminal judgment.

(4) In no event shall a prisoner be prohibited from bringing a civil action or appealing a civil or criminal judgment for the reason that the prisoner has no assets and no means by which to pay the initial partial filing fee.

(c) Upon the filing of an affidavit in accordance with subsections (a) and (b) and the prepayment of any partial filing fee as may be required under subsection (b), the court may direct payment by the United States of the expenses of (1) printing the record on appeal in any civil or criminal case, if such printing is required by the appellate court; (2) preparing a transcript of proceedings before a United States magistrate in any civil or criminal case, if such transcript is required by the district court, in the case of proceedings conducted under section 636(b) of this title or under section 3401(b) of title 18, United States Code; and (3) printing the record on appeal if such printing is required by the appellate court, in the case of proceedings conducted pursuant to section 636(c) of this title. Such expenses shall be paid when authorized by the Director of the Administrative Office of the United States Courts.

(d) The officers of the court shall issue and serve all process, and perform all duties in such cases. Witnesses shall attend as in other cases, and the same remedies shall be available as are provided for by law in other cases.

(e) **(1)** The court may request an attorney to represent any person unable to afford counsel.

(2) Notwithstanding any filing fee, or any portion thereof, that may have been paid, the court shall dismiss the case at any time if the court determines that—

(A) the allegation of poverty is untrue; or

(B) the action or appeal—

(i) is frivolous or malicious;

(ii) fails to state a claim on which relief may be granted; or

(iii) seeks monetary relief against a defendant who is immune from such relief.

(f) **(1)** Judgment may be rendered for costs at the conclusion of the suit or action as in other proceedings, but the United States shall not be liable for any of the costs thus incurred. If the United States has paid the cost of a stenographic transcript or printed record for the prevailing party, the same shall be taxed in favor of the United States.

(2) **(A)** If the judgment against a prisoner includes the payment of costs under this subsection, the prisoner shall be required to pay the full amount of the costs ordered.

(B) The prisoner shall be required to make payments for costs under this subsection in the same manner as is provided for filing fees under subsection (a)(2).

(C) In no event shall the costs collected exceed the amount of the costs ordered by the court.

(g) In no event shall a prisoner bring a civil action or appeal a judgment in a civil action or proceeding under this section if the prisoner has, on 3 or more prior occasions, while incarcerated or detained in any facility, brought an action or appeal in a court of the United States that was dismissed on the grounds that it is frivolous, malicious, or fails to state a claim upon which relief may be granted, unless the prisoner is under imminent danger of serious physical injury.

(h) As used in this section, the term 'prisoner' means any person incarcerated or detained in any facility who is accused of, convicted of, sentenced for, or adjudicated delinquent for, violations of criminal law or the terms and conditions of parole, probation, pretrial release, or diversionary program.

§ 1917. District Courts; Fee on Filing Notice of or Petition for Appeal

Upon the filing of any separate or joint notice of appeal or application for appeal or upon the receipt of any order allowing, or notice of the allowance of, an appeal or of a writ of certiorari $5 shall be paid to the clerk of the district court, by the appellant or petitioner.

§ 1920. Taxation of Costs

A judge or clerk of any court of the United States may tax as costs the following:

(1) Fees of the clerk and marshal;

(2) Fees for printed or electronically recorded manuscripts necessarily obtained for use in the case;

(3) Fees and disbursements for printing and witnesses;

(4) Fees for exemplification and the costs of making copies of any materials where copies are necessarily obtained for use in the case;

(5) Docket fees under section 1923 of this title;

(6) Compensation of court appointed experts, compensation of interpreters, and salaries, fees, expenses, and costs of special interpretation services under section 1828 of this title.

A bill of costs shall be filed in the case and, upon allowance, included in the judgment or decree.

§ 1924. Verification of Bill of Costs

Before any bill of costs is taxed, the party claiming any item of cost or disbursement shall attach thereto an affidavit, made by himself or by his duly authorized attorney or agent having knowledge of the facts, that such item is correct and has been necessarily incurred in the case and that the services for which fees have been charged were actually and necessarily performed.

§ 1927. Counsel's Liability for Excessive Costs

Any attorney or other person admitted to conduct cases in any court of the United States or any Territory thereof who so multiplies the proceedings in any case unreasonably and vexatiously may be required by the court to satisfy personally the excess costs, expenses, and attorneys' fees reasonably incurred because of such conduct.

§ 1961. Interest

(a) Interest shall be allowed on any money judgment in a civil case recovered in a district court. Execution therefor may be levied by the marshal, in any case where, by the law of the State in which such court is held, execution may be levied for interest on judgments recovered in the courts of the State. Such interest shall be calculated from the date of the entry of the judgment, at a rate equal to the weekly average 1-year constant maturity Treasury yield, as published by the Board of Governors of the Federal Reserve System, for the calendar week preceding the date of the judgment. The Director of the Administrative Office of the United States Courts shall distribute notice of that rate and any changes in it to all Federal judges.

(b) Interest shall be computed daily to the date of payment except as provided in section 2516(b) of this title and section 1304(b) of title 31, and shall be compounded annually.

(c) **(1)** This section shall not apply in any judgment of any court with respect to any internal revenue tax case. Interest shall be allowed in such cases at the underpayment rate or overpayment rate (whichever is appropriate) established under section 6621 of the Internal Revenue Code of 1986.

(2) Except as otherwise provided in paragraph (1) of this subsection, interest shall be allowed on all final judgments against the United States in the United States Court of Appeals for the Federal circuit,[4] at the rate provided in subsection (a) and as provided in subsection (b).

(3) Interest shall be allowed, computed, and paid on judgments of the United States Court of Federal Claims only as provided in paragraph (1) of this subsection or in any other provision of law.

(4) This section shall not be construed to affect the interest on any judgment of any court not specified in this section.

§ 1963. Registration of Judgments for Enforcement in Other Districts

A judgment in an action for the recovery of money or property entered in any court of appeals, district court, bankruptcy court, or in the Court of International Trade may be registered by filing a certified copy of the judgment in any other district or, with respect to the Court of International Trade, in any judicial district, when the judgment has become final by appeal or expiration of the time for appeal or when ordered by the court that entered the judgment for good cause shown. Such a judgment entered in favor of the United States may be so registered any time after judgment is entered. A judgment so registered shall have the same effect as a judgment of the district court of the district where registered and may be enforced in like manner.

A certified copy of the satisfaction of any judgment in whole or in part may be registered in like manner in any district in which the judgment is a lien.

The procedure prescribed under this section is in addition to other procedures provided by law for the enforcement of judgments.

§ 1964. Constructive Notice of Pending Actions

Where the law of a State requires a notice of an action concerning real property pending in a court of the State to be registered, recorded, docketed, or indexed in a particular manner, or in a certain office or county or parish in order to give constructive notice of the action as it relates to the real property, and such law authorizes a notice of an action concerning real property pending in a United States district court to be registered, recorded, docketed, or indexed in the same manner, or in the same place,

[4] So in original. Probably should be "Circuit,".

those requirements of the State law must be complied with in order to give constructive notice of such an action pending in a United States district court as it relates to real property in such State.

§ 2071. Rule-Making Power Generally

(a) The Supreme Court and all courts established by Act of Congress may from time to time prescribe rules for the conduct of their business. Such rules shall be consistent with Acts of Congress and rules of practice and procedure prescribed under section 2072 of this title.

(b) Any rule prescribed by a court, other than the Supreme Court, under subsection (a) shall be prescribed only after giving appropriate public notice and an opportunity for comment. Such rule shall take effect upon the date specified by the prescribing court and shall have such effect on pending proceedings as the prescribing court may order.

(c) **(1)** A rule of a district court prescribed under subsection (a) shall remain in effect unless modified or abrogated by the judicial council of the relevant circuit.

(2) Any other rule prescribed by a court other than the Supreme Court under subsection (a) shall remain in effect unless modified or abrogated by the Judicial Conference.

(d) Copies of rules prescribed under subsection (a) by a district court shall be furnished to the judicial council, and copies of all rules prescribed by a court other than the Supreme Court under subsection (a) shall be furnished to the Director of the Administrative Office of the United States Courts and made available to the public.

(e) If the prescribing court determines that there is an immediate need for a rule, such court may proceed under this section without public notice and opportunity for comment, but such court shall promptly thereafter afford such notice and opportunity for comment.

(f) No rule may be prescribed by a district court other than under this section.

§ 2072. Rules of Procedure and Evidence; Power to Prescribe

(a) The Supreme Court shall have the power to prescribe general rules of practice and procedure and rules of evidence for cases in the United States district courts (including proceedings before magistrates thereof) and courts of appeals.

(b) Such rules shall not abridge, enlarge or modify any substantive right. All laws in conflict with such rules shall be of no further force or effect after such rules have taken effect.

(c) Such rules may define when a ruling of a district court is final for the purposes of appeal under section 1291 of this title.

§ 2101. Supreme Court; Time for Appeal or Certiorari; Docketing; Stay

(a) A direct appeal to the Supreme Court from any decision under section 1253 of this title, holding unconstitutional in whole or in part, any Act of Congress, shall be taken within thirty days after the entry of the interlocutory or final order, judgment or decree. The record shall be made up and the case docketed within sixty days from the time such appeal is taken under rules prescribed by the Supreme Court.

(b) Any other direct appeal to the Supreme Court which is authorized by law, from a decision of a district court in any civil action, suit or proceeding, shall be taken within thirty days from the judgment, order or decree, appealed from, if interlocutory, and within sixty days if final.

(c) Any other appeal or any writ of certiorari intended to bring any judgment or decree in a civil action, suit or proceeding before the Supreme Court for review shall be taken or applied for within ninety days after the entry of such judgment or decree. A justice of the Supreme Court, for good cause shown, may extend the time for applying for a writ of certiorari for a period not exceeding sixty days.

(d) The time for appeal or application for a writ of certiorari to review the judgment of a State court in a criminal case shall be as prescribed by rules of the Supreme Court.

(e) An application to the Supreme Court for a writ of certiorari to review a case before judgment has been rendered in the court of appeals may be made at any time before judgment.

(f) In any case in which the final judgment or decree of any court is subject to review by the Supreme Court on writ of certiorari, the execution and enforcement of such judgment or decree may be stayed for a reasonable time to enable the party aggrieved to obtain a writ of certiorari from the Supreme Court. The stay may be granted by a judge of the court rendering the judgment or decree or by a justice of the Supreme Court, and may be conditioned on the giving of security, approved by such judge or justice, that if the aggrieved party fails to make application for such writ within the period allotted therefor, or fails to obtain an order granting his application, or fails to make his plea good in the Supreme Court, he shall answer for all damages and costs which the other party may sustain by reason of the stay.

(g) The time for application for a writ of certiorari to review a decision of the United States Court of Appeals for the Armed Forces shall be as prescribed by rules of the Supreme Court.

§ 2104. Reviews of State Court Decisions

A review by the Supreme Court of a judgment or decree of a State court shall be conducted in the same manner and under the same regulations, and shall have the same effect, as if the judgment or decree reviewed had been rendered in a court of the United States.

§ 2106. Determination

The Supreme Court or any other court of appellate jurisdiction may affirm, modify, vacate, set aside or reverse any judgment, decree, or order of a court lawfully brought before it for review, and may remand the cause and direct the entry of such appropriate judgment, decree, or order, or require such further proceedings to be had as may be just under the circumstances.

§ 2107. Time for Appeal to Court of Appeals

(a) Except as otherwise provided in this section, no appeal shall bring any judgment, order or decree in an action, suit or proceeding of a civil nature before a court of appeals for review unless notice of appeal is filed, within thirty days after the entry of such judgment, order or decree.

(b) In any such action, suit, or proceeding, the time as to all parties shall be 60 days from such entry if one of the parties is—

> **(1)** the United States;
>
> **(2)** a United States agency;
>
> **(3)** a United States officer or employee sued in an official capacity; or
>
> **(4)** a current or former United States officer or employee sued in an individual capacity for an act or omission occurring in connection with duties performed on behalf of the United States, including all instances in which the United States represents that officer or employee when the judgment, order, or decree is entered or files the appeal for that officer or employee.

(c) The district court may, upon motion filed not later than 30 days after the expiration of the time otherwise set for bringing appeal, extend the time for appeal upon a showing of excusable neglect or good cause. In addition, if the district court finds—

> **(1)** that a party entitled to notice of the entry of a judgment or order did not receive such notice from the clerk or any party within 21 days of its entry, and
>
> **(2)** that no party would be prejudiced,

the district court may, upon motion filed within 180 days after entry of the judgment or order or within 14 days after receipt of such notice, whichever is earlier, reopen the time for appeal for a period of 14 days from the date of entry of the order reopening the time for appeal.

(d) This section shall not apply to bankruptcy matters or other proceedings under Title 11.

§ 2111. Harmless Error

On the hearing of any appeal or writ of certiorari in any case, the court shall give judgment after an examination of the record without regard to errors or defects which do not affect the substantial rights of the parties.

§ 2201. Creation of Remedy

(a) In a case of actual controversy within its jurisdiction, except with respect to Federal taxes other than actions brought under section 7428 of the Internal Revenue Code of 1986, a proceeding under section 505 or 1146 of title 11, or in any civil action involving an antidumping or countervailing duty proceeding regarding a class or kind of merchandise of a free trade area country (as defined in section 516A(f)(10) of the Tariff Act of 1930), as determined by the administering authority, any court of the United States, upon the filing of an appropriate pleading, may declare the rights and other legal relations of any interested party seeking such declaration, whether or not further relief is or could be sought. Any such declaration shall have the force and effect of a final judgment or decree and shall be reviewable as such.

(b) For limitations on actions brought with respect to drug patents see section 505 or 512 of the Federal Food, Drug, and Cosmetic Act, or section 351 of the Public Health Service Act.

§ 2202. Further Relief

Further necessary or proper relief based on a declaratory judgment or decree may be granted, after reasonable notice and hearing, against any adverse party whose rights have been determined by such judgment.

§ 2283. Stay of State Court Proceedings

A court of the United States may not grant an injunction to stay proceedings in a State court except as expressly authorized by Act of Congress, or where necessary in aid of its jurisdiction, or to protect or effectuate its judgments.

§ 2284. Three-Judge Court; When Required; Composition; Procedure

(a) A district court of three judges shall be convened when otherwise required by Act of Congress, or when an action is filed challenging the constitutionality of the apportionment of congressional districts or the apportionment of any statewide legislative body.

(b) In any action required to be heard and determined by a district court of three judges under subsection (a) of this section, the composition and procedure of the court shall be as follows:

(1) Upon the filing of a request for three judges, the judge to whom the request is presented shall, unless he determines that three judges are not required, immediately notify the chief judge of the circuit, who shall designate two other judges, at least one of whom shall be a circuit judge. The judges so designated, and the judge to whom the request was presented, shall serve as members of the court to hear and determine the action or proceeding.

(2) If the action is against a State, or officer or agency thereof, at least five days' notice of hearing of the action shall be given by registered or certified mail to the Governor and attorney general of the State.

(3) A single judge may conduct all proceedings except the trial, and enter all orders permitted by the rules of civil procedure except as provided in this subsection. He may grant a temporary restraining order on a specific finding, based on evidence submitted, that specified irreparable damage will result if the order is not granted, which order, unless previously revoked by the district judge, shall remain in force only until the hearing and determination by the district court of three judges of an application for a preliminary injunction. A single judge shall not appoint a master, or order a reference, or hear and determine any application for a preliminary or permanent injunction or motion to vacate such an injunction, or enter judgment on the merits. Any action of a single judge may be reviewed by the full court at any time before final judgment.

§ 2361. Process and Procedure

In any civil action of interpleader or in the nature of interpleader under section 1335 of this title, a district court may issue its process for all claimants and enter its order restraining them from instituting or prosecuting any proceeding in any State or United States court affecting the property, instrument or obligation involved in the interpleader action until further order of the court. Such process and order shall be returnable at such time as the court or judge thereof directs, and shall be addressed to and served by the United States marshals for the respective districts where the claimants reside or may be found.

Such district court shall hear and determine the case, and may discharge the plaintiff from further liability, make the injunction permanent, and make all appropriate orders to enforce its judgment.

§ 2401. Time for Commencing Action Against United States

(a) Except as provided by chapter 71 of title 41, every civil action commenced against the United States shall be barred unless the complaint is filed within six years after the right of action first accrues. The action of any person under legal disability or beyond the seas at the time the claim accrues may be commenced within three years after the disability ceases.

(b) A tort claim against the United States shall be forever barred unless it is presented in writing to the appropriate Federal agency within two years after such claim accrues or unless action is begun within six months after the date of mailing, by certified or registered mail, of notice of final denial of the claim by the agency to which it was presented.

§ 2402. Jury Trial in Actions Against United States

Subject to chapter 179 of this title, any action against the United States under section 1346 shall be tried by the court without a jury, except that any action against the United States under section 1346(a)(1) shall, at the request of either party to such action, be tried by the court with a jury.

§ 2403. Intervention by United States or a State; Constitutional Question

(a) In any action, suit or proceeding in a court of the United States to which the United States or any agency, officer or employee thereof is not a party, wherein the constitutionality of any Act of Congress affecting the public interest is drawn in question, the court shall certify such fact to the Attorney General, and shall permit the United States to intervene for presentation of evidence, if evidence is otherwise admissible in the case, and for argument on the question of constitutionality. The United States shall, subject to the applicable provisions of law, have all the rights of a party and be subject to all liabilities of a party as to court costs to the extent necessary for a proper presentation of the facts and law relating to the question of constitutionality.

(b) In any action, suit, or proceeding in a court of the United States to which a State or any agency, officer, or employee thereof is not a party, wherein the constitutionality of any statute of that State affecting the public interest is drawn in question, the court shall certify such fact to the attorney general of the State, and shall permit the State to intervene for presentation of evidence, if evidence is otherwise admissible in the case, and for argument on the question of constitutionality. The State shall, subject to the applicable provisions of law, have all the rights of a party and be subject to all liabilities of a party as to court costs to the extent necessary for a proper presentation of the facts and law relating to the question of constitutionality.

§ 2404. Death of Defendant in Damage Action

A civil action for damages commenced by or on behalf of the United States or in which it is interested shall not abate on the death of a defendant but shall survive and be enforceable against his estate as well as against surviving defendants.

§ 2408. Security Not Required of United States

Security for damages or costs shall not be required of the United States, any department or agency thereof or any party acting under the direction of any such department or agency on the issuance of process or the institution or prosecution of any proceeding.

Costs taxable, under other Acts of Congress, against the United States or any such department, agency or party shall be paid out of the contingent fund of the department or agency which directed the proceedings to be instituted.

§ 2411. Interest

In any judgment of any court rendered (whether against the United States, a collector or deputy collector of internal revenue, a former collector or deputy collector, or the personal representative in case of death) for any overpayment in respect of any internal-revenue tax, interest shall be allowed at the overpayment rate established under section 6621 of the Internal Revenue Code of 1986 upon the amount of the overpayment, from the date of the payment or collection thereof to a date preceding the date of the refund check by not more than thirty days, such date to be determined by the Commissioner of Internal Revenue. The Commissioner is authorized to tender by check payment of any such judgment, with interest as herein provided, at any time after such judgment becomes final, whether or not a claim for such payment has been duly filed, and such tender shall stop the running of interest, whether or not such refund check is accepted by the judgment creditor.

§ 2412. Costs and Fees

(a) **(1)** Except as otherwise specifically provided by statute, a judgment for costs, as enumerated in section 1920 of this title, but not including the fees and expenses of attorneys, may be awarded to the prevailing party in any civil action brought by or against the United States or any agency or any official of the United States acting in his or her official capacity in any court having jurisdiction of such action. A judgment for costs when taxed against the United States shall, in an amount established by statute, court rule, or order, be limited to reimbursing in whole or in part the prevailing party for the costs incurred by such party in the litigation.

(2) A judgment for costs, when awarded in favor of the United States in an action brought by the United States, may include an amount equal to the filing fee prescribed under section 1914(a) of this title. The preceding sentence shall not be construed as requiring the United States to pay any filing fee.

(b) Unless expressly prohibited by statute, a court may award reasonable fees and expenses of attorneys, in addition to the costs which may be awarded pursuant to subsection (a), to the prevailing party in any civil action brought by or against the United States or any agency or any official of the United States acting in his or her official capacity in any court having jurisdiction of such action. The United States shall be liable for such fees and expenses to the same extent that any other party would be liable under the common law or under the terms of any statute which specifically provides for such an award.

(c) (1) Any judgment against the United States or any agency and any official of the United States acting in his or her official capacity for costs pursuant to subsection (a) shall be paid as provided in sections 2414 and 2517 of this title and shall be in addition to any relief provided in the judgment.

(2) Any judgment against the United States or any agency and any official of the United States acting in his or her official capacity for fees and expenses of attorneys pursuant to subsection (b) shall be paid as provided in sections 2414 and 2517 of this title, except that if the basis for the award is a finding that the United States acted in bad faith, then the award shall be paid by any agency found to have acted in bad faith and shall be in addition to any relief provided in the judgment.

(d) (1) (A) Except as otherwise specifically provided by statute, a court shall award to a prevailing party other than the United States fees and other expenses, in addition to any costs awarded pursuant to subsection (a), incurred by that party in any civil action (other than cases sounding in tort), including proceedings for judicial review of agency action, brought by or against the United States in any court having jurisdiction of that action, unless the court finds that the position of the United States was substantially justified or that special circumstances make an award unjust.

(B) A party seeking an award of fees and other expenses shall, within thirty days of final judgment in the action, submit to the court an application for fees and other expenses which shows that the party is a prevailing party and is eligible to receive an award under this subsection, and the amount sought, including an itemized statement from any attorney or expert witness representing or appearing in behalf of the party stating the actual time expended and the rate at which fees and other expenses were computed. The party shall also allege that the position of the United States was not substantially justified. Whether or not the position of the United States was substantially justified shall be determined on the basis of the record (including the record with respect to the action or failure to act by the agency upon which the civil action is based) which is made in the civil action for which fees and other expenses are sought.

(C) The court, in its discretion, may reduce the amount to be awarded pursuant to this subsection, or deny an award, to the extent that the prevailing party during the course of the proceedings engaged in conduct which unduly and unreasonably protracted the final resolution of the matter in controversy.

(D) If, in a civil action brought by the United States or a proceeding for judicial review of an adversary adjudication described in section 504(a)(4) of title 5, the demand by the United States is substantially in excess of the judgment finally obtained by the United States and is unreasonable when compared with such judgment, under the facts and circumstances of the case, the court shall award to the party the fees and other expenses related to defending against the excessive demand, unless the party has committed a willful violation of law or otherwise acted in bad faith, or special circumstances make an award unjust. Fees and expenses awarded under this subparagraph shall be paid only as a consequence of appropriations provided in advance.

(2) For the purposes of this subsection—

(A) "fees and other expenses" includes the reasonable expenses of expert witnesses, the reasonable cost of any study, analysis, engineering report, test, or project which is found by the court to be necessary for the preparation of the party's case, and reasonable attorney fees (The amount of fees awarded under this subsection shall be based upon prevailing market rates for the kind and quality of the services furnished, except that (i) no expert witness shall be compensated at a rate in excess of the highest rate of compensation for expert witnesses paid by the United States; and (ii) attorney fees shall not be awarded in excess of $125 per hour unless the court determines that an increase in the cost of living or a special factor, such as the limited availability of qualified attorneys for the proceedings involved, justifies a higher fee.);

(B) "party" means (i) an individual whose net worth did not exceed $2,000,000 at the time the civil action was filed, or (ii) any owner of an unincorporated business, or any partnership, corporation, association, unit of local government, or organization, the net worth of which did not exceed $7,000,000 at the time the civil action was filed, and which had not more than 500 employees at the time the civil action was filed; except that an organization described in section 501(c)(3) of the Internal Revenue Code of 1986 (26 U.S.C. 501(c)(3)) exempt from taxation under section 501(a) of such Code, or a cooperative association as defined in section 15(a) of the Agricultural Marketing Act (12 U.S.C. 1141j(a)), may be a party regardless of the net worth of such organization or cooperative association or for purposes of subsection (d)(1)(D), a small entity as defined in section 601 of title 5;

(C) "United States" includes any agency and any official of the United States acting in his or her official capacity;

(D) "position of the United States" means, in addition to the position taken by the United States in the civil action, the action or failure to act by the agency upon which the civil action is based; except that fees and expenses may not be awarded to a party for any portion of the litigation in which the party has unreasonably protracted the proceedings;

(E) "civil action brought by or against the United States" includes an appeal by a party, other than the United States, from a decision of a contracting officer rendered pursuant to a disputes clause in a contract with the Government or pursuant to chapter 71 of title 41;

(F) "court" includes the United States Court of Federal Claims and the United States Court of Appeals for Veterans Claims;

(G) "final judgment" means a judgment that is final and not appealable, and includes an order of settlement;

(H) "prevailing party", in the case of eminent domain proceedings, means a party who obtains a final judgment (other than by settlement), exclusive of interest, the amount of which is at least as close to the highest valuation of the property involved that is attested to at trial on behalf of the property owner as it is to the highest valuation of the property involved that is attested to at trial on behalf of the Government; and

(I) "demand" means the express demand of the United States which led to the adversary adjudication, but shall not include a recitation of the maximum statutory penalty (i) in the complaint, or (ii) elsewhere when accompanied by an express demand for a lesser amount.

(3) In awarding fees and other expenses under this subsection to a prevailing party in any action for judicial review of an adversary adjudication, as defined in subsection (b)(1)(C) of section 504 of title 5, or an adversary adjudication subject to chapter 71 of title 41, the court shall include in that award fees and other expenses to the same extent authorized in subsection (a) of such section, unless the court finds that during such adversary adjudication the position of the United States was substantially justified, or that special circumstances make an award unjust.

(4) Fees and other expenses awarded under this subsection to a party shall be paid by any agency over which the party prevails from any funds made available to the agency by appropriation or otherwise.

(5) **(A)** Not later than March 31 of the first fiscal year beginning after the date of enactment of the John D. Dingell, Jr. Conservation, Management, and Recreation Act, and every fiscal year thereafter, the Chairman of the Administrative Conference of the United States shall submit to Congress and make publicly available online a report on the amount of fees and other expenses awarded during the preceding fiscal year pursuant to this subsection.

(B) Each report under subparagraph (A) shall describe the number, nature, and amount of the awards, the claims involved in the controversy, and any other relevant information that may aid Congress in evaluating the scope and impact of such awards.

(C) (i) Each report under subparagraph (A) shall account for all payments of fees and other expenses awarded under this subsection that are made pursuant to a settlement agreement, regardless of whether the settlement agreement is sealed or otherwise subject to a nondisclosure provision.

(ii) The disclosure of fees and other expenses required under clause (i) shall not affect any other information that is subject to a nondisclosure provision in a settlement agreement.

(D) The Chairman of the Administrative Conference of the United States shall include and clearly identify in each annual report under subparagraph (A), for each case in which an award of fees and other expenses is included in the report—

(i) any amounts paid under section 1304 of title 31 for a judgment in the case;

(ii) the amount of the award of fees and other expenses; and

(iii) the statute under which the plaintiff filed suit.

(6) As soon as practicable, and in any event not later than the date on which the first report under paragraph (5)(A) is required to be submitted, the Chairman of the Administrative Conference of the United States shall create and maintain online a searchable database containing, with respect to each award of fees and other expenses under this subsection made on or after the date of enactment of the John D. Dingell, Jr. Conservation, Management, and Recreation Act, the following information:

(A) The case name and number, hyperlinked to the case, if available.

(B) The name of the agency involved in the case.

(C) The name of each party to whom the award was made as such party is identified in the order or other court document making the award.

(D) A description of the claims in the case.

(E) The amount of the award.

(F) The basis for the finding that the position of the agency concerned was not substantially justified.

(7) The online searchable database described in paragraph (6) may not reveal any information the disclosure of which is prohibited by law or a court order.

(8) The head of each agency (including the Attorney General of the United States) shall provide to the Chairman of the Administrative Conference of the United States in a timely manner all information requested by the Chairman to comply with the requirements of paragraphs (5), (6), and (7).

(e) The provisions of this section shall not apply to any costs, fees, and other expenses in connection with any proceeding to which section 7430 of the Internal Revenue Code of 1986 applies (determined without regard to subsections (b) and (f) of such section). Nothing in the preceding sentence shall prevent the awarding under subsection (a) of this section of costs enumerated in section 1920 of this title (as in effect on October 1, 1981).

(f) If the United States appeals an award of costs or fees and other expenses made against the United States under this section and the award is affirmed in whole or in part, interest shall be paid on the amount of the award as affirmed. Such interest shall be computed at the rate determined under section 1961(a) of this title, and shall run from the date of the award through the day before the date of the mandate of affirmance.

§ 2413. Executions in Favor of United States

A writ of execution on a judgment obtained for the use of the United States in any court thereof shall be issued from and made returnable to the court which rendered the judgment, but may be executed in any other State, in any Territory, or in the District of Columbia.

§ 2414. Payment of Judgments and Compromise Settlements

Except as provided by chapter 71 of title 41, payment of final judgments rendered by a district court or the Court of International Trade against the United States shall be made on settlements by the Secretary of the Treasury. Payment of final judgments rendered by a State or foreign court or tribunal against the United States, or against its agencies or officials upon obligations or liabilities of the United States, shall be made on settlements by the Secretary of the Treasury after certification by the Attorney General that it is in the interest of the United States to pay the same.

Whenever the Attorney General determines that no appeal shall be taken from a judgment or that no further review will be sought from a decision affirming the same, he shall so certify and the judgment shall be deemed final.

Except as otherwise provided by law, compromise settlements of claims referred to the Attorney General for defense of imminent litigation or suits against the United States, or against its agencies or officials upon obligations or liabilities of the United States, made by the Attorney General or any person authorized by him, shall be settled and paid in a manner similar to judgments in like causes and appropriations or funds available for the payment of such judgments are hereby made available for the payment of such compromise settlements.

§ 2415. Time for Commencing Actions Brought by the United States

(a) Subject to the provisions of section 2416 of this title, and except as otherwise provided by Congress, every action for money damages brought by the United States or an officer or agency thereof which is founded upon any contract express or implied in law or fact, shall be barred unless the complaint is filed within six years after the right of action accrues or within one year after final decisions have been rendered in applicable administrative proceedings required by contract or by law, whichever is later: *Provided,* That in the event of later partial payment or written acknowledgment of debt, the right of action shall be deemed to accrue again at the time of each such payment or acknowledgment: *Provided further,* That an action for money damages brought by the United States for or on behalf of a recognized tribe, band or group of American Indians shall not be barred unless the complaint is filed more than six years and ninety days after the right of action accrued: *Provided further,* That an action for money damages which accrued on the date of enactment of this Act in accordance with subsection (g) brought by the United States for or on behalf of a recognized tribe, band, or group of American Indians, or on behalf of an individual Indian whose land is held in trust or restricted status, shall not be barred unless the complaint is filed sixty days after the date of publication of the list required by section 4(c) of the Indian Claims Limitation Act of 1982: *Provided,* That, for those claims that are on either of the two lists published pursuant to the Indian Claims Limitation Act of 1982, any right of action shall be barred unless the complaint is filed within (1) one year after the Secretary of the Interior has published in the Federal Register a notice rejecting such claim or (2) three years after the date the Secretary of the Interior has submitted legislation or legislative report to Congress to resolve such claim or more than two years after a final decision has been rendered in applicable administrative proceedings required by contract or by law, whichever is later.

(b) Subject to the provisions of section 2416 of this title, and except as otherwise provided by Congress, every action for money damages brought by the United States or an officer or agency thereof which is founded upon a tort shall be barred unless the complaint is filed within three years after the right of action first accrues: *Provided,* That an action to recover damages resulting from a trespass on lands of the United States; an action to recover damages resulting from fire to such lands; an action to recover for diversion of money paid under a grant program; and an action for conversion of property of the United States may be brought within six years after the right of action accrues, except that such actions for or on behalf of a recognized tribe, band or group of American Indians, including actions relating to allotted trust or restricted Indian lands, may be brought within six years and ninety days after the right of action accrues, except that such actions for or on behalf of a recognized tribe, band or group of American Indians, including actions relating to allotted trust or restricted Indian lands, or on behalf of an individual Indian whose land is held in trust or restricted status which accrued on the date of enactment of this Act in accordance with subsection (g) may be brought on or before sixty days after the date of the publication of the list required by section 4(c) of the Indian Claims Limitation Act of 1982: *Provided,* That, for those claims that are on either of the two lists published pursuant to the Indian Claims Limitation Act of 1982, any right of action shall be barred unless the complaint is filed within (1) one year after the Secretary of the Interior has published in the Federal Register a notice rejecting such claim or (2) three years after the Secretary of the Interior has submitted legislation or legislative report to Congress to resolve such claim.

(c) Nothing herein shall be deemed to limit the time for bringing an action to establish the title to, or right of possession of, real or personal property.

(d) Subject to the provisions of section 2416 of this title and except as otherwise provided by Congress, every action for the recovery of money erroneously paid to or on behalf of any civilian employee of any agency of the United States or to or on behalf of any member or dependent of any member of the uniformed services of the United States, incident to the employment or services of such employee or member, shall be barred unless the complaint is filed within six years after the right of action accrues: *Provided,* That in the event of later partial payment or written acknowledgment of debt, the right of action shall be deemed to accrue again at the time of each such payment or acknowledgment.

(e) In the event that any action to which this section applies is timely brought and is thereafter dismissed without prejudice, the action may be recommenced within one year after such dismissal, regardless of whether the action would otherwise then be barred by this section. In any action so recommenced the defendant shall not be barred from interposing any claim which would not have been barred in the original action.

(f) The provisions of this section shall not prevent the assertion, in an action against the United States or an officer or agency thereof, of any claim of the United States or an officer or agency thereof against an opposing party, a co-party, or a third party that arises out of the transaction or occurrence that is the subject matter of the opposing party's claim. A claim of the United States or an officer or agency thereof that does not arise out of the transaction or occurrence that is the subject matter of the opposing party's claim may, if time-barred, be asserted only by way of offset and may be allowed in an amount not to exceed the amount of the opposing party's recovery.

(g) Any right of action subject to the provisions of this section which accrued prior to the date of enactment of this Act shall, for purposes of this section, be deemed to have accrued on the date of enactment of this Act.

(h) Nothing in this Act shall apply to actions brought under the Internal Revenue Code or incidental to the collection of taxes imposed by the United States.

(i) The provisions of this section shall not prevent the United States or an officer or agency thereof from collecting any claim of the United States by means of administrative offset, in accordance with section 3716 of title 31.

§ 2416. Time for Commencing Actions Brought by the United States—Exclusions

For the purpose of computing the limitations periods established in section 2415, there shall be excluded all periods during which—

(a) the defendant or the res is outside the United States, its territories and possessions, the District of Columbia, or the Commonwealth of Puerto Rico; or

(b) the defendant is exempt from legal process because of infancy, mental incompetence, diplomatic immunity, or for any other reason; or

(c) facts material to the right of action are not known and reasonably could not be known by an official of the United States charged with the responsibility to act in the circumstances; or

(d) the United States is in a state of war declared pursuant to article I, section 8, of the Constitution of the United States.

PART IX

THE CONSTITUTION OF THE UNITED STATES

1787

Preamble

We the People of the United States, in Order to form a more perfect Union, establish Justice, insure domestic Tranquility, provide for the common defence, promote the general Welfare, and secure the Blessings of Liberty to ourselves and our Posterity, do ordain and establish this Constitution for the United States of America.

Article I

Section 1. All legislative Powers herein granted shall be vested in a Congress of the United States, which shall consist of a Senate and House of Representatives.

Section 2. The House of Representatives shall be composed of Members chosen every second Year by the People of the several States, and the Electors in each State shall have the Qualifications requisite for Electors of the most numerous Branch of the State Legislature.

No Person shall be a Representative who shall not have attained to the Age of twenty five Years, and been seven Years a Citizen of the United States, and who shall not, when elected, be an Inhabitant of that State in which he shall be chosen.

Representatives and direct Taxes shall be apportioned among the several States which may be included within this Union, according to their respective Numbers, which shall be determined by adding to the whole Number of free Persons, including those bound to Service for a Term of Years, and excluding Indians not taxed, three fifths of all other Persons. The actual Enumeration shall be made within three Years after the first Meeting of the Congress of the United States, and within every subsequent Term of ten Years, in such Manner as they shall by Law direct. The Number of Representatives shall not exceed one for every thirty Thousand, but each State shall have at Least one Representative; and until such enumeration shall be made, the State of New Hampshire shall be entitled to chuse three, Massachusetts eight, Rhode Island and Providence Plantations one, Connecticut five, New York six, New Jersey four, Pennsylvania eight, Delaware one, Maryland six, Virginia ten, North Carolina five, South Carolina five, and Georgia three.

When vacancies happen in the Representation from any State, the Executive Authority thereof shall issue Writs of Election to fill such Vacancies.

The House of Representatives shall chuse their Speaker and other Officers; and shall have the sole Power of Impeachment.

Section 3. The Senate of the United States shall be composed of two Senators from each State, chosen by the Legislature thereof, for six Years; and each Senator shall have one Vote.

Immediately after they shall be assembled in Consequence of the first Election, they shall be divided as equally as may be into three Classes. The Seats of the Senators of the first Class shall be vacated at the Expiration of the Second Year, of the second Class at the Expiration of the fourth Year, and of the third Class at the Expiration of the sixth Year, so that one third may be chosen every second Year; [and if Vacancies happen by Resignation, or otherwise, during the Recess of the Legislature of any State, the Executive thereof may make temporary Appointments until the next Meeting of the Legislature, which shall then fill such Vacancies.

No Person shall be a Senator who shall not have attained to the Age of thirty Years, and been nine Years a Citizen of the United States, and who shall not, when elected, be an Inhabitant of that State for which he shall be chosen.

The Vice President of the United States shall be President of the Senate, but shall have no Vote, unless they be equally divided.

The Senate shall chuse their other Officers, and also a President pro tempore, in the Absence of the Vice President, or when he shall exercise the Office of President of the United States.

The Senate shall have the sole Power to try all Impeachments. When sitting for that Purpose, they shall be on Oath or Affirmation. When the President of the United States is tried, the Chief Justice shall preside: And no Person shall be convicted without the Concurrence of two thirds of the Members present.

Judgment in Cases of Impeachment shall not extend further than to removal from Office, and disqualification to hold and enjoy any Office of honor, Trust, or Profit under the United States: but the Party convicted shall nevertheless be liable and subject to Indictment, Trial, Judgment, and Punishment, according to Law.

Section 4. The Times, Places and Manner of holding Elections for Senators and Representatives, shall be prescribed in each State by the Legislature thereof; but the Congress may at any time by Law make or alter such Regulations, except as to the Places of chusing Senators.

The Congress shall assemble at least once in every Year, and such Meeting shall be on the first Monday in December, unless they shall by Law appoint a different Day.

Section 5. Each House shall be the Judge of the Elections, Returns, and Qualifications of its own Members, and a Majority of each shall constitute a Quorum to do Business; but a smaller Number may adjourn from day to day, and may be authorized to compel the Attendance of absent Members, in such Manner, and under such Penalties as each House may provide.

Each House may determine the Rules of its Proceedings, punish its Members for disorderly Behaviour, and, with the Concurrence of two thirds, expel a Member.

Each House shall keep a Journal of its Proceedings, and from time to time publish the same, excepting such Parts as may in their Judgment require Secrecy; and the Yeas and Nays of the Members of either House on any question shall, at the Desire of one fifth of those Present, be entered on the Journal.

Neither House, during the Session of Congress, shall, without the Consent of the other, adjourn for more than three days, nor to any other Place than that in which the two Houses shall be sitting.

Section 6. The Senators and Representatives shall receive a Compensation for their Services, to be ascertained by Law, and paid out of the Treasury of the United States. They shall in all Cases, except Treason, Felony and Breach of the Peace, be privileged from Arrest during their Attendance at the Session of their respective Houses, and in going to and returning from the same; and for any Speech or Debate in either House, they shall not be questioned in any other Place.

No Senator or Representative shall, during the Time for which he was elected, be appointed to any civil Office under the Authority of the United States, which shall have been created, or the Emoluments whereof shall have been increased during such time; and no Person holding any Office under the United States, shall be a Member of either House during his Continuance in Office.

Section 7. All Bills for raising Revenue shall originate in the House of Representatives; but the Senate may propose or concur with Amendments as on other Bills.

Every Bill which shall have passed the House of Representatives and the Senate, shall, before it become a Law, be presented to the President of the United States; If he approve he shall sign it, but if not he shall return it, with his Objections to the House in which it shall have originated, who shall enter the Objections at large on their Journal, and proceed to reconsider it. If after such Reconsideration two thirds of that House shall agree to pass the Bill, it shall be sent together with the

Objections, to the other House, by which it shall likewise be reconsidered, and if approved by two thirds of that House, it shall become a Law. But in all such Cases the Votes of both Houses shall be determined by Yeas and Nays, and the Names of the Persons voting for and against the Bill shall be entered on the Journal of each House respectively. If any Bill shall not be returned by the President within ten Days (Sundays excepted) after it shall have been presented to him, the Same shall be a Law, in like Manner as if he had signed it, unless the Congress by their Adjournment prevent its Return in which Case it shall not be a Law.

Every Order, Resolution, or Vote, to Which the Concurrence of the Senate and House of Representatives may be necessary (except on a question of Adjournment) shall be presented to the President of the United States; and before the Same shall take Effect, shall be approved by him, or being disapproved by him, shall be repassed by two thirds of the Senate and House of Representatives, according to the Rules and Limitations prescribed in the Case of a Bill.

Section 8. The Congress shall have Power to lay and collect Taxes, Duties, Imposts and Excises, to pay the Debts and provide for the common Defence and general Welfare of the United States; but all Duties, Imposts and Excises shall be uniform throughout the United States;

To borrow money on the credit of the United States;

To regulate Commerce with foreign Nations, and among the several States, and with the Indian Tribes;

To establish an uniform Rule of Naturalization, and uniform Laws on the subject of Bankruptcies throughout the United States;

To coin Money, regulate the Value thereof, and of foreign Coin, and fix the Standard of Weights and Measures;

To provide for the Punishment of counterfeiting the Securities and current Coin of the United States;

To Establish Post Offices and Post Roads;

To promote the Progress of Science and useful Arts, by securing for limited Times to Authors and Inventors the exclusive Right to their respective Writings and Discoveries;

To constitute Tribunals inferior to the supreme Court;

To define and punish Piracies and Felonies committed on the high Seas, and Offenses against the Law of Nations;

To declare War, grant Letters of Marque and Reprisal, and make Rules concerning Captures on Land and Water;

To raise and support Armies, but no Appropriation of Money to that Use shall be for a longer Term than two Years;

To provide and maintain a Navy;

To make Rules for the Government and Regulation of the land and naval Forces;

To provide for calling forth the Militia to execute the Laws of the Union, suppress Insurrections and repel Invasions;

To provide for organizing, arming, and disciplining, the Militia, and for governing such Part of them as may be employed in the Service of the United States, reserving to the States respectively, the Appointment of the Officers, and the Authority of training the Militia according to the discipline prescribed by Congress;

To exercise exclusive Legislation in all Cases whatsoever, over such District (not exceeding ten Miles square) as may, by Cession of particular States and the Acceptance of Congress, become the Seat of the Government of the United States, and to exercise like Authority over all Places purchased by the Consent of the Legislature of the State in which the Same shall be, for the Erection of Forts, Magazines, Arsenals, dock-Yards, and other needful Buildings;—And

To make all Laws which shall be necessary and proper for carrying into Execution the foregoing Powers, and all other Powers vested by this Constitution in the Government of the United States, or in any Department or Officer thereof.

Section 9. The Migration or Importation of Such Persons as any of the States now existing shall think proper to admit, shall not be prohibited by the Congress prior to the Year one thousand eight hundred and eight, but a Tax or duty may be imposed on such Importation, not exceeding ten dollars for each Person.

The privilege of the Writ of Habeas Corpus shall not be suspended, unless when in Cases of Rebellion or Invasion the public Safety may require it.

No Bill of Attainder or ex post facto Law shall be passed.

No Capitation, or other direct, Tax shall be laid, unless in Proportion to the Census or Enumeration herein before directed to be taken.

No Tax or Duty shall be laid on Articles exported from any State.

No Preference shall be given by any Regulation of Commerce or Revenue to the Ports of one State over those of another: nor shall Vessels bound to, or from, one State be obliged to enter, clear, or pay Duties in another.

No money shall be drawn from the Treasury, but in Consequence of Appropriations made by Law; and a regular Statement and Account of the Receipts and Expenditures of all public Money shall be published from time to time.

No Title of Nobility shall be granted by the United States: And no Person holding any Office of Profit or Trust under them, shall, without the Consent of the Congress, accept of any present, Emolument, Office, or Title, of any kind whatever, from any King, Prince, or foreign State.

Section 10. No State shall enter into any Treaty, Alliance, or Confederation; grant Letters of Marque and Reprisal; coin Money; emit Bills of Credit; make any Thing but gold and silver Coin a Tender in Payment of Debts; pass any Bill of Attainder, ex post facto Law, or Law impairing the Obligation of Contracts, or grant any Title of Nobility.

No State shall, without the Consent of the Congress, lay any Imposts or Duties on Imports or Exports, except what may be absolutely necessary for executing it's inspection Laws: and the net Produce of all Duties and Imposts, laid by any State on Imports or Exports, shall be for the Use of the Treasury of the United States; and all such Laws shall be subject to the Revision and Controul of the Congress.

No State shall, without the Consent of Congress, lay any Duty of Tonnage, keep Troops, or Ships of War in time of Peace, enter into any Agreement or Compact with another State, or with a foreign Power or engage in War, unless actually invaded, or in such imminent Danger as will not admit of delay.

Article II

Section 1. The executive Power shall be vested in a President of the United States of America. He shall hold his Office during the Term of four Years, and, together with the Vice President, chosen for the same Term, be elected, as follows:

Each State shall appoint, in such Manner as the Legislature thereof may direct, a Number of Electors, equal to the whole Number of Senators and Representatives to which the State may be entitled in the Congress; but no Senator or Representative, or Person holding an Office of Trust or Profit under the United States, shall be appointed an Elector.

The Electors shall meet in their respective States, and vote by Ballot for two Persons, of whom one at least shall not be an Inhabitant of the same State with themselves. And they shall make a List of all the Persons voted for, and of the Number of Votes for each; which List they shall sign and certify, and transmit sealed to the Seat of the Government of the United States, directed to the President of the Senate. The President of the Senate shall, in the Presence of the Senate and House of Representatives, open all the Certificates, and the Votes shall then be counted. The Person having the greatest Number of Votes shall be the President, if such Number be a Majority of the whole Number of Electors appointed; and if there be more than one who have such Majority, and have an equal Number of Votes, then the House of Representatives shall immediately chuse by Ballot one of them for President; and if no Person have a Majority, then from the five highest on the List the said House shall in like Manner chuse the President. But in chusing the President, the Votes shall be taken by States, the Representation from each State having one Vote; A quorum for this Purpose shall consist of a Member or Members from two thirds of the States, and a Majority of all the States shall be necessary to a Choice. In every Case, after the Choice of the President, the Person having the greater Number of Votes of the Electors shall be the Vice President. But if there should remain two or more who have equal Votes, the Senate shall chuse from them by Ballot the Vice President.

The Congress may determine the Time of chusing the Electors, and the Day on which they shall give their Votes; which Day shall be the same throughout the United States.

No person except a natural born Citizen, or a Citizen of the United States, at the time of the Adoption of this Constitution, shall be eligible to the Office of President; neither shall any Person be eligible to that Office who shall not have attained to the Age of thirty five Years, and been fourteen Years a Resident within the United States.

In case of the removal of the President from Office, or of his Death, Resignation or Inability to discharge the Powers and Duties of the said Office, the Same shall devolve on the Vice President and the Congress may by Law provide for the Case of Removal, Death, Resignation or Inability, both of the President and Vice President, declaring what Officer shall then act as President, and such Officer shall act accordingly, until the Disability be removed, or a President shall be elected.

The President shall, at stated Times, receive for his Services, a Compensation, which shall neither be increased nor diminished during the Period for which he shall have been elected, and he shall not receive within that Period any other Emolument from the United States, or any of them.

Before he enter on the Execution of his Office, he shall take the following Oath or Affirmation: "I do solemnly swear (or affirm) that I will faithfully execute the Office of President of the United States, and will to the best of my Ability, preserve, protect and defend the Constitution of the United States."

Section 2. The President shall be Commander in Chief of the Army and Navy of the United States, and of the militia of the several States, when called into the actual Service of the United States; he may require the Opinion, in writing, of the principal Officer in each of the Executive Departments, upon any Subject relating to the Duties of their respective Offices and he shall have Power to grant Reprieves and Pardons for Offenses against the United States, except in Cases of Impeachment.

He shall have Power, by and with the Advice and Consent of the Senate, to make Treaties, provided two thirds of the Senators present concur; and he shall nominate, and by and with the Advice and Consent of the Senate, shall appoint Ambassadors, other public Ministers and Consuls, Judges of the supreme Court, and all other Officers of the United States, whose Appointments are not herein otherwise provided for, and which shall be established by Law; but the Congress may by Law vest the Appointment of such inferior Officers, as they think proper, in the President alone, in the Courts of Law, or in the Heads of Departments.

The President shall have Power to fill up all Vacancies that may happen during the Recess of the Senate, by granting Commissions which shall expire at the End of their next Session.

Section 3. He shall from time to time give to the Congress Information of the State of the Union, and recommend to their Consideration such Measures as he shall judge necessary and expedient; he may, on extraordinary Occasions, convene both Houses, or either of them, and in Case of Disagreement between them, with Respect to the Time of Adjournment, he may adjourn them to such Time as he shall think proper; he shall receive Ambassadors and other public Ministers; he shall take Care that the Laws be faithfully executed, and shall Commission all the Officers of the United States.

Section 4. The President, Vice President and all civil Officers of the United States, shall be removed from Office on Impeachment for, and Conviction of, Treason, Bribery, or other high Crimes and Misdemeanors.

Article III

Section 1. The judicial Power of the United States, shall be vested in one supreme Court, and in such inferior Courts as the Congress may from time to time ordain and establish. The Judges, both of the supreme and inferior Courts, shall hold their Offices during good Behaviour, and shall, at stated Times, receive for their Services a Compensation, which shall not be diminished during their Continuance in Office.

Section 2. The judicial Power shall extend to all Cases, in Law and Equity, arising under this Constitution, the Laws of the United States, and Treaties made, or which shall be made, under their Authority;—to all Cases affecting Ambassadors, other public Ministers and Consuls;—to all Cases of admiralty and maritime Jurisdiction;—to Controversies to which the United States shall be a Party;—to Controversies between two or more States;—between a State and Citizens of another State;—between Citizens of different States;—between Citizens of the same State claiming Lands under the Grants of different States, and between a State, or the Citizens thereof, and foreign States, Citizens or Subjects.

In all Cases affecting Ambassadors, other public Ministers and Consuls, and those in which a State shall be a Party, the supreme Court shall have original Jurisdiction. In all the other Cases before mentioned, the supreme Court shall have appellate Jurisdiction, both as to Law and Fact, with such Exceptions, and under such Regulations as the Congress shall make.

The trial of all Crimes, except in Cases of Impeachment, shall be by Jury; and such Trial shall be held in the State where the said Crimes shall have been committed; but when not committed within any State, the Trial shall be at such Place or Places as the Congress may by Law have directed.

Section 3. Treason against the United States, shall consist only in levying War against them, or, in adhering to their Enemies, giving them Aid and Comfort. No Person shall be convicted of Treason unless on the Testimony of two Witnesses to the same overt Act, or on Confession in open Court.

The Congress shall have Power to declare the Punishment of Treason, but no Attainder of Treason shall work Corruption of Blood, or Forfeiture except during the Life of the Person attainted.

Article IV

Section 1. Full Faith and Credit shall be given in each State to the public Acts, Records, and judicial Proceedings of every other State. And the Congress may by general Laws prescribe the Manner in which such Acts, Records and Proceedings shall be proved, and the Effect thereof.

Section 2. The Citizens of each State shall be entitled to all Privileges and Immunities of Citizens in the several States.

A Person charged in any State with Treason, Felony, or other Crime, who shall flee from Justice, and be found in another State, shall on demand of the executive Authority of the State from which he fled, be delivered up, to be removed to the State having Jurisdiction of the Crime.

No Person held to Service or Labour in one State, under the Laws thereof, escaping into another, shall, in Consequence of any Law or Regulation therein, be discharged from such Service or Labour, but shall be delivered up on Claim of the Party to whom such Service or Labour may be due.

Section 3. New States may be admitted by the Congress into this Union; but no new State shall be formed or erected within the Jurisdiction of any other State; nor any State be formed by the Junction of two or more States, or Parts of States, without the Consent of the Legislatures of the States concerned as well as of the Congress.

The Congress shall have Power to dispose of and make all needful Rules and Regulations respecting the Territory or other Property belonging to the United States; and nothing in this Constitution shall be so construed as to Prejudice any Claims of the United States, or of any particular State.

Section 4. The United States shall guarantee to every State in this Union a Republican Form of Government, and shall protect each of them against Invasion; and on Application of the Legislature, or of the Executive (when the Legislature cannot be convened) against domestic Violence.

Article V

The Congress, whenever two thirds of both Houses shall deem it necessary, shall propose Amendments to this Constitution, or, on the Application of the Legislatures of two thirds of the several States, shall call a Convention for proposing Amendments, which, in either Case, shall be valid to all Intents and Purposes, as part of this Constitution, when ratified by the Legislatures of three fourths of the several States, or by Conventions in three fourths thereof, as the one or the other Mode of Ratification may be proposed by the Congress; Provided that no Amendment which may be made prior to the Year One thousand eight hundred and eight shall in any Manner affect the first and fourth Clauses in the Ninth Section of the first Article; and that no State, without its Consent, shall be deprived of its equal Suffrage in the Senate.

Article VI

All Debts contracted and Engagements entered into, before the Adoption of this Constitution, shall be as valid against the United States under this Constitution, as under the Confederation.

This Constitution, and the Laws of the United States which shall be made in Pursuance thereof; and all Treaties made, or which shall be made, under the Authority of the United States, shall be the supreme Law of the Land; and the Judges in every State shall be bound thereby, any Thing in the Constitution or Laws of any State to the Contrary notwithstanding.

The Senators and Representatives before mentioned, and the Members of the several State Legislatures, and all executive and judicial Officers, both of the United States and of the several States, shall be bound by Oath or Affirmation, to support this Constitution; but no religious Test shall ever be required as a Qualification to any Office or public Trust under the United States.

Article VII

The Ratification of the Conventions of nine States shall be sufficient for the Establishment of this Constitution between the States so ratifying the Same.

DONE in Convention by the Unanimous Consent of the States present the Seventeenth Day of September in the Year of Our Lord one thousand seven hundred and Eighty seven and of the Independence of the United States of America the Twelfth. IN WITNESS whereof We have hereunto subscribed our Names,

Go. WASHINGTON—
Presidt.
and deputy from Virginia

New Hampshire

JOHN LANGDON — NICHOLAS GILMAN

Massachusetts

NATHANIEL GORHAM — RUFUS KING

Connecticut

WM. SAML. JOHNSON — ROGER SHERMAN

New York

ALEXANDER HAMILTON

New Jersey

WIL: LIVINGSTON
DAVID BREARLEY
WM. PATERSON
JONA: DAYTON

Pennsylvania

B. FRANKLIN
THOMAS MIFFLIN
ROBT. MORRIS
GEO. CLYMER
THOS. FITZSIMONS
JARED INGERSOLL
JAMES WILSON
GOUV MORRIS

Delaware

GEO: READ
GUNNING BEDFORD JUN
JOHN DICKINSON
RICHARD BASSETT
JACO: BROOM

Maryland

JAMES MCHENRY
DAN OF ST THOS. JENIFER
DANL. CARROLL

Virginia

JOHN BLAIR
JAMES MADISON, JR.

North Carolina

WM. BLOUNT
RICHD. DOBBS SPAIGHT
HU WILLIAMSON

South Carolina

J. RUTLEDGE
CHARLES COTESWORTH PINCKNEY
CHARLES PINCKNEY
PIERCE BUTLER

Georgia

WILLIAM FEW
ABR BALDWIN

Attest
WILLIAM JACKSON
Secretary

ARTICLES IN ADDITION TO, AND AMENDMENT OF, THE CONSTITUTION OF THE UNITED STATES OF AMERICA, PROPOSED BY CONGRESS, AND RATIFIED BY THE LEGISLATURES OF THE SEVERAL STATES PURSUANT TO THE FIFTH ARTICLE OF THE ORIGINAL CONSTITUTION.

Amendment [I] [1791]

Congress shall make no law respecting an establishment of religion, or prohibiting the free exercise thereof; or abridging the freedom of speech, or of the press; or the right of the people peaceably to assemble, and to petition the Government for a redress of grievances.

Amendment [II] [1791]

A well regulated Militia, being necessary to the security of a free State, the right of the people to keep and bear Arms, shall not be infringed.

Amendment [III] [1791]

No Soldier shall, in time of peace be quartered in any house, without the consent of the Owner, nor in time of war, but in a manner to be prescribed by law.

Amendment [IV] [1791]

The right of the people to be secure in their persons, houses, papers, and effects, against unreasonable searches and seizures, shall not be violated, and no Warrants shall issue, but upon probable cause, supported by Oath or affirmation, and particularly describing the place to be searched, and the persons or things to be seized.

Amendment [V] [1791]

No person shall be held to answer for a capital, or otherwise infamous crime, unless on a presentment or indictment of a Grand Jury, except in cases arising in the land or naval forces, or in the Militia, when in actual service in time of War or public danger; nor shall any person be subject for the same offence to be twice put in jeopardy of life or limb; nor shall be compelled in any criminal case to be a witness against himself, nor be deprived of life, liberty, or property, without due process of law; nor shall private property be taken for public use, without just compensation.

Amendment [VI] [1791]

In all criminal prosecutions, the accused shall enjoy the right to a speedy and public trial, by an impartial jury of the State and district wherein the crime shall have been committed, which district shall have been previously ascertained by law, and to be informed of the nature and cause of the accusation; to be confronted with the witnesses against him; to have compulsory process for obtaining witnesses in his favor, and to have the Assistance of Counsel for his defence.

Amendment [VII] [1791]

In Suits at common law, where the value in controversy shall exceed twenty dollars, the right of trial by jury shall be preserved, and no fact tried by jury, shall be otherwise re-examined in any Court of the United States, than according to the rules of the common law.

Amendment [VIII] [1791]

Excessive bail shall not be required, nor excessive fines imposed, nor cruel and unusual punishments inflicted.

Amendment [IX] [1791]

The enumeration in the Constitution, of certain rights, shall not be construed to deny or disparage others retained by the people.

Amendment [X] [1791]

The powers not delegated to the United States by the Constitution, nor prohibited by it to the States, are reserved to the States respectively, or to the people.

Amendment [XI] [1798]

The Judicial power of the United States shall not be construed to extend to any suit in law or equity, commenced or prosecuted against one of the United States by Citizens of another State, or by Citizens or Subjects of any Foreign State.

Amendment [XII] [1804]

The Electors shall meet in their respective states and vote by ballot for President and Vice-President, one of whom, at least, shall not be an inhabitant of the same State with themselves; they shall name in their ballots the person voted for as President, and in distinct ballots the person voted for as Vice-President, and they shall make distinct lists of all persons voted for as President, and of all persons voted for as Vice-President, and of the number of votes for each, which lists they shall sign and certify, and transmit sealed to the seat of the government of the United States, directed to the President of the Senate;—The President of the Senate shall, in the presence of the Senate and House of Representatives, open all the certificates and the votes shall then be counted;—The person having the greatest number of votes for President, shall be the President, if such number be a majority of the whole number of Electors appointed; and if no person have such majority, then from the persons having the highest numbers not exceeding three on the list of those voted for as President, the House of Representatives shall choose immediately, by ballot, the President. But in choosing the President, the votes shall be taken by states, the representation from each State having one vote; a quorum for this purpose shall consist of a member or members from two-thirds of the states, and a majority of all the states shall be necessary to a choice. And if the House of Representatives shall not choose a President whenever the right of choice shall devolve upon them before the fourth day of March next following, then the Vice-President shall act as President, as in the case of the death or other constitutional disability of the President.—The person having the greatest number of votes as Vice-President, shall be the Vice-President, if such number be a majority of the whole number of Electors appointed, and if no person have a majority, then from the two highest numbers on the list, the Senate shall choose the Vice-President; a quorum for the purpose shall consist of two-thirds of the whole number of Senators, and a majority of the whole number shall be necessary to a choice. But no person constitutionally ineligible to the office of President shall be eligible to that of Vice-President of the United States.

Amendment XIII [1865]

Section 1. Neither slavery nor involuntary servitude, except as a punishment for crime whereof the party shall have been duly convicted, shall exist within the United States, or any place subject to their jurisdiction.

Section 2. Congress shall have power to enforce this article by appropriate legislation.

Amendment XIV [1868]

Section 1. All persons born or naturalized in the United States, and subject to the jurisdiction thereof, are citizens of the United States and of the State wherein they reside. No State shall make or enforce any law which shall abridge the privileges or immunities of citizens of the United States; nor shall any State deprive any person of life, liberty, or property, without due process of law; nor deny to any person within its jurisdiction the equal protection of the laws.

Section 2. Representatives shall be apportioned among the several States according to their respective numbers, counting the whole number of persons in each State, excluding Indians not taxed. But when the right to vote at any election for the choice of electors for President and Vice President of the United States, Representatives in Congress, the Executive and Judicial officers of a State, or the members of the Legislature thereof, is denied to any of the male inhabitants of such State, being twenty-one years of age, and citizens of the United States, or in any way abridged, except for participation in rebellion, or other crime, the basis of representation therein shall be reduced in the proportion which the number of such male citizens shall bear to the whole number of male citizens twenty-one years of age in such State.

Section 3. No person shall be a Senator or Representative in Congress, or elector of President and Vice President, or hold any office, civil or military, under the United States, or under any State, who having previously taken an oath, as a member of Congress, or as an officer of the United States, or as a member of any State legislature, or as an executive or judicial officer of any State, to support the Constitution of the United States, shall have engaged in insurrection or rebellion against the same, or given aid or comfort to the enemies thereof. But Congress may by a vote of two-thirds of each House, remove such disability.

Section 4. The validity of the public debt of the United States, authorized by law, including debts incurred for payment of pensions and bounties for services in suppressing insurrection or rebellion, shall not be questioned. But neither the United States nor any State shall assume or pay any debt or obligation incurred in aid of insurrection or rebellion against the United States, or any claim for the loss or emancipation of any slave; but all such debts, obligations and claims shall be held illegal and void.

Section 5. The Congress shall have power to enforce, by appropriate legislation, the provisions of this article.

Amendment XV [1870]

Section 1. The right of citizens of the United States to vote shall not be denied or abridged by the United States or by any State on account of race, color, or previous condition of servitude.

Section 2. The Congress shall have power to enforce this article by appropriate legislation.

Amendment XVI [1913]

The Congress shall have power to lay and collect taxes on incomes, from whatever source derived, without apportionment among the several States, and without regard to any census or enumeration.

Amendment [XVII] [1913]

The Senate of the United States shall be composed of two Senators from each State, elected by the people thereof, for six years; and each Senator shall have one vote. The electors in each State shall have the qualifications requisite for electors of the most numerous branch of the State legislatures.

When vacancies happen in the representation of any State in the Senate, the executive authority of such State shall issue writs of election to fill such vacancies: Provided, That the legislature of any State may empower the executive thereof to make temporary appointments until the people fill the vacancies by election as the legislature may direct.

This amendment shall not be so construed as to affect the election or term of any Senator chosen before it becomes valid as part of the Constitution.

Amendment [XVIII] [1919]

Section 1. After one year from the ratification of this article the manufacture, sale, or transportation of intoxicating liquors within, the importation thereof into, or the exportation thereof from the United States and all territory subject to the jurisdiction thereof for beverage purposes is hereby prohibited.

Section 2. The Congress and the several States shall have concurrent power to enforce this article by appropriate legislation.

Section 3. This article shall be inoperative unless it shall have been ratified as an amendment to the Constitution by the legislatures of the several States, as provided in the Constitution, within seven years from the date of the submission hereof to the States by the Congress.

Amendment [XIX] [1920]

The right of citizens of the United States to vote shall not be denied or abridged by the United States or by any State on account of sex.

Congress shall have power to enforce this article by appropriate legislation.

Amendment [XX] [1933]

Section 1. The terms of the President and Vice President shall end at noon on the 20th day of January, and the terms of Senators and Representatives at noon on the 3d day of January, of the years in which such terms would have ended if this article had not been ratified; and the terms of their successors shall then begin.

Section 2. The Congress shall assemble at least once in every year, and such meeting shall begin at noon on the 3d day of January, unless they shall by law appoint a different day.

Section 3. If, at the time fixed for the beginning of the term of the President, the President elect shall have died, the Vice President elect shall become President. If the President shall not have been chosen before the time fixed for the beginning of his term, or if the President elect shall have failed to qualify, then the Vice President elect shall act as President until a President shall have qualified; and the Congress may by law provide for the case wherein neither a President elect nor a Vice President elect shall have qualified, declaring who shall then act as President, or the manner in which one who is to act shall be selected, and such person shall act accordingly until a President or Vice President shall have qualified.

Section 4. The Congress may by law provide for the case of the death of any of the persons from whom the House of Representatives may choose a President whenever the right of choice shall have devolved upon them, and for the case of the death of any of the persons from whom the Senate may choose a Vice President whenever the right of choice shall have devolved upon them.

Section 5. Sections 1 and 2 shall take effect on the 15th day of October following the ratification of this article.

Section 6. This article shall be inoperative unless it shall have been ratified as an amendment to the Constitution by the legislatures of three-fourths of the several States within seven years from the date of its submission.

Amendment [XXI] [1933]

Section 1. The eighteenth article of amendment to the Constitution of the United States is hereby repealed.

Section 2. The transportation or importation into any State, Territory, or possession of the United States for delivery or use therein of intoxicating liquors, in violation of the laws thereof, is hereby prohibited.

Section 3. This article shall be inoperative unless it shall have been ratified as an amendment to the Constitution by conventions in the several States, as provided in the Constitution, within seven years from the date of the submission hereof to the States by the Congress.

Amendment [XXII] [1951]

Section 1. No person shall be elected to the office of the President more than twice, and no person who has held the office of President, or acted as President, for more than two years of a term to which some other person was elected President shall be elected to the office of President more than once. But this Article shall not apply to any person holding the office of President when this Article was proposed by the Congress, and shall not prevent any person who may be holding the office of President, or acting as President, during the term within which this Article becomes operative from holding the office of President or acting as President during the remainder of such term.

Section 2. This article shall be inoperative unless it shall have been ratified as an amendment to the Constitution by the legislatures of three-fourths of the several States within seven years from the date of its submission to the States by the Congress.

Amendment [XXIII] [1961]

Section 1. The District constituting the seat of Government of the United States shall appoint in such manner as the Congress may direct:

A number of electors of President and Vice President equal to the whole number of Senators and Representatives in Congress to which the District would be entitled if it were a State, but in no event more than the least populous state; they shall be in addition to those appointed by the states, but they shall be considered, for the purposes of the election of President and Vice President, to be electors appointed by a state; and they shall meet in the District and perform such duties as provided by the twelfth article of amendment.

Section 2. The Congress shall have power to enforce this article by appropriate legislation.

Amendment [XXIV] [1964]

Section 1. The right of citizens of the United States to vote in any primary or other election for President or Vice President, for electors for President or Vice President, or for Senator or Representative in Congress, shall not be denied or abridged by the United States or any State by reason of failure to pay any poll tax or other tax.

Section 2. The Congress shall have power to enforce this article by appropriate legislation.

Amendment [XXV] [1967]

Section 1. In the case of the removal of the President from office or of his death or resignation, the Vice President shall become President.

Section 2. Whenever there is a vacancy in the office of the Vice President, the President shall nominate a Vice President who shall take office upon confirmation by a majority vote of both Houses of Congress.

Section 3. Whenever the President transmits to the President pro tempore of the Senate and the Speaker of the House of Representatives his written declaration that he is unable to discharge the powers and duties of his office, and until he transmits to them a written declaration to the contrary, such powers and duties shall be discharged by the Vice President as Acting President.

Section 4. Whenever the Vice President and a majority of either the principal officers of the executive departments or of such other body as Congress may by law provide, transmit to the President pro tempore of the Senate and the Speaker of the House of Representatives, their written declaration that the President is unable to discharge the powers and duties of his office, the Vice President shall immediately assume the powers and duties of the office as Acting President.

Thereafter, when the President transmits to the President pro tempore of the Senate and the Speaker of the House of Representatives his written declaration that no inability exists, he shall resume the powers and duties of his office unless the Vice President and a majority of either the principal officers of the executive department or of such other body as Congress may by law provide, transmit within four days to the President pro tempore of the Senate and the Speaker of the House of Representatives their written declaration that the President is unable to discharge the powers and duties of his office. Thereupon Congress shall decide the issue, assembling within forty-eight hours for that purpose if not in session. If the Congress, within twenty-one days after receipt of the latter written declaration, or, if Congress is not in session, within twenty-one days after Congress is required to assemble, determines by two-thirds vote of both Houses that the President is unable to discharge the powers and duties of his office, the Vice President shall continue to discharge the same as Acting President; otherwise, the President shall resume the powers and duties of his office.

Amendment [XXVI] [1971]

Section 1. The right of citizens of the United States, who are eighteen years of age or older, to vote shall not be denied or abridged by the United States or by any State on account of age.

Section 2. The Congress shall have power to enforce this article by appropriate legislation.

Amendment [XXVII] [1992]

No law, varying the compensation for the services of the Senators and Representatives, shall take effect, until an election of Representatives shall have intervened.